Historic Documents of 2004

Historic Documents of 2004

Includes Cumulative Index, 2000–2004

A Division of Congressional Quarterly Inc.
Washington, D.C.

CQ Press
1255 22nd Street, NW, Suite 400
Washington, DC 20037

Phone, 202-729-1900; toll-free, 1-866-427-7737 (1-866-4CQ-PRESS)

Web: www.cqpress.com

Printed and bound in the United States of America
09 08 07 06 05 1 2 3 4 5

∞ The paper used in this publication exceeds the requirements of the American National Standard for Information Sciences—Permanence of Paper for Printed Library Materials, ANSI Z39.48-1992.

Historic Documents of 2004
Editors: Martha Gottron, John Felton, Bruce Maxwell
Production and Associate Editor: Kerry V. Kern
Indexer: Victoria Agee

The Library of Congress cataloged the first issue of this title as follows:

Historic documents. 1972—
Washington. Congressional Quarterly Inc.

1. United States—Politics and government—1945- —Yearbooks.
2. World politics—1945- —Yearbooks. I. Congressional Quarterly Inc.
E839.5H57 917.3'03'9205 72-97888
ISSN 0892-080X
ISBN 1-56802-948-9

Contents

April

May

June

July

December

Thematic Table of Contents

Health Care, Social Services, Housing, and Education

International Affairs—Africa

International Affairs—Asia

International Affairs—Europe

International Affairs—Latin America

International Affairs—Middle East

International Affairs—Russia and Former Soviet Republics

International Affairs—World Issues

List of Documents

White House and President

Executive Departments and Agencies

Governmental Commissions

Congress

Judiciary

U.S. Nongovernmental Organizations

Non-U.S. Governments

International Nongovernmental Organizations

Preface

The continuing turmoil in Iraq and the Middle East, a natural disaster of epic proportions, and a contentious presidential election year in America are only some of the topics of national and international interest chosen for *Historic Documents of 2004.* This edition marks the thirty-third volume of a CQ Press project that began with *Historic Documents of 1972.* This series allows students, librarians, journalists, scholars, and others to research and understand the most important issues and events of the year through primary source documents. These primary sources have often been excerpted to highlight the most important parts of lengthy documents written for a specialized audience. In our judgment, the official statements, news conferences, speeches, special studies, and court decisions presented here will be of lasting interest.

This edition also includes a new thematic table of contents (page xvi) and a new list of documents by type or source (page xx). For more details on how these new features can help you locate the events and documents you need, please see "How to Use This Book" (page xxviii).

Historic Documents of 2004 begins with "Overview of 2004," which puts key events and issues from around the world in political, historical, or social context. The balance of the book is organized chronologically, with each "article" comprising an introduction and one or more related documents on a specific event, issue, or topic. The introduction preceding each document provides context, background, and an account of continuing developments during the year, when relevant.

As events, issues, and consequences become more complex and far-reaching, these introductions and documents yield important information and deepen understanding about the world in which we live. The editors of this series believe these introductions will become increasingly useful as memories of current events fade.

How to Use This Book

The seventy-eight articles in this edition contain two sections: a comprehensive introduction, followed by one or more primary source documents. The articles are arranged in chronological order. There are several ways to find events and documents of interest:

By date: If you know the approximate date of the event or document you are looking for, glance through the titles for that month in the table of contents or in the monthly tables of contents that appear at the start of each month's introductions and documents.

By theme: If you are interested in a particular topic or area, review the new thematic table of contents to find articles on the subjects of interest.

By document type or source: If you are interested in a particular type or source of document, review the new list of documents, which will take you to the start of the document you need.

By index: The five-year index at the end of the book will help you find references not only to the particular event or document you seek but also to other entries on the same or a related subject. The index in this volume is a five-year cumulative index of *Historic Documents* covering the years 2000–2004. There is a separate volume, *Historic Documents Index, 1972–2002,* which may also be useful.

Each article begins with the heading "Introduction," and the discussion that directly follows provides the historical and intellectual context for the selected document(s). A rule designates the start of the official document, followed by the document's formal title (designated with quotation marks or italics) or informal title. The documents are reproduced with the spelling, capitalization, and punctuation of the original or official copy. Where the full text is not given, omissions of material are indicated by the customary ellipsis points. Insertions within the documents by the editors to clarify information are enclosed within brackets.

Full citations to the official print and online sources, including the Internet URL addresses noting where the documents have been obtained, appear at the end of each document, as necessary, allowing you to find original documents in either format. If documents were not available on the Internet, this also has been noted.

Overview of 2004

For much of 2004 it appeared possible that President George W. Bush would join his father, President George H.W. Bush (1989–1993), in the ranks of one-term presidents—each man denied reelection in part by an ambivalent economy and despite having led the nation to an overwhelming military victory in Iraq. The younger Bush was buffeted by so many problems, and endured so many weeks of bad news during an election year, that he was widely seen as vulnerable politically, just as his father had proved to be in 1992. Indeed, on election day, many pundits believed Bush's Democratic challenger, Sen. John F. Kerry of Massachusetts, had a fifty-fifty chance of becoming the next president. The president's victory, while certainly no landslide, was a convincing one that not only upset conventional wisdom but also helped Republicans consolidate their control of Congress. Bush was thus in a potentially strong position to impose elements of his conservative agenda that had stalled in Congress during his first term and to deepen his imprint on the federal court system, perhaps even with one or more appointments to the Supreme Court.

In historical terms, Democrats had every reason to believe Bush could be beaten. The war in Iraq, which a year earlier had been so successful in the initial stage of ousting Saddam Hussein from power in Baghdad, had dragged on, leading some critics to compare it to the "quagmire" of the Vietnam War more than three decades earlier. Economists, and officials in the president's administration, produced all sorts of technical evidence that the economy was recovering nicely from a brief recession. But many ordinary Americans remained nervous about their personal economic prospects, mainly because the so-called jobless recovery was failing to produce an abundance of new employment. Moreover, Bush had become a deeply polarizing figure after nearly four years in office, reviled by some critics as ignorant and intolerant, but admired by many supporters as a determined man of righteous principle. The political fates of such controversial presidents have tended to be decided by their ability to mobilize their supporters and to convince enough of those in the middle that the critics were misguided.

Guided by his political mentor, Karl Rove, Bush waged an extraordinarily focused campaign that put his accomplishments in the most positive light possible and planted seeds of doubt in the voters' minds about the character of Kerry, the opponent. Kerry ultimately contributed to his own defeat. While polls showed that Kerry "won" the three televised debates, he was never able to effectively refute Republican charges that he had lied about his military record in the Vietnam War and had flip-flopped on important issues.

Bush also benefited politically from a sudden surge of gay marriages. The sight of men marrying men, and women marrying women, at churches and courthouses in

Massachusetts and San Francisco may have heartened those who saw gay rights as the next stage of the nation's civil rights struggle—but it also energized millions of Americans who were repelled by what they saw as further evidence of decline in the nation's moral values. Polls showed that those in the latter category outnumbered the former and that they voted overwhelmingly for Bush.

The Iraq War, Chapter II

By 2004 there no longer was doubt that the Bush administration had laid brilliant plans for a successful short-term war in Iraq but had failed to consider the possibility that the war would continue long after Saddam Hussein, the Iraqi leader, had been toppled from power. An anti-U.S. insurgency, which at first was an annoyance to the American occupiers, quickly developed into a serious threat to all of Washington's plans for a democratic, prosperous, and stable Iraq. Rather than withdrawing U.S. forces at the end of 2003, as Pentagon plans had envisioned, the administration found itself scrambling desperately to keep enough troops in Iraq so the insurgents would not win by default. At the end of 2004 the Pentagon was ready to boost the U.S. troop level in Iraq to about 150,000 for the weeks before and after the country's parliamentary elections, scheduled for January 2005.

The depth and breadth of the insurgency forced the administration to rethink the political, as well as the military, aspects of its occupation of Iraq. The original plan to turn Iraq over to a coalition of Iraqi exiles favored by the Pentagon was the first idea to fall by the wayside, shortly after the war in 2003. One by one other schemes for governing Iraq succumbed to reality, until by early 2004 the Bush administration was forced to turn for help to the United Nations. After UN-mediated negotiations that often seemed ready to collapse, leaders of Iraq's numerous political and religious factions settled on a multistep process beginning with formation of an interim government by July 1, followed by elections for another interim government early in 2005, and leading up to the adoption of a constitution and elections for a permanent government by the end of 2005.

The threat of insurgent attacks upon an official ceremony led the U.S. occupiers to hand over nominal political authority to the new interim Iraqi government three days early, on June 28. The hurried handover ceremony, held in secret in a heavily fortified compound in Baghdad, said more about the dangers faced by the new government, which relied for its survival on the U.S. military, than about the opportunities for a democratic and stable Iraq. The interim government represented a delicate balance among the country's three main factions: the majority Shi'ite Muslims, and the two largest minorities, the Sunni Muslims and the Kurds. Whether that balance could be maintained, in the face of an insurgency apparently determined to upset it, was the main question facing Iraq in its new era.

The Bush administration had portrayed its policy in Iraq as a jump-start for a broader campaign to encourage democracy in the Middle East, particularly in Arab lands long dominated by repressive regimes. The purity of Washington's motives became questionable, in Arab eyes, beginning in April when news organizations published photographs showing U.S. soldiers abusing Iraqis at a notorious Baghdad prison. The Pentagon insisted the abuses were committed by a handful of soldiers acting contrary to established policy. However, a continuing wave of photographs and other evidence, along with some of the official investigations launched by the military, appeared to show a broader pattern of abuse by soldiers who had reason to believe they were acting with official approval. The prison abuse scandal deepened in June when news organizations reported that the Justice Department in 2002 had appeared to endorse the use of torture against terrorism suspects. Embarrassed, administration officials withdrew the memoranda authorizing torture and, in December, produced a new legal rationale against torture.

Another continuing source of embarrassment for the administration was its failure to locate in Iraq the biological, chemical, and nuclear weapons programs that Bush had said posed a mortal danger to the United States, thus justifying the 2003 war. A broad CIA search came to a close in 2004 with a report to Congress saying Iraq's weapons were eliminated during or shortly after the 1991 Persian Gulf War and that Saddam's government had done virtually nothing to rebuild them.

Rethinking Intelligence

The apparently conclusive evidence about Iraq's lack of weapons of mass destruction was one of two recent cases of major failures by the U.S. intelligence community, including its flagship agency, the CIA. The other failure involved the government's inability to assess the risks that a small group of terrorists would or could hijack several airliners and deliberately fly them into large and symbolically important buildings—as was done on September 11, 2001, when nineteen members of the al Qaeda terrorist network destroyed the two World Trade Center towers in New York and damaged the Pentagon.

After studying the matter for nearly two years, a high-level commission issued a report in July saying U.S. intelligence agencies, along with the rest of the government, failed to comprehend the nature of Islamist-driven terrorism. The commission called for a sweeping overhaul of the intelligence community, starting with appointment of a single director who had the authority to hold all its fifteen agencies accountable. Despite resistance from the Pentagon, which jealously guarded the privileges of its own intelligence agencies, Congress responded in December by passing the most fundamental revision of the U.S. intelligence structure since it was created after World War II.

The "War on Terrorism"

Although there was no evidence that Iraq had been involved, even indirectly, in any recent terrorist attacks against the United States, Bush had portrayed the war in Iraq as a central front in his post-September 11 "global war on terror" (known at the White House and Pentagon as GWOT). The first front of that war was in Afghanistan, where U.S. and allied forces in October 2001 ousted from power the Taliban regime, which had provided sanctuary for al Qaeda and its leader, Osama bin Laden. By 2004 a certain degree of stability had developed in Afghanistan, where an interim government headed by Hamid Karzai, with the support of U.S. and NATO troops, struggled to assert authority in the country's lawless provinces that were largely controlled by tribal warlords. Karzai won Afghanistan's first-ever free election, held October 9, and then set about the task of unifying his country so parliamentary elections could be held in 2005. The political process seemed to be moving faster than the process of reconstructing a country that had been battered by more than two decades of war, however, creating a situation in which unfulfilled economic aspirations potentially could endanger the fragile new democracy.

Another unfinished piece of business in the terrorism war was the fate of hundreds of terrorism suspects the Bush administration had imprisoned at various locations, including the Guantanamo Bay naval base in Cuba. With only a handful of exceptions, the suspects were being held indefinitely, without being charged with any crime and without the benefit of legal counsel. The Supreme Court entered the fray in June, rebuking the administration in its handling of nearly 600 detainees at Guantanamo Bay and of a U.S. citizen, of Saudi Arabian descent, who had been held at a U.S. Navy brig in South Carolina. The Court's action forced the administration to accord the Guantanamo detainees a modest degree of legal recourse and to negotiate a deal under which the man held in South Carolina was sent back to his native Saudi Arabia.

Global terrorism did surface during 2004, notably in Spain, where a coordinated series of bombings onboard Madrid commuter trains on March 11 killed 191 people and wounded more than 1,600. Those bombings had immediate political ramifications. Three days later, Spanish voters ousted the conservative government of Prime Minister José Marìa Aznar, replacing it with the center-left Socialist Workers Party and its leader, José Luis Rodriguez Zapatero. Aznar's supporters claimed voters had given in to al Qaeda terrorists, who appeared to be responsible for the bombings and who may have targeted Spain in part because of Aznar's support for the U.S. war in Iraq. Most independent analysts, however, said Spanish voters punished Aznar and his government for a clumsy effort to lie about who had carried out the bombings.

A Mideast Peace Opportunity?

A pair of developments in 2004 offered at least a modest degree of hope that the decades-long conflict between Israelis and Palestinians might be entering a more positive phase. The first was a plan by Israeli prime minister Ariel Sharon to withdraw Israel's settlements and military posts from the tiny Palestinian territory along the Mediterranean known as the Gaza strip. Sharon, who had been a political sponsor of Jewish settlements in Palestinian territories, portrayed his plan as a unilateral action to rid Israel of the burden of protecting about 8,000 settlers living among 1.3 million Palestinians. Settlers and their allies in the Israeli right wing and religious partners condemned Sharon as a traitor and threatened to block the Gaza withdrawal, scheduled for the summer of 2005. But most Palestinians, after initially expressing skepticism about Sharon's motives, grew to embrace his plan as a way of asserting their authority over a territory that Israel had seized in 1967.

The year's other development, of potentially even greater significance, was the death on November 11, from unknown causes, of longtime Palestinian leader Yasir Arafat at age seventy-five. Arafat had founded the cause of Palestinian nationalism in the 1960s and had become a one-man symbol of Palestinian national identity. He had been unable or unwilling to lead his people into permanent peace and reconciliation with Israel, however. Both Israel and the United States considered Arafat an obstacle to peace, and so his death created what many observers considered the best opportunity in years for a renewal of the long-stalled peace process. Arafat was succeeded by a former aide, Mahmoud Abbas, who appeared determined to seize the new opportunity. Although he had no real personal following among the Palestinian populace, Abbas was expected to win an election to succeed Arafat in January 2005.

Other Key International Developments

The year saw significant developments on several other international fronts—none of them conclusive but each serving as indicators of where the world was headed in the early years of the twenty-first century.

Perhaps of greatest importance over the long-term was the rapid rise of China as an economic and even political power. By 2004 free-market economic principles had come to dominate many important aspects of Chinese life, and the country responded with astonishing growth that put China on course to overtake Japan as the world's second-biggest economic power (after the United States) by around 2020. China's pace of growth was so torrid (clocking in at around 9 percent a year) that the government intervened with small steps to cool things off, in hopes of avoiding an overheating that might lead to a crash. The prospect of a sudden "hard landing" by China had become a serious source of concern around Asia, where many countries were hitching their own economic futures to China's.

In keeping with its new economic clout, the government in Beijing was becoming an increasingly important player on the world stage. One of many notable examples was a twelve-day visit to Latin America in November by President Hu Jintao, who showered billions of dollars of investment in the region and began negotiating free-trade deals in a part of the world Washington considered its backyard. In another area of possible tension with the United States, China late in the year began crafting the legal basis for a move to halt the independence of Taiwan. Voters on that island—claimed by China—in March reelected a president committed to independence from the mainland. Although President Chen Shui-bian made subsequent efforts to play down the prospect of a formal break, alarmed leaders in Beijing said they would draft an "anti-secession" law barring Taiwanese independence. Any conflict over Taiwan likely would draw in the United States, which was formally committed to defending the island.

Two other areas of potential international conflict, each with ramifications just as broad as the China-Taiwan issue, appeared little closer to resolution at the end of 2004 than at the beginning. One was Iran's seeming determination to develop a capability of building nuclear weapons, and possibly the weapons themselves. European diplomats, with grudging support from the Bush administration, negotiated with Iran in hopes of reaching a deal under which Tehran would give up its weapons program in exchange for economic and political concessions. Those negotiations produced a tentative agreement in November, but the prospects for a more solid deal were questionable, at best. Likewise, international efforts to convince the reclusive government of North Korea to give up its nuclear weapons program were proceeding on an uncertain course. In this case, China was the key interlocutor because of its historic patronage of the communist regime in Pyongyang. North Korea said it already had built some nuclear weapons, and most Western analysts tended to believe that claim, although given the recent experience of intelligence assessments about Iraq, it was impossible to know the truth for certain.

Three more positive developments, at least potentially, concerned the future of Europe. On May 1 ten new countries joined the European Union (EU), boosting the economic and trade consortium to twenty-five countries encompassing most of the continent. Eight of the new members had been under communist rule during the cold war, and three of them (the Baltic states of Estonia, Latvia, and Lithuania) had been part of the Soviet Union until its collapse in 1991. Just in time to receive its new members, the EU adopted a constitution replacing an outdated patchwork of laws and treaties; a key element was a new voting procedure intended to promote harmony in a union with members ranging in size from tiny Malta to giant Germany. The constitution was to be submitted to referendums in several countries during 2005–2006, including several where it was unpopular; in theory and possibly in practice, rejection by a single country would nullify the constitution and force EU leaders to return to the drawing board. The EU took a third important step in December, formally inviting Turkey to begin negotiations, in October 2005, leading toward eventual membership. The question of Turkey's membership, with its overwhelmingly Muslim population, raised a host of questions of great economic, historical, and political significance in Europe and was expected to generate controversy for years to come.

Another international union of sorts—the United Nations—confronted its own questions about the future during 2004. At the request of Secretary General Kofi Annan, a panel of well-known international figures debated the entire range of issues facing the United Nations and gave Annan a long list of recommended actions in late November. Among them was a call for revamping the Security Council, the one UN body with legal authority to order countries to take certain actions. But in an implicit recognition of the political difficulty of making such a change, the panel could not agree on a single solution and instead offered Annan two choices. Annan was expected to come up with his own recommendations early in 2005. The secretary general, who had been extraordinarily popular and influential, came under fire himself because of the alleged involvement of his son, Kojo, in a UN-administered program that sold Iraqi oil on world markets. An investigation was under way.

Finally, the world watched in horror late in December as India, Indonesia, Sri Lanka, Thailand, and a half-dozen other Indian Ocean countries suffered the consequences of a series of giant tsunami waves, generated December 26 by a huge underwater earthquake off the Indonesian island of Sumatra. The waves, in some cases more than thirty feet high, roared onto beaches and devastated everything in their paths. At year's end more than 100,000 people had died as an immediate result of the destruction; tens of thousands more were still missing, and health authorities feared epidemics of disease resulting from the lack of food and clean water. Relief agencies rushed tons of supplies to the affected countries, but some of the hardest-hit communities were in remote areas where transportation facilities were inadequate even before the tsunami wrought its destruction.

Other U.S. Domestic Issues

Because the presidential election was expected to be an exceptionally close one, partisan politics dominated much of the domestic scene in the United States during 2004. The federal government accomplished little of substance, as the two parties sought to gain political advantage before November 2—each expecting to be the victor.

The economy was the year's dominant domestic issue, both politically and in daily life for many Americans. The economy continued to grow at a relatively strong pace—4.4 percent over the course of the year—but polls showed that many Americans were not persuaded that the recovery from the 2000–2001 recession was a strong and lasting one. The lagging job market was perhaps the chief source of concern. Unemployment was fairly low by historic standards, hovering around 5.5 percent throughout the year. But in most months since President Bush took office the economy failed to create enough new jobs to make up for jobs that were lost, let alone satisfy those entering the workforce. Rapidly rising energy prices—stimulated by an oil market that shot past the $50-a-barrel mark—caused concern about a possible rise in inflation and contributed to a tightening of monetary policy by the Federal Reserve Board.

The year was the third in a row that brought significant revelations of wrongdoing by major corporations. More than a dozen top-level corporate figures were being prosecuted on various fraud charges, the latest being Kenneth Lay, the former chairman and chief executive of Enron Corporation—the energy company whose bankruptcy in late 2001 set off the current round of business scandals. Lay was indicted on fraud charges on July 8, the same day that a jury convicted John J. Rigas, the former chairman of Adelphia Communications, on fraud charges and that a federal judge denied a new trial for the most famous of those caught up in the scandals: Martha Stewart, the guru of homemakers who had been convicted on charges related to insider trading. New York state's crusading attorney general, Elliot L. Spitzer, took aim at fraudulent activities in the insurance business, the third industry (after Wall Street investment banks and mutual funds) to feel the heat of his reformist zeal.

The nation's pharmaceutical industry had not been touched by similar allegations of financial wrongdoing, but late in the year two industry giants—Merck and Pfizer—came under intense market and public pressure because of concerns about the safety of some of their best-selling medicines. Merck on September 30 pulled Vioxx, a financially lucrative painkiller, off the market after studies showed it could cause increased risk of heart attack and stroke. Pfizer stopped marketing a competing drug, Celebrex, to consumers because of similar concerns. These events stimulated questions about the regulatory prowess of the Food and Drug Administration, which was supposed to monitor the safety and efficacy of drugs both before and after they went to market.

The FDA also came under fire after contamination forced the closing of a vaccine factory, depriving the nation of one half of the year's supply of flu vaccine. The sudden shortage at the beginning of the flu season sparked alarm and panic among patients as doctors and the government scrambled to find alternative sources of the vaccine. Fortunately, the flu season was mild, but the incident pointed up the vulnerability of the health care system to serious attack, whether from natural causes such as the bird flu that the World Health Organization feared could turn into a human flu pandemic or from manmade causes such as a bioterrorism attack.

The legal gay marriages in Massachusetts and illegal ones in San Francisco, Oregon, and a few other places touched off a backlash that conservative leaders turned to great advantage politically. Although both chambers of Congress failed by wide margins to approve a constitutional amendment barring gay marriages, voters in eleven states came out en masse to support state constitutional bans at the November elections. The turnout might have cost John Kerry the election. In the pivotal state of Ohio, 62 percent of the voters supported a referendum banning gay marriage. Had that issue not been on the ballot, many social conservatives might not have bothered coming to the polls, where Bush edged out Kerry by less than 2 percent of the vote to win the state and clinch a majority in the electoral college.

Moral values also continued to be front and center for the American Roman Catholic Church, which had been wracked by widespread allegations of sexual abuse of minors by priests. Three reports published under the auspices of the church gave some reason to believe that the worst period of abuse might be past and that most dioceses around the country were taking steps to prevent abuses in the future. But it was clear that the scandal had not run its course. New allegations of past abuse arose in hundreds of lawsuits filed around the country, the board that issued the reports accused the leaders of the church of backtracking on their efforts to protect children, and victims' rights groups were highly skeptical that the church was dealing with the problem openly and in good faith.

John Felton and Martha Gottron

January

2004 HISTORIC DOCUMENTS

NASA on the Mars Rovers

January 4, 2004

INTRODUCTION

Two golf cart-size robots landed on Mars in January, where they began uncovering what scientists said was conclusive evidence that the Red Planet once contained large quantities of salty water. The findings, by NASA's rovers *Opportunity* and *Spirit*, opened the possibility that Mars once had some form of life. The rovers were still exploring Mars at year's end—more than seven months beyond their planned lifetimes. The success of the missions stood in sharp contrast to a failed European attempt in late 2003 to land a robot on Mars, the *Beagle 2*. That rover disappeared shortly after it headed to the Martian surface and was never heard from again. *(Space Probe Launch, Historic Documents of 2003, p. 301)*

Encouraged by the international enthusiasm generated by the U.S. rover missions, President George W. Bush on January 14, 2004, outlined a bold plan to build a station on the moon that would serve as a staging platform for later manned missions to Mars and possibly even more distant planets. Although the plan generated little excitement on Capitol Hill or among space enthusiasts, Bush's election victory in November gave him the political muscle to force the first-year spending for it through Congress. *(Bush plan, p. 773)*

Rovers Land on Mars

NASA launched the two rovers toward Mars in mid-2003 to take advantage of the unusual closeness of Earth and Mars in their orbit around the sun. The missions cost a total of $820 million, about three-fourths of which was to build the spacecraft and equip them with scientific instruments. The United States had successfully landed three earlier robots on Mars: the *Viking I* and *Viking II* in 1976 and the *Mars Sojourner* in 1997. Along with scientific surveys by orbiting satellites, these missions had exploded long-held myths about Mars, notably that a perceived lacework pattern represented "canals" that had been dug by intelligent beings. *(Background, Historic Documents of 1997, p. 509)*

As with all space missions, the rover missions were plagued with problems at all stages. To hold down costs, NASA scientists and engineers used designs, equipment, and software left over from previous missions, notably the highly successful *Pathfinder* mission of 1997, which sent the *Sojourner* rover to the Martian surface. Some elements from the previous models did not fit the new rovers, however, and engineers repeatedly had to redesign such things as the airbags and parachutes that would protect the rovers during their landings.

Spirit and *Opportunity* were lifted into space from Cape Canaveral, Florida, on June 10 and July 7, 2003, respectively. The flights to Mars went well, until the final days when engineers discovered through repeated testing that the airbags might not inflate and the rockets used to slow the descent of the landing vehicles might not fire properly. Those problems turned out to be caused by minor differences between the clocks at mission control and those aboard the spacecrafts. Engineers finished synchronizing the clocks just a few hours before *Spirit* was scheduled to land. These technical discrepancies were reminiscent of an engineering flaw that doomed the *Climate Orbiter* mission to Mars in 1999. *(Background, Historic Documents of 1999, p. 711)*

NASA scientists chose landing places for the two rovers because they appeared to be safe and offered evidence that water once existed, and might still exist, which could have made some form of life possible on Mars. *Spirit*'s landing site was near the center of Gusev Crater, a giant depression (larger than the state of Connecticut) south of the Martian equator. It appeared that the crater might once have held a large lake, and scientists believed that sediment from the lake might still be present. *Opportunity*'s target was the Meridiani Planum, one of the planet's flattest and smoothest places, located nearly halfway around Mars from the *Spirit* landing site. Meridiani interested scientists because the *Mars Global Surveyor* had detected sizable deposits there of gray hematite, a type of iron oxide mineral that on Earth typically formed in the presence of liquid water.

Spirit landed on January 3 and took several bounces around the Gusev Crater. Within hours, the robot was sending back its first pictures, including some that gave scientists the most detailed views ever of the Martian landscape. NASA published a mosaic, combining the first dozen pictures, on the Internet on January 6, making *Spirit* an instant global celebrity. The excitement was quickly tempered by the first signs of trouble, however. A deflated airbag apparently was caught in *Spirit*'s landing vehicle, posing an obstacle to the rover before it could roll onto the Martian surface. Over the next week NASA engineers put *Spirit* through a complex series of maneuvers that got the lander untangled from the airbag. Spirit successfully rolled off its lander, and onto Martian soil, on January 15, three days later than had been planned. Its first trip was a short one, just ten feet in a little over a minute.

Spirit continued sending back spectacular pictures of the Martian landscape, along with scientific readings. Suddenly on January 21 *Spirit* stopped communicating with Earth. NASA communications engineers repeatedly tried to get the rover to send back a signal—any kind of signal—but got nothing in return. After more than a day of effort, *Spirit* responded with gibberish, date-stamped with the year 2038. Buried in the gibberish was valid information indicating that the rover's computer was constantly resetting itself, a process that was running down its batteries and causing its internal temperatures to rise to dangerous levels.

Spirit's computer malfunction appeared to threaten both missions because *Opportunity* contained the same equipment and software and presumably would also fail once it reached Mars. Uppermost in the minds of all NASA officials were previous failures of missions to Mars, including the loss of the European *Beagle 2* rover less than a month earlier and the failure of two NASA missions in 1999, the *Climate Orbiter* and the *Polar Lander*.

Engineers were still working frantically to reset *Spirit*'s computer code by long distance when *Opportunity* landed on schedule on January 24. *Opportunity* landed just fifteen miles from the dead center of its target range, in the Eagle crater in the Meridiani plain. After bouncing several times on the surface, *Opportunity* came to rest amid a pile of rocks. The rover's first photographs, showing an exposed slice of bedrock on the slope of a small crater, excited scientists, who had never had a close-up view of the Martian bedrock.

By January 29 engineers decided *Spirit* was recovered enough to resume some of its scientific missions, and they instructed the robot to take pictures of some of the nearby rocks, along with readings that two of its scientific instruments had taken of a rock dubbed Adirondack. *Opportunity* was not plagued by the same airbag problem that delayed *Spirit*, and it rolled off its lander on January 31. Initial readings from *Opportunity*'s instruments indicated that its landing site was rich in crystalline hematite, the water-indicating mineral that was a key goal of both rover missions. NASA announced on February 6 that *Spirit* once again appeared "healthy," its computer having been purged of thousands of files that had clogged the rover's system.

The Rovers' First Observations

The first major discovery of the joint mission was announced on March 2, when NASA said rocks at the *Opportunity*'s home, the Eagle crater, showed signs of past water. "Liquid water once flowed through these rocks. It changed their texture, and it changed their chemistry," Cornell University professor Steve Squyres, the principal investigator for the scientific instruments on the rovers, said. "We've been able to read the tell-tale clues the water left behind, giving us confidence in that conclusion." Scientists pointed in particular to pictures of a rock they called El Capitan because its shape was similar to that of the famed formation in Yosemite National Park. The rock contained features, such as pitting, that likely were caused by the presence of water, NASA said.

Each rover was scheduled to work on Mars for ninety Martian days (equal to about ninety-two Earth days), which meant their original missions were accomplished in April. With both rovers still healthy and functioning at peak capacity, NASA announced in April that the rovers had successfully met all their objectives, so their missions would be extended through September. Engineers and scientists continued sending instructions to the rovers and receiving photographs and scientific readings in response. NASA in mid-September extended the missions for another six months, provided that the machines kept working properly and sending back valuable information.

Both rovers experienced mechanical problems as their missions progressed. For *Spirit*, the most serious problem was that one of its six hollow wheels began to show signs of wear. *Opportunity* experienced problems with its rock abrasion tool, which extracted samples from rocks, and with a cable on its arm that carried a microscopic camera. Both rovers also were idle for twelve days in September because the position of the sun interfered with radio transmissions between Mars and Earth.

NASA took its biggest gamble of the year on June 8 when it sent *Opportunity* into a crater, informally dubbed Endurance, the size of a football stadium. There was a risk the rover would not be able to climb back out again, but scientists were eager to get a close-up look at exposed layers of rock that *Opportunity* had photographed within the crater. NASA's plan was to have *Opportunity* explore the rock for a few days, then head back out of the crater. The rover kept finding more layers of exposed rock, however, and so its masters kept urging it on, deeper into the crater. By September, scientists began worrying that *Opportunity* might get stuck in the crater, and they plotted an exit strategy. For a while it appeared that planning might have come too late; by late November *Opportunity* had reached an apparent impasse, unable to find any acceptable route out of the crater. After several weeks of work, NASA eventually found a route, and *Opportunity* climbed back onto the plain surrounding the crater on December 12.

Spirit, meanwhile, spent its time examining layers of rocks in an area NASA called the Columbia Hills. Scientists announced in November that *Spirit* had discovered sedimentary layers of rock that had been formed either of volcanic ash or dust thrown up by the impact of a meteor. Whatever the original source, the rock layers showed clear evidence of past presence of water, NASA said.

On December 3 the journal *Science* published the first detailed scientific studies from the rovers' initial three-month missions. Eleven reports, written by a total of 122 scientists, described evidence that, billions of years ago, both parts of Mars explored by the rovers contained significant amounts of water. While highly salty and acidic, the water might have sustained some form of life, the scientists said. Even so, they added, no direct evidence had yet been found that any kind of life ever existed on Mars.

The Fate of the *Beagle 2*

The successes of the two rovers served as a bitter reminder for European scientists of the failure of their own attempt to land a robot on Mars. On December 19, 2003, the *Beagle 2* robot was ejected from an orbiter, the *Mars Express*, and was intended to land on Mars on Christmas day. *Beagle 2* was never heard from again, despite frantic efforts by European and U.S. space officials to contact it. On February 11 the European Space Agency and the British National Space Center—which cosponsored the mission—gave up the rover as lost.

The cosponsors conducted an inquiry into the loss of *Beagle 2* but refused to make public any conclusions of what went wrong and why. On May 24, 2004, the two agencies published a set of recommendations for similar missions in the future. Many observers drew conclusions from the recommendations that the project had not been managed carefully enough and that the various technical components of the mission should have been more rigorously tested.

A committee of the British House of Commons on November 2 made public a report saying the mission had been endangered by an "amateurish" management arrangement and lack of funding. Government agencies wanted a project "on the cheap," committee chairman Ian Gibson said. "As a result, the scientists had to go chasing celebrities for sponsorship when they might have been testing rockets," he added.

The loss of the *Beagle 2* did not directly affect the *Mars Express* orbiter, which continued its mission of taking three-dimensional photographs and other scientific readings of the planet. The orbiter sent back numerous observations during 2004, including a finding that one-time lakes on Mars left behind deep layers of salt deposits. On December 22 scientists published photographs from *Mars Express* suggesting the possible presence of active volcanoes on Mars. The scientists said some Martian volcanoes showed signs of geological activity as recently as 4 million years ago, indicating that the volcanoes might still be active.

Other Space Findings

The year was a rich one for other discoveries about space, including:

- The *Cassini* spacecraft on December 24 sent a robot, called *Huygens*, on a mission that was to end with a crash-landing on Titan, a giant moon of the planet Saturn. *Huygens*'s mission was to collect and send back information on Titan's thick atmosphere and surface, which had never been observed.

Cassini began orbiting Saturn on June 30 and sent back detailed observations of the planet's famed rings before focusing its attention on Titan in late October. One of *Cassini*'s first findings was that Titan's atmosphere appeared to rotate faster than the moon; this also was the case with the planet Venus. A joint venture between NASA, the European Space Agency, and the Italian Space Agency, *Cassini* was to continue exploring Saturn and its vicinity for another three years.

- Two teams of astronomers announced early in the year that they had found evidence of galaxies that appeared to be the most distant objects ever identified in space. The first announcement came February 16 from U.S. astronomers who said images from the Hubble space telescope and giant telescopes in Hawaii had provided evidence of a faint galaxy, much smaller than the Milky Way, 13 billion light-years from Earth. Then on March 2 a team of French and Swiss astronomers said they had identified another galaxy 13.23 billion light-years from Earth. The latter discovery was based on images from a European telescope in Chile, along with those from Hubble and the Hawaii telescope.
- The most distant object discovered so far in the solar system was announced on March 16. Called Sedna, after an Inuit goddess, the object was said by scientists at the California Institute of Technology to have an orbit that took it as far as 84 billion miles from the sun. Astronomers called the object a "planetoid," indicating that it was not technically a planet. Sedna was larger than another distant subplanet, Quaoar, discovered in 2002.
- NASA's *Stardust* spacecraft began its two-year return trip to Earth early in January after collecting samples from a comet, Wild 2, about 230 million miles in space. *Stardust* passed through the comet's long tail, trapping thousands of particles of dust and sending photographs back to Earth. NASA scientists said they believed particles in the comet's tail could be left over from the early years of the solar system. *Stardust* was expected to return to Earth in 2006. Scientists who studied *Stardust*'s photographs said in June the comet appeared to have a surprising variety of features, including cliffs, peaks, and a large overhang. These features indicated that Wild 2 was more cohesive, and made of harder material, than scientists previously had thought was likely in such comets.

Following is the January 4, 2004, press release from NASA's Jet Propulsion Laboratory announcing the safe landing on Mars of the Spirit *rover.*

"*Spirit* Lands on Mars and Sends Postcards"

A traveling robotic geologist from NASA has landed on Mars and returned stunning images of the area around its landing site in Gusev Crater.

Mars Exploration Rover *Spirit* successfully sent a radio signal after the spacecraft had bounced and rolled for several minutes following its initial impact at 11:35 p.m. EST (8:35 p.m. Pacific Standard Time) on January 3.

"This is a big night for NASA," said NASA Administrator Sean O'Keefe. "We're back. I am very, very proud of this team, and we're on Mars."

Members of the mission's flight team at NASA's Jet Propulsion Laboratory, Pasadena, Calif., cheered and clapped when they learned that NASA's Deep Space Network had received a post-landing signal from *Spirit*. The cheering resumed about three hours later when the rover transmitted its first images to Earth, relaying them through NASA's Mars *Odyssey* orbiter.

"We've got many steps to go before this mission is over, but we've retired a lot of risk with this landing," said JPL's Pete Theisinger, project manager for the Mars Exploration Rover Project.

Deputy project manager for the rovers, JPL's Richard Cook, said, "We're certainly looking forward to *Opportunity* landing three weeks from now." *Opportunity* is *Spirit*'s twin rover, headed for the opposite side of Mars.

Dr. Charles Elachi, JPL director, said, "To achieve this mission, we have assembled the best team of young women and men this country can put together. Essential work was done by other NASA centers and by our industrial and academic partners.

Spirit stopped rolling with its base petal down, though that favorable position could change as airbags deflate, said JPL's Rob Manning, development manager for the rover's descent through Mars' atmosphere and landing on the surface.

NASA chose *Spirit*'s landing site, within Gusev Crater, based on evidence from Mars orbiters that this crater may have held a lake long ago. A long, deep valley, apparently carved by ancient flows of water, leads into Gusev. The crater itself is basin the size of Connecticut created by an asteroid or comet impact early in Mars' history. *Spirit*'s task is to spend the next three months exploring for clues in rocks and soil about whether the past environment at this part of Mars was ever watery and suitable to sustain life.

Spirit traveled 487 million kilometers (302.6 million) miles to reach Mars after its launch from Cape Canaveral Air Force Station, Fla., on June 10, 2003. Its twin, Mars Exploration Rover *Opportunity,* was launched July 7, 2003, and is on course for a landing on the opposite side of Mars on Jan. 25 (Universal Time and EST; 9:05 p.m. on Jan. 24, PST).

The flight team expects to spend more than a week directing *Spirit* through a series of steps in unfolding, standing up and other preparations necessary before the rover rolls off of its lander platform to get its wheels onto the ground. Meanwhile, *Spirit*'s cameras and a mineral-identifying infrared instrument will begin examining the surrounding terrain. That information will help engineers and scientists decide which direction to send the rover first. . . .

Source: U.S. National Aeronautics and Space Administration. Jet Propulsion Laboratory. "*Spirit* Lands on Mars and Sends Postcards." January 4, 2004. News release 2004–003. http://marsrovers.jpl.nasa.gov/newsroom/pressreleases/20040104a.html (accessed January 5, 2005).

President Bush on Missions to the Moon and Mars

January 14, 2004

INTRODUCTION

President George W. Bush on January 14, 2004, announced the most ambitious plan for manned space missions since 1961, when President John F. Kennedy first proposed to send astronauts to the moon. Kennedy's plan succeeded eight years later, when U.S. astronauts first set foot on the moon. The last mission to the moon took place in 1972. The only subsequent plan to return there was put forward in 1989 by Bush's father, President George H. W. Bush, who was unable to win sufficient congressional or public support for the proposal when its estimated cost soared. *(Background, Historic Documents of 1989, p. 649)*

The proposal came eleven days after NASA's *Spirit* rover landed on Mars. The rover's extraordinarily vivid photographs of the Martian surface generated intense interest and enthusiasm worldwide—enthusiasm the president clearly hoped to use to boost his space plan and possibly even his reelection campaign later in the year. Bush quickly appeared to lose interest in his space plan, however, failing even to mention it in his State of the Union address or to highlight it in his campaign speeches. Working behind the scenes later in the year, key Republicans ensured that Congress included nearly all the money Bush had requested for the first year of the space program—guaranteeing that work would start but leaving the plan's ultimate success to future years. *(Mars rovers, p. 1; State of the Union address, p. 17)*

Bold Plan, Few Details

A panel of experts that investigated the disintegration of the *Columbia* space shuttle in 2003—an accident that killed all seven astronauts on board—had bemoaned the lack of a long-term "vision" for the U.S. space program and called for a national debate on the matter. Within weeks of that panel's report, in August 2003, Bush administration officials began talking of a "new direction" for the space program, one that would focus on manned flights deeper into space while abandoning some existing programs, possibly including the space shuttle. White House officials said the *Columbia* investigation report provided the impetus for a new approach to space endeavors. The impending presidential election in 2004 offered a political reason for the president to advocate a bold venture that would make him appear to be a man of vision, his aides said. (Columbia *accident, Historic Documents of 2003, p. 631*)

Bush made his proposal public on January 14, speaking at NASA headquarters in Washington, D.C. Two astronauts aboard the International Space Station, orbiting 240 miles above the Earth's surface, joined Bush's presentation by television hookup: Commander C. Michael Foale, an American, and flight engineer Alexander Kaleri, a Russian.

Bush set a series of goals, beginning with long-term robotic missions on the moon no later than 2008. Astronauts would return to the moon as early as 2015 (but no later than 2020). The astronauts would build a permanent station there that would be used for scientific experiments and as a launching platform for further explorations deeper into space, starting with a manned visit to Mars. A key assumption of the plan was that enough water would be found on the moon for conversion to hydrogen fuel and oxygen for the subsequent missions. Bush gave no prospective dates for the first Mars mission.

"We may discover resources on the moon or Mars that will boggle the imagination, that will test our limits to dream," Bush said. "We do not know where this journey will end, yet we know this: Human beings are headed into the cosmos."

Bush sought to contrast his space plan with Kennedy's earlier initiative, which launched an expensive cold war-era "race" to the moon between the United States and the Soviet Union, one the United States won eight years later. "The vision I outline today is a journey, not a race, and I call on other nations to join us in this journey in a spirit of cooperation and friendship," Bush said.

A vague summary of Bush's plan, provided by the White House, gave no total cost estimates beyond an initial five-year projection of $12 billion, all but $1 billion of which would be diverted from other NASA programs. Officials said history dictated the decision not to give long-term cost estimates: The senior Bush's 1989 space plan had foundered primarily because its cost eventually was put at more than $400 billion, a figure that Congress found unacceptable.

Chief among the programs to be cut to make room for Bush's plan was the space shuttle. Bush proposed retiring the shuttle fleet after 2010, when the shuttles were to have finished their missions of ferrying equipment, people, and supplies to the International Space Station. The shuttle fleet would be replaced in 2014 with what NASA called a "crew exploration vehicle," which would carry astronauts to the moon. NASA officials said they had developed no specific plans for the vehicle and could not say, for example, whether it would be used repeatedly (as were the shuttles) or would be used just one time (as were earlier space vehicles in the 1960s and 1970s). At this early stage, "we have to avoid getting fond of a design," NASA administrator Sean O'Keefe told reporters.

Reaction

As could be expected, enthusiasts of manned space travel greeted Bush's plan warmly. Many scientists who wanted more emphasis on science-based missions (most of which were unmanned) were less enthusiastic, as were the general public and members of Congress who worried about the budget implications.

Typical of comments from those who wanted the return of manned missions was that of Eugene Cernan, the commander of the last Apollo mission to the moon in 1972. "No new technology has come out of NASA in twenty-five years," he told the *Chicago Tribune*. "Today, NASA was changed. We now have a goal in life." Several space-exploration advocates concurred, saying they hoped Bush's high-profile goal would energize the nation's engineering and scientific communities, just as earlier space programs had.

Many other observers were more skeptical, noting that Bush's plan was short on details and light on funding—the two elements that had bedeviled several previous, ambitious space plans. "The success rate for bold new visions in human spaceflight is about the same as that for missions to Mars, namely, two out of three fail," said Howard E. McCurdy, a historian of the space program at American University in Washington.

Other skeptics noted that the goals Bush articulated were so far in the future that the public—which would have to pay the costs—was unlikely to get excited any time soon about a return to space. Indeed, a *Washington Post*-ABC News poll conducted two days after Bush's announcement found more than 60 percent of those surveyed opposed the space plan as too expensive. The moon-Mars concept barely registered in opinion polls conducted during the election campaign, possibly because the president himself rarely mentioned it.

Bush took one step to help build support for his proposal, appointing a nine-member committee headed by retired astronaut Edward C. "Pete" Aldridge Jr. That panel, the President's Commission on Implementation of U.S. Space Exploration Policy, issued a report on June 16 calling for much of the government's space program to be transferred to commercial industry. Adopting some, but not all, of the commission's recommendations, O'Keefe on June 24 announced a reorganization of the space agency's bureaucracy. O'Keefe's changes included shrinking NASA's seven "strategic enterprises" down to four "mission directorates" dealing with aeronautics, exploration, operations, and science.

Many space scientists expressed concerns that money for NASA's long-planned scientific missions would be diverted to more expensive manned missions. The most detailed criticism of Bush's plan, from a scientific point of view, was published on November 22 by a committee of the American Physical Society, which represented the nation's academic and research physicists. That report said Bush's plan "has not been well defined, its long-term cost has not been adequately addressed, and no budgetary mechanisms have been established to avoid causing major irreparable damage to the agency's scientific program."

Bush's plan disappeared not only from public view but also from spending and policy debates on Capitol Hill, where many members worried about the potential costs. During the early stages of work on annual appropriations bills, most congressional panels reacted skeptically, trimming funding for the moon-Mars missions when the administration failed to provide specific details. That changed during the postelection "lame duck" session, however, when House Majority Leader Tom DeLay, a Texas Republican whose district abutted the Johnson Space Center, brought his influence to bear. Reportedly at DeLay's insistence, an omnibus appropriations bill (PL 108–447) for government agencies, cleared by Congress on November 20, approved nearly all of Bush's $16.24 billion request for NASA programs in fiscal year 2005, including early work on the moon-Mars plan. In a highly unusual step, the bill gave NASA "unrestrained" authority to transfer money within its accounts—in effect allowing the administration to switch priorities as the year progressed.

Space Shuttle and Hubble

An announcement by the NASA administrator, two days after Bush laid out his moon-Mars plan, generated significant controversy all through the rest of the year. O'Keefe said he was canceling a planned mission by the space shuttle in 2005 or 2006 to service the Hubble space telescope. The mission was supposed to install replacement batteries and gyroscopes, along with two major new instruments that cost more than $150 million to build. Without the replacement batteries and gyroscopes, Hubble was expected to stop functioning within a few years. Scientists said the giant telescope would fall back to Earth—probably by 2012—unless it could be fitted with a module that would guide it safely out of orbit.

O'Keefe said none of the three remaining shuttles could safely undertake the Hubble repair mission. Once the shuttles resumed flying, possibly in 2005, they would be assigned only to servicing the International Space Station until it was completed in 2010, he said. O'Keefe insisted that he made his decision solely on the basis of safety and that saving money for Bush's moon-Mars plan had not been a factor.

The unexpected cancellation of the Hubble-servicing mission shocked many of the nation's scientists, who had come to depend on the space telescope for clear, spectacular images of objects deep in space. Images from the Hubble had reshaped long-held assumptions about the universe, including such basic questions as its age. The Hubble photographs also became highly popular among the general public; millions of copies had been downloaded from the Internet as of early 2004. A replacement for the Hubble—the James Webb Telescope, named after a former NASA administrator—was not due in orbit until about 2012, meaning that scientists would be without a working deep-space telescope for about five years. *(Hubble background, Historic Documents of 2002, p. 212)*

Responding to criticism from Congress and the scientific community, O'Keefe agreed in May to investigate the possibility of servicing the Hubble by robots, rather than humans carried on a space shuttle. Such a mission would be the most complex task ever assigned to robots, but some scientists said it might be possible. As part of his review, O'Keefe asked the National Academy of Sciences to consider all the options. An academies panel issued an "interim report" on July 13 urging O'Keefe to reverse his decision because of the "compelling scientific returns" to be gained by keeping the Hubble in service. The panel expressed extreme doubts about the prospects for having robots fix the Hubble.

Despite that advice, O'Keefe in August said NASA would attempt to service the Hubble with robots. NASA in October awarded contracts to two firms to design and build a space ship and robots for such a mission.

The final report of the National Academies of Science, made public on December 8, again criticized the plan for a robotic mission. The report, "Assessment of Options for Extending the Life of the Hubble Space Telescope," strongly urged returning to NASA's original plan to service Hubble with a manned space shuttle mission. In essence, the report said a robotic mission to Hubble would be more likely to fail than a manned mission. Robots capable of replacing batteries and other components on the Hubble had not been designed as of 2004, the panel noted, making it improbable that a robotic mission could be launched in time to save the telescope. The panel also noted that NASA planned to resume the use of shuttles to ferry supplies and astronauts to the International Space Station; a mission to Hubble would be no more risky than one to the space station, the panel said.

In the meantime, NASA during the year revealed increasingly high price tags for fixing the problems with the shuttle fleet that had been identified after the *Columbia* disaster. NASA officials suggested in August that costs had risen about $900 million above the $1 billion initial projections given to Congress in late 2003. In September O'Keefe told a Senate committee that the total cost might be $2.2 billion, more than twice the initial amount. In October NASA announced that the shuttle flight had been moved back from March 2005 until at least May 2005.

O'Keefe submitted his resignation as NASA chief on December 13, saying he intended to pursue the job of chancellor of Louisiana State University in Baton Rouge. The university's board of supervisors hired O'Keefe four days later. Bush had not announced a replacement as of year's end.

In his final news conference as NASA administrator, on December 17, O'Keefe defended his original decision to scrap the shuttle mission to Hubble. O'Keefe also discounted the criticism from the panel of scientists, noting that many experts had suggested in the early 1990s that original design flaws on Hubble—discovered only after the telescope was in space—could never be corrected. "Well, I guess if we had listened to that wisdom, we would never have repaired it, or never given it the first [shuttle service] mission that it needed," O'Keefe said.

Following are excerpts from a speech by President George W. Bush, delivered at NASA headquarters in Washington, D.C., on January 14, 2004, in which he announced plans for a series of manned space missions, first to the moon and later to Mars and possibly deeper into space.

"Remarks at the National Aeronautics and Space Administration"

Thanks for the warm welcome. I'm honored to be with the men and women of NASA. I thank those of you who have come in person. I welcome those who are listening by video. This agency and the dedicated professionals who serve it have always reflected the finest values of our country, daring, discipline, ingenuity, and unity in the pursuit of great goals.

America is proud of our space program. The risktakers and visionaries of this agency have expanded human knowledge, have revolutionized our understanding of the universe, and produced technological advances that have benefited all of humanity.

Inspired by all that has come before and guided by clear objectives, today we set a new course for America's space program. We will give NASA a new focus and vision for future exploration. We will build new ships to carry man forward into the universe, to gain a new foothold on the moon, and to prepare for new journeys to worlds beyond our own.

I am comfortable in delegating these new goals to NASA, under the leadership of Sean O'Keefe. He's doing an excellent job. . . .

Two centuries ago, Meriwether Lewis and William Clark left St. Louis to explore the new lands acquired in the Louisiana Purchase. They made that journey in the spirit of discovery, to learn the potential of vast new territory and to chart a way for others to follow. America has ventured forth into space for the same reasons. We have undertaken space travel because the desire to explore and understand is part of our character.

And that quest has brought tangible benefits that improve our lives in countless ways. The exploration of space has led to advances in weather forecasting, in communications, in computing, search and rescue technology, robotics, and electronics. Our investment in space exploration helped to create our satellite telecommunications network and the Global Positioning System. Medical technologies that help prolong life, such as the imaging processing used in CAT scanners and MRI machines, trace their origins to technology engineered for the use in space.

Our current programs and vehicles for exploring space have brought us far, and they have served us well. The space shuttle has flown more than a hundred missions. It has been used to conduct important research and to increase the sum of human knowledge. Shuttle crews and the scientists and engineers who support them have helped build the International Space Station.

Telescopes, including those in space, have revealed more than 100 planets in the last decade alone. Probes have shown us stunning images of the rings of Saturn and the outer planets of our solar system. Robotic explorers have found evidence of water, a key ingredient for life, on Mars and on the moons of Jupiter. At this very hour, the Mars Exploration Rover *Spirit* is searching for evidence of life beyond the Earth.

Yet for all these successes, much remains for us to explore and to learn. In the past 30 years, no human being has set foot on another world or ventured farther upward into space than 386 miles, roughly the distance from Washington, D.C., to Boston, Massachusetts. America has not developed a new vehicle to advance human exploration in space in nearly a quarter-century. It is time for America to take the next steps.

Today I announce a new plan to explore space and extend a human presence across our solar system. We will begin the effort quickly, using existing programs and personnel. We'll make steady progress, one mission, one voyage, one landing at a time.

Our first goal is to complete the International Space Station by 2010. We will finish what we have started. We will meet our obligations to our 15 international partners on this project. We will focus our future research aboard the station on the long-term effects of space travel on human biology. The environment of space is hostile to human beings. Radiation and weightlessness pose dangers to human health, and we have much to learn about their long-term effects before human crews can venture through the vast voids of space for months at a time. Research onboard the station and here on Earth will help us better understand and overcome the obstacles that limit exploration. Through these efforts, we will develop the skills and techniques necessary to sustain further space exploration.

To meet this goal, we will return the space shuttle to flight as soon as possible, consistent with safety concerns and the recommendations of the Columbia Accident Investigation Board. The shuttle's chief purpose over the next several years will be to help finish assembly of the International Space Station. In 2010, the space shuttle, after nearly 30 years of duty, will be retired from service.

Our second goal is to develop and test a new spacecraft, the crew exploration vehicle, by 2008 and to conduct the first manned mission no later than 2014. The crew exploration vehicle will be capable of ferrying astronauts and scientists to the space station after the shuttle is retired. But the main purpose of this spacecraft will be to carry astronauts beyond our orbit to other worlds. This will be the first spacecraft of its kind since the *Apollo Command Module.*

Our third goal is to return to the moon by 2020, as the launching point for missions beyond. Beginning no later than 2008, we will send a series of robotic missions to the lunar surface to research and prepare for future human exploration. Using the crew exploration vehicle, we will undertake extended human missions to the moon as early as 2015, with the goal of living and working there for increasingly extended periods of time. Eugene Cernan, who is with us today, the last man to set foot on the lunar surface, said this as he left, "We leave as we came, and God willing as we shall return, with peace and hope for all mankind." America will make those words come true.

Returning to the moon is an important step for our space program. Establishing an extended human presence on the moon could vastly reduce the costs of further space exploration, making possible ever more ambitious missions. Lifting heavy spacecraft and fuel out of the Earth's gravity is expensive. Spacecraft assembled and provisioned on the moon could escape its far lower gravity using far less energy, and thus, far less cost. Also, the moon is home to abundant resources. Its soil contains raw materials that might be harvested and processed into rocket fuel or breathable air. We can use our time on the moon to develop and test new approaches and technologies and systems that will allow us to function in other, more challenging environments. The moon is a logical step toward further progress and achievement.

With the experience and knowledge gained on the moon, we will then be ready to take the next steps of space exploration, human missions to Mars and to worlds beyond. Robotic missions will serve as trailblazers, the advanced guard to the unknown. Probes, landers, and other vehicles of this kind continue to prove their worth, sending spectacular images and vast amounts of data back to Earth. Yet the human thirst for knowledge ultimately cannot be satisfied by even the most vivid pictures or the most detailed measurements. We need to see and examine and touch for ourselves. And only human beings are capable of adapting to the inevitable uncertainties posed by space travel.

As our knowledge improves, we'll develop new power generation propulsion, life support, and other systems that can support more distant travels. We do not know where this journey will end, yet we know this: Human beings are headed into the cosmos.

And along this journey, we'll make many technological breakthroughs. We don't know yet what those breakthroughs will be, but we can be certain they'll come and that our efforts will be repaid many times over. We may discover resources on the moon or Mars that will boggle the imagination, that will test our limits to dream. And the fascination generated by further exploration will inspire our young people to study math and science and engineering and create a new generation of innovators and pioneers.

This will be a great and unifying mission for NASA, and we know that you'll achieve it. I have directed Administrator O'Keefe to review all of NASA's current spaceflight and exploration activities and direct them toward the goals I have outlined. I will also form a commission of private and public sector experts to advise on implementing the vision that I've outlined today. This commission will report to me within 4 months of its first meeting. I'm today naming former Secretary of the Air Force Pete Aldridge to be the chair of the commission. Thank you for being here today, Pete. He has tremendous experience in the Department of Defense and the aerospace industry. He is going to begin this important work right away.

We'll invite other nations to share the challenges and opportunities of this new era of discovery. The vision I outline today is a journey, not a race, and I call on other nations to join us on this journey, in a spirit of cooperation and friendship.

Achieving these goals requires a long-term commitment. NASA's current 5-year budget is $86 billion. Most of the funding we need for the new endeavors will come from reallocating $11 billion within that budget. We need some new resources, however. I will call upon Congress to increase NASA's budget by roughly a billion dollars, spread out over the next 5 years. This increase, along with refocusing of our space agency, is a solid beginning to meet the challenges and the goals that we set today.

It's only a beginning. Future funding decisions will be guided by the progress we make in achieving these goals.

We begin this venture knowing that space travel brings great risks. The loss of the Space Shuttle *Columbia* was less than one year ago. Since the beginning of our space program, America has lost 23 astronauts and one astronaut from an allied nation, men and women who believed in their mission and accepted the dangers. As one family member said, "The legacy of *Columbia* must carry on—for the benefit of our children and yours." *Columbia*'s crew did not turn away from the challenge, and neither will we.

Mankind is drawn to the heavens for the same reason we were once drawn into unknown lands and across the open sea. We choose to explore space because doing so improves our lives and lifts our national spirit. So let us continue the journey.

May God bless.

Source: U.S. Executive Office of the President. "Remarks at the National Aeronautics and Space Administration." *Weekly Compilation of Presidential Documents* 40, no. 3 (January 19, 2004): 66–68. www.gpoaccess.gov/wcomp/v40no3.html (accessed January 6, 2005).

State of the Union Address and Democratic Response

January 20, 2004

INTRODUCTION

In 2003 President George W. Bush used his annual State of the Union address to strengthen his case for going to war in Iraq. In 2004 he used the occasion to start shaping the campaign stump speech that in November would help him win a closely contested election to a second term in office.

In a near hour-long speech interrupted frequently by applause and standing ovations from GOP lawmakers, Bush sought to project an image of a strong president leading the nation, contrasting himself with the seven Democratic presidential contenders whose attacks on each other and on the president were driving up negative poll ratings. According to several White House aides, the speech was deliberately scheduled for the night after the Iowa caucuses to refocus people's attention away from the contest for the Democratic presidential nomination. One Republican close to the Bush campaign told the *New York Times* that the timing of the State of the Union was designed "to get people to focus on the president's positive agenda after two weeks of people beating his brains in and criticizing every aspect of his policies."

How well the strategy succeeded was debatable. The surprisingly strong victory of Massachusetts senator John Kerry in the Iowa caucus and the almost total collapse of former Vermont governor John Dean's campaign kept attention riveted on the Democratic race. But the State of the Union speech gave the president's campaign an opportunity to try out several themes that would form the foundation of his campaign message. The speech also gave Bush an opportunity to challenge many of the criticisms the Democrats were lodging against him, particularly on his handling of the war and the economy. Although he never used the word *Democrats,* they were clearly whom Bush meant when he described "some in this chamber" and "critics" who voted against the Iraq war and to "skeptics" of his domestic policies, including "defenders of the status quo" on education.

"We have faced serious challenges together—and now we face a choice," Bush told the lawmakers gathered in the chamber of the House of Representatives—and the estimated 60 million Americans watching the nationally televised speech. "We can go forward with confidence and resolve—or we can turn back to the dangerous illusion that terrorists are not plotting and outlaw regimes are no threat to us. We can press on with economic growth and reforms in education and Medicare—or we can turn back to the old policies and old divisions. We have not come all this way—through tragedy, and trial, and war—only to falter and leave our work unfinished."

Delivering a Calculated Message

Virtually every modern State of the Union speech has been a thinly veiled political message, with the president touting his and his party's accomplishments while deflecting attention from controversial policies and actions. Bush's speech was all of that intensified. Stephen Hess, a former staff aide to Republican presidents and a longtime watcher of presidents, said the speech was "more of a campaign speech" than he had ever before heard in a State of the Union address.

The president laid out a list of accomplishments that he said made the world safer and the American economy stronger—among them the fall of Iraqi dictator Saddam Hussein, continuing success in hunting down and capturing or killing terrorists around the globe, substantial tax cuts that Bush said gave Americans more control of their money, an overhaul of Medicare to help pay for prescription drug costs for seniors, and a revamping of federal education aid to ensure that—in the president's words—no child is left behind.

In emphasizing themes that registered as the highest priorities of voters in opinion polls, Bush glossed over or ignored issues that troubled many Americans. He spoke with pride of Saddam's capture but skirted the administration's failure to find weapons of mass destruction in Iraq, the existence of which he had used to justify the U.S. invasion of that country in March 2003. Nor did he mention Osama bin Laden, the al Qaeda leader responsible for the September 11, 2001, attacks on the World Trade Center and the Pentagon. Bush had vowed to hunt down bin Laden, but the terrorist had so far eluded capture and was thought to be hiding somewhere along the Afghan-Pakistani border.

While the president acknowledged Libyan leader Muammar Qaddafi for voluntarily giving up his weapons of mass destruction, he made only passing reference to North Korea and Iran. In his 2002 speech the president had said that Iraq, Iran, and Korea comprised an "axis of evil" that threatened the United States and the rest of the world because of their support for terrorism and their efforts to acquire weapons of mass destruction. Diplomatic efforts to persuade North Korea and Iran to abandon their weapons programs made little headway during the year. *(Libya, p. 168; North Korea, p. 323; 2002 speech, Historic Documents of 2002, p. 33)*

The speech was also notable for other subjects the president did not discuss. The Israeli Palestinian conflict was not mentioned at all, even though most experts said there could be no lasting peace or democracy in the Middle East until that troublesome issue was resolved. The president also made no mention of AIDS; in 2003 Bush's request for $15 billion over five years to fund anti-AIDS programs in Africa and the Caribbean was one of the most dramatic moments of his state of the union speech. Nor did the president mention an ambitious plan to build a manned space base on the moon and eventually to send humans to Mars. Formally announced just a week earlier, that initiative had been panned by Democrats and Republicans in Congress and had met with little enthusiasm by the public. *(Space missions, p. 3; AIDS, p. 429; Palestinian-Israeli conflict, p. 806; 2003 speech, Historic Documents of 2003, p. 18)*

The War in Iraq

On those subjects the president did discuss, he appeared to be honing the pattern, and the patter, that he would use throughout the election campaign. Bush, for example, sought to portray the war in Iraq as an integral part of the U.S.

post–9/11 war on terror. He reminded his listeners that the United States was "on the offensive" against terrorists, who had "started this war" when they attacked the country in 2001, and against those who harbored terrorists and could supply them with weapons of mass destruction. He declared that, with the collapse of the Iraqi regime and the December capture of Saddam Hussein, the Iraqi people were free and preparing for a transition to democracy. He said America would never be intimidated by insurgents battling the U.S. occupation forces, whom he described as "violent Saddam supporter . . . joined by foreign terrorists," that were battling the U.S. occupation forces. *(Saddam's capture, Historic Documents of 2003, p. 1189)*

Bush refused to acknowledge the failure to find any weapons of mass destruction in Iraq. Instead, using careful phrasing to imply that such weapons had been in the country, he said searchers had "identified dozens of weapons of mass destruction-related program activities and significant amounts of equipment that Iraq concealed from the United Nations." At the same time, he sought to shift the administration's justification for invading Iraq from finding and destroying Saddam's weapons of mass destruction to ending the regime of a brutal dictator who had killed many of his own citizens. "For all who love freedom and peace, the world without Saddam Hussein's regime is a better and safer place," he said. Preserving Iraqi freedom and the country's move toward democracy was a theme that Bush would retreat to again and again throughout the year, even in the face of a growing insurgency in Iraq that threatened the stability of the country and the security of Iraqi citizens.

On another issue that would arise repeatedly on the campaign trail, Bush suggested that those who complained that the administration had acted unilaterally in Iraq were ill informed. "Some critics have said our duties in Iraq must be internationalized," the president said with a hint of derision. "This particular criticism is hard to explain to our partners in Britain, Australia, Japan, South Korea, the Philippines, Thailand, Italy, Spain, Poland, Denmark Hungary, Bulgaria, Ukraine, Romania, the Netherlands. . . ." At this point he was interrupted by cheers from the Republican side of the aisle. As those died down, he pressed on: ". . . Norway, El Salvador, and the 17 other countries that have committed troops to Iraq." At the same time, Bush made clear that that the United States would act to defend against threats without waiting for international approval. "America will never seek a permission slip to defend the security of our people," the president said.

Economy and Domestic Issues

On the domestic front, Bush's primary proposal was to make permanent the tax cuts Congress passed during the first three years of his term. The tax relief measures, which primarily benefited individual taxpayers and small businesses, totaled more than $2 trillion over ten years. Parts of those laws expired as early as 2005, while most of the cuts would expire at the end of 2010. (Expiration dates were included to hold down the long-term cost of the tax cuts and to give the legislation protection from filibusters in the Senate.) Bush credited the tax cuts with stimulating the economy and argued that permanent tax relief would result in even stronger economic growth and more job creation. "Unless you act, Americans face a tax increase. What the Congress has given, the Congress should not take away," Bush said, in a reference to Democratic calls to repeal at least some of the tax cuts received by the wealthy.

Making the tax cuts permanent was expected to cost at least $1.6 trillion over ten years. Given the high federal budget deficit, projected to reach $450 billion in fiscal 2004, and the opposition of many Democrats and some Republicans, Congress did not seriously consider the president's request. But Congress gave Bush the next best thing. Six weeks before the election it voted to extend through 2010 several popular tax cuts, including lower tax brackets, relief from the so-called marriage penalty, and an increase in the child tax credit. Although Democrats had initially opposed the extensions because they were not offset by any revenue raisers, election-year politics proved overwhelming. From the campaign trail, Kerry endorsed the tax cuts as a means to help the middle class that was being "squeezed by the weak Bush economy." Senate Minority Leader Tom Daschle of South Dakota, who was locked in a tight and ultimately unsuccessful fight for reelection, also voted for the bill.

On two other economic topics of concern to voters, Bush had little specific to offer. On the mounting budget deficit, Bush called on Congress to "cut wasteful spending and be wise with the people's money." On the loss of jobs in the first three years of his administration, Bush said only that job creation was important and that the nation "must continue to pursue an aggressive pro-growth economic agenda."*(Economy, p. 56)*

Having just signed a controversial overhaul of Medicare that provided prescription drug coverage to seniors, Bush offered few new initiatives on health care, relying instead on past proposals, such as tax credits to help individuals purchase medical insurance. He asked Congress to make catastrophic health insurance premiums fully tax deductible for individuals who bought coverage as part of health savings accounts authorized in the Medicare overhaul measure. He repeated his call for limits on damages in medical malpractice lawsuits, contending that excessive awards were driving up health care costs and putting a strain on the federal budget. The House had passed a medical malpractice bill, but Democratic opposition blocked the measure in the closely divided Senate. Bush used that opposition to his advantage during the campaign against Kerry and his running mate, North Carolina senator John Edwards, a trial lawyer who had grown wealthy representing victims of medical malpractice.

One new initiative the president offered was a temporary worker program that would allow undocumented workers already in the United States to obtain three-year visas for jobs that employers found hard to fill. The proposal, intended among other things to help Bush's standing among Hispanics, met resistance from some Republicans who said it would reward workers for entering the country illegally and from some Democrats who said it did not go far enough. Congress did not give it serious consideration during the year.

Bush also vigorously defended the "No Child Left Behind" program, which required elementary and secondary schools to meet strict new testing and accountability standards to ensure that children were learning or face loss of their federal funding. Democrats had criticized Bush for not fully funding the program and thus leaving school districts and teachers without the means to achieve the new standards.

Social Values

President Bush used the State of the Union to reinforce his support for so-called traditional values, issues that were important to conservatives whose turnout was critical to Republicans in close elections—and would be a key factor in the Bush's victory in November. "The values we try to live by never change," Bush declared, in what would become a common theme of his election campaign. Bush proposed additional funding for drug testing in schools and a doubling of the federal funding for sexual abstinence programs in schools. Both programs were popular among many conservative families. Bush also called on professional sports to set an example for the nation's youth by ending the use of performance-enhancing steroids.

Bush issued his strongest statement to date against gay marriage, which many social conservatives had come to oppose as fervently as they opposed abortion. He stopped short of calling for a constitutional amendment defining marriage as the union of a man and a woman, but he declared that the nation "must defend the sanctity of marriage" and indicated that if "activist judges" continued to define marriage "by court order, without regard for the will of the people," the only recourse would be "the constitutional process." Bush was referring to a decision in November 2003 by the Massachusetts supreme court holding a state ban on gay marriage to be unconstitutional. *(Ruling, Historic Documents of 2003, p. 401)*

Although some conservatives expressed disappointment that Bush did not explicitly endorse a constitutional amendment banning gay marriage, most were pleased by his remarks. "I am thrilled, and our public is thrilled," said the Rev. Louis P. Sheldon of the Traditional Values Coalition. "While you have most of the Democratic candidates not supporting marriage in this emphatic way, it really leaves them on the wrong side of the issue."

In February, after a handful of cities began to allow gays to marry, Bush formally endorsed a constitutional ban on gay marriage. Republican leaders in both chambers of Congress forced votes on the issue, but neither chamber came close to the two-thirds majority required to approve a constitutional amendment. *(Gay marriage, p. 37)*

Democratic Response

The official Democratic response was given by the Democratic leaders in the House and Senate, who also sounded the campaign themes the party would run on. Rep. Nancy Pelosi of California spoke first, attacking bush for mishandling American security both at home and abroad. "The president led us into the Iraq war on the basis of unproven assertions without evidence," she said. "He embraced a radical doctrine of preemptive war unprecedented in our history; and he failed to build a true international coalition." Pelosi also said the administration had not done anywhere near enough to protect homeland security. She called for more funding to inspect cargo on ships and airplanes, to ensure the security of nuclear power and chemical plants, and to keep track of uranium and other materials that could be used in weapons of mass destruction. "We know what we must do to protect America," she said, "but this administration is failing to meet the challenge."

Pelosi was followed by Senator Daschle, who put forth the Democratic platform for improving the economy, providing quality education and affordable health care, and strengthening Social Security. Referring to the loss of American jobs to countries where wages were lower, Daschle called for policies that would support the manufacturing sector and create good jobs at decent wages for American workers. "America can't afford to keep rewarding the accumulation of wealth over the dignity of work," he declared. Daschle also called for legislation that would allow the importation of cheaper drugs from Canada and that would allow the federal government to negotiate lower drug prices for Medicare. Although the House passed a measure allowing some drug imports, splits among Republicans and resistan from the administration sidetracked the legislation in 2004. *(Drug imports, p. 981; Medicare overhaul, Historic Documents of 2003, p. 1119)*

Following are the texts of the State of the Union address, delivered January 20, 2004, by President George W. Bush to a joint session of Congress and the Democratic response by House Minority Leader Nancy Pelosi of California and Senate Minority Leader Tom Daschle of South Dakota.

President Bush's 2004 State of the Union Address

To the Congress of the United States:

Mr. Speaker, Vice President [Dick] Cheney, Members of Congress, distinguished guests, and fellow citizens:

America this evening is a Nation called to great responsibilities. And we are rising to meet them.

As we gather tonight, hundreds of thousands of American service men and women are deployed across the world in the war on terror. By bringing hope to the oppressed, and delivering justice to the violent, they are making America more secure.

Each day, law enforcement personnel and intelligence officers are tracking terrorist hreats; analysts are examining airline passenger lists; the men and women of our new Iomeland Security Department are patrolling our coasts and borders. And their vignce is protecting America.

Americans are proving once again to be the hardest working people in the world. American economy is growing stronger. The tax relief you passed is working.

onight, Members of Congress can take pride in great works of compassion and reform keptics had thought impossible. You are raising the standards of our public schools; u are giving our senior citizens prescription drug coverage under Medicare.

have faced serious challenges together—and now we face a choice. We can go with confidence and resolve—or we can turn back to the dangerous illusion orists are not plotting and outlaw regimes are no threat to us. We can press conomic growth, and reforms in education and Medicare—or we can turn e old policies and old divisions.

not come all this way—through tragedy, and trial, and war—only to fale our work unfinished. Americans are rising to the tasks of history, and the same of us. In their efforts, their enterprise, and their character, the ple are showing that the state of our Union is confident and strong.

t responsibility is the active defense of the American people. Twentyave passed since September 11, 2001—over 2 years without an attack il—and it is tempting to believe that the danger is behind us. That ndable, comforting—and false. The killing has continued in Bali, a, Riyadh, Mombassa, Jerusalem, Istanbul, and Baghdad. The terrorists continue to plot against America and the civilized world. And by our will and courage, this danger will be defeated.

Inside the United States, where the war began, we must continue to give homeland security and law enforcement personnel every tool they need to defend us. And one of those essential tools is the PATRIOT Act, which allows Federal law enforcement to better share information, to track terrorists, to disrupt their cells, and to seize their assets. For years, we have used similar provisions to catch embezzlers and drug traffickers. If these methods are good for hunting criminals, they are even more important for hunting terrorists. Key provisions of the PATRIOT Act are set to expire next year. The terrorist threat will not expire on that schedule. Our law enforcement needs this vital legislation to protect our citizens—you need to renew the PATRIOT Act.

America is on the offensive against the terrorists who started this war. Last March, Khalid Shaikh Mohammed, a mastermind of September 11th, awoke to find himself in the custody of U.S. and Pakistani authorities. Last August 11th brought the capture of the terrorist Hambali, who was a key player in the attack in Indonesia that killed over 200 people. We are tracking al-Qaida around the world—and nearly two-thirds of their known leaders have now been captured or killed. Thousands of very skilled and determined military personnel are on a manhunt, going after the remaining killers who hide in cities and caves—and, one by one, we will bring the terrorists to justice.

As part of the offensive against terror, we are also confronting the regimes that harbor and support terrorists, and could supply them with nuclear, chemical, or biological weapons. The United States and our allies are determined: We refuse to live in the shadow of this ultimate danger.

The first to see our determination were the Taliban, who made Afghanistan the primary training base of al-Qaida killers. As of this month, that country has a new constitution, guaranteeing free elections and full participation by women. Businesses are opening, healthcare centers are being established, and the boys and girls of Afghanistan are back in school. With help from the new Afghan Army, our coalition is leading aggressive raids against surviving members of the Taliban and al-Qaida. The men and women of Afghanistan are building a nation that is free, and proud, and fighting terror—and America is honored to be their friend.

Since we last met in this chamber, combat forces of the United States, Great Britain, Australia, Poland, and other countries enforced the demands of the United Nations, ended the rule of Saddam Hussein—and the people of Iraq are free. Having broken the Baathist regime, we face a remnant of violent Saddam supporters. Men who ran away from our troops in battle are now dispersed and attack from the shadows.

These killers, joined by foreign terrorists, are a serious, continuing danger. Yet we are making progress against them. The once all-powerful ruler of Iraq was found in a hole, and now sits in a prison cell. Of the top 55 officials of the former regime, we have captured or killed 45. Our forces are on the offensive, leading over 1,600 patrol a day, and conducting an average of 180 raids every week. We are dealing with thes thugs in Iraq, just as surely as we dealt with Saddam Hussein's evil regime.

The work of building a new Iraq is hard, and it is right. And America has alwa been willing to do what it takes for what is right. Last January, Iraq's only law w the whim of one brutal man. Today our coalition is working with the Iraqi Gover ing Council to draft a basic law, with a bill of rights. We are working with Iraqis a the United Nations to prepare for a transition to full Iraqi sovereignty by the end

June. As democracy takes hold in Iraq, the enemies of freedom will do all in their power to spread violence and fear. They are trying to shake the will of our country and our friends—but the United States of America will never be intimidated by thugs and assassins. The killers will fail, and the Iraqi people will live in freedom.

Month by month, Iraqis are assuming more responsibility for their own security and their own future. And tonight we are honored to welcome one of Iraq's most respected leaders: the current President of the Iraqi Governing Council, Adnan Pachachi. Sir, America stands with you and the Iraqi people as you build a free and peaceful nation.

Because of American leadership and resolve, the world is changing for the better. Last month, the leader of Libya voluntarily pledged to disclose and dismantle all of his regime's weapons of mass destruction programs, including a uranium enrichment project for nuclear weapons. Colonel Qadhafi correctly judged that his country would be better off, and far more secure, without weapons of mass murder. Nine months of intense negotiations involving the United States and Great Britain succeeded with Libya, while 12 years of diplomacy with Iraq did not. And one reason is clear: for diplomacy to be effective, words must be credible—and no one can now doubt the word of America.

Different threats require different strategies. Along with nations in the region, we are insisting that North Korea eliminate its nuclear program. America and the international community are demanding that Iran meet its commitments and not develop nuclear weapons. America is committed to keeping the world's most dangerous weapons out of the hands of the world's most dangerous regimes.

When I came to this rostrum on September 20, 2001, I brought the police shield of a fallen officer, my reminder of lives that ended, and a task that does not end. I ave to you and to all Americans my complete commitment to securing our country d defeating our enemies. And this pledge, given by one, has been kept by many. u in the Congress have provided the resources for our defense, and cast the diffi- votes of war and peace. Our closest allies have been unwavering. America's intel- ce personnel and diplomats have been skilled and tireless.

d the men and women of the American military—they have taken the hardest We have seen their skill and courage in armored charges, and midnight raids, nely hours on faithful watch. We have seen the joy when they return, and felt ow when one is lost. I have had the honor of meeting our service men and ut many posts, from the deck of a carrier in the Pacific, to a mess hall in Bagh- ny of our troops are listening tonight. And I want you and your families to erica is proud of you. And my Administration, and this Congress, will give ources you need to fight and win the war on terror.

hat some people question if America is really in a war at all. They view re as a crime—a problem to be solved mainly with law enforcement and After the World Trade Center was first attacked in 1993, some of the dicted, tried, convicted, and sent to prison. But the matter was not set- rists were still training and plotting in other nations, and drawing up plans. After the chaos and carnage of September 11th, it is not enough nies with legal papers. The terrorists and their supporters declared war ates—and war is what they got.

hamber, and in our country, did not support the liberation of Iraq. often come from principled motives. But let us be candid about the consequences of leaving Saddam Hussein in power. We are seeking all the facts—already the Kay Report identified dozens of weapons of mass destruction-related program activities and significant amounts of equipment that Iraq concealed from the United Nations. Had we failed to act, the dictator's weapons of mass destruction programs would continue to this day. Had we failed to act, Security Council resolutions on Iraq would have been revealed as empty threats, weakening the United Nations and encouraging defiance by dictators around the world. Iraq's torture chambers would still be filled with victims—terrified and innocent. The killing fields of Iraq—where hundreds of thousands of men, women, and children vanished into the sands—would still be known only to the killers. For all who love freedom and peace, the world without Saddam Hussein's regime is a better and safer place.

Some critics have said our duties in Iraq must be internationalized. This particular criticism is hard to explain to our partners in Britain, Australia, Japan, South Korea, the Philippines, Thailand, Italy, Spain, Poland, Denmark, Hungary, Bulgaria, Ukraine, Romania, the Netherlands, Norway, El Salvador, and the 17 other countries that have committed troops to Iraq. As we debate at home, we must never ignore the vital contributions of our international partners, or dismiss their sacrifices. From the beginning, America has sought international support for operations in Afghanistan and Iraq, and we have gained much support. There is a difference, however, between leading a coalition of many nations, and submitting to the objections of a few. America will never seek a permission slip to defend the security of our people.

We also hear doubts that democracy is a realistic goal for the greater Middle East, where freedom is rare. yet it is mistaken, and condescending, to assume that whole cultures and great religions are incompatible with liberty and self-government. I believe that God has planted in every heart the desire to live in freedom. And even when that desire is crushed by tyranny for decades, it will rise again.

As long as the Middle East remains a place of tyranny, despair, and anger, it will continue to produce men and movements that threaten the safety of America and our friends. So America is pursuing a forward strategy of freedom in the greater Middle East. We will challenge the enemies of reform, confront the allies of terror, and expect a higher standard from our friends. To cut through the barriers of hateful propaganda, the Voice of America and other broadcast services are expanding their programming in Arabic and Persian—and soon, a new television service will begin providing reliable news and information across the region. I will send you a proposal to double the budget of the National Endowment for Democracy, and to focus its new work on the development of free elections, free markets, free press, and free labor unions in the Middle East. And above all, we will finish the historic work of democracy in Afghanistan and Iraq, so those nations can light the way for others, and help transform a troubled part of the world.

America is a Nation with a mission—and that mission comes from our most basic beliefs. We have no desire to dominate, no ambitions of empire. Our aim is a democratic peace—a peace founded upon the dignity and rights of every man and woman. America acts in this cause with friends and allies at our side, yet we understand our special calling: This great Republic will lead the cause of freedom.

In these last 3 years, adversity has also revealed the fundamental strengths of the American economy. We have come through recession, and terrorist attack, and corporate scandals, and the uncertainties of war. And because you acted to stimulate our economy with tax relief, this economy is strong, and growing stronger.

You ha'e doubled the child tax credit from $500 to $1,000, reduced the marriage penalty, ɔegun to phase out the death tax, reduced taxes on capital gains and stock dividends, cut taxes on small businesses, and you have lowered taxes for every American who pays income taxes.

mericans took those dollars and put them to work, driving this economy forward. The pace of economic growth in the third quarter of 2003 was the fastest in nearly 0 years. New home construction: the highest in almost 20 years. Home ownership rates: the higher ever. Manufacturing activity is increasing. Inflation is low. Interest rates are low. Exports are growing. Productivity is high. And jobs are on the rise.

These numbers confirm that the American people are using their money far better than Government would have—and you were right to return it.

America's growing economy is also a changing economy. As technology transforms the way almost every job is done, America becomes more productive, and workers need new skills. Much of our job growth will be found in high-skilled fields like health care and biotechnology. So we must respond by helping more Americans gain the skills to find good jobs in our new economy.

All skills begin with the basics of reading and math, which are supposed to be learned in the early grades of our schools. Yet for too long, for too many children, those skills were never mastered. By passing the No Child Left Behind Act, you have made the expectation of literacy the law of our country. We are providing more funding for our schools—a 36 percent increase since 2001. We are requiring higher standards. We are regularly testing every child on the fundamentals. We are reporting sults to parents, and making sure they have better options when schools are not perming. We are making progress toward excellence for every child.

But the status quo always has defenders. Some want to undermine the No Child Behind Act by weakening standards and accountability. Yet the results we require eally a matter of common sense: We expect third graders to read and do math at grade level—and that is not asking to much. Testing is the only way to identify elp students who are falling behind.

Nation will not go back to the days of simply shuffling children along from grade without them learning the basics. I refuse to give up on any child—and Child Left Behind Act is opening the door of opportunity to all of America's

same time, we must ensure that older students and adults can gain the skills to find work now. Many of the fastest growing occupations require strong cience preparation, and training beyond the high school level. So tonight series of measures called Jobs for the 21st Century. This program will prolp to middle- and high school students who fall behind in reading and Advanced Placement programs in low-income schools, and invite math ofessionals from the private sector to teach part-time in our high schools. er Pell Grants for students who prepare for college with demanding school. I propose increasing our support for America's fine commuthey can train workers for the industries that are creating the most these actions, we will help more and more Americans to join in the y of our country.

mportant, and so is job creation. We must continue to pursue and vth economic agenda.

Congress has some unfinished business on the issue of taxes. The tax reductions you passed are set to expire. Unless you act, the unfair tax on marriage will go back up. Unless you act, millions of families will be charged $300 more in Federal taxes for every child. Unless you act, small businesses will pay higher taxes. Unless you act, the death tax will eventually come back to life. Unless you act, Americans face a tax increase. What the Congress has given, the Congress should not take away: For the sake of job growth, the tax cuts you passed should be permanent.

Our agenda for jobs and growth must help small business owners and employees with relief from needless Federal regulation, and protect them from junk and frivolous lawsuits. Consumers and businesses need reliable supplies of energy to make our economy run—so I urge you to pass legislation to modernize our electricity system, promote conservation, and make America less dependent on foreign sources of energy. My Administration is promoting free and fair trade, to open up new markets for America's entrepreneurs, and manufacturers, and farmers, and to create jobs for America's workers. Younger workers should have the opportunity to build a nest egg by saving part of their Social Security taxes in a personal retirement account. We should make the Social Security system a source of ownership for the American people.

And we should limit the burden of Government on this economy by acting as good stewards of taxpayer dollars. In 2 weeks, I will send you a budget that funds the war, protects the homeland, and meets important domestic needs, while limiting the growth in discretionary spending to less than 4 percent. This will require that Congress focus on priorities, cut wasteful spending, and be wise with the people's money. By doing so, we can cut the deficit in half over the next 5 years.

Tonight I also ask you to reform our immigration laws, so they reflect our values and benefit our economy. I propose a new temporary worker program to match willing foreign workers with willing employers, when no Americans can be found to fill the job. This reform will be good for our economy—because employers will find needed workers in an honest and orderly system. A temporary worker program will help protect our homeland—allowing border patrol and law enforcement to focus on true threats to our national security. I oppose amnesty, because it would encourage further illegal immigration, and unfairly reward those who break our laws. My temporary worker program will preserve the citizenship path for those who respect the law, while bringing millions of hardworking men and women out from the shadows of American life.

Our Nation's healthcare system, like our economy, is also in a time of change. Amazing medical technologies are improving and saving lives. This dramatic progress has brought its own challenge, in the rising costs of medical care and health insurance. Members of Congress, we must work together to help control those costs and extend the benefits of modern medicine throughout our country.

Meeting these goals requires bipartisan effort—and 2 months ago, you showed the way. By strengthening Medicare and adding a prescription drug benefit, you kept a basic commitment to our seniors: You are giving them the modern medicine they deserve.

Starting this year, under the law you passed, seniors can choose to receive a drug discount card, saving them 10 to 25 percent off the retail price of most prescription drugs—and millions of low-income seniors can get an additional $600 to buy medicine. Beginning next year, seniors will have new coverage for preventive screenings against diabetes and heart disease, and seniors just entering Medicare can receive wellness exams.

In Janu ry of 2006, seniors can get prescription drug coverage under Medicare. For a month premium of about $35, most seniors who do not have that coverage today can exp ct to see their drug bills cut roughly in half. Under this reform, senior citizens ll be able to keep their Medicare just as it is, or they can choose a Medicare plar hat fits them best—just as you, as Members of Congress, can choose an insuran plan that meets your needs. And starting this year, millions of Americans will be e to save money tax-free for their medical expenses, in a health savings account.

I signed this measure proudly, and any attempt to limit the choices of our seniors, or to take away their prescription drug coverage under Medicare, will meet my veto.

On the critical issue of health care, our goal is to ensure that Americans can choose and afford private healthcare coverage that best fits their individual needs. To make insurance more affordable, Congress must act to address rapidly rising healthcare costs. Small businesses should be able to band together and negotiate for lower insurance rates, so they can cover more workers with health insurance—I urge you to pass Association Health Plans. I ask you to give lower-income Americans a refundable tax credit that would allow millions to buy their own basic health insurance. By computerizing health records, we can avoid dangerous medical mistakes, reduce costs, and improve care. To protect the doctor-patient relationship, and keep good doctors doing good work, we must eliminate wasteful and frivolous medical lawsuits. And tonight I propose that individuals who buy catastrophic healthcare coverage, as part of our new ealth savings accounts, be allowed to deduct 100 percent of the premiums from their xes.

A Government-run healthcare system is the wrong prescription. By keeping costs ler control, expanding access, and helping more Americans afford coverage, we will erve the system of private medicine that makes America's health care the best in vorld.

e are living in a time of great change—in our world, in our economy, and in e and medicine. Yet some things endure—courage and compassion, reverence tegrity, respect for differences of faith and race. The values we try to live by hange. And they are instilled in us by fundamental institutions, such as families, schools, and religious congregations. These institutions—the unseen pillars of n—must remain strong in America, and we will defend them.

ıst stand with our families to help them raise healthy, responsible children. it comes to helping children make right choices, there is work for all of us

ıe worst decisions our children can make is to gamble their lives and futures ur Government is helping parents confront this problem, with aggressive eatment, and law enforcement. Drug use in high school has declined by er the past 2 years. Four hundred thousand fewer young people are using ıan in the year 2001. In my budget, I have proposed new funding to gressive, community- based strategy to reduce demand for illegal drugs. our schools has proven to be an effective part of this effort. So tonight litional $23 million for schools that want to use drug testing as a tool lives. The aim here is not to punish children, but to send them this you, and we don't want to lose you.

n make right choices, they need good examples. Athletics play such n our society, but, unfortunately, some in professional sports are not setting much of an example. The use of performance-enhancing drugs like steroids in baseball, football, and other sports is dangerous, and it sends the wrong message—that there are shortcuts to accomplishment, and that performance is more important than character. So tonight I call on team owners, union representatives, coaches, and players to take the lead, to send the right signal, to get tough, and to get rid of steroids now.

To encourage right choices, we must be willing to confront the dangers young people face—even when they are difficult to talk about. Each year, about three million teenagers contract sexually transmitted diseases that can harm them, or kill them, or prevent them from ever becoming parents. In my budget, I propose a grassroots campaign to help inform families about these medical risks. We will double Federal funding for abstinence programs, so schools can teach this fact of life: Abstinence for young people is the only certain way to avoid sexually transmitted diseases. Decisions children make now can affect their health and character for the rest of their lives. All of us—parents, schools, government—must work together to counter the negative influence of the culture, and to send the right messages to our children.

A strong America must also value the institution of marriage. I believe we should respect individuals as we take a principled stand for one of the most fundamental, enduring institutions of our civilization. Congress has already taken a stand on this issue by passing the Defense of Marriage Act, signed in 1996 by President Clinton. That statute protects marriage under Federal law as the union of a man and a woman, and declares that one State may not redefine marriage for other States. Activist judges, however, have begun redefining marriage by court order, without regard for the will of the people and their elected representatives. On an issue of such great consequence, the people's voice must be heard. If judges insist on forcing their arbitrary will upon the people, the only alternative left to the people would be the constitutional process. Our Nation must defend the sanctity of marriage.

The outcome of this debate is important—and so is the way we conduct it. The same moral tradition that defines marriage also teaches that each individual has dignity and value in God's sight.

It is also important to strengthen our communities by unleashing the compassion of America's religious institutions. Religious charities of every creed are doing some of the most vital work in our country—mentoring children, feeding the hungry, taking the hand of the lonely. Yet government has often denied social service grants and contracts to these groups, just because they have a cross or Star of David or crescent on the wall. By Executive Order, I have opened billions of dollars in grant money to competition that includes faith-based charities. Tonight I ask you to codify this into law, so people of faith can know that the law will never discriminate against them again.

In the past, we have worked together to bring mentors to the children of prisoners, and provide treatment for the addicted, and help for the homeless. Tonight I ask you to consider another group of Americans in need of help. This year, some 600,000 inmates will be released from prison back into society. We know from long experience that if they can't find work, or a home, or help, they are much more likely to commit more crimes and return to prison. So tonight, I propose a 4-year, $300 million Prisoner Re-Entry Initiative to expand job training and placement services, to provide transitional housing, and to help newly released prisoners get mentoring, including from faith-based groups. America is the land of the second chance—and when the gates of the prison open, the path ahead should lead to a better life.

For all Americans, the last 3 years have brought tests we did not ask for, and achievements shared by all. By our actions, we have shown what kind of Nation we are. In grief, we found the grace to go on. In challenge, we rediscovered the courage and daring of a free people. In victory, we have shown the noble aims and good heart of America. And having come this far, we sense that we live in a time set apart.

I have been a witness to the character of the American people, who have shown calm in times of danger, compassion for one another, and toughness for the long haul. All of us have been partners in a great enterprise. And even some of the youngest understand that we are living in historic times. Last month a girl in Lincoln, Rhode Island, sent me a letter. It began, "Dear George W. Bush." "If there is anything you know, I Ashley Pearson age 10 can do to help anyone, please send me a letter and tell me what I can do to save our country." She added this P.S.: "If you can send a letter to the troops please put, 'Ashley Pearson believes in you.'"

Tonight, Ashley, your message to our troops has just been conveyed. And yes, you have some duties yourself. Study hard in school, listen to your mom and dad, help someone in need, and when you and your friends see a man or woman in uniform, say "thank you." And while you do your part, all of us here in this great chamber will do our best to keep you and the rest of America safe and free.

My fellow citizens, we now move forward, with confidence and faith. Our Nation is strong and steadfast. The cause we serve is right, because it is the cause of all mankind. The momentum of freedom in our world is unmistakable—and it is not carried forward by our power alone. We can trust in that greater power Who guides the unfolding of the years. And in all that is to come, we can know that His purposes are just and true. May God bless the United States of America. Thank you.

Source: U.S. Congress. House. *State of the Union Message: Message from the President of the United States Transmitting a Report on the State of the Union.* 108th Cong., 2nd sess., January 20, 2004. H. Doc. 108–144. http://purl.access.gpo.gov/GPO/LPS44731 (accessed December 16, 2004).

Democratic Response to the State of the Union Address

"A Question of Priorities"

Part 1: Protecting American Security at Home and Abroad By House Democratic Leader Nancy Pelosi

The state of our union is indeed strong, due to the spirit of the American people—the creativity, optimism, hard work, and faith of everyday Americans.

The State of the Union address should offer a vision that unites us as a people—and priorities that move us toward the best America. For inspiration, we look to our brave young men and women in uniform, especially those in Iraq and Afghanistan.

Their noble service reminds us of our mission as a nation—to build a future worthy of their sacrifice.

Tonight, from the perspective of ten years of experience on the Intelligence Committee working on national security issues, I express the Democrats' unbending determination to make the world safer for America—for our people, our interests and our ideals.

Iraq and Afghanistan

Democrats have an unwavering commitment to ensure that America's armed forces remain the best trained, best led, best equipped force for peace the world has ever known. Never before have we been more powerful militarily. But even the most powerful nation in history must bring other nations to our side to meet common dangers.

The President's policies do not reflect that. He has pursued a go-it-alone foreign policy that leaves us isolated abroad and that steals the resources we need for education and health care here at home.

The President led us into the Iraq war on the basis of unproven assertions without evidence; he embraced a radical doctrine of pre-emptive war unprecedented in our history; and he failed to build a true international coalition.

Therefore, American taxpayers are bearing almost all the cost—a colossal $120 billion and rising. More importantly, American troops are enduring almost all the casualties—tragically, 500 killed and thousands more wounded.

Making America Safer and More Secure

As a nation, we must show our greatness, not just our strength. America must be a light to the world, not just a missile.

Forty three years ago today, as a college student standing in the freezing cold outside this Capitol Building, I heard President Kennedy issue this challenge in his Inaugural Address: "My fellow citizens of the world," he said, "ask not what America will do for you, but what together we can do for the freedom of man."

There is great wisdom in that, but in it there is also greater strength for our country and the cause of a safer world.

Instead of alienating our allies, let us work with them and international institutions so that together we can prevent the proliferation of weapons of mass destruction and keep them out of the hands of terrorists.

Instead of billions of dollars in no-bid contracts for politically-connected firms such as Halliburton, and an insistence on American dominance in Iraq, let us share the burden and responsibility with others, so that together we can end the sense of American occupation and bring our troops home safely when their mission is completed.

Instead of the diplomatic disengagement that almost destroyed the Middle East peace process and aggravated the danger posed by North Korea, let us seek to forge agreements and coalitions—so that, together with others, we can address challenges before they threaten the security of the world.

Terrorism and Homeland Security

We must remain focused on the greatest threat to the security of the United States—the clear and present danger of terrorism. We know what we must do to protect America, but this Administration is failing to meet the challenge. Democrats have a better way to ensure our homeland security.

One hundred percent of containers coming into our ports or airports must be inspected. Today, only 3 percent are inspected. One hundred percent of chemical and nuclear plants in the United States must have high levels of security. Today, the Bush Administration has tolerated a much lower standard.

One hundred percent communication in real time is needed for our police officers, firefighters, and all our first responders to prevent or respond to a terrorist attack. Today, the technology is there, but the resources are not. One hundred percent of the enriched uranium and other material for weapons of mass destruction must be secured. Today, the Administration has refused to commit the resources necessary to prevent it from falling into the hands of terrorists.

America will be far safer if we reduce the chances of a terrorist attack in one of our cities than if we diminish the civil liberties of our own people.

The Armed Forces and Veterans

As a nation, we must do better to keep faith with our armed forces, their families and our veterans. Our men and women in uniform show their valor every day. On the battlefield, our troops pledge to leave no soldier behind. Here at home, we must leave no veteran behind. We must ensure their health care, their pensions, and their survivors' benefits.

'The Future of Our Children Is at Stake'

The year ahead offers great opportunity for progress and perhaps new perils still hidden in the shadows of an uncertain world. But you, the American people, have shown again and again that you are equal to any test. Now your example summons all of us in government, Republicans and Democrats, to a higher standard.

This is personal for all of us, in every community across this land. As a mother of five, and now as a grandmother of five, I came into government to help make the future brighter for all of America's children. As much as at any time in my memory, the future of our country and our children is at stake.

Democrats are committed to strengthening the state of our union—to reach for a safer, more prosperous America.

Together, let us make America work for all Americans—let us restore our rightful role of leadership in the world, working with others for "the freedom of man."

I'm now proud to introduce my colleague, the outstanding Senate Democratic leader, Tom Daschle.

Part 2: Building an Opportunity Society for the American People By Senate Democratic Leader Tom Daschle

Let there be no doubt: the state of our union is strong—stronger than the terrorists who seek to harm us and stronger than the challenges that confront us. At the same time, we know that our union can be stronger still.

The President spoke of great goals, and America should never hesitate to push the boundaries of exploration. But neither should we shrink from the great goal of creating a more perfect union here at home.

An Opportunity Society

In his speech, the President asked us to make permanent the tax cuts already passed. He asked us to create more tax shelters for the wealthy, and he asked us to use Social Security money to pay for it. For the last couple of weeks, I've been traveling through my home state of South Dakota, visiting the people and small towns that are America's backbone. And the folks I met were asking something, too: what about us? When do our priorities become America's priorities?

Rather than a society that restricts its rewards to a privileged few, we need an "opportunity society" that allows all Americans to succeed. Our "opportunity society" has at its foundation good jobs, a solid education and quality health care that is affordable and available. We believe that we have to honor the promises we've made to the millions of families who worked hard, played by the rules and have earned a retirement of dignity.

Jobs and the Economy

Our first challenge is to strengthen the economy—the right way. The true test of America's economic recovery is not measured simply in quarterly profit reports, it's measured in jobs. The massive tax cuts that were supposed to spark an economic expansion have instead led to an economic exodus. To make up for the three million private-sector jobs that have been lost on President Bush's watch, the economy would have to create 226,000 jobs a month through the end of his term. Last month, the economy created only 1,000 new jobs. That's not good enough.

America can't afford to keep rewarding the accumulation of wealth over the dignity of work. Instead of borrowing even more money to give more tax breaks to companies so that they can export even more jobs, we propose tax cuts and policies that will strengthen our manufacturing sector and create good jobs at good wages here at home. We can also show our patriotism while strengthening agriculture and rural America by labeling all food products with their country of origin.

Education

Education is the second key to our "opportunity society." Two years ago, the President signed a new education law. The heart of that law was a promise. The federal government would set high standards for every student, and hold schools responsible for results. In exchange, schools would receive the resources to meet the new standards. America's schools are holding up their end of the bargain—the President has not held up his. Millions of children are being denied the better teachers, smaller classes, and extra help they were promised.

At the same time, the President's tax cuts have put states in such a bind that they're being forced to raise the cost of college. Since President Bush took office, the average tuition at a four-year public college has increased by nearly $600. The America our parents gave us was a place in which everyone had a chance to go to a good school, and then to college, community college or vocational school, regardless of family income. Our children deserve nothing less.

Health Care and Medicare Prescription Drugs

Third, our "opportunity society" is built on the belief that affordable, available health care is not a luxury, but a basic foundation of a truly compassionate society.

Today, 43.6 million Americans—almost all of them from working families—have no health insurance. That's over 3.8 million more than when President Bush took office. Those Americans lucky enough to have health insurance have seen their premiums go up each of the last three years. The increase in premiums that middle-income families have seen over the past three years is larger than the four-year tax cut they've been promised. This is an invisible tax increase on middle class families.

Tonight, three years into his Administration, the President acknowledged that the rapidly rising cost of health care, and the increasing number of Americans with no health coverage, are problems. But the solutions he proposed—more tax cuts—are not the right ones. More tax cuts will do little to make health care more affordable or reduce the number of people without insurance, and they will weaken health coverage for those who now have it.

When I was driving around South Dakota this summer, I met a nurse in Sioux Falls who has cancer. She told me that she couldn't afford the $1,500 a month her drugs cost. She told me that she was going to die—that she was a lost cause. But, she said, we must solve this problem; don't turn more people into lost causes.

We believe that the federal government should use the power of 40 million Americans to lower prescription drug prices and to allow us to get more affordable drugs from Canada—instead of forbidding both. Drug companies and insurance companies are the only ones who benefit from that restriction—not the American people—and that's why we want to change it.

Retirement

And in our vision of an "opportunity society," promises made to those who have worked a lifetime will be honored in retirement. That's why we believe that America's pension system needs to be strengthened, and that Social Security's benefit should be a guarantee, not a gamble.

Only when every American who wants to work, can, when every child goes to a good school and has the opportunity to go further, only when health care is available and affordable for every American, when a lifetime of work guarantees a retirement with dignity and when America is secure at home and our strength abroad is respected and not resented—only then will we have a union as strong as the American people. That's the America we want to build, because that's the union the American people deserve. Thank you for listening, good night, and God bless America.

Source: U.S. Congress. House. Office of Congresswoman Nancy Pelosi. *Pelosi and Daschle Official State of the Union Response.* January 20, 2004. house.gov/pelosi/press/releases/Jan04/STOU_Response012004.html (accessed December 16, 2004).

February

2004 HISTORIC DOCUMENTS

Massachusetts Supreme Court on Gay Marriage

February 3, 2004

INTRODUCTION

A ruling by the Massachusetts Supreme Judicial Court on February 3, 2004, cleared the way for same-sex marriages to begin in that state on May 17, 2004. Massachusetts thus became the first state to legalize gay marriage. One other state, Vermont, recognized civil unions between same-sex couples; these unions conferred most of the benefits and obligations of marriage but not the right to marry. Three other states—California, Hawaii, and New Jersey—offered some spousal benefits to same-sex couples. Most of the rest of the states had laws defining marriage as the union of a man and a woman. *(Vermont civil unions, Historic Documents of 2000, p. 158)*

Whether states and the federal government should recognize gay marriage remained an emotional question. Gay rights advocates and their supporters said that denying gays the fundamental right of marriage made them second-class citizens and deprived them of the benefits and obligations accorded opposite-sex couples, including those involving children, taxation, health care, insurance, and inheritance. Opponents of gay marriage were appalled by what they perceived to be a threat to traditional moral values, religious teachings, and the sanctity of marriage as the union of a man and a woman.

Even before the legal weddings began in Massachusetts, the mayor of San Francisco authorized the issuance of marriage licenses to gay couples from across the country. More than 4,000 same-sex couples were married in that city before the weddings were stopped in March 2004. The court ruling in Massachusetts and the weddings themselves outraged religious and socially conservative groups who mobilized to push amendments to the federal and state constitutions banning gay marriage. Although both the House and Senate fell far short of procuring the two-thirds majority vote needed to approve a constitutional amendment, voters in eleven states supported constitutional bans at the November elections. Opposition to gay marriage was widely thought to have been a major factor in the increased turnout of social conservatives whose votes helped President George W. Bush win a second term in the White House.

Despite the apparent voter support for prohibiting gay marriage, the issue was still far from resolved. Bush promised to push for enactment of a federal constitutional amendment during his second term, and some gay rights groups indicated that they might revamp their political strategy for legalizing gay marriage in the face of the voter backlash. Other activists were pushing ahead with lawsuits challenging the constitutionality of marriage bans in several states. They also were challenging such policies as the military's "don't ask, don't tell" policy, which allowed gays and lesbians to serve in the military so long as they did not make their homosexuality known and refrained from homosexual conduct. "The nation is not at rest on this issue," Yale law professor William Eskridge said. "We should let Mississippi be Mississippi and Vermont be Vermont, and let's see where we are in another ten years. At that point, there will be another generation of voters and more experience."

Massachusetts Ruling

The Massachusetts Supreme Judicial Court ruling on February 3 followed its historic decision in November 2003 declaring that the state's ban on gay marriage was discriminatory and thus a violation of the state constitution. In handing down that decision in the case of *Goodridge v. Department of Public Health,* the court gave the state legislature 180 days to "take such action as it may deem appropriate" with regard to the ruling. If the legislature failed to take appropriate action, gay couples could legally marry in the state starting on May 17, 2004. *(Court ruling, Historic Documents of 2003, p. 401)*

Massachusetts legislators appeared to have three options—permit same-sex marriages, try to pass a constitutional amendment banning same-sex marriages, or permit civil unions. The heavily Democratic and Roman Catholic legislature did not appear likely to endorse gay marriage outright, so the legislature began a two-track process. One track laid the groundwork for a constitutional convention where the legislature would consider an amendment defining marriage solely as the union of a man and a woman. Under state law, the legislature had to approve a constitutional amendment two years in a row; the amendment then had to win support from a majority of the voters. That meant the earliest an amendment banning gay marriage could receive approval was in November 2006.

The second track was to ask the Massachusetts Supreme Judicial Court for its advisory opinion on whether a comprehensive civil union law would pass constitutional muster. In a 4–3 opinion announced February 3, the court said no. By differentiating between civil unions for same-sex couples and marriage for opposite-sex couples, the proposed legislation violated both the equal protection and due process requirements of the state constitution and maintained "an unconstitutional, inferior, and discriminatory status for same-sex couples," the majority wrote.

That decision threw the ball directly into the constitutional convention, where legislators voted 105–92 on March 29 to approve a constitutional amendment that would prohibit gays from marrying but allow them to enter civil unions with all the rights and obligations of marriage. Republican governor Mitt Romney, who opposed both gay marriage and civil unions, immediately said he would ask the state's high court to stay the May 17 date for the start of same-sex marriages until after the voters had an opportunity to vote on the issue in 2006. But the state attorney general, Thomas F. Reilly, refused to ask for the stay because he said there were no legal grounds on which to base his request. A spokesman for Reilly said that the state had "already been before the court twice and made just about every potential argument that one can make and all of the arguments have been soundly rejected." Reilly, a Democrat who also opposed gay marriage, was considered a potential candidate to run for governor in 2006 against Romney, who was expected to seek reelection. Romney was also considered a potential Republican presidential candidate in 2008.

Romney and Reilly agreed that a 1913 state law prohibited the state from issuing marriage licenses to same-sex couples whose marriages would not be recognized in their home states. "Massachusetts should not become the Las Vegas of same-sex marriage," Romney said in an interview with the *New York Times* published on April 24. "We do not intend to export our marriage confusion to the entire nation." Cease-and-desist orders were issued to town clerks in at least four jurisdictions, requiring them to stop giving marriage licenses to out-of-state couples.

One last hurdle to same-sex marriages in Massachusetts was cleared away on May 15, when the U.S. Supreme Court refused without comment to issue an emergency stay barring the marriages. The injunction had been sought by opponents of gay marriage, including eleven state legislators and the Florida-based Liberty Counsel, who were challenging the *Goodridge* ruling on the grounds that the state supreme court had usurped legislative and executive branch powers when it ruled that gay marriage was unconstitutional. That argument failed in lower federal courts, and on November 30 the Supreme Court refused to hear the case, again without comment. On May 17 hundreds of gay and lesbian couples flocked to city halls across Massachusetts to exchange their wedding vows in civil ceremonies. By the end of the year more than 4,200 same-sex couples had legally married.

The Massachusetts ruling legalizing same-sex marriage had an impact that stretched far beyond state borders. In February San Francisco mayor Gavin Newsome ordered city officials to grant marriage licenses to same-sex couples despite California's ban on same-sex marriage. Newsome argued that he had authority to act because he believed the law to be unconstitutional. More than 4,000 marriage licenses were issued to same-sex couples in San Francisco before the California Supreme Court ordered an immediate stop to the marriages on March 11. On August 12 the court ruled that Newsome had exceeded his authority and that the marriage licenses issued to same-sex couples were "void and of no legal effect." The court indicated that it might be willing to decide the underlying issue of whether the ban on gay marriage was constitutional but only if that question came to it after passing through the lower courts. Lawyers for the city and county of San Francisco and more than a dozen same-sex couples subsequently filed suit in San Francisco Superior Court challenging the constitutionality of the ban. The ban was being defended by the state attorney general and several Christian and conservative groups that opposed gay marriage. Arguments in the case began December 22.

The mayor of New Paltz, New York, also defied state law when he married twenty-five same-sex couples in late February. Criminal charges were brought against the mayor but later dropped.

Backlash in the States

Thirty-nine states and the federal government had laws barring same-sex marriages. But the Massachusetts rulings, as well as the same-sex weddings in San Francisco and New Paltz, energized groups and organizations opposed to gay marriage to step up political pressure on politicians in Washington and in state capitals to write constitutional bans on same-sex marriages and in some cases same-sex civil unions.

When the year began, only four states had constitutional amendments banning same-sex marriage. By the end of the year, voters in thirteen other states had approved constitutional amendments banning gay marriage (although a state court ruled Louisiana's new amendment unconstitutional for technical reasons). Missouri passed its law in August, and voters in eleven states—Arkansas, Georgia, Kentucky, Michigan, Mississippi, Montana, North Dakota, Ohio, Oklahoma, Oregon, and Utah—all approved constitutional amendments barring same-sex marriages. In all but three states—Mississippi, Montana, and Oregon—the constitutional amendments also barred civil unions or domestic partnership benefits. The amendments passed by wide margins in all eleven states. The narrowest margins were in Michigan and Oregon, where the amendment passed with about 59 percent of the vote.

Groups that supported the amendments were ecstatic with the voting results. "I think it's a real warning shot across the bow of politicians, but also a warning shot across the bow to activist judges," said Gary Bauer, chairman of the Campaign for Working Families, a political action committee that supported socially conservative causes. Predictably, gay rights advocates were disappointed, but for the most part philosophical. "Backlash simply means that you're making forward progress," said Josh Friedes, spokesman for the Massachusetts Freedom to Marry Coalition. "I think that people who say it suddenly seems like the radical right has momentum on their side, they're not looking at the broad brushstroke of history."

Federal Constitutional Amendment

Gay marriage opponents were less satisfied with the outcome of their efforts to get Congress to add a ban on gay marriage to the federal constitution. In the Senate the proposed amendment was killed July 14 on a procedural vote. Only forty-eight senators voted to cut off debate, twelve short of the sixty votes needed to stop a filibuster and nineteen short of the two-thirds majority needed to pass the amendment. The House supported a constitutional ban on gay marriage by a vote of 227–186 on September 30, well-short of the two-thirds majority of those present and voting—276 in this instance—needed to pass a constitutional amendment. The House approved a bill in July that would bar federal courts from hearing challenges to a provision of the 1996 Defense of Marriage law that gave states the option of not recognizing same-sex marriages performed in other states. But the Senate took no action, and the measure died at the end of the session.

Although President Bush had endorsed a constitutional amendment, the votes in the House and Senate appeared to reflect the American public's ambivalence on the issue. Public opinion polls showed that somewhere between 36 percent and 60 percent of those surveyed favored a constitutional amendment barring gay marriage, according to an analysis by the Pew Research Center released in July. Support was higher if the question was phrased positively—"Do you favor an amendment defining marriage as a union of a man and a woman?"—and lower if the question was phrased negatively—"Do you support a prohibition on same-sex marriage?" Support was also lower when respondents were given an alternative to amending the constitution, such as leaving the matter to the states to decide. "The polls tell us that most people oppose gay marriage," Andrew Kohut of the Pew center told the *New York Times.* "They also tell us that the public is pretty conservative when it comes to fiddling with the old Constitution."

Gay Marriage and the Presidential Election

It was evident in the closely contested presidential race that the issue of gay marriage made both Republican George Bush and Democrat John Kerry uncomfortable. Both candidates opposed gay marriage, but both had to finesse the issue in a way that would satisfy their respective political bases without offending voters who took a more tolerant view of the matter.

President Bush resisted endorsing a constitutional amendment even after the first Massachusetts court ruling in November 2003. But the second ruling in February 2004, and the sight of same-sex couples marrying on the steps of city hall in San Francisco, raised a clamor from Republican conservatives that Bush could no longer ignore. On February 24 he announced his support for a constitutional amendment that defined marriage as the union of a man and a woman but allowed state legislatures to make their own choices about legal arrangements for gay couples other than marriage. "America's a free society which limits the role of government in the lives of our citizens," the president said. "This commitment of freedom, however, does not require the redefinition of one of our own most basic social institutions."

Having announced his position, Bush did not go out of his way to make it a central issue in his campaign. The issue was downplayed for several reasons. First, polls showed that most voters were more concerned about the war in Iraq, terrorism, and the economy than about gay marriage. Second, Bush's vice president, Dick Cheney, whose daughter Mary was a lesbian, did not support a federal constitutional amendment banning gay marriage and indicated that the individual states should bear the responsibility for determining whether and what kind of government recognition should be given to gay relationships. Third, Bush could not afford to discourage moderates who might lean toward him on such issues as Iraq and the economy but find his views on gay marriage intolerant. Finally, Bush campaign operatives calculated that the campaigns in several states to enact state constitutional amendments banning gay marriage were already energizing conservatives who might not otherwise have voted to come to the polls.

John Kerry opposed gay marriage, but he also opposed a constitutional amendment banning it, saying it was a matter for the states to decide. Like Bush, Kerry downplayed the issue for several reasons. For one, he was from Massachusetts and did not want to emphasize that his state was the first to allow gay marriage. For another, he was vulnerable to Republican challenges that he was once again taking both sides of an issue. The Bush campaign had already used that tactic to great effect in deriding Kerry's stand on supporting funding for the war on Iraq. *(2004 presidential campaigns, pp. 478, 675, 773)*

In the aftermath of the election, which Bush won by about 3.5 million votes, conservative Republicans, many Democrats, and even some gay rights activists said the backlash from the push for same-sex marriage in Massachusetts and San Francisco cost Kerry the election. Senator Dianne Feinstein, D-Calif., said the thousands of weddings in San Francisco "did energize a very conservative vote," adding that she thought the "whole issue has been too much, too fast, too soon. And people aren't ready for it."

Others said that the issue did not have a substantial impact on the outcome of the presidential vote. For example, Kerry carried both Oregon and Michigan, where voters at the same time approved by wide margins constitutional amendments banning gay marriage. The picture was not so clear in the pivotal state of Ohio, where voters approved a constitutional amendment barring same-sex marriage by 62 percent but Bush defeated Kerry by only 120,000 votes—less than 2 percent of the votes cast. Robert T. Bennett, chairman of the Ohio Republican Party, said he would be "naïve" not to think the same-sex marriage referendum had helped increase the turnout. "And it helped most in what we refer to as the Bible Belt area of southeastern and southwestern Ohio, where we had the largest percentage increase in support or the president."

"Don't Ask, Don't Tell"

In a related development, twelve men and women expelled from the military because they were homosexual filed suit in a federal district court in Boston on December 6 challenging the constitutionality of the Pentagon's "don't ask, don't tell" policy. The lawsuit said that the Pentagon policy conflicted with the Supreme Court ruling in *Lawrence v. Texas,* which struck down state sodomy laws. In that landmark 2003 decision, the Court majority said there was a "zone of privacy" for sexual relationships involving consenting adults that was beyond the reach of government intervention. The "don't ask, don't tell" policy allowed gays and lesbians to serve in the military so long as they did not reveal their sexual orientation and abstained from homosexual activity. "We think the gay ban can no longer survive constitutionally," said C. Dixon Osburn, executive director of Servicemembers Legal Defense Network, a advocacy group for gays in the military. "You do not ban an entire class of people just to accommodate prejudice." (Lawrence v. Texas, *Historic Documents of 2003, p. 403*)

A ruling by the U.S. Army Court of Criminal Appeals, handed down the first week in December but not reported until December 8, seemed to lend strength to that argument. Citing *Lawrence,* the military court overturned the conviction of a soldier for engaging in consensual sodomy. Although the case involved a male soldier and a female civilian, legal experts said that the principles cited by the military judges were equally applicable to homosexual conduct. The appeals court ruling was believed to be the first time that a military court had upheld the right of consenting adults to engage in oral sex in private.

Canadian Law

Rather than banning same-sex marriage, Canada appeared to be condoning it. At the end of 2004, the high courts of six provinces and one territory, altogether representing 85 percent of the population, had ruled that defining marriage solely as the union of a man and a woman was discriminatory and unconstitutional. On December 9 the Canadian Supreme Court gave a green light to legislative efforts to redefine marriage throughout the country to include same-sex couples, although it did not rule that the traditional definition of marriage was unconstitutional. Provincial laws permitting same-sex marriages had drawn little protest, but the national legislation was provoking opposition from rural areas and some immigrant and Muslim populations in the larger cities. The legislation redefining marriage was expected to be taken up early in 2005.

If Canada approved same-sex marriages, it would join Belgium and the Netherlands as the only countries to permit such marriages. France and Germany had laws permitting civil union laws and Britain was considering such a law. In the Netherlands, which in 2001 became the first country to sanction gay marriage, the number of same-sex couples seeking marriage licenses was falling and the first same-sex divorces were being registered.

Gays and the Clergy

Gay clergy, rather than gay marriage, was threatening to split apart three major religious denominations in the United States in 2004. The consecration of an openly gay Episcopalian bishop in New Hampshire in November 2003 was causing an uproar within both the Episcopal Church in the United States and the global

Anglican Communion to which it belonged. In January 2004 a handful of Episcopalian congregations and dioceses formed the Network of Anglican Communion Dioceses and Parishes to protest ordination of gay clergy. Formation of the group was backed by leaders of Anglican churches in Africa, Asia, and Latin America representing more than half of the 77 million Anglicans worldwide. In August three churches in the Los Angeles diocese announced they were breaking with the Episcopal Church and aligning themselves with the Anglican Church in Uganda.

In October a special Anglican panel, known as the Lambeth Commission, released a report reprimanding the Episcopal Church USA for ordaining V. Gene Robinson as bishop of New Hampshire and for blessing same-sex marriages. The report called on the three dozen bishops who presided at Robinson's consecration to consider withdrawing from church "functions" until they offered "an expression of regret." The commission also criticized conservatives in the U.S. church and the leaders of Anglican churches outside the United States who had "broken or impaired communion" with the American church, asking them to "express regret for the consequences of their action." Although the commission stopped short of saying what would happen if the church leaders both in the United States and abroad ignored its advice, it warned that "there remains a very real danger that we will not choose to walk together. Should [this] call to halt and find ways to continuing in our present Communion not be heeded, then we shall have to begin to learn to walk apart."

The council of bishops of the Episcopal Church was scheduled to meet in January 2005 to discuss the commission's recommendations. The presiding bishop of the church, the Most Rev. Frank T. Griswold told the *New York Times* that he thought the report was "nuanced and balanced," but he also indicated he was unlikely to change his position on ordination of gay clergy. Noting that the report asked for "an expression of regret," rather than an apology, Griswold said "I can regret the effects of something, but at the same time be clear about the integrity of what I've done." African Anglican leaders reacted even more forcefully, announcing in November that they would stop sending African clergy for training in Western seminaries and indicating that the future of the Anglican Communion depended on whether the Episcopalian Church in the United States reversed its position on ordination of gay clergy.

In other U.S. action, the legislative assembly of the Presbyterian Church in July narrowly rejected an effort that would have allowed regional governing bodies to ordain gay clergy and lay officers. The vote was 255–259 and left in place current church law that prohibited the ordination of gay clergy. Conservative Presbyterians had warned that a vote in favor of gay ordination would split the church. Some 1,300 congregations with 450,000 members were reported to be ready to break away from the main church if the ban on gay ordination had been relaxed.

The United Methodist Church also found itself caught up in the debate over the gay clergy. In March a church jury made up of thirteen ministers acquitted a Washington state minister who had openly acknowledged being in a lesbian relationship. The jury based its acquittal of the well-liked minister on what it said were unclear and contradictory passages in church law about homosexuality in the ministry. The ambiguity was subsequently eliminated from Methodist law, and in December a church jury in Pennsylvania defrocked a lesbian minister for violating the law banning "self-avowed, practicing homosexuals" from the ministry. The minister's congregation had agreed that if she were convicted she could continue to work as a lay employee but would be unable to celebrate the rites of baptism and communion. The ruling, however, was unlikely to end the debate between those in the church who believed in a traditional interpretation of the Bible condemning homosexuality as sinful and those who argued that Christian values should extend equal rights and protections to everyone, regardless of their sexual status.

Following are excerpts from the majority and minority advisory opinions to the Massachusetts Senate from the justices of the Massachusetts Supreme Judicial Court, issued February 3, 2004, in which the majority concluded that differentiating between civil unions for same-sex couples and marriage for opposite-sex couples would violate the equal protection and due process requirements of the Massachusetts constitution. The opinion cleared the way for legal same-sex marriages to begin in the state on May 17, 2004.

"Opinions of the Justices to the Senate"

On February 3, 2004, the Justices submitted the following answer to a question propounded to them by the Senate.

To the Honorable the Senate of the Commonwealth of Massachusetts:

The undersigned Justices of the Supreme Judicial Court respectfully submit their answers to the question set forth in an order adopted by the Senate on December 11, 2003, and transmitted to the Justices on December 12, 2003. The order indicates that there is pending before the General Court a bill, Senate No. 2175, entitled "An Act relative to civil unions." A copy of the bill was transmitted with the order. As we describe more fully below, the bill . . . provides for the establishment of "civil unions" for same-sex "spouses," provided the individuals meet certain qualifications described in the bill.

The order indicates that grave doubt exists as to the constitutionality of the bill if enacted into law and requests the opinions of the Justices on the following "important question of law":

> Does Senate, No. 2175, which prohibits same-sex couples from entering into marriage but allows them to form civil unions with all 'benefits, protections, rights and responsibilities' of marriage, comply with the equal protection and due process requirements of the Constitution of the Commonwealth and articles 1, 6, 7, 10, 12 and 16 of the Declaration of Rights? . . .

Under . . . the Constitution of the Commonwealth, as amended by art. 85 of the Amendments, "[e]ach branch of the legislature, as well as the governor or the council, shall have authority to require the opinions of the justices of the supreme judicial court, upon important questions of law, and upon solemn occasions." "[A] solemn occasion exists 'when the Governor or either branch of the Legislature, having some action in view, has serious doubts as to their power and authority to take such action, under the Constitution, or under existing statutes.' " The pending bill involves an important question of law and the Senate has indicated "grave doubt" as to its constitutionality. We therefore address the question.

1. Background of the Proposed Legislation

In *Goodridge v. Department of Pub. Health* (2003) (*Goodridge*), the court considered the const*itutio*nal question "[w]hether the Commonwealth may use its formidable regulatory authority to bar same-sex couples from civil marriage. . . ." The court concluded that it may not do so, determining that the Commonwealth had failed to articulate a rational basis for denying civil marriage to same-sex couples. The court stated that the Massachusetts Constitution "affirms the dignity and equality of all individuals" and "forbids the creation of second-class citizens." The court concluded that in "[l]imiting the protections, benefits, and obligations of civil marriage to opposite-sex couples," the marriage licensing law, "violates the basic premises of individual liberty and equality under law protected by the Massachusetts Constitution."

In so concluding, the court enumerated some of the concrete tangible benefits that flow from civil marriage, including, but not limited to, rights in property, probate, tax, and evidence law that are conferred on married couples. The court also noted that "intangible benefits flow from marriage," intangibles that are important components of marriage as a "civil right." The court stated that "[m]arriage also bestows enormous private and social advantages on those who choose to marry . . . [and] is at once a deeply personal commitment to another human being and a highly public celebration of the ideals of mutuality, companionship, intimacy, fidelity, and family." "Because it fulfils yearnings for security, safe haven, and connection that express our common humanity, civil marriage is an esteemed institution, and the decision whether and whom to marry is among life's momentous acts of self-definition." Therefore, without the right to choose to marry, same-sex couples are not only denied full protection of the laws, but are "excluded from the full range of human experience."

The court stated that the denial of civil marital status "works a deep and scarring hardship on a very real segment of the community for no rational reason." These omnipresent hardships include, but are by no means limited to, the absence of predictable rules of child support and property division, and even uncertainty concerning whether one will be allowed to visit one's sick child or one's partner in a hospital. . . . All of these stem from the status of same-sex couples and their children as "outliers to the marriage laws."

After reviewing the marriage ban under the deferential rational basis standard, the court concluded that the Department of Public Health "failed to identify any relevant characteristic that would justify shutting the door to civil marriage to a person who wishes to marry someone of the same sex." The *Goodridge* decision by the court made no reference to the concept of "civil unions," nor did the separate concurring opinion of Justice Greaney. Rather, it was the lawfulness under the Massachusetts Constitution of the bar to civil marriage itself, "a vital social institution," that the court was asked to decide. The court decided the question after extensively reviewing the government's justifications for the marriage ban.

In response to the plaintiffs' specific request for relief, the court preserved the marriage licensing statute, but refined the common-law definition of civil marriage to mean "the voluntary union of two persons as spouses, to the exclusion of all others." The entry of judgment was stayed "for 180 days to permit the Legislature to take such action as it may deem appropriate." The purpose of the stay was to afford the Legislature an opportunity to conform the existing statutes to the provisions of the *Goodridge* decision.

2. Provisions of the Bill

The order of the Senate plainly reflects that Senate No. 2175 is proposed action in response to the *Goodridge* opinion. The bill states that the "purpose" of the act is to provide "eligible same-sex couples the opportunity to obtain the benefits, protections, rights and responsibilities afforded to opposite sex couples by the marriage laws of the commonwealth, without entering into a marriage," declares that it is the "public policy" of the Commonwealth that "spouses in a civil union" "shall have all the benefits, protections, rights and responsibilities afforded by the marriage laws," and recites "that the Commonwealth's laws should be revised to give same-sex couples the opportunity to obtain the legal protections, benefits, rights and responsibilities associated with civil marriage, while preserving the traditional, historic nature and meaning of the institution of civil marriage." To that end, the bill proposes [to amend the marriage licensing law] which establishes the institution of "civil union," eligibility for which is limited to "[t]wo persons . . . [who] are of the same sex. . . ."

The proposed law states that "spouses" in a civil union shall be "joined in it with a legal status equivalent to marriage." The bill expressly maintains that "marriage" is reserved exclusively for opposite-sex couples. . . . Notwithstanding, the proposed law purports to make the institution of a "civil union" parallel to the institution of civil "marriage." For example, the bill provides that "spouses in a civil union shall have all the same benefits, protections, rights and responsibilities under law as are granted to spouses in a marriage." In addition, terms that denote spousal relationships, such as "husband," "wife," "family," and "next of kin," are to be interpreted to include spouses in a civil union "as those terms are used in any law." The bill goes on to enumerate a nonexclusive list of the legal benefits that will adhere to spouses in a civil union, including property rights, joint State income tax filing, evidentiary rights, rights to veteran benefits and group insurance, and the right to the issuance of a "civil union" license, identical to a marriage license . . . "as if a civil union was a marriage."

3. Analysis

As we stated above, in *Goodridge* the court was asked to consider the constitutional question "whether the Commonwealth may use its formidable regulatory authority to bar same-sex couples from civil marriage." The court has answered the question. We have now been asked to render an advisory opinion on Senate No. 2175, which creates a new legal status, "civil union," that is purportedly equal to "marriage," yet separate from it. The constitutional difficulty of the proposed civil union bill is evident in its stated purpose to "preserv[e] the traditional, historic nature and meaning of the institution of civil marriage." Preserving the institution of civil marriage is of course a legislative priority of the highest order, and one to which the Justices accord the General Court the greatest deference. We recognize the efforts of the Senate to draft a bill in conformity with the *Goodridge* opinion. Yet the bill, as we read it, does nothing to "preserve" the civil marriage law, only its constitutional infirmity. This is not a matter of social policy but of constitutional interpretation. As the court concluded in *Goodridge,* the traditional, historic nature and meaning of civil marriage in Massachusetts is as a wholly secular and dynamic legal institution, the governmental aim of which is to encourage stable adult relationships for the good of the individual and of the community, especially its children. The very nature and purpose of civil marriage, the court concluded, renders unconstitutional any attempt to ban all same-sex couples, as same-sex couples, from entering into civil marriage.

The same defects of rationality evident in the marriage ban considered in *Goodridge* are evident in, if not exaggerated by, Senate No. 2175. Segregating same-sex unions from opposite-sex unions cannot possibly be held rationally to advance or "preserve" what we stated in *Goodridge* were the Commonwealth's legitimate interests in procreation, child rearing, and the conservation of resources. Because the proposed law by its express terms forbids same-sex couples entry into civil marriage, it continues to relegate same-sex couples to a different status. The holding in *Goodridge,* by which we are bound, is that group classifications based on unsupportable distinctions, such as that embodied in the proposed bill, are invalid under the Massachusetts Constitution. The history of our nation has demonstrated that separate is seldom, if ever, equal.

In *Goodridge,* the court acknowledged, as we do here, that "[m]any people hold deep-seated religious, moral, and ethical convictions that marriage should be limited to the union of one man and one woman, and that homosexual conduct is immoral. Many hold equally strong religious, moral, and ethical convictions that same-sex couples are entitled to be married, and that homosexual persons should be treated no differently than their heterosexual neighbors." The court stated then, and we reaffirm, that the State may not interfere with these convictions, or with the decision of any religion to refuse to perform religious marriages of same-sex couples. These matters of belief and conviction are properly outside the reach of judicial review or government interference. But neither may the government, under the guise of protecting "traditional" values, even if they be the traditional values of the majority, enshrine in law an invidious discrimination that our Constitution, "as a charter of governance for every person properly within its reach," forbids.

The bill's absolute prohibition of the use of the word "marriage" by "spouses" who are the same sex is more than semantic. The dissimilitude between the terms "civil marriage" and "civil union" is not innocuous; it is a considered choice of language that reflects a demonstrable assigning of same-sex, largely homosexual, couples to second-class status. The denomination of this difference by the separate opinion of Justice Sosman as merely a "squabble over the name to be used" so clearly misses the point that further discussion appears to be useless. If, as the separate opinion posits, the proponents of the bill believe that no message is conveyed by eschewing the word "marriage" and replacing it with "civil union" for same-sex "spouses," we doubt that the attempt to circumvent the court's decision in *Goodridge* would be so purposeful. For no rational reason the marriage laws of the Commonwealth discriminate against a defined class; no amount of tinkering with language will eradicate that stain. The bill would have the effect of maintaining and fostering a stigma of exclusion that the Constitution prohibits. It would deny to same-sex "spouses" only a status that is specially recognized in society and has significant social and other advantages. The Massachusetts Constitution, as was explained in the *Goodridge* opinion, does not permit such invidious discrimination, no matter how well intentioned.

The separate opinion maintains that, because same-sex civil marriage is not recognized under Federal law and the law of many States, there is a rational basis for the Commonwealth to distinguish same-sex from opposite-sex "spouses." There is nothing in the bill, including its careful and comprehensive findings, to suggest that the rationale for the bill's distinct nomenclature was chosen out of deference to other jurisdictions. This is but a post hoc, imaginative theory created in the separate opinion to justify different treatment for a discrete class. Even if the different term were used for the reason the separate opinion posits, and not in order to label the unions of same-sex couples as less worthy than those of opposite sex couples, we would remain unpersuaded. "Our concern," as the court stated in *Goodridge,* "is with the Massachusetts Constitution as a charter of governance for every person properly within its reach."

We are well aware that current Federal law prohibits recognition by the Federal government of the validity of same-sex marriages legally entered into in any State, and that it permits other States to refuse to recognize the validity of such marriages. The argument in the separate opinion that, apart from the legal process, society will still accord a lesser status to those marriages is irrelevant. Courts define what is constitutionally permissible, and the Massachusetts Constitution does not permit this type of labeling. That there may remain personal residual prejudice against same-sex couples is a proposition all too familiar to other disadvantaged groups. That such prejudice exists is not a reason to insist on less than the Constitution requires. We do not abrogate the fullest measure of protection to which residents of the Commonwealth are entitled under the Massachusetts Constitution. Indeed, we would do a grave disservice to every Massachusetts resident, and to our constitutional duty to interpret the law, to conclude that the strong protection of individual rights guaranteed by the Massachusetts Constitution should not be available to their fullest extent in the Commonwealth because those rights may not be acknowledged elsewhere. We do not resolve, nor would we attempt to, the consequences of our holding in other jurisdictions. But, as the court held in *Goodridge,* under our Federal system of dual sovereignty, and subject to the minimum requirements of the Fourteenth Amendment to the United States Constitution, "each State is free to address difficult issues of individual liberty in the manner its own Constitution demands."

We recognize that the pending bill palliates some of the financial and other concrete manifestations of the discrimination at issue in *Goodridge.* But the question the court considered in *Goodridge* was not only whether it was proper to withhold tangible benefits from same-sex couples, but also whether it was constitutional to create a separate class of citizens by status discrimination, and withhold from that class the right to participate in the institution of civil marriage, along with its concomitant tangible and intangible protections, benefits, rights, and responsibilities. Maintaining a second-class citizen status for same-sex couples by excluding them from the institution of civil marriage *is* the constitutional infirmity at issue.

4. Conclusion

We are of the opinion that Senate No. 2175 violates the equal protection and due process requirements of the Constitution of the Commonwealth and the Massachusetts Declaration of Rights. Further, the particular provisions that render the pending bill unconstitutional . . . are not severable from the remainder. The bill maintains an unconstitutional, inferior, and discriminatory status for same-sex couples, and the bill's remaining provisions are too entwined with this purpose to stand independently.

The answer to the question is "No."

The foregoing answer and opinion are submitted by the Chief Justice and the Associate Justices subscribing hereto on the third day of February, 2004.

Margaret H. Marshall
John M. Greaney
Roderick L. Ireland
Judith A. Cowin

In response to this court's decision in *Goodridge* v. *Department of Pub. Health,* the Senate is considering a bill that would make available to same-sex couples all of the protections, benefits, rights, responsibilities, and legal incidents that are now available to married opposite-sex couples, but would denominate the legal relationship thus created as a "civil union" instead of a civil "marriage." The question submitted to us by the Senate thus asks, in substance, whether the Massachusetts Constitution would be violated by utilizing the term "civil union" instead of "marriage" to identify the otherwise identical package of State law rights and benefits to be made available to same-sex couples.

In response to the court's invitation to submit amicus briefs on this question, we have received, from both sides of the issue, impassioned and sweeping rhetoric out of all proportion to the narrow question before us. Both sides appear to have ignored the fundamental import of the proposed legislation, namely, that same-sex couples who are civilly "united" will have literally every single right, privilege, benefit, and obligation of every sort that our State law confers on opposite-sex couples who are civilly "married." Under this proposed bill, there are no substantive differences left to dispute—there is only, on both sides, a squabble over the name to be used. There is, from the amici on one side, an implacable determination to retain some distinction, however trivial, between the institution created for same-sex couples and the institution that is available to opposite-sex couples. And, from the amici on the other side, there is an equally implacable determination that no distinction, no matter how meaningless, be tolerated. As a result, we have a pitched battle over who gets to use the "m" word.

This does not strike me a dispute of any constitutional dimension whatsoever, and today's response from the Justices—unsurprisingly—cites to no precedent suggesting that the choice of differing titles for various statutory programs has ever posed an issue of constitutional dimension, here or anywhere else. And, rather than engage in any constitutional analysis of the claimed statutory naming rights, today's answer to the Senate's question merely repeats the impassioned rhetoric that has been submitted to us as if it were constitutional law, opining that any difference in names represents an "attempt to circumvent" the court's decision in *Goodridge.*

A principle premise of the Justices's answer is that this specific issue has somehow already been decided by *Goodridge.* It has not. In *Goodridge,* the court was presented with a statutory scheme that afforded same-sex couples absolutely *none* of the benefits, rights, or privileges that same-sex couples could obtain under Massachusetts law by way of civil marriage. At length, the *Goodridge* opinion identified the vast array of benefits, rights, and privileges that were effectively withheld from same-sex couples (and their children), and concluded that "[l]imiting the protections, benefits, and obligations of civil marriage to opposite-sex couples violates the basic premises of individual liberty and equality under law protected by the Massachusetts Constitution." The ostensible reasoning behind that conclusion was that there was no "rational basis" for depriving same-sex couples (and their children) of those protections, benefits, and obligations.

Today's question presents the court with the diametric opposite of the statutory scheme reviewed in *Goodridge.* Where the prior scheme accorded same-sex couples (and their children) absolutely *none* of the benefits, rights, or privileges that State law confers on opposite-sex married couples (and their children), the proposed bill would accord them *all* of those substantive benefits, rights, and privileges. Nothing in *Goodridge* addressed the very limited issue that is presented by the question now before us, i.e., whether the Constitution mandates that the license that qualifies same-sex couples for that identical array of State law benefits, rights, and privileges be called a "marriage" license. In other words, where *Goodridge* addressed whether there was any rational basis for the enormous substantive difference between the treatment of same-sex couples and the treatment of opposite-sex couples, the present question from the Senate asks whether a single difference in form alone—the name of the licensing scheme—would violate the Constitution. Repeated quotations of dicta from *Goodridge*—which is essentially all that today's answer to the Senate consists of—simply does not answer the question that is before us.

Rather, according to *Goodridge* itself, we must consider whether there is any "rational basis" for giving the licensure program for same-sex couples a different name from the licensure program for opposite-sex couples, despite the fact that the two programs confer identical benefits, rights, and privileges under State law. Nowhere does today's answer to the Senate actually analyze whether there is or is not a conceivable rational basis for that distinction in name. Instead, the answer pays lip service to the rational basis test in a footnote and, in conclusory fashion, announces that, because the different name would still connote "a different status," it somehow lacks a rational basis and is contrary to *Goodridge.*

While we have no precedent for the application of the rational basis test (or the strict scrutiny test, for that matter) to as insignificant an issue as what a statutory program is to be called, it would seem logical that the Legislature could call a program by a different name as long as there was any difference between that program and the other program in question. . . .

At first blush, one would say that the very identity between the package of benefits, rights, and privileges accorded same-sex couples under the proposed bill and the package of benefits, rights, and privileges accorded opposite-sex couples under existing State law means that there is no reason to give those two packages different names. Where the stated purpose of the proposed bill is to eliminate all substantive differences between those two types of couples, what conceivable purpose is served by retaining a different title for their respective licensing schemes?

The problem, however, is simple: it is beyond the ability of the Legislature—and even beyond the ability of this court, no matter how activist it becomes in support of this cause—to confer a package of benefits and obligations on same-sex "married" couples that would be truly identical to the entire package of benefits and obligations that being "married" confers on opposite-sex couples. That difference stems from the fact that, *Goodridge* notwithstanding, neither Federal law nor the law of other States will recognize same-sex couples as "married" merely because Massachusetts has given them a license called a "marriage" license. That fact, by itself, will result in many substantive differences between what it would mean for a same-sex couple to receive a Massachusetts "marriage" license and what it means for an opposite-sex couple to receive a Massachusetts "marriage" license. Those differences are real, and, in some cases, quite stark. Their very existence makes it rational to call the license issued to same-sex couples by a different name, as it unavoidably—and, to many, regrettably—cannot confer a truly equal package of rights, privileges, and benefits on those couples, no matter what name it is given.

Just as *Goodridge* identified the vast array of State benefits, rights, and privileges that are conferred based on marital status, a vast array of Federal benefits, rights, and privileges are also conferred based on marital status. However, whatever Massachusetts chooses to call the license it grants to same-sex couples, the Federal government will not, for purposes of *any* Federal statute or program, treat it as a "marriage." . . . As such, same-sex "married" couples will not be treated as "married" for such purposes as Federal taxation (both income taxes and, even more significantly, estate taxes), Social Security benefits (of any kind), immigration, or Federal programs providing health care or nursing home care benefits, to name but a few. And, where those Federal programs set the eligibility requirements for many of our federally funded State programs, those corresponding State programs will not be allowed to treat same-sex couples as married either, thus excluding them from (or profoundly affecting the calculation of) entitlement to benefits under many such State programs. State officials—not just Federal officials—will, of necessity, have to differentiate between same-sex and opposite-sex couples for all of these State programs. One may decry the unfairness of this different treatment at the hands of the Federal government and its programs, just as the plaintiffs in *Goodridge* decried the unfairness of different treatment under State law, but neither this court nor the Legislature has any power to eradicate those differences or to obviate the need that will arise to distinguish between same-sex and opposite-sex couples for many purposes.

Yet another significant difference stems from the fact that, at present, most States will refuse to recognize a "marriage" license issued by Massachusetts to a same-sex couple. . . . Not only would such a couple be deprived of any benefits of being "married" if that couple moved to another State, but such a couple would not have access to that State's courts for purposes of obtaining a divorce or separation and the necessary orders (with respect to alimony, child support, or child custody) that accompany a divorce or separation. . . . Ironically, a "marriage" license issued to a same-sex couple will not only fail to entitle that couple to the same array of benefits that normally attend the marriage of opposite-sex couples, but it will not subject them to the same obligations, either—their status as a "married" couple, and therefore all of the obligations that attend that status, can be made to disappear by the simple expedient of moving to another State that will not recognize them as "married." Opposite-sex couples, once "married" in Massachusetts, cannot shed that status and its significant obligations so easily.

It would be rational for the Legislature to give different names to the license accorded to these two groups, when the obligations they are undertaking and the benefits they are receiving are, in practical effect, so very different, and where, for purposes of the vast panoply of federally funded State programs, State officials will have to differentiate between them. That these differences stem from laws and practices outside our own jurisdiction does not make those differences any less significant. They will have a very real effect on the everyday lives of same-sex couples, and the lives of their children, that will unavoidably make their ostensible "marriage" a very different legal institution from the "marriage" enjoyed by opposite-sex couples. That lack of recognition in other jurisdictions is not simply a matter affecting the intangibles of "status" or "personal residual prejudice," but is a difference that gives rise to a vast assortment of highly tangible, concrete consequences. It is not the naming of the legal institution that confers "a different status" on same-sex couples; rather, that difference in terminology reflects the reality that, for many purposes, same-sex couples will have "a different status."

Not only will the institution itself be different, but those very differences would, in many areas, justify (and, in some cases, require) modifications of our own State law in ways that are unique to same-sex couples in order to address those differences. Such modifications range from the mundane (and almost automatic) to very substantive and complex. To begin with the mundane, while the proposed bill specifies that same-sex couples in "civil unions" can file joint Massachusetts income tax returns, such couples will not be allowed to file joint Federal income tax returns; when, on their Massachusetts returns, they encounter the numerous cross-references to what was entered on a particular line of their Federal return, what figure are they to use? Some regulation or instruction, applicable only to the tax returns of same-sex couples, will inevitably have to be promulgated. On a more substantive level, would it not be permissible (and, in the view of many, appropriate) for the Legislature to provide some form of tax benefit to same-sex couples to recognize that they have been deprived of certain deductions, credits, or other benefits on their Federal income taxes or Federal estate taxes? . . . Would it not also be permissible (and, in the view of many, appropriate) to establish a program of benefits for same-sex couples and their children to offset the hardship they will encounter as a result of being denied Social Security benefits, health care benefits, and the many other benefits that opposite-sex married couples (and their children) receive under Federal programs and federally funded State programs? . . . And, would it not be desirable to try and formulate some mechanism—admittedly complex and difficult to fashion—by which same-sex couples who move out of State could still have resort to Massachusetts courts to enforce the obligations of their union in the event one party or the other wished to dissolve it?

I recognize that the proposed bill does not contain any measures addressing any of these problems. The question, however, is whether it is rational to envision a need to differentiate between these two types of licenses—after all, the 180-day deadline imposed by *Goodridge* does not realistically allow for a review of every one of the "hundreds of statutes" in Massachusetts alone that are "related to marriage and to marital benefits," let alone review how differences in Federal law and the law of other States will frustrate the goal of complete equality and require separate statutory or regulatory remedies for same-sex couples in Massachusetts. It is understandable, therefore, that the proposed bill sets forth as its initial goal the overarching proposition that these two programs should be equal and leaves to another day the painstaking task of revising the "hundreds" of provisions that might, in order to obtain equality in a more pragmatic sense, need substantial revision. Moreover, it makes eminent sense to obtain some direct experience with this first in the nation proposed program of "civil unions" that are to be the complete functional equivalent of "marriage"; that experience will both identify where the theoretically identical treatment is not identical in reality and simultaneously inform those seeking genuine equality what remedies might best be fashioned to "close the gap." Indeed, once the euphoria of *Goodridge* subsides, the reality of the still less than truly equal status of same-sex couples will emerge, and it will emerge in pragmatic ways far beyond the purely symbolic issue of what their legal status is to be named. There will surely be more to address than mere "administrative details."

Where the rights and obligations conferred on same-sex couples by *Goodridge* will not in fact be identical to the rights and obligations of opposite-sex married couples, where State officials will have to differentiate between them under essentially all federally funded State programs, and where it is rational to envision different, yet constitutional, treatment of same-sex couples in the future to address those remaining differences, it is eminently rational to give a different name to the legal status being conferred on same-sex couples by the proposed bill. It is not enough to say that eligibility for current federally funded State programs, or for some future programs or statutory modifications unique to same-sex couples, could be confirmed by some other means; under the rational basis test, the sole question is whether a different name for the license being issued is a rational method of identifying those persons who would be eligible for constitutionally permissible differing treatment in future. It clearly is.

It is of no consequence that the actual purpose that has motivated the proposed bill may be different from that just articulated. The criticism that my articulated rationale "is but a post hoc, imaginative theory created . . . to justify different treatment," and not the actual rationale of the bill's proponents, is therefore beside the point. The rational basis test asks whether there is any conceivable basis for the distinction at issue. The test does not require that the Legislature disclose its actual motives or that those motives be pure. Nor does the test even place the burden on the Commonwealth to demonstrate the existence of a rational basis—rather, it is on those seeking to challenge the legislation to demonstrate the absence of *any* conceivable basis. In my view, the proposed difference in name passes muster under the rational basis test.

A more fundamental problem with the answer given to the Senate today is that it does not apply the rational basis test, but instead announces, without qualification, that the Massachusetts Constitution prohibits "invidious discrimination" or "status discrimination" against, or the imposition of a "different status," "second-class status" or "stigma" on, same-sex couples. Of course, if the Massachusetts Constitution contained any "equal rights amendment" making sexual orientation the equivalent of the prohibited categories of "sex, race, color, creed or national origin," I would readily agree with those general pronouncements. However, our Constitution contains no such amendment, and *Goodridge* itself did not go so far as to accept the plaintiffs' argument that the court itself, absent such an amendment, should nevertheless treat sexual orientation as a suspect classification for purposes of equal protection analysis. Nor did *Goodridge* rely on the alternative claim that a "fundamental right" was at stake, such that a "strict scrutiny" analysis was to be applied. Rather, the court purported to apply a mere rational basis analysis, the extremely deferential test that is applied to any classification that does not impinge on fundamental rights or employ a suspect classification.

The *Goodridge* opinion employed repeated analogies to cases involving fundamental rights and suspect classifications, while ostensibly not adopting either predicate for strict scrutiny. Today's answer to the Senate's question discards the fig leaf of the rational basis test and, relying exclusively on the rhetoric rather than the purported reasoning of *Goodridge,* assumes that discrimination on the basis of sexual orientation is prohibited by our Constitution as if sexual orientation were indeed a suspect classification. If that is the view of a majority of the Justices, they should identify the new test they have apparently adopted for determining that a classification ranks as "suspect"—other types of persons making claims of a denial of equal protection will need to know whether they, too, can qualify as a "suspect" classification under that new test and thereby obtain strict scrutiny analysis of any statute, regulation, or program that uses that classification. No analysis of why sexual orientation should be treated as a suspect classification was provided in *Goodridge,* and none is provided today. Yet that is, apparently, the interpretation that is now being given to *Goodridge.* The footnote disclaimer of any resort to "suspect classification" and corresponding "strict scrutiny" analysis, rings hollow in light of the sweeping text of today's answer.

Here, as in *Goodridge,* I remain of the view that the rational basis test is the test to be applied to this issue and, at least in theory, all but one of the Justices in *Goodridge* applied that test. That same test should be applied to the question before us, and, because this proposed legislation passes that test, I would advise the Senate that Senate No. 2175 does not violate the equal protection or due process requirements of the Constitution of the Commonwealth and the Massachusetts Declaration of Rights.

Martha B. Sosman

I agree with the opinion of Justice Sosman.

Francis X. Spina

"Shorn of [its] emotion-laden invocations," *Goodridge* v. *Department of Pub. Health,* and reduced to its legal essence, the court's *Goodridge* decision held that "[l]imiting the protections, benefits, and obligations of civil marriage to opposite-sex couples violates the basic premises of individual liberty and equality under law protected by the Massachusetts Constitution." This holding, while monumental in effect, rested on the slender reed of the court's conclusion that the Department of Public Health had failed to articulate a rational basis for denying civil marriage to couples of the same sex, while permitting civil marriage under Massachusetts law for similarly situated heterosexual couples.

What was before the court, in fairness, was a yawning chasm between hundreds of protections and benefits provided under Massachusetts law for some, and none at all for others. That a classification with such attendant advantages afforded to one group over another could not withstand scrutiny under the rational basis standard does little to inform us about whether an entirely different statutory scheme, such as the one pending before the Senate, that provides all couples similarly situated with an identical bundle of legal rights and benefits under licenses that differ in name only, would satisfy that standard. A mere difference in name, that does not differentiate on the basis of a constitutionally protected or suspect classification or create any legally cognizable advantage for one group over another under Massachusetts law, may not even raise a due process or equal protection claim under our Constitution, and the rational basis test may be irrelevant to the court's consideration of such a statute, once enacted.

Assuming, however, that a difference in statutory name would itself have to rest on a rational basis, I would withhold judgment until such time as the Legislature completed its deliberative process before concluding that there was or was not such a basis. . . .

In sum, if the new statutory scheme is subjected to and passes the rational basis test, it would be constitutional, and while one could speculate now as to what conceivable bases might exist to justify the difference, there is no reason to prejudge the point, and no basis on which to pronounce the task to be impossible.

Robert J. Cordy

Source: Commonwealth of Massachusetts. Supreme Judicial Court. *Opinions of the Justices to the Senate.* SJC-09163, February 3, 2004. news.findlaw.com/nytimes/docs/conlaw/marriage20304.html (accessed January 20, 2005).

President's Economic Report, Economic Advisers' Report

February 9, 2004

INTRODUCTION

The 2004 presidential election campaign, with its focus on the "jobless recovery" and record federal budget deficits, tended to mask the solid performance turned in by the American economy in 2004. Preliminary estimates put annual economic growth at 4.4 percent for the year, the highest growth rate since 1999. Consumer spending, business investment, and corporate profits all remained strong despite a record increase in world oil prices and a slide in the value of the dollar. Inflation, interest rates, and the overall jobless rate all stayed relatively low. By most indicators, the country appeared to have emerged from the mild recession of 2001 and the slow recovery that followed.

The one area that had not recovered was job creation. For Democratic policymakers and many American workers, the slow pace of job creation since the end of the recession had come to symbolize all that was wrong with economic policy during President George W. Bush's first term in office.

World economic growth set a strong pace of 5 percent in 2004, its highest in nearly thirty years. Forecasters generally expected world economic growth to slow in 2005 but to remain above 4 percent. China continued to outpace the rest of the world, growing at a rate of 9 percent or better. Other parts of Asia and parts of Eastern Europe also grew swiftly as investors and companies sought to take advantage of new markets and cheaper labor.

The declining value of the dollar, however, caused uneasiness around the world. While most analysts agreed that a gradual decline was necessary to correct large exchange rate imbalances, they warned that a sudden drop in the dollar's value, perhaps triggered by increasing concerns about the high U.S. trade and budget deficits, could jeopardize economic growth around the globe. *(Declining dollar and the trade deficit, p. 235)*

2004 Economic Overview

Consumer spending, which accounted for two-thirds of economic activity, continued to underpin economic growth in 2004. According to the Federal Reserve, consumer debt was hovering around $2 trillion, including credit card debt and car loans but not mortgages. U.S. households owned more than $14 trillion in real estate assets, almost twice as much as they held in stock and mutual funds. That was the result largely of the biggest boom ever in housing prices, which had gone up nearly 7 percent a year for four straight years. Refinancings and the rise in home values helped bolster consumer spending during both the recession and the recovery.

Economic analysts continued to question how long consumer spending could continue to rise. "At some point consumer spending has to come into line with income growth, and in 2004 income did not rise as fast as spending," said Brian Moulton of the Bureau of Economic Analysis, the agency within the Commerce Department that produced the quarterly reports on economic growth. The housing boom was showing signs of slowing toward the end of the year. Although construction of new homes appeared to be continuing apace, houses were taking longer to sell, owners were running into price resistance, and more deals were falling through. The median price for an existing house fell back from a high of $191,000 in June to $187,000 in October.

One factor slowing the housing market might have been rising interest rates. Although inflation remained low in 2004, at an annual average of 3.5 percent, the sudden spike in energy prices, coupled with two years of record high federal budget deficits and signs of slowing labor productivity, put upward pressure on prices. To keep inflation in check, the Federal Reserve, after steadily reducing interest rates from 2001 through June 2003, announced that it planned gradual rate increases. Starting in June it raised the short-term federal funds rate on overnight loans five times, each time by a quarter of a percentage point. At the end of the year, the rate was 2.25 percent, still well below historical levels. *(Oil prices, p. 186)*

Overall, the stock markets gained during the year, continuing a rally that began in 2003. The Dow Jones industrial average was somewhat disappointing; it finished the year with a 3.15 percent increase, in large part because several highly profitable drugs were pulled off the market for safety reasons at the end of the year, sending stocks of pharmaceutical companies plummeting. But the NASDAQ composite index ended the year up 8.6 percent and the Standard and Poor's 500 Index (S&P 500) finished at 9 percent above its endpoint in 2003. Most of the growth occurred after President Bush won a second term in the White House. Before November 2, the Dow Jones industrial average and the NASDAQ composite were both down for the year, while the S&P 500 was up less than 2 percent. Analysts generally predicted continued growth for 2005.

Similarly, while the overall annual figures for many economic indicators were strong in 2004, the month-to-month and quarter-to-quarter changes were often erratic, leading to a pervasive sense of unease about the course of the economy. For example, while the growth rate for the year was 4.4 percent, it would move above 4 percent in one quarter only to fall back near 3 percent the next.

This up-and-down pattern was particularly apparent in the job statistics. Overall, according to preliminary figures, the economy added 2.2 million jobs in 2004, for a net gain of 119,000 jobs for the period from January 2001 to January 2005. That saved Bush from becoming the first president since Herbert Hoover (1929–1933) to preside over a net loss of jobs, but it fell 400,000 short of the number the president's Council of Economic Advisers had predicted would be added. The small increase also fell far short of the hopes of many American workers who had been laid off and were unable to find new work. The jobless rate, which had been hovering around 6 percent in 2003, fell to around 5.4 percent in 2004, but the decline had as much to do with discouraged workers dropping out of the formal labor market as it did with new jobs being created.

Manufacturing companies, which lost more than 2 million jobs from 2000 to the end of 2003, gained back just 96,000 jobs in 2004—the weakest rebound in factory jobs of any recent economic recovery in the United States. Moreover, most of the growth in manufacturing jobs took place at the beginning of the year; relatively few were added in the last quarter. Most of the new jobs in 2004 were in the services industry, where business and professional service jobs rose by 546,000 and jobs in health care services rose by 342,000.

There was some expectation that job creation would pick up in 2005. Labor productivity—worker output per hour—slowed from its 5 percent pace in 2003 to 4.1 percent in 2004, its slowest rate of growth since 2001. Slower productivity meant companies might have to take on more workers to meet production requirements. Companies already appeared to be slowing or stopping layoffs. In addition, a tax depreciation benefit that had been accelerated to give companies an incentive to buy computers, software, and other machinery that helped improve labor productivity was expiring. At the same time, analysts were expecting more mergers among big companies; such mergers almost inevitably led to layoffs of redundant workers. Although the Council of Economic Advisers predicted in its 2004 report, released February 9, that a net of 3.6 million jobs would be added in 2005, in December it pared back that prediction to 2.1 million.

Not surprisingly, given the number of people who had lost their jobs or could not find work, the government reported that the numbers of people living in poverty and without health insurance had increased in 2003 for the third year in a row. The Census Bureau said in August that about 1.3 million people fell into poverty in 2003, for a total of 35.8 million people, or 12.5 percent of the population. The number of people without health insurance rose by 1.4 million to 45 million, or 15.6 percent of the population. At the same time, the number of Americans on welfare declined by 149,000 in 2003 to a total of 4.9 million people. Many experts and policymakers suggested this seeming anomaly resulted from the overhaul of the federal welfare system in 1996, which they said helped thousands of single mothers obtain and stay in paying jobs. Others disagreed, arguing that the overhaul was designed to reduce welfare, not poverty, and that many people in need were simply not being helped. *(Welfare overhaul, Historic Documents of 1996, p. 450)*

Elections and Job Creation

Several factors accounted for the 2 million-plus jobs lost in manufacturing since 2000, according to experts. One was a drop in demand resulting from the recession and weak recovery. A second was the shift over time of demand away from manufactured goods and toward services. According to the Congressional Budget Office, the percentage of total consumer spending on manufactured goods fell from 67 percent in 1950 to 42 percent in 2000. At the same time, investments in better and more efficient manufacturing tools and techniques led to an improvement in manufacturing labor productivity. Overall, that was a benefit because it led to higher profits, lower prices, and higher real wages. But strong productivity growth combined with lower demand also meant companies did not need as many workers. In recent years manufacturers were increasingly dealing with short-term upswings in demand by hiring temporary workers, who were not counted in government measurements of manufacturing employment. Finally, a portion of the lost manufacturing jobs were attributable to trade expansion, as consumers turned away from higher priced domestic goods to lower-priced imports for everything from clothing to computers and other electronic equipment.

Although it accounted for a relatively small portion of the lost jobs (3–10 percent by some estimates), this last factor proved most contentious. When the government reported job losses month after month, workers blamed their employers for laying off American workers in favor of lower-paid foreign workers. Such outsourcing or offshoring had started in the 1970s for many sectors in manufacturing that found it more profitable to move their production facilities overseas. With the advent of high-speed computers and communications technology, information-based service industries also began to outsource some of their operations, such as call centers and bookkeeping functions, to foreign countries. *(Outsourcing, Historic Documents of 2003, p. 441)*

Democrats seeking to make Bush a one-term president like his father focused on outsourcing as evidence that the president was doing little to help stimulate job creation or stop the flow of jobs overseas. They received some unintended help early in the year from the president's own Council of Economic Advisers. At a February 9 news conference releasing the annual economic report of the president, Gregory N. Mankiw, the chairman of the council, touched off a major controversy when he described outsourcing as "just a new way of doing international trade. More things are tradable than were tradable in the past and that's a good thing."

Most economists would agree with Mankiw that the expansion of free trade in goods and services benefited all participating countries over the long run. Democrats, however, immediately seized on Mankiw's remarks as confirming that Bush was insensitive to the plight of American workers. "The Bush administration said that sending American jobs overseas is a good thing for America and for the economy," Sen. John Kerry of Massachusetts, the leading contender for the Democratic presidential nomination, said the next day. "What could they be thinking?" he asked rhetorically. Even Republicans sought to separate themselves from Mankiw's remarks. "I understand that Mr. Mankiw is a brilliant economic theorist, but his theory fails a basic test of real economics. We can't have a healthy economy unless we have more jobs here in America," House Speaker J. Dennis Hastert of Illinois said.

A week later the administration began backing away from the Council of Economic Advisers' projection that the economy would add 2.6 million new jobs in 2004. Few outside analysts expected that many jobs to be created, and administration officials were apparently worried that failure to meet the projection would only give Democrats another opportunity to attack Bush on his jobs record.

In March the administration suffered yet another embarrassment, when it was revealed that Bush's first choice for the new position of assistant secretary of manufacturing and services, Anthony Raimondo, headed a manufacturing firm in Nebraska that had laid off workers in 2002 and then built a new factory in China. The administration abandoned the Raimondo nomination and in April named California businessman Al Frink to be the nation's first "manufacturing czar."

Throughout his presidential campaign, Kerry tried to keep the focus on Bush's vulnerability on job creation and on his own plans for dealing with outsourcing. Kerry said he would close tax loopholes that he said encouraged companies to move work overseas. He proposed tax incentives that would encourage companies to keep manufacturing jobs in the United States. But Kerry also suffered some embarrassing moments. In May, for example, while out on the campaign trail, the senator missed a vote in the Senate on a Democratic amendment to the corporate tax bill that would have extended unemployment benefits for an additional thirteen weeks for some jobless workers. The amendment lost by a single vote, and Kerry was the only senator who did not cast a vote. He was immediately criticized for undermining his own campaign message. *(Presidential debates, p. 675; election results, p. 773)*

Following are the text of President George W. Bush's annual report to Congress, The Economic Report of the President, *and excerpts from chapter 1, "Lessons from the Recent Business Cycle," of* The Annual Report of the Council of Economic Advisers, *both released February 9, 2004.*

The Economic Report of the President

To the Congress of the United States:

As 2004 begins, America's economy is strong and getting stronger. Over the past several years, this Nation has faced major economic challenges resulting from the decline of the stock market beginning in early 2000, a recession that began shortly after, revelations about corporate governance scandals, slow growth among many of our major trading partners, terrorist attacks, and the war against terror, including in Afghanistan and Iraq. These challenges affected business and consumer confidence and resulted in hardship for people in many industries and regions of our Nation. Americans have responded to each challenge, and now we have the results: renewed confidence, strong growth, new jobs, and a mounting prosperity that will reach every corner of America.

This Report, prepared by my Council of Economic Advisers, describes the economic challenges we faced, the actions we took, and the results we are seeing. It also discusses our plan to continue growing the economy and creating jobs.

In May 2003, I signed a Jobs and Growth bill that focused on three key goals. First, we accelerated previously passed tax relief and let American households keep more of their own money to save, invest, and spend. Second, we increased incentives for small businesses to invest in new equipment and plant expansions. Third, we enacted important tax relief on dividend income and capital gains to help investors and businesses. These actions were designed to promote investment, job creation, and income growth. By all three measures of performance, we are seeing signs of success.

Since May 2003, we have seen the economy grow at its fastest pace in nearly 20 years. Consumers and businesses have gained confidence. Retail sales are strong, and Americans are buying, building, and renovating houses at a record pace. Investment has strengthened, with spending on business equipment the best in 5 years. The unemployment rate has fallen from its peak of 6.3 percent last June to 5.7 percent in December, and employment is beginning to rise as new jobs are created, especially in small business. Productivity growth has been strong, leading to higher incomes for workers, while the tax relief we passed means that American families keep more of their money instead of sending it to Washington.

We are moving in the right direction, but have more to do. I will not be satisfied until every American who wants a job can find one. I have outlined a six-point plan to promote job creation and strong economic growth. This plan includes initiatives to help manage rising health care costs to make health care more affordable and accessible for American workers and families; reduce the burden of junk lawsuits on the economy; ensure a reliable and affordable energy supply; simplify and streamline government regulations; open foreign markets for American goods and services; and allow businesses and families to keep more of their hard-earned money and plan with confidence by making our tax relief permanent. This year, I will work with the Congress to achieve these goals.

I will also continue to work with the Congress on another important shared goal: controlling federal spending and reducing the deficit. The federal budget is in deficit, foremost because of the economic slowdown and then recession that began in 2000 and the additional costs of fighting the war on terror and protecting the homeland. We are continuing to take action to restrain spending and bring the deficit down. By carefully evaluating priorities and being good stewards of the taxpayer's money, we will cut the budget deficit in half over the next five years.

The task of reducing the deficit will become easier because America's economy is growing. We have taken the actions needed to restore growth, and we are pursuing additional policies to help create jobs for American workers and families. I'm optimistic about the future of our economy because I know the values of America and the decency and entrepreneurial spirit of our people.

George W. Bush
The White House
February 2004

Source: U.S. Executive Office of the President. *Economic Report of the President.* February 9, 2004. www.gpoaccess.gov/eop (accessed January 20, 2005).

The Annual Report of the Council of Economic Advisers

Lessons from the Recent Business Cycle

Economic conditions in the United States improved substantially during 2003, with real gross domestic product (GDP), the most comprehensive measure of the output of the U.S. economy, expanding at an annual rate of more than 8 percent in the third quarter of the year. Based on data available through the middle of January, a further solid gain appears likely in the fourth quarter (the GDP estimate for the fourth quarter was released after this Report went to press). The improvement in the economy over the course of the year stemmed largely from faster growth in household consumption, extraordinary gains in residential investment, and a sharp acceleration of investment in equipment and software by businesses. Payroll employment bottomed out in July and increased 278,000 over the remainder of the year. Financial markets responded favorably to the strengthening of the economy, with the total value of the stock market rising more than $3 trillion, or 31 percent, over the course of 2003.

Despite this improvement, the U.S. economy has further to go to make up for the weakness that began showing even before the economy slipped into recession roughly three years ago. Until recently, the recovery has been slow and uneven. Employment has lagged behind gains in other areas. Strong fiscal policy actions by this Administration and the Congress, together with the Federal Reserve's stimulative monetary policy, have softened the impact of the recession and have also put the economy on an upward trajectory. The Administration's pro-growth tax policy, in particular, has laid the groundwork for sustainable rapid growth in the years ahead. This chapter discusses the distinctive features of the recent recession and recovery, and it draws lessons for the future. The key points in this chapter are:

- Structural imbalances, such as the "capital overhang" that developed in the late 1990s, can take some time to resolve.
- Uncertainty matters for economic decisions, and was likely a factor weighing on investment in recent years.
- Aggressive monetary policy can reduce the depth of a recession.
- Tax cuts can boost economic activity by raising after-tax income and enhancing incentives to work, save, and invest.
- Strong productivity growth raises standards of living but means that much faster economic growth is needed to raise employment.

Overview of the Recent Business Cycle

The recent recession and recovery mark the seventh business cycle in the U.S. economy since 1960. This cycle shares some common features with previous business cycles. According to the National Bureau of Economic Research (NBER), the unofficial arbiter of U.S. business cycles, a recession is "a period of falling economic activity spread across the economy, lasting more than a few months, normally visible in real GDP, real income, employment, industrial production, and wholesale-retail sales." The recent recession, like others, has involved a downturn in economic activity of sufficient depth, duration, and breadth to be judged a recession by the NBER.

The NBER also identifies the peaks and troughs of economic activity that mark when recessions begin and end. In November 2001, the NBER determined that the economy had peaked in March 2001. However, revisions to economic data since the NBER's initial decision suggest that the peak in activity was actually months earlier. In July 2003, the NBER determined that the economy had reached a trough in November 2001.

Despite the similarities between the recent business cycle and previous ones, this most recent cycle was distinctive in important and instructive ways. One noteworthy difference is that real GDP fell much less in this recession than has been typical. . . .

This relatively mild decline in output can be attributed to unusually resilient household spending. Consumer spending on goods and services held up well throughout the slowdown, and investment in housing increased at a fairly steady pace rather than declining as has been typical in past recessions. In contrast, business investment in capital equipment and structures has been quite soft in this cycle. As discussed below, business spending during the past few years has likely been held down by overinvestment in the late 1990s, as well as by heightened business caution owing to terrorism and corporate scandals. As a result of these forces, investment weakened sooner and has recovered more slowly than in the typical cycle.

Another distinguishing feature of this cycle has been the weakness in labor markets relative to output. In particular, the recovery in employment—although now under way—lagged the upturn in output by a much longer period than in prior recessions. This difference was associated with unusually large productivity gains. . . .

Lesson 1: Structural Imbalances Can Take Some Time to Resolve

Business investment in equipment and software surged in the late 1990s. Real investment increased at an average annual rate of roughly 13 percent between the fourth quarter of 1994 and the fourth quarter of 1999, compared with an average annual rate of less than 7 percent over the preceding three decades. The surge in investment was led by purchases of high-tech capital goods—computers, software, and communications equipment—which increased at an average annual rate of 20 percent over the period.

Economic theory implies that businesses invest when they believe that there are profits to be made from that investment. In the late 1990s, several developments fed a perception that the expected future return from newly installed capital would be considerably greater than the cost of this capital. Rapid advances in technology had lowered the price of high-tech capital goods dramatically throughout the 1990s and especially in the second half of the decade. For example, the quality-adjusted price index for business computers and peripheral equipment fell at an average annual rate of 22 percent between late 1994 and late 1999. In addition, rapidly growing demand for business output led firms to believe that newly installed capital would be used productively, boosting the expected return to investment.

Moreover, technological progress and legislation provided incentives for strong investment in high-tech equipment. The development of the World Wide Web enabled new and established firms to enter e-commerce, and rapidly increasing household and business access to the Internet provided a large base of potential customers for these firms. The Telecommunications Act of 1996 provided for substantial deregulation of the telecommunications industry and may have spurred investment in that sector. In addition, concern that some computer systems might be inoperable after December 1999 caused a wave of so-called Y2K-related investment. Some analysis indicates that Y2K spending alone boosted the growth rate of real equipment and software investment by more than $3\frac{1}{2}$ percentage points per year in the latter part of the 1990s.

Optimism about the potential gains from new capital, and from high-tech capital in particular, was reflected not only in investment decisions but also in a sharp rise in stock prices. From late 1994 to late 1999, the Wilshire 5000—a broad index of U.S. stock prices—nearly tripled. The NASDAQ stock price index, which is heavily weighted toward high-tech industries, registered an even more dramatic ascent, increasing more than fourfold over this period. The increase in stock prices stimulated investment by reducing the cost of equity capital. In addition, the rise in stock prices fueled a consumption boom by boosting the wealth of a growing number of Americans and more generally signaling better future economic conditions. This consumption boom encouraged further business investment.

In mid-2000, business equipment investment abruptly slowed. After rising at an annual rate of 15 percent in the first half of the year, real spending on business equipment and software inched up at about a $\frac{1}{4}$ percent annual rate in the second half. The slowdown in high-tech equipment investment was especially dramatic. For example, real outlays for computers had skyrocketed at an annual rate of 40 percent in the first half of the year, but grew at less than one-quarter of that pace in the second half. This stalling of investment preceded the downturn in the overall economy; by contrast, in the typical business cycle, investment has turned down at the same time as overall economic activity. The unusual timing of the investment slowdown in this recession is the reason that the recent business cycle has been widely viewed as an "investment-led" recession.

The sharp break in investment occurred in parallel with an apparent reevaluation of future corporate profitability among financial market participants. By the end of 2000, the Wilshire 5000 index of stock prices was down 13 percent from its peak, and analysts had substantially marked down their forecasts for S&P 500 earnings over the coming year. The movements were even more dramatic in the high-tech sector. The NASDAQ index of stock prices dropped nearly 50 percent from its peak in March 2000 to the end of the year. The prices of technology, telecommunications, and Internet shares fell particularly sharply, along with near-term earnings estimates. The elevated valuations of many such companies also declined markedly. Indeed, the price-earnings ratio (where "earnings" are those expected over the next year) for the technology component of the S&P 500 fell from a peak of more than 50 in early 2000 to less than 35 by the end of the year.

These facts and considerable anecdotal evidence suggest that business managers and investors sharply revised downward the expected gains from new capital investment during this period. One factor that may have contributed to the downward revision is a possible slowing of the pace of technological advance—the rate at which computer prices were declining eased (from more than 20 percent in the late 1990s to about half that in 2000), and the software industry reportedly developed no new so-called "killer applications" that required or spurred purchases of new hardware. In addition, firms may have been disappointed by the response of households to e-commerce opportunities and to new communications technologies such as broadband. Finally, previous investments had not uniformly translated into higher profitability, perhaps because the true potential of new forms of capital could be realized only by changing other aspects of production processes. For example, new computer systems designed to lower inventory management costs might have required an expensive reconfiguration of warehouses.

This reassessment of the gains from capital investment also implied that existing stocks of some types of equipment exceeded the amount of equipment that firms could put to profitable use. Such an excess of the existing capital stock relative to the desired stock (often called a capital overhang) is one type of *structural imbalance* that can slow or reverse economic expansion. In the case of an excess supply of capital, investment would be expected to slow until the capital overhang dissipates through a combination of depreciation in the existing stock and an increase in the desired stock due to lower costs of capital or stronger final demand.

Resolving the structural imbalance that developed in the late 1990s took considerable time. Real business spending on equipment and software dropped more than 9 percent during the four quarters of 2001 and posted less than a 2 percent gain during the four quarters of 2002. The high-tech categories showed especially sharp breaks in their upward trends. In these categories, the effects of the capital overhang were likely exacerbated by a reduction in normal replacement demand following the Y2K-related investment spurt. The prolonged period of sluggishness in business investment is another distinctive feature of this business cycle. Real investment in equipment and software typically has fallen less and has recovered more quickly than it did in the current recession and recovery. . . .

Lesson 2: Uncertainty Matters for Economic Decisions

The U.S. economy has been hit hard in the past few years by a number of unexpected developments, including the tragic terrorist attacks of September 11, 2001, the corporate governance and accounting scandals of 2002, and the geopolitical tensions surrounding the war with Iraq in 2003. In addition to having direct effects on the economy, each of these events contributed to a climate of uncertainty that weighed on household and business confidence and thereby affected spending decisions.

The terrorist attacks have had substantial consequences for many aspects of the U.S. economy. The heightened focus on security at home, together with the determined efforts against terrorism around the world, have required increases in some types of government spending. The attacks hurt some industries directly: for example, fear of new attacks and the inconveniences associated with heightened airport security reduced air travel and tourism. Beyond these direct economic effects, the unprecedented attacks on the United States also generated uncertainty about future economic conditions.

Another setback for the economy was the series of revelations during 2002 regarding incomplete or misleading corporate financial reporting and, in some cases, wrongful conduct by corporate management. The number of financial restatements—that is, corrections to previous statements of earnings—by U.S. public corporations reached a record high in 2002. Although most of the restatements were not linked to misconduct, they raised questions about the reliability of accounting practices and the credibility of corporate financial disclosures. The combination of these concerns and allegations of misconduct by high-profile executives heightened investors' uncertainty about the quality of corporate governance and the reliability of earnings reports and projections.

In early 2003, uncertainty about the economic outlook increased during the period leading up to the war with Iraq. One source of this uncertainty was the potential effect of the conflict on the capacity for producing and transporting oil in the Persian Gulf, and thus on the future supply and price of oil. Observers were also concerned about the amount of additional government spending that would be needed to finance military operations and subsequent reconstruction, as well as the danger of retaliatory terrorist attacks on the United States. Finally, consumer confidence fell sharply in early 2003, raising concerns that the consumer demand that had supported the economy over the previous couple of years might falter. Such concerns were plausible, given that the 1990 Gulf War roughly coincided with a marked drop in consumer confidence and the start of the 1990–1991 recession.

The uncertainties created by the three developments described above had significant effects on financial markets. Stock prices dipped noticeably in September 2001, recovered subsequently, but moved down during the summer of 2002 and fell again in early 2003. *Risk spreads* (the difference between interest rates on corporate bonds and on comparable Treasury bonds) jumped temporarily after the terrorist attacks and rose again in late 2002 during the peak of concerns about corporate governance. Because risk spreads generally reflect the extra return investors require to hold riskier corporate assets, the rise in spreads in 2002 indicated investors' greater perceived probability of default, lesser willingness to take on risk, or both. Investor uncertainty also was reflected in measures of the expected volatility of stock prices based on option prices, which were elevated during each of the episodes noted above. . . .

Reductions in share prices and increases in bond yields raised the cost of funding capital expenditures and thus directly discouraged business investment. Increased uncertainty likely also had *direct* effects on business decisions about investment and hiring: uncertainty may cause firms to wait until they have more information before committing to an investment. In this case, firm managers hesitate to respond to a change in demand. Anecdotal evidence from the past few years as well as some statistical analyses suggest that uncertainty has a noticeable damping effect on investment. Anecdotal evidence also suggests that uncertainty has held back hiring in the past few years.

Household spending may also have been affected by uncertainty. Economic theory and empirical evidence suggest that greater uncertainty about future economic conditions may lead households to raise saving and reduce spending. However, such effects are not immediately apparent in the recent cyclical downturn—as will be explained shortly, household spending has shown remarkable resiliency over the past few years. A possible explanation for the seeming discrepancy between this pattern and empirical work based on earlier data is that the negative effects of greater uncertainty were offset by lower taxes and the effects of lower interest rates.

While the uncertainty created by these unexpected developments has hampered the economic recovery, household and business confidence strengthened considerably during the second half of 2003. This Administration and the Congress moved swiftly to address problems with corporate governance. In March 2002, the President proposed a set of reforms aimed at a wide range of corporate governance issues, and in July 2002, Congress passed the landmark Sarbanes-Oxley Act. As concerns about corporate governance have abated, and the durability of the recovery has become more apparent, firms have begun to invest and hire.

Lesson 3: Aggressive Monetary Policy Can Reduce the Depth of a Recession

When the economy showed signs of weakening three years ago, the Federal Reserve moved decisively to reduce interest rates to stimulate the economy. During 2001, the Federal Reserve cut the Federal funds rate eleven times for a total reduction of $4\frac{3}{4}$ percentage points. When the economy failed to gain much forward momentum, the Federal Reserve reduced the funds rate another $\frac{1}{2}$ percentage point in November 2002 and a further $\frac{1}{4}$ percentage point last June, to 1 percent. The decline in the Federal funds rate in this economic downturn was larger and occurred more rapidly than in previous downturns. One factor that likely contributed to the Federal Reserve's willingness to cut the funds rate so sharply was the low level of inflation. Core consumer price inflation, as measured by the 12-month change in the consumer price index excluding food and energy, was around $2\frac{3}{4}$ percent in early 2001 and fell to just over 1 percent by late last year. Thus, the Federal Reserve was able to lower the Federal funds rate and keep it low with little apparent risk of triggering an undesirably high inflation rate.

Long-term interest rates on government securities and high-grade corporate securities began falling in late 2000, likely in part reflecting an anticipated decline in the Federal funds rate in response to a weaker economic outlook. Throughout 2001, short-term and medium-term interest rates declined along with the Federal funds rate. However, long-term rates changed little, on net, because market participants apparently expected the downturn to be short-lived and believed that the Federal Reserve would soon begin raising the funds rate. Then, in 2002, persistently weak economic conditions, combined with the Federal Reserve's decisions to hold the funds rate steady for much of the year and cut it further in November, persuaded market participants that short-term rates were likely to stay low for some time. As a result, long-term rates fell substantially, on balance, in 2002. Long-term rates fluctuated in 2003, but finished the year a little above where they started.

Interest rates on fixed-rate mortgages tracked long-term government yields over this period, as they typically have. In 2003, the interest rate on 30-year fixed-rate mortgages averaged more than 2 percentage points below the average in 2000. Low and falling mortgage rates have provided strong support for housing demand over the past few years. Indeed, residential investment has increased at a fairly steady pace throughout the period of overall economic weakness—a stark contrast to the pattern in past recessions, when residential investment tended to fall sharply.

Declining mortgage interest rates have also fueled an enormous wave of mortgage refinancing. (The response has been particularly strong because technological and institutional advances in mortgage markets have reduced the costs of such transactions.) In many refinancing transactions, homeowners have "cashed out" some of their accumulated home equity by taking out new mortgages that are larger than the remaining balance on their previous mortgages. According to a survey of households, more than half of the liquefied equity funded either home renovations or household consumption and thus may have helped to sustain aggregate demand. Another substantial portion reportedly was used to pay down credit card debt, which generally carries a higher interest rate than mortgage debt and, unlike mortgage debt, is not tax-deductible. By moving from a high-cost form of debt to a lower-cost one, households have been better able to cope with their debt burdens. In particular, the transition has held down the fraction of their income committed to regular debt service payments, and thus has increased the amount of income available for spending on discretionary items.

Low long-term interest rates have also reduced the cost of funds to businesses. In some cases, this lower cost has been passed directly to households. For example, motor vehicle manufacturers made low-interest-rate loans available to car buyers in late 2001 and have generally maintained a high level of financing incentives since then. These incentives have bolstered consumer outlays for motor vehicles.

More generally, lower interest rates make it cheaper for firms to finance new investment projects. The aggressive easing of monetary policy since early 2001 has likely helped to support business investment, even though the forces discussed earlier have, on balance, caused investment to be weak.

Firms have also taken advantage of low long-term interest rates to restructure their balance sheets. Net issuance of commercial paper and net borrowing from banks were both negative in each of the past three years, while net bond issuance was strong. By issuing longer-term bonds and paying down short-term debt, businesses have substantially lengthened the overall maturity of their debt. This restructuring reduced firms' near-term repayment obligations and locked in low rates for longer periods. The strengthening of businesses' financial positions means that financial constraints are less likely to restrain a further pickup in hiring and investment.

Lesson 4: Tax Cuts Can Boost Economic Activity by Raising After-Tax Income and Enhancing Incentives to Work, Save, and Invest

The use of *discretionary fiscal policy*—explicit changes in taxes and government spending, as opposed to those that occur automatically as economic activity changes—to reduce cyclical fluctuations in the economy has fallen out of favor with many economists over the past several decades. Some have pointed to the difficulties of crafting and implementing discretionary policy quickly enough to provide stimulus while the economy is still weak rather than accentuating an upturn that is already under way. It has also been noted that a temporary reduction in taxes might be mostly saved by households and thus encourage relatively little additional spending. Moreover, some have argued that expansionary fiscal policy can push up interest rates and thereby "crowd out" interest-sensitive spending. All told, before the recent business cycle, many economists believed that monetary policy made the use of discretionary fiscal policy unnecessary to stabilize the economy.

The experience of the past three years, however, shows that well-designed and well-timed tax cuts are a useful complement to expansionary monetary policy. Over this period, three bills have made significant changes to the personal and corporate tax systems. The President came into office with proposals for permanently reducing taxes on work and saving. With the budget surplus having reached its highest level relative to GDP in half a century, the proposals were aimed predominantly at reducing tax-based impediments to long-term growth. The proposals resulted in the Economic Growth and Tax Relief Reconciliation Act (EGTRRA), which the President signed into law in June 2001. In the wake of the terrorist attacks of September 2001 and continuing softness in the economy, the Congress passed the Job Creation and Worker Assistance Act (JCWAA), which the President signed into law in March 2002. And, in early 2003, with the pace of economic growth still falling below its potential and the labor market lagging behind, the President proposed and the Congress enacted the Jobs and Growth Tax Relief Reconciliation Act (JGTRRA), which the President signed into law in May.

These three bills provided substantial short-term stimulus to economic activity and helped put the economy on the road to recovery. One source of stimulus has been the large boost to after-tax personal income stemming from lower marginal tax rates, a larger child tax credit, reduced tax rates on dividends and capital gains, and other changes in the tax law. Real after-tax income has increased much more than before-tax income over the past three years. Over the preceding five years, average annual growth in real after-tax income was more than $\frac{1}{2}$ percentage point below the growth rate of real before-tax income. Numerous studies have shown that long-term tax cuts foster higher consumer spending. Thus, the additional income provided by the tax cuts is likely to have substantially boosted aggregate demand since 2000.

The tax cuts provided further stimulus by increasing incentives for business investment. Some of these incentives came in the form of bonus depreciation for business investment, an expansion in the amount of expensing of investment available for small businesses. The bonus depreciation was introduced in the 2002 tax cut (JCWAA), which specified that 30 percent of the price of investments made by September 10, 2004 could be treated as an immediate expense under the corporate profits tax and the remaining 70 percent depreciated over time according to the regular depreciation schedules. Moving the depreciation closer to the time of new investment increased the present value of depreciation allowances and the net after-tax return on investment. The 2003 tax cut (JGTRRA) raised the bonus depreciation to 50 percent of the price of new equipment and extended the period of eligibility so that investments made by the end of 2004 would be covered. It also increased the cap on small-business expensing from $25,000 to $100,000 per year through 2005, effectively lowering the cost of investment for small businesses. These tax changes lowered firms' cost of capital and likely provided support for investment at a crucial time.

The tax cuts also reduced the cost of capital and increased incentives for business investment by lowering tax rates on personal capital income. The 2001 tax cut (EGTRRA) phased out the estate tax and reduced marginal tax rates on all forms of income. These steps lowered the tax burden on capital income received from corporations and also on income received through sole proprietorships, partnerships, and S corporations (corporations for which income is taxed through individual tax returns). In addition, the 2003 tax cut (JGTRRA) reduced taxes on corporate dividends and capital gains.

Altogether, these three tax bills provided $68 billion in tax stimulus in fiscal year 2001, $89 billion in fiscal year 2002, $159 billion in fiscal year 2003, and $272 billion in fiscal year 2004. However, the bills were designed not only to provide short-term stimulus, but also to encourage stronger economic growth over the long run. Lower tax rates on labor income provide an incentive to increase work effort. Lower tax rates on capital income—the reward for saving and investment—provide an incentive to do more of these activities. Investment increases the amount of capital for each worker and also increases the rate at which new technology embodied in capital can be put to use. According to one study, the cut in taxes on capital income in the 2003 tax package (JGTRRA) reduced the marginal effective total tax rate on income from corporate investment by 2 to 4 percentage points. Lower taxes on dividends and capital gains also move the tax system toward a more equal treatment of debt and equity, of dividends and capital gains, and of corporate and noncorporate capital. This move increases economic efficiency because it promotes the allocation of capital based on business fundamentals rather than a desire for tax avoidance.

In sum, the tax cuts supported by this Administration provided a substantial short-term stimulus to consumption and investment and promoted strong and sustainable long-term growth. In weighing the merits of countercyclical monetary and fiscal policy, the stimulus provided by discretionary fiscal policy may be especially important in the low-inflation, low-interest-rate environment the country now enjoys. Under these circumstances, the Federal Reserve may have less room to cut interest rates, and direct stimulus to demand from fiscal policy may be needed to ensure that the Nation's resources are fully utilized in the face of cyclical weakness.

Lesson 5: Strong Productivity Growth Raises Standards of Living but Means That Much Faster Economic Growth Is Needed to Raise Employment

One distinctive feature of this recession and recovery has been the remarkably fast growth of *labor productivity*—the amount of goods and services that a worker with given skills produces from each hour of work. The late 1990s had already witnessed an acceleration of productivity growth from an average annual rate of around $1\frac{1}{2}$ percent between the fourth quarters of 1972 and 1995 to a roughly $2\frac{1}{2}$ percent rate between the fourth quarters of 1995 and 2000. Productivity growth then picked up further, contrary to the usual experience in which productivity growth has typically softened in the quarters surrounding business-cycle peaks. In the latest recession, productivity growth leveled off for just one quarter before beginning to rise rapidly. Since the fourth quarter of 2000, productivity has increased at an exceptional annual rate of more than 4 percent per year.

Labor productivity growth can be decomposed into the skills of the workforce (*labor quality*), increases in the amount of capital services per worker-hour (*capital deepening*), and increases in *total factor productivity*—a residual category that captures the change in aggregate output not explained by changes in capital and labor inputs. According to this framework . . . productivity growth stepped up in the mid-1990s partly because the rapid pace of business investment generated large increases in the amount of capital available to each worker. Yet a larger part of this acceleration owes to faster growth in the unexplained residual category of total factor productivity.

The explanation for faster productivity growth in the past couple of years is not clear (especially since the information needed to decompose productivity growth over this period is quite limited). One possibility is that weaker profits and skepticism about the return to new physical investment have encouraged firms to make better use of the resources they already had rather than investing in new technology and capacity. This effort to increase what is sometimes called *organizational capital* might involve, for example, restructuring production processes and retraining workers to take maximum advantage of new information-technology equipment installed in the late 1990s. Another possibility is that firms somehow induced extra work effort for a time because they were hesitant to hire new workers until they were more confident that increases in final demand would persist. A third possibility is that the slower recent pace of gross investment may have been accompanied by slower depreciation of the existing capital stock so that firms lengthened replacement cycles and held on to their existing equipment for longer periods. If this were the case, net investment and the growth rate of the capital stock would have been stronger than indicated by measures based on historical depreciation rates.

In the long run, productivity growth is the key determinant of growth in living standards. Without labor productivity growth, our nation's output and income would grow only at the rate at which the labor force expands; if the labor force grows proportionally with population, this would mean that income per person would be unchanged. With productivity growth, income per person increases. Indeed, U.S. average income is close to eight times as high as it was one hundred years ago, similar to the increase in productivity over this period. The recent robust gains in productivity have boosted both corporate profits and employees' compensation. Corporate profits declined sharply during the recession, but turned around and rose briskly in 2003 (based on data through the first three quarters). Average hourly earnings of production workers in private industry have risen at an average annual rate of close to 3 percent over the past three years. Moreover, productivity growth has reduced inflationary pressures by holding down growth in unit labor costs. As a result, wage gains after adjusting for inflation have been even more impressive by historical standards. In this recession, real average hourly earnings, published in the Bureau of Labor Statistics employment release, never fell below their pre-recession levels, and increased nearly 3 percent in the eleven quarters after the recession began. The experiences in past recessions have been diverse, but many show a net decline in real hourly earnings or much weaker growth even eleven quarters after the start of the recession.

By definition, labor productivity multiplied by hours worked equals output. Thus, in an arithmetic sense, faster productivity growth generally implies that output must expand more rapidly to generate employment gains. The same principle explains why the rapid pace of productivity growth over the past couple of years has meant that gains in output occurred without gains in employment, until recently.

Indeed, the performance of employment over the past couple of years has been appreciably weaker than in past business cycles. Employment was slow to pick up in the average previous recovery, perhaps because employers delayed hiring until they became confident that the increases in demand were sustainable. However, such sluggishness typically has been short-lived (a quarter or two) and followed by vigorous expansion. In contrast, in the current business cycle, employment did not begin its recovery until nearly two years after the upturn in real GDP. The performance of employment in this cycle has lagged even that of the so-called "jobless recovery" from the 1990–1991 recession. . . .

Nonetheless, one should not conclude that rapid productivity growth causes low employment growth. Rapid productivity growth means that output must increase faster for employment to expand, but it also means that the economy is capable of growing faster. In the long run, the faster rate of *potential output growth* is undoubtedly a good thing for living standards. . . .

Conclusion

The U.S. economy is much stronger now than it was a year ago and . . . prospects for the coming year look solid. Nonetheless, the experiences of the past several years remain relevant for the future. Understanding the negative forces that weighed against the economy, as well as the policies that contributed to the recovery, can help policy makers ensure that economic activity maintains a strong upward trend in the years ahead.

Source: Council of Economic Advisers. *The Annual Report of the Council of Economic Advisers.* February 9, 2004. www.gpoaccess.gov/eop (accessed January 20, 2005).

Georgian President Saakashvili on the Transition to Democracy

February 24, 2004

INTRODUCTION

Georgia's thirty-six-year-old firebrand opposition leader, Mikhail Saakashvili, won an overwhelming election as the country's new president on January 4, 2004. He then embarked on an ambitious agenda to end the corruption that had dominated the country's sagging economy and to reassert control over three breakaway provinces. Saakashvili had led a nonviolent revolution the previous November, which led to the ouster of President Eduard Shevardnadze after he tried to rig parliamentary elections. *(Background, Historic Documents of 2003, p. 1039)*

An Overwhelming Electoral Victory

Saakashvili and two colleagues, all three of whom had been protégés of Shevardnadze, had masterminded the street protests in late 2004 that had sapped the strength of the longtime president's autocratic regime and led to his ignominious departure from power. As mayor of Tbilisi, the Georgian capital, Saakashvili clearly was the dominant figure in the opposition—a dynamic, U.S.-educated lawyer who spoke his mind, tended to be arrogant and emotional, and was not troubled by diplomatic niceties. His colleague Nino Burdhanadze, speaker of the old parliament, became acting president after Shevardnadze left office but readily gave way to Saakashvili as the opposition presidential candidate; so, too, did the third member of the opposition leadership, Zhurab Zvania.

The next presidential election had not been due until 2005, but after ousting Shevardnadze the opposition moved the voting up to January 4, 2004. A key step in the preelection process was an agreement by Aslan Abashidze, the leader of the Adzharia region in southwest Georgia, to participate in the voting. Abashidze had backed Shevardnadze in the disputed November polling, had refused to acknowledge the opposition's rise to power, and had threatened to take his "autonomous" region into formal independence. However, after persuasion by the U.S. ambassador to Georgia, Richard M. Miles, Abashidze lifted a state of emergency that had closed borders with the rest of Georgia, allowed the voting to proceed in his region, and even showed up to vote himself.

The voting proceeded peacefully and with little rancor—a sharp contrast to the tension that had surrounded the disputed parliamentary election two months earlier. The former ruling party of Shevardnadze chose not to contest the election, and Saakashvili faced only token opposition from five rivals. Shevardnadze himself was among those who said they cast ballots for the young, new leader. "He has a lot of energy and is well educated," Shevardnadze said of his former protégé. "He should talk less and work more. Enough of populism. There is a great deal that needs to be done."

The final tally was more like those customary in the days of the old Soviet Union, of which Georgia had been a part: Saakashvili won 96 percent of the 1.5 million votes cast, out of a total population of 5 million. Even some supporters warned of the dangers inherent in such an outcome: that some might consider the vote fraudulent, that Saakashvili might misinterpret the victory as a blanket endorsement of everything he wanted to do, or that public expectations might be so high that Saakashvili could never meet them. "Now he faces the most difficult task of his life," Alexander Rondeli, president of he Georgian Foundation for Strategic and International Studies, told the *Los Angeles Times.* "To make many people happy is not easy."

Even before Saakashvili took office, he received another vote of confidence—from the Bush administration, which had tried and failed to ensure fairness in the 2003 parliamentary elections. U.S. officials said informally on January 18 that a Pentagon training mission in Georgia, which had been due to leave in March, would be extended indefinitely. The mission had begun in 2002, with the stated intent of training Georgian soldiers to battle Islamist fighters in the Pankisi Gorge region, adjacent to the troubled Chechnya region of Russia. The presence of some 150 U.S. Special Forces trainers quickly took on broader significance as Washington's implicit guarantee of Georgia's independence from Russia, which still maintained two military bases on Georgian soil. Saakashvili had made removal of Russian troops a high priority during his campaign.

Saakashvili took office on January 25 in a ceremony featuring red rose petals, symbolizing the single rose he carried as he led opposition forces into parliament the day before Shevardnadze stepped aside. In his inaugural address Saakashvili reached out to Russia, saying: "Today, as my first act, I am offering a friendly hand to Russia and I am waiting for a friendly response." He made it clear, however, that the United States was his preferred partner. Secretary of State Colin Powell attended the inauguration and participated in a public meeting at the Tbilisi town hall and a news conference at the parliament building. Russian foreign minister Igor Ivanov also attended the inauguration but was not invited to the other meetings.

Although he looked to the West for inspiration, Saakashvili clearly recognized that good relations with Russia were vital to Georgia's future. His first foreign trip, therefore, was to Moscow, where he had a cordial meeting with Russian president Vladimir Putin. A month later, Saakashvili traveled to Washington for meetings with President George W. Bush and other officials. In a February 24 speech at the School for Advanced International Studies at Johns Hopkins University's Washington campus, Saakashvili appealed for U.S. financial aid and diplomatic support to help Georgia take advantage of a "special window of opportunity" that, he said, was opened by political revolution there. The next day, after their meeting at the White House, Bush told reporters: "I'm impressed by this leader, I'm impressed by his vision. I'm impressed by his courage."

The coalition of opposition parties that Saakashvili and his colleagues had put together in late 2003 dominated new parliamentary elections, held on March 28. Only one other party gained enough of the vote to win any of the 150 seats that were up for election in the 235-seat parliament.

Tackling Corruption

Although big power politics may have gotten the attention of Moscow and Washington when Saakashvili took office, for the Georgian people the central promises the new president offered were to battle endemic corruption and attract the foreign investment needed to jump-start Georgia's anemic economy. Both were considered enormous long-term challenges, but going after high-profile symbols of corruption was one task that promised immediate results. The interim government had fired cabinet officials responsible for the energy and railroads, generally considered by Georgians to be among the most corrupt aspects of society. Other officials of Shevardnadze's government were arrested in February, and for a time there even were hints that Saakashvili might target the former president himself. Saakashvili sought to set a new tone on February 17, when he met with ministers in the new cabinet. "Don't take bribes and don't give jobs to your relatives," he said. "And if you do, you will go straight to prison."

Most Georgians applauded the anticorruption campaign, but some also were quoted as worrying about a downside because corruption had been one of the few efficient sectors of society. "You know, corruption reached so deep that just about every inhabitant of the country could be put in prison for this or that infraction," a doctor, Kote Gvetadze, told the Associated Press in February. "So, we're going to put at least half of Georgia in prison? People are afraid."

Among Saakashvili's corruption targets were several mass media outlets that were raided or threatened with closure for failing to pay taxes and other crimes. These steps brought protests from Amnesty International, the British human rights organization, and others, including the general secretary of Saakashvili's own National Movement Party, who resigned, expressing disgust.

International concerns that Saakashvili might be taking too much power into his own hands escalated in February when the lame-duck parliament adopted a constitutional amendment giving the president expanded influence over all branches of government. The amendment was modeled after the emerging system in Russia, where Putin had consolidated control over a weak parliament and subservient judiciary. *(Russian politics, p. 564)*

Criticism of Saakashvili's often heavy-handed tactics against remnants of the old regime—and even against some of his own supporters—continued throughout the year. On October 18 fourteen nongovernmental groups published an open letter challenging the president for prosecuting his opponents, seeking to marginalize the news media, and what they called his "intolerance toward people with different opinions." In interviews late in the year with Western news media, Saakashvili acknowledged that he had made mistakes but insisted he needed to run risks and take strong action to root out corruption and get the economy moving again.

Confronting Adzharia

Saakashvili's first major crisis emerged in mid-March, when he got into the inevitable confrontation with Abashidze, the leader of Adzharia province, who had defied central Georgian authority for more than a decade. Abashidze on March 15 prevented Saakashvili and some of his aides from entering the province; Saakashvili responded by mounting a blockade of Batumi, Adzharia's capital and chief port on the Black Sea. The crisis briefly threatened to bring Russian intervention on behalf of Abashidze, but it was defused in just a few days with a Russian-mediated agreement that appeared to represent a partial victory for Saakashvili's campaign to gain control of the province.

The dispute over Adzharia flared up again just six weeks later when Saakashvili accused Abashidze of reneging on the earlier agreement and ordered him to dissolve the militias that he had used to control his province. Abashidze responded by blowing up the three bridges that connected the province to Georgia proper. That step set off large street protests in Batumi, with the demonstrators demanding that the autocratic Abashidze give up power. Once again, a senior Russian official stepped in, but rather than negotiate an agreement he apparently persuaded Abashidze to leave his province and head to the safety of Russia. The departure of Abashidze on May 6 was greeted with large celebrations in Batumi and gave Saakashvili an opportunity to proclaim victory: "Georgians, Aslan has fled. Adzharia is free." Saakashvili immediately made a triumphant visit to Batumi and thanked the crowds for their support in the country's second peaceful revolution in six months. News reports later said Saakashvili had orchestrated the street protests against Abashidze, using supporters who had learned their skills in Tbilisi the previous November.

Abkhazia and South Ossetia

Chasing Abashidze from Adzharia proved to be an unexpectedly easy task for the popular Saakashvili, but carrying out the other elements of his campaign promise to "unify Georgia" brought him into more direct conflict with Russian interests. Two other provinces technically remained part of Georgia, under the lasting legacy of Moscow's tinkering with geography during the Soviet era. The larger of the two was Abkhazia, in the northwest, which had declared independence from Georgia shortly after the collapse of the Soviet Union. A bloody civil war there during the early 1990s killed as many as 10,000 people and was a major factor leading to Georgia's decline. By 2004 Abkhazia depended almost entirely upon Russia; nearly all its 250,000 people spoke Russian and held Russian passports, and Moscow kept several thousand troops at a base there. The United Nations for more than a decade had mediated fruitless peace talks between Russia and Georgia on the Abkhazia question.

South Ossetia, in north central Georgia, was the southern portion of a region in the Caucasus mountains known as Ossetia. Its twin, North Ossetia, had been part of Russia, and most Ossetians in both regions considered themselves Russian. South Ossetia's leaders declared independence from Georgia in 1991 but settled temporarily for autonomy when Shevardnadze pledged not to interfere in the region's affairs.

Saakashvili waited until the summer to make good on his pledge to bring Abkhazia and South Ossetia back into Georgia's fold. First, in July, the Georgian army seized two Russian trucks that were delivering helicopter missiles and other weapons to South Ossetia. Saakashvili's government said the seizure was part of a campaign to crack down on the smuggling of guns, vodka, and drugs in the region. Moscow angrily denounced the action, saying the weapons were for a contingent of Russian troops. Moscow called the troops "peacekeepers," but their real mission was to guarantee the region's autonomy against Georgia. That incident led to several outbreaks of shootings, which were tempered in mid-August with the signing of a European-mediated cease-fire. Saakashvili then sought to lure Ossetians back into the Georgian fold with promises of improved schools and even vacations at a Black Sea resort.

Saakashvili escalated his antiseparatist campaign dramatically at the end of July, when a Georgian coast guard vessel fired on a Russian cargo ship as it approached a Black Seat port in Abkhazia. On August 3 Saakashvili said he had ordered the Georgian coast guard to intercept—and, if necessary, sink—all ships entering the country's Black Sea waters without government permission, including ships carrying Russian tourists to coastal resorts in Abkhazia. Addressing Russian tourists directly, he said of Abkhazia: "It is not a place for you to put out deck chairs, because it is stained with Georgian blood." This was a reference to the brief civil war over the region in the early 1990s. Once again, Russia responded with angry words, saying the interception of Russian ships would be a "hostile act, with all the ensuing consequences." Saakashvili followed his threats with another long-planned trip to Washington, where he sought support for his position but instead found the Bush administration deeply reluctant to confront Moscow on such a matter. A month later, on September 21, Saakashvili was back in the United States for a speech to the UN General Assembly, in which he pledged to deal with Abkhazia and South Ossetia "through solely peaceful means."

For all practical purposes Saakashvili then put his confrontation with Abkhazia on hold, pending the outcome of an election the local government there had scheduled to choose a replacement for longtime leader, Vladislav Ardzinba. The outcome of the October 3 election was contested, however, causing a political crisis that led to a rerun on January 12, 2005. The winner of that vote, Sergey Bagapsh, immediately pledged to continue aligning Abkhazia with Russia, rather than Georgia—indicating that the long-running dispute was likely to continue even longer.

Following are excerpts from a speech delivered February 24, 2004, by Georgian president Mikhail Saakashvili to a forum at the Johns Hopkins University School for Advanced International Studies in Washington, D.C., in which he appealed for U.S. help for his country's transition to democracy.

"Georgia after the Rose Revolution"

A Few Thoughts on the Rose Revolution . . .

By now, everyone in this room is familiar with the dramatic events that took place in Georgia during the month of November. Those events so eloquently labeled as the Revolution of Roses. Revolutions are strange in a way—when the processes that contribute to their creation are underway one becomes consumed by a special energy—an energy that in our case was underlined by both *hope* and *apprehension. Hope* that we could reverse Georgia's tragic decline and build a better future. *Apprehension* over how events would unfold—could violence be avoided? Would the Georgian people and the Georgian dream succeed?

Three months have passed since our Revolution took place. What have we learned?

I think we have learned three important lessons. Lessons that only now are becoming clear as my government and me set about the task of re-building Georgia.

The first lesson is that we could survive the succession challenge. What is arguably the single greatest challenge to any transitional nation and in particular, those states of the former Soviet Union.

Many members of our neighborhood seem to have trouble with this issue—with President's not knowing when to leave and political opposition unable to unite or imagine a better future outside the context of inside deal-making. In Georgia—we proved that succession can be peaceful. It can occur—if dramatically—within the framework of the Constitution. It can occur under the banner of a united opposition. And most importantly, it can occur with the strong and genuine support of the people.

Passing the succession test—we have showed at home and abroad—that Georgia has matured and that the State, while weakened during the previous era, nonetheless exists. For anyone who ever thought, or hoped, that Georgia was a failed State—our Revolution and our people, proved them forever wrong. Emerging from the Rose Revolution—Georgia is stronger than ever, more united than ever—and more resolute in its commitment to build a stabile and prosperous State than ever.

The second lesson of the Rose Revolution is that Georgians are very much members of Europe and the European family of nations. In reflecting on this point, I am not simply looking to geography, but rather, to national identity. What we saw in November was a population mobilized in defense of the principles of liberal democracy. What we saw was a population that refused to have their voice—their choice—and their future stolen from them by a corrupt and incompetent government.

The Revolution was not a protest against low wages or electricity shortages, or the lack of basic security guarantees. Nor was it about people coming out to support me.

Rather, our Revolution was about people fighting for their freedom and their desire to live in a democratic society. A society that respects human rights, freedom of speech, the rule of law and the belief that citizens—*and citizens alone*—have the right to choose their leaders and their destiny.

What the former government never understood—never grasped, and never believed in—was that democracy—in order to succeed and be genuine—must be derived from the people *and* be responsible to the people. Otherwise it will not be a true democracy.

The Georgian people proved that they have the courage, wisdom, and universal desire to live in a democracy. I am extremely proud of my people today and deeply honored to be their President.

I am the President of a democracy! This is a democracy whose national identity and destiny is rooted in Europe—as a full and contributing Member to Euro-Atlantic institutions—to regional security, and economic development.

The third lesson of the Revolution is that Georgia has a special relationship with the United States of America.

I make this claim—this evaluation—based on the realization that Georgians and Americans share a common set of values. That we share common beliefs and common aspirations to make our societies more free and more prosperous.

That we believe in government working to serve the people. That we believe in the sacred principle that the power of the State derives from its citizens and that no man is above the law.

These values—which were at the very core of the Revolution—have served to re-enforce the bonds that unites our countries and our peoples!

During this trip to Washington my goal is to strengthen those bonds. . . .

To those who believe our Revolution was somehow covertly supported by special American interests—I can only say that they fail to understand our culture and our values. The values of freedom and democracy are not established through grants or loans. They are not the product of assistance programs or negotiations. While that assistance was absolutely crucial in building our skills and capacities . . . and was used extremely well.

. . . It was our values—which are a reflection of our culture and our identity—that have allowed us to succeed. . . . That Georgia has contributed from *day one* to the war on terrorism in Afghanistan and Iraq—and is ready to contribute even more—is because we share a common belief in freedom.

To be Georgian is to be part of the family of democratic nations—composed of our European brothers and our American friends and partners.

Confronting Georgia's Challenges

Looking at Georgia today—it is easy to see that we are located on the frontlines of some of the most pressing challenges facing Europe and our increasingly interconnected world. We live in a neighborhood that contains numerous geo-political and geo-strategic threats.

We live in a country where reconstruction and reform is a national security imperative. We also stand on the edge of enormous opportunities—opportunities to help the world fight global terrorism, increase its energy security *and* open new and untapped markets.

Under my leadership—during my Presidency—I intend to realize these opportunities, to take advantage of those opportunities—so that Georgia will re-gain its rightful place in the democratic community of nations. So that Georgia will prosper. So that Georgia will always be welcome in Washington with the words told to me this morning at the U.S. Senate—*That Georgia Is a Breath of Fresh Air for All Freedom Loving People.* . . .

What are the Specific Challenges?

Georgia nevertheless faces some very specific challenges. These challenges are in: governance reform; security reform; and economic reform.

This trio of sectors represents the principle avenues that we intend to address and focus our reform efforts on.

1. The First Step Is Governance Reform—Setting the Example for Georgia and the Region. We must eliminate corruption (Visible and Institutional forms).

We must make government more efficient and responsive. But How?

- By reducing bureaucracy and red tape.
- By downsizing government and increasing professionalism and transparency.
- By reforming our civil service.
- By providing real salaries, establishing new standards and enforcing the rule of law.

All of these steps will require courage and strong political will. We must move forward swiftly to take advantage of public support.

The whole region is watching us—some hope we will fail—but I know that the vast majority hopes we will succeed!

As Georgia succeeds in strengthening its governance—in establishing *a model of good governance*—we have the ability to bring positive change to an entire region. Not through exporting Revolution—because Revolutions don't work that way. But rather, by providing an example that democracy and stability—prosperity and respect for human dignity—are possible in our region of the world—in that interconnected space linking Europe with the greater Middle East.

When Georgia succeeds, the region succeeds. In that respect, what is good for Georgia is good for Europe, the US and more than 400 million inhabitants of the region.

2. The Second Step Is Security Reform—What Keeps Georgia Strong and Stable. Internally we plan to introduce civilian control over *all* power Ministries. We plan to create *and fund* the capability to defend against all threats to Georgia.

To bring lasting stability we must and we will restore Georgia's full territorial integrity using peaceful means—I think the Revolution proves that we can create great change without violence.

That means taking the necessary steps and creating the right conditions to peacefully return Abkhazia. Returning Abkhazia and confirming Georgia's territorial integrity will take time and great effort—*My government and I view this effort as one of our top priorities.*

We must make Georgia a country that *all* citizens will want to be a part of and live in.

Here I want to emphasize how important it is for Georgia to restore good relations with our neighbors—in particular Russia.

Russia is a special case due to our historic ties and the last decade of less than perfect relations. Russia is a special case because of its vast markets and the role that Russia *can* play in promoting or reducing regional stability.

After my trip to Moscow I have hope that a new era in relations is commencing—one that is based on pragmatism and the mutual recognition of shared common interests. While I have no illusions that our relationship will be transformed overnight—I do see that the door is open for new and more positive relations. Georgia is ready to cooperate with Russia and is ready to meet the Russians half-way on many issues.

Just as Georgia has legitimate interests in the region—so too does Russia (i.e. border security, fighting terrorism, economic growth). As long as Russia remembers and respects our national sovereignty. As long as Russia abides by its international commitments to remove its bases. As long as Russia realizes that we cannot and will not become a battlefield between two *great* powers.

I am ready for a new era.

I believe Mr. Putin understands this and is prepared to continue the good start that we began a few weeks ago in Moscow. I intend to continue down the path of new and improved relations with Moscow.

Our challenge—Georgia's challenge—is to work cooperatively with all our partners to advance lasting security and stability.

3. The Next Step Is Economic Reform—What Will Re-build Georgia. We need to strengthen and improve the investment climate in Georgia. How?

- Tax liberalization
- Elimination of corruption and harassment by State officials
- Provision of greater personal security for investors and businesses
- Creation of one-stop-shop for foreign investors
- Development of natural comparative advantage: Agriculture, trade, transport, wine, tourism, light manufacturing, etc.

We need to ensure access to regional markets. We need to find new sources of financing for entrepreneurs. We need to develop new public/private partnerships.

We need to strengthen infrastructure. *In particular—we need to do all we can to build the energy corridor—of which Georgia is such an important participant.*

This means fulfilling our obligations for the BTC and South Caucasus pipelines—pipelines of stability, prosperity and security.

Energy projects in our region are not just about economics—rather they represent concrete vehicles for promoting human development, regional integration and lasting peace. Georgia is proud and I am proud to contribute to this process.

It is clear to me, that the investments we make in Georgia's economic development are actually investments in Georgia's future.

Improving Georgia's economic strength will improve Georgia's governance. It will give real and powerful reasons for separatists to seek a joint future inside Georgia. Improvements in governance will in turn strengthen stability and lasting security.

This is an inter-connected, inter-dependent cycle. We see and recognize these critical relationships—and plan to take advantage of them.

Results So Far

I have always believed that actions speak louder than words. That deeds and results are the only way to judge and evaluate progress.

After only 100 days we have succeeded in delivering some impressive results—defying the skeptics.

- Increased tax revenues
- Arrests of some of the most corrupt officials and a visible crackdown on smuggling
- Renewed relations with the IMF
- The creation of the most competent and progressive government in Eastern Europe

We also know that expectations are very high—perhaps unreasonably so. We also know that we will make mistakes from time to time. And we also know that we will learn from any mistakes we might make.

What is important in this respect is maintaining the pace of change and providing—*for the first time in a decade*—leadership that sets an example.

The Georgia of the past was a nation where neither the leaders nor the people could believe in the future—

I believe we have succeeded in changing that perception.

I believe we have succeeded in offering hope.

I believe we have succeeded in showing strength in the face of enormous challenges.

And I believe that we have a vision that can transform a nation and an entire region! . . .

We know that many challenges lie waiting in the future—we know that re-building our State will not be romantic and that it will take very hard work, sacrifice, focus—and commitment. We know that we have to deliver with concrete actions and measurable results.

I believe that we won't disappoint. I believe that step-by-step we will succeed.

Today—there is a special window of opportunity in Georgia. This is a unique time. Georgians and people all around the world have been energized by our positive example.

While this special window of opportunity is open—we will need to rely on the collective efforts of all of us—and here I mean the international community in general and AMERICA in particular—in order to succeed.

Let none of us in this room underestimate just how much we can achieve when we work together—when we continue to deepen and expand our cooperation.

Tonight, I wish to issue an appeal to all of you—to help us take advantage of this historic opportunity. That together we can advance stability and democracy in one of the world's most complex and important geo-strategic regions.

Georgia has benefited greatly from its partnership with the United States in the past—and I *have* argued—and *I believe* that this success is due to our shared system of values and beliefs.

I am sure that our cooperation in the future will be even more robust—even more close—and even more fruitful—*for the very same reasons.*

Georgia and the United States are partners—we are allies and we are friends. By working together—honestly and openly, for Georgia—for Europe—and for the entire region—we can build a brighter, safer and more prosperous future.

Thank you.

Source: Georgia. Embassy of Georgia (in the United States). "Georgia after the Rose Revolution: Rebuilding Democracy and Stability." Prepared remarks of Mikhail Saakashvili, president of Georgia, at Johns Hopkins University. February 24, 2004. www.georgiaemb.org/Print.asp?id=310 (accessed January 20, 2005).

National Review Board on Sexual Abuse in the Catholic Church

February 27, 2004

INTRODUCTION

Three reports issued early in 2004 under the auspices of America's Roman Catholic bishops began to outline the scope of child sexual abuse by priests over the last half century, investigate its causes, and determine whether individual dioceses were complying with new rules aimed at preventing such abuse. The reports found that 4 percent of all priests since 1950 had been accused of sexually abusing minors and that bishops bore a large share of the blame for the continuing crisis because they had failed to report the allegations to civil authorities, had kept many of the alleged abusers in the ministry where they continued to come into contact with children, and had spent hundreds of millions of dollars to keep the accusations hidden rather than reach out to the victims of the abuse.

Taken together, the reports gave some reason to believe that the worst period of abuse might be over and that most dioceses were taking steps to prevent it in the future. But new allegations of past abuse continued to arise as dioceses around the country coped with dozens, in some cases hundreds, of lawsuits from victims seeking damages. The board that issued the reports accused the bishops of back-tracking on its efforts to protect children. The most vocal victims' rights groups continued to be highly skeptical that the church was dealing with the problem openly and in good faith.

Although there had long been reported isolated incidents of abuse in the church, the current scandal erupted in January 2002, when Cardinal Bernard F. Law of Boston was forced to admit that he had moved a priest from parish to parish despite evidence that the priest was a child molester. Later evidence showed that Law had dealt with several other cases similarly, moving priests to other parishes without notifying either the parish or law enforcement officials of the suspected abuse.

Similar revelations quickly came from other Catholic dioceses around the country. Over the next few months, at least 200 priests suspected of sexual abuse had either resigned or been removed from their duties. Hundreds of lawsuits alleging abuse and seeking financial settlement had been filed, and thousands of Catholic parishioners had joined reform groups demanding that the church take steps to stop the abuse.

In November 2002 the United States Conference of Catholic Bishops approved a "zero-tolerance" policy that barred all priests found to have committed sexual abuse from parish work and the public ministry. The reforms also created a procedure for deciding whether to defrock abusive priests and required each diocese to set up procedures for preventing abuse and for dealing with allegations of abuse.

The bishops also set up a National Review Board for the Protection of Children and Young People, made up of prominent lay Catholics, to assess whether individual dioceses were complying with the new rules. The review board was directed to make a "comprehensive study of the causes and context of the current crisis." As part of that broader study, the review board commissioned researchers at the John Jay College of Criminal Justice in New York to determine the number and nature of the allegations of clerical abuse occurring between 1950 and 2002. The first annual audit of dioceses as well as the two studies on the scope and causes of the abuse were issued early in 2004. *(Background, Historic Documents of 2002, p. 867; Historic Documents of 2003, p. 523)*

National Review Board Audit

The audit of 191 of the 195 Roman Catholic dioceses, released on January 6, 2004, found that 90 percent of them had complied with the new rules. Among those that had not were the archdioceses of New York, Anchorage, and Omaha, as well as dioceses in several large cities, including Arlington and Richmond, Virginia; Honolulu; Lincoln, Nebraska; and Memphis, Tennessee. The report said that a lack of resources, rather than negligence, explained the lack of compliance. "These twenty dioceses . . . have substantial work to do. But this doesn't mean they haven't started," said Kathleen McChesney, a former FBI official who headed the Office of Child and Youth Protection for the bishops' conference.

McChesney said that dioceses were most successful in forming lay review boards to work with bishops on handling accusations of abuse, appointing victims' assistance coordinators, erasing the requirement that victims sign confidentiality agreements, and referring accusations to the police or civil authorities. The most common shortcomings were failure to reach out and meet with victims and their families, failure to implement abuse prevention programs, failure to establish codes of conduct for church workers that had regular contact with children, and failure to conduct background checks on diocesan workers.

The audit was conducted by fifty-four investigators, most of them former FBI agents, employed by the Gavin Group in Boston, at a cost of $1.8 million. The study was based largely on interviews with church officials, although a few local prosecutors and victims were also interviewed. Bishop Wilton D. Gregory, president of the Conference of Catholic Bishops, said in a news conference: "The audit results represent solid progress on the journey toward fulfilling the vision set out in the charter. I believe these findings show that we bishops are keeping our word." Victims' advocacy groups were not convinced. "Essentially, bishops have defined the rules of the game, decided who plays, paid the umpires, and are now declaring themselves the winner," Survivors Network of those Abused by Priests (SNAP) said in a statement.

In a letter accompanying the audit, McChesney urged the bishops to create a longer-term plan for accountability and response to the abuse crisis. Failure to do so, she said, would "undermine the substantial efforts that have been made thus far." She recommended that annual reports be issued giving the number of allegations of clergy abuse of minors reported during the year, the number of actions taken against those found to have committed abuse, and the financial costs associated with the cases. She also asked that the bishops implement measures for determining the effectiveness of their abuse prevention programs no later than 2006.

Scope of the Abuse

The report by researchers at John Jay College of Criminal Law showed that 10,667 individuals had made credible allegations of sexual abuse of minors against 4,392 priests between 1950 and 2002. This represented 4 percent of the estimated 109,694 active priests during the time period. Dioceses reported that they were aware of another 3,000 people who said they had been abused but had not filed formal complaints. The findings, released on February 27, were based on surveys sent to all Roman Catholic dioceses and religious communities in the United States; the researchers received responses that covered 98 percent of all diocesan priests and 80 percent of all religious priests during that time period.

Overall, 81 percent of the victims were boys under eighteen, with 50 percent of the boys between the ages of eleven and fourteen; 19 percent were girls. Fifty-six percent of the priests were alleged to have abused only a single victim. A relatively small number of priests, 149, were alleged to have abused ten or more minors each, accounting for 2,960 victims, or 26 percent of the allegations. Nearly half the alleged abuses occurred over two more or years. The report said that individual victims experienced multiple types of abuse and that "relatively few priests committed only the most minor acts," such as verbal abuse or the use of pornography.

Less than 13 percent of the allegations were made in the year in which the abuse allegedly occurred, while more than 25 percent of the claims were made more than thirty years after the alleged abuse began. The distribution of reported cases by year showed that more abuse occurred in the 1970s, peaking in 1980. Only about 11 percent of the allegations involved priests who were ordained after 1979. But the report cautioned that future allegations could affect that conclusion.

The report also said that only about 25 percent of the alleged abuses had been reported to police. Nearly all those cases led to investigations. Criminal charges were brought in 384 cases, at least 252 priests were convicted, and at least 100 of those served some time in jail. Only 37 percent of priests involved in alleged abuses received any sort of treatment program.

According to the surveys, the Catholic Church had paid out $472 million in settlements with victims, legal expenses, and treatment for priests. That figure did not include any costs for settlements reached after the surveys were conducted, including the $85 million settlement the Archdiocese of Boston agreed to pay alleged victims early in 2003, the report said.

The "Causes and Context" of the Crisis

A broader study on the "causes and context" of the crisis called the number of incidents of clergy abuse revealed by the surveys "significant and disturbing" and said the failure of the bishops and other church leaders to take effective action to stop the abuse was "shameful." This national review board study was also issued February 27. Headed by prominent Washington attorney Robert S. Bennett, the research committee of the national review board interviewed eight-five people, including church leaders in the United States and the Vatican, priests, former priests, seminarians, theologians, psychiatrists, lawyers, law enforcement officers, and victims of clergy abuse.

The study said it sought to answer two questions:

- How did men with "a disposition" to abuse minors gain admission to the priesthood?
- How did they remain in the priesthood even after allegations of their abuse came to the attention of their bishops and other church leaders?

On the first question, the panel concluded that while there was no one "cause" of the clergy abuse, there were two "overarching" contributing factors. First, a failure to properly screen candidates for the priesthood resulted in the admission into seminaries of "many sexually dysfunctional and immature" men. Second, the report said, seminaries did not adequately prepare their seminarians for the "challenges of the priesthood, particularly the challenge of living a chaste, celibate life." Although it drew no conclusions, the board said homosexuality in the priesthood and the requirement of celibacy deserved further study.

As to why abusive priests remained in the priesthood, the review board placed the blame squarely on "the failure of some bishops to respond to the abuse" in a manner that was "consistent with their position as leaders of the flock with a duty to protect the most vulnerable among us from possible predators." The board listed several causes of this failure, including the failure of bishops and other church leaders to understand the broad nature of the problem as well as the "extent and magnitude" of the harm done to victims of clergy abuse; the tendency for some bishops to try to avert scandal through secrecy and concealment; the overreliance on psychiatrists and lawyers to deal with a problem that was "at its heart a problem of faith and morality"; and a tendency to place the interests of accused priests above those of the victims. The board also said that bishops and other church leaders did not engage in enough "fraternal correction" to ensure that their colleagues dealt with the allegations effectively.

The board offered five key recommendations to help restore the trust between the Catholic Church and its members:

- Enhanced screening and oversight, to ensure that candidates for the priesthood were "mature, well-adjusted individuals" and that seminaries were capable of training seminarians to meet the challenges of priesthood, including a life of celibacy.
- Increased sensitivity in responding to allegations of abuse, including more openness in dealing with victims and the "avoidance of harsh litigation tactics" such as defenses that could be construed as blaming the victim and disclaiming responsibility for the actions of priests.
- Greater accountability for bishops and other church leaders. "The Church must choose bishops who see themselves first and foremost as pastors; and the bishops must ensure that their brother bishops act accordingly," the review board wrote.
- Greater interaction with law enforcement, including reporting all allegations of sexual abuse, regardless of the age or credibility of the accuser.
- Increased responsiveness to the concerns of the laity, by acting with "less secrecy, more transparency, and a greater openness."

On the same day, Bishop Gregory, the outgoing president of the U.S. Conference of Catholic Bishops, issued a statement announcing that about 700 priests and deacons had been removed from the Catholic ministry since January 2002 in direct response to the abuse scandal. "As far as it is humanly possible to know such things, I assure you that known offenders are not in ministry," Gregory said. "The terrible history recorded here is history."

That did not satisfy many victims and others in the church, who said bishops should release the names and parishes of accused priests. As of the end of 2004, only three archdioceses had released the names of accused priests—Baltimore, Los Angeles, and Tucson. Church leaders said they were reluctant to take such steps for fear of naming priests who had been wrongly accused and of breaking the confidentiality of victims. Other critics said that bishops should be held accountable for knowingly transferring pedophile priests from one parish to another. One of those was Robert Bennett of the national review board. Asked on NBC's *Meet the Press* on February 29 if he thought some bishops should resign, he said, "Yes. There are bishops who have totally failed as pastors and shepherds of their flock."

Although Bennett did not name any specific bishops, the national review board singled out four whose actions they criticized. These included Cardinal Law, whose role in the Boston abuse scandal had triggered the crisis, and Bishop Thomas J. O'Brien of Phoenix, both of whom the report said transferred abusive priests rather than deal with the problem. Both men had already resigned as head of their respective archdiocese. The review board also cited Cardinal Edward M. Egan of New York for failing in his former post in Bridgeport, Connecticut, to remove a priest despite allegations of abuse from several victims. It cited Cardinal Roger M. Mahoney, archbishop of Los Angeles, for refusing to turn over personnel records and other church documents to a grand jury probe of abuses in that city. "This argument did little to enhance the reputation of the church . . . for transparency and cooperation," the review board said of Mahoney's actions.

Accusations of Backsliding

Cardinal Egan was one of "many bishops" who in February and March asked for a postponement of the second round of audits until after the bishops' annual meeting in November. In late March Anne M. Burke, an appellate court judge in Illinois and the interim chairman of the national review board, wrote a letter protesting the delay. In her letter, which was not made public until early May, Burke chastised the bishops for taking a "business-as-usual" approach to the abuse scandal. "Those who said the bishops were never serious about breaking free from the sins, crimes and bad judgments of the past will be vindicated," she wrote. She also accused the bishops of "manipulating" the review board by not informing it that a delay in the 2004 audits was under discussion. Keeping that knowledge from the board ensured that the delay would not become a public issue at the board's February 27 high-profile national news conference where it released its reports on the crisis. The review board had strongly urged that annual audits continue. In response, the bishops took up the issue of the audits at a closed-door meeting in June and approved a second round of audits for 2004.

The controversy was not over, however. At its November meeting, the bishops agreed to a third audit in 2005 but limited on-site visits to those dioceses that had not yet complied with all the requirements or that voluntarily requested one. The bishops said that the paring back was intended only to make the process more efficient, but SNAP complained that without independent on-site audits, the situation was "back to square one" of trusting the church leaders who had hidden the scandal for so long.

Another potential controversy was brewing over a review and possible revision of the Charter for the Protection of Children and Young People. The review was mandated when the charter was adopted in 2002. Among the most controversial provisions of the charter were its zero-tolerance policy and its definition of sexual abuse. Some critics had said that barring priests accused of sexual abuse from active ministry was too harsh. Under canon law, priests were assumed guilty and removed from the ministry until proven innocent, a process that could take years. Some critics also said the definition of abuse was too broad. The head of the review committee, Cardinal Francis George, the vice president of the bishops conference, said in November that the bishops were unlikely to change the zero-tolerance policy but that they might "tighten" the definition of sexual abuse. Revisions to the charter were expected to be finalized in June 2005.

In October Bishop Gregory announced the appointment of five new members and a new chairman of the national review board. The new chairman was Nicholas P. Cafardi, dean of the Duquesne University Law School who had been serving as a board member. Among the members departing because their terms had expired were Burke and Bennett.

Other Developments

The sexual abuse scandal continued to affect Catholic dioceses across the country. Following are some of the major developments of 2004.

- In Boston, the archdiocese was facing at least 140 new sexual abuse claims less than a year after it paid $85 million to settle more than 500 claims. In September the church said it could not afford to settle the claims, in part because it had not been able to recoup money from its insurance polices to cover the initial settlement. Archbishop Sean P. O'Malley announced that it would close at least sixty-five parishes as part of a massive restructuring due to declining attendance and donations that had been aggravated by the scandal. At year end, members of several parishes were holding twenty-four hour vigils in their parishes to prevent their closure. In February the archdiocese reported that 162 priests that had served there between 1950 and 2002—nearly 7 percent—had been accused of abusing 815 minors. Seven priests accounted for "slightly more than half" of those allegations. One of the priests, John J. Geoghan, was murdered in his prison cell in August 2003; he was serving a ten-year sentence for indecent assault and battery. A second priest, Paul R. Shanley, was scheduled to go on trial for rape in January 2005. In May Pope John Paul II named Cardinal Law archpriest of St. Mary Major Basilica in Rome, a largely ceremonial position. Law had resigned as archbishop of Boston on December 13, 2002,
- In December the Roman Catholic Diocese of Orange County, California, reached a $100 million settlement agreement with eighty-seven plaintiffs who had alleged clergy abuse. The average payout of $1.1 million made it the largest settlement to date. The settlement had implications for the neighboring Archdiocese of Los Angeles, which was trying to settle some 544 abuse claims. The Orange Country diocese also promised not to fight the release of confidential personnel files of accused priests, which some said could undercut Los Angeles Archbishop Mahoney's efforts to keep such files secret.
- In July the archdiocese of Portland, Oregon, became the first to file for bankruptcy, seeking protection from having to pay millions of dollars in claims. Churches had avoided taking that step in the past in part because it placed a civilian authority, the bankruptcy court, over diocesan affairs, including any schools operated by the diocese. Archbishop John G. Vlazny said he had decided to file for bankruptcy because "the pot of gold is pretty much empty right now." He added that he was not trying to avoid compensating abuse victims but rather to ensure that the available funds to pay claims were distributed fairly.
- Two other dioceses, Tucson and Spokane, also filed for bankruptcy in 2004. The Spokane filing, on December 6, was particularly sensitive because its bishop, William Skylstad, was the president-elect of the national bishops conference.

Skylstad said declaring bankruptcy was the best way to ensure that all abuse victims were treated fairly and still enable the church to continue its mission. Critics said Skylstad was trying to cover up the diocese's protection of serial pedophile priests.

Following are excerpts from the introduction and summary of A Report on the Crisis in the Catholic Church in the United States, *issued February 27, 2004, by the National Review Board for the Protection of Children and Young People, an independent lay board of prominent Catholics appointed by the United States Conference of Catholic Bishops to monitor the church's response to allegations of widespread sexual abuse of minors by priests.*

A Report on the Crisis in the Catholic Church in the United States

I. Introduction

The National Review Board for the Protection of Children and Young People (the "Review Board" or "Board"), composed of lay Catholics and chartered by the United States Conference of Catholic Bishops (the "Conference" or "USCCB"), issues this Report as part of its mandate to evaluate the "causes and context" of the crisis that has beset the Catholic Church in the United States as a result of the sexual abuse of minors by some members of the Catholic clergy and the inadequate response of bishops and other Church leaders to that abuse.

The Charter for the Protection of Children and Young People (the "Charter"), which the Conference adopted in June 2002, created the Review Board and directed it to "commission a comprehensive study of the causes and context of the current crisis." In response, the Board, acting through its Research Committee, has interviewed more than eighty-five individuals in sixty separate interviews, including: cardinals, archbishops, bishops, and other Church leaders in the United States and the Vatican; priests, former priests, seminarians, and theologians; victims of clergy abuse; psychiatrists, psychologists, and other medical professionals; civil lawyers, canon lawyers, and law enforcement officials; and other knowledgeable lay people. Further, the Board has consulted numerous articles and studies written or conducted by experts in pertinent fields, as well as various public records relating to reported cases of abuse. In addition, the Board commissioned a study by the John Jay College of Criminal Justice of the City University of New York to develop empirical data on the nature and scope of the problem that precipitated the crisis.

The purpose of the Report is to share the Review Board's findings and recommendations based upon its evaluation of the current crisis. Those findings seek to describe the problem and to address two fundamental questions posed by it. First, why did individuals with a disposition to prey sexually upon minors gain admission to the priesthood? Second, how did they manage to remain in the priesthood even after allegations and evidence of such abuse became known to their bishops and other Church leaders?

Concerning the first of these questions, the Report provides the Review Board's findings with respect to the process of selecting and then forming candidates for the priesthood, with special attention to issues relating to sexual orientation, celibacy, and spiritual life. Concerning the second of these questions, the Report provides the Board's findings with respect to a number of shortcomings on the part of some bishops and Church officials, including: (i) a failure to grasp the gravity of the problem of sexual abuse of minors by priests; (ii) deficiencies in the response to victims; (iii) unwarranted presumptions in favor of accused priests; (iv) reliance on secrecy and an undue emphasis on the avoidance of scandal; (v) excessive reliance on the therapeutic model in dealing with priest offenders; (vi) undue reliance upon legal advice that placed a premium on adversarial defense tactics at the expense of concern for victims of abuse; and (vii) a failure to hold themselves and other bishops accountable for mistakes, including a failure to make use of lay consultative bodies and other governance structures.

This Report also offers the Review Board's recommendations based on those findings. These include recommendations for enhanced screening, formation, and oversight of candidates for the priesthood; for increased sensitivity in responding to allegations of abuse; for greater accountability of bishops and Church leaders; for improved interaction with civil authorities; and for greater participation by the laity in the life of the Church.

The Review Board is pleased that the bishops asked a group of lay Catholics to address these important issues. The Board also appreciates the nearly uniform cooperation it received from the bishops and other Church leaders, without which this Report would not have been possible. We join Pope John Paul II in earnest prayer that from this "pain" and "sorrow" might emerge "a holier priesthood, a holier episcopate, and a holier Church."

II. Summary

The Review Board believes that the overwhelming majority of priests serving the Church in the United States fulfill their roles honorably and chastely. According to Church records, however, there were credible allegations that several thousand priests, comprising four percent of priests in ministry over the last half-century, committed acts of sexual abuse of minors. There appears to have been a significant surge in acts of abuse beginning in the 1960s and continuing into the mid-1980s. The fallout resulting from this epidemic of abuse and the shortcomings in the response of a number of bishops and other Church leaders to that misconduct continues to this day.

The crime of sexual abuse of minors is not a problem unique to the Catholic clergy. As Pope John Paul II stated prior to the adoption of the Charter, "Abuse of the young is a grave symptom of a crisis affecting not only the Church but society as a whole." (April 23, 2002 Address of Pope John Paul II to the United States Cardinals.) Indeed, it is a contemporary societal problem that affects numerous families and many secular organizations as well as other churches and ecclesial communities. Although some evidence suggests that the abuse epidemic afflicted many institutions and organizations in our country, it is beyond the Board's mission to determine whether the problem was more pervasive among Catholic clergy than it was in other sectors of society or in the general population. Reliable statistical evidence of the sexual abuse of minors is particularly difficult to obtain because, according to experts, many if not most acts of abuse occur within families and often are not reported.

Nevertheless, the number of incidents of sexual abuse of minors by Catholic clergy, at least over the past fifty years, is significant and disturbing. This is a failing not simply on the part of the priests who sexually abused minors but also on the part of those bishops and other Church leaders who did not act effectively to preclude that abuse in the first instance or respond appropriately when it occurred. These leadership failings have been shameful to the Church as both a central institution in the lives of the faithful and a moral force in the secular world, and have aggravated the harm suffered by victims and their families. The bishops themselves recognized in the Charter that both the abuse itself and the response of some of the bishops to that abuse "caused enormous pain, anger, and confusion." The bishops acknowledged that "in the past, secrecy has created an atmosphere that has inhibited the healing process and, in some cases, enabled sexually abusive behavior to be repeated." Finally, the bishops stated, "As bishops, we acknowledge our mistakes and our role in that suffering, and we apologize and take responsibility for too often failing victims and our people in the past." (Charter, Preamble.)

The bishops were right to recognize their part in the crisis and the extent and gravity of the crisis. The Review Board believes, however, that effective measures have been taken to ensure the safety of minors in the Church today. Actions taken by many, but not all, dioceses in the 1980s and early 1990s significantly reduced the number of reported incidents of abuse. More recently, in the wake of the Charter, several hundred abusers who had not yet been removed from ministry were laicized or otherwise removed from ministry over the last two years. Many bishops have met with victims and their families, even if belatedly, and have seen first-hand the horrific impact abuse can have on victims and their families. In addition, most dioceses have implemented safe-environment policies that train adults to recognize the signs of abuse and teach children to report it.

Moreover, the "zero-tolerance" policy embodied in the Essential Norms adopted in 2002 by the bishops in response to the crisis specifies that no priest who has sexually abused a minor will continue in ministry. To ensure that the zero-tolerance policy is applied consistently, bishops must consult with lay review boards in assessing allegations of sexual abuse of minors and making determinations about a priest's suitability for ministry.

The policies and procedures put in place over the last two years do not remediate, nor can they excuse, the multitude of preventable acts of abuse that preceded them. But in acknowledgment of those acts of abuse as crimes and sins lies hope for the future. That hope can be fulfilled, however, only if the bishops maintain a commitment to meaningful reforms and vigilant enforcement that outlasts the immediate crisis and becomes ingrained in the character of the Church itself.

What is the Nature of the Current Crisis?

Narrowly defined, the nature of the current crisis is twofold: It consists both of the sexual abuse of minors by clergy and the failure of many Church leaders to respond appropriately to that abuse. But the crisis also has a spiritual dimension, for, as is the case with all sinful conduct, it represents a failure to comport with divine law and the teachings of the Church. Unless all aspects of the crisis are addressed forthrightly, any steps to remedy it will bear only the patina of reform and renewal.

Why did so Many Priests Sexually Abuse Minors?

Although it is not possible to pinpoint any one "cause" of the problem of sexual abuse of minors by priests, there were two overarching contributing factors:

- Dioceses and orders did not screen candidates for the priesthood properly. As a result, many sexually dysfunctional and immature men were admitted into seminaries and later ordained into the priesthood.
- Seminaries did not form candidates for the priesthood adequately. As a result, seminarians were not prepared for the challenges of the priesthood, particularly the challenge of living a chaste, celibate life.

In addition, although neither the presence of homosexually-oriented priests nor the discipline of celibacy caused the crisis, an understanding of the crisis is not possible without reference to these issues. There are, no doubt, many outstanding priests of a homosexual orientation who live chaste, celibate lives, but any evaluation of the causes and context of the current crisis must be cognizant of the fact that more than eighty percent of the abuse at issue was of a homosexual nature. Likewise, celibacy does not cause sexual abuse; but the Church did an inadequate job both of screening out those individuals who were destined to fail in meeting the demands of the priesthood, and of forming others to meet those demands, including the rigors of a celibate life.

Why did Church Leaders Respond to the Problem of Sexual Abuse so Poorly for so Many Years?

Perhaps even more troubling than the criminal and sinful acts of priests who engaged in abuse of minors was the failure of some bishops to respond to the abuse in an effective manner, consistent with their positions as leaders of the flock with a duty to protect the most vulnerable among us from possible predators. Sexual abuse of minors is an evil and, as one priest told the Board, knowingly allowing evil conduct to continue is "cooperation with evil." Causes of this failure include the following:

- Bishops and other Church leaders did not understand the broad nature of the problem but treated allegations as sporadic and isolated.
- Some bishops and other Church leaders often put what they erroneously believed to be the institutional concerns of the local Church above the concerns of the universal Church. The fear of scandal caused them to practice secrecy and concealment.
- The threat of litigation caused some bishops to disregard their pastoral role and adopt an adversarial stance not worthy of the Church.
- Some bishops and other Church leaders failed to comprehend fully the extent and magnitude of the harm suffered by victims of sexual abuse by priests.
- Bishops and other Church leaders relied too heavily on psychiatrists, psychologists, and lawyers in dealing with a problem that, while it undoubtedly has psychological causes and legal implications, is at its heart a problem of faith and morality.

- Bishops and other Church leaders did not do enough in the way of "fraternal correction" to ensure that their brethren dealt with the problem in an effective manner.
- Some bishops and other Church leaders placed the interests of the accused priests above those of the victims and too often declined to hear from victims directly, relying instead on denials and assurances from those accused of abuse.
- Canon law and canonical procedures made it too difficult to remove a predator priest from ministry, and bishops did not make sufficient use of what canonical authority they did have to take action against such priests and protect the children and young people of the Church.

As a result, priests who had engaged in sexual abuse of minors were, with distressing frequency, allowed to remain where they had abused, reassigned to other parishes within the same dioceses, or allowed to live in other dioceses where they posed a further threat to children that predictably materialized into additional incidents of abuse.

The leniency afforded predator priests by some bishops may in some instances have been a misguided act of forgiveness. Nevertheless, the failure of some bishops to temper forgiveness with responsible actions to insulate minors from additional acts of abuse has seriously undermined the confidence of the laity in the leadership of the Church as a whole.

What can we as a Church do to Ensure that this Never Happens Again?

Ultimately, the crisis besetting the Church is not a legal crisis, a media crisis, or a personnel crisis, but a crisis of trust and faith; and it is only by the living out of their faith by bishops, priests, and the laity that the Church will be able to regain trust and fulfill its mission. By enacting the Charter and the Essential Norms, the bishops have laid a framework for restoring the trust of the laity in the Church hierarchy in the United States and ensuring the safety of minors in the Church. The Review Board's most urgent hope is that the bishops zealously enforce and adhere to the Charter and the Essential Norms, which then can serve as a beacon for the Church in other countries, for other churches and ecclesial communities, and for secular organizations.

But in order for the Church to achieve the goal set out by the bishops of "restoring the bonds of trust that unite us," more must be done, through a process that involves both transparency and substantial participation by the laity. To that end, this Report offers a number of recommendations, including the following:

- *Enhanced screening, formation, and oversight.* The Church must ensure that the men selected as candidates for the priesthood in the Catholic Church are mature, well-adjusted individuals with a clear understanding of the challenges of the priesthood, including the challenge of celibacy; that candidates undergo proper formation as seminarians to meet those challenges through a process for which responsible bishops take personal ownership; and that the seminaries themselves are capable of accomplishing this mission.
- *Increased sensitivity in responding to allegations of abuse.* Church leaders must not let concerns about the rights of accused priests, the threat of scandal, and the potential adverse consequences of litigation keep them from their primary duty when faced with allegations of abuse–seeing to the welfare of victims of abuse.

More openness regarding allegations and evidence of abuse, and the response thereto, is needed. Greater sensitivity to victims also requires the avoidance of harsh litigation tactics that tend to compound the pain that already has been inflicted.

- *Greater accountability of bishops and other church leaders.* The Church must choose bishops who see themselves first and foremost as pastors; and the bishops must ensure that their brother bishops act accordingly. Diocesan and presbyteral councils should be revitalized to provide an increased measure of advice and oversight for bishops; and other mechanisms, such as strengthened metropolitans, accreditation-type visitations of the dioceses, and lay diocesan consultative boards, should be considered as a means of providing greater accountability on the part of bishops and other Church leaders.
- *Improved interaction with civil authorities.* Dioceses and orders should report all allegations of sexual abuse to the civil authorities, regardless of the circumstances or the age or perceived credibility of the accuser, and should endeavor to resolve government investigations and civil claims on reasonable terms and in a manner that minimizes the potential intrusion of civil authorities into the governance of Church matters.
- *Meaningful participation by the Christian faithful in the Church.* The bishops and other Church leaders must listen to and be responsive to the concerns of the laity. To accomplish this, the hierarchy must act with less secrecy, more transparency, and a greater openness to the gifts that all members of the Church bring to her. . . .

Source: United States Conference of Catholic Bishops. The National Review Board for the Protection of Children and Young People. *A Report on the Crisis in the Catholic Church in the United States.* February 27, 2004. www.usccb.org/nrb/nrbstudy/nrbreport.pdf (accessed January 20, 2005).

UN Security Council on the Post-Aristide Era in Haiti

February 29, 2004

INTRODUCTION

A plague of locusts was just about the only type of disaster not to befall Haiti during 2004. The desperately poor Caribbean nation of 8.4 million people endured an armed rebellion, the ousting in February of democratically elected president Jean-Bertrand Aristide, a drought in some regions, massive floods in May and September that killed thousands of people and left tens of thousands homeless, and repeated outbreaks of violence that hampered relief operations and endangered the fragile new government that had promised a return to democracy in 2005. Haiti was effectively in international receivership, its minimal security provided by a United Nations peacekeeping force, its government barely functioning, and its economy barely kept afloat with international aid. Haiti's chances of recovery appeared marginal, at best. In a hard-hitting report issued on November 18, the International Crisis Group, a Brussels-based think tank, said Haiti "seems to be heading toward anarchy" because of failures by both its interim government and the international community. Haiti's troubles could spread far beyond its borders, the report warned, if the country became a "permanently failed state hemorrhaging instability throughout the Caribbean in the form of refugees, violence, and drugs."

Haiti's year of misery came in what should have been a year of celebration: the two hundredth anniversary of its independence from France. Haiti was the second nation in the Western Hemisphere to become independent, after the United States, and it was the world's first republic governed by blacks. Very little in the country's two centuries of independence was cause for celebration, however, The majority of its leaders, especially in the twentieth century, had been dictatorial or corrupt or both; none succeeded in fostering a climate of economic development and social progress. The United States intervened repeatedly in Haiti's affairs—including occupying the country for nineteen years early in the twentieth century—but undertook no enduring work to improve the lives of citizens there. By 2004 Haiti was by far the poorest country in the Western Hemisphere, with an estimated average per capita income of less than $1 a day. The United Nations Development Programme in 2003 ranked Haiti at the bottom of all Western Hemisphere countries on its scale of economic and social well-being and number 150 out of 173 countries worldwide.

On March 30 the United Nations special advisor for Haiti at the time, Reginald Dumas, said Haiti would need substantial international help for at least twenty years. "We cannot continue . . . with the stop-start cycle that has characterized relations between the international community and Haiti," he said. Dumas noted that in the previous decade the UN and the Organization of American States had mounted ten aid or peacekeeping missions in Haiti, none of which had produced any significant long-term improvements.

Aristide Ousted, Again

Long dominated by dictators, Haiti held its first free democratic election in 1990. The victor was Aristide, a former priest who had won a devoted following among the country's impoverished majority. Seven months into his term, in September 1991, the military ousted Aristide from power and forced him into exile in the United States. The United States in 1994 led an international military invasion that restored Aristide to office. *(U.S. invasion, Historic Documents of 1994, p. 433)*

Rather than returning Haiti to democracy, however, Aristide's renewed tenure was plagued by increasing tensions and frequent bouts of violence. The turning point came in 2000 when Aristide's political party, *Fanmi Lavalas* ("Family Lavalas"), won legislative elections that were disputed by the opposition and questioned by most international observers. Aristide himself won another presidential term in an election boycotted by most opposition groups. President Bill Clinton in late 2000 extracted a promise from Aristide to allow democratic reforms and new elections, but those promises were never kept. Attempting to pressure Aristide to keep his promises, the United States and other donors withheld about $500 million in aid to Haiti. *(Aristide promises, Historic Documents of 2000, p. 959)*

Opposition to Aristide continued to grow, and by 2003 armed groups—some backing the government and some composed of former military personnel who opposed Aristide—were terrorizing many parts of the country. A key event was the brutal murder in September 2003 of a gang leader aligned with Aristide. That killing set off a series of demonstrations and violent clashes between the president's supporters and opponents that killed an estimated fifty people by the end of January.

The Organization of American States (OAS) and the Caribbean Community attempted unsuccessfully to broker a political agreement among Haiti's factions. The security situation deteriorated in February when anti-Aristide rebels stepped up attacks in outlying areas. Among the rebels were former soldiers and officers of the army that Aristide had disbanded in 1994 and members of gangs that the government had accused of engaging in drug trafficking and death-squad killings. The rebels, united only in their hatred for Aristide, made swift progress because the government had no formal military to stop them and relied instead on its own armed gangs and poorly equipped police.

The rebels seized control of Gonaives, Haiti's fourth-largest city, on February 5, leading to uprisings in more than ten other towns. In some cases police units fled when attacked by rebels; other policemen joined the rebels. Aristide's belated offers of reconciliation were rejected by the rebels, who appeared emboldened by their ability to seize control of large sections of the country. Some areas came under the control of one side only to fall days later to the other. On February 15 two rebel leaders announced formation of a joint Resistance Front; they were Guy Philippe, a former police official who had been accused of plotting against Aristide, and Louis Jodel Chamblain, the who led one of the most violent anti-Aristide gangs.

Cap Haitien, Haiti's second-largest city, fell to the rebels on February 22, the day after an international diplomatic delegation failed to negotiate a political solution to the crisis. Three days later the French government called for an international force to stabilize Haiti and called on Aristide to resign. As rebels approached Port au Prince on February 25, pro-Aristide gangs began setting up barricades to block their advance—a sign that a pitched battle for the capital was about to begin.

After weeks of internal debate about what to do, the Bush administration intervened on February 28, calling on Aristide to surrender power and leave Haiti. Shortly after midnight on February 29, U.S. Ambassador James B. Foley persuaded Aristide to sign a statement resigning as president. Escorted by armed U.S. guards, Aristide climbed aboard a U.S. chartered airplane, not knowing where he would be taken. After a quick stop in Antigua, the plane headed toward the Central Africa Republic—the only country that would immediately accept the deposed Haitian leader. On March 15 Aristide was flown to Jamaica, where he stayed briefly before heading into permanent exile in South Africa.

Aristide later said he was forced to resign by the U.S. ambassador, then "kidnapped" and taken to the Central African Republic against his will. Aristide's charge fell on sympathetic ears elsewhere in the Caribbean, a region accustomed to frequent U.S. interventions, few of which had happy endings. U.S. Secretary of State Colin Powell, who had frantically sought to find a host country willing to accept Aristide, called the former president's claims "absolutely baseless" and "absurd."

Hours after Aristide left Haiti, President George W. Bush announced that he was sending about 250 marines to help provide security during a transition period. "This is the beginning of a new chapter in the country's history," Bush said. "I would urge the people of Haiti to reject violence to give this break from the past a chance to work. The United States is prepared to help."

Guy Philippe, who by then had emerged as the chief rebel leader, arrived in Port-au-Prince on March 1 and proclaimed himself head of the Haitian army. He was unable to take control of government offices, which were protected by the U.S. marines. Most of the rest of Haiti remained in the grip of chaos, however, as armed gangs ravaged the countryside and cities. The violence during the previous month had resulted in the deaths of at least 300 people, according to most estimates.

An Interim Government

Hours after Aristide left, the chief justice of the country's Supreme Court, Boniface Alexandre, was sworn in as interim president. In New York that same day, the UN Security Council hastily adopted resolution 1529 authorizing a multinational peacekeeping force—led by the United Sates with additional troops from Canada, Chile, and France—to take control of the security situation and restore order.

Gerard Latortue, a former Haitian foreign minister who had served as a UN official, was selected by a seven-member advisory council to serve as prime minister. Latortue was living in Florida at the time, one of thousands of Haitian exiles there. He arrived in Haiti on March 10 and took office on March 12 with a promise of elections in 2005. Latortue selected fellow cabinet ministers who also were technocrats.

Subsequent efforts during 2004 to produce agreement on a political process leading to the promised elections had little success. An eighteen member "transitional" committee was formed in July, with representatives from many of Haiti's civil society groups and political parties—except for Aristide's Lavalas party. Most outsider observers said that committee had almost no influence on the government, however.

Although the interim government was backed by the United States and had at least tacit support from the United Nations, it was greeted with little warmth by Haiti's Caribbean neighbors, most of whom objected to what they perceived as the U.S.-led ouster of Aristide.

Foreign Peacekeepers

By early March about 3,600 troops from the United States, Canada, and France were patrolling Port au Prince and other major cities—serving as the only effective security force in Haiti. The Bush administration had made clear that the U.S. military presence was only temporary and that replacements would have to be found from other countries. The UN Security Council on April 30 adopted resolution 1542 creating the UN Stabilization Mission in Haiti (known by its French acronym MINUSTAH). Led by Brazil, members of that force began arriving in Haiti on June 1 and took over from the U.S.-led mission on June 25. The UN force was given the assignments of providing security, supporting the government and elections, and supervising short-term reconstruction aid to Haiti.

MINUSTAH had an authorized strength of 6,700 soldiers and 1,622 civilian police officers, but the UN was forced to issue repeated pleas during the year for countries to fulfill their pledges of personnel. Some countries, notably Brazil, kept their promises to provide troops for Haiti, but others did not. By early November only about 4,500 troops had reached Haiti, about two-thirds of the authorized total. Just under 1,000 police officers had arrived, only about 60 percent of the authorized total. The UN force had an initial six-month mandate, and in mid-November UN Secretary General Kofi Annan asked the Security Council to renew the mandate for another eighteen months, arguing that a long-term commitment was necessary. Several Security Council member countries objected to such a long term, however, and on November 29 extended the force's mandate for only another six months. The peacekeeping force finally reached its full strength in late December, but the international police force remained understaffed at year's end.

The presence of foreign troops calmed the situation for several months but failed to eliminate the threats to stability. Both the initial U.S.-led force and the later UN force acted as peacekeepers rather than peacemakers; they made little effort to disarm—and no serious effort to disband—any of the armed groups. Months after Aristide left, anti-Aristide rebels continued to control much of the country, including the city of Petit-Goave just forty miles west of the capital, while pro-Aristide gangs controlled the large slums of Port au Prince. In August groups of former soldiers began taking over police stations in many towns—often with the overt cooperation of the national police. In an August 30 report to the Security Council, Annan estimated that some 25,000 people were members of armed groups in Haiti.

The Latortue government set a September 15 deadline for armed groups to turn in their weapons, but neither the government nor the UN mission took any effective action to carry out this decree. The challenge they faced was illustrated by the defiant stance of Remissainthe Ravix, an ex-army sergeant who was one of the leaders of the groups composed of former soldiers. "We will never hand over our weapons; we'd rather die with them," Reuters quoted him as saying on November 19. Ravix in December briefly took over Aristide's former home in a wealthy suburb, but was forced out by UN troops after a few days.

In its November 18 report, the International Crisis Group said the UN mission had been too "passive" in its attempts to deal with the armed groups, notably the anti-Aristide rebel forces. The group also warned Haiti's government against the temptation to staff the national police with former military personnel. Such a step "would be a tremendous mistake that would generate extensive clashes with armed pro-Aristide groups, leaving the Haitian people caught in the middle," the report said.

Restoration Efforts

Aristide fled a country that was bankrupt in just about every conceivable way. Haiti's governments historically had provided few public services, and any pretense of governmental service had been dropped during the conflict of the previous months. The new government reported that the treasury was bare, millions of dollars having been taken in the previous five months with little or no accounting. The United States and other donors announced plans for generous aid packages for Haiti, but even the promises that were kept soon were overwhelmed by the new disasters that befell Haiti.

The Bush administration in late May announced a $100 million aid package for Haiti, including $35 million for a partial subsidy of the government's budget and $22 million to reconstitute a national police and provide security for government leaders. An international donors conference held in Washington, D.C., on July 20 produced $1.1 billion in pledges for short-term and long-term aid to Haiti. That total fell significantly short of the $1.4 billion that Annan had said Haiti needed just to survive through September 2006. U.S. pledges totaled $230 million, including the previously announced $122 million. Annan on July 15 appointed Chilean diplomat Juan Gabriel Valde to head the UN mission and serve as his personal representative in Haiti.

A measure of Haiti's desperate situation was the set of goals the Haitian government established for itself over the summer: the creation of 44,000 jobs, the collection and disposal of half of the garbage in rural areas, the upgrading of 500 slum dwellings in Port-au-Prince, and providing 12 hours a day of electricity in the capital. None of these goals had been met by year's end, largely because Latortue's government appeared overwhelmed by the many challenges it faced. Criticism of the government's failures became so widespread late in the year that some business leaders called on the United Nations to take over formal control of Haiti temporarily, just as the world body had done in East Timor and the Balkan regions of Bosnia and Kosovo.

Impunity for Abuses

Latortue's government also came under strong international criticism in mid-2004 for a series of actions that appeared to favor anti-Aristide rebels, including former military officials who had been charged with crimes and human rights abuses. By far the most important case was the acquittal on August 16 of Louis Jodel Chamblain, a former army sergeant, who had been accused of a 1993 murder of a key Aristide supporter. Chamblain led a gang that international human rights groups long had considered one of Haiti's most notorious death squads.

A Haitian court freed Chamblain and a codefendant following an overnight trial at which the government's prosecutor failed to present any evidence or witnesses to describe their alleged crimes. Amnesty International and other human rights groups called the trial a "sham" and suggested that Latortue's government exonerated Chamblain in a deal for the support of former army officers and supporters who formed the core of anti-Aristide forces. UN Secretary General Annan also expressed dismay, saying in a report to the Security Council: "The sudden acquittal of a former paramilitary leader accused of murder at a trial during which the proper procedures were not respected stands in sharp contrast with a commitment [by the government] to tackle impunity effectively."

Haiti's Natural Disasters

Governmental incompetence and political violence were just the beginning of the scourges Haitians suffered in 2004. Two waves of floods, and even a drought, killed thousands of people, destroyed what little remained of public services in several parts of the country, and strained local and international relief efforts to the maximum.

The first flood came on May 24–25, when more than two weeks of heavy rains swept villages off denuded hillsides and sent rivers surging over their banks. The most severe damage was in southeastern Haiti, particularly around the cities of Mapou and Fonds Verrettes. The floods killed 1,261 people, with another 1,414 missing and presumed dead, according to UN agencies. An estimated 16,000 people lost their homes. For weeks after the flood, survivors were totally dependent on food, water, and other supplies airlifted by U.S. and Canadian military helicopters. In contrast to the flood, the northwestern section of Haiti continued to suffer the effects of a severe drought in 2003 and the early months of 2004.

Yet another calamity struck Haiti in September when Hurricane Jeanne raced through the Caribbean. Heavy rains from the hurricane caused massive mudslides in the northwest of Haiti on September 17–18, especially Gonaives and surrounding localities where mountains had been deforested. Gonaives, a city of 250,000, was hit by an enormous wall of muddy water that came off the surrounding hills. The water and mud swept away buildings hundreds of people. In the wake of the flood, the city's sewer system collapsed, spewing raw sewage into streets that remained flooded for several weeks afterwards.

Trucks delivering food and water stalled, and some overturned, in a deep lake of water that covered the highway between Gonaives and Port au Prince. Once the delivery trucks arrived in the city they often were attacked by armed gangs. UN peacekeepers attempted to restore order but had to deal with large crowds of people fighting over food that aid workers were attempting to deliver. As of year's end, Haitian officials estimated that 2,826 people died as a result of the flood and several thousand remained homeless.

Both storms caused substantially more devastation and misery in Haiti than in neighboring Dominican Republic, its neighbor on the island of Hispaniola. A major reason was that Haiti had been almost totally deforested because wood was the principal source of fuel, and the government lacked any environmental controls. Massive amounts of rainwater rushed off mountainsides unimpeded by trees or other vegetation, carrying vast quantities of mud that buried low-lying cities and towns. The Dominican Republic, by contrast, retained the bulk of its forests. An estimated 500 people died there in the May storms, most of them in an area along the border with Haiti.

Renewed Violence

Less than two weeks after Hurricane Jeanne, a new outbreak of political violence posed yet another danger to Haiti's immediate future. The violence began with a large pro-Aristide demonstration in Port-au-Prince on September 30—the anniversary of the coup that ousted Aristide in 1991. The demonstration turned violent and resulted in the deaths of two demonstrators and the beheading of three policemen. That violence in turn led to weeks of killings and mob activity that left scores of people dead, including nearly a dozen policemen. Government officials attributed the violence to pro-Aristide groups, and Latortue later suggested that Aristide had fomented the uprising from his South African exile. The government received support from the U.S. State Department, which said Aristide partisans were attempting to "destabilize" the government. As the fighting escalated, police arrested three members of Arisitide's political party and a prominent pro-Aristide priest, who was held without charges for six weeks. The arrests fueled even more violence and boosted the popularity of the priest, Gerard Jean-Juste, who was expected to run for president in the 2005 elections. Aristide's allies accused the government of provoking the violence to justify its crackdown. International human rights groups also accused the police of carrying out executions in poor neighborhoods that provided the base of Aristide's support.

Whatever the causes, the new wave of violence further endangered Haiti's desperate push for progress, and it created an even more immediate problem by hampering the delivery of post-Jeanne relief supplies to Gonaives and other areas.

Secretary of State Powell received a first-hand taste of the instability during a brief visit to Haiti December 1. As Powell was meeting with political figures in the national palace, gunfire broke out near a high school in a nearby neighborhood—an almost daily occurrence in the capital. An ensuing battle pitted police, international peacekeepers, and Powell's security forces on one side, against a group suspected to be Aristide loyalists. A hospital said three people died and nine were injured in the fights. Powell emerged from the government building after the shooting stopped and called for more forceful action to disarm the rebels.

Two weeks later, on December 14, UN troops launched their first large-scale incursion into a pro-Aristide stronghold, the slum of Cite Soleil along the waterfront in the northern section of Port-au-Prince. The force of several hundred troops successfully took over two police stations and, for the moment at least, seized the initiative from the gangs that had terrorized the capital. Attempting a longer-term solution to at least some of the violence, Haiti's interim government on December 28 announced that it would pay some 6,000 former members of the army that Aristide had disbanded. The government said payments would average $4,800 a person. Officials said they hoped the payments would soothe the grievances of former soldiers, who had led the uprising that drove Aristide from power and kept Haiti in turmoil for months afterward.

Following is the text of United Nations Security Council Resolution 1529, adopted February 29, 2004, authorizing an international peacekeeping force, led by the United States, to stabilize the situation in Haiti following the resignation of President Jean-Bertrand Aristide.

Resolution 1529

The Security Council,

Recalling its previous resolutions and statements by its President on Haiti, in particular the statement of 26 February 2004 (S/PRST/2004/4),

Deeply concerned by the deterioration of the political, security and humanitarian situation in Haiti and *deploring* the loss of life that has already occurred,

Expressing its utmost concern at the continuing violence in Haiti, as well as the potential for a rapid deterioration of the humanitarian situation in that country, and its destabilizing effect on the region,

Stressing the need to create a secure environment in Haiti and the region that enables respect for human rights, including the well-being of civilians, and supports the mission of humanitarian workers,

Commending the Organization of American States (OAS) and the Caribbean Community (CARICOM) for their lead efforts to advance a peaceful solution and for attempting to establish confidence among the parties, in particular through their Plan of Action,

Taking note of the resignation of Jean-Bertrand Aristide as President of Haiti and the swearing-in of President Boniface Alexandre as the acting President of Haiti in accordance with the Constitution of Haiti,

Acknowledging the appeal of the new President of Haiti for the urgent support of the international community to assist in restoring peace and security in Haiti and to further the constitutional political process now under way,

Determined to support a peaceful and constitutional solution to the current crisis in Haiti,

Determining that the situation in Haiti constitutes a threat to international peace and security, and to stability in the Caribbean especially through the potential outflow of people to other States in the subregion,

Acting under Chapter VII of the Charter of the United Nations,

1. *Calls on* Member States to support the constitutional succession and political process now under way in Haiti and the promotion of a peaceful and lasting solution to the current crisis;

2. *Authorizes* the immediate deployment of a Multinational Interim Force for a period of not more than three months from adoption of this resolution:

(a) To contribute to a secure and stable environment in the Haitian capital and elsewhere in the country, as appropriate and as circumstances permit, in order to support Haitian President Alexandre's request for international assistance to support the constitutional political process under way in Haiti;

(b) To facilitate the provision of humanitarian assistance and the access of international humanitarian workers to the Haitian people in need;

(c) To facilitate the provision of international assistance to the Haitian police and the Haitian Coast Guard in order to establish and maintain public safety and law and order and to promote and protect human rights;

(d) To support establishment of conditions for international and regional organizations, including the United Nations and the Organization of American States, to assist the Haitian people;

(e) To coordinate, as needed, with the OAS Special Mission and with the United Nations Special Adviser for Haiti, to prevent further deterioration of the humanitarian situation;

3. *Declares* its readiness to establish a follow-on United Nations stabilization force to support continuation of a peaceful and constitutional political process and the maintenance of a secure and stable environment, and in this regard requests the Secretary-General, in consultation with the Organization of American States, to submit to the Council recommendations, preferably by 30 days from adoption of this resolution, for the size, structure and mandate of such a force, including the role of international police and means of coordination with the OAS Special Mission, and for subsequent deployment of the United Nations force not later than three months from adoption of this resolution;

4. *Welcomes* the Secretary-General's February 27 appointment of a Special Adviser for Haiti, and *requests* the Secretary-General to elaborate a programme of action for the United Nations to assist the constitutional political process and support humanitarian and economic assistance and promote the protection of human rights and the development of the rule of law;

5. *Calls on* Member States to contribute personnel, equipment and other necessary financial and logistic resources on an urgent basis to the Multinational Interim Force and invites contributing Member States to inform the leadership of the force and the Secretary-General of their intent to participate in the mission; and *stresses* the importance of such voluntary contributions to help defray the expenses of the Multinational Interim Force that participating Member States will bear;

6. *Authorizes* the Member States participating in the Multinational Interim Force in Haiti to take all necessary measures to fulfil its mandate;

7. *Demands* that all the parties to the conflict in Haiti cease using violent means, and reiterates that all parties must respect international law, including with respect to human rights and that there will be individual accountability and no impunity for violators; *further demands* that parties respect the constitutional succession and the political process under way to resolve the current crisis, and enable legitimate Haitian security forces and other public institutions to perform their duties and provide access to humanitarian agencies to carry out their work;

8. *Further calls* on all parties in Haiti and on Member States to cooperate fully with the Multinational Interim Force in Haiti in the execution of its mandate and to respect the security and freedom of movement of the Multinational Interim Force, as well as to facilitate the safe and unimpeded access of international humanitarian personnel and aid to populations in need in Haiti;

9. *Requests* the leadership of the Multinational Interim Force in Haiti to report periodically to the Council, through the Secretary-General, on the implementation of its mandate;

10. *Calls upon* the international community, in particular the United Nations, the Organization of American States, and the Caribbean Community, to work with the people of Haiti in a long-term effort to promote the rebuilding of democratic institutions and to assist in the development of a strategy to promote social and economic development and to combat poverty;

11. *Decides* to remain seized of the matter.

Source: United Nations. Security Council. *Resolution 1529.* S/RES/1529 (2004), February 29, 2004. http://daccess-ods.un.org/access. nsf/Get?Open&DS=S/RES/1529%20(2004)&Lang=E&Area=UNDOC (accessed January 5, 2005). Reprinted with the permission of the United Nations Security Council.

March

2004 HISTORIC DOCUMENTS

Spanish Leaders on the Terrorist Bombings in Madrid

March 11, 2004

INTRODUCTION

Spain suffered its single largest and deadliest terrorist attack ever on March 11, 2004, one that had broad repercussions both domestically and internationally. Ten bombs placed aboard four commuter trains in Madrid killed 191 people and wounded more than 1,600. The bombings came just three days before national elections, and Spanish voters quickly punished the center-right party then in power—not because of its failure to prevent the attack but primarily because its leaders were perceived to have lied about who was responsible.

The government of President José María Aznar at first blamed the bombings on *Euskadi Ta Askatasuna* (Basque Homeland and Freedom, known as ETA), a group that often had used bombings and assassinations to advance the cause of independence for the Basque region of northern Spain and southern France. Evidence quickly mounted, however, that an Islamist group, possibly associated with the al Qaeda terrorist network, more likely had been responsible and had targeted Spain because Aznar had aligned the country with the U.S. invasion and occupation of Iraq. Voters defeated Aznar's hand-picked successor, Mariano Rajoy, and instead turn to the center-left Socialist Workers Party and its leader, José Luis Rodriguez Zapatero. The new government then pulled Spain's troops out of Iraq and became a critic, rather than an ally, of the policies of U.S. president George W. Bush. *(Iraq, p. 399)*

Months later ETA appeared to be responsible for five simultaneous bomb blasts at gasoline stations in the Madrid area. Two police offices were injured in the December 3 bombings, which caused only limited damage but created enormous traffic jams. ETA had been blamed for more than 800 deaths since the late 1960s but had been severely damaged by years of government retaliation. The December bombings coincided with a drive by the civilian, non-ETA leadership of the Basque regional parliament for a referendum on virtual independence for the region—a concept the central government refused to consider.

The Madrid Bombings

Madrid's morning rush hour was still under way at 7:39 a.m. when three explosions went off in a train at the Atocha train station, Madrid's main commuter terminal just one block from the Prado Museum near the city center. Almost simultaneously, four more explosions occurred on another train that had been held up just outside the same station. Eighty-nine people were killed on those two trains. Even more people probably would have died if—as the bombers apparently intended—all the bombs had gone off while both trains were in the station, and if police had not quickly located and safely detonated two other bombs on the train just outside the station.

About three minutes later, explosions went off in trains at two other stations southeast of the city center: two explosions in a double-decker train at El Pozo station and one explosion in a train that was passing through Santa Eugenia station. All together, 191 people died and more than 1,600 people were wounded in the ten explosions on four separate trains. Investigators later determined that bombers had loaded backpacks and plastic bags containing their deadly cargo onto the trains as they passed through the station in Alcala de Henares, a suburb east of downtown Madrid. The trains were used predominantly by working class people and students living in Alcala de Henares.

The explosions ripped giant holes in each of the trains and sent pieces of metal, glass, and plastic firing off in all directions. Dozens of people were killed outright by the force of the blasts; others were burned to death or died of their wounds in subsequent days. Original estimates were that more than 200 people had been killed; the final figure of 191 was determined two weeks later. Authorities set up emergency hospitals near each of the stations for the wounded; some were able to crawl from the wreckage of the trains, while others had to be removed from the rubble. Typical of stories told by survivors was the account of Amet Oulabid, a carpenter who left the front of the train inside Atocha station seconds before the first bomb went off. "I saw bodies flying," he said. "There was a security guard dripping with blood. People were pushing and running. I saw a woman who had fallen on the tracks because people were pushing so hard."

Government Blames Basques

Senior government officials immediately laid responsibility for the bombings on ETA. "It is absolutely clear that the terrorist organization ETA was seeking an attack with wide repercussions," Interior Minister Angel Acebes told reporters shortly after the attacks. ETA was a logical suspect in some ways because it had often used bombs to advance its separatist cause. But in other respects ETA did not seem a likely candidate for this particular incident, as the group had never before carried out such a broad-scale attack against ordinary citizens, having focused nearly all its fatal attention on policemen, judges, and other government officials. ETA typically claimed responsibility for its attacks, but in this case it heatedly denied responsibility. Additionally, the unexploded bombs found by police did not match any devices ETA had used in the past.

Several hours after the bombings, investigators discovered a stolen van near the Alcala de Henares station containing seven bomb detonators and an audiotape with verses from the Qur'an. An Arabic-language newspaper in London, *al-Quds al-Arabi,* also said it had received an e-mail message, reportedly from a group linked to al Qaeda, claiming responsibility for the bombings. "This is part of settling old accounts with Spain, the crusader, and America's ally in the war against Islam," the letter said in part. Al Qaeda often had used the London newspaper to publicize its messages.

Interior Minister Acebes then said the government was open to the possibility that a group other than ETA was responsible but still believed the Basque group was the likely culprit. To bolster their case against ETA, authorities noted that a van containing a half-ton of explosives had been intercepted as it headed toward Madrid in late February; two suspected ETA militants were arrested. Spanish police had also foiled the planned bombing of a train in Madrid the previous December and arrested a suspect in Basque territory.

The question of who was responsible held obvious import for Spanish politics, with national elections only three days away. If ETA was to blame, Aznar's government clearly stood to benefit politically because its hard-line position against the Basque movement would appear to be justified, if not fully successful. But if al Qaeda or some other Islamist terrorist group was to blame, many Spaniards were sure to fault the government for its backing of the U.S. war in Iraq, which had aroused Arab opposition in many lands and helped make Spain a potential target for Islamist terrorism.

Later in the day, King Juan Carlos I and President Aznar made separate appearances on national television to express the nation's grief. The king's speech was historic in and of itself, marking his first address to the nation (other than on symbolic occasions) since he blocked an attempted coup in 1981. "Your king suffers with all of you, shares your indignation and places his trust in the strength and effectiveness of the rule of law so that such despicable and cowardly murderers may fall into the hands of justice and serve in prison all of the sentences that the courts issue," he said to the families of those killed in the attack. "They must be irremissibly accountable for their crimes."

Aznar promised a hard line against "the terrorist group," the government's standard reference to ETA. He pledged their "complete and total defeat, their unconditional surrender. There is no possible or desirable negotiation with these murders who have so often spread death all over Spain." Spaniards understood this last line as another clear reference to ETA.

Mass Demonstrations

Responding to the united urgings of the government and opposition leaders, millions of Spaniards crowded into streets and public plazas on the day after the bombings. The Madrid newspaper, *El Mundo,* estimated that about 11.4 million people—a fourth of the country's population—took part in the demonstrations. Taken together, the demonstrations were considered by many observers to be the largest one-day public gathering anywhere in recent world history.

In Madrid about 2 million people crowded onto flag-draped Castellana Avenue, the central Colon Square, and other open spaces. Many carried flags or banners with such messages as "We were all on that train" and chanted "No to terrorism" and other slogans. Thousands of Spaniards also had painted the palms of their hands white (to symbolize resistance to terrorism) or red (to symbolize the blood of victims). It was a rainy day in Spain, but a student, Jorge Mendez, seemed to speak for others: "It is not raining. Madrid is crying." Dignitaries from across Europe came to pay their respects, including French prime minister Jean Pierre Raffarin and Italian prime minister Silvio Berlusconi. Aznar and Crown Prince Felipe led the demonstration in Madrid; it was the prince's first participation in a public demonstration.

First Arrests

Even as the demonstrations were under way, Spanish officials continued to debate who was responsible for the bombings. Police released photographs of five ETA militants, suggesting they might have been planning several attacks on Madrid. Aznar said all possibilities were being investigated, even as he again pointed to ETA as the likely culprit. The Foreign Ministry sent cables instructing Spain's ambassadors to "use any opportunity" to make the case overseas that ETA was to blame. Responding to Madrid's lobbying, the United Nations Security Council quickly adopted Resolution 1530 directly blaming ETA. Despite the assertions from Madrid, many counterterrorism experts in Europe and the United States expressed doubts about ETA's role and suggested that al Qaeda or some other Islamist faction was the more likely culprit.

A key discovery came on March 12, when police found a bag on one of the trains containing an unexploded bomb, a detonator, and a cell phone. The phone turned out to be a central piece of evidence, enabling the government to make its first arrests the following day: three Moroccans and two Indians were held on charges related to the sale of the phone. One of the Moroccan suspects, Jamal Zougam, had been linked—in an indictment issued the previous fall against al Qaeda leader Osama bin Laden—to Imad Eddin Barakat Yarkas (also known as Abu Dadah), the alleged leader of an al Qaeda cell in Spain.

The government announced these arrests in the evening of March 13, the day before the election. Acebes, the interior minister, said it was "too early to make a determination that they [the suspects] are linked to Islamist groups such as al Qaeda," but he acknowledged that some of the suspects might have links to "Moroccan extremist groups." Coming against other evidence pointing toward al Qaeda, this stance added to a growing public impression that the government had something to hide.

Also on March 13 the Telemadrid television station received a call alerting it to a videotape placed in a trash can near a mosque in Madrid. In the tape, a man speaking Arabic claimed responsibility for the bombings on behalf of "al Qaeda in Europe." He said the bombings were in response to Spain's "collaboration" with the "the criminal Bush and his allies" in Afghanistan and Iraq. The man also said the attack was timed for exactly two-and-a-half years after the September 11, 2001, attacks in the United States. Spanish police verified two days later that the tape was authentic.

Election

Aznar had been prime minister since 1996 and had firmly affixed a conservative stamp on a government that had been dominated for a decade by the Socialist Party and its dynamic former leader, Felipe Gonzalez.

Aznar's free-market policies boosted the economy, but Aznar himself had become a polarizing figure because of his seemingly arrogant manner and his insistence on supporting the U.S. war in Iraq, which was opposed by the vast majority of Spaniards, according to polls. Aznar chose to step aside for the 2004 elections and selected Mariano Rajoy, a Popular Party functionary, as his successor. Until shortly before the bombings, Rajoy and the Popular Party had enjoyed a comfortable lead over Zapatero and the Socialists. Zapatero, a lawyer from the region of Castile, had led his party for just three years. Until the election campaign he had failed to make much of an impression nationally. He ran an aggressive campaign, however, harshly criticizing Aznar's Iraq policy and the government's handling of a giant oil spill off the northern coast in 2002.

Rajoy and Zapatero differed on many issues, but their sharpest clash was on the question of Spain's role in Iraq. Rajoy said he was committed to Aznar's policy of supporting the U.S. role there, while Zapatero pledged to withdraw Spain's 1,300 troops unless the United Nations took command of the foreign military presence in Iraq.

The race had tightened just a week before the election, with opinion surveys showing strong gains by the Socialist Party, although not enough for victory. Politicians suspended their campaigning immediately after the bombings—leaving voters to draw their own conclusions about how to respond to Spain's latest, and deadliest, experience with terrorism.

On election day, March 14, Spanish voters turned against Aznar's party, giving it just 38 percent of the overall vote, compared to 43 percent for the Socialists. The Socialists gained nearly 3 million votes over their totals in the 2000 elections, and the Popular Party lost nearly 1 million. In terms of seats in the parliament, the 350-seat Cortes, or Chamber of Deputies, the Socialists captured 164 seats (a gain of 39) but fell just short of a working majority, meaning they would have to form a coalition with minor left-leaning parties. The Popular Party captured only 148 seats, a loss of 35.

Claiming victory at his party's headquarters, Zapatero said he would take a tough line against terrorism. However, he pledged a different style of governing from Aznar, who was often accused of cold arrogance. "I will lead a quiet change. I will govern for all in unity, and power will not change me, I promise you that," he said.

Most Spanish political analysts said the bombings provided the crucial boost for the Socialists, for two reasons: They reminded voters, even conservatives, that Spain's vulnerability to terrorism had increased as a result of its participation in the Iraq war, and they stimulated left-leaning voters to go to the polls rather than stay at home—as many had done in the 2000 elections. Important support for the latter supposition was that turnout jumped eight points to 77 percent of the electorate.

Supporters of Aznar—and conservative political commentators in many other countries, including the United States—portrayed Zapatero's victory as a setback for the U.S.-led war against Islamist terrorism. Al Qaeda, according to this line of argument, had been able to sway the Spanish election by frightening the voters.

Many other observers, however, said the political outcome in Spain resulted from a much more complicated set of circumstances, starting with voter anger at Aznar's government for appearing to manipulate information about the bombings for its own political benefit. Voter anger emerged from fertile soil: lingering public resentment that Aznar had disregarded the near-universal opposition in Spain to the country's military role in Iraq. Citing these factors, the *Financial Times* newspaper editorialized on March 16: "There are no grounds for concluding that Spain flinched when confronted with terror on this scale."

Two days after the election, Zapatero made it clear that he intended to stand by his campaign promise to withdraw Spain's troops from Iraq. "The war has been a disaster, the occupation continues to be a great disaster," he told reporters. "It hasn't generated anything but more violence and hate. What simply cannot be is that after it became so clear how badly it was handled there be no consequences." In language unusually strong for a top politician, Zapatero also took direct aim at Bush and British prime minister Tony Blair, saying: "You cannot organize a war with lies. Bush and Blair should do some self-criticism to avoid repeating what has happened." He promised a "pro-European" policy for Spain and said Madrid would look for solidarity to France and Germany, rather than the United States.

Zapatero made good on his promise to disengage from Iraq. His new government took office on April 17. The next day he said he as ordering the withdrawal of all Spanish military personnel in Iraq.

The Investigation

The three Moroccans and two Indians who had been arrested on March 13 were charged six days later: the Moroccans on 190 charges of murder (reflecting the death toll at the time), and the Indians on charges of collaborating with a terrorist group. Authorities on March 23 arrested several other people in connection with the bombings, including a Spaniard who was charged with 190 counts of murder for providing the explosives for the bombs. On April 1 police discovered and dismantled a bomb placed aboard a high-speed train from Madrid to Seville, renewing concerns that Spain might be subject to multiple terrorist attacks. Authorities said the bomb was made of the same brand of dynamite that had been used in the Madrid attacks.

On April 3, when police entered an apartment building in Leganes, a suburb of Madrid, to arrest four bombing suspects, the suspects exploded a bomb, killing themselves and a policeman and wounding eleven other policemen. One of the dead suspects, a Tunisian, was thought to have been an organizer of the Madrid bombings, and police found a videotape threatening additional attacks against Spain unless it withdrew its troops from Iraq.

The investigation stretched to the United States early in May, with embarrassing consequences for the FBI. Federal agents on May 6 arrested an attorney, Brandon Mayfield, in West Slope, Oregon, and held him as a material witness in the Madrid bombings case. The FBI said Mayfield's fingerprint had been found on one of the bags containing detonating devices the day of the bombings. Mayfield was released May 21 after the FBI acknowledged that the fingerprint had been mistakenly identified as his and apologized for the error. An internal investigation later found that FBI fingerprint experts feared disagreeing with their superiors, who had become convinced that Mayfield, a Muslim, had some connection to the Madrid bombings.

An alleged ringleader of the bombings was arrested June 8 in Milan, Italy. Italian police held Rabei Osman el Sayed Ahmed on charges of belonging to a terrorist organization, but Spanish authorities said he was the mastermind of the Madrid plot. He was extradited to Spain in December. Also accused of helping plan the bombings was Hasan al-Haski, a Moroccan who was arrested in December in the Canary Islands. On December 22 a judge charged him with 191 counts of murder and said he belonged to the Moroccan Islamic Combat Group, which international police authorities believe carried out May 2003 bombings in Casablanca that killed thirty-three people in addition to a dozen suicide bombers.

By year's end, the Interior Ministry said sixty-two people had been arrested and jailed at one point or another in connection with the case; most had been charged. Nineteen of these people were still being held on various "provisional" charges that fell short of formal indictments. A judge supervising the case was planning to complete the investigation by March 2005, the ministry said.

Parliamentary Hearings

In July a special committee of parliament began an inquiry into all aspects of the Madrid bombings, focusing in particular on the actions of Aznar's government at the time. The early days of the inquiry were spiced with revelations from leaked documents, including one appearing to show that Aznar had contracted with a public relations firm in Washington for a variety of services, including arranging for him to receive a gold medal from Congress.

Aznar testified on November 29 and staunchly defended both his handling of the attacks and the public statements of his government. "We told the truth about what we knew," he said, adding that Zapatero himself had said at the time there was "no difference" whether the bombings had been commited by ETA or al Qaeda. Aznar also said he believed a theory, which had gained popularity in conservative circles in Spain, that ETA was linked to al Qaeda.

Zapatero appeared before the committee on December 13 and offered sensational charges that Aznar's government had deleted all official records concerning the days immediately after the Madrid bombings. "There was not a single paper, not a single piece of data in computer form or in paper, absolutely nothing in the executive offices of the presidency, because there was a massive erasing [of computers]," he said. The prime minister's office was referred to as the "presidency" of the government.

Demonstrating that political wounds were still raw, Zapatero accused Aznar and his government of lying about who was responsible for the bombings. "It was all deceit," he said. "It was massive deceit." He also heatedly denied lingering charges that Spanish voters had given into terrorism when they ousted the Popular Party. Noting that Spanish politicians of both the right and left had dealt forcefully with terrorism for decades, he said: "It is inconceivable that someone can imagine that the citizens of Spain bowed to the wishes of terrorists. It is brutal, it is unacceptable, to call a brave people cowards."

The continued squabbling among politicians brought a rebuke on December 15 from Pilar Manujon, whose son died in the bombings and who was spokeswoman for the Association of Victims of March 11. She charged that the hearings had turned into "playground politics" and had failed to investigate why the police had not prevented the bombings.

Following are the texts of two televised statements to the people of Spain by King Juan Carlos I and President of the Government José María Aznar on the afternoon of March 11, 2004, hours after 191 people were killed and more than 1,600 were injured by bomb explosions on commuter trains in Madrid.

"King Juan Carlos on the March 11 Madrid Bombings"

Today, terrorist savagery has plunged Spain into the deepest grief, condemnation and indignation. Men, women and children, free citizens of all ages and occupations, even from other countries, who were arriving at their destinations, schools and jobs brutally faced death and suffering.

A nightmarish scenario has seized all Spanish households to display the cruelest and most murderous face of terrorism. In these tragic times, I wish to convey to the families of the victims my most profound sympathy and that of my entire family. I would like to clasp all of you in an embrace full of comfort and grief.

We will always be with you, with all who suffer from the consequences of an impossibly justifiable macabre madness. These repulsive attacks only deserve the most vigorous and absolute condemnation.

I would also like to address the wounded victims and their families to express to them our affection, closeness and our desire for a speedy recovery. Your King suffers with all of you, shares your indignation and places his trust in the strength and effectiveness of the Rule of Law so that such despicable and cowardly murderers may fall into the hands of justice and serve in prison all of the sentences that the courts issue. They must be irremissibly accountable for their crimes.

The public agencies and citizens of Madrid, always generous, have risen to the occasion amidst the tragedy to show their dedicated support, effort and collaboration. The Armed Forces and police corps are indefatigable in the defense of our liberties.

The good-hearted Spain has once again vibrated, offering its material aid and moral support. To all of you, our most profound appreciation.

Discouragement is unheard of for Spaniards. We are a great country which has exceeding proven its capability to overcome challenges and difficulties. A country which knows all to well that, in the face of injustice and barbarity, there is no other option but unity, firmness and serenity.

Unity, firmness and serenity in the fight against terrorism, with all of the instruments which the Rule of Law provides us, stepping up our joint efforts to do away with this blight, relying on police actions, the endeavor of the judicial system and international cooperation.

Unity, firmness and serenity above all of the legitimate differences in opinion, regarding the strongest willingness for peaceful and democratic coexistence, guaranteed by our Constitution, which is the sovereign expression of the Spanish people.

In these hours of immense pain, we Spaniards are called to reaffirm, more than ever, our determination to put an end to terrorist violence. Let there be no mistake. Terrorism will never attain its objectives. It will not crush our faith in democracy or our trust in the future of Spain.

Source: Kingdom of Spain. Embassy of Spain in the United States. "Speech Delivered by H.M. the King Due to the Terrorist Attacks Perpetrated in Madrid." English translation. March 11, 2004.

"President José María Aznar on the March 11 Madrid Bombings"

Good Afternoon to all of you.

March 11, 2004 already holds its place in the annals of infamy. This morning, in Madrid, terrorists have detonated several bombs placed in commuter trains full of people.

At this moment of such profound sadness, my first words go out to the victims of these unspeakable attacks. There are already more than 100 people dead and many more wounded; for hundreds of families, mourning has arrived unannounced; thousands are living through hours of anxiety and uncertainty. I wish to tell them that I feel their terrible anguish as if it were my own. I would like them to know that, in this time of pain and democratic strength, the Nation's Government stands by them, as do the immense majority of Spaniards.

I know all too well that, today, words are not enough to ease their pain. We stand by them and are going to be standing by them for all that they may need, today and always, and we will not forget what has happened.

We are undergoing difficult times but we have also had the chance to notice how many anonymous people have given the best they have to give of themselves. The response of our citizens has been exceptional. Spontaneous collaborations in order to aid the victims, transport the wounded or donate blood is worthy of the utmost acknowledgement. On behalf of the Government, I wish to express my deepest gratitude to these people.

Likewise, I would like to thank the members of the emergency health services, fire fighters, municipal police officers and members of the Armed Forces and police corps, in addition to the judicial, local, regional and Government authorities for their selfless work, efficiency and sense of responsibility and duty.

The Government of Spain has undertaken all of the measures within its scope to guarantee the security of its citizens and re-establish the public services affected. In collaboration with Madrid city agencies, the mechanism to evacuate wounded victims and treat victims and their families has been initiated. Of course, police investigations have immediately commenced in order to hunt down the murderers.

I have informed His Majesty the King. I have spoken with the leaders of the major political parties, as well as with representatives from different institutions. I have issued a decree for three official days of mourning as a public expression of the distress that, today, all law-abiding Spaniards share.

I have received displays of solidarity and grief from numerous leaders of allied and friendly governments. On behalf of the Spanish people, I have thanked them for their statements and I have underscored the importance of a firmly determined international fight to defeat terrorism.

The terrorists wanted to cause the largest damage possible. This is a mass murder which, as all terrorist attacks, lacks any justification. But terrorism is not blind. They have slain many people just because they are Spaniards.

We are all aware of the fact that this is not the first time that a mass murder has been attempted. The Armed Forces and police corps have prevented us from experiencing this tragedy several times. Today, I wish to express the Government's greatest support to the people who comprise them and to the heads of the anti-terrorist forces. Thanks to their splendid work, the operational capability of the terrorists is weaker than ever. However, their murdering instinct and their drive to subjugate Spain to their rule remain, tragically, active.

We will defeat them. Let there be no mistake. We will finish off the terrorist group with the strength of the Rule of Law and with the unity of all Spaniards. We will eradicate them with strong laws, with security forces and with courts firmly backed and decidedly resolved to enforce the law.

The criminals who have caused, today, so many deaths will be captured. They will be tried and sentenced by courts which are only ruled by law. They will serve their entire sentences and will have no other horizon but that of seeing the sun rise from within prison walls everyday.

We are standing by the victims. It is they whom we have to support and whose voice we must provide. The families of those who, today, have been murdered can always count on the support and aid of the Government and its institutions. They will also have the sympathy of the immense majority of Spaniards. No institution or social group can spare them the acknowledgement or respect that the will always deserve.

We are standing by the Constitution. It is the pact of the immense majority of Spaniards which guarantees the liberties and rights of all. It is also the grand accord regarding our political regime, and it is the expression of our united and plural Spain. We are not going to change the regime because terrorists kill or because they will stop killing.

This is why I am telling all Spaniards that we must not yearn for anything less than the complete defeat of terrorism, the complete and total defeat; their unconditional surrender. There is no possible or desirable negotiation with these murders who have so often spread death all over Spain. Do not be deceived: it is only through firmness that we can make the attacks stop; a firmness which must be present in the fight against terrorism as well as in the whole-hearted opposition to the final goals that the terrorists are attempting to achieve.

In order to defend these causes, the Government is asking Spaniards to demonstrate, tomorrow, along the streets of Spain. Under the heading "Standing by the Victims and the Constitution and for the Defeat of Terrorism," demonstrations have been scheduled in all Spanish cities, tomorrow, Friday, at 7:00 p.m. I hope that these demonstrations will be as overwhelming as the pain we feel today; as civic as the patriotism which makes us sympathize with all of those who suffer from the consequences of terrorist acts.

We are a great nation. We are a great nation whose sovereignty resides in all Spaniards. It is the Spanish people who decide. We will never allow, are never going to allow, a minority of fanatics to impose our decisions regarding our national future.

Thank you all very much for your attention and Good Afternoon.

Source: Kingdom of Spain. Embassy of Spain in the United States. "Statement Made by the President of the Government Regarding the ETA Terrorist Attacks in Madrid." English translation. March 11, 2004.

UN Secretary General on Remembering the Rwanda Genocide

March 26, 2004

INTRODUCTION

The world confronted in 2004—as it never had before—the failure to prevent the genocide in Rwanda a decade earlier. Commemorations were held around the world in late March and early April, marking the tenth anniversary of the outbreak of the most horrific ten weeks of killings in modern history. Between April 7 and early June 1994 at least 800,000 Rwandans were slaughtered with machetes, knives, guns, or grenades. The vast majority were Tutsi, a minority group in Rwanda that traditionally held much of the country's economic and political power. Thousands, however, were moderates among the majority Hutu, some of whom lost their lives trying to protect the Tutsi from fellow Hutu extremists who were intent on ridding Rwanda of the Tutsi. The Rwandan genocide led indirectly to an even bigger and deadlier conflict in neighboring Congo, during which as many as 3 million people may have lost their lives. That conflict, largely initiated by the post-genocide government of Rwanda, was still sputtering to a close in 2004. *(Congo war, p. 505; genocide background, Historic Documents of 1999, p. 860)*

The Rwandan government on April 2 announced that a detailed census had counted 937,000 genocide victims. Even that figure was not complete, the government said, because more deaths were still being brought to light in village-based trials that were just getting under way.

The Rwanda genocide even became the subject of a major Hollywood moving, released in late 2004. *Hotel Rwanda* told the true story of a hotel manager in Kigali who shielded hundreds of people from the killings.

Making good on its pledge to try to stop other potential genocides, Rwanda in August sent several hundred soldiers to take part in a peacekeeping mission in Sudan, where militias armed and aligned with the government were accused of driving more than 2 million people from their homes. U.S. secretary of state Colin Powell said the conflict in Sudan was a case of genocide—a finding that was still under review by a UN panel at year's end. *(Sudan, p. 588)*

Remembering the Genocide

The rest of the world averted its eyes as the rampage of murder was occurring in Rwanda. The United Nations Security Council, which had been warned of potential conflict between the Hutu and the Tutsi, refused to intervene until after it was too late. Indeed, at the height of the killings, the Security Council—at the urging of

France and the United States—ordered the almost total withdrawal of an undermanned, poorly equipped peacekeeping force in Rwanda. Rwanda's neighbors in Africa took no action, either; many had been plagued by their own internal wars that lasted years or even decades.

The first major world leader to apologize for his failure to act was U.S. president Bill Clinton, who traveled to Rwanda in 1998 and said he had not taken seriously the reports from Rwanda. A year later, the United Nations acknowledged its failure. A report published under the auspices of Secretary General Kofi Annan said the world body failed to recognize the extent of the killings.

The UN's failure to act appeared to weigh especially heavy on Annan, an African who had headed the world body's peacekeeping bureau in 1994. Speaking to a memorial conference in New York on March 26, 2004, Annan recalled that he had asked "dozens of countries for troops" for the peacekeeping mission in Rwanda. "I believed at that time I was doing my best," he said. "But I realized after the genocide that there was more that I could and should have done to sound the alarm and rally support." The "painful memory" of Rwanda, along with the concurrent war in Bosnia, "has influenced much of my thinking, and many of my actions, as secretary general," he said.

Another conference on the genocide was held in Rwanda's capital, Kigali, beginning on April 4. Many speakers offered personal remembrances of the terror a decade earlier, while others who had watched from afar admitted that they—along with the rest of the world—had stood by in silence. Speaking at the opening session, François Garambe, chairman of a genocide survivors group called Ibuka, squarely blamed the rest of the world for failing to act. "With the information that the international community had on preparations for the genocide and the means it had as its disposal, the international community could have prevented the genocide," he said. "The international community still continues after the genocide to display total indifference to the survivors' unspeakable moral and physical suffering."

Another speaker at the conference was retired Canadian general Romeo Dallaire, who had commanded the UN peacekeeping force in Rwanda that was unable to stop the genocide. Weeks before the killing broke out, Dallaire had pleaded unsuccessfully with UN headquarters for permission to seize a weapons cache assembled by the Hutu militants who were about to launch the genocide. "The international community didn't give one damn for Rwandans because Rwanda was a country of no strategic importance," Dallaire told the conference.

On April 7 about 65,000 people gathered at a stadium in Kigali to hear Rwandan president Paul Kagame castigate Western nations for blocking UN intervention at the outbreak of the genocide. Also addressing the crowd was Guy Verhofstadt, the prime minister of Belgium, which in 1994 had the largest and best equipped military unit in the UN's peacekeeping force in Rwanda. Belgium withdrew its troops after ten of them were killed on the first day of the genocide. Acknowledging the failures of his country, which had been Rwanda's colonial power, Verhofstadt spoke to the crowd in Kinyarwanda, the national language: "We must correct the mistakes we made in our history."

At the UN on April 7, diplomats from across the globe spoke at a special session of the General Assembly devoted to remembering the events in Rwanda. Kagame addressed the session by a television hookup and challenged the world to consider whether it would again stand by as a genocide occurred. In Geneva, Annan warned the UN Human Rights Commission that another potential genocide was unfolding in Sudan. "We cannot afford to wait until the worst has happened, or is already happening, or end up with little more than futile hand-wringing or callous indifference," Annan said.

Recovering in Rwanda

Rwanda ten years after the killing was in some ways a very different place, and in others much the same as it had been. International guilt in the wake of the genocide had brought hundreds of millions of dollars in foreign aid that stimulated the economy and built new schools, medical clinics, roads, power stations, and other essentials. Although lacking many of the natural resources that offered potential wealth to some of its neighbors (notably Congo), Rwanda by 2004 was a relatively prosperous nation in the Great Lakes region of east-central Africa.

Another major change was that the Tutsi were in charge of post-genocide Rwanda. Ever since Kagame's Rwandan Patriotic Front guerrillas drove out the genocidal government, he and other Tutsi were the undisputed leaders. The only Hutu with any significant role in the post-genocide government was Pasteur Bizimungu, who served as a figurehead president while Kagame ran the government as vice president. Bizimungu was forced to resign in 2000. In 2004 he was convicted on charges of embezzlement, inciting violence, and associating with criminals; on June 7 he was sentenced to fifteen years in prison.

Kagame banned all distinctions between Hutu and Tutsi, which he said were "divisive" in society. Critics said he was trying to play down the fact that the Tutsi minority was running the country. Rwanda held elections in 2003, but Kagame allowed only token opposition. Opposition parties were banned, and the news media operated under tight restrictions that made independent reporting almost impossible. In that respect, many observers said, the Rwanda of 2004 bore some similarity to Rwanda before the genocide. "Such is Rwanda's irony," journalist Stefan Lovgren wrote for *National Geographic News* on April 6. "Just as the genocide was made possible because of the government's absolute authority over its citizenry, so is peace maintained today."

UN War Crimes Tribunal

The slow-moving legal process of bringing the leaders of the genocide to justice continued at the United Nations War Crimes Tribunal based in Arusha, Tanzania. The tribunal began work in 1996 and had rendered several ground-breaking judgments, including the first-ever conviction on genocide charges and the first conviction of journalists on charges of instigating mass killings. The tribunal had been widely criticized for the slowness of its work; it held sixty-six suspects but after eight years had completed only about one-third of their cases. Another sixteen suspects charged with major crimes remained at large; among them was Felicien Kabuga, who was accused of financing the genocide and who had narrowly escaped capture in Kenya in 2003. *(Background, Historic Documents of 2003, p. 1069)*

The most prominent defendant before the court in 2004 was Colonel Theoneste Bagosora, who in 1994 was a senior official of the Rwandan defense minister and was described by many observers as the principal mastermind of the genocide. Dramatic testimony in that case came on January 19 from Dallaire, the head of the UN peacekeeping mission. Dallaire testified that Bagosora had physically threatened him if he tried to intervene in the killings. "I had a very tense meeting with him and he threatened me with a pistol, saying that next time we met he would shoot me," Dallaire said. Dallaire also testified that he had warned UN headquarters in January 1994 that Hutu militias aligned with the government were stockpiling weapons, but he was denied permission to raid the weapons. Bagosora's case was still pending at year's end.

Among the judgments rendered by the tribunal in 2004 was the conviction of a former minister for culture and higher education to two life sentences. Jean de Dieu Kamuhanda was convicted on charges of genocide and extermination but found not guilty on eight other charges. Witnesses had said Kamuhanda on April 12, 1994, had delivered armed militiamen to a church where Tutsis had taken refugee. The militiamen used machetes, guns, and grenades to kill the Tutsis. The tribunal gave Kamuhanda two life sentences. The tribunal on June 17 convicted a former mayor of Rusumo, Sylvestre Gacumbitsi, on charges of genocide, extermination, and rape for ordering the executions of as many as 20,000 Tutsi and sentenced him to thirty years in prison.

Rwandan Hutus complained that the tribunal had yet to bring to justice a single Tutsi despite evidence that Kagame's Rwandan Patriotic Front guerrillas had killed tens of thousands of people as they took over the county in the closing phase of the genocide. The tribunal's chief prosecutor, Hassan Jallow, said in April that he was still investigating charges against former Tutsi guerrillas.

Rwanda Court Cases

After the genocide more than 130,000 people were imprisoned in Rwanda on charges of having participated in the killings. In the late 1990s the government began putting the cases of many of those suspects into a traditional system of justice known as *gacaca,* in which they were judged by village elders. Several dozen gacaca courts had been held around the country as an experiment, but they had dealt with only about 750 cases as of mid-2004. On June 24 Kagame said gacaca courts were to be held nationwide in more than 9,000 local jurisdictions.

The slow pace of dispensing justice put the government under intense criticism, both domestically and internationally. In response, the government began offering leniency for those who admitted to crimes. Some 25,000 suspects took advantage of that offer early in 2003; they were released from prison, sent to "solidarity camps" for education in how to live in civil society, then allowed to return to their former homes. More than 5,000 of those suspects were arrested again when new evidence was presented against them. Thousands more genocide suspects confessed early in 2004 prior to a government deadline of March 15.

Rwanda's system of justice was further troubled by cases in which genocide witnesses were killed or threatened, allegedly by those they were prepared to testify against. A Rwandan court on February 27 sentenced to death five people for killing a genocide survivor the previous November. A parliamentary commission in June attributed the killings to what it called a "genocide ideology," which it said was being spread by several political, religious, human rights, and nongovernmental groups. Amnesty International, the Britain-based international human rights group, on July 6 expressed concern that the government was "manipulating the concept of genocide" to silence organizations that had criticized the government. Representatives of several groups cited by the parliamentary commission fled Rwanda, saying they feared for their lives.

Other Developments

There were other developments during the year relating to the genocide. Hundreds of Rwandans who had taken refugee in neighboring Uganda during or immediately after the 1994 genocide began returning to their homes in January under the sponsorship of the UN High Commissioner for Refugees (UNHCR). Some 25,000 Rwandans had been living in UNHCR camps in Uganda ever since the genocide. They were the latest wave of Rwandans who had taken refugee in Uganda (and other countries, as well) as a result of periodic violence after Rwanda gained is independence from Belgium in 1962. The first 242 of the genocide-era refugees returned home on January 31.

The Paris newspaper *Le Monde* reported on April 10 that French investigators had compiled evidence alleging that Kagame was behind the incident that triggered the genocide. On April 6, 1994, an airplane carrying the presidents of Rwanda and Burundi crashed, killing both presidents. Rwandan government officials and Hutu extremists used the crash as the excuse for the murderous attacks against the Tutsi. The cause of the crash had never been explained or even fully investigated, and a host of explanations had been offered over the years. *Le Monde* reported that investigators for French antiterrorism judge Jean-Louis Brugiere had concluded that Kagame—who was then the leader of the Rwandan Patriotic Front guerrillas based in Uganda—had ordered a rocket attack that downed the plane. *Le Monde* said Brugiere was investigating the crash because the pilots were French citizens. Kagame, who was visiting Belgium when the report was published, said he had "nothing to do with" the plane crash and instead blamed the French government for complicity in the genocide. "The French knew about it," Kagame told Radio France International. "They supported it, they provided the weapons, they gave orders and instructions to those who carried out the genocide."

Following is the text of "Rwanda Genocide 'Must Leave Us Always with a Sense of Bitter Regret and Abiding Sorrow,' Says Secretary-General to New York Memorial Conference," a March 30, 2004, press release of a statement by United Nations Secretary General Kofi Annan on March 26 at a conference in New York City commemorating the Rwanda genocide.

"Rwanda Genocide"

The genocide in Rwanda should never, ever have happened. But it did. The international community failed Rwanda, and that must leave us always with a sense of bitter regret and abiding sorrow.

If the international community had acted promptly and with determination, it could have stopped most of the killing. But the political will was not there, nor were the troops.

If the United Nations, government officials, the international media and other observers had paid more attention to the gathering signs of disaster, and taken timely action, it might have been averted. Warnings were missed. I recall a 1993 report by a United Nations special rapporteur that spoke specifically of an impending catastrophe.

The international community is guilty of sins of omission. I myself, as head of the UN's peacekeeping department at the time, pressed dozens of countries for troops. I believed at that time that I was doing my best. But I realized after the genocide that there was more that I could and should have done to sound the alarm and rally support.

This painful memory, along with that of Bosnia and Herzegovina, has influenced much of my thinking, and many of my actions, as secretary-general.

None of us must ever forget, or be allowed to forget, that genocide did take place in Rwanda, or that it was highly organized, or that it was carried out in broad daylight. No one who followed world affairs or watched the news on television, day after sickening day, could deny that they knew a genocide was happening, and that it was happening on an appalling scale.

Some brave individuals tried to stop the killing, above all General Romeo Dallaire of Canada, who is here with us today, the force commander of the small UN peacekeeping force that was on the ground at the time. They did all they could. They were entitled to more help.

Eight hundred thousand men, women and children were abandoned to the most brutal and callous of deaths, as neighbour killed neighbour. Sanctuaries such as churches and hospitals were turned into slaughterhouses. An entire country was shattered. A terrible chain of events gradually engulfed the entire region in conflict.

Ten years later, we are trying to pick up the pieces.

In Rwanda itself, the United Nations is doing its utmost to help people recover and reconcile. We are present throughout the country—clearing mines, repatriating refugees, rehabilitating clinics and schools, building up the judicial system, and much else.

In Tanzania, a United Nations criminal tribunal continues to pursue the main perpetrators of the genocide. The tribunal has handed down pioneering verdicts: the first conviction for genocide by an international court; the first to hold a former head of government responsible for genocide; the first to determine that rape was used as an act of genocide; and the first to find journalists guilty of genocide—because they helped create the state of mind in which thousands of people could set aside the most fundamental moral instincts of all human society, and embark on the wholesale massacre of fellow human beings.

With these and other steps, the United Nations is doing what it can to help Rwanda find a path to lasting security and peace, with itself and its neighbours. We cannot undo the past. But we can help Rwandans, especially the young generation who are the future of the country, build a new society together.

The genocide in Rwanda raised questions that affect all humankind—fundamental questions about the authority of the Security Council, the effectiveness of United Nations peacekeeping, the reach of international justice, the roots of violence, and the responsibility of the international community to protect people threatened by genocide and other grave violations of human rights. There has been intense debate, and some genuine advances—practical and philosophical—on some of these questions over the past decade. But still one must ask, are we confident that, confronted by a new Rwanda today, we can respond effectively, in good time? We can by no means be certain we would.

I have suggested a number of measures that would better equip the United Nations and its Member States to meet genocide with resolve, including a special rapporteur or adviser on the subject. More can and must be done, and I am currently analysing what further steps could be taken. The silence that has greeted genocide in the past must be replaced by a global clamour—a clamour and a willingness to call what is happening by its true name.

The General Assembly has designated 7 April as the International Day of Reflection on the Genocide in Rwanda. The Government of Rwanda, for its part, has asked that the world's observance of the Day include a minute of silence at noon local time in each time zone.

Such a minute of silence has the potential to unite the world, however fleetingly, around the idea of global solidarity. I have written to all the world's heads of State and government, asking them, and especially their public servants, to honour it. I have also instructed all UN offices, throughout the world, to take part. Here today, I would like to urge all people, everywhere, no matter what their station in life, whether in crowded cities or remote rural areas, to set aside whatever they might be doing at noon on that day, and pause to remember the victims. Let us be united in a way we were not 10 years ago. And let us, by what we do in one single minute, send a message—a message of remorse for the past, resolve to prevent such a tragedy from ever happening again—and let's make it resound for years to come.

May the victims of the Rwandan genocide rest in peace. May our waking hours be lastingly altered by their sacrifice. And may we all reach beyond this tragedy, and work together to recognize our common humanity. If we can accept that everyone on this earth, regardless of colour, creed, language or ethnicity is fully human—and, as such, fully worthy of our interest, sympathy and acceptance—we will have taken a giant step forward from dehumanization and toward a stronger sense of global kinship.

Source: United Nations. "Rwanda Genocide 'Must Leave Us Always with a Sense of Bitter Regret and Abiding Sorrow,' Says Secretary-General to New York Memorial Conference." Press Release SG/SM/9223, AFR/870, HQ631. March 26, 2004. www.un.org/News/Press/docs/2004/sgsm9223.doc.htm (accessed January 5, 2005).

Congressional Research Service Report on Human Trafficking

March 26, 2004

INTRODUCTION

Slavery was made illegal in the United States in 1865, but reports released in 2004 offered new evidence that slavery remained a problem in much of the country. The federal government estimated that at least 14,500 people were trafficked into the United States each year by criminal gangs and individual employers. The first-ever modern study of U.S. slavery provided detailed evidence that at least 10,000 people were forced laborers at any given time—most of them in the sex industry or in domestic service.

By 2004 modern-day slavery and the international trafficking in people had received increased attention from governments and the public worldwide for more than a decade. United Nations treaties attempted to provide the legal basis for prosecuting those who forced people into slavery and trafficked them across international borders. The U.S. Congress in 2000 passed landmark legislation to step up prosecutions of human traffickers, to provide aid to victims in the United States, and to hold other nations accountable for failures to act against the international trade in human beings. *(Background, Historic Documents of 2002, p. 232)*

A report prepared for Congress by the Congressional Research Service and made public on March 26, 2004, cited several reasons for the apparent increase in global trafficking of people, including:

- International organized crime had taken advantage of the globalization of the world economy, which had increased the movement of people across borders.
- The "subordination of women in many societies" continued to encourage poor families to sell their daughters to brothels or traffickers.
- Girls and women in Eastern Europe and the former Soviet Union were vulnerable to entrapment by traffickers as a result of economic dislocations since the collapse of communism in the region.
- Most countries did not have adequate laws or regulations to deal with human trafficking, and even countries with tough laws, such as the United States, tended to treat victims as criminals.

Slavery in the United States

Free the Slaves, a Washington, D.C.-based antislavery organization, on September 23 released a report, "Hidden Slaves: Forced Labor in the United States," which estimated that at least 10,000 people were forced to work in slave-like conditions in the United States at any given time. The actual figure could be much higher, the report said, but getting precise numbers was difficult because virtually all forced labor was hidden from public view.

Much of the background work for the publication was done by the Human Rights Center at the University of California at Berkeley. Researchers gathered details of existing forced labor conditions in the United States through interviews with forty-nine social service agencies, eight case studies in different regions, and news accounts of 131 incidents of forced labor—most of them involving legal prosecutions.

Cases of forced labor had been documented over the previous five years in at least ninety cities, the report said, with the greatest number in or near large cities in California, Florida, New York, and Texas—the main transit points for the trafficking of people into the United States. Most of the forced laborers came from overseas, with China, Mexico, and Vietnam being the largest points of origin. Victims typically were enticed into forced labor through fraudulent means, such as promises of good jobs with high pay, and then forced to work to pay off alleged "debts" to those who trafficked them into the United States. Other victims were coerced into labor through threats or actual violence.

Not surprisingly, 46 percent of the forced laborers identified in the survey were engaged in prostitution and other sex services. Domestic service accounted for 27 percent, followed by agriculture (10 percent), sweatshop and other factory work (5 percent), and hotel and restaurant work (4 percent). Forced labor was most prevalent in these sectors, the report said, because they were characterized by cheap labor and minimal regulation of working conditions. "These conditions enable unscrupulous employers and criminal networks to gain virtually complete control over workers' lives," the report said.

The report praised recent efforts by the federal government to crack down on forced labor in the United States, notably the Victims of Trafficking and Violence Protection Act (PL 106–386). Passed in 2000, the act gave law enforcement agencies new authority to combat the crime. Among its provisions, the law made it a federal crime to traffick in people or force anyone into labor, authorized limited social services for victims of forced labor, authorized temporary visas for victims who cooperated in investigations of traffickers, and established a State Department bureau to monitor forced labor internationally. The law made the United States one of the most proactive countries in the world when it came to battling forced labor, the report said.

Even so, the report said the new law had several shortcomings, notably the requirement that forced labor victims could obtain benefits, such as food stamps and temporary visas, only by cooperating in the prosecution of those who victimized them. This requirement, the report said, "creates the perception that survivors are primarily instruments of law enforcement rather than individuals who are, in and of themselves, deserving of protection and restoration of their human rights."

Governmentwide Assessment

In 2003 and 2004 federal government agencies with responsibilities for dealing with human trafficking issued a joint report assessing the extent of the problem and the government's attempts to deal with it. The 2004 report, made public on July 7, estimated that 14,500 to 17,500 people were trafficked into the United States annually. The report said this estimate was based on law enforcement figures and reports by intelligence agencies, none of which were cited directly.

Three broad geographic regions accounted for nearly all the people in that figure, the report said: East Asia and the Pacific (5,000–7,000), Latin America (3,500–5,500), and Europe and Eurasia (3,500–5,500). Using a "weighted average" of figures from data from U.S. government agencies and other sources, the report estimated that 600,000 to 800,000 people are trafficked worldwide. Because of changes in methodology, the report said the range was not comparable to a widely quoted U.S. estimate made in 1997 that some 700,000 people were trafficked worldwide. East Asia and the Pacific provided 43 percent of the people being trafficked globally, the report said. About 29 percent came from Europe and Eurasia, 17 percent from Africa, and the rest from the Western hemisphere, South Asia, and the Near East.

The report also detailed the rapid escalation of criminal cases, at the federal level, involving human trafficking. In 1993 the Justice Department began 12 investigations into cases involving human trafficking; a decade later 82 new cases were opened. Likewise, in fiscal years 2001–2003, the government prosecuted 110 traffickers (nearly three times the number of the previous three years) and secured 78 convictions or guilty pleas, the report said. About three-fourths of the prosecutions and convictions were for crimes related to the sex industry. In most of the cases, victims were smuggled into the United States, forced to engage in menial labor or prostitution, and threatened with physical violence or deportation if they refused to comply. The people who held them were charged with a variety of crimes, such as transporting a minor for prostitution, money laundering, racketeering, and subjecting workers to involuntary servitude. The report attributed much of the increase in criminal prosecutions to the opening in 2000 of a telephone complaint line that victims, witnesses, and others could use to report potential cases.

Other government antitrafficking programs cited in the report included the training of personnel in government and nongovernmental agencies to recognize potential trafficking cases and public service announcements informing the public about the problem and offering help to victims. The United States also offered grants and training programs to foreign governments to help them combat human trafficking. For example, the Labor Department worked with the Brazilian government to end forced labor in agriculture, and the government funded programs to help women in West Africa who had been forced to serve as wives of guerrillas during the civil war in Sierra Leone. *(Sierra Leone war, Historic Documents of 2002, p. 247)*

T Visas

The United States in 2002 began offering temporary visas (known as T visas), good for three years, to victims of trafficking who agreed to cooperate with law enforcement agencies investigating trafficking rings. In the first year of the program, 601 people applied for the visas; of those, 297 were granted the visas, 30 applications were denied, and the remainder were still pending as of September 30, 2003, according to the July 7 government report. After holding a T visa for three years, a victim could apply for permanent residency in the United States; those applications were expected in 2005, the government said.

The government report said the number of T visas that had been granted was low, compared to the estimated number of forced workers in the United States, because few victims knew of the visas. New efforts were under way to publicize the availability of visas, the report said.

The September report by Free the Slaves offered another potential reason for what would appear to be the relative lack of use of the new visas: Victims were afraid to make any contact with government agencies out of fear that their "employers" might find out and exact retribution. Since the government typically took several months to process applications for the visas, the victims were afraid of persecution during the lengthy waits. Quoting agencies that worked to help forced-labor victims, the report said that "for some victims the dependency on federal authorities for immigration relief, compounded by the pain and discomfort of testifying about their experience, does not serve their needs and dissuades them from cooperating with law enforcement."

Trafficking Worldwide

Another outgrowth of the 2000 trafficking act was a mandate for the State Department to compile annual reports on various aspects of human trafficking around the world, including steps taken by other governments to curtail it. The law required the president to use this information as the basis for deciding whether to impose sanctions against governments that were not acting to stem the problem.

In its reports beginning in 2001, the State Department categorized each country into one of three "tiers." Tier one consisted of countries that met certain minimum standards defined by the 2000 law, such as criminalizing human trafficking and making sustained efforts to eliminate it. Tier two consisted of countries that did not meet the minimum standards but were making "significant efforts" to do so. Tier three countries were those that neither met the minimum standards nor were making significant efforts to do so. Congress amended the Trafficking Act in 2003 to add a "special watch list" within the first two tiers, signifying countries whose actions barely qualified for the status given.

In each of the first three years of the report, the division of countries into these tiers led to controversies. Critics said the administration used diplomatic or political considerations in some of its grades, such as giving higher grades than justified to U.S. allies and assigning lower grades to countries at odds with various U.S. policies.

Most of the attention was focused on the tier three countries because the law required the president to consider imposing economic or other sanctions against them. The 2004 report, released June 14, put ten countries in that category: Bangladesh, Burma (Myanmar), Cuba, Ecuador, Equatorial Guinea, Guyana, North Korea, Sierra Leone, Sudan, and Venezuela.

Two months later, on September 10, the White House issued its determinations for sanctions, based on actions each of the tier-three governments had taken since the work on the report was complete. The White House document concluded that Bangladesh, Ecuador, Guyana, and Sierra Leone had each begun to make significant efforts to combat trafficking and would be moved to the tier-two special watch list, thereby escaping such sanctions as a cut-off of some U.S. aid programs. The White House said Burma, Cuba, Equatorial Guinea, North Korea, Sudan, and Venezuela were not taking steps against trafficking. The United States already had various sanctions in place against Burma, Cuba, and North Korea, so President George W. Bush took no further steps against them. Extensive U.S. economic and political sanctions also were in effect against Sudan because of its civil wars and support for international terrorism; Bush added a new sanction barring Sudanese government officials from participating in U.S.-funded cultural and educational exchange programs. In the case of Equatorial Guinea, Bush stopped a U.S. military training program. In the case of Venezuela, Bush prohibited subsidized financing of arms sales to the government. Bush did not stop other U.S. programs in Venezuela, however, including aid to build political parties there. The government of Hugo Chavez had accused the Bush administration of supporting an attempted military coup against him. *(Cuba, p. 246; North Korea, p. 323; Sudan, p. 588; Venezuela, p. 548)*

Several countries escaped a tier-three listing even though they had been widely criticized, both in the United States and internationally, for failing to take strong steps against trafficking. Examples were India and Thailand, both of which were major sources of women and children for the international sex trade. The State Department said both countries were taking steps to curb human trafficking, and it put them on the tier-two watch list.

Chile was typical of the fifty-four countries placed by the State Department in the standard tier two. The report said Chile was both a destination for and source of children, men, and women who were trafficked for the sex trade and forced labor. A Chilean government report in 2003 estimated that more than 3,700 adolescents were victims of sexual exploitation. Chile recently had begun to take steps to curb the sex trade and trafficking. For example, in late 2003 Chile raised the minimum age for sexual consent from twelve to fourteen. Even so, the State Department said Chile should adopt the international standard of eighteen as the age of consent and should outlaw prostitution.

Following are excerpts from "Trafficking in Women and Children: The U.S. and International Response," a report released March 26, 2004, by the Congressional Research Service, an arm of the Library of Congress.

"Trafficking in Women and Children"

Scope of the Problem Worldwide

Trafficking in people, especially women and children, for prostitution and forced labor is one of the fastest growing areas of international criminal activity and one that is of increasing concern to the U.S. Administration, Congress, and the international community. Although men are also victimized, the overwhelming majority of those trafficked are women and children. According to the latest U.S. Government estimates, some 800,000 to 900,000 people are trafficked across borders each year worldwide for forced labor, domestic servitude, or sexual exploitation. Trafficking is considered one of the largest sources of profits for organized crime, generating seven to ten billion dollars annually according to United Nations estimates.

Trafficking is a problem that affects virtually every country in the world. Generally, the flow of trafficking is from less developed countries to industrialized nations, including the United States, or toward neighboring countries with marginally higher standards of living. Since trafficking is an underground criminal enterprise, there are no precise statistics on the extent of the problem and all estimates are unreliable. The largest number of victims trafficked internationally are still believed to come from South and Southeast Asia. The former Soviet Union may be the largest new source of trafficking for prostitution and the sex industry. Many people are also trafficked to Eastern Europe. Other main source regions include Latin America and the Caribbean, and Africa. Most of the victims are sent to Asia, the Middle East, Western Europe and North America. They usually end up in large cities, vacation and tourist areas, or near military bases, where the demand is highest.

Causes of Rise in Trafficking

The reasons for the increase in trafficking are many. In general, the criminal business feeds on poverty, despair, war, crisis, and ignorance. The globalization of the world economy has increased the movement of people across borders, legally and illegally, especially from poorer to wealthier countries. International organized crime has taken advantage of the freer flow of people, money, goods and services to extend its own international reach.

Other contributing factors include:

- the continuing subordination of women in many societies, as reflected in economic, educational, and work opportunity disparities between men and women. Many societies still favor sons and view girls as an economic burden. Desperate families in some of the most impoverished countries sell their daughters to brothels or traffickers for the immediate payoff and to avoid having to pay the dowery to marry off daughters;
- the hardship and economic dislocations caused by the transition following the collapse of Communism in the former Soviet Union and Eastern Europe, as well as the wars in the former Yugoslavia. The lack of opportunity and the eagerness for a better life abroad have made many women and girls especially vulnerable to entrapment by traffickers. With the weakening of law enforcement in post-Communist societies, criminal organizations have grown and established themselves in the lucrative business of international trafficking;
- the high demand, worldwide, for trafficked women and children as sex workers, cheap sweatshop labor, and domestic workers. Traffickers are encouraged by large tax-free profits and continuing income from the same victims, until recently at very low risk;
- The inadequacy of laws and law enforcement in most origin, transit, and destination countries hampers efforts to fight trafficking. Even in the United States, more effective legal remedies are only now being implemented. Prostitution is legal or tolerated in many countries, and widespread in most. When authorities do crack down, it is usually against prostitutes, themselves. Penalties for trafficking humans for sexual exploitation are often relatively minor compared with those for other criminal activities like drug and gun trafficking.
- The priority placed on stemming illegal immigration in many countries, including the United States, has resulted in treatment of trafficking cases as a problem of illegal immigration, thus treating victims as criminals. When police raid brothels, women are often detained and punished, subjected to human rights abuses in jail, and swiftly deported. Few steps have been taken to provide support, health care, and access to justice. Few victims dare testify against the traffickers or those who hold them, fearing retribution for themselves and their families since most governments do not offer stays of deportation or adequate protection for witnesses.
- The disinterest and in some cases even complicity of governments is another big problem. Many law-enforcement agencies and governments ignore the plight of trafficking victims and downplay the scope of the trafficking problem. In some cases, police and other governmental authorities accept bribes and collude with

> traffickers by selling fake documentation, etc. [For instance, according to Global Survival Network, an NGO [nongovernmental organization] group, Russian traffickers can obtain false documentation in order to enable a minor to travel to destination countries to work as a prostitute from corrupt officials in the Ministry of Foreign Affairs for approximately $800.] In addition, local police often fear reprisals from criminal gangs so they find it easier to deny knowledge of trafficking. Many countries have no specific laws aimed at trafficking in humans.

Traffickers and Their Victims

Chinese, Asian, Mexican, Central American, Russian and other former Soviet Union gangs are among the major traffickers of people. Chinese and Vietnamese Triads, the Japanese Yakuza, South American drug cartels, the Italian mafia, and Russian gangs increasingly interact with local networks to provide transportation, safe houses, local contacts, and documentation.

Traffickers acquire their victims in a number of ways. Sometimes women are kidnapped outright in one country and taken forcibly to another. In other cases, victims are lured with phony job offers. Traffickers entice victims to migrate voluntarily with false promises of well-paying jobs in foreign countries as au pairs, models, dancers, domestic workers, etc. Traffickers advertise these "jobs" as well as marriage opportunities abroad in local newspapers. Russian crime gangs reportedly use marriage agency databases and match-making parties to find victims. In some cases, traffickers approach women or their families directly with offers of lucrative jobs elsewhere. After providing transportation and false documents to get victims to their destination, they subsequently charge exorbitant fees for those services, often creating life-time debt bondage.

While there is no single victim stereotype, a majority of trafficked women are under the age of 25, with many in their mid to late teens. The fear of infection with HIV and AIDS among customers has driven traffickers to recruit younger women and girls, some as young as seven, erroneously perceived by customers to be too young to have been infected.

Trafficking victims are often subjected to cruel mental and physical abuse in order to keep them in servitude, including beating, rape, starvation, forced drug use, confinement, and seclusion. Once victims are brought into destination countries, their passports are often confiscated. Victims are forced to have sex, often unprotected, with large numbers of partners, and to work unsustainably long hours. Many victims suffer mental breakdowns and are exposed to sexually-transmitted diseases, including HIV and AIDS. They are often denied medical care and those who become ill are sometimes even killed.

Regional Trends

Asia and the Pacific

The largest number of victims are trafficked from Southeast Asia annually according to the U.S. Department of State. The growth of sex tourism in this region is one of the main contributing factors. Large-scale child prostitution occurs in many countries. Thailand, Cambodia, and the Philippines are popular travel destinations for "sex tourists," including pedophiles, from Europe, North America, Japan, and Australia.

Japan is the considered the largest market for Asian women trafficked for sex. Victims are believed to come mainly from the Philippines and Thailand. Victims are also trafficked in increasing numbers to Taiwan, Malaysia, Hong-Kong, and Thailand. Cross-border trafficking is prevalent in the Mekong region of Thailand, Burma, Laos, Cambodia, Vietnam, and the Southern Yunan province of China. Vietnamese women are trafficked to China and Cambodia. According to various NGO sources, hundreds of thousands of foreign women and children have been sold into the Thai sex industry since 1990, with most coming from Burma, Southern China, Laos, and Vietnam. East Asia, especially Japan, is also a destination for trafficked women from Russia and Eastern Europe.

Victims from Southeast Asia, especially China, Burma, the Philippines, Thailand, Cambodia, and Vietnam, are also sent to Western Europe, the United States, Australia, and the Middle East.

South Asia may be the second highest source region for trafficking victims according to the State Department. The low status of women in some societies as well as the growth of sex tourism contribute significantly to trafficking in this region. Sri Lanka and India are among the favored destinations of sex tourists from other parts of the world. Bangladesh and Nepal, the poorest countries in the region, are the main source countries. India and Pakistan are key destination countries. Thousands of Nepalese girls and young women are lured or abducted to India for sexual exploitation each year. The total number of Nepalese working as prostitutes in India are believed to be in the tens of thousands. Thousands of women and children from Bangladesh are trafficked to Pakistan each year. Also, according to Amnesty International, Afghan women have been sold into prostitution in Pakistan.

Thousands of Nepalese women and children are believed to be trafficked for prostitution to the Asia Pacific region, especially Hong Kong. Bangladeshi women and children have also been trafficked to the Middle East in large numbers, over the last 20 years. India is a source, transit, and destination country, receiving women and children from Bangladesh, Nepal, Bhutan, Sri Lanka, and Pakistan and sending victims to Europe and the Middle East.

Australia has been a prime source of sex tourists in Asia. The Philippines, Thailand, South Korea, Sri Lanka, and Hong Kong are some of the primary Asian destinations for organized sex tours. Indonesia and Taiwan are secondary destinations. Australians also travel to Europe and Latin America. To counteract this problem, the Australian government has developed extraterritorial legislation and public awareness campaigns aimed at travelers.

International criminal organizations traffic hundreds of Thai women yearly to Australia for prostitution. Australia is developing tougher laws including long jail terms to stop the trafficking of Asian women to Australia.

Europe

The former Soviet Union and Central and Eastern Europe have replaced Asia as the main source of women trafficked to Western Europe. Victims come from Russia,

Ukraine, and other East European countries. With the economic and political turmoil after the collapse of the Soviet Union, trafficking from the region has escalated from a minor problem before 1991 into a major crisis. As criminal organizations have grown, especially in Russia, they have gravitated to this lucrative business. Russian organizations now play a dominant role not just in the trafficking of Russian women but also women from throughout Eastern Europe. Russian organized crime groups and others including Albanian, Estonian, Chechen, Serb, and Italian gangs are involved in human trafficking in Europe. Furthermore, Russian organized crime is starting to take over the sex industry in a number of West European countries. Russian criminal groups reportedly are also gaining control of prostitution in Israel, and parts of the United States.

The largest number of victims trafficked annually from the former Soviet Union and Eastern Europe come from Russia and Ukraine. In addition, several Central and East European countries are reported to be source, receiving, and transit countries. The conflicts in Bosnia and Kosovo provided new opportunities for traffickers in the former Yugoslavia and the Balkans. Traffickers targeted refugee women who fled Kosovo. According to the Women's Commission for Refugee Women and Children, Albanian traffickers have smuggled thousands of Kosovo women into Italy by boat for the sex trade.

Most Russian and East European victims are believed to be sent to West European countries (especially Germany, Italy, France, Switzerland, the Netherlands, Greece, Austria, and England). A substantial number are also sent to the Middle East (especially Israel and Saudi Arabia) and the Far East (especially Japan and Thailand). Many wind up in the United States or Canada. The remainder are sent to Central European countries, especially Poland, Hungary, the Czech Republic.

Western European countries are also destination points for victims from other parts of the world, including Africa (Ghana, Nigeria, Morocco), Latin America (Brazil, Colombia, the Dominican Republic), and Southeast Asia (the Philippines, Thailand).

Middle East

The sexual exploitation of women and children in the Middle East usually involves the importation of women from other regions. The exploitation of Middle Eastern women tends to have less of a commercial dimension.

Women and children, mostly from Asia (Thailand, the Philippines, Indonesia), are trafficked as prostitutes or brides to the Middle East (Saudi Arabia, The United Arab Emirates). Women from the former Soviet Republics are sent to Israel. According to the Israel Women's Network, every year several hundred women from Russia and the former Soviet Union are brought to Israel by well-organized criminal groups.

Latin America and the Caribbean

Tens of thousands of Latin American and Caribbean women and children are believed to be trafficked for sexual exploitation each year. Impoverished children are particularly vulnerable to trafficking for prostitution. Victims from Latin America and the Caribbean are trafficked to Western Europe and the United States. The Central American countries and Mexico are also transit countries for trafficking to the United States.

The presence of sex tourists from Europe, North America, and Australia has significantly contributed to the trafficking of women and children. A growing number of sex tourists are going to Latin America, partly as a result of recent restrictions placed on sex tourism in Thailand, Sri Lanka, and other Asian countries. Favored sex tourism destinations are Brazil, Argentina, the Dominican Republic, Mexico, Honduras, Costa Rica, Trinidad and Tobago. Brazil has one of the worst child prostitution problems in the world.

Africa

In Africa, tens of thousands of victims are believed to be trafficked annually according to the U.S. Department of State, although the extent of trafficking is not well documented. Like elsewhere, poverty and the low status of women are major contributing factors. In addition, wars and civil strife engulfing countries like Sudan and Rwanda, as well as the indifference of some governments make women and children vulnerable to trafficking.

Trafficking in children for labor is a serious problem in Togo and Benin as well as Botswana, Zaire, Somalia, Ethiopia, Zambia, Nigeria, Algeria. Victims are trafficked to Nigeria, Gabon, Ghana, and South Africa. Africans, especially women from Nigeria, are trafficked to Western Europe and the Middle East.

Trafficking to the United States

Some 18,000 to 20,000 people are trafficked to the United States each year, according to the most recent Department of State estimates. Most come from Southeast Asia and the former Soviet Union. About half of those are forced into sweatshop labor and domestic servitude. The rest are forced into prostitution and the sex industry, or in the case of young children, kidnapped and sold for adoption. While many victims come willingly, they are not aware of the terms and conditions they will face. Women trafficked to the United States most often wind up in the larger cities in New York, Florida, North Carolina, California, and Hawaii. But the problem is also migrating to smaller cities and suburbs. Russian crime groups are said to be actively involved in trafficking and the sex industry in the United States.

The United States is also the major destination country for young children kidnapped and trafficked for adoption by childless couples unwilling to wait for a child through legitimate adoption procedures and agencies. The largest source country is Mexico. Mexican children are also kidnapped and trafficked to the United States for child prostitution.

American men, along with Europeans and Australians, are reportedly the most numerous sex tourists in Central America (Costa Rica, Honduras), South East Asia (The Philippines, Thailand), and South Asia (India, Sri Lanka). Many companies operating in a number of large cities reportedly specialize in sex tours.

Until recently, U.S. laws were widely believed to be inadequate to deal with trafficking in women and children. Nor were there thought to be adequate laws and services to protect and assist victims. With the implementation of anti-trafficking legislation and programs, the hope is that the situation will improve significantly. . . .

The International Response

The United States and other countries are also pursuing a number of bilateral and multilateral programs and initiatives to combat trafficking. The steps taken by the United States internationally include the following:

- The Departments of State and Justice are training foreign law enforcement and immigration officers to better identify and crackdown on traffickers and their victims at the border.
- U.S. embassies and consulates worldwide are working with other countries to stop international trafficking in women and children. The United States has expanded its program to heighten public awareness about trafficking in source countries, targeting the messages to potential victims.
- The United States is also working with the European Union, the Group of Eight, the United Nations, and the Organization for Security and Cooperation in Europe (OSCE). The United States supported some 240 programs in 75 countries to combat trafficking in FY [fiscal year] 2002.

The United States and the European Union agreed on a joint initiative to combat trafficking in November 1997. U.S. and EU officials met in Luxembourg to launch a jointly funded initiative against trafficking in women from Russia and Eastern Europe. It is primarily an information campaign, warning potential victims and an education program for law enforcement, customs and consular officials to heighten their awareness of the problem. Pilot projects were launched in Poland by the EU and in Ukraine by the United States. The United States initiated bilateral cooperation programs in a number of countries, including Russia, other former Soviet Republics, Bosnia, Albania, Poland, Bulgaria, Hungary, Thailand, and the Philippines to fight trafficking.

In 2002, the Council of the European Union took a major further step in the fight against human trafficking, reaching agreement on a broad new framework decision. The decision sought to strengthen police and judicial cooperation and to harmonize the laws and policies of member states in areas such as criminalization, penalties, sanctions, aggravating circumstances, jurisdiction, and extradition. The deadline for implementation of the decision by Member States was set for August 1, 2002.

At the OSCE Summit Meeting in Istanbul in November 1999, leaders of the 55 OSCE member states from Europe, Central Asia, and North America, agreed to make combating trafficking in the OSCE area (where some 200,000 people are trafficked annually) a priority issue. A follow up meeting on trafficking was held in Vienna on June 19, 2000. The participating states agreed on steps to increase their efforts and better coordinate actions to fight the problem. The OSCE sponsored conference in Bangkok in June 2002 to deal with the trafficking issues. Speaking at the conference, Helga Konrad who heads the OSCE task force on human trafficking said that the approach taken to date to fighting trafficking has failed. She argued that closer collaboration between source and destination countries was vital.

The international community began meeting in 1999 to draft a Protocol to Prevent, Suppress, and Punish Trafficking in Persons, especially Women and Children in conjunction with the U.N. Convention Against Transnational Organized Crime. The United States, along with Argentina, introduced the draft protocol in January 1999.

Negotiations were concluded in 2000 on a revised draft. On November 15, 2000, the U.N. General Assembly adopted the Convention on Transnational Crime, including the Protocol on Trafficking. The Convention and Protocols formally signed in Palermo, Italy, in December 2000, were designed to enable countries to work together more closely against criminals engaged in crossborder crimes. The United States signed the U.N. protocol on Trafficking in December 2000, but has not yet ratified it.

The United States is party to two other international agreements that have been adopted to address aspects of trafficking in children. The International Labor Organization (ILO) Convention 182 concerning the Prohibition and Immediate Action for the Elimination of the Worst Forms of Child Labor was ratified by United States in December 1999. The Protocol to the Convention on the Rights of the Child on Sale of Children, Child Prostitution and Child Pornography was signed by the United States July 2000 and ratified in December 2002. In January, 2002, the Protocol went into force, having been signed by 88 countries and ratified by 16.

The Organization of American States (OAS) has also placed the issue of trafficking on its agenda. In November 2002, its Inter-American Commission on Women is scheduled to meet in Washington to discuss trafficking in the Americas. . . .

Policy Issues

A broad consensus seems to be shared in Congress and the policy community on the need for decisive action to curb trafficking. And the general framework of "prevention, protection, and prosecution" also has widespread support. Questions have been raised about implementation.

How will the war on terrorism and the emphasis on homeland security affect the efforts to combat human trafficking? Since the terrorist attacks on the United States on September 11, 2001, there has been concern among those advocating strong policies to counter human trafficking that momentum might be lost in that battle. The concern diminished in early 2002 when both the Administration and Congress were seen as renewing their attention to the trafficking problem. However, there is still some question about whether the emphasis on homeland security and the war on terrorism might sap financial, law enforcement, and judicial resources from other efforts, including the campaign against human trafficking. Some observers also wonder if the U.S. need for support in the war on terrorism from certain governments will make it more difficult to pressure those governments if their anti-trafficking efforts are inadequate.

Should sanctions against foreign governments be used as a policy instrument to combat trafficking? Most agree that extensive international cooperation will be needed to stop international trafficking and that both "carrots" and "sticks" may be needed to encourage other governments, including assisting governments in their efforts to curb trafficking. The Clinton Administration argued against sanctions language in P.L. 106–386 as unnecessary and counterproductive since very few, if any, governments favor or support trafficking. Instead, it was argued, the focus should be on cooperation. In the Bush Administration, Secretary of State Powell has expressed concern in general that sanctions are an overused policy tool. On the other side, some see the sanctions language contained in the anti-trafficking legislation as being too weak since sanctions can be easily waived and a broad range of programs are exempted. The

Administration must make a determination by October 1, 2003, about whether to impose sanctions against certain governments. The Tier 3 list of non-cooperating countries includes a number of key U.S. allies and front-line states in the war on terrorism, as well as some of the largest recipients of U.S. assistance. How will the Administration decide against which Tier Three countries to impose sanctions?

Who is eligible for protection as a victim of trafficking? Are the standards of eligibility for benefits as a victim of trafficking the right ones? At present, protection is limited to victims of "severe forms of trafficking" and victims must prove that they are in the United States as a direct result of trafficking and that they have a well founded fear of retribution if they are returned to their country of origin. They must be willing and needed to help identify and prosecute their traffickers. Some critics argue that the standards are too high to help many deserving victims. Critics also argue that the line between pure victims and those who have a degree of complicity in being brought to the United States may be difficult to draw. Such distinctions, they argue, will leave some victims unprotected. P.L. 106–386 gives the executive branch some discretion in determining who qualifies.

More broadly, differing perspectives on what constitutes trafficking could make international cooperation more difficult. In the United States, some politicians, religious groups, as well as feminist and other organizations, have campaigned to broaden the definition of trafficking to include all prostitution, whether forced or voluntary, with the prostitutes are always victims, and that traffickers will simply force their victims to claim to be acting voluntarily. However, a number of countries including some western democracies with otherwise strong human rights records have legal and regulated prostitution, believing that the "world's oldest profession" cannot be stamped out and that a carefully regulated sex industry is the best protection for those involved.

Are the links between human trafficking and HIV/AIDS receiving adequate attention? Trafficking victims in the sex industry are exposed to sexually transmitted diseases, including HIV/AIDS, at much higher rates than the general population. Very often they have no access to medical care. In addition, the fear of infection with HIV/AIDS among customers has driven traffickers to recruit younger women and girls, erroneously perceived by customers to be too young to have been infected. Some question whether existing legislation, policies, and programs address these issues.

Source: U.S. Congress. Library of Congress. Congressional Research Service. "Trafficking in Women and Children: The U.S. and International Response." RL30545, March 26, 2004. http://fpc.state.gov/documents/organization/31990.pdf (accessed February 8, 2005).

President Bush on NATO Expansion

March 29, 2004

INTRODUCTION

Seven formerly communist nations of eastern Europe joined the North Atlantic Treaty Organization (NATO) alliance on March 29, 2004, thereby putting Western military power right at the border of Russia, once the heart of the Soviet Union. This expansion, the fifth and by far the largest in the five-decade history of the alliance, brought total NATO membership to twenty-six countries. It was the second to incorporate countries once under Soviet control. The additions did nothing, however, to change the lopsided nature of the alliance, which was dominated in all important respects by the United States.

The expansion did nothing, however, to resolve lingering questions about NATO's raison d'etre; since the collapse of communism more than a decade earlier, NATO often had appeared to be a military alliance in search of an enemy, or at least a new purpose in life beyond several peacekeeping missions that were still under way in 2004. *(NATO background, Historic Documents of 2002, p. 885)*

The NATO expansion coincided with a parallel growth in the European Union (EU). That economic and political alliance was in the early stages of developing a military capability independent of NATO, and thus of U.S. control. Five of NATO's new members also joined the EU on May 1. *(EU expansion, p. 197)*

In addition to new members, NATO got a new secretary general in 2004: former Dutch foreign minister Jaap de Hoop Scheffer. A conservative political leader who received strong support for the post from the Bush administration, Scheffer replaced Lord George Robertson, a former British defense secretary who had held NATO's top civilian post since 1999. Because of his military background, Robertson had spent much of his tenure trying to persuade NATO's European members to boost their defense budgets so the United States and Britain would not have to bear all of the alliance's burden. Scheffer came to office months after the wrenching conflict during 2002–2003 among NATO members over the U.S.-led war in Iraq. He spent much of his time in 2004 trying to repair frayed relations on both sides of the Atlantic. Ignoring critics who said NATO was no longer necessary, the alliance on December 8 signed an agreement with Belgium for construction of a new headquarters building in Brussels. NATO's military arm would continue to be based in nearby Mons, Belgium. *(Iraq war disputes, Historic Documents of 2003, p. 40)*

Seven New Members

NATO was founded in the years after World War II as a military bulwark against a perceived drive by the Soviet Union to control Europe. From the outset the alliance was dominated by the United States, which contributed the bulk of troops, weapons, and money. Starting with twelve members in 1949, NATO gradually expanded to sixteen during the closing years of the cold war in the 1980s. The Czech Republic, Hungary, and Poland became the first formerly communist countries to join NATO, in 1999. *(Historic Documents of 1999, p. 119)*

In November 2002 NATO leaders invited another seven formerly communist countries—Bulgaria, Estonia, Latvia, Lithuania, Romania, Slovakia, and Slovenia—to join as members, effective in 2004. Three of them—the Baltic states of Estonia, Latvia, and Lithuania—had been forcibly incorporated into the Soviet Union in 1940, and they had been the among the first members of the Soviet empire to flee Moscow's clutches when communism collapsed between 1989 and 1991. Bulgaria generally had been a loyal ally of the Soviet Union during the cold war, but Romania had exercised a small degree of independence from Moscow during communism's last two decades, the 1970s and 1980s. Slovakia (also known as the Slovak Republic) had been part of Czechoslovakia for most of the twentieth century. A brief reform experiment in Czechoslovakia was brutally crushed by Soviet military might in 1968; once they were free of Moscow's control, the Czech and Slovak republics divorced amicably in 1992. Slovenia was one of the seven constituent republics of Yugoslavia until that multiethnic empire began its bloody disintegration in 1990; while its sister republics were mired in conflict, Slovenia prospered and became the most glittering success story of eastern Europe.

Five of these new NATO members also won admission into the EU, as of May 1. The exceptions were Bulgaria and Romania, which lagged far behind the others in reforming their economic and political systems to meet the EU's minimum standards. They hoped to join by 2007.

The seven nations officially joined NATO on March 29, when their prime ministers deposited ratification documents with the U.S. government at a ceremony held in the ornate Cash Room of the Treasury building in Washington. Later, in a speech marking the occasion on the South Lawn of the White House, President George W. Bush welcomed the new allies as "full and equal partners." Bush said the new members brought "moral clarity" to NATO because tyranny "is still a fresh memory" for them. "These nations know that when great democracies fail to confront danger, far worse peril can follow," he said. "They know that aggression, left unchecked, can rob millions of their liberty and their lives."

Bush noted that all seven new members had aided U.S. military operations in Afghanistan or Iraq. The contingents of Bulgaria and Romania were among the largest in Iraq, at 500 and 700 soldiers, respectively, at the time. *(Iraq stabilization, p. 399)*

A flag-raising ceremony at NATO headquarters in Brussels on April 2 offered another ceremonial occasion for celebration by the new members. Foreign ministers from the seven countries each made speeches praising the alliance. Latvian foreign minister Rihards Piks expressed a common view: "In the past, Latvia lost its freedom because it had to look for security on its own. Now, Latvia stands shoulder to shoulder in the company of twenty-five other nations guaranteeing the liberty of each other and sharing the values and ideals that unite us."

Three other eastern European countries remained active applicants for NATO membership: Albania, Croatia, and Macedonia. In his March 29 speech welcoming the new seven members, Secretary of State Colin Powell said to the three others: "We recognize your countries' commitment to achieve NATO membership and I can assure you that we support your aspirations." Scheffer echoed these words at NATO headquarters on April 2, saying "the NATO door is open" to other potential members.

NATO and Russia

During the previous decade Russia had watched in alarm (and occasionally in anger) as NATO marched eastward to incorporate countries that Moscow had dominated during the Soviet era. Beginning in the mid-1990s NATO leaders tried repeatedly to assuage Moscow's fears, first with rhetorical reassurances, then with an invitation to Russian representatives to participate in some NATO meetings, and finally with the creation in 2002 of a formal NATO-Russia Council. The idea was to give Moscow a forum to express its views on important matters considered by NATO without bestowing upon it the veto power enjoyed by all official NATO members. *(Background, Historic Documents of 2002, p. 886)*

The expanded twenty-seven member council (the NATO members plus Russia) held its first meeting in Brussels on April 2, the day the new NATO nations raised their flags at alliance headquarters. The council's one official achievement was the adoption of a resolution pledging cooperation to battle international terrorism. The formation of this council appeared to foster improved relations among top diplomatic and military officials on both sides, but it did not erase Moscow's concerns about the alliance, or vice versa. Russian membership in NATO was not even on the table, and prospects for genuinely close cooperation were undermined by Russian president Vladimir Putin's increasingly authoritarian posture. *(Russia, p. 564)*

Despite Russia's participation in NATO forums, Moscow was still nervous about the expansion of the alliance to its borders. One concrete reason was that NATO jets began patrolling the skies of the three Baltic states on April 2—a not-so-subtle reminder that NATO still considered Russia a potential threat.

NATO's Twenty-First Century Missions

Ever since the implosion of the Soviet Union at the end of 1991, many observers in Europe and North America had questioned the continued need for NATO. Some critics had gone so far as to suggest the dissolution of the alliance, which, after all, had achieved its original stated purpose of defending Western Europe against a communist threat. NATO's political and military leaders suggested new roles for the alliance, starting in 1995 with a large peacekeeping mission in Bosnia following the civil war there. By 2004 troops under NATO command were operating in Afghanistan, Bosnia, Iraq, and Kosovo. From late 2002 to early 2003 NATO troops also had performed peacekeeping functions in Macedonia following a brief but bloody civil conflict there. NATO handed off that assignment to a EU force in March 2003.

Following the September 11, 2001, terrorist attacks against the United States, the Bush administration sought to focus NATO efforts on the "war against terrorism," which the administration defined broadly to incorporate a variety of U.S. aims. In his March 29 speech, Bush focused on confronting terrorism as the major new challenge for NATO. His speech came just two weeks after 191 people were killed, and about 1,800 wounded, in the bombings of commuter trains in Madrid—an act attributed to the same al Qaeda terrorist organization that sponsored the attacks against the United States. Noting that NATO's "core mission" remained mutual defense, Bush said: "Today, our alliance faces a new enemy, which has brought death to innocent people from New York to Madrid. Terrorists hate everything this alliance stands for. They despise our freedom, they fear our unity, they seek to divide. They will fail." *(Madrid bombings, p. 105)*

NATO's first involvement in the U.S. antiterror war came in August 2003, when it assumed command of a multinational peacekeeping force in Afghanistan, known as the International Security Assistance Force (ISAF). Ever since the U.S.-led ouster of the Taliban regime in Afghanistan, ISAF had operated primarily in Kabul and the surrounding region. During 2004 NATO gradually expanded ISAF's role in other areas of Afghanistan but encountered sharp criticism that it had failed to provide adequate security for the fledgling government in Kabul. *(Afghan developments, p. 912; background, Historic Documents of 2003, p. 1093)*

The Afghanistan operation had broad political support within NATO member countries, but the next request for an alliance operation linked to the Bush administration's antiterrorism campaign caused sparks to fly. This was an appeal by Washington for additional soldiers to help train military forces in Iraq. U.S. diplomats began discussing the request in European capitals early in 2004 and encountered immediate resistance. Countries that had opposed the war in Iraq, such as Belgium and Germany, flatly refused to consider the request. Even some of the countries that had supported the war and had originally sent troops to Iraq were having second thoughts because foreign troops were targets for insurgents.

Under continued U.S. pressure, NATO leaders on June 28 agreed to the concept of a NATO training program in Iraq. A small "assessment mission" went to Iraq in August. NATO ambassadors on September 22 approved the mission's recommendations, then on November 17 adopted an "operation plan" calling for 200–300 military officers from NATO countries to be assigned to the program. Even then, Belgium, France, Germany, Greece, and Spain refused to allow any of their officers to participate. Several countries refused to help pay for the Iraqi training, provoking cries of outrage from U.S. officials. Another indication that the cross-Atlantic anxieties over Iraq had not totally died down was that six of the NATO nations that had sent troops to Iraq in 2003—Hungary, Italy, Latvia, the Netherlands, Poland, and Spain—announced in 2004 that they would withdraw or reduce their contingents there.

NATO'S first-ever peacekeeping mission had begun in Bosnia in 1995, and it finally wound down in 2004. That mission succeeded in its major task of keeping the former warring parties in Bosnia—the Croats, Muslims, and Serbs—militarily separated and at peace. But NATO failed spectacularly in its most important secondary mission, that of capturing the two highest-ranking Bosnian Serb leaders charged with war crimes by a United Nations tribunal: political leader Radovan Karadzic and general Ratko Mladic. NATO forces tried and failed several times to catch them.

In 2003 the European Union offered to take over Bosnia peacekeeping, marking the most significant mission yet for the EU's newly constituted military capability. Negotiations between the two Brussels-based organizations produced an agreement for a handover of responsibility in Bosnia effective December 2, 2004. In a February 17 speech to a European security conference in Munich, Scheffer called the planned Bosnia handover "a litmus test for the relationship between NATO and the EU. It is a litmus test for our ability to put behind the theological debates of the past and move toward pragmatic cooperation." This last remark was a clear reference to U.S. and European differences over the war in Iraq. *(Balkans developments, p. 949)*

NATO forces were still deeply involved in Kosovo, which had been the scene of the alliance's only active war, in 1999. A NATO peacekeeping unit known as the Kosovo Force continued to patrol the small province of Serbia, where the majority population of Albanian Muslims had taken control from the ethnic Serbian minority.

Following are excerpts from a speech by President George W. Bush at the White House on March 29, 2004, welcoming seven new member nations into the North Atlantic Treaty Organization.

"Remarks Honoring Seven Nations on Accession to NATO"

Thank you all. Good afternoon, and welcome to the White House.

Fifty-five years ago, the representatives of 12 nations gathered here in Washington to sign the North Atlantic Treaty, which established the most successful military alliance in history. Today we proudly welcome Bulgaria, Estonia, Latvia, Lithuania, Romania, Slovakia, and Slovenia. We welcome them into the ranks of the North Atlantic Treaty Organization.

When NATO was founded, the people of these seven nations were captives to an empire. They endured bitter tyranny. They struggled for independence. They earned their freedom through courage and perseverance, and today they stand with us as full and equal partners in this great Alliance.

It has been my honor to host the prime ministers of each new NATO member in the Oval Office. I want to thank them for their friendship. I want to thank them for their leadership. I look forward to working with them to make the world more peaceful and more free. Welcome to America.

I want to thank the foreign and defense ministers of the new NATO members who are with us today. I want to thank the Prime Ministers of Albania, Croatia, and Macedonia, who are with us today. Jaap de Hoop Scheffer is with us today, who is the Secretary General of NATO. Thank you for coming, Mr. Secretary General. I thank the Ambassadors of all the members of NATO, both old and new.

I want to thank the Vice President [Dick Cheney], Secretary of State [Colin] Powell, Secretary of Defense [Donald] Rumsfeld, General Dick Myers [chairman of the Joint Chiefs of Staff], General [James L.] Jones [Supreme Commander of NATO], members of my administration. I want to thank the Members of Congress who are with us today: Majority Leader Bill Frist [R-Tenn.] of the United States Senate; Members of the Senate which voted unanimously in support of the admission of the new members that we welcome today. I want to thank the Members of the House of Representatives who have joined us today. I want to thank those who are here today whose vision years ago helped make this moment a reality. I want to thank other distinguished guests. Welcome.

Today marks a great achievement for each of the nations joining our Alliance. All member nations of NATO must be free and democratic and fully committed to defending the principles of liberty. All member nations must be willing and able to contribute to the common defense of our Alliance. Our seven new members have built free institutions. They've increased their military capabilities in the span of a decade. They are stronger nations because of that remarkable effort, and the NATO Alliance is made stronger by their presence.

Since NATO's founding, the assurance of mutual defense has been a safeguard for peace. As President Truman said, "By this treaty, we are not only seeking to establish freedom from aggression and from the use of force in the North Atlantic community, but we are also actively striving to promote and preserve peace throughout the world."

Under NATO's banner, the nations of Europe put aside rivalries that had divided the Continent for centuries. NATO members stood watch on freedom's borders for two generations of the cold war. Because of NATO's vigilance, free people lifted the Iron Curtain and tore down the Berlin Wall and replaced dictators with democratic governments.

In the aftermath of this victory, some questioned whether NATO could or should survive the end of the cold war. Then the Alliance proved its enduring worth by stopping ethnic cleansing in Bosnia and by ousting the armies of a tyrant in Kosovo. Some wondered whether NATO could adapt to the new threats of the 21st century. Those doubts were laid to rest on September the 12th, 2001, when NATO invoked for the first time in its history Article 5 of our Charter, which states that an attack against one NATO Ally is an attack against all.

NATO's core mission remains the same, the defense of its members against any aggression. Today, our Alliance faces a new enemy, which has brought death to innocent people from New York to Madrid. Terrorists hate everything this Alliance stands for. They despise our freedom. They fear our unity. They seek to divide us. They will fail. We will not be divided. We will never bow to the violence of a few. We will never—we will face the mortal danger of terrorism, and we will overcome it together.

The countries we welcome today were friends before they were Allies, and they were allies in action before becoming Allies by treaty. Today, all seven of these nations are helping to bring lasting freedom to Afghanistan and Iraq. Bulgaria provided refueling facilities during the early days of Operation Enduring Freedom [the 2001 invasion of Afghanistan] and has deployed more than 400 soldiers to Iraq. Military engineers from Estonia and Latvia are helping to clear explosive devices from Iraq. Forces from Lithuania and Slovakia are helping to secure Iraq. Romanian troops have sacrificed their lives fighting terrorists in Afghanistan. And troops from Slovenia are serving in the international force that is protecting the city of Kabul in Afghanistan.

Forces from Albania and Croatia and Macedonia are also contributing in Afghanistan or Iraq, proving their mettle as they aspire to NATO membership. These three nations, joined together under the Adriatic Charter, are building strong democracies at home that can contribute to NATO efforts abroad. The United States supports these efforts. The door to NATO will remain open until the whole of Europe is united in freedom and in peace.

As witness to some of the great crimes of the last century, our new members bring moral clarity to the purposes of our Alliance. They understand our cause in Afghanistan and in Iraq, because tyranny for them is still a fresh memory. These nations know that when great democracies fail to confront danger, far worse peril can follow. They know that aggression left unchecked can rob millions of their liberty and their lives. And so now, as members of NATO, they are stepping forward to secure the lives and freedom of others.

The NATO Alliance now flies seven new flags and reaches from the Bay of Biscay to the Black Sea. And Europe, once the source of global conflict, is now a force for stability and peace. Our great Transatlantic Alliance has met and overcome great dangers in the past, and our work in NATO is not done. In the past, many assumed that NATO represented a pledge that America would come to the aid of Europe. Today, by our words and by our actions, we know that NATO means much more. It is a solemn commitment that America and Europe are joined together to advance the cause of freedom and peace.

NATO is acting to meet the challenges of our time. NATO forces are securing Afghanistan. NATO ships are patrolling the Mediterranean, and NATO is supporting the Polish-led division in Iraq. NATO is widening the circle of its friends by creating a new chapter in our relationship with Russia. NATO members are reaching out to the nations of the Middle East to strengthen our ability to fight terror and to provide for our common security. And we're discussing how we can support and increase the momentum of freedom in the greater Middle East.

Our unity and our commitment to freedom carried us to victory in the cold war, and they showed us the way to victory in the war on terror. Together, Europe and America can lead peaceful nations against the dangers of our time. Europe and America can advance freedom and give hope and support to those who seek to lift the yoke of isolation and fear and oppression. That is the mission that history has set for NATO—this great and confident alliance of 26 nations—and we proudly accept this mission.

May God bless you all.

Source: U.S. Executive Office of the President. "Remarks at a Ceremony Honoring Seven Nations on Accession to the North Atlantic Treaty Organization." *Weekly Compilation of Presidential Documents* 40, no. 14 (April 5, 2004): 495–497. www.gpoaccess.gov/wcomp/v40no14.html (accessed January 7, 2005).

General Accounting Office on Federal Aviation Security Efforts

March 30, 2004

INTRODUCTION

Three years after the September 11, 2001, terrorist attacks, in which hijacked airplanes were used to destroy the World Trade Center towers in New York City and damage the Pentagon outside Washington, D.C., the United States continued to struggle with the nearly impossible task of securing commercial aviation against terrorism. The federal government had reorganized its aviation security bureaucracies—in some cases multiple times—and spent billions of dollars on equipment, personnel, and procedures.

As of the end of 2004 there had been no successful terrorist attacks in the United States in three years. Terrorism experts said it was only a matter of time, however, before terrorists would be able to exploit continuing security weaknesses in the nation's enormous aviation industry, with its hundreds of airports and thousands of flights each day. Some experts also argued that the government was focusing too much attention on preventing another September 11-style hijacking and was failing to address different tactics by terrorists, notably an attack using bombs placed in the cargo holds of airplanes or ships. *(Background, Historic Documents of 2003, p. 720)*

Passenger Screening

For much of the general public, aviation security meant the screening of passengers and their carry-on luggage before they boarded commercial airplanes. This was one requirement that every passenger endured, and in recent years it often had become a true test of endurance as passengers at many airports were forced to wait in long lines and undergo increasingly intrusive checks that forced them to remove their jackets and shoes—and even submit to body pat-downs.

Passenger screening of some kind had been standard at most major airports internationally ever since the outbreak of airplane hijackings in the 1960s and 1970s. In most cases passengers simply were required to pass through a metal detector. The inadequacy of these screenings was made evident by the ability of nineteen al Qaeda terrorists to board, and then hijack, four airplanes on September 11, 2001, armed only with knives used to open cardboard boxes. In the wake of September 11, the U.S. government toughened screening requirements, and Congress passed sweeping legislation taking passenger screening out of the hands of private contractors and putting the responsibility under a new Transportation Security Administration (TSA). In 2002 that agency was incorporated into the massive new Homeland Security Department. *(Background, Historic Documents of 2002, p. 746)*

During 2002 and 2003 investigations by government watchdog agencies and reports by news organizations generally found that the new screening procedures were working well but were still plagued by numerous problems. In September 2003, for example, the General Accounting Office (GAO, renamed the Government Accountability Office on July 7, 2004), found that the TSA was not adequately monitoring the performance of screeners and their supervisors.

Follow-up investigations in 2004 by the GAO, the inspector general of the Homeland Security Department, and other government and nongovernmental organizations found that some problems had been fixed but that others continued to plague nearly every aspect of U.S. aviation security.

In a report to Congress on March 30, the GAO said flaws remained in several aspects of the TSA screening program. Some airports had unacceptably high turnover rates among screeners; some airports still had too few screeners, while others had too many for the workload; and the agency had difficulty attracting qualified personnel, notably for part-time work. In testimony to a House subcommittee on February 12, GAO homeland security director Cathleen A. Berrick said eleven of the fifteen busiest airports did not have enough screeners. Annual turnover of screeners at some high-volume airports was as high as 36 percent, she said, citing low pay and erratic work schedules among the main causes.

A February 3 report by the Homeland Security Department's inspector general found that contractors hired by the TSA had conducted more than 360,000 background checks on 55,600 screeners and applicants for screening jobs, but the TSA had not carefully monitored the work of the contractors. Some screeners were allowed to begin working even though their background checks had not been completed, and applications for those whose background checks found problems were held in bureaucratic limbo for weeks or even months, the report said. Another report by the inspector general, published in September, found lapses in the training and supervision of screeners at a range of airports nationwide during 2003. That report recommended what it called "recurrent" training, with standardized testing, of all scanners to make sure they remained familiar with standard procedures. The TSA began the suggested follow-up training later in 2004.

Since 2002 any passenger who set off an alarm as he or she went through a metal detector was then required to submit to a secondary search by a screener using a hand-held metal detector and, in some cases, a body pat-down using the back of the hand. About 15 percent of passengers, selected at random, also were required to undergo these secondary searches even if they did not set off a metal detector alarm.

The TSA authorized more intrusive body searches following the simultaneous bombings on August 24 of two Russian airliners, in which ninety people died, including two suspected suicide bombers. Under the new procedures, which took effect September 22, all passengers were required to take off their jackets before passing through metal detectors, and screeners were authorized to use the palms of their hands to pat down passengers who raised suspicions. As in the past, male passengers were to be searched only by male screeners and female passengers by female screeners.

Almost immediately the new procedure led to incidents in which passengers alleged that searches had been unduly intrusive. Most of the complaints came from women who said they had been fondled by screeners or forced to take off too much of their clothing. The TSA reported in December that the number of passenger complaints about screeners more than doubled in October, the first full month the new procedures were in effect. Responding to the complaints, the TSA on December 23 announced several revised procedures, including telling screeners to avoid touching female passengers between their breasts.

Even body searches were not guaranteed to spot one danger that security experts were increasingly worried about: a suicide bomber, wearing a belt packed with plastic explosives, boarding a plane and setting off the bombs once the plane was in the air. The Homeland Security Department's inspector general reported early in September that investigators had been able to sneak bombs past security checkpoints at fifteen airports in 2003. The danger was further highlighted by the double suicide bombing of the Russian planes, reportedly by female terrorists associated with Islamist groups in Chechnya. In the wreckage of both planes Russian officials found traces of the explosive material hexogen (also known as RDX), a component of the easily hidden plastic explosive C-4. *(Russia, p. 564)*

U.S. airports in 2003 began screening checked luggage for explosives, but as of 2004 none were equipped to conduct that type of screening for passengers. The TSA in September began testing walk-through explosive-scanners, known as "portals," at airports in Chicago, Los Angeles, New York City, and Washington, D.C. Installing the devices, which cost tens of thousands of dollars apiece, at all airports was a major recommendation of the commission that studied the September 11 attacks. *(Commission report, p. 450)*

Identifying "High Risk" Passengers

Ever since the mid-1990s the government and airlines had used a database system known as the Computer Assisted Passenger Prescreening System (CAPPS) to compare the names of passengers with some of the government's numerous terrorism "watch lists" and lists of suspicious behavioral characteristics—such as paying by cash for a one-way ticket. The CAPPS program had failed to catch the September 11 hijackers, however, and the government in 2002 began working on an upgraded program called CAPPS II. Because it would use many personal details about passengers—including information gathered from commercial databases of questionable reliability—the proposed new system came under fire from a broad range of groups, including conservatives and civil libertarians. Congress in 2003 ordered both the TSA and the GAO to study eight questions relating to the effectiveness of CAPPS II and its potential impact on passenger privacy.

In reports to Congress on February 12 and March 30, the GAO said the Transportation Security Administration had not yet addressed seven of the eight questions dealing with such matters as protection of privacy and the ability of passengers to correct inaccurate information about them. The only matter that had been resolved at that time was the creation of an internal oversight board to monitor the CAPPS II program and related matters, the GAO said.

Homeland Security officials acknowledged in August that much of the proposed CAPPS II program had proved so unworkable and fraught with controversy that it was undergoing a major revision, including a new name: Secure Flight. The TSA announced on August 26 that the new program would be a stripped-down version of the CAPPS II system, matching information about passengers only against the government's lists of suspected terrorists. The new system would not rely on information from commercial databases, such as reports by credit bureaus, nor would it attempt to identify passengers who had committed nonterrorism-related crimes or who simply were wanted for violations of immigration laws.

Critics of the CAPPS II proposal said they were pleased the government had eliminated some aspects that had raised privacy concerns. Even so, they said the new system relied on terrorism watch lists, which numerous investigations had found to be flawed. "If the watch lists are no good, the program is not going to make us more secure or protect our civil liberties," Lara Flint, staff counsel for the Center for Democracy and Technology, said. *(Watch lists, Historic Documents of 2003, p. 155)*

Another civil liberties group that had objected to the CAPPS II system, the Electronic Privacy Information Center (EPIC), said the Secure Flight proposal was "disturbingly similar" to CAPPS II. In a report issued in October, EPIC noted that the TSA planned the same broad exemptions for the Secure Flight program as it had for the CAPPS II program, from the 1974 Privacy Act, which was intended to limit the government's use of private information about U.S. citizens. EPIC also said government agencies had refused its requests for details about how the Secure Flight program would use passenger information.

The TSA in November ordered airlines to turn over one month's worth of their computerized databases of passenger information—including addresses, telephone numbers, credit card information, and even meal requests—for a test of the new Safe Flight system. That test began November 30 and was expected to continue into early 2005. Demonstrating continued political concern about privacy issues, Congress ordered another report from the GAO on the results of the Safe Flight testing; that report was due in March 2005.

One high-profile demonstration of the flaws in the government's databases came in mid-August. Sen. Edward M. Kennedy, D-Mass., one of the most famous and recognizable members of Congress, told colleagues at a Judiciary Committee hearing that he had twice been told he could not board commuter shuttle planes between Washington and Boston because his name appeared on the government's "no-fly" list. Kennedy said he was able to board the planes only after he made several phone calls to government officials. Kennedy said he also had to make three phone calls to Tom Ridge, secretary of homeland security, over a period of several weeks before his name was removed from the no-fly list. Rep. John Lewis, D-Ga., also said he had been flagged by the no-fly list dozens of times because his name was similar to that of someone on the list.

Government documents released October 8 in connection with a San Francisco court case showed that agencies had no uniform rules for determining whose name appeared on the no-fly list. News reports said at least 20,000 names, and possibly as many as 100,000 names, appeared on the list and that the TSA had received more than 2,000 complaints from passengers, like Kennedy and Lewis, who had been barred from flights.

Congress responded to these complaints by requiring the TSA to correct the no-fly list and create a standard procedure enabling passengers to fix inaccurate information about them on the list. Those provisions were included in the intelligence overhaul legislation (PL 108–458) incorporating many of the recommendations of the September 11 commission.

Air Marshal Program

In its March 30 report, the GAO identified several problems with the government's program of placing armed "air marshals" aboard many of the nation's commercial air flights. Before the September 11 attacks the government had fewer than fifty air marshals, who rode incognito to thwart airplane hijackings. Congress boosted funding for the program starting in late 2001, and by 2004 several thousand marshals were placed aboard airplanes—the exact number was classified.

The GAO said the rapid escalation of the air marshal program led the government to make many compromises, notably by reducing training. The effect of these compromises was compounded by budget cutbacks mandated by the Bush administration and Congress, the GAO said. As a result, the number of marshals had not reached the government's targets "and may be declining," the GAO said.

On August 27 the inspector general for the Homeland Security Department reported a different set of problems with the air marshal program: More than 700 cases of misconduct by air marshals were reported in 2002, and more than 100 air marshals had been cited for misconduct during their previous jobs with the U.S. Bureau of Prisons. Many of the misconduct cases involved relatively minor matters, such as tardiness for work or rudeness to airline employees, and some marshals were fired, the Homeland Security Department said. Many of the cases of misconduct by marshals during their work in the federal prison system involved more serious matters, including security breaches, physical and verbal abuse of prisoners, and misuse of government property.

The inspector general's report suggested—but did not say directly—that some problems with the air marshal program may have resulted from bureaucratic shuffling. Overall responsibility for the Federal Air Marshal Service was transferred three times in three years. In November 2001 the service was shifted from the Federal Aviation Administration to the new TSA (then part of the Transportation Department). Along with the rest of the TSA, the air marshal service was shifted again to the Homeland Security Department when it was created in March 2003. In November 2003 the air marshal service was transferred to the Bureau of Immigration and Customs Enforcement (also within the Homeland Security Department) so that some 5,000 immigration agents could be trained as backup air marshals.

Missiles and Lasers

The aviation industry and the government issued new warnings in 2004 about two relatively new threats to the security of airplanes: portable antiaircraft missiles and lasers. The United States, the Soviet Union, and other countries had produced tens of thousands of shoulder-fired antiaircraft missiles in the 1970s and 1980s, many of which ended up on international black markets. The first known use of such a missile to attack a commercial airliner came in 2002, when terrorists fired a shoulder-launched antiaircraft missile at an Israeli civilian airplane in Kenya in 2002—missing the plane. The Bush administration then mounted an effort to equip U.S. civilian airplanes with a version of an antimissile system that was widely used to protect military aircraft. In its March 30 report, and in another report issued in April, the GAO said the government faced "significant challenges" to protecting civilian airliners against portable missiles.

Two men accused of plotting to sell antiaircraft missiles to al Qaeda pleaded guilty to narcotics and terrorism charges in San Diego on March 3. The two men admitted in federal court that they had conspired to provide al Qaeda with four U.S.-made "Stinger" missiles as part of a deal involving the sale of five metric tons of hashish and six hundred kilograms of heroin.

Federal agencies in November warned of potential danger from the use of lasers deliberately aimed at pilots in the air. During 2004 pilots reported several cases in which laser beams entered their cockpits; in at least one case a pilot reported an eye injury from a laser beam as he made a landing approach into the Salt Lake City airport.

Following are excerpts from "Aviation Security: Improvement Still Needed in Federal Aviation Security Efforts," a report to Congress by the General Accounting Office, issued March 30, 2004, assessing government programs to improve aviation security.

"Aviation Security: Improvement Still Needed in Security Efforts"

Background

The security of the U.S. commercial aviation system has been a long-standing concern. Over the years, numerous initiatives have been implemented to strengthen aviation security. However, as we and others have documented in numerous reports and studies, weaknesses continue to exist. It was due in part to these weaknesses that terrorists were able to hijack four commercial aircraft on September 11, 2001, with tragic results. Concerns continue to exist regarding the security of the aviation system, as evidenced by the cancellations of several, mostly transatlantic flights to and from the United States in response to intelligence information regarding specific threats to those flights.

With hundreds of commercial airports, thousands of commercial aircraft, tens of thousands of daily flights, and millions of passengers using the system daily, providing security to the nation's commercial aviation system is a daunting task. In an effort to strengthen the security of commercial aviation, the President signed into law the Aviation and Transportation Security Act (ATSA) on November 19, 2001. ATSA created TSA [Transportation Security Administration] and mandated actions designed to strengthen aviation security, including the federalization of passenger and baggage screening at over 440 commercial airports in the United States by November 19, 2002, and the screening of all checked baggage using explosive detection systems. On March 1, 2003, pursuant to the Homeland Security Act of 2002, TSA was transferred from the Department of Transportation to the newly created Department of Homeland Security [DHS].

Virtually all aviation security responsibilities now reside within DHS, and most of these are with TSA, including conducting passenger and baggage screening, and overseeing security measures for airports, commercial aircraft, air cargo, and general aviation. Only the Federal Air Marshal Service, which was recently moved from TSA to DHS's Bureau of Immigration and Customs Enforcement, is not within the responsibilities of TSA. Taken together, these programs are intended to form a layered system that maximizes the security of passengers, aircraft, and other elements of the aviation infrastructure.

Significant Challenges Face Implementation of Computer-Assisted Passenger Prescreening System

One effort under way to strengthen aviation security is TSA's development of a Computer-Assisted Passenger Prescreening System, known as CAPPS II, to replace the current prescreening system now in use. CAPPS II will evaluate each passenger's level of risk before they reach the check-in counter at the airport by accessing commercial and government databases to authenticate the passenger's identity and generate a risk score. The risk scores will be used to determine if passengers need additional security measures or, if warranted, be denied boarding and/or detained by law enforcement.

However . . . TSA faces numerous challenges that could affect CAPPS II's successful development and implementation. Key activities in the development of CAPPS II are behind schedule and TSA has not developed critical system plans; numerous developmental, operational, and privacy issues of concern to the Congress remain unresolved by TSA; and other significant challenges exist that could affect the successful implementation of CAPPS II. As a result, the potential for CAPPS II to improve aviation security remains questionable until TSA addresses the numerous concerns raised and challenges facing the program.

Program Delays and Critical Plans Incomplete

Key activities in the development of CAPPS II have been delayed and TSA has not yet completed critical system planning activities. TSA is developing CAPPS II in nine increments, with each increment providing increased functionality. As each increment reached completion, TSA planned to conduct tests that would ensure the system meets the objectives of that increment before proceeding to the next increment. The development of CAPPS II began in March 2003 with increments 1 and 2 being completed in August and October 2003, respectively. However, TSA has not completely tested these initial two increments because it was unable to obtain the necessary passenger data for testing from air carriers. Air carriers have been reluctant to provide passenger data due to privacy concerns. As a result, TSA deferred completing these tests until increment 3.

Completion of increment 3, however, has been delayed. Due to the continued inability to secure passenger data for testing, TSA delayed the completion of increment 3 from October 2003 until the end of March 2004. Moreover, the functionality that this increment was expected to achieve has been reduced. Increment 3 was originally intended to provide a functioning system that could handle live passenger data from one air carrier in a test environment to demonstrate that the system can satisfy operational and functional requirements. However, TSA officials reported that they recently modified increment 3 to instead provide a functional application of the system in a simulated test environment that is not actively connected to an airline reservation system, and they are uncertain when testing that was deferred from increments 1 and 2 to increment 3 will be completed. As a result, all succeeding increments of CAPPS II have been delayed.

Further, TSA has not yet developed critical elements associated with sound project planning, including a plan for what specific functionality will be delivered, by when, and at what cost throughout the development of the system. For example, although TSA established plans for the initial increments of the system, it lacks a comprehensive plan identifying the specific functions that will be delivered during the remaining increments; such as, which government and commercial databases will be incorporated, the date when these functions will be delivered, and an estimated cost of the functions. In addition, TSA officials are uncertain when CAPPS II will achieve initial operating capability—the point at which the system will be ready to operate with one airline. Project officials also said that because of testing delays, they are unable to plan for future increments with any certainty. Until project officials develop a plan that includes scheduled milestones and cost estimates for key deliverables, CAPPS II is at increased risk of not providing the promised functionality, not being fielded when planned, and being fielded at an increased cost.

Issues Identified by Congress Remain Unresolved

TSA has not fully addressed seven of eight issues identified by the Congress as key areas of interest related to the development and implementation of CAPPS II. At this time, only one issue—the establishment of an internal oversight board to review the development of major systems that includes CAPPS II—has been addressed. DHS and TSA are taking steps to address the remaining seven issues; however, they have not yet:

- determined and verified the accuracy of the databases to be used by CAPPS II,
- stress tested and demonstrated the accuracy and effectiveness of all search tools to be used by CAPPS II,
- developed sufficient operational safeguards to reduce the opportunities for abuse,
- established substantial security measures to protect CAPPS II from unauthorized access by hackers and other intruders,
- adopted policies to establish effective oversight of the use and operation of the system,
- identified and addressed all privacy concerns, and
- developed and documented a process under which passengers impacted by CAPPS II can appeal decisions and correct erroneous data.

Although TSA is in various stages of progress to address each of these issues, TSA has not established milestones for some and delayed others without estimating a new completion date. For example, TSA planned to conduct stress and system tests by August 2003; however, stress testing was delayed several times due to TSA's inability to obtain the passenger data needed to test the system. Completion of stress testing was moved to March 31, 2004, but this testing has been postponed again and currently no estimate exists for when these tests will be conducted. Although TSA program officials contend that their ongoing efforts will ultimately address each issue, program officials were unable to identify a time frame for when all remaining issues will be fully addressed. . . .

Efforts to Improve Screening Face Challenges

One of the critical layers of our nation's aviation security system is passenger and baggage screening. All passengers on commercial airliners must pass through airport screening checkpoints and have their carry on and checked baggage screened. TSA manages the screening operations and uses electronic searches, manual searches, and other measures to determine if threat objects, including explosives, are in the possession of the passengers or in their baggage. Following the events of September 11, 2001, airline passenger and baggage screening became a federal responsibility and is now carried out by TSA employees or, in the case of five airports, by private screening companies under the direction of TSA.

Our recent work on screening has found that numerous challenges impede TSA's progress in improving screening. Four key areas of concern include TSA's efforts to (1) hire and deploy passenger and baggage screeners, (2) train the screening workforce, (3) measure screener performance in detecting threat objects, and (4) leverage and deploy screening equipment and technologies.

Concerns Remain Regarding Hiring and Deploying the Screener Workforce

TSA accomplished a significant goal by hiring and deploying more than 55,000 screeners by November 19, 2002. However, its initial staffing efforts created imbalances in the screener workforce. While some airports had too many screeners, others had too few. To address these imbalances, as well as congressional concerns regarding overall screener-staffing levels, TSA began attempting to right-size its screener workforce. Specifically, TSA established a goal to reduce its screener workforce by 3,000 screeners by June 1, 2003, and an additional 3,000 screeners by September 30, 2003. These reductions were achieved through attrition, voluntary transfers from full to part-time, and involuntary transfers to part-time or terminations based on screeners' scores on competency-based examinations.

However, TSA continues to struggle to achieve the right number of screeners at airport passenger and baggage checkpoints and has not yet achieved a stable screener workforce. To accomplish its security mission, TSA needs a sufficient number of screeners trained and certified in TSA security procedures and technologies. Currently, TSA's screener staffing level is below a congressionally imposed staffing cap of 45,000 full-time equivalents. According to TSA officials, TSA has experienced an average annual attrition rate of 14 percent for screeners, with some of the larger airports reportedly experiencing annual attrition rates ranging from 15 to 36 percent. TSA has also experienced difficulties in hiring new staff. TSA's hiring process is designed to ensure that its hiring practices are standardized and consistent throughout all airports. However, this process has hindered the ability of some Federal Security Directors (FSD) to adequately staff passenger and baggage screening checkpoints. In addition, TSA has also experienced challenges in attracting needed part-time screeners. As a result, FSDs at some of the larger airports we visited had to frequently require mandatory overtime, particularly during the holiday season, to accomplish screening functions. . . .

Screener Training Programs Enhanced, but Access to Programs Is Sometimes Limited

TSA has taken steps to enhance its training programs for screeners. However, staffing shortages and lack of high-speed connectivity at airport training facilities have made it difficult for screeners to fully utilize these programs. Specifically, TSA recently revamped its screener training program to include three main components: (1) training all screeners in the skills necessary for both passenger and baggage screening (replaces basic screener training); (2) recurrent (skills refresher) screener training; and (3) technical screener training/certification for EDS. In addition to strengthening its basic and recurrent training programs, TSA is enhancing and standardizing remedial training for screeners who fail testing conducted by TSA's Office of Internal Affairs and Program Review. TSA has also established leadership and technical training programs for screening supervisors.

Despite these efforts, however, some FSDs said that ensuring screeners received required training continued to be a challenge. For example, FSDs at 5 of the largest airports said that due to staffing shortages, they were unable to let screeners take training because it would impact FSDs' ability to provide adequate screener coverage. Consequently, screeners received an average of only 3 hours of recurrent training per month, far less than the required 3 hours per week. In an attempt to ensure screeners receive required training, several FSDs provided training through overtime, or established training relief teams with the sole purpose of staffing screening checkpoints while screeners participated in training. . . .

Expansion of the Federal Air Marshal Service Has Experienced Problems

Although measures are taken to keep dangerous individuals and items off aircraft, the possibility still exists that terrorists and dangerous objects can still get on board aircraft. Consequently, a number of other layers of security are in place to enhance the security of commercial aircraft while in transit. One such layer is the Federal Air Marshal Service, which places specially trained and armed teams of civil aviation security specialists on board aircraft to protect passengers, crew, and aircraft from terrorist activities on both domestic and international flights.

Following the September 11, 2001, terrorist attacks, the Service rapidly expanded. The organization grew from about 50 air marshals to 1,000s [the exact number was classified], as the Deputy Secretary of the Department of Transportation—the Service's then parent agency—established a goal of hiring, training, and deploying the new air marshals by July 2002. The Service's budget grew commensurately, from $4.4 million in fiscal year 2001 to $545 million in fiscal year 2003. The rapid expansion led to a number of operational and management control issues for the Service. These included reviewing nearly 200,000 applications for federal air marshal positions, initiating thousands of background investigations for top-secret clearances, training the new workforce, and scheduling the air marshals for flight duty.

These operational and management control issues have caused a number of problems. As we discussed in a November 2003 report, to deploy the requisite number of air marshals by July 2002, the Service revised and abbreviated its training program. . . .

Ongoing work that examines the funding of the Service indicates that problems may be continuing. Specifically, the number of air marshals has not reached established target levels and may be declining. . . . Officials from the Service have said that if budget trends continue, they expect that at the end fiscal year 2004 they will have fewer air marshals than they had at any point since mid-2002. . . .

Concerns Exist in Other Aviation Security Areas

In addition to the concerns with the CAPPS II program, passenger and baggage screening, and the expansion of the Federal Air Marshal Service, TSA and DHS face a number of other programmatic and management concerns in strengthening aviation security. The concerns include developing measures to counter the Man-Portable Anti-aircraft Defense Systems (MANPADS) threat against commercial aircraft, implementing commercial airport perimeter and access controls, developing effective measures for ensuring the security of air cargo, and strengthening general aviation security. We have ongoing work that is examining DHS's and TSA's efforts in all of these areas.

MANPADS

The threat of terrorists using MANPADS—shoulder-launched surface-to-air missiles—against commercial aviation has increased in recent years, as many thousands of these missiles have been produced and are in national arsenals and black markets throughout the world. In late 2002, terrorists fired surface-to-air missiles at an airliner departing from an airport in Kenya, marking the first time they had been used to attack commercial aircraft in a non-combat zone. Following the attack, the White House convened a task force to develop a strategy to reduce the MANPADS threat against commercial aircraft, and the Congress directed DHS to submit a plan to develop and demonstrate a counter-MANPADS device for commercial aircraft. In January 2004, DHS initiated a 2-year program to migrate existing military counter-MANPADS systems to the civil aviation environment and minimize the total lifecycle cost of such systems.

DHS faces significant challenges in adapting current military counter-MANPADS systems to commercial aircraft. These challenges include establishing system requirements, maturing the counter-MANPADS technology and design, and setting reliable cost estimates. For example, DHS has to account for a wide variety of aircraft types in designing and integrating the system. Further, the current generation of missile warning systems have high false alarm rates and high maintenance costs. In a January 2004 report, we noted the benefits of following the knowledge-based approach used by leading developers in industry and government to reduce program risks and increase the likelihood of success and recommended that the department adopt this approach to develop a counter-MANPADS system for commercial aviation. DHS concurred with our recommendation and said that it will be using knowledge-based evaluations throughout the program. . . .

Perimeter and Access Controls

Prior to September 2001, work performed by us and others highlighted the vulnerabilities in controls for limiting access to secure airport areas. In one report, we noted that our special agents were able to use fictitious law enforcement badges and credentials to gain access to secure areas, bypass security checkpoints, and walk unescorted to aircraft departure gates. The agents, who had been issued tickets and boarding passes, could have carried weapons, explosives, or other dangerous objects onto aircraft. Concerns over the adequacy of the vetting process for airport workers who have unescorted access to secure airport areas have also arisen, in part, as a result of federal agency airport security sweeps that uncovered hundreds of instances in which airport workers lied about their criminal history, or immigration status, or provided false or inaccurate Social Security numbers on their application for security clearances to obtain employment. . . .

Although progress has been made, challenges remain with perimeter security and access controls. Specifically, ATSA contains numerous requirements for strengthening perimeter security and access controls, some of which contained deadlines that TSA is working to meet. A number of technologies could be used to secure and monitor airport perimeters, including barriers, motion sensors, and closed-circuit television. Airport representatives have cautioned that as security enhancements are made to airport perimeters, it will be important for TSA to coordinate with the Federal Aviation Administration and the airport operators to ensure that any enhancements do not pose safety risks for aircraft. . . .

Air Cargo Security

As we and the Department of Transportation's Inspector General have reported, vulnerabilities exist in ensuring the security of cargo carried aboard commercial passenger and all-cargo aircraft. The Federal Aviation Administration has reported that an estimated 12.5 million tons of cargo are transported each year—9.7 million tons on all-cargo planes and 2.8 million tons on passenger planes. Potential security risks are associated with the transport of air cargo—including the introduction of undetected explosive and incendiary devices in cargo placed aboard aircraft. To reduce these risks, ATSA requires that all cargo carried aboard commercial passenger aircraft be screened and that TSA have a system in place as soon as practicable to screen, inspect, or otherwise ensure the security of cargo on all-cargo aircraft. However, according to a September 2003 report by the Congressional Research Service, less than 5 percent of cargo placed on passenger airplanes is physically screened. TSA's primary approach to ensuring air cargo security and safety is to ensure compliance with the "known shipper" program—which allows shippers that have established business histories with air carriers or freight forwarders to ship cargo on planes. However, we and the Department of Transportation's Inspector General have identified weaknesses in the known shipper program and in TSA's procedures for approving freight forwarders, such as possible tampering with freight at various handoff points before it is loaded into an aircraft. . . .

General Aviation Security

Not only are commercial aircraft a concern, but general aviation aircraft can be a security concern. TSA has taken limited action to improve general aviation security, leaving general aviation far more open and potentially vulnerable than commercial aviation. General aviation is vulnerable because general aviation pilots and passengers are not screened before takeoff and the contents of general aviation planes are not screened at any point. General aviation includes more than 200,000 privately owned airplanes, which are located in every state at more than 19,000 airports. In the last 5 years, about 70 aircraft have been stolen from general aviation airports, indicating a potential weakness that could be exploited by terrorists. This vulnerability was demonstrated in

January 2002, when a teenage flight student stole and crashed a single-engine airplane into a Tampa, Florida, skyscraper. Moreover, general aviation aircraft could be used in other types of terrorist acts. It was reported that the September 11th hijackers researched the use of crop dusters to spread biological or chemical agents.

We reported in September 2003 that TSA chartered a working group on general aviation within the existing Aviation Security Advisory Committee. The working group consists of industry stakeholders and is designed to identify and recommend actions to close potential security gaps in general aviation. On October 1, 2003, the working group issued a report that included a number of recommendations for general aviation airport operators' voluntary use in evaluating airports' security requirements. These recommendations are both broad in scope and generic in their application, with the intent that every general aviation airport and landing facility operators may use them to evaluate that facility's physical security, procedures, infrastructure, and resources. TSA will use these recommendations as a baseline to develop a set of federally endorsed guidelines for enhancing airport security at general aviation facilities throughout the nation. TSA is taking some additional action to strengthen security at general aviation airports, including developing a risk-based self-assessment tool for general aviation airports to use in identifying security concerns. . . .

Source: U.S. Congress. General Accounting Office. "Aviation Security: Improvement Still Needed in Federal Aviation Security Efforts." Prepared testimony of Norman J. Rabkin for a hearing by the Subcommittee on Aviation of the Senate Committee on Commerce, Science and Transportation. GAO–04–592T, March 30, 2004. http://purl.access.gpo.gov/GPO/LPS48431 (accessed January 25, 2005).

2004 HISTORIC DOCUMENTS

Presidential Council on the Ethics of Cloning

April 1, 2004

INTRODUCTION

The successful cloning of a human embryo, fears that the United States might be losing its edge in biotechnology to other countries, and the deaths of two popular figures—Ronald Reagan and Christopher Reeve—all put pressure on President George W. Bush to relax the restrictions he had placed on human embryonic stem cell research in 2002. Controversy over the ethics of using such cells in research also became a major issue in the presidential campaign—and an even bigger issue in California, where voters approved a ballot initiative calling for $3 billion over ten years in state funding to support stem cell research.

Stem cells were unspecialized master cells capable of transforming themselves into the specialized cells that made up the various elements of the human body, such as blood, bone, muscle, nerve, and organs. Embryonic stem cells began to form about four days after a human egg was fertilized and quickly differentiated into specialized cells. For some years, scientists had been researching the possibility that these cells, which were capable of endless division in the laboratory, might be used to grow replacement tissues and organs for the human body and thus allow scientists to develop cures for numerous degenerative diseases and conditions, including diabetes, Parkinson's disease, Alzheimer's disease, and spinal cord injuries. Stem cells had also been found in adults and in umbilical cord blood, and researchers were also investigating the potential of these cells in treating degenerative diseases.

Embryos left over from in vitro, or assisted, fertilization therapies were one source of human embryonic stem cells. Some medical researchers favored using cloned human embryos, which were created when scientists removed the nucleus of individual egg cells and replaced it with one from an adult cell. The restructured egg cell was then induced to begin dividing and, if the process was successful, would eventually produce an embryo with stem cells that were genetic replicas of the adult from whom the adult cell was taken. Using cloned stem cells that genetically matched a human being had the benefit of reducing the possibility of organ rejection. Scientists also thought they might better understand the causes of, and possible treatments for, various diseases if they could study stem cells cloned from people with those disorders to determine how genes cause disease.

Embryonic stem cell research was highly controversial, however, because the embryos had to be destroyed to obtain the stem cells. Cloned embryonic stem cells were even more controversial because they potentially could be used to create human life. Researchers had already successfully cloned various species of animals, including sheep and other mammals. Most mainstream scientists opposed cloning for purposes of human reproduction, saying that the procedure was both unethical and unsafe. Abortion foes, who equated the destruction of human embryos—however formed—with the taking of life, said it was impossible to ensure that cloned human embryos would not be used for reproductive purposes. At least one organization had already claimed to have created a cloned human baby, although it never offered any proof of its claims. *(Animal cloning, Historic Documents of 1997, p. 212; background on human cloning, Historic Documents of 2002, p. 512)*

Human Embryos Cloned

The controversy over cloning humans was reignited early in 2004 when South Korean scientists announced that they had successfully cloned human embryos. The first cloned human embryos had been made in 2001 by researchers at Advanced Cell Technology, a Massachusetts bioresearch firm, but the embryos died almost immediately. The South Korean scientists, Woo Suk Hwang and Shin Yong Moon of Seoul National University, reported in February that they had cloned human embryos and successfully started a line, or colony, of stem cells from one of the embryos.

Researchers examining the findings of the South Koreans called the work "stunning" and "fantastic" but cautioned that much more research had to be undertaken before any therapies based on cloned stem cells could be developed. Opponents of cloning quickly renewed their calls for a federal ban on human cloning for any purpose. One of these was Leon R. Kass, chairman of the President's Council on Bioethics. "The age of human cloning has apparently arrived: today, cloned [embryos] for research, tomorrow cloned [embryos] for babymaking. In my opinion, and that of a majority of the council, the only way to prevent this from happening here is for Congress to enact a comprehensive ban or moratorium on all human cloning," he said in an e-mail message to the *New York Times.*

On April 1 the bioethics council released a report that did not directly address the controversy on cloning for therapeutic purposes but recommended closer monitoring of the fast-growing but largely unregulated fertility business. The report, "Reproduction and Responsibility: The Regulation of New Biotechnologies," called for expanded data collection from fertility clinics on the use of genetic tests that could help parents choose their children's sex and other traits, such as eye color. It also called for government-financed, long-term studies on the health effects of assisted reproduction for both the mothers and their children.

The council also urged Congress to act quickly to ban procedures that almost everyone could agree were unethical, such as creating human-animal hybrids and implanting human embryos in the wombs of animals. It also urged Congress to ban the use of cloned human embryos for reproductive purposes, but it tacitly approved use of human embryos for therapeutic purposes so long as they were not used beyond a designated stage of their development, which the council defined as ten to fourteen days. A note accompanying that recommendation said that "some" members of the council were opposed to any experimentation that destroyed human embryos, but "recognizing that it is legal and active, see value in limiting the practice." On this issue the council seemed no closer to resolving its differences than it had been in 2002 , when it released its first report. The council, which Bush had established to advise him on the issue, said it favored a ban on human cloning for reproductive purposes but was almost evenly divided on the ethics of human cloning for therapeutic purposes. *(First council report, Historic Documents of 2002, p. 512)*

The report was released in the wake of a political controversy over the dismissal by the White House, in late February, of two members of the council who were outspoken advocates of research on human embryonic stem cells and their replacement with members who seemed more likely to support a ban on such work. One of two members dismissed was Elizabeth Blackburn, a well-known and well-respected biologist at the University of California, San Francisco, sometimes mentioned as a potential Nobel Prize nominee for her work. Blackburn was one of the few scientists on the council, which also included ethicists and moral philosophers. She told news agencies that she thought the president was "stacking the council with the compliant."

Blackburn's dismissal came little more than a week after the Union of Concerned Scientists, a liberal organization advocating strict environmental standards, among other causes, issued a statement accusing the administration of manipulating science to suit its ideological or moral views. Blackburn's dismissal prompted a letter to the president that was signed by about 170 scholars, clinicians, and researchers protesting the dismissals and warning that the credibility of the council had been "severely compromised." The White House denied that Blackburn's dismissal had anything to do with her policy views. *(Bush and science, p. 841)*

Organizations representing fertility doctors and clinics said the controversy had contributed to a softening of the council's initial draft on regulating assisted reproduction, including backing away from requiring fertility patients to participate in government studies and eliminating language that some members construed as moralistic rather than scientific. "In this report, an embryo is an embryo, it is no longer 'nascent human life,' or 'a person to be.' They took out the recommendation to track every embryo made, which again felt like it had a political agenda," a spokeswoman for a fertility patient advocacy group told the *Washington Post.*

Stem Cells in the Presidential Campaign

Even as some organizations and individuals pushed for a federal ban on human embryonic research for any purposes, others pressed the president to relax the funding restrictions he had placed on embryonic stem cell research. In August 2001 Bush surprised his conservative supporters by permitting limited federal funding for the research. Bush, an opponent of abortion, limited the funding to about sixty lines of stem cells that had already been extracted from human embryos "where the life and death decision had already been made." (The restrictions did not affect federal funding for research into adult stem cells. The National Institutes of Health [NIH] made research grants in fiscal 2003 totaling about $25 million for embryonic stem cell research and slightly more than $190 million for adult stem cell research.) *(Funding limits, Historic Documents of 2001, p. 539)*

For a number of reasons, about two-thirds of the stem cell lines President Bush referred to in his speech never became available for research, and by 2004 researchers were encountering almost insurmountable problems with the rest. Several lines were so difficult to keep alive that they had little potential as research tools. Many, if not all, of the federal stem cell lines were contaminated by being cultivated initially in laboratory dishes that also contained mouse cells, and all of them shared a trait that made it likely they would be rejected by immune systems—thus eroding their potential as medical treatments. Scientists were also beginning to discover that different stem cell lines behaved in different ways, suggesting that research on a broad range of stem cell lines was more likely to produce benefits.

In addition to pressure from the scientific community to expand the sources of stem cells available for research, the president was coming under increasing pressure from legislators, patients, and their families who said the federal funding restrictions were stifling promising research and slowing development of new medical treatments. On April 28, 2004, more than 200 members of the House of Representatives sent Bush a letter asking that he loosen the funding restrictions. Although the letter did not make specific recommendations, leaders of the effort said they would like to see federal funding for research on the unused embryos that were stored at fertility clinics and ultimately slated for destruction. About three dozen signers of the letter were Republicans, including some, like Rep. Dana Rohrabacher of California, who were outspoken opponents of abortion. A similar petition was sent to the president on June 7 by 58 senators, including 14 Republicans.

Advocates for policy change were joined in May by former first lady Nancy Reagan, whose husband, Ronald Reagan, suffered from Alzheimer's disease. For years, Nancy Reagan had quietly and indirectly lobbied the Bush administration to change its funding policy. On May 8 she spoke out publicly for the first time. At a fundraising dinner for the Juvenile Diabetes Research Foundation, Mrs. Reagan said she believed stem cell research "may provide our scientists with many answers that for so long have been beyond our grasp. . . . I just don't see how we can turn our backs on this. . . ." Ronald Reagan died from Alzheimer's on June 5. Another tireless advocate for federal support of stem cell research, actor Christopher Reeve, died in October 2004 from complications of the paralysis he sustained in a fall from a horse in 1995. Best known for his movie role as Superman, Reeve was a relentless advocate for embryonic stem cell research. *(Reagan death, p. 316)*

Reagan's death triggered an outpouring of public support for loosening the federal funding restriction. With public opinion polls showing roughly 70 percent of Americans in favor of expanded federal funding for embryonic stem cell research, Democratic presidential candidate John Kerry stepped up his attacks on the policy, calling on the president to "tear down every wall" blocking the research. Ronald Reagan's son, Ron, also was enlisted to give a prime-time speech at the Democratic National Convention in support of the research. Kerry promised to lift the funding restrictions if he was elected and to increase federal funding for embryonic stem cell studies to more than $100 million a year. Surrogates for Bush said Kerry was misrepresenting both the federal funding restrictions (which Kerry had referred to as a ban on the research) and the major scientific hurdles that had to be cleared before cures from embryonic stem cells became widely available. "Scientific research is too important to play politics with, and John Kerry should stop cynically trying to manipulate voters' emotions," said Senate Majority Leader Bill Frist, a doctor from Tennessee. *(Democratic convention, p. 478)*

President Bush, speaking through his wife, Laura, and White House spokesman Scott McClellan, rejected the calls for change. At several campaign appearances Laura Bush maintained the need to balance scientific interests with moral issues. Despite the rejections, some members of Congress said they thought they saw a small hint that Bush might be willing to explore a possible compromise if he won a second term. They referred specifically to the letter written in May by NIH director Elias A. Zerhouni responding, at Bush's request, to the House petition. In that letter, Zerhouni acknowledged that "from a purely scientific perspective more cell lines may well speed some areas of human embryonic stem cell research."

In October the Bush administration unsuccessfully pushed the United Nations to adopt a total ban on human embryonic cloning. The United States joined with about sixty other countries calling for the ban, saying that cloning for any purpose was "unethical and morally reproachable." All 191 member nations of the UN supported a ban on cloning embryos for reproductive purposes, but many countries—including Britain and other important U.S. allies—were not willing to ban cloning for therapeutic purposes. As a result of the impasse, further discussion of a ban was deferred for the third year in a row.

California Initiative

Frustration with the federal funding restrictions prompted some scientists to relocate to countries in Europe, Asia, and Latin America whose governments supported embryonic stem cell research. Great Britain, for example, in 2004 opened the first national stem cell bank to grow embryonic stem cells and distribute them to researchers around the world. In 2001 Britain was the first country to authorize the cloning of human embryos for research, but as of the end of 2004 it had not yet licensed anyone to conduct the research. The team of researchers at the Roslin Institute, near Edinburgh, Scotland, who created Dolly the sheep, the first cloned mammal, were reported to be considering applying for a license.

Fears that the United States would lose its researchers—and thus its biotechnological edge as well as any potential profits to foreign companies and governments—prompted some states, several universities, and private philanthropies to support and set up stem cell research laboratories that were totally privately funded. In January New Jersey became the second state, after California, to enact legislation explicitly permitting research on stem cells derived from human embryos. Legislators hoped that the measure would encourage biotechnology companies in this rapidly developing and potentially lucrative field to set up research labs in the state. "If you were a biotech, would you invest millions of dollars and jobs in a state that might outlaw what you're doing?" asked Michael Manganiello, vice president for government relations at the Christopher Reeve Paralysis Foundation.

In April Harvard University set up a stem cell institute with funding from the Howard Hughes Medical Institute and quickly developed seventeen lines of stem cells. In October the Harvard researchers applied to the university's ethics board for permission to create cloned human embryos from patients with juvenile onset diabetes, Parkinson's disease, and Alzheimer's disease. Scientists wanted to extract stem cells from these genetically flawed embryos and then watch their development in petri dishes to try to isolate the causes of the three diseases and perhaps even to test drugs that might cure them. Northwestern University, the University of Chicago, the University of Wisconsin, John Hopkins University, and the University of Maryland were among the other major academic institutions seeking private or state funding for embryonic stem cell research.

In California backers of stem cell research mounted a $25 million campaign to pass Proposition 71, which required the state to devote a total of $3 billion over ten years to fund a new institute of "regenerative medicine." The ballot initiative was the brainchild of real estate developer Robert N. Klein II, whose son had diabetes. The campaign included endorsements from Republican governor Arnold Schwarzenegger and glitzy ad campaigns featuring Nobel Prize winners and Hollywood actors lauding the potential benefits of stem cell research. Although opponents said the campaign was glossing over complex ethical, scientific, and financial issues involved in creating the institute, on election day nearly 60 percent of California's voters supported the initiative.

Once the campaign was over, however, some Californians began questioning various aspects of the initiative, including its funding, which could cost the state

$6 billion in interest payments on the bonds it was mandated to sell to finance the institute. Others raised concerns about whether state officials would have any oversight of the institute, although Klein, who was named to head the institute, said there were safeguards to prevent conflict of interests. Still others were dismayed to learn that the institute did not have to devote all its funding to stem cell research but could also conduct research on other medical technologies. Charles Krauthammer, a syndicated columnist and a member of the President's Council on Bioethics, called the initiative "an unbelievable rip-off by people with an interest in the business of stem cells."

Following are excerpts from the executive summary of Reproduction and Responsibility: The Regulation of New Biotechnologies, *released April 1, 2004, by the President's Council on Bioethics, which called for closer monitoring of fertility clinic procedures and long-term studies of the health effects of assisted reproduction.*

Reproduction and Responsibility

Advances in biotechnology in recent decades have made available an increasing capacity to intervene in the beginnings of human life, especially life initiated outside the body, whether in the clinic or in the laboratory. This capacity emerges from a confluence of work in reproductive biology, developmental biology, and human genetics, and raises ethical issues involving a number of important human goods. There is little question that the way these new technologies are used could have far-reaching consequences, not only for the individuals involved but also for society as a whole.

Yet it is not clear just how the interests of those individuals and of the public at large can best be served as these new technologies are developed and applied. What challenges and public policy concerns arise together with the use of new technologies affecting human reproduction? Whose responsibility is it to monitor, review, and offer guidance where guidance is needed, in order to safeguard the diverse human goods at stake? Should there be more or less oversight and regulation? Should there be any? Just how much is there now? Only partial answers are available to these questions, and much basic data remain to be gathered before they could be answered.

Since its very first meeting, in January of 2002, the President's Council on Bioethics has taken an interest in these subjects, and the Council has sought a way to advance public understanding of the challenges that confront us in this arena—beginning with the most basic information regarding what is being done and with what results. In the Council's report, Human Cloning and Human Dignity (2002), members observed that, with regard to assisted reproduction, genetic testing, and human embryo research,

> we lack comprehensive knowledge about what is being done, with what success, at what risk, under what ethical guidelines, respecting which moral boundaries, subject to what oversight and regulation, and with what sanctions for misconduct or abuse. If we are to have wise public policy regarding these scientifically

> and medically promising but morally challenging activities, we need careful study and sustained public moral discourse on this general subject, and not only on specific narrowly defined pieces of the field.

Following the release of that report, the Council decided to undertake a thoroughgoing inquiry into the current regulation of those biotechnologies that touch on human reproduction. This report is the fruit of that inquiry. Its principal aim is to describe and critically assess the various oversight and regulatory measures that now govern the biotechnologies and practices at the intersection of assisted reproduction, human genetics, and human embryo research.

I. What Is at Stake?

The Council saw a number of powerful reasons for taking up this subject. It involves some of the key concerns of bioethics and is likely to be an area of increasing importance, one in which both public understanding and public policy lag well behind the rapid advance of technological developments. Among the goods and ideals that are at stake, and that led the Council to point the public's attention toward this subject, are the following:

- The health and well-being of the human subjects directly affected by these technologies, not only the individuals or couples seeking their use, but also and especially the children who may be born with their aid.
- Relief of the suffering and sorrow of those afflicted with infertility.
- Compassion for children with serious genetic diseases, and relief of the sorrows and burdens that they and those who love and care for them must bear.
- The intrinsic value of new knowledge of human development and genetic function in addition to the inestimable practical value of new treatments for diseases and disabilities.
- Privacy of genetic information and reproductive practice.
- The foundational value of human life and the respect owed to it in its various stages.
- Several expressions and avenues of human freedom, including the freedom of parents to make their own reproductive decisions or to use or refuse genetic screening, and the freedom of scientists to conduct research. As important, as well, is the necessity to protect the freedom of children from improper attempts to manipulate their lives through control of their genetic make-up or from unreasonable expectations that could accompany such manipulations.
- The promotion of justice and equality, including equitable access to the use and benefits of new technologies, equal respect and opportunity in a world that places great emphasis on genetic distinctions, and the prevention of discrimination against or contempt for genetic "defectiveness" or "inferiority."
- The protection of human dignity, including the dignity of the human body and its parts, the dignity of important human relationships (parent and child, one generation and the next), and the humanity of human procreation

The Council's review of the field has been guided and motivated by these concerns.

II. A Diagnostic Overview

This report is fundamentally a diagnostic document, and even most of the recommendations with which it concludes aim largely at improving the nation's capacity for future diagnosis of the state of this field. The diagnosis begins by examining policies and practices related to assisted reproduction. This is our starting point because assisted reproduction is, in practice, the necessary gateway to all the newer technologies—present and projected—that affect human reproduction. Preimplantation genetic diagnosis (including sex selection), germ-line genetic modification, human embryo research, and similar techniques all presuppose in vitro fertilization and the existence of developing human life in vitro. As a consequence, any oversight or regulation of the use of genetic technologies in human reproduction will necessarily depend on the systems that oversee and regulate assisted reproduction itself. Also, the addition of genetic technologies to existing techniques of assisted reproduction has made it clear—if it had not been clear before—that we are dealing here with a most unusual branch of medicine. In no other area of medicine does the treatment of an ailment—in this case, infertility—call for the creation of another human being. Our deep concern for the safety and well-being of children suggests to us the need for special attention to the uses and outcomes of these new biotechnologies.

The report then proceeds to review the regulatory policies and practices involved in screening and selecting for genetic conditions and traits; modification of traits and characteristics; research involving in vitro human embryos; and commercial and financial interests in this arena.

In discussing each area we review the relevant techniques and practices, the principal ethical issues, and (especially) the existing regulatory activities. This extended diagnostic discussion explores in detail precisely who currently provides oversight and guidance in each area, pursuant to what authority, according to what principles and values, and with what ultimate practical effect.

III. The Council's Findings

The Council's diagnostic review of these areas has led us to several general conclusions:

- The fields of assisted reproduction, human genetics, and embryo research are increasingly converging with one another.
- There is no uniform, comprehensive, and enforceable system of data collection, monitoring, or oversight for the biotechnologies affecting human reproduction.
- There is minimal direct governmental regulation of the practice of assisted reproduction.
- There is extensive professional self-regulation of the practice of assisted reproduction, but compliance with the standards invoked is purely voluntary.
- There is no comprehensive, uniform, and enforceable mechanism for data collection, monitoring, or oversight of how the new reproductive biotechnologies affect the well-being of the children conceived with their aid, the egg donors, or the gestational mothers.

- There are no nationally uniform laws or policies relating to access to assisted reproduction.
- Given the present framework of regulation, novel technologies and practices that are successful move from the experimental context to clinical practice with relatively little oversight or deliberation. Once in practice, these techniques are used at clinicians' discretion, with little or no external oversight. Use of effective technologies becomes widespread rapidly.
- As in other areas of medicine, there is no uniform system for public review and deliberation regarding the larger human or social significance of new reproductive biotechnologies.
- Preimplantation genetic diagnosis is an unregulated practice.
- Gene transfer research, by contrast, is regulated robustly.
- There is no comprehensive, uniform, and enforceable mechanism for data collection, monitoring, or oversight regarding the use and disposition of in vitro human embryos in the context of clinical practice or research.
- There is no comprehensive mechanism for regulation of commerce in gametes, embryos, and assisted reproductive technology services.
- Patenting of embryonic or fetal human organisms is prohibited for the fiscal year 2004.

The Council does not take these findings in and of themselves to mean that any public policy response is called for, but any consideration of potential public policies in this area must take these basic facts into account.

IV. Policy Options and Recommendations

The Council's findings, combined with the concerns that animate our interest in this area, point toward a fairly wide array of possible regulatory approaches. In this report, the Council considers these options in some detail, laying out a range of potential institutional options—from doing nothing to developing entirely new regulatory institutions—and offering a number of possible aims and principles that might guide future regulators.

However, given the preliminary character of this report, and the fact that our review of the field has turned up a number of areas where crucial data are simply lacking, the Council was not prepared to recommend any sweeping institutional reform or innovation. Rather, members agreed upon a series of modest measures to alleviate some clear and significant present problems, including especially the lack of information on certain key practices and their consequences.

The report concludes, therefore, with a set of recommendations that the Council agrees should be adopted immediately. These recommendations are not for structural or institutional changes; we do not propose the wholesale creation of new regulatory institutions or even the reform of existing ones. Rather, we offer these recommendations as interim measures with two goals in mind: first, to strengthen existing legislation and regulatory mechanisms in order to gather more complete and useful information; and, second, to erect certain legislative safeguards against a small number of boundary-crossing practices, at least until there can be further deliberation and debate about both the human goods at stake and the best way to protect them.

The recommendations fall into three general categories: studies and data collection, oversight and self-regulation by professional societies, and targeted legislative measures. In each case, the Council has detailed its precise recommendations in the report and has offered extensive supporting arguments and reasons. The recommendations are as follows.

A. Federal Studies, Data Collection, Reporting, and Monitoring Regarding the Uses and Effects of These Technologies

As the Council's findings demonstrate, the incompleteness of basic information on the uses and impact of new reproductive technologies makes any conclusive policy judgments very difficult to formulate. The Council therefore recommends that the federal government take a number of specific steps to improve our knowledge and understanding:

- Undertake a federally funded longitudinal study of the impact of assisted reproductive technologies on the health and development of children born with their aid.
- Undertake federally funded studies on the impact of assisted reproductive technologies on the health and well-being of women.
- Undertake federally funded comprehensive studies on the uses of reproductive genetic technologies, and on their effects on children born with their aid.
- Strengthen and augment the Fertility Clinic Success Rate and Certification Act to better protect consumers and patients:
    - Provide more user-friendly reporting of data.
    - Require the publication of all reported adverse health effects.
    - Require the reporting of the average prices of the procedures and the average cost (to patients) of a successful assisted pregnancy.
    - Include information on novel and experimental procedures.
    - Require more specific reporting and publication of the frequency of, and reasons for, uses of specialized techniques such as ICSI, preimplantation genetic diagnosis, and sperm sorting for sex-selection.
    - Provide model forms for decision-making.
    - Provide stronger penalties to enhance compliance with the Act's reporting requirements.
    - Increase funding for implementation of the Act

B. Increased Oversight by Professional Societies and Practitioners

Most oversight in this area currently takes the form of self-regulation by professional societies, and as far as the Council can determine the vast majority of practitioners abide by these guidelines and standards and are dedicated to the welfare of their patients. Yet the Council has identified a few ways in which self-regulation could be meaningfully improved:

- Strengthen informed patient decision-making.
- Treat the child born with the aid of assisted reproductive procedures as a patient.
- Improve enforcement of existing guidelines.

- Improve procedures for movement of experimental procedures into clinical practice.
- Create and enforce minimum uniform standards for the protection of human subjects affected by assisted reproduction.
- Develop additional self-imposed ethical boundaries

C. Targeted Legislative Measures

In the course of its review, discussion, and findings, the Council encountered and highlighted several particular practices and techniques (some already in use, others likely to be tried in the foreseeable future) touching human reproduction that raise new and distinctive challenges. Given the importance of the matter, we believe these require special attention, and we therefore recommend that Congress should consider some limited targeted measures that might institute a moratorium on certain particularly questionable practices. The report includes an extensive discussion of the reasons for these recommendations as well as the aims we hope they might serve. The Council recommends that the Congress should, at least for a limited time:

- Prohibit the transfer, for any purpose, of any human embryo into the body of any member of a non-human species.
- Prohibit the production of a hybrid human-animal embryo by fertilization of human egg by animal sperm or of animal egg by human sperm.
- Prohibit the transfer of a human embryo (produced ex vivo) to a woman's uterus for any purpose other than to attempt to produce a live-born child.
- Prohibit attempts to conceive a child by any means other than the union of egg and sperm.
- Prohibit attempts to conceive a child by using gametes obtained from a human fetus or derived from human embryonic stem cells.
- Prohibit attempts to conceive a child by fusing blastomeres from two or more embryos.
- Prohibit the use of human embryos in research beyond a designated stage in their development (between 10 and 14 days after fertilization).
- Prohibit the buying and selling of human embryos.
- Prohibit the issuing of patents on claims directed to or encompassing human embryos or fetuses at any stage of development; and amend Title 35, United States Code, section 271(g) (which extends patent protections to products resulting from a patented process) to exclude these items from patentability

Source: U.S. Executive Office of the President. President's Council on Bioethics. *Reproduction and Responsibility: The Regulation of New Biotechnologies.* April 1, 2004. http://purl.access.gpo.gov/GPO/LPS49455 (accessed February 24, 2005).

Bush Administration on Lifting Economic Sanctions against Libya

April 23, 2004

INTRODUCTION

Libya during 2004 allowed U.S., British, and international experts to dismantle the chemical and nuclear weapons programs it had built secretly during the previous two decades. In return, the United States and the European Union (EU) lifted nearly all the economic sanctions that had been imposed against Libya since the mid-1980s because of its sponsorship of several high-profile terrorist attacks. These steps went much of the way toward removing Libya's pariah status in the international community and enabled the country's leader, Muammar Qaddafi, to return to his favorite platform: the world stage.

Qaddafi kept busy hosting a succession of foreign dignitaries at his Bedouin tent in Tripoli, beginning in January with the first of several delegations from the U.S. Congress. Then followed Italian prime minister Silvio Berlusconi in February; European Union Commission president Romano Prodi (on the first of several visits during the year) and British prime minister Tony Blair, both in March; German chancellor Gerhard Schroeder in mid-October; French president Jacques Chirac in November; and Canadian prime minister Paul Martin in December. Qaddafi in April traveled to Brussels for a meeting with EU officials; it was his first international trip outside Africa or the Middle East in fifteen years, as his travel had been curtailed by international sanctions.

For the Western leaders who visited Tripoli, part of the attraction might have been meeting one of the world's most mercurial and mysterious figures on his exotic home turf. However, economic interests—especially the revival of Libya's oil production—certainly headed the agendas of the high-profile officials who lined up for private sessions with Qaddafi. Blair's visit, for example, coincided with the signing of a $700 million deal under which Royal Dutch Shell, a British-Dutch company, would develop a natural gas field off the coast of Libya. BAE, a British defense contractor, was negotiating a potential aviation deal, and U.S. oil companies hoped to reenter the lucrative Libyan market that sanctions had long closed to them. Each of the leaders brought with him a delegation of business executives anxious to win contracts. "It is a promising market. We must do the maximum to support it," Chirac said.

The Western rush toward better relations with Libya continued despite the revelation that Libya in 2003 had plotted to assassinate Crown Prince Abdullah of Saudi Arabia. The Saudi plot attracted little attention in the United States, but some critics said it illustrated the Bush administration's double standard on terrorism. "[T]he Saudis must wonder how serious the administration is when it lionizes a man who plotted to kill their ruler," *Washington Post* columnist David Ignatius wrote on October 26.

Background

After years of hints that he wanted to shed his bad-boy image, Qaddafi in 2003 launched secret negotiations with the United States and Great Britain, leading to a startling announcement on December 19, 2003, that Libya was giving up all its weapons of mass destruction. The announcement set in motion an intense U.S.-led process during the first half of 2004 in which Libya turned over tons of equipment, supplies, and technology for chemical and nuclear weapons that it had bought secretly on the world market since the 1970s. In September U.S. officials announced that all of Libya's so-called weapons of mass destruction had been located and destroyed, shipped to the United States for examination and storage, or were put under international control. *(Background, Historic Documents of 2003, p. 1218)*

The process of uncovering Libya's weapons programs revealed many details of an international black market in nuclear weapons supplies run by Abdul Qadeer Kahn, who was largely responsible for Pakistan's successful development of nuclear weapons. U.S. officials said that starting in 1997 Libya had paid Kahn more than $100 million for equipment, weapons designs, and even several thousand tons of partially processed uranium. The year's investigations reportedly showed that Libya had received nuclear weapons supplies through a clandestine network of companies around the world, including in Dubai, Germany, Japan, Malaysia, South Africa, and Turkey. The probes also verified long-held Western suspicions that Libya had traded information on missiles and nuclear weapons with Egypt. *(Kahn network, p. 323)*

Dismantling Libya's Weapons

Qaddafi's surprise announcement in December 2003 that he was giving up Libya's chemical and nuclear weapons—along with the missiles to deliver them throughout much of the Middle East and into southern Europe—presented the world's greatest disarmament challenge since the collapse of the Soviet Union a dozen years earlier. In that earlier case, the United States mounted a major program to help Russia and the other former Soviet republics dismantle and secure the biological, chemical, and nuclear weapons they inherited. Three countries—Belarus, Kazakhstan, and Ukraine—agreed to give up all their weapons, which were either destroyed or returned to Russia. The only other country that had willingly given up its nuclear weapons was South Africa, following the dissolution of its white-minority government. *(Soviet weapons dismantlement, Historic Documents of 2002, p. 437)*

Qaddafi had negotiated his agreement to give up the weapons with the United States and Britain, and Washington took the lead in locating, securing, and dismantling the weapons programs. Much of the actual equipment and material was shipped to the United States for examination and safekeeping. Two United Nations agencies were involved in verifying the dismantlement efforts: the International Atomic Energy Agency (IAEA), which supervised compliance with the Nuclear Nonproliferation Treaty, and the Organization for the Prevention of Chemical Weapons, which monitored compliance with the UN Chemical Weapons Convention. Libya in 1975 had ratified the nonproliferation treaty, which banned the development of nuclear weapons, but obviously it had not fully complied with it. Until 2003 Libya was one of a handful of countries that had refused to sign the treaty banning chemical weapons.

U.S. experts removed weapons equipment and supplies from Libya in two stages. The first phase consisted of what U.S. officials said were items of the greatest "proliferation concern"—easily transportable parts and materials that were in demand in countries seeking to build weapons. The United States on January 22 removed technical design materials, including Chinese-origin blueprints (reportedly provided by Kahn) for a 1,000-pound nuclear weapon. On January 26 a U.S. plane shipped from Libya 55,000 pounds of equipment and supplies, including components of centrifuges to enrich uranium, key parts for the five medium-range Scud-C missiles Libya had bought from North Korea, and unprocessed uranium gas.

In the second stage, during March and April, U.S. and British experts removed remaining parts and material for Libya's nuclear weapons and missiles. In one of the most complicated maneuvers, U.S. and IAEA experts removed about 35 pounds of highly enriched uranium, which was shipped to Russia for processing into fuel that could not be used for nuclear weapons. Libya had bought the uranium from the Soviet Union in the 1980s for a research reactor. Libya also destroyed more than 3,000 empty bombs intended to carry chemical weapons, and it turned over to a UN agency 23 tons of mustard gas, a deadly chemical weapon.

On March 15 Bush administration officials displayed, at the government's Oak Ridge, Tennessee, nuclear complex, casings for a dozen centrifuges. Officials said these casings were among the 4,000 centrifuges found at Libyan weapon facilities. Centrifuges were used to process uranium hexafluoride gas (UF_6) into highly enriched uranium, one of the fuels for nuclear weapons.

This event was timed to coincide with the one-year anniversary of the start of the U.S. war to dislodge Iraqi leader Saddam Hussein. President George W. Bush and his aides had claimed that Qaddafi gave up his weapons because he feared that the United States might next turn its attention to him. Many foreign policy experts were skeptical about that claim, noting that the administration had never threatened Libya directly or indirectly, and that lifting sanctions appeared to be Qaddafi's chief concern.

Most U.S. weapons experts said the material removed from Libya demonstrated that Qaddafi's regime had been much further along in its work on nuclear weapons than had been assumed internationally before late 2003. Particularly surprising was Libya's acquisition of the centrifuges and the Chinese blueprints for a bomb. Even so, several important pieces of evidence appeared to demonstrate that Libya's nuclear weapons program was far from complete. For example, the IAEA quoted Libyan officials as saying no one in the country had the technical expertise to assemble a weapon from the Chinese blueprints. The Institute for Science and International Security, in Washington, also noted that few, if any, of the 4,000 centrifuge casings displayed at Oak Ridge actually had the internal rotors needed to make the machines work. Institute director David Albright, a former United Nations weapons inspector, said Libya appeared to be "several years from being able to produce enough highly enriched uranium for a bomb."

By contrast, Libya's handing over of 23 tons of mustard gas settled any question of whether the country had developed chemical weapons. U.S. officials and private experts long had suggested that Libya was using a secret facility at Rabta, in the Sahara Desert south of Tripoli, to produce chemical weapons. Until 2003, however, Libya had claimed the Rabta plant was producing pharmaceuticals. After the weapons and components for them were removed early in 2004, Libya began the process of converting the laboratories at Rabta into a genuine pharmaceuticals plant, this time under the supervision of the UN's chemical weapons agency.

Even as U.S. experts were busy dismantling nuclear facilities in Libya, Qaddafi's government moved quickly to prove to the rest of the world that it in fact was giving up its program to develop nuclear weapons. On March 9 Libya signed an agreement called the Additional Protocol that gave the IAEA broad access—including the right of unannounced inspections—to all of the country's nuclear sites. Previously, the IAEA had been able to visit only sites specifically authorized by the Libyan government.

IAEA director general Mohamed ElBaradei submitted reports to the agency's board of governors in February and May documenting the progress of the work to dismantle Libya's nuclear weapons. In its summary, the February report said: "Starting in the early 1980s and continuing until the end of 2003, Libya imported nuclear material and conducted a wide variety of nuclear activities which it had failed to report" to the IAEA under the agreements it had signed. Libya had agreed to report all that material and bring itself into compliance with its agreements, ElBaradei said.

Testifying to Congress on September 22, a senior State Department official said the United States had verified "with reasonable certainty that Libya has eliminated, or set in place the elimination" of, all its chemical and nuclear weapons programs and its medium-range missiles. Paula A. DeSutter, the assistant secretary of verification and compliance, also paid tribute to what she called the "momentous changes taken by Libya" in dismantling its weapons programs. "It could not have been an easy decision to abandon weapons programs in which it had invested untold amounts of money," she told a House International Relations subcommittee.

U.S., EU Relations with Libya

Qaddafi clearly expected rewards from the international community in return for his sudden about-face, and the rewards were quick in coming. In steps throughout the year, the United States and the EU lifted nearly all the sanctions and embargoes that they had imposed against Libya since the 1980s in retaliation for its sponsorship of several major terrorist attacks. Chief among those attacks had been the 1986 bombing of a discotheque in Berlin; the bombing of Pan Am flight 103 over Lockerbie, Scotland, in December 1988, killing all 259 passengers and 11 people on the ground; and the bombing of a French airliner over Niger in 1989, killing 170 people

Libya in 2003 formally acknowledged its sponsorship of the Lockerbie bombing and agreed to pay the families of the victims $10 million each in compensation, for a total payout of $2.7 billion. The size of that settlement encouraged families of victims of the French airliner bombing to demand a larger payment than the $34 million Libya previously had agreed to; as a result, Libya upped that agreement to $170 million in January 2004. Finally, Libya agreed in August 2004 to pay $35 million to the non-U.S. victims of the 1986 bombing of La Belle disco in Berlin; 2 U.S. servicemen and a Turkish woman were killed and 230 people were wounded in that attack, which a German court later ruled was mounted by the Libyan secret service.

Responding to Qaddafi's concessions on the weapons, and to the admission of responsibility for the Lockerbie bombing, the Bush administration took four significant steps during 2004 to lift restrictions on U.S. official and private dealings with Libya:

- On February 26 the administration lifted all restrictions on U.S. travel to Libya, authorized U.S. companies that had done business in Libya before sanctions were imposed to begin negotiations for their return, and authorized U.S. educational and humanitarian organizations to hold meetings with their counterparts in Libya.

- On April 23 Bush lifted the bulk of U.S. sanctions against Libya, which had been in effect since 1986. The president's action meant that U.S. companies could resume doing business in Libya, including importing Libyan oil and investing in Libyan businesses. In a statement, the White House said Bush acted "in recognition of the steps [Libya] has taken over the last two months to repudiate WMD [weapons of mass destruction] and to build the foundation for Libya's economic growth and reintegration with the international community."
- On June 28 the United States formally reestablished diplomatic relations with Libya. William Burns, the assistant secretary of state for Near Eastern affairs, visited Tripoli and officially opened a "liaison office" (the step below an embassy) that had been functioning for about two months. The United States had closed its embassy in Tripoli in 1980; since 1986 U.S. interests in Libya had been handled through the embassy of Malta. Secretary of State Colin Powell met with Libyan foreign minister Abdel-Rahman Shalqam at the United Nations on September 23; it was the highest level official meeting between the two countries in more than twenty-five years.
- On September 20 the Bush administration lifted the remaining sanctions against Libya. This step eliminated the need for businesses to obtain licenses from the Treasury Department for all trade with Libya; allowed direct air service between the United States and Libya; made U.S. businesses eligible for government export-promotion programs, such as loans from the Export-Import Bank and insurance through the Overseas Private Insurance Corporation; and freed up about $1.25 billion worth of Libyan government bank accounts, securities, and other financial assets that the Reagan administration had frozen in 1986. Libya withdrew those assets in December.

At each step during the year, the administration left in place the long-standing U.S. designation of Libya as a "state sponsor" of terrorism. Although Libya had made statements foreswearing terrorism, U.S. officials said they remained concerned about evidence that Tripoli in 2003 had planned the assassination of Crown Prince Abdullah of Saudi Arabia. In July a prominent Muslim activist in the United States, Abdurahman Alamoudi, pleaded guilty in federal court to accepting several hundred thousand dollars from high-ranking Libyan officials. According to affidavits filed in the case, Alamoudi served as an intermediary in a plot to kill Abdullah. Alamoudi was not formally charged in connection with the alleged plot, but prosecutors cited his role in successfully asking the court to impose a maximum twenty-three-year prison sentence.

Keeping Libya on the terrorism list had some practical implications, including the continued prohibition on sales by the U.S. government or any U.S. businesses to Libya of weapons or so-called dual use equipment with military or nonmilitary uses, such as some aviation and communications equipment. Another consequence was that each family of the Lockerbie bombing victims would have to wait even longer for the final $2 million of the promised $10 million payout. This was because a provision of the settlement withheld that amount until Libya was removed from the list.

The EU lifted all its remaining economic sanctions on September 22. The key to this step had been Libya's agreement to pay compensation for victims of the Berlin disco bombing. The EU lifted its arms embargo against Libya on October 11. Italy had pressed for the action, wanting to sell Libya helicopters, night-vision goggles, and other equipment to patrol its shores to prevent illegal immigrants from North Africa heading to Italy.

For Western businesses, the principal attraction of Libya was its oil reserves, said to be the largest and most marketable in Africa. Significant reserves of natural gas also were located just off the Libyan coast in the Mediterranean Sea. Libyan oil was relatively easy to produce, and because Libya was far from the often-troubled Persian Gulf, its oil was considered relatively inexpensive to transport to world markets. As of early 2004 Libya's production was only about one-half of its 1970 peak of 3.3 million barrels a day.

Four U.S. oil companies had operated in Libya before the sanctions were imposed, all in conjunction with the Libyan national oil company that controlled the country's oil business. Three of them—Marathon Oil Co., Amerada Hess Corp., and ConocoPhillips—were minority partners, along with Libya's national oil company, in a joint operation called the Oasis Group; the fourth company was Occidental Petroleum Corp. All four companies began negotiations with the government on the terms of their return, and other oil producers expressed interest in Libya, as well.

Despite the remarkable series of steps that reopened commercial and governmental cooperation between Libya and the rest of the world, Qaddafi said late in the year that he had hoped for more. "To tell you the truth, we have been a little disappointed by the reaction of Europe, the United States and Japan. They haven't really rewarded Libya for its contribution to international peace," he told the French newspaper *Le Figaro* in an interview published November 24. "And we're still waiting. If we are not recompensed, other countries will not follow our example and dismantle their own programs." Qaddafi was vague about what else he had expected, saying only that he wanted Western help in adapting military technologies for civilian purposes and should have been given "guarantees from the international community on its [Libya's] national security."

Following is the text of a statement released April 23, 2004, by the Office of the Press Secretary announcing that President George W. Bush had lifted most U.S. economic sanctions against Libya in recognition of that country's willingness to give up its programs to develop chemical and nuclear weapons.

"U.S. Eases Economic Embargo against Libya"

Since December 19, Libya has taken significant steps eliminating weapons of mass destruction programs and longer range missiles, and has reiterated its pledge to halt all support for terrorism. In the last two months, the Government of Libya has removed virtually all elements of its declared nuclear weapons program, signed the IAEA [International Atomic Energy Agency] Additional Protocol, joined the Chemical Weapons Convention, destroyed all of its declared unfilled chemical munitions, secured its chemical agent pending destruction under international supervision, submitted a declaration of its chemical agents to the Organization for the Prevention of Chemical Weapons, eliminated its Scud-C missile force, and undertaken to modify its Scud-B missiles.

Officials from the United States, United Kingdom, OPCW [Organization for the Prevention of Chemical Weapons, a UN agency], and IAEA, invited by the Libyan government to assist in and verify the elimination of its WMD [weapons of mass destruction] programs, have received excellent cooperation and support.

Through its actions, Libya has set a standard that we hope other nations will emulate in rejecting weapons of mass destruction and in working constructively with international organizations to halt the proliferation of the world's most dangerous systems. Libyan actions since December 19 have made our country and the world safer.

The President made clear on December 19 that Libya's actions to voluntarily dismantle its WMD and longer range missile programs, as well as renounce terrorism, would open the path to better relations with the United States.

In recognition of the steps it has taken over the last two months to repudiate WMD and to build the foundation for Libya's economic growth and reintegration with the international community, the United States will take the following steps:

Today, the President has terminated the application of the Iran and Libya Sanctions Act with respect to Libya, and the Treasury Department has modified sanctions imposed on U.S. firms and individuals under the authority of the International Emergency Economic Powers Act to allow the resumption of most commercial activities, financial transactions, and investments. U.S. companies will be able to buy or invest in Libyan oil and products. U.S. commercial banks and other financial service providers will be able to participate in and support these transactions.

Controls on exports with respect to Libya will be maintained consistent with Libya's continued presence on the State Sponsors of Terrorism List. Restrictions will continue to apply to exports of dual-use items with military potential, including potential for WMD or missile applications. Exports to Libya of defense articles and services on the U.S. Munitions List remain prohibited. Direct air service between the U.S. and Libya and third country code-sharing are not yet authorized, nor is the release of frozen Libyan Government assets.

In conjunction with our enhanced economic relations, we will begin a dialogue on trade, investment, and economic reform, and will take steps to encourage Libya's reintegration with the global market. In particular, we will drop our objection to Libyan efforts to begin WTO accession process.

In recognition of our deepening dialogue and diplomatic engagement on a broader range of issues, the Department of State intends to establish a U.S. Liaison Office in Tripoli, pending Congressional notification. Our protecting power relationship with Belgium, whose support in Tripoli over the years has been greatly appreciated, would end. Direct diplomatic dealings with Libya will reflect the reality on the ground over the last several months of bilateral cooperation and dialogue.

The U.S. will continue to promote humanitarian and joint programs that advance people-to-people ties between America and Libya. As a result of the lifting of commercial restrictions on Libya, Libyan students will be eligible to study in the United States, subject to admission to an American educational institute and meeting the eligibility requirements for a student visa.

A U.S. education delegation will travel to Libya on April 23, to begin consultations on cooperation in the education sector and in educational exchanges.

The United States has underscored to Libya the importance of a complete renunciation of all ties to terrorism. The President's certification to Congress under ILSA [the Iran-Libya Sanctions Act, of 1996] that Libya has fulfilled the requirements of relevant United Nations Security Council resolutions relating to the bombing of Pan Am 103 does not prejudge the removal of Libya from the Terrorism List or detract from Libya's obligation to fulfill its continuing Pan Am 103 commitments. The necessity of ending any tie to terrorist groups or activities will continue to be a central issue in relations with Libya.

Assistant Secretary of State for Near Eastern Affairs William Burns will continue our political and economic dialogue with Libya on issues that include terrorism, human rights, political and economic modernization, and foreign policy in Africa.

Source: U.S. Executive Office of the President. Office of the Press Secretary. "U.S. Eases Economic Embargo against Libya." Statement by the press secretary. April 23, 2004. www.whitehouse.gov/news/releases/2004/04/20040423-9.html (accessed January 18, 2005).

General Accounting Office on Missile Defense Systems

April 23, 2004

INTRODUCTION

The Bush administration missed its September 30, 2004, deadline for deployment of a missile defense system that was supposed to protect the United States against a potential missile attack by North Korea. Eight interceptor missiles were placed in their silos in Alaska and California during the last half of the year, but they were not activated by year's end—and the first test of the system in two years failed even to get off the ground. Other key components of the antimissile system were still being developed.

President George W. Bush campaigned in 2000 on a promise of pressing ahead with a long-discussed, long-delayed system to shoot down ballistic missiles before they could reach U.S. territory. Congress appropriated $8–$10 billion annually to develop such a system, and Bush in late 2002 set a goal of having the first part in place by the end of September 2004. The initial system was aimed exclusively at North Korea, which the Bush administration said was developing nuclear weapons and had medium-range missiles potentially able to reach parts of the United States.

The administration envisioned what it called a "layered" missile defense system using components based on land, at sea, in the air, and in space. The land-based components included missiles that would fly into space and then intercept and destroy any missiles before they could reach their targets. This was an expanded version of a defense system the Clinton administration had begun to develop in the 1990s. A new generation of space-based satellites was being developed to send word of the attacking missiles to U.S. military command centers. Radars based on land and at sea would guide the interceptor missiles to their targets. One of these radars, called the X-band, was to be placed on an enormous mobile platform rising some 300 feet above the Pacific Ocean near the far-western extremity of the Aleutian Islands.

Within a few years, a half-dozen Aegis-class destroyers armed with interceptor missiles known as the Standard Missle-3 would patrol the world to defend the continental United States, U.S. military installations overseas, and U.S. allies. Another future component of the missile defense system was what the Pentagon called an airborne laser—a set of high-intensity lasers to be mounted on Boeing 747 airplanes that would patrol the skies in the vicinity of a potential enemy and then destroy short- or medium-range missiles launched toward the United States or its allies. The airborne laser was not intended to attack larger, longer-range intercontinental ballistic missiles such as those deployed by China or Russia. Antimissile lasers mounted on satellites in space also were a possibility for the distant future.

As of 2004 the Clinton and Bush administrations had spent a total of more than $25 billion on missile defense systems. Bush administration projections called for an additional $50.3 billion through fiscal year 2009. *(Background, Historic Documents of 2003, p. 817)*

Testing the Systems

Traditionally, the Pentagon built complex military systems through a rigorous set of procedures that started with research, then proceeded to development, testing, construction, further testing of the completed product, and, finally, actual deployment. In Pentagon terms, this was known as "buy after you build." For its missile defense system, the Bush administration in 2002 developed a new approach to deploy key components of the system as they were being developed, even if they had not been fully tested. Administration officials called this new approach "buy as you build" and defended it on the grounds that the system had to be built before it could be fully tested, and that the looming threat of a missile attack demanded urgent action. Even a system that had not been fully tested would be "better than nothing," argued Lt. Gen. Ronald Kadish, who was head of the Pentagon's Missile Defense Agency (MDA) until mid-2004.

As of the start of 2004 the Pentagon had conducted eight tests of the partial system it planned and claimed five of those tests to have been successful. Critics noted, however, that none of the tests had simulated a realistic attack; for example, the "attacking" missiles had flown at relatively low altitudes and speeds, and the interceptor missiles had not confronted decoys that an attacking nation was likely to use. All tests had taken place over an identical course in the Pacific and none had used the actual components that were to be part of the functioning system; for example, these tests used surrogates for the interceptor missile (which the Pentagon called the "kill vehicle") and the booster rocket that was intended to lift it into space. The actual interceptor missile and booster rocket were still in development when those tests were conducted. The booster rocket, being built by Lockheed Martin Corp., had proven particularly problematic.

Concerns expressed by many critics about the inadequacy of the Pentagon's testing appeared to be shared by at least some officials within the Pentagon. On January 21 the Defense Department's official in charge of weapons testing issued a report saying the small number and rudimentary nature of tests that had been conducted made it difficult to determine if the system actually would work. "At this point it is not clear what mission capability will be demonstrated" by the time the administration planned to put the system into operation, said Thomas P. Christie, chief of the Pentagon's office of operational testing and evaluation. Christie told Congress during the summer that he estimated the system, as currently configured, might be only about 20–30 percent effective in blocking an attacking missile. That estimate was the direct opposite of the MDA's claim of 80 percent effectiveness.

In January Pentagon officials said that two more sets of tests were scheduled, one for May and another for July. Later, the Pentagon announced that the initial components of the missile defense system would be deployed by late summer, even before the latter test had been conducted. The plan was to install six interceptor missiles in their silos at Fort Greely, an army base near Fairbanks, Alaska. During 2005 another ten interceptors were to be installed at Fort Greely and four were to be placed at Vandenberg Air Force Base in California. Ten more missiles were to be stationed at Fort Greely in later years, making a total there of twenty-six.

The tests scheduled for midyear fell by the wayside, however, because of continuing technical problems. Just before the planned test in May engineers found a faulty circuit board in the warhead of the interceptor missile. That problem led Pentagon officials to undertake what they called a "top-to-bottom review" of all electronic and mechanical systems in the missiles.

Despite the continuing problems, the Pentagon went ahead with what was little more than a symbolic step of placing the first of six interceptor missiles into a silo at Fort Greely on July 22. Although the missile simply sat in the silo and was not ready to be launched, Bush used that step to claim during campaign appearances that he had kept his promise. "It's a beginning of a missile defense system that was envisioned by Ronald Reagan—a system necessary to protect us against the threats of the twenty-first century," Bush said on August 17 at an appearance at a Boeing Co. defense plant near Philadelphia. Defense Secretary Donald H. Rumsfeld described the missile defense as "the triumph of hope and vision over pessimism and skepticism." For the moment, some senior military officers appeared to be among the skeptics. News organizations reported that the Strategic Air Command, which eventually would take over command of the missile defense system, was operating on the assumption that it could not yet be relied on in the case of an attack.

Another test was scheduled in August, but then the computer in the booster rocket was found to have a problem. That test was rescheduled for September but once again was postponed when senior Pentagon officials discovered that recently made modifications to the interceptor missile had not gone through preliminary testing procedures.

Although the repeated testing delays pushed actual deployment of the system further behind schedule, White House and Pentagon officials remained upbeat and denied any serious problems. Rumsfeld and top officials of the Pentagon's Missile Defense Agency said all aspects of the system had been subjected to ground testing and computer simulations, and no serious design flaws had yet been discovered.

Lt. Gen. Henry A. Obering, the new director of the MDA, told reporters early in December that the system had an "emergency" capability of shooting down an enemy missile. The system still needed to go through a "shakedown cruise" to make sure everything would work as intended, he said.

On December 15 the first test of the defense system in two years failed. A target warhead launched on schedule from Alaska, but the interceptor missile that was supposed to destroy it shut down automatically and never made it off the launch pad at its testing site in the Marshall Islands. A Pentagon spokesman blamed "an unknown anomaly" for the failure and insisted the event, which cost $85 million, had been "a very good training exercise" even though the missile never left the ground.

Two days later a Pentagon spokesman said the system would not be activated by the end of the year, as the White House had planned, but he insisted the delay was unrelated to the test failure. Also in December, the Pentagon placed the first two interceptor missiles in their silos at Vandenberg Air Force Base in California. Two other missiles were to be put in place early in 2005.

GAO Criticisms

Over the previous three years the Pentagon's rapid work on the missile defense system had come under repeated criticism from arms control advocates, who feared it might fuel another arms race, and from several scientific groups, which said key elements would not work as planned. Perhaps the strongest and most important criticism during 2004 came from two congressional watchdog groups: the General Accounting Office (GAO, later renamed the Government Accountability Office), and the Congressional Budget Office. The GAO issued three reports during the year warning that the Pentagon was rushing the missile defense system without adequate management plans or clear goals. The budget office weighed in with a detailed criticism of the administration's futuristic plans to destroy attacking missiles shortly after they left the ground.

The GAO's most extensive examination of the missile defense program was issued April 23. It carried a typically understated title that nevertheless summarized the problems the agency found: "Missile Defense: Actions Are Needed to Enhance Testing and Accountability."

In essence, the GAO said the administration was building a system that was more expensive than planned, had not been tested as rigorously as it should have been, and might not work as intended when it was activated. The GAO said the Pentagon's Missile Defense Agency did not have firm milestones for measuring its progress; this made it difficult for the agency or anyone else to judge the quality and cost of the work being done, most of it by major defense contractors. The overall performance goals, the GAO said, "are based on assumptions regarding the system's capability against certain threats under various engagement conditions. Neither the engagement conditions nor critical assumptions about the threat [such as the type of incoming missile and whether it was accompanied by decoys] used in establishing these goals are explicitly stated as part of MDA's program goals. Without these implicit assumptions being explained, the operational capability of the fielded system is difficult to fully understand."

Another GAO report, sent to Congress on May 17, warned that costs were escalating rapidly for the airborne laser system, to be carried aboard Boeing 747 airplanes. The total cost to date for the system had doubled from $1 billion to $2 billion, the GAO said, and the contractors working on it faced a "bow wave" of unfinished work from previous years. Furthermore, GAO said, the Pentagon's predictions of the military utility of the one laser-plane in production were "highly uncertain" because they were "based on modeling, simulations, and analysis rather than the demonstrated capability of the system," which had yet to be tested.

In a study released in July, the Congressional Budget Office raised significant questions about the Pentagon's attempt to develop a system to destroy enemy missiles in the first three to five minutes after launch—during the so-called boost phase. Pentagon plans assumed that the system would be used to deter missile threats from Iran or North Korea, or even an accidental launch by China or Russia. The budget office study said the Pentagon was counting on technology that pressed the limits of what was currently available—and what might be physically possible. The study estimated that such a system based on land (using interceptor missiles fired from silos) would cost $16 billion to $37 billion to develop, produce, and operate over a twenty-year period. To work, however, such a system would have to be built very close to the enemy. In the case of Iran that would mean basing the system in a neighboring country, such as Iraq or Turkmenistan, both subject to instability. A system based on satellites might cost $27 billion to $78 billion, the budget office said.

A detailed criticism, on scientific grounds, of the administration's plans to destroy enemy missiles during the boost phase was offered on October 5 by a panel of the American Physical Society—the professional association of physicists. Expanding on similar findings of a year earlier, the panel said defending the entire United States with such a system "is unlikely to be practical when all factors are considered." The panel cited numerous technical limitations that, it said, would severely undermine the effectiveness of the system. Even if an effective system could be devised, destroying a missile immediately after its launch would create another danger: debris from the warhead would fall back to Earth and pose a potential danger to populated areas.

Despite these and other concerns, the Republican-controlled Congress in 2004 gave Bush nearly all the money he requested for the missile defense program during the 2005 fiscal year. At the urging of Senate Democrats, however, Congress included language in the Defense Department authorization bill (PL 108–375) requiring "operationally realistic" testing of the system by October 2005. The bill also required the Pentagon to give Congress more specific information than in the past on the costs and schedules for the missile defense program.

Other Nations Join Missile Defense Drive

While it was building its missile defense system, the Bush administration launched an equally ambitious diplomatic initiative to gain support for the idea from other countries. Much of the attention focused on countries bordering on the Pacific Ocean because North Korea was the principal threat the administration foresaw and China was seen as a potential missile threat. Australia in December 2003 agreed to accept new U.S. radar installations that would be part of the missile defense system.

Japan also agreed to take part in the system, for reasons that were far from theoretical. North Korea in 1998 launched a medium-range missile that flew over part of Japan before crashing into the ocean. The missile was intended to carry a broadcast satellite into space, but that attempt failed. U.S. officials said the missile was capable of carrying a small nuclear warhead.

The Japanese government announced in December 2003 that it planned to develop a limited missile defense system based on weapons it already had purchased from the United States or would purchase and modify for its own use. In late March the Japanese parliament approved the $1 billion first step in a multiyear, $10 billion program to build two layers of a shield against a missile attack from North Korea. One layer was to consist of four U.S.-made Aegis destroyers carrying the Standard Missile-3, which would try to shoot down any missiles fired toward Japan from North Korea. A backup layer was to consist of sixteen land-based Patriot missiles, also purchased from the United States, that were to be based in the vicinity of large Japanese cities.

Japan's participation was significant for another reason: Japan's constitution—drafted by the United States after World War II—enshrined a pacifist tradition that many Japanese had come to cherish. The constitution barred offensive operations by the Japanese military but allowed Japan to defend itself against potential attack, thus appearing to allow a missile defense program. Even so, the constitution did not allow Japan to export weapons—and under the system envisioned jointly by Tokyo and Washington Japan would develop some components that technically would be exported to the United States and possibly other countries.

Several European countries also were engaged in various aspects of the missile defense program. Early warning radars in Britain and Greenland—both dating from the cold war—were being modernized to provide better notice of missile launches. In September the United States, Italy, and Germany signed an agreement to develop a mobile system, called the Medium Extended Air Defense System or MEADS, that would be a new generation of defense against short-range missile attacks, including those against military forces in the field. The Pentagon also was considering installing radar installations in the Czech Republic, Poland, or Romania to monitor the launching of ballistic missiles from Russia and the Middle East.

The Bush administration encountered more resistance in Canada, where opinion polls showed strong public resistance to participation in the U.S. system. Bush met with Canadian prime minister Paul Martin on December 1 and pressed him to support the defense system. Martin on December 14 announced several conditions for his support, including that no missiles would be based in Canada and that space-based weapons would not be part of the system.

Bush and Russian president Vladimir Putin agreed in 2002, and again in 2003, to explore mutual cooperation on missile defense issues. By 2004 little cooperation appeared to have come out of those declarations, however, and a senior State Department official acknowledged to Congress on December 17 that "progress has been extremely slow." Putin in February announced that Russia was developing a new ballistic missile that, he said, was capable of overwhelming any planned missile defense system.

Following are excerpts from "Missile Defense: Actions Are Needed to Enhance Testing and Accountability," a report submitted to Congress April 23, 2004, by the General Accounting Office.

"Missile Defense"

Background

MDA [Missile Defense Agency] has the mission to develop and field a Ballistic Missile Defense System capable of defeating ballistic missiles of all ranges in all phases of flight. In particular, the system is intended to defend the U.S. homeland against intercontinental ballistic missile (ICBM) attacks and to protect deployed U.S. armed forces, which are operating in or near hostile territories, against short-and medium-range ballistic missiles. Additionally, the BMDS is to evolve into a system that is capable of defending friends and allies of the United States. . . .

Much of the operational capability of the Block 2004 BMDS [the portions of work on the Ballistic Missile Defense System to be done in fiscal year 2004] results from capabilities developed in legacy programs. These include the GMD [ground-based missile defense], Aegis BMD [missile defense system aboard Aegis cruisers and destroyers], and Patriot elements. Existing space-based sensors would also be available, including Defense Support Program satellites, for the early warning of missile launches. The Block 2004 BMDS can be viewed as a collection of semi-autonomous missile defense systems interconnected and coordinated through the Command, Control, Battle Management, and Communications (C2BMC) element. Functional pieces of system elements, such as radars or interceptors, are referred to as "components."

Block 2004 program goals involve developmental activities of five MDA elements: Aegis BMD, ABL [airborne laser], C2BMC [command, control, battle management, and communications], GMD [ground-based mid-course defense], and Theater High

Altitude Area Defense (THAAD). As indicated above, three of these five elements—GMD, Aegis BMD, and C2BMC—comprise the Block 2004 defensive capability that is currently being fielded. MDA is also funding the development of two other elements—Space Tracking and Surveillance System (STSS) and Kinetic Energy Interceptors (KEI)—but these elements are part of future blocks of the MDA missile defense program.

During Block 2006, MDA will focus on fielding additional hardware and enhancing the performance of the BMDS. For example, MDA plans to field additional GMD interceptors at Fort Greely, add new radars that can be deployed overseas, and incorporate enhanced battle management capabilities into the C2BMC element.

For Blocks 2008 and 2010, MDA plans to augment the Block 2006 capability with boost phase capabilities being developed in the ABL and KEI programs. Additionally, MDA plans to field the THAAD element for protecting deployed U.S. forces against short-and medium-range ballistic missiles.

According to MDA officials, the integrated BMDS offers more than simply the deployment of individual, autonomous elements. A synergy results from information sharing and enhanced command and control, yielding a layered defense with multiple shot opportunities. This preserves interceptor inventory and increases the opportunities to engage ballistic missiles. . . .

Results in Brief

MDA completed many activities in fiscal year 2003—such as software development, ground and flight testing, and facility construction at various BMDS sites—leading to the planned initial fielding of the BMDS by September 2004. During this time, however, MDA experienced significant schedule delays, conducted little testing of the integrated BMDS, and incurred cost overruns. Also, as a result of testing shortfalls, the predicted effectiveness of the Block 2004 system will be largely unproven. Furthermore, between its budget requests for fiscal years 2004 and 2005, MDA revised the goals for its first fielded block of missile defense capability by increasing costs by $1.12 billion and decreasing the number of fielded components.

Our overall assessment of MDA's progress in fiscal year 2003 toward meeting its schedule, testing, performance, and cost goals is discussed below. Key risks associated with the development and fielding of system elements are summarized as well.

- **Schedule and testing.** Primary system elements that make up the fielded Block 2004 defensive capability—Ground-based Midcourse Defense (GMD) and Aegis Ballistic Missile Defense (BMD)—are executing aggressive schedules to meet the fielding dates prescribed under the President's directive. These elements completed a number of activities that MDA expects will lead to the achievement of its program goals. For example, construction activities for facilities at Fort Greely, Alaska, and other GMD sites were completed on or ahead of schedule. However, based on progress made in fiscal year 2003, the actual defensive system to be fielded by September 2004 will have fewer components than planned. For example, we found that MDA will not meet its upper-end goal of fielding 10 GMD interceptors by September 2004. In addition, the agency will be hard-pressed to achieve its goal of producing and delivering an inventory of 20 GMD interceptors by December 2005, because GMD contractors have yet to meet the planned production rate.

MDA completed many activities toward the completion of the BMDS Test Bed, the venue in which system elements are integrated and tested. However, some element-level testing did not progress as planned. During fiscal year 2003, MDA achieved a 50-percent success rate on hit-to-kill intercepts—one success out of two attempts for each of the GMD and Aegis BMD elements. Also during this time period, delays in GMD interceptor development and delivery caused flight tests (intercept attempts) leading up to IDO to slip 10 months or more. Furthermore, unanticipated problems in system-integration efforts caused key Airborne Laser (ABL) demonstration events to slip over a year.

- **Performance.** MDA predicts with confidence that the September 2004 defensive capability will provide protection of the United States against limited attacks from Northeast Asia. However, testing in 2003 did little to demonstrate the predicted effectiveness of the system's capability to defeat ballistic missiles as an integrated system. None of the components of the defensive capability have yet to be flight tested in their fielded configuration (i.e., using production-representative hardware).
- **Cost.** We assessed prime contractor cost performance for six BMDS elements funded under the Block 2004 program. Four of the six elements completed fiscal year 2003 work at or near budgeted costs. However, work on ABL and GMD cost much more than budgeted. The ABL contractor overran budgeted costs by $242 million and the GMD contractor by $138 million.
- **Key risks.** Our analysis of fiscal year 2003 activities indicates there are key risks associated with the development and fielding of elements of the Block 2004 program. For example, significant uncertainty remains about how much more time and money are required to complete ABL integration activities and whether ABL can be proven to work effectively. MDA recently announced that a new contract structure is being implemented to more efficiently demonstrate the technology.

Also, as a result of testing shortfalls and the limited time available to test the BMDS being fielded, system effectiveness will be largely unproven when the initial capability goes on alert at the end of September 2004. Delays in flight testing presented MDA with limited opportunities to demonstrate the operation of hardware and software being fielded and to resolve any problems that may be uncovered during flight testing before September 2004. In addition, although MDA is attempting to make flight tests as realistic as possible, these tests will not be conducted under the unscripted conditions that characterize operational testing. Independent, operational testing through an operational test agent outside of the program being developed, and through the input of DOD's [Department of Defense] independent operational test and evaluation office, is intended to demonstrate objectively how capable a system truly is and whether the warfighter can trust it to be suitable and effective.

During our review, we observed shortcomings in how MDA defines its Block 2004 program goals. As discussed below, program goals do not serve as a reliable and complete baseline for oversight and investment decision-making because they can vary year-to-year, do not include life-cycle costs, and are based on assumptions about performance not explicitly stated.

- **Variable program goals.** MDA's methodology for establishing program goals—both cost and block content—allows for variations from one year to the next. MDA recognized that the first BMDS block will cost more and deliver fewer fielded components than originally planned. As reported in DOD budget submissions for fiscal years 2004 and 2005, the Block 2004 cost goal increased from $6.24 billion to $7.36 billion, the Aegis BMD interceptor inventory decreased from 20 to 9, the number of Aegis BMD ships upgraded for the long-range surveillance and tracking mission decreased from 15 to 10, and the potential operational use of ABL and the sea-based radar as sensors is no longer part of Block 2004. The variability weakens accountability because the goals cannot serve as a reliable baseline for measuring cost, schedule, and performance status over time.
- **Reporting life-cycle costs.** DOD categorizes the BMDS as a Research, Development, Testing, and Evaluation (RDT&E)-only program costing $53 billion between fiscal years 2004 and 2009. Accordingly, the BMDS Selected Acquisition Report does not specify costs for procurement, military construction, and operations and maintenance that are part of a full life-cycle cost estimate. Given the imminent fielding of a missile defense capability, procurement of inventory, and funding of operation and sustainment costs, this Selected Acquisition Report provides an incomplete cost picture to decision makers in DOD and Congress. MDA officials told us that they are working to include life-cycle cost estimates in future Selected Acquisition Reports for the BMDS.
- **Assumptions about performance.** BMDS performance goals, such as the probability of engagement success, are based on assumptions regarding the system's capability against certain threats under various engagement conditions. Neither the engagement conditions nor critical assumptions about the threat—such as the enemy's type and number of decoys—used in establishing these goals are explicitly stated as part of MDA's program goals. Without these implicit assumptions being explained, the operational capability of the fielded system is difficult to fully understand.

To more independently test the BMDS and give the warfighter greater confidence that the system will perform as intended, we are recommending that independent, operationally realistic testing and evaluation be conducted for each BMDS block configuration being fielded. Also, to enhance accountability and the ability of decision makers in Congress and DOD to provide oversight, we are recommending that cost, schedule, and performance baselines, including full life-cycle costs, be established for each block configuration being fielded and that year-to-year variations in baselines be explained. DOD concurred with our recommendations regarding cost, schedule, and performance baselines but non-concurred with our recommendations for operational testing.

In commenting on the draft report, DOD stated that there is no statutory requirement to conduct operational testing of developmental items and that it will conduct formal operational test and evaluation when an element of the BMDS matures and transitions from MDA to a military service and before entry into full-rate production. We retain our recommendation that DOD conduct independent, operational testing of block configurations being fielded. Given that inventory is being procured and the system is being fielded, decision makers considering further investments in the system should have an independent, objective assessment of whether the fielded system can be trusted to perform as intended. . . .

Source: U.S. Congress. General Accounting Office. "Missile Defense: Actions Are Needed to Enhance Testing and Accountability." GAO-04-409, April 23, 2004. www.gao.gov/new.items/d04409.pdf (accessed February 4, 2005).

Federal Reserve Board Chairman on Rising Energy Prices

April 27, 2004

INTRODUCTION

Instability in Iraq, supply problems, and booming demand for energy as a result of economic revivals worldwide contributed to the sharpest rise in oil prices in a quarter-century. For the first time ever Americans found themselves paying more than $2 for a gallon of gasoline. Although the spike in prices came as a shock and may have moderated economic growth in some places, in historical terms the year's energy prices were not extraordinary. Federal Reserve Board Chairman Alan Greenspan, in an April 27 speech, noted that—when inflation was taken into account—the price of crude oil at the time was only half of the level a quarter-century earlier.

Greenspan and others warned, however, that the world could not be complacent about the supply of energy, which was coming under increasing pressure because large developing countries such as China and India were beginning to compete with the longtime industrialized countries for oil and natural gas. Energy production was growing but at a much slower rate than demand. Rising demand had long-term consequences for world economies and the environment.

Worldwide Supply and Demand

The rapid rise in energy prices focused new public attention on what had been an academic argument among oil industry experts over one seemingly simple question: When, if ever, would the demand for oil significantly exceed the supply? At least through 2004, worldwide supply was keeping up with, and possibly even exceeding, demand, when new discoveries and new production techniques were taken into account. Energy pessimists argued that demand would begin to outrun supply within a decade or so; optimists foresaw several more decades in which new sources would keep supplies running ahead of the growing demand. In particular, the optimists pointed to new technology that enabled the oil industry to discover deposits that had been missed before and to extract more oil from old wells. Improved technology also made it economical for the industry to develop sources that in the past had been considered marginal, such as the oil-laden sands in Canada.

On the demand side, the single most important factor since the 1990s was the booming demand for energy in China, which for more than a decade had the world's fastest-growing economy. China was a net exporter of oil until 2001, when its own demands made it reach out for oil imports. By 2004 China had become the second largest importer of oil (after the United States), surpassing Japan. The rapid growth of industrial production was the major cause of China's increased demand, closely followed by the country's rapid adoption of the automobile as a form of individual transportation, replacing more energy-efficient bicycles. The Chinese were expected to buy more than 4.5 million cars in 2004.

In his April 27 speech to a conference on U.S.-Saudi Arabian energy relations at the Center for Strategic and International Studies in Washington, Greenspan said rising oil prices might dampen U.S. economic growth, but he expressed cautious optimism about the future of energy supplies and the long-term ability of the U.S. economy to deal with energy price increases. While demand in the United States continued to rise, he said, it had been moderated since the 1970s by conservation measures, such as fuel efficiency standards for automobiles. Improved technology, Greenspan said, also was likely "to make existing energy reserves stretch much further and to keep long-term energy costs lower than they otherwise would have been." And while the recent surge in oil prices (then to about $27 a barrel) had been dramatic, he said, "the price of crude oil in real terms [after inflation was taken into account] is only half of what it was in December 1979." That was the date of a major spike in oil prices resulting from the taking of hostages at the U.S. embassy in Tehran. *(Iran hostage crisis, Historic Documents of 1979, p. 867)*

The Year's Oil Price Fluctuations

Oil prices rose sharply during the first three quarters of 2004, then generally stabilized in the last quarter of the year, largely in response to world events and trends in the oil industry. Continuing instability in the Middle East—especially the ongoing violence in oil-exporting Iraq—was one factor, as was uncertainty about oil production in Russia, where the Kremlin used criminal prosecutions and other legal tactics to take over the country's largest private oil company. Questions about supply often were enough to cause prices to rise, but the effect of these questions was magnified by booming demand, which during most of the year exceeded expectations. The gradual economic recovery in Western industrialized countries, coupled with rapid economic growth in China, put even more pressure on prices.

The first major stimulus to prices came on February 10 when the Organization of Petroleum Exporting Countries (OPEC) announced a production cut of 1 million barrels a day, or about 5 percent of current production, saying the step was needed to stabilize prices. That announcement pushed prices for U.S. crude oil to $33.45 a barrel. After weeks of hesitation, OPEC confirmed its production cut decision on March 30, setting off another round of price increases and pushing oil costs to levels not seen since Iraq invaded Kuwait in 1990. *(Kuwait invasion, Historic Documents of 1990, p. 533)*

For Americans, the most visible sign of rising world oil prices was the rapid escalation of prices at the gasoline pumps. In fact, gasoline prices rose even more rapidly than oil prices because of differences in the gasoline marketplace. By mid-March the average price of a gallon of self-serve unleaded regular reached $1.74 in the United States, exceeding a record set in the summer of 2003 when demand also reached an all-time peak. Prices in mid-March jumped above $2 in California, where gasoline prices typically were 15–25 cents higher than national averages because of that state's tougher environmental regulations, higher taxes, and unique supply problems. U.S. gasoline prices were still far below those in most other countries.

The spike in gas prices pushed energy questions onto the election-year political agenda. President George W. Bush and his supporters called for Congress to pass his proposed energy legislation that emphasized increased production, including opening up the Alaska National Wildlife Refuge to drilling. The presumptive Democratic presidential candidate, Sen. John Kerry of Massachusetts, insisted the longer-term answer lay in greater focus on energy conservation and renewable energy sources.

The political debate did not address some of the underlying causes of the sharp increase in gasoline prices. Industry experts noted that the United States was becoming increasingly dependent on foreign sources for finished gasoline (as well as oil generally) because no new refineries had been built in the United States since the late 1970s. By 2004 about 10 percent of the gasoline used by Americans came from overseas. Venezuela was one of the largest foreign suppliers of finished gasoline; its production fell sharply early in 2003, and continued to be inconsistent into 2004, because of political turmoil there. The United States also had some of the world's toughest environmental regulations for gasoline, and that raised costs both for domestic and foreign suppliers. *(Venezuela, p. 548)*

As oil prices touched the $40-a-barrel level and average U.S. gasoline prices finally exceeded $2 a gallon in mid-May, some economists began warning about potential damage to economic recoveries in the United States and Europe. Apparently fearing negative consequences for the oil business, Saudi Arabia said it wanted OPEC to raise production. Other OPEC nations at first rejected that call but on June 2 agreed to boost production back to 25.5 million barrels a day, roughly where it had been before the earlier cutback. Even so, oil industry analysts noted that most OPEC countries already were pumping at close to their full capacity; Saudi Arabia was the major exception.

Economists had warned that rising energy prices might slow economic growth, and they appeared to be correct, at least on a temporary basis. Commerce Department figures released at the end of July showed that U.S. economic growth slowed to 3 percent in the second quarter of 2004, about one-third below the level of the first three months. Most economists said rising energy prices had led consumers to cut back their spending, which was the principal engine behind the U.S. economy. Major industries also reported that energy prices had cut into their profits, further dampening enthusiasm about the nation's economic recovery. *(Economic issues, p. 235)*

Oil prices continued to rise intermittently over the summer months, hitting $45 a barrel for the first time on August 11. Gasoline prices, by contrast, fell back below the $2 a gallon level in most of the country as inventories rose.

On October 1 instability in the oil-producing regions of Nigeria and hurricane damage to oil wells in the Gulf of Mexico finally drove oil prices over the $50-a-barrel mark, a symbolic milestone that previously had seemed almost beyond reach. The immediate cause was an outbreak of fighting between the government of Nigeria and Muslim rebels in the Niger River delta region who demanded a greater share of the nation's oil profits. Nigeria was a relatively small oil producer, but the temporary threat to its production threatened to add to the strain on an international oil industry that was having trouble keeping ahead of demand. Gulf of Mexico oil production also fell by about 20 percent when hurricane Ivan damaged several oil drilling platforms in September.

Oil prices briefly hit $55 a barrel in mid-to-late October, sparking some concerns that even a $60 price might be within reach. The $55 figure proved to be a high-water mark, however. On October 27 the Energy Department released figures showing a higher-than-expected increase in U.S. inventories of crude oil, and oil prices began what turned out to be an extended slide. Within a month oil prices had fallen back to $43 a barrel, and OPEC was again talking of cutting production to maintain what it called "stability" in the market. At year's end oil prices were still about $43 a barrel—nearly twice the level at the beginning of the year.

Cheney's Energy Task Force

The Supreme Court on June 24 effectively ended a long struggle over the Bush administration's reliance on private advice from energy industry officials to help it produce an "energy policy" in 2001. A task force headed by Vice President Dick Cheney met for months shortly after the Bush administration took office and produced a series of proposals calling for increased oil drilling and the lifting of environmental regulations on the energy industry. The Cheney task force report served as the basis for legislation Bush submitted to Congress and was still pending at the end of 2004. *(Background, Historic Documents of 2001, p. 331; Historic Documents of 2003, p. 1017)*

Environmental and public interest groups sued the administration to obtain information about the operations of Cheney's task force, most importantly the names of energy industry executives and lobbyists who had participated in its work. That suit worked its way through the judicial system and finally reached the Supreme Court in 2004. In its decision, the Court said a lower court in Washington, D.C., had acted prematurely in ordering Cheney to turn over the information. On a 7–2 vote, the Supreme Court sent the case, *Cheney v. United States District Court,* back to the appellate court for the District of Columbia, which took no further action during the year.

U.S. Energy Policy

Partisan and philosophical differences for years had stalled proposals by Bush and previous presidents for a coordinated federal policy on energy supply and demand. The Bush administration's emphasis on boosting production of coal, natural gas, and oil was popular with the energy industry but raised deep concerns among environmentalists. Both chambers of Congress approved legislation incorporating most elements of Bush's proposals, but Democrats managed to block final passage in the Senate.

An unusual attempt to develop a bipartisan compromise on energy matters was mounted by the National Commission on Energy Policy, which after two years of deliberations issued on December 8 a detailed report, "Ending the Energy Stalemate: A Bipartisan Strategy to Meet America's Energy Challenges." The commission was funded by several foundations and was composed of business executives, labor union leaders, environmentalists, academics, and others whose views often were sharply at odds on these issues. The panel was cochaired by John W. Rowe, chairman and chief executive office of Exelon Corp. (a public power utility), and John Holdren, professor of environmental policy at Harvard University.

As could be expected with such a diverse group, the commission's recommendations represented significant compromises and some were relatively noncontroversial, such as the need to diversify sources of energy supplies to avoid disruptions from terrorism and persistent crises in the Middle East. The panel reached consensus agreement on several recommendations that were routinely opposed by one or the other side in U.S. energy policy debates. Among these were proposals to enact mandatory limits on emissions of the so-called greenhouse gases that were said to contribute to global climate change; significantly boost fuel efficiency requirements for automobiles; fund construction of one or two nuclear power reactors using advanced technology; extend federal tax credits for wind, solar, and other renewable power sources; and provide federal financial incentives for construction of a pipeline to supply Alaskan natural gas to the lower forty-eight states. *(Climate change, p. 827)*

Final Report on 2003 Blackout

A U.S.-Canadian joint task force on April 5 issued its final report on the causes of a massive power blackout that darkened much of North America on August 14, 2003. The task force of energy officials from the U.S. and Canadian governments had issued a preliminary report in November 2003 describing how downed power lines near Akron, Ohio, had led to a cascading series of events that eventually deprived electrical power to about 50 million people. *(Background, Historic Documents of 2003, p. 1014)*

The final report essentially confirmed the findings of the earlier version, notably concerning failings of the main utility company in northeast Ohio, FirstEnergy Corporation, and the regional energy coordinator, Midwest Independent System Operator. Those two entities used computer systems that could not adequately monitor their transmission systems and failed to respond in time to the power failures resulting from the downed lines. The new report added several details, one of which was a conclusion that the broader blackout could have been averted if FirstEnergy had quickly responded by blacking out the Cleveland area. A FirstEnergy official disputed that argument, saying the company had no reason to "interrupt local customers in favor of long-distance transactions."

The final ask force report also raised questions about some consequences of the deregulation of the energy industry during the 1990s. In particular, the report said a major factor in the 2003 blackout was a lack of what engineers called "reactive power"—the component of electricity that maintained magnetic fields around electrical equipment. FirstEnergy and some energy analysts had said recent changes in the electrical power industry fostered by deregulation, notably the nation's increasing reliance on long-distance transmissions, had led to a reduction in reactive power. In its preliminary report, the joint task force had played down the role of reactive power in the 2003 blackout, but the final version said diminished reactive power had been a significant contributing factor.

Following is the text of an address April 27, 2004, by Alan Greenspan, chairman of the Federal Reserve Board, to a conference on U.S.-Saudi Arabian energy relations, held at the Center for Strategic and International Studies in Washington, D.C., in which he described the economic challenges posed by increased energy prices.

"Remarks by Chairman Alan Greenspan: Energy"

The dramatic rise in six-year forward futures prices for crude oil and natural gas over the past few years has received relatively little attention for an economic event that can significantly affect the long-term path of the U.S. economy. Six years is a period long enough to seek, discover, drill, and lift oil and gas, and hence futures prices at that horizon can be viewed as effective long-term supply prices.

These elevated long-term prices, if sustained, could alter the magnitude of and manner in which the United States consumes energy. Until recently, long-term expectations of oil and gas prices appeared benign. When choosing capital projects, businesses could mostly look through short-run fluctuations in prices to moderate prices over the longer haul. The recent shift in expectations, however, has been substantial enough and persistent enough to influence business investment decisions, especially for facilities that require large quantities of natural gas. Although the effect of these developments on energy-related investments is significant, it doubtless will fall far short of the large changes in our capital stock that followed the 1970s surge in crude oil prices.

The energy intensity [a measure of energy use as a percentage of the gross domestic product] of the United States economy has been reduced by almost half since the early 1970s. Much of the energy displacement occurred by 1985, within a few years of the peak in the real price of oil. Progress in reducing energy intensity has continued since then, but at a lessened pace. This more-modest pace should not be surprising, given the generally lower level of real oil and natural gas prices that prevailed between 1985 and 2000 and that carried over into electric power prices.

The production side of the oil and gas markets also has changed dramatically over the past decade. Technological changes taking place are likely to make existing energy reserves stretch further and to keep long-term energy costs lower than they otherwise would have been. Seismic techniques and satellite imaging, which are facilitating the discovery of promising new reservoirs of crude oil and natural gas worldwide, have nearly doubled the success rate of new-field wildcat wells in the United States during the past decade. New techniques allow far deeper drilling of promising fields, especially offshore. The newer innovations in recovery are reported to have increased significantly the average proportion of oil and, to a lesser extent, gas reserves eventually brought to the surface.

One might expect that, as a consequence of what has been a dramatic shift from the hit-or-miss wildcat oil and gas exploration and development of the past to more-advanced technologies, the cost of developing new fields and, hence, the long-term supply price of new oil and gas would have declined. And, indeed, these costs have declined, but by less than might otherwise have been the case. Much of the innovation in oil development outside OPEC [Organization of Petroleum Exporting Countries], for example, has been directed at overcoming an increasingly inhospitable and costly exploratory environment, the consequence of more than a century of draining the more immediately accessible sources of crude oil.

Still, distant futures prices for crude oil moved lower, on net, during the 1990s as a result of declining long-term marginal costs of extraction. The most-distant futures prices fell from a bit more than $20 per barrel just before the first Gulf War [1991] to $16 to $18 a barrel in 1999. Distant futures for natural gas, which were less than $2 per million Btu at the time of the first Gulf War drifted up to $2.50 per million Btu by 1999, although those prices remained below the prices of oil on an equivalent Btu basis.

Such long-term price tranquility has faded noticeably over the past four years. Between 1990 and 2000, although spot prices ranged between $11 and $35 per barrel, distant futures exhibited little variation. Currently prices for delivery in 2010 of light sweet crude, roughly equal to West Texas intermediate, have risen to more than $27 per barrel. A similar pattern is evident in natural gas. Even the spikes in the spot price in 2000 had only a temporary effect on distant natural gas futures prices. That situation changed in 2001, however, when the distant futures prices for gas delivery at the Henry Hub [a natural gas port in Louisiana; its prices were the benchmark for U.S. natural gas prices] began a rise from $3.20 per million Btu to almost $5 today.

The reasons for the sharp increases in both crude and gas distant futures prices seem reasonably straightforward, though they differ in important respects. The strength of crude oil prices presumably reflects fears of long-term supply disruptions in the Middle East that have resulted in an increase in risk premiums being added to the cost of capital. Although there are competitive spillovers from the higher price of oil, the causes of the rise in the long-term supply price of natural gas appear related primarily to supply and demand in North America.

Today's tight natural gas markets have been a long time in coming. Little more than a half-century ago, drillers seeking valuable crude oil bemoaned the discovery of natural gas. Given the lack of adequate transportation, wells had to be capped or the gas flared. As the U.S. economy expanded after World War II, the development of a vast interstate transmission system facilitated widespread consumption of natural gas in our homes and business establishments. By 1970, natural gas consumption, on a heat-equivalent basis [a measure of energy use], had risen to three-fourths that of oil. But in the following decade consumption lagged because of competitive inroads made by coal and nuclear power. Since 1985, natural gas has gradually increased its share in total energy use and, owing to its status as a clean-burning fuel, is projected by the Energy Information Administration of the United States to maintain that higher share over the next quarter century.

Dramatic changes in technology in recent years, while making existing natural gas reserves stretch further, have been unable, in the face of inexorably rising demand, to keep the underlying long-term price for natural gas in the United States from rising.

Over the past few decades, short-term movements in domestic prices in the markets for crude oil have been determined largely by international market participants, especially OPEC. But that was not always the case.

In the early years of oil development, pricing power was firmly in the hands of Americans, predominately John D. Rockefeller and Standard Oil. Reportedly appalled by the volatility of crude oil prices in the early years of the petroleum industry, Rockefeller endeavored with some success to control those prices. After the breakup of Standard Oil in 1911, pricing power remained with the United States—first with the U.S. oil companies and later with the Texas Railroad Commission, which raised allowable output to suppress price spikes and cut output to prevent sharp declines. Indeed, as late as 1952 U.S. crude oil production still accounted for more than half of the world total. However, that historical role came to an end in 1971, when excess capacity in the United States was finally absorbed by rising demand.

At that point, the marginal pricing of oil, which for so long had been resident on the gulf coast of Texas, moved to the Persian Gulf. To capitalize on their newly acquired pricing power, many producing nations in the Middle East nationalized their oil companies. But the full magnitude of their pricing power became evident only in the aftermath of the oil embargo of 1973. During that period, posted crude oil prices at Ras Tanura [the main oil port in Saudi Arabia, north of Dhahran] rose to more than $11 per barrel, significantly above the $1.80 per barrel that had been unchanged from 1961 to 1970.

The sharp price increases of the early 1970s brought to an abrupt end the extraordinary period of growth in U.S. oil consumption and the increased intensity of its use that was so evident in the decades immediately following World War II. Between 1945 and 1973, consumption of oil products rose at a startling $4\frac{1}{2}$ percent average annual rate, well in excess of growth of real gross domestic product. However, since 1973, oil consumption has grown, on average, only $\frac{1}{2}$ percent per year, far short of the rise in real GDP.

Although OPEC production quotas have been a significant factor in price determination for a third of a century, the story since 1973 has been as much one of the power of markets as of power over markets. The signals provided by market prices have eventually resolved even the most seemingly insurmountable difficulties of inadequate domestic supply in the United States. The gap projected between supply and demand in the immediate post-1973 period was feared by many to be so large that rationing would be the only practical solution.

But the resolution did not occur quite that way. To be sure, mandated fuel-efficiency standards for cars and light trucks accompanied slower growth of gasoline demand. Some observers argue, however, that, even without government-enforced standards, market forces would have produced increased fuel efficiency. Indeed, the number of small, fuel-efficient Japanese cars that were imported into the United States markets grew significantly in the late 1970s after the Iranian Revolution drove up crude oil prices to nearly $40 per barrel.

Moreover, at that time, prices were expected to go still higher. Projections of $50 per barrel or more were widely prevalent. Our Department of Energy had baseline projections showing prices reaching $60 per barrel—the equivalent of more than twice that in today's prices.

The failure of oil prices to rise as projected in the late 1970s is a testament to the power of markets and the technologies they foster. Today, despite its recent surge, the price of crude oil in real terms is only half of what it was in December 1979.

As I indicated earlier, the rise in six-year oil and gas futures prices is almost surely going to affect the growth of oil and gas consumption in the United States and the nature of the capital stock investments currently under contemplation. However, the responses are likely to differ somewhat between plans for oil and those for gas usage.

OPEC, the source of greatest supply flexibility, has endeavored to calibrate crude oil liftings to price. They fear that significant supply excesses will drive down prices and revenues, whereas too low a level of output will elevate prices to a point that will induce long-term reductions in demand for oil and in the associated long-term revenues to be earned from oil.

Natural gas pricing, on the other hand, is inherently far more volatile than oil, doubtless reflecting, in part, less-developed, price-damping global trade. Because gas is particularly challenging to transport in its cryogenic form as a liquid, imports of liquefied natural gas (LNG) into the United States to date have been negligible, accounting for only 2 percent of U.S. gas supply in 2003. Environmental and safety concerns and cost considerations have limited the number of terminals available for importing LNG. Canada, which has recently supplied a sixth of our consumption, has little capacity to significantly expand its exports, in part because of the role that Canadian gas plays in supporting growing oil production from tar sands.

Given notable cost reductions for both liquefaction and transportation of LNG, significant global trade is developing. And high natural gas prices projected by distant futures prices have made imported gas a more attractive option for us. According to the tabulations of BP, worldwide imports of natural gas in 2002 were only 23 percent of world consumption, compared with 57 percent for oil. Clearly, the gas trade has a long way to go.

The gap in the behaviors of the markets for oil and for natural gas is readily observable. The prices of crude oil and products are subject to much price arbitrage, which has the effect of encouraging the transportation of supplies from areas of relative surplus to those of relative shortage and of thereby containing local price spikes. This effect was most vividly demonstrated in 2003, when Venezuelan oil production was essentially shut down. American refiners with unlimited access to world supplies were able to replace lost oil with diversions from Europe, Asia, and the Middle East.

If North American natural gas markets are to function with the flexibility exhibited by oil, more extensive access to the vast world reserves of gas is required. Markets need to be able to adjust effectively to unexpected shortfalls in domestic supply in the same way that they do in oil. Access to world natural gas supplies will require a major expansion of LNG terminal import capacity and the development of the newer offshore regasification technologies. Without the flexibility such facilities impart, imbalances in supply and demand must inevitably engender price volatility.

As the technology of LNG liquefaction and shipping has improved and as safety considerations have lessened, a major expansion of U.S. import capability appears to be under way. These movements bode well for widespread natural gas availability in North America in the next decade and beyond. The near term, however, is apt to continue to be challenging.

Source: U.S. Federal Reserve Board. "Remarks by Chairman Alan Greenspan: Energy." Speech presented at the Center for Strategic and International Studies, Washington, D.C. April 27, 2004. www.federalreserve.gov/boarddocs/speeches/2004/20040427/default.htm (accessed January 24, 2005).

May

2004 HISTORIC DOCUMENTS

EU Officials on the Addition of Ten New Member Nations

May 1, 2004

INTRODUCTION

Ten countries—most of them former communist societies in central and eastern Europe—swelled the membership of the European Union (EU) to twenty-five on May 1, 2004. With a few exceptions, the new EU members all were significantly poorer than the fifteen existing members of the world's largest economic, political, and trade grouping.

The biggest single expansion in EU history was the most dramatic of a series of major events during the year for the union. After years of debate, the EU in October adopted a new constitution; steps were taken to encourage the future membership of three other countries, including Turkey, which had knocked at Europe's door for four decades; and the union's executive body, the European Commission, underwent its first wholesale change in five years—but only after a nasty feud over the qualifications of some of the commissioners. On December 2 the EU took its most important step yet toward exercising its own military capability, independent of NATO, by assuming full responsibility for peacekeeping in Bosnia. The EU took over from NATO, which had been enforcing a 1995 peace treaty that ended the biggest war in Europe since World War II. *(Turkey, p. 973)*

Ten New EU Members

The EU traced its history to the years after World War II, when six countries (Belgium, France, Germany, Italy, Luxembourg, and the Netherlands) founded the European Coal and Steel Community to stimulate industrial development in lands still devastated by the war. By 1973 the name had been changed to the European Economic Community, and three new members were added: Britain, Denmark, and Ireland. Greece joined in 1981; Portugal and Spain joined five years later. After the collapse of communism in eastern Europe and the Soviet Union, the European Community adopted the name European Union and became committed to broadening its membership and deepening its role in the economic and political affairs of all member countries. The admission of Austria, Finland, and Sweden brought the EU's membership to fifteen in 1995. Another key step came in 1999 when most EU members began a phased adoption of the euro as a common currency, replacing such familiar national denominations as the franc, the Deutschmark, and the lira. *(Background, Historic Documents of 1999, p. 75)*

By the mid-1990s the leaders of nearly all the formerly communist countries of central and eastern Europe realized that turning westward—toward Europe—held a much greater promise of economic and social progress than continuing to lean eastward—toward a Russia still trying to shake off its own legacy of decades of communist corruption, dictatorship, and mismanagement. A dozen countries applied for EU membership, and in 2002 ten of them were invited into membership by 2004: Cyprus, the Czech Republic, Estonia, Hungary, Latvia, Lithuania, Malta, Poland, Slovakia, and Slovenia. All but the Mediterranean islands of Cyprus and Malta had been under the domination of the Soviet Union during the cold war. The Czech Republic, Hungary, and Poland had joined the NATO alliance in 1997, and all the others except Cyprus and Malta officially joined NATO on March 29, 2004—a little over a month before their accession to the EU. *(NATO expansion, p. 135; Background, Historic Documents of 2002, p. 885, Historic Documents of 2003, p. 492)*

Voters in nine of the ten new member countries had approved EU membership in referendums, most of which passed by wide margins. However, these votes had disguised deep unease in some of the countries. Poland's farmers were worried about their ability to compete with the more industrialized agricultural sectors in western Europe, and the ethnic Russian minorities in the three Baltic states (Estonia, Latvia, and Lithuania) feared being left in the lurch as those countries turned their backs on Russia.

By 2004 sentiment about EU expansion also was mixed in the fifteen "old" member countries. Polls showed that support for the EU itself had fallen sharply in most of those countries, and many people worried about losing their jobs to low-wage immigrants from Poland or their city streets being taken over by criminal gangs from eastern Europe. Moreover, some of the current EU countries were beset by long-term economic woes (notably low growth rates and high unemployment). French and German citizens, in particular, seemed concerned that these troubles were likely to be exacerbated, rather than reduced, by a broader European Union. Voters and leaders in the three poorest EU nations—Greece, Portugal, and Spain—also worried that the new members would siphon off much of the subsidies they had been receiving under the union's programs to equalize the economies of its members.

These complaints were set aside temporarily on May 1, the day the ten countries officially joined the EU, bringing the union's total population to about 450 million. May Day traditionally was regarded in Europe as a celebration of workers' rights, but this May Day put a cap on the transformation of central and eastern Europe from communism and dictatorship to capitalism and democracy. At midnight in Lithuania thousands of bonfires lit up the night sky in celebration. In Estonia volunteers planted more than 20,000 trees. Former enemies during Europe's many wars, ancient and modern, greeted each other in peace. Germany's president, Johannes Rau, addressed Poland's parliament and said: "For Germany and Poland a completely new chapter in our relationship as neighbors is beginning, a new epoch with great possibilities and wide-reaching perspectives." In Slovakia, parliament chairman Pavol Hrusovsky gave this graphic reminder to his fellow legislators of the progress made since the fall of the Berlin Wall nearly fifteen years earlier: "In 1989, we cut up the barbed wire," he said. "Pieces of this wire have for us become a symbol of the end of the totalitarian regime. For the generation which lived in captivity of the barbed wire, the EU means a fulfillment of a dream." *(Fall of the Berlin Wall, Historic Documents of 1989, p. 625)*

The official celebration took place in Dublin, not for any historical reason but because Irish prime minister Bertie Ahern happened to hold the six-month presidency of the European Council, the EU's highest decision-making body. On a sunny day, thousands of people crowded into the city center for a celebration called the European Fair, featuring food, drink, and products from across the EU. As the leaders of all EU nations watched in a park, young people raised the twenty-five national flags and a choir sang the "Ode to Joy" from Beethoven's Ninth Symphony. Ahern said Europe was now at peace and would remain so. "From hatred there is now respect, from division there is union, and from dictatorship and oppression there is democracy."

The May 1 celebrations marked just the beginning, not the end, of the road for the EU's new members. As the price of membership, each country had pledged to bring its laws and regulations into line with EU standards, known as the *acquis communitaire,* and some aspects of that complex process were still under way in 2004. The new members also were required to reform their budget processes and to reduce their budget deficits before they could adopt the euro in place of their currencies. The European Central Bank, which administered the euro, on October 20 issued a report warning that most of the ten new members were falling behind the schedule to join the "euro zone" by the goal of 2010. Budget reforms were "too slow" and budget deficits were "not sustainable in the medium term" for the new members, the bank warned. Estonia was in the best shape overall, and Hungary was the worst performer, with inflation at 6.5 percent and a budget deficit of 5.5 percent of gross domestic product—nearly twice the 3 percent maximum, the bank said.

Bulgaria and Romania: Next in Line

Along with Turkey, Bulgaria and Romania were awaiting formal invitations for EU membership. Both had been communist dictatorships during the cold war, and both had experienced political upheaval and uneven economic progress since the collapse of communism. In 2002 both were invited to join the NATO alliance, and their NATO membership became official on March 29, 2004.

Of these two prospective entries, Romania's appeared to be the more difficult case for the EU, largely because the country's political situation remained unstable. Since the collapse of its communist regime in 1989, Romania had lurched from one political extreme to another. In the late 1990s an upsurge of nationalism threatened to open long-suppressed divisions between the country's ethnic Romanian majority and ethnic Hungarian minority.

Parliamentary and presidential elections on November 28, 2004, fell short of international standards, according to most official observers, but probably were no more fraudulent than previous ones in the country. The ruling Social Democrat Party (the renamed and somewhat reformed former Communist Party) claimed 37 percent of the vote in parliamentary elections, five points ahead of the center-right opposition, the Alliance for Justice and Truth. Presidential elections in the first round were inconclusive, with outgoing prime minister Adrian Nastaste of the Social Democrat Party finishing with 41 percent of the vote, seven points ahead of opposition candidate Traian Basescu, the mayor of Bucharest. Basescu narrowly won the runoff on December 12 with slightly more than 51 percent of the vote.

Three days before the final presidential vote, EU and Romanian negotiators settled on a plan under which Romania would become an EU member in 2007. However, the agreement provided for a fail-safe mechanism for the Europeans: Romania's entry could be delayed by a year if the country failed to make sufficient reforms in curbing corruption, allowing freedom of expression, and providing for independence of the court system.

Several of the Balkan countries that had been torn by civil conflict during the 1990s also were hoping for invitations to discuss possible EU membership. Croatia appeared to be at the head of the list, but continuing turmoil in Bosnia, Macedonia, and Serbia-Montenegro limited their chances to join the EU anytime soon. Albania also hoped for membership but was deeply mired in corruption. *(Balkan nations, p. 949)*

New EU Constitution

For several years the prospective addition of ten new members had forced the EU to confront the question of how to manage such an unwieldy organization—with twenty-five member countries ranging in size from Luxembourg to Germany. The numerous governing bodies of the fifteen-member EU often had difficulty reaching agreement on common policies and laws, and it long had been clear that bringing ten new voices to the table would make consensus even more difficult to achieve. Even simple tasks—such as giving each of the twenty-five leaders a chance to speak at meetings—posed logistical hurdles.

Meeting in Nice in late 2000, EU leaders had hammered out a governing structure that gave the smaller countries a near-equal voice to the larger ones. But that accord merely papered over fundamental disagreements and came under strong attack almost as soon as it was signed. Just one year later the EU leaders decided to try to develop a more permanent solution: a formal constitution to replace the network of treaties that served as the union's legal underpinning. A constitutional convention, headed by former French president Valery Giscard d'Estaing, worked all through 2002 and produced a draft document in February 2003. That draft satisfied few and was replaced by a new one in June 2003, which also failed to produce the required consensus among EU leaders at the December 2003 summit. *(EU constitution, Historic Documents of 2003, p. 492)*

Several issues plagued the constitution-writing process, the most vexing of which involved allocating political power among the twenty-five member countries, defining the boundaries between the laws and regulations of each member country and those of the union as a whole, and the union's taxing and spending powers. Large countries—especially Britain, France, and Germany—had fundamentally different views on each of these matters from those held by the union's numerous smaller countries.

Negotiators went back to the drawing board early in 2004 and produced yet another draft, which EU leaders accepted on June 28 after two days of hard bargaining in Brussels. The key compromise came on the question of political power—how many votes it would take to pass legislation in the EU's law-making bodies. Under the compromise, new laws need to be supported by at least 55 percent of the member states (or fourteen of the twenty-five members) representing at least 65 percent of the union's total population of about 450 million. Together, these provisions offered some assurance both to small countries and to large ones because the votes of the more numerous small countries would be needed to reach the 55 percent majority, but if the four largest EU nations (Britain, France, Germany, and Italy) voted together, they could block legislation through the population requirement.

The new draft retained the complex system under which the EU had two "presidents," one of whom headed the executive branch (the European Commission) while the other headed the most powerful legislative body, the European Council, which was composed of the leaders of the member nations. The role of the latter president underwent significant change. Previously, the council presidency rotated among the EU's national leaders every six months, thus severely limiting the position's influence. Under the new setup, the presidency would be a full-time job, with a term of two-and-a-half years that could be renewed once. Although the powers of the office were not significantly expanded, the new nature of the job offered the prospect that a dynamic leader could exercise great influence as Europe's single most visible leader.

The constitution also sought to end some of the ambiguity over the EU's role in international affairs. Previously, two separate officials appeared to be authorized to speak for the union on the world stage: the high representative for the common foreign and security policy and the commissioner for external affairs. The constitution merged these roles into that of a union minister for foreign affairs—a position with the potential authority of the U.S. secretary of state but without some of the American's administrative powers. The new minister's main handicap was that he or she could speak for the union only when all twenty-five countries agreed to a common policy; any dissent and his or her hands would be tied.

EU leaders formally signed the new constitution during a meeting in Rome on October 29. Even that step did not finally resolve the matter, however. A key provision was that the constitution would take legal effect in two years (by the end of October 2006) unless it had been rejected by any one of the union's twenty-five member states. In effect, that provision gave veto power over the new constitution to all countries. Bowing to public demands for votes, nine of the twenty-five had scheduled referendums: the Czech Republic, Denmark, France, Ireland, Luxembourg, the Netherlands, Portugal, Spain, and the United Kingdom. Putting the constitution to a public vote was a risky step, as demonstrated by several previous referendums on EU-related questions; for example, voters in Denmark and Ireland had initially rejected important EU treaties in the past but then voted yes in later votes. As of the end of 2004, EU leaders had failed to address the question of what would happen in the likely event that one or more countries rejected the new constitution.

New European Commission Leadership

The tussle over the new constitution was resolved fairly amicably in mid-2004, but another dispute illuminated even more clearly the political fractures in an institution of twenty-five diverse countries: who would succeed Romano Prodi, who was scheduled to step down after five years as president of the European Commission, the main executive body? A former Italian prime minister, Prodi planned to return to his home country to mount an eventual challenge to the incumbent, Silvio Berlusconi. Prodi's tenure at the helm of the commission had been marked by numerous controversies, and the general consensus in Europe appeared to be that he had been a lackluster and uncertain leader.

By June a half-dozen potential candidates had emerged to succeed Prodi, including Belgian prime minister Guy Verhofstadt (supported by France and Germany but opposed by Britain) and Chris Patten, the union's commissioner of external affairs (supported by Britain, his home country, but opposed by France). Blackballed by major powers, each of these candidates pulled out of the race in late June, presenting the EU leaders with the ticklish task of finding a consensus candidate. This was a challenge for several reasons, notably the lingering division over the Iraq war, which had split Europe more deeply than any other issue in decades.

Eventually, a consensus candidate emerged: José Manuel Barroso, the center-right prime minister of Portugal. Barroso had not been the first choice of any EU leader, but more important he was not strongly opposed by any of them. Several commentators suggested that Barroso thus was a "least common denominator" candidate. EU leaders agreed on him during their Brussels summit on June 28, and the European Parliament ratified his selection on July 22.

Barroso's noncontroversial stature may have helped him win a coveted post, but it also meant that he entered office lacking real political clout—the currency of power. This became abundantly clear in October, when his nominees for the twenty-four European Commission cabinet posts came up for confirmation by the European Parliament. By far the most controversial was Rocco Buttiglione, an Italian politician nominated to be commissioner for justice and home affairs, one of the most important commission posts. Buttiglione's disparaging comments about women and homosexuals raised the hackles of many in the parliament, where a committee voted to oppose his nomination. Italian prime minister Berlusconi, who had sponsored Buttiglione for the job, refused to withdraw his colleague's name, forcing Barroso to stand by him as well. In the resulting turmoil parliamentarians challenged several other nominees for commission posts.

The climax came October 27, when the parliament was scheduled to vote on the full slate of twenty-four nominees Barroso had submitted. Moments before the vote was to occur, Barroso addressed the parliament and withdrew his slate, acknowledging that he lacked the votes to win approval. Three days later Buttiglione withdrew his own name, although insisting that his views on women and homosexuals had been distorted by the news media.

Barroso went back to work to negotiate a new lineup for his commission, and by mid-November had replaced Buttiglione with Italy's outgoing foreign minister, Franco Frattini. Barroso made two other changes involving slightly less controversial nominees, and the result was approval of the entire slate by the parliament on November 18—nearly three weeks after the commission was supposed to have taken office. Barroso insisted he emerged from this political struggle with great political strength because he demonstrated a willingness to listen to his critics. Even so, his critics in the parliament also appeared buoyed by their unusual demonstration of political muscle.

Following are excerpts of speeches delivered May 1, 2004, at the official ceremonies in Dublin, Ireland, commemorating the addition of ten new member nations to the European Union. The speeches were delivered by Bertie Ahern, the prime minister of Ireland and the current president of the European Council; Pat Cox, president of the European Parliament; and Romano Prodi, president of the European Commission.

Presidents Address European Union Accession Day Conference

Remarks by Bertie Ahern, President of the European Council

I am delighted and honoured to be here today as President-in-Office of the European Council. I am joined by the President of the European Parliament, Pat Cox, and the President of the European Commission, Romano Prodi. We are here together as representatives of the main institutions of the European Union to mark a hugely significant moment in Europe's history.

We are welcoming ten new Member States into the European Union.

Today marks a new beginning for Europeans. I would like to take this opportunity to acknowledge the many millions of people across Europe for whom this day—the first of May 2004—is a day of hope and opportunity.

To the people of Europe who are joining us today in the European Union, I extend the hand of friendship. It was your democratic choice and your own efforts that made this day happen. Today marks the triumph of your determination and perseverance over the legacy of history.

Over the past years, you have been knocking on the door of Europe's biggest family. Today, we open it and in the great Irish tradition, bid you a "céad míle fáilte"—a hundred, thousand welcomes.

We feel honoured that you are joining us. We feel pride that the European Union has attracted, and continues to attract, new members. Enlargement is a testament to the European Union's success.

Our Union will change with twenty-five members. That is inevitable. But that change will be for the better. The Union has been strengthened and enhanced by the contributions of each of its current members. Ten more members will enhance and strengthen the Union that much more.

We look forward to the unique contributions that the new members will make to the European Union. Each of us brings our own culture. We bring a particular history and a unique vision.

The sheer range and scale of our historical experience and our different perspectives are enormous assets. With these assets, we can promote the values of the European Union together. Working together will benefit us all. And, what is more, working together we will help to reinforce Europe as an area united in peace and stability, acting as a force for good in the world.

To the new Member States, I want to stress that the European Union poses no threat to your uniqueness. On the contrary. The Union enables us to celebrate our diversity. At the same time, working together, we can succeed for all the people of Europe.

Our first major task together will be to agree a new Constitutional Treaty. In March, we decided to reach agreement, at the latest, by the June European Council meeting. President Cox and President Prodi share my hope that agreement will be achieved at the earliest possible opportunity.

Although there are significant issues to be resolved in the negotiations on the Constitutional Treaty, there are very large parts of it that are agreed. On the more difficult and sensitive issues which remain, I firmly believe a way forward can be found with the necessary political will.

The Constitutional Treaty will help to ensure that the new needs and circumstances of the European Union are reflected in its basic law. It will improve the foundations for democratic discourse in the European Union. It will build on the success of the European Union and it will make the work of the Union more accessible and effective.

And there remain other challenges. We will have to continue our work to protect our citizens from the scourge of terrorism. We must work harder to create jobs and growth. And many outside the European Union look to us to assist them in building the peace and prosperity we enjoy. There is indeed much work to be done.

But for now, we pause to reflect—and to celebrate! . . .

We are hosting this ceremony because we believe that it is important for the democratic leaders of Europe to acknowledge what the European Union has achieved for the people of Europe. . . .

For Europe, today marks the closure of one chapter and the opening of another new and exciting chapter in its long history.

The European Union that the new Member States are joining has been a resounding success. It has delivered prosperity for its people by providing a framework within which economies can grow and people thrive. It has promoted democracy and equality and tackled poverty and exclusion. Now we must ensure that the Union continues to achieve success for its citizens into the future.

Thank you.

Remarks by Pat Cox, President of the European Parliament

. . . This new continent-wide Europe, stretching from Dublin in the west to Lublin in the east, from the Connemara to Latgale, is witness to the success of the new Member States and those societies which have undergone a radical transformation over the last 15 years. It is also the result of the determined and consistent effort by successive Presidencies, Member States and the European institutions, who have overcome obstacles on the road and provided sustained leadership for the earliest possible enlargement.

Fifty years ago a generation of European leaders, after a devastating war that divided our continent, saw all too clearly what was, but were prepared to dream of what could be. They had the courage of their European convictions. They opened for Europe a pathway to creative reconciliation and progress which none had walked before. We are the beneficiaries of that legacy and of their foresight. With the ceremony today we give a new meaning, a new raison d'être to and a new vindication of that vision.

I acknowledge today the leadership and determination of peoples and successive governments in the new member states. Today the transforming generation of leaders is awarded a glittering prize.

Now a new challenge faces leaders to spread the benefits of accession, to use the access to markets to engender prosperity and prepare for entry into the EMU. To achieve this, the new members need to be able to count on the solidarity of others.

The new member states will now be firmly anchored in the community of values, which inform and permeate the public purpose of the Union. Their rightful place at the heart of this community will also give them new confidence, new dynamism, which will generate positive effects on the whole Union.

In time, it will help us to rediscover of the spirit of 1989, that annus mirabilis, which has since yielded in some places to feelings of uncertainty, and some economic hardship. The dynamic young societies of many member states, their courage to transform, their entrepreneurial spirit will, I hope, help us all to strengthen the dynamic of the Union itself and reinforce its global role, including and perhaps especially towards our new neighbours in the South and in the East. . . .

Remarks by Romano Prodi, President of the European Commission

This is truly an historic and a happy day. It gives me great pleasure to be here in Dublin on this occasion and to be able to celebrate with you the achievement of the key goal of my Presidency of the European Commission.

For many long years we have been preparing the ground for the accession to the European Union of these 10 countries from central and eastern Europe and the Mediterranean. The negotiations we have conducted, while difficult at times, bear witness to our common commitment to unify our continent and finally to end the artificial division the Iron Curtain imposed on us for more than half a century.

First, I want to pay tribute to the peoples of Europe who are joining us today. Even in the darkest days of Stalinism, they never lost hope. Since the fall of the Berlin Wall, they have carried out a quiet revolution based on the democratic values that are our common heritage today.

I also want to pay tribute to the leaders of these countries—to the Governments and Parliaments that have followed since the fall of the Berlin Wall. Despite difficulties of all sorts, they have managed to mobilise the whole population in their countries and implement courageous reforms. And I also want to pay tribute to the peoples of the 15 older members for welcoming in the new countries and sharing their area of prosperity and security with them.

These reforms now mean the new members can join our institutions with their heads held high, with equal rights and responsibilities. . . .

Although the Union is now closer to becoming geographically coterminous with our continent, we still have much unfinished business to attend to.

Last weekend's disappointing referendum result in Cyprus demonstrates that the achievement of the grand goal of a broad-based European unification can still be undermined by unresolved regional concerns.

Throughout its history, the European Union has already demonstrated its capacity to act as a reliable and trustworthy broker in overcoming such problems. Indeed the Union's capacity to accommodate diversity is one of its strengths.

With this enlargement, the Union has grown one third geographically and one fifth in population, but we cannot and must not rest on our laurels. There are other candidates whose aspirations must be given due consideration. Since negotiations with 10 new members were completed, the Commission has recommended opening negotiations with Croatia.

Negotiations are progressing well with Bulgaria and Romania. And the Council will take a decision on Turkey at the end of the year on the basis of the recommendation that my Commission will adopt in the autumn.

The Union must also assume its responsibilities towards the other neighbouring countries with whom, from today, we share a land border of over 5,000 kilometres. This has brought a new dimension to our strategic thinking.

In order to meet this challenge, the Commission I lead has proposed a New Neighbourhood Policy. And I am happy to say it has received strong support from the Member States. The goal is to create a ring of friends, stretching from Russia to Morocco, with whom we share common concerns, both political and economic, and thereby prevent new dividing lines being drawn across Europe and barriers across the Mediterranean.

In a sense, this is another concept of enlargement—enlargement without sharing our institutions.

Another awesome challenge we must face together at present is the need to combat terrorism, the evil spectre that haunts all of us who strive for peace. No country can stand alone against this sinister phenomenon, not even a Union of the size and sophistication we have been fortunate enough to build.

There are two further challenges which the new Europe must meet in a spirit of solidarity.

These are the interlinked issues of how best to manage economic globalisation and the concerns and opportunities it entails and, in an increasingly multipolar world, how best to ensure systems of political governance that are both efficient and equitable.

That is why the constitution we are working on is crucially important. A good constitution needs to be adopted quickly to send a strong, clear message of confidence in the future and to lay down arrangements that allow us to work effectively.

In an increasingly complex world, the enlarged Union, based on democratic values, economic openness and a strong social model, can achieve far more than any country can ever hope to achieve on its own. It can provide a reference for all those across the world who seek their own path, from Latin America to Africa and to Asia.

This does not mean that Europeans want to impose their model on others. Particularly as our "model" is based on the recognition and safeguarding of our diversity. But Europe has a great responsibility to help build a world based on the principles of partnership, fairness and justice. . . .

Source: Ireland. Department of Foreign Affairs. Irish Presidency of the European Union. "Mr. Bertie Ahern, Mr. Pat Cox and Mr. Romano Prodi Address Accession Day Conference of the Three Presidents." Dublin, Ireland. May 1, 2004. http://www.eu2004.ie/templates/news.asp?sNavlocator=66&version=printerfriendly&list_id=638 (accessed January 6, 2005).

U.S. Army Report on Abuses of Iraqi Prisoners

May 3, 2004

INTRODUCTION

The publication in April 2004 of photographs of Iraqi prisoners being abused by American soldiers at a Baghdad prison sent shock waves around the world, led to numerous official and unofficial investigations, and severely damaged U.S. prestige in Arab lands. President George W. Bush, Defense Secretary Donald H. Rumsfeld, and other senior U.S. officials insisted the abuses were isolated incidents carried out by a few soldiers who violated military rules. Human rights groups and other critics rejected that claim and said the abuses appeared to flow from administration policies that gave prison guards and military interrogators the impression that even torture was acceptable in the U.S. war against terrorists and their allies.

The photographs, first made public on April 28 by CBS News, showed soldiers in an army reserve military police unit abusing and humiliating Iraqis being held at a prison known as Abu Ghraib. Among the most shocking photographs were those showing a grinning female soldier hunched over a pile of naked male prisoners; a hooded prisoner, dressed in a tattered robe, standing on a box with wires attached to his hands and feet; and naked prisoners cowering at the sight of menacing dogs. Ironically, Abu Ghraib had been the prison where Iraq's dictator Saddam Hussein held opponents of his regime. The United States ousted Saddam from power in April–May 2003. *(Iraq invasion, Historic Documents of 2003, p. 135)*

The prison abuses in Iraq drew new attention to the treatment by the U.S. military and intelligence agencies of so-called enemy combatants held at more than two dozen other locations around the world since the September 11, 2001, terrorist attacks against the United States. More than 500 of these people were in detention at a U.S. naval base at Guantanamo Bay, Cuba. The Supreme Court on June 28 overturned the administration's contention that these detainees were beyond the reach of U.S. courts because they were in Cuba. Several dozen terrorist suspects also were held in Afghanistan, which the United States had invaded in October 2001, and an unknown number reportedly were held at other locations in Asia and the Middle East. *(Guantanamo ruling, p. 375)*

The Bush administration's contention that the abuses could be blamed on just a few errant soldiers was undermined June 22, 2004, with the publication of an August 2002 Justice Department legal opinion appearing to condone the use of torture against terrorist suspects. The Justice Department rewrote the opinion to prohibit torture late in 2004, but critics said the original language demonstrated that the administration had lowered the standards of acceptable behavior, thus creating the atmosphere that made the abuses at Iraq prisons and elsewhere possible. *(Torture memo, p. 336)*

Abuse Scandal Emerges

In the months after a U.S.-led coalition took power in Iraq in 2003, U.S. military and civilian leaders were given several confidential warnings—by the International Committee of the Red Cross, the United Nations, Amnesty International and other human rights groups, and internal investigations—that abuses were occurring at some of its detention facilities there. The Red Cross, which had access to the Iraq prisons, gave the U.S. occupation office (known as the Coalition Provisional Authority) several verbal reports and written reports in May and July 2003 on abuses, which it said were "tantamount to torture." The United Nations also said that its special envoy to Iraq, Sergio Vieira de Mello, expressed concerns in May to the U.S. Coalition Provisional Authority about abuses of detainees (de Mello later was killed in a massive suicide bombing of the UN compound in Baghdad). The Pentagon conducted at least three investigations during 2003 into its handling of Iraqi prisoners, two of which identified some of the operational flaws that contributed to the abuses.

What was to become the public scandal began to unfold on January 13, 2004, when Spc. Joseph M. Darby, a military policeman at Abu Ghraib, gave army investigators a computer disk containing graphic photographs showing abuses at the prison. Three days later the Pentagon's Central Command—which had overall responsibility for U.S. military operations in the Middle East—issued a vague, five-sentence news release saying an investigation was being conducted into "reported incidents of detainee abuse at a Coalition Forces detention facility" in Iraq. This news release attracted virtually no public attention at the time, but Rumsfeld was told of the abuses within days, and Bush was alerted by early February. Lt. Gen. Ricardo S. Sanchez, the senior U.S. commander in Iraq, ordered a high-level investigation, which was conducted by Maj. Gen. Antonio M. Taguba. Taguba handed in his report on March 12. It was approved on April 6 by Lt. Gen. David D. McKiernan, the commander of ground forces in Iraq, and on May 1 by Sanchez.

On March 30 the army announced that six members of the 372d Military Police Company, an army reserve unit based in Cresaptown, Maryland, had been charged with abusing prisoners at Abu Ghraib. The charges included assault, cruelty, dereliction of duty, and indecent acts with another person. As with the announcement of the investigation two months earlier, this statement received little news coverage.

In mid-April someone at the Pentagon gave CBS News copies of some of the photographs from Abu Ghraib. When CBS asked the Pentagon for comment, Gen. Richard Myers, chairman of the Joint Chiefs of Staff, appealed to the network to delay its broadcast because the anti-U.S. insurgency in Iraq was especially active at the time. CBS agreed and withheld its broadcast until April 28—the same day that Rumsfeld privately briefed congressional leaders about the abuses. The CBS broadcast included an interview with one of the soldiers who had been charged with abuses, Staff Sgt. Ivan L. Frederick II. Also in April, investigative journalist Seymour Hersh obtained copies of the photographs and a copy of Taguba's report. The *New Yorker* magazine on April 30 posted on the Internet the first of several detailed accounts by Hersh of Iraq prison abuses; the account included excerpts from the Taguba report.

After the CBS broadcast, much of the rest of the U.S. news media took another day or two to catch onto the significance of what had happened at Abu Ghraib. By April 30 the photographs of naked prisoners had begun to generate an enormous worldwide scandal. Bush sought to contain the damage with a statement portraying the abuse as an aberration. "I shared a deep disgust that those prisoners were treated in the way they were treated," he said on April 30. "Their treatment does not reflect the nature of the American people." The next day General Myers said he was "appalled" by the photographs but said the abuses had been committed by "just a handful" of soldiers. In May 5 interviews with two Arabic-language television networks (one of them financed by the U.S. government), Bush again decried the abuses, which he said were committed by "a few people." Bush went further the following day, saying during a White House news conference with Jordan's King Abdullah that had he had apologized to the king during a private meeting. "I told him I was sorry for the humiliation suffered by the Iraqi prisoners, and the humiliation suffered by their families," he said.

The administration's attempt to contain the public relations damage done to the United States in the Arab world appeared to have little effect. Arab television networks showed the photographs for weeks, along with commentary claiming the actions showed in them were representative of U.S. behavior toward the Arab world. The damage was most severe in Iraq, where many people said the tyranny of Saddam's regime had been replaced by an American one. "People feel their dignity has been insulted," the *Chicago Tribune* quoted Ahmad al-Samaree, the imam of a large Sunni mosque in Baghdad. "What will a father tell his son when an American soldier comes and handcuffs him, then makes him lay down and then a female soldier comes and steps on his head?" This reference to "a female soldier" reflected the fact that many of the abuse photographs showed naked Iraqi prisoners being humiliated by grinning American women, an insult of special potency in the Islamic world.

Taguba Report

The *Los Angeles Times,* the *New York Times,* and other newspapers on May 2–3 published stories based on information from the Taguba report, which the Pentagon then posted on its Web site for about one week. Also on May 3 the Pentagon announced that General Sanchez had issued strong reprimands for six supervisors at Abu Ghraib and a milder reprimand for a seventh. Among those reprimanded and removed from their posts were Brig. Gen. Janis Karpinski, who commanded the 800th Military Police Brigade; and Lt. Col. Jerry L. Phillabaum, commander of the 320th Military Police Battalion.

Taguba's report provided details about the events at Abu Ghraib, focusing on the abuses that had taken place on the overnight shift in cell block one at Abu Ghraib—where the photographs had been taken. In its most attention-getting paragraph, the report said that between October and December 2003 "numerous incidents of sadistic, blatant, and wanton criminal abuses were inflicted on several detainees. This systemic and illegal abuse of detainees was intentionally perpetrated by several members of the military police guard force" in the 372nd Military Police Company. The report said the army reserve military police soldiers had not been trained for their duties, had worked under minimal supervision, had been under stress themselves because of overcrowding at the prison and repeated insurgent attacks on the prison, and had been told to "soften up" prisoners so they would be more cooperative with the military intelligence officers who questioned them.

Taguba's report also provided the first official confirmation that abuses had occurred over a period of several months in 2003 and had not been limited to the one cell block where the photographs had been taken. Other units cited in the report were the 325th Military Intelligence Battalion, the 205th Military Intelligence Brigade, and a unit known as the Joint Interrogation and Debriefing Center. Taguba reported that three army reserve military policemen had beaten prisoners at a detention site known as Camp Bucca in May 2003. The soldiers were court martialed and discharged from the army.

Taguba blamed many of the problems at Abu Ghraib on what he called "clear friction and lack of communication" between Karpinski, who commanded the military police, and the intelligence officers who were in charge of getting information from the prisoners. Taguba said Karpinski blamed the military intelligence officers for pressuring her troops, but he said she had failed to supervise the troops or instill military discipline.

Taguba challenged a key recommendation that Maj. Gen. Geoffrey D. Miller had made after a visit to the Iraqi prison system in 2003. Miller, who then ran the U.S. detention center in Guantanamo Bay, had suggested that military intelligence officers be given effective control of the prisoners so they could extract more "actionable intelligence" from them. This suggestion, which had been implemented, was "not doctrinally sound" and had led, at least indirectly, to the abuses, Taguba said. Miller later was transferred from Guantanamo Bay to Iraq, where he was put in charge of the U.S.-run prisons.

The Taguba report also shed some light on the activities of private contractors the military had hired to help with the interrogations at Abu Ghraib. Taguba said he suspected that Steven Stephanowicz and John Israel, employees of two private security firms, were among those who were "either directly or indirectly responsible for the abuses" at Abu Ghraib.

Focus on Rumsfeld

In his initial public responses to the Abu Ghraib scandal, Defense Secretary Rumsfeld at first appeared to play down the significance of the event, telling reporters "I'm not one for instant history." That stance was denounced by Democrats in Congress and numerous newspaper editorials, some calling for his resignation. Facing a sudden fire storm of criticism, an uncharacteristically chastened Rumsfeld appeared before the House and Senate Armed Services committees on May 7. "To those Iraqis who were mistreated by members of the U.S. armed forces, I offer my deepest apology," he said. The mistreatment "was inconsistent with the values of our nation, it was inconsistent with the teachings of the military to the men and women of the armed forces, and it was certainly fundamentally un-American." Rumsfeld insisted the abuses had been "perpetrated by a small number of the U.S. military."

Rumsfeld acknowledged that he had not examined the photographs or read the Taguba report until the scandal broke publicly and had failed to alert Bush to the potential significance of what had happened at Abu Ghraib. "I failed to recognize how important it was to elevate a matter of such gravity to the highest levels, including the president and the members of Congress," he said. Rumsfeld also warned the committees that the Pentagon had obtained additional photographs and evidence showing "sadistic, cruel, and inhuman" activities at Abu Ghraib. "It's going to get still more terrible, I'm afraid," he said of the scandal.

Asked by congressional Democrats whether he had considered resigning, Rumsfeld said he had "given a lot of thought" to the matter. "Needless to say, if I felt I could not be effective, I'd resign in a minute. I would not resign simply because people try to make an issue out of it." Rumsfeld already had the public backing of the president, who said he wanted his defense secretary to stay on the job.

Six days later, on May 13, Rumsfeld traveled to Iraq and toured the Abu Ghraib prison and promised that those responsible would be brought to justice "with no cover up." Rumsfeld did not speak with any of the detainees, some of whom held signs as he passed by with badly spelled but powerful messages, including "What are you going to do about scandl" and "Most of us are innocents." The next day the army released more than 300 detainees from the prison; it was the first of several mass releases during the year. Several of those released told reporters they had been abused or humiliated by the guards.

International Red Cross Report

On the same day Rumsfeld testified on Capitol Hill, the *Wall Street Journal* published substantial excerpts from a confidential report that had been submitted to the Pentagon in February by the International Committee of the Red Cross. The Red Cross was the only nongovernmental organization that routinely was given access to prisoners of war and other detainees in combat zones.

The report, based on visits to detention centers in Iraq between March and November 2003, detailed "a number of serious violations of international humanitarian law," including brutality that "in some cases caused death or serious injury, physical or psychological coercion, prolonged solitary confinement" and "excessive and disproportionate use of force." The report drew particular attention to the treatment by U.S. military intelligence officers of prisoners "deemed to have 'intelligence' value." These detainees, the report said, "were at high risk of being subjected to a variety of harsh treatments ranging from insults, threats, and humiliations to both physical and psychological coercion, which in some cases was tantamount to torture, in order to force cooperation with their interrogators."

Pierre Kraehenbuehl, director of Red Cross operations in Geneva, confirmed that the excerpts published by the *Journal* were authentic and reflected previous reports given U.S. occupation officials in Iraq during 2003. He said the newspaper had obtained and printed the report without Red Cross consent. The Red Cross "has repeatedly made its concerns known to the Coalition Forces and requested corrective measures prior to the submission of this particular report," Kraehenbuehl told reporters. He also noted that the Red Cross had observed "a broader pattern and a system, as opposed to individual acts" of abuse.

Pentagon Investigations

As the scandal continued to grow in intensity, both domestically and internationally, the Bush administration launched seven additional investigations, including internal reviews by the military of the procedures at U.S.-run detention centers in Iraq and elsewhere. The Senate Armed Services Committee began its own investigation but held no hearings after mid-May and effectively stopped its work on the matter by early July. Committee chairman John Warner, R-Va., had come under sharp criticism from fellow Republicans for providing a forum for Democrats to criticize the administration.

The first of the military's follow-up inquiries to be made public was by the army inspector general, Lt. Gen. Paul T. Mikolashek. Released July 22, the report discussed ninety-four incidents of abuse, which it said were made possible by poor training, a lack of experienced interrogators, and faulty command procedures. In contrast to Taguba and the Red Cross, Mikolashek did not find any systemic problems. The abuses, the report said, "are not representative of policy, doctrine, or soldier training. These abuses were unauthorized actions taken by a few individuals, coupled with the failure of a few leaders to provide adequate monitoring, supervision, and leadership over those soldiers." In a pattern that was becoming increasingly evident, Republicans in Congress praised the report while several Democrats called it a "whitewash" and said it failed to examine responsibility at higher levels of the military and government.

Rumsfeld on May 12 named a high-profile commission—a political obligation for all such scandals—to investigate the Pentagon's recent handling of detainees in Afghanistan, Guantanamo Bay, and Iraq. Chaired by former defense secretary James Schlesinger, its members included another former defense secretary, Harold Brown; former representative Tillie K. Fowler (a Florida Republican); and retired air force general Charles A. Horner. Called the Independent Panel to Review DOD Detention Operations, the Schlesinger panel visited Iraq once in June, interviewed military personnel at all levels (but no detainees), and reviewed the military's numerous other reports on the matter.

In its report, made public August 24, the Schlesinger panel said the abuses resulted from failures at all levels of the military. "The abuses were not just the failure of some individuals to follow known standards, and they are more than the failure of a few leaders to enforce proper discipline," the panel said, in a statement that directly contradicted the Bush administration's earlier assertions. "There is both institutional and personal responsibility at higher levels." However, the panel did not say specifically who bore that responsibility at higher levels. Schlesinger rebuffed the question of whether Rumsfeld should accept the responsibility by resigning, saying such a step "would be a boon for all of America's enemies."

The panel painted a picture of a military detention operation that was plagued with problems from the start—in effect, it said, a microcosm of the Bush administration's failure to plan adequately for its work in Iraq after the war ended. Both the military police and military intelligence units that took over detention facilities in Iraq were short-staffed and ill-equipped, the panel said, noting that for the 800th Military Police Brigade in particular "improvisation was the order of the day." At Abu Ghraib, staffing and logistical problems "were heightened by friction between military intelligence and military police personnel, including the brigade commanders themselves." Once it became apparent in mid-2003 that the Iraqi insurgency was growing, the military should have ensured that detention facilities there were staffed adequately, but it did not, the panel said.

Moreover, the panel reported that the Pentagon gave army personnel inconsistent, even conflicting, information about what types of interrogation techniques had been authorized for Iraq. In August 2003 General Miller arrived in Iraq to conduct an assessment of the interrogation work there. He brought with him a copy of guidelines Rumsfeld had approved four months earlier for use only in Guantanamo, where conditions were more "carefully controlled," the panel said. The commanders in Iraq apparently used those guidelines to authorize similar procedures at Abu Ghraib. Central Command headquarters later rescinded those procedures, but the Schlesinger panel said "the existence of confusing and inconsistent interrogation technique policies contributed to the belief that additional interrogation techniques were condoned."

Interrogation policies used in Afghanistan also "migrated" to Iraq, even though Bush himself specifically had set different standards for the treatment of prisoners in those two conflicts, the panel said. In the case of Afghanistan, Bush had decided on February 7, 2002, that the United States was not obligated to apply the Geneva Conventions (which guaranteed certain human rights protections to prisoners of war) to captured guerrillas from the former Taliban regime and the al Qaeda terrorist network. Bush argued that these fighters were not uniformed soldiers and therefore were not covered by the Geneva Conventions and should be considered as "illegal combatants." By contrast, the administration determined that the Geneva Conventions did apply to those captured during and after the Iraq war. Even so, the Schlesinger panel said, the military tended to apply, without authorization, the lesser protections from the Afghanistan conflict to the later situation in Iraq. Several of the soldiers accused of abuses at Abu Ghraib said they had never been told about the Geneva Conventions—a contention confirmed in the reports by Taguba and other investigators.

Despite the widely publicized abuses at Abu Ghraib—and less well-known abuses at detention centers in Afghanistan and Guantanamo Bay—the "vast majority" of those detained by the United States since late 2001 "were treated appropriately," the panel said. The panel also noted that interrogations at those detention centers "yielded significant amounts of actionable intelligence" for the United States, some of which was noted in the July 22 report of the commission that investigated the September 11 terrorist attacks. *(September 11 report, p. 450)*

A small portion of another broad-scale report was made public the following day, August 25. It was conducted, for the most part, by Maj. Gen. George R. Fay (and was generally referred to as the Fay Report), but was led by Gen. Paul Kern. Officials said the full report ran to several thousand pages, of which 177 pages were made public. The report catalogued, in a greater level of detail than any previous reports, forty-four incidents of prisoner abuse by army military intelligence units at Abu Ghraib during the last four months of 2003. It said twenty-three military intelligence soldiers, four civilian contractors, three military policemen, and two medics were among those who participated in the abuses or failed to stop them. Kern said some of the practices uncovered in the investigation amounted to "torture" and violated all established military rules. "The abuses spanned from direct physical assault, such as delivering head blows rendering detainees unconscious, to sexual posing and forced participation in group masturbation," the report's summary said. "At the extremes were the death of a detainee and an alleged rape committed by a U.S. translator and observed by a female soldier, and the alleged sexual assault of an unknown female."

The most senior official identified in the report was General Sanchez. "While senior-level officers did not commit the abuse at Abu Ghraib, they did bear responsibility for lack of oversight at the facility, failing to respond in a timely manner to reports from the International Committee of the Red Cross, and for issuing policy memos that failed to provide clear, consistence guidance," the report said, in a reference to Sanchez and other top commanders in Iraq. The *New York Times* reported on August 27 that classified portions of the report said Sanchez in the fall of 2003 had issued confusing and contradictory rules for interrogations, including at one point allowing methods (such as threatening prisoners with dogs) that the Pentagon had not approved for use in Iraq. Even so, the report's authors said they were not recommending disciplinary actions against Sanchez or his top deputies.

This report offered the most explicit information of any of the year's investigations, on the role at Abu Ghraib of the Central Intelligence Agency. The report said the CIA held prisoners, known as "ghost detainees," who were not accounted for under normal military procedures. CIA officials also "convinced military leaders that they should be allowed to operate outside the local rules and procedures," the report said.

At least a half-dozen other investigations into specific aspects of prisoner treatment in Iraq were conducted by various Pentagon units. Most resulted in classified reports that were not made public, and two probes were said to be continuing at year's end.

The *New York Times* reported on December 7 that Vice Adm. Lowell E. Jacoby, the head of the Defense Intelligence Agency, had sent the Pentagon a memorandum in June reporting that two agency employees recently had witnessed brutal treatment of prisoners at U.S. intelligence centers in Iraq. These incidents allegedly took place weeks after the Abu Ghraib scandal became public. Several news reports indicated that conditions had been greatly improved at Abu Ghraib, however, including much tighter supervision of prisoner interrogations by senior officers.

Criticisms of Administration Policies

The Abu Ghraib scandal broke early in the election year, and embarrassing revelations continued almost up until election day in November. Leading Democrats, including presidential candidate John Kerry, cited the scandal primarily as a means of criticizing Rumsfeld, whom they also blamed for U.S. failures to anticipate the insurgency in Iraq. Kerry and other Democrats were careful not to place blame on U.S. enlisted personnel in Iraq, however.

Nongovernmental organizations that had been highly critical of Bush administration policies generally used the scandal to reinforce their criticisms. Among the most active in this regard were the American Civil Liberties Union (ACLU), which used Freedom of Information Act requests to win release of numerous documents, including internal e-mails that shed light on some of the abuses at Abu Ghraib and other detention centers; Amnesty International, which had been denouncing U.S. detention policies in Iraq since shortly after the war began in March 2003; and Human Rights Watch, which challenged the administration's legal justification for its detention policies.

In a detailed report released July 16, Human Rights Watch said the administration was trying to play down the extent of the abuse problem by consistently blaming "a few bad apples" who broke the military's rules. In fact, Human Rights Watch said, the abuses resulted from "decisions made by the Bush administration to bend, ignore, or cast rules aside." Administration policies—including the Justice Department's torture memo and a temporary decision by Rumsfeld to allow coercive interrogation methods that were not part of standard procedures—"created the climate for Abu Ghraib," the report said. Low-level soldiers apparently came to believe that abusive techniques were acceptable: "The brazenness with which some soldiers conducted themselves at Abu Ghraib, snapping photographs and flashing the 'thumbs-up' sign as they abused prisoners, confirms that they felt they had nothing to hide from their superiors," the report said.

Punishments

Over the course of the year the military took action to punish more than 100 military personnel—but no senior civilian officials in Washington—in connection with prisoner abuses at Abu Ghraib and other detention centers. Nearly sixty soldiers and marines were referred to court-martial proceedings, only a handful of which had been completed by year's end. More than fifty others were given lesser disciplinary actions, including demotions or less-than-honorable discharges from service.

The highest-ranking officer to pay a price was Lt. Gen. Sanchez, the senior U.S. commander in Iraq, who was replaced on July 1 by a more senior officer, Gen. George W. Casey, who had been the army vice chief of staff. The Schlesinger panel criticized Sanchez by name, saying he "should have taken stronger action in November [2003] when he realized the extent of the leadership problems at Abu Ghraib." Before the Abu Ghraib scandal broke there had been speculation that

Sanchez—one of the army's highest ranking and most prominent Hispanic officers—was in line to head the Southern Command, one of the military's top command assignments, entitling him to a fourth star. In the fallout from the prison abuse scandal Sanchez lost that post, however, and instead was given command of the U.S. Army 5th Corps in Germany.

The second-highest-ranking officer to be caught up in the scandal was Maj. Gen. Barbara Fast, who commanded all army military intelligence operations in Iraq at the time of the Abu Ghraib abuses. The Schlesinger panel had faulted her for failing to give Sanchez appropriate information on interrogation methods and for not monitoring the CIA's interrogations at the prison. Before the Abu Ghraib scandal broke, Fast had been chosen to head the army's intelligence training school at Fort Huachuca in Arizona. The army delayed that assignment because of questions about Fast's actions, and it was still on hold as of year's end.

Maj. Gen. Karpinksi, a reserve officer who commanded the military police units in Iraq, was reprimanded and removed from her post. She said in numerous interviews during the year that higher-ups had engaged in a "conspiracy" to blame all the abuses on her and the soldiers under her command. Among others reprimanded included Col. Thomas M. Pappas, of the 205th Military Intelligence Brigade, who assumed command of Abu Ghraib in November 2003; and Captain Donald J. Reese, commander of the 372nd Military Police Company, whose soldiers committed most of the abuses shown in the photographs.

As of year's end the army had charged seven soldiers of the 372nd Military Police Company in connection with the photographed abuses at Abu Ghraib. The first court-martial trial resulted in the conviction, on May 19, of Spc. Jeremy Sivits. He had pleaded guilty to mistreating prisoners and agreed to testify against his colleagues. He was sentenced to one year in prison and given a "bad conduct" discharge from the army. His trial took place in Baghdad and was widely publicized in the Arab world, where many opinion leaders said it demonstrated the Bush administration's determination to pin the blame on low-ranking soldiers.

Sergeant Frederick on October 20 became the second member to plead guilty. He accepted eight charges of abusing prisoners and gave a court martial in Baghdad detailed accounts of some of the scenes depicted in the famous photographs. Frederick was sentenced to eight years in prison, his rank was reduced to private, and he was given a dishonorable discharge from the army. On October 30 Spc. Megan M. Ambuhl pleaded guilty to one charge of abuse and was sentenced to a reduction in rank to private and the forfeiture of a half-month's salary. She had witnessed some of the abuses but said she did not participate in them; prosecutors said she failed to report the abuses.

Spc. Charles A. Grainer Jr., who by most accounts was the ringleader of the Abu Ghraib abuses shown in the photographs, was charged on May 14 with seven counts of abuse. His court-martial trial was scheduled for 2005, as was that of Sgt. Javal C. Davis.

The soldier who gained the most notoriety from the pictures was Private First Class Lynndie R. England, a clerk who appeared in several of the abuse pictures, including a widely publicized one showing her holding a dog leash that was wrapped around the neck of a naked Iraqi man lying outside a prison cell. She was charged with nineteen counts of abuse and underwent a preliminary hearing in August at Fort Bragg, North Carolina. Her case was transferred in December to Fort Hood, Texas, but she had not gone on trial as of year's end.

The navy said on September 3 that four special forces personnel had been charged in connection with the abuse of one prisoner who died at Abu Ghraib the previous November. A picture of the prisoner's body, wrapped in plastic and packed in ice, had been among those that brought the prison abuses to public attention five months earlier.

Abuses Elsewhere in Iraq

News reports and independent investigations by human rights organizations focused attention on several other abuses of Iraqi prisoners by U.S. and other coalition troops. One case involved the death in November 2003, at a U.S.-run camp in southern Iraq, of Maj. Gen. Abed Hamed Mowhoush, the former chief of Iraqi air defenses. The U.S. military initially reported that Mowhoush had died of natural causes, but after the Abu Ghraib scandal broke the Pentagon acknowledged that he had died of asphyxiation "due to smothering and chest compression." According to an investigation, intelligence officers put Mowhoush in a sleeping bag, and one sat on his chest while questioning him. The army on October 4 charged four soldiers with murder and dereliction of duty in the case.

Mowhoush's death was the most widely publicized of about thirty deaths among detainees at U.S. facilities in Afghanistan and Iraq between 2002 and 2004. The Pentagon, and the investigations commissioned by the Pentagon, said most of the deaths were from natural causes or the result of external violence, such as mortar attacks against the Abu Ghraib prison by Iraqi insurgents.

Internal Pentagon documents released December 14—as the result of an ACLU lawsuit—described abuses of prisoners elsewhere in Iraq, including by marines. A summary of cases prepared for the Pentagon inspector general listed ten substantiated cases of marines abusing detainees. Eleven marines had been convicted on various charges related to the abuses, the documents showed.

Detainees in Afghanistan and Elsewhere

The Abu Ghraib prison in Iraq was just one of several places where the U.S. military and the CIA had detained suspected terrorists in the years after the September 11 attacks. Scores, and possibly hundreds, of men also were being held in Afghanistan and at several undisclosed locations—reportedly including the Indian Ocean island of Diego Garcia and aboard U.S. naval ships in international waters. The military also turned an unknown number of suspected terrorists over to the security services in Egypt and Jordan, where the use of torture was routine, according to Amnesty International, Human Rights Watch, and other human rights groups. The Pentagon called these cases "renditions."

Aside from Guantanamo Bay and Iraq, the largest number of detainees was in Afghanistan, where the military said it ran twenty-two detention facilities. Two of these were long-term facilities, one at Bagram air base north of Kabul, and the other in the southern city of Kandahar. The remaining twenty sites were what the Pentagon called "field holding sites" where prisoners were processed before being sent to Bagram or Kandahar.

In a December 13 letter to Defense Secretary Rumsfeld, Human Rights Watch said it had compiled evidence that six detainees had died in Afghanistan—four of them under circumstances that appeared to have been murder or manslaughter. Human Rights Watch said "the failure to investigate and prosecute abuses had created a culture of impunity among some interrogators, and allowed abuse to spread." Hours after

Human Rights Watch publicized its letter, the army's Criminal Investigation Command released a list of eight deaths among detainees in Afghanistan. The army said charges had been filed in three cases, three other cases remained under investigation, and two cases had been investigated and closed.

Two days later, on December 15, an army spokesman in Afghanistan said an inspection of U.S. detention facilities there, conducted in May by Brig. Gen. Charles Jacoby Jr. of the army, had found "no evidence of abuse." Briefing reporters in Kabul, army Maj. Mark McCann said Jacoby had found "deficiencies" that "were either corrected on the spot, or policy and procedure changes were implemented to ensure any potential abuse in the future was eliminated." Jacoby's report had not been made public by year's end.

The military refused to allow journalists to inspect any of the facilities in Afghanistan, saying such an inspection would violate the privacy of detainees. The two main facilities at Bagram and Kandahar (but not the twenty field centers) had been subject to regular inspections by the International Committee of the Red Cross; in keeping with its standard procedures, the Red Cross did not publish its findings.

Following are excerpts from "Article 15-6 Investigation of the 800th Military Police Brigade," a report submitted to the U.S. Army in March 2004 by Maj. Gen. Antonio M. Taguba. The report dealt with General Taguba's investigation into abuses by U.S. military personnel of Iraqi prisoners at the Abu Ghraib prison in Baghdad and at other U.S.-run detention facilities in Iraq. Excerpts of the report were first published by U.S. newspapers on May 3, 2004.

"Article 15-6 Investigation of the 800th Military Police Brigade"

Background

1. On 19 January 2004, Lieutenant General (LTG) Ricardo S. Sanchez, Commander, Combined Joint Task Force Seven (CJTF-7) requested that the Commander, US Central Command, appoint an Investigating Officer (IO) in the grade of Major General (MG) or above to investigate the conduct of operations within the 800th Military Police (MP) Brigade. LTG Sanchez requested an investigation of detention and internment operations by the Brigade from 1 November 2003 to present. LTG Sanchez cited recent reports of detainee abuse, escapes from confinement facilities, and accountability lapses, which indicated systemic problems within the brigade and suggested a lack of clear standards, proficiency, and leadership. LTG Sanchez requested a comprehensive and all-encompassing inquiry to make findings and recommendations concerning the fitness and performance of the 800th MP Brigade. . . .

[Sections that followed reviewed a report written in 2003 by Major General Tom Miller and Major General Donald Ryder.]

Preliminary Investigative Actions

1. Following our review of MG Ryder's Report and MG Miller's Report, my investigation team immediately began an in-depth review of all available documents regarding the 800th MP Brigade. We reviewed in detail the voluminous CID investigation regarding alleged detainee abuses at detention facilities in Iraq, particularly the Abu Ghraib (BCCF) Detention Facility. We analyzed approximately fifty witness statements from military police and military intelligence personnel, potential suspects, and detainees. We reviewed numerous photos and videos of actual detainee abuse taken by detention facility personnel, which are now in the custody and control of the US Army Criminal Investigation Command and the CJTF-7 prosecution team. The photos and videos are not contained in this investigation. We obtained copies of the 800th MP Brigade roster, rating chain, and assorted internal investigations and disciplinary actions involving that command for the past several months. . . .

Findings and Recommendations (Part One)

The investigation should inquire into all of the facts and circumstances surrounding recent allegations of detainee abuse, specifically, allegations of maltreatment at the Abu Ghraib Prison (Baghdad Central Confinement Facility).

1. The US Army Criminal Investigation Command (CID), led by COL Jerry Mocello, and a team of highly trained professional agents have done a superb job of investigating several complex and extremely disturbing incidents of detainee abuse at the Abu Ghraib Prison. They conducted over 50 interviews of witnesses, potential criminal suspects, and detainees. They also uncovered numerous photos and videos portraying in graphic detail detainee abuse by Military Police personnel on numerous occasions from October to December 2003. Several potential suspects rendered full and complete confessions regarding their personal involvement and the involvement of fellow Soldiers in this abuse. Several potential suspects invoked their rights under Article 31 of the Uniform Code of Military Justice (UCMJ) and the 5th Amendment of the U.S. Constitution.

2. In addition to a comprehensive and exhaustive review of all of these statements and documentary evidence, we also interviewed numerous officers, NCOs, and junior enlisted Soldiers in the 800th MP Brigade, as well as members of the 205th Military Intelligence Brigade working at the prison. We did not believe it was necessary to reinterview all the numerous witnesses who had previously provided comprehensive statements to CID, and I have adopted those statements for the purposes of this investigation.

Regarding Part One of the Investigation, I Make the Following Specific Findings of Fact

1. That Forward Operating Base (FOB) Abu Ghraib (BCCF) provides security of both criminal and security detainees at the Baghdad Central Correctional Facility, facilitates the conducting of interrogations for CJTF-7 [the U.S. military command in Iraq], supports other CPA operations at the prison, and enhances the force protection/quality of life of Soldiers assigned in order to ensure the success of ongoing operations to secure a free Iraq.

2. That the Commander, 205th Military Intelligence Brigade, was designated by CJTF-7 as the Commander of FOB Abu Ghraib (BCCF) effective 19 November 2003. That the 205th MI Brigade conducts operational and strategic interrogations for CJTF-7. That from 19 November 2003 until Transfer of Authority (TOA) on 6 February 2004, COL Thomas M. Pappas was the Commander of the 205th MI Brigade and the Commander of FOB Abu Ghraib (BCCF).

3. That the 320th Military Police Battalion of the 800th MP Brigade is responsible for the Guard Force at Camp Ganci, Camp Vigilant, & Cellblock 1 of FOB Abu Ghraib (BCCF). That from February 2003 to until he was suspended from his duties on 17 January 2004, LTC Jerry Phillabaum served as the Battalion Commander of the 320th MP Battalion. That from December 2002 until he was suspended from his duties, on 17 January 2004, CPT Donald Reese served as the Company Commander of the 372nd MP Company, which was in charge of guarding detainees at FOB Abu Ghraib. I further find that both the 320th MP Battalion and the 372nd MP Company were located within the confines of FOB Abu Ghraib.

4. That from July of 2003 to the present, BG Janis L. Karpinski was the Commander of the 800th MP Brigade.

5. That between October and December 2003, at the Abu Ghraib Confinement Facility (BCCF), numerous incidents of sadistic, blatant, and wanton criminal abuses were inflicted on several detainees. This systemic and illegal abuse of detainees was intentionally perpetrated by several members of the military police guard force (372nd Military Police Company, 320th Military Police Battalion, 800th MP Brigade), in Tier (section) 1-A of the Abu Ghraib Prison (BCCF). The allegations of abuse were substantiated by detailed witness statements and the discovery of extremely graphic photographic evidence. Due to the extremely sensitive nature of these photographs and videos, the ongoing CID investigation, and the potential for the criminal prosecution of several suspects, the photographic evidence is not included in the body of my investigation. The pictures and videos are available from the Criminal Investigative Command and the CTJF-7 prosecution team. In addition to the aforementioned crimes, there were also abuses committed by members of the 325th MI Battalion, 205th MI Brigade, and Joint Interrogation and Debriefing Center (JIDC). Specifically, on 24 November 2003, SPC Luciana Spencer, 205th MI Brigade, sought to degrade a detainee by having him strip and returned to cell naked.

6. I find that the intentional abuse of detainees by military police personnel included the following acts:

a. Punching, slapping, and kicking detainees; jumping on their naked feet;
b. Videotaping and photographing naked male and female detainees;
c. Forcibly arranging detainees in various sexually explicit positions for photographing;
d. Forcing detainees to remove their clothing and keeping them naked for several days at a time;
e. Forcing naked male detainees to wear women's underwear;
f. Forcing groups of male detainees to masturbate themselves while being photographed and videotaped;
g. Arranging naked male detainees in a pile and then jumping on them;
h. Positioning a naked detainee on a MRE [meal-ready-to-eat] Box, with a sandbag on his head, and attaching wires to his fingers, toes, and penis to simulate electric torture;

i. Writing "I am a Rapest" (sic) on the leg of a detainee alleged to have forcibly raped a 15-year old fellow detainee, and then photographing him naked;
j. Placing a dog chain or strap around a naked detainee's neck and having a female Soldier pose for a picture;
k. A male MP guard having sex with a female detainee;
l. Using military working dogs (without muzzles) to intimidate and frighten detainees, and in at least one case biting and severely injuring a detainee;
m. Taking photographs of dead Iraqi detainees.

7. These findings are amply supported by written confessions provided by several of the suspects, written statements provided by detainees, and witness statements. In reaching my findings, I have carefully considered the pre-existing statements of the following witnesses and suspects:

a. SPC Jeremy Sivits, 372nd MP Company—**Suspect**
b. SPC Sabrina Harman, 372nd MP Company—**Suspect**
c. SGT Javal S. Davis, 372nd MP Company—**Suspect**
c. PFC Lynndie R. England, 372nd MP Company—**Suspect**
d. Adel Nakhla, Civilian Translator, Titan Corp., Assigned to the 205th MI Brigade—**Suspect**
e. SPC Joseph M. Darby, 372nd MP Company
f. SGT Neil A. Wallin, 109th Area Support Medical Battalion
g. SGT Samuel Jefferson Provance, 302nd MI Battalion
h. Torin S. Nelson, Contractor, Titan Corp., Assigned to the 205th MI Brigade
j. CPL Matthew Scott Bolanger, 372nd MP Company
k. SPC Mathew C. Wisdom, 372nd MP Company
l. SSG Reuben R. Layton, Medic, 109th Medical Detachment
m. SPC John V. Polak, 229th MP Company

8. In addition, several detainees also described the following acts of abuse, which under the circumstances, I find credible based on the clarity of their statements and supporting evidence provided by other witnesses:

a. Breaking chemical lights and pouring the phosphoric liquid on detainees;
b. Threatening detainees with a charged 9mm pistol;
c. Pouring cold water on naked detainees;
d. Beating detainees with a broom handle and a chair;
e. Threatening male detainees with rape;
f. Allowing a military police guard to stitch the wound of a detainee who was injured after being slammed against the wall in his cell;
g. Sodomizing a detainee with a chemical light and perhaps a broom stick.
h. Using military working dogs to frighten and intimidate detainees with threats of attack, and in one instance actually biting a detainee.

9. I have carefully considered the statements provided by the following detainees, which under the circumstances I find credible based on the clarity of their statements and supporting evidence provided by other witnesses:

a. Amjed Isail Waleed, Detainee # 151365
b. Hiadar Saber Abed Miktub-Aboodi, Detainee # 13077
c. Huessin Mohssein Al-Zayiadi, Detainee # 19446
d. Kasim Mehaddi Hilas, Detainee # 151108
e. Mohanded Juma Juma (sic), Detainee # 152307

f. Mustafa Jassim Mustafa, Detainee # 150542
g. Shalan Said Alsharoni, Detainee, # 150422
h. Abd Alwhab Youss, Detainee # 150425
i. Asad Hamza Hanfosh, Detainee # 152529
j. Nori Samir Gunbar Al-Yasseri, Detainee # 7787
k. Thaar Salman Dawod, Detainee # 150427
l. Ameen Sa'eed Al-Sheikh, Detainee # 151362
m. Abdou Hussain Saad Faleh, Detainee # 18470

10. I find that contrary to the provision of AR 190-8, and the findings found in MG Ryder's Report, Military Intelligence (MI) interrogators and Other US Government Agency's (OGA) [a reference to the CIA] interrogators actively requested that MP guards set physical and mental conditions for favorable interrogation of witnesses. Contrary to the findings of MG Ryder's Report, I find that personnel assigned to the 372nd MP Company, 800th MP Brigade were directed to change facility procedures to "set the conditions" for MI interrogations. I find no direct evidence that MP personnel actually participated in those MI interrogations.

11. I reach this finding based on the actual proven abuse that I find was inflicted on detainees and by the following witness statements:

a. **SPC Sabrina Harman, 372nd MP Company,** stated in her sworn statement regarding the incident where a detainee was placed on a box with wires attached to his fingers, toes, and penis, "that her job was to keep detainees awake." She stated that MI was talking to CPL Grainer. She stated: **"MI wanted to get them to talk. It is Grainer and Frederick's job to do things for MI and OGA to get these people to talk."**

b. **SGT Javal S. Davis, 372nd MP Company,** stated in his sworn statement as follows: **"I witnessed prisoners in the MI hold section, wing 1A being made to do various things that I would question morally. In Wing 1A we were told that they had different rules and different SOP for treatment. I never saw a set of rules or SOP for that section just word of mouth. The Soldier in charge of 1A was Corporal Granier. He stated that the Agents and MI Soldiers would ask him to do things, but nothing was ever in writing he would complain (sic)."** When asked why the rules in 1A/1B were different than the rest of the wings, SGT Davis stated: **"The rest of the wings are regular prisoners and 1A/B are Military Intelligence (MI) holds."** When asked why he did not inform his chain of command about this abuse, SGT Davis stated: **"Because I assumed that if they were doing things out of the ordinary or outside the guidelines, someone would have said something. Also the wing belongs to MI and it appeared MI personnel approved of the abuse."** SGT Davis also stated that he had heard MI insinuate to the guards to abuse the inmates. When asked what MI said he stated: **"Loosen this guy up for us." Make sure he has a bad night." "Make sure he gets the treatment."** He claimed these comments were made to CPL Granier and SSG Frederick. Finally, SGT Davis stated that (sic): **"the MI staffs to my understanding have been giving Granier compliments on the way he has been handling the MI holds. Example being statements like, "Good job, they're breaking down real fast. They answer every question. They're giving out good information, Finally, and Keep up the good work. Stuff like that."**

c. **SPC Jason Kennel, 372nd MP Company,** was asked if he were present when any detainees were abused. He stated: **"I saw them nude, but MI would tell us to take away their mattresses, sheets, and clothes."** He could not recall who in MI had instructed him to do this, but commented that, "if they wanted me to do that they needed to give me paperwork." He was later informed that "we could not do anything to embarrass the prisoners."

d. **Mr. Adel L. Nakhla,** a US civilian contract translator was questioned about several detainees accused of rape. He observed (sic): **"They (detainees) were all naked, a bunch of people from MI, the MP were there that night and the inmates were ordered by SGT Granier and SGT Frederick ordered the guys while questioning them to admit what they did. They made them do strange exercises by sliding on their stomach, jump up and down, throw water on them and made them some wet, called them all kinds of names such as "gays" do they like to make love to guys, then they handcuffed their hands together and their legs with shackles and started to stack them on top of each other by insuring that the bottom guys penis will touch the guy on tops butt."**

e. **SPC Neil A Wallin, 109th Area Support Medical Battalion,** a medic testified that: **"Cell 1A was used to house high priority detainees and cell 1B was used to house the high risk or trouble making detainees. During my tour at the prison I observed that when the male detainees were first brought to the facility, some of them were made to wear female underwear, which I think was to somehow break them down."**

12. **I find that prior to its deployment to Iraq for Operation Iraqi Freedom, the 320th MP Battalion and the 372nd MP Company had received no training in detention/internee operations.** I also find that very little instruction or training was provided to MP personnel on the applicable rules of the Geneva Convention Relative to the Treatment of Prisoners of War, FM 27-10, AR 190-8, or FM 3-19.40. Moreover, I find that few, if any, copies of the Geneva Conventions were ever made available to MP personnel or detainees.

13. Another obvious example of the Brigade Leadership not communicating with its Soldiers or ensuring their tactical proficiency concerns the incident of detainee abuse that occurred at Camp Bucca, Iraq, on May 12, 2003. Soldiers from the 223rd MP Company reported to the 800th MP Brigade Command at Camp Bucca, that four Military Police Soldiers from the 320th MP Battalion had abused a number of detainees during inprocessing at Camp Bucca. An extensive CID investigation determined that four soldiers from the 320th MP Battalion had kicked and beaten these detainees following a transport mission from Talil Air Base.

14. Formal charges under the UCMJ were preferred against these Soldiers and an Article-32 Investigation conducted by LTC Gentry. He recommended a general court martial for the four accused, which BG Karpinski supported. Despite this documented abuse, there is no evidence that BG Karpinski ever attempted to remind 800th MP Soldiers of the requirements of the Geneva Conventions regarding detainee treatment or took any steps to ensure that such abuse was not repeated. Nor is there any evidence that LTC(P) Phillabaum, the commander of the Soldiers involved in the Camp Bucca abuse incident, took any initiative to ensure his Soldiers were properly trained regarding detainee treatment.

Recommendations as to Part One of the Investigation

1. Immediately deploy to the Iraq Theater an integrated multi-discipline Mobile Training Team (MTT) comprised of subject matter experts in internment/resettlement operations, international and operational law, information technology, facility management, interrogation and intelligence gathering techniques, chaplains, Arab cultural awareness, and medical practices as it pertains to I/R activities. This team needs to oversee and conduct comprehensive training in all aspects of detainee and confinement operations.

2. That all military police and military intelligence personnel involved in any aspect of detainee operations or interrogation operations in CJTF-7, and subordinate units, be immediately provided with training by an international/operational law attorney on the specific provisions of The Law of Land Warfare FM 27-10, specifically the Geneva Convention Relative to the Treatment of Prisoners of War, Enemy Prisoners of War, Retained Personnel, Civilian Internees, and Other Detainees, and AR 190-8.

3. **That a single commander in CJTF-7 be responsible for overall detainee operations throughout the Iraq Theater of Operations.** I also recommend that the Provost Marshal General of the Army assign a minimum of two (2) subject matter experts, one officer and one NCO, to assist CJTF-7 in coordinating detainee operations.

4. That detention facility commanders and interrogation facility commanders ensure that appropriate copies of the Geneva Convention Relative to the Treatment of Prisoners of War and notice of protections be made available in both English and the detainees' language and be prominently displayed in all detention facilities. Detainees with questions regarding their treatment should be given the full opportunity to read the Convention.

5. That each detention facility commander and interrogation facility commander publish a complete and comprehensive set of Standing Operating Procedures (SOPs) regarding treatment of detainees, and that all personnel be required to read the SOPs and sign a document indicating that they have read and understand the SOPs.

6. That in accordance with the recommendations of MG Ryder's Assessment Report, and my findings and recommendations in this investigation, all units in the Iraq Theater of Operations conducting internment/confinement/detainment operations in support of Operation Iraqi Freedom be OPCON for all purposes, to include action under the UCMJ, to CJTF-7.

7. Appoint the C3, CJTF as the staff proponent for detainee operations in the Iraq Joint Operations Area (JOA). (MG Tom Miller, C3, CJTF-7, has been appointed by COMCJTF-7).

8. That an inquiry UP AR 381-10, Procedure 15 be conducted to determine the extent of culpability of Military Intelligence personnel, assigned to the 205th MI Brigade and the Joint Interrogation and Debriefing Center (JIDC) regarding abuse of detainees at Abu Ghraib (BCCF).

9. That it is critical that the proponent for detainee operations is assigned a dedicated Senior Judge Advocate, with specialized training and knowledge of international and operational law, to assist and advise on matters of detainee operations.

Findings and Recommendations (Part Two)

The Investigation inquire into detainee escapes and accountability lapses as reported by CJTF-7, specifically allegations concerning these events at the Abu Ghraib Prison.

Regarding Part Two of the Investigation, I Make the Following Specific Findings of Fact

1. The 800th MP Brigade was responsible for theater-wide Internment and Resettlement (I/R) operations.

2. The 320th MP Battalion, 800th MP Brigade was tasked with detainee operations at the Abu Ghraib Prison Complex during the time period covered in this investigation.

3. The 310th MP Battalion, 800th MP Brigade was tasked with detainee operations and Forward Operating Base (FOB) Operations at the Camp Bucca Detention Facility until TOA on 26 February 2004.

4. The 744th MP Battalion, 800th MP Brigade was tasked with detainee operations and FOB Operations at the HVD Detention Facility until TOA on 4 March 2004.

5. The 530th MP Battalion, 800th MP Brigade was tasked with detainee operations and FOB Operations at the MEK holding facility until TOA on 15 March 2004.

6. Detainee operations include accountability, care, and well being of Enemy Prisoners of War, Retained Person, Civilian Detainees, and Other Detainees, as well as Iraqi criminal prisoners.

7. The accountability for detainees is doctrinally an MP task IAW FM 3-19.40.

8. There is a general lack of knowledge, implementation, and emphasis of basic legal, regulatory, doctrinal, and command requirements within the 800th MP Brigade and its subordinate units.

9. The handling of detainees and criminal prisoners after in-processing was inconsistent from detention facility to detention facility, compound to compound, encampment to encampment, and even shift to shift throughout the 800th MP Brigade AOR.

10. Camp Bucca, operated by the 310th MP Battalion, had a "Criminal Detainee In- Processing SOP" and a "Training Outline" for transferring and releasing detainees, which appears to have been followed.

11. Incoming and outgoing detainees are being documented in the National Detainee Reporting System (NDRS) and Biometric Automated Toolset System (BATS) as required by regulation at all detention facilities. However, it is underutilized and often does not give a "real time" accurate picture of the detainee population due to untimely updating.

12. There was a severe lapse in the accountability of detainees at the Abu Ghraib Prison Complex. The 320th MP Battalion used a self-created "change sheet" to document the transfer of a detainee from one location to another. For proper accountability, it is imperative that these change sheets be processed and the detainee manifest be updated within 24 hours of movement. At Abu Ghraib, this process would often take as long as 4 days to complete. This lag-time resulted in inaccurate detainee Internment Serial Number (ISN) counts, gross differences in the detainee manifest and the actual occupants of an individual compound, and significant confusion of the MP Soldiers. The 320th MP Battalion S-1, CPT Theresa Delbalso, and the S-3, MAJ David DiNenna, explained that this breakdown was due to the lack of manpower to process change sheets in a timely manner.

13. The 320th Battalion TACSOP requires detainee accountability at least 4 times daily at Abu Ghraib. However, a detailed review of their operational journals revealed that these accounts were often not done or not documented by the unit. Additionally,

there is no indication that accounting errors or the loss of a detainee in the accounting process triggered any immediate corrective action by the Battalion TOC.

14. There is a lack of standardization in the way the 320th MP Battalion conducted physical counts of their detainees. Each compound within a given encampment did their headcounts differently. Some compounds had detainees line up in lines of 10, some had them sit in rows, and some moved all the detainees to one end of the compound and counted them as they passed to the other end of the compound.

15. FM 3-19.40 outlines the need for 2 roll calls (100% ISN band checks) per day. The 320th MP Battalion did this check only 2 times per week. Due to the lack of real-time updates to the system, these checks were regularly inaccurate.

16. The 800th MP Brigade and subordinate units adopted non-doctrinal terms such as "band checks," "roll-ups," and "call-ups," which contributed to the lapses in accountability and confusion at the soldier level.

17. Operational journals at the various compounds and the 320th Battalion TOC contained numerous unprofessional entries and flippant comments, which highlighted the lack of discipline within the unit. There was no indication that the journals were ever reviewed by anyone in their chain of command.

18. Accountability SOPs were not fully developed and standing TACSOPs were widely ignored. Any SOPs that did exist were not trained on, and were never distributed to the lowest level. Most procedures were shelved at the unit TOC, rather than at the subordinate units and guards mount sites.

19. Accountability and facility operations SOPs lacked specificity, implementation measures, and a system of checks and balances to ensure compliance.

20. Basic Army Doctrine was not widely referenced or utilized to develop the accountability practices throughout the 800th MP Brigade's subordinate units. Daily processing, accountability, and detainee care appears to have been made up as the operations developed with reliance on, and guidance from, junior members of the unit who had civilian corrections experience.

21. Soldiers were poorly prepared and untrained to conduct I/R operations prior to deployment, at the mobilization site, upon arrival in theater, and throughout their mission.

22. The documentation provided to this investigation identified 27 escapes or attempted escapes from the detention facilities throughout the 800th MP Brigade's AOR. Based on my assessment and detailed analysis of the substandard accountability process maintained by the 800th MP Brigade, it is highly likely that there were several more unreported cases of escape that were probably "written off" as administrative errors or otherwise undocumented. 1LT Lewis Raeder, Platoon Leader, 372nd MP Company, reported knowing about at least two additional escapes (one from a work detail and one from a window) from Abu Ghraib (BCCF) that were not documented. LTC Dennis McGlone, Commander, 744th MP Battalion, detailed the escape of one detainee at the High Value Detainee Facility who went to the latrine and then outran the guards and escaped. Lastly, BG Janis Karpinski, Commander, 800th MP Brigade, stated that there were more than 32 escapes from her holding facilities, which does not match the number derived from the investigation materials.

23. The Abu Ghraib and Camp Bucca detention facilities are significantly over their intended maximum capacity while the guard force is undermanned and under resourced. This imbalance has contributed to the poor living conditions, escapes, and

accountability lapses at the various facilities. The overcrowding of the facilities also limits the ability to identify and segregate leaders in the detainee population who may be organizing escapes and riots within the facility.

24. The screening, processing, and release of detainees who should not be in custody takes too long and contributes to the overcrowding and unrest in the detention facilities. There are currently three separate release mechanisms in the theater-wide internment operations. First, the apprehending unit can release a detainee if there is a determination that their continued detention is not warranted. Secondly, a criminal detainee can be released after it has been determined that the detainee has no intelligence value, and that their release would not be detrimental to society. BG Karpinski had signature authority to release detainees in this second category. Lastly, detainees accused of committing "Crimes Against the Coalition," who are held throughout the separate facilities in the CJTF-7 AOR, can be released upon a determination that they are of no intelligence value and no longer pose a significant threat to Coalition Forces. The release process for this category of detainee is a screening by the local US Forces Magistrate Cell and a review by a Detainee Release Board consisting of BG Karpinski, COL Marc Warren, SJA, CJTF-7, and MG Barbara Fast, C-2, CJTF-7. MG Fast is the "Detainee Release Authority" for detainees being held for committing crimes against the coalition. According to BG Karpinski, this category of detainee makes up more than 60% of the total detainee population, and is the fastest growing category. However, MG Fast, according to BG Karpinski, routinely denied the board's recommendations to release detainees in this category who were no longer deemed a threat and clearly met the requirements for release. According to BG Karpinski, the extremely slow and ineffective release process has significantly contributed to the overcrowding of the facilities.

25. After Action Reviews (AARs) are not routinely being conducted after an escape or other serious incident. No lessons learned seem to have been disseminated to subordinate units to enable corrective action at the lowest level. The Investigation Team requested copies of AARs, and none were provided.

26. Lessons learned (i.e. Findings and Recommendations from various 15-6 Investigations concerning escapes and accountability lapses) were rubber stamped as approved and ordered implemented by BG Karpinski. There is no evidence that the majority of her orders directing the implementation of substantive changes were ever acted upon. Additionally, there was no follow-up by the command to verify the corrective actions were taken. Had the findings and recommendations contained within their own investigations been analyzed and actually implemented by BG Karpinski, many of the subsequent escapes, accountability lapses, and cases of abuse may have been prevented.

27. The perimeter lighting around Abu Ghraib and the detention facility at Camp Bucca is inadequate and needs to be improved to illuminate dark areas that have routinely become avenues of escape.

28. Neither the camp rules nor the provisions of the Geneva Conventions are posted in English or in the language of the detainees at any of the detention facilities in the 800th MP Brigade's AOR, even after several investigations had annotated the lack of this critical requirement.

29. The Iraqi guards at Abu Ghraib (BCCF) demonstrate questionable work ethics and loyalties, and are a potentially dangerous contingent within the Hard-Site. These

guards have furnished the Iraqi criminal inmates with contraband, weapons, and information. Additionally, they have facilitated the escape of at least one detainee.

30. In general, US civilian contract personnel (Titan Corporation, CACI, etc . . .), third country nationals, and local contractors do not appear to be properly supervised within the detention facility at Abu Ghraib. During our on-site inspection, they wandered about with too much unsupervised free access in the detainee area. Having civilians in various outfits (civilian and DCUs) in and about the detainee area causes confusion and may have contributed to the difficulties in the accountability process and with detecting escapes.

31. SGM Marc Emerson, Operations SGM, 320th MP Battalion, contended that the Detainee Rules of Engagement (DROE) and the general principles of the Geneva Convention were briefed at every guard mount and shift change on Abu Ghraib. However, none of our witnesses, nor our personal observations, support his contention. I find that SGM Emerson was not a credible witness.

32. Several interviewees insisted that the MP and MI Soldiers at Abu Ghraib (BCCF) received regular training on the basics of detainee operations; however, they have been unable to produce any verifying documentation, sign-in rosters, or soldiers who can recall the content of this training.

33. The various detention facilities operated by the 800th MP Brigade have routinely held persons brought to them by Other Government Agencies (OGAs) without accounting for them, knowing their identities, or even the reason for their detention. The Joint Interrogation and Debriefing Center (JIDC) at Abu Ghraib called these detainees "ghost detainees." On at least one occasion, the 320th MP Battalion at Abu Ghraib held a handful of "ghost detainees" (6-8) for OGAs that they moved around within the facility to hide them from a visiting International Committee of the Red Cross (ICRC) survey team. This maneuver was deceptive, contrary to Army Doctrine, and in violation of international law.

34. The following riots, escapes, and shootings have been documented and reported to this Investigation Team. Although there is no data from other missions of similar size and duration to compare the number of escapes with, the most significant factors derived from these reports are twofold. First, investigations and SIRs lacked critical data needed to evaluate the details of each incident. Second, each investigation seems to have pointed to the same types of deficiencies; however, little to nothing was done to correct the problems and to implement the recommendations as was ordered by BG Karpinski, nor was there any command emphasis to ensure these deficiencies were corrected. . . .

[Sections that followed listed seven cases of escapes from Abu Ghraib or other detention facilities in Iraq; some of the cases resulted in shootings of detainees; in one incident three detainees were shot to death.]

36. As I have previously indicated, this investigation determined that there was virtually a complete lack of detailed SOPs at any of the detention facilities. Moreover, despite the fact that there were numerous reported escapes at detention facilities throughout Iraq (in excess of 35), AR 15-6 Investigations following these escapes were simply forgotten or ignored by the Brigade Commander with no dissemination to other facilities. After-Action Reports and Lessons Learned, if done at all, remained at individual facilities and were not shared among other commanders or soldiers throughout the Brigade. The Command never issued standard TTPs for handling escape incidents.

Recommendations Regarding Part Two of the Investigation

1. **ANNEX 100** of this investigation contains a detailed and referenced series of recommendations for improving the detainee accountability practices throughout the OIF area of operations.

2. Accountability practices throughout any particular detention facility must be standardized and in accordance with applicable regulations and international law.

3. The NDRS and BATS accounting systems must be expanded and used to their fullest extent to facilitate real time updating when detainees are moved and or transferred from one location to another.

4. "Change sheets," or their doctrinal equivalent must be immediately processed and updated into the system to ensure accurate accountability. The detainee roll call or ISN counts must match the manifest provided to the compound guards to ensure proper accountability of detainees.

5. Develop, staff, and implement comprehensive and detailed SOPs utilizing the lessons learned from this investigation as well as any previous findings, recommendations, and reports.

6. SOPs must be written, disseminated, trained on, and understood at the lowest level.

7. Iraqi criminal prisoners must be held in separate facilities from any other category of detainee.

8. All of the compounds should be wired into the master manifest whereby MP Soldiers can account for their detainees in real time and without waiting for their change sheets to be processed. This would also have the change sheet serve as a way to check up on the accuracy of the manifest as updated by each compound. The BATS and NDRS system can be utilized for this function.

9. Accountability lapses, escapes, and disturbances within the detainment facilities must be immediately reported through both the operational and administrative Chain of Command via a Serious Incident Report (SIR). The SIRs must then be tracked and followed by daily SITREPs until the situation is resolved.

10. Detention Rules of Engagement (DROE), Interrogation Rules of Engagement (IROE), and the principles of the Geneva Conventions need to be briefed at every shift change and guard mount.

11. AARs must be conducted after serious incidents at any given facility. The observations and corrective actions that develop from the AARs must be analyzed by the respective MP Battalion S-3 section, developed into a plan of action, shared with the other facilities, and implemented as a matter of policy.

12. There must be significant structural improvements at each of the detention facilities. The needed changes include significant enhancement of perimeter lighting, additional chain link fencing, staking down of all concertina wire, hard site development, and expansion of Abu Ghraib (BCCF).

13. The Geneva Conventions and the facility rules must be prominently displayed in English and the language of the detainees at each compound and encampment at every detention facility IAW AR 190-8.

14. Further restrict US civilians and other contractors' access throughout the facility. Contractors and civilians must be in an authorized and easily identifiable uniform to be more easily distinguished from the masses of detainees in civilian clothes.

15. Facilities must have a stop movement/transfer period of at least 1 hour prior to every 100% detainee roll call and ISN counts to ensure accurate accountability.

16. The method for doing head counts of detainees within a given compound must be standardized.

17. Those military units conducting I/R operations must know of, train on, and constantly reference the applicable Army Doctrine and CJTF command policies. The references provided in this report cover nearly every deficiency I have enumerated. Although they do not, and cannot, make up for leadership shortfalls, all soldiers, at all levels, can use them to maintain standardized operating procedures and efficient accountability practices.

Findings and Recommendations (Part Three)

Investigate the training, standards, employment, command policies, internal procedures, and command climate in the 800th MP Brigade, as appropriate.

Pursuant to Part Three of the Investigation, select members of the Investigation team (Primarily COL La Fate and I) personally interviewed the following witnesses. . . .

[Forty-eight witnesses were listed.]

Regarding Part Three of the Investigation, I Make the Following Specific Findings of Fact

1. I find that BG Janis Karpinski took command of the 800th MP Brigade on 30 June 2003 from BG Paul Hill. BG Karpinski has remained in command since that date. The 800th MP Brigade is comprised of eight MP battalions in the Iraqi TOR: 115th MP Battalion, 310th MP Battalion, 320th MP Battalion, 324th MP Battalion, 400th MP Battalion, 530th MP Battalion, 724th MP Battalion, and 744th MP Battalion.

2. Prior to BG Karpinski taking command, members of the 800th MP Brigade believed they would be allowed to go home when all the detainees were released from the Camp Bucca Theater Internment Facility following the cessation of major ground combat on 1 May 2003. At one point, approximately 7,000 to 8,000 detainees were held at Camp Bucca. Through Article-5 Tribunals and a screening process, several thousand detainees were released. Many in the command believed they would go home when the detainees were released. In late May-early June 2003 the 800th MP Brigade was given a new mission to manage the Iraqi penal system and several detention centers. This new mission meant Soldiers would not redeploy to CONUS when anticipated. Morale suffered, and over the next few months there did not appear to have been any attempt by the Command to mitigate this morale problem.

3. There is abundant evidence in the statements of numerous witnesses that soldiers throughout the 800th MP Brigade were not proficient in their basic MOS skills, particularly regarding internment/resettlement operations. Moreover, there is no evidence that the command, although aware of these deficiencies, attempted to correct them in any systemic manner other than ad hoc training by individuals with civilian corrections experience.

4. I find that the 800th MP Brigade was not adequately trained for a mission that included operating a prison or penal institution at Abu Ghraib Prison Complex. As the

Ryder Assessment found, I also concur that units of the 800th MP Brigade did not receive corrections-specific training during their mobilization period. MP units did not receive pinpoint assignments prior to mobilization and during the post mobilization training, and thus could not train for specific missions. The training that was accomplished at the mobilization sites were developed and implemented at the company level with little or no direction or supervision at the Battalion and Brigade levels, and consisted primarily of common tasks and law enforcement training. However, I found no evidence that the Command, although aware of this deficiency, ever requested specific corrections training from the Commandant of the Military Police School, the US Army Confinement Facility at Mannheim, Germany, the Provost Marshal General of the Army, or the US Army Disciplinary Barracks at Fort Leavenworth, Kansas.

5. I find that without adequate training for a civilian internee detention mission, Brigade personnel relied heavily on individuals within the Brigade who had civilian corrections experience, including many who worked as prison guards or corrections officials in their civilian jobs. Almost every witness we interviewed had no familiarity with the provisions of AR 190-8 or FM 3-19.40. It does not appear that a Mission Essential Task List (METL) based on in-theater missions was ever developed nor was a training plan implemented throughout the Brigade.

6. I also find, as did MG Ryder's Team, that the 800th MP Brigade as a whole, was understrength for the mission for which it was tasked. Army Doctrine dictates that an I/R Brigade can be organized with between 7 and 21 battalions, and that the average battalion size element should be able to handle approximately 4000 detainees at a time. This investigation indicates that BG Karpinski and her staff did a poor job allocating resources throughout the Iraq JOA. Abu Ghraib (BCCF) normally housed between 6000 and 7000 detainees, yet it was operated by only one battalion. In contrast, the HVD Facility maintains only about 100 detainees, and is also run by an entire battalion.

7. Reserve Component units do not have an individual replacement system to mitigate medical or other losses. Over time, the 800th MP Brigade clearly suffered from personnel shortages through release from active duty (REFRAD) actions, medical evacuation, and demobilization. In addition to being severely undermanned, the quality of life for Soldiers assigned to Abu Ghraib (BCCF) was extremely poor. There was no DFAC, PX, barbershop, or MWR facilities. There were numerous mortar attacks, random rifle and RPG attacks, and a serious threat to Soldiers and detainees in the facility. The prison complex was also severely overcrowded and the Brigade lacked adequate resources and personnel to resolve serious logistical problems. Finally, because of past associations and familiarity of Soldiers within the Brigade, it appears that friendship often took precedence over appropriate leader and subordinate relationships.

8. With respect to the 800th MP Brigade mission at Abu Ghraib (BCCF), I find that there was clear friction and lack of effective communication between the Commander, 205th MI Brigade, who controlled FOB Abu Ghraib (BCCF) after 19 November 2003, and the Commander, 800th MP Brigade, who controlled detainee operations inside the FOB. There was no clear delineation of responsibility between commands, little coordination at the command level, and no integration of the two functions. Coordination occurred at the lowest possible levels with little oversight by commanders.

9. I find that this ambiguous command relationship was exacerbated by a CJTF-7 Fragmentary Order (FRAGO) 1108 issued on 19 November 2003. Paragraph 3.C.8,

Assignment of 205th MI Brigade Commander's Responsibilities for the Baghdad Central Confinement Facility, states as follows:

> **3.C.8. A. 205 MI Brigade.**
> **3.C.8. A. 1. Effective Immediately Commander 205 MI Brigade Assumes Responsibility for the Baghdad Confinement Facility (BCCF) and Is Appointed the FOB Commander. Units Currently at Abu Ghraib (BCCF) Are TACON to 205 MI Brigade for "Security of Detainees and FOB Protection."**

Although not supported by BG Karpinski, FRAGO 1108 made all of the MP units at Abu Ghraib TACON to the Commander, 205th MI Brigade. This effectively made an MI Officer, rather than an MP Officer, responsible for the MP units conducting detainee operations at that facility. This is not doctrinally sound due to the different missions and agendas assigned to each of these respective specialties.

10. Joint Publication 0-2, Unified Action Armed Forces (UNAAF), 10 July 2001 defines Tactical Control (TACON) as the detailed direction and control of movements or maneuvers within the operational area necessary to accomplish assigned missions or tasks.

> **"TACON is the command authority over assigned or attached forces or commands or military capability made available for tasking that is limited to the detailed direction and control of movements or maneuvers within the operational area necessary to accomplish assigned missions or tasks. TACON is inherent in OPCON and may be delegated to and exercised by commanders at any echelon at or below the level of combatant commander."**

11. Based on all the facts and circumstances in this investigation, I find that there was little, if any, recognition of this TACON Order by the 800th MP Brigade or the 205th MI Brigade. Further, there was no evidence if the Commander, 205th MI Brigade clearly informed the Commander, 800th MP Brigade, and specifically the Commander, 320th MP Battalion assigned at Abu Ghraib (BCCF), on the specific requirements of this TACON relationship.

12. It is clear from a comprehensive review of witness statements and personal interviews that the 320th MP Battalion and 800th MP Brigade continued to function as if they were responsible for the security, health and welfare, and overall security of detainees within Abu Ghraib (BCCF) prison. Both BG Karpinski and COL Pappas clearly behaved as if this were still the case.

13. With respect to the 320th MP Battalion, I find that the Battalion Commander, LTC (P) Jerry Phillabaum, was an extremely ineffective commander and leader. Numerous witnesses confirm that the Battalion S-3, MAJ David W. DiNenna, basically ran the battalion on a day-to-day basis. At one point, BG Karpinski sent LTC (P) Phillabaum to Camp Arifjan, Kuwait for approximately two weeks, apparently to give him some relief from the pressure he was experiencing as the 320th Battalion Commander. This movement to Camp Arifjan immediately followed a briefing provided by LTC (P) Phillabaum to the CJTF-7 Commander, LTG Sanchez, near the end of October 2003. BG Karpinski placed LTC Ronald Chew, Commander of the 115th MP Battalion, in charge of the 320th MP Battalion for a period of approximately two weeks. LTC Chew was also in command of the 115th MP Battalion

assigned to Camp Cropper, BIAP, Iraq. I could find no orders, either suspending or relieving LTC (P) Phillabaum from command, nor any orders placing LTC Chew in command of the 320th. In addition, there was no indication this removal and search for a replacement was communicated to the Commander CJTF-7, the Commander 377th TSC, or to Soldiers in the 320th MP Battalion. Temporarily removing one commander and replacing him with another serving Battalion Commander without an order and without notifying superior or subordinate commands is without precedent in my military career. LTC (P) Phillabaum was also reprimanded for lapses in accountability that resulted in several escapes. The 320th MP Battalion was stigmatized as a unit due to previous detainee abuse which occurred in May 2003 at the Bucca Theater Internment Facility (TIF), while under the command of LTC (P) Phillabaum. Despite his proven deficiencies as both a commander and leader, BG Karpinski allowed LTC (P) Phillabaum to remain in command of her most troubled battalion guarding, by far, the largest number of detainees in the 800th MP Brigade. LTC (P) Phillabaum was suspended from his duties by LTG Sanchez, CJTF-7 Commander on 17 January 2004.

14. During the course of this investigation I conducted a lengthy interview with BG Karpinski that lasted over four hours, and is included verbatim in the investigation Annexes. BG Karpinski was extremely emotional during much of her testimony. What I found particularly disturbing in her testimony was her complete unwillingness to either understand or accept that many of the problems inherent in the 800th MP Brigade were caused or exacerbated by poor leadership and the refusal of her command to both establish and enforce basic standards and principles among its soldiers.

15. BG Karpinski alleged that she received no help from the Civil Affairs Command, specifically, no assistance from either BG John Kern or COL Tim Regan. She blames much of the abuse that occurred in Abu Ghraib (BCCF) on MI personnel and stated that MI personnel had given the MPs "ideas" that led to detainee abuse. In addition, she blamed the 372nd Company Platoon Sergeant, SFC Snider, the Company Commander, CPT Reese, and the First Sergeant, MSG Lipinski, for the abuse. She argued that problems in Abu Ghraib were the fault of COL Pappas and LTC Jordan because COL Pappas was in charge of FOB Abu Ghraib.

16. BG Karpinski also implied during her testimony that the criminal abuses that occurred at Abu Ghraib (BCCF) might have been caused by the ultimate disposition of the detainee abuse cases that originally occurred at Camp Bucca in May 2003. She stated that **"about the same time those incidents were taking place out of Baghdad Central, the decisions were made to give the guilty people at Bucca plea bargains. So, the system communicated to the soldiers, the worst that's gonna happen is, you're gonna go home."** I think it important to point out that almost every witness testified that the serious criminal abuse of detainees at Abu Ghraib (BCCF) occurred in late October and early November 2003. The photographs and statements clearly support that the abuses occurred during this time period. The Bucca cases were set for trial in January 2004 and were not finally disposed of until 29 December 2003. There is entirely no evidence that the decision of numerous MP personnel to intentionally abuse detainees at Abu Ghraib (BCCF) was influenced in any respect by the Camp Bucca cases.

17. Numerous witnesses stated that the 800th MP Brigade S-1, MAJ Hinzman and S-4, MAJ Green, were essentially dysfunctional, but that despite numerous complaints, these officers were not replaced. This had a detrimental effect on the Brigade Staff's effectiveness and morale. Moreover, the Brigade Command Judge Advocate, LTC

James O'Hare, appears to lack initiative and was unwilling to accept responsibility for any of his actions. LTC Gary Maddocks, the Brigade XO did not properly supervise the Brigade staff by failing to lay out staff priorities, take overt corrective action when needed, and supervise their daily functions.

18. In addition to poor morale and staff inefficiencies, I find that the 800th MP Brigade did not articulate or enforce clear and basic Soldier and Army standards. I specifically found these examples of unenforced standards:

a. There was no clear uniform standard for any MP Soldiers assigned detention duties. Despite the fact that hundreds of former Iraqi soldiers and officers were detainees, MP personnel were allowed to wear civilian clothes in the FOB after duty hours while carrying weapons.

b. Some Soldiers wrote poems and other sayings on their helmets and soft caps.

c. In addition, numerous officers and senior NCOs have been reprimanded/disciplined for misconduct during this period. Those disciplined include;

1). BG Janis Karpinski, Commander, 800th MP Brigade
- Memorandum of Admonishment by LTG Sanchez, Commander, CJTF-7, on 17 January 2004.

2). LTC (P) Jerry Phillabaum, Commander, 320th MP Battalion
- GOMOR from BG Karpinski, Commander 800th MP Brigade, on 10 November 2003, for lack of leadership and for failing to take corrective security measures as ordered by the Brigade Commander; filed locally
- Suspended by BG Karpinski, Commander 800th MP Brigade, 17 January 2004; Pending Relief for Cause, for dereliction of duty

3). LTC Dale Burtyk, Commander, 400th MP Battalion
- GOMOR from BG Karpinski, Commander 800th MP Brigade, on 20 August 2003, for failure to properly train his Soldiers. (Soldier had negligent discharge of M-16 while exiting his vehicle, round went into fuel tank); filed locally. . . .

[Eight additional officers or noncommissioned officers were cited.]

20. In addition I find that psychological factors, such as the difference in culture, the Soldiers' quality of life, the real presence of mortal danger over an extended time period, and the failure of commanders to recognize these pressures contributed to the pervasive atmosphere that existed at Abu Ghraib (BCCF) Detention Facility and throughout the 800th MP Brigade.

21. As I have documented in other parts of this investigation, I find that there was no clear emphasis by BG Karpinski to ensure that the 800th MP Brigade Staff, Commanders, and Soldiers were trained to standard in detainee operations and proficiency or that serious accountability lapses that occurred over a significant period of time, particularly at Abu Ghraib (BCCF), were corrected. AR 15-6 Investigations regarding detainee escapes were not acted upon, followed up with corrective action, or disseminated to subordinate commanders or Soldiers. Brigade and unit SOPs for dealing with detainees if they existed at all, were not read or understood by MP Soldiers assigned the difficult mission of detainee operations. Following the abuse of several detainees at Camp Bucca in May 2003, I could find no evidence that BG Karpinski ever directed corrective training for her soldiers or ensured that MP Soldiers throughout Iraq clearly understood the requirements of the Geneva Conventions relating to the treatment of detainees.

22. On 17 January 2004 BG Karpinski was formally admonished in writing by LTG Sanchez regarding the serious deficiencies in her Brigade. LTG Sanchez found that the performance of the 800th MP Brigade had not met the standards set by the Army or by CJTF-7. He found that incidents in the preceding six months had occurred that reflected a lack of clear standards, proficiency and leadership within the Brigade. LTG Sanchez also cited the recent detainee abuse at Abu Ghraib (BCCF) as the most recent example of a poor leadership climate that "permeates the Brigade." I totally concur with LTG Sanchez' opinion regarding the performance of BG Karpinski and the 800th MP Brigade. . . .

[The following section gave specific recommendations for reprimands and other actions to be taken against Brigadier General Karpinski, Colonel Pappas, and other officers and soldiers.]

Conclusion

1. Several US Army Soldiers have committed egregious acts and grave breaches of international law at Abu Ghraib/BCCF and Camp Bucca, Iraq. Furthermore, key senior leaders in both the 800th MP Brigade and the 205th MI Brigade failed to comply with established regulations, policies, and command directives in preventing detainee abuses at Abu Ghraib (BCCF) and at Camp Bucca during the period August 2003 to February 2004.

2. Approval and implementation of the recommendations of this AR 15-6 Investigation and those highlighted in previous assessments are essential to establish the conditions with the resources and personnel required to prevent future occurrences of detainee abuse.

Source: U.S. Department of Defense. U.S. Army. U.S. Central Command. Coalition Forces Land Component Command. "Article 15-6 Investigation of the 800th Military Police Brigade." May 3, 2004. www.lib.umich.edu/govdocs/pdf/taguba.pdf (accessed February 18, 2005).

Federal Reserve Chairman on Trade and Budget Deficits

May 6, 2004

INTRODUCTION

The value of the dollar relative to other major currencies continued to slide downward in 2004, raising concerns about the stability of the world economy. Much of the dollar's decline was blamed on the U.S. federal budget and trade deficits, which ran record highs in 2003 and 2004 and were largely financed by foreign investors, including foreign governments. An apparent slowing of foreign investments in American capital and financial assets toward the end of the year heightened concerns that foreign lenders might be getting nervous about the ability of the United States to carry its massive debt.

Opinion on that question was divided. Virtually all economists and analysts agreed that the dollar was overvalued relative to other currencies and needed to be brought back into balance. The concern was whether the realignment could be managed gradually, with time for investors, businesses, and consumers to adjust. Some analysts thought the world economy could—and would—finance the U.S. deficits for many years, while market forces helped realign the global currency and trade imbalances. At the other extreme were those who worried that the realignment might instead happen suddenly. They pictured scenarios in which the continuing fall of the dollar would spark foreign investors to cut their losses by selling off dollar assets. Under one scenario, the results were significantly higher inflation and interest rates and a slowdown in economic growth. Other scenarios envisioned recession, or even depression, worldwide.

Which outcome was most likely was the subject of great debate in policy, business, and academic circles throughout 2004. The Bush administration sided with the more optimistic versions, arguing that foreigners saw investment in the United States as an opportunity rather than a great risk and would continue to be willing to invest in U.S. Treasury securities and stock markets. The administration professed to support a strong dollar but showed no inclination to prop up the dollar either by raising interest rates or intervening in the currency exchange markets. Analysts read the disinterest in intervention as a signal that the administration was willing to see the value of the dollar decline even further.

Federal Budget Deficits

Whatever their views on the precariousness of the dollar, most analysts agreed that the federal budget deficit, which reached $378 billion in fiscal 2003 and $412 billion in fiscal 2004, was too high and needed to be reduced. Those were by far the highest dollar values for the budget deficit ever recorded. The highest previous budget deficit measured in dollars was $290 billion in 1992, posted as the country was emerging from a short but painful recession.

As a share of the economy, however, the current budget deficit did not appear so out of balance. The fiscal 2003 and 2004 budget deficits were 3.5 percent and 3.6 percent, respectively, of gross domestic product (the value of all goods and services produced in the United States). That was well within the range recorded for budget deficits since 1975 and far below the all-time high of 6 percent posted in 1983 after the tax cut and cold war defense buildup championed by President Ronald Reagan took hold.

Tax cuts and defense spending also accounted for much of the budget deficit that the country was experiencing in 2004. When George W. Bush entered the White House in 2001, the country had been running a budget surplus for four years, and government analysts were predicting surpluses for years to come. Bush seized the opportunity to push his central campaign promise through Congress, winning passage of a ten-year, $1.3 trillion cut in individual income taxes. Three months later, al Qaeda terrorists attacked the World Trade Center in New York and the Pentagon in Washington, sending the economy into a short, mild recession and spurring the United States into Afghanistan to destroy al Qaeda leaders thought to be hiding there and the extremist Taliban regime that was harboring them. *(Tax cuts, Historic Documents of 2001, p. 400; terrorist attacks, Historic Documents of 2001, p. 614; invasion of Afghanistan, Historic Documents of 2001, p. 686)*

In March 2003 Bush invaded Iraq to oust the repressive regime of Iraqi dictator Saddam Hussein and quell that country's threat of weapons of mass destruction. No weapons of mass destruction were found, but the United States and its allies found themselves in a long, deadly, and expensive operation to quell an insurgency and install a democratic government in the war-ravaged country. By the end of 2004 the war on terror and the invasions of Afghanistan and Iraq had cost at least $200 billion. *(Situation in Iraq, pp. 399, 711, 874; invasion of Iraq, Historic Documents of 2003, p. 135)*

Meanwhile, at Bush's urging, Congress in 2003 passed another substantial tax reduction measure, this one for $330 billion. The Bush administration argued that accelerating many of the tax cuts that were part of the 2001 tax relief package, allowing fast write-offs for business investment and cutting dividends and capital gains, would help jump start the economy, which was recovering only slowly from the 2001 recession. Most analysts agreed that the tax cuts did have a stimulatory effect, but tax revenues fell significantly in 2001 through 2003 and began to grow again only in 2004. *(Economy in 2003, Historic Documents of 2003, p. 68)*

In 2004 the Republican-led Congress extended some expiring individual tax breaks and approved major cuts in corporate taxes. The corporate tax cuts were offset by revenue increases from closing existing loopholes, but most observers cynically assumed that new loopholes would be found quickly.

As he prepared for his second term in office in late 2004, President Bush again pledged to cut the federal budget deficit in half in five years. Many observers, however, were skeptical that Bush would succeed or even that he meant it. They pointed to his continuing request to make the tax cuts permanent, a move that analysts estimated would cost the government as much $1.3 trillion over ten years; the U.S. military's continuing involvement in Iraq and Afghanistan; and the start of a prescription drug benefit for Medicare that was expected to cost at least $534 billion over ten years. Bush was also expected to propose an overhaul of the Social Security program that would allow young workers to invest part of their payroll taxes in personal savings account. Analysts said the government would need to borrow as much as $2 trillion to cover the transition costs of such a change at the very time that the baby-boom generation was starting to retire and draw down the surplus in the Social Security trust funds. *(Medicare, p. 577)*

In its annual September forecast, the Congressional Budget Office (CB0) estimated that under the federal laws and policies currently in place, the cumulative federal budget deficit for 2005 through 2014 would add $2.3 trillion of new debt. If the tax cuts were made permanent, CBO estimated that the cumulative deficit would climb to $3.6 trillion. The CBO estimate did not include any estimates for Bush's proposal to change Social Security. The nonpartisan budget office also estimated that the total federal debt held by the public—the amount that was financed through the sale of Treasury bonds—would increase from $4.3 trillion in 2004 to nearly $6.8 trillion in 2014.

At the end of the year, nearly 40 percent of the federal debt was held by foreign-based investors, up from an average of about 18 percent in the early 1980s. Central banks, foreign ministries, and other official institutions held about three-fifths of the foreign-held public debt. Between them, Japan and China held about $900 billion in U.S. Treasury securities. At year's end indications that foreign central banks were beginning to trade off their dollar holdings for reserves denominated in euros sent shivers through the financial markets.

The Trade Deficit

The other growing deficit was in goods and services traded with other countries. Preliminary estimates put the 2004 trade deficit in goods and services at $617.7 billion, compared with a deficit of $496.5 billion in 2003. Aided by the slide in the dollar, exports of goods and services increased in 2004, to a total of $1.1 trillion, but imports increased at an even faster pace, rising to $1.8 trillion. Rising petroleum prices accounted for some of the increase, but much of it was driven by American consumers' seemingly insatiable appetite for everything from foreign cars to foreign cheeses. Some economists suggested that December statistics showing a narrowing trade gap indicated that consumers were beginning to slow their spending as a result of higher import prices. *(Oil price increases, p. 186)*

Not surprisingly, the current account deficit for 2004—the combined balance on trade, international investment income, and other international financial transactions—was even higher, at an estimated $650 billion or so in 2004 (final figures were scheduled to come in out June 2005). Altogether the trade deficit equaled 5.3 percent of gross domestic product, the broader current account deficit represented about 5.7 percent.

Aided in part by the strong dollar, American willingness to import foreign goods helped drive world economic growth in recent years. Europe, still struggling to stimulate domestic demand and end rising unemployment, was dependent on its export markets for a large share of its economic growth. Japan's exports to the United States also helped keep its faltering economy from worsening further. America's biggest trade deficit was with China, the fastest growing major economy in the world, in part because of its thriving export market. In 2004 the United States imported $162 billion more from China than it exported.

Although American consumers benefited by being able to buy cheaper goods from China and elsewhere, American workers complained that those cheaper goods were costing them their jobs. For several years American manufacturers had been moving some of their factory jobs to foreign countries where labor was cheaper; more recently, American companies had been moving service jobs overseas, particularly to India where there was an abundance of educated, English-speaking workers who could perform a range of tasks from staffing call centers to reading medical X-rays to preparing income tax returns—all for wages well below those for the same work performed in the United States. Still other jobs were "exported" when factories closed down altogether because they could no longer compete with foreign manufacturers of similar products. Although economists said that productivity gains were the main reason that employers were slow to hire new workers after the mild recession of 2001, many factory workers and others blamed this job "outsourcing" for the "jobless" recovery. *(Jobless recovery, p. 56; Historic Documents of 2003, p. 441)*

Decline of the Dollar

The weakening dollar was both a sign that the global economy was badly out of alignment and an important element for moving the world economy back into a more stable balance. Long the strongest currency in the world, the dollar reached a peak relative to other currencies in April 2002 and then declined more or less steadily through the end of 2004 as analysts and investors grew increasingly wary of the rising U.S. trade and budget deficits. At the end of the year the euro, the common currency used by twelve European countries, including France and Germany, was worth about $1.35—roughly 30 percent more than it had been when Bush came into office in 2001. When the euro was first introduced in 1999, it began trading at about $1.17 but sank to about parity with the dollar by the end of the year. A British pound was worth $1.92, a 7 percent change from the end of 2003. European leaders, distressed with the drop in their exports caused by the upward valuation in the euro, urged the Bush administration to stop the dollar from falling further.

The dollar also declined against Japan's currency. At the end of the year a dollar was worth 102.63 Japanese yen, its lowest level against the yen since 1999. The drop would likely have been lower if foreign governments, namely Japan and China, had not stepped in to support the dollar by buying U.S. Treasury securities. *(Introduction of the euro, Historic documents of 1999, p. 75)*

In the short run, the declining dollar was likely to help restore some balance in the U.S. trade deficit. Although foreign imports and vacations in Europe were more expensive for Americans to buy, U.S. exports of goods and services were more competitive in foreign markets, and the domestic tourism industry was likely to experience some growth as foreigners took advantage of the weak dollar. The declining dollar could also contribute to higher employment in the United States, as some foreign manufacturers, such as foreign automakers, sought to cut their costs by expanding their production into the United States rather than exporting the finished product.

But the question remained whether the falling dollar would lead to enough balance and a smooth realignment. One issue was whether and when China would ease its decade-long policy of tying its currency, the yuan, at a fixed exchange rate to the dollar. Keeping the yuan pegged to the dollar gave China what many said was an unfair advantage by making its exports relatively cheaper in global trade markets. If the yuan was allowed to float, it was likely to increase in value against the dollar, sending the dollar still lower but pricing Chinese exports closer to their real market value and thus helping to close the trade gap. The European Union, the International Monetary Fund, and the Bush administration had all been pressing the Chinese government to let the yuan float, but to no apparent avail.

At a meeting of leaders of Pacific Rim countries in Santiago, Chile, in November, Bush reported that Chinese president Hu Jintao had given "a clear commitment" to move toward "a flexible exchange rate that reflects the market factors." But the Chinese refused to be pinned down on when they might unpeg the yuan from the dollar. At a meeting in Berlin of top finance ministers and central bankers the same weekend, Zhou Xiaochuan, governor of the People's Bank of China, said it was "still not the stage to talk about specific technical arrangements."

The Bush administration also argued that Europe and Japan could help reduce the trade imbalance by doing more to stimulate their own domestic demand. Treasury Secretary John W. Snow repeatedly said "the euro zone is growing below its potential."

Foreign leaders and many Americans, however, said the Bush administration could make a much stronger case if it worked to get its own house in order. "The U.S. will be in a much better position to demand that the Europeans grow faster and the Chinese revalue their currency if the U.S. did something to deal with its underlying problem," C. Fred Bergsten, director of the Institute for International Economics, a research group in Washington, told the *New York Times* in December. If the president is unwilling to deal with the deficits, Bergsten added, then "the dollar tanks, interest rates soar, the economy weakens, and his own agenda is at stake."

One person who took a longer view of the deficit-dollar dilemma was Alan Greenspan, the chairman of the Federal Reserve Board. In a speech to bankers in Chicago on May 6, elements of which he repeated throughout the year, Greenspan suggested that the process of globalization—the expansion of trade and investment across national borders—was the primary reason that America's twin deficits had not been a major drag on the world economy. So far, he said, the economic forces that were allowing the United States to run ever-larger deficits without substantial increases in interest rates or other interventions showed little signs of diminishing. But he cautioned that, at some point, investors were likely to turn away from dollar assets if only to diversify their risks. He warned that protectionism, signs of which were evident in the United States and elsewhere, could undermine the global adjustment process.

Following are excerpts from the text of "Globalization and Innovation," a speech delivered May 6, 2004, by Federal Reserve Board chairman Alan Greenspan at the Conference on Bank Structure and Competition in Chicago.

"Globalization and Innovation"

The United States economy appears to have been pressing a number of historic limits in recent years without experiencing the types of financial disruption that almost surely would have arisen in decades past. This observation raises some key questions about the longer-term stability of the U.S. and global economies that bear significantly on future economic developments, including the future competitive shape of banking.

Among the limits we have been pressing against are those in our external and budget balances. We in the United States have been incurring ever larger trade deficits, with the broader current account measure having reached 5 percent of our gross domestic product (GDP). Yet the dollar's real exchange value, despite its recent decline, remains close to its average of the past two decades. Meanwhile, we have lurched from a budget surplus in 2000 to a deficit that is projected by the Congressional Budget Office to be $4\frac{1}{4}$ percent of GDP this year. In addition, we have legislated commitments to our senior citizens that, given the inevitable retirement of our huge baby-boom generation, will create significant fiscal challenges in the years ahead. Yet the yield on Treasury notes maturing a decade from now remain at low levels. Nor are we experiencing inordinate household financial pressures as a consequence of record high household debt as a percent of income.

Has something fundamental happened to the U.S. economy and, by extension, U.S. banking, that enables us to disregard all the time-tested criteria of imbalance and economic danger? Regrettably, the answer is no. The free lunch has still to be invented. We do, however, seem to be undergoing what is likely, in the end, to be a one-time shift in the degree of globalization and innovation that has temporarily altered the specific calibrations of those criteria. Recent evidence is consistent with such a hypothesis of a transitional economic paradigm, a paradigm somewhat different from that which fit much of our earlier post-World War II experience.

Globalization has altered the economic frameworks of both advanced and developing nations in ways that are difficult to fully comprehend. Nonetheless, the largely unregulated global markets, with some notable exceptions, appear to move effortlessly from one state of equilibrium to another. Adam Smith's "invisible hand" remains at work on a global scale.

Because of a lowering of trade barriers, deregulation, and increased innovation, cross-border trade in recent decades has been expanding at a far faster pace than GDP. As a result, domestic economies are increasingly exposed to the rigors of international competition and comparative advantage. In the process, lower prices for some goods and services produced by our trading partners have competitively suppressed domestic price pressures.

Production of traded goods has expanded rapidly in economies with large, low-wage labor forces. Most prominent are China and India, which over the past decade have partly opened up to market capitalism, and the economies of central and eastern Europe that were freed from central planning by the fall of the Soviet empire. The consequent significant additions to world production and trade have clearly put downward pressure on domestic prices, though somewhat less so over the past year. Moreover, the pronounced fall in inflation, virtually worldwide, over the past two decades has doubtless been a key factor in the notable decline in world economic volatility.

In tandem with increasing globalization, monetary policy, to most observers, has become increasingly effective in achieving the objective of price stability. But because we have not experienced a sufficient number of economic turning points to judge the causal linkages among increased globalization, improved monetary policy, significant disinflation, and greater economic stability, the structure of the transitional paradigm is necessarily sketchy.

Nonetheless, a paradigm encompassing globalization and innovation, far more than in earlier decades, appears to explain the events of the past ten years better than other conceptual constructs. If this is indeed the case, because there are limits to how far globalization and the speed of innovation can proceed, the current apparent rapid pace of structural shift cannot continue indefinitely. A couple of weeks ago, I indicated in testimony to the Congress that the outlook for the next year or two has materially brightened. But the outlook for the latter part of this decade remains opaque because it is uncertain whether this transitional paradigm, if that is what it is, is already far advanced and about to slow, or whether it remains in an early, still vibrant stage of evolution.

Globalization—the extension of the division of labor and specialization beyond national borders—is patently a key to understanding much of our recent economic history. With a deepening of specialization and a growing population free to take risks over a widening area, production has become increasingly international.

The pronounced structural shift over the past decade to a far more vigorous competitive world economy than that which existed in earlier postwar decades apparently has been adding significant stimulus to world economic activity. That stimulus, like that which resulted from similar structural changes in the past, is likely a function of the rate of increase of globalization and not its level. If so, such impetus would tend to peter out, as we approach the practical limits of globalization.

Full globalization, in which trade and finance are driven solely by risk-adjusted rates of return and risk is indifferent to distance and national borders, will likely never be achieved. The inherent risk aversion of people, and the home bias implied by that aversion, will limit how far globalization can proceed. But because so much of our recent experience has little precedent, as I noted earlier, we cannot fully determine how long the current globalization dynamic will take to play out.

The increasing globalization of the post-war world was fostered at its beginnings by the judgment that burgeoning prewar protectionism was among the primary causes of the depth of the Great Depression of the 1930s. As a consequence, trade barriers began to fall after the war. Globalization was enhanced further when the inflation-ridden 1970s provoked a rethinking of the philosophy of economic policy, the roots of which were still planted in the Depression era. In the United States, that rethinking led to a wave of bipartisan deregulation of transportation, energy, and finance. At the same time, there was a growing recognition that inflation impaired economic performance. Indeed, Group of Seven world leaders at their 1977 Economic Summit identified inflation as a cause of unemployment. Moreover, monetary policy tightening, and not increased regulation, came to be seen by the end of that decade as the only viable solution to taming inflation. Of course, the startling recovery of war-ravaged West Germany following Ludwig Erhard's postwar reforms, and Japan's embrace of global trade, were early examples of the policy reevaluation process.

It has taken several decades of experience with markets and competition to foster an unwinding of regulatory rigidities. Today, privatization and deregulation have become almost synonymous with "reform."

By any number of measures, globalization has expanded markedly in recent decades. Not only has the ratio of international trade in goods and services to world GDP risen inexorably over the past half-century, but a related measure—the extent to which savers reach beyond their national borders to invest in foreign assets—has also risen.

Through much of the post-World War II years, domestic saving for each country was invested predominantly in its domestic capital assets, irrespective of the potential for superior risk-adjusted returns to be available from abroad. Because a country's domestic saving less its domestic investment is equal to its current account balance, such balances, positive or negative, with the exception of the mid-1980s, were therefore generally modest. But in the early 1990s, "home bias" began to diminish appreciably, and, hence, the dispersion of current account balances among countries has increased markedly. The widening current account deficit in the United States has come to dominate the tail of that distribution of external balances across countries.

Thus, the decline in home bias, or its equivalent, expanding globalization, has apparently enabled the United States to finance and, hence, incur so large a current account deficit. As a result of these capital flows, the ratio of foreign net claims against U.S. residents to our annual GDP has risen to approximately one-fourth. While some other countries are far more in debt to foreigners, at least relative to their GDPs, they do not face the scale of international financing that we require.

A U.S. current account deficit of 5 percent or more of GDP would probably not have been readily fundable a half-century ago or perhaps even a couple of decades ago. The ability to move that much of world saving to the United States in response to relative rates of return almost surely would have been hindered by the far-lesser degree of both globalization and international financial flexibility that existed at the time. Such large transfers would presumably have induced changes in the prices of assets that would have proved inhibiting.

Nonetheless, we have little evidence that the economic forces that are fostering international specialization, and hence cross-border trade and increasing dispersion of current account balances, are as yet diminishing. At some point, however, international investors, private and official, faced with a concentration of dollar assets in their portfolios, will seek diversification, irrespective of the competitive returns on dollar assets. That shift, over time, would likely induce contractions in both the U.S. current account deficit and the corresponding current account surpluses of other nations.

Can market forces incrementally defuse a buildup in a nation's current account deficit and net external debt before a crisis more abruptly does so? The answer seems to lie with the degree of market flexibility. In a world economy that is sufficiently flexible, as debt projections rise, product and equity prices, interest rates, and exchange rates presumably would change to reestablish global balance.

We may not be able to usefully determine at what point foreign accumulation of net claims on the United States will slow or even reverse, but it is evident that the greater the degree of international flexibility, the less the risk of a crisis.

Should globalization continue unfettered and thereby create an ever more flexible international financial system, history suggests that current account imbalances will be defused with modest risk of disruption. A Federal Reserve study of large current account adjustments in developed countries, the results of which are presumably applicable to the United States, suggests that market forces are likely to restore a more long-term sustainable current account balance here without measurable disruption. Indeed, this was the case in the second half of the 1980s.

I say this with one major caveat. Protectionism, some signs of which have recently emerged, could significantly erode global flexibility and, hence, undermine the global adjustment process. We are already experiencing pressure to slow down the expansion of trade. The current Doha Round of trade negotiations is in some difficulty owing largely to the fact that the low-hanging fruit of trade negotiation has already been picked in the trade liberalizations that have occurred since the Kennedy Round.

Augmenting the dramatic effect of increased globalization on economic growth, and perhaps at some times, fostering it, have been the remarkable technological advances of recent decades. In particular, information and communication technologies have propelled the processing and transmission of data and ideas to a level far beyond our capabilities of a decade or two ago.

The advent of real-time information systems has enabled managers to organize a workforce without the redundancy required in earlier decades to ensure against the type of human error that technology has now made far less prevalent. Real-time information, by eliminating much human intervention, has markedly reduced scrappage rates on production lines, lead times on purchases, and errors in all forms of record-keeping. Much data transfer is now electronic and far more accurate than possible in earlier times.

The long-term path of technology and growth is difficult to discern. Indeed, innovation, by definition, is not forecastable. Nonetheless, the overall pace of productivity growth that has recently been near 5 percent at an annual rate is highly likely to slow because we have rarely exceeded 3 percent for any protracted period. In the United States, we have always employed technologies at, or close to, the cutting edge, and we have created much of our innovative technologies ourselves. The opportunities of many developing economies to borrow innovation is not readily available to us. Thus, even though the longer-term prospects for innovation and respectable productivity growth are encouraging, some near-term slowing in the pace of advance to a rate closer to productivity's long-term average seems likely.

We have, I believe, a reasonably good understanding of why Americans have been able to reach farther into global markets, incur significant increases in debt, and yet fail to produce the disruptions so often observed as a consequence. However, a widely held alternative view of the past decade cannot readily be dismissed. That view holds that the postwar paradigm is still largely in place, and key financial ratios, rather than suggesting a moving structure, reflect extreme values of a fixed structure that must eventually adjust, perhaps abruptly.

To be sure, even with the increased flexibility implied in a paradigm of expanding globalization and innovation, the combination of exceptionally low saving rates and historically high ratios of household debt to income can be a concern if incomes unexpectedly fall. Indeed, there is little doubt that virtually any debt burden becomes oppressive if incomes fall significantly.

But rising debt-to-income ratios can be somewhat misleading as an indicator of stress. Indeed the ratio of household debt to income has been rising sporadically for more than a half-century, a trend that partly reflects the increased capacity of ever-wealthier households to service debt. Moreover, a significant part of the recent rise in the debt-to-income ratio also reflects the remarkable gain in homeownership. Over the past decade, for example, the share of households that owns homes has risen from 64 percent to 69 percent. During the decade a significant number of renters bought homes, thus increasing the asset side of their balance sheets as well as increasing their debt. It can scarcely be argued that the substitutions of debt service for rent materially impaired the financial state of the new homeowner. Yet the process over the past decade added more than 10 percent to outstanding mortgage debt and accounted for more than one-seventh of the increase in total household debt over that period.

Thus, short of a period of overall economic weakness, households, with the exception of some highly leveraged subprime borrowers, do not appear to be faced with significant financial strain. With interest rates low, debt service costs for households are average, or only marginally higher than average. Adding other fixed charges such as rent, utilities, and auto-leasing costs does not materially alter the change in the degree of burden.

Even should interest rates rise materially further, the effect on household expenses will be stretched out because four-fifths of debt is fixed rate of varying maturities, and it will take time for debt to mature and reflect the higher rates. Despite the almost two percentage point rise in mortgage rates on new originations from mid-1999 to mid-2000, the average interest rate on outstanding mortgage debt rose only slightly, as did debt service.

In a related concern, a number of analysts have conjectured that the extended period of low interest rates is spawning a bubble in housing prices in the United States that will, at some point, implode. Their concern is that, if this were to occur, highly leveraged homeowners will be forced to sharply curtail their spending. To be sure, indexes of house prices based on repeat sales of existing homes have outstripped increases in rents, suggesting at least the possibility of price misalignment in some housing markets. A softening in housing markets would likely be one of many adjustments that would occur in the wake of an increase in interest rates.

But a destabilizing contraction in nationwide house prices does not seem the most probable outcome. Indeed, nominal house prices in the aggregate have rarely fallen and certainly not by very much.

Still, house prices, like those of many other assets, are difficult to predict, and movements in those prices can be of macroeconomic significance. Moreover, because these transactions often involve considerable leverage, they need to be monitored by those responsible for fostering financial stability.

There appears, at the moment, to be little concern about corporate financial imbalances. Debt-to-equity ratios are well within historical ranges, and the recent prolonged period of low long-term interest rates has enabled corporations to fund short-term liabilities and stretch out bond maturities. Even the relatively narrow spreads on below-investment-grade corporate debt appear to reflect low expected losses rather than an especially small aversion to risk.

The resolution of our current account deficit and household debt burdens does not strike me as overly worrisome, but that is certainly not the case for our yawning fiscal deficit. Our fiscal prospects are, in my judgment, a significant obstacle to long-term stability because the budget deficit is not readily subject to correction by market forces that stabilize other imbalances.

One issue that concerns most analysts, especially in the context of a widening structural federal deficit, is inadequate national saving. Fortunately, our meager domestic savings, and those attracted from abroad, are being very effectively invested in domestic capital assets. The efficiency of our capital stock thus has been an important offset to what, by any standard, has been an exceptionally low domestic saving rate in the United States. Although saving is a necessary condition for financing the capital investment required to engender productivity, it is not a sufficient condition. The very high saving rates of the Soviet Union, of China, and of India in earlier decades, often did not foster significant productivity growth in those countries. Saving squandered in financing inefficient technologies does not advance living standards. It is thus difficult to judge how significant a problem our relatively low gross domestic saving rate is to the future growth of an efficient capital stock. The high productivity growth rate of the past decade does not suggest a problem. But our success in attracting savings from abroad may be masking the full effect of deficient domestic saving.

Our day-by-day experiences with the effectiveness of flexible markets as they adjust to, and correct, imbalances can readily lead us to the conclusion that once markets are purged of rigidities, macroeconomic disturbances will become a historical relic. However, the penchant of humans for quirky, often irrational, behavior gets in the way of this conclusion. A discontinuity in valuation judgments, often the cause or consequence of a building and bursting of a bubble, can occasionally destabilize even the most liquid and flexible of markets. I do not have much to add on this issue except to reiterate our need to better understand it.

The last three decades have witnessed a significant coalescing of economic policy philosophies. Central planning has been judged as ineffective and is now generally avoided. Market flexibility has become the focus, albeit often hesitant focus, of reform in most countries. All policymakers are struggling to understand global and technological changes that appear to have profoundly altered world economic developments. For most economic participants, these changes appear to have had positive effects on their economic well-being. But a significant minority, trapped on the adverse side of creative destruction, are suffering. This is an issue that needs to be addressed if globalization is to sustain the necessary public support. . . .

Source: U.S. Federal Reserve Board. "Remarks by Chairman Alan Greenspan: Globalization and Innovation." Speech presented at the Conference on Bank Structure and Competition in Chicago, Illinois. May 6, 2004. www.federalreserve.gov/boarddocs/speeches/2004/200405062/default.htm (accessed January 24, 2005).

Bush Administration Commission on Policies toward Cuba

May 6, 2004

INTRODUCTION

The Bush administration stepped up pressure on the communist government of Cuba by announcing a broad set of new policies aimed at encouraging dissidents and depriving the government of foreign hard currency. The new policies appeared to have little immediate impact on the regime of Cuban president Fidel Castro, who had been in power since 1959 and had survived U.S. economic sanctions since 1962. Castro, who turned seventy-eight in 2004, could not beat back the ravages of time, however. He fell from a stage on October 21 and broke a leg; he was forced to spend several weeks in a wheelchair. The incident, which was publicized widely around the world, increased speculation about how long the communist government might last once the charismatic Cuban leader passed from the scene. *(Background, Historic Documents of 2002, p. 232)*

Powell Commission Report

During much of the 1990s and into 2000, the United States took modest steps to ease its economic sanctions against Cuba—largely because of a growing consensus in Washington that U.S. policy toward Cuba had failed and a new approach was needed. The most important manifestation of this new approach was congressional action in 2000 to allow the cash sale of U.S. food and other agricultural products to Cuba. *(Historic Documents of 2000, p. 266)*

President George W. Bush entered office in 2001 determined to reverse what he viewed as concessions to Castro's government. Bush may have owed his presidency to conservative Cuban American voters in Florida, who gave him overwhelming support in the 2000 election, which Bush won by carrying Florida with a 531-vote margin. *(Background, Historic Documents of 2000, p. 999)*

In October 2003 Bush named a commission of government officials, headed by Secretary of State Colin Powell, to examine U.S. policy toward Cuba with an eye toward increasing pressure on the Castro government. Administration officials acknowledged that appointment of the commission was motivated at least in part by politics—the need for the president to maintain his solid base of support among Cuban American voters in Florida.

The Commission for Assistance to a Free Cuba held meetings and hearings over the winter and produced a 500-page report that Powell presented to the president on May 3. The White House released it three days later and said President Bush had endorsed the findings and recommendations. The report offered a two-pronged strategy against the Cuban government: another ratcheting up of U.S. economic and political pressure, coupled with a public effort to encourage Cubans to prepare a new government that could take power when the Castro regime fell. The report did not advocate a military invasion of Cuba; that had been tried once, with CIA support for an army of Cuban exiles in 1961, and failed miserably at the Bay of Pigs. Instead, the report advocated measures to encourage democracy before Castro died, thereby frustrating what the report insisted was the Cuban leader's "succession strategy" of handing power to his younger brother Raul.

One item of contention within the commission as it deliberated involved the transfer of money by Cuban Americans to their relatives back in Cuba. Current U.S. regulations allowed each Cuban American age eighteen or older to send cash remittances of up to $300 per household each quarter—or $1,200 a year. The only restriction was that remittances could not be sent to households of senior Cuban government or Communist Party officials. The report said these remittances provided $400 million to $800 million a year to Cuba, with an unknown percentage of that reaching the Cuban government through fees and the government's control of couriers—known as "mules"—who transferred much of the cash to Cuba.

Some commission members reportedly wanted to freeze or even cut back the amount of remittances as one way of putting additional pressure on the Castro government. Others said such a step would cause more pain to the relatives of Cuban Americans than to Castro. In the end, the commission recommended, and Bush approved, limiting the remittances to immediate family members and cracking down on the use of couriers to deliver the money. Bush also approved limits on gift parcels (called *paquetes*) that Cuban Americans shipped to their relatives in Cuba via U.S.-based delivery services. The Powell commission said these parcels helped Cubans but also benefited the Castro government, which charged fees for their delivery. The new policy barred several items from the parcels that formerly had been permitted, including soaps and other personal hygiene supplies, seeds, hospital supplies, veterinary medicines, and fishing equipment.

The panel also called for stricter limits on visits to Cuba by Cuban Americans, another source of income for Havana. Under the plan, which Bush also approved, Cuban Americans could visit only immediate family members in Cuba (parents, grandparents, siblings, and children, but not cousins, aunts or uncles) once every three years (rather than once a year) and could spend no more than $50 a day on food and lodging while in Cuba (less than one-third of the current $164 per diem limit).

Bush also approved a recommendation for direct political pressure on Castro in the form of radio and television broadcasts to Cuba via a communications airplane known as "Commando Solo." The plane would send broadcasts directly to Cuba of the federal government's Spanish language, anti-Castro stations Radio Marti and TV Marti, both named after Cuban hero Jose Marti. Cuba had been jamming broadcasts of TV Marti since the station's inception in 1990, but experts said the Commando Solo plane might be able to overcome the jamming and offer Cubans an alternative source of news. The plane began its broadcasts on August 21.

The Bush administration put the new policies—including the cutbacks on remittances and gift packages—into effect on June 30. In the rush to get the policies in place, the administration bypassed public comment periods that were standard for most new regulations. To ease the burden on Cuban Americans who had previously scheduled trips to Cuba, the limit on family visits was postponed until the end of July.

The new approach outlined in the Powell commission report won endorsements from many of the conservative Cuban Americans who had long advocated a tough policy against Castro; generally, these tended to be people who had left Cuba in the first decade or two after Castro took power in 1959. Rep. Ileana Ros-Lehtinen, a Republican who represented a heavily Cuban American district in Miami, praised the new limits on remittances and travel permits to Cuba as helping "to ensure the Castro regime does not plunder the Cuban American exile community's hard work and contributions to their family members suffering on the island." A diametrically opposing view came from the only Cuban American Democrat in Congress, Rep. Robert Menendez of New Jersey, who said the restrictions would hurt Cubans, not Castro, and were a "politically transparent" attempt to help Bush carry Florida in the November election.

Other Cuban Americans expressed concerns about the provisions that directly affected them and their relatives in Cuba, notably the limits on remittances and gift packages. Among them was Jose Garcia, executive director of the Cuban American National Foundation, who said he supported most of the Powell commission recommendations but faulted others for "affecting family relationships between exiles and Cubans on the island." The foundation once demanded a no-compromise line toward Castro but since the late 1990s had advocated U.S. policies—such as allowing remittances—that eased the lives of ordinary Cubans.

Garcia's ambivalence turned out to be shared widely, not only among Cuban Americans but also among political leaders in Washington. The House of Representatives on July 8 voted 221–194 to reject the new limits on gift parcels. Forty-six Republicans joined nearly all Democrats in this rebuff of administration policy—the latest of several votes in the Republican-controlled House in recent years that went against a rigidly hard-line stance toward Cuba. The Bush administration responded to that vote by allowing soap and other personal hygiene products to be included in the Cuban family gift packages. The Senate also added provisions to appropriations bills that sought to lift the ban on travel to Cuba by U.S. citizens and to ease the sale to Cuba of agricultural good and medical supplies. Conference committees deleted both provisions, however, in the face of administration opposition.

The Cuban government responded to the new U.S. policies in two ways. First, on May 10, the government announced the closing of most so-called dollar stores—retail establishments that sold goods in dollars, rather than in Cuba pesos, primarily to relatives of Cuban Americans, tourists, workers in tourism businesses, and others who had access to dollars. The closure did not apply to stores selling food and medicine. The Castro government broadened its crackdown in late October, ordering an end to all transactions in dollars.

Castro also protested the U.S. policies on May 15 by leading a parade of several hundred thousand people past the U.S. diplomatic mission, called an "interest section," in downtown Havana. Castro said the parade was a protest of "the brutal, merciless, and cruel measures" the Bush administration had taken against Cuba. Many of the marchers carried posters showing Bush with an Adolph Hitler-type mustache and wearing a German Nazi uniform.

Other Administration Actions

The Bush administration took several other steps during the early months of 2004 to crack down on the Cuban government. Among the steps:

- On January 7 the State Department announced the suspension of what had been regular talks with Cuba on immigration matters. Spokesman Richard

Boucher said Cuba had refused to discuss "serious matters," such as the monitoring of dissidents and the granting of exit visas to Cuba citizens. The United States and Cuba had conducted the twice-annual talks since 1994, when there was a surge of Cubans trying to reach Florida using rafts and small boats. The talks had offered one of the few venues for direct discussions between the two governments, which had not had formal diplomatic relations for forty-five years.
- On February 9 the Treasury Department took action against ten foreign companies that it said were owned or controlled by the Cuban government or Cuban nationals connected to the government. Most were involved in the travel business and had arranged travel between the United States and Cuba, which was subject to strict limitations under a U.S. government travel ban. The February 9 action sought to freeze any assets in the United States belonging to the ten companies and barred U.S. individuals or companies from doing business with those firms. Both houses of Congress had voted to ease the travel ban in 2003, but the proposal never made it into law because of a White House veto threat. Later in 2003 the administration began enforcing the travel ban more rigorously, curtailing trips that were advertised as "educational" but, the administration said, in fact were for leisure travel.
- On February 26 the administration again tightened the travel ban, by expanding the powers of U.S. law enforcement agencies to prevent ships bound for Cuba from leaving U.S. waters. An order signed by Bush allowed U.S. authorities to board, inspect, and even seize any ships believed to be destined for Cuba.
- On March 18—the one-year anniversary of a Cuban crackdown against dissidents in Cuba—the State Department announced that it would deny visas to anyone who "participated" in trials of the dissidents. That announcement was expected to have little practical effect because few Cuban officials, other than diplomats, sought to travel to the United States.

Despite the strained relations, Cuba and the United States continued to do a brisk business in agricultural trade. In the first three years after Congress eased restrictions on food exports to Cuba, U.S. companies had sold more than $700 million worth of dairy products, grains, meat, rice, and other food. A trade fair in Havana in mid-April resulted in additional sales of more than $100 million, according to U.S. business executives.

Cuba's 2003 Crackdown

The Bush administration said its tough policy toward Cuba was a justified response to Cuba's May 2003 crackdown on dissidents—the toughest action the Castro government had taken against its opponents in many years. Cuba arrested and then convicted seventy-five human rights activists, journalists, librarians, and others on charges of conspiring with the United States against the Cuban government. They were sentenced to prison for terms that ranged between six and twenty-eight years; the average sentence was about twenty years. Among those prosecuted were several of the leaders of a petition drive, known as the Varela Project, that asked the government to honor Cuba's constitutional guarantees of democracy. Critics said Castro acted at that time because the rest of the world was focused on the war in Iraq, which was just getting under way. *(Varela project, Historic Documents of 2002, p. 234)*

The *Washington Post* reported on February 14, 2004, that at least twenty of the imprisoned dissidents were in poor health and being held in inhumane conditions, according to their relatives. The *Post* quoted Cuban dissidents as saying many of the seventy-five were being kept in tiny, isolated cells. Many of the allegations appeared to be confirmed in a report submitted later in February to the UN Human Rights Commission by French judge Christine Chanet, who had investigated the human rights situation in Cuba but had been denied permission to visit that country. Cuba on March 25 rejected the charges as "a lie" and showed reporters a videotape purporting to show relatives of seven of the detainees, who said the detainees had been treated well.

The UN Human Rights Commission voted April 15, by a 22–21 margin, to "deplore" the Cuban crackdown and demand that Cuba allow a visit by UN monitors. That vote produced an angry exchange between Cuba and Mexico, which for years had enjoyed friendly relations. Mexico voted for the UN resolution. Two weeks later Castro denounced the vote, and Mexico responded by withdrawing its ambassador from Havana and expelled the Cuban counterpart. A similar dispute erupted between Cuba and Peru, which also had voted for the UN measure. Cuba and Mexico returned their ambassadors on May 27.

Following are excerpts from the executive summary of "Report to the President: Commission for Assistance to a Free Cuba," compiled by U.S. government officials under the chairmanship of Secretary of State Colin Powell. The report was presented to President George W. Bush on May 3, 2004, and made public on May 6.

"Report to the President: Commission for Assistance to a Free Cuba"

Chapter 1: Hastening Cuba's Transition

As an essential part of America's commitment to stand with the Cuban people against the tyranny of Fidel Castro's regime, President George W. Bush mandated that the Commission for Assistance to a Free Cuba identify additional means by which the United States can help the Cuban people bring about an expeditious end to the Castro dictatorship.

In the past, the United States has tended to initiate policies towards Cuba that were implemented in isolation from each other. For instance, economic sanctions were initially imposed with little, if any, support to Cuban civil society, and were not coupled with initiatives to break the regime's information blockade or proactively engage the international community. In addition, well-meaning humanitarian policies were authorized without thorough consideration of the relationship they would have to the fundamental policy objective of assisting the Cuban people regain their freedom and their right to determine their way of life and their future.

The Commission sought a more proactive, integrated, and disciplined approach to undermine the survival strategies of the Castro regime and contribute to conditions that will help the Cuban people hasten the dictatorship's end. The recommendations focus on actions available to the United States Government, allowing us to establish a strong foundation on which to build supportive international efforts. This comprehensive framework is composed of six inter-related tasks considered central to hastening change:

> **Empower Cuban Civil Society:** The Castro dictatorship has been able to maintain its repressive grip on the Cuban people by intimidating civil society and preventing the emergence of a credible alternative to its failed policies. As a result of Castro's 45-year strategy of co-opting or crushing independent actors, Cuban civil society is weak and divided, its development impeded by pervasive and continuous repression. Through absolute control of the Cuban economy and the manipulation of U.S. migration policy, the Castro regime has made it all but impossible for human rights activists and reformers to operate and has forced many into exile.
>
> Now, the tide of public opinion has turned and Castro's loyalists must constantly work to restrain the Cuban people from organizing and expressing demands for change and freedom. Cubans are increasingly losing their fear and vocalizing their desire to be architects of their own destinies. By continuing to isolate the Castro regime while supporting the democratic opposition and empowering an emerging civil society, the United States can help the Cuban people in their efforts to effect positive political and social change in their country. Cuban civil society is not lacking spirit, desire, or determination; it is hampered by a lack of materials and support needed to bring about these changes.
>
> **Break the Cuban Dictatorship's Information Blockade:** The Castro regime controls all formal means of mass media and communication on the island. The Cuban Communist Party exerts strict editorial control over newspapers, television, and radio through the regime's pervasive apparatus of repression, preventing the Cuban people from obtaining accurate information on such issues as the regime's systematic violations of human rights and fundamental freedoms, and the state of the Cuban economy. Consistent with its fear of an uncontrolled information flow to the Cuban people, the regime has set up technological, administrative, and intelligence structures to impede the ability of pro-democracy groups and the larger civil society, both on and off the island, to effectively communicate their message to the Cuban people. In concert with efforts to strengthen Cuban civil society, and building on the excellent work already underway by U.S. Government broadcasting entities, the means exist to increase the availability to the Cuban people of reliable information on events in Cuba and around the world and to assist in the effort to present a democratic alternative to the failed policies of the Castro regime.
>
> **Deny Resources to the Cuban Dictatorship:** The policies of the Castro regime have debilitated the Cuban economy and impoverished the Cuban people. Rather than address the deprivation confronting Cubans, the regime cynically ignores its obligations and seeks to exploit external engagement with the island and humanitarian assistance to the Cuban people in order to maintain its grip on power. The economic lifelines of the Castro regime are tourism; access to subsidized Venezuelan oil; commodities; and revenues and other support generated by those with family on the island, with the vast majority of such support coming from the United States. Over the past decade, the regime has built an apparatus designed to exploit humanitarian aspects of U.S. policy, specifically to siphon off hundreds of millions of dollars for itself. Remittances, gift parcels and travel-related revenues from those

in exile with family on the island, especially those Cubans who have come to the United States since the early 1990s, are avenues through which the regime has franchised out the subsistence of a significant portion of the Cuban population. The dollars made available to the regime through these means permit it to divert resources to the maintenance and strengthening of its repressive apparatus and away from meeting the basic needs of the Cuban people. Dollars and donated goods, although provided with good intentions by U.S. persons, are effectively helping keep the regime afloat. U.S. initiatives should maintain avenues by which Americans can engage the Cuban people, and by which those with family on the island can reasonably assist immediate relatives, while minimizing the regime's manipulation and exploitation of the plight of the Cuban people.

Illuminate the Reality of Castro's Cuba: The current survival of the regime is, in part, dependent upon its projection of a benign international image. Cuba presents itself internationally as a prime tourist destination, as a center for bio-technological innovation, and as a successful socialist state that has improved the standard of living of its people and that is a model for education, health care, and race relations for the world. This image belies the true state of Cuba's political, economic, and social conditions, its status as a state sponsor of terrorism, and the increasingly erratic behavior of its leadership.

Encourage International Diplomatic Efforts to Support Cuban Civil Society and Challenge the Castro Regime: There is a growing international consensus on the nature of the Castro regime and the need for fundamental political and economic change on the island. This consensus coalesced, in large part, after the regime's brutal March-April 2003 crackdown on peaceful pro-democracy advocates, an act properly characterized as the most severe repression of peaceful political activists in the history of Cuba, and certainly the most significant act of political repression in Latin America in a decade. Infuriated by, and fearful of, the valiant effort by these same activists to continue to reach out to the Cuban people and the international community, the regime reacted; Castro's political attacks against the European Union (EU) and other nations also reveal his regime's continuing trepidation in the face of peaceful Cubans calling for their fundamental rights. Many of those who once stood by Castro have now begun to speak out publicly against the regime's abuses. However, while this same international consensus has limits, encouraging multilateral diplomatic efforts to challenge the regime in international organizations and to strengthen policies of proactive support for pro-democracy groups in Cuba should form a cornerstone of our policy to hasten an end to the Castro regime. The International Labor Organization and the Inter-American Commission on Human Rights, amongst other international organizations, are natural fora for highlighting the conditions under which Cubans live and struggle to survive.

Undermine the Regime's "Succession Strategy": The Castro dictatorship is pursuing every means at its disposal to survive and perpetuate itself through a "succession strategy" from Fidel Castro to Raul Castro and beyond; its goal is that the unelected and undemocratic communist elite now in power remain so indefinitely. The United States rejects the continuation of a communist dictatorship in Cuba, and this Commission recommends measures to focus pressure and attention on the ruling elite so that succession by this elite or any one of its individuals is seen as what it would be: an impediment to a democratic and free Cuba.

Selected Recommendations

- Provide an additional $29 million (to augment the current Cuba program budget of $7 million) to the State Department, USAID, and other appropriate U.S. Government agencies to:
  - Work with willing third-country allies to support creation of an international fund for the protection and development of civil society in Cuba, to engage, train, and provide resources for volunteers of different nationalities to travel to Cuba to provide assistance to independent libraries, professional organizations, charity organizations, journalists, educators, nurses, and medical doctors working independently of the regime;
  - Fund programs to provide educational opportunities to family members of the political opposition and, working with the Organization of American States (OAS), to establish a university scholarship program for the children of Cuban dissidents to study at Latin American universities; and
  - Fund programs to support democracy-building efforts by youth, women, and Afro-Cubans to train, develop, and organize these disaffected and marginalized segments of Cuban society to take greater action in support of democracy and human rights in Cuba.
- Direct the immediate deployment of the C-130 COMMANDO SOLO airborne platform and make available funds to acquire and refit a dedicated airborne platform for the transmission of Radio and Television Martái into Cuba, consistent with U. S. international telecommunications obligations;
- Support efforts by NGOs in selected third countries to highlight human rights abuses in Cuba, as part of a broader effort to discourage tourist travel and reinforce international attention on the plight of the Cuban people, including political prisoners and civil society;
- Eliminate abuses of educational travel by limiting it to undergraduate or graduate degree granting institutions and for full-semester study programs, or shorter duration only when the program directly supports U.S. policy goals;
- Direct U.S. law enforcement authorities to conduct "sting" operations against "mule" networks and others who illegally carry money and offer rewards to those who report on illegal remittances that lead to enforcement actions;
- Reduce the regime's manipulation of family visits to generate hard currency—while preserving efforts to promote legitimate family ties and humanitarian relief for the Cuban people by:
  - Limiting family visits to Cuba to one (1) trip every three years under a specific license; individuals would be eligible to apply for a specific license three years after their last visit to Cuba; new arrivals from Cuba would be eligible to apply for a specific license three years after leaving Cuba;
  - Limiting the definition of "family" for the purposes of family visits to immediate family (including grandparents, grandchildren, parents, siblings, spouses, and children); and

    - Reducing the current authorized per diem amount (the authorized amount allowed for food and lodging expenses for travel in Cuba) from $164 per day to $50 per day (i.e., approximately eight times what a Cuban national would expect to earn during a 14-day visit) for all family visits to Cuba, based on the presumption that travelers will stay with family in Cuba.
- The process for implementation of Title III of the Cuban Liberty and Democratic Solidarity (LIBERTAD) Act should ensure that the full range of policy options are made available to the President, and that a detailed, rigorous, and complete country-by-country analysis of policies and actions with respect to Cuba is provided to the President for use in assessing whether the suspension is necessary to the national interests of the United States and will expedite a transition to democracy in Cuba;
- To deter foreign investment in Cuba in confiscated properties, claims to which are owned by U.S. nationals, aggressively pursue Title IV visa sanctions against those foreign nationals trafficking in (e.g., using or benefiting from) such property, including devoting additional personnel and resources to application and enforcement;
- Neutralize Cuban government front companies by establishing a Cuban Asset Targeting Group, comprised of appropriate law enforcement authorities, to investigate and identify new ways in which hard currency is moved in and out of Cuba;
- Provide an additional $5 million for U.S. Embassy public diplomacy initiatives to:
    - Disseminate information abroad about U.S. foreign policy, specifically regarding human rights and other developments in Cuba, including Castro's record of harboring terrorists, committing espionage against the United States and other countries, fomenting subversion of democratically elected governments in Latin America, and the U.S. Government's belief that Cuba has at least a limited developmental offensive biological weapons research and development effort; and
    - Fund and promote international or third-country national conferences to disseminate information abroad about U.S. policies on transition planning efforts related to Cuba.
- Increase direct efforts with willing third-country governments to implement a robust, proactive policy to (1) support Cuban civil society, including the opposition, and (2) develop policy frameworks for assistance to a post-dictatorship Cuba;
- Work with NGOs and other interested parties to assure that a Cuban independent labor representative or labor representative in exile is able to speak at ILO conferences;
- Encourage efforts by NGOs to draw attention to exploitative labor conditions in Cuba and assist Cuban workers in obtaining redress for that wrong;
- Fund NGO projects designed to help Cuban citizens obtain effective access to the Inter-American Commission on Human Rights and provide in-country training, through appropriate NGOs, to Cuban human rights activists in collecting and preparing information in order to file claims with the IACHR;
- Target regime officials for visa denial if they (1) are or were involved in torture or other serious human rights abuses or (2) provided assistance to fugitives from U.S. justice; and

- Establish a Transition Coordinator at the State Department to facilitate expanded implementation of pro-democracy, civil-society building, and public diplomacy projects for Cuba and to continue regular planning for future transition assistance contingencies.

Chapter 2: Meeting Basic Human Needs in Health, Education, Housing, and Human Services

Cuba's transition from the Castro regime to a democratic society with a free economy will be a challenging process. The task of meeting the basic human needs of the Cuban population involves the removal of the manifestations of Castro's communism; the introduction of the values and practices of democracy and free enterprise; and the building of institutions and services that will improve the health, nutrition, education, housing, and social services available to the Cuban people.

The fundamental goal of any assistance to a free Cuba must be to empower the Cuban people by improving their economic and social well-being, ensuring that adequate health and social services are maintained, reconstructing a democratic civic culture through education and institution-building, dealing with the human cost of the totalitarian police state, and supporting the Cuban people as they cope with these issues and work to transform themselves.

The international community, especially organizations in the Western Hemisphere, can play a leading role in assisting the Cuban transition process. The U.S. Government can work through the Organization of American States and regional agencies, and with the United Nations and its agencies, and other organizations and individual countries.

Improving Cubans' condition will require dramatic reforms to ensure that democratic values and a civic culture return, that important democratic institutions—including private and faith-based organizations—are able to flourish, and that helping agents such as schools, clinics, and community centers can respond to real needs and be accountable to the citizenry.

Some of the effort to meet basic human needs will involve immediate, short-term assistance to ensure that critical health, nutrition, and social services issues are addressed; that schools are kept open and provided with new instructional materials and staff; that any housing emergencies are addressed; that comprehensive needs assessments and data collection are begun; and that food and medical aid is distributed as needed.

As a new Cuban government initiates the process of establishing the rule of law, safeguarding human rights, and creating a new climate of opportunity, a variety of programs and services are identified that U.S. public and private sources could provide to the Cuban people over the medium- and long-term. It is expected that such assistance would come not only from U.S. Government agencies and contractors, but also from philanthropic foundations, non-profit expert organizations, and businesses investing in Cuba's future. Cuban-American and other U.S. citizens and organizations would be involved in these efforts.

Both short- and long-term issues will involve the work of many players and will need to be coordinated. The Cuban people are educated to a good basic standard and, despite the repression of the Castro regime, they have shown themselves to be remarkably resilient, savvy, and entrepreneurial. They will need the resources (including short- and long-term loans), technical assistance, and general support to enable them to improve health standards, manage the change to a market economy, and maintain and improve their infrastructure and basic services.

Selected Recommendations

The U.S. Government, if requested by the transition government, should be prepared:

- To conduct a hands-on needs assessment to provide objective data and observations on the state of health care, nutrition, education, housing, and social services;
- For the immediate immunization of all children under five who have not been already immunized under the existing health system for the major childhood diseases;
- To distribute food aid as needed and as feasible, and consider a food aid monetization program for merchants to maintain the price of food at a reasonable level;
- To work with Cuban churches and their external supporting church institutions to use local religious networks and structures to assist with humanitarian relief;
- Prepare to keep all schools open during an emergency phase of the transition in order to keep children and teenagers off the streets and learning during this unstable period;
- To institute large-scale public works projects using local Cuban labor to provide immediate jobs and help with aid efforts; and
- To provide support to Cuban small farmers to supplement food aid and to encourage self-reliance. Use the humanitarian aid program to encourage the democratic transition by empowering Cuban churches, free libraries, civic centers, the media, and small businesses to assist in the effort.

Chapter 3: Establishing Democratic Institutions, Respect For Human Rights, Rule Of Law, And National Justice And Reconciliation

The United States is committed to assist a post-Castro transition government in the promotion and consolidation of representative democratic processes and institutions that will respect the human rights and personal freedoms of all Cuban citizens.

Only when the Castro regime's authoritarian institutions and practices are abandoned, its instruments of repression dismantled, and a popularly based democratic process initiated, will Cubans be able to begin governing themselves through the exercise of their own free will. Such a liberation from Fidel Castro's brutal communist dictatorship will inspire a new political order based on national reconciliation, the rule of law, personal choice, and equal justice and opportunity for all.

Leaders of a transition government will likely move urgently to address a number of immediate priorities. Political prisoners will be freed because they have been unjustly incarcerated for exercising their fundamental freedoms. The large segment of the population that has been subjugated and silenced by government intimidation and violence will fear no more. The many forms of violence that have characterized the Castro regime's behavior at home and abroad will be abandoned. The Cuban people will have reason once again to be proud as they take collective responsibility for restoring their country to a respected, peaceful, and constructive role in the international community. . . .

Source: U.S. Department of State. Bureau of Western Hemisphere Affairs. "Report to the President: Commission for Assistance to a Free Cuba." May 6, 2004. www.state.gov/p/wha/rt/cuba/commission/2004/c12237.htm (accessed February 6, 2005).

Chen Shui-bian on His Reelection as President of Taiwan

May 20, 2004

INTRODUCTION

Taiwan's pro-independence president, Chen Shui-bian, narrowly won reelection on March 20, 2004—but only after a dramatic election-eve shooting that he called an assassination attempt but opponents insisted was staged to win sympathy for him. The slightly wounded Chen overcame opposition protests that the election was illegitimate, and he went on during the year to pursue policies that annoyed Beijing—which claimed Taiwan as part of Chinese territory—and that frustrated Washington, Taiwan's most important patron.

Chen's agenda suffered a potentially important setback on December 11, when Taiwan's voters rebuffed his effort to gain control of parliament. Opposition parties, which had decried the president's anti-China rhetoric, picked up 3 seats in the quadrennial elections to retain a slim working majority of the 225-seat parliament. The results of that election, coupled with the narrowness of the earlier presidential election, appeared to represent a "go slow" message from Taiwan's voters to Chen and those who wanted to make Taiwan officially independent from China.

Background

Ever since the communist takeover of mainland China in 1949, Taiwan had enjoyed an ambiguous de facto independence. China's last noncommunist leader, Chiang Kai-shek, and thousands of his supporters had fled to Taiwan from the mainland, and for years Chiang claimed his government, which he called the Republic of China, still ruled all of China. Chiang's pretense began to collapse in 1971 when the United Nations stripped Taiwan of China's seat at the UN Security Council and awarded it instead to the Peoples Republic of China, on the mainland. In 1979 the United States withdrew diplomatic recognition from the Taiwan government but continued unofficial relations through a nongovernmental entity. As of 2004 only twenty-seven countries officially recognized the Republic of China. *(U.S. recognition of China, Historic Documents of 1979, p. 669)*

Chiang had ruled Taiwan as a dictator through his Kuomintang (Nationalist) Party. A decade after his death in 1975 his son, Chiang Ching-kuo, abolished martial law and initiated economic and political reforms that led to parliamentary and presidential elections in the 1990s. In 2000 Chen Shui-bian, a former mayor of Taipei, ended the Nationalist Party's control with his victory in Taiwan's first seriously contested presidential election. His surprise victory was made possible by a split in the Nationalist Party. Then-president Lee Teng-hui ran for reelection under the Nationalist Party banner, but a former ally, James Soong, split from the party and ran independently. Chen came in first in the three-way race, with just over 39 percent of the vote, and took office as Taiwan's first president from an opposition party. *(Chen's first election, Historic Documents of 2000, p. 190)*

Before the 2000 election, Chen and his Democratic Progressive Party had advocated independence for Taiwan but had been vague about the details. Once in office Chen took no overt steps to declare independence and through a series of statements and proposals appeared to be taking an incremental approach to reaching that goal. He denounced Beijing's "one China" policy that implied Taiwan was part of China even if it had a different political system from the mainland. In 2002 Chen proposed drafting a new constitution to replace the one imposed by Chiang's regime in 1949. These steps angered the Chinese government, which issued periodic threats to take military action if Taiwan moved too far toward official independence.

Chen had to be cautious during his first term, however, because his party held only a minority of seats in the national legislature, even after it scored gains in 2001 elections. The legislature continued to be dominated by the Nationalist Party and its allies.

In general, Chen and his Democratic Progressive Party presented a fundamentally different view of Taiwan's status from what had been Nationalist Party policy. The Nationalist Party long had been dominated by those who fled mainland China in 1949, and later by their descendants; for years many nursed dreams of returning home when the communist regime collapsed. Others still thought of themselves as Chinese rather than Taiwanese. In recent years there had been a growing willingness among Nationalist leaders to consider some form of eventual reunification with China. Chen's party drew support from native Taiwanese and from those descendants of mainlanders who feared that Taiwan's hard-won economic and political freedoms would be lost if the island was taken over by Beijing. Some of these people advocated outright independence for Taiwan, while others simply sought a more assertive policy that opposed any reunification with China. Still others on the island—particularly the younger generation—appeared to view themselves as Taiwanese but with a Chinese heritage; in polls they expressed pride in China's long history and traditions but also in Taiwan's achievements over the previous half-century. The growing economic interdependence between China and Taiwan was another important factor. Many Taiwanese companies had invested in the mainland, and had even moved large manufacturing operations there, and so had a vested interest in smooth relations.

By 2004 opinion polls showed that most of Taiwan's people were comfortable with the status quo and had reservations about either aligning the island more closely with China or declaring its formal independence. The status quo also was the position most favored by Washington, which increasingly found itself torn between historic ties to Taiwan (including a long-standing promise to defend the island against an attack from China) and the growing economic and political strength of China. Successive U.S. administrations had accepted Beijing's mantra of "one China" but had favored postponing any reckoning with the logical consequence of that phrase: that Taiwan one day would again come under the control of China.

A Dramatic Election

Taiwan's status vis-à-vis China had been the major issue in the island's 2000 presidential campaign, and that was the case again in 2004. Determined to avoid a replay of the earlier election, the Nationalist Party convinced third-party candidate

James Soong to join the ticket as the vice presidential candidate, with Lien Chan running as the presidential candidate. The Nationalist Party chairman, Lien was born on the mainland and represented the generation of Taiwan residents who came to the island with Chiang.

The 2004 election campaign was a rerun of the earlier one, except that the focus now was on Chen's tenure rather than the Nationalist Party's long grip on power. Chen continued to appeal to voters who feared China's eventual takeover of the island, while Lien tried to portray Chen as a dangerous and irresponsible demagogue whose policies would provoke a military attack by Beijing.

Most opinion polls taken before the election showed the two candidates running almost neck-and-neck. Some analysts suggested in mid-March that only a dramatic incident could shift the election one way or another. That incident came March 19, the day before the election, when Chen and Vice President Annette Lu were campaigning in the southern city of Tainan. While standing in an open-air jeep traveling in a motorcade, the two suddenly collapsed and where rushed to a hospital. Doctors said a bullet had grazed Chen's stomach, and the same bullet or a different one hit one of Lu's knees. Possibly because firecrackers had been set off in the area, no one had noticed a gunshot.

Within hours, rumors flew across the island that the shooting had been staged to win public sympathy for Chen. According to some rumors, an ally of Chen's carried out the shooting and was allowed to flee the scene; another rumor even suggested that Chen had shot himself and his vice president. Nationalist candidate Lien seemed determined to reinforce the rumors, saying there were "doubts" about what actually happened. Hoping to quell the speculation, the government released photographs of Chen's stomach wound being sewn up. A team of U.S. forensics experts later concluded that Chen's wound likely was the result of a shooting and not self-inflicted. A government investigation uncovered evidence that rumors of an attack against the president were reported to authorities beforehand but were not taken seriously.

On election day, Taiwan's voters appeared to be almost evenly divided. According to official figures, Chen defeated his challenger by fewer than 30,000 votes out of nearly 13.5 million cast. More than 300,000 ballots were voided—some deliberately in response to a call by Nationalist politicians for voters to reject both Chen and his opposition. Chen narrowly won a majority of the vote, in contrast to his 39 percent plurality four years earlier, but his margin of victory was much smaller than before. The opposition immediately denounced the voting as unfair, citing what it called hundreds of "irregularities." In particular, the opposition said the government used the shootings as an excuse to put thousands of security forces on special alert, thus depriving them of the chance to vote.

The government's initial explanations of the shooting, and its defense of the final vote tally, failed to satisfy the opposition, which mounted enormous public protests in Taipei for more than a week after the voting. On March 27 an estimated 300,000 people crowded around the presidential palace. Dressed in black as a sign of mourning, Nationalist candidate Lien told the crowd that protests would continue "until our goal is achieved." In response, Chen said he would support a recounting of votes if the opposition filed a legal challenge to the election. Opposition protests continued sporadically for several more weeks, then gradually faded out as the Nationalist Party turned to the courts, filing a lawsuit charging Chen with staging the shooting and undermining the election process. A mid-level court on November 4 ruled against the opposition, and that ruling was upheld by the country's High Court on December 31.

Chen's Referendum

Also as part of the election, Taiwan's voters acted on two controversial referendum proposals. Chen in November 2003 had said he would ask Taiwan's voters to vote on proposals calling on China to withdraw its ballistic missiles that were aimed at Taiwan and demanding that China renounce the use of force against Taiwan. China denounced the proposals, and U.S. president George W. Bush had warned Chen against them, saying in December 2003 that the United States opposed any "unilateral" actions that would "change the status quo." *(Background, Historic Documents of 2003, p. 1181)*

Taiwan's parliament authorized a referendum but put limits on what Chen could propose. Chen then watered down the language he proposed putting before the voters. The proposal on missiles was changed to ask voters if they agreed that Taiwan "should acquire more advanced antimissile weapons" if China refused to withdraw its missiles pointed at the island. The other proposal asked voters to support an unspecified "peace and stability framework" to be negotiated by China and Taiwan. The moderate wording of these proposals failed to satisfy China, which continued to denounce what it called Chen's penchant for "confrontation."

The war of words across the Taiwan Strait over these proposals may have influenced some of Taiwan's voters and possibly confused others. In any event, the outcome was ambiguous. A majority of voters, 7.4 million, supported the two proposals, but that fell short of the requirement for a majority all 16 million eligible voters. Along with the close presidential vote, this result appeared to indicate that the Taiwanese people remained deeply divided about the island's underlying relationship with China.

Chen's Inauguration

Chen was inaugurated for a second four-year term on May 20. The Nationalist Party boycotted the event and instead held a rally elsewhere in Taipei. Reputedly under strong pressure from the Bush administration to tone down his often-fiery rhetoric, Chen in his inaugural speech adopted a moderate stance on Taiwan's relationship with China.

In particular, Chen appeared to modify his position on the subject of a new constitution. Chen had first proposed a new constitution in September 2003, saying he wanted to have such a document completed by 2006 and put into effect by 2008. At that point Chen offered no specifics on what he wanted, but he said in October 2003 that a new constitution would make Taiwan a "normal, complete, great country"—language that appeared to indicate his intention to add an official gloss to Taiwan's de facto independence. Chinese officials said Chen appeared ready to risk war. They noted that Taiwan's existing constitution stated that the island's sovereignty rested with "China"—an implicit recognition that the island was part of China. Chen, however, had said Taiwan's people held the island's sovereignty, and he implied that a new constitution would recognize that fact.

At his inauguration, Chen appeared to try to allay China's concerns about a new constitution. "I am fully aware that consensus has yet to be reached on issues related to national sovereignty, territory and the subject of unification-independence," he said in his inaugural speech. "Therefore, let me explicitly propose that these particular issues be excluded from the present constitutional re-engineering project." Chen outlined numerous specific matters he said he wanted to address in a new constitution—all having to do with the machinery of Taiwan's government, such as lowering the voting age from twenty to eighteen and eliminating the provincial layer of government.

The Bush administration appeared pleased by Chen's statements. White House spokesman Scott McClellan called the speech "responsible and constructive." Official Chinese spokesmen rejected Chen's language but used relatively moderate language themselves. "The root of tensions in the Taiwan Strait has not been eliminated," Zhang Mingqing, spokesman for Beijing's Taiwan Affairs Office, told reporters on May 24. "The peril affecting peace and stability in the Asia-Pacific region still exists." Noting that Chen continued to describe Taiwan as a "country" and its people as "sovereign," Zhang said: "He is riding near the edge of the cliff, and there is no sign that he is going to rein in his horse."

Chen made one other significant effort during the year to address the issue. In the president's traditional National Day address on October 10, he suggested a return to the direct talks that Taiwan and China had conducted between 1992 and 1999. In what some observers considered a subtle shift of his policy, Chen appeared to suggest that any new talks could be held on the same basis as the old ones—a mutual recognition of the "one China" policy but with the understanding that each side had its own interpretation of what the term meant. If he intended to signal such a shift, Chen did not make it clear—and China continued to reject his statements as "provocative" and said his actions would "only bring great catastrophe."

After meeting with top Chinese officials in Beijing on October 25, U.S. Secretary of State Colin Powell said he had urged them to consider the "positive" nature of Chen's speech. "The United States thought there might be some elements [in the speech] the Chinese could work with in improving cross-straits dialogue," Powell said. "The response I received from Chinese leadership today was that they are still concerned about President Chen Shui-bian's actions and they did not find his statement to be that forthcoming."

Legislative Elections

Taiwan's electoral calendar meant that the island's voters had two opportunities during the year to express themselves on Chen's policies toward China and other matters. Any ambiguities created by the close results of the presidential election and the accompanying referendum could be cleared up with legislative elections scheduled for December 11. Early polls suggested that Chen might succeed in gaining control of parliament, which had remained in the hands of the Nationalist Party and its allies during his first term. But in the closing weeks of the campaign, Chen came under pressure not just from the opposition but from some of his own allies, who said he was not moving fast enough to confirm Taiwan's independence from China. Pulled in this direction, Chen sharpened his anti-China rhetoric—shoring up support among his base but apparently alarming voters who feared jeopardizing Taiwan's status quo.

The elections appeared to confirm that Taiwan's voters remained deeply divided and that neither Chen nor the opposition had swung the electorate decisively. Overall, the Nationalist Party and its allies in opposition gained 3 seats to retain a slim working majority of 114 seats in the 225-seat legislature. This result was widely seen as a defeat for Chen because he had failed to gain control of parliament for his Democratic Progressive Party and its allies. "The result did not meet our expectations, and we deeply regret this," Chen said. Three days later he resigned as party chairman and accepted personal responsibility for the outcome. The results were widely viewed as handicapping Chen's ability to forge an entirely new relationship between Taiwan and China. Even so, some observers said the results could not be interpreted as an absolute rebuff of Chen because the party most opposed to his China policies—the pro-Beijing People First Party—lost 12 seats, more than one-fourth of its previous total.

A week after the election, news organizations reported that the Chinese government was preparing legislation to block Taiwan's "secession" from the mainland. Details were still unclear at year's end, but legal analysts in China said the proposed law reflected continuing concern by Beijing authorities that Chen remained determined to press for a formal declaration of independence.

Following are excerpts from the inaugural address on May 20, 2004, by Chen Shui-bian, the reelected president of Taiwan (Republic of China).

"Paving the Way for a Sustainable Taiwan"

... In the final year of the twentieth century, Taiwan crossed a historic doorsill, completing an unprecedented transfer of power between political parties, and ushering in a new era in our nation's democratic development. In that time of change over—between the old and the new century—our fledgling democracy found itself stumbling down a rugged path of trial and tribulation. Taiwan's maiden voyage into the new century came wrought with turbulence as the old and the new, the weak and the strong, the emergence of crisis and the rise of opportunity—all came clashing into co-existence.

In the eyes of Chinese societies and other emerging democratic states, Taiwan's democracy embodies not merely a democratic experimentation; it signifies an exemplary success. The standard of democracy achieved in Western nations is the tried result through the test of time. In comparison, Taiwan's newfound democracy, after weathering rough waters, has burgeoned into an even more precious accomplishment. Our experience also serves as testament that democracy does not come ready-made, nor is it a Utopian ideal. There is no express train to transport us to the final destination. Democratic advancement occurs only through constant and gradual endeavor, one step at a time.

In the initial stage of Taiwan's democratization—from lifting of the martial law, complete re-election of the national legislature to direct presidential election—we have vested sovereignty with the people and began fostering Taiwan's national identity. In the second stage, a greater emphasis is placed on the establishment of a civil society and on the rebuilding of unity through a sense of shared destiny.

From increased community and civic consciousness to broader participation in public affairs and national policymaking—including the holding of a referendum, the rights and duties of citizens in a civil society have been affirmed and further improved; and thereby, the development towards a more matured, rational, and responsive democracy. We must seek to establish a civil society, and through joint participation and collective efforts, to create an identity with this land and a common memory if we are to transcend the limitations of ethnicity, lineage, language and culture, and to build a new and unified sense of shared destiny.

In today's society, issues of identity and ethnicity are a serious matter that cannot be denied or deliberately overlooked. My colleagues and I, in the Democratic Progressive Party (DPP) as the governing party, will lead the way in addressing such issues. We will take the first step and begin with candid self-reflection. . . .

The fabric of Taiwan society today is comprised mainly of diverse immigrant groups. It is not a minority-ruled colonial state; hence, no single ethnic group alone should undeservingly bear the burden of history. Presently, regardless of one's birthplace—be it Guangdong or Taitung, regardless of the origin of one's mother—be it Vietnam or Tainan, and regardless of whether an individual identifies with Taiwan or with the Republic of China, per se, a common destiny has bequeathed upon all of us the same parity and dignity. Therefore, let us relinquish our differentiation between native and foreign, and between minority and majority, for the most complimentary and accurate depiction of present-day Taiwan is of a people "ethnically diverse, but one as a nation." A shared sense of belonging has become the common denominator among all the 23 million people of Taiwan.

This year's presidential election was marked by an exceedingly spirited campaign, hitherto unseen in history. The close results have prompted opposition parties to question the process and file legal charges contesting the results of the vote. As the incumbent president, I have, with the utmost sincerity, expressed my highest respect for the independence and fairness of our judicial system. I have also vowed to accept the result of its investigation regardless of the final outcome. It is my firm belief that abiding by and acceptance of the rule of law is the only conduit through which we can resolve conflicts—for, if we were to rebuke the trust placed by the people in Taiwan's democracy and independent judiciaries, then the end result would be that "everyone loses." Today's timely spring shower will calm our spirits and clear our minds. . . .

Unite Taiwan, stabilize cross-strait relations, seek social harmony, and reinvigorate the economy. These are the earnest hopes of the people and the preeminent mission of my new administration. But none of these objectives can be accomplished through an individual effort, nor can one political party do it alone. I shall go to the people with my plea for support, just as I stand here today, calling on the opposition parties and the voices of public opinion to join me in this historic endeavor. . . .

The Constitution stands as the supreme legal basis of a nation, symbolizing a paramount contract between the government and the people. Our current Constitution was promulgated under circumstances that were very different from the society we know today, and the majority of the articles in the Constitution no longer address the present—much less the future—needs of Taiwan. The promotion of constitutional re-engineering and the re-establishment of the constitutional order are tasks that correspond with the expectations of the people and are in accordance with the consensus shared by all political parties.

The constitutional re-engineering project aims to enhance good governance and increase administrative efficiency, to ensure a solid foundation for democratic rule of law, and to foster long-term stability and prosperity of the nation. There are many problems in our current Constitution that need to be tackled, amongst which the more immediate and obvious include: whether to have a three-branch or five-branch separation of power; whether to adopt a presidential or parliamentary system of government;

whether the president should be elected by a relative majority or an absolute majority; reform of the national legislature and relevant articles; the role of the National Assembly and its retainment versus abolishment; whether to suspend or abolish the provincial government; lowering of voting age; modification of compulsory military service requirements; protection of basic human rights and the rights of the disadvantaged; and, principles governing the running of the national economy. Indeed, this will be a project of grand scale that is certain to have significant impact.

To avoid repeating the same mistakes by past administrations—six rounds of constitutional amendments in ten years time—the proposed constitutional reform project must not be monopolized by one person or by a single political party, nor should it be undertaken merely for the short-term. In the future, we will invite members of the ruling party and the opposition parties, as well as legal experts, academic scholars and representatives from all fields and spanning all social classes, to collaborate in forming a "Constitutional Reform Committee." Our aim will be to generate the highest level of social consensus on the scope and procedure of the constitutional reform, all of which are to be open to public scrutiny.

By the time I complete my presidency in 2008, I hope to hand to the people of Taiwan and to our country a new version of our Constitution—one that is timely, relevant and viable—this is my historic responsibility and my commitment to the people. In the same context, I am fully aware that consensus has yet to be reached on issues related to national sovereignty, territory and the subject of unification/independence; therefore, let me explicitly propose that these particular issues be excluded from the present constitutional re-engineering project. . . .

Taiwan's long-term friendship with the United States, Japan and our allies in the world has been founded on the safeguarding of our common interests. More importantly, it is an alliance of core values that we share: freedom, democracy, human rights and peace.

Taiwan's democratic development, and peace and stability in the Taiwan Strait, remains a focal point of international attention. On behalf of our government and people, I would like to once again express our heartfelt gratitude for the friendship that has been extended to us—reminding me of the old adage "together though apart." The people of Taiwan embrace peace. Needless to say, Taiwan's national security is of greater concern to us than to anyone else in the world. Faced with an ever-increasing military threat from across the Strait, it is imperative for all the people, including political adversaries, to forge a strong will to defend ourselves, proactively strengthening our defense equipment and upgrading our self-defense capabilities. It is our sincere hope that our friends in the international arena will continue to render their valuable attention and assistance to the cause of peace in the Taiwan Strait and stability in the Asia-Pacific Region. Let us take this opportunity to give a warm round of applause to our international allies for their friendship and dedication. . . .

Not long ago, the European Union (EU) welcomed the accession of ten new member states. Following several decades of effort, with respect to each individual country and by the free choice of citizens, the EU has successfully integrated the common interests of the people of Europe. Such a valuable experience has far-reaching implications and will impact world order in this new century. From this we see that regional integration is not merely an ongoing but also a future trend. This trend, in addition to globalization, has led to fundamental changes in the conventional thinking of national sovereignty and territorial boundaries, such that envisioning "universal harmony" will no longer be an intangible ideal.

With the new century upon us, let the leaders on both sides of the Strait, in striving to attain the greatest welfare for their peoples, heed this new trend by adopting a brand new frame of mind—together, let us take a fresh, unparalleled approach in addressing future cross-strait issues.

The peoples on both sides share a common ancestral, cultural and historical heritage. In the past century, both have endured the repression of foreign powers and the domination of authoritarian rule. Both our peoples now share an indomitable resolve to stand up and be the masters of their own destiny, a sentiment that is worthy of our full, mutual understanding.

We can understand why the government on the other side of the Strait, in light of historical complexities and ethnic sentiments, cannot relinquish the insistence on the "One China Principle." By the same token, the Beijing authorities must understand the deep conviction held by the people of Taiwan to strive for democracy, to love peace, to pursue their dreams free from threat, and, to embrace progress. But if the other side is unable to comprehend that this honest and simple wish represents the aspiration of Taiwan's 23 million people, if it continues to threaten Taiwan with military force, if it persists in isolating Taiwan diplomatically, if it keeps up irrational efforts to blockade Taiwan's rightful participation in the international arena, this will only serve to drive the hearts of the Taiwanese people further away and widen the divide in the Strait.

The Republic of China now exists in Taiwan, Penghu (The Pescadores), Kinmen and Matsu. This is a fact. Taiwan's existence as a member of international society is also a fact. Such realities cannot be negated by anyone for any reason—for therein lies the collective will of the people of Taiwan. A half century of toil and labor by the people of this land has culminated in what is now known as the "Taiwan Experience," the fruits of which validate the existence of the Republic of China and, what is more, have become the proud assets, not only of the peoples on both sides of the Taiwan Strait, but of all Chinese societies.

History has given rise to the development of two very different political systems as well as two dissimilar ways of life on either side of the Taiwan Strait. However, if we make a concerted effort to find some positive aspect of our differences and commonalities, perhaps we shall discover a wonderful opportunity, a catalyst for building a cooperative and mutually beneficial relationship. Taiwan is a completely free and democratic society. Neither single individual nor political party can make the ultimate choice for the people. If both sides are willing, on the basis of goodwill, to create an environment engendered upon "peaceful development and freedom of choice," then in the future, the Republic of China and the People's Republic of China—or Taiwan and China—can seek to establish relations in any form whatsoever. We would not exclude any possibility, so long as there is the consent of the 23 million people of Taiwan.

For more than a decade, interaction between the peoples on both sides has grown closer and more intense. This development bears great significance and increases the importance of furthering cross-strait relations. In the future, we hope to continue pushing forth current liberalization measures while expanding cross-strait exchange across the spectrum—from journalism and information to education and culture, to economics and trade—and to promote the establishment of channels for resuming cross-strait dialogue and communication. By building bridges, we will aim to close gaps and establish a foundation for mutual trust.

The first two decades of this century will be a crucial time for Taiwan to pursue a comprehensive program of upgrading and transformation; it also represents an opportune moment in history for Mainland China to move forward with democratization and liberalization. Therefore, governments on both sides should seize this timely opportunity to take on the challenges of global competition, advocating for progress and development instead of dwelling on the impasse of political debate. We have taken note that Chinese Communist Party leaders repeatedly emphasize the importance of steady development for the welfare of Mainland China's 1.3 billion people, hence, the espousal of "peaceful emergence" as its tone for developing international relations. We have no doubt the Beijing authorities recognize that maintaining the peaceful status quo in the Taiwan Strait is of vital importance to sustainable development for our respective sides and for the stability of the Asia-Pacific region as a whole.

It is my belief that both sides must demonstrate a dedicated commitment to national development, and through consultation, establish a dynamic "peace and stability framework" for interactions; that we must work together to guarantee there will be no unilateral change to the status quo in the Taiwan Strait; and, additionally, we must further promote cultural, economic and trade exchanges—including the three links—for only in so doing can we ensure the welfare of our peoples while fulfilling the expectations of the international community.

As the President of the Republic of China, I have been mandated by the people of Taiwan to defend the sovereignty, security and dignity of this nation, to chart our country's sustainable development, to safeguard peace and stability in the Taiwan Strait, to seek consensus and garner the collective support of all the people, and to carefully manage future relations across the Strait. Today I would like to reaffirm the promises and principles set forth in my inaugural speech in 2000. Those commitments have been honored—they have not changed over the past four years, nor will they change in the next four years. Upon this foundation, my next step will be to invite both the governing and opposition parties, in conjunction with representatives from various walks of the society, to participate in the establishment of a "Committee for Cross-Strait Peace and Development," combining the collective insight and wisdom of all parties and our citizenry, to draft the "Guidelines for Cross-Strait Peace and Development." The goal will be to pave the way for formulating a new relationship of cross-strait peace, stability and sustainable development. . . .

Source: Republic of China. Government Information Office. "President Chen's Inaugural Speech 'Paving the Way for a Sustainable Taiwan.'" May 20, 2004. www.gio.gov.tw/taiwan-website/4-oa/20040520/2004052001.html (accessed January 12, 2005).

Attorney General and FBI Director on the Terrorism Threat

May 26, 2004

INTRODUCTION

The Bush administration gave Americans urgent warnings in 2004 that the al Qaeda terrorist network was planning a major attack against the United States, possibly during the Democratic and Republican national conventions during the summer. Attorney General John Ashcroft and FBI director Robert Mueller on May 26 cited al Qaeda's reported sponsorship of the bombing of commuter trains in Madrid two months earlier and suggested that al Qaeda had nearly completed its plans for a similar "large scale attack" in the United States. Homeland Security Secretary Tom Ridge issued another warning on August 1 that al Qaeda was planning to attack some of the country's major financial centers. Al Qaeda had claimed responsibility for the September 11, 2001, terrorist attacks in New York City and Washington, D.C., which had resulted in nearly 3,000 deaths. *(Madrid bombings, p. 105; September 11 attacks, Historic Documents of 2001, p. 614)*

There were no terrorist attacks of any size in the United States during 2004, although the poison ricin had been discovered in a Capitol Hill mailroom in January, causing a brief flurry of concern. The political conventions took place in Boston and New York safely, under heavy security. The Bush administration said its "war" against terrorism had headed off any planned attack and seriously weakened al Qaeda, but many terrorism experts outside the government said al Qaeda might simply be taking time to complete its plans for an attack, as it had often done in the past. The almost daily carnage of terrorist attacks in Iraq—despite, or possibly because of, the presence there of thousands of U.S. troops—also served as a constant reminder of the symbiotic relationship between the United States and Islamist terrorism. *(Bioterrorism concerns, p. 450; al Qaeda network, p. 534; Iraq violence, p. 874)*

Color-coded Alerts

The Bush administration in March 2002 established a color-coded system to alert the public and government agencies to the potential threat of a terrorist attack. Red signified that an attack was likely, orange that there was a "high" possibility of an attack, yellow that the threat was "elevated," and green that a threat was not likely.

The level had been raised to orange (for the fifth time) on December 21, 2003, when Ridge cited intelligence reports of a potential attack during the holiday season. That alert had led to cancellation of several flights between Europe and the United States, but there were no attacks. The threat level was lowered to yellow (elevated) on January 9 except for Las Vegas, Los Angeles, New York City, and

Washington, D.C., and the airline and nuclear power industries. This was the first time the government had set different threat levels for specific areas or industries.

By 2004 the administration's repeated public warnings of potential attacks unnerved millions of Americans—and led millions of others eventually to ignore the warnings, according to opinion polls. The aviation industry was affected more often than any other sector of society, with commercial airlines and airports often being forced to cancel or delay flights when the government issued its alerts. The warnings also caused stress for state and local law enforcement agencies, many of which had been on a high state of alert almost continuously since the September 2001 attacks. The federal government provided millions of dollars in funding to help these agencies buy equipment, such as night-vision goggles and high-tech radios, but offered virtually no financial help for hiring or paying personnel to be on guard against terrorism.

A report sent to Congress by the General Accounting Office (GAO, later renamed the General Accountability Office) on June 25 said the Homeland Security Department was not adequately notifying other authorities of changes in the alert levels. The report quoted authorities in eight federal, local, and state agencies as saying they had learned about changes in threat levels from the news media. The report also faulted the department for lacking written standards for determining when to change the threat levels.

The senior Republican and Democratic members of the House Homeland Security Committee said the GAO report showed problems in the alert system. The government needed to "make it work better or get rid of it," committee chairman Christopher Cox, a California Republican, said. The ranking Democrat, Jim Turner of Texas, added: "I'm afraid if we don't make improvements in the system, the public's going to lose trust and confidence in that system."

Ashcroft, Mueller Warning

Top intelligence officials told Congress in late February that al Qaeda had supporters in the United States and was continuing to recruit new members worldwide. Mueller told the Senate Intelligence Committee on February 24 that al Qaeda remained able to "strike in the United States and to strike United States citizens abroad with little or no warning." Mueller also warned that al Qaeda tended to "revisit missed targets until they succeed." This appeared to be a suggestion that al Qaeda might again target the Capitol building and White House, which apparently were among the intended targets on September 11.

CIA director George Tenet added his own warning to the Intelligence Committee: "We are still at war against a movement. People who say it's [the threat] exaggerated don't look at the same world I look at. It's not going away anytime soon."

Al Qaeda issued its own reminder that same day, with a broadcast in the Arab world of two audiotapes reportedly by Ayman al-Zawahiri, the senior aide to Osama bin Laden. "Bush, fortify your defenses and intensify your security measures because the Muslim nation, which sent brigades to New York and Washington, has decided to send you one brigade after another, carrying death and seeking paradise," a voice, said to be that of al Zawahiri, said on one of the tapes. U.S. officials said the tapes appeared genuine.

After the Madrid bombings on March 11, Mueller and other officials made new statements warning that al Qaeda was determined to attack the United States. In a March 25 interview with the Associated Press, Mueller said: "We understand that between now and the election, there is a window of time in which terrorists may well wish to influence events, whether it's in the United States or overseas." As the

United States stepped up security at airports and other traditional targets, he said, terrorists were looking for "soft targets," as the train attacks in Madrid demonstrated. In several statements during March and April, officials warned that buses and trains were potential terrorist targets.

The year's most specific warning from government agencies came on May 26—just before the Memorial Day weekend—when Ashcroft and Mueller issued their warning of a potential al Qaeda attack during the political conventions or possibly during the early June summit meeting in Sea Island, Georgia, of the leaders of the Group of Eight nations (the seven leading industrialized nations plus Russia). Ashcroft said the administration had received "credible evidence from multiple sources that al Qaeda plans to attempt an attack on the United States in the next few months." He added that al Qaeda's plan was "to hit the United States hard." Even so, Ashcroft acknowledged that he knew of no specific plans by al Qaeda—just the general threat that an attack was possible.

Ashcroft and Mueller also asked Americans to be on the lookout for seven suspected al Qaeda members; five of the suspects had lived for periods in either Canada or the United States. Two of the five held Canadian citizenship and one was a U.S. citizen. Two others were suspects in the August 1998 bombing of U.S. embassies in Kenya and Tanzania. Mueller said each of them "is known to have a desire and the ability to undertake planning, facilitation and attack against the United States, whether it be in the United States itself or overseas." Mueller said he had no information indicating that any of the seven actually were in the United States at the time.

Oddly, Secretary Ridge did not appear at the news conference, nor did his agency raise the threat level. Ridge said in a television interview that there was no need to "put the entire country on [an elevated] national alert," although there was a need to increase security. Some news reports quoted senior aides to Ridge as saying they were surprised by Ashcroft's statements.

Local officials in some jurisdictions expressed confusion about the warning, saying they were not sure exactly how to respond when the threat level had not been raised. The New York City police commissioner said he had been aware "for a while" of the information cited by Ashcroft and Mueller. "This is not information that just broke yesterday." Some Democrats said they suspected a political motive behind the warning. Illinois senator Dick Durbin suggested that the administration was hoping to divert attention from bad news in Iraq, where insurgent bombings and other attacks were imperiling the U.S. plan to build an Iraqi government. Most other Democrats, including the presumptive presidential candidate, Sen. John Kerry, did not accuse the administration of having a political motive for its action, however.

On July 8 Ridge became the first senior administration official to say al Qaeda was planning an attack aimed at disrupting the November elections. The government had no specific information on when or where such an attack might take place, he said, but added: "These are not conjectures or mythical statements that we're making; these are pieces of information that we can trace comfortably to sources that we deem to be credible." Once again, however, Ridge said it was unnecessary to raise the terrorism alert level, which remained at yellow for most of the country.

Financial Centers Put on Alert

Three weeks later, on Sunday, August 1, Ridge raised the alert level to orange, but only for the nation's major financial centers in New York City; Newark, New Jersey; and Washington, D.C. Ridge said he issued this "targeted" alert because U.S.

intelligence had obtained "new and unusually specific information," which he called "alarming," about potential al Qaeda attacks on financial centers. He cited in particular the Citigroup buildings and the New York Stock Exchange in Manhattan, the Prudential Financial headquarters in Newark, and the International Monetary Fund and World Bank headquarters in the nation's capital. Ridge said he had no information about a "specific time" other than that any attacks likely would take place before election day.

The *New York Times* immediately reported that Ridge's warning was based on information obtained from Muhammad Naeem Noor Khan, an al Qaeda operative captured two weeks earlier in Pakistan. The newspaper said Khan had helped operate an Internet-based communications system for al Qaeda, and his capture led to the retrieval of documentary evidence indicating the potential attack cited by Ridge. Because of the reported quality of the information, this terrorist alert appeared to be taken very seriously by government officials at all levels. New York City mayor Michael R. Bloomberg said the city's police would step up security, which would include random searches of trucks and other large vehicles. Even so, Bloomberg urged New Yorkers to go about their daily business, and he rang the opening bell at the stock exchange the next day. In Washington, police blocked traffic in key areas and said they had installed surveillance cameras near the locations cited by Ridge as potential targets.

The excitement level dropped considerably the next day, August 2, when news reports quoted administration officials as saying the information cited by Ridge did not contain specific warnings, and in fact much of it was several years old. Frances Fragos Townsend, the White House homeland security adviser, told the PBS *News Hour* program that information about al Qaeda's surveillance of the U.S. financial centers had been "gathered in 2000 and 2001" but might have been updated as recently as the previous January. That statement, and similar ones by other officials, led to news reports saying the administration had used old information to warn of a new threat. Attempting to combat those reports, intelligence officials on August 3 said Ridge's warning was based on "multiple streams of intelligence"—not just the old reports. Officials also said a terrorism suspect arrested the previous week in Britain, Abu Issa al-Hindi, had supervised the surveillance of U.S. financial institutions in 2000 and 2001.

Ridge defended his alert, saying it had led to increased security steps, which in turn "make it much more difficult for the terrorists to achieve their broad objectives." A former Republican member of the House of Representatives and governor of Pennsylvania, Ridge also insisted that the administration had no political motives in issuing its alert, which came just days after the Democratic National Convention ended in Boston. "We don't do politics in the Department of Homeland Security," he said on August 3. That line rankled some Democrats, who noted that Ridge had claimed three days earlier that the information behind the alert had resulted from "the president's leadership in the war against terror."

Yet another conflicting signal to the public came on August 3. Even as security was being tightened in Manhattan, the Statue of Liberty in New York harbor was reopened to visitors. The iconic monument had been closed since the September 11 attacks for major renovations upgrading its security and safety.

The uproar over Ridge's alert had barely died down when al Qaeda's deputy chief reappeared with another taped warning against the United States. A videotape broadcast by Arab-language networks on September 9 said the United States was facing defeat in both Afghanistan and Iraq. "The Americans in both countries are between two fires," Zawahiri said in the tape. "If they continue they will bleed until death, and if they withdraw, they will lose everything." Another audiotape, reportedly by Zawahiri, surfaced on October 1, repeating al Qaeda's longstanding calls for Muslin resistance against the United States.

Al Qaeda's most potent message of the year appeared to be timed to influence the elections. A videotape aired October 29 by the Arabic al Jazeera network showed bin Laden—who had not been seen on tape for more than a year—speaking to the American people and denouncing Bush in florid terms. "I am surprised by you," bin Laden said on the tape. "Despite entering the fourth year after September 11, Bush is still deceiving you and hiding the truth from you and therefore the reasons are still there to repeat what happened." The tape contained no specific threats, however.

Experts on terrorism in the United States said it was unclear exactly what bin Laden was trying to accomplish with the tape, except possibly to remind Americans that he remained at large and had eluded Bush's 2001 promise to capture him "dead or alive." Some experts suggested the tape—possibly the thirteen minutes of it that al Jazeera did not broadcast—might have contained a signal for al Qaeda loyalists to mount a planned attack.

Bush and Kerry reacted aggressively to the tape, each saying it reinforced the messages they had been giving about fighting terrorism. After the November 2 election, which Bush won by a broader margin than many polls had predicted, political pundits differed on whether the tape had swayed many voters one way or another. *(Election, p. 773)*

Two days after the election, federal officials offered details of some of the steps they had taken during the year to head off a potential terrorist attack. The FBI had interviewed about 10,000 Muslims and Arab-Americans, seeking information about potential terrorism; more than 700 people were arrested on immigration violations, and most were later deported. "It's very hard to prove a negative," Michael Garcia, head of the U.S. Immigration and Customs Enforcement agency told the Associated Press on November 4, when asked if these steps had foiled an attack. "We did cases and operations for people we thought posed national security concerns. We didn't arrest anyone who had a bomb."

On November 9, a week after the election, Ridge's deputy, James M. Loy, said the alert level had been lowered from orange to yellow for the financial centers in the New York and Washington areas. Loy said the government had received no new intelligence about potential threats, but he said the targets cited by Ridge had improved security enough to justify lowering the threat level. Loy and other security officials said they were turning their attention to possible threats for events in upcoming months, including the December holiday season and the next football Super Bowl, scheduled for February 6, 2005. Loy said it would be "very dangerous" to assume that the threat of terrorism was in the past.

Ridge announced November 30 that he was resigning as Homeland Security secretary—the position he had held since shortly after Congress created the agency in a massive reorganization in 2002. Ridge at times had been ridiculed for his terrorism alerts, notably in 2003 when the Homeland Security Department urged Americans to buy plastic sheeting and duct tape to safeguard their homes against chemical weapons. Even so, members of Congress from both parties generally praised his work in assembling a cabinet department from twenty-two agencies. Bush quickly named Bernard Kerick, who had been New York police chief at the time of the September 11 attacks, as Ridge's successor. Kerick withdrew his nomination a week later, on December 10, after news reports raised numerous ethical questions about his personal conduct since leaving the New York job at the end of 2001. Bush had not named a replacement as of year's end.

Terrorism Convictions Thrown Out

The Bush administration and local law enforcement agencies had arrested hundreds of people in the United States since the September 11 attacks, but after three years only a handful of people had been convicted on terrorism-related charges, and none had been convicted in connection with September 11. In September the Justice Department acknowledged that the first important convictions had been gained through the misuse of evidence, and the convictions were set aside.

The case involved two Moroccan men, Abdel-Ilah Elmardoudi and Karim Koubriti, who were convicted in federal court in Detroit on charges of document fraud and conspiring to provide material support to terrorists. A third Moroccan man, Ahmed Hannan, was convicted of document fraud, but a fourth defendant, an Algerian, was acquitted. Federal prosecutors had said the men were part of a terrorism "sleeper cell" in the Detroit area.

Lawyers for the defendants had questioned the actions of the chief federal prosecutor, Richard G. Covertino, and forced his removal from the case. An outside review basically agreed with the defense lawyers and showed that Covertino had refused to turn evidence over to the defense and had engaged in a "pattern of mistakes and oversights" that tainted the convictions. The Justice Department on September 1 asked the court to set aside the convictions, and Judge Gerald E. Rosen agreed to do so. New prosecutors said they would request a new trial on the document fraud charges but would drop the terrorism-related charges on which two of the defendants had been wrongfully convicted.

Judge Rosen on October 12 released Koubriti from prison and sent him to a halfway house. His two codefendants remained in custody, and all three awaited a new trial on the pared-down charges, but no date had been set as of year's end.

Following are excerpts from a news conference held at the Justice Department in Washington, D.C., on May 26, 2004, in which Attorney General John Ashcroft and FBI director Robert Mueller warned of potential terrorist attacks against the United States.

"Attorney General and FBI Director on Summer Terrorist Threat"

Statement by Attorney General Ashcroft

Good afternoon. Today, Director Mueller and Deputy Attorney General [James] Comey and I want to announce developments in the war on terror.

First, credible intelligence from multiple sources indicates that al Qaeda plans to attempt an attack on the United States in the next few months. This disturbing intelligence indicates al Qaeda's specific intention to hit the United States hard.

Beyond this intelligence, al Qaeda's own public statements suggest that it's almost ready to attack the United States. Just after New Year's, al Qaeda announced openly that preparations for an attack on the United States were 70 percent complete.

After the March 11th attack in Madrid, Spain, an al Qaeda spokesman announced that 90 percent of the arrangements for an attack in the United States were complete. The Madrid railway bombings were perceived by Osama bin Laden and al Qaeda to have advanced their cause. Al Qaeda may perceive that a large-scale attack in the United States this summer or fall would lead to similar consequences.

Several upcoming events over the next few months may suggest especially attractive targets for such an al Qaeda attack. These events include the G-8 Summit, hosted by the United States in Georgia, the Democratic Party Convention in Boston this summer, or the Republican Party Convention in New York City.

Second, in addition to making this announcement on the war on terror, we are seeking help from the American people. We ask our fellow citizens to be on the lookout for individuals, and in specific, for each of these seven individuals that are associated with al Qaeda. They all are sought in connection with the possible terrorist threats in the United States; they all pose a clear and present danger to America; they all should be considered armed and dangerous. And if anyone has any information about any one of them, please report it immediately to law enforcement.

Adnan Shukrijumah, for example, could be a future facilitator of terrorist attacks for al Qaeda. He speaks English well. He lived in the United States for years and has tried to get back into the United States using various passports. We know that he has been involved in terrorist planning with senior al Qaeda leaders overseas and has scouted sites across America that might be vulnerable to terrorist attack.

We also ask for public assistance as we conduct interviews nationwide to gather intelligence to disrupt potential threats. Now, a similar FBI-led interview program that was launched prior to the Iraq war developed valuable intelligence that protected American lives.

In addition, we ask citizens to be aware of their surroundings. Public awareness may cause terrorists to change their plans or targets, or cause terrorists to disrupt or delay their plans. If you see suspicious activity, report it to your local police department sheriff's office or to the FBI.

Third, let me say that the face of al Qaeda may be changing. It is possible al Qaeda will attempt to infiltrate young Middle Eastern extremists into America, as they did before September 11th. Al Qaeda is a resilient and adaptable organization, known for altering tactics in the face of new security measures.

Intelligence sources suggest that ideal al Qaeda operatives may now be in their late 20s or early 30s and may travel with a family to lower their profile.

Our intelligence confirms al Qaeda is seeking recruits who can portray themselves as Europeans. Al Qaeda also attracts Muslim extremists among many nationalities and ethnicities, including North Africans and South Asians, as well as recruiting young Muslim converts of any nationality inside target countries.

Fourth, the FBI has established a 2004 threat task force to focus on this developing threat over this summer and fall period. The task force will coordinate our intelligence, analysis and field operations.

Analysts at FBI headquarters and in every field office are reviewing previously collected intelligence to re-analyze it and determine what additional information we need to collect in order to be best positioned to disrupt attacks.

We have asked the 84 joint terrorism task forces, that is our partners with state and local law enforcement, to collect specific information, to develop additional intelligence sources and to report that information to the 2004 threat task force for further analysis.

Director Mueller and I review personally the threat intelligence daily and it is shared throughout the government. When intelligence is properly collected and shared, government agencies can then act to prevent terrorist acts to protect the American people.

Specific intelligence is the foundation for effective counterterrorism strategies such as hardening targets, intercepting terrorist communications, disrupting cells, elevating threat levels and alerting state and local law enforcement.

May I be clear on this: We seek unprecedented levels of cooperation with state and local law enforcement in collecting intelligence to enable America's entire terror-fighting apparatus to act decisively to disrupt any al Qaeda presence in the United States. And we will appropriately share unprecedented access to precisely what our intelligence needs and findings are.

It is imperative that all law enforcement and intelligence agencies be enlisted to assist in identifying al Qaeda operatives and activities; activities such as surveillance of buildings, bridges, tunnels, ports of entry, et cetera.

For 32 months now, we have not had a major terrorist attack on American soil. We are winning the war on terror, but we should never forget that it is a war. Fighting terrorists is a tough business. I have faith that Americans will continue to be equal to the task.

Thank you.

Statement by FBI Director Mueller

Good afternoon, everyone.

This summer and fall, our nation will celebrate a number of events that serve as powerful symbols of our free and democratic society. As the attorney general has pointed out, they include the 4th of July celebrations, the Democratic and Republican conventions, and the November presidential election amongst others.

And unfortunately, the same events that fill most of us with hope and pride are seen by terrorists as possible opportunities for attack. So today I want to talk briefly about three things: first, the threat; second, our response; and third, what you can do to help.

Over the next few months, we have reason to believe that there will be a heightened threat to United States interests around the world. Unfortunately, we currently do not know what form the threat may take.

And that is why it is so important that we locate the seven individuals shown to my right. Though we do not have any reason at this time to believe that they are working in concert, we will not take any chances. And in light of the March terrorist bombings in Madrid, we must be prepared for any plans to launch attacks in the next several months.

Now, let me take a moment if I could to review why we are interested in each of these individuals.

Abderraouf Jdey appears in a martyrdom video that was seized in Afghanistan. His tape and the tape of four others is the last will and testament of five possible jihad martyrs. He was reportedly selected to get flight training in preparation for a second attack in the United States. He is a Canadian citizen born in Tunisia.

Adnan Shukrijumah, as has been mentioned by the attorney general, is a trained operative who poses an operational threat to the United States. As was pointed out, he's English-speaking, spent 15 years in the United States, left the United States when he was led to believe that we were interested in his activities. He was born in Saudi Arabia and carries a Guyanese passport.

Adam Gadahn is a U.S. citizen who converted to Islam, is associated with Abu Zubaydah in Pakistan, and he attended the training camps in Afghanistan. He is known to have performed translations for al Qaeda as part of the services he has provided to al Qaeda.

Aafia Siddiqui is an al Qaeda operative and facilitator, she attended colleagues in the Boston area, and is believed to have left Boston in January of 2003.

Amer El-Maati, an al Qaeda member and a licensed pilot, is believed to have discussed hijacking a plane in Canada and flying it into a building into the United States. He is a Canadian citizen of Egyptian and Syrian origin.

The last two individuals are Fazul Abdullah Mohammed and Ahmed Khalfan Ghailani. These individuals were participants in the 1998 East Africa bombings. These individuals were indicted in the Southern District of New York and have been fugitives since.

They are known to have participated in the 1998 East Africa embassy bombings and have the wherewithal, the skill, the ability, to undertake attacks both against American interests overseas as well as in the United States.

These are the seven individuals whom we are seeking. Each of these seven individuals is known to have a desire and the ability to undertake planning, facilitation and attack against the United States whether it be within the United States itself or overseas.

Now, in reissuing these "be on the lookouts for"—also known as BOLOs in trade—we want to emphasize the need for vigilance against our terrorist enemies, particularly al Qaeda.

The FBI and the entire intelligence community continues to seek information as to the whereabouts and activities of these seven individuals in connection to possible terrorist threats or attacks in the United States or against American interests overseas.

Now, we in the FBI have established a task force. We are operating around the clock to increase our collection of human intelligence, to identify any gaps in our knowledge and to develop new information sources.

We're working closely with our counterparts and our partners in the intelligence community, with the Department of Homeland Security and with state and local law enforcement in a worldwide effort to gather relevant information.

Last week, I talked with our special agents in charge of every FBI field office, explained the heightened threat and the importance of devoting the time and resources necessary to our increased intelligence collection and our investigative efforts over the next several months.

We also need the support of the American people.

First, we ask for your cooperation as we launch a nationwide series of interviews to gather information and intelligence on these potential threats and on these individuals.

And second, we need the public, both in the United States and—I'll emphasize—overseas to be on the lookout for these seven individuals. We want to know whether you've seen them in your communities, or that someone might be hiding them. Have any idea where they might be, we need you to come forward, whether it be here or oversees.

And finally, we ask you to simply be aware of your surroundings. Remain vigilant. Take note of any suspicious activities. And if you do observe anything suspicious, please contact your local police or your local FBI office.

I want to thank you for your continued support, and rest assured that there are thousands of FBI agents, Homeland Security agents, other law enforcement and intelligence officials who will be working day and night over the coming months to ensure America's continued safety.

Thank you.

Question and Answer Session

Question: Gentlemen, for either of you. What is it about these seven? There are clearly other people that are on your seeking information list or on your most wanted terror list. Is there intelligence that indicates they might be involved in any pending attacks, or is it more analysis of who'd be the most likely? And is there any information you have that any of them are in the U.S.?

Ashcroft: Well, we know some of them to be very adept at the variety of things that are necessary for the achievement of an attack in the United States. Some of them very familiar with the United States. Obviously, several of them by having lived here, been educated here, speak English well, understand the country well. Those are very important things. Other of the individuals would have other core competencies, so to speak, that they would bring to an operation. . . .

Question: You've been looking for these folks for some time. What makes you think that re-issuing these alerts will make a difference; and why the timing, today, in particular?

Ashcroft: Well, we believe that the public, like all of us, needs a reminder.

Secondly, we have gone out, as the director indicated, to every FBI office. And we're going to law enforcement authorities across America at every level of law enforcement to ask them to renew their efforts. As I indicated in my remarks, it is to re-invigorate and revitalize our contact with all our sources of information, to query those sources to generate additional intelligence that would provide us the kind of information upon which we could take further action to defend. . . .

Question: Is this threat information causing you to go to specific cities and ask them to heighten their procedures? And also, are you taking other additional extraordinary measures surrounding the G-8 or the World War II Memorial ceremonies or other events that are taking place beyond what had already been planned?

Ashcroft: Well, this is intelligence that is developing intelligence. It continues to be a subject of our interest. I think it's fair to say that this is intelligence that has come in over time. So this isn't a one shot or other thing. And as we have intelligence, we adjust our behavior.

I want to address the first aspect of your question, though. You asked about specific cities. And I think it's fair to say that we do not have intelligence that leads us to specific location in regard to this threat which we see this summer and fall. . . .

Question: Would it not make sense for people in Boston and New York to get out of those cities during the conventions?

Ashcroft: We certainly don't come to that conclusion.

Mueller: Can I add one thing to that, if I could? In response to the question here and the question with regard to Boston and New York, there are—extraordinary precautions are being taken in both those cities for the conventions as there are the G-8.

And the police chiefs in New York and Boston have undertaken extraordinary efforts to protect those sites during both the conventions as well as the G-8.

And so, we have every expectation that they will be free from any terrorist attacks by reason of the fact of the efforts that have been undertaken to protect those sites.

Question: In this (inaudible) that you've outlined here, do you have any reason to believe, first, that any of these seven are in the United States? And does the intelligence indicate that there's a new wave of people who have been attempting to enter the United States?

Ashcroft: I said in my remarks that al Qaeda had indicated that it was at one point 70 percent complete in its planning and at another point 90 percent. You might interpret that as including its own sort of projections of the human resources necessary.

I don't think we could go beyond those kinds of assessments at this moment.

As to these individuals, we know a number of them have spent a considerable amount of time in the United States. We know of their familiarity. We know of their attempts both successful and unsuccessful in the past that have resulted in their being here.

We are not able to say with certainty where they are at this particular time. . . .

Question: General Ashcroft, with all of these events this summer, I'm wondering if you are planning any series of periodic announcements such as this? And how do you balance the need to discuss a serious threat with the inevitable criticisms that you're scaring people unnecessarily and that you're covering your own bases for purely defensive purposes?

Ashcroft: Well, we don't have a specific plan.

We plan to make announcements whenever they would be in the national interest to make announcements. And one of the reasons we make announcements is that the American people can help us reduce the risk by participating in an aggressive approach to disruption.

Over and over again in the intelligence which I read on a daily basis, I find it said that activities in law enforcement and by an alert population disrupt and prevent and cause the discontinuance of terrorism. These are statements that are part of the intelligence we receive, and it indicates to me that the activities, both of the American people and of the American law enforcement community, can be very valuable in saving American lives by virtue of disrupting terrorism.

So we do not have a specific schedule. We don't have any next planned announcement at any time, scheduled or unscheduled, except to say that whenever—if it's later this afternoon or if it's later this month or next month or later in the summer, whenever it becomes in the national interest for us to make an announcement, we would make such an announcement.

Question: But there are inevitably skeptics who say you're overdoing it or you're scaring people or you're just protecting your behind, or what have you. Do you worry about those?

Ashcroft: No.

Question: You can't overdo it, in other words.

Ashcroft: Well, no. I just don't think my job is to worry about what skeptics say. My job is to do everything I can to protect the American people and to help the American people protect themselves.

In a country as substantial, as large and as free as the United States is, it takes the coordinated effort of law enforcement officials with their feet on the street, 670,000 state and local law enforcement officials, and an alert American population and everything we do, I think, to preserve that liberty and that freedom by being alert.

And so, my job is to do that. My job isn't to worry about whether someone will be second guessing. I'd far prefer that they second guess a plan which led us to safety than a plan which somehow provided us with risk. . . .

Source: Congressional Quarterly. "Attorney General John Ashcroft and FBI Director Robert Mueller Hold News Conference on Summer Terrorist Threat." May 26, 2004. Newsmaker Transcripts, CQ.com (accessed February 21, 2005).

Surgeon General on the Dangers of Smoking

May 27, 2004

INTRODUCTION

Several developments, both in the United States and abroad, advanced the cause of those trying to persuade smokers to give up the habit. In the United States, the latest U.S. surgeon general's report on the dangers of smoking added several diseases—including cataracts, leukemia, gum disease, and cancers of the cervix, kidney, pancreas, and stomach—to an already long list of illnesses caused by smoking. Congress approved legislation ending federal subsidies to farmers who grew tobacco, although an effort to authorize the Food and Drug Administration (FDA) to regulate tobacco and tobacco products failed. A federal district court judge began hearing testimony in a civil racketeering trial brought by the federal government alleging that the tobacco industry had knowingly misled the American public about the dangers of smoking. The suit, which was expected to last six months, sought to recover $280 billion in profits.

An international treaty, the Framework Convention on Tobacco Control, reached a significant milestone late in the year when Peru became the fortieth country to ratify it. Once forty countries had ratified the treaty, it became legally binding on the signatories. The treaty, aimed at reducing the number of smokers worldwide, was the first internationally binding health treaty to come into force. Several countries also took steps to ban smoking in public places. Secondhand smoke—the smoke from burning cigarettes—was widely thought to be nearly as harmful to health as smoking itself.

Worldwide, tobacco use killed 4.9 million people a year, according to the World Health Organization, which sponsored the treaty. That worked out to one death from a tobacco-related disease every six and one-half seconds. Most of the deaths occurred in the developing world, where 84 percent of the world's 1.3 billion smokers lived, and where death and disease from preventable tobacco-related illnesses placed a heavy burden on health care costs and services that poor countries could ill afford.

Surgeon General's Report

"We've known for decades that smoking is bad for your health, but this report shows that it's even worse [than we realized]," Surgeon General Richard H. Carmona said at a May 27, 2004, news conference. "The toxins from cigarette smoke go everywhere the blood flows." According to the 960-page report, entitled "The Health Consequences of Smoking," smoking remained the single largest cause of preventable death, killing an estimated 440,000 Americans each year, cutting life expectancy for smokers typically by thirteen or fourteen years and costing the country $157 billion annually in direct medical care and lost productivity.

Declaring that "the only way to avoid the health hazards of smoking is to quit completely or never start smoking," Carmona emphasized that quitting reduced the risk of disease caused by smoking and led to improved overall health. "Within minutes and hours after smokers inhale that last cigarette, their bodies begin a series of changes that continue for years," he said. "Among these health improvements are a drop in heart rate, improved circulation, and reduced risk of heart attack, lung cancer, and stroke. By quitting today a smoker can assure a healthier tomorrow." Carmona revealed that he himself had smoked until he began working on the report.

The report was the twenty-eighth on smoking to be issued by the U.S. surgeon general since 1964, when the federal government first linked smoking to lung cancer. Since then smoking had been found to be a cause of several other cancers, as well as chronic heart and cardiovascular disease, respiratory illnesses, and reproductive problems. The new report added cervical, kidney, pancreatic, and stomach cancer to the list of diseases, as well as abdominal aortic aneurysm, acute myeloid leukemia, cataracts, pneumonia, and a gum disease called periodontitus. It also said that so-called light cigarettes, with lower levels of tar and nicotine, provided "no clear" health benefits. "There is no safe cigarette," Carmona said, "whether it is called 'light,' ultralight,' or any other name."

For the first time, Carmona said, the number of former smokers slightly exceeded the number of smokers in 2002, the last year for which figures were available. An estimated 46 million people had kicked the habit, but 45.8 million Americans, slightly more than 22 percent of the population, continued to light up regularly. Although the proportion of smokers had dropped from 42 percent in 1964, the rate of decline in recent years was about half a percent a year. At that rate, Carmona said, the country was unlikely to meet the government's goal of reducing the smoking population to less than 12 percent of the total population by 2010. Carmona also expressed concern about the relatively high levels of smoking among poor Americans; nearly one-third of adults living below the poverty line smoked in 2002.

The surgeon general said that Tommy G. Thompson, secretary of the Health and Human Services Department, had earmarked $25 million for a national "quit-smoking" telephone line to lend information and support for smokers trying to stop. But neither Carmona nor the report offered any policy recommendations for further reducing the number of smokers.

Teenage Smoking

The federal Centers for Disease Control and Prevention (CDC) reported June 17 that smoking among high school teenagers had fallen to its lowest level in a generation, largely as a result of antismoking campaigns and higher cigarette prices. Just under 22 percent of high school students said they smoked in 2003, down from more than 36 percent in 1997 and the lowest level since the CDC began keeping records in 1975. For the first time, the percentage of high school smokers was lower than the percentage of adult smokers, which was just under 23 percent.

CDC officials and others found the new statistics encouraging. They showed "probably the most dramatic progress which has been made in terms of any public health problem, at least in recent memory," said John Banzhaf III, a professor of public interest law at George Washington University Law School who played an active role in the recent state lawsuits against the tobacco industry. Terry Pechanek, associate director of science for the CDC's Office on Smoking and Health, agreed that important progress was being made but warned that the battle was not over. Pechanek noted that the amount of money the tobacco industry spent to promote smoking had doubled in just five years, from $5.7 billion in 1997 to $11.2 billion in 2001, and that many states were cutting back on their antismoking campaigns because of budget constraints.

One new product being heavily promoted was flavored cigarettes, including such flavors as mint, chocolate, citrus, and coffee. Spokesmen for the tobacco companies said that the premium-priced cigarettes were fulfilling a demand among adults for flavored products and denied that their advertising was aimed at children under age eighteen. But antismoking organizations and others disagreed. "We clearly see them [the tobacco companies] repositioning themselves to go after the youth market," Greg Connally, a scientific adviser to the Massachusetts Department of Public Health, told the *Boston Globe.* "By masking the natural toxic products of smoke with these candy flavors, they're basically trying to turn a blow torch into rice pudding. It's unconscionable."

Meanwhile, a coalition of antismoking and health groups reported in December that the states were falling woefully short of funding smoking prevention programs. Only three states—Delaware, Maine, and Mississippi—were spending the minimum level of money on antismoking campaigns that the CDC had recommended. Altogether, the report said, states were planning to spend $538 million on smoking prevention in fiscal 2005, just one-third of the $1.6 billion that the CDC recommended be spent nationwide. Ironically, the states stood to receive about $20 billion in tobacco-related revenue in 2005—$7.1 billion in payments from the tobacco industry as a result of the massive settlement states reached with cigarette makers in 1998 and nearly $13 billion in tobacco tax revenues. "The states are receiving more and more revenue related to tobacco but doing far too little to fund programs to reduce tobacco use, particularly among children," said Matthew Myers, president of the Campaign for Tobacco Free Kids. "They're using the money to fill short-term budget shortfalls, build roads and every other conceivable political purpose." The other members of the coalition included the American Heart Association, American Cancer Society, and American Lung Association.

Subsidies and Regulation

Congress came closer than it ever had to giving the Food and Drug Administration authority to regulate tobacco and tobacco products, but strong opposition from the House Republican leadership and strong incentives for Democrats to vote for the underlying corporate tax breaks in an election year ended up carrying the day. Public health and antismoking groups had been lobbying for the FDA authority since 2000, when the Supreme Court ruled, 5–4, that the FDA could regulate tobacco and tobacco products only with the express authority of Congress. *(Supreme Court decision, Historic Documents of 2000, p. 556)*

Although the antismoking lobby continued to press for the FDA authority, little action was taken until 2003, when passage of FDA authority was linked to a plan for the federal government to buy out the tobacco quota program, which determined who could grow tobacco and how much they could sell. Originally enacted during the New Deal, the subsidy program had stabilized prices over the years for one of the South's main agricultural products. But in recent years tobacco farmers had complained that the quota program inflated the price of American-grown tobacco and restricted farmers' ability to compete with foreign growers. While big tobacco growers were expected to use their buyout proceeds to upgrade and modernize their growing operations, many small farmers said they would use the money to retire from tobacco growing altogether.

An agreement linking FDA regulation to a tobacco buyout was worked out in the Senate in July 2003, but negotiations later fell apart, largely over the scope of the authority to be given to the FDA. In 2004 the issue came up again, when House Ways and Means Committee Chairman Bill Thomas, R-Calif., added a $10 billion tobacco buyout to the corporate tax overhaul legislation. That legislation was considered a "must pass" because it repealed a subsidy to U.S. exporters that had triggered international sanctions of as much as $4 billion a year.

In response to Thomas's move, the Senate reopened the version of the bill it had already passed and added provisions authorizing FDA regulation. Among other things the Senate measure would allow the FDA to ban vending machine sales and cigarette advertising aimed at children and require more conspicuous warning labels. The FDA regulatory authority was strongly opposed by the House Republican leadership, as well as by most of the big tobacco companies. House leaders made it clear during the negotiations on the final bill that they might be willing to forgo the tobacco buyout if it continued to be linked to the FDA regulatory authority. Although Senate Democrats initially insisted on the FDA provisions, enough other enticements had been included in the corporate tax break bill that several finally caved in and accepted the buyout without the FDA authority. Both chambers then easily passed the corporate tax bill. Disappointed advocates of FDA regulatory authority lamented their loss. "The only way we were ever going to get FDA regulation was to hook it to a buyout," said Sen. Tom Harkin, D-Iowa. "I don't know how and when we'll ever get FDA regulation."

(In April the European Union decided to stop subsidizing its tobacco farmers. Tobacco, grown primarily in Greece and Italy, was the most heavily subsidized crop in Europe.)

Federal Lawsuit

The long-awaited trial of six tobacco companies on federal racketeering charges began September 21 in a federal district court in Washington, D.C., presided over by Judge Gladys Kessler. The companies charged with racketeering were Altria Group Inc.'s Philip Morris; R. J. Reynolds and Brown & Williamson, which had merged into Reynolds America Inc.; British American Tobacco; Liggett Groups, Inc., owned by Vector Group, Ltd; and Loew Corp.'s Lorillard Tobacco Co. The Justice Department, which filed the suit in 1999, sought to prove that the six companies had engaged in a conspiracy since 1953 to defraud the public about the health risks associated with smoking through misleading research and deceptive marketing and that the fraud was continuing. The federal suit was filed after forty-six states and the District of Columbia reached a settlement in 1998 with the four largest cigarette makers. The companies agreed to pay $206 billion over twenty-five years to compensate the states for Medicaid funds used to treat tobacco-related illnesses and to refrain from directing advertising and marketing at teenagers, among other things. *(State settlement, Historic Documents of 1998, p. 842)*

The federal government was seeking forfeiture of $280 billion in profits. In a pretrial ruling, Kessler said that the court could legally order the companies to "disgorge" the $280 billion if the government proved that fraud had occurred in the past and was likely to continue into the future. Claiming that a $280 billion judgment would bankrupt them, the tobacco companies challenged that ruling in a federal appeals court; a decision was still pending at the end of the year. Earlier Judge Kessler had thrown out a Justice Department claim seeking reimbursement for Medicare funds spent on tobacco-related illnesses.

In their opening statements, attorneys for the tobacco companies conceded that the companies had made mistakes and shown poor judgment about the health risks of smoking. But they flatly denied there was a conspiracy and insisted that they were now acknowledging the dangers of smoking. Public health advocates disputed those claims, noting that the companies still did not admit the dangers of secondhand smoke and pointing out that at least one company had been fined for violating the settlement restriction on advertising to minors.

Tobacco Control Treaty

The Framework Convention on Tobacco Control was drafted by the World Health Organization to attack tobacco use on several fronts. It called for a banning tobacco advertising, placing warning labels that covered at least 30 percent of the packaging on all smoking products, and listing all ingredients on the package. The treaty also committed governments to pass laws banning smoking indoors, to put high taxes on tobacco products to discourage their use, and to crack down on tobacco smuggling, some of the profits of which were thought to be financing terrorist operations.

The treaty, which supporters predicted would save millions of lives, was unanimously approved by the World Health Assembly in May 2003. Over the next year, 167 countries signed it. But the treaty would not take effect until ninety days after forty countries had ratified it. Peru became that country on November 30, and the treaty was scheduled to enter into force on February 28, 2005. Among the countries that had ratified the treaty were Canada, France, India, Japan, Mexico, and Thailand, as well as several countries in Latin America and Africa. An adviser to the minister of health in South Africa, which was expected to ratify the treaty early in 2005, said the new international standards would be particularly helpful in Africa, which the tobacco industry "has turned to as a potentially lucrative market" in the wake of declining smoking and legal obstacles in many developed countries such as the United States.

The United States signed the treaty on May 10, amid considerable skepticism about how hard the Bush administration would push for ratification; as of the end of the year, President George W. Bush still had not submitted the treaty to the Senate for ratification. The U.S. delegation to the treaty negotiations had been sharply criticized for trying to weaken the pact at the behest of tobacco companies; it denied the charges. White House spokesman Trent Duffy told the *Christian Science Monitor* in early December that the Bush administration was considering the best time to submit the treaty to the Senate. "The administration signed on to the treaty, and the president believed we do need to take measures to stop young people from smoking," Duffy said. *(Treaty negotiations, Historic Documents of 2000, p. 538; treaty approval, Historic Documents of 2003, p. 260)*

Secondhand Smoke

With the dangers to health from smoking now generally accepted, public health officials and others were trying to focus attention on the dangers of secondhand smoke. In April the CDC warned people at risk of heart disease to avoid all public places that allowed indoor smoking. The CDC said that as little as thirty minutes' exposure to passive smoke could have a serious, perhaps lethal, effect for some people with heart disease. Evidence showed that secondhand smoke increased the tendency for blood to clot, which could restrict the flow of blood to the heart.

Governments throughout the United States and worldwide enacted bans on smoking in public places because of the potential risks to health from secondhand smoke. These included:

- Kentucky, where the state supreme court upheld a ban on smoking in bars, restaurants, and other public places in Lexington. The ban was notable because Kentucky, a major tobacco-producing state, also had the highest rate of smoking of any state—about one-third of Kentucky's adults smoked .
- India, which was the second most populous country in the world and which ratified the tobacco control treaty. It passed legislation in February to implement a ban on smoking in public places as well as to prohibit advertising directed at children.
- Ireland , where a ban on smoking in bars, pubs, and enclosed workplaces went into effect on March 30. Although bar and pub owners warned that the ban would be impossible to enforce, officials appeared pleased with the level of compliance with the ban, and a leading cigarette maker said its sales had declined sharply. Ireland was the first country in the world to ban smoking in enclosed workplaces nationwide.
- Bhutan, a small Himalayan kingdom, which on December 17 became the first country to ban tobacco sales and all smoking in public.
- Italy, where a ban on smoking in restaurants and all other indoor places without a separate smoking area was set to go into effect on January 10, 2005.

In the Norwegian municipality of Levanger, however, a law that banned employees from smoking at all during their working hours, even within the confines of their own cars, was ruled to be a violation of human rights. The country administrator who issued the ruling in April said that the right to smoke was implicit in the right to a private life.

Following are excerpts from the executive summary of "The Health Consequences of Smoking," a report released May 27, 2004, by Surgeon General Richard H. Carmona.

"The Health Consequences of Smoking"

This report of the Surgeon General on the health effects of smoking returns to the topic of active smoking and disease, the focus of the first Surgeon General's report published in 1964. The first report established a model of comprehensive evidence evaluation for the 27 reports that have followed: for those on the adverse health effects of smoking, the evidence has been evaluated using guidelines for assessing causality of smoking with disease. Using this model, every report on health has found that smoking causes many diseases and other adverse effects. Repeatedly, the reports have concluded that smoking is the single greatest cause of avoidable morbidity and mortality in the United States.

Of the Surgeon General's reports published since 1964, only a few have comprehensively documented and updated the evidence on active smoking and disease. The 1979 report provided a broad array of information, and the 1990 report on smoking cessation also investigated major diseases caused by smoking. Other volumes published during the 1980s focused on specific groups of diseases caused by smoking, and the 2001 report was devoted to women and smoking. Because there has not been a recent systematic review of the full sweep of the evidence, the topic of active smoking and health was considered an appropriate focus for this latest report. Researchers have continued to identify new adverse effects of active smoking in their ongoing efforts to investigate the health effects of smoking. Lengthy follow-ups are now available for thousands of participants in long-term cohort (follow-up) studies.

This report also updates the methodology for evaluating evidence that the 1964 report initiated. Although that model has proved to be effective, this report establishes a uniformity of language concerning causality of associations so as to bring greater specificity to the findings of the report. Beginning with this report, conclusions concerning causality of association will be placed into one of four categories with regard to strength of the evidence: (1) sufficient to infer a causal relationship, (2) suggestive but not sufficient to infer a causal relationship, (3) inadequate to infer the presence or absence of a causal relationship, or (4) suggestive of no causal relationship.

This approach separates the classification of the evidence concerning causality from the implications of that determination. In particular, the magnitude of the effect in the population, the attributable risk, is considered under "implications" of the causal determination. For example, there might be sufficient evidence to classify smoking as a cause of two diseases but the number of attributable cases would depend on the frequency of the disease in the population and the effects of other causal factors.

This report covers active smoking only. Passive smoking was the focus of the 1986 Surgeon General's report and subsequent reports by other entities. The health effects of pipes and cigars, also not within the scope of this report, are covered in another report.

In preparing this report, the literature review approach was necessarily selective. For conditions for which a causal conclusion had been previously reached, there was no attempt to cover all relevant literature, but rather to review the conclusions from previous Surgeon General's reports and focus on important new studies for that topic. The enormous scope of the evidence precludes such detailed reviews. For conditions for which a causal conclusion had not been previously reached, a comprehensive search strategy was developed. Search strategies included reviewing previous Surgeon General's reports on smoking, publications originating from the largest observational studies, and reference lists from important publications; consulting with content experts; and conducting focused literature searches on specific topics. For this report, studies through 2000 were reviewed.

In addition, conclusions from prior reports concerning smoking as a cause of a particular disease have been updated and are presented in this new format based on the evidence evaluated in this report. Remarkably, this report identifies a substantial number of diseases found to be caused by smoking that were not previously causally associated with smoking: cancers of the stomach, uterine cervix, pancreas, and kidney; acute myeloid leukemia; pneumonia; abdominal aortic aneurysm; cataract; and periodontitis. The report also concludes that smoking generally diminishes the health of smokers. . . .

Despite the many prior reports on the topic and the high level of public knowledge in the United States of the adverse effects of smoking in general, tobacco use remains the leading preventable cause of disease and death in the United States, causing approximately 440,000 deaths each year and costing approximately $157 billion in annual health-related economic losses. Nationally, smoking results in more than 5.6 million years of potential life lost each year. Although the rates of smoking continue to decline, an estimated 46.2 million adults in the United States still smoked cigarettes in 2001. In 2000, 70 percent of those who smoked wanted to quit. An increasingly disturbing picture of widespread organ damage in active smokers is emerging, likely reflecting the systemic distribution of tobacco smoke components and their high level of toxicity. Thus, active smokers are at higher risk for cataract, cancer of the cervix, pneumonia, and reduced health status generally.

This new information should be an impetus for even more vigorous programs to reduce and prevent smoking. Smokers need to be aware that smoking carries far greater risks than the most widely known hazards. Health care providers should also use the new evidence to counsel their patients. For example, ophthalmologists may want to warn patients about the increased risk of cataract in smokers, and geriatricians should counsel their patients who smoke, even the oldest, to quit. This report shows that smokers who quit can lower their risk for smoking-caused diseases and improve their health status generally. Those who never start can avoid the predictable burden of disease and lost life expectancy that results from a lifetime of smoking.

Preparation of the Report

This report of the Surgeon General was prepared by the Office on Smoking and Health, National Center for Chronic Disease Prevention and Health Promotion, CDC, USDHHS. Initial chapters were written by 19 experts who were selected because of their expertise and familiarity with the topics covered in this report. Their various contributions were summarized into six major chapters that were then reviewed by more than 60 peer reviewers. The entire manuscript was then sent to more than 20 scientists and experts, who reviewed it for its scientific integrity. After each review cycle was completed, the drafts were revised by the editors on the basis of the experts' comments. Subsequently, the report was reviewed by various institutes and agencies within USDHHS.

Publication lags, even short ones, prevent an up-to-the-minute inclusion of all recently published articles and data. Therefore, by the time the public reads this report, there may be additional published studies or data. To provide published information as current as possible, this report includes an appendix of more recent studies that represent major additions to the literature.

This report is also accompanied by a companion database of key evidence that is accessible through the Internet (see http://www.cdc.gov/tobacco). The database includes a uniform description of the studies and results on the risks of smoking that were presented in a format compatible with abstraction into standardized tables. Readers of the report may access these data for additional analyses, tables, or figures. The Office on Smoking and Health at CDC intends to maintain this database and will periodically update its contents as new reports are published. . . .

Major Conclusions

Forty years after the first Surgeon General's report in 1964, the list of diseases and other adverse effects caused by smoking continues to expand. Epidemiologic studies are providing a comprehensive assessment of the risks faced by smokers who continue to smoke across their life spans. Laboratory research now reveals how smoking causes disease at the molecular and cellular levels. Fortunately for former smokers, studies show that the substantial risks of smoking can be reduced by successfully quitting at any age. The evidence reviewed in this and prior reports of the Surgeon General leads to the following major conclusions:

1. Smoking harms nearly every organ of the body, causing many diseases and reducing the health of smokers in general.
2. Quitting smoking has immediate as well as long-term benefits, reducing risks for diseases caused by smoking and improving health in general.
3. Smoking cigarettes with lower machine-measured yields of tar and nicotine provides no clear benefit to health.
4. The list of diseases caused by smoking has been expanded to include abdominal aortic aneurysm, acute myeloid leukemia, cataract, cervical cancer, kidney cancer, pancreatic cancer, pneumonia, periodontitis, and stomach cancer.

Chapter Conclusions

Chapter 2. Cancer

Lung Cancer

1. The evidence is sufficient to infer a causal relationship between smoking and lung cancer.
2. Smoking causes genetic changes in cells of the lung that ultimately lead to the development of lung cancer.
3. Although characteristics of cigarettes have changed during the last 50 years and yields of tar and nicotine have declined substantially, as assessed by the Federal Trade Commission's test protocol, the risk of lung cancer in smokers has not declined.
4. Adenocarcinoma has now become the most common type of lung cancer in smokers. The basis for this shift is unclear but may reflect changes in the carcinogens in cigarette smoke.
5. Even after many years of not smoking, the risk of lung cancer in former smokers remains higher than in persons who have never smoked.
6. Lung cancer incidence and mortality rates in men are now declining, reflecting past patterns of cigarette use, while rates in women are still rising.

Laryngeal Cancer

7. The evidence is sufficient to infer a causal relationship between smoking and cancer of the larynx.
8. Together, smoking and alcohol cause most cases of laryngeal cancer in the United States.

Oral Cavity and Pharyngeal Cancers

9. The evidence is sufficient to infer a causal relationship between smoking and cancers of the oral cavity and pharynx.

Esophageal Cancer

10. The evidence is sufficient to infer a causal relationship between smoking and cancers of the esophagus.
11. The evidence is sufficient to infer a causal relationship between smoking and both squamous cell carcinoma and adenocarcinoma of the esophagus.

Pancreatic Cancer

12. The evidence is sufficient to infer a causal relationship between smoking and pancreatic cancer.

Bladder and Kidney Cancers

13. The evidence is sufficient to infer a causal relationship between smoking and renal cell, renal pelvis, and bladder cancers.

Cervical Cancer

14. The evidence is sufficient to infer a causal relationship between smoking and cervical cancer.

Ovarian Cancer

15. The evidence is inadequate to infer the presence or absence of a causal relationship between smoking and ovarian cancer.

Endometrial Cancer

16. The evidence is sufficient to infer that current smoking reduces the risk of endometrial cancer in postmenopausal women.

Stomach Cancer

17. The evidence is sufficient to infer a causal relationship between smoking and gastric cancers.
18. The evidence is suggestive but not sufficient to infer a causal relationship between smoking and noncardia gastric cancers, in particular by modifying the persistence and/or the pathogenicity of *Helicobacter pylori* infections.

Colorectal Cancer

19. The evidence is suggestive but not sufficient to infer a causal relationship between smoking and colorectal adenomatous polyps and colorectal cancer.

Prostate Cancer

20. The evidence is suggestive of no causal relationship between smoking and risk for prostate cancer.
21. The evidence for mortality, although not consistent across all studies, suggests a higher mortality rate from prostate cancer in smokers than in nonsmokers.

Acute Leukemia

22. The evidence is sufficient to infer a causal relationship between smoking and acute myeloid leukemia.
23. The risk for acute myeloid leukemia increases with the number of cigarettes smoked and with duration of smoking.

Liver Cancer

24. The evidence is suggestive but not sufficient to infer a causal relationship between smoking and liver cancer.

Adult Brain Cancer

25. The evidence is suggestive of no causal relationship between smoking cigarettes and brain cancer in men and women.

Breast Cancer

26. The evidence is suggestive of no causal relationship between active smoking and breast cancer.
27. Subgroups of women cannot yet be reliably identified who are at an increased risk of breast cancer because of smoking, compared with the general population of women.
28. Whether women who are at a very high risk of breast cancer because of mutations in BRCA1 or BRCA2 genes can lower their risks by smoking has not been established.

Chapter 3. Cardiovascular Diseases

Smoking and Subclinical Atherosclerosis

1. The evidence is sufficient to infer a causal relationship between smoking and subclinical atherosclerosis.

Smoking and Coronary Heart Disease

2. The evidence is sufficient to infer a causal relationship between smoking and coronary heart disease.
3. The evidence suggests only a weak relationship between the type of cigarette smoked and coronary heart disease risk.

Smoking and Cerebrovascular Disease

4. The evidence is sufficient to infer a causal relationship between smoking and stroke.

Smoking and Abdominal Aortic Aneurysm

5. The evidence is sufficient to infer a causal relationship between smoking and abdominal aortic aneurysm.

Chapter 4. Respiratory Diseases

Acute Respiratory Illnesses

1. The evidence is sufficient to infer a causal relationship between smoking and acute respiratory illnesses, including pneumonia, in persons without underlying smoking-related chronic obstructive lung disease.
2. The evidence is suggestive but not sufficient to infer a causal relationship between smoking and acute respiratory infections among persons with preexisting chronic obstructive pulmonary disease.
3. In persons with asthma, the evidence is inadequate to infer the presence or absence of a causal relationship between smoking and acute asthma exacerbation.

Chronic Respiratory Diseases

4. The evidence is sufficient to infer a causal relationship between maternal smoking during pregnancy and a reduction of lung function in infants.
5. The evidence is suggestive but not sufficient to infer a causal relationship between maternal smoking during pregnancy and an increase in the frequency of lower respiratory tract illnesses during infancy.
6. The evidence is suggestive but not sufficient to infer a causal relationship between maternal smoking during pregnancy and an increased risk for impaired lung function in childhood and adulthood.
7. Active smoking causes injurious biologic processes (i.e., oxidant stress, inflammation, and a protease-antiprotease imbalance) that result in airway and alveolar injury. This injury, if sustained, ultimately leads to the development of chronic obstructive pulmonary disease.
8. The evidence is sufficient to infer a causal relationship between active smoking and impaired lung growth during childhood and adolescence.
9. The evidence is sufficient to infer a causal relationship between active smoking and the early onset of lung function decline during late adolescence and early adulthood.
10. The evidence is sufficient to infer a causal relationship between active smoking in adulthood and a premature onset of and an accelerated age-related decline in lung function.
11. The evidence is sufficient to infer a causal relationship between sustained cessation from smoking and a return of the rate of decline in pulmonary function to that of persons who had never smoked.
12. The evidence is sufficient to infer a causal relationship between active smoking and respiratory symptoms in children and adolescents, including coughing, phlegm, wheezing, and dyspnea.
13. The evidence is sufficient to infer a causal relationship between active smoking and asthma-related symptoms (i.e., wheezing) in childhood and adolescence.
14. The evidence is inadequate to infer the presence or absence of a causal relationship between active smoking and physician-diagnosed asthma in childhood and adolescence.
15. The evidence is suggestive but not sufficient to infer a causal relationship between active smoking and a poorer prognosis for children and adolescents with asthma.

16. The evidence is sufficient to infer a causal relationship between active smoking and all major respiratory symptoms among adults, including coughing, phlegm, wheezing, and dyspnea.
17. The evidence is inadequate to infer the presence or absence of a causal relationship between active smoking and asthma in adults.
18. The evidence is suggestive but not sufficient to infer a causal relationship between active smoking and increased nonspecific bronchial hyper-responsiveness.
19. The evidence is sufficient to infer a causal relationship between active smoking and poor asthma control.
20. The evidence is sufficient to infer a causal relationship between active smoking and chronic obstructive pulmonary disease morbidity and mortality.
21. The evidence is suggestive but not sufficient to infer a causal relationship between lower machine-measured cigarette tar and a lower risk for cough and mucus hypersecretion.
22. The evidence is inadequate to infer the presence or absence of a causal relationship between a lower cigarette tar content and reductions in forced expiratory volume in one second decline rates.
23. The evidence is inadequate to infer the presence or absence of a causal relationship between a lower cigarette tar content and reductions in chronic obstructive pulmonary disease-related mortality.
24. The evidence is inadequate to infer the presence or absence of a causal relationship between active smoking and idiopathic pulmonary fibrosis.

Chapter 5. Reproductive Effects

Fertility

1. The evidence is inadequate to infer the presence or absence of a causal relationship between active smoking and sperm quality.
2. The evidence is sufficient to infer a causal relationship between smoking and reduced fertility in women.

Pregnancy and Pregnancy Outcomes

3. The evidence is suggestive but not sufficient to infer a causal relationship between maternal active smoking and ectopic pregnancy.
4. The evidence is suggestive but not sufficient to infer a causal relationship between maternal active smoking and spontaneous abortion.
5. The evidence is sufficient to infer a causal relationship between maternal active smoking and premature rupture of the membranes, placenta previa, and placental abruption.
6. The evidence is sufficient to infer a causal relationship between maternal active smoking and a reduced risk for preeclampsia.
7. The evidence is sufficient to infer a causal relationship between maternal active smoking and preterm delivery and shortened gestation.
8. The evidence is sufficient to infer a causal relationship between maternal active smoking and fetal growth restriction and low birth weight.

Congenital Malformations, Infant Mortality, and Child Physical and Cognitive Development

9. The evidence is inadequate to infer the presence or absence of a causal relationship between maternal smoking and congenital malformations in general.
10. The evidence is suggestive but not sufficient to infer a causal relationship between maternal smoking and oral clefts.
11. The evidence is sufficient to infer a causal relationship between sudden infant death syndrome and maternal smoking during and after pregnancy.
12. The evidence is inadequate to infer the presence or absence of a causal relationship between maternal smoking and physical growth and neurocognitive development of children.

Chapter 6. Other Effects

Diminished Health Status

1. The evidence is sufficient to infer a causal relationship between smoking and diminished health status that may manifest as increased absenteeism from work and increased use of medical care services.
2. The evidence is sufficient to infer a causal relationship between smoking and increased risks for adverse surgical outcomes related to wound healing and respiratory complications.

Loss of Bone Mass and the Risk of Fractures

3. The evidence is inadequate to infer the presence or absence of a causal relationship between smoking and reduced bone density before menopause in women and in younger men.
4. In postmenopausal women, the evidence is sufficient to infer a causal relationship between smoking and low bone density.
5. In older men, the evidence is suggestive but not sufficient to infer a causal relationship between smoking and low bone density.
6. The evidence is sufficient to infer a causal relationship between smoking and hip fractures.
7. The evidence is inadequate to infer the presence or absence of a causal relationship between smoking and fractures at sites other than the hip.

Dental Diseases

8. The evidence is sufficient to infer a causal relationship between smoking and periodontitis.
9. The evidence is inadequate to infer the presence or absence of a causal relationship between smoking and coronal dental caries.
10. The evidence is suggestive but not sufficient to infer a causal relationship between smoking and root-surface caries.

Erectile Dysfunction

11. The evidence is suggestive but not sufficient to infer a causal relationship between smoking and erectile dysfunction.

Eye Diseases

12. The evidence is sufficient to infer a causal relationship between smoking and nuclear cataract.
13. The evidence is suggestive but not sufficient to infer that smoking cessation reduces the risk of nuclear opacity.
14. The evidence is suggestive but not sufficient to infer a causal relationship between current and past smoking, especially heavy smoking, with risk of exudative (neovascular) age-related macular degeneration.
15. The evidence is suggestive but not sufficient to infer a causal relationship between smoking and atrophic age-related macular degeneration.
16. The evidence is suggestive of no causal relationship between smoking and the onset or progression of retinopathy in persons with diabetes.
17. The evidence is inadequate to infer the presence or absence of a causal relationship between smoking and glaucoma.
18. The evidence is suggestive but not sufficient to infer a causal relationship between ophthalmopathy associated with Graves' disease and smoking.

Peptic Ulcer Disease

19. The evidence is sufficient to infer a causal relationship between smoking and peptic ulcer disease in persons who are *Helicobacter pylori* positive.
20. The evidence is inadequate to infer the presence or absence of a causal relationship between smoking and peptic ulcer disease in nonsteroidal anti-inflammatory drug users or in those who are *Helicobacter pylori* negative.
21. The evidence is suggestive but not sufficient to infer a causal relationship between smoking and risk of peptic ulcer complications, although this effect might be restricted to nonusers of nonsteroidal anti-inflammatory drugs.
22. The evidence is inadequate to infer the presence or absence of a causal relationship between smoking and the treatment and recurrence of *Helicobacter pylori*-negative ulcers.

Chapter 7. The Impact of Smoking on Disease and the Benefits of Smoking Reduction

1. There have been more than 12 million premature deaths attributable to smoking since the first published Surgeon General's report on smoking and health in 1964. Smoking remains the leading preventable cause of premature death in the United States.
2. The burden of smoking attributable mortality will remain at current levels for several decades. Comprehensive programs that reflect the best available science on tobacco use prevention and smoking cessation have the potential to reduce the adverse impact of smoking on population health.
3. Meeting the *Healthy People 2010* goals for current smoking prevalence reductions to 12 percent among persons aged 18 years and older and to 16 percent among youth aged 14 through 17 years will prevent an additional 7.1 million premature deaths after 2010. Without substantially stronger national and state efforts, it is unlikely that this health goal can be achieved. However, even with more modest reductions in tobacco use, significant additional reductions in premature death can be expected.

4. During 1995–1999, estimated annual smoking attributable economic costs in the United States were $157.7 billion, including $75.5 billion for direct medical care (adults), $81.9 billion for lost productivity, and $366 million for neonatal care. In 2001, states alone spent an estimated $12 billion treating smoking attributable diseases.

A Vision for the Future

. . . The courses of action highlighted below are potential next steps presented by the Surgeon General. Given his role as the nation's spokesman on matters of public health, these recommendations represent a vision for the future built on information available today. They do not constitute formal policy statements, but are intended to inform and guide policymakers, public health professionals, professional and advocacy organizations, researchers, and most important, the American people, to ensure that efforts to prevent and control tobacco use are proportionate to the harmful effects it causes.

Tremendous Progress Since 1964

The publication of the first Surgeon General's report on smoking and health in January of 1964 was a landmark and pivotal event in the history of public health. By that time, there was a rapidly accumulating amount of evidence on the dangers of smoking, and it was inevitable that action would follow the publication of a comprehensive expert report with the powerful conclusion that smoking causes disease. Since 1964, there has been a broad societal shift in the acceptability of tobacco use and in the public's knowledge about the accompanying health risks. In 1963, per capita annual adult consumption in the United States peaked at 4,345 cigarettes, a figure that included both smokers and nonsmokers. By 2002, per capita annual consumption in this country had declined to 1,979 cigarettes, the lowest level since before the start of World War II. In 1964, the majority of men smoked and an increasing number of women were becoming smokers. Today, there are more former smokers than current smokers, and each year over half of all daily smokers try to quit. In 1964, smoking a cigarette was viewed as a "rite of passage" by almost all adolescents. Today, only about half of all high school seniors have ever smoked a cigarette and less than one in four is a current smoker, the lowest level since researchers started monitoring smoking rates among high school seniors in the mid-1970s.

In 1964, smoking was permitted almost everywhere, and even the U.S. Public Health Service had logo ashtrays on its conference tables. Today, secondhand tobacco smoke is widely accepted as a public health hazard and levels of exposure among nonsmokers have declined dramatically over the last decade. In fact, there is an unprecedented level of activity to achieve clean indoor air quality at both the local and state levels. More communities and states are considering and adopting laws that are even more comprehensive in the range of venues they cover. The 1964 Surgeon General's report on smoking and health started this country on an epic process of change toward a society free of tobacco-related disease and death. Yet many challenges remain . . . .

The Need for a Comprehensive Approach

The 2000 Surgeon General's report, *Reducing Tobacco Use,* provided a detailed framework for comprehensive tobacco use prevention and control efforts: educational, clinical, regulatory, economic, and social approaches. That report noted that ". . . our recent lack of progress in tobacco control is attributable more to the failure to implement proven strategies than it is to a lack of knowledge about what to do." A comprehensive approach—one that optimizes synergy from a mix of educational, clinical, regulatory, economic, and social strategies—has emerged as the guiding principle for effective efforts to reduce tobacco use.

There is a very strong scientific base to guide these sustained efforts. In addition to recent Surgeon General's reports, the Community Preventive Services Task Force, the U.S. Public Health Service, and other professional bodies have reviewed the efficacy of specific strategies. Additionally, CDC's *Best Practices for Comprehensive Tobacco Control Programs* provides a broad framework for comprehensive statewide tobacco control programs. Recent analyses of evidence from these state programs conclude that the magnitude and rate of change in smoking behaviors are significantly related to the level and continuity of investments in comprehensive program efforts. The results from these programs indicate that reducing youth initiation rates, promoting smoking cessation, and increasing protections for nonsmokers from secondhand tobacco smoke exposure necessitate changing many facets of the social and policy environments. Thus, Best Practices provides effective guidance for efforts at the state level, but a comprehensive national tobacco control effort requires strategies that go beyond guidance to the states. Based on the evidence reviewed in *Reducing Tobacco Use,* a comprehensive national effort should involve a broad mix of strategies. That report also noted that some of the program and policy changes needed within these strategies can be most effectively addressed at the national level.

There is a need for a continuing and sustained national tobacco use prevention and control effort. Many factors encourage tobacco use in this country: the positive imagery of smoking in movies and in the popular culture, the billions of dollars spent by the tobacco industry to advertise and promote cigarettes, acceptance of secondhand smoke in public places, and the perception by some that the problem has been solved. Additionally, funding levels for many effective state and national counter-advertising campaigns were recently reduced. We know enough to take action. As in many areas of public health, there is a need to improve the dissemination, adoption, and implementation of effective, evidence-based interventions, and to continue to investigate new methods to prevent and reduce tobacco use.

Continuing to Build the Scientific Foundation

Progress in tobacco control always has been built upon a foundation of conclusive scientific knowledge. . . .

One major topic in need of more research is to complete the understanding of the mechanisms by which tobacco-related diseases are caused. A greater understanding of these causal mechanisms should have implications for disease prevention that extend to agents other than smoking. This report reviews the association between smoking and cancer, cardiovascular diseases, respiratory diseases, reproductive effects, and other health consequences, and defines a variety of specific research questions and issues related to the biologic mechanisms by which the multiple toxic agents in tobacco products and tobacco smoke cause specific adverse health outcomes. For example, the lung remains the primary site for elevated tobacco-related cancer risk; however, during the past 40 years, the type of lung cancer caused by smoking has changed for reasons still unknown. Similarly, as the evidence that smoking damages the heart and circulatory system and is a primary preventable cause of heart disease and stroke continues to expand, important research questions remain about how smoking interacts with other cardiovascular risk factors and accelerates the atherosclerotic disease process. With respect to these and the other research questions, the public health message remains the same: smoking greatly increases the risk of many adverse health effects. Therefore, never start smoking or quit as soon as possible.

For several organ sites, there is a need for more evidence regarding the possible causal role of smoking on cancer risk. For prostate and colorectal cancers, the evidence is suggestive but not sufficient to determine a possible causal relationship. For breast cancer, even though there is no evidence overall for a causal role of smoking, on a genetic basis some evidence suggests that some women may be at an increased risk if they smoke. For other sites such as the liver, confounding exposures to other risk factors have made the evaluation of the risk of smoking very complex, but this report finds the evidence to be suggestive of causation. There should be further research on those sites where the evidence is suggestive but not yet sufficient to warrant a causal conclusion. . . .

. . . More research emphasis needs to be placed on the broad health consequences of smoking—namely, how smoking has a negative impact on many aspects of the body at the same time, and how these multiple adverse health effects combine to produce an overall reduced quality of life and greater health care costs prior to causing premature death. Recently, preliminary estimates indicated that for every premature death caused each year by smoking, there were at least 20 smokers living with a smoking-related disease.

This report highlights the diversity of the health effects caused by smoking, and how dramatically smoking affects the risk of the leading causes of death in this country (e.g., cancer, heart disease, respiratory disease). These findings emphasize that tobacco prevention and control should be key elements in a national prevention strategy for all of these major causes of death. Additionally, there is great disparity in tobacco-related disease and death among populations and the need to address the research gaps that exist for many special populations. Research is needed not only on disease outcome but also on the development of more effective strategies to reach and involve high risk populations (e.g., race/ethnicity, low income, low education, the unemployed, blue-collar and service workers, and heavily addicted smokers).

Finally, more research is needed on how changing tobacco products, as well as pharmaceutical products, have affected and could continue to affect health. In this report, one major conclusion finds that cigarettes with lower machine-measured yields of tar and nicotine (i.e., low-tar/nicotine cigarettes) have not produced a lower risk of smoking-related diseases. Yet there are rapidly growing numbers of modified tobacco products characterized as Potentially Reduced Exposure Products (PREPs). Research has demonstrated that with the expectation of reducing risk, many smokers switched to low machine-measured tar/nicotine cigarettes, and may thus have been deterred from quitting. Therefore, it is critically important that the health risks of the emerging PREPs be evaluated comprehensively and quickly to avoid a replication of that unfortunate low-tar/nicotine cigarette experience. Research on the biologic mechanisms by which the multiple toxic agents in tobacco products and tobacco smoke cause specific adverse health outcomes can help establish an important scientific foundation for evaluating the potential health effects of PREPs. Similarly, the public health and policy implications of changes in manufactured cigarettes, other tobacco-containing products, and pharmaceutical products will require the continued attention of public health researchers and policymakers.

Tobacco Control in the New Millennium

As the world enters this new millennium, it is faced with many new public health challenges even as many of the old risks to good health remain. During the last 40 years, people have become increasingly more aware of the adverse health consequences of tobacco use. Currently, tobacco use is the leading cause of preventable illness and death in this nation, in the majority of other high-income nations, and increasingly in low- and middle-income nations. Unfortunately, the high rates of tobacco-related illnesses and deaths will continue until tobacco prevention and control efforts worldwide are commensurate with the harm caused by tobacco use. At the start of the last century, lung cancer was a very rare disease. Now lung cancer is the leading cause of cancer deaths in both men and women in this country. Our success in reducing tobacco use during the last 40 years has led to a reversal in the epidemic of lung cancer among men; nationwide, rates of lung cancer deaths among men have declined since the early 1990s. In California, where there has been a comprehensive tobacco control program in place since 1989, reductions in rates of tobacco-related disease and deaths already have been observed. If we apply what we know works, we can make lung cancer a rare disease again by the end of this century!

Source: U.S. Department of Health and Human Services. Centers for Disease Control and Prevention. National Center for Chronic Disease Prevention and Health Promotion. Office on Smoking and Health. "The Health Consequences of Smoking: A Report of the Surgeon General." May 27, 2004. Washington, D.C.: Government Printing Office. http://purl.access.gpo.gov/GPO/LPS49585 (accessed January 29, 2005).

June

Israeli Plan to Withdraw Troops and Settlers from the Gaza Strip

June 6, 2004

INTRODUCTION

Israeli prime minister Ariel Sharon pressed ahead in 2004 with a plan to withdraw Jewish settlements and Israeli military outposts from the Gaza Strip by mid-2005—leaving the tiny region to the direct control of Palestinians. Sharon called his plan a unilateral "disengagement," and he intended it to rid Israel of the burden of providing security for some 8,000 Jews who lived in settlements adjacent to 1.2 million Palestinians in Gaza. The withdrawal would have great political significance, representing Israel's first return of Palestinian territories that it had occupied since the 1967 Six Day War. For that reason, the plan was bitterly opposed by right-wing and ultra-religious factions, including prominent figures in Sharon's own Likud Party.

Sharon had fashioned the general concept of his disengagement policy in late 2003, citing what he said was the lack of a reliable Palestinian "partner" for long-stalled peace talks. With full support from U.S. president George W. Bush and his administration, Sharon had refused to deal with Palestinian leader Yasir Arafat, who, Sharon said, ultimately was responsible for the violent Palestinian uprising that by 2004 had led to the deaths of some 3,000 Palestinians and 1,000 Israelis.

That entire picture underwent dramatic change in November when Arafat died and was succeeded by Mahmoud Abbas, a senior Palestinian leader who opposed the use of violence and appeared determined to resume negotiations with the Israelis. Abbas appeared on course to win a January 2005 election to succeed Arafat, giving him the mandate he needed to dampen conflict in favor of a return to peace.

Earlier in the year Sharon's government had taken direct action to rid itself of another Palestinian leader, Sheikh Ahmed Yassin, the spiritual head of the militant Hamas movement, which had carried out some of the largest attacks against Israel. An Israeli missile strike killed Yassin on March 22; less than a month later the Israeli military killed Yassin's successor, Abdel Aziz Rantisi, in a similar missile strike. Hamas drew most of its strength from within the Gaza Strip. *(Arafat death and the year's violence, p. 806)*

Sharon Outlines His Plan

In December 2003, as the violence between Israelis and Palestinians continued and there appeared to be little hope for a return to the long-stalled "peace process," Sharon made a bold move on his own. Speaking to an annual conference on security topics, Sharon proposed what he described as a unilateral Israeli disengagement from the Palestinians. He suggested, but did not spell out with exact details, that this step would mean "relocating" some settlements and perhaps military posts from the Palestinian territories, starting with Gaza. Sharon's December speech was the latest in a series of statements indicating he was reconsidering some of his core beliefs. Earlier in 2003 he for the first time had expressed a willingness to accept a Palestinian state and had even used the word "occupation" to describe Israel's hold on the Gaza strip and West Bank. Sharon did not say so himself at the time, but many Israeli leaders, including Deputy Prime Minister Ehud Olmert, had suggested a demographic reason for evacuating some Palestinian lands: Under current population projections, within a decade Israel would be governing more Palestinian Arabs than Jews, thus throwing into question the country's identity as a democratic, Jewish state. *(Background, Historic Documents of 2003, p. 1200)*

By mid-January 2004 Sharon was becoming somewhat more specific, speaking of withdrawing at least some of the twenty-one Jewish settlements that the government had encouraged and financed in Gaza over the previous three decades. These comments increasingly unnerved the settlers and conservative Israelis, who long had viewed Sharon as the virtual founder of the settlement movement when he held previous government posts in the 1970s.

Sharon finally unveiled his ground-breaking plan in an interview with the liberal newspaper *Haaretz,* published on February 2. "I am working on the assumption that in the future there will be no Jews in Gaza," Sharon said in a characteristically blunt summary of one of the most dramatic policy reversals in Israeli history. "It is my intention to carry out an evacuation—sorry, a relocation—of settlements that cause us problems and of places that we will not hold onto anyway in a final settlement [peace agreement with the Palestinians], like the Gaza settlements." Sharon reportedly repeated his statements during a private meeting with Likud Party colleagues. In addition to pulling out from Gaza, Sharon said he expected to close a handful of settlements on the West Bank.

Despite Sharon's earlier hints that he was considering a major change in Gaza, the sweeping nature of his statement shocked Israelis across the political spectrum. Even Sharon's foreign minister, Silvan Shalom, said he was taken by surprise and disapproved of what his boss was quoted as saying. A Likud Party member who stood even to the right of Sharon on some issues, Shalom said he opposed "unilateral steps" by Israel. Gaza settlers expressed outrage and accused Sharon of betraying their cause and giving into Palestinian terrorism. Palestinian spokesmen also seemed puzzled but suggested that Sharon was not really serious and instead was engaging in a feinting movement, just as he had in years past as one of Israel's most successful generals. "If Israel wants to leave Gaza, no Palestinian will stand in its way," Saeb Erekat, a Palestinian cabinet member told Reuters.

Despite increasingly harsh criticism from the settlers and his colleagues in the Israeli right-wing, Sharon bulled ahead with his plan. Even continued violence from Palestinian militants did not deter him. His February 2 statement came just four days after a suicide bombing in Jerusalem killed eleven Israelis. Sharon also continued his political maneuvering on the plan after the February 22 suicide bombing of a bus in Jerusalem killed another eight Israelis. Sharon's method of dealing with such challenges was just as direct as his language often was. He ordered continued military reprisals, including large-scale army raids into the Gaza strip and frequent helicopter missile strikes against Palestinian militants, including what Israel called the "targeted" assassinations of Hamas leaders Yassin and Rantisi in March and April. Aides said these steps showed that Sharon was not "giving in" to Palestinian terrorism.

To put his plan into action, Sharon faced a series of legal and political hurdles that might have been daunting to a man of lesser determination. Evacuation of Jewish settlements and military bases in the Gaza strip required adoption of legislation by his cabinet and the Knesset (the parliament). Sharon also needed at least some kind of consent from his own Likud Party.

Sharon survived the first of what would be many political challenges on February 9, when the Knesset narrowly rejected four "no confidence" motions against his government. The votes were on budget matters not directly related to the Gaza pullout, but Sharon lost the support of two pro-settler parties that were part of his governing coalition. One of the parties threatened to leave the government if Sharon carried out his plan.

In addition to support within his own government, Sharon needed backing from the United States—Israel's closest ally and strongest financial supporter—if he was to take the dramatic step he planned. At least initially, Sharon's plan proved to be nearly as divisive among top echelons of the Bush administration as it was at home. Some White House and Pentagon officials reportedly favored backing Sharon, while others (notably in the State Department) feared Sharon's plan might further undermine a stalled peace plan, known as the "roadmap," that Bush had endorsed in 2003 and that Sharon had accepted only with strong reservations. Bush administration officials met with Sharon in Israel on February 19 and received assurances that the Israeli leader was not trying to kill the roadmap plan. *(Roadmap, Historic Documents of 2003, p. 191)*

Sharon in March also took the first of several steps to win support for his plan from Egypt, whose cooperation would be necessary because the Gaza strip was under de facto Egyptian control before the 1967 war and Egyptian security forces would have to continue patrolling the Egyptian-Gaza border. Israeli foreign minister Shalom—who by this point was officially supporting his boss's plan despite his personal misgivings—met on March 11 with Egyptian president Hosni Mubarak and won a promise of cooperation. Shalom was the highest-ranking Israeli to visit Egypt in the three years Sharon had been in office. Mubarak's backing may have contributed to a concurrent decision by Arafat to endorse the Gaza plan, but only as part of a broader Israeli withdrawal from Palestinian territories.

Bush Endorsement

Although support for his Gaza plan remained shaky at home, Sharon on April 14 won crucial public backing from President Bush. After the two leaders met at the White House, Bush appeared to give a blanket endorsement to Sharon's policies, starting with the Gaza plan and extending to some of the longer-term questions that still had not been resolved in negotiations between the Israelis and Palestinians. Bush called the Gaza plan a "bold and courageous decision."

The president went further and appeared to reverse long-standing U.S. policy on two of the major "final status" questions that would need to be resolved before Israel and the Palestinians could reach a complete peace agreement. One question involved Israel's settlements on the West Bank, where more than 230,000 Jews lived in territory that Palestinians claimed (these were in addition to the Gaza settlements and to the 200,000 Israelis who had moved into former Palestinian neighborhoods in East Jerusalem). For more than thirty years U.S. administrations had officially opposed the West Bank settlements as an obstacle to peace and said they would have to be considered in any final Israeli-Palestinian negotiations. Endorsing the Israeli position, Bush jumped past any future negotiations and said it was clear Israel would retain large blocks of settlements in any agreement. Bush also said Palestinian refugees, who had fled or been forced from Israel proper during the 1947–1948 Arab-Israeli conflict, should give up their hopes of returning to Israel and should instead move into a Palestinian state, once it was created. In essence, Bush rejected what Palestinians had long claimed was a "right of return" to Israel under international law.

"Realities on the ground and in the region have changed greatly," Bush said in explaining his positions. Bush set out his stance in letters he and Sharon exchanged during the White House meeting. Administration officials later insisted Bush's stance was not a dramatic policy shift. They pointed to a peace proposal that President Bill Clinton (1993–2001) had offered just before he left office in January 2001, which included similar ideas. Clinton had made his proposal contingent on a much broader set of concessions by both Israelis and Palestinians, however.

Sharon beamed as he accepted public praise from Bush, and he left the White House saying he was encouraged by his reception. Back in Israel, most public commentary suggested Sharon had strengthened his hand considerably in what was certain to be a long struggle with his domestic critics.

Predictably, Bush's statements brought no smiles among Palestinians. Prime Minister Ahmed Qureia said: "Bush is the first U.S. president to give legitimacy to Jewish settlements on Palestinian land. We reject this."

Putting the Plan in Place

Before his trip to Washington, Sharon had offered only a general description of his Gaza withdrawal plan. Fortified with U.S. backing, he published the first detailed version on April 18. Its main elements were unambiguous:

- Israel "will evacuate the Gaza strip," the plan said, including all towns and villages. Buildings and other "immovable" property would be left intact for the use of Palestinians, subject to future negotiations on compensation. Also subject to negotiation was the future of an Israeli-owned industrial zone near the Erez border crossing, which employed about 4,000 Palestinians. All permanent military installations also would be evacuated, except for a roadway, known as the "Philadelphi route" along the border between the Gaza strip and Egypt. Ultimately, Israel would leave even the Philadelphi route if Egypt provided security there. Israel would retain control of the airspace over Gaza, would patrol the Mediterranean coast, and would reserve the right to reenter the strip in "self-defense," but would no longer have a permanent civilian or military presence there.
- Israel would withdraw four settlements and several military installations from an area of the northern West Bank, which Israelis called Northern Samaria (after its biblical name). Israel would continue to build a wall, which it called a security fence, around much of the West Bank to prevent terrorists from entering Israeli proper, but it would make adjustments to the route to "take into account humanitarian considerations." Palestinians complained that the wall split farmland and even villages and made it difficult, in some cases impossible, for them to travel to jobs, schools, or public services.

Officially, the April 18 plan was silent on a timetable for these changes. Sharon's aides said the Gaza withdrawal could begin in the first half of 2005 and be completed within a few months.

The first of several large-scale public demonstrations against Sharon's plan came on April 27, when tens of thousands of people—many of them settlers from Gaza and the West Bank—crowded into a beachfront Gaza settlement. Many of the protesters carried banners accusing Sharon of betrayal.

Public opinion polls showed that nearly two-thirds of all Israelis supported Sharon's plan, but the minority included his political base in the settler movement and many in his own Likud Party. To bolster support, Sharon agreed to submit the plan to a referendum among party members. Early indications were that a narrow majority would back the prime minister, but the actual vote on May 2 resulted in a stunning rebuff, with 60 percent of the nearly 100,000 party members voting against his plan. Sharon said he would "respect" the vote but made it clear he had not been deterred, telling fellow Likud parliamentarians the next day that he would not resign and instead would "come up with a plan that will get wider support." Sharon quickly got support from a group of Israelis who had rarely backed him before—the more than 100,000 leftists, who crowded into downtown Tel Aviv on May 15 to praise the Gaza withdrawal.

As Sharon was negotiating details of a new Gaza plan, another round of violence engulfed the Gaza strip. The Israeli army moved into the southern part of the strip on May 11 to destroy what it said were "workshops" where Palestinians built short-range rockets that were used to attack nearby villages in Israel. Eleven Israeli soldiers died in the first two days, but the army launched a series of retaliatory attacks that killed dozens of Palestinians by the time the troops withdrew on May 24. The Palestinian Red Cross said more than 120 Palestinians died during the offensive; the Israeli Army said 40 armed Palestinians and 14 civilians were killed.

Sharon submitted a revised Gaza withdrawal plan to his cabinet on May 30 but did not seek a formal vote because he still lacked the votes to pass it. The new plan retained most of the basics of the original but said the settlers would be withdrawn in four groups rather than all at once. It also said Israel would demolish the settlers' homes and synagogues so Palestinians could not occupy them. Among the resisters were key Likud Party members, including Foreign Minister Shalom and Finance Minister Benjamin Netanyahu, a former prime minister who was angling to regain his old post. Sharon eventually won over these members by including vague language saying none of the settlement withdrawals would occur until the government had taken further action. Sharon also engaged in Chicago-style hardball tactics, firing two conservative cabinet members whose no votes might have doomed the plan.

These steps enabled Sharon to win on June 6 a convincing 14–7 cabinet vote in favor of his plan. Despite the qualifying language Shalom and Netanyahu had demanded, Sharon expressed no uncertainty. "The disengagement is underway," he said after the vote. "Today the government decided that by the end of 2005 Israel intends to leave Gaza and four settlements in Samaria [the West Bank]." Sharon said the vote was of "immense importance" to Israel, and indeed it was only the second time Israel had agreed to withdraw from any lands it captured during the 1967 war. The first withdrawal, from the Sinai peninsula, resulted from the 1979 peace treaty between Egypt and Israel. *(Historic Documents of 1979, p. 223)*

The hard-fought vote failed to produce unity, however. Two cabinet members from the conservative National Religious Party quit in protest two days later, and Gaza settlers said they would resist any move to force them to leave.

Sharon Escapes Prosecution

All through the early debate over the Gaza plan, one major cloud had hung over Sharon: the threat of prosecution on corruption charges. Sharon and his son, Gilad, had been under investigation for their alleged role in two scandals. The more important of the two involved a failed development on a Greek island. A developer, David Appel, had been indicted on charges of paying bribes of nearly $700,000 to the two Sharons for their help in promoting the project. Israel's chief prosecutor had recommended an indictment of both Sharons, a development that would have forced Ariel Sharon to resign as prime minister. Attorney General Menachem Mazuz announced on June 15 that he was dropping the case for lack of evidence. In addition to easing Sharon's legal troubles, the announcement gave Sharon the option of turning to the opposition Labor Party to help form a future governing coalition if his own coalition collapsed. Labor leader Shimon Peres had refused to consider joining the government while Sharon was under the threat of indictment.

Sharon still faced another investigation into his acceptance of a loan from a South African businessman that he allegedly used to refund illegal campaign contributions he had received in 1999. That investigation was still under way at year's end

Growing Dissension in Israel

Sharon began negotiations with Labor leader Peres about a potential coalition government in mid-July, but he was still in a delicate position politically. Because of defections by right-wing coalition partners, Sharon lacked a working majority in the parliament and had to govern on an ad hoc basis—surviving periodic no-confidence votes and getting legislation passed courtesy of abstentions and other legislative maneuvers. The Labor Party's nineteen seats would give him a nominal majority, but at the risk of prompting a revolt by some of his more conservative Likud Party colleagues.

Meanwhile, the Palestinian government was even more at risk, with militants attacking Palestinian police stations in Gaza and young political leaders demanding the ouster of longtime politicians whom they said were corrupt and incompetent. After repeatedly threatening to do so, Prime Minister Qureia resigned in the midst of a political crisis on July 17, only to retract his resignation ten days later when he said the crisis had been resolved.

Sharon again appealed to his Likud Party for unity, asking on August 18 for support of his plan to enter into a coalition government with Labor. To his embarrassment, the party's 1,450-member central committee rebuffed the leader. The vote was nonbinding, but it again demonstrated that Likud was deeply divided and that Sharon no longer had firm control of his own party. An angry Sharon said his party was on "the verge of division and disintegration," but aides said he would press ahead, both with his Gaza plan and his drive to secure broader parliamentary support.

Ironically, Sharon's troubles again were mirrored that same day on the Palestinian side. Faced with a petition from Palestinian legislators demanding changes to curb corruption and cronyism, Arafat gave a speech acknowledging the need for reform. Arafat refused to back the specific changes the protesting legislators wanted, however.

Less than two weeks after being rebuffed by fellow Likud leaders, Sharon made it clear that he was not deterred. Returning from a summer vacation, Sharon on August 30 reneged on the phased-withdrawal portion of the Gaza plan approved by the cabinet on June 6. The prime minister reportedly told senior cabinet officials that a drawn-out process would not work. "You want me to hold a vote every day about each bunch of settlements?" he was quoted as saying. "How about every hour?" Sharon's cabinet colleagues voted to stick with the phased plan, but Sharon had again taken the offensive and appeared determined to have his way.

Groups representing the settlers raised the political stakes early in September, publishing statements calling Sharon's plan a "Nazi act" and warning that it might lead to civil war. Another mass demonstration against the Gaza plan, this one in Jerusalem on September 12, featured personal attacks on Sharon. Sharon fumed to his cabinet that not enough of his colleagues were speaking out in his support, and he denounced what he called the "grave incitement" of settlers who once were at the core of his political support. The intensity of the rhetoric led Israeli commentators across the political spectrum to warn of potential dangers, including threats to Sharon's life. A right-wing Israeli had assassinated Prime Minister Yitzhak Rabin in 1995 after he had signed peace agreements with the Palestinians and Jordan; that act caused deep anguish in Israel and led many moderates to wonder how far extremist forces would go to advance their causes. *(Rabin assassination, Historic Documents of 1995, p. 689)*

New complications came the next day, September 13, when Finance Minister Netanyahu publicly called, for the first time, for a general referendum of all Israeli voters on the Gaza withdrawal. Netanyahu said such a vote would strengthen Sharon's hand, but Netanyahu's own lukewarm support for the plan appeared to indicate that he really wanted to stall it. His specific proposal called for a vote on a "phased disengagement," meaning he wanted to lock Sharon into the step-by-step approach approved by the cabinet in June. Sharon rebuffed the referendum call—and similar ones from other cabinet colleagues later in the year—saying he wanted no further delays in carrying out his plan.

In the first formal government action on the plan in three months, Sharon's security cabinet (consisting of senior cabinet ministers) on September 14 approved compensation for the settlers to be displaced from Gaza. The compensation would range from $200,000 to $300,000 for each family based on several factors. Many settlers called the amounts inadequate. Again trying to appease conservatives, Sharon gave an interview to an Israeli newspaper, published on September 15, in which he said his Gaza plan was not part of the U.S.-backed peace roadmap. The roadmap remained highly controversial in Israel because of its call for an eventual Palestinian state.

The Israeli Army mounted a major new military operation in the Gaza strip on September 29, for the first time occupying parts of the large Jebaliya refugee camp, a stronghold for Palestinian militant groups. The incursion was in response to the killing of two Israeli children, ages two and four, by Palestinian rockets. In the first day, 28 Palestinians were killed, and more than 130 were wounded; it was the bloodiest day in the current three-year cycle of violence. By the time the army withdrew two weeks later, more than 100 Palestinians had been killed. The military said most were armed fighters, but Palestinians said most were civilians. On October 7, as heavy fighting was still under way in Gaza, bombs planted at Red Sea resorts in Egypt, just south of the Israeli border, killed 32 people, including 12 Israelis. Responsibility for the bombings had not been determined by year's end.

Once again, external events did not deter Sharon, who continued maneuvering to win approval of his Gaza plan. Sharon suffered a temporary setback on October 11, when the Knesset rejected his opening speech to the winter session. The vote was nonbinding but again demonstrated deep divisions within the government.

The divisions within the broader Israeli society were deepened on October 14, when a senior rabbi, Avraham Shapira, urged army soldiers to disobey orders to carry out the Gaza withdrawal. Other rabbis had made similar statements, but Shapira's comments carried special weight because he was the former chief rabbi of the community of Ashkenazi Jews—those who came to Israel from Europe and had led Israel during its first decades since independence. These comments brought an angry response from military leaders, who accused the rabbis of trying to tear apart the army and even Israeli society as a whole.

Knesset Approval

In that environment of toxic rhetoric, Sharon returned to his full cabinet on October 24 and won approval of the plan to compensate the Gaza settlers. The next day, he went before the full Knesset to ask its approval. Sharon's opening remarks established the gravity of the occasion: "This is a fateful hour for Israel. We are on [the] threshold of a difficult decision, the likes of which we have seldom faced, the significance of which, for the future of our country in the region is consistent with the difficulty, pain, and dispute it arouses within us."

Sharon's motives for what he called the "unbearably difficult decision" to abandon Gaza had been much debated, and Sharon himself had offered only vague explanations. In this speech to the Knesset, however, Sharon suggested at least three reasons. One was shedding the responsibility of governing the 1.2 million-plus Palestinians in Gaza, a duty that also required enormous effort and expense to protect the 8,000 Jews in the settlements there. A second, and possibly more important, reason was enabling Israel to concentrate on expanding and protecting the large Israeli towns and villages—known as "settlement blocks"—on the West Bank, most in the neighborhood of Jerusalem. Sharon said leaving Gaza "will strengthen Israel's hold over territory which is essential to our existence," a clear reference to the West Bank areas Israel was determined to keep in any future peace agreement with the Palestinians. A third rationale was breaking the stalemate in the Israeli-Palestinian conflict, a step Sharon said "will be welcomed and appreciated by those near and far" and might lead to the end of Arab "boycotts and sieges" of Israel. Others had suggested Sharon's intent was not to return to the long-stalled peace talks with Palestinians, but was in fact to ease U.S. and European pressure to do so. This view was expressed bluntly a week earlier by one of his top advisers, Dov Weissglas, who called the Gaza plan "formaldehyde" that would smother the political negotiations that lead to a Palestinian state.

A typically raucous debate followed Sharon's speech, putting on display all the passions of Israeli politics. In the end, on October 26, Sharon got what he wanted: a vote of 67–45, with 7 abstentions, in favor of his plan to withdraw the settlements from Gaza. Israeli commentators said the significance of the vote could not be overstated. It was the first time the parliament had voted to remove settlements from territories that many Israelis viewed as being part of the country's biblical heritage. Many observers said the issue was much broader than the fate of a couple dozen Jewish settlements. "Is Israel a secular democratic state or a state governed by Jewish religious law?" was the question posed by Asher Susser, director of the Moshe Dayan Center for Middle East Studies. "We are debating the borders of Israel, its long-term survivability, and the very nature of the Jewish state."

The climactic vote in the Knesset certainly did not resolve such existential questions, nor did it even guarantee that the day would come when the 8,000-some Gaza settlers would have to pack their belongings and move elsewhere. Netanyahu and three cabinet colleagues again demanded a voter referendum on the plan and threatened to resign within two weeks if Sharon did not agree. Sharon emphatically did not agree, and the ministers eventually withdrew their ultimatum. Even so, the calls for a referendum—and other attempts to delay or defeat the Gaza plan—continued to arise. The Knesset on November 3 gave preliminary approval to the compensation plan for Gaza settlers. Five days later the National Religious Party withdrew its four ministers from Sharon's coalition, cementing the government's minority position within the Knesset. Sharon on December 17 reached a deal with the Labor Party to form a new coalition government, but final arrangements were still pending at year's end.

The long history of the Israeli-Palestinian conflict was rich with irony and strikingly parallel events, and one of the most remarkable of those events occurred in the wake of the Knesset's historic vote on the Gaza plan. The very next day, October 27, was the ninth anniversary of Rabin's assassination. It also was the day that Palestinian officials reported that Arafat had fallen deathly ill. Two days later, on October 29, Arafat was flown to a Paris hospital for treatment. Arafat's death there on November 11 set in motion an upheaval in the Palestinian community that in some ways mirrored the turmoil within Israel.

Court Rulings on West Bank "Wall"

If Israelis were focusing much of their attention on the Gaza Strip during 2004, many Palestinians were concerned about events on the West Bank, notably Israeli's continued construction of an enormous wall intended to separate the West Bank from the rest of Israel. The government called the wall a "security barrier" and said it was necessary to prevent Palestinian suicide bombers from crossing into Israel from crowded cities and refugee camps on the West Bank, such as Jenin and Nablus. Sharon and other officials noted that a similar wall surrounding the Gaza strip had for years bottled up Palestinian militants there. Israel began building the West Bank wall in 2002 and by early 2004 had finished large sections of it in the Jerusalem area.

Palestinians compared the barrier to the Berlin Wall, which had divided Germany for four decades after World War II. They said its construction damaged farmland and villages and split some Palestinian communities in two. Because the planned route of the wall cut deeply into the West Bank at several points, to insulate large Israeli settlements from Palestinian areas, the Palestinians also viewed the wall as a land grab by Israel.

The Palestinian Authority took its case against the wall to the United Nations General Assembly, which in December 2003 requested an advisory opinion from the International Court of Justice (better known as the World Court) on whether the wall violated international law. Concurrently, the West Bank Palestinian village of Beit Surik challenged the legality of the wall before the Israeli Supreme Court. The Israeli court heard arguments on February 9, and the World Court began its hearings three days later—but with Israel boycotting the proceedings.

The Israeli court acted first, issuing an opinion on June 30 that portions of the wall would pose an undue hardship on Palestinians, putting many of them in "a veritable chokehold, which will severely stifle daily life." The court ordered a rerouting of about twenty miles of the wall near Jerusalem. The Defense Ministry responded to the ruling a week later with a modified route intended to ease the burdens the court had found unacceptable. It was the second major change in the wall's route in six months. The government in February had postponed the construction of major sections that were to enclose several large Israeli settlements.

The World Court ruling, issued July 9, went much further than the Israeli court judgment, saying that the entire wall violated international law and should be torn down. "The Court considers that the construction of the wall and its associate regime creates a 'fait accompli' on the ground that could well become permanent, in which case, and notwithstanding the formal characterization by Israel, it would be tantamount to de facto annexation," the ruling said. Israel's claim that the wall was a military necessity did not trump international law, it added. Only one of the fifteen judges—the American representative, Thomas Burgenthal—dissented from the basic ruling. However, he was joined by Dutch judge Pieter Kooijmans in opposing an associated call by the court for member nations of the UN General Assembly to take unspecified actions against the wall.

Palestinian officials said the ruling represented a moral victory that proved their contention that the wall was illegal. The Palestinians returned to the General Assembly, which on July 20 overwhelmingly adopted a resolution demanding that Israel comply with the ruling. The Israeli government shrugged off both the court ruling and the General Assembly resolution and said neither would affect its determination to proceed.

In parallel to its construction of the wall, the Israeli government accelerated its expansion of settlements on the West Bank. In August the government announced plans for about 2,200 new housing units, more than twice as many as had been built in any of the three previous years. That step brought strong protests from the Palestinians and United Nations Secretary General Kofi Annan, but not from the Bush administration, which reportedly had given its advance consent on the grounds that Sharon needed to appease the settler movement.

Destruction of Palestinian Homes

The year also brought increasing international attention to Israel's long-standing practice of demolishing Palestinian homes in the territories. By 2004 hundreds of Palestinian homes had been demolished over the years, forcing thousands of occupants to move in with relatives, to rebuild, or to find housing in crowded cities or UN-run refugee camps.

The government said it demolished Palestinian homes in three types of circumstances: when they were being used for "terrorism" against Israel, such as when militants hid in houses to shoot at passing Israeli troops or used them to disguise entrances to tunnels in which they smuggled arms and other contraband from Egypt into the southern Gaza strip; when Palestinian homes stood in the way of construction projects, such as the West Bank wall or highways, that the government said were necessary for security purposes; or when Palestinians were discovered to have built their homes without government permits (which were nearly impossible for most Palestinians to obtain, especially in the West Bank and East Jerusalem).

Israeli and international human rights groups had criticized the home demolitions for years. A new surge of demolitions in Gaza during 2004 heightened the criticism and brought expressions of international concern from the United Nations and even from the Bush administration. The year's first major demolitions began January 16, when the Israeli army bulldozed several dozen houses and a mosque in the Rafah refugee camp in southern Gaza, leaving about 600 Palestinians homeless, according to the United Nations Relief and Works Agency for Palestine Refugees.

Amnesty International, the British human rights advocacy group, issued a report May 18 accusing Israel of "war crimes" in its demolition of Palestinian homes. The report catalogued the destruction of 3,000 homes, most in the Gaza strip, and the destruction of 226,000 fruit and olive trees owned by Palestinians there. The UN Security Council added its voice on the issue the next day, adopting 14–0 (with the United States abstaining) a resolution expressing "grave concern" about the humanitarian situation of Palestinians whose homes had been demolished during a large-scale Israeli military operation in Gaza. The U.S. abstention was widely seen as a rare rebuke to Israel, since the United States regularly vetoed Security Council resolutions that criticized Israel but not the Palestinians.

Following is an excerpt from "The Cabinet Resolution Regarding the Disengagement Plan," approved June 6, 2004, by the Israeli cabinet incorporating the elements of a proposal by Prime Minister Ariel Sharon to withdraw all Jewish settlements from, and end the military occupation of, the area known as the Gaza Strip. The plan also envisioned the withdrawal of four small Jewish settlements and military outposts from a portion of the northern West Bank.

"The Cabinet Resolution Regarding the Disengagement Plan"

Addendum A: Revised Disengagement Plan—Main Principles

1. Background—Political and Security Implications

The State of Israel is committed to the peace process and aspires to reach an agreed resolution of the conflict based upon the vision of US President George Bush.

The State of Israel believes that it must act to improve the current situation. The State of Israel has come to the conclusion that there is currently no reliable Palestinian partner with which it can make progress in a two-sided peace process. Accordingly, it has developed a plan of revised disengagement (hereinafter—the plan), based on the following considerations:

One. The stalemate dictated by the current situation is harmful. In order to break out of this stalemate, the State of Israel is required to initiate moves not dependent on Palestinian cooperation.

Two. The purpose of the plan is to lead to a better security, political, economic and demographic situation.

Three. In any future permanent status arrangement, there will be no Israeli towns and villages in the Gaza Strip. On the other hand, it is clear that in the West Bank, there are areas which will be part of the State of Israel, including major Israeli population centers, cities, towns and villages, security areas and other places of special interest to Israel.

Four. The State of Israel supports the efforts of the United States, operating alongside the international community, to promote the reform process, the construction of institutions and the improvement of the economy and welfare of the Palestinian residents, in order that a new Palestinian leadership will emerge and prove itself capable of fulfilling its commitments under the Roadmap.

Five. Relocation from the Gaza Strip and from an area in Northern Samaria [northern West Bank] should reduce friction with the Palestinian population.
Six. The completion of the plan will serve to dispel the claims regarding Israel's responsibility for the Palestinians in the Gaza Strip.
Seven. The process set forth in the plan is without prejudice to the relevant agreements between the State of Israel and the Palestinians. Relevant arrangements shall continue to apply.
Eight. International support for this plan is widespread and important. This support is essential in order to bring the Palestinians to implement in practice their obligations to combat terrorism and effect reforms as required by the Roadmap, thus enabling the parties to return to the path of negotiation.

2. Main Elements

A. The Process

The required preparatory work for the implementation of the plan will be carried out (including staff work to determine criteria, definitions, evaluations, and preparations for required legislation).

Immediately upon completion of the preparatory work, a discussion will be held by the Government in order to make a decision concerning the relocation of settlements, taking into consideration the circumstances prevailing at that time–whether or not to relocate, and which settlements.

The towns and villages will be classified into four groups, as follows:

1) Group A—Morag, Netzarim, Kfar Darom
2) Group B—the villages of Northern Samaria (Ganim, Kadim, Sa-Nur and Homesh)
3) Group C—the towns and villages of Gush Katif
4) Group D—the villages of the Northern Gaza Strip (Elei Sinai, Dugit and Nissanit)

It is clarified that, following the completion of the aforementioned preparations, the Government will convene periodically in order to decide separately on the question of whether or not to relocate, with respect to each of the aforementioned groups.

The continuation of the aforementioned process is subject to the resolutions that the Government will pass, as mentioned above in Article 2, and will be implemented in accordance with the content of those resolutions.

The Gaza Strip. The State of Israel will evacuate the Gaza Strip, including all existing Israeli towns and villages, and will redeploy outside the Strip. This will not include military deployment in the area of the border between the Gaza Strip and Egypt ("the Philadelphi Route") as detailed below.

Upon completion of this process, there shall no longer be any permanent presence of Israeli security forces in the areas of Gaza Strip territory which have been evacuated.

The West Bank. The State of Israel will evacuate an area in Northern Samaria (Ganim, Kadim, Sa-Nur and Homesh), and all military installations in this area, and will redeploy outside the vacated area.

Upon completion of this process, there shall no longer be any permanent presence of Israeli security forces in this area.

The move will enable territorial contiguity for Palestinians in the Northern Samaria area.

The State of Israel will assist, together with the international community, in improving the transportation infrastructure in the West Bank in order to facilitate the contiguity of Palestinian transportation.

The process will facilitate normal life and Palestinian economic and commercial activity in the West Bank.

The intention is to complete the planned relocation process by the end of 2005.

B. The Security Fence

The State of Israel will continue building the Security Fence [surrounding much of the West Bank], in accordance with the relevant decisions of the Government. The route will take into account humanitarian considerations.

3. Security Situation Following the Relocation

One: The Gaza Strip

1) The State of Israel will guard and monitor the external land perimeter of the Gaza Strip, will continue to maintain exclusive authority in Gaza air space, and will continue to exercise security activity in the sea off the coast of the Gaza Strip.
2) The Gaza Strip shall be demilitarized and shall be devoid of weaponry, the presence of which does not accord with the Israeli-Palestinian agreements.
3) The State of Israel reserves its fundamental right of self-defense, both preventive and reactive, including where necessary the use of force, in respect of threats emanating from the Gaza Strip.

Two: The West Bank

1) Upon completion of the evacuation of the Northern Samaria area, no permanent Israeli military presence will remain in this area.
2) The State of Israel reserves its fundamental right of self-defense, both preventive and reactive, including where necessary the use of force, in respect of threats emanating from the Northern Samaria area.
3) In other areas of the West Bank, current security activity will continue. However, as circumstances require, the State of Israel will consider reducing such activity in Palestinian cities.
4) The State of Israel will work to reduce the number of internal checkpoints throughout the West Bank.

4. Military Installations and Infrastructure in the Gaza Strip and Northern Samaria

In general, these will be dismantled and evacuated, with the exception of those which the State of Israel decides to transfer to another party.

5. Security Assistance to the Palestinians

The State of Israel agrees that by coordination with it, advice, assistance and training will be provided to the Palestinian security forces for the implementation of their obligations to combat terrorism and maintain public order, by American, British, Egyptian, Jordanian or other experts, as agreed therewith.

No foreign security presence may enter the Gaza Strip and/or the West Bank without being coordinated with and approved by the State of Israel.

6. The Border Area Between the Gaza Strip and Egypt (Philadelphi Route)

The State of Israel will continue to maintain a military presence along the border between the Gaza Strip and Egypt (Philadelphi Route). This presence is an essential security requirement. At certain locations, security considerations may require some widening of the area in which the military activity is conducted.

Subsequently, the evacuation of this area will be considered. Evacuation of the area will be dependent, inter alia, on the security situation and the extent of cooperation with Egypt in establishing a reliable alternative arrangement.

If and when conditions permit the evacuation of this area, the State of Israel will be willing to consider the possibility of the establishment of a seaport and airport in the Gaza Strip, in accordance with arrangements to be agreed with Israel.

7. Real Estate Assets

In general, residential dwellings and sensitive structures, including synagogues, will not remain. The State of Israel will aspire to transfer other facilities, including industrial, commercial and agricultural ones, to a third, international party which will put them to use for the benefit of the Palestinian population that is not involved in terror.

The area of the Erez industrial zone will be transferred to the responsibility of an agreed upon Palestinian or international party.

The State of Israel will explore, together with Egypt, the possibility of establishing a joint industrial zone on the border of the Gaza Strip, Egypt and Israel.

8. Civil Infrastructure and Arrangements

Infrastructure relating to water, electricity, sewage and telecommunications will remain in place.

In general, Israel will continue, for full price, to supply electricity, water, gas and petrol to the Palestinians, in accordance with current arrangements.

Other existing arrangements, such as those relating to water and the electro-magnetic sphere shall remain in force.

9. Activity of Civilian International Organizations

The State of Israel recognizes the great importance of the continued activity of international humanitarian organizations and others engaged in civil development, assisting the Palestinian population.

The State of Israel will coordinate with these organizations arrangements to facilitate their activities.

The State of Israel proposes that an international apparatus be established (along the lines of the AHLC), with the agreement of Israel and international elements which will work to develop the Palestinian economy.

10. Economic Arrangements

In general, the economic arrangements currently in operation between the State of Israel and the Palestinians shall remain in force. These arrangements include, inter alia:

One. The entry and exit of goods between the Gaza Strip, the West Bank, the State of Israel and abroad.
Two. The monetary regime.
Three. Tax and customs envelope arrangements.
Four. Postal and telecommunications arrangements.
Five. The entry of workers into Israel, in accordance with the existing criteria.

In the longer term, and in line with Israel's interest in encouraging greater Palestinian economic independence, the State of Israel expects to reduce the number of Palestinian workers entering Israel, to the point that it ceases completely. The State of Israel supports the development of sources of employment in the Gaza Strip and in Palestinian areas of the West Bank, by international elements.

11. International Passages

A. The International Passage Between the Gaza Strip and Egypt

1) The existing arrangements shall continue.
2) The State of Israel is interested in moving the passage to the "three borders" area, south of its current location. This would need to be effected in coordination with the Government of Egypt. This move would enable the hours of operation of the passage to be extended.

B. The International Passages Between the West Bank and Jordan:
The existing arrangements shall continue.

12. Erez Crossing Point

The Erez crossing point will be moved to a location within Israel in a time frame to be determined separately by the Government.

13. Conclusion

The goal is that implementation of the plan will lead to improving the situation and breaking the current deadlock. If and when there is evidence from the Palestinian side of its willingness, capability and implementation in practice of the fight against terrorism, full cessation of terrorism and violence and the institution of reform as required by the Road Map, it will be possible to return to the track of negotiation and dialogue.

Source: State of Israel. Ministry of Foreign Affairs. "The Cabinet Resolution Regarding the Disengagement Plan." June 6, 2004. www.mfa.gov.il/MFA/Peace+Process/Reference+Documents/Revised+Disengagement+Plan+6-June-2004.htm (accessed February 25, 2005).

President Bush on the Death of Former President Reagan

June 11, 2004

INTRODUCTION

Ronald W. Reagan, a former movie actor whose sunny optimism and rock-solid beliefs in a few core principles made him one of the most popular and successful presidents of the twentieth century, died on June 5, 2004, at the age of ninety-three. Reagan had been out of office for more than fifteen years, but the United States and much of the broader world remained shaped by his actions as president, from cutting taxes to confronting the Soviet Union in the closing years of the cold war. Few presidents in modern history had been as beloved, or as reviled, as Ronald Reagan. It also was undeniable that few presidents had left as enduring a legacy.

A former Democrat turned conservative Republican, Reagan served two terms (1981–1989) after defeating incumbent Jimmy Carter (1977–1981) in 1980. He was the first president since Dwight D. Eisenhower (1953–1961) to win a second term, and he did so with a landslide win of historic proportions over former vice president Walter Mondale in 1984.

Reagan was succeeded by his vice president, George H. W. Bush (1989–1993). Bush proved to be not nearly as skilled a politician and lost his reelection bid in 1992 to Bill Clinton (1993–2001), a southern Democrat who nearly matched Reagan in charisma and popularity.

Five years after leaving office and returning to his home in California, Reagan revealed that he suffered from Alzheimer's disease. He quickly faded from public view and by the late 1990s was unable to recognize even close friends and family members. His wife, Nancy, remained loyally by his side and became a prominent advocate for the cause of helping Alzheimer's patients. She choreographed a week-long series of funeral events for him just as carefully as his political advisers had stage-managed his presidency, with an eye toward shaping her husband's place in history. *(Reagan elections, Historic Documents of 1980, p. 959; Historic Documents of 1984, p. 953)*

From B-Movies to the White House

Reagan was born in Tampico, Illinois, in 1911 and after graduating from college worked as a radio announcer in Iowa during the 1930s. He found his way to Hollywood and made his film debut in 1937. Through the 1940s he had parts in more than fifty lackluster movies, including a football tear-jerker called *Knute Rockne—All American,* in which he received the nickname of the "Gipper," which would stick with him the rest of his life. A Democrat and labor union activist, Reagan served as president of the Screen Actors Guild in 1947 but switched allegiances starting in 1952 when retired general and World War II hero Eisenhower first ran for president as a Republican. Reagan later claimed he, too, had served in World War II—an apparent blending in his mind of reality with propaganda movies he made during the war. In the 1950s and early 1960s Reagan worked in the new mass medium, television, and honed the communications skills that would later serve him well as a politician.

A turning point in Reagan's life came in October 1964 when he gave a televised speech endorsing Barry Goldwater, the Republican presidential candidate. Goldwater's campaign failed, but Reagan's apparently sincere speech on behalf of conservative values won the hearts of millions of Republicans. Two years later he ran for governor of California and defeated the incumbent, Edmund G. "Pat" Brown. Reagan served two terms as governor, putting into practice the conservative ideals that he would later bring to the presidency, notably a strong belief in free enterprise and opposition to government social programs. Although his convictions were strong, Reagan as governor, and later as president, proved capable of reaching compromises and shifting course to stay ahead of his opponents.

The only significant political defeat of Reagan's career came in 1976 when he unsuccessfully challenged President Gerald R. Ford (1974–1977) in the Republican primaries. His second chance came four years later, and he made the best of it, defeating Carter with 51.6 percent of the vote. Riding on Reagan's coattails, Republicans gained control of the Senate, although not the House. Carter was troubled by a stagnant economy and high inflation, but even more so by the long "hostage crisis" in Iran: Islamist students, with support from the Iranian leadership, held fifty-two Americans hostage at the U.S. embassy in Tehran. Reagan portrayed the crisis as a sign of Carter's weak leadership. During the campaign he failed to propose an alternative to Carter's actions, insisting he had a "secret" plan—one he never revealed. Under a deal negotiated by Carter's aides, Iran released the hostages on January 20, 1981, just moments after Reagan took the oath of office as president. *(Hostage crisis, Historic Documents of 1981, p. 137)*

Two months after the inauguration, a deranged American attempted to assassinate Reagan. The new president suffered a bullet wound but recovered fully.

Domestic Priorities

Throughout his political career Reagan was highly successful in articulating a handful of straightforward beliefs and convincing the public that he was acting on them. His approach to governing could not have been simpler: except for defense against enemies foreign and domestic, he said, "Government is the problem, not the solution." His first and single most important step to follow through on that rhetoric was to propose a massive tax cut, which Congress passed overwhelmingly just seven months after Reagan took office. Many Democrats in Congress had misgivings about the tax cut but voted for it anyway, having listened to voters back home who were persuaded by the president's direct appeals for support in televised speeches. Reagan promised in those appeals that he also would cut federal spending to put the budget back in balance after years of deficits. That promise proved harder to keep, however, because the voters and members of Congress (of both parties) liked funding popular programs, even when the money for them was not at hand. After a brief recession, the economy improved, although not nearly to the extent Reagan's advisers had predicted would result from the tax cut.

Budget deficits nearly tripled to more than $200 billion in the third year of Reagan's presidency, but by then Reagan had set aside his long-time aversion to deficits.

Although continuing to denounce government spending, Reagan vetoed few appropriations bills sent him by Congress. Reagan also accepted a tax increase in 1982 and got around his aversion to taxes by calling them "revenue enhancers."

Taxation was again a major theme in Reagan's second term, this time as tax "reform." Again with important help from Democrats, Reagan in 1986 pushed legislation through Congress that simplified the tax code. That bill was a prime example of Reagan's willingness to compromise; it cut tax rates and the number of categories (his priorities) but also eliminated some of the complex schemes that the wealthiest Americans had used to avoid paying taxes (a priority of Democrats).

Reagan's administration took some steps to follow through on his promise to cut the size of government, but many of them were blocked in Congress or carried out only in part. For Democrats and other critics, the Reagan administration's approach was symbolized by an early action taken by the Agriculture Department; seeking to cut spending on school lunch programs for poor children, the department declared that ketchup and relish qualified as vegetables. Public protests forced the administration to back down.

Despite his failure to rein in the size of government, Reagan did succeed in encouraging new generations of conservative Republicans, who shared his vision, to seek public office. The ultimate fruit of that vision came in two stages: the Republican takeover of the House of Representatives in 1994, ending forty years of Democratic rule; and the presidency of George W. Bush, who carried out many of Reagan's policies.

Battling Communism

Reagan's straightforward domestic policies were matched by an equally simple approach to the rest of the world. The president declared, at every opportunity, that the U.S. military needed to be strengthened to ensure that it remained the strongest on the planet, and that the Soviet Union and communism had to be opposed at all costs. Reagan appeared to view all the world's other problems in the context of those core beliefs.

Under Reagan the Defense Department was the one part of government with a virtual carte blanche for its spending requests. The Pentagon's plans for new generations of tanks, helicopters, planes, and ships were taken off the drawing boards and put into production. The navy even returned to service two giant battleships from World War II. Over the opposition of some Democrats in Congress—and to the chagrin of many in Europe—Reagan also pressed ahead with a giant new nuclear-tipped intercontinental ballistic missile—the MX, which he called the "Peacekeeper."

All these weapons paled in comparison, however, to the president's dream of a high-tech shield that would protect the United States from missiles launched by any enemy. Reagan in 1983 spelled out a vision for what he called the Strategic Defense Initiative and promised it would begin taking shape within a few years. Critics called the plan "Star Wars," after a popular series of space-age movies. The Pentagon spent billions of dollars chasing Reagan's vision before his successor, Bush, gave up on it and sought a more modest program. It fell to Bush's son, George W. Bush, to try to begin putting in place an even more modest defense against some enemy missiles. *(Missile defense, p. 176)*

An extraordinarily effective communicator, Reagan believed deeply in the power of words to convey ideas and move people. Just two of his words made crystal clear his view that the Soviet Union was the principal challenge facing the world in the last half of the twentieth century. Those words were *evil empire,* Reagan's characterization of the six-decade-old communist regime in Moscow that had taken control of most of Eastern Europe and appeared to threaten much of the rest of the world as well. When he uttered those words in 1983, Reagan inspired dissidents in communist countries worldwide but irritated many leaders and intellectuals in the West, who believed he oversimplified communism and was heightening the risk of a nuclear conflict.

What neither Reagan nor his critics appeared to fully comprehend at the time was that the Soviet Union and its empire were rapidly disintegrating. Corruption, stagnant economies, political gridlock, overspending on bloated militaries, and sullen populations were among the afflictions that by the 1980s had brought European communism to the brink of collapse. In 1985 the man who would push it over the brink took office in Moscow. Mikhail Gorbachev sought to breathe new life into the communist system with *glasnost* (openness) and *perestroika* (restructuring). After several difficult experiences, Reagan found he could deal with Gorbachev, and the two men resumed in earnest the process of negotiating nuclear arms reduction treaties that Reagan formerly had spurned as a sign of weakness. Even so, Reagan gave one final rhetorical kick to the Soviet empire in 1987. Visiting the Berlin Wall (then dividing Germany into two parts), he demanded: "Mr. Gorbachev, tear down this wall."

Ten months after Reagan left office, Gorbachev gave the signal that led to the destruction of that wall and all other barriers between communist Eastern Europe and the noncommunist West. Two years after that, Gorbachev himself was forced out of power as the Soviet Union imploded. *(Fall of Berlin Wall, Historic Documents of 1989, p. 625; Soviet collapse, Historic Documents of 1991, p. 808)*

In the days and weeks after Reagan died, many of his advocates—and even some of his former adversaries—gave him much of the credit for the collapse of the Soviet Union. "Reagan bolstered the U.S. military might to ruin the Soviet economy, and he achieved his goal," Gennady Gerasimov, the chief spokesman of the Kremlin's foreign ministry during the 1980s, said upon hearing of Reagan's death. Some historians, however, said Reagan merely nudged an increasingly hollow communist system that would have collapsed sooner or later.

Lebanon and Iran-Contra

Two other significant foreign initiatives by the Reagan administration were widely perceived as enormous blunders. Both involved the Middle East, where Jimmy Carter's presidency had run aground.

Reagan's most serious misadventure—foreign or domestic— as president took place in Lebanon. Seeking to end a civil war that had raged for seven years, Israel–with Reagan's blessing—invaded Lebanon in 1982. Israel succeeded in ousting the Palestine Liberation Organization, a central actor in the civil war, but found itself bogged down in the fighting. Hoping to stabilize the situation, the United States (along with France, Italy, and other nations) sent peacekeeping forces into Lebanon. A terrorist bomb destroyed much of the U.S. embassy in Beirut in April 1983. Six months later, on October 23, two separate truck bombs attacked U.S. and French military installations in Beirut, killing 241 marines and 58 French soldiers. U.S. and Israeli intelligence agencies later determined the attacks were carried out by groups funded and organized by the Islamist government of Iran. Reagan withdrew the remaining U.S. troops from Lebanon early in 1984, and the Europeans withdrew as well. The U.S.-led intervention was widely perceived in the Arab world as intended to bolster Israel and a Christian-led government in Lebanon—a perception that fostered anti-American terrorism throughout the region during the next two decades. The conflict continued in Lebanon, on and off, for another seven years until Syria brought it under control. Many historians considered the Lebanon intervention the second biggest single foreign fiasco for the United States in the second half of the twentieth century after the war in Vietnam. *(Background, Historic Documents of 1983, p. 933)*

Also in the mid-1980s, the Reagan administration intervened in the long and bloody war between Iran and Iraq. First, the administration backed the Iraqi regime of Saddam Hussein, giving it credits to buy U.S. food (thus freeing up money for weapons) and intelligence information on Iranian troop movements. In 1985 the administration began selling missiles to Iran, a country still the subject of a U.S. arms embargo because of the embassy hostage crisis. The administration's internal rationale was that Iran would then use its influence to free seven American citizens then being held hostage in Lebanon. Tehran did free some hostages, but only to the extent that the United States kept providing missiles. Reagan never acknowledged that he had secretly violated his oft-stated policy of refusing to make deals with the hostage-takers. Making matters even more complicated, the White House turned profits from the missile sales over to guerrillas, known as the contras, who were battling the leftist government in Nicaragua. Reagan had supported the contras militarily, through the CIA, in the early 1980s until Congress blocked further funding to them. The diversion of money from the Iran arms sales was a way to get around Congress.

A Lebanese newspaper published details of Reagan's arms sales to Iran in November 1986, setting in motion a scandal that came to be known as the Iran-contra affair. A joint congressional committee investigated the affair in 1987 and issued a damning report charging the White House with abuse of power. Reagan said "mistakes were made" but never acknowledged personal responsibility for what he said were the actions of his aides, several of whom were forced to resign and faced criminal charges. *(Iran-contra affair, Historic Documents of 1987, p. 891)*

Remembering Reagan

For five days after Reagan's death, more than 200,000 people filed past his coffin, first at the Ronald Reagan Presidential Library in Simi Valley, California, then in the Rotunda of the U.S. Capitol. Among those paying respects was former Soviet leader Gorbachev. The ceremonies ended on June 11 with an elaborate state funeral at the National Cathedral in Washington and then a sunset burial back in California just outside Los Angeles. Twenty-five heads of state and eleven former heads of state (including four former U.S. presidents) were among those who gathered for the final tributes to the nation's fortieth president. Among the tributes was a videotaped statement by former British prime minister Margaret Thatcher, a close friend and ideological soul mate whose tenure overlapped Reagan's. In his eulogy, the sitting U.S. president, George W. Bush, said: "Ronald Reagan belongs to the ages now, but we preferred it when he belonged to us." It was Bush's father, however, who might have come closest to describing why the man he had served as vice president had been so popular with the public and fellow politicians, even those who disagreed strongly with him. Choking up as he spoke, George H. W. Bush recalled that Reagan "fought hard for his beliefs. But he . . . never made an adversary into an enemy."

Following are excerpts from the eulogy given by President George W. Bush on June 11, 2004, at the state funeral in Washington, D.C., for former president Ronald W. Reagan.

"Eulogy at the Funeral Service for President Ronald Reagan"

. . . We lost Ronald Reagan only days ago, but we have missed him for a long time. We have missed his kindly presence, that reassuring voice, and the happy ending we had wished for him. It has been 10 years since he said his own farewell, yet it is still very sad and hard to let him go. Ronald Reagan belongs to the ages now, but we preferred it when he belonged to us. . . .

When the sun sets tonight off the coast of California and we lay to rest our 40th President, a great American story will close. . . .

Along the way, certain convictions were formed and fixed in the man. Ronald Reagan believed that everything happens for a reason and that we should strive to know and do the will of God. He believed that the gentleman always does the kindest thing. He believed that people were basically good and had the right to be free. He believed that bigotry and prejudice were the worst things a person could be guilty of. He believed in the Golden Rule and in the power of prayer. He believed that America was not just a place in the world but the hope of the world. . . .

As soon as Ronald Reagan became California's Governor, observers saw a star in the West, tanned, well-tailored, in command, and on his way. In the 1960s, his friend Bill Buckley wrote, "Reagan is indisputably a part of America, and he may become a part of American history."

Ronald Reagan's moment arrived in 1980. He came out ahead of some very good men, including one from Plains and one from Houston. What followed was one of the decisive decades of the century, as the convictions that shaped the President began to shape the times.

He came to office with great hopes for America and more than hopes. Like the President he had revered and once saw in person, Franklin Roosevelt, Ronald Reagan matched an optimistic temperament with bold, persistent action. President Reagan was optimistic about the great promise of economic reform, and he acted to restore the rewards and spirit of enterprise. He was optimistic that a strong America could advance the peace, and he acted to build the strength that mission required. He was optimistic that liberty would thrive wherever it was planted, and he acted to defend liberty wherever it was threatened.

And Ronald Reagan believed in the power of truth in the conduct of world affairs. When he saw evil camped across the horizon, he called that evil by its name. There were no doubters in the prisons and gulags where dissidents spread the news, tapping to each other in code what the American President had dared to say. There were no doubters in the shipyards and churches and secret labor meetings where brave men and women began to hear the creaking and rumbling of a collapsing empire. And there were no doubters among those who swung hammers at the hated wall that the first and hardest blow had been struck by President Ronald Reagan.

The ideology he opposed throughout his political life insisted that history was moved by impersonal tides and unalterable fates. Ronald Reagan believed instead in the courage and triumph of free men, and we believe it all the more because we saw that courage in him.

As he showed what a President should be, he also showed us what a man should be. Ronald Reagan carried himself, even in the most powerful office, with a decency and attention to small kindnesses that also defined a good life. He was a courtly, gentle, and considerate man, never known to slight or embarrass others.

Many people across the country cherish letters he wrote in his own hand to family members on important occasions, to old friends dealing with sickness and loss, to strangers with questions about his days in Hollywood. A boy once wrote to him requesting Federal assistance to help clean up his bedroom. [Laughter] The President replied that, "Unfortunately, funds are dangerously low." [Laughter] He continued, "I'm sure your mother was fully justified in proclaiming your room a disaster. Therefore, you are in an excellent position to launch another volunteer program in our Nation. Congratulations."

See, our 40th President wore his title lightly, and it fit like a white Stetson. In the end, through his belief in our country and his love for our country, he became an enduring symbol of our country. We think of his steady stride, that tilt of the head and snap of the salute, the big-screen smile, and the glint in his Irish eyes when a story came to mind.

We think of a man advancing in years with the sweetness and sincerity of a Scout saying the Pledge. We think of that grave expression that sometimes came over his face, the seriousness of a man angered by injustice and frightened by nothing. We know, as he always said, that America's best days are ahead of us, but with Ronald Reagan's passing, some very fine days are behind us, and that is worth our tears.

Americans saw death approach Ronald Reagan twice, in a moment of violence and then in the years of departing light. He met both with courage and grace. In these trials, he showed how a man so enchanted by life can be at peace with life's end.

And where does that strength come from? Where is that courage learned? It is the faith of a boy who read the Bible with his mom. It is the faith of a man lying in an operating room who prayed for the one who shot him before he prayed for himself. It is the faith of a man with a fearful illness who waited on the Lord to call him home.

Now death has done all that death can do. And as Ronald Wilson Reagan goes his way, we are left with the joyful hope he shared. In his last years, he saw through a glass darkly. Now he sees his Savior face to face.

And we look for that fine day when we will see him again, all weariness gone, clear of mind, strong and sure and smiling again, and the sorrow of this parting gone forever.

May God bless Ronald Reagan and the country he loved.

Source: U.S. Executive Office of the President. "Eulogy at the National Funeral Service for President Ronald Reagan." June 11, 2004. *Weekly Compilation of Presidential Documents* 40, no. 25 (June 21, 2004): 1057–1060. Washington, D.C.: National Archives and Records Administration. www.gpoaccess.gov/wcomp/v40no25. html (accessed December 16, 2004).

IAEA Director on Halting the Spread of Nuclear Weapons

June 21, 2004

INTRODUCTION

Weaknesses in the international systems to thwart illegal trading in biological, chemical, and nuclear weapons—the so-called weapons of mass destruction—became more obvious than ever during 2004. A major reason was the discovery of the progress Libya had made in building chemical weapons and beginning a program to develop nuclear weapons. Libya's leader, Muammar Qaddafi, had agreed in late 2003 to end his weapons programs. U.S. and other international inspectors uncovered new evidence that Libya had acquired substantial material for its nuclear weapons program from an international black market run by Pakistani scientist Abdul Qadeer Kahn. *(Libyan weapons, p. 168)*

The dismantling of Libya's weapons and the unmasking of Kahn's network prompted several new initiatives to strengthen treaties and informal agreements, all dating from the last decades of the twentieth century, that had attempted to halt the spread of weapons of mass destruction. Those treaties and agreements had produced some notable successes, but the Libya case demonstrated that they were far from perfect.

Bush Proposal for Tighter Standards

The year's first proposal for a new approach came from President George W. Bush. When he entered office in 2001, Bush paid little attention to U.S. and international programs to stem the proliferation of weapons of mass destruction. One of the new president's first actions, in fact, had been to order cutbacks in U.S. programs that helped Russia protect and dispose of the weapons it had inherited from the former Soviet Union. The September 11, 2001, terrorist attacks against the United States quickly changed the attitude of the president and his administration. Starting in late 2001 the administration devoted new attention, and government resources, to combating weapons proliferation, especially the possibility that terrorists might obtain weapons of mass destruction. The issue took on new urgency in 2003 when Libya gave up its weapons programs, revealing the extent of the international arms trade. *(Background, Historic Documents of 2001, p. 1218)*

Seeking to capitalize on the attention generated by the Libyan disclosures, Bush on February 11 went to the National Defense University in Washington, D.C., armed with a speech outlining an extensive series of proposals to curtail the international trade in biological, chemical, and nuclear weapons. Key proposals in Bush's speech involved such issues as producing fissile material, enacting a new program called the Proliferation Security Initiative, and adding a measure known as the "additional protocol" to the Nuclear Non-Proliferation Treaty (NPT).

Producing Fissile Material. For years many arms control advocates had said the only guaranteed way to halt the spread of nuclear weapons was by cutting off all international trade in equipment and raw materials needed to produce enriched uranium and reprocessed plutonium—the two so-called fissile materials that could serve as fuel for an atomic bomb but were unnecessary for civilian nuclear power. In his speech, however, Bush rejected this approach, choosing instead to target only those countries that did not already have the capability of producing the dangerous fuel. Under his proposal the Nuclear Suppliers Group—the forty nations that had nuclear power programs—would agree not to sell uranium reprocessing equipment or technology to "any state that does not already possess full-scale, functioning" plants. He said this step would close a "loophole" in the NPT that allowed countries, such as Iran, to buy uranium reprocessing equipment by claiming it was for civilian purposes. Bush said Iran and North Korea had used that loophole to "produce nuclear material that can be used to build bombs under the cover of civilian nuclear programs."

Critics said Bush's proposal was inadequate because it failed to address the dangers posed by all nuclear weapons programs, not just those of so-called rogue states such as Iran and North Korea. "So long as one state continues to possess nuclear weapons, the danger that they will be stolen or deliberately or accidentally used will persist," Daryl G. Kimball, executive director of the Arms Control Association in Washington, D.C., said. "In addition, other states will be compelled or justified to seek nuclear, chemical, or biological weapons and the means to deliver them."

Bush won an endorsement for this proposal in June from his fellow leaders at the Group of Eight summit, which met in Sea Island, Georgia. The leaders said they planned to have "appropriate measures" to enforce the proposal in place by the time of the 2005 summit; in the meantime, as a measure of "prudence," they called on international nuclear suppliers to impose a one-year moratorium on sales of fissile material or equipment to new customers.

Proliferation Security Initiative. Bush also proposed a major expansion of a program intended to make it easier for countries to block international shipments of equipment or supplies to produce weapons of mass destruction. Called the Proliferation Security Initiative, the program was started by the United States in 2003 with support from ten other countries: Australia, France, Germany, Italy, Japan, the Netherlands, Poland, Portugal, Spain, and the United Kingdom. These countries pledged to interdict boats or planes that were carrying illegal shipments of equipment or supplies destined for countries or terrorist groups suspected of trying to develop weapons of mass destruction. Bush announced that Canada, Norway, Russia, and Singapore agreed to join the program. The program's greatest success so far was the October 2003 seizure of a ship headed to Libya with a cargo of centrifuges to enrich uranium; that seizure reportedly helped convince Qaddafi to give up his nuclear weapons program.

In his speech, Bush said the program would be expanded to "bring to justice those who traffic in deadly weapons." Participating nations would use their police and intelligence-gathering resources to track down weapons proliferators "to shut down their labs, to seize their materials, to freeze their assets," he said.

"Additional protocol." Another Bush proposal called on all countries to sign a measure known as the "additional protocol" to the nonproliferation treaty. This protocol gave the International Atomic Energy Agency (IAEA) broad authority to investigate the nuclear activities of countries that adhered to the treaty. Bush proposed to enforce his demand by urging the Nuclear Suppliers Group to refuse further sales of equipment or supplies to countries that had not signed the protocol. Bush faced a diplomatic hurdle in advancing this proposal because the United States had signed such a protocol but had never put it in force by ratifying it. Recognizing this problem, Bush urged the Senate to pass legislation approving the protocol "immediately," and the Senate acted on March 31.

Bush won important endorsements for his proposal on the additional protocol from two advisory panels appointed by UN Secretary General Kofi Annan. The proposal also was expected to be discussed in 2005 during a UN conference reviewing the status of the nonproliferation treaty.

Reviewing the NPT

Recent revelations that Iran, Libya, and North Korea had violated their obligations under the nonproliferation treaty had raised new questions internationally about the treaty's effectiveness. The 1968 treaty was an ambitious—some critics said overly idealistic—attempt by the nations of the world to halt the spread of nuclear weapons beyond the five countries that acknowledged having them at the time: Britain, China, France, the Soviet Union (later Russia), and the United States. In essence, the nations that had nuclear weapons, along with the nations that used nuclear power but did not have nuclear weapons, agreed under the treaty to help other countries develop civilian nuclear energy programs if they would agree never to try to acquire nuclear weapons.

The nonproliferation treaty had many successes over the years, notably its encouragement to Argentina and Brazil to give up their ambitions for nuclear weapons and South Africa's dismantling of its small weapons program in the early 1990s. At the turn of the twentieth century, it became obvious that nations determined to acquire weapons could do so even while pretending to abide by the treaty's provisions. North Korea long had violated its commitments and ultimately withdrew from the treaty in late 2002. Investigations during 2003 showed that both Iran and Libya had acquired key components for nuclear weapons programs but kept them hidden from the IAEA. Moreover, the Bush administration, both in word and deed, made clear that it found the treaty's provisions inadequate to the task and the IAEA incapable of enforcing the treaty. Bush articulated some of the criticisms in a February 11 speech, saying that nations should no longer be allowed "to cynically manipulate the NPT to acquire the material and infrastructure necessary for manufacturing illegal weapons." The State Department's chief arms control negotiator, John Bolton, was even more direct, arguing in a September 6 column in the *Financial Times* that previous nonproliferation efforts had produced "decades of stillborn plans, wishful thinking, and irresponsible passivity." *(Iran and North Korea, p. 867)*

A formal debate about the treaty's future got under way in 2004 as diplomats met at the United Nations to prepare for a conference in 2005 reviewing the treaty provisions and enforcement. These reviews were held every five years. Previous ones, in 1995 and 2000, had produced sharp clashes between the nuclear weapons states (principally the United States and Russia) and countries that did not have the weapons. The latter nations demanded that the United States and Russia take seriously their commitments under the treaty to move toward giving up their weapons. Washington and Moscow made vague promises along those lines but, in the view of many other nations, took no serious action to follow through. *(Background, Historic Documents of 2000, p. 201)*

A five-week session of the UN's Disarmament Committee, in November and December, appeared to show that the old debates about the treaty would dominate again at the 2005 review conference. Two votes in early November illustrated the divide. By a margin of 135–5, the committee supported a resolution by a coalition of countries, called the New Agenda, which included a nuclear disarmament agenda among a series of goals for the 2005 conference. The five "no" votes came from four countries that had nuclear weapons (Britain, France, Israel, and the United States) plus Latvia. Another proposal by Japan calling for the eventual "total elimination of nuclear weapons" was opposed by India and the United States.

ElBaradei's Proposals

Another set of proposals for strengthening international controls on nuclear weapons development was offered repeatedly during the year by Mohamed ElBaradei, who for ten years had headed UN nuclear weapons inspections. An Egyptian scientist and director general of the IAEA, ElBaradei was a cautious diplomat who strongly advocated the importance of his agency's inspections, but who also, by 2004, had experienced the frustration of failed attempts to halt nuclear programs in Iran, Libya, and North Korea. As the head of one of the UN's weapons inspection teams in Iraq, ElBaradei also had incurred the wrath of the Bush administration, which rejected his contention in February 2003 that Iraq had not been able to reconstitute weapons programs that the UN had dismantled in the 1990s. The administration's anger at ElBaradei was not diminished when U.S. inspectors later found that he had been correct in his assessment. *(Iraq weapons, p. 711)*

In speeches and newspaper commentaries during 2004 ElBaradei laid out a series of proposals that he said were needed to strengthen the nonproliferation treaty and other arms control agreements. ElBaradei summarized his case for change in a June 21 speech to the Carnegie Endowment for International Peace, in Washington, D.C. "Some estimates indicate that forty countries or more now have the know-how to produce nuclear weapons, which means that if they have the required fissile material—high enriched uranium or plutonium—we are relying primarily on the good intentions of these countries, intentions which in turn are based on their sense of security or insecurity, and could therefore be subject to rapid change," he said. "Clearly, the margin of security this affords is thin, and worrisome."

To fix the system, ElBaradei proposed tighter controls on the exports of sensitive nuclear material and technology, including making compliance mandatory, rather than voluntary, as it had been. In one of his most controversial proposals ElBaradei suggested that all new production of weapons-grade nuclear material should be done "exclusively under multinational controls," in other words under the supervision of his agency. The Bush administration rejected this idea, saying the U.S. weapons program should not be subjected to the same kind of scrutiny as countries such as Iran.

ElBaradei also called on the nuclear weapons states—primarily the United States and Russia—to take more seriously their promises, under the nonproliferation treaty, to dismantle their nuclear weapons. He noted that the Bush administration instead was considering developing a new generation of more powerful nuclear weapons. Under such circumstances, he said, "it is hard to understand how we can continue to ask the nuclear have-nots to accept additional nonproliferation obligations, and to renounce any sensitive nuclear capability as being adverse to their security."

Global Threat Reduction Initiative

Potentially, one of the Bush administration's most important nonproliferation actions during the year was the May 26 announcement by the Energy Department of a new program called the Global Threat Reduction Initiative. This initiative consolidated and expanded several U.S. government programs to secure potentially dangerous nuclear material at civilian installations around the world. The major new component in the initiative was a stepped-up campaign, led by the United States, to remove highly enriched uranium from an estimated 130 research reactors in forty countries. U.S. officials estimated that these reactors contained about twenty metric tons of enriched uranium, enough to make several hundred crude nuclear weapons. Most of this material was protected at high-security installations in industrialized countries, but experts estimated that several tons in such countries as Colombia and the Congo potentially could be vulnerable to theft by well-organized terrorist groups.

Mainly in cooperation with Russia, the United States had been working to secure some of this nuclear material for more than a decade. During the 1990s, for example, the United States paid to move enriched uranium and plutonium at nuclear installations throughout the former Soviet Union and eastern Europe to Russia, where it was placed in secure storage financed by Washington. However, these programs had dealt with only a tiny fraction of the nuclear material considered vulnerable worldwide, and they had come under sharp criticism for bureaucratic inefficiency both in the United States and Russia. Energy Department officials said the May 26 announcement was intended both to speed up the pace of work and cut the red tape.

A related goal of the new program was to convince other countries to eliminate the use of highly enriched uranium in all research reactors worldwide, replacing the fuel with low-enriched uranium, which could not be used for weapons. Energy Secretary Spencer Abraham said the United States would convert all its research reactors to the less dangerous fuel by 2013.

Fissile Material Cut-Off

Arms control advocates in the United States and internationally said one key action by the Bush administration later in the year undermined the president's plan to control nuclear exports. On July 29 the State Department suggested that the United States would oppose efforts to include verification provisions in a UN agreement, the Fissile Material Cut-Off Treaty, that was first proposed by President Dwight Eisenhower in the 1950s and had been under sporadic negotiation since 1995. The treaty would require all countries to stop producing fissile material; the United States halted its own production in 1989.

While stopping international production of this material was a "desirable goal," measures to verify compliance by dozens of countries would be too intrusive and too costly, the department said. The administration previously had opposed attempts to write verification provisions into other international treaties, most recently the 1972 Biological Weapons Convention, which banned production of those weapons.

Tracing the Kahn Network

In his February 11 speech, Bush provided the first extensive official account of the weapons-smuggling activities over several decades by Kahn, the Pakistani scientist. Bush said Kahn, while supposedly living on a modest salary from the Pakistan government, "financed lavish lifestyles through the sale of nuclear technologies and equipment to outlaw regimes stretching from north Africa to the Korean peninsula."

Specifically, Bush said Kahn sold designs, components, and even complete uranium-enrichment equipment to Iran, Libya, and North Korea.

Kahn, a metallurgist, first came to public attention in 1983, when he was convicted, *in abstentia,* in a Dutch court on charges of stealing designs for uranium enrichment while he had been employed at a nuclear plant in the Netherlands during the early 1970s. Kahn had returned to Pakistan in 1976 and reportedly began work on developing a nuclear weapon for his country. His conviction in the Netherlands later was overturned on a legal technicality. In 1998 Pakistan exploded its first nuclear weapon and Kahn won renown at home as the "father" of Pakistan's bomb.

Investigations found that Kahn bought supplies and equipment from companies worldwide and was aided by merchants from Britain, France, Germany, and the Netherlands. The Persian Gulf emirate of Dubai reportedly was the key transshipment point, where supplies such as natural uranium from Africa and sophisticated equipment from Europe were repackaged and sent to Pakistan. Much of this trade was known to U.S. and other Western intelligence agencies at the time, but Washington had little success in getting governments to block the work of the companies involved.

Kahn's dealings were exposed and ended in late 2003 when Qaddafi opened Libya's illicit weapons facilities to U.S. and British inspection. The Libyan purchases were more extensive than Western intelligence agencies had expected, including even a Chinese-origin design for a complete nuclear weapon. Also in 2003, IAEA inspectors found traces of enriched uranium on centrifuges that Iran had previously hidden. Under questioning, Iranian officials suggested the machines had come from Pakistan in 1987—a clear indication that Kahn had been the source.

Under U.S. pressure, Pakistan fired Kahn from his government job and placed him under house arrest. Kahn went on Pakistani television to apologize and take "full responsibility." The next day Pakistan's president, Pervez Musharraf pardoned Kahn of any wrongdoing. Musharraf insisted Kahn had acted on his own, without the knowledge of the Pakistani military or government—a claim that few international experts took seriously. Musharraf also refused to make Kahn available to international investigators—even those from the United Nations—or to open Pakistan's weapons facilities to any kind of a review that might determine how closely the equipment in Iran or Libya matched Kahn's originals. Musharraf said he could not act against Kahn because he was a "national hero."

The investigations during 2004 showed that the second key figure in Kahn's networks was Buhari Sayed Abu Tahir, a native of Sri Lanka with operations in Dubai and Malaysia. In his speech, Bush described Tahir as the "chief financial officer and money launderer" for Kahn's network. As was the case in Pakistan, the Malaysian government refused to allow the investigators from the IAEA or other international agencies to interview Tahir, who was being held incommunicado. The *Los Angeles Times* reported on December 5 that investigations into Kahn's network had stalled, in large part because neither Kahn nor Tahir were available for interviews.

Western intelligence and law enforcement agencies took satisfaction that Kahn's network had been disrupted, but they warned that other criminal enterprises almost certainly were attempting to duplicate Kahn's work. "There may never be another A. Q. Khan network quite like this one, but equally it would be very surprising if there weren't some criminals or potential criminals out there looking to take advantage of this kind of trade again in the future," David Landsman, head of counterproliferation at the British Foreign Office, told the BBC in December.

Following are excerpts from "Nuclear Non-Proliferation: Global Security in a Rapidly Changing World," a speech delivered June 21, 2004, by Mohamed ElBaradei, director general of the International Atomic Energy Agency, at the Carnegie Endowment for International Peace in Washington, D.C., in which he offered proposals for reforming the international system to halt the spread of nuclear weapons.

"Nuclear Non-Proliferation: Global Security in a Rapidly Changing World"

It has been nearly a year and a half since I spoke at the Carnegie International Non-Proliferation Conference. Already at that time—November 2002—it seemed clear to me that we needed to revisit some of the basic assumptions and features of the current nuclear non-proliferation regime, and equally to consider new approaches to international security.

Since that time, the need for substantive change—to the international security system in general and to the nuclear non-proliferation regime in particular—has become even more obvious and urgent.

Today, I will outline for you my views on what we face, what we have learned, and the nature of the required reforms.

Non-Proliferation: Changes in the Security Landscape

The Treaty on the Non-Proliferation of Nuclear Weapons (NPT) remains the global anchor for nuclear non-proliferation and nuclear disarmament. Despite flaws in the system, implementation of the NPT continues to provide important security benefits—by providing assurance that, in the great majority of non-nuclear-weapon States, nuclear energy is not being misused for weapon purposes. Although the NPT is sometimes perceived as a Western project, its benefits extend across any North-South or East-West geopolitical divide. The NPT is also the only binding agreement in which all five of the nuclear-weapon States have committed themselves to move forward on disarmament. . . .

In the past decade and a half, the international security landscape has changed. With the dissolution of the Soviet Union, the Cold War rivalry disappeared. But the failure to establish the once much vaunted 'new world order'—by effectively addressing security concerns that persisted after the disappearance of the bipolar world or emerged in its aftermath—has resulted instead in a sort of "new world instability". Many ethnic and religious tensions, held in check during the Cold War, have erupted to the fore—and in many cases have turned into civil wars, further complicated by multiple protagonists from the outside. Yugoslavia is but one stark example.

Longstanding conflicts have also continued to fester, most notably on the Korean Peninsula, in the Middle East and in South Asia, with escalating tensions and in some cases increasing hostilities. Violence by sub-State actors has also risen to appalling new levels, as we have witnessed recently in Chechnya, Spain and elsewhere, and has resulted in the emergence of new types of conflicts that cannot easily be deterred by traditional means. An increasing polarization between the Western and Muslim cultures has emerged in the wake of September 2001. And while more than 30 States continue to be party to NATO or other alliances that contribute to their security and explicitly depend upon nuclear weapons, many other countries continue to face a sense of insecurity because of these and other new security threats.

Rather than trying to understand these changes in the international security landscape and adapting to the new threats and challenges—and harnessing the opportunities afforded by an increasingly globalized world to build an equally global security system—the trend has been towards inaction or late action on the part of the international community, selective invocation of norms and treaties, and unilateral and "self-help" solutions on the part of individual States or groups of States. Against this backdrop of insecurity and instability, it should not come as a surprise to witness a continued interest, particularly in regions of tension, in the acquisition of nuclear weapons or other weapons of mass destruction. Four undeclared nuclear programmes have come to the fore since the early 1990s.

Lessons from Recent Experience

Before I discuss specific proposals for moving forward, I would like to focus briefly on some of the lessons we at the IAEA have learned from our recent experience in verifying these undeclared nuclear programmes—in Iraq, Iran, Libya and North Korea.

Perhaps the most important lesson is the confirmation that verification and diplomacy, used in conjunction, can be effective. When inspections are given adequate authority, aided by all available information, backed by a credible compliance mechanism, and supported by international consensus, the system works. The Iraq experience demonstrated that inspections—while requiring time and patience—can be effective even when the country under inspection was providing less than active cooperation. . . .

But our experience in Iraq before the first Gulf War, and our recent experience in Iran and Libya, have also highlighted the importance to verification of the "additional protocol"—that is, the supplement to a safeguards agreement with the IAEA that provides the Agency with significant additional authority with regard to both information and physical access. Without the authority provided by the protocol, our ability to draw conclusions is mostly limited to the non-diversion of material already declared, with little authority to verify the absence of undeclared nuclear material or activities.

Perhaps the most disturbing lesson to emerge from our work in Iran and Libya is the existence of an extensive illicit market for the supply of nuclear items, which clearly thrived on demand. The relative ease with which A.Q. Khan and associates were able to set up and operate a multinational illicit network demonstrates clearly the inadequacy of the present export control system. Nuclear components designed in one country could be manufactured in another, shipped through a third (which may have appeared to be a legitimate user), assembled in a fourth, and designated for eventual turnkey use in a fifth.

The fact that so many companies and individuals could be involved is extremely worrying. And the fact that, in most cases, this could occur apparently without the knowledge of their own governments, clearly points to the inadequacy of national systems of oversight for sensitive equipment and technology.

The present system of nuclear export controls is clearly deficient. The system relies on informal arrangements that are not only non-binding, but also limited in membership, and many countries with growing industrial capacity are not included. Moreover, at present there is no linkage between the export control system and the verification system. Export control information is not systematically shared with the IAEA, nor even fully among the members of the Nuclear Suppliers Group.

Let me be clear: even a verification system making use of the authority under the additional protocol may not reliably detect low levels of clandestine nuclear activity, such as that conducted in Iran and Libya for many years, unless at the very least supported and supplemented by the sharing of actionable information from an effective system of export controls—as well as by intelligence information, where applicable.

Our recent experience has also taught us a clear lesson regarding the accessibility of nuclear technology. The technical barriers to mastering the essential steps of uranium enrichment—and to designing weapons—have eroded over time, which inevitably leads to the conclusion that the control of technology, in and of itself, is not an adequate barrier against further proliferation.

Some estimates indicate that 40 countries or more now have the know-how to produce nuclear weapons, which means that if they have the required fissile material—high enriched uranium or plutonium—we are relying primarily on the continued good intentions of these countries, intentions which are in turn based on their sense of security or insecurity, and could therefore be subject to rapid change. Clearly, the margin of security this affords is thin, and worrisome.

Finally, the evolution of the North Korean situation over the past 18 months carries an equally disturbing lesson. For 12 years, the Democratic People's Republic of Korea (DPRK) has been in non-compliance with its NPT obligations. In January 2003, the DPRK capped its non-compliance by declaring its withdrawal from the NPT. Naturally, the Agency reported the situation to the United Nations Security Council. But now, more than a year later, the Security Council has not even reacted. This lack of response, this inaction, may be setting the worst precedent of all, if it conveys the message that acquiring a nuclear deterrent, by whatever means, will neutralize any compliance mechanism and guarantee preferred treatment.

On the other hand, I would note that verification and diplomacy have been an important part of the success so far in Iran and Libya, and in that sense I can only hope that the continuation of the six-party talks on the DPRK nuclear programme will yield results".

The Need For New Non-Proliferation and Security Initiatives: Control, Commitment and Collective Security

With what I have covered so far as a backdrop, it should be clear that we are well beyond the point where a few quick fixes will adequately address the new and emerging threats. . . .

But I find it encouraging that both governments and civil society are beginning to come forward with proposals on how to address these challenges—including the draft report recently released by the Carnegie Endowment. We are seeing some degree of overlap and complementarity in these proposals. In my view, this could be the beginning of a much needed discussion on non-proliferation and security—and we should do all we can to stimulate this dialogue, move it forward, and keep it in public focus.

In my view, these proposals fall into three categories: control, commitment and collective security—that is, strengthening the controls of the nuclear non-proliferation regime, and plugging existing gaps; re-affirming and in some ways expanding the commitments of all parties to this regime; and reforming the existing system of collective security in a manner that addresses the concerns of all.

Better Control

The first set of proposals should ensure that peaceful uses of nuclear technology are controlled in such a way that they do not lend themselves to further weapons proliferation. There are five aspects to this improved control.

First, we must tighten controls over the export of sensitive nuclear material and technology. The nuclear export control system should be binding rather than voluntary, and should be made more widely applicable, to include all countries with the capability of manufacturing sensitive nuclear related items. It should strike a balance between ensuring effective control and preserving the rights of States to peaceful nuclear technology. And as prescribed in April by Security Council resolution 1540, it should ensure effective national control over sensitive items, and criminalize the actions of individuals and companies involved in efforts to acquire nuclear weapons.

Second, it is time that we revisit the availability and adequacy of controls provided over sensitive portions of the nuclear fuel cycle under the current non-proliferation regime. We should consider limitations on the production of new nuclear material through reprocessing and enrichment, possibly by agreeing to restrict these operations to being exclusively under multinational controls. These limitations would need to be accompanied by proper rules of transparency and, above all, by international guarantees of supply to legitimate would-be users. . . .

Third, we should work to help countries stop using weapon-usable material (separated plutonium and high enriched uranium—HEU) in their civilian nuclear programmes. Approximately 100 facilities in 40 countries, primarily research reactors, still use HEU for peaceful purposes—for example, to produce radioisotopes for medicine. Research reactors and critical assemblies in use worldwide should be converted to use only low enriched uranium.

Fourth, we should eliminate the weapon-usable nuclear material now in existence. Around the globe, stocks of HEU—which could be converted for weapons use by State or sub-State actors—should be eliminated, by "down-blending" these stocks to low enriched uranium for use in civilian reactors to generate electricity—a "megatons to megawatts" approach that builds on the successful Russia-US model. . . .

Fifth, until these HEU and plutonium stocks have been eliminated, we should take steps to better protect the existing sensitive nuclear material around the world, with physical security measures that will ensure that such material does not fall into the wrong hands. Despite our best efforts, adequate physical protection is still lacking in many such facilities in various parts of the world. As Sam Nunn stated last November, "the most effective, least expensive way to prevent nuclear terrorism is to lock down and secure weapons and fissile materials in every country and in every facility that has them."

Just last month in Vienna, US Secretary of Energy Spencer Abraham announced an expanded "Global Threat Reduction Initiative," with objectives very much in line with some aspects of these proposals, and the IAEA is in dialogue with the US Department of Energy to see how we can contribute to, support and broaden this initiative.

Renewed and Expanded Commitment

My second set of proposals involves guaranteeing and strengthening the commitment of all parties—nuclear-weapon States, non-nuclear-weapon States, and those currently outside the regime—to the basic tenets of nuclear arms control and disarmament. There are four essential aspects to this commitment.

First, a concrete roadmap for verified, irreversible nuclear disarmament, complete with a timetable, should be put in place. Thirty years after the enactment of the NPT, with the Cold War ended and over 30,000 nuclear weapons still available for use, it should be understandable that many non-nuclear-weapon States are no longer willing to accept as credible the commitment of nuclear-weapon States to their NPT disarmament obligations. . . .

In July 1996, the International Court of Justice (ICJ) declared unanimously that the obligation of nuclear-weapon States, under Article VI of the NPT, to "pursue [disarmament] negotiations in good faith," is a dual obligation that also includes the obligation "to bring to a conclusion" these negotiations. "The obligation involved here is an obligation to achieve a precise result—nuclear disarmament in all its aspects."

By contrast, a report recently presented to the US Congress by the US Departments of State, Defense and Energy advocated research on the development of advanced nuclear weapons, declaring that such a move was needed to increase the "credibility" of nuclear deterrence for the US and its allies. . . .

To my mind, it is hard to reconcile the opinion of the ICJ, underscoring the obligation to "bring to a conclusion" negotiations on disarmament, with these statements supporting the exploration of new types of nuclear weapons more than 30 years after entry into force of the Treaty establishing this obligation. But more importantly, if such efforts proceed, it is hard to understand how we can continue to ask the nuclear "have-nots" to accept additional non-proliferation obligations—and to renounce any sensitive nuclear capability as being adverse to their security. As I have often stated, the continuing pursuit of asymmetric and divisive policies—such as "the early bird gets the nukes"; pitting the interests of so-called "civilized" nations against "uncivilized"; failing to bridge the gap between those inside and outside the regime; and promoting policies that do not take into account the security of all—is unsustainable and counterproductive. . . .

Second, any new adjustment to the regime must include India, Pakistan and Israel at the negotiating table. Without their inclusion in and commitment to this broad non-proliferation and security reform, our efforts will fail. None of the three States has joined the NPT, and their development of nuclear weapons or nuclear weapon capability has been outside of the current nuclear non-proliferation regime. Yet their status as known or presumed holders of nuclear weapons has clearly contributed to tensions in their respective regions.

Third, the integrity of the NPT should be ensured. The Treaty now allows any member to withdraw with three months notice. Any nation invoking this escape clause is almost certainly signaling its intent to develop nuclear weapons, which inevitably has serious implications for international peace and security. This provision of the Treaty should be curtailed. At a minimum, notice of NPT withdrawal should prompt an automatic review by the Security Council. And France has recently advanced a number of proposals for the development of a set of pre-agreed actions that would automatically be taken by the Security Council in such a case.

Fourth, the IAEA's additional protocol should be made the verification standard. Much effort was recently expended—and rightly so—to persuade Iran and Libya to give the IAEA broader rights of inspection, by accepting the authority provided to the Agency by the additional protocol. But the Agency should have the right to conduct these broader inspections in all countries. As I mentioned before, experience has shown that verification of the NPT's safeguards obligations in a credible manner requires the authority provided by the additional protocol. However, to date, only 56 States, out of the 184 non-nuclear-weapon States party to the NPT, have accepted the protocol.

Collective Security: Reforming the System

My third set of proposals relates to reforming the system for international security. It has four aspects.

First, we can only hope to make meaningful progress if we continue to keep our eyes focused on the security picture—seeking a comprehensive solution that addresses the security concerns of all. As a starting point, we must recognize that the current crisis of international insecurity will not be resolved by anything short of a functional system of collective security, as clearly hoped for in the United Nations Charter.

The Security Council must be able and ready to engage effectively in both preventive diplomacy and enforcement measures, with the tools and methods in place necessary to cope with existing and emerging threats to international peace and security. These should include: mechanisms for preventive diplomacy to settle emerging disputes; "smart" sanctions that can target a government without adding misery to its citizens; and adequate forces to deal with the foreseeable range of situations—from maintaining law and order, to monitoring borders, to combating aggression.

In that context, I believe the Security Council should under certain circumstances authorize pre-emptive measures—collective pre-emptive measures—to address extreme threats to international peace and security, such as to prevent genocide, or to counter an imminent threat to use weapons of mass destruction in an act of aggression.

Second, once these non-proliferation and security measures are in place, we should aim for our legal regime related to nuclear weapons to emerge into a "peremptory norm" of international law—a norm that is part of our collective conscience—not dependent on any particular treaty. In short, as with the ban on slavery or genocide, the renunciation of such weapons should be universal and permanent. This legal norm, however, cannot be contemplated without an agreed disarmament roadmap, and clear subscription to that roadmap by all States possessing nuclear weapons.

Third, we must work collectively to address not only the symptoms but also the root causes of insecurity and instability, including: the regional rivalries and conflicts I have already mentioned; the widening divide between rich and poor, in which two-fifths of the world's population lives on less than two dollars per day; the chronic lack of good governance and respect for human rights; and the increasing schisms between cultures and civilizations. We should not forget that nearly all efforts to acquire nuclear weapons are to be found in the Middle East and other areas of instability. Effective amelioration of these causes of global insecurity will require political resolve and more balanced "North-South" relations.

Consider the current imbalance: as a global community, we spend $900 billion every year on armaments, $300 billion on subsidies to farmers in wealthy nations, and only $60 billion on development assistance to the developing world. Improving our performance in this "global distributive justice" will go a long way towards pre-empting many of the security threats—let alone the social ills—that affect our planet.

Finally, our work to achieve consensus on these proposals should proceed with the initiation of an expanded public dialogue. Organizations like your own, the Carnegie Endowment for International Peace, should work to refine these proposals and ideas, and to bring them to the attention of governments and opinion leaders. As I indicated earlier, we should work to further stimulate public discourse on these ideas, at all levels of civil society, to make the global community understand that our survival is at stake—but that we can, in fact, solve the international security dilemma, including the nuclear dilemma, within our generation and within our own time.

Conclusion

As I see it, we have before us two possible courses of action. We can wait for the unthinkable to happen; or we can take notice of the writing on the wall and begin to act today.

With the continuing erosion of the effectiveness and even the legitimacy of the present arms control and security structure, we must have the wisdom and the foresight to understand—as has been aptly stated—that "as we are collectively menaced, so we must collectively act." I repeat that it is time to abandon the unworkable notion that it is morally reprehensible for some countries to pursue nuclear weapons, but morally acceptable for others to rely on them. Our aim must be clear: a security structure that is based on our shared humanity and not on the ability of some to destroy us all.

Source: United Nations. International Atomic Energy Agency. "Nuclear Non-Proliferation: Global Security in a Rapidly Changing World." Speech by IAEA director general Dr. Mohamed ElBaradei at the Carnegie International Non-Proliferation Conference, Washington, D.C. June 21, 2004. www.iaea.org/PrinterFriendly/NewsCenter/Statements/2004/ebsp2004n004.html (accessed January 18, 2004).

Justice Department on the Use of Torture in Terrorism Interrogations

June 22 and December 30, 2004

INTRODUCTION

Controversy over the abuse of Iraqis by U.S. soldiers at a prison in Baghdad deepened in June 2004 when it was revealed that Bush administration lawyers in 2002 and 2003 had approved the use of torture to extract information from suspected terrorists. The Bush administration insisted it had never used torture, but critics said the legal advice authorizing torture had created an atmosphere that made the Iraqi prison abuses possible.

Six months after the legal opinions were made public, the administration produced new legal guidance that sought to end the controversy by reversing some of the earlier judgments. That guidance, issued December 30, said torture was prohibited by U.S. domestic law and international treaties and was not justified. *(Iraq prison scandal, p. 207)*

Evolution of the Bush Administration Position

After the September 11, 2001, terrorist attacks against the United States, President George W. Bush declared war against what he called "global terrorism," starting with the al Qaeda network that, he said, was responsible for those attacks. The first major element of that war was the U.S.-led invasion of Afghanistan in October 2002. That invasion ousted the Taliban regime that had governed Afghanistan for six years, along with al Qaeda militants who operated from camps in the country. By late 2001 the United States and its allies, including Pakistan, had captured hundreds of al Qaeda and Taliban fighters. Many senior-level militants were held at various facilities in Afghanistan, but starting in January 2002 the Pentagon transferred several hundred of the captured fighters to the U.S. naval base at Guantanamo Bay, Cuba. *(Guantanamo Bay detentions, p. 375)*

The detention of these fighters gave the United States a potential bonanza of intelligence information about al Qaeda, but it also raised questions about how the fighters were to be treated and what techniques could be used to interrogate them. On January 9, 2002, Justice Department lawyers John C. Yoo and Robert J. Delahunty produced a lengthy memorandum setting out reasons why fighters captured in Afghanistan were not entitled to prisoner-of-war status under the 1949 Geneva Conventions, which governed the rules of war. The memo, titled "Application of Treaties and Laws to Al Qaeda and Taliban Detainees," was addressed to lawyers at the White House and the Pentagon. Like other administration documents on the matter, this memo was kept secret until the disclosures in June 2004. It laid out several legal arguments justifying a U.S. refusal to treat the hundreds of Taliban and al Qaeda fighters captured in Afghanistan as prisoners of war; that status would have entitled them to legal rights under the Geneva Conventions, including freedom from coercive interrogations.

Alberto Gonzales, the White House counsel, on January 25, 2002, sent Bush a memo endorsing the Justice Department's position and urging the president to treat the Afghanistan detainees as "enemy combatants" rather than as prisoners of war. "The nature of the new war [against terrorism] places a high premium on other factors such as the ability to quickly obtain information from captured terrorists and their sponsors in order to avoid further atrocities against American civilians," Gonzales wrote. "The same reason," he added, "renders obsolete Geneva's strict limitations on questioning of enemy prisoners and renders quaint some of its provisions." This last phrase was a reference to such requirements of the Geneva Conventions that prisoners of war be given commissary privileges and scrip in lieu of pay.

The Gonzales memo was referred to the State Department, where Secretary of State Colin Powell argued that the United States stood to gain more, over the long term, by adhering to the international rules of war. Following the Gonzales advice, Powell said in a January 26, 2002, memo to Bush, would "reverse over a century of U.S. policy and practice in supporting the Geneva Conventions and undermine the protections of the laws of war for our troops." Mindful of the need to build international support for the antiterrorism war Bush had declared, the State Department said departing from the Geneva Conventions also would "undermine public support among critical allies."

The State Department's arguments reportedly led Bush to adopt a middle ground. In a memorandum dated February 7, 2002, Bush decreed that former Taliban fighters would be given the protections of the Geneva Conventions but did not qualify as prisoners of war. Fighters for al Qaeda were not covered by the Geneva Conventions because al Qaeda was not a state, Bush said, and so they would not receive any of its protections, including prisoner-of-war status. As a practical matter, this distinction between the Taliban and al Qaeda made little difference in how the two kinds of fighters were treated.

Bush's memo also said all detainees should be "treated humanely and, to the extent appropriate and consistent with military necessity, in a manner consistent with the principals of Geneva." When questions about treatment of detainees arose over the next two years, administration officials repeatedly emphasized Bush's order that they be treated "humanely." When the full text of Bush's order was made public in June 2004, human rights organizations and other critics pointed to the qualifying phrase as evidence that Bush had opened the door to treatment outside the rules of the Geneva Conventions on the vague grounds of being "appropriate" and a "military necessity."

Justice Department "Torture Memo"

As the United States continued to capture al Qaeda and Taliban fighters in Afghanistan in 2002, the Bush administration saw an increasing need to extract as much information as possible from the prisoners, especially information about the operations of al Qaeda and its plans for future terrorist attacks. According to later investigations and news reports, U.S. interrogators were uncertain how far they could go in using coercive methods to extract that information. In the summer of 2002 the Central Intelligence Agency asked for guidance on the matter. CIA interrogators were responsible for interviewing so-called high-value detainees—those who were believed to have the most useful types of information about terrorist activities.

White House counsel Gonzales passed the CIA request on to the Justice Department, which responded on August 1, 2002, with a fifty-page formal legal opinion, written by Jay S. Bybee, the assistant attorney general who headed the department's Office of Legal Counsel. Later in 2002 Bush nominated Bybee for a seat on the U.S. Ninth Circuit Court of Appeals, and the Senate confirmed him in 2003.

Bybee's memo made three basic arguments. First, it offered narrow definitions of physical and mental torture. To constitute torture, the memo said, physical abuse would have to cause pain of "an extreme nature" equivalent in intensity to that "accompanying serious physical injury, such as organ failure, impairment of bodily function, or even death." Similarly, the memo said, mental abuse would qualify as torture only if it resulted in "significant psychological harm of significant duration, e.g., lasting for months or even years."

The memo's second argument was that the president had the constitutional right, as commander in chief of U.S. armed forces, to override U.S. laws and international treaties prohibiting the use of torture. "The president enjoys complete discretion in the exercise of his commander-in-chief authority," the memo said. "Congress may no more regulate the president's ability to detain and interrogate enemy combatants than it may regulate his ability to direct troop movements on the battlefield." Among the laws the president could override, Bybee said, was the United Nations Convention Against Torture and Other Cruel, Inhuman and Degrading Treatment, which the United States had ratified in 1994, and the related 1994 Anti-Torture Act (PL 103–322) that made it a criminal offense for anyone to engage in torture.

A third argument was that U.S. interrogators could be legally defended against later prosecution, under the Anti-Torture Act, for using torture. Such a legal defense could be based on the "military necessity" of protecting the United States against an attack by al Qaeda, the memo said.

Interrogations at Guantanamo

In a related development in late 2002, officials in charge of the Guantanamo prison asked for permission, in the cases of "exceptionally resistant detainees," to use stronger interrogation techniques than those allowed by the *Army Field Manual.* Defense Secretary Donald H. Rumsfeld responded to that request on December 2, 2002, with a decision authorizing the use of additional interrogation tactics, including putting prisoners into "stress positions" and interrogating them for up to twenty consecutive hours, intimidating them with dogs, forcing them to wear hoods while being interrogated, shaving their beard and heads, and keeping them naked. The most extreme method was described as "mild, non-injurious physical contact." Pentagon officials later said these additional techniques were used on two detainees at Guantanamo before Rumsfeld rescinded his authorization on January 15, 2003, after the navy's general counsel expressed concern about the matter.

Rumsfeld also ordered the creation of a "review panel" to recommend rules for interrogating prisoners at Guantanamo. That panel, headed by air force general counsel Mary Walker, on March 6, 2003, sent Rumsfeld a detailed memo that essentially adopted the Justice Department reasoning from the previous August on what constituted torture. The panel also argued that the president's "inherent constitutional authority to manage a military campaign" allowed him to approve whatever types of interrogations were necessary—specifically including torture—to obtain "intelligence vital to the protection of untold thousands of American citizens." International treaties and even U.S. laws barring torture "must be construed as inapplicable to interrogation undertaken pursuant" to the president's authority, the memo argued.

Rumsfeld issued his order for Guantanamo interrogations on April 16, 2003. It did not specifically adopt the sweeping arguments put forward by Pentagon lawyers. Instead, Rumsfeld's order approved a new list of two dozen interrogation techniques for Guantanamo, but not at other facilities where detainees were held. Seventeen of the techniques (for example, yelling at a detainee) were taken from the *Army Field Manual,* but four could be used only when Rumsfeld was told about them in advance: extended solitary confinement, attacking or insulting a detainee's ego, using rewards or removing privileges, and alternating the use of friendly and harsh interrogators ("good cop" versus "bad cop").

Secret Detentions

Late in 2002 U.S. and international news organizations began reporting that the CIA and the U.S. military were holding dozens, perhaps hundreds, of suspected terrorists in secret locations in Afghanistan, on the Indian Ocean island of Diego Garcia (a British territory), and aboard ships in international waters. Many of these detainees were subjected to what military officials called "stress and duress" interrogation tactics, which were described as stopping short of actual torture.

The *Washington Post* reported December 26, 2002, that detainees at the U.S.-run Bagram air base north of Kabul at times were held "in awkward, painful positions and deprived of sleep with a 24-hour bombardment of lights." The *Post* quoted one official, who had supervised the capture and transfer of accused terrorists, as saying: "If you don't violate someone's human rights some of the time, you probably aren't doing your job. I don't think we want to be promoting a view of zero tolerance on this." The newspaper also quoted CIA director George Tenet and other officials as saying the interrogations in Afghanistan had produced useful intelligence for the U.S. war against terrorism.

The *New York Times* reported in May 2004 that among the detainees held at these secret locations was Khalid Sheikh Mohammed, described by U.S. officials as the "mastermind" of al Qaeda's September 11, 2001, terrorist attacks in New York City and Washington, D.C. The *Times* reported that Mohammed had been subjected to a technique known as "water boarding," in which the prisoner was strapped to a board and forced under water until he believed he might drown. At least some of the techniques used on Mohammed appeared to have been effective. The commission that investigated the September 11 attacks said, in its July 22, 2004, report, that Mohammed had provided useful information on al Qaeda and its plans. *(September 11 commission report, p. 450)*

News reports also said the United States had turned some detainees over to countries in the Middle East or Central Asia where the security services were known to use torture. The *Washington Post* report in December 2002, for example, quoted unnamed officials as saying detainees had been transferred to Egypt, Jordan, Morocco, Pakistan, Saudi Arabia, and Uzbekistan for questioning. The military called these transfers "renditions." The UN anti-torture convention specifically barred sending detainees to countries known to use torture.

Growing Criticism

The detentions at Guantanamo Bay and other places, plus the reports suggesting that some detainees were being subjected to abusive interrogation, led to broad international criticism of the United States in late 2002 and early 2003. Representatives of several major civil liberties and human rights organizations met privately with senior administration officials in the early months of 2003 and received assurances that the United States was not using torture or otherwise abusing its detainees.

Some Democrats on Capitol Hill also began raising alarms, among them Senator Patrick J. Leahy, of Vermont, the ranking Democrat on the Judiciary Committee. On June 2, 2003, Leahy wrote to Bush's national security adviser, Condoleeza Rice, to express concern about reports that detainees were being beaten and deprived of food. William J. Haynes II, general counsel for the Pentagon, responded to Leahy on June 25, 2003, with a letter saying all U.S.-held detainees were being treated in accordance with the United Nations antitorture convention. The United States, Haynes said, "does not permit, tolerate, or condone any such torture by its employees under any circumstances." Haynes went even further in his letter, saying the U.S. government would not tolerate "other acts of cruel, inhuman, or degrading treatment or punishment which do not amount to torture."

The following day, June 26, 2003, the White House issued a statement under Bush's name denouncing the use of torture in unequivocal terms. "Freedom from torture is an inalienable human right," the statement said, adding that the UN convention "forbids governments from deliberately inflicting severe physical or mental pain or suffering on those within their custody or control." The statement singled out "notorious human rights abusers" as current practitioners of torture, including Burma, Cuba, Iran, North Korea, and Zimbabwe. It also said the United States was "committed to the world-wide elimination of torture and we are leading this fight by example."

Torture Memos Disclosed

The revelation in late April 2004 that U.S. soldiers had been abusing detainees at a notorious Baghdad prison, Abu Ghraib, brought new scrutiny to the administration's policies toward detainees. Almost inevitably, the previously secret documents that underpinned the administration's actions came into public view.

The first major revelation came June 7, when the *Wall Street Journal* disclosed the March 2003 memo to Rumsfeld from Pentagon lawyers laying out legal grounds for aggressive questioning of detainees and arguing that the president had legal powers to overrule laws and treaties barring torture. The next day the *Washington Post* revealed the existence of the Justice Department's August 1, 2002, memo justifying the use of torture in some circumstances. The *Post* noted that the Pentagon lawyers had adopted the Justice Department's reasoning in their March 2003 memo to Rumsfeld.

These disclosures deepened the furor of the Abu Ghraib scandal. Human rights groups, lawyers for Guantanamo detainees, and other critics said the memos appeared to provide the legal basis for the extreme interrogation techniques used at the prison in Iraq and at Guantanamo. "It is by leaps and bounds the worst thing I've seen since this whole Abu Ghraib scandal broke," Human Rights Watch lawyer Tom Malinowski told the *Post.* "It appears that what they were contemplating was the commission of war crimes and looking for ways to avoid legal accountability. The effect is to throw out years of military doctrine and standards on interrogation." News reports also quoted unidentified U.S. military lawyers as saying they opposed the administration's legal reasoning because it could undermine Washington's demands that American service personnel be treated humanely when they were captured by enemy forces.

As in the past, the administration responded by saying Bush had ordered that detainees be treated humanely. Testifying to the Senate Judiciary Committee on the day the *Post* disclosed the torture memo, Attorney General John Ashcroft refused to comment on his department's memo or to release it publicly. Instead, he said Bush "has not directed or ordered any conduct that would violate the Constitution of the United States, that would violate any one of these enactments of the United States Congress or that would violate the provisions of any of the treaties as they have been entered into by the United States." Under questioning by Leahy and other Democrats, Ashcroft included the 1994 Anti-Torture Act among those laws and said "this administration rejects torture." A Pentagon spokesman told the *Post* that the crafting of legal justifications for torture did not mean that torture was being practiced.

Editorial comment on the matter broke largely along predictable lines, with most conservative-leaning newspapers arguing that the administration was justified in taking harsh action against terrorists and liberal-leaning newspapers decrying the administration's legal arguments. The *Wall Street Journal* editorialized that the arguments advanced in the memos were "standard lawyerly fare, routine legal stuff." The *Washington Post* took a sharply different view, arguing in a June 9 editorial: "There is no justification, legal or moral, for the judgments made by Mr. Bush's political appointees at the Justice and Defense departments. Theirs is the logic of criminal regimes, of dictatorships around the world that sanction torture on grounds of 'national security.'"

Asked by reporters on June 10 whether he had sanctioned torture, Bush repeatedly said he had ordered that "anything we did would conform to the U.S. law and would be consistent with international treaty obligations." Bush said he could not recall seeing the Justice Department's memo on the matter.

The assurances by Bush and Ashcroft failed to dampen the controversy generated by the revelation of the administration memos. On Capitol Hill, Democratic members of the Senate Judiciary Committee tried unsuccessfully to get chairman Orrin G. Hatch, R-Utah, to issue a subpoena for twenty-three administration memos on the subject. Even so, Hatch and other Republicans informally called on the White House to give them to Congress.

Responding to intense pressure, the administration on June 22 gave reporters copies of some of the key internal memos on the legal issues, including Bush's February 2002 order, the August 2002 Justice Department's memo on torture, and the March 2003 memo by Pentagon lawyers. A senior Justice Department official, speaking on background, also said the 2002 torture memo was being withdrawn because the legal theories it suggested were "unnecessary" for the actual interrogation of al Qaeda members and other detainees.

At a separate news conference on June 22, Bush appeared to reject the legal reasoning of the 2002 memo. "Let me make very clear the position of my government and our country: We do not condone torture," he said. "I have never ordered torture. I will never order torture. The values of this country are such that torture is not a part of our soul and our being."

The Justice Department's action failed to satisfy critics. "This selective release of documents raises more questions than it answers," Human Rights Watch executive director Kenneth Roth said. "We need an independent investigation, not a selective self-investigation."

Roth and other critics also expressed concern that the administration had not specifically renounced the reasoning in the torture memo that the president had the constitutional right to set aside laws and treaties. Critics noted, for example, that the August 2002 memo had failed to take into account a landmark Supreme Court decision saying the president could not use his commander-in-chief authority to set aside U.S. laws. That 1952 decision came in a case, *Youngstown Sheet and Tube Co. v. Sawyer,* in which the Court ruled that President Harry Truman (1945–1953) could not use the Korean War to justify taking over steel companies to end a crippling strike.

Senate Democrats tried again on June 23 to force the administration to release all its legal opinions on the treatment of detainees. The Senate rejected the Democratic proposal on a 50–46 vote, largely along party lines.

On June 26 the *New York Times* reported that the CIA had suspended the use of what it called "enhanced interrogation techniques" on al Qaeda and other detainees pending a new administration policy on torture.

On June 28, six days after the administration memos were made public, the Supreme Court rebuffed the administration on another key aspect of its antiterrorism war: the indefinite detention of suspects without any review by the courts. *(Court rulings, p. 375)*

In August, the administration's contention that the Justice Department's memo and other legal arguments did not lead to the abuses at Abu Ghraib came under challenge from two official reports. A high-level army investigation of the Abu Ghraib abuses and a Pentagon commission headed by former defense secretary James Schlesinger both concluded that coercive interrogation techniques approved by the administration for very narrow circumstances in Afghanistan ultimately were used at the Abu Ghraib prison, as well.

A New Position on Torture

The furor over the Abu Ghraib abuses and the torture memo died down during the presidential campaign, only to arise two weeks after the election when Bush nominated Gonzales to succeed Ashcroft as attorney general. Noting that the Justice Department's torture memo had been addressed to Gonzales, Democrats said they would question him about his role in the matter when his nomination came before the Senate in January 2005. Further controversy arose in mid-December when the American Civil Liberties Union (ACLU) obtained, and posted on its Web site, e-mails and other messages from FBI agents who said they had witnessed abuses by military interrogators of detainees at Guantanamo Bay and in Iraq.

On December 30 the Justice Department released a revised document explicitly disavowing torture as "abhorrent both to American law and values and to international norms." Release of the revised memo came just a week before the Senate Judiciary Committee was to begin hearings on Bush's nomination of Gonzales as attorney general.

In contrast to the August 2002 opinion, the new memo said U.S. officials were barred from using torture under any circumstances. It also defined torture in much broader terms as physical suffering "even if it does not involve severe physical pain." Damage done to a detainee "need not be permanent, but it must continue for a prolonged period of time" to qualify as torture, the memo added. The memo did not address the argument, made in the August 2002 opinion, that the president had the constitutional right to override laws and treaties barring torture.

Anthony D. Romero, executive director of the ACLU, said the new memo "is certainly an improvement over the government's previous policies." However, Romero and other critics said the administration had not adequately explained why the original memo was drafted in the first place or why it took the Abu Ghraib scandal to bring it to light and force its reversal. These critics said they remained concerned that the administration had not explicitly renounced the doctrine that the president could use his commander-in-chief power to set aside laws and treaties.

Following are excerpts from two documents. The first, made public by the White House on June 22, 2004, is a memorandum submitted to White House legal counsel Alberto Gonzales on August 1, 2002, by the Office of Legal Counsel in the Justice Department, headed by Assistant Attorney General Jay S. Bybee. The memorandum laid out legal justifications for the possible use of torture by U.S. interrogators when questioning suspected members of the al Qaeda terrorist network. The second document is a memorandum submitted to Deputy Attorney General James B. Comey by Daniel Levin, the acting assistant attorney general in charge of the Justice Department Office of Legal Counsel. This memorandum, dated December 30, 2004, and made public that same day, rejected as unlawful the use of torture by U.S. interrogators.

"Memorandum for Alberto R. Gonzales, Counsel to the President"

Re: Standards of Conduct for Interrogation under 18 U.S.C. Sections 2340–2340A

You have asked for our Office's views regarding the standards of conduct under the Convention Against Torture and Other Cruel, Inhuman and Degrading Treatment or Punishment as implemented by Sections 2340–2340A of title 18 of the United States Code [the Anti-Torture Act of 1994, as amended]. As we understand it, this question has arisen in the context of interrogations outside of the United States. We conclude below that Section 2340A proscribes acts inflicting, and that are specifically intended to inflict, severe pain or suffering, whether mental or physical. Those acts must be of an extreme nature to rise to the level of torture within the meaning of Section 2340A and the Convention. We further conclude that certain acts may be cruel, inhuman or degrading, but still not produce pain and suffering of the requisite intensity to fall within Section 2340A's proscription against torture. We conclude by examining possible defenses that would negate any claim that certain interrogation methods violate the statute.

[*Editor's note:* Sections 2340 and 2340A read:

Section 2340:

(a) Offense.—Whoever outside the United States commits or attempts to commit torture shall be fined under this title or imprisoned not more than 20 years, or both, and if death results to any person from conduct prohibited by this subsection, shall be punished by death or imprisoned for any term of years or for life.

(b) Jurisdiction.—There is jurisdiction over the activity prohibited in subsection (a) if—
   (1) the alleged offender is a national of the United States; or
   (2) the alleged offender is present in the United States, irrespective of the nationality of the victim or alleged offender.

(c) Conspiracy.—A person who conspires to commit an offense under this section shall be subject to the same penalties (other than the penalty of death) as the penalties prescribed for the offense, the commission of which was the object of the conspiracy.

Section 2340A:

"(a) Offense.—Whoever outside the United States commits or attempts to commit torture shall be fined under this title or imprisoned not more than 20 years, or both, and if death results to any person from conduct prohibited by this subsection, shall be punished by death or imprisoned for any term of years or for life.

(b) Jurisdiction.—There is jurisdiction over the activity prohibited in subsection (a) if—
   (1) the alleged offender is a national of the United States; or
   (2) the alleged offender is present in the United States, irrespective of the nationality of the victim or alleged offender."]

In Part I, we examine the criminal statute's text and history. We conclude that for an act to constitute torture as defined in Section 2340, it must inflict pain that is difficult to endure. Physical pain amounting to torture must be equivalent in intensity to the pain accompanying serious physical injury, such as organ failure, impairment of bodily functions, or even death. For purely mental pain or suffering to amount to torture under Section 2340, it must result in significant psychological harm of significant duration, e.g., lasting for months or even years. We conclude that the mental harm also must result from one of the predicate acts listed in the statute, namely: threats of imminent death; threats of infliction of the kind of pain that would amount to physical torture; infliction of such physical pain as a means of psychological torture; use of drugs or other procedures designed to deeply disrupt the senses, or fundamentally alter an individual's personality; or threatening to do any of these things to a third party. The legislative history simply reveals that Congress intended for the statute's definition to track the Convention's definition of torture and the reservations, understandings, and declarations that the United State submitted with its ratification. We conclude that the statute, taken as a whole, makes plain that it prohibits only extreme acts.

[*Editor's note:* In its reservations, the United States said it was bound by the obligation to prevent "cruel, inhuman or degrading treatment or punishment" only insofar as the term meant the cruel, unusual and inhumane treatment or punishment prohibited by the Fifth, Eighth, and Fourteenth Amendments to the U.S. Constitution. The U.S. reservations also said that mental pain or suffering meant prolonged mental harm from: (1) the intentional infliction or threatened infliction of severe physical pain or suffering; (2) the use or threat of mind altering substances; (3) the threat of imminent death; or (4) that another person will imminently be subjected to the above mistreatment.]

In Part II, we examine the text, ratification history, and negotiating history of the Torture Convention. We conclude that the treaty's text prohibits the most extreme acts by reserving criminal penalties solely for torture and declining to require such penalties for "cruel, inhuman, or degrading treatment or punishment." This confirms our view that the criminal statute penalizes only the most egregious conduct. Executive branch interpretations and representations to the Senate at the time of ratification further confirm that the treaty was intended to reach only the most extreme conduct.

In Part III, we analyze the jurisprudence of the Torture Victims Protection Act, 28 U.S.C. Section 1350 note (2000), which provides civil remedies for torture victims, to predict the standards that courts might follow in determining what actions might reach the threshold of torture in the criminal context. We conclude from these cases that courts are likely to take a totality-of-the-circumstances approach, and will look to an entire course of conduct, to determine whether certain acts will violate Section 2340A. Moreover, these cases demonstrate that most often torture involves cruel and extreme physical pain. In Part IV, we examine international decisions regarding the use of sensory deprivation techniques. These cases make clear that while many of these techniques may amount to cruel, inhuman, or degrading treatment, they do not produce pain or suffering of the necessary intensity to meet the definition of torture. From these decisions, we conclude that there is a wide range of such techniques that will not rise to the level of torture.

In Part V, we discuss whether Section 2340A may be unconstitutional if applied to interrogations undertaken of enemy combatants pursuant to the President's Commander-in-Chief powers. We find that in the circumstances of the current war against al Qaeda and is allies, prosecution under Section 2340A may be barred because enforcement of the statute would represent an unconstitutional infringement of the President's authority to conduct war. In Part VI, we discuss defenses to an allegation that an interrogation method might violate the statute. We conclude that, under the current circumstances, necessity or self-defense may justify interrogation methods that might violate Section 2340A. . . .

[Parts I–IV omitted.]

V. The President's Commander-in-Chief Power

Even if an interrogation method arguably were to violate Section 2340A, the statute would be unconstitutional if it impermissibly encroached on the President's constitutional power to conduct a military campaign. As Commander-in-Chief, the president has the constitutional authority to order interrogation of enemy combatants to gain intelligence information concern the military plans of the enemy. The demands of the Commander-in-Chief power are especially pronounced in the middle of a war in which the nation has already suffered a direct attack. In such a case, the information gained from interrogations may prevent future attacks by foreign enemies. Any effort to apply Section 2340A in a manner that interferes with the President's direction of such core war matters as the detention and interrogation of enemy combatants thus would be unconstitutional." . . .

[Section A omitted.]

B. Interpretation to Avoid Constitutional Problems

As the Supreme Court has recognized, and as we will explain further below, the President enjoys complete discretion in the exercise of his Commander-in-Chief authority and in conducting operations against hostile forces. Because both "[t]he executive power and the commander of the military naval forces is vested in the President," the conduct of operations during war. . . . As we discuss below, the President's power to detain and interrogate enemy combatants arises out of his constitutional authority as Commander in Chief. A construction of Section 2340A that applied the provision to regulate the President's authority as Commander in Chief to determine the interrogation and treatment of enemy combatants would raise serious constitutional questions. Congress may no more regulate the President's ability to detain and interrogate enemy combatants than it may regulate his ability to direct troop movements on the battlefield. Accordingly, we would construe Section 2340A to avoid this constitutional difficulty, and conclude that it does not apply to the President's detention and interrogation of enemy combatants pursuant to his Commander-in-Chief authority. . . .

Source: U.S. Department of Justice. Office of Legal Counsel. Office of the Assistant Attorney General. "Memorandum for Alberto R. Gonzales, Counsel to the President." August 1, 2002. Declassified and released June 22, 2004. www.aclu.org/torturefoia/released/DOJ_Memo_080102.pdf (accessed February 28, 2005).

Memorandum for James B. Comey, Deputy Attorney General

Re: Legal Standards Applicable under 18 U.S.C. Sections 2340–2340A

Torture is abhorrent both to American law and values and to international norms. This universal repudiation of torture is reflected in our criminal aw, for example, 18 U.S.C. Sections 234—2340A; international agreements, exemplified by the United Nations Convention Against Torture (the "CAT"); customary international law; centuries of Anglo-American law; and the longstanding policy of the United States, repeatedly and recently reaffirmed by the President. . . .

[A deleted paragraph in the full document reviewed the circumstances of the August 1, 2002 memorandum.]

Questions have since been raised, both by this Office and by others, about the appropriateness and relevance of the non-statutory discussion in the August 2002 Memorandum, and also about various aspects of the statutory analysis, in particular the statement that "severe" pain under the statute was limited to pain "equivalent in intensity to the pain accompanying serious physical injury, such as organ failure, impairment of bodily function, or even death." We decided to withdraw the August 2002 Memorandum, a decision you announced in June 2004. At that time, you directed this

Office to prepare a replacement memorandum. Because of the importance of—and public interest in—these issues, you asked that this memorandum be prepared in a form that could be released so that interested parties could understand our analysis of the statute.

This memorandum supersedes the August 2002 Memorandum in its entirety. Because the discussion of that memorandum concerning the President's Commander-in-Chief power and the potential defenses to liability was—and remains—unnecessary, it has been eliminated from the analysis that follows. Considerations of the bounds of any such authority would be inconsistent with the President's unequivocal directive that United States personnel not engage in torture. [This refers to statements issued by the White House on June 26, 2003, and July 5, 2004, condemning the use of torture.]

We have also modified in some important respects our analysis of the legal standards applicable under 18 U.S.C. Sections 234—2340A. For example, we disagree with statements in the August 2002 Memorandum limiting "severe" pain under the statute to "excruciating and agonizing pain", or to pain "equivalent in intensity to the pain accompanying serious physical injury, such as organ failure, impairment of bodily function, or even death." There are additional areas where we disagree with or modify the analysis in the August 2002 Memorandum. . . .

The Criminal Division of the Department of Justice has reviewed this memorandum and concurs in the analysis. . . .

Source: U.S. Department of Justice. Office of Legal Counsel. Office of the Assistant Attorney General. "Memorandum for James B. Comey, Deputy Attorney General." December 30, 2004. www.justice.gov/olc/18usc23402340a2.htm (accessed February 28, 2005).

India's New Prime Minister on Programs and Priorities

June 24, 2004

INTRODUCTION

India faced two giant shocks to its political system within a few days in May 2004. First, in parliamentary elections held between April 20 and May 10, voters turned out of power a coalition government led by the Hindu nationalist party, the Bharatiya Janata Party (BJP), in favor of the once-dominant Indian Congress Party. Five days later, Sonia Gandhi, the latest in a succession of Gandhi family members to lead the Congress Party, suddenly renounced the post of prime minister, which would have been hers by right of her party's victory. Instead, she and her party turned to Manmohan Singh, a respected economist with little experience as a politician. He took office on May 22, becoming the first member of the Sikh minority to hold India's top political post. Even so, Sonia Gandhi remained as head of the Congress Party—filling a key advisory role and, some said, serving as de facto prime minister behind the scenes.

Another shock, this one administered by nature, came December 26 when an earthquake off the coast of Indonesia sent a giant tsunami wave roaring through the Indian Ocean, shattering coastlines. The southeast coast of India was among those hit by the devastating waves, which killed more than 170,000 people throughout the region. At least 10,000 Indians died. *(Tsunami, p. 991)*

Surprise Election Result

The Congress Party led India for nearly all of the first five decades after the country's 1947 independence from Britain. For most of that time the party's leadership was a family affair: first, Jawaharlal Nehru, who led India to independence and served as prime minister until his death in 1964; then after a gap of two years in the mid-1960s his daughter, Indira Gandhi, who served until she was assassinated in 1984; and then her son Rajiv Gandhi, who served until the Congress Party lost power temporarily in 1989 (he also was assassinated, in 1991). Congress regained power after Rajiv Gandhi's death but lost it again five years later amid charges of widespread corruption in its government.

A new era for India began in 1998 when a coalition (the National Democratic Alliance) took office headed by the Bharatiya Janata Party and its leader, Atal Bahari Vajpayee. It was India's first government dominated by a political party dedicated primarily to the interests of just one of the country's many sectarian groups, the Hindus, who made up about 80 percent of the population of more than 1 billion. Vajpayee himself espoused moderation in all things, but key figures in his government were fierce advocates of *Hindutva* (oneness), the vague concept that sought to define India as a Hindu nation despite the presence of more than 150 million Muslims, Christians, Sikhs, and other minorities. Vajpayee's first government lasted eighteen months, but he then won elections in 1999 and served the standard five-year term, heading the first government not led by the Congress Party.

In contrast to some previous elections—when several of India's thirty major parties often battled for potential leadership of parliament—only the Congress Party and the BJP appeared to have the potential national strength to form a government. A soft-spoken poet who had shown a remarkable ability to navigate India's rough political waters, Vajpayee generally was seen as a strong candidate for yet another term. By contrast, Sonia Gandhi, the leader of the Congress Party, was a lightening rod of controversy. The widow of Rajiv Gandhi, she was born in Italy but had lived in India for most of her adult life and had become a citizen in 1983. Millions of Indians revered her simply as the inheritor of the Gandhi family tradition, but millions, in a land with a deep xenophobic tradition, also considered her a foreigner.

Before the four stages of voting began April 20, nearly all analysts predicted a repeat victory by the BJP because of India's recent economic growth and the controversy over Sonia Gandhi's background. The BJP claimed full credit for the country's booming economy, which was aided by better-than-average monsoon rains in 2003 and a rapid growth in computer technology industries. The party's upbeat slogan, "India Shining," was an attempt to capitalize on an optimistic mood, at least among urban, educated Indians. Another supposedly good omen for the government was India's victory over Pakistan in a first-ever series of cricket matches.

Exit polling while the voting was still under way in dozens of constituencies showed that the BJP coalition was lagging well behind expectations, however. The Mumbai (Bombay) stock market began a deep slide in late April on fears of political instability.

Even with these early warnings, the tallies of the 370 million votes made public May 13 came as a shock. The two main parties won an almost identical number of seats in the 545-seat lower house (the Lok Sabha): 145 for the Congress Party and 138 for the BJP. Both of the major parties actually fell slightly below the 1999 results in terms of the percentage of votes cast. The more important difference was the trend in the number of seats: the Congress Party gained thirty-two seats, while the BJP lost forty-four seats—a full one-fifth of its previous total. As a result, neither party could form a government on its own. The likely allies of Congress won many more seats in parliament than did any potential grouping of allies for the BJP, and so Congress was the obvious choice to lead a new government.

Analysts from across India's vast political spectrum suggested several important reasons why BJP lost and Congress won. Perhaps most important was the nation's long-running "anti-incumbency factor"—the tendency of Indian voters to throw out the incumbents, especially at the state level. As always, local and state issues topped the list of concerns for many voters, and in 2004 the Congress and its allies appeared better positioned because they were not the incumbents. The BJP's "India Shining" campaign might also have backfired, at least among the estimated 700 million rural poor, who had yet to see personally any shining results from the country's high-tech boom. The very nature of the BJP—and especially some of its most extreme Hindu nationalist leaders—also appeared to concern millions of voters who wanted to think of India as a broad secular society rather than as a collection of competing ethnic or religious communities. These concerns had been heightened by violent clashes between Hindus and Muslims in 2002 in the far-western state of Gujarat; according to various estimates as many as 2,000 people were killed in that violence, the worst since the mass slaughter that ensued when India and Pakistan achieved independence five decades earlier.

Vajpayee himself seemed characteristically philosophical about his defeat. Announcing his resignation on May 14, he said: "Victory and defeat are a part of life which are to be viewed with equanimity."

Sonia Gandhi's Reversal

Sonia Gandhi and fellow Congress Party leaders quickly assembled the main elements of a multiparty coalition, and on May 15 she was selected to lead that coalition as the next prime minister. Because she had led the party during the campaign and was considered largely responsible for its strong showing, Gandhi was the logical choice. In response, BJP politicians—including Deputy Prime Minister L. K. Advani—attacked Gandhi as a foreigner and said they would mount massive street protests and boycott her swearing-in ceremony as prime minister. India's combative, partisan news media outlets filled with reports either praising her party leadership during the campaign or reviling her background as an Italian, even including a controversy about the subject of her studies at Cambridge University. Some reports said her two children opposed her taking the government post out of fear that she might be assassinated, as her mother-in-law and husband had been.

Amid the mounting furor, Gandhi appeared to waver, holding lengthy meetings with colleagues for several days. When word leaked out on May 18 that she had decided to reject the prime ministership, emotional supporters gathered outside her home and pleaded for her to reconsider. One former member of parliament even held a gun to his head and threatened to shoot himself if she rejected the post; police prevented him from carrying out his threat.

Despite these pleadings, Gandhi stepped before the microphones on May 18 and said her "inner voice" had told her not to take the government post. "I never wanted to be prime minister," she said.

Gandhi said Singh should be the prime minister, and the following day India's president, Abdul Kalam, asked him to form a new government. "I feel humbled," Singh said after receiving the directive. "The nation has given this mandate for Sonia Gandhi."

Although she gave up the opportunity to hold power officially, Gandhi clearly retained significant influence as the leader who had made victory possible for the Congress Party. Political commentators portrayed her decision to step aside as a shrewd one that defanged the BJP opposition and enhanced her own standing. "Having made her point, the Italian-born Congress president . . . has grown enormously in political and moral stature," the national newspaper, *Hindu,* editorialized on May 19.

Assembling a Coalition

As the architect of India's economic reforms in the early 1990s, Singh was well known and highly respected, both domestically and internationally, but he was not an experienced politician. He served at the time in the upper chamber of parliament (the Rajya Sabha) but had never won a direct popular election.

For Singh and his party, assembling and holding together a multiparty coalition was difficult for several reasons, not the least of which was that Congress and some of its potential partners also were political rivals in several states, whose governments exercised much of India's real power. Eleven parties were more or less natural allies of Congress; altogether they won seventy-two seats, not enough to enable Congress to form a working majority. This coalition took the name United

Progressive Alliance. To get a majority, Congress had to turn to leftist parties, especially the two communist parties with near-identical names: the Communist Party of India-Marxist, which had won forty-three seats, and the Communist Party of India, which had ten seats. Those parties added their votes to the Congress coalition for purposes of supporting a new government but remained officially outside the government and did not take posts in the cabinet; this stance gave them maximum flexibility to criticize and make demands of the government.

Despite its name and the Marxist rhetoric of its platform, the larger Communist Party of India-Marxist essentially had become a social democratic party that promoted capitalism and democracy. The party had governed the state of West Bengal and had followed the lead of the national government, selling off more than a dozen state-owned businesses and encouraging foreign investment in the region's high-technology industry.

Except for the extraordinary events that brought it to power, the Congress coalition found itself in a position similar to when it last took office, in 1991. In both cases, the Congress Party and its natural coalition partners fell far short of a majority in parliament and had to rely on the communists to assemble a government. Also in both cases, Singh emerged as the driving force for economic reform. The first time around, Singh was finance minister, while the government was headed by P. V. Narasimha Rao, another of India's poet-politicians. Singh had moved aggressively in the 1990s to reduce the regulations and bureaucratic red tape that had stifled economic growth; he also began what was to become a lengthy process of selling off state-run enterprises and opening the economy to foreign investment. That Congress-led government lasted for a full five-year term, only to lose power in the elections that ultimately brought the BJP coalition into office.

Congress Party loyalists took most of the major positions in the sixty-eight-member cabinet that Singh assembled, with Gandhi's help. Several of the key figures were in their sixties and seventies, as was Singh, who was sixty-nine at the time of his appointment.

Economic Issues

Maintaining India's rapid economic growth clearly was the highest priority for the new government, which needed to demonstrate that it could produce real benefits for the millions of Indians who had been left out of the boom of the previous decade. Doing so would require a balancing act: pushing forward with economic reforms that had stimulated billions of dollars in new investment, while somehow keeping millions of jobs in state-run industries that, under Singh's reforms, were candidates for privatization.

Among the challenges, according to Indian and foreign economists, were reducing the subsides that enabled many businesses to skate by with inefficient practices; extending the process of privatization to sectors that the government had dominated because of national pride, including banks, the energy industry, and the national airline, Air India; and cutting government spending, which had produced an annual budget deficit of about 10 percent of the nation's gross domestic product (a figure most economists considered unsustainable for more than a few years). Singh and his BJP successors as finance minister also had begun, but had not yet finished, dismantling the complex system of permits and regulations, known as the "license raj," that made starting and running even a small business in India a seemingly monumental task.

Singh also faced pressure to do something to aid the rural poor. About 700 million people—more than two-thirds of the total population—remained poor and lived outside India's huge urban centers. They lived far different lives than the urban elite who had come to enjoy the Internet cafes, foreign sports cars, and other symbols of India's emergence onto the global economic scene.

In his first comments as prime minister-designate, Singh on May 20 acknowledged the conflicting priorities he would face, describing his mandate as carrying out "economic reforms with an emphasis on the human element." Singh appeared to retreat from his reform platform on one score, however. He said he had "no intention" of selling the state-run oil and natural gas companies, which employed millions of people.

Singh returned to these themes on June 24 in his first nationally televised speech. Sigh turned to this forum after the BJP prevented him from addressing parliament because he had not yet been elected to the lower house. Many Indians had prospered from economic reforms and foreign investment, he said, but "millions of our citizens are still plagued by illiteracy, disease, want, hunger, and malnutrition." Singh said reforming government to deal with the problems of ordinary people would be "my main concern and challenge" as prime minister. "I am convinced that the government, at every level, is today not adequately equipped to deal with this challenge and meet the aspirations of the people," he said.

In his first months in office, Singh was stymied by opposition from the BJP-led minority coalition and by criticism from some of the leftist parties whose votes he needed to stay in power. He acknowledged, at his first news conference on September 4, that his government had a "rough start" but insisted he was determined to press ahead with economic and government reforms and to serve a full five years in office.

Despite his stated intentions to aid the nation's poor, Singh had no control over nature, which undermined the government's efforts. The year's vital monsoon rains between July and September were about 13 percent below the long-term average. The resulting loss of agriculture production—which accounted for about one-fourth of the total Indian economy—led forecasters to trim more than a full percentage point off the country's projected growth rate for 2004. The tsunami in December caused loss of life and isolated damage along the southeast coast but was not expected to have a major economic impact. India also faced a threat from the rapid spread of the deadly disease AIDS. *(AIDS, p. 429)*

Negotiations with Pakistan

In his last year as prime minister Vajpayee had appeared to be making some progress in resolving India's longest running and most dangerous foreign policy problem: the conflict with Pakistan over the province of Kashmir, which both countries claimed. The two had fought three wars over the province and had come close to conflict on other occasions, including in 1999, by which time both possessed nuclear weapons. *(Pakistan, p. 1009; Kashmir background, Historic Documents of 2003, p. 209)*

Vajpayee in 2003 had reached out to Pakistan and appeared to assume that reaching an accommodation—or at least the initial stages of one—would be his most important legacy. The guns went silent in November 2003 as both sides honored a cease-fire, which held throughout 2004. Vajpayee met with Pakistan's military president, Pervez Musharraf, in January and the two leaders made optimistic statements about keeping a "peace process" alive. Vajpayee then moved up the date of Indian election, putting that process on hold for several months.

Once he took office, Singh pledged to continue his predecessor's policy of seeking peace with Pakistan. However, Singh lacked some of the political cover Vajpayee had enjoyed as the representative of a Hindu nationalist party. Singh and Musharraf (along with new Pakistani prime minister Shaukat Aziz), held their first meeting in September while attending the opening session of the United Nations General Assembly. The leaders issued a joint statement promising to explore a "peaceful, negotiated settlement" of the Kashmir issue.

What at first seemed another potential lurch forward in the peace process occurred in October, when Musharraf gave a speech hinting he might be willing to drop one of Pakistan's chief demands: a plebiscite, sponsored by the United Nations, giving Kashmiri citizens the right to choose the region's future political status. Musharraf outlined what he said where several "options" for a settlement, including demilitarizing Kashmir and giving the region autonomy from both India and Pakistan, establishing joint Indian-Pakistani control of Kashmir, and dividing some parts between the two countries.

In what was widely viewed as a small peace gesture, India on November 17 withdrew 1,000 of its estimated 500,000 troops from Kashmir, citing the reduced level of tension there. The next day Singh made his first visit to Kashmir since becoming prime minister. Apparently referring to pro-Pakistan militants who had been battling India since 1989, he called on the region's "misled youth" to give up violence. However, Singh clearly rejected Musharraf's offer of the previous month. "I have made it clear to President Musharraf that any redrawing of the international border is not acceptable to us," he said in Kashmir's summer capital, Srinigar. "Any proposal which smacks of further division is not going to be acceptable to us."

Musharraf retreated, saying his earlier comment had been intended only to provoke internal debate in Pakistan. This back-and-forth thus eliminated any prospect that a second scheduled meeting between Singh and Aziz would produce any movement on Kashmir. The two leaders met in Delhi on November 23–24 and discussed economic issues and other matters of mutual interest, including plans for a pipeline that would carry natural gas from Iran to India through Pakistan, but they had nothing new to offer on Kashmir. A follow-up meeting between the Indian and Pakistani foreign ministers was scheduled for late December but was postponed after the tsunami hit the Indian coast. In an address to the nation on December 30, Musharraf said he would "show flexibility if India also reciprocates." He left unclear, however, his precise stance on Pakistan's demand for a plebiscite in Kashmir.

Following are excerpts from a nationally televised speech on June 24, 2004, by Manmohan Singh, who had taken office the previous month as prime minister of India, laying out the new government's program.

"Address to the Nation by Prime Minister Dr. Manmohan Singh"

My Fellow Citizens,

I speak to you with a deep sense of humility, fully conscious of the sacred responsibility entrusted to me. You have assigned the task of governance of our country to the United Progressive Alliance and its supporting parties. You have delivered your verdict and the verdict is clear. You have sought a change in the manner in which this country is run, a change in national priorities, and a change in the processes and focus of governance. You have, through your mandate, made it clear that economic growth has to be accompanied by equity and social justice. You have expressed concern for the poor and disadvantaged sections of our society and for minorities and backward regions to be at the heart of all policies of the government.

As I share with you the priorities of our government, I am reminded of the Father of our Nation, Mahatma Gandhi. Gandhiji had said that his mission in life was "to wipe every tear from every eye." Think of the poorest person you have ever seen, Gandhiji would say, "and ask if your next act will be of any use to him." That message of Bapu resonates in our ears as we settle down to the business of government.

The National Common Minimum Program has been prepared by us keeping in mind the priorities brought into focus by your mandate. The Address of the President of India to Parliament outlines a comprehensive agenda for the nation to which our government is committed. The country would have benefited if Parliament had been allowed to discuss the President's Address. I was eagerly looking forward to contributions from all parties in this discussion. Unfortunately, this was not allowed to happen. It should be a matter of deep concern for all of us when established mechanisms for a constructive dialogue and critique, which are vital for a parliamentary democracy, are disrupted and not allowed to operate.

Parliament is a forum which is sacred and it must be our collective endeavor to ensure that we maximize its effectiveness. I request parties across the entire political spectrum to respect Parliament as an essential forum for public debate so that we can move forward on the task of nation building which is a common goal for one and all.

We can justly take pride in the fact that since Independence we have been able, with our efforts, to build the foundations of a modern economy and record an acceleration in the rate of economic growth. There have been impressive gains in terms of the educational and health status of the nation. However, the benefits of this performance have not touched all our citizens in equal measure. Growth is not an end in itself. It is a means to generate employment, banish poverty, hunger and homelessness and improve the standard of living of the mass of our people. It must also be environmentally sustainable.

Equity and efficiency are complimentary, not contradictory, and we must move forward on both these while maintaining a high degree of fiscal and financial discipline, and a robust external economic profile.

To be able to devote our attention and energy to economic development that improves the lives of our people, we must ensure social and political stability, communal harmony and respect for the rule of law. We must put in place policies and programs which empower all our citizens to lead a life of dignity and self-respect. Our government is committed to the security and welfare of all minorities, the protection of the interests of the scheduled castes and scheduled tribes, of backward classes and all weaker sections. Equally we are committed to the empowerment of women. We will ensure equal participation of all in the processes of governance.

The essence of the National Common Minimum Program is the recognition that policies that are aimed at promoting economic growth must also advance the cause of distributive justice and create new employment opportunities. Economic reform is not only about freeing private enterprise from the shackles of bureaucratic control. It is also about making the government more effective, efficient and people friendly so that it can handle better the many tasks that only Governments can perform. And, it is also about ensuring fair and transparent regulation of the market where this is necessary. While many in our country are benefiting from their integration into the market and the global economy, millions of our citizens are still plagued by illiteracy, disease, want, hunger and malnutrition. Gender disparities are high and educational, nutritional and health levels of women are much lower than of men. Chronic poverty afflicts millions who lack income and food security. This is particularly acute among the scheduled castes, other backward castes and scheduled tribes. At a regional level, too, the disparities are high and while some regions of the country seem to be on an accelerating growth path, there is a concern that other regions are not only lagging but are also falling behind. Regrettably, minorities suffer from not only economic insecurity but also a sense of marginalization from political and governance processes.

As a nation, we cannot accept such disparities. We have been given a mandate which enjoins us to be sensitive to the concerns of these deprived sections and regions. We have an obligation to ensure that they too benefit from growth in full measure. Our commitment to investments in the social sectors is rooted in this reality. It is the responsibility of government, at all levels, at the Centre, in the States and at the level of the community, to address each of these economic and social challenges. However, I am convinced that the government, at every level, is today not adequately equipped and attuned to deal with this challenge and meet the aspirations of the people. To be able to do so, we require the reform of government and of public institutions. Much of the focus of economic reforms in the past decade has been on reducing the role of the government in controlling the Private Sector; controls that hampered entrepreneurial dynamism and often bred corruption. This was necessary. Yet, there are many areas, critical areas, that directly affect the quality of life of every citizen, where the government has a role, and is expected by every citizen to have a role. These include the provision of social and physical infrastructure for development, the provision of elementary education and public health, providing drinking water and sanitation. They also include economic infrastructure which in our country in large part must be provided by the Government such as irrigation, power, roads and railways. Our people expect the government to be pro-active and sensitive to their needs. In each of these areas, at every level of governance, the reform of government is today an urgent task before us.

We will pursue economic reform and widen the space for individual initiative and enterprise, but even as we do so, we cannot forsake the obligation of running a government that works, and works for the people. The reform of administration and of public institutions to improve efficiency and the quality of delivery services will be our immediate priority. . . .

Our economy has been rapidly integrating with the global economy over the past decade, with a growing sense of self-confidence. However, domestic enterprise needs world class and cost-effective infrastructure. Better roads, better connectivity, modern airports and railways, efficient ports and affordable and reliable power are all the basic requirements for a competitive economy. For centuries India has been a trading nation, actively engaged in the movement of goods and people across continents and high seas. We will pursue policies that enable our economy to be better integrated with the world economy without hurting the interests of our people. We will create an environment conducive to the utilization of the talent pool of the vast and diverse Indian Diaspora. We greatly value their participation in the development of our nation.

No objective in this development agenda can be met if we do not reform the instrument in our hand with which we have to work, namely the government and public institutions. Clearly, this will be my main concern and challenge in the days to come.

We will maintain our tradition of an independent foreign policy, built on a national consensus and based on our supreme national interests. We will expand our network of international relationships–preserving solidarity with traditional allies and strengthening new partnerships. We will work with like-minded nations for an equitable, multi-polar world order, which takes into account the legitimate aspirations of developing countries.

We desire to live in a neighborhood of peace and prosperity. We will actively pursue the composite dialogue with Pakistan. We are sincere about discussing and resolving all issues, including Jammu & Kashmir. We recognize that resolution of major issues requires national consensus and accommodation of public sentiment in both countries. It is self-evident that terrorism and violence would cast a dark shadow over this process. With our other South Asian neighbors, it will be our sincere effort to jointly realize the vast potential for cooperation, and to ensure mutual security, stability and development.

In our relations with China, we are encouraged by positive developments, which we are committed to strengthening. Bilateral economic cooperation has shown remarkable growth and diversification. We shall carry forward the process of discussion to resolve the boundary question from the political perspective of our bilateral relations.

As two of the world's great democracies, our strengthened relationship with U.S.A is a fact of considerable importance. The transformation of our relations with USA has been supported by the expansion of economic links and people to people ties, including the presence of almost a million people of Indian origin in that country. We will welcome the expansion of cooperation between the two Governments to include new and mutually beneficial areas, particularly high technology. . . .

We will maintain a credible minimum nuclear deterrent, along with a policy of 'no first use' in our nuclear doctrine. India is a responsible nuclear power, and we will continue to work to prevent proliferation of weapons of mass destruction. At the same time, we remain committed to the goal of universal nuclear disarmament.

Internal security remains an important challenge. Terrorism poses a grave threat to the unity and progress of our nation. We shall combat it with all the resources at our command. There shall be no doubt whatsoever about our resolve to deal with this insidious threat to our nation.

The government will continue the process of dialogue with the Hurriyat and all other groups in Jammu and Kashmir. The Government is willing to talk with all disaffected groups provided they shun the path of violence.

We will adopt a comprehensive approach to the problem of national security, to create greater synergy between our intelligence agencies, closer coordination between internal security structures, more efficient civil-military interface and more effective harnessing of technology to national security management.

My fellow citizens, I share the feeling of well-meaning citizens when they express pained concern about the decline of morals and ethics in public life. There is, however, no better way to deal with this incipient threat to our democracy than to meet it head on by joining public life ourselves.

When I chose to enter public life I did so because I was convinced that our democracy needs more professionals to become more engaged and active in politics.

I, therefore, now appeal to each one of you to also participate in our public life so that governments at all levels—central, state and local—are all constantly put on notice and not just tested once in five years.

When I travel across the country I am always heartened by the increasing number of young and idealistic people I meet who work with voluntary organizations, empowering the dispossessed and the dis-enfranchised. We shall make effective use of the resources of the civil society to improve the quality of governance and delivery of important public services.

Fellow citizens, I urge you to come forward and take an active role in the nation's public affairs. Each one of you can make a difference. I seek your support to restore to our public life a greater sense of purpose and a renewed commitment to decency, morality and the hard work needed to take our country and every one of our citizens forward. We must re-capture the spirit of idealism and self-sacrifice which characterized the high noon of our freedom struggle. Working together, we shall ensure that this ancient sacred land of ours regains its rightful place in the comity of nations.

Source: Republic of India. Prime Minister's Office. "Address to the Nation by Prime Minister Dr. Manmohan Singh." New Delhi, June 24, 2004. http://pmindia.nic.in/speech/content.asp?id=3 (accessed February 14, 2005).

Supreme Court on Sentencing Guidelines

June 24, 2004

INTRODUCTION

A divided Supreme Court handed down a decision on June 24, 2004, that threw criminal federal sentencing guidelines used by the federal government and several states into a constitutional limbo that had not been resolved by year's end. By a 5–4 vote, the Court overturned Washington state's sentencing guidelines because they allowed a state judge to lengthen a defendant's sentence based on factors not considered by a jury or admitted by the defendant as part of a plea bargain. The guidelines, the Court said, violated the Sixth Amendment guarantee of a right to trial by jury.

The ruling was a direct outgrowth of the Court's decision in 2000 in which it declared unconstitutional a New Jersey hate crime law that permitted a judge to double the penalty if the judge found that the crime had been motivated by racial, ethnic, religious, or other hatred. "Other than the fact of a prior conviction," the Court majority ruled then in the case of *Apprendi v. New Jersey,* "any fact that increases the penalty for a crime beyond the prescribed statutory maximum must be submitted to a jury, and proved beyond a reasonable doubt."

Like the guidelines struck down in Washington, sentencing guidelines for the federal judiciary and at least nine states allowed judges to make factual findings, such as whether the convicted criminal carried a gun or used it to threaten someone, in setting sentences. Justice Antonin Scalia, the author of the majority opinion in 2004, said that the federal guidelines were not before the Court and that the majority justices "express no opinion on them." But it was difficult to see how sentencing guidelines nearly identical to those in Washington state could now pass constitutional muster. "What I have feared most [since the *Apprendi* ruling] has now come to pass," Justice Sandra Day O'Connor wrote in her dissenting opinion, which she read from the bench. "Over 20 years of sentencing reform are all but lost, and tens of thousands of criminal judgments are in jeopardy."

Less than a month later, the Justice Department said that the ruling in *Blakely v. Washington* had created "a wave of instability in the federal sentencing system" and asked the Supreme Court to clarify its ruling as soon as possible. The Court agreed and heard oral arguments in two federal cases on the sentencing guidelines on October 4, the first day of its 2004–2005 term, but did not issue a ruling by the end of the year.

Background

Until federal sentencing guidelines took effect in 1987, federal judges had great latitude in imposing sentences. They could sentence a convicted criminal to the maximum penalty allowed under the law or give him probation (except in those cases where federal law set a mandatory minimum penalty). As a result two offenders who committed similar crimes under similar circumstances but in different jurisdictions could receive very different punishments. Moreover, sentencing decisions could not be appealed. Another source of inconsistency was the possibility that a federal prisoner might be released on parole, usually only after serving at least one-third of the sentence.

Concerns about inconsistency and unfairness in the sentencing system spawned calls for federal guidelines in the late 1970s and early 1980s. Patrick J. Leahy of Vermont, ranking Democrat on the Senate Judiciary Committee, summarized the motivations behind the guidelines at a July 13 hearing on possible fixes to them: "The guidelines as originally conceived were about fairness, consistency, predictability, reasoned discretion, and minimizing the role of congressional policies and the ideology of the individual judge in sentencing."

In 1984 Congress enacted criteria for federal sentencing and established a seven-member commission to promulgate specific guidelines. As approved by Congress, those guidelines consisted of a complicated matrix of forty-three "offense levels" that gave judges a narrow range of possible punishments for a given crime. A judge could go above or below the range but had to specify aggravating or mitigating factors to justify the decision to depart from the range specified by the guideline. All sentences by federal trial judges could be appealed, and parole was abolished. Thus the sentence issued by the judge was the sentence the offender would serve, shortened only by time off for good behavior.

Critics said the sentencing guidelines were a key factor accounting for the sharp rise in the federal prison population since the mid-1980s. Other factors included mandatory minimum sentences set by Congress and the designation of several offenses as federal crimes. The federal prison population nearly quadrupled between 1985 and 2003, moving from just under 36,000 to just below 160,000. *(Crime report, p. 761)*

The guidelines had been revised many times since they went into effect in 1987, generally to stiffen the sentences meted out. For example, in 2003 Republican lawmakers added provisions to a sweeping child crimes bill (PL 108–21) that limited judges' discretion in handing down sentences lighter than those in the guidelines for crimes against children. Among the more controversial changes made by Congress were mandatory minimum sentences for various drug offenses.

Judges and civil rights organizations complained that many mandatory sentences enacted by Congress were too long and too inflexible, forcing judges to hand out harsher penalties than they deemed appropriate. Several judges began to advocate that judges be given more latitude in sentencing. Among them were Supreme Court Justices Anthony M. Kennedy and Stephen G. Breyer. As chief counsel of the Senate Judiciary Committee in the late 1970s, Breyer had helped write the legislation calling for the federal guidelines. He also served on the U.S. Sentencing Commission that drafted the original guidelines. Conservatives, however, were wary of judges who "departed downward" from the guidelines to hand out milder sentences. Attorney General John Ashcroft stirred up a heated controversy in 2003 when he asked federal prosecutors to report the names of judges who issued sentences lighter than the mandatory minimums. Ashcroft said these downward departures were undermining fairness and uniformity in sentencing across the system; critics said the Ashcroft order was an attempt to intimidate judges. *(Sentencing controversy, Historic Documents of 2003, p. 982)*

The *Blakely* Ruling

The issue in *Blakely v. Washington* was not downward departures, but upward ones. The case concerned Ralph Howard Blakely Jr., who kidnapped his estranged wife in 1998. Blakely struck a deal with Washington state prosecutors whereby he pleaded guilty to second-degree kidnapping involving domestic violence and the use of a firearm. Prosecutors recommended a sentence of forty-nine to fifty-three months, consistent with the state's sentencing guidelines for the offense. But the judge in the case sentenced Blakely to ninety months, after finding that Blakely had acted with "deliberate cruelty." The ninety-month sentence was within the defined range for first-degree kidnapping; the state's statutory maximum penalty for kidnapping was ten years.

An unusual alliance of conservative and more liberal justices joined to hold that under the *Apprendi* rule, the Washington state judge had violated Blakely's right to trial by jury. "That right is no mere procedural formality, but a fundamental reservation of power in our constitutional structure," wrote Scalia, in an opinion that was signed by Justices John Paul Stevens, David H. Souter, Clarence Thomas, and Ruth Bader Ginsburg—the same five who had been in the majority in the *Apprendi* case. "The jury could not function as a circuitbreaker in the State's machinery of justice if it were relegated to making a determination that the defendant at some point did something wrong, a mere preliminary to a judicial inquisition into the facts of the crime the State *actually* seeks to punish."

In a sharp dissent, Justice O'Connor argued that Blakely's rights had not been violated. He "was informed in the charging document, his plea agreement, and during his plea hearing that he faced a potential statutory maximum of 10 years in prison. . . . The guidelines served due process by providing notice to petitioner of the consequences of his acts; they vindicated his jury trial right by informing him of the stakes of risking trial; they served equal protection by ensuring petitioner that invidious characteristics such as race would not impact his sentence." Given all this, O'Connor said, "it is difficult for me to discern what principle besides doctrinaire formalism actually motivates today's decision." O'Connor's opinion was signed by Breyer and joined in all but one part by Chief Justice William H. Rehnquist and Justice Kennedy.

In a separate opinion, Breyer described three alternatives that sentencing was likely to take in the wake of the majority's ruling. He found them to be either impractical, unfair, or harmful to the right of trial by jury. "The simple fact is that the design of any fair sentencing system must involve efforts to make practical compromises among competing goals," Breyer wrote. "The majority's reading of the Sixth Amendment makes the effort to find those compromises—already difficult—virtually impossible."

In addition to the federal government, ten states had sentencing guidelines that could be affected by the ruling: Alaska, Arkansas, Florida, Michigan, Minnesota, North Carolina, Ohio, Oregon, Pennsylvania, and Tennessee. The decision was expected to affect thousands of criminal cases where sentences were still being appealed. In a note to her opinion, O'Connor said that more than 8,300 such cases were pending in federal courts alone, and that more than 272,000 defendants had been sentenced in federal court since the *Apprendi* ruling in 2000. But, in a second decision issued June 24, the Court indicated that it might not apply the *Apprendi* rule retroactively. That case involved a 2002 ruling in *Ring v. Arizona* in which the Court applied the *Apprendi* law to hold that juries, not judges, must decide the facts that determine whether a capital defendant is sentenced to death. In the case of *Schriro v. Summerlin,* a five-justice majority ruled that *Ring* was not retroactive. The ruling affected about

100 death row inmates, whose hopes of reprieve were dashed by the decision. *(Ring ruling, Historic Documents of 2002, p. 357)*

Call for Clarification

Just as O'Connor predicted, the decision roiled the federal courts, with federal judges around the country reaching different conclusions about how to proceed. Less than a week after the *Blakely* ruling, U.S. District Judge Thomas Penfield Jackson in Washington, D.C., cited it when he commuted the sentence of Dwight Watson, a North Carolina farmer who engaged police in a forty-seven-hour standoff in 2003, after driving a tractor into a pond on the National Mall. On June 23, the day before the Supreme Court ruling, Jackson sentenced Watson to six years in prison. On July 3 he lowered the sentence to sixteen months. "The Supreme Court has told me that what I did a week ago was plainly illegal," said Jackson, adding that he had considered factors in the original sentencing that had not been presented to a jury.

Federal appeals courts were handing down conflicting decisions. The U.S. Court of Appeals for the 7th Circuit found judicial fact-finding under federal guidelines unconstitutional. The 5th Circuit upheld the guidelines. The 4th Circuit, widely regarded as the most conservative federal appellate court, instructed its judges to issue two sentences in criminal cases—one according to the sentencing guidelines and another that treated the guidelines as merely advisory, in case the Supreme Court struck them down.

On July 22 the Justice Department asked the Court to review, as soon as possible, two cases that could clarify the status of the sentencing guidelines. One was the 7th Circuit decision holding that a trial judge had violated Freddie Booker's Sixth Amendment rights when he enhanced Booker's sentence to thirty years, based on the amount of drugs involved and the judge's conclusion that Booker had obstructed justice. That was eight years more than the maximum sentence Booker could have received for the crimes he was convicted of committing. The second case involved a federal district judge in Maine who said he had been prepared to sentence Ducan Fanfan to sixteen years based on information the judge received after a jury convicted Fanfan of conspiracy to distribute cocaine. The judge instead imposed a six-year term, saying that he could not legally consider the new information in light of the *Blakely* decision.

The Court agreed on August 2 to an expedited review and heard arguments in the cases on October 4, where it seemed clear from the questioning that the federal sentencing guidelines were unlikely to survive. Although the Court had not handed down its decision by the end of the year, members of Congress were already considering alternatives to the existing guidelines. One proposal that seemed to be garnering favor was offered by Frank O. Bowman III, a law professor at Indiana University. Under Bowman's proposal, the top of the sentencing range for any offense would automatically equal the maximum possible sentence allowed under law. Judges would thus be prevented from imposing a sentence harsher than one envisioned by either a guilty plea or a guilty verdict.

Following are excerpts from the majority and two minority opinions in the case of Blakely v. Washington, *in which the Supreme Court, by a vote of 5–4, ruled on June 24, 2004, that a judge had violated a defendant's Sixth Amendment right to trial by jury when he lengthened the defendant's sentence based on factors that had not been considered by a jury or admitted by the defendant as part of a plea agreement.*

Blakely v. Washington

No. 02–1632

Ralph Howard Blakely, Jr., Petitioner *v.* Washington	}	On writ of certiorari to the Court of Appeals of Washington, Division 3

[June 24, 2004]

JUSTICE SCALIA delivered the opinion of the Court.

Petitioner Ralph Howard Blakely, Jr., pleaded guilty to the kidnaping of his estranged wife. The facts admitted in his plea, standing alone, supported a maximum sentence of 53 months. Pursuant to state law, the court imposed an "exceptional" sentence of 90 months after making a judicial determination that he had acted with "deliberate cruelty." We consider whether this violated petitioner's Sixth Amendment right to trial by jury.

I

Petitioner married his wife Yolanda in 1973. He was evidently a difficult man to live with, having been diagnosed at various times with psychological and personality disorders including paranoid schizophrenia. His wife ultimately filed for divorce. In 1998, he abducted her from their orchard home in Grant County, Washington, binding her with duct tape and forcing her at knifepoint into a wooden box in the bed of his pickup truck. In the process, he implored her to dismiss the divorce suit and related trust proceedings.

When the couple's 13-year-old son Ralphy returned home from school, petitioner ordered him to follow in another car, threatening to harm Yolanda with a shotgun if he did not do so. Ralphy escaped and sought help when they stopped at a gas station, but petitioner continued on with Yolanda to a friend's house in Montana. He was finally arrested after the friend called the police.

The State charged petitioner with first-degree kidnaping. Upon reaching a plea agreement, however, it reduced the charge to second-degree kidnaping involving domestic violence and use of a firearm. Petitioner entered a guilty plea admitting the elements of second-degree kidnaping and the domestic-violence and firearm allegations, but no other relevant facts.

The case then proceeded to sentencing. In Washington, second-degree kidnaping is a class B felony. State law provides that "[n]o person convicted of a [class B] felony shall be punished by confinement . . . exceeding . . . a term of ten years." Other provisions of state law, however, further limit the range of sentences a judge may impose. Washington's Sentencing Reform Act specifies, for petitioner's offense of second-degree kidnaping with a firearm, a "standard range" of 49 to 53 months. A judge may impose a sentence above the standard range if he finds "substantial and compelling reasons justifying an exceptional sentence." The Act lists aggravating factors that justify such a departure, which it recites to be illustrative rather than exhaustive. Nevertheless, "[a] reason offered to justify an exceptional sentence can be considered only if it takes into account factors other than those which are used in computing the standard range sentence for the offense." When a judge imposes an exceptional sentence, he must set forth findings of fact and conclusions of law supporting it. A reviewing court will reverse the sentence if it finds that "under a clearly erroneous standard there is insufficient evidence in the record to support the reasons for imposing an exceptional sentence."

Pursuant to the plea agreement, the State recommended a sentence within the standard range of 49 to 53 months. After hearing Yolanda's description of the kidnaping, however, the judge rejected the State's recommendation and imposed an exceptional sentence of 90 months—37 months beyond the standard maximum. He justified the sentence on the ground that petitioner had acted with "deliberate cruelty," a statutorily enumerated ground for departure in domestic-violence cases.

Faced with an unexpected increase of more than three years in his sentence, petitioner objected. The judge accordingly conducted a 3-day bench hearing featuring testimony from petitioner, Yolanda, Ralphy, a police officer, and medical experts. . . .

The judge adhered to his initial determination of deliberate cruelty.

Petitioner appealed, arguing that this sentencing procedure deprived him of his federal constitutional right to have a jury determine beyond a reasonable doubt all facts legally essential to his sentence. The State Court of Appeals affirmed, relying on the Washington Supreme Court's rejection of a similar challenge. . . . The Washington Supreme Court denied discretionary review. We granted certiorari.

II

This case requires us to apply the rule we expressed in *Apprendi v. New Jersey* (2000): "Other than the fact of a prior conviction, any fact that increases the penalty for a crime beyond the prescribed statutory maximum must be submitted to a jury, and proved beyond a reasonable doubt." This rule reflects two longstanding tenets of common-law criminal jurisprudence: that the "truth of every accusation" against a defendant "should afterwards be confirmed by the unanimous suffrage of twelve of his equals and neighbours," and that "an accusation which lacks any particular fact which the law makes essential to the punishment is . . . no accusation within the requirements of the common law, and it is no accusation in reason." These principles have been acknowledged by courts and treatises since the earliest days of graduated sentencing. . . .

Apprendi involved a New Jersey hate-crime statute that authorized a 20-year sentence, despite the usual 10-year maximum, if the judge found the crime to have been committed "'with a purpose to intimidate . . . because of race, color, gender, handicap, religion, sexual orientation or ethnicity.'" In *Ring v. Arizona* (2002), we applied *Apprendi* to an Arizona law that authorized the death penalty if the judge found one of ten aggravating factors. In each case, we concluded that the defendant's constitutional rights had been violated because the judge had imposed a sentence greater than the maximum he could have imposed under state law without the challenged factual finding.

In this case, petitioner was sentenced to more than three years above the 53-month statutory maximum of the standard range because he had acted with "deliberate cruelty." The facts supporting that finding were neither admitted by petitioner nor found by a jury. The State nevertheless contends that there was no *Apprendi* violation because the relevant "statutory maximum" is not 53 months, but the 10-year maximum for class B felonies. . . . It observes that no exceptional sentence may exceed that limit. Our precedents make clear, however, that the "statutory maximum" for *Apprendi* purposes is the maximum sentence a judge may impose *solely on the basis of the facts reflected in the jury verdict or admitted by the defendant.* In other words, the relevant "statutory maximum" is not the maximum sentence a judge may impose after finding additional facts, but the maximum he may impose without any additional findings. When a judge inflicts punishment that the jury's verdict alone does not allow, the jury has not found all the facts "which the law makes essential to the punishment," and the judge exceeds his proper authority.

The judge in this case could not have imposed the exceptional 90-month sentence solely on the basis of the facts admitted in the guilty plea. Those facts alone were insufficient because, as the Washington Supreme Court has explained, "[a] reason offered to justify an exceptional sentence can be considered only if it takes into account factors other than those which are used in computing the standard range sentence for the offense," which in this case included the elements of second-degree kidnaping and the use of a firearm. Had the judge imposed the 90-month sentence solely on the basis of the plea, he would have been reversed. The "maximum sentence" is no more 10 years here than it was 20 years in *Apprendi* (because that is what the judge could have imposed upon finding a hate crime) or death in Ring (because that is what the judge could have imposed upon finding an aggravator). . . .

Because the State's sentencing procedure did not comply with the Sixth Amendment, petitioner's sentence is invalid.

III

Our commitment to *Apprendi* in this context reflects not just respect for longstanding precedent, but the need to give intelligible content to the right of jury trial. That right is no mere procedural formality, but a fundamental reservation of power in our constitutional structure. Just as suffrage ensures the people's ultimate control in the legislative and executive branches, jury trial is meant to ensure their control in the judiciary. . . . *Apprendi* carries out this design by ensuring that the judge's authority to sentence derives wholly from the jury's verdict. Without that restriction, the jury would not exercise the control that the Framers intended.

Those who would reject *Apprendi* are resigned to one of two alternatives. The first is that the jury need only find whatever facts the legislature chooses to label elements of the crime, and that those it labels sentencing factors—no matter how much they may increase the punishment— may be found by the judge. This would mean, for example, that a judge could sentence a man for committing murder even if the jury convicted him only of illegally possessing the firearm used to commit it—or of making an illegal lane change while fleeing the death scene. Not even *Apprendi*'s critics would advocate this absurd result. The jury could not function as circuitbreaker in the

State's machinery of justice if it were relegated to making a determination that the defendant at some point did something wrong, a mere preliminary to a judicial inquisition into the facts of the crime the State *actually* seeks to punish.

The second alternative is that legislatures may establish legally essential sentencing factors within limits—limits crossed when, perhaps, the sentencing factor is a "tail which wags the dog of the substantive offense." What this means in operation is that the law must not go *too far*—it must not exceed the judicial estimation of the proper role of the judge.

The subjectivity of this standard is obvious. Petitioner argued below that second-degree kidnaping with deliberate cruelty was essentially the same as first-degree kidnaping, the very charge he had avoided by pleading to a lesser offense. The court conceded this might be so but held it irrelevant. Petitioner's 90-month sentence exceeded the 53-month standard maximum by almost 70%; the Washington Supreme Court in other cases has upheld exceptional sentences 15 times the standard maximum. Did the court go *too far* in any of these cases? There is no answer that legal analysis can provide. With *too far* as the yardstick, it is always possible to disagree with such judgments and never to refute them.

Whether the Sixth Amendment incorporates this manipulable standard rather than *Apprendi*'s bright-line rule depends on the plausibility of the claim that the Framers would have left definition of the scope of jury power up to judges' intuitive sense of how far is *too far.* We think that claim not plausible at all, because the very reason the Framers put a jury-trial guarantee in the Constitution is that they were unwilling to trust government to mark out the role of the jury.

IV

By reversing the judgment below, we are not, as the State would have it, "find[ing] determinate sentencing schemes unconstitutional." This case is not about whether determinate sentencing is constitutional, only about how it can be implemented in a way that respects the Sixth Amendment. Several policies prompted Washington's adoption of determinate sentencing, including proportionality to the gravity of the offense and parity among defendants. Nothing we have said impugns those salutary objectives.

Justice O'Connor argues that, because determinate sentencing schemes involving judicial factfinding entail less judicial discretion than indeterminate schemes, the constitutionality of the latter implies the constitutionality of the former. This argument is flawed on a number of levels. First, the Sixth Amendment by its terms is not a limitation on judicial power, but a reservation of jury power. It limits judicial power only to the extent that the claimed judicial power infringes on the province of the jury. Indeterminate sentencing does not do so. It increases judicial discretion, to be sure, but not at the expense of the jury's traditional function of finding the facts essential to lawful imposition of the penalty. Of course indeterminate schemes involve judicial factfinding, in that a judge (like a parole board) may implicitly rule on those facts he deems important to the exercise of his sentencing discretion. But the facts do not pertain to whether the defendant has a legal *right* to a lesser sentence—and that makes all the difference insofar as judicial impingement upon the traditional role of the jury is concerned. In a system that says the judge may punish burglary with 10 to 40 years, every burglar knows he is risking 40 years in jail. In a system that punishes burglary with a 10-year sentence, with another 30 added for use of a gun, the burglar who enters a home unarmed is *entitled* to no more than a 10-year sentence—and by reason of the Sixth Amendment the facts bearing upon that entitlement must be found by a jury.

But even assuming that restraint of judicial power unrelated to the jury's role is a Sixth Amendment objective, it is far from clear that *Apprendi* disserves that goal. Determinate judicial-factfinding schemes entail less judicial power than indeterminate schemes, but more judicial power than determinate *jury*-factfinding schemes. Whether *Apprendi* increases judicial power overall depends on what States with determinate judicial-factfinding schemes would do, given the choice between the two alternatives. JUSTICE O'CONNOR simply assumes that the net effect will favor judges, but she has no empirical basis for that prediction. Indeed, what evidence we have points exactly the other way: When the Kansas Supreme Court found *Apprendi* infirmities in that State's determinate-sentencing regime in *State v. Gould* (2001), the legislature responded not by reestablishing indeterminate sentencing but by applying *Apprendi*'s requirements to its current regime. The result was less, not more, judicial power.

JUSTICE BREYER argues that *Apprendi* works to the detriment of criminal defendants who plead guilty by depriving them of the opportunity to argue sentencing factors to a judge. But nothing prevents a defendant from waiving his *Apprendi* rights. When a defendant pleads guilty, the State is free to seek judicial sentence enhancements so long as the defendant either stipulates to the relevant facts or consents to judicial factfinding. If appropriate waivers are procured, States may continue to offer judicial factfinding as a matter of course to all defendants who plead guilty. Even a defendant who stands trial may consent to judicial factfinding as to sentence enhancements, which may well be in his interest if relevant evidence would prejudice him at trial. We do not understand how *Apprendi* can possibly work to the detriment of those who are free, if they think its costs outweigh its benefits, to render it inapplicable.

Nor do we see any merit to JUSTICE BREYER'S contention that *Apprendi* is unfair to criminal defendants because, if States respond by enacting "17-element robbery crime[s]," prosecutors will have more elements with which to bargain. Bargaining already exists with regard to sentencing factors because defendants can either stipulate or contest the facts that make them applicable. If there is any difference between bargaining over sentencing factors and bargaining over elements, the latter probably favors the defendant. Every new element that a prosecutor can threaten to charge is also an element that a defendant can threaten to contest at trial and make the prosecutor prove beyond a reasonable doubt. Moreover, given the sprawling scope of most criminal codes, and the power to affect sentences by making (even nonbinding) sentencing recommendations, there is already no shortage of *in terrorem* tools at prosecutors' disposal.

Any evaluation of *Apprendi*'s "fairness" to criminal defendants must compare it with the regime it replaced, in which a defendant, with no warning in either his indictment or plea, would routinely see his maximum potential sentence balloon from as little as five years to as much as life imprisonment based not on facts proved to his peers beyond a reasonable doubt, but on facts extracted after trial from a report compiled by a probation officer who the judge thinks more likely got it right than got it wrong. We can conceive of no measure of fairness that would find more fault in the utterly speculative bargaining effects JUSTICE BREYER identifies than in the regime he champions. Suffice it to say that, if such a measure exists, it is not the one the Framers left us with.

The implausibility of JUSTICE BREYER'S contention that *Apprendi* is unfair to criminal defendants is exposed by the lineup of amici in this case. It is hard to believe that the National Association of Criminal Defense Lawyers was somehow duped into arguing for the wrong side. JUSTICE BREYER'S only authority asking that defendants be protected from *Apprendi* is an article written not by a criminal defense lawyer but by a law professor and former prosecutor.

JUSTICE BREYER also claims that *Apprendi* will attenuate the connection between "real criminal conduct and real punishment" by encouraging plea bargaining and by restricting alternatives to adversarial factfinding. The short answer to the former point (even assuming the questionable premise that *Apprendi* does encourage plea bargaining) is that the Sixth Amendment was not written for the benefit of those who choose to forgo its protection. It guarantees the *right* to jury trial. It does not guarantee that a particular number of jury trials will actually take place. That more defendants elect to waive that right (because, for example, government at the moment is not particularly oppressive) does not prove that a constitutional provision guaranteeing *availability* of that option is disserved.

JUSTICE BREYER'S more general argument—that *Apprendi* undermines alternatives to adversarial factfinding—is not so much a criticism of *Apprendi* as an assault on jury trial generally. His esteem for "non-adversarial" truth-seeking processes, post, at 12, supports just as well an argument against either. Our Constitution and the common-law traditions it entrenches, however, do not admit the contention that facts are better discovered by judicial inquisition than by adversarial testing before a jury. JUSTICE BREYER may be convinced of the equity of the regime he favors, but his views are not the ones we are bound to uphold.

Ultimately, our decision cannot turn on whether or to what degree trial by jury impairs the efficiency or fairness of criminal justice. One can certainly argue that both these values would be better served by leaving justice entirely in the hands of professionals; many nations of the world, particularly those following civil-law traditions, take just that course. There is not one shred of doubt, however, about the Framers' paradigm for criminal justice: not the civil-law ideal of administrative perfection, but the common-law ideal of limited state power accomplished by strict division of authority between judge and jury. As *Apprendi* held, every defendant has the right to insist that the prosecutor prove to a jury all facts legally essential to the punishment. Under the dissenters' alternative, he has no such right. That should be the end of the matter.

* * *

Petitioner was sentenced to prison for more than three years beyond what the law allowed for the crime to which he confessed, on the basis of a disputed finding that he had acted with "deliberate cruelty." The Framers would not have thought it too much to demand that, before depriving a man of three more years of his liberty, the State should suffer the modest inconvenience of submitting its accusation to "the unanimous suffrage of twelve of his equals and neighbours," rather than a lone employee of the State.

The judgment of the Washington Court of Appeals is reversed, and the case is remanded for further proceedings not inconsistent with this opinion.

It is so ordered.

JUSTICE O'CONNOR, with whom JUSTICE BREYER joins, and with whom THE CHIEF JUSTICE and JUSTICE KENNEDY join as to all but Part IV–B, dissenting.

The legacy of today's opinion, whether intended or not, will be the consolidation of sentencing power in the State and Federal Judiciaries. The Court says to Congress and state legislatures: If you want to constrain the sentencing discretion of judges and bring some uniformity to sentencing, it will cost you—dearly. Congress and States, faced with the burdens imposed by the extension of *Apprendi* to the present context, will either trim or eliminate altogether their sentencing guidelines schemes and, with them, 20 years of sentencing reform. It is thus of little moment that the majority does not expressly declare guidelines schemes unconstitutional. . . . The "effect" of today's decision will be greater judicial discretion and less uniformity in sentencing. Because I find it implausible that the Framers would have considered such a result to be required by the Due Process Clause or the Sixth Amendment, and because the practical consequences of today's decision may be disastrous, I respectfully dissent.

I

One need look no further than the history leading up to and following the enactment of Washington's guidelines scheme to appreciate the damage that today's decision will cause. Prior to 1981, Washington, like most other States and the Federal Government, employed an indeterminate sentencing scheme. . . . Sentencing judges, in conjunction with parole boards, had virtually unfettered discretion to sentence defendants to prison terms falling anywhere within the statutory range, including probation—i.e., no jail sentence at all.

This system of unguided discretion inevitably resulted in severe disparities in sentences received and served by defendants committing the same offense and having similar criminal histories. . . . Indeed, rather than reflect legally relevant criteria, these disparities too often were correlated with constitutionally suspect variables such as race.

To counteract these trends, the state legislature passed the Sentencing Reform Act of 1981. The Act had the laudable purposes of "mak[ing] the criminal justice system accountable to the public," and "[e]nsur[ing] that the punishment for a criminal offense is proportionate to the seriousness of the offense . . . [and] commensurate with the punishment imposed on others committing similar offenses." The Act . . . placed meaningful constraints on discretion to sentence offenders within the statutory ranges, and eliminated parole. There is thus no evidence that the legislature was attempting to manipulate the statutory elements of criminal offenses or to circumvent the procedural protections of the Bill of Rights. Rather, lawmakers were trying to bring some much-needed uniformity, transparency, and accountability to an otherwise "'labyrinthine' sentencing and corrections system that 'lack[ed] any principle except unguided discretion.'"

II

Far from disregarding principles of due process and the jury trial right, as the majority today suggests, Washington's reform has served them. Before passage of the Act, a defendant charged with second degree kidnaping, like petitioner, had no idea whether he would receive a 10-year sentence or probation. The ultimate sentencing determination could turn as much on the idiosyncrasies of a particular judge as on the specifics of the defendant's crime or background. A defendant did not know what facts, if any, about his offense or his history would be considered relevant by the sentencing judge or by the parole board. After passage of the Act, a defendant charged with second degree kidnaping knows what his presumptive sentence will be; he has a good idea of the types of factors that a sentencing judge can and will consider when deciding whether to sentence him outside that range; he is guaranteed meaningful appellate review to protect against an arbitrary sentence. Criminal defendants still face the same statutory maximum sentences, but they now at least know, much more than before, the real consequences of their actions.

Washington's move to a system of guided discretion has served equal protection principles as well. Over the past 20 years, there has been a substantial reduction in racial disparity in sentencing across the State. The reduction is directly traceable to the constraining effects of the guidelines—namely, its "presumptive range[s]" and limits on the imposition of "exceptional sentences" outside of those ranges. For instance, sentencing judges still retain unreviewable discretion in first-time offender cases and in certain sex offender cases to impose alternative sentences that are far more lenient than those contemplated by the guidelines. To the extent that unjustifiable racial disparities have persisted in Washington, it has been in the imposition of such alternative sentences. . . .

The majority does not, because it cannot, disagree that determinate sentencing schemes, like Washington's, serve important constitutional values. Thus, the majority says: "[t]his case is not about whether determinate sentencing is constitutional, only about how it can be implemented in a way that respects the Sixth Amendment.". . .

The costs are substantial and real. Under the majority's approach, any fact that increases the upper bound on a judge's sentencing discretion is an element of the offense. Thus, facts that historically have been taken into account by sentencing judges to assess a sentence within a broad range—such as drug quantity, role in the offense, risk of bodily harm—all must now be charged in an indictment and submitted to a jury, simply because it is the legislature, rather than the judge, that constrains the extent to which such facts may be used to impose a sentence within a pre-existing statutory range. . . .

III

Washington's Sentencing Reform Act did not alter the statutory maximum sentence to which petitioner was exposed. Petitioner was informed in the charging document, his plea agreement, and during his plea hearing that he faced a potential statutory maximum of 10 years in prison. As discussed above, the guidelines served due process by providing notice to petitioner of the consequences of his acts; they vindicated his jury trial right by informing him of the stakes of risking trial; they served equal protection by ensuring petitioner that invidious characteristics such as race would not impact his sentence.

Given these observations, it is difficult for me to discern what principle besides doctrinaire formalism actually motivates today's decision. The majority chides the *Apprendi* dissenters for preferring a nuanced interpretation of the Due Process Clause and Sixth Amendment jury trial guarantee that would generally defer to legislative labels while acknowledging the existence of constitutional constraints . . . indeed the choice is between adopting a balanced case-by-case approach that takes into consideration the values underlying the Bill of Rights, as well as the history of a particular sentencing reform law, and adopting a rigid rule that destroys everything in its path, I will choose the former. . . .

IV

A

The consequences of today's decision will be as far reaching as they are disturbing. Washington's sentencing system is by no means unique. Numerous other States have enacted guidelines systems, as has the Federal Government. Today's decision casts constitutional doubt over them all and, in so doing, threatens an untold number of criminal judgments. Every sentence imposed under such guidelines in cases currently pending on direct appeal is in jeopardy. And, despite the fact that we hold in *Schriro v. Summerlin,* that *Ring* (and a fortiori *Apprendi*) does not apply retroactively on habeas review, all criminal sentences imposed under the federal and state guidelines since *Apprendi* was decided in 2000 arguably remain open to collateral attack.

The practical consequences for trial courts, starting today, will be equally unsettling: How are courts to mete out guidelines sentences? Do courts apply the guidelines as to mitigating factors, but not as to aggravating factors? Do they jettison the guidelines altogether? The Court ignores the havoc it is about to wreak on trial courts across the country.

[B omitted.]

* * *

What I have feared most has now come to pass: Over 20 years of sentencing reform are all but lost, and tens of thousands of criminal judgments are in jeopardy. I respectfully dissent.

JUSTICE BREYER, with whom JUSTICE O'CONNOR joins, dissenting. . . .

[Introduction omitted.]

I

The majority ignores the adverse consequences inherent in its conclusion. As a result of the majority's rule, sentencing must now take one of three forms, each of which risks either impracticality, unfairness, or harm to the jury trial right the majority purports to strengthen. This circumstance shows that the majority's Sixth Amendment interpretation cannot be right.

A

A first option for legislators is to create a simple, pure or nearly pure "charge offense" or "determinate" sentencing system. In such a system, an indictment would charge a few facts which, taken together, constitute a crime, such as robbery. Robbery would carry a single sentence, say, five years' imprisonment. And every person convicted of robbery would receive that sentence—just as, centuries ago, everyone convicted of almost any serious crime was sentenced to death.

Such a system assures uniformity, but at intolerable costs. First, simple determinate sentencing systems impose identical punishments on people who committed their crimes in very different ways. When dramatically different conduct ends up being punished the same way, an injustice has taken place. Simple determinate sentencing has the virtue of treating like cases alike, but it simultaneously fails to treat different cases differently. . . .

Second, in a world of statutorily fixed mandatory sentences for many crimes, determinate sentencing gives tremendous power to prosecutors to manipulate sentences through their choice of charges. Prosecutors can simply charge, or threaten to charge, defendants with crimes bearing higher mandatory sentences. Defendants, knowing that they will not have a chance to argue for a lower sentence in front of a judge, may plead to charges that they might otherwise contest. Considering that most criminal cases do not go to trial and resolution by plea bargaining is the norm, the rule of *Apprendi,* to the extent it results in a return to determinate sentencing, threatens serious unfairness.

B

A second option for legislators is to return to a system of indeterminate sentencing, such as California had before the recent sentencing reform movement. . . . Under indeterminate systems, the length of the sentence is entirely or almost entirely within the discretion of the judge or of the parole board, which typically has broad power to decide when to release a prisoner.

When such systems were in vogue, they were criticized, and rightly so, for producing unfair disparities, including race-based disparities, in the punishment of similarly situated defendants. The length of time a person spent in prison appeared to depend on "what the judge ate for breakfast" on the day of sentencing, on which judge you got, or on other factors that should not have made a difference to the length of the sentence. And under such a system, the judge could vary the sentence greatly based upon his findings about how the defendant had committed the crime—findings that might not have been made by a "preponderance of the evidence," much less "beyond a reasonable doubt."

Returning to such a system would diminish the "reason" the majority claims it is trying to uphold. It also would do little to "ensur[e] [the] control" of what the majority calls "the peopl[e,]" . . . since "the peopl[e]" would only decide the defendant's guilt, a finding with no effect on the duration of the sentence. While "the judge's authority to sentence" would formally derive from the jury's verdict, the jury would exercise little or no control over the sentence itself. It is difficult to see how such an outcome protects the structural safeguards the majority claims to be defending.

C

A third option is that which the Court seems to believe legislators will in fact take. That is the option of retaining structured schemes that attempt to punish similar conduct similarly and different conduct differently, but modifying them to conform to *Apprendi*'s dictates. Judges would be able to depart downward from presumptive sentences upon finding that mitigating factors were present, but would not be able to depart upward unless the prosecutor charged the aggravating fact to a jury and proved it beyond a reasonable doubt. The majority argues, based on the single example of Kansas, that most legislatures will enact amendments along these lines in the face of the oncoming *Apprendi* train. It is therefore worth exploring how this option could work in practice, as well as the assumptions on which it depends.

1

This option can be implemented in one of two ways. The first way would be for legislatures to subdivide each crime into a list of complex crimes, each of which would be defined to include commonly found sentencing factors such as drug quantity, type of victim, presence of violence, degree of injury, use of gun, and so on. A legislature, for example, might enact a robbery statute, modeled on robbery sentencing guidelines, that increases punishment depending upon (1) the nature of the institution robbed, (2) the (a) presence of, (b) brandishing of, (c) other use of, a firearm, (3) making of a death threat, (4) presence of (a) ordinary, (b) serious, (c) permanent or life threatening, bodily injury, (5) abduction, (6) physical restraint, (7) taking of a firearm, (8) taking of drugs, (9) value of property loss, etc.

This possibility is, of course, merely a highly calibrated form of the "pure charge" system discussed [earlier]. And it suffers from some of the same defects. The prosecutor, through control of the precise charge, controls the punishment, thereby marching the sentencing system directly away from, not toward, one important guideline goal: rough uniformity of punishment for those who engage in roughly the same real criminal conduct. The artificial (and consequently unfair) nature of the resulting sentence is aggravated by the fact that prosecutors must charge all relevant facts about the way the crime was committed before a presentence investigation examines the criminal conduct, perhaps before the trial itself, i.e., before many of the facts relevant to punishment are known. . . .

2

The second way to make sentencing guidelines *Apprendi*-compliant would be to require at least two juries for each defendant whenever aggravating facts are present: one jury to determine guilt of the crime charged, and an additional jury to try the disputed facts that, if found, would aggravate the sentence. Our experience with bifurcated trials in the capital punishment context suggests that requiring them for run-of-the-mill sentences would be costly, both in money and in judicial time and resources. In the context of noncapital crimes, the potential need for a second indictment alleging aggravating facts, the likely need for formal evidentiary rules to prevent prejudice, and the increased difficulty of obtaining relevant sentencing information, all will mean greater complexity, added cost, and further delay.

The majority refers to an *amicus curiae* brief filed by the Kansas Appellate Defender Office, which suggests that a two-jury system has proved workable in Kansas. And that may be so. But in all likelihood, any such workability reflects an uncomfortable fact, a fact at which the majority hints, but whose constitutional implications it does not seem to grasp. The uncomfortable fact that could make the system seem workable—even desirable in the minds of some, including defense attorneys—is called "plea bargaining." The Court can announce that the Constitution requires at least two jury trials for each criminal defendant—one for guilt, another for sentencing—but only because it knows full well that more than 90% of defendants will not go to trial even once, much less insist on two or more trials.

What will be the consequences of the Court's holding for the 90% of defendants who do not go to trial? The truthful answer is that we do not know. Some defendants may receive bargaining advantages if the increased cost of the "double jury trial" guarantee makes prosecutors more willing to cede certain sentencing issues to the defense. Other defendants may be hurt if a "single-jury-decides-all" approach makes them more reluctant to risk a trial—perhaps because they want to argue that they did not know what was in the cocaine bag, that it was a small amount regardless, that they were unaware a confederate had a gun, etc.

At the least, the greater expense attached to trials and their greater complexity, taken together in the context of an overworked criminal justice system, will likely mean, other things being equal, fewer trials and a greater reliance upon plea bargaining—a system in which punishment is set not by judges or juries but by advocates acting under bargaining constraints. At the same time, the greater power of the prosecutor to control the punishment through the charge would likely weaken the relation between real conduct and real punishment as well. Even if the Court's holding does not further embed plea-bargaining practices (as I fear it will), its success depends upon the existence of present practice. I do not understand how the Sixth Amendment could require a sentencing system that will work in practice only if no more than a handful of defendants exercise their right to a jury trial. . . .

D

Is there a fourth option? Perhaps. Congress and state legislatures might, for example, rewrite their criminal codes, attaching astronomically high sentences to each crime, followed by long lists of mitigating facts, which, for the most part, would consist of the absence of aggravating facts. But political impediments to legislative action make such rewrites difficult to achieve; and it is difficult to see why the Sixth Amendment would require legislatures to undertake them.

It may also prove possible to find combinations of, or variations upon, my first three options. But I am unaware of any variation that does not involve (a) the shift of power to the prosecutor (weakening the connection between real conduct and real punishment) inherent in any charge offense system, (b) the lack of uniformity inherent in any system of pure judicial discretion, or (c) the complexity, expense, and increased reliance on plea bargains involved in a "two-jury" system. The simple fact is that the design of any fair sentencing system must involve efforts to make practical compromises among competing goals. The majority's reading of the Sixth Amendment makes the effort to find those compromises—already difficult—virtually impossible.

[II omitted.]

III

The majority also overlooks important institutional considerations. Congress and the States relied upon what they believed was their constitutional power to decide, within broad limits, whether to make a particular fact (a) a sentencing factor or (b) an element in a greater crime. They relied upon McMillan as guaranteeing the constitutional validity of that proposition. They created sentencing reform, an effort to change the criminal justice system so that it reflects systematically not simply upon guilt or innocence but also upon what should be done about this now-guilty offender. Those efforts have spanned a generation. They have led to state sentencing guidelines and the Federal Sentencing Guideline system. These systems are imperfect and they yield far from perfect results, but I cannot believe the Constitution forbids the state legislatures and Congress to adopt such systems and to try to improve them over time. Nor can I believe that the Constitution hamstrings legislatures in the way that JUSTICE O'CONNOR and I have discussed.

IV

Now, let us return to the question I posed at the outset. Why does the Sixth Amendment permit a jury trial right (in respect to a particular fact) to depend upon a legislative labeling decision, namely, the legislative decision to label the fact a *sentencing fact,* instead of an *element of the crime?* The answer is that the fairness and effectiveness of a sentencing system, and the related fairness and effectiveness of the criminal justice system itself, depends upon the legislature's possessing the constitutional authority (within due process limits) to make that labeling decision. To restrict radically the legislature's power in this respect, as the majority interprets the Sixth Amendment to do, prevents the legislature from seeking sentencing systems that are consistent with, and indeed may help to advance, the Constitution's greater fairness goals.

To say this is not simply to express concerns about fairness to defendants. It is also to express concerns about the serious practical (or impractical) changes that the Court's decision seems likely to impose upon the criminal process; about the tendency of the Court's decision to embed further plea bargaining processes that lack transparency and too often mean nonuniform, sometimes arbitrary, sentencing practices; about the obstacles the Court's decision poses to legislative efforts to bring about greater uniformity between real criminal conduct and real punishment; and ultimately about the limitations that the Court imposes upon legislatures' ability to make democratic legislative decisions. Whatever the faults of guide-lines systems—and there are many—they are more likely to find their cure in legislation emerging from the experience of, and discussion among, all elements of the criminal justice community, than in a virtually unchangeable constitutional decision of this Court. . . .

Source: U.S. Supreme Court of the United States. *Blakely v. Washington.* 542 U.S. ___ (2004), slip opinion. June 24, 2004. www.supremecourtus.gov/opinions/03pdf/02-1632.pdf (accessed February 21, 2005).

Supreme Court on Detentions in Terrorism Cases

June 28, 2004

INTRODUCTION

The Supreme Court ruled June 28, 2004, that U.S. courts—not the Bush administration—had the final say on the status of hundreds of men who had been detained for two years or more for their alleged involvement in terrorism against the United States. In two separate but related rulings, the Court said the detainees—nearly all of whom were Muslim men picked up in the Middle East or South Asia—were entitled to a neutral hearing on their status. The rulings essentially refuted the administration's contention that the detainees could be held indefinitely—without recourse to any legal proceedings—because they were "enemy combatants" in the ongoing U.S. war against terrorism, which began after the September 11, 2001, terrorist attacks in New York City and Washington, D.C.

While the Court's decisions represented a significant setback for the Bush administration on procedural grounds, they by no means prevented the administration from continuing its policy of keeping hundreds of suspects locked up indefinitely at the U.S. naval base in Guantanamo Bay, Cuba. By year's end, the military had held more than 500 hearings in response to the Court's rulings but had released only two detainees as a result. Another man held in a U.S. Navy brig—a Saudi Arabian who held U.S. citizenship—eventually was freed and sent back to Saudi Arabia after he renounced his U.S. citizenship and promised never to return.

The Court decisions came in the midst of an even more widely publicized controversy over the U.S. military's treatment of detainees at a prison, Abu Ghraib, in occupied Iraq. Photographs of military police officers mistreating Iraqi detainees raised serious legal and moral questions and caused a storm of anti-American protests in the Middle East. Later in the year, substantial evidence emerged that some Guantanamo detainees also had been abused, and possibly even tortured, in ways similar to what had happened at the Abu Ghraib prison. During the height of the Iraq prison controversy, news organizations published Justice Department legal opinions, written in 2002, that appeared to endorse the use of torture in some circumstances. In December the administration produced new opinions banning the use of torture. *(Iraq detainees, p. 207; torture memos, p. 336)*

In a case with some similarities to the Guantanamo detentions, Britain's highest court ruled on December 16 that the British government could not indefinitely detain foreigners on grounds that they posed a terrorist threat. The judges overturned an antiterrorism law that allowed the government to detain foreigners, but not citizens, indefinitely without access to regular courts. The government had not disclosed, by year's end, how it intended to respond to the decision.

Background

In the wake of the September 11 terrorist attacks, the Bush administration rounded up nearly 2,000 people—both in the United States and overseas—on grounds that they might somehow be involved in international terrorism. Most of the 1,100 or so people who were detained in the United States were foreigners, and most of them eventually were deported for immigration law violations, such as having overstayed their visas. The Supreme Court on January 12, 2004, let stand a lower court decision rejecting a suit by the Center for National Security Studies (a civil liberties group) that sought to force the Justice Department to make public the names of the foreigners it had held in the United States after September 11. On March 20 the Justice Department released an updated report by Inspector General Glenn A. Fine on conditions at a detention center in Brooklyn, New York. Fine had issued reports in 2003 saying that guards had abused dozens of post–September 11 detainees at the center. Fine's latest report said the Bureau of Prisons subsequently had taken "reasonable and responsible steps" to improve conditions but further improvements were still needed. *(September 11 detainees, Historic Documents of 2002, p. 830; Historic Documents of 2003, p. 310)*

The U.S. military also captured or detained hundreds of people overseas—most of them in the wake of the U.S.-led invasion of Afghanistan in late 2001. Starting in January 2002, many of these people were transferred to the U.S. naval base at Guantanamo Bay, where, the administration argued, they were beyond the reach of U.S. law because the base was in sovereign Cuban territory. In 2003 the military built permanent facilities to accommodate more than 600 of these detainees, reportedly on the assumption that many of them would be held there for the rest of their lives. Defense Secretary Donald H. Rumsfeld announced February 14, 2004, that military panels would review the case of each Guantanamo detainee annually to determine whether he was still a threat to the United States.

Between late 2002 and the end of 2004 the military released more than 150 of the Guantanamo detainees; most were returned to Afghanistan or Pakistan, where they had been arrested in the first place. The largest mass release of 2004 came in mid-September, when thirty-five Pakistani detainees were released and sent to their home country. About sixty other Guantanamo detainees were transferred to the custody of their home governments, nearly half of them to Pakistan. *(Guantanamo detainee background, Historic Documents of 2003, p. 106)*

In separate but related cases, U.S. officials held incommunicado two U.S. citizens on grounds that they were enemy combatants in the war against terrorism. One, Yaser Esam Hamdi, had been captured in Afghanistan in 2001, then taken to Guantanamo Bay, where he was discovered to be a U.S. citizen by virtue of his birth in Louisiana; he had been raised in Saudi Arabia, where his parents lived. Eventually he was transferred to a U.S. Navy brig in South Carolina. The other U.S. citizen, Jose Padilla, was arrested in Chicago in May 2002 on suspicion that he had plotted with the al Qaeda terrorist network to develop a "dirty bomb" mixing radiological material and conventional explosives. He was held at a military base in South Carolina. Neither man had been charged with a crime, and neither was allowed to see a lawyer until the Supreme Court in December 2003 agreed to review rulings in a lawsuit brought by a lawyer hired by Hamdi's father. Early in 2004 the administration allowed lawyers to see both Hamdi and Padilla as their cases were heard by the courts. *(Background, Historic Documents of 2003, p. 107)*

The administration had announced in 2002 that the Geneva Conventions, which gave certain rights to prisoners of war, did not apply to any of the "combatants" held as a result of U.S. antiterrorism operations worldwide. Along with requiring humane treatment of prisoners of war, the Geneva Conventions required that anyone captured in battle was entitled to a hearing by a "competent tribunal" to determine his or her status. Although saying it had no intention of providing such hearings, the administration said the detainees would be treated respectfully.

The Hamdi Case

In 2002 Hamdi's father filed a habeas corpus petition on his behalf, essentially demanding that the government prove that it was justified in holding him. That case wound its way through the federal court system in 2002 and 2003, eventually reaching the Fourth Circuit Court of Appeals, which in July 2003 ruled that the government was justified in holding Hamdi indefinitely, without any charges, under the president's powers as commander-in-chief of U.S. armed forces. In December 2003, while the Supreme Court was deciding whether to hear an appeal of that decision, the administration suddenly decided to allow Hamdi to see an attorney for the first time. The Supreme Court agreed on January 10, 2004, to hear the case and held a formal hearing on April 28.

The Court's 8–1 decision, issued June 28 in the case of *Hamdi v. Rumsfeld,* held that the administration had the right to hold a U.S. citizen as an enemy combatant in detention during the course of a conflict. Even so, the ruling said, the detainee must be given an opportunity to challenge his detention before a "neutral" tribunal, with the aid of legal counsel. This opinion was written by Justice Sandra Day O'Connor, who was joined by Chief Justice William H. Rehnquist and Justices Stephen G. Breyer and Anthony M. Kennedy. "A state of war is not a blank check for the president when it comes to the rights of the nation's citizens," O'Connor wrote. Although the ruling gave Hamdi the opportunity for a hearing, it said a hearing before a military tribunal at which hearsay evidence was permitted would be sufficient.

Four other justices—Antonin Scalia, Ruth Bader Ginsburg, David H. Souter, and John Paul Stevens—concurred in the opinion, though with different reasoning. In perhaps the most remarkable opinion in the case, Scalia and Stevens (who rarely agreed on controversial matters) argued that the government could not hold Hamdi indefinitely unless Congress had suspended the writ of habeas corpus, which it had not done. Hamdi and other U.S. citizens either should be tried for treason or released, they argued. Clarence Thomas was the sole justice arguing that the Court had no power to challenge the detention of Hamdi, which he said "falls squarely within the federal government's war powers, and we lack the expertise and capacity to second-guess that decision."

The Court's ruling sent the case back to the U.S. District Court in Richmond, Virginia, where Hamdi's father's suit had originated. On September 22, before that Court could act, the government and Hamdi's lawyers reached a settlement under which Hamdi gave up his U.S. citizenship, renounced terrorism, pledged not to sue the government for wrongful imprisonment, agreed to be sent back to Saudi Arabia, and promised never to return to the United States. Saudi Arabia at first refused to accept Hamdi because the agreement called for the Saudi government to monitor him for five years. Saudi officials later relented and Hamdi was flown to Saudi Arabia to reunite with his family on October 11, just shy of three years after he was captured in Afghanistan.

The Padilla Case

In a similar case decided the same day, the Supreme Court rebuffed Padilla on technical grounds, arguing that his lawyer had filed suit in the wrong court—in New York, where Padilla originally had been held, rather than in South Carolina, where he currently was being held. This decision, in the case of *Padilla v. Rumsfeld,* came in a 5–4 vote. Rehnquist wrote the decision and was joined by Justices Scalia, O'Connor, Kennedy, and Thomas. The minority of four justices, in a decision written by Justice Stevens, faulted the majority for its "slavish application" of a procedural rule and noted that the government had moved Padilla to South Carolina only after a New York court had assumed jurisdiction in his case.

Padilla's lawyers on July 2 filed a new habeas corpus lawsuit in federal court in South Carolina. That suit was still pending at year's end.

The Rasul Case

In 2002 lawyers representing sixteen detainees filed three separate habeas corpus suits challenging their detention at the Guantanamo prison; the sixteen included two Australian citizens, two British citizens, and twelve Kuwaiti citizens. Those cases worked their way through the court system and eventually were consolidated into one case, *Rasul v. Bush,* named after one of the British detainees, Shafiq Rasul, who had been held at Guantanamo since late November 2001. Rasul himself was released and returned to Britain (along with two other British detainees) in March 2004, before the Supreme Court had a chance to issue its decision. The Supreme Court held a hearing on the issue on April 20 and released its decision on June 28, along with the *Hamdi* and *Padilla* rulings.

On a 6–3 vote, the Court determined that the Guantanamo detainees had the right to challenge their detentions. The majority decision was written by Justice Stevens, who was joined by Breyer, Ginsburg, Kennedy, O'Connor, and Souter.

The ruling hinged on the interpretation of a 1950 Supreme Court decision, in the case of *Johnson v. Eisentrager,* in which the Court had ruled that Germans held prisoner after World War II by U.S. forces in Germany did not have the right to appeal their detention to U.S. courts because they were held in foreign territory. The Bush administration contended—and some lower courts had agreed—that the *Eisentrager* case meant that detainees at Guantanamo Bay also were beyond the reach of U.S. courts because the naval base was in Cuban territory. This was the case, the administration said, even though the United States occupied the base and exercised total control there, under a permanent lease granted by the Cuban government in 1903.

In his decision, Stevens argued that the United States "exercises exclusive jurisdiction and control" over Guantanamo Bay even if the base technically was in Cuban territory. Stevens also argued that the *Eisentrager* ruling did not apply in the Guantanamo case because of subsequent Supreme Court decisions.

A dissent, written by Scalia and supported by Rehnquist and Thomas, argued that the Court's ruling was too broad, was potentially dangerous to U.S. security, and tied the administration's hands. The ruling, the dissenters said, was "forcing the courts to oversee one aspect of the executive's [the administration's] conduct of a foreign war." The minority also said the majority ruling effectively meant that detainees held in similar circumstances anywhere in the world could sue for habeas corpus in U.S. courts.

Terry Hicks, the father of David Hicks, one of the Australians held at Guantanamo, issued a statement thanking the Court "for standing up for the principle of justice for all." David Hicks was one of four detainees the Bush administration had chosen to face a full-scale military tribunal; his father said he had been in solitary confinement at Guantanamo since July 2003.

Although the Court's decision made it clear that federal courts had jurisdiction over the Guantanamo detainees, it left unclear virtually all other questions about their status. Most important, the ruling gave no guidance to lower courts on how they should handle cases brought by the detainees.

Attempting to follow through on the ruling, civil liberties groups recruited lawyers from prestigious firms in New York, Washington, and other cities to file lawsuits demanding that the Pentagon accord legal privileges to the detainees when they went before the hearings the Supreme Court had ordered. Among other things, the suits sought to require that detainees have the right to be represented by lawyers and be allowed to examine and dispute evidence against them. By year's end nineteen suits, on behalf of sixty-nine detainees, had been filed in U.S. district court in Washington. That court's judges at first decided to consolidate all the cases before a single judge, but a dissenting judge later assumed control over two of the cases. The administration asked the judges to throw out the suits, but a decision had not been issued by year's end.

Hearings at Guantanamo

In response to the Court's ruling, the Bush administration announced on July 7 that it would review the case of each of the detainees then held at Guantanamo. The reviews began on July 30 in the form of what the Pentagon called "combatant status-review tribunals"—panels of three military officials responsible for deciding whether each detainee should remain in prison. The tribunals, held at Guantanamo Bay, had none of the legal trappings of a regular court. Detainees were not allowed to examine the evidence against them (most of it based on classified information), and few of the hearing officers were lawyers or had any legal training. The detainees were represented by military officers, none of whom were lawyers. Journalists were allowed to attend some of the hearings; typical news accounts described sessions at which detainees struggled to understand the evidence against them and were frustrated because they could offer no concrete evidence or witnesses in their defense. Several detainees refused to appear before the review panels.

As of year's end the Guantanamo Bay tribunals had heard the cases of more than 525 of the 550 detainees still held at the base; Pentagon officials said remaining detainees were to receive hearings by the end of January 2005. Only two detainees had been released as a result of the hearings: both were found to have been held improperly for more than two years.

In December, while the hearings were still under way, the Pentagon gave each of the detainees a three-paragraph statement informing them that they had the right to challenge their detentions in a federal court. The statement listed the address of the U.S. District Court in Washington. Lawyers for groups critical of administration policy said the letter failed to provide any useful guidance for the detainees, most of whom had no legal representation.

In a separate development, the Pentagon in November began formal military trials at Guantanamo of the only four Guantanamo detainees who had been formally charged with crimes. On November 8 pretrial hearings in the first case—involving Salim Ahmed Hamdan, a Yemeni accused of being al Qaeda leader Osama bin Laden's bodyguard and driver—were just getting under way when U.S. District Court

Judge James Robertson, in Washington, ruled the proceedings illegal. Robertson said that before trying Hamden the government was required to give him a hearing to determine if he had prisoner-of-war-rights under the Geneva Conventions—something the administration had refused to do for any of its detainees. The administration heatedly disputed Robertson's ruling and appealed to the Washington, D.C., circuit court. The issue had not been resolved as of year's end and was considered likely to go to the Supreme Court. Hamden was represented by a military lawyer, Navy Lt. Cmdr. Charles Swift, who had attracted wide attention for his aggressive pursuit of justice for his client.

On December 17 the *Washington Post* disclosed that the Central Intelligence Agency maintained a separate detention facility at Guantanamo Bay that held what were called "high value" members of al Qaeda. The newspaper said interrogations of those prisoners "could last for years." The government refused to make public any information about the CIA facility, which the *Post* said was located in a section of the naval base known as Camp Echo. The newspaper quoted a statement by the International Committee of the Red Cross indicating that it was aware of the facility and had regularly visited detainees there. The *Post* said the detainees were among some three dozen al Qaeda leaders the CIA was holding in various facilities around the world.

Charges of Abuse at Guantanamo

Many of the detainees who had been released from Guantanamo and sent back to their home countries subsequently claimed they had been tortured while in U.S. custody. Most of the claims included such treatment as beatings, deprivation of sleep or food, and sexual abuse. Despite heated Pentagon denials, these claims gained some credence in the spring after the revelations of abuse by U.S. military police officers at the Abu Ghraib prison in Iraq.

On August 4 lawyers for three British citizens who had been held at Guantanamo, and then released in March, published a lengthy report alleging that the men had been beaten, injected with drugs against their will, and pressured into making false confessions. The men also said they had seen other detainees beaten, and some had been threatened by dogs. The Pentagon denied the charges. "We do not use any kind of coercive or physically harmful techniques," Col. David McWilliams, said. More claims of torture were made in some of the lawsuits filed on behalf of detainees following the Supreme Court decision.

On November 30 the *New York Times* published what it said were details from a report submitted to the military in July by the International Committee of the Red Cross. In that report, the Red Cross said that during its visits to Guantanamo it had found cases of "cruel, inhumane, and degrading" treatment of detainees. Some interrogation tactics—such as subjecting detainees to severe temperature extremes—stopped just short of physical torture, the *Times* quoted the report as saying. Reacting to the report, a spokesman said Pentagon officials "vehemently deny any allegations of torture at Guantanamo, and reject categorically allegations that the treatment of detainees at Guantanamo is improper."

Additional information came to light on December 20, when the American Civil Liberties Union (ACLU) released copies of e-mails exchanged by FBI agents and officials describing severe interrogation techniques used on some Guantanamo detainees over a two-year period. The ACLU obtained the e-mails as a result of a Freedom of Information Act filing. In one e-mail, an FBI agent said a detainee had been wrapped in an Israeli flag and blasted with loud music and strobe lights.

Another agent said he witnessed "numerous physical abuse incidents," including the beating and choking of detainees, and even the placing of lit cigarettes inside ears. One agent said that in a "couple" of cases detainees were shackled to the floor in a fetal position for more than twenty-four hours and deprived of food and water. In the e-mails, the FBI agents expressed disapproval of the interrogations, reportedly carried out by military personnel posing as FBI agents.

The *New York Times* on January 1, 2005, published another detailed report quoting interrogators who had worked at Guantanamo Bay as confirming many of the abuses reported by FBI agents. In one case, the *Times* said, a Saudi Arabian detainee, Mohamed al-Kahtani, in mid-2003 was flown in an airplane for several hours, then returned to Guantanamo Bay and subjected to "harsh interrogation procedures that he was encouraged to believe were being conducted by Egyptian national security operatives." Red Cross inspectors were not allowed to visit Kahtani, the newspaper said, "in order to carry on the charade that he was not at Guantanamo" and instead was in Egypt. U.S. officials reportedly believed that Kahtani might have intended to join the hijackers who commandeered four airplanes for the September 11, 2001, terrorist attacks against the United States.

Following are excerpts from the majority and minority decisions in two cases decided by the Supreme Court on June 28, 2004. In the first case, Hamdi v. Rumsfeld, *the Court ruled 8–1 that a U.S. citizen held as an "enemy combatant" was entitled to a hearing before a federal court. In the second case,* Rasul v. Bush, *the Court ruled 6–3 that the government was required to provide a legal forum for foreigners detained at the U.S. Naval Base in Guantanamo Bay, Cuba, to challenge their detentions.*

Hamdi v. Rumsfeld

No. 03–6696

Yaser Esam Hamdi and Esam Fouad Hamdi, as Next Friend of Yaser Esam Hamdi, Petitioners *v.* Donald H. Rumsfeld, Secretary of Defense, et al.	On writ of certiorari to the United States Court of Appeals for the Fourth Circuit

[June 28, 2004]

JUSTICE O'CONNOR announced the judgment of the Court and delivered an opinion, in which THE CHIEF JUSTICE, JUSTICE KENNEDY, and JUSTICE BREYER join.

At this difficult time in our Nation's history, we are called upon to consider the legality of the Government's detention of a United States citizen on United States soil as an "enemy combatant" and to address the process that is constitutionally owed to one who seeks to challenge his classification as such. The United States Court of Appeals for the Fourth Circuit held that petitioner's detention was legally authorized and that he was entitled to no further opportunity to challenge his enemy-combatant label. We now vacate and remand. We hold that although Congress authorized the detention of combatants in the narrow circumstances alleged here, due process demands that a citizen held in the United States as an enemy combatant be given a meaningful opportunity to contest the factual basis for that detention before a neutral decisionmaker. . . .

[Part I omitted.]

II

The threshold question before us is whether the Executive has the authority to detain citizens who qualify as "enemy combatants." There is some debate as to the proper scope of this term, and the Government has never provided any court with the full criteria that it uses in classifying individuals as such. It has made clear, how-ever, that, for purposes of this case, the "enemy combatant" that it is seeking to detain is an individual who, it alleges, was "'part of or supporting forces hostile to the United States or coalition partners'" in Afghanistan and who "'engaged in an armed conflict against the United States'" there. We therefore answer only the narrow question before us: whether the detention of citizens falling within that definition is authorized. The Government maintains that no explicit congressional authorization is required, because the Executive possesses plenary authority to detain pursuant to Article II of the Constitution. We do not reach the question whether Article II provides such authority, however, because we agree with the Government's alternative position, that Congress has in fact authorized Hamdi's detention, through the AUMF [Authorization for Use of Military Force]. . . .

III

Even in cases in which the detention of enemy combatants is legally authorized, there remains the question of what process is constitutionally due to a citizen who disputes his enemy-combatant status. Hamdi argues that he is owed a meaningful and timely hearing and that "extra-judicial detention [that] begins and ends with the submission of an affidavit based on third-hand hearsay" does not comport with the Fifth and Fourteenth Amendments. The Government counters that any more process than was provided below would be both unworkable and "constitutionally intolerable." Our resolution of this dispute requires a careful examination both of the writ of habeas corpus, which Hamdi now seeks to employ as a mechanism of judicial review, and of the Due Process Clause, which informs the procedural contours of that mechanism in this instance.

A

Though they reach radically different conclusions on the process that ought to attend the present proceeding, the parties begin on common ground. All agree that, absent suspension, the writ of habeas corpus remains available to every individual detained within the United States. Only in the rarest of circumstances has Congress seen fit to suspend the writ. At all other times, it has remained a critical check on the Executive, ensuring that it does not detain individuals except in accordance with law. All agree suspension of the writ has not occurred here. Thus, it is undisputed that Hamdi was properly before an Article III court to challenge his detention under 28 U.S.C. §2241 Further, all agree that §2241 and its companion provisions provide at least a skeletal outline of the procedures to be afforded a petitioner in federal habeas review. Most notably, §2243 provides that "the person detained may, under oath, deny any of the facts set forth in the return or allege any other material facts," and §2246 allows the taking of evidence in habeas proceedings by deposition, affidavit, or interrogatories.

The simple outline of §2241 makes clear both that Congress envisioned that habeas petitioners would have some opportunity to present and rebut facts and that courts in cases like this retain some ability to vary the ways in which they do so as mandated by due process. The Government recognizes the basic procedural protections required by the habeas statute, but asks us to hold that, given both the flexibility of the habeas mechanism and the circumstances presented in this case, the presentation of the Mobbs Declaration to the habeas court completed the required factual development [a reference to a statement by Michael Mobbs, special advisor to the under secretary of defense for policy, giving the government's case against Hamdi]. It suggests two separate reasons for its position that no further process is due.

B

First, the Government urges the adoption of the Fourth Circuit's holding below—that because it is "undisputed" that Hamdi's seizure took place in a combat zone, the habeas determination can be made purely as a matter of law, with no further hearing or factfinding necessary. This argument is easily rejected. As the dissenters from the denial of rehearing en banc noted, the circumstances surrounding Hamdi's seizure cannot in any way be characterized as "undisputed," as "those circumstances are neither conceded in fact, nor susceptible to concession in law, because Hamdi has not been permitted to speak for himself or even through counsel as to those circumstances." Further, the "facts" that constitute the alleged concession are insufficient to support Hamdi's detention. Under the definition of enemy combatant that we accept today as falling within the scope of Congress' authorization, Hamdi would need to be "part of or supporting forces hostile to the United States or coalition partners" and "engaged in an armed conflict against the United States" to justify his detention in the United States for the duration of the relevant conflict. The habeas petition states only that "[w]hen seized by the United States Government, Mr. Hamdi resided in Afghanistan." An assertion that one *resided* in a country in which combat operations are taking place is not a concession that one was "*captured* in a zone of active combat operations in a foreign theater of war," and certainly is not a concession that one was "part of or supporting forces hostile to the United States or coalition partners" and "engaged in an armed conflict against the United States." Accordingly, we reject any argument that Hamdi has made concessions that eliminate any right to further process.

C

The Government's second argument requires closer consideration. This is the argument that further factual exploration is unwarranted and inappropriate in light of the extraordinary constitutional interests at stake. Under the Government's most extreme rendition of this argument, "[r]espect for separation of powers and the limited institutional capabilities of courts in matters of military decision-making in connection with an ongoing conflict" ought to eliminate entirely any individual process, restricting the courts to investigating only whether legal authorization exists for the broader detention scheme. At most, the Government argues, courts should review its determination that a citizen is an enemy combatant under a very deferential "some evidence" standard Under this review, a court would assume the accuracy of the Government's articulated basis for Hamdi's detention, as set forth in the Mobbs Declaration, and assess only whether that articulated basis was a legitimate one.

In response, Hamdi emphasizes that this Court consistently has recognized that an individual challenging his detention may not be held at the will of the Executive without recourse to some proceeding before a neutral tribunal to determine whether the Executive's asserted justifications for that detention have basis in fact and warrant in law. He argues that the Fourth Circuit inappropriately "ceded power to the Executive during wartime to define the conduct for which a citizen may be detained, judge whether that citizen has engaged in the proscribed conduct, and imprison that citizen indefinitely," and that due process demands that he receive a hearing in which he may challenge the Mobbs Declaration and adduce his own counter evidence. The District Court, agreeing with Hamdi, apparently believed that the appropriate process would approach the process that accompanies a criminal trial. It therefore disapproved of the hearsay nature of the Mobbs Declaration and anticipated quite extensive discovery of various military affairs. Anything less, it concluded, would not be "meaningful judicial review."

Both of these positions highlight legitimate concerns. And both emphasize the tension that often exists between the autonomy that the Government asserts is necessary in order to pursue effectively a particular goal and the process that a citizen contends he is due before he is deprived of a constitutional right. The ordinary mechanism that we use for balancing such serious competing interests, and for determining the procedures that are necessary to ensure that a citizen is not "deprived of life, liberty, or property, without due process of law," is the test that we articulated in *Mathews* v. *Eldridge* (1976). *Mathews* dictates that the process due in any given instance is determined by weighing "the private interest that will be affected by the official action" against the Government's asserted interest, "including the function involved" and the burdens the Government would face in providing greater process. The *Mathews* calculus then contemplates a judicious balancing of these concerns, through an analysis of "the risk of an erroneous deprivation" of the private interest if the process were reduced and the "probable value, if any, of additional or substitute safeguards." We take each of these steps in turn.

1

It is beyond question that substantial interests lie on both sides of the scale in this case. Hamdi's "private interest . . . affected by the official action," *ibid.*, is the most elemental of liberty interests—the interest in being free from physical detention by one's own government. "In our society liberty is the norm," and detention without trial "is the carefully limited exception." "We have always been careful not to 'minimize the importance and fundamental nature' of the individual's right to liberty," and we will not do so today.

Nor is the weight on this side of the *Mathews* scale offset by the circumstances of war or the accusation of treasonous behavior, for "[i]t is clear that commitment for *any* purpose constitutes a significant deprivation of liberty that requires due process protection," and at this stage in the *Mathews* calculus, we consider the interest of the *erroneously* detained individual. Indeed, as *amicus* briefs from media and relief organizations emphasize, the risk of erroneous deprivation of a citizen's liberty in the absence of sufficient process here is very real. Moreover, as critical as the Government's interest may be in detaining those who actually pose an immediate threat to the national security of the United States during ongoing international conflict, history and common sense teach us that an unchecked system of detention carries the potential to become a means for oppression and abuse of others who do not present that sort of threat. Because we live in a society in which "[m]ere public intolerance or animosity cannot constitutionally justify the deprivation of a person's physical liberty," *O'Connor* v. *Donaldson* (1975), our starting point for the *Mathews* v. *Eldridge* analysis is unaltered by the allegations surrounding the particular detainee or the organizations with which he is alleged to have associated. We reaffirm today the fundamental nature of a citizen's right to be free from involuntary confinement by his own government without due process of law, and we weigh the opposing governmental interests against the curtailment of liberty that such confinement entails.

2

On the other side of the scale are the weighty and sensitive governmental interests in ensuring that those who have in fact fought with the enemy during a war do not return to battle against the United States. . . . [T]he law of war and the realities of combat may render such detentions both necessary and appropriate, and our due process analysis need not blink at those realities. Without doubt, our Constitution recognizes that core strategic matters of warmaking belong in the hands of those who are best positioned and most politically accountable for making them.

The Government also argues at some length that its interests in reducing the process available to alleged enemy combatants are heightened by the practical difficulties that would accompany a system of trial-like process. In its view, military officers who are engaged in the serious work of waging battle would be unnecessarily and dangerously distracted by litigation half a world away, and discovery into military operations would both intrude on the sensitive secrets of national defense and result in a futile search for evidence buried under the rubble of war. To the extent that these burdens are triggered by heightened procedures, they are properly taken into account in our due process analysis.

3

Striking the proper constitutional balance here is of great importance to the Nation during this period of on-going combat. But it is equally vital that our calculus not give short shrift to the values that this country holds dear or to the privilege that is American citizenship. It is during our most challenging and uncertain moments that our Nation's commitment to due process is most severely tested; and it is in those times that we must preserve our commitment at home to the principles for which we fight abroad.

With due recognition of these competing concerns, we believe that neither the process proposed by the Government nor the process apparently envisioned by the District Court below strikes the proper constitutional balance when a United States citizen is detained in the United States as an enemy combatant. That is, "the risk of erroneous deprivation" of a detainee's liberty interest is unacceptably high under the Government's proposed rule, while some of the "additional or substitute procedural safeguards" suggested by the District Court are unwarranted in light of their limited "probable value" and the burdens they may impose on the military in such cases.

We therefore hold that a citizen-detainee seeking to challenge his classification as an enemy combatant must receive notice of the factual basis for his classification, and a fair opportunity to rebut the Government's factual assertions before a neutral decisionmaker. These essential constitutional promises may not be eroded.

At the same time, the exigencies of the circumstances may demand that, aside from these core elements, enemy combatant proceedings may be tailored to alleviate their uncommon potential to burden the Executive at a time of ongoing military conflict. Hearsay, for example, may need to be accepted as the most reliable available evidence from the Government in such a proceeding. Likewise, the Constitution would not be offended by a presumption in favor of the Government's evidence, so long as that presumption remained a rebuttable one and fair opportunity for rebuttal were provided. Thus, once the Government puts forth credible evidence that the habeas petitioner meets the enemy-combatant criteria, the onus could shift to the petitioner to rebut that evidence with more persuasive evidence that he falls outside the criteria. A burden-shifting scheme of this sort would meet the goal of ensuring that the errant tourist, embedded journalist, or local aid worker has a chance to prove military error while giving due regard to the Executive once it has put forth meaningful support for its conclusion that the detainee is in fact an enemy combatant. In the words of *Mathews*, process of this sort would sufficiently address the "risk of erroneous deprivation" of a detainee's liberty interest while eliminating certain procedures that have questionable additional value in light of the burden on the Government.

We think it unlikely that this basic process will have the dire impact on the central functions of warmaking that the Government forecasts. The parties agree that initial captures on the battlefield need not receive the process we have discussed here; that process is due only when the determination is made to *continue* to hold those who been seized. The Government has made clear in its briefing that documentation regarding battlefield detainees already is kept in the ordinary course of military affairs. Any factfinding imposition created by requiring a knowledgeable affiant to summarize these records to an independent tribunal is a minimal one. Likewise, arguments that military officers ought not have to wage war under the threat of litigation lose much of their steam when factual disputes at enemy-combatant hearings are limited to the alleged combatant's acts. This focus meddles little, if at all, in the strategy or conduct of war, inquiring only into the appropriateness of continuing to detain an individual claimed to have taken up arms against the United States. While we accord the greatest respect and consideration to the judgments of military authorities in matters relating to the actual prosecution of a war, and recognize that the scope of that discretion necessarily is wide, it does not infringe on the core role of the military for the courts to exercise their own time-honored and constitutionally mandated roles of reviewing and resolving claims like those presented here.

In sum, while the full protections that accompany challenges to detentions in other settings may prove unworkable and inappropriate in the enemy-combatant setting, the threats to military operations posed by a basic system of independent review are not so weighty as to trump a citizen's core rights to challenge meaningfully the Government's case and to be heard by an impartial adjudicator.

D

In so holding, we necessarily reject the Government's assertion that separation of powers principles mandate a heavily circumscribed role for the courts in such circumstances. Indeed, the position that the courts must forgo any examination of the individual case and focus exclusively on the legality of the broader detention scheme cannot be mandated by any reasonable view of separation of powers, as this approach serves only to *condense* power into a single branch of government. We have long since made clear that a state of war is not a blank check for the President when it comes to the rights of the Nation's citizens. Whatever power the United States Constitution envisions for the Executive in its exchanges with other nations or with enemy organizations in times of conflict, it most assuredly envisions a role for all three branches when individual liberties are at stake. Likewise, we have made clear that, unless Congress acts to suspend it, the Great Writ of habeas corpus allows the Judicial Branch to play a necessary role in maintaining this delicate balance of governance, serving as an important judicial check on the Executive's discretion in the realm of detentions. Thus, while we do not question that our due process assessment must pay keen attention to the particular burdens faced by the Executive in the context of military action, it would turn our system of checks and balances on its head to suggest that a citizen could not make his way to court with a challenge to the factual basis for his detention by his government, simply because the Executive opposes making available such a challenge. Absent suspension of the writ by Congress, a citizen detained as an enemy combatant is entitled to this process.

Because we conclude that due process demands some system for a citizen detainee to refute his classification, the proposed "some evidence" standard is inadequate. Any process in which the Executive's factual assertions go wholly unchallenged or are simply presumed correct without any opportunity for the alleged combatant to demonstrate otherwise falls constitutionally short. As the Government itself has recognized, we have utilized the "some evidence" standard in the past as a standard of review, not as a standard of proof. That is, it primarily has been employed by courts in examining an administrative record developed after an adversarial proceeding—one with process at least of the sort that we today hold is constitutionally mandated in the citizen enemy-combatant setting. This standard therefore is ill suited to the situation in which a habeas petitioner has received no prior proceedings before any tribunal and had no prior opportunity to rebut the Executive's factual assertions before a neutral decisionmaker.

Today we are faced only with such a case. Aside from unspecified "screening" processes, and military interrogations in which the Government suggests Hamdi could have contested his classification, Hamdi has received no process. An interrogation by one's captor, however effective an intelligence-gathering tool, hardly constitutes a constitutionally adequate factfinding before a neutral decisionmaker. . . . Plainly, the "process" Hamdi has received is not that to which he is entitled under the Due Process Clause.

There remains the possibility that the standards we have articulated could be met by an appropriately authorized and properly constituted military tribunal. Indeed, it is notable that military regulations already provide for such process in related instances, dictating that tribunals be made available to determine the status of enemy detainees who assert prisoner-of-war status under the Geneva Convention. In the absence of such process, however, a court that receives a petition for a writ of habeas corpus from an alleged enemy combatant must itself ensure that the minimum requirements of due process are achieved. Both courts below recognized as much, focusing their energies on the question of whether Hamdi was due an opportunity to rebut the Government's case against him. The Government, too, proceeded on this assumption, presenting its affidavit and then seeking that it be evaluated under a deferential standard of review based on burdens that it alleged would accompany any greater process. As we have discussed, a habeas court in a case such as this may accept affidavit evidence like that contained in the Mobbs Declaration, so long as it also permits the alleged combatant to present his own factual case to rebut the Government's return. We anticipate that a District Court would proceed with the caution that we have indicated is necessary in this setting, engaging in a factfinding process that is both prudent and incremental. We have no reason to doubt that courts faced with these sensitive matters will pay proper heed both to the matters of national security that might arise in an individual case and to the constitutional limitations safeguarding essential liberties that remain vibrant even in times of security concerns.

IV

Hamdi asks us to hold that the Fourth Circuit also erred by denying him immediate access to counsel upon his detention and by disposing of the case without permitting him to meet with an attorney. Since our grant of certiorari in this case, Hamdi has been appointed counsel, with whom he has met for consultation purposes on several occasions, and with whom he is now being granted unmonitored meetings. He unquestionably has the right to access to counsel in connection with the proceedings on remand. No further consideration of this issue is necessary at this stage of the case.

* * *

The judgment of the United States Court of Appeals for the Fourth Circuit is vacated, and the case is remanded for further proceedings.

It is so ordered.

JUSTICE SOUTER, with whom JUSTICE GINSBURG joins, concurring in part, dissenting in part, and concurring in the judgment.

According to Yaser Hamdi's petition for writ of habeas corpus, brought on his behalf by his father, the Government of the United States is detaining him, an American citizen on American soil, with the explanation that he was seized on the field of battle in Afghanistan, having been on the enemy side. It is undisputed that the Government has not charged him with espionage, treason, or any other crime under domestic law. It is likewise undisputed that for one year and nine months, on the basis of an Executive designation of Hamdi as an "enemy combatant," the Government denied him the right to send or receive any communication beyond the prison where he was held and, in particular, denied him access to counsel to represent him. The Government asserts a right to hold Hamdi under these conditions indefinitely, that is, until the Government determines that the United States is no longer threatened by the terrorism exemplified in the attacks of September 11, 2001.

In these proceedings on Hamdi's petition, he seeks to challenge the facts claimed by the Government as the basis for holding him as an enemy combatant. And in this Court he presses the distinct argument that the Government's claim, even if true, would not implicate any authority for holding him that would satisfy 18 U. S. C. §4001(a) (Non-Detention Act), which bars imprisonment or detention of a citizen "except pursuant to an Act of Congress."

The Government responds that Hamdi's incommunicado imprisonment as an enemy combatant seized on the field of battle falls within the President's power as Commander in Chief under the laws and usages of war, and is in any event authorized by two statutes. Accordingly, the Government contends that Hamdi has no basis for any challenge by petition for habeas except to his own status as an enemy combatant; and even that challenge may go no further than to enquire whether "some evidence" supports Hamdi's designations; if there is "some evidence," Hamdi should remain locked up at the discretion of the Executive. At the argument of this case, in fact, the Government went further and suggested that as long as a prisoner could challenge his enemy combatant designation when responding to interrogation during incommunicado detention he was accorded sufficient process to support his designation as an enemy combatant. Since on either view judicial enquiry so limited would be virtually worthless as a way to contest detention, the Government's concession of jurisdiction to hear Hamdi's habeas claim is more theoretical than practical, leaving the assertion of Executive authority close to unconditional.

The plurality rejects any such limit on the exercise of habeas jurisdiction and so far I agree with its opinion. The plurality does, however, accept the Government's position that if Hamdi's designation as an enemy combatant is correct, his detention (at least as to some period) is authorized by an Act of Congress. . . . Here, I disagree and respectfully dissent. The Government has failed to demonstrate that the Force Resolution authorizes the detention complained of here even on the facts the Government claims. If the Government raises nothing further than the record now shows, the Non-Detention Act entitles Hamdi to be released. . . .

[Part I omitted.]

II

. . . The defining character of American constitutional government is its constant tension between security and liberty, serving both by partial helpings of each. In a government of separated powers, deciding finally on what is a reasonable degree of guaranteed liberty whether in peace or war (or some condition in between) is not well entrusted to the Executive Branch of Government, whose particular responsibility is to maintain security. For reasons of inescapable human nature, the branch of the Government asked to counter a serious threat is not the branch on which to rest the Nation's entire reliance in striking the balance between the will to win and the cost in liberty on the way to victory; the responsibility for security will naturally amplify the claim that security legitimately raises. A reasonable balance is more likely to be reached on the judgment of a different branch, just as Madison said in remarking that "the constant aim is to divide and arrange the several offices in such a manner as that each may be a check on the other—that the private interest of every individual may be a sentinel over the public rights." Hence the need for an assessment by Congress before citizens are subject to lockup, and likewise the need for a clearly expressed congressional resolution of the competing claims.

III

Under this principle of reading §4001(a) robustly to require a clear statement of authorization to detain, none of the Government's arguments suffices to justify Hamdi's detention. . . .

IV

Because I find Hamdi's detention forbidden by §4001(a) and unauthorized by the Force Resolution, I would not reach any questions of what process he may be due in litigating disputed issues in a proceeding under the habeas statute or prior to the habeas enquiry itself. For me, it suffices that the Government has failed to justify holding him in the absence of a further Act of Congress, criminal charges, a showing that the detention conforms to the laws of war, or a demonstration that §4001(a) is unconstitutional. I would therefore vacate the judgment of the Court of Appeals and remand for proceedings consistent with this view.

Since this disposition does not command a majority of the Court, however, the need to give practical effect to the conclusions of eight members of the Court rejecting the Government's position calls for me to join with the plurality in ordering remand on terms closest to those I would impose. Although I think litigation of Hamdi's status as an enemy combatant is unnecessary, the terms of the plurality's remand will allow Hamdi to offer evidence that he is not an enemy combatant, and he should at the least have the benefit of that opportunity. . . .

JUSTICE SCALIA, with whom JUSTICE STEVENS joins, dissenting.

Petitioner, a presumed American citizen, has been imprisoned without charge or hearing in the Norfolk and Charleston Naval Brigs for more than two years, on the allegation that he is an enemy combatant who bore arms against his country for the Taliban. His father claims to the contrary, that he is an inexperienced aid worker caught in the wrong place at the wrong time. This case brings into conflict the competing demands of national security and our citizens' constitutional right to personal liberty. Although I share the Court's evident unease as it seeks to reconcile the two, I do not agree with its resolution.

Where the Government accuses a citizen of waging war against it, our constitutional tradition has been to prosecute him in federal court for treason or some other crime. Where the exigencies of war prevent that, the Constitution's Suspension Clause, allows Congress to relax the usual protections temporarily. Absent suspension, however, the Executive's assertion of military exigency has not been thought sufficient to permit detention without charge. No one contends that the congressional Authorization for Use of Military Force, on which the Government relies to justify its actions here, is an implementation of the Suspension Clause. Accordingly, I would reverse the decision below.

I

The very core of liberty secured by our Anglo-Saxon system of separated powers has been freedom from indefinite imprisonment at the will of the Executive. . . .

[Parts II–V omitted.]

VI

Several limitations give my views in this matter a relatively narrow compass. They apply only to citizens, accused of being enemy combatants, who are detained within the territorial jurisdiction of a federal court. This is not likely to be a numerous group; currently we know of only two, Hamdi and Jose Padilla. Where the citizen is captured outside and held outside the United States, the constitutional requirements may be different. Moreover, even within the United States, the accused citizen-enemy combatant may lawfully be detained once prosecution is in progress or in contemplation. The Government has been notably successful in securing conviction, and hence long-term custody or execution, of those who have waged war against the state.

I frankly do not know whether these tools are sufficient to meet the Government's security needs, including the need to obtain intelligence through interrogation. It is far beyond my competence, or the Court's competence, to determine that. But it is not beyond Congress's. If the situation demands it, the Executive can ask Congress to authorize suspension of the writ—which can be made subject to whatever conditions Congress deems appropriate, including even the procedural novelties invented by the plurality today. To be sure, suspension is limited by the Constitution to cases of rebellion or invasion. But whether the attacks of September 11, 2001, constitute an "invasion," and whether those attacks still justify suspension several years later, are questions for Congress rather than this Court. If civil rights are to be curtailed during wartime, it must be done openly and democratically, as the Constitution requires, rather than by silent erosion through an opinion of this Court.

* * *

The Founders well understood the difficult tradeoff between safety and freedom. . . .

The Founders warned us about the risk, and equipped us with a Constitution designed to deal with it. Many think it not only inevitable but entirely proper that liberty give way to security in times of national crisis—that, at the extremes of military exigency, *inter arma silent leges.* Whatever the general merits of the view that war silences law or modulates its voice, that view has no place in the interpretation and application of a Constitution designed precisely to confront war and, in a manner that accords with democratic principles, to accommodate it. Because the Court has proceeded to meet the current emergency in a manner the Constitution does not envision, I respectfully dissent.

JUSTICE THOMAS, dissenting.

The Executive Branch, acting pursuant to the powers vested in the President by the Constitution and with explicit congressional approval, has determined that Yaser Hamdi is an enemy combatant and should be detained. This detention falls squarely within the Federal Government's war powers, and we lack the expertise and capacity to second-guess that decision. As such, petitioners' habeas challenge should fail, and there is no reason to remand the case. The plurality reaches a contrary conclusion by failing adequately to consider basic principles of the constitutional structure as it relates to national security and foreign affairs and by using the balancing scheme of *Mathews* v. *Eldridge* (1976). I do not think that the Federal Government's war powers can be balanced away by this Court. Arguably, Congress could provide for additional procedural protections, but until it does, we have no right to insist upon them. But even if I were to agree with the general approach the plurality takes, I could not accept the particulars. The plurality utterly fails to account for the Government's compelling interests and for our own institutional inability to weigh competing concerns correctly. I respectfully dissent. . . .

Source: U.S. Supreme Court of the United States. *Hamdi v. Rumsfeld.* 542 U.S. ___ (2004), Docket 03-6696. June 28, 2004. www.supremecourtus.gov/opinions/03pdf/ 03-6696.pdf (accessed February 15, 2005).

Rasul v. Bush

Nos. 03–334 and 03–343

Shafiq Rasul, et al., Petitioners 03–334 *v.* George W. Bush, President of the United States, et al. Fawzi Khalid Abdullah Fahad Al Odah, et al., Petitioners 03–343 *v.* United States et al.	On writs of certiorari to the United States Court of Appeals for the District of Columbia Circuit

[June 28, 2004]

JUSTICE STEVENS delivered the opinion of the Court.

These two cases present the narrow but important question whether United States courts lack jurisdiction to consider challenges to the legality of the detention of foreign nationals captured abroad in connection with hostilities and incarcerated at the Guantanamo Bay Naval Base, Cuba. . . .

I

. . . Petitioners in these cases are 2 Australian citizens and 12 Kuwaiti citizens who were captured abroad during hostilities between the United States and the Taliban. Since early 2002, the U.S. military has held them—along with, according to the Government's estimate, approximately 640 other non-Americans captured abroad—at the Naval Base at Guantanamo Bay. Brief for United States. The United States occupies the Base, which comprises 45 square miles of land and water along the southeast coast of Cuba, pursuant to a 1903 Lease Agreement executed with the newly independent Republic of Cuba in the aftermath of the Spanish-American War. . . .

In 2002, petitioners, through relatives acting as their next friends, filed various actions in the U.S. District Court for the District of Columbia challenging the legality of their detention at the Base. All alleged that none of the petitioners has ever been a combatant against the United States or has ever engaged in any terrorist acts. They also alleged that none has been charged with any wrongdoing, permitted to consult with counsel, or provided access to the courts or any other tribunal. . . .

Construing [court filings by the detainees] as petitions for writs of habeas corpus, the District Court dismissed them for want of jurisdiction. The court held, in reliance on our opinion in *Johnson v. Eisentrager* (1950), that "aliens detained outside the sovereign territory of the United States [may not] invok[e] a petition for a writ of habeas corpus." The Court of Appeals affirmed. Reading *Eisentrager* to hold that "'the privilege of litigation' does not extend to aliens in military custody who have no presence in 'any territory over which the United States is sovereign,'" it held that the District Court lacked jurisdiction over petitioners' habeas actions, as well as their remaining federal statutory claims that do not sound in habeas. We granted certiorari and now reverse.

II

Congress has granted federal district courts, "within their respective jurisdictions," the authority to hear applications for habeas corpus by any person who claims to be held "in custody in violation of the Constitution or laws or treaties of the United States.". . .

Consistent with the historic purpose of the writ, this Court has recognized the federal courts' power to review applications for habeas relief in a wide variety of cases involving Executive detention, in wartime as well as in times of peace. The Court has, for example, entertained the habeas petitions of an American citizen who plotted an attack on military installations during the Civil War, and of admitted enemy aliens convicted of war crimes during a declared war and held in the United States, and its insular possessions.

The question now before us is whether the habeas statute confers a right to judicial review of the legality of Executive detention of aliens in a territory over which the United States exercises plenary and exclusive jurisdiction, but not "ultimate sovereignty."

III

Respondents' primary submission is that the answer to the jurisdictional question is controlled by our decision in *Eisentrager.* In that case, we held that a Federal District Court lacked authority to issue a writ of habeas corpus to 21 German citizens who had been captured by U.S. forces in China, tried and convicted of war crimes by an American military commission headquartered in Nanking, and incarcerated in the Landsberg Prison in occupied Germany. The Court of Appeals in *Eisentrager* had found jurisdiction, reasoning that "any person who is deprived of his liberty by officials of the United States, acting under purported authority of that Government, and who can show that his confinement is in violation of a prohibition of the Constitution, has a right to the writ." *Eisentrager v. Forrestal* (CADC 1949). In reversing that determination, this Court summarized the six critical facts in the case:

> "We are here confronted with a decision whose basic premise is that these prisoners are entitled, as a constitutional right, to sue in some court of the United States for a writ of habeas corpus. To support that assumption we must hold that a prisoner of our military authorities is constitutionally entitled to the writ, even though he (a) is an enemy alien; (b) has never been or resided in the United States; (c) was captured outside of our territory and there held in military custody as a prisoner of war; (d) was tried and convicted by a Military Commission sitting outside the United States; (e) for offenses against laws of war committed outside the United States; (f) and is at all times imprisoned outside the United States."

On this set of facts, the Court concluded, "no right to the writ of habeas corpus appears."

Petitioners in these cases differ from the *Eisentrager* detainees in important respects: They are not nationals of countries at war with the United States, and they deny that they have engaged in or plotted acts of aggression against the United States; they have never been afforded access to any tribunal, much less charged with and convicted of wrongdoing; and for more than two years they have been imprisoned in territory over which the United States exercises exclusive jurisdiction and control.

Not only are petitioners differently situated from the *Eisentrager* detainees, but the Court in *Eisentrager* made quite clear that all six of the facts critical to its disposition were relevant only to the question of the prisoners' constitutional entitlement to habeas corpus. The Court had far less to say on the question of the petitioners' statutory entitlement to habeas review. Its only statement on the subject was a passing reference to the absence of statutory authorization: "Nothing in the text of the Constitution extends such a right, nor does anything in our statutes.". . .

IV

. . . Whatever traction the presumption against extraterritoriality might have in other contexts, it certainly has no application to the operation of the habeas statute with respect to persons detained within "the territorial jurisdiction" of the United

States. By the express terms of its agreements with Cuba, the United States exercises "complete jurisdiction and control" over the Guantanamo Bay Naval Base, and may continue to exercise such control permanently if it so chooses. Respondents themselves concede that the habeas statute would create federal-court jurisdiction over the claims of an American citizen held at the base. Considering that the statute draws no distinction between Americans and aliens held in federal custody, there is little reason to think that Congress intended the geographical coverage of the statute to vary depending on the detainee's citizenship. Aliens held at the base, no less than American citizens, are entitled to invoke the federal courts' authority under §2241.

Application of the habeas statute to persons detained at the base is consistent with the historical reach of the writ of habeas corpus. At common law, courts exercised habeas jurisdiction over the claims of aliens detained within sovereign territory of the realm, as well as the claims of persons detained in the so-called "exempt jurisdictions," where ordinary writs did not run, and all other dominions under the sovereign's control. As Lord Mansfield wrote in 1759, even if a territory was "no part of the realm," there was "no doubt" as to the court's power to issue writs of habeas corpus if the territory was "under the subjection of the Crown." Later cases confirmed that the reach of the writ depended not on formal notions of territorial sovereignty, but rather on the practical question of "the exact extent and nature of the jurisdiction or dominion exercised in fact by the Crown."

In the end, the answer to the question presented is clear. Petitioners contend that they are being held in federal custody in violation of the laws of the United States. No party questions the District Court's jurisdiction over petitioners' custodians. We therefore hold that §2241 confers on the District Court jurisdiction to hear petitioners' habeas corpus challenges to the legality of their detention at the Guantanamo Bay Naval Base. . . .

[V omitted.]

VI

Whether and what further proceedings may become necessary after respondents make their response to the merits of petitioners' claims are matters that we need not address now. What is presently at stake is only whether the federal courts have jurisdiction to determine the legality of the Executive's potentially indefinite detention of individuals who claim to be wholly innocent of wrongdoing. Answering that question in the affirmative, we reverse the judgment of the Court of Appeals and remand for the District Court to consider in the first instance the merits of petitioners' claims.

It is so ordered.

JUSTICE KENNEDY, concurring in the judgment.

The Court is correct, in my view, to conclude that federal courts have jurisdiction to consider challenges to the legality of the detention of foreign nationals held at the Guantanamo Bay Naval Base in Cuba. While I reach the same conclusion, my analysis follows a different course. . . . In my view, the correct course is to follow the framework of *Eisentrager*.

Eisentrager considered the scope of the right to petition for a writ of habeas corpus against the backdrop of the constitutional command of the separation of powers. The issue before the Court was whether the Judiciary could exercise jurisdiction over the claims of German prisoners held in the Landsberg prison in Germany following the cessation of hostilities in Europe. The Court concluded the petition could not be entertained. The petition was not within the proper realm of the judicial power. It concerned matters within the exclusive province of the Executive, or the Executive and Congress, to determine. . . .

The decision in *Eisentrager* indicates that there is a realm of political authority over military affairs where the judicial power may not enter. The existence of this realm acknowledges the power of the President as Commander in Chief, and the joint role of the President and the Congress, in the conduct of military affairs. A faithful application of *Eisentrager*, then, requires an initial inquiry into the general circumstances of the detention to determine whether the Court has the authority to entertain the petition and to grant relief after considering all of the facts presented. A necessary corollary of *Eisentrager* is that there are circumstances in which the courts maintain the power and the responsibility to protect persons from unlawful detention even where military affairs are implicated.

The facts here are distinguishable from those in *Eisentrager* in two critical ways, leading to the conclusion that a federal court may entertain the petitions. First, Guantanamo Bay is in every practical respect a United States territory, and it is one far removed from any hostilities. . . . At the same time, this lease is no ordinary lease. Its term is indefinite and at the discretion of the United States. What matters is the unchallenged and indefinite control that the United States has long exercised over Guantanamo Bay. From a practical perspective, the indefinite lease of Guantanamo Bay has produced a place that belongs to the United States, extending the "implied protection" of the United States to it.

The second critical set of facts is that the detainees at Guantanamo Bay are being held indefinitely, and without benefit of any legal proceeding to determine their status. In *Eisentrager*, the prisoners were tried and convicted by a military commission of violating the laws of war and were sentenced to prison terms. Having already been subject to procedures establishing their status, they could not justify "a limited opening of our courts" to show that they were "of friendly personal disposition" and not enemy aliens. Indefinite detention without trial or other proceeding presents altogether different considerations. It allows friends and foes alike to remain in detention. It suggests a weaker case of military necessity and much greater alignment with the traditional function of habeas corpus. Perhaps, where detainees are taken from a zone of hostilities, detention without proceedings or trial would be justified by military necessity for a matter of weeks; but as the period of detention stretches from months to years, the case for continued detention to meet military exigencies becomes weaker.

In light of the status of Guantanamo Bay and the indefinite pretrial detention of the detainees, I would hold that federal-court jurisdiction is permitted in these cases. This approach would avoid creating automatic statutory authority to adjudicate the claims of persons located outside the United States, and remains true to the reasoning of *Eisentrager*. For these reasons, I concur in the judgment of the Court.

JUSTICE SCALIA, with whom THE CHIEF JUSTICE and JUSTICE THOMAS join, dissenting.

The Court today holds that the habeas statute, 28 U.S.C. §2241, extends to aliens detained by the United States military overseas, outside the sovereign borders of the United States and beyond the territorial jurisdictions of all its courts. This is not only a novel holding; it contradicts a half-century-old precedent on which the military undoubtedly relied, *Johnson v. Eisentrager* (1950). The Court's contention that *Eisentrager* was somehow negated by *Braden v. 30th Judicial Circuit Court of Ky.* (1973)—a decision that dealt with a different issue and did not so much as mention *Eisentrager*—is implausible in the extreme. This is an irresponsible overturning of settled law in a matter of extreme importance to our forces currently in the field. I would leave it to Congress to change §2241, and dissent from the Court's unprecedented holding. . . .

I

. . . The reality is this: Today's opinion, and today's opinion alone, overrules *Eisentrager*; today's opinion, and today's opinion alone, extends the habeas statute, for the first time, to aliens held beyond the sovereign territory of the United States and beyond the territorial jurisdiction of its courts. No reasons are given for this result; no acknowledgment of its consequences made. By spurious reliance on *Braden* the Court evades explaining why stare decisis can be disregarded, and why *Eisentrager* was wrong. Normally, we consider the interests of those who have relied on our decisions. Today, the Court springs a trap on the Executive, subjecting Guantanamo Bay to the oversight of the federal courts even though it has never before been thought to be within their jurisdiction—and thus making it a foolish place to have housed alien wartime detainees.

II

In abandoning the venerable statutory line drawn in *Eisentrager*, the Court boldly extends the scope of the habeas statute to the four corners of the earth. Part III of its opinion asserts that Braden stands for the proposition that "a district court acts 'within [its] respective jurisdiction' within the meaning of §2241 as long as 'the custodian can be reached by service of process.'" . . .

The consequence of this holding, as applied to aliens outside the country, is breathtaking. It permits an alien captured in a foreign theater of active combat to bring a §2241 petition against the Secretary of Defense. Over the course of the last century, the United States has held millions of alien prisoners abroad. A great many of these prisoners would no doubt have complained about the circumstances of their capture and the terms of their confinement. The military is currently detaining over 600 prisoners at Guantanamo Bay alone; each detainee undoubtedly has complaints—real or contrived—about those terms and circumstances. The Court's unheralded expansion of federal-court jurisdiction is not even mitigated by a comforting assurance that the legion of ensuing claims will be easily resolved on the merits. To the contrary, the Court says that the "[p]etitioners' allegations . . . unquestionably describe 'custody in violation of the Constitution or laws or treaties of the United States.'" From this point forward, federal courts will entertain petitions from these prisoners, and others like them around the world, challenging actions and events far away, and forcing the courts to oversee one aspect of the Executive's conduct of a foreign war. . . .

Source: U.S. Supreme Court of the United States. *Rasul v. Bush.* 542 U.S. ___ (2004), Docket 03–334. June 28, 2004. www.supremecourtus.gov/opinions/03/pdf/03-334.pdf (accessed February 15, 2005).

Leaders on Transfer of Power to Interim Iraqi Government

June 28, 2004

INTRODUCTION

The United States gave an interim Iraqi government sovereignty for the country on June 28, 2004, but more than 150,000 soldiers from the United States and other countries remained in Iraq, which was deeply unstable and plagued by daily violence. Iraq's new leaders reached agreement during the year on plans for elections in January 2005 that would chart the country's political future. At year's end, however, it appeared likely that a significant minority—the Sunni Muslims, who for decades had held a monopoly on power in Iraq—would boycott the elections.

A coalition led by the United States invaded Iraq in March 2003 and one month later overthrew the dictatorial regime of longtime leader Saddam Hussein. For the next fourteen-plus months, Iraq was governed by a U.S.-appointed entity called the Coalition Provisional Authority (CPA), backed with the might of the U.S.-led occupying army. U.S. administrators had expected an easy task, with U.S.-backed exiles quickly taking charge of the government and Iraqis eagerly volunteering to put their country back together after decades of repression and war. Those expectations proved grossly unrealistic, however, in the face of a rapidly growing insurgency that targeted the U.S. occupation and Iraqis who cooperated with it. By 2004 the prevailing question was whether Iraq was slipping into all-out civil war or simply was becoming mired in a debilitating conflict with no end in sight.

Thousands of Iraqis—many of them security personnel—and more than 700 U.S. soldiers died in the year's violence, which featured almost daily suicide bombings, roadside bombings, shootings, and other attacks. The United States military, with limited support from a new Iraqi army, mounted several major military operations during the year, the last of which succeeded, in November, in taking control of Falluja, where key leaders of the anti-U.S. insurgency were said to be based. *(Iraq's security situation, p. 874)*

Popular support for the U.S. presence, never high to begin with, was undermined in April and May by revelations that American soldiers had cruelly abused Iraqi prisoners at a notorious prison in Baghdad. Back in the United States, support for President George W. Bush's decision to launch the war in Iraq was undermined by confirmation that Iraq had not possessed the weapons of mass destruction that Bush had claimed posed a mortal danger to the United States.

Bush steadfastly defended the war and remained relentlessly upbeat about the prospects for success in Iraq. Acknowledging for the first time that the insurgents were "having an effect" in Iraq, Bush on December 21 said: "I'm confident of the result. I'm confident the terrorists will fail, the elections will go forward."

The president's confidence apparently was not uniformly shared within his government. Two reports written by the Central Intelligence Agency in June and December—partial contents of which were leaked to the news media—warned that instability in Iraq could last for years. *(Prison abuses, p. 207; weapons, p. 711; background, Historic Documents of 2003, pp. 135, 933, 1189)*

Creating a New Government

A little over a month after Saddam Hussein was pushed from power in April 2003, a senior U.S. diplomat, L. Paul Bremer III, arrived in Baghdad to take over as head of the CPA, a vaguely defined entity that was to handle the political side of the military occupation of Iraq. For the next fourteen months, Bremer was in charge of everything in Iraq except security, which was in the hands of the U.S. military, led by Lt. Gen. Ricardo Sanchez. Bremer was advised by a committee of Iraqis he had selected, the Iraqi Governing Council, the chief roles of which were to add an Iraqi gloss to the occupation and to help produce a plan for a new Iraqi government.

After two previous plans for postwar governance of Iraq fell by the wayside, Bremer on November 15, 2003, produced a new plan under which the Iraqi Governing Council would draft an interim constitution, known as a "fundamental law" by the end of February 2004, then caucuses around the country would select members of a transitional assembly. That assembly then would appoint an interim government to take office and assume sovereignty over the country by the end of June 2004. Elections for a constitutional convention were to be held on March 15, 2005, followed by the drafting of a constitution, and then elections for a permanent government by the end of 2005. That plan ran into immediate opposition, most importantly from Iraq's senior cleric representing the Shi'ite Muslim majority, Ayatollah Ali al-Sistani, who demanded earlier elections to establish Shi'ite dominance.

In the early months of 2004, the key political questions involved the method of selecting the transitional assembly and the date of the actual handover. Bremer's caucus system was complicated, and Sistani wanted to replace it with direct elections. The plans of both Bremer and Sistani ultimately were set aside, however, after UN Secretary General Kofi Annan sent retired Algerian diplomat Lakhdar Brahimi to Iraq in February. Brahimi was Annan's top troubleshooter who had brokered an agreement leading to Afghanistan's new government a year earlier. *(Afghanistan, p. 912)*

After meeting with Sistani and other key leaders, Brahimi produced a report on February 23 saying it would be impossible to organize a legitimate election in Iraq until late in the year or early 2005. Sistani seized on that report to demand elections by the end of the year. Brahimi also rejected the caucuses as unrealistic, and Bremer dropped the idea.

Some critics, both inside and outside Iraq, said the June 30 handover date was unrealistic because it was doubtful that a functioning interim government—however selected—could be put in place by then. In the United States, some Democrats also suspected the Bush administration had selected the date for the domestic political reason of enabling Bush to declare a success just as his election campaign got under way, with Iraq having been turned over to Iraqis. Despite these questions, the date took on a symbolic importance that could not be denied, and officials from Bush on down said it had to be honored.

Parallel to these matters was the requirement for an interim constitution, which was being drafted by the Iraqi Governing Council. One of the major disputes involved the rights of women. Late in December 2003 the council had voted secretly to repeal parts of the Iraqi civil code that gave a broad series of rights to women. That sparked protests when it became public knowledge early in January.

The council produced its draft constitution on March 1, just a day behind schedule. It called for an election by January 31, 2005, for a 275-seat assembly to write a permanent constitution, restored some of the rights for women that had been deleted two months earlier, and set aside 25 percent of the seats in the assembly for women. One of the document's most controversial provisions was a virtual veto power for the Kurds over a permanent constitution.

Bremer hailed the agreement, but it immediately became ensnared in a dispute when five Shi'ite members of the Iraqi Governing Council refused to sign it. The council ultimately signed the document on March 8, but Sistani continued to criticize it because of the provision giving Kurds veto power.

On April 22 Bremer's office announced a significant reversal of one of his first acts after taking over eleven months earlier: the banning of all members of Saddam's Ba'ath Party from public affairs. This step had been widely criticized as depriving Iraq of the services of thousands of capable government officials, along with Saddam's corrupt and venal inner circle. Under the new rule, former Ba'ath Party members who were found to be "innocent" of crimes during Saddam's regime would be allowed to participate in the government.

Much of April and May was taken up with intense bargaining over the makeup on the transitional government that would take office at the end of June. Leading Iraqi politicians jockeyed for position among themselves but also had to negotiate with Brahimi (representing the UN) and with Bremer (representing the United States). They also had to consider the potential reaction of Ayatollah Sistani, whose objection would make any government untenable. The result was the naming on May 27 of Ayad Allawi, a hard-nosed secular Shi'ite who clearly had been favored by the United States, as the interim prime minister A medical doctor, Allawi had joined the ruling Ba'ath Party as a young man but had a falling out with Saddam's regime in the 1970s and fled to London, where he was attacked with an ax in an attempted assassination in 1978. Allawi had gained support from the CIA for a coup attempt in 1996, but it failed. Allawi returned to Iraq only after the U.S. invasion in 2003. In the summer of 2003 he was named one of the twenty-five members of the Iraqi Governing Council, but he did not take a lead role. Allawi's past ties to the CIA reportedly concerned Brahimi, who had opposed his appointment on the grounds that Allawi lacked credibility among Iraqis at large. In a nod to Sunni Muslims, a tribal leader from central Iraq, Sheik Ghazi al-Yawar, was given the largely ceremonial post as interim president. Allawi and the rest of his thirty-three member cabinet took office June 1, serving at first in an advisory capacity to Bremer.

Allawi appeared on Iraqi television on June 4 and said restoring security was the country's first priority. For that reason, he defended the presence of U.S. forces and denounced insurgent attacks against them. "Targeting the multinational forces, led by the United States, to force them out of Iraq would be a catastrophe for Iraq, especially before the completion of the building of security and military institutions," he said.

The UN Security Council blessed the transition on June 8 in Resolution 1546, the third since mid-2003 establishing international legitimacy for Iraq's postwar governance. That measure endorsed the interim government and a timetable that included elections no later than January 31, 2005, for a Transitional National Assembly that would appoint a transitional government and write a permanent constitution leading to an elected government by the end of 2005. Left unclear in the resolution was the status of the interim constitution negotiated just three months earlier; that document was not mentioned in the UN resolution, reportedly because of Ayatollah Sistani's continued objections to some of its provisions. The resolution also endorsed the continued presence of the U.S.-led armed forces in Iraq (referred to in the resolution as the "multinational force") through the end of 2005. That force was given broad power to "take all necessary measures to contribute to the maintenance of security and stability of Iraq."

Another important element of the transition fell into place on April 19, when Bush appointed veteran diplomat John Negroponte as the U.S. ambassador to Iraq. Negroponte, who had been serving as U.S. ambassador to the United Nations, was to assume Bremer's post as the top U.S. official in Iraq—but in a behind-the-scenes consultative role, not as the upfront decisionmaker Bremer had been.

As he prepared to give up the sweeping power he had exercised for more than a year, Bremer in late June signed a series of decrees intended to preserve key elements of U.S. policy in Iraq. Some of Bremer's decrees involved such ordinary matters as requiring drivers to obtain licenses and obey traffic laws. Others were more significant, including a provision shielding U.S. and other Western contractors from Iraqi law and another appointing inspectors to review the actions of Iraqi government ministries. Bremer also transferred responsibility for government ministries to Allawi's cabinet members in June.

It was widely expected that the transition to official Iraqi sovereignty would take place on June 30—the date specified by the interim constitution and the UN resolution. The prospect of violence on that date led Allawi and Bremer to settle on an earlier handover, which was accomplished on June 28 during a low-key ceremony at Allawi's new office in the U.S.-protected government zone in Baghdad. Two hours later, again with no fanfare, Bremer strode up the steps of a U.S. transport plane at Baghdad International Airport, waved to a small crowd, and disappeared into the plane without saying a word. His departure—which one aide described as a "tail-between-your-legs-exit"—ended a brief era of neocolonialism for the United States in Iraq.

Meeting in Istanbul with leaders of NATO countries, Bush said the handover of sovereignty "marks a proud moral achievement for members of our coalition." In a joint appearance with British prime minister Tony Blair—the most steadfast U.S. ally throughout the Iraq enterprise—Bush added: "We pledged to end a dangerous regime, to free the oppressed and to restore sovereignty. We have kept our word." The two leaders pledged support for Allawi and his government and said they understood the extent of the challenges ahead in Iraq.

A Difficult Transition

The tasks facing Allawi's government appeared almost insurmountable. Perhaps the most vital task was establishing its credibility in the eyes of Iraqis, many of whom understandably believed the United States still controlled all important levers of power. Allawi's first effort in that regard was a brief speech to the nation on June 28, in which he promised that "a national unity and tolerance and brotherly behavior and spirit of peace and prosperity will prevail." Allawi and his ministers also had to take control of the daily functions of government, supplanting the U.S. bureaucrats who had been in charge for more than a year. Part of this task was gradually assuming some authority over the country's security, which still remained almost entirely in the hands of the U.S.-led military. Finally, and perhaps most difficult of all, Allawi and his colleagues needed to manage the transition to a future government without precedent in Iraq, one that was elected by the people, who in turn had no experience with democracy and who were divided by ethnic and cultural differences into groups that rarely had gotten along throughout history.

Under the interim constitution and the UN resolution, the next step in the process of building Iraq's government was the holding of a broad-based national conference to form a 100-member National Council, which would have the power to veto decisions by Allawi's government. The conference was to have been held at the end of June, but it was postponed because of a surge of violence and kidnappings. It got under way on August 1 and, after four days of sometimes rancorous debate and backroom deal-making, selected the council. For a country with no experience in participatory democracy, the delegates demonstrated a remarkable ability to engage in the coalition building that would be necessary in the future.

Preparing for Elections

The major task facing the government was preparing for elections, scheduled for January 30, 2005. Organizing the elections posed an enormous logistical hurdle, starting with the task of identifying the electorate (there had been no accurate census in Iraq in decades) and continuing with the process of arranging for political candidates and parties to compete for the 275 seats that were to be filled. The United Nations was responsible for handling many of the details, but Secretary General Annan refused to send more than a handful of election experts to Iraq because of the lack of security there. About twenty UN officials had been killed in the bombing of the UN headquarters in Baghdad in August 2003, and Annan had vowed not to put his subordinates into dangerous situations again without adequate security. Adding to the difficulties was a tight timetable for the various steps leading up to the election; the first step was the opening on November 1 of voter registration and candidate declarations, and the campaign itself was to begin on December 15.

Beyond these logistical hurdles were two related matters of even greater importance: improving the overall security environment so voters would feel safe enough to go to the polls and getting the minority Sunni Muslim population to participate as candidates and as voters. To provide security, the Pentagon announced early in December that U.S. forces in Iraq would be boosted by 12,000 troops to a total of 150,000 for the first three months of 2005. U.S. officials also said Iraqi units would be given the primary responsibility of guarding polling places. An early lesson in the troubles to be faced during the election cycle came on December 19, when a group of about thirty insurgents pulled three Iraqi election workers from their car in central Baghdad and executed them on the spot. That attack came on the same day that car bombs were set off in Karbala and Najaf, killing sixty-six people. Those largely Shi'ite cities in southern Iraq had been relatively quiet in recent months, and the attacks there fanned fears of sectarian violence during the election campaign.

Encouraging Sunni participation appeared to be just as difficult a task as providing security. On November 9 the Association of Muslim Scholars, representing

Iraq's Sunni clerics, called for a boycott of the elections in response to a U.S.-led offensive then under way in Falluja. The group's director said the election "is to be held over the bodies of the dead and the blood of the wounded in cities like Falluja." That same day one of the main Sunni political parties, the Iraqi Islamic Party, said it was withdrawing from Allawi's government to protest the Falluja invasion. Early in December that party mounted a petition drive calling for postponement of the election, but the three men with the most to say about the matter rejected that call and insisted elections would be held on schedule: President Bush, Ayatollah Sistani, and Prime Minister Allawi. Faced with that insistence, the Sunni leadership announced December 27 that it was withdrawing from the election.

In political terms, the most important preelection development was the creation of a broad coalition dominated by Shi'ite parties under Sistani's sponsorship. Known as the United Iraqi Alliance, that coalition included such disparate leaders as Ahmed Chalabi, the former exile who had been the Pentagon's favorite before the war to head Iraq but had since fallen from favor in Washington; Moqtada al-Sadr, a militant cleric who had led two uprisings against U.S. forces in southern Iraq and Baghdad; Abdul Aziz al-Hakim, who inherited the leadership of the Iranian-backed Supreme Council for the Islamic Revolution in Iraq (a Shi'ite party) when his elder brother, Muhammad Bakir al-Hakim, was killed in a bomb attack in August 2003; Hussein Shahristani, a prominent nuclear scientist who had been jailed by Saddam's regime; and Ibrahim al-Jaafari, a leader of the radical Shi'ite Dawa Party who was serving as one of two vice presidents in the interim government.

As expected, the two major Kurdish parties in northern Iraq set aside years of often-bitter dissension and announced plans to run a unified slate in hopes of retaining the de facto autonomy they had achieved for their region. On December 15, the opening day of the campaign, Allawi announced that he was heading a 240-candidate coalition of Sunnis and Shi'ites called the Iraqi List. Another significant coalition, the Independent Democratic Gathering, was headed by Adnan Pachachi, a prominent Sunni Muslim elder statesman who had been Iraq's foreign minister in the late 1950s.

These and dozens of other parties presented a total of more than 19,000 candidates for Iraqi voters to choose from when they went to the polls. Most of these candidates were running for assemblies in each of the eighteen provinces, but 6,239 of them were competing for the 275 seats in the National Assembly. Because of the danger, few of the candidates planned to campaign actively in person and were instead relying on the lure of their coalitions and well-known leaders. Fourteen million Iraqis were eligible to vote.

Saddam in Custody

On July 1 Iraqis and the rest of the world got the first look at Saddam Hussein, the deposed leader, since his capture by U.S. forces the previous December. Saddam was brought into a heavily guarded courtroom to face a young Iraqi magistrate who was preparing criminal charges that Saddam had ordered tens of thousands of Iraqis killed for political reasons.

Somewhat shrunken after nearly seven months of captivity, Saddam remained defiant, challenging the magistrate's authority and denying all charges against him. The proceedings were televised live in Iraq, where millions of people watched their once-dominant leader attempt to reassert his authority. The government planned a trial in 2005.

Reconstruction Lags

After the war ended in April 2003, there were great expectations both among Iraqis and officials in Washington that Iraq's infrastructure would be repaired quickly and the country's economy would be revived with the help of revenues from the country's formerly booming oil industry. As with most other prewar expectations, these proved wildly unrealistic for two reasons: Iraq's public utilities and public services were in much worse shape than U.S. officials had imagined, and the oil industry was decrepit and subject to repeated attacks by the insurgents. Senior Bush administration officials had told Congress before the war that Iraq's oil revenues would pay most of the cost of rebuilding Iraq. By late 2003 Bush was forced to return to Congress to ask for about $18 billion in U.S. tax dollars to pay those costs because oil revenues were less than one-third of prewar projections.

Even with that large budget in hand, U.S. officials discovered that rebuilding electric power grids and water treatment plants, repairing schools and health clinics, and reconstructing elements of Iraq's economy would be a lengthy, time-consuming process. As of the June 28 handover, only $5 billion of the $18.4 billion appropriated by Congress had been allocated, and only about $400 million of that amount actually had been spent. Much of the money had gone to contractors from the United States and other countries; little of it was spent to put Iraqis to work, one of the stated goals of U.S. aid.

On September 14 U.S. officials said $3.5 billion of the remaining aid would be shifted from reconstruction to a higher priority: recruiting, training, equipping, and paying an estimated 60,000 new members of Iraq's security forces. "The security situation represents the most serious obstacle to reconstruction and economic and political development in Iraq," Marc Grossman, the undersecretary of state for political affairs said in announcing the shift. Congress quickly approved the step, but not before some members in both parties said it represented an acknowledgment that U.S. reconstruction efforts in Iraq had failed to make much headway. Noting that only 6 percent of the money had been spent ten months after Congress approved it, Sen. Chuck Hagel, R-Neb., said: "It's beyond pitiful, it's beyond embarrassing, it's now in the zone of dangerous."

The administration sent a follow-up report to Congress on October 1 acknowledging that about half the money it had spent under the reconstruction budget actually went for law enforcement and security projects. This meant that less than $600 million had gone for work of direct benefit to ordinary Iraqis, with nearly half of that total going for work on the electrical system.

During a visit to Iraq on December 13, Andrew Natsios, administrator of the U.S. Agency for International Development, defended the pace of reconstruction work. Natsios noted that many of the infrastructure projects involved such work as building water treatment plants, power stations, and schools—all of which took time. "I know people are impatient," he said. "They have a right to be impatient, but I think progress is being made and the money is being spent appropriately.

Largely because of the insecurity in Iraq, many of the international aid and relief organizations that worked in Iraq before or immediately after the war pulled out during the course of 2003 and 2004. Of the organizations that remained, most worked in the relatively safe areas of southern Iraq or the Kurdish-controlled north. Few aid workers ventured into the violence-prone areas of central Iraq, where about 40 percent of the population lived.

Also because of the insecurity, few independent assessments were made of the reconstruction effort. Journalists and other monitors reported occasionally on a handful of reconstruction projects in Baghdad and other cities, but it was difficult for outsiders to judge the Bush administration's claims of progress in improving everyday life for the Iraqi people. Many Iraqis made just the opposite claim, that life was even worse than under Saddam's rule.

Perhaps the broadest independent assessment of the reconstruction came in a report issued in September by the Washington-based Center for Strategic and International Studies. The report was written by experts in post-conflict situations who visited Iraq in both 2003 and 2004. Entitled "Progress or Peril? Measuring Iraq's Reconstruction," the report found that U.S. aid had initially improved education and health care in Iraq through such projects as rebuilding more than 2,000 schools and inoculating several million children against life-threatening diseases. But the lack of security and the stalled economy "continue to overshadow and undermine efforts across the board," the report said.

Another assessment by a British medical organization warned that Iraq was facing an enormous public health crisis because of the years of mismanagement under Saddam's regime, the ongoing violence, and continuing mismanagement in the aftermath of the war. Medact, an organization that had opposed the war, issued a report November 30 calling Iraq's medical system woefully inadequate and arguing that failed water and sanitation systems, inadequate food supplies, and lack of reliable electricity were factors creating a potential breakdown in public health.

Two major international efforts provided some financial help for the U.S.-led reconstruction effort. The first was a donor's conference on February 29, which produced pledges of about $1 billion for reconstruction. This was in addition to $33 billion that had been pledged at a conference in Madrid in October 2003, most of it from the United States. As in many similar cases, however, the pledges came faster than the actual money. One U.S. government report in October said only about $1 billion of $13 billion pledged by countries other than the United States had made its way to Iraq.

Another significant move to boost Iraq's economy came November 11 when nineteen creditor nations agreed to write off 80 percent (or about $31 billion) of Iraq's $39 billion in external debt. The Bush administration had pushed for a 95 percent debt write-down but praised the less generous agreement by members of the Paris Club, which included France, Germany, Russia, and other creditors, in addition to the United States. Still unclear at year's end was the status of Iraq's even larger debt, totaling about $80 billion, to other Arab countries, notably Kuwait and Saudi Arabia.

Following are two documents, released June 28, 2004, the date that the United States transferred sovereignty over Iraq from the U.S.-led Coalition Provisional Authority (CPA) to an interim Iraqi government. The first is an exchange of letters by L. Paul Bremer III, the administrator of the CPA; Ayad Allawi, the interim prime minister of Iraq; and U.S. president George W. Bush. The second document consists of excerpts of statements on the transition in Iraq by Bush and British prime minister Tony Blair at a news conference in Istanbul, Turkey.

"Texts of Letters on Iraq Sovereignty"

This letter was given to the judge in the presence of Prime Minister [Ayad] Allawi and President Ghazi al-Yawer at approximately 10:35 a.m. Baghdad time:

Judge Medhat al Mahmood
Court of Cassation
Baghdad, Iraq

Dear Judge Mahmood:

As recognized in U.N. Security Council Resolution 1546 (2004), the Coalition Provisional Authority will cease to exist on June 28, at which point the occupation will end, and the Iraqi Interim Government will assume and exercise full sovereign authority on behalf of the Iraqi people. We welcome Iraq's steps to take its rightful place of equality and honor among the nations of the world.

Sincerely,
L. Paul Bremer III
Administrator

This letter is from the president to Prime Minister Allawi proposing the establishment of diplomatic relations between the United States and Iraq. . . .

June 27, 2004

His Excellency
Ayad Allawi
Prime Minister of the Republic of Iraq
Baghdad

Dear Mr. Prime Minister:

Congratulations on your recent appointment and to the Iraqi people on the great strides that have been made in the past year toward freedom and democracy in Iraq. The United States is a committed partner in this endeavor, and it is my honor to propose the establishment of diplomatic relations between the United States and Iraq with permanent missions, effective immediately upon the assumption of sovereign authority by the Iraqi Interim Government.

The United States reiterates its commitment to support your government as it leads Iraq toward national elections. I look forward to your response confirming the establishment of diplomatic relations between our two countries and to pursuing our shared vision for Iraq's journey to freedom.

Sincerely,
George W. Bush

The letter in response from Prime Minister Allawi:

Dear President Bush

I have received your letter of June 27, 2004 and have the honor of confirming the establishment of diplomatic relations with full diplomatic mission between Iraq and the United States.

Sincerely,
Ayad Allawi
Prime Minister

Source: U.S. Executive Office of the President. Office of the Press Secretary. "Texts of Letters on Iraq Sovereignty as Read by Scott McClellan." Hilton International Hotel, Istanbul, Turkey. June 28, 2004. www.whitehouse.gov/news/releases/2004/06/20040628-10.html (accessed March 4, 2005).

"President's News Conference with Prime Minister Blair"

Transfer of Sovereignty in Iraq

President Bush. Good afternoon. Earlier today, 15 months after the liberation of Iraq, and 2 days ahead of schedule, the world witnessed the arrival of a free and sovereign Iraqi Government. Iraqi officials informed us that they are ready to assume power, and Prime Minister Allawi believes that making this transition now is best for his country. After decades of brutal rule by a terror regime, the Iraqi people have their country back.

This is a day of great hope for Iraqis and a day that terrorist enemies hoped never to see. The terrorists are doing all they can to stop the rise of a free Iraq. But their bombs and attacks have not prevented Iraqi sovereignty, and they will not prevent Iraqi democracy. Iraqi sovereignty is a tribute to the will of the Iraqi people and the courage of Iraqi leaders.

This day also marks a proud moral achievement for members of our coalition. We pledged to end a dangerous regime, to free the oppressed, and to restore sovereignty. We have kept our word.

Fifteen months ago, Saddam's regime was an enemy of America and the civilized world. Today Iraq's Government is an ally of both. Fifteen months ago, Iraq was a state sponsor of terrorism. Today Iraq's leaders, with our support, are systematically fighting terrorists across their country. Fifteen months ago, we faced the threat of a dictator with a history of using weapons of mass destruction. Today the dictator is a threat to no one, from the cell he now occupies. Fifteen months ago, the regime in Baghdad was the most aggressive in the Middle East and a constant source of fear and alarm for Iraq's neighbors. Today Iraq threatens no other country, and its democratic progress will be an example to the broader Middle East. Fifteen months ago, Iraq was ruled by a regime that brutalized and tortured its own people, murdered hundreds of thousands, and buried them in mass graves. Today Iraqis live under a Government that strives for justice, upholds the rule of law, and defends the dignity of every citizen.

Iraq today still has many challenges to overcome. We recognize that. But it is a world away from the tormented, exhausted, and isolated country we found last year. Now the transfer of sovereignty begins a new phase in Iraq's progress toward full democracy. Together with the Iraqi Government, we're moving forward on every element of our five-part plan for Iraqi self-government.

Iraq's Interim Government has gained broad international support and has been endorsed by the U.N. Security Council. The United States and our coalition partners are helping prepare Iraqis for the defense of their own country, and we appreciate NATO's decision to approve Prime Minister Allawi's request for assistance in training Iraqi security forces—in training the Iraqi security forces. We're helping Iraqis rebuild their country's infrastructure, and Iraq will move—continue moving toward free elections, with important assistance from the United Nations.

All this progress is being attacked by foreign terrorists and by thugs from the fallen regime. The terrorists know they face defeat unless they break the spirit and commitment of the civilized world. The civilized world will not be frightened or intimidated. And Iraq's new leaders have made their position clear: Prime Minister Allawi recently said that "The insurgents are trying to destroy our country, and we're not going to allow this."

The struggle is, first and foremost, an Iraqi struggle. The Prime Minister said of his people, "We're prepared to fight and, if necessary, die for these objectives." America, Great Britain, our coalition respect that spirit, and the Iraqi people will not stand alone.

The United States military and our coalition partners have made a clear, specific, and continuing mission in Iraq. As we train Iraqi security forces, we'll help those forces to find and destroy the killers. We'll protect infrastructure from the attacks. We'll provide security for the upcoming elections. Operating in a sovereign nation, our military will act in close consultation with the Iraqi Government. Yet coalition forces will remain under coalition command. Iraq's Prime Minister and President have told me that their goal is to eventually take full responsibility for the security of their country, and America wants Iraqi forces to take that role. Our military will stay as long as the stability of Iraq requires and only as long as their presence is needed and requested by the Iraqi Government.

Today, at the moment sovereignty was transferred, the mission of the Coalition Provisional Authority came to an end. Ambassador Jerry Bremer has been tireless and dedicated, and he returns home with the thanks of his country. Thousands of American civilians have labored for progress in Iraq under difficult and sometimes dangerous conditions. They also have our gratitude.

From the first hours of Operation Iraqi Freedom and to this very hour, in their battles against the terrorists, America's men and women in uniform have been unrelenting in the performance of their duty. They've had staunch allies, like Great Britain, at their side. We asked a lot of our military, and there's still much hard work ahead. We're grateful for the sacrifice of all who've served. We honor the memory of all who've died. The courage of our military has brought us to this hopeful day, and the continued service of our military assures the success of our cause.

In Iraq, we're serving the cause of liberty, and liberty is always worth fighting for. In Iraq, we're serving the cause of peace by promoting progress and hope in the Middle East as the alternative to stagnation and hatred and violence for export. In Iraq, we're serving the cause of our own security, striking the terrorists where we find them, instead of waiting for them to strike us at home.

For all these reasons, we accepted a difficult task in Iraq, and for all these reasons, we will finish that task.

Mr. Prime Minister.

Prime Minister Blair. Thank you, Mr. President.

Today is, obviously, an important staging post on the journey of the people of Iraq towards a new future, one in which democracy replaces dictatorship, in which freedom replaces repression, and of which all the people of Iraq can look forward to the possibility and the hope of an Iraq that genuinely guarantees a future for people from whatever part of Iraq they come.

I think it's just worth reflecting for a moment on what we now have before us, because today, of course, is extremely important. It's the transfer of real and full sovereignty to the people and the Government of Iraq. From now on, the coalition changes. We are there in support of the Iraqi Government and the Iraqi people.

And what you have very clearly, therefore, is on one side you have the Iraqi Government, the Iraqi people, the international community that has now spoken through the United Nations, who want a free, stable, pluralist, democratic Iraq. And on the other hand you have some of the former Saddam supporters; you have outside terrorists; you have fanatics and extremists of one sort or another who want to stop the possibility of that new Iraq happening.

And of course, it's going to carry on being difficult and dangerous. There was the tragic loss of a British soldier today, and many American servicemen have died. Many Iraqi civilians have died. Many of those who are joining up to the new Iraqi security services have died, have given their lives. But they've all given their lives in the cause of trying to provide a different and better future for the people of Iraq.

And I think what is interesting about this situation is that for those people who are there in Iraq causing this death and destruction, they have a very, very clear and simple objective. And the objective is not just to destabilize Iraq, to produce chaos, to produce bloodshed, to try and prevent democracy. The strategy of these terrorists is to try and prevent Iraq becoming a symbol of hope not just for the Iraqi people but, actually, for that region and the wider world.

And that is why, in a very real sense, because Al Qaida and other terrorist groups are actually there in Iraq now, what is happening in Iraq, the battle in Iraq, the battle for Iraq and its future, if you like, is, in a genuine sense, the frontline of the battle against terrorism and the new security threat that we face.

And that security threat is what has dominated our discussion here at the NATO Summit. And that security threat, which is about this new and poisonous and evil form of extremism linked to a perversion of the true faith of Islam and repressive, unstable states that proliferate in and deal in chemical, biological, nuclear weapons—that security threat is the threat of our times. . . .

Possibility of Martial Law in Iraq

Q. Mr. President, Iraq's new Prime Minister has talked in recent days about the possibility of imposing martial law there as a way of restoring security. Is that something that you think a new, emerging Government should do, and particularly with the use of U.S. forces, who would have to be instrumental in doing it?

President Bush. You know, Prime Minister Allawi has fought tyranny. He's a guy that stood up to Saddam Hussein. He's a patriot, and every conversation I've had with him has been one the recognizes human liberty, human rights. I mean, he's a man who is willing to risk his life for a democratic future for Iraq.

Having said that, he may take tough security measures to deal with [Abu Masud] Zarqawi [a leader of Iraqi insurgents], but he may have to. Zarqawi is the guy who beheads people on TV. He's the person that orders suiciders to kill women and children. And so Prime Minister Allawi, as the head of a sovereign Government, may decide he's going to have to take some tough measures to deal with a brutal, coldblooded killer. And our job is to help the Iraqis stand up forces that are able to deal with these thugs.

I mean, it's tough; there's no question about it. Look, they can't whip our militaries. They can't whip our militaries. What they can do is get on your TV screens and stand in front of your TV cameras and cut somebody's head off, in order to try to cause us to cringe and retreat. That's their strongest weapon. And we just—as Prime Minister Allawi has said publicly many times, he will not cower in the face of such brutal murder, and neither will we—neither will we.

Prime Minister Blair. I think you've got to distinguish very carefully between two separate things. The first is, undoubtedly, the new Iraqi Government will want to take tough security measures. They have to. They've got a situation where they've got these terrorists who are prepared to kill any number of innocent people. And remember, the innocent Iraqis who are dying in Iraq today are dying because of these terrorist acts.

On the other hand, I know perfectly well from the discussions I've had not just with the Prime Minister but with the other Iraqi ministers, their purpose is to take tough security measures but in order to guarantee freedom for people, not to take it away. So they're not going to be wanting to introduce martial law that takes away the basic freedoms of the people. On the contrary, they will be wanting to take tough security measures, and we will want to help train their forces able to guard and get after the people doing this killing. But it's not going to be about taking away people's freedoms. It's going to be about allowing those freedoms to happen.

Source: U.S. Executive Office of the President. "The President's News Conference with Prime Minister Tony Blair of the United Kingdom in Istanbul." *Weekly Compilation of Presidential Documents* 40, no. 27 (March 5, 2004): 1170–1177. www.gpoaccess.gov/wcomp/v40no27.html (accessed March 4, 2005).

2004 HISTORIC DOCUMENTS

Justice Department on Indictment of Former Enron CEO

July 8, 2004

INTRODUCTION

The wave of scandals at major corporations that began in late 2001 with the collapse of Enron Corporation continued all through 2004 and even expanded in scope. More than a dozen senior corporate officials faced criminal prosecution for financial misdeeds, and for the third year in a row an entire industry—this time the insurance industry—came under intense legal scrutiny initiated by New York state attorney general Elliot L. Spitzer. In 2002 Spitzer had revealed improper dealings by many of the nation's major investment banks, and in 2003 he had uncovered practices by mutual funds that benefited a minority of customers at the expense of most others.

July 8, 2004, may have been a watershed date in the current round of corporate misdeeds. On that day, the federal government unsealed an indictment of Kenneth L. Lay, the former board chairman and chief executive officer (CEO) of Enron; a jury convicted John J. Rigas, the founder of the cable television firm Adelphia Communications, on fraud charges; and a federal judge denied a new trial for Martha Stewart, who had built a business empire based on advice to homemakers but also had been convicted in March on charges related to insider trading. Stewart in December began serving a five-month sentence at a low-security prison in Virginia, becoming by far the most famous person in recent years to don prison garb for financial wrongdoing.

The high-profile prosecutions put business executives on notice that they might pay a personal price for stretching the limits of propriety in managing their companies. Behind the scenes, however, many business leaders were lobbying Congress and the Bush administration to water down laws and regulations that had been put in place after the collapse of Enron and several other major companies. Some leaders said the new rules went too far in governing corporate behavior. *(Background, Historic Documents of 2002, pp. 391, 1032; Historic Documents of 2003, pp. 332, 693)*

Indictment of Enron's Lay

Before it fell into bankruptcy in December 2001, Houston-based Enron had become the model for a new type of business based on buying and selling services provided by other companies. After its collapse revealed that Enron's business was based more on hype and financial manipulation than on substance, the company name became a synonym for corporate shenanigans. Shareholders lost tens of billions of dollars they had invested in the company, and more than 30,000 employees lost their jobs and their retirement savings based on Enron stock. *(Enron bankruptcy, Historic Documents of 2001, p. 857)*

Among the out-of-work former Enron employees were the top executives who had used a complex series of schemes to make it appear the company was busier, and more profitable, than it actually was. The top three were Lay, who had guided the firm since its creation in a 1985 merger of two natural gas companies; Jeffrey K. Skilling, Enron's former president who briefly served as CEO before its collapse; and Andrew S. Fastow, the former chief financial officer (CFO) who allegedly developed the financial maneuvers that enhanced Enron's appearance of success.

Fastow was the first of the three to be indicted, in 2003, and on January 14, 2004, he pleaded guilty to two charges of conspiracy to commit fraud. He agreed to a sentence of ten years in prison, forfeited $23.8 million in personal holdings, and was barred from ever again holding an executive position in a publicly traded company. Fastow's wife, Lea, also pleaded guilty on the same day to a tax misdemeanor; she had served as an assistant treasurer at Enron. The judge in the case challenged the five-month prison sentence that prosecutors had accepted for Lea Fastow, however, and on May 6 she again pleaded guilty under an arrangement providing for her to serve one year in prison and one year of supervision after her release.

Skilling was charged with thirty-five financial misdeeds on February 19, 2004, and he pleaded not guilty to all of them. His case was still pending at year's end. Also on February 19 the government expanded its case against former Enron chief accounting officer Richard A. Causey to a total of thirty-one charges.

In symbolic terms, the July 8 indictment of Lay was one of the most important actions taken by the government during the three-plus years of the current wave of corporate scandals. Lay was charged with eleven counts of fraud and making false statements. A Republican Party insider who had boasted of his friendship with President George W. Bush and other top administration officials, Lay had come to symbolize the powerful corporate chief executive who used political contacts and questionable maneuverings to build a company. Lay cashed in more than $20 million worth of Enron shares in the summer and fall of 2001, even as he assured employees and investors that the company remained sound.

Lay pleaded not guilty to all eleven charges and then, in a highly unusual move, held a news conference and gave several interviews to declare his innocence. Lay said he had not been aware of the dealings that had led to Enron's downfall and that only a "superman" could have kept track of everything at the giant firm. On October 19 U.S. District Court Judge Sim Lake, in Houston, split the charges against Lay into two groups, meaning that Lay would face two separate trials: one dealing with four charges of fraud in his personal banking affairs and another dealing with seven charges of conspiracy and fraud in connection with Lay's official acts at Enron. The first case involving Lay and co-defendants Skilling and Causey was expected to go to trial in late 2005 or early 2006.

As of the end of 2004 fifteen former Enron officials (including the Fastows) had pleaded guilty to civil or criminal charges, and another six had been convicted. Among those who pleaded guilty during 2004 was John M. Forney, a senior energy trader, who on August 5 admitted to charges of manipulating energy markets in California from 1999 to 2001. The first Enron-related criminal case to go to trial resulted in a mixed verdict on November 3. The case involved allegations that Enron had manipulated its books in 1999 to enhance its reported profits through a sham deal with Merrill Lynch involving electricity-generating barges off the coast of Nigeria. A jury found former Enron accountant Sheila Kahanek not guilty in the case but convicted former Enron vice president Dan Boyle and four Merrill Lynch investment bankers. *(California energy crisis, Historic Documents of 2001, p. 332)*

The prosecutions of Enron executives were widely publicized, but less attention was paid to the ongoing process of selling off and reorganizing the pieces of Enron that still had some business value. First to go was the energy trading business that Skilling and other executives had claimed represented Enron's future but that proved to be more talk than actual business. UBS-Paine Webber, the investment banking firm, took over that business in 2002 and promptly closed most of it. Under the supervision of U.S. Bankruptcy Judge Arthur Gonzalez in New York, other Enron assets gradually were sold off. Among them was an entity known as Cross Country, which owned all or part of three natural gas pipelines in the United States; Cross Country was bought in September 2004 by a joint venture of Southern Union Co. and GE Commercial Finance Energy Financial Services. Judge Gonzalez in July 2004 also approved the sale of Portland General Electric, a major utility company, to a holding company that included Texas Pacific Group, but the deal was held up by the Oregon public utilities commission.

After those sales, all that was left of Enron was a business named Prisma Energy International Inc., which owned twenty-two energy-related business in fourteen countries, most of them in South America. Once the reorganization was complete—possibly early in 2005—Enron's creditors, who had filed $67 billion in claims against the company, were expected to receive between 18 and 22 cents on the dollar. Enron's shareholders were to receive nothing for their stock, which at one point traded for $90 a share but had become worthless.

WorldCom

The 2001 bankruptcy of Enron was exceeded, in terms of financial size, a year later by the bankruptcy of WorldCom, a telecommunications company created through an aggressive series of acquisitions by company founder Bernard J. Ebbers. The firm collapsed in July 2002 when an investigation by the Securities and Exchange Commission (SEC) discovered that the empire Ebbers built was riddled with financial manipulations intended to bolster the appearance of profitability, and thus WorldCom's share price. At the time of its bankruptcy, WorldCom had accumulated debts of $42 billion. Subsequent investigations by the company showed that its earnings had been overstated by about $11 billion between 1999 and early 2002.

Ebbers was indicted on March 2, 2004, on three criminal counts of securities fraud and filing false statements with the SEC. He pleaded not guilty to all three charges. The government's case was strengthened by a guilty plea, on the same day to similar charges, by Scott D. Sullivan, WorldCom's former CFO, who also agreed to cooperate with federal investigators; the extent of his cooperation was expected to determine how much time he would spend in prison. Ebbers on May 24 was indicted on six more charges of filing false statements with the SEC. He was expected to go on trial in 2005.

The indictment of Ebbers and the guilty plea by Sullivan were hailed by former SEC chairman Richard Breeden, who had been appointed by the federal court in New York to monitor WorldCom's bankruptcy proceedings. "This is a great day for the justice system," he said. "It was impossible for us to believe that distortions of this scale could take place without Ebbers' knowledge."

Ebbers, other WorldCom officials, and several investment banks that had financed the company also faced a shareholder class action lawsuit, which was pending before a federal district court in New York. Documents filed in connection with that suit in March indicated that analysts at several major investment banks had become concerned about WorldCom's financial health early in 2001, but the banks had not made those concerns public. One of the banks, Citigroup, reached a settlement in the case on May 10, under which it agreed to pay $2.6 billion to holders of WorldCom bonds and shares. It was the second largest settlement in a securities fraud case in U.S. history, topped only by a $3.2 billion settlement by Cendant in an accounting fraud case in 2000. The cases of three other banks named in the class action lawsuit were expected to go to trial early in 2005.

WorldCom on March 12 restated its losses for the years 2000 through 2002, saying the total net loss for the period was $73.7 billion. Until its financial irregularities were uncovered in 2002, the company had claimed to be profitable for that period. Also on March 12 WorldCom reached a settlement with the state of Oklahoma on criminal charges that had been brought by attorney general Drew Edmondson. Under the agreement, WorldCom pledged to create 1,600 jobs in the state over a ten-year period—nearly doubling its employment there.

As part of its emergence from bankruptcy, the company put $500 million in cash, and stock valued at $250 million, into a court-administered fund for a partial reimbursement of investors who had been defrauded. The company also changed its name to MCI, which had been the name of the long-distance carrier Ebbers had acquired during his spending spree in 1999.

Spitzer Takes on Insurance Giants

Late in 2004 New York attorney general Spitzer trained his sights on the insurance industry and forced a series of revelations of financial irregularities, followed by corporate changes, that were certain to have repercussions for years to come. Spitzer's first target was a big one: Marsh Inc., the world's largest insurance broker, which also was a subsidiary of the Marsh & McLennan Companies. Spitzer filed a lawsuit on October 14 accusing Marsh of rigging prices and sending business to favored insurers in exchange for kickbacks. Spitzer said in a statement that his investigation would extend to many other companies because "virtually every line of insurance is implicated" in the kinds of practices he had found at Marsh. Spitzer also filed suit on the same day against two executives of American International Group (AIG) and one executive of Ace Ltd.

In less than two weeks, Spitzer's probe resulted in a major corporate reshuffling. Jeffrey W. Greenberg, chairman and CEO of Marsh & McLennan, resigned on October 25 and was succeeded by Michael G. Cherkasky, whose selection appeared motivated primarily by the fact that he had once been Spitzer's boss. On November 18 Marsh & McLennan announced that five senior company officials, including a vice chairman, were leaving the board of directors.

Spitzer's probe added urgency to a long-running investigation by the Securities and Exchange Commission of AIG, run by Maurice Greenberg, the father of the ousted Marsh & McLennan chairman. That probe was still under way at year's end but was expected to force major changes at the company during 2005. Late in December the SEC also requested documents and other information from General Re, a reinsurance subsidiary of Berkshire Hathaway, the giant investment conglomerate run by Wall Street legend Warren Buffett. News reports suggested the SEC was expanding its investigation into several aspects of the insurance business.

Mutual Funds

The mutual funds industry—long considered the most important bastion of safe investing for ordinary Americans—experienced significant changes in the sixteen months following the first charges brought in September 2003 by Spitzer. More than a dozen companies agreed to pay nearly $2.5 billion in fines and reimbursements and pledged to cut the fees they charged investors in the future; leaders of several major mutual funds had been forced from office and a half-dozen of them were indicted; and federal regulators adopted a series of new rules intended to ensure that mutual funds conducted their business to benefit all investors, not just favored ones.

The scandal over mutual funds began when Spitzer accused four large funds of allowing a New Jersey company to use special profit-making deals that harmed the interests of most other investors. Spitzer, other state regulators, and the SEC conducted broad-ranging investigations that showed that many other funds—but not all of them—had engaged in similar practices.

The year's largest financial settlement in the mutual funds scandal came on March 15, when Bank of America and FleetBoston Financial Corp. agreed to pay a total of $675 million in fines and reimbursements resulting from Spitzer's charges that they had favored some clients at the expense of others. That agreement removed a hurdle to the merger of the two banks, which had been announced in 2003. An important element of the agreement was the forced resignation of eight trustees of Bank of America's mutual fund known as Nations Fund. Another major settlement came on April 8, when Putnam Investments agreed to pay $110 million to settle federal and Massachusetts state charges. Putnam, based in Boston, had been the first major mutual fund caught up in the scandal over improper activities in the industry.

The largest financial penalty assessed against an individual in the mutual funds scandal was levied on May 20 against Richard S. Strong, the founder of Strong Capital Management Inc., a Wisconsin firm. Strong agreed to pay $140 million in fines and restitution to settle federal, New York, and Wisconsin charges that he shortchanged investors while profiting personally from his deals.

The SEC adopted a series of new rules for the mutual fund industry during 2004. On February 11 the commission required mutual funds to disclose more clearly the fees they charged investors. The rules, adopted unanimously, required mutual funds to disclose its fees in two ways: first, the fund's fees for each $1,000 investment; second, the total costs for each $1,000 investment based on the fund's expense ratio and an assumed annual rate of return of 5 percent. The latter disclosure was intended to enable investors to compare the fees of various mutual funds. Other rules adopted by the SEC barred mutual funds from paying higher commissions to brokers who promoted them and required the boards of mutual funds to disclose to investors how they hired and evaluated the work of fund managers.

On February 25 the SEC proposed another rule requiring mutual funds to charge a 2 percent fee on rapid-fire transactions—known as "market timing"—that were intended to take advantage of short-term fluctuations in market prices. Most mutual funds had rules prohibiting these types of transactions, but investigations by Spitzer and the SEC turned up numerous cases in which funds had allowed favored customers to engage in market timing, to the detriment of most other investors. SEC officials said the proposed 2 percent fee would discourage market timing.

More controversial was another SEC proposal requiring the boards of mutual funds to be led by independent chairmen—a proposal that would require about

80 percent of U.S. mutual funds to replace their chairmen. After the commission proposed the rule in March, leaders of several major mutual funds, including Fidelity Investments, T. Rowe Price, and Vanguard Group Inc., lobbied against it, arguing that requiring board chairmen to be independent of fund management would not, by itself, ensure that funds were managed properly. Even so, the commission adopted the rule on June 23 on a 3–2 vote, with Chairman William H. Donaldson siding with the two commission Democrats in favor of the rule. Mutual fund executives kept up the pressure against the rule, however, and in November Congress included a provision in an omnibus spending bill (PL 108–447) requiring the SEC to justify the need for it.

Fannie Mae's Tumble

Fannie Mae, the nation's largest source of money for home mortgages, came under intense scrutiny late in 2004 and—for the first time in years—was unable to rely for protection on its extensive Washington political connections. Chief executive officer Franklin D. Raines and chief financial officer J. Timothy Howard were forced to resign on December 21 after the SEC required the company to correct its books in a way that reduced its claimed revenues by $9 billion over a period of three-and-a half years. Fannie Mae's regulator, the Office of Federal Housing Enterprise Oversight, on December 27 said it was investigating a $19 million severance package for Raines and asked Fannie Mae to suspend any payments until its investigation was complete.

That regulator had brought the company's problems to light with a report in September accusing the company of engaging in "cookie jar" accounting. Among other things, the report said Fannie Mae in 1998 had deliberately delayed booking expenses so Raines and other executives could get bonuses. Raines denied that charge, and others, during a full day of testimony before a House committee on October 6.

Martha Stewart Conviction

In terms of public interest, all other business scandals of recent years paled in comparison to the legal woes of Martha Stewart. She had built a media empire, called Martha Stewart Living Omnimedia, on a magazine and television show that offered advice for homemakers on cooking and home decor. Stewart was one of the most famous businesswomen in the United States, and her legal troubles generated enormous public interest. Many supporters said she had been targeted by prosecutors simply because she was a famous woman; others came to the opposite conclusion, that even someone as famous and powerful as Stewart could be brought to justice.

Stewart fell afoul of the law not because of her own business but because of her sale of 4,000 shares in ImClone Systems on December 27, 2001—one day before the biotechnology company announced that its application for approval of a new cancer drug had been rejected by the Food and Drug Administration. Stewart insisted that her sale of the shares was based on a previous agreement with her broker, Peter E. Bacanovic, relating to the value of the stock. Federal prosecutors disagreed, saying she had benefited from inside information resulting from her friendship with ImClone chief Samuel D. Waksal. Stewart was charged with conspiracy, obstruction of justice, making false statements, and securities fraud. The latter charge—the most serious Stewart faced—was dismissed by a judge on

February 27, but a jury on March 2 convicted Stewart on the other charges. The jury also found Bacanovic guilty on four charges related to Stewart's stock sale.

Stewart had resigned as CEO of her company when she was indicted on June 4, 2003. On March 15, 2004, she resigned as a director and CEO but said she would continue working on projects, including two books she was writing. Stewart maintained her innocence, and her lawyers filed a motion requesting a new trial. That motion was denied on July 8, the same day Enron's Lay was indicted. On July 16 Stewart was sentenced to five months in prison, plus five months of home detention, two years of supervised probation, and a $30,000 fine. Stewart said the "small, personal matter" had been "blown out of all proportion." Although Stewart appealed her conviction, she voluntarily began serving her five-month sentence on October 8, checking into a women's prison in Alderson, West Virginia; reports said the prison was known locally as "Camp Cupcake." A message on her Web site said she was confident of overturning the verdict on appeal but had decided "to serve my sentence now because I want to put this nightmare behind me as quickly as possible for the good of my family and my company."

Backlash against Reforms

In the two years after the collapse of Enron, many corporate leaders had found themselves on the defensive as they endured relentless negative publicity about financial irregularities and numerous investigations by state and federal regulators. Even as those developments continued into 2004, business groups began lobbying Congress and the Bush administration in hopes of rolling back some of the new rules that were put in place as a result of the current wave of scandals.

Business leaders were most vocal in their complaints about some provisions of the Sarbanes-Oxley Act (PL 107–204), passed by Congress in 2002 in response to the Enron bankruptcy and other scandals. The law established numerous requirements intended to improve financial controls at, and give investors better information about, publicly traded companies. A main target was a provision known as section 404, which required companies to disclose in annual reports details about their internal financial controls.

Business lobbying during 2004 resulted in at least the postponement of another proposed rule by the Financial Accounting Standards Board requiring companies to show on their books the expense of granting stock options to executives and employees. Many companies, especially in the computer business, had used these stock options to reward executives without having to write off the cost of providing them—a practice that many critics said resulted in misleading balance sheets. Business groups lobbied intensely against the rule, and the Republican-led House of Representatives voted in July to apply it only to each company's top five executives. The accounting board in October delayed implementation of the rule until June 2005.

In a similar case, the SEC retreated from a proposal it made in October 2003 that would have allowed shareholders, in some instances, to nominate their own candidates for boards of directors. The SEC's two Democratic members supported the proposal, but the two Republicans opposed it, putting chairman Donaldson in the middle. After initially supporting the proposal, Donaldson backed down in the face of staunch opposition from business groups.

The *Wall Street Journal* reported on December 20 that some business leaders were hoping Donaldson would retire before his term expired in 2007—or even would be forced out by the Bush administration. The *Journal* said business leaders had a long list of complaints about SEC rules and enforcement actions, notably the proposed rule requiring that the boards of mutual funds have independent chairmen.

Other Major Corporate Scandals

Dozens of other U.S. and international companies were charged with or found guilty of some form of financial irregularity during the year. Among them were:

- **The New York Stock Exchange.** Chairman Richard Grasso was fired in 2003, and a series of sweeping reforms were initiated, when it became known that the board had given Grasso pay packages valued at nearly $190 million. Spitzer on May 24 filed a lawsuit demanding that Grasso return more than $100 million. That suit was still pending at year's end.
- **Adelphia Communications Corp.** Founder John J. Rigas and his sons Michael and Timothy went on trial February 23 on charges of stealing more than $1 billion from the publicly traded company, which was the nation's sixth largest cable television operator. John and Timothy Rigas (who had been the company's CFO) were found guilty on July 8, but the jury deadlocked on most charges against Michael Rigas. Sentencing of John and Timothy Rigas and a retrial of Michael Rigas were scheduled for 2005.
- **Tyco International.** A New York state judge on April 2 declared a mistrial in the case of two former executives of Tyco International, an industrial conglomerate that had become a premier symbol of personal abuse of corporate coffers. L. Dennis Kozlowski, Tyco's former chairman and CEO, and Mark H. Swartz, the former CFO, had been charged with stealing $170 million from the company and gaining about $430 million by secretly selling company shares, which had been artificially inflated. On March 26, as the jury was deliberating in the case, one of the jurors appeared to flash an "okay" sign to Kozlowski. That set off an intense frenzy in the news media, leading the judge to declare a mistrial a week later. A new trial was scheduled for 2005. Kozlowski had become something of a poster boy for corporate corruption. Previous reports, and evidence made public during the trial, showed that he dipped into corporate accounts to finance an extraordinarily lavish lifestyle. Much of the public attention focused on a weeklong birthday party for Kozlowski's wife held on the island of Sardinia, costing $2 million, and the purchase, with company funds, of such items as a $6,000 shower curtain for his Manhattan luxury apartment.
- **Rite Aid Corp.** Martin L. Grass, former CEO of the nationwide drugstore chain, on May 14 accepted a ten-year prison term as part of an arrangement with federal prosecutors. Grass in 2003 had pleaded guilty to fraud and obstruction of justice charges stemming from a real estate deal and other financial misdealings in the late 1990s. He was the first CEO convicted of criminal charges during the current round of corporate scandals.
- **The Frank P. Quattrone case.** The former managing director and head of global technology at Credit Suisse First Boston, Quattrone was convicted on May 3 on charges of obstructing an SEC investigation into his firm's practices in allocating shares of initial public offering securities. A jury had deadlocked on the case in October 2003, and the conviction came after a second, month-long trial. Quattrone had been one of the country's most prominent boosters of Internet-related businesses during the boom of that industry in the late

1990s. U.S. District Court Judge Richard Owen on September 8 sentenced Quattrone to eighteen months in prison. Owen said Quattrone had committed perjury when he testified during his trial.

- **Newspaper circulation.** Several major newspapers were forced to repay advertisers millions of dollars after it was disclosed that they had inflated their circulation figures. The first newspapers affected were Long Island's *Newsday*, the Hoy chain of newspapers, the Chicago *Sun-Times*, and the Dallas *Morning News*. The *New York Times* reported on October 13 that the SEC had begun a broad probe of newspaper circulation practices by asking for information from the *Times* and thirty other major newspapers.
- **Royal Dutch/Shell.** The Anglo-Dutch firm—the world's third largest oil company—acknowledged in January, and again in statements later in the year, that its oil and gas reserves had been overstated by about 23 percent. Several senior executives were forced to resign, and pressure for more resignations followed. On July 29 the company agreed to pay $150 million in fines to settle charges by British and U.S. regulators that it had misled investors.
- **Computer Associates.** Sanjay Kumar, the former chairman and CEO of Computer Associates International, was indicted on September 22 on charges of securities fraud and obstruction of justice. Stephen Richards, the former executive vice president for worldwide sales, also was indicted on similar charges. The Long Island-based company had been one of the country's largest computer firms, but it had been dogged for years by questions about its business practices. The indictment accused Kumar and Richards of backdating billions of dollars in contracts so the firm could meet Wall Street estimates and then encouraging employees to mislead investigators once the problems came to light.
- **Disney.** Chairman and CEO Michael D. Eisner was forced to step down as chairman in March after investors representing 45 percent of the company shares withheld their votes in his reelection bid. Eisner also agreed to leave his CEO post by 2005. Former Maine Democratic senator George Mitchell, who had served on the Disney board, took over as chairman. Disney had been in trouble on numerous fronts, the most important of which was its poor financial performance as a result of questionable business decisions. Infighting in the company's executive suites also came into public view as a result of a challenge to Eisner by a former friend, Michael S. Ovitz, who Eisner had hired as Disney president and fired after less than a year. Ovitz's suit against Disney reached Delaware Chancery Court in 2004 and produced embarrassing revelations about the inside operations of the major media corporation.
- **The "Big Four" accounting firms.** The new federal agency responsible for monitoring accounting firms—the Public Company Accounting Oversight Board—said on August 26 that it had found "significant audit and accounting issues" at the four national firms: Deloitte & Touche, Ernst & Young, KPMG, and PricewaterhouseCoopers. The board had reviewed sixteen audits each firm had conducted in 2003 and found numerous mistakes, including misapplication of rules that led clients to restate their earnings. Despite the findings, oversight board chairman William J. McDonough said all four accounting firms were "capable of the highest quality auditing." Congress had established McDonough's board in the wake of the accounting scandal at Enron, which had led to the collapse of another large auditing firm, Arthur Andersen.
- **Hollinger International.** Conrad M. Black, a Canadian-born businessman who built an international newspaper empire, developed close friendships with diplomats and politicians on both sides of the Atlantic, and secured a British

peerage, was booted from his company, Hollinger International, amid allegations of mismanagement and fraud. The company owned the Chicago *Sun-Times*, the British *Telegraph* newspaper chain, the *Jerusalem Post*, and other news media properties. A report issued by the company's board on August 30 accused Black of running Hollinger as a "corporate kleptocracy." In addition to denouncing Black's personal misuse of company funds, the report said board members—who had been hand-picked by Black—had failed to exercise their fiduciary responsibilities to shareholders. In particular, the report cited Richard Perle, who had been a senior official in the Pentagon during the Reagan administration and was serving as chairman of a Pentagon advisory committee for the Bush administration. The report said Perle should return $5.4 million in pay he had received from Hollinger because he had put "his own interests" above those of company investors. Perle denied any wrongdoing.

Following is the text of "Former Enron Chairman and Chief Executive Officer Kenneth L. Lay Charged with Conspiracy, Fraud, False Statements," an announcement by the Justice Department, on July 8, 2004, that two former officers of Enron Corporation had been indicted on eleven counts of fraud and making false statements.

"Enron Chairman and CEO Charged with Conspiracy, Fraud"

Deputy Attorney General James B. Comey, Assistant Attorney General Christopher A. Wray of the Criminal Division, FBI Director Robert Mueller, and Enron Task Force Director Andrew Weissmann announced today that a federal grand jury in Houston has indicted former Enron Corp. Chairman and Chief Executive Officer Kenneth L. Lay on charges of conspiracy, securities fraud, wire fraud, bank fraud and making false statements.

A superseding indictment returned by the grand jury in Houston Wednesday, and unsealed today, charges Lay, 62, of Houston, with conspiracy to commit securities fraud, four counts of securities fraud and two counts of wire fraud, one count of bank fraud and three counts of making false statements to a bank. The superseding indictment joins Lay as a defendant in a case pending against former Enron CEO Jeffrey K. Skilling and former Enron Chief Accounting Officer Richard Causey. Causey was originally indicted in January 2004, and Skilling was added to the case in February 2004. The new indictment also adds a money laundering conspiracy count and four counts of money laundering against Causey in connection with fraudulent hedging vehicles, and expands certain factual allegations against Causey in connection with the securities fraud conspiracy. The case is pending before U.S. District Judge Sim Lake in Houston, Texas.

Lay surrendered this morning to FBI agents in Houston and the indictment was unsealed. Lay had an initial appearance this morning before Magistrate Judge Mary Milloy.

"The indictment charges that Lay, Skilling, Causey and others oversaw a massive conspiracy to cook the books at Enron and to create the illusion that it was a robust, growing company with limitless potential when, in fact, Enron was an increasingly troubled business kept afloat only by a series of deceptions," said Deputy Attorney General James B. Comey, who heads the President's Corporate Fraud Task Force. "These charges demonstrate the Department's commitment to the rule of law, its commitment to the principle that no one is above the law, and its commitment to unravel even the most complex of fraudulent schemes."

"This indictment alleges that every member of Enron's senior management participated in a criminal conspiracy to commit one of the largest corporate frauds in American history," said Assistant Attorney General Wray. "Kenneth Lay is charged with abusing his powerful position as Chairman of the Board and CEO and repeatedly lying in an effort to cover up the financial collapse that caused devastating harm to millions of Americans. The progress of this investigation shows that the Department of Justice will work tirelessly to hold corporate America to the high standards imposed by federal law."

"The collapse of Enron was devastating to tens of thousands of people and shook the public's confidence in corporate America," said FBI Director Mueller. "The FBI and our partners on the President's Corporate Fraud Task Force responded with a concerted effort to uncover the truth and to bring those responsible to justice. The charges against Ken Lay, Jeffrey Skilling and Richard Causey take us one step closer to restoring the public confidence in our financial markets."

The indictment alleges that at various times between at least 1999 and 2001, Lay, Skilling, Causey and other Enron executives engaged in a wide-ranging scheme to deceive the investing public, the U.S. Securities and Exchange Commission and others about the true performance of Enron's businesses. The alleged scheme was designed to make it appear that Enron was growing at a healthy and predictable rate, consistent with analysts' published expectations, that Enron did not have significant write-offs or debt and was worthy of investment-grade credit rating, that Enron was comprised of a number of successful business units, and that the company had an appropriate cash flow. It had the effect of inflating artificially Enron's stock price, which increased from approximately $30 per share in early 1998 to over $80 per share in January 2001, and artificially stemming the decline of the stock during the first three quarters of 2001.

The indictment alleges that Lay had a significant profit motive for participating in the scheme. As stated in the indictment, between 1998 and 2001, Lay received approximately $300 million from the sale of Enron stock options and restricted stock, netting over $217 million in profit, and was paid more than $19 million in salary and bonuses. During 2001 alone, Lay received a salary of over $1 million, a bonus of $7 million and $3.6 million in long term incentive payments. Additionally, during the period of August 21 through Oct. 26, 2001, Lay sold 918,104 shares of Enron stock to repay advances totaling $26,025,000 he had received from a line of credit extended to Lay by Enron.

As a part of the alleged scheme, unrealistic and unattainable earnings goals were set for Enron, based on analysts' expectations rather than on actual or reasonably achievable business results. When, as expected within the company, Enron consistently fell short of those goals, Lay, Skilling, Causey and others allegedly orchestrated a series of accounting gimmicks designed to make up the shortfall between actual and predicted results. Enron then announced publicly that it had met or exceeded analysts' expectations when, as Lay, Skilling and Causey allegedly knew, it made its numbers only by engaging in fraud. The indictment also alleges that Lay, Skilling and Causey made false and misleading representations about Enron's finances and business operations to analysts, at press conferences, in SEC filings and elsewhere.

Lay is principally charged for his conduct during the third quarter of 2001. As the indictment alleges, upon Skilling's abrupt departure from Enron in August 2001, Lay resumed his position as CEO of the company, intensified his oversight of Enron's day-to-day operations, and took control as leader of the conspiracy. Starting in August, according to the indictment, Lay was briefed extensively about mounting and undisclosed financial and operational problems, including overvaluation of Enron's assets and business units by several billion dollars. As a result of these and other issues confronting Enron, Lay privately considered a range of potential solutions, including mergers, restructurings, and even divestiture of Enron's pipelines, assets that Lay considered to be the crown jewels of the company. However, the indictment alleges he failed to disclose Enron's problems to the investing public and affirmatively misled the investing public about Enron's financial condition, while falsely claiming that he was disclosing everything that he had learned.

For example, the indictment states that during August 2001, Lay participated in Management Committee meetings at which reports were presented showing earnings shortfalls in virtually every Enron business unit, totaling approximately $1 billion. During early September 2001, Lay attended a Management Committee retreat in the Woodlands, Texas, at which the serious problems besetting Enron, including underperforming business units and troubled assets, were further discussed. Among other things, executives discussed the need to take in the third quarter of 2001 at least a $1 billion charge and that Enron had committed an accounting error in the amount of $1.2 billion.

The indictment alleges that throughout the remainder of September 2001, Lay engaged in a series of high-level meetings to discuss the growing financial crisis at Enron and the likely impact on Enron's credit rating. Among other things, Lay knew that the total amount of losses embedded in Enron's assets and business units was, at a minimum, $7 billion. Lay also knew that Enron's auditors had changed their position concerning the accounting treatment of four off-balance sheet vehicles called the Raptors, which required Enron to determine in short order whether an acceptable alternative methodology existed or whether, instead, Enron would have to restate its earnings and admit the error.

Despite knowing these negative facts, on Sept. 26, 2001, in an online forum with thousands of Enron employees, many of whom were investors in Enron stock, Lay allegedly stated that Enron was going to "hit [its] numbers." Lay allegedly created the false impression that his confidence in Enron's stock was such that he had increased his personal ownership of Enron stock in the past two months as a sign of his belief in what he was espousing. As the indictment alleges, during the prior two months, Lay actually purchased $4 million in Enron stock while also selling $24 million in Enron stock through nonpublic transactions.

The indictment states that in the weeks leading up to Enron's third quarter earnings release on Oct. 16, 2001, Lay determined that Enron could not publicly report a loss in excess of $1 billion without triggering negative action by Enron's credit rating agencies. Lay thus artificially capped Enron's losses to that amount. Also during this time, Lay learned that changes to the accounting rules governing goodwill (i.e., the difference between what Enron paid for an entity and the book value of that entity's net assets) would require Enron to disclose impairments to certain of its assets, including its interest in Wessex Water, a business located in Bath, England. In order to hide the impact of asset impairment, Lay allegedly claimed, falsely, that Enron was committed to engaging in a "water growth strategy," which would have required Enron to expend between $1 billion and $28 billion in capital investments in the water industry. Lay allegedly knew that Enron had no intention of pursuing such a strategy and did not have the capital to support it.

According to the indictment, on Oct. 16, 2001, when Enron announced losses of approximately $1 billion, Lay allegedly sought to minimize the import of the reported losses by falsely describing the losses as "nonrecurring," that is, a one-time or unusual earnings event. Enron also disclosed the same day an approximate $1.2 billion reduction in shareholder equity, which Lay again sought to minimize by falsely attributing it to the unwind of the Raptor vehicles, rather than to an accounting error. According to the indictment, on October 12, Lay misled a representative of a national credit rating agency about the need to take additional writedowns and the extent of Enron's goodwill problems. On both October 16 and 23, Lay told the investing public that Enron had determined that its goodwill impairment was up to $200 million. However, he failed to disclose the impact on Enron of an additional goodwill impairment of up to $700 million in connection with Wessex. Also on October 23, Lay allegedly espoused faith in Elektro, a Brazilian power plant which Enron carried on its books as worth in excess of $2 billion. In fact, as Lay allegedly knew, Elektro was overvalued by up to $1 billion. Lay also allegedly distributed materials at the road shows that misleadingly described the value of the international portfolio as $6.5 billion. In reality, as Lay knew, this vastly overstated the true value of the international assets by billions of dollars.

These and other schemes alleged in the indictment quickly unraveled, and on Dec. 2, 2001, Enron filed for bankruptcy, making its stock, which less than a year earlier had been trading at over $80 per share, virtually worthless.

Lay was also charged in four counts with bank fraud and making false statements to three banks arising out of his obtaining and using four personal lines of credit worth over $60 million. Lay allegedly promised the banks that the loans would not be used to purchase stock. As a result of these false representations, the banks extended far greater loans to Lay than they otherwise would. The indictment alleges that in spite of his promises, Lay repeatedly used the lines of credit to buy the stock. The lines of credit were collateralized mainly by artificially inflated shares of Enron stock and were repaid with the same.

If convicted of all the charges in the indictment, Lay faces a maximum sentence of 175 years in prison and millions of dollars in fines.

Criminal indictments are only charges and not evidence of guilt. A defendant is presumed to be innocent unless and until proven guilty.

The investigation into Enron's collapse is being conducted by the Enron Task Force, a team of federal prosecutors supervised by the Justice Department's Criminal Division and agents from the FBI and the IRS Criminal Investigations Division. The Task Force also has coordinated with and received considerable assistance from the Securities and

Exchange Commission. The Enron Task Force is part of President Bush's Corporate Fraud Task Force, created in July 2002 to investigate allegations of fraud and corruption at U.S. corporations.

Thirty-one defendants have been charged to date, including 21 former Enron executives. Eleven defendants have been convicted to date, including former CFO Andrew Fastow and former Treasurer Ben Glisan. To date, the Enron Task Force has restrained more than $161 million in proceeds derived from criminal activity. The Task Force investigation is continuing.

Source: U.S. Department of Justice. "Former Enron Chairman and Chief Executive Officer Kenneth L. Lay Charged with Conspiracy, Fraud, False Statements." Press release, July 8, 2004. www.justice.gov/opa/pr/2004/July/04_crm_470.htm (accessed March 28, 2004).

Bush Administration on the U.S. AIDS Program

July 14, 2004

INTRODUCTION

Despite record levels of international funding, increased political commitment, and expanded access to treatment, the acquired immunodeficiency syndrome (AIDS) pandemic continued to spread in 2004. The disease continued its deadly sweep through sub-Saharan Africa, where 25 million people were estimated to be infected with the human immunodeficiency virus (HIV), which caused AIDS. But infection rates were now growing alarmingly fast in other regions of the world, with international experts fearing that HIV/AIDS was nearing a critical point in China, India, and Russia, which together accounted for nearly half the world's population. "The virus is running faster than all of us," Peter Piot said July 6. Piot, a Belgian physician and epidemiologist, was executive director of UNAIDS, the United Nations program that sought to coordinate the international response to the epidemic. Piot's assessment came while releasing the program's annual report on the global AIDS epidemic.

Amid the bleak news, there were a few small signs of progress. Prominent leaders in a handful of African countries publicly acknowledged the loss of family members to AIDS. Among the leaders were Zimbabwe's president, Robert Mugabe, and Mangosuthu Buthelezi, the head of South Africa's Inkatha Freedom Party. AIDS experts welcomed these acknowledgments, saying they helped break the stigma that surrounded AIDS and the accompanying taboo about discussing the disease and its causes in public.

In Malawi, political leaders went one step further, openly competing for votes among HIV/AIDS victims and their families and promising to provide free medical treatment. In Botswana, where nearly four of every ten adults were infected with HIV, the government ordered routine HIV testing for every person coming into a health clinic or hospital in an effort to help control the spread of the disease.

In a major policy shift, China announced in April that it would offer free HIV testing to all its citizens. The health ministry also promised to cover the treatment costs for poor people found to have the virus. It was unclear whether China would have the resources to follow through on its promise, however, particularly in rural areas where most of the people were poor and health care was inadequate.

Quickening Pace of the Epidemic

Almost 5 million people were newly infected with HIV in 2003, the greatest number in a single year since the epidemic began in the 1980s, according to UNAIDS. The number of people living with HIV had grown from 35 million in 2001 to 38 million in 2003. About 3 million people died from AIDS in 2003; more than 20 million had died since 1981. In its November update, the agency estimated about the same number of new infections and deaths for 2004, bringing the number of people living with HIV to 39.4 million. (The numbers reported were slightly lower than in the past, UNAIDS said, because it had revised its estimates for 2001 and 2003 based on improved methodologies. It cautioned that comparing the 2003 estimates with any estimates for previous years other than the revised 2001 estimates could be misleading.)

More than one-fifth of the new infections came in Asia, where an estimated 8.2 million people, most of them in India, were living with HIV. The disease was spreading fastest in East Asia, with the rate of new infections rising by almost 50 percent in just two years. Countries most at risk were China, where HIV had spread to all thirty-one provinces; Indonesia; and Vietnam. Eastern Europe and Central Asia were also experiencing quickly expanding epidemics, fueled by injecting drug use among young adults.

The worst-hit region continued to be sub-Saharan Africa, where 25 million were living with HIV; in other words, the region had 10 percent of the world's population but two-thirds of all people living with HIV. Although HIV prevalence rates appeared to have stabilized, UNAIDS said that was deceptive, caused by a rise in AIDS deaths coupled with a continued increase in new infections.

Speaking at the Woodrow Wilson International Center in Washington on November 30, Piot warned that the AIDS epidemics in China, India, and Russia were "perilously close to a tipping point" that could turn them "from a series of concentrated outbreaks and hot spots into a generalized explosion across the entire population," much like the way AIDS spread across sub-Saharan Africa. Piot observed that HIV prevalence was still low in those countries and still largely confined to high-risk populations. But, he said, "the tipping point is not a hypothetical construct. In South Africa, it took five years for prevalence rates to move from 0.5 percent to 1 percent. Then, in only seven years, it jumped from 1 percent to 20 percent." He added, "If the epidemic gains a foothold even in a few states or provinces in China and India, and spreads there as it has in some African countries, the global resources now available for Africa could easily diminish or perhaps even vanish."

"Feminization" of the Epidemic

International AIDS officials also sought to focus attention on the vulnerability of women to HIV infection and AIDS. Since 1985 the percentage of women HIV/AIDS patients had risen from 35 percent to 48 percent, as an increasing number of apparently low-risk women were infected by men who had been infected through high-risk behavior, perhaps years before. "This is an emerging pattern [that] has profound implications," Piot said. "We have to put women at the heart of the response to AIDS if we want to stop this epidemic." Piot was speaking on November 23 as UNAIDS released its latest update on the epidemic in anticipation of World AIDS Day, December 1. The problem was most evident in sub-Saharan Africa, where 57 percent of adult HIV victims were women, and 75 percent of those ages fifteen to twenty-four were women. From 2002 to 2004, the report said, infection rates among women either rose or stayed the same in all regions.

Women's financial dependence on men, their inferior social status, the infidelity of husbands, and fear of violence from the men in their lives made it more difficult for women in many regions of the world to negotiate safe sex; thus they were more vulnerable to infection. At the same time, women also bore much of the burden of caring for family members with the disease. Girls were withdrawn from school to provide care or because the family could no longer afford school fees; widows and others often turned to the sex trade as a much-needed source of income.

Although awareness had increased substantially, ignorance about the disease was still high throughout the world. Even where women were aware of prevention strategies, they often did not have the power to use them. "The prevention strategies are missing the point. Women do not have the economic power or social choices over their lives to put the information into practice," said Kathleen Cravero, deputy director of UNAIDS. "We tell women to abstain when they have no right. We tell them to be faithful when they cannot ask their partners to be faithful. We tell them to use a condom when they have no power to do so," Cravero said, referring to the "ABC principles" (abstain, be faithful, use a condom) that had been deployed to some effect in Uganda's successful campaign to control AIDS. The controversial ABC principles had also been adopted as part of the Bush administration's initiative to fight AIDS in fifteen developing countries in Africa, Asia, and the Caribbean.

One example of women's second-class status was preliminary evidence that indicated women received anti-AIDS drugs less often than men, particularly where there was a charge for the drugs. According to Piot, women often either did not have the money or could not get it from their husbands. Piot said that microbicides—substances that could kill the HIV virus during intercourse and that women could use without their partner's knowledge—would be essential in protecting women. Although not yet available, three types of microbicides were entering their final testing phase. Piot also said that protecting women from HIV would require societies to address not only sexual norms but also laws such as those governing property ownership and inheritance that kept women dependent on men.

Funding and AIDS Drugs

One bright spot in the AIDS story was a significant increase in global resources in 2004. Spending on prevention and treatment in developing countries grew 30 percent, to $6.1 billion, in 2004. Half of that came from the stricken countries themselves, the other half was contributed by wealthier countries. Projections of how much was needed to fight the epidemic were climbing along with the infection rate, however. In 2002 UNAIDS said $10 billion a year would be needed by 2005; that estimate was raised in 2004 to $12 billion, in part because funding delays in fighting the disease meant more people were stricken and needed care, and in part because the planned campaign was more comprehensive than it once was.

One breakthrough that made treatment dollars go further came late in 2003 when former president Bill Clinton announced that the Clinton Foundation had negotiated a deal with four generic drug manufacturers to bring the per-patient cost of the combination drug antiretrovirals (ARVs) down to about $140 a year, from about $300, in return for a guaranteed customer base. In January 2004 Clinton announced new deals that would sharply discount the price of two tests that diagnosed HIV/AIDS in the thirteen countries of Africa and the Caribbean where the Clinton Foundation was working. The tests, routinely used in the West, help to determine when to start ARV treatment for AIDS patients and to monitor the effectiveness of the drug therapy. In April Clinton announced that his foundation would negotiate contracts for the inexpensive generic drugs with any country that had UN or World Bank grants to fight AIDS, even if the country was not one where the foundation currently worked. *(Generic drugs, Historic Documents of 2002, p. 780)*

The Clinton Foundation's action may have hastened a change in the Bush administration's policy on AIDS drugs that had been sharply criticized in forums around the world. That policy prevented U.S. tax dollars from being spent to buy drugs whose safety and quality had not been approved by the federal Food and Drug Administration (FDA), even though the World Health Organization (WHO) had listed several generics that met its quality and safety standards. In essence, the policy meant that U.S. funds could be used only to buy patented medicines produced by the giant pharmaceutical companies; those drugs cost about four times as much as generics. As a result, far fewer people would receive ARV treatment under the U.S. program. Critics noted that the head of President Bush's Emergency Plan for AIDS Relief, Randall Tobias, was a former chief executive of the drug maker Eli Lilly. They said the policy was a thinly disguised means of throwing business to the politically powerful American drug industry.

After several months of adverse criticism, the administration relented. On May 16 Tommy G. Thompson, secretary of the Health and Human Services Department (HHS), announced "an expedited review process" in which generic companies could seek approval for their combination drugs from the FDA. "Drug patent issues that apply in developed nations should not impede purchase of these drugs for developing countries," Thompson said in a statement. He added that FDA approval should take between two and six weeks and that the $500,000 approval fee could be waived. In addition to making U.S. funding for generics available, the announcement was likely to spur collaboration among major pharmaceutical companies on producing combination ARVs, something the companies currently did not do because no one company held all the patents on the drugs used in the combination.

Stephen Lewis, the UN special envoy on HIV/AIDS in Africa, said the announcement was "an unexpected and excellent move." But other elements of the administration's program for fighting AIDS remained controversial. An announcement by HHS that it was cutting back significantly on the government experts it sent to the 2004 international AIDS conference in Bangkok in July was seen by many as payback for the heckling Thompson endured in 2002 at the last international AIDS conference in Barcelona, Spain. Denying those allegations, HHS officials said the department was simply attempting to cut travel expenses. One government official who declined to be identified told the *Washington Post* that the cutback sent the message "that the U.S. wants to be engaged, but the U.S. wants to call the shots." *(2002 conference, Historic Documents of 2002, p. 469)*

Other critics took issue with the administration's insistence on earmarking a substantial portion of its international AIDS funding for abstinence campaigns, saying that these campaigns often depicted condoms as unreliable and withheld practical information on their use. "Governments should be promoting condom use, not treating condoms like contraband," said Jonathan Cohen of Human Rights Watch. "The clear result of restricting access to condoms will be more lives lost to AIDS." Speaking on July 14 at the international AIDS conference in Bangkok, Tobias defended the effectiveness of abstinence campaigns but said no one method was enough to prevent the spread of AIDS. "Abstinence works, being faithful works, condoms work. Each has its place," Tobias said during his speech at the Bangkok conference. Tobias further stressed the need for donor countries and organizations to work with local officials to find the prevention and treatment strategies that were likely to be most effective given each individual country's cultural mores and health care capacity.

The World Health Organization also came in for some harsh criticism in 2004, as questions arose about whether it could meet its goal of providing ARV treatment to 3 million HIV patients in poor countries by the end of 2005. According to WHO, about 440,000 people were receiving the treatment in mid-2004. That was twice as many as in 2002 but 60,000 fewer than WHO had hoped to be treating by midyear. The program, known as 3 by 5 (for 3 million by 2005), was announced in 2003, and some observers said even then that it was too ambitious. A more damning view came July 9 when Joep Lange, cochair of the Bangkok conference and president of the International AIDS Society, told the BBC news agency that the target was "inflated" and "totally unrealistic." WHO's general director, Lee Jong Wook, said that WHO could not fail to meet the target because "the collective response to the HIV/AIDS pandemic is the benchmark by which our generation will be judged."

AIDS in the United States

In the United States, 950,000 people were living with HIV in 2003, up 50,000 from 2001, according to the UNAIDS report released in July. A federal government program was launched in 2001 to "break the back" of the AIDS epidemic by 2005 by cutting the number of new infections in half. Even so, infection rates remained about the same in the United States, at roughly 40,000 a year. More than 18,000 Americans died of AIDS in 2003.

HIV infection rates appeared to be rising again among young gay men who were not practicing safe sex, apparently lulled into complacency by "prevention fatigue" and the availability of antiretroviral drugs that allowed many HIV patients to lead healthy, productive lives. But the biggest increases were among African American women. They accounted for 72 percent of new HIV cases among women from 1999 to 2002, according to government statistics for twenty-nine states. Black woman accounted for half of all HIV infections in men and women acquired through heterosexual sex during the time period.

Researchers said black women were more likely than other women to be infected because there was a higher rate of HIV infection in the black population compared with the general population. Blacks made up 12 percent of the population but 42 percent of all people living with HIV. Blacks also were the least likely ethnic group to have partners of different races. "A high prevalence of infection in the pool of potential partners can spread sexually transmitted infections rapidly within the ethnic group and keep it there," said Adaora Adimora, an infectious disease physician at the University of North Carolina.

One reason for the high incidence of HIV in African American women, according to some researchers, was the high HIV infection rate in gay and bisexual black men, which was six times that of whites and four times that of Hispanics, according to a 2001 report from the federal Centers for Disease Control and Prevention. Because homosexuality was frowned upon in the black community, many bisexual black men lived on "the down-low"—conducting secret relationships with men and public relationships with women. Other studies showed that 30 percent of all black bisexual men might be infected with HIV, and as many as 90 percent of them might be unaware of their infection. "Most women don't even know they're at risk," said one observer. "They find out when their spouse dies, or when they deliver a sick baby."

Following are excerpts from a speech delivered July 14, 2004, by Randall Tobias, head of President Bush's Emergency Plan for AIDS Relief, at the 2004 international conference on HIV/AIDS in Bangkok, Thailand.

"Global Fight Against HIV/AIDS"

Good afternoon.

The theme of this Conference is Access for All.

I have been thinking a great deal about that theme over the past week as I have met with different people coming from very different perspectives. . . .

But Access for All is not just about this conference, it is a challenge that we must carry forward in our work every day. The United States is working to involve people living with HIV and AIDS in the work of our country teams implementing the President's Emergency Plan, and we have exercised our leadership in the Global Fund to help ensure that Country Coordinating Mechanisms will have not just representation, but the true involvement of people living with AIDS and HIV around the world. . . .

The involvement of small local organizations in the President's global effort, such as those representing people living with AIDS and HIV, is vital to the Emergency Plan's effectiveness. For that reason, we will soon be launching pilot programs in a number of countries that will allow small groups to apply directly to the U.S. Embassies' country teams for rapid approval on small grants. The idea of this program is to ensure that small and effective organizations that are doing some of the best work on the ground, can get money fast to address urgent needs within their communities.

Speaking of access for all, listening to one another and hearing what those on the ground are saying to us about the fight against this disease brings me to another point. When we say we are listening, and we say those on the ground know best, then we must surely listen and learn from the man who has led one of the most successful and pivotal battles against this disease.

Ugandan President Yoweri Museveni has, largely by sheer leadership and will, fought back this disease in his country with an A-B-C prevention focus. We must learn from his leadership in the fight against AIDS. Abstinence works . . . Being Faithful works . . . Condoms work. Each has its place.

I want to get something straight about the U.S. position on prevention, because there seems to be a lot of confusion and misinformation. Preventing AIDS is not a multiple-choice test—there is no one right answer to preventing the spread of this pandemic. Those who want to simplify the solution to just one method—any one method—do not understand the complexity of the problem.

And let me go further. Anyone who believes AIDS can be defeated by *just* these three means of prevention alone surely underestimates the challenges we as a world community face in trying to save people from the ravages of this disease.

The years ahead are going to require exceptional leadership to meet the special needs of individual countries. Prevention will require us to empower women. Prevention will require us to compassionately assist drug users in liberating themselves from their dark addictions. Prevention will require us to find many ways to give hope to communities devastated by pain, suffering and loss.

The President's Emergency Plan itself cannot be reduced to simplistic descriptions. It was designed to adapt to the needs of different nations, the trend of the epidemic in each nation and the needs of individuals within those nations.

From its foundational principles, our plan will grow and integrate into each nation and community, as host governments, local leaders, people living with AIDS and HIV, aid workers and activists help us to define the implementation of the plan for their people.

The President's Emergency Plan for AIDS Relief, from the very beginning, has recognized that to implement an effective prevention strategy, our approach must be based very specifically on what works in each place we are working, with the individuals and groups we are targeting.

For instance, unlike most of our other focus nations, Vietnam's HIV/AIDS epidemic has been fueled by intravenous drug use. As we develop our country plan, we will be looking at ways to educate those who inject drugs about the added risk of HIV/AIDS, and exploring means to support drug abuse prevention and treatment.

On another key issue, trafficking and prostitution facilitate the spread of HIV/AIDS. The U.S. Government is opposed to prostitution and related activities, which are inherently harmful and dehumanizing, and contribute to the phenomenon of trafficking in persons.

But to address another matter of some confusion, it is important to note that U.S. law—and the President's Emergency Plan—*do* allow the provision of HIV/AIDS prevention, treatment and care services to the victims of prostitution or sex trafficking. . . .

So, you see, this initiative is not simply a matter of money—although $15 billion over five years is the largest financial commitment ever, by any nation, for any major international health initiative dedicated to a single disease.

This initiative is about action. President Bush has insisted that we stop talking about the reasons we couldn't do anything to stop AIDS, that we figure out what we can do, and then do it—with urgency. He has made crystal clear to me that "business as usual" can no longer be the order of the day. And stamping out business as usual includes many things—including the need to stop thinking about prevention in single-minded, one-approach-fits-all simplistic terms.

For instance, we believe that prevention messages are most effective when delivered in culturally appropriate ways. That is one reason why the President's Emergency Plan emphasizes working with indigenous organizations as partners. I am very pleased that at this point, 61% of the current partners we're working with on the ground are indigenous organizations.

When we speak of access for all, we must think about how we can best reach the places and people who most need access to our help. They cannot always find us.

When you think of the people who live in the most remote regions and in the most hopeless slums—who has been there to help them?

Who already has people on the ground who are trusted?

Who will help those who must persevere in the face of being stigmatized in their own communities?

And who will help replace stigma with compassion and understanding?

The fact is that among those indigenous organizations, the Buddhist temples and the monasteries, the churches, the mosques and the synagogues are among those who have gone where no one else would go. They have built trust and provided hope to generations of individuals in places where hope is scarce.

Last week I met with a Buddhist Monk in Vietnam who has started a home for children in Ho Chi Minh City. Many of those children are living with AIDS. He talked with me about the children's desperate need for treatment, but he also talked about how these children are finding hope and some relief through the work of his program.

Yesterday, I visited the Mercy Center to spend time with the HIV-positive children who have been taken off the streets of Bangkok by Father Joe's enormous compassion. While I was there, I also spent some time with people who are benefiting from a very innovative program. . . . With funding assistance from a United States initiative, this program is providing micro-loans for start up businesses in the Bangkok slums. What's also different about this program is that to qualify, the businesses have to involve a partnership between one person who is HIV positive and another who is HIV negative.

In Ethiopia, I met with the Patriarch of the Ethiopian Orthodox Church. About 40 million people are members of the Church—more than one-half of the people in the country. We're partnering with them because they represent a highly motivated way to reach people, including young people, with prevention messages, and because they have a level of credibility in the country that foreigners simply don't have.

If we were to work in developing countries but refuse to work with faith-based organizations, we would be harming our ability to save lives—and that is just incomprehensible to us.

Another reason to rely heavily on indigenous partners in all facets of our work is to ensure sustainability of the program. We will increasingly ask our large international NGO [nongovernmental organization] partners to provide "exit strategies"—plans for including training and capacity building in their work so they will eventually be able to turn over their efforts to local providers and move on to other projects. Local ownership of this fight is essential if the programs we build are to be sustainable in the long term, as they must be. As someone said to me very recently, we must provide both fish and fishing poles. And we intend to promote this philosophy in our own programs, and to advocate it through our leadership in the Global Fund and other international organizations.

But local ownership must be supported by local leadership, and the United States will continue to support leadership on this issue from public officials at all levels. I have a personal story that shows how what seems like a small, unique gesture can become a significant show of leadership.

Ethiopia is one of the focus countries in which America is making an especially large investment of resources and attention. On a recent visit there, I was invited to "cut the ribbon" at a new HIV testing center that has been established with U.S. support in a public hospital operated by the city of Addis Ababa. I was delighted to do so, because reducing the stigma around testing, and making it more widely available and a routine part of health care in severely affected countries, is simply essential.

In order to draw the attention of community leaders to their role in eliminating stigma, in my remarks, I reported that I had been tested myself the day before, in another center in Ethiopia. I urged the local leaders to do the same, and then to make it known that they had been tested, and that it was the thing to do.

The Mayor of Addis Ababa, who is a tremendous leader on HIV/AIDS, was there with me at the event. He promptly announced that he was going to be tested himself following the ceremony, and he encouraged all the other political leaders there to do the same. Now a visiting American getting tested might be an interesting curiosity to the local media. But when the Mayor of the capital, one of the most important people in the whole country, got tested—and publicly said so—well, that was a big story! It was all over the local media. And because of his leadership example, the effects multiplied as more and more leaders came forward to be tested in the days that followed.

On one level, that's a story about encouraging testing. But I see it as even more a story of leadership—leadership from within a society making the decision to fight the stigma and taboo that surround HIV/AIDS.

More money is necessary. Wise programming is critical. But without real leadership—on the part of everyone involved—we will lose this fight.

I believe any fair-minded person, looking at the history of the response over the last 20 years, would conclude that the world was far too slow to take up this fight with the focus it deserves. And when I say "the world," I mean in particular the developed world, including the United States.

In the past, we in the developed world displayed ignorance, or even apathy, about the global dimensions and intricacies of the AIDS crisis. Over time, I believe awareness grew and apathy turned to empathy. Empathy is important—but it is really not enough.

So I believe we all need to acknowledge the inadequacy of the world's response. But I also believe that it is time—in fact, it is past time—to move forward from this point. Too much time has been lost already.

At this point, perhaps the most critical mistake we can make is to allow this pandemic to divide us. We are striving toward the same goal—a world free of HIV/AIDS. When 8,000 lives are lost to AIDS every day, division is a luxury we cannot afford.

I recently visited Mozambique, one of the countries where the U.S. is dramatically increasing our investment. I visited a woman living in a very resource-poor setting. Tragically, she was on the verge of passing away from AIDS. Sitting on the edge of her mother's mattress was the woman's daughter, perhaps 5 years old. I asked the home-care volunteer who was present during my visit who would be taking care of that little girl when her mother was gone. She told me no one had an answer. Her father had also passed away from AIDS, and it was not clear that anyone in her extended family would be able to help.

A mother passes away.

A child is orphaned.

One family's tragedy reflects the devastation that this epidemic is bringing to bear. Every day, thousands are suffering and dying like that woman, but each one has a name. Thousands are losing their parents—and much of their hope for a better life—like that little girl.

When I insist that we put our differences aside and focus on the real enemy, I do not ask that we do it for our own benefit. I ask that we do it for that woman, that little girl. They deserve nothing less.

Let me say this as directly as I can: HIV/AIDS is the real enemy. The denial, stigma, and complacency that fuel HIV/AIDS—these too are real enemies. It is morally imperative that we direct our energies at these enemies, not at one another. We may not agree on every tactic employed by every donor and we may have passionate opinions about how things can be done better, but we must work with each other to find the best solutions, while knowing that every person in this fight simply wants to save lives. That is a noble calling, and should be appreciated and respected.

The United States has decisively turned the corner, from the eras of apathy and empathy, to a new era of compassionate action. We have willingly assumed the leadership role in this fight.

The President's budget to fight global HIV and AIDS for next year, Fiscal Year 2005, reflects an increase of almost three and a half times from that of Fiscal Year 2001.

And we're moving with urgency. Almost exactly a year ago, the President asked me to become the United States Global AIDS Coordinator. Five months ago, we received the first funding from Congress. Three weeks later we began to commit those funds. Already we are seeing results.

We have not even hit our first reporting period, but we do have some anecdotal information—so please do not consider this to be all inclusive of our activities.

Within days of receiving funding, we were traveling by motor scooter to deliver antiretroviral drugs to people in their homes in rural Uganda. Within weeks, we were doubling the number of patients on ARVs [antiretroviral drugs] in urban Uganda. We put 500 people on therapy at just one site in Kenya. One of our treatment partners has begun therapy for another 500 hundred patients in just two countries, and they are enrolling more patients at a rate of 220 per week. Another partner mentioned to us just yesterday that they will begin delivering ARVs at multiple centers next week, expanding to nine countries rapidly. We have ordered and are receiving drug treatments in nearly all of our focus countries.

America is providing leadership in the fight to keep HIV-positive people alive by providing anti-retroviral drugs. Not just any drugs, but safe and effective drugs. I have consistently and repeatedly expressed our intent to provide, through the Emergency Plan, AIDS drugs that are acquired at the lowest possible cost, regardless of origin or who produces them, as long as we know they are safe, effective, and of high quality. These drugs may include brand name products, generics, or copies of brand name products.

The United States has a stringent regulatory authority to assess the safety and efficacy of the drugs sold within its borders. It is a moral imperative that families in programs funded by the United States in the developing world have the same assurances as American families that the drugs they use are safe and effective. America will not have one health standard for her own citizens and a lower standard of "good enough" for those suffering elsewhere.

In order to speed drugs to the fight against HIV/AIDS, the Bush Administration has taken action to allow any drug company in the world to seek accelerated review of AIDS drugs from the U.S. Food and Drug Administration (FDA).

This new FDA process includes the review of applications from companies who are manufacturing copies of antiretroviral drugs—alone or in fixed dose combinations—for sale in developing nations, as well as applications from the research-based companies that developed the already-approved individual therapies and want to put them into fixed dose combinations. The FDA has reached out to manufacturers in both categories and will even waive the application fee when necessary, in light of the global AIDS emergency.

When a new combination drug for AIDS treatment receives a positive outcome under this expedited FDA review, I will recognize that result as evidence of the safety and efficacy of that drug. Thus the drug will be eligible for funding by the President's

Emergency Plan, so long as international patent agreements and local government policies allow their purchase.

I call on each of you today to urge every company manufacturing these drugs to file their applications as soon as possible so we can begin funding these drugs as soon as possible.

At this point in the development of our bilateral plan, as well as the multilateral programs we support, the availability of drugs—though very important—is far from being the main constraint on our work. The major challenge is one that is becoming widely recognized: the need for human capacity and infrastructure that can accommodate our investment. Ignoring those limitations means wasting money and failing to solve problems.

In places like Africa, the Caribbean, and Southeast Asia, there is a desperate lack of health care workers and infrastructure. African leaders understand this, sometimes better than we from the developing world do. All the AIDS drugs in the world won't do any good if they're stuck in warehouses with no place to go to actually be part of the delivery of treatment to those in need.

In the U.S., we have 279 physicians for every 100,000 people.

In Mozambique, however, there are only 2.6 physicians for every 100,000 people. That means that just 500 physicians serve the needs of the entire country—a population of 18 million.

In some countries, the "brain-drain" of trained medical personnel is an enormous problem. In Ethiopia, where there are only 2.9 physicians for every 100,000 people, a physician there told me recently that there are more Ethiopian-trained physicians practicing today in Chicago than in all of Ethiopia.

We have to find solutions for these human resource issues, including the development of new models for the treatment and care of patients. Obviously, without making progress on the capacity issue, our ability to deliver prevention, treatment and care is quite limited. That's why, especially in these early years, the President's Emergency Plan is making a tremendous investment in training and infrastructure. Improving capacity is essential for all efforts to be sustainable in these countries for the long term.

After 20 years fighting HIV/AIDS worldwide, America has a wealth of experience, infrastructure and relationships. Thus we are in a particularly strong position to help address the capacity issue. Our experience on the ground is allowing us both to implement our own Emergency Plan with urgency, and to assist our multinational partners, such as the Global Fund, in building their programs.

To cite just one example, the U.S. has quickly trained 14,700 health workers and built capacity at over 900 different health care sites, as part of our "prevention of mother-to-child transmission" programs in just 18 months. But let's look beyond the numbers, at what that training and capacity-building has meant to one woman in Guyana.

Brenda, already a mother of one child, attended her first antenatal visit in her second pregnancy. During group counseling, her health visitor—trained by the United States—discussed transmission of HIV from mothers to infants and ways to reduce the risk of this transmission. In the individual session, Brenda who was about twelve weeks pregnant, went through pre-test counseling on HIV, and agreed to be tested.

Brenda did not attend the clinic for two months, because she was experiencing great difficulties in finding a stable place to live, since she had severed her relationship with her partner. During her second visit, the nurse shared her HIV test result. Unfortunately, the form was stamped "HIV antibodies detected."

That was a difficult moment—one that I know many in this room have experienced. Brenda reacted with disbelief and then hurt, as anyone would. But caring health workers calmed her, reassuring her that she could live a healthy life with HIV. When Brenda told her mother and siblings, they overcame their shock and encouraged her to go through the U.S.-supported program to protect against transmission to her child.

Brenda received further counseling at the clinic and joined a support group of HIV positive mothers. Four hours before delivery, Brenda received the single-dose antiretroviral prophylaxis, and the baby received a pediatric dose of nevirapine. Her baby is now HIV free.

After giving birth, Brenda became an advocate and community educator for the Network of People Living with HIV/AIDS in Guyana. Brenda says, "Today, I can use myself as an example to talk to other women about HIV/AIDS. I am not ashamed of my condition, and I feel that I can use my experience to help others."

Once again, it all started with training health visitors—without those people, and the places for them to work, none of this would have been possible. That's exactly the kind of effect we want our capacity-building work to have—to save people from HIV and its effects, and to build sustainable leadership in their communities. America is proud to be a partner in building a better life for people like Brenda—and her baby.

Since I mentioned our multinational partners, let me note that bilateral U.S. programs, while a critical part of the President's Emergency Plan, are by no means all of it. Our strategy aims to increase the overall chances of success by pursuing multiple approaches to this complex emergency—supporting and partnering with individuals, community and faith-based organizations, host governments, and multilateral institutions like the Global Fund and the United Nations. We want to use every means at our disposal to address this crisis, and that is what we are doing.

The Bush Administration took the lead in helping to found the Global Fund. The U.S. Secretary of Health and Human Services, Tommy Thompson, serves as the Chairman of its Board. The Global Fund is a young venture and still maturing, but we consider it a very promising vehicle and a critically important part of the work that all of us are doing—including the implementation of the President's Emergency Plan. The U.S. is working with the Global Fund to build capacity on the ground so that more of the Fund's money can begin to flow and to reach those who need it.

America is the world's largest contributor to the Fund—making thirty-six percent of all pledges to date. The Fund offers a vehicle for other donors to substantially increase their commitment to this fight, as the United States has done.

Once again, I must speak directly. This year America is spending nearly twice as much to fight global AIDS as the rest of the world's donor governments combined. By its actions, the United States has challenged the rest of the world to take action.

Please—join with us in our deepened commitment to the global fight against HIV/AIDS.

My hope is that in the future, we will look back at the year 2004, and this Bangkok conference, as a turning point into an era of compassionate action—not only by America, but by the whole world.

All of us share a great responsibility, and time is short.

May we all come together, in a spirit of heightened commitment and cooperation, to focus our energies on doing what we must to win this fight—on behalf of the people of the world who so desperately need our help.

Thank you very much.

Source: U.S. Department of State. "Global Fight Against HIV/AIDS: What Do We Need to Do Differently?" Prepared remarks of Ambassador Randall L. Tobias, U.S. Global AIDS Coordinator. July 14, 2004, Bangkok, Thailand. www.state.gov/s/gac/rl/rm/2004/34366.htm (accessed April 5, 2005).

President Bush on Signing Project BioShield Act

July 21, 2004

INTRODUCTION

Three years after a small but deadly anthrax attack alerted the nation to the dangers of terrorism carried out by biological weapons, the federal government in 2004 took a potentially significant step to guarantee the availability of vaccines and other medicines to respond to a future attack. Project BioShield, legislation proposed in 2003 by President George W. Bush and enacted by Congress in July, provided $5.6 billion over ten years for medicines and equipment to treat Americans in the event of a terrorist attack using anthrax or some other biological weapon.

The legislation was not an immediate or full cure for the nation's vulnerability to bioterrorism, however. The first new anthrax vaccines were not scheduled to be delivered until 2006, and it was unclear whether the promise of federal funding would be enough to encourage private industry to enter the risky field of developing medicines that might not be needed for years, if ever.

New studies released during the year said the federal and state governments were becoming better prepared to respond to a terrorist attack using biological weapons, but more progress was needed. *(Background, Historic Documents of 2003, p. 903)*

Ricin Fears

Congress received an unwanted spur to action on bioterrorism when the deadly poison ricin was discovered in the mailroom of the Senate Majority Leader Bill Frist, R-Tenn. On February 2, 2004, an intern working in Frist's mailroom in the Dirksen Senate Office Building noticed a tiny amount of an unusual powder, ordered his colleagues out of the room, and called Capitol police. The powder was quickly identified as ricin, a poison made from castor beans that could be fatal if injected under the skin (and could cause illness if inhaled or eaten); there was no known antidote for it.

The police ordered the temporary evacuation of the three Senate office buildings just north of the Capitol. No one was injured, but Frist, a medical doctor, immediately said that "somebody in all likelihood manufactured it with intent to harm." Subsequent tests by government laboratories produced few clues as to the ricin's origin, reportedly because the amount found in Frist's office was so small. No real progress in the investigation had been reported by year's end.

Officials said ricin had also been discovered at two other locations in late 2003. In October a small vial of ricin was found in a mail facility in South Carolina. The ricin was included in an envelope marked with a warning, "RICIN POISON." The envelope also contained a letter, signed "Fallen Angel," complaining about new federal regulations on the long-distance trucking industry. In November a vial of ricin was sent to, but did not reach, the White House.

The ricin discovery in Frist's office revived fears on Capitol Hill, where dozens of staffers had been among those exposed in late 2001 to an even deadlier anthrax poison, which someone had mailed to congressional and news media offices. Five people died, and more than a dozen other people were sickened, after handling anthrax-laden letters. The suburban Maryland postal facility that had processed mail for Congress and other government agencies had reopened in December 2003 after an extensive fumigation and installation of new equipment. A large-scale investigation had failed to identify the perpetrator of the anthrax attack, which authorities attributed to domestic, rather than foreign, terrorism. In fact, FBI officials said in 2004 that the investigation had been hindered by an inability to recreate the exact anthrax powder used in that attack. *(Anthrax attack, Historic Documents of 2001, p. 674)*

The FBI had devoted much of its investigation of the anthrax attacks to locating U.S. scientists who had worked on programs to develop biological weapons or defenses against them. Steven J. Hatfill, a former army scientist who was subjected to repeated searches in the case, on July 14 sued the *New York Times* and columnist Nicholas D. Kristof, saying he had been defamed as the "likely culprit." Kristof had written columns pointing toward Hatfill, even while saying there was no physical evidence linking him to the anthrax attacks. Hatfill in 2003 had sued Attorney General John Ashcroft and the FBI on similar grounds after Ashcroft identified him as a "person of interest" in the case. At an October 7 hearing on Hatfill's suit agains the government, U.S. District Court Judge Reggie B. Walton appeared to side with the former scientist, telling prosecutors in an angry voice: "If you don't have enough to indict this man, then it's wrong to drag his name through the mud." Walton also said he had read a sealed FBI affidavit that offered little hope the anthrax case would be resolved "in the near future." Both of Hatfill's suits were still pending at the end of 2004.

Suggestions that government-funded scientists might be involved in terrorism led the Department of Health and Human Services (HHS) to announce on March 4 the creation of a National Science Advisory Board for Biosecurity. That panel would develop recommendations for the conduct of biomedical research in ways that would guard against misuse, HHS secretary Tommy G. Thompson said.

Lack of Preparation for Bioterrorism

Concerns about U.S. vulnerability to bioterrorism had first been heightened after the 1991 Persian Gulf War, when United Nations weapons inspectors found evidence that Iraq had developed a large arsenal of biological weapons, including anthrax. Subsequent investigations in 2003–2004 determined that Iraq had destroyed those weapons shortly after that war, but in the intervening years it had been widely assumed outside Iraq that the weapons were still there. *(Iraqi weapons, p. 771)*

A small library of official and unofficial reports, starting in 1993 and continuing into 2004, concluded that the United States remained woefully ill-prepared to deal with attacks by biological weapons. These reports identified weaknesses both in military preparedness—for example, in the training and equipping of troops overseas—and in the protection and potential treatment of civilians within U.S. borders. *(Background, Historic Documents of 2002, p. 240)*

A congressionally mandated report, made public on January 22, focused on the Pentagon's preparations to counter bioterrorism. Conducted by the Institute of Medicine and the National Research Council, the report said the Pentagon had failed over the previous dozen years to develop any new vaccines against biological weapons and had made little progress in developing therapeutic drugs and antitoxins to protect armed forces personnel. President Bush had ordered troops immunized against anthrax and smallpox before the 2003 invasion of Iraq, but some service personnel resisted the shots on the grounds that the medicine was ineffective or even dangerous.

The General Accounting Office (GAO, later renamed the Government Accountability Office) reported to Congress on February 12 that most states had taken some steps since the 2001 anthrax scare to prepare for a major health emergency, such as a bioterror attack for an influenza pandemic. In most cases, however, these steps were limited to creating advisory committees and systems for alerting the public to broad health threats. Few states had developed regional or statewide plans to deal with a major health emergency, the GAO reported.

Another study of readiness at the state level was published on December 14 by a Washington, D.C., research organization, Trust for America's Health, headed by former senator and Connecticut governor Lowell P. Weicker Jr. The study ranked the states according to their abilities to respond to bioterrorism, natural disasters, and other public health emergencies. Florida and North Carolina—both of which regularly dealt with hurricanes, and were forced to do so in 2004—were ranked at the top. Alaska and Massachusetts were ranked at the bottom. The report said most states lacked adequate budgets to deal with bioterrorism and other threats, and it noted that one-third of the states had recently cut their spending on public health systems. "More than three years after 9/11 and the anthrax tragedies, we've made only baby steps toward better bioterrorism preparedness, rather than the giant leaps required to adequately protect the American people," Weicker said. Representatives of several of the states ranked low in the report took issue with the findings, insisting they were acting responsibly to protect their citizens.

Bush Executive Order

The *New York Times* reported on April 28 that Bush had signed a secret executive order a week earlier mandating a series of steps to counter biological terrorism. Among the actions, the *Times* said, was the creation of a common surveillance system to collect and analyze information about bioterror threats and a requirement for the Department of Homeland Security to conduct an assessment every two years on the risk of new biological threats, including genetically modified agents. Portions of Bush's order were made public at a news conference on April 29 with administration officials. The order resulted from a lengthy assessment of the government's bioterrorism responses, triggered by the 2001 anthrax attack.

Bush's executive order brought praise from some experts as a useful step, but some long-time critics of government preparedness said it failed to mandate necessary changes to make Americans safer. "It's not a strategy but a list of projects and goals," Tara O'Toole, a bioterrorism expert at the University of Pittsburgh Medical Center told the *Washington Post.* Rep. Jim Turner, D-Texas, the ranking Democrat on the House Select Committee on Homeland Security, said Bush's order also failed to specify "who is in charge of implementing a biodefense strategy."

Project BioShield

Bush had first proposed Project BioShield in his January 2003 State of the Union address. He said he would propose spending nearly $6 billion over a decade "to quickly make available effective vaccines and treatments against agents like anthrax, botulinum toxin, Ebola, and plague. We must assume that our enemies would use these diseases as weapons, and we must act before the dangers are upon us." *(Bush address, Historic Documents of 2003, p. 18)*

In a reversal of its usual procedures, Congress in 2003 included a $5.6 billion, ten-year appropriation for Bush's proposal in the fiscal 2004 separate spending bill for the Homeland Security Department, PL 108–90. However, crucial legislation authorizing the money and setting out the specifics of how it was to be used was delayed. The House passed a bill containing a version of Bush's proposal in July 2003, but in the Senate members of both parties raised concerns about congressional control of the spending, coordination of the program, and whether soldiers would be forced to test experimental medicines. After the ricin scare, a bipartisan coalition of senators worked in 2004 to make changes addressing those concerns, and on May 19 the Senate adopted the revised measure by a 99–0 vote. Majority Leader Frist recalled the anthrax attack and the discovery of ricin in his mailroom as evidence that the bill was needed. "Bioterror is here," he said. "It's on our own soil, hit this nation, hit this Capitol, hit the entire East Coast, and indeed it was deadly."

The House approved the Senate version on July 14, and Bush signed it into law (PL 108–276) on July 21. Its central provision authorized $5.6 billion over ten years, including $885 million for the first fiscal year (2004) to purchase and stockpile vaccines, antidotes, and diagnostic devices for dealing with biological weapons.

In signing the BioShield bill, Bush noted that the threat of bioterrorism had brought "new challenges" both to the government and to those who would deal with the results first-hand, including medical and emergency-response personnel. "Not long ago, few of these men and women could have imagined duties like monitoring the air for anthrax or delivering antibiotics on a massive scale," he said. "Yet, this is the world as we find it."

The legislation was considered a potential major boost for the biomedical industry, which did not have a commercial market for the medicines and equipment to combat biological terrorism. Some industry spokesmen said they would speed research, development, and production of treatments, some of which had been on hold pending adoption of the bill. Others, however, said they would move cautiously because the bill failed to resolve such questions as protection of patents and potential legal liability for side effects patients might experience after the emergency use of experimental medical products. Health care industry representatives also said the bill provided no funding or other incentives for hospitals to train personnel to administer new medicines in a bioterror emergency.

The first critical assessment of the new bill came in a report released October 12. Conducted by the Center for Biosecurity at the University of Pittsburgh Medical Center and the Sarnoff Corporation of Princeton, New Jersey, the study quoted a variety of experts in the field as saying the bill did not provide enough incentive for industry to create new vaccines and drugs to protect Americans against either a biological weapons attack or a major epidemic of a natural disease. The thirty academic, government, and industry experts consulted for the report said there was a "virtual certainty" of a natural epidemic of a new disease for which no drugs or vaccines yet existed. The experts were less certain about the odds of a biological weapons attack, but agreed, in any event, that the Project BioShield legislation was "not efficient to engage industry or to produce the countermeasures that will be ultimately needed." The study was funded by the army and the Alfred P. Sloan Foundation.

The first contract executed under the Project BioShield legislation was announced on November 3, when HHS secretary Thompson said the government would buy 75 million doses of a new generation anthrax vaccine. The purchase had been in the planning stages for more than a year while Congress worked on the bill. Under an $877.5 million contract, VaxGen Inc., of Brisbane, California, was to deliver doses to treat 25 million people by 2006, and doses for another 50 million people by 2007. The company had not yet obtained approval for its new drug from the Food and Drug Administration (FDA) and said it did not plan to seek approval until after it had delivered the full shipment in 2007. The Project BioShield law allowed use of the vaccine beforehand if the Centers for Disease Control and Prevention declared a health emergency. If successful, the vaccine would replace a much older one that had been used by the U.S. military. VaxGen was a spinoff from a much larger biotechnology company, Genentech Inc. Its vaccine had been developed by researchers at the Army's Medical Research Institute of Infectious Diseases.

Food as a Bioterror Weapon

As he announced his resignation on December 3, Secretary Thompson gave Americans yet another potential threat to worry about: the possibility that terrorists might inject poisons into the nation's food supply. "For the life of me, I cannot understand why the terrorists have not attacked our food supply because it is so easy to do," he said. Thompson said he worried about such an attack "every single night," and noted, as an example, the prospect that infected food might be imported from the Middle East.

Thompson's remark was greeted by both alarm and derision. Some terrorism experts said he voiced a legitimate fear that long had concerned them, as well, while food industry spokesmen sought to assure the public that the nation's food supply was safe. President Bush joined in the latter chorus, saying the government was "doing everything we can to protect the American people."

By coincidence, the FDA on December 6 announced long-planned regulations aimed at making it easier for the government to trace the source of food contamination—once it had occurred. The regulations required many of those involved in manufacturing, processing, transporting, and marketing foods to keep accurate records on the chain of supply and to present those records to the FDA upon request. Farmers and restaurants were exempted from the requirement. *(Food safety issues, p. 850)*

Thompson used the announcement of the new FDA rules to soften his earlier remark. "Our nation is now more prepared than ever before to protect the public against threats to the food supply," he said.

New Biolabs

A handful of experts began raising concerns in 2004 about the government's funding of fourteen new research laboratories to develop vaccines and other countermeasures against biological weapons. The new labs, called "hot labs" because they would conduct experiments with dangerous pathogens, were being funded by the National Institute of Allergy and Infectious Diseases (a part of the National Institutes of Health) and other federal agencies as part of the government's antiterrorism programs.

Two of the new labs were designated as "BioSafety Level 4" because they would handle the most dangerous germs. Those high-security labs were to be built at the Boston University School of Public Health, just outside of Boston, and at the University of Texas Medical Branch at Galveston. A dozen other laboratories were to be constructed or upgraded at other universities and government research centers.

Anthony Fauci, director of the National Institute of Allergy and Infectious Diseases, said the new labs were a vital addition to the nation's battle against bioterrorism. "We're training people who are going to be making vaccines, who are going to be looking at pathogenesis of microbes," he said.

Several prominent critics warned that the new laboratories would vastly increase the number of people studying pathogens and thus increase the risk that some of the dangerous material might escape or fall into the wrong hands. The most vocal critic was Richard H. Ebright, a chemistry professor at Rutgers University's Waksman Institute of Microbiology. "This does not make sense, no more than increasing the number of flight schools, increasing the number of flight-school trainees, and enveloping advanced tactics for air piracy would make sense as a response to 9/11," he told the *Boston Globe,* for an article published August 8. "We're spending money to increase our vulnerability." Ebright cited a 2001 study reporting on twenty-one biological weapons attacks around the world in recent decades, most of which were carried out by research or medical personnel. Fauci and other officials dismissed such worries. Even so, there was significant local opposition to the Boston University lab, construction of which was expected to begin in mid-2005.

Following are excerpts from remarks by President George W. Bush on July 21, 2004, upon signing the Project BioShield Act of 2004, which authorized $5.6 billion over ten years for the purchase of vaccines and other medicines and equipment to protect Americans in the event of a terrorist attack using biological weapons.

"Remarks on Signing the Project BioShield Act of 2004"

. . . On September the 11th, 2001, America saw the destruction and grief terrorists could inflict with commercial airlines turned into weapons of mass murder. Those attacks revealed the depth of our enemies' determination but not the extent of their ambitions. We know that the terrorists seek an even deadlier technology. And if they acquire chemical, biological, or nuclear weapons, we have no doubt they will use them to cause even greater harm.

The bill I am about to sign is an important element in our response to that threat. By authorizing unprecedented funding and providing new capabilities, Project BioShield will help America purchase, develop, and deploy cutting-edge defenses against catastrophic attack.

This legislation represents the collective foresight and considered judgment of United States Senators and Members of the House of Representatives from both political parties, many of whom experienced bioterror firsthand when anthrax and ricin were found on Capitol Hill. It reflects 18 months of hard work and cooperation by many dedicated public servants in Congress and in the White House. It sends a message about our direction in the war on terror: We refuse to remain idle while modern technology might be turned against us; we will rally the great promise of American science and innovation to confront the greatest danger of our time.

I want to thank the Vice President [Dick Cheney] for his hard work. He was the point man in the White House on this piece of legislation and did an excellent job. I appreciate Secretaries Tommy Thompson [Health and Human Services, HHS] and Tom Ridge [Homeland Security] for their leadership on this important piece of legislation as well.

I appreciate the [House] Speaker [J. Dennis Hastert, R-Ill.] and [Senate] Leader [Bill] Frist [R-Tenn.] for making this bill a priority. I want to thank Senator [Judd] Gregg [R-N.H.] and Senator [Edward M.] Kennedy [D-Mass.] and Senator [Thad] Cochran [R-Miss.] for working on this bill. I appreciate the efforts. I appreciate Congressmen [Joe] Barton [R-Texas], Billy Tauzin [R-La.], Chris Cox [R-Calif.], and Henry Waxman [D-Calif.] as well for their hard work.

I appreciate the members of my administration who are here. Thanks for coming. These will be the implementers of this important piece of legislation.

Project BioShield will transform our ability to defend the Nation in three essential ways. First, Project BioShield authorizes $5.6 billion over 10 years for the Government to purchase and stockpile vaccines and drugs to fight anthrax, smallpox, and other potential agents of bioterror. The Department of Health and Human Services has already taken steps to purchase 75 million doses of an improved anthrax vaccine for the Strategic National Stockpile. Under Project BioShield, HHS is moving forward with plans to acquire a safer, second-generation smallpox vaccine, an antidote to botulinum toxin, and better treatments for exposure to chemical and radiological weapons.

Private industry plays a vital role in our biodefense efforts by taking risks to bring new treatments to the market, and we appreciate those efforts.

By acting as a willing buyer for the best new medical technologies, the Government ensures that our drug stockpile remains safe, effective, and advanced. The Federal Government and our medical professionals are working together to meet the threat of bioterrorism; we're making the American people more secure in doing so.

Second, Project BioShield gives the Government new authority to expedite research and development on the most promising and time-sensitive medicines to defend against bioterror. We will waste no time putting those new powers to use. Today Secretary Thompson will direct the NIH to launch two initiatives, one to speed the development of new treatments for victims of a biological attack and another to expedite development of treatments for victims of a radiological or nuclear attack. Under the old rules, grants of this kind of research often took 18 to 24 months to process. Under Project BioShield, HHS expects the process to be completed in about 6 months. Our goal is to translate today's promising medical research into drugs and vaccines to combat a biological attack in the future, and now we will not let bureaucratic obstacles stand in the way.

Third, Project BioShield will change the way the Government authorizes and deploys medical defenses in a crisis. When I sign this bill, the Food and Drug

Administration (FDA) will be able to permit rapid distribution of promising new drugs and antidotes in the most urgent circumstances. This will allow patients to quickly receive the best treatments in an emergency. Secretary Thompson has directed the FDA to prepare guidelines and procedures for implementing this new authority. By acting today, we are making sure we have the best medicine possible to help the victims of a biological attack.

Project BioShield is part of a broader strategy to defend America against the threat of weapons of mass destruction. Since September the 11th, we've increased funding for the Strategic National Stockpile by a factor of 5, increased funding for biodefense research at NIH by a factor of 30, secured enough smallpox vaccine for every American, worked with cities on plans to deliver antibiotics and chemical antidotes in an emergency, improved the safety of our food supply, and deployed advanced environmental detectors under the BioWatch Program to provide the earliest possible warning of a biological attack.

The threat of bioterrorism has brought new challenges to our Government, to our first-responders, and to our medical personnel. We are grateful for their service. Not long ago, few of these men and women could have imagined duties like monitoring the air for anthrax or delivering antibiotics on a massive scale. Yet, this is the world as we find it. This Nation refuses to let our guard down.

Tomorrow the 9/11 Commission will issue its findings and recommendations to help prevent future terrorist attacks. I look forward to receiving the report. I will continue to work with the Congress and State and local governments to build on the homeland security improvements we have already made. Every American can be certain that their Government will continue doing everything in our power to prevent a terrorist attack. And if the terrorists do strike, we'll be better prepared to defend our people because of the good law I sign today.

It's my honor to invite the Members of the Congress to join me as I sign the Project BioShield Act of 2004. Thanks for coming.

Source: U.S. Executive Office of the President. "Remarks on Signing the Project BioShield Act of 2004." *Weekly Compilation of Presidential Documents* 40, no. 30 (July 26, 2004): 1346–1348. www.gpoaccess.gov/wcomp/v40no30.html (accessed February 23, 2005).

Final Report of the National Commission on Terrorist Attacks

July 22, 2004

INTRODUCTION

The September 11, 2001, terrorist attacks against the United States were made possible by the government's failure to comprehend the true danger of Islamist terrorism and an institutional inability to take effective action to counter it. These were the main conclusions of a landmark report released July 22, 2004, by a federal commission that devoted nearly two years to studying all aspects of the terrorist attacks, which killed nearly 3,000 people, damaged the U.S. economy, and led to major U.S. wars in Afghanistan and Iraq. The commission recommended a revamping of the government's intelligence-gathering agencies and a broad series of programs to defeat terrorists and make the United States more secure against their attacks.

The ten-member commission was composed of five Republicans and five Democrats, headed by Chairman Thomas Kean, a former Republican governor of New Jersey, and Vice Chairman Lee H. Hamilton, a former Democratic member of the House of Representatives from Indiana. Despite its partisan composition and the controversial nature of the issues it dealt with, the commission adopted its findings unanimously—a unity that members hoped would serve as an example for Congress and the Bush administration.

The commission's report was extraordinary for two unusual reasons: Congress adopted many of its key recommendations within a matter of months, and a commercial publication of the report was released and became a national best seller. Both of these results stood in sharp contrast to the fate of most reports authored by government commissions, which were often given some fanfare upon release, then largely ignored. This report was nominated for, but failed to receive, a National Book Award for nonfiction—the first time a government document had been accorded that honor.

In both the report and in their public comments, commissioners gave much of the credit for their work to a group of relatives of the September 11 victims. The relatives had applied political pressure on Congress and a reluctant Bush administration to create the commission. A core group, known as the September 11 Family Steering Committee, attended every commission public hearing—applauding tough questioning by commissioners and expressing disapproval when officials claimed they had done all they could to prevent the attacks.

On January 23 the *New York Times* reported that three names had been removed from the list of those reported killed in the September 11 attack on the World Trade Center towers—putting the figure at 2,749. Officials had pared forty names from the list the previous October and produced a number, 2,752 that was believed at the time to be final. In late January the city's medical examiner removed the names of three additional people from the list because there was no confirmation they had been killed. *(September 11 background, Historic Documents of 2001, p. 614)*

Political Hurdles

Members of Congress began calling for a commission to investigate the September 11 attacks in late 2001, but the Bush administration resisted that move for more than a year. Under pressure from the September 11 families, Bush agreed to the commission in 2002 and named as its chairman former secretary of state Henry Kissinger. Kissinger withdrew before the panel could begin work, however, as did vice chairman George Mitchell, a former Democratic senator from Maine. Kissinger objected to a legal provision requiring him to disclose the clients of a consulting firm he headed, and Mitchell said he concluded he could not devote enough time to the commission.

The commission's report was the second major examination of the September 11 attacks and the failures that made it possible. The first was by a joint panel of the House and Senate Intelligence committees, which issued a preliminary report in December 2002 and a final version in July 2003. That report found that numerous bureaucratic failings had made the United States vulnerable to the attacks. *(Background, Historic Documents of 2003, p. 544)*

Once Kean and Hamilton took over, the commission faced numerous delays as the Bush administration balked at its requests for government documents, including thousands of pages from the Clinton administration. Congressional Democrats, and even some Republicans, accused the administration of "slow-walking" the commission to prevent the disclosure of details that might be embarrassing in an election year. White House officials insisted the administration was providing all the information the commission wanted.

In the most publicized case, between late 2003 and mid-2004 the commission and the White House wrestled over release of the text of documents for an intelligence briefing that had been given to Bush on August 6, 2001, warning that al Qaeda was planning terrorist attacks against the United States. After the commission threatened to issue a subpoena, the White House allowed four commission representatives to review the documents and take notes on them—but on the condition that the information was not to be shared with the rest of the commission. Negotiations to give the full commission access to the documents stalled early in 2004, and on February 9 commissioners threatened again to issue a subpoena. The White House relented the next day, allowing the full commission access to summaries of the documents. Kean told reporters the documents contained "no smoking guns," in other words no information proving that Bush had been clearly warned about the September 11 attacks.

Yet another dispute involved the deadline for the commission to complete its work. The law creating the commission set a May 27, 2004, deadline for the commission to issue its report, with another sixty days to wrap up its administrative duties. By late 2003 commission leaders began complaining that the administration's lack of cooperation had made meeting the May 27 deadline difficult. White House officials and congressional leaders opposed an extension, fearing that a report issued later in the 2004 election year might damage the president politically. The commission on January 27 formally asked for a time extension. A week later the White House relented and agreed to support an extension until late July. House

Speaker J. Dennis Hastert delayed final approval of the extension for three weeks, however, during which the commission began to examine options for scaling back its planned hearings and one Democratic member, former senator Bob Kerrey, threatened to resign. Hastert relented on February 27 and agreed to give the panel until July 26 to complete its report.

The commission also was dogged by controversy early in 2004 after news organizations reported that commission executive director Philip D. Zelikow and commission member Jamie S. Gorelick had been interviewed by the other commission members. Zelikow had worked for Bush's transition office before the president's inauguration in January 2001 and had participated in discussions on antiterrorism policy. Gorelick was deputy attorney general during the Clinton administration in the 1990s. Both had recused themselves from discussions on matters in which they had been involved while serving in those posts. The September 11 Family Steering Committee on March 20 wrote the commission a letter calling on Zelikow to resign, but the panel rebuffed the request.

Public Hearings

Between March 31, 2003, and June 17, 2004, the commission conducted twelve sets of public hearings, most focused on specific topics, such as border security, the growth of terrorist groups, and various aspects of counterterrorism policy. All hearings were in Washington except for two in New York City (including the first hearing, which focused on the actual attacks on the Trade Center towers) and one held at Drew University in Madison, New Jersey, where chairman Kean was the president.

Fifteen detailed staff reports, based on private testimony and research conducted by the commission, were made public at these hearings and offered a wealth of new information. These staff reports formed the backbone of the final commission report.

A staff report released January 26, for example, suggested that government agencies missed numerous opportunities to catch some of the nineteen September 11 hijackers. Eight of the hijackers carried passports that showed evidence of "fraudulent manipulation," the report said, while at least six had violated U.S. immigration laws, and five had aroused the suspicion of customs or immigration inspectors but were allowed to enter the country after brief interviews. Nine of the hijackers had been flagged by a government computer system when they arrived at airports on the morning of September 11, but all were allowed to board their planes because procedures in place at the time merely required scanning their baggage for explosives. Another staff report, made public June 17, offered the most detailed glimpse ever given the public about the two-and-a-half hours during which the September 11 attacks were carried out. The report painted a picture of the federal government, the domestic aviation industry, and the military unable to comprehend what was occurring, much less react fast enough to prevent the attacks.

The commission's most publicized hearings came in March and April, when senior officials of the Clinton and Bush administration testified. All the officials said they had understood that Islamist terrorists posed a threat to the United States, but all said they were unprepared for the type of attack al Qaeda launched on September 11. William S. Cohen, a Republican who served as defense secretary in President Clinton's second term, said Americans still did not fully appreciate the threat of terrorism. "Even now, after September 11, I think it's far from clear that our society truly understands the gravity of the threat that we face or is yet willing to do what I believe is going to be necessary to counter it."

In many ways the most widely anticipated testimony was that of Richard A. Clarke, who had been the White House counterterrorism chief during much of the Clinton administration and the first two years of the Bush administration. Clarke on March 22 published a book, *Against All Enemies: Inside America's War on Terror,* in which he said the incoming Bush administration turned a deaf ear to his pleas for "urgent" action to counter the al Qaeda terrorist network. Clarke's book was filled with embarrassing anecdotes and observations, including a suggestion that the immediate response of Defense Secretary Donald Rumsfeld to the September 11 attacks was to focus on Iraq as a potential target, even though Iraq had no link to the attacks. The White House launched a multipoint attack on Clarke's book the day it was published, including a statement by Vice President Dick Cheney that Clarke "wasn't in the loop, frankly, on a lot of this stuff." That attack did not prevent Clarke's book from becoming an instant best seller.

On March 24, two days after his book was published, Clarke appeared before the September 11 commission as part of a panel with Samuel R. Berger, Clinton's national security adviser, and Richard L. Armitage, Bush's deputy secretary of state. Clarke opened his testimony with the single most dramatic moment of all the commission hearings. Addressing the families of September 11 victims, Clark said: "Your government failed you, those entrusted with protecting you failed you, and I failed you. We tried hard, but that doesn't matter, because we failed. And for that failure, I would ask, once all the facts are out, for your understanding and your forgiveness." That statement—the most direct apology offered by any current or former official during the commission hearings—brought praise from representatives of the September 11 families.

Clarke's testimony also brought out the latent partisanship among September 11 commission members. Republican members James R. Thompson, a former Illinois governor, and John Lehman, who had been navy secretary in the Reagan administration, grilled Clarke and suggested that he had political motives for his attack on the Bush administration, noting that he was a friend of the foreign policy adviser to Democratic presidential contender John Kerry. Clarke responded that he was a registered Republican, and said he would not accept a government position if Kerry won the presidency. Several Democratic commissioners praised Clarke and defended him against the Republican attacks.

In his testimony, Clarke said fighting terrorism was an "extraordinarily high priority" during the Clinton administration but was regarded as "an important issue, but not an urgent issue" by the Bush administration before the September 11 attacks. Clarke told the panel he had written Bush's national security adviser, Condoleeza Rice, a memo on January 25, 2001 (five days after Bush took office) asking for a cabinet-level "urgent" meeting to discuss proposals he had drafted for countering al Qaeda. Clarke said Rice and other administration officials appeared not to share his sense of urgency; the meeting he requested finally was held on September 4, exactly one week before the attacks.

Apparently alarmed by the forcefulness of Clarke's testimony, the White House arranged for Bush to make a campaign appearance in New Hampshire the next day, accompanied by the widow of a pilot whose plane was hijacked on September 11. "Had I known that the enemy was going to use airplanes to strike America, to attack us, I would have used every resource, every asset, every power of this government to protect the American people," he said.

In the wake of Clarke's testimony, attention turned to Rice, his former boss, who had testified to the commission in private but for weeks had refused to appear in public. She cited a tradition that holders of her office did not testify on Capitol

Hill—even though Rice and her predecessors were major public figures who appeared frequently on television talk shows. Under intense political pressure generated by Clarke's testimony, Rice eventually relented and appeared before the commission on the morning of April 8. Rice gave no ground, insisting that the Bush administration had taken the threat of terrorism seriously, had acted aggressively against it, and had been given no specific indication that al Qaeda was about to carry out the kind of attack it did on September 11. Rice specifically refuted a contention by commissioner Richard Ben-Veniste that the intelligence briefing given Bush on August 6, 2001, had warned that al Qaeda was prepared to launch attacks in the United States. "It did not warn of attacks inside the United States," she said. "It was historical information based on old reporting. There was no new threat information."

The White House released the briefing document on April 10, nearly two years after its existence was first disclosed. Titled "Bin Laden Determined to Strike in U.S.," the paper cited numerous reports on al Qaeda activities since the bombing of U.S. embassies in Kenya and Tanzania in 1998 and suggested that al Qaeda leader Osama bin Laden was planning attacks on U.S. territory. FBI information since 1998 "indicates patterns of suspicious activity in this country consistent with preparations for hijackings or other types of attacks, including recent surveillance of federal buildings in New York," the document said. It added that the FBI was conducting seventy field investigations in the United States that were "bin Laden-related." Bush said on April 11 that the document had told him "nothing about an attack on America."

Bush-Cheney Testimony

As it was preparing for its work, the commission asked President Bush to testify both privately and publicly. The White House refused the request for public testimony but in January agreed to allow the commission to question Bush in private under strict conditions. The president would be accompanied by Vice President Cheney and would testify for only one hour. Those restrictions subjected the president to public ridicule, with late-night television comedians suggesting Bush needed Cheney's help to get through the questioning. John Kerry also chided the president for spending hours at a rodeo but refusing to give the commission more than an hour of his time. Repeating its pattern on other procedural issues, the White House eventually relented and agreed to allow the commission as much time as it needed.

Bush and Cheney met with the commission on April 29 in the Oval Office at the White House. The session was neither tape recorded nor transcribed, and Bush and Cheney were not under oath. A White House statement called the meeting a "conversation," not testimony. Bush told reporters afterwards that the meeting was "cordial" and that he had answered "every question I was asked." White House officials and commission members refused to divulge any substantive details of the meeting. Commission chairman Kean said he learned important information from Bush about the events on September 11 but had not been surprised by anything either Bush or Cheney said.

One more controversy erupted in the closing weeks of the commission's work. A staff report made public June 16 said the commission had found no "collaborative relationship" between al Qaeda and the former Iraqi leader Saddam Hussein. This appeared to contradict frequent allegations by Cheney and other Bush administration officials, who had used the supposed links between al Qaeda and Saddam's regime as one justification for the 2003 invasion of Iraq. In response, Cheney said the commission might not have learned all the relevant information about the matter. The commission invited Cheney to offer additional evidence, but he declined the invitation. On July 6 the commission issued a statement saying it had access to the same information as Cheney but stood by its earlier finding about the lack of ties between Iraq and al Qaeda. *(Iraq war justifications, Historic Documents of 2003, p. 136)*

Major Findings

The commission released its 567-page report, completed with detailed footnotes and graphics, on July 22—four days ahead of the new deadline set by Congress. The report offered a gripping, almost minute-by-minute accounting of what happened on September 11 and the events that led up to the attacks. It examined numerous "missed opportunities" when the plot might have been uncovered and foiled, and it offered sweeping recommendations for changing government intelligence agencies and procedures to bolster the future fight against terrorism.

For many readers, the most compelling sections of the report were the pages describing al Qaeda's planning for the September 11 attacks, and then the attacks themselves. Written in the narrative style of a fictional thriller—but without the need for overheated adjectives to make fiction appear real—the report traced a series of events, beginning with al Qaeda's 1998 bombing of two U.S. embassies in Africa, that led three years later to nineteen hijackers boarding four airliners on the east coast of the United States. On the morning of September 11, 2001, three teams of five hijackers flew two of the planes into the twin towers of the World Trade Center and one into the Pentagon. The four hijackers on the fourth plane had planned to fly it into either the Capitol building or the White House, the report said, but were thwarted by passengers who rebelled; the hijackers ultimately crashed that plane into a field in Shanksville, Pennsylvania, southeast of Pittsburgh.

Fascinating as this narrative was, the meat of the report was a series of conclusions about how the United States government—with the strongest military, the most sophisticated intelligence-gathering operation, and the most advanced system of computer technology in the world at the time—could have overlooked the September 11 plot. The commission said it found major failings in four key areas: imagination, policy, capabilities, and management.

"The most important failure was one of imagination," the commission reported. "We do not believe leaders understood the gravity of the threat" posed by al Qaeda. Because the government failed to understand the threat, it did not adopt appropriate policies to deal with it, the report said, noting that terrorism "was not the overriding national security concern" during either the Clinton or the Bush administration. No division of the government had developed the appropriate capabilities to deal with al Qaeda and large-scale terrorism, the commission said—not the CIA, the military, the FBI, or the Federal Aviation Administration (FAA). The report pointed in particular to the FBI, which failed "to link the collective knowledge of agents in the field to national priorities," a reference to the fact that field agents had uncovered elements of the September 11 plot but had not been able to get the attention of decision makers at national headquarters. The FAA's capabilities also were "weak," the commission said, as a result of the agency's inability to confront threats "other than those experienced in the past." The FAA had based its aviation security regulations on preventing terrorists from loading bombs on airplanes but was unprepared to deal with the suicide hijackers willing to use airplanes as missiles, the report said.

Finally, the report cited management failures across the government, notably the inability to pool information and resources to deal with challenges different from those of the past. As an example, the commission noted that CIA director George Tenet in December 1998 issued a directive saying "we are at war" with al Qaeda and that he wanted "no resources or people spared in this effort." Despite its strong language, the report said, Tenet's directive "had little overall effect on mobilizing the CIA or the intelligence community."

Commission Recommendations

No commission report would be complete without recommendations for changes, and the September 11 commission complied with that implicit mandate by offering a series of proposals calling for fundamental shifts in the ways government business was conducted in Washington, D.C. The underlying thrust of the commission's recommendations was to provide a new answer to what vice chairman Hamilton said were the critical questions. "Who is in charge? Who oversees the massive integration and unity of effort necessary to keep America safe?" he asked at the news conference when the report was released. "Too often, the answer is, no one."

The commission divided its recommendations into three categories: attacking terrorists and their organizations, preventing the continued growth of Islamist terrorism, and protecting against future attacks. In the first category, the commission said the United States needed a better strategy for attacking terrorist "sanctuaries" in the Islamic world. One answer, it said, was bolstering support for the antiterrorism efforts by the governments of Afghanistan and Pakistan; another was building a more "open" relationship, not based simply on oil, with Saudi Arabia, which had been the home of fifteen of the nineteen of the hijackers and was the major source of funding for extreme Islamist factions worldwide. Preventing the spread of Islamist terrorism meant such steps as improving U.S. relations with the Islamic world, promoting public education in countries (such as Pakistan) where Islamic schools had taken over that function, and building coalitions among Islamic countries willing to confront terrorism.

The commission's most specific recommendations dealt with measures by the government to guard against future terrorist attacks. The commission called for "a different way of organizing the government." This meant not only revising government organizational charts but also changing the deeper institutional cultures that determined how agencies did their jobs. The panel's keystone recommendation was for the appointment of a national intelligence director who would have budgetary and operational authority over all the government's numerous intelligence agencies. This director would have more authority than the current head of the CIA, who both ran that agency and was the nominal head of the "intelligence community" but had no real power over the other agencies. This recommendation was not a new one. Dozens of experts and committees had offered similar proposals over the years. The idea had never gone anywhere, however, primarily because of resistance from the Defense Department, which ran most of the government's fifteen intelligence agencies and was reluctant to give up that institutional power.

Another major commission proposal called for creation of a national counterterrorism center, responsible for collecting and analyzing in one central place all the government's information about threats posed by terrorist groups. The center would take the lead in planning government actions to counter those threats but would leave the actual implementation to specific operational agencies, such as the CIA or the Pentagon. The commission said its goal was to break a tendency in government agencies known as "stovepiping"—the passing of information and orders up and down the chain of command in an agency or office, often bypassing those best positioned to take the necessary action.

Five of the commission members, including its vice chairman, had served in Congress and were familiar with the limitations of congressional oversight of intelligence gathering and counterterrorism. As a result, the commission proposed significant organizational changes to Congress, including the creation of a single committee in each chamber to oversee the new Department of Homeland Security and a reform of the committees that monitored the intelligence agencies. The commission offered two alternatives for the latter: either a single joint House-Senate committee modeled after the Joint Committee on Atomic Energy, which operated in the 1950s and 1960s; or a single committee in each chamber that wrote both the annual authorization and appropriations legislation for intelligence agencies. Currently, these responsibilities were handled by two panels in each chamber, the Intelligence committee (which wrote authorizing legislation), and an Appropriations subcommittee (which decided how much money to spend).

In making the report public, commission members sought to impart a sense of urgency, noting the prediction in the report that another major terrorist attack against the United States was all but certain. "We're in danger of just letting things slide," Kean said. "We believe unless we implement these recommendations, we're more vulnerable to another terrorist attack."

Reaction

The commission report won immediate praise from groups representing families of the September 11 victims, from Democrats and many Republicans, and from most experts who had studied the problems examined by the commission. The Bush administration, however, reacted cautiously at first. Bush invited Kean and Hamilton to the White House, patted each of them on the back, and called the report "very constructive," but he hesitated to endorse any of the specific findings or recommendations. Apparently sensing that this response was falling flat with the public, the White House quickly moved to adopt a more positive approach, announcing on July 26 that Bush already was moving to adopt some of the recommendations and was giving favorable consideration to others. Five days later the White House issued a twenty-three page "fact sheet" purporting to show that the administration was attempting to implement key recommendations of the report or was considering how to do so.

Perhaps the most enthusiastic response came from the September 11 families, who saw in the report a vindication of their long-held contention that the government's inattention had made the success of the attacks possible. "The report shows there was a catastrophic failure that day, and had the hijackers wanted to take twenty planes that day, they could have," said Terry McGovern, whose mother Anne died at the World Trade Center. Others said they would use the report to keep up the pressure on Congress and the administration to take new steps against terrorism. "The families know that this is an election year," said Debra Burlingame, sister of a pilot on the plane that crashed into the Pentagon. "We're going to hold these people's feet to the fire."

One of the few critics of the report was the man who long had been at the center of U.S. counterterrorism policy: Richard Clarke. In a column published in the *New York Times* on July 25, Clarke called the proposals for revamping the intelligence community "incremental" and suggested instead a sweeping overhaul of government agencies, starting with recruitment of "new blood"—people who had not spent their entire careers in the intelligence agencies and so might have new ideas and viewpoints.

Senator Kerry immediately embraced most of the report's recommendations, notably the call for a powerful new national intelligence director. "That's overdue, and when I'm president, it's going to happen," he said. Two of Kerry's Senate colleagues who had sponsored the legislation creating the commission—Republican John McCain of Arizona and Democrat Joseph I. Lieberman of Connecticut—said they were creating a "bipartisan congressional caucus" to push for approval of the recommendations.

Others on Capitol Hill appeared less enthusiastic. Among them was House Speaker Hastert, who at first said he doubted Congress could write and pass legislation implementing the commission recommendations before the November elections, or even in a lame duck session afterward. Hastert quickly relented, however, and agreed to allow hearings during the traditional August recess on legislation dealing with the recommendations.

Promoting the Report

One of the most remarkable things about the September 11 commission was its apparent determination to see its recommendations put into action. Typically in the past, government commissions issued their reports, held a news conference, gave a few interviews, and then faded into history, their reports quickly forgotten. Kean, Hamilton, and their colleagues said they were determined not to let that happen to their report.

As a first step, the commission members traveled around the country in bipartisan pairs to publicize their recommendations. The commission raised private donations to pay for those trips and for a small office in Washington to serve as the headquarters for lobbying Capitol Hill and continuing the public relations push by the commissioners. On September 18 the commission said it had received pledges of nearly $1 million from several foundations for a lobbying effort called the 9/11 Public Discourse Project.

Following is the text of the executive summary of The 9/11 Commission Report: The Final Report of the National Commission on Terrorist Attacks upon the United States, *released July 22, 2004. The commission was composed of Thomas H. Kean, chairman; Lee H. Hamilton, vice chairman; and members Richard Ben-Veniste, Fred F. Fielding, Jamie S. Gorelick, Slade Gorton, Bob Kerrey, John F. Lehman, Timothy J. Roemer, and James R. Thompson.*

The 9/11 Commission Report

We present the narrative of this report and the recommendations that flow from it to the President of the United States, the United States Congress, and the American people for their consideration. Ten Commissioners—five Republicans and five Democrats chosen by elected leaders from our nation's capital at a time of great partisan division—have come together to present this report without dissent.

We have come together with a unity of purpose because our nation demands it. September 11, 2001, was a day of unprecedented shock and suffering in the history of the United States. The nation was unprepared.

A Nation Transformed

At 8:46 on the morning of September 11, 2001, the United States became a nation transformed.

An airliner traveling at hundreds of miles per hour and carrying some 10,000 gallons of jet fuel plowed into the North Tower of the World Trade Center in Lower Manhattan. At 9:03, a second airliner hit the South Tower. Fire and smoke billowed upward. Steel, glass, ash, and bodies fell below. The Twin Towers, where up to 50,000 people worked each day, both collapsed less than 90 minutes later.

At 9:37 that same morning, a third airliner slammed into the western face of the Pentagon. At 10:03, a fourth airliner crashed in a field in southern Pennsylvania. It had been aimed at the United States Capitol or the White House, and was forced down by heroic passengers armed with the knowledge that America was under attack.

More than 2,600 people died at the World Trade Center; 125 died at the Pentagon; 256 died on the four planes. The death toll surpassed that at Pearl Harbor in December 1941.

This immeasurable pain was inflicted by 19 young Arabs acting at the behest of Islamist extremists headquartered in distant Afghanistan. Some had been in the United States for more than a year, mixing with the rest of the population. Though four had training as pilots, most were not well-educated. Most spoke English poorly, some hardly at all. In groups of four or five, carrying with them only small knives, box cutters, and cans of Mace or pepper spray, they had hijacked the four planes and turned them into deadly guided missiles.

Why did they do this? How was the attack planned and conceived? How did the U.S. government fail to anticipate and prevent it? What can we do in the future to prevent similar acts of terrorism?

A Shock, Not a Surprise

The 9/11 attacks were a shock, but they should not have come as a surprise. Islamist extremists had given plenty of warning that they meant to kill Americans indiscriminately and in large numbers. Although Osama Bin Laden himself would not emerge as a signal threat until the late 1990s, the threat of Islamist terrorism grew over the decade.

In February 1993, a group led by Ramzi Yousef tried to bring down the World Trade Center with a truck bomb. They killed six and wounded a thousand. Plans by Omar Abdel Rahman and others to blow up the Holland and Lincoln tunnels and other New York City landmarks were frustrated when the plotters were arrested. In October 1993, Somali tribesmen shot down U.S. helicopters, killing 18 and wounding 73 in an incident that came to be known as "Black Hawk down." Years later it would be learned that those Somali tribes-men had received help from al Qaeda.

In early 1995, police in Manila uncovered a plot by Ramzi Yousef to blow up a dozen U.S. airliners while they were flying over the Pacific. In November 1995, a car bomb exploded outside the office of the U.S. program manager for the Saudi National Guard in Riyadh, killing five Americans and two others. In June 1996, a truck bomb demolished the Khobar Towers apartment complex in Dhahran, Saudi Arabia, killing 19 U.S. servicemen and wounding hundreds. The attack was carried out primarily by Saudi Hezbollah, an organization that had received help from the government of Iran.

Until 1997, the U.S. intelligence community viewed Bin Laden as a financier of terrorism, not as a terrorist leader. In February 1998, Osama Bin Laden and four others issued a self-styled fatwa, publicly declaring that it was God's decree that every Muslim should try his utmost to kill any American, military or civilian, anywhere in the world, because of American "occupation" of Islam's holy places and aggression against Muslims.

In August 1998, Bin Laden's group, al Qaeda, carried out near-simultaneous truck bomb attacks on the U.S. embassies in Nairobi, Kenya, and Dar es Salaam, Tanzania. The attacks killed 224 people, including 12 Americans, and wounded thousands more. In December 1999, Jordanian police foiled a plot to bomb hotels and other sites frequented by American tourists, and a U.S. Customs agent arrested Ahmed Ressam at the U.S. Canadian border as he was smuggling in explosives intended for an attack on Los Angeles International Airport.

In October 2000, an al Qaeda team in Aden, Yemen, used a motorboat filled with explosives to blow a hole in the side of a destroyer, the USS *Cole*, almost sinking the vessel and killing 17 American sailors.

The 9/11 attacks on the World Trade Center and the Pentagon were far more elaborate, precise, and destructive than any of these earlier assaults. But by September 2001, the executive branch of the U.S. government, the Congress, the news media, and the American public had received clear warning that Islamist terrorists meant to kill Americans in high numbers.

Who Is the Enemy?

Who is this enemy that created an organization capable of inflicting such horrific damage on the United States? We now know that these attacks were carried out by various groups of Islamist extremists. The 9/11 attack was driven by Osama Bin Laden.

In the 1980s, young Muslims from around the world went to Afghanistan to join as volunteers in a jihad (or holy struggle) against the Soviet Union. A wealthy Saudi, Osama Bin Laden, was one of them. Following the defeat of the Soviets in the late 1980s, Bin Laden and others formed al Qaeda to mobilize jihads elsewhere.

The history, culture, and body of beliefs from which Bin Laden shapes and spreads his message are largely unknown to many Americans. Seizing on symbols of Islam's past greatness, he promises to restore pride to people who consider themselves the victims of successive foreign masters. He uses cultural and religious allusions to the holy Quran and some of its interpreters. He appeals to people disoriented by cyclonic change as they confront modernity and globalization. His rhetoric selectively draws from multiple sources—Islam, history, and the region's political and economic malaise. Bin Laden also stresses grievances against the United States widely shared in the Muslim world. He inveighed against the presence of U.S. troops in Saudi Arabia, which is the home of Islam's holiest sites, and against other U.S. policies in the Middle East.

Upon this political and ideological foundation, Bin Laden built over the course of a decade a dynamic and lethal organization. He built an infrastructure and organization in Afghanistan that could attract, train, and use recruits against ever more ambitious targets. He rallied new zealots and new money with each demonstration of al Qaeda's capability. He had forged a close alliance with the Taliban, a regime providing sanctuary for al Qaeda.

By September 11, 2001, al Qaeda possessed

- leaders able to evaluate, approve, and supervise the planning and direction of a major operation;
- a personnel system that could recruit candidates, indoctrinate them, vet them, and give them the necessary training;
- communications sufficient to enable planning and direction of operatives and those who would be helping them;
- an intelligence effort to gather required information and form assessments of enemy strengths and weaknesses;
- the ability to move people great distances; and
- the ability to raise and move the money necessary to finance an attack.

1998 to September 11, 2001

The August 1998 bombings of U.S. embassies in Kenya and Tanzania established al Qaeda as a potent adversary of the United States.

After launching cruise missile strikes against al Qaeda targets in Afghanistan and Sudan in retaliation for the embassy bombings, the Clinton administration applied diplomatic pressure to try to persuade the Taliban regime in Afghanistan to expel Bin Laden. The administration also devised covert operations to use CIA-paid foreign agents to capture or kill Bin Laden and his chief lieutenants. These actions did not stop Bin Laden or dislodge al Qaeda from its sanctuary.

By late 1998 or early 1999, Bin Laden and his advisers had agreed on an idea brought to them by Khalid Sheikh Mohammed (KSM) called the "planes operation." It would eventually culminate in the 9/11 attacks. Bin Laden and his chief of operations, Mohammed Atef, occupied undisputed leadership positions atop al Qaeda. Within al Qaeda, they relied heavily on the ideas and enterprise of strong-willed field commanders, such as KSM, to carry out worldwide terrorist operations.

KSM claims that his original plot was even grander than those carried out on 9/11—ten planes would attack targets on both the East and West coasts of the United States. This plan was modified by Bin Laden, KSM said, owing to its scale and complexity. Bin Laden provided KSM with four initial operatives for suicide plane attacks within the United States, and in the fall of 1999 training for the attacks began. New recruits included four from a cell of expatriate Muslim extremists who had clustered together in Hamburg, Germany. One became the tactical commander of the operation in the United States: Mohamed Atta.

U.S. intelligence frequently picked up reports of attacks planned by al Qaeda. Working with foreign security services, the CIA broke up some al Qaeda cells. The core of Bin Laden's organization nevertheless remained intact. In December 1999, news about the arrests of the terrorist cell in Jordan and the arrest of a terrorist at the

U.S.-Canadian border became part of a "millennium alert." The government was galvanized, and the public was on alert for any possible attack.

In January 2000, the intense intelligence effort glimpsed and then lost sight of two operatives destined for the "planes operation." Spotted in Kuala Lumpur, the pair were lost passing through Bangkok. On January 15, 2000, they arrived in Los Angeles. Because these two al Qaeda operatives had spent little time in the West and spoke little, if any, English, it is plausible that they or KSM would have tried to identify, in advance, a friendly contact in the United States. We explored suspicions about whether these two operatives had a support network of accomplices in the United States. The evidence is thin—simply not there for some cases, more worrisome in others.

We do know that soon after arriving in California, the two al Qaeda operatives sought out and found a group of ideologically like-minded Muslims with roots in Yemen and Saudi Arabia, individuals mainly associated with a young Yemeni and others who attended a mosque in San Diego. After a brief stay in Los Angeles about which we know little, the al Qaeda operatives lived openly in San Diego under their true names. They managed to avoid attracting much attention.

By the summer of 2000, three of the four Hamburg cell members had arrived on the East Coast of the United States and had begun pilot training. In early 2001, a fourth future hijacker pilot, Hani Hanjour, journeyed to Arizona with another operative, Nawaf al Hazmi, and conducted his refresher pilot training there. A number of al Qaeda operatives had spent time in Arizona during the 1980s and early 1990s.

During 2000, President Bill Clinton and his advisers renewed diplomatic efforts to get Bin Laden expelled from Afghanistan. They also renewed secret efforts with some of the Taliban's opponents—the Northern Alliance—to get enough intelligence to attack Bin Laden directly. Diplomatic efforts centered on the new military government in Pakistan, and they did not succeed. The efforts with the Northern Alliance revived an inconclusive and secret debate about whether the United States should take sides in Afghanistan's civil war and support the Taliban's enemies. The CIA also produced a plan to improve intelligence collection on al Qaeda, including the use of a small, unmanned airplane with a video camera, known as the Predator.

After the October 2000 attack on the USS *Cole,* evidence accumulated that it had been launched by al Qaeda operatives, but without confirmation that Bin Laden had given the order. The Taliban had earlier been warned that it would be held responsible for another Bin Laden attack on the United States. The CIA described its findings as a "preliminary judgment"; President Clinton and his chief advisers told us they were waiting for a conclusion before deciding whether to take military action. The military alternatives remained unappealing to them.

The transition to the new Bush administration in late 2000 and early 2001 took place with the *Cole* issue still pending. President George W. Bush and his chief advisers accepted that al Qaeda was responsible for the attack on the *Cole,* but did not like the options available for a response.

Bin Laden's inference may well have been that attacks, at least at the level of the *Cole,* were risk free.

The Bush administration began developing a new strategy with the stated goal of eliminating the al Qaeda threat within three to five years.

During the spring and summer of 2001, U.S. intelligence agencies received a stream of warnings that al Qaeda planned, as one report put it, "something very, very,

very big." Director of Central Intelligence George Tenet told us," The system was blinking red."

Although Bin Laden was determined to strike in the United States, as President Clinton had been told and President Bush was reminded in a Presidential Daily Brief article briefed to him in August 2001, the specific threat information pointed overseas. Numerous precautions were taken overseas. Domestic agencies were not effectively mobilized. The threat did not receive national media attention comparable to the millennium alert.

While the United States continued disruption efforts around the world, its emerging strategy to eliminate the al Qaeda threat was to include an enlarged covert action program in Afghanistan, as well as diplomatic strategies for Afghanistan and Pakistan. The process culminated during the summer of 2001 in a draft presidential directive and arguments about the Predator aircraft, which was soon to be deployed with a missile of its own, so that it might be used to attempt to kill Bin Laden or his chief lieutenants. At a September 4 meeting, President Bush's chief advisers approved the draft directive of the strategy and endorsed the concept of arming the Predator. This directive on the al Qaeda strategy was awaiting President Bush's signature on September 11, 2001.

Though the "planes operation" was progressing, the plotters had problems of their own in 2001. Several possible participants dropped out; others could not gain entry into the United States (including one denial at a port of entry and visa denials not related to terrorism). One of the eventual pilots may have considered abandoning the planes operation. Zacarias Moussaoui, who showed up at a flight training school in Minnesota, may have been a candidate to replace him.

Some of the vulnerabilities of the plotters become clear in retrospect. Moussaoui aroused suspicion for seeking fast-track training on how to pilot large jet airliners. He was arrested on August 16, 2001, for violations of immigration regulations. In late August, officials in the intelligence community realized that the terrorists spotted in Southeast Asia in January 2000 had arrived in the United States.

These cases did not prompt urgent action. No one working on these late leads in the summer of 2001 connected them to the high level of threat reporting. In the words of one official, no analytic work foresaw the lightning that could connect the thundercloud to the ground.

As final preparations were under way during the summer of 2001, dissent emerged among al Qaeda leaders in Afghanistan over whether to proceed. The Taliban's chief, Mullah Omar, opposed attacking the United States. Although facing opposition from many of his senior lieutenants, Bin Laden effectively overruled their objections, and the attacks went forward.

September 11, 2001

The day began with the 19 hijackers getting through a security checkpoint system that they had evidently analyzed and knew how to defeat. Their success rate in penetrating the system was 19 for 19. They took over the four flights, taking advantage of air crews and cockpits that were not prepared for the contingency of a suicide hijacking.

On 9/11, the defense of U.S. air space depended on close interaction between two federal agencies: the Federal Aviation Administration (FAA) and North American

Aerospace Defense Command (NORAD). Existing protocols on 9/11 were unsuited in every respect for an attack in which hijacked planes were used as weapons. What ensued was a hurried attempt to improvise a defense by civilians who had never handled a hijacked aircraft that attempted to disappear, and by a military unprepared for the transformation of commercial aircraft into weapons of mass destruction.

A shootdown authorization was not communicated to the NORAD air defense sector until 28 minutes after United 93 had crashed in Pennsylvania. Planes were scrambled, but ineffectively, as they did not know where to go or what targets they were to intercept. And once the shootdown order was given, it was not communicated to the pilots. In short, while leaders in Washington believed that the fighters circling above them had been instructed to "take out' hostile aircraft, the only orders actually conveyed to the pilots were to "ID type and tail."

Like the national defense, the emergency response on 9/11 was necessarily improvised.

In New York City, the Fire Department of New York, the New York Police Department, the Port Authority of New York and New Jersey, the building employees, and the occupants of the buildings did their best to cope with the effects of almost unimaginable events—unfolding furiously over 102 minutes. Casualties were nearly 100 percent at and above the impact zones and were very high among first responders who stayed in danger as they tried to save lives. Despite weaknesses in preparations for disaster, failure to achieve unified incident command, and inadequate communications among responding agencies, all but approximately one hundred of the thousands of civilians who worked below the impact zone escaped, often with help from the emergency responders.

At the Pentagon, while there were also problems of command and control, the emergency response was generally effective. The Incident Command System, a formalized management structure for emergency response in place in the National Capital Region, overcame the inherent complications of a response across local, state, and federal jurisdictions.

Operational Opportunities

We write with the benefit and handicap of hindsight. We are mindful of the danger of being unjust to men and women who made choices in conditions of uncertainty and in circumstances over which they often had little control.

Nonetheless, there were specific points of vulnerability in the plot and opportunities to disrupt it. Operational failures—opportunities that were not or could not be exploited by the organizations and systems of that time—included

- not watchlisting future hijackers Hazmi and Mihdhar, not trailing them after they traveled to Bangkok, and not informing the FBI about one future hijacker's U.S. visa or his companion's travel to the United States;
- not sharing information linking individuals in the *Cole* attack to Mihdhar;
- not taking adequate steps in time to find Mihdhar or Hazmi in the United States;
- not linking the arrest of Zacarias Moussaoui, described as interested in flight training for the purpose of using an airplane in a terrorist act, to the heightened indications of attack;
- not discovering false statements on visa applications;
- not recognizing passports manipulated in a fraudulent manner;

- not expanding no-fly lists to include names from terrorist watchlists;
- not searching airline passengers identified by the computer-based CAPPS screening system; and
- not hardening aircraft cockpit doors or taking other measures to pre-pare for the possibility of suicide hijackings.

General Findings

Since the plotters were flexible and resourceful, we cannot know whether any single step or series of steps would have defeated them. What we can say with confidence is that none of the measures adopted by the U.S. government from 1998 to 2001 disturbed or even delayed the progress of the al Qaeda plot. Across the government, there were failures of imagination, policy, capabilities, and management.

Imagination

The most important failure was one of imagination. We do not believe leaders understood the gravity of the threat. The terrorist danger from Bin Laden and al Qaeda was not a major topic for policy debate among the public, the media, or in the Congress. Indeed, it barely came up during the 2000 presidential campaign.

Al Qaeda's new brand of terrorism presented challenges to U.S. governmental institutions that they were not well-designed to meet. Though top officials all told us that they understood the danger, we believe there was uncertainty among them as to whether this was just a new and especially venomous version of the ordinary terrorist threat the United States had lived with for decades, or it was indeed radically new, posing a threat beyond any yet experienced.

As late as September 4, 2001, Richard Clarke, the White House staffer long responsible for counterterrorism policy coordination, asserted that the government had not yet made up its mind how to answer the question: "Is al Qaeda a big deal?"

A week later came the answer.

Policy

Terrorism was not the overriding national security concern for the U.S. government under either the Clinton or the pre-9/11 Bush administration. The policy challenges were linked to this failure of imagination. Officials in both the Clinton and Bush administrations regarded a full U.S. invasion of Afghanistan as practically inconceivable before 9/11.

Capabilities

Before 9/11, the United States tried to solve the al Qaeda problem with the capabilities it had used in the last stages of the Cold War and its immediate aftermath. These capabilities were insufficient. Little was done to expand or reform them.

The CIA had minimal capacity to conduct paramilitary operations with its own personnel, and it did not seek a large-scale expansion of these capabilities before 9/11. The CIA also needed to improve its capability to collect intelligence from human agents.

At no point before 9/11 was the Department of Defense fully engaged in the mission of countering al Qaeda, even though this was perhaps the most dangerous foreign enemy threatening the United States.

America's homeland defenders faced outward. NORAD itself was barely able to retain any alert bases at all. Its planning scenarios occasionally considered the danger of hijacked aircraft being guided to American targets, but only aircraft that were coming from overseas.

The most serious weaknesses in agency capabilities were in the domestic arena. The FBI did not have the capability to link the collective knowledge of agents in the field to national priorities. Other domestic agencies deferred to the FBI.

FAA capabilities were weak. Any serious examination of the possibility of a suicide hijacking could have suggested changes to fix glaring vulnerabilities—expanding no-fly lists, searching passengers identified by the CAPPS screening system, deploying federal air marshals domestically, hardening cockpit doors, alerting air crews to a different kind of hijacking possibility than they had been trained to expect. Yet the FAA did not adjust either its own training or training with NORAD to take account of threats other than those experienced in the past.

Management

The missed opportunities to thwart the 9/11 plot were also symptoms of a broader inability to adapt the way government manages problems to the new challenges of the twenty-first century. Action officers should have been able to draw on all available knowledge about al Qaeda in the government. Management should have ensured that information was shared and duties were clearly assigned across agencies, and across the foreign-domestic divide.

There were also broader management issues with respect to how top leaders set priorities and allocated resources. For instance, on December 4, 1998, DCI Tenet issued a directive to several CIA officials and the DDCI for Community Management, stating: "We are at war. I want no resources or people spared in this effort, either inside CIA or the Community." The memorandum had little overall effect on mobilizing the CIA or the intelligence community. This episode indicates the limitations of the DCI's authority over the direction of the intelligence community, including agencies within the Department of Defense.

The U.S. government did not find a way of pooling intelligence and using it to guide the planning and assignment of responsibilities for joint operations involving entities as disparate as the CIA, the FBI, the State Department, the military, and the agencies involved in homeland security.

Specific Findings

Unsuccessful Diplomacy

Beginning in February 1997, and through September 11, 2001, the U.S. government tried to use diplomatic pressure to persuade the Taliban regime in Afghanistan to stop being a sanctuary for al Qaeda, and to expel Bin Laden to a country where he could face justice. These efforts included warnings and sanctions, but they all failed.

The U.S. government also pressed two successive Pakistani governments to demand that the Taliban cease providing a sanctuary for Bin Laden and his organization and, failing that, to cut off their support for the Taliban. Before 9/11, the United States could not find a mix of incentives and pressure that would persuade Pakistan to reconsider its fundamental relationship with the Taliban.

From 1999 through early 2001, the United States pressed the United Arab Emirates, one of the Taliban's only travel and financial outlets to the outside world, to break off ties and enforce sanctions, especially those related to air travel to Afghanistan. These efforts achieved little before 9/11.

Saudi Arabia has been a problematically in combating Islamic extremism. Before 9/11, the Saudi and U.S. governments did not fully share intelligence information or develop an adequate joint effort to track and disrupt the finances of the al Qaeda organization. On the other hand, government officials of Saudi Arabia at the highest levels worked closely with top U.S. officials in major initiatives to solve the Bin Laden problem with diplomacy.

Lack of Military Options

In response to the request of policymakers, the military prepared an array of limited strike options for attacking Bin Laden and his organization from May 1998 onward. When they briefed policymakers, the military presented both the pros and cons of those strike options and the associated risks. Policymakers expressed frustration with the range of options presented.

Following the August 20, 1998, missile strikes on al Qaeda targets in Afghanistan and Sudan, both senior military officials and policymakers placed great emphasis on actionable intelligence as the key factor in recommending or deciding to launch military action against Bin Laden and his organization. They did not want to risk significant collateral damage, and they did not want to miss Bin Laden and thus make the United States look weak while making Bin Laden look strong. On three specific occasions in 1998–1999, intelligence was deemed credible enough to warrant planning for possible strikes to kill Bin Laden. But in each case the strikes did not go forward, because senior policymakers did not regard the intelligence as sufficiently actionable to offset their assessment of the risks.

The Director of Central Intelligence, policymakers, and military officials expressed frustration with the lack of actionable intelligence. Some officials inside the Pentagon, including those in the special forces and the counterterrorism policy office, also expressed frustration with the lack of military action. The Bush administration began to develop new policies toward al Qaeda in 2001, but military plans did not change until after 9/11.

Problems within the Intelligence Community

The intelligence community struggled throughout the 1990s and up to 9/11 to collect intelligence on and analyze the phenomenon of transnational terrorism. The combination of an overwhelming number of priorities, flat budgets, an outmoded structure, and bureaucratic rivalries resulted in an insufficient response to this new challenge.

Many dedicated officers worked day and night for years to piece together the growing body of evidence on al Qaeda and to understand the threats. Yet, while there were many reports on Bin Laden and his growing al Qaeda organization, there was no comprehensive review of what the intelligence community knew and what it did not know, and what that meant. There was no National Intelligence Estimate on terrorism between 1995 and 9/11.

Before 9/11, no agency did more to attack al Qaeda than the CIA. But there were limits to what the CIA was able to achieve by disrupting terrorist activities abroad and by using proxies to try to capture Bin Laden and his lieutenants in Afghanistan. CIA officers were aware of those limitations.

To put it simply, covert action was not a silver bullet. It was important to engage proxies in Afghanistan and to build various capabilities so that if an opportunity presented itself, the CIA could act on it. But for more than three years, through both the late Clinton and early Bush administrations, the CIA relied on proxy forces, and there was growing frustration within the CIA's Counterterrorist Center and in the National Security Council staff with the lack of results. The development of the Predator and the push to aid the Northern Alliance were products of this frustration.

Problems in the FBI

From the time of the first World Trade Center attack in 1993, FBI and Department of Justice leadership in Washington and New York became increasingly concerned about the terrorist threat from Islamist extremists to U.S. interests, both at home and abroad. Throughout the 1990s, the FBI's counterterrorism efforts against international terrorist organizations included both intelligence and criminal investigations. The FBI's approach to investigations was case-specific, decentralized, and geared toward prosecution. Significant FBI resources were devoted to after-the-fact investigations of major terrorist attacks, resulting in several prosecutions.

The FBI attempted several reform efforts aimed at strengthening its ability to prevent such attacks, but these reform efforts failed to implement organization-wide institutional change. On September 11, 2001, the FBI was limited in several areas critical to an effective preventive counterterrorism strategy. Those working counterterrorism matters did so despite limited intelligence collection and strategic analysis capabilities, a limited capacity to share information both internally and externally, insufficient training, perceived legal barriers to sharing information, and inadequate resources.

Permeable Borders and Immigration Controls

There were opportunities for intelligence and law enforcement to exploit al Qaeda's travel vulnerabilities. Considered collectively, the 9/11 hijackers

- included known al Qaeda operatives who could have been watchlisted;
- presented passports manipulated in a fraudulent manner;
- presented passports with suspicious indicators of extremism;
- made detectable false statements on visa applications;
- made false statements to border officials to gain entry into the United States; and
- violated immigration laws while in the United States.

Neither the State Department's consular officers nor the Immigration and Naturalization Service's inspectors and agents were ever considered full partners in a national counterterrorism effort. Protecting borders was not a national security issue before 9/11.

Permeable Aviation Security

Hijackers studied publicly available materials on the aviation security system and used items that had less metal content than a handgun and were most likely permissible. Though two of the hijackers were on the U.S.TIPOFF terrorist watchlist, the FAA did not use TIPOFF data. The hijackers had to beat only one layer of security—the security checkpoint process. Even though several hijackers were selected for extra screening by the CAPPS system, this led only to greater scrutiny of their checked baggage. Once on board, the hijackers were faced with aircraft personnel who were trained to be nonconfrontational in the event of a hijacking.

Financing

The 9/11 attacks cost somewhere between $400,000 and $500,000 to execute. The operatives spent more than $270,000 in the United States. Additional expenses included travel to obtain passports and visas, travel to the United States, expenses incurred by the plot leader and facilitators outside the United States, and expenses incurred by the people selected to be hijackers who ultimately did not participate.

The conspiracy made extensive use of banks in the United States. The hijackers opened accounts in their own names, using passports and other identification documents. Their transactions were unremarkable and essentially invisible amid the billions of dollars flowing around the world every day.

To date, we have not been able to determine the origin of the money used for the 9/11 attacks. Al Qaeda had many sources of funding and a pre-9/11 annual budget estimated at $30 million. If a particular source of funds had dried up, al Qaeda could easily have found enough money elsewhere to fund the attack.

An Improvised Homeland Defense

The civilian and military defenders of the nation's airspace—FAA and NORAD—were unprepared for the attacks launched against them. Given that lack of preparedness, they attempted and failed to improvise an effective home-land defense against an unprecedented challenge.

The events of that morning do not reflect discredit on operational personnel. NORAD's Northeast Air Defense Sector personnel reached out for information and made the best judgments they could based on the information they received. Individual FAA controllers, facility managers, and command center managers were creative and agile in recommending a nationwide alert, ground-stopping local traffic, ordering all aircraft nationwide to land, and executing that unprecedented order flawlessly.

At more senior levels, communication was poor. Senior military and FAA leaders had no effective communication with each other. The chain of command did not function well. The President could not reach some senior officials. The Secretary of Defense did not enter the chain of command until the morning's key events were over. Air National Guard units with different rules of engagement were scrambled without the knowledge of the President, NORAD, or the National Military Command Center.

Emergency Response

The civilians, firefighters, police officers, emergency medical technicians, and emergency management professionals exhibited steady determination and resolve under horrifying, overwhelming conditions on 9/11. Their actions saved lives and inspired a nation.

Effective decisionmaking in New York was hampered by problems in command and control and in internal communications. Within the Fire Department of New York, this was true for several reasons: the magnitude of the incident was unforeseen; commanders had difficulty communicating with their units; more units were actually dispatched than were ordered by the chiefs; some units self-dispatched; and once units arrived at the World Trade Center, they were neither comprehensively accounted for nor coordinated. The Port Authority's response was hampered by the lack both of standard operating procedures and of radios capable of enabling multiple commands to respond to an incident in unified fashion. The New York Police Department, because of its history of mobilizing thousands of officers for major events requiring crowd control, had a technical radio capability and protocols more easily adapted to an incident of the magnitude of 9/11.

Congress

The Congress, like the executive branch, responded slowly to the rise of transnational terrorism as a threat to national security. The legislative branch adjusted little and did not restructure itself to address changing threats. Its attention to terrorism was episodic and splintered across several committees. The Congress gave little guidance to executive branch agencies on terrorism, did not reform them in any significant way to meet the threat, and did not systematically perform robust oversight to identify, address, and attempt to resolve the many problems in national security and domestic agencies that became apparent in the aftermath of 9/11.

So long as oversight is undermined by current congressional rules and resolutions, we believe the American people will not get the security they want and need. The United States needs a strong, stable, and capable congressional committee structure to give America's national intelligence agencies oversight, sup-port, and leadership.

Are We Safer?

Since 9/11, the United States and its allies have killed or captured a majority of al Qaeda's leadership; toppled the Taliban, which gave al Qaeda sanctuary in Afghanistan; and severely damaged the organization. Yet terrorist attacks continue. Even as we have thwarted attacks, nearly everyone expects they will come. How can this be?

The problem is that al Qaeda represents an ideological movement, not a finite group of people. It initiates and inspires, even if it no longer directs. In this way it has transformed itself into a decentralized force. Bin Laden may be limited in his ability to organize major attacks from his hideouts. Yet killing or capturing him, while extremely important, would not end terror. His message of inspiration to a new generation of terrorists would continue.

Because of offensive actions against al Qaeda since 9/11, and defensive actions to improve homeland security, we believe we are safer today. But we are not safe. We therefore make the following recommendations that we believe can make America safer and more secure.

Recommendations

Three years after 9/11, the national debate continues about how to protect our nation in this new era. We divide our recommendations into two basic parts: What to do, and how to do it.

What To Do? A Global Strategy

The enemy is not just "terrorism." It is the threat posed specifically by Islamist terrorism, by Bin Laden and others who draw on a long tradition of extreme intolerance within a minority strain of Islam that does not distinguish politics from religion, and distorts both.

The enemy is not Islam, the great world faith, but a perversion of Islam. The enemy goes beyond al Qaeda to include the radical ideological movement, inspired in part by al Qaeda, that has spawned other terrorist groups and violence. Thus our strategy must match our means to two ends: dismantling the al Qaeda network and, in the long term, prevailing over the ideology that con-tributes to Islamist terrorism.

The first phase of our post-9/11 efforts rightly included military action to topple the Taliban and pursue al Qaeda. This work continues. But long-term success demands the use of all elements of national power: diplomacy, intelligence, covert action, law enforcement, economic policy, foreign aid, public diplomacy, and homeland defense. If we favor one tool while neglecting others, we leave ourselves vulnerable and weaken our national effort.

What should Americans expect from their government? The goal seems unlimited: Defeat terrorism anywhere in the world. But Americans have also been told to expect the worst: An attack is probably coming; it may be more devastating still.

Vague goals match an amorphous picture of the enemy. Al Qaeda and other groups are popularly described as being all over the world, adaptable, resilient, needing little higher-level organization, and capable of anything. It is an image of an omnipotent hydra of destruction. That image lowers expectations of government effectiveness.

It lowers them too far. Our report shows a determined and capable group of plotters. Yet the group was fragile and occasionally left vulnerable by the marginal, unstable people often attracted to such causes. The enemy made mistakes. The U.S. government was not able to capitalize on them.

No president can promise that a catastrophic attack like that of 9/11 will not happen again. But the American people are entitled to expect that officials will have realistic objectives, clear guidance, and effective organization. They are entitled to see standards for performance so they can judge, with the help of their elected representatives, whether the objectives are being met.

We propose a strategy with three dimensions: (1) attack terrorists and their organizations, (2) prevent the continued growth of Islamist terrorism, and (3) protect against and prepare for terrorist attacks.

Attack Terrorists and Their Organizations

- Root out sanctuaries. The U.S. government should identify and prioritize actual or potential terrorist sanctuaries and have realistic country or regional strategies for

each, utilizing every element of national power and reaching out to countries that can help us.
- Strengthen long-term U.S. and international commitments to the future of Pakistan and Afghanistan.
- Confront problems with Saudi Arabia in the open and build a relation-ship beyond oil, a relationship that both sides can defend to their citizens and includes a shared commitment to reform.

Prevent the Continued Growth of Islamist Terrorism

In October 2003, Secretary of Defense Donald Rumsfeld asked if enough was being done "to fashion a broad integrated plan to stop the next generation of terrorists." As part of such a plan, the U.S. government should

- Define the message and stand as an example of moral leadership in the world. To Muslim parents, terrorists like Bin Laden have nothing to offer their children but visions of violence and death. America and its friends have the advantage—our vision can offer a better future.
- Where Muslim governments, even those who are friends, do not offer opportunity, respect the rule of law, or tolerate differences, then the United States needs to stand for a better future.
- Communicate and defend American ideals in the Islamic world, through much stronger public diplomacy to reach more people, including students and leaders outside of government. Our efforts here should be as strong as they were in combating closed societies during the Cold War.
- Offer an agenda of opportunity that includes support for public education and economic openness.
- Develop a comprehensive coalition strategy against Islamist terrorism, using a flexible contact group of leading coalition governments and fashioning a common coalition approach on issues like the treatment of captured terrorists.
- Devote a maximum effort to the parallel task of countering the proliferation of weapons of mass destruction.
- Expect less from trying to dry up terrorist money and more from following the money for intelligence, as a tool to hunt terrorists, understand their networks, and disrupt their operations.

Protect against and Prepare for Terrorist Attacks

- Target terrorist travel, an intelligence and security strategy that the 9/11 story showed could be at least as powerful as the effort devoted to terrorist finance.
- Address problems of screening people with biometric identifiers across agencies and governments, including our border and transportation systems, by designing a comprehensive screening system that addresses common problems and sets common standards. As standards spread, this necessary and ambitious effort could dramatically strengthen the world's ability to intercept individuals who could pose catastrophic threats.
- Quickly complete a biometric entry-exit screening system, one that also speeds qualified travelers.

- Set standards for the issuance of birth certificates and sources of identification, such as driver's licenses.
- Develop strategies for neglected parts of our transportation security system. Since 9/11, about 90 percent of the nation's $5 billion annual investment in transportation security has gone to aviation, to fight the last war.
- In aviation, prevent arguments about a new computerized profiling system from delaying vital improvements in the "no-fly" and "automatic selectee" lists. Also, give priority to the improvement of check-point screening.
- Determine, with leadership from the President, guidelines for gathering and sharing information in the new security systems that are needed, guidelines that integrate safeguards for privacy and other essential liberties.
- Underscore that as government power necessarily expands in certain ways, the burden of retaining such powers remains on the executive to demonstrate the value of such powers and ensure adequate supervision of how they are used, including a new board to oversee the implementation of the guidelines needed for gathering and sharing information in these new security systems.
- Base federal funding for emergency preparedness solely on risks and vulnerabilities, putting New York City and Washington, D.C., at the top of the current list. Such assistance should not remain a program for general revenue sharing or pork-barrel spending.
- Make homeland security funding contingent on the adoption of an incident command system to strengthen teamwork in a crisis, including a regional approach. Allocate more radio spectrum and improve connectivity for public safety communications, and encourage wide-spread adoption of newly developed standards for private-sector emergency preparedness—since the private sector controls 85 percent of the nation's critical infrastructure.

How To Do It? A Different Way of Organizing Government

The strategy we have recommended is elaborate, even as presented here very briefly. To implement it will require a government better organized than the one that exists today, with its national security institutions designed half a century ago to win the Cold War. Americans should not settle for incremental, ad hoc adjustments to a system created a generation ago for a world that no longer exists.

Our detailed recommendations are designed to fit together. Their purpose is clear: to build unity of effort across the U.S. government. As one official now serving on the front lines overseas put it to us: "One fight, one team." We call for unity of effort in five areas, beginning with unity of effort on the challenge of counterterrorism itself:

- unifying strategic intelligence and operational planning against Islamist terrorists across the foreign-domestic divide with a National Counterterrorism Center;
- unifying the intelligence community with a new National Intelligence Director;
- unifying the many participants in the counterterrorism effort and their knowledge in a network-based information sharing system that transcends traditional governmental boundaries;

- unifying and strengthening congressional oversight to improve quality and accountability; and
- strengthening the FBI and homeland defenders.

Unity of Effort: A National Counterterrorism Center

The 9/11 story teaches the value of integrating strategic intelligence from all sources into joint operational planning—with *both* dimensions spanning the foreign-domestic divide.

- In some ways, since 9/11, joint work has gotten better. The effort of fighting terrorism has flooded over many of the usual agency boundaries because of its sheer quantity and energy. Attitudes have changed. But the problems of coordination have multiplied. The Defense Department alone has three unified commands (SOCOM, CENTCOM, and NORTHCOM) [the three regional commands, Southern Command, Central Command, and Northern Command] that deal with terrorism as one of their principal concerns.
- Much of the public commentary about the 9/11 attacks has focused on "lost opportunities." Though characterized as problems of "watch-listing," "information sharing," or "connecting the dots," each of these labels is too narrow. They describe the symptoms, not the disease.
- Breaking the older mold of organization stovepiped purely in executive agencies, we propose a National Counterterrorism Center (NCTC) that would borrow the joint, unified command concept adopted in the 1980s by the American military in a civilian agency, combining the joint intelligence function alongside the operations work.
- The NCTC would build on the existing Terrorist Threat Integration Center and would replace it and other terrorism "fusion centers" with-in the government. The NCTC would become the authoritative knowledge bank, bringing information to bear on common plans. It should task collection requirements both inside and outside the United States.
- The NCTC should perform joint operational planning, assigning lead responsibilities to existing agencies and letting them direct the actual execution of the plans.
- Placed in the Executive Office of the President, headed by a Senate-confirmed official (with rank equal to the deputy head of a cabinet department) who reports to the National Intelligence Director, the NCTC would track implementation of plans. It would be able to influence the leadership and the budgets of the counterterrorism operating arms of the CIA, the FBI, and the departments of Defense and Homeland Security.
- The NCTC should *not* be a policymaking body. Its operations and planning should follow the policy direction of the president and the National Security Council.

Unity of Effort: A National Intelligence Director

Since long before 9/11—and continuing to this day—the intelligence community is not organized well for joint intelligence work. It does not employ common standards and practices in reporting intelligence or in training experts overseas and at home. The expensive national capabilities for collecting intelligence have divided management. The structures are too complex and too secret.

- The community's head—the Director of Central Intelligence—has at least three jobs: running the CIA, coordinating a 15-agency confederation, and being the intelligence analyst-in-chief to the president. No one person can do all these things.
- A new National Intelligence Director should be established with two main jobs: (1) to oversee national intelligence centers that combine experts from all the collection disciplines against common targets—like counterterrorism or nuclear proliferation; and (2) to oversee the agencies that contribute to the national intelligence program, a task that includes setting common standards for personnel and information technology.
- The national intelligence centers would be the unified commands of the intelligence world—a long-overdue reform for intelligence comparable to the 1986 Goldwater-Nichols law that reformed the organization of national defense. The home services—such as the CIA, DIA [Defense Intelligence Agency], NSA [National Security Agency], and FBI—would organize, train, and equip the best intelligence professionals in the world, and would handle the execution of intelligence operations in the field.
- This National Intelligence Director (NID) should be located in the Executive Office of the President and report directly to the president, yet be confirmed by the Senate. In addition to overseeing the National Counterterrorism Center described above (which will include both the national intelligence center for terrorism and the joint operations planning effort), the NID should have three deputies:
  - For foreign intelligence (a deputy who also would be the head of the CIA)
  - For defense intelligence (also the under secretary of defense for intelligence)
  - For homeland intelligence (also the executive assistant director for intelligence at the FBI or the under secretary of homeland security for information analysis and infrastructure protection)
- The NID should receive a public appropriation for national intelligence, should have authority to hire and fire his or her intelligence deputies, and should be able to set common personnel and information technology policies across the intelligence community.
- The CIA should concentrate on strengthening the collection capabilities of its clandestine service and the talents of its analysts, building pride in its core expertise.
- Secrecy stifles oversight, accountability, and information sharing. Unfortunately, all the current organizational incentives encourage overclassification. This balance should change; and as a start, open information should be provided about the overall size of agency intelligence budgets.

Unity of Effort: Sharing Information

The U.S. government has access to a vast amount of information. But it has a weak system for processing and using what it has. The system of "need to know" should be replaced by a system of "need to share."

- The President should lead a government-wide effort to bring the major national security institutions into the information revolution, turning a mainframe system into a decentralized network. The obstacles are not technological. Official after official has urged us to call attention to problems with the unglamorous "back office" side of government operations.
- But no agency can solve the problems on its own—to build the net-work requires an effort that transcends old divides, solving common legal and policy issues in ways that can help officials know what they can and cannot do. Again, in tackling information issues, America needs unity of effort.

Unity of Effort: Congress

Congress took too little action to adjust itself or to restructure the executive branch to address the emerging terrorist threat. Congressional oversight for intelligence—and counterterrorism—is dysfunctional. Both Congress and the executive need to do more to minimize national security risks during transitions between administrations.

- For intelligence oversight, we propose two options: either a joint committee on the old model of the Joint Committee on Atomic Energy or a single committee in each house combining authorizing and appropriating committees. Our central message is the same: the intelligence committees cannot carry out their oversight function unless they are made stronger, and thereby have both clear responsibility and accountability for that oversight.
- Congress should create a single, principal point of oversight and review for homeland security. There should be one permanent standing committee for homeland security in each chamber.
- We propose reforms to speed up the nomination, financial reporting, security clearance, and confirmation process for national security officials at the start of an administration, and suggest steps to make sure that incoming administrations have the information they need.

Unity of Effort: Organizing America's Defenses in the United States

We have considered several proposals relating to the future of the domestic intelligence and counterterrorism mission. Adding a new domestic intelligence agency will not solve America's problems in collecting and analyzing intelligence within the United States. We do not recommend creating one.

- We propose the establishment of a specialized and integrated national security workforce at the FBI, consisting of agents, analysts, linguists, and surveillance specialists who are recruited, trained, rewarded, and retained to ensure the development of an institutional culture imbued with a deep expertise in intelligence and national security. At several points we asked: Who has the responsibility for defending us at home? Responsibility for America's national defense is shared by the Department of Defense, with its new Northern Command, and by the Department of Homeland Security. They must have a clear delineation of roles, missions, and authority.

- The Department of Defense and its oversight committees should regularly assess the adequacy of Northern Command's strategies and planning to defend against military threats to the homeland.
- The Department of Homeland Security and its oversight committees should regularly assess the types of threats the country faces, in order to determine the adequacy of the government's plans and the readiness of the government to respond to those threats.

* * *

We call on the American people to remember how we all felt on 9/11, to remember not only the unspeakable horror but how we came together as a nation—one nation. Unity of purpose and unity of effort are the way we will defeat this enemy and make America safer for our children and grandchildren. We look forward to a national debate on the merits of what we have recommended, and we will participate vigorously in that debate.

Source: U.S. National Commission on Terrorist Attacks upon the United States. *The 9/11 Commission Report: Final Report of the National Commission on Terrorist Attacks upon the United States.* July 22, 2004. Washington, D.C.: Government Printing Office. ISBN 0-16-072304-3. http://purl.access.gpo.gov/GPO/LPS51934 (accessed February 15, 2005).

Kerry, Bush Presidential Nomination Acceptance Speeches

July 29 and September 2, 2004

INTRODUCTION

The presidential election campaign of 2004 was the longest, most expensive, and perhaps most negative in recent memory. Yet most voters had apparently made up their minds before the campaign actually began, and the rallies, speeches, attack ads, position papers, innuendo, and allegations pumped out day after day for nearly ten months did relatively little to change their minds. From early February, when it became clear that John F. Kerry, the junior senator from Massachusetts, would win the Democratic nomination to challenge the incumbent Republican president, George W. Bush, until Election Day, the two candidates ran virtually neck-and-neck in the public opinion polls, with one pulling ahead for a few days or weeks only to drop back a few points before moving forward again.

Bush was judged to be vulnerable going into the campaign, with voters expressing deep doubts about his handling both of the economy and the war in Iraq. Kerry tried to take advantage of those doubts, challenging Bush for giving mammoth tax cuts to wealthy Americans while failing to provide jobs and health care for the middle class and for rushing the war in Iraq and diverting attention from the war on terror. But Bush kept Kerry on the defensive, skillfully portraying him as the epitome of a Massachusetts liberal and a "flip-flopper" on the issues. The Bush campaign also managed to raise questions about Kerry's Vietnam War record, in an effort to undermine the Democrat's credibility as a potential commander-in-chief.

On the campaign trail, voters often found it easier to see the difference in style between Bush and Kerry than the differences in policy. Bush was amiable and relaxed. Kerry often appeared distant and cool. Bush's penchant for simple, declarative statements helped voters see him as decisive and a strong leader. Kerry's tendency to overexplain himself, particularly early in the campaign, left voters uncertain what he had said and contributed to the Bush camp's charge that Kerry changed his position on the issues for political expediency.

In the end, the presidential campaign posed a choice that was shaped not so much by the candidates' stands on the economy or Iraq but by the uncertainties that had gripped the country since the terrorist attacks of September 11, 2001: Was it better in a time of tumult for voters to stick with a sitting president even though they disagreed with many of his policies, or should the country take a chance on a candidate whose policies might be more agreeable but whose leadership was largely untested? A majority of the voters decided to stay with the president. On Election Day, November 2, Bush won with 51 percent of the vote to Kerry's 48.5 percent. *(Election results, p. 773)*

Bush's Vulnerability

As Congressional Quarterly reporter John Cochran observed, when it mattered most, Bush pushed hard to make the most of the hand he had been dealt. He did that in 2000 in the presidential race against Democratic vice president Al Gore. Although Bush lost the popular vote in that election by more than half a million votes, he nonetheless won the presidency in the electoral college, first by mounting an aggressive campaign to be certified the winner of the contested Florida vote and then by prevailing in the Supreme Court on the question of a recount.

With his legitimacy in doubt, Bush in his first five months in office was able to leverage his position as president, a huge budget surplus, and a narrow Republican majority in Congress to win the deep tax cut that became his signature legislative achievement. Three months later, a country traumatized by the September 11 terrorist attacks turned to the president for leadership, granting him almost everything he wanted to fight his broadly defined war on terrorism.

Throughout his first term, Bush exerted extraordinary control over the agenda in Washington. He won enactment of two of the three biggest tax cuts in American history, brokered deals on his terms to revamp Medicare and federal education policy, and presided over the implementation of the so-called doctrine of preemption that led the nation to wage simultaneous wars in Afghanistan and Iraq.

As the 2004 presidential campaign got under way, Bush was judged to be once again at a vulnerable point. His job approval ratings were plummeting as public concerns about the war in Iraq and the state of the economy mounted. A majority of Americans said the country was on the wrong track. Bumper stickers reading "Anybody but Bush" became popular.

Democratic Primary Campaign

The first question for Democrats was who the "anybody" would be. In addition to Kerry, eight other Democrats sought the nomination, including former Vermont governor Howard Dean; former House leader Richard A. Gephardt of Missouri; Joseph I. Lieberman, a senator from Connecticut and the Democratic vice presidential candidate in 2000; John R. Edwards, a successful trial lawyer and a first-term senator from North Carolina; and retired army general Wesley Clark, the former head of NATO. The long shots in the race were Rep. Dennis J. Kucinich, a maverick politician from Ohio; former Illinois senator Carol Moseley-Braun, and the Rev. Al Sharpton, an outspoken Democratic activist from New York. Bob Graham, a senator and former governor of Florida, had dropped out of the race in October 2003.

Kerry entered the fray in the fall of 2003 as the early favorite of the Democratic establishment. But he quickly fell behind former Vermont governor Howard Dean, who had announced his candidacy early in 2002 and spent the next year and a half using the Internet to raise a record $41 million and solicit supporters who were attracted to his anti-Washington, antiwar message. In the months leading up to the first two major primary events—the Iowa caucuses on January 19 and the New Hampshire primary on January 27, Kerry's candidacy was nearly written off as dead. Kerry was said to be spending too much time tending to his disorganized and unfocused campaign organization instead of campaigning. His campaign financing had dried up, and he was having trouble raising more.

With the campaign all but lost, Kerry began to turn things around in mid-November 2003. He replaced his campaign manager with longtime Democratic operative Mary Beth Cahill, mortgaged his Boston townhouse, and ran a series of ads that portrayed the candidate as someone who understood and would deal with the problems of ordinary Americans. He also decided to focus his campaign almost entirely on the Iowa caucuses, abandoning for the time being New Hampshire, where he was badly trailing Dean. And he turned to fellow Vietnam veterans, who began turning out in force at his campaign rallies, praising Kerry's leadership and bravery during that war and applauding wildly when Kerry challenged his Democratic rivals and President Bush to "bring it on!"

At the same time the Kerry campaign was gathering new energy, the Dean campaign ran into trouble. Dean won endorsement in early December 2003 from Al Gore, the party's standard-bearer in 2000. But that strengthened the attacks on the front-runner from the other Democratic candidates, his campaign began to run out of money, and the news media began to ask harder questions. One question that was particularly troublesome for Dean was why he had sealed more than half of his gubernatorial records for a decade after he left office. Dean also got into a negative war of attack ads with Gephardt in the week before the Iowa caucuses, which damaged both candidates. Even before then, Dean made a series of intemperate comments that raised questions about his temperament and electability—doubts that were solidified by a notorious screaming rant after Dean came in third behind Kerry and Edwards in the Iowa caucuses.

A week later, Kerry won New Hampshire, with Dean coming in second but still twelve percentage points behind. From that point on, Kerry was unstoppable. On February 3 Edwards and Clark each won a primary, but Kerry won the other five held that day and all but clinched the nomination. Dean focused his attention on winning the Wisconsin primary on February 17, but after coming in third, behind Kerry and Edwards, he effectively ended his candidacy. Edwards, easily the most likable Democrat on the campaign stump with his boyish good looks and his insistence on running a positive campaign, slogged on for another two weeks but retired from the campaign after Kerry swept nine of ten primaries held on March 2. (The tenth was Vermont, which backed its former governor even though he had pulled out of the race.)

Kerry's Vice Presidential Selection

Kerry named Senator Edwards as his choice for a running mate on July 6, ending a search that included Gephardt, Iowa governor Tom Vilsack, and Republican senator John McCain of Arizona, a close friend of Kerry's who ultimately campaigned for Bush against Kerry. In naming Edwards, Kerry reached for qualities that many Democrats feared the presidential candidate lacked: charisma, youthful energy, and an instinctively deft touch with ordinary people. Edwards also was a sharp contrast to the often dour Republican vice president, Dick Cheney, who assumed the role of "hit man" in the Bush campaign.

Despite differences of personality and style, both Kerry and Edwards saw eye-to-eye on nearly every major issue. Their records in the Senate were similar enough to suggest that they shared plenty of common ground and were unlikely to differ significantly on matters of policy in a Kerry administration. Democratic campaign strategists also hoped this similarity of views would help the ticket state clearly what Democrats stood for and what they would do with a governing majority—something the party had failed to do in either the 2000 presidential election or the midterm election in 2002, when the Republicans managed to widen their lead in the House and regain control, albeit narrow, in the Senate.

The two men already had domestic messages that were easy to mesh. When he announced that he had picked Edwards, Kerry embraced, word for word, his vanquished rival's pledge to bridge the "great divide" between the "two Americas, one of wealth and one of work." That blended neatly with Kerry's campaign speeches about the "middle-class squeeze": ordinary working people were suffering, Kerry said, while President Bush rewarded his wealthy supporters with tax breaks and other favors.

The Campaign Trail

With polls showing that a majority of the states were already firmly in the Republican "red" column or the Democratic "blue" one, the campaigns concentrated their energies on a handful of "battleground" states, including Florida, Ohio, and Pennsylvania, where the presidential and vice presidential candidates each made multiple appearances. Bush often appeared at carefully scripted "town hall" meetings where the audiences consisted wholly of supporters who asked preplanned questions and applauded on cue. The TV news clips that followed such appearances usually showed a jovial and sincere President Bush, shirt-sleeves rolled up, giving an optimistic assessment of both the economy and the war in Iraq, while raising questions about Kerry's policy proposals and leadership capabilities. Vice President Cheney, in contrast, led a harsher assault on Kerry in a not-so-subtle effort to raise fears that the country would be vulnerable to terrorist attack if Kerry were elected—a message that was underscored by attack ads and surrogates speaking in behalf of the Republican candidates.

Kerry tried to keep his campaign focused on economic and domestic issues where the president was clearly vulnerable. But the dominant issue during much of the campaign was the war in Iraq and the underlying war on terrorism. It was the first time a foreign policy matter had been at the center of the nation's politics since the Vietnam War during the late 1960s and early 1970s. As with much of the year's campaign rhetoric, however, voters often found it difficult to discern the actual differences in the positions Bush and Kerry took. Kerry often was harshly critical of Bush's handling of Iraq and other foreign affairs matters, but his policy differences often were so subtle as to be indistinguishable to the average voter.

One of Kerry's chief problems was that the Bush campaign—and conservative groups supporting the president—had succeeded in defining him in negative terms before he was able to make his case as the Democratic nominee. As soon as Kerry's rivals dropped out, the Bush campaign began running negative television ads portraying him as weak and indecisive. Bush, Cheney, and campaign surrogates cited Kerry's votes during his twenty years in the Senate in such a way that Kerry appeared to have repeatedly shifted positions on controversial matters and had constantly voted for budget-busting spending programs and tax increases.

Perhaps even more damaging to Kerry were attacks challenging his service in the Vietnam War. Kerry served for fourth months in Vietnam as a navy lieutenant, where he was awarded the Silver Star, the Bronze Star, and three Purple Hearts. Upon his return home, Kerry became a prominent leader in the antiwar movement, and his heroism and then his opposition to the war had been the hallmarks of his political life. The first attacks, which surfaced in February, focused on Kerry's antiwar activities. Kerry was charged with throwing away his medals, a charge he denied, and for impugning the honor of troops serving in Vietnam by describing the actions of some as "crimes."

The real damage came after the Democratic National Convention in July, when a group calling itself the "Swift Boat Veterans for Truth" claimed that Kerry had lied about his dramatic rescue under fire of a fellow sailor and other elements of his navy career. Kerry was slow to respond to these ads, which ran in only a few markets but generated enormous controversy nationwide. By the time he did respond, millions of voters had come to question the reputation he had carefully nurtured as a decisive, even heroic, military figure.

Questions also arose about Bush's Vietnam-era service but appeared to cause less damage to the president. Bush had joined the Texas Air National Guard in 1968, just before he graduated from Yale and at the height of the Vietnam War. Bush trained as a fighter pilot and was honorably discharged from service in 1973. Over the course of his political career, however, critics had alleged that Bush's father, George H. W. Bush, had used political connections to get his son the national guard post. Questions also had been raised about a period of Bush's service when he transferred to an Alabama guard unit while working on a senatorial campaign but appeared not to have shown up for duty at least part of the time.

These questions arose again early in the 2004 campaign and were calmed after the White House released documents indicating that Bush had served during the disputed period but still leaving some questions unanswered. The controversy flared again in early September, when a CBS television program reported that it had documents purportedly showing that Bush had shirked his guard duty and later lied about it. CBS later retracted that report, acknowledging that the documents it cited had been forgeries. The end result was that CBS was damaged more than Bush, who gained some sympathy because of what many supporters alleged was a partisan attack by the news media.

Iraq

In addition to the economy, Bush appeared vulnerable on Iraq, where nearly all his optimistic statements about what would happen there had proven wrong. By 2004 the United States had gotten bogged down fighting an increasingly strong insurgency throughout much of Iraq, in sharp contrast to Bush's prewar predictions that most U.S. forces would be back home by the end of 2003. Some critics were beginning to call the U.S. occupation of Iraq a "quagmire"—the term used to describe the later years of the Vietnam War.

It was natural, then, that Iraq would become the dominant issue of the campaign. Ironically, this focus on Iraq ultimately became more of a problem for Kerry, the challenger, than for Bush the defender. Bush was able to use the conflict in Iraq to remind voters of his leadership in what he called the ongoing "war against terrorism" and to plant doubts in voters' minds about what kind of a leader Kerry would be. Kerry accused Bush and his administration of "incompetence" in Iraq but failed to articulate a clear alternative strategy.

Kerry criticized Bush for failing to plan for the postwar occupation of that country—a failure that had been documented in numerous academic studies and news accounts since shortly after the war. But on the fundamental question of whether Bush was justified in taking the nation to war in Iraq, Kerry waffled. In what he described as a major foreign speech, delivered in Seattle on May 27, Kerry suggested that Bush and his aides rushed into war without gaining adequate support from allies. "They looked to force before exhausting diplomacy," he said. "They bullied when they should have persuaded." Later in the campaign, Kerry defended his vote in October 2002 to authorize the war, and he offered a confusing, procedural explanation for his apparently conflicting votes in November 2003 on Bush's request for $87 billion to fund military operations and foreign aid in Iraq and Afghanistan. Bush used Kerry's statement about voting for the $87 billion before he voted against it to great affect on the campaign trail; Bush's political adviser Karl Rove later referred to the Kerry statement as "the gift that kept on giving."

For his part, Bush repeatedly shifted his justification for the war to suit the circumstances. Early in the year, Bush stood by his contention that Iraq's leader Saddam Hussein had or was developing weapons of mass destruction and thus posed a threat to the United States and its allies. As more and more evidence emerged that Iraq did not have those weapons, Bush fell back on vague terms that implied the same thing: Iraq had "weapons of mass destruction-related program activities" or simply the "capability" to produce those weapons, he said. Ultimately, Bush adopted a democracy and human rights rationale for the war, arguing that Saddam was a dictator whose removal laid the ground for democracy in Iraq and perhaps elsewhere in the Middle East.

In their first debate, on September 30, the candidates offered voters a choice of two different world views, if not the specific policies to put them into practice. Kerry emphasized the need to work with allies. "I believe we're strongest when we reach out and lead the world and build strong alliances," he said, noting that recruiting broader international support was the basis for his plan to defeat the insurgency in Iraq. Bush, in turn, emphasized determination. "The way to win this [in Iraq] is to be steadfast and resolved and to follow through on the plan" to back the new Iraqi government and promote elections, he said. *(Debates, p. 675)*

Democratic National Convention

In recent election seasons, the national nominating conventions had lost much of their interest for the public. With no decisions to be made about the nominees, virtually no controversy over the party platforms, and little live coverage by the broadcast networks, the conventions were little more than rallying grounds for the faithful and launching pads for the fall campaigns. Still, both parties spent a great deal of time and money orchestrating speakers and speeches to present their candidate and their campaign messages in the most positive light possible.

For the Democrats, meeting July 26–29 at the Fleet Center in Kerry's home town of Boston, the convention was an opportunity to showcase solid party support for their candidate. Party dignitaries speaking on Kerry's behalf included former presidents Jimmy Carter and Bill Clinton, and former vice president Al Gore. Senators Edward M. Kennedy of Massachusetts, the elder statesman of Democratic liberalism, and Hillary Rodham Clinton of New York, a potential prospect for the Democratic nomination in 2008, spoke. The keynote address was given by Barack Obama, a candidate for the U.S. Senate from Illinois and a rising star in the Democratic Party. Obama, the son of a Kenyan father and a Kansan woman, eloquently called for a united and tolerant America, to the great pleasure of applauding delegates.

Democrats believed they scored a coup with the appearance of Ron Reagan, the son of former president and Republican icon Ronald Reagan, who had died in June of Alzheimer's disease. The younger Reagan urged delegates to vote for candidates who would support embryonic stem cell research, which scientists believed held great promise for curing degenerative diseases such as juvenile diabetes, Parkinson's disease, and perhaps even Alzheimer's. President Bush had limited federal funding for such research. *(Stem cell research, p. 157; Reagan's death, p. 316)*

Kerry's speech on July 29 accepting the Democratic nomination, and the biographical film leading up to it, emphasized the senator's service in Vietnam in hopes that he could convince voters that he would be a strong commander in chief. As the film concluded, Kerry strode on stage, turned to the audience, saluted, and said. "I'm John Kerry and I'm reporting for duty." Noting that he had "defended this country as a young man," Kerry promised to "defend it as President." Kerry also excoriated Bush for a litany of mistakes: "I will be a commander in chief who will never mislead us into war. I will have a vice president who will not conduct secret meetings with polluters to rewrite our environmental laws. I will have a secretary of defense who will listen to the advice of the military leaders. And I will appoint an attorney general who upholds the Constitution of the United States."

Republican National Convention

The Republicans held their convention August 30–September 2 in New York City's Madison Square Garden, just four miles north of the ruins of the World Trade Center. The first night of the convention focused on the September 11 attack and on Bush's declaration of a new war on terrorism in response. One of the featured speakers was former New York mayor Rudolph Giuliani, a moderate Republican whose stewardship of the city after the attacks was widely admired.

On August 31 the emphasis turned to the party's themes of hope and optimism, with speeches by California governor Arnold Schwarzenegger, Secretary of Education Rod Paige, and first lady Laura Bush all promising that with President Bush in the White House, the nation's best days still lay ahead. On September 1 the gloves came off as Vice President Cheney and Democratic senator Zell Miller of Georgia laced into Kerry. Cheney said Kerry still did "not appear to understand how the world has changed" since the September 11 attacks, while Miller accused him of being "more wrong, more weak, and more wobbly than any other national figure" on the "great issues of freedom and security." Miller, who in recent years had increasingly aligned himself with Senate Republicans, said that "George Bush wants to grab terrorists by the throat and not let them go to get a better grip. From John Kerry, they get a 'yes-no-maybe' bowl of mush that can only encourage our enemies and confuse our friends."

Accepting the Republican nomination on September 2, Bush promised to "build a safer world and a more hopeful America." He devoted the first half of his speech to a broad outline of his plans for a second term, including overhauling Social Security and Medicare, reducing the deficit, and making tax cuts permanent. He spoke of an "ownership society" and promised to transform fundamental government systems such as health coverage, pension plans, and worker training "so that all citizens are equipped, prepared—and thus truly free—to make your own choices and follow your own dreams." But the core of his message was that he was the candidate best suited to lead the country in time of great threat: "We have fought the terrorists across the Earth—not for pride, not for power, but because the lives of our citizens are at stake. We are staying on the offensive—striking terrorists abroad—so we do not have to face them here at home."

Following are texts of speeches by Massachusetts senator John F. Kerry, accepting the Democratic presidential nomination on July 29, 2004, and by President George W. Bush, accepting the Republican presidential nomination on September 2, 2004.

"Speech to the 2004 Democratic National Convention: Remarks of John Kerry"

We are here tonight because we love our country.

We are proud of what America is and what it can become.

My fellow Americans: we are here tonight united in one simple purpose: to make America stronger at home and respected in the world.

A great American novelist wrote that you can't go home again. He could not have imagined this evening. Tonight, I am home. Home where my public life began and those who made it possible live. Home where our nation's history was written in blood, idealism, and hope. Home where my parents showed me the values of family, faith, and country.

Thank you, all of you, for a welcome home I will never forget.

I wish my parents could share this moment. They went to their rest in the last few years, but their example, their inspiration, their gift of open eyes, open mind, and endless world are bigger and more lasting than any words.

I was born in Colorado, in Fitzsimmons Army Hospital, when my dad was a pilot in World War II.

Now, I'm not one to read into things, but guess which wing of the hospital the maternity ward was in? I'm not making this up. I was born in the West Wing!

My mother was the rock of our family as so many mothers are. She stayed up late to help me do my homework. She sat by my bed when I was sick, and she answered the questions of a child who, like all children, found the world full of wonders and mysteries.

She was my den mother when I was a Cub Scout and she was so proud of her fifty year pin as a Girl Scout leader. She gave me her passion for the environment. She taught me to see trees as the cathedrals of nature. And by the power of her example, she showed me that we can and must finish the march toward full equality for all women in our country.

My dad did the things that a boy remembers. He gave me my first model airplane, my first baseball mitt and my first bicycle. He also taught me that we are here for something bigger than ourselves; he lived out the responsibilities and sacrifices of the greatest generation to whom we owe so much.

When I was a young man, he was in the State Department, stationed in Berlin when it and the world were divided between democracy and communism. I have unforgettable memories of being a kid mesmerized by the British, French, and American troops, each of them guarding their own part of the city, and Russians standing guard on the stark line separating East from West. On one occasion, I rode my bike into Soviet East Berlin. And when I proudly told my dad, he promptly grounded me.

But what I learned has stayed with me for a lifetime. I saw how different life was on different sides of the same city. I saw the fear in the eyes of people who were not free. I saw the gratitude of people toward the United States for all that we had done.

I felt goose bumps as I got off a military train and heard the Army band strike up "Stars and Stripes Forever." I learned what it meant to be America at our best. I learned the pride of our freedom. And I am determined now to restore that pride to all who look to America.

Mine were greatest generation parents. And as I thank them, we all join together to thank that whole generation for making America strong, for winning World War II, winning the Cold War, and for the great gift of service which brought America fifty years of peace and prosperity.

My parents inspired me to serve, and when I was a junior in high school, John Kennedy called my generation to service. It was the beginning of a great journey—a time to march for civil rights, for voting rights, for the environment, for women, and for peace. We believed we could change the world. And you know what? We did.

But we're not finished. The journey isn't complete. The march isn't over. The promise isn't perfected. Tonight, we're setting out again. And together, we're going to write the next great chapter of America's story.

We have it in our power to change the world again. But only if we're true to our ideals—and that starts by telling the truth to the American people. That is my first pledge to you tonight. As President, I will restore trust and credibility to the White House.

I ask you to judge me by my record: As a young prosecutor, I fought for victim's rights and made prosecuting violence against women a priority. When I came to the Senate, I broke with many in my own party to vote for a balanced budget, because I thought it was the right thing to do. I fought to put a 100,000 cops on the street.

And then I reached across the aisle to work with [Sen.] John McCain [R-Ariz.], to find the truth about our POW's and missing in action, and to finally make peace with Vietnam.

I will be a commander in chief who will never mislead us into war. I will have a Vice President who will not conduct secret meetings with polluters to rewrite our environmental laws. I will have a Secretary of Defense who will listen to the best advice of our military leaders. And I will appoint an Attorney General who actually upholds the Constitution of the United States.

My fellow Americans, this is the most important election of our lifetime. The stakes are high. We are a nation at war—a global war on terror against an enemy unlike any we have ever known before. And here at home, wages are falling, health care costs are rising, and our great middle class is shrinking. People are working weekends; they're working two jobs, three jobs, and they're still not getting ahead.

We're told that outsourcing jobs is good for America. We're told that new jobs that pay $9,000 less than the jobs that have been lost is the best we can do. They say this is the best economy we've ever had. And they say that anyone who thinks otherwise is a pessimist. Well, here is our answer: There is nothing more pessimistic than saying America can't do better.

We can do better and we will. We're the optimists. For us, this is a country of the future. We're the can do people. And let's not forget what we did in the 1990s. We balanced the budget. We paid down the debt. We created 23 million new jobs. We lifted millions out of poverty and we lifted the standard of living for the middle class. We just need to believe in ourselves—and we can do it again.

So tonight, in the city where America's freedom began, only a few blocks from where the sons and daughters of liberty gave birth to our nation—here tonight, on behalf of a new birth of freedom—on behalf of the middle class who deserve a champion, and those struggling to join it who deserve a fair shot—for the brave men and women in uniform who risk their lives every day and the families who pray for their return—for all those who believe our best days are ahead of us—for all of you—with great faith in the American people, I accept your nomination for President of the United States.

I am proud that at my side will be a running mate whose life is the story of the American dream and who's worked every day to make that dream real for all Americans—Senator John Edwards of North Carolina. And his wonderful wife Elizabeth and their family. This son of a mill worker is ready to lead—and next January, Americans will be proud to have a fighter for the middle class to succeed Dick Cheney as Vice President of the United States.

And what can I say about Teresa? She has the strongest moral compass of anyone I know. She's down to earth, nurturing, courageous, wise and smart. She speaks her mind and she speaks the truth, and I love her for that, too. And that's why America will embrace her as the next First Lady of the United States.

For Teresa and me, no matter what the future holds or the past has given us, nothing will ever mean as much as our children. We love them not just for who they are and what they've become, but for being themselves, making us laugh, holding our feet to the fire, and never letting me get away with anything. Thank you, Andre, Alex, Chris, Vanessa, and John.

And in this journey, I am accompanied by an extraordinary band of brothers led by that American hero, a patriot named Max Cleland. Our band of brothers doesn't march together because of who we are as veterans, but because of what we learned as soldiers. We fought for this nation because we loved it and we came back with the deep belief that every day is extra. We may be a little older now, we may be a little grayer, but we still know how to fight for our country.

And standing with us in that fight are those who shared with me the long season of the primary campaign: Carol Moseley Braun, General Wesley Clark, Howard Dean, Dick Gephardt, Bob Graham, Dennis Kucinich, Joe Lieberman and Al Sharpton.

To all of you, I say thank you for teaching me and testing me—but mostly, we say thank you for standing up for our country and giving us the unity to move America forward.

My fellow Americans, the world tonight is very different from the world of four years ago. But I believe the American people are more than equal to the challenge.

Remember the hours after September 11th, when we came together as one to answer the attack against our homeland. We drew strength when our firefighters ran up the stairs and risked their lives, so that others might live. When rescuers rushed into smoke and fire at the Pentagon. When the men and women of Flight 93 sacrificed themselves to save our nation's Capitol. When flags were hanging from front porches all across America, and strangers became friends. It was the worst day we have ever seen, but it brought out the best in all of us.

I am proud that after September 11th all our people rallied to President Bush's call for unity to meet the danger. There were no Democrats. There were no Republicans. There were only Americans. How we wish it had stayed that way.

Now I know there are those who criticize me for seeing complexities—and I do—because some issues just aren't all that simple. Saying there are weapons of mass destruction in Iraq doesn't make it so. Saying we can fight a war on the cheap doesn't make it so. And proclaiming mission accomplished certainly doesn't make it so.

As President, I will ask hard questions and demand hard evidence. I will immediately reform the intelligence system—so policy is guided by facts, and facts are never distorted by politics. And as President, I will bring back this nation's time-honored tradition: the United States of America never goes to war because we want to, we only go to war because we have to.

I know what kids go through when they are carrying an M-16 in a dangerous place and they can't tell friend from foe. I know what they go through when they're out on patrol at night and they don't know what's coming around the next bend. I know what it's like to write letters home telling your family that everything's all right when you're not sure that's true.

As President, I will wage this war with the lessons I learned in war. Before you go to battle, you have to be able to look a parent in the eye and truthfully say: "I tried everything possible to avoid sending your son or daughter into harm's way. But we had no choice. We had to protect the American people, fundamental American values from a threat that was real and imminent." So lesson one, this is the only justification for going to war.

And on my first day in office, I will send a message to every man and woman in our armed forces: You will never be asked to fight a war without a plan to win the peace.

I know what we have to do in Iraq. We need a President who has the credibility to bring our allies to our side and share the burden, reduce the cost to American taxpayers, and reduce the risk to American soldiers. That's the right way to get the job done and bring our troops home. Here is the reality: that won't happen until we have a president who restores America's respect and leadership—so we don't have to go it alone in the world.

And we need to rebuild our alliances, so we can get the terrorists before they get us.

I defended this country as a young man and I will defend it as President. Let there be no mistake: I will never hesitate to use force when it is required. Any attack will be met with a swift and certain response. I will never give any nation or international institution a veto over our national security. And I will build a stronger American military.

We will add 40,000 active duty troops—not in Iraq, but to strengthen American forces that are now overstretched, overextended, and under pressure. We will double our special forces to conduct anti-terrorist operations. We will provide our troops with the newest weapons and technology to save their lives—and win the battle. And we will end the backdoor draft of National Guard and reservists.

To all who serve in our armed forces today, I say, help is on the way.

As President, I will fight a smarter, more effective war on terror. We will deploy every tool in our arsenal: our economic as well as our military might; our principles as well as our firepower.

In these dangerous days there is a right way and a wrong way to be strong. Strength is more than tough words. After decades of experience in national security, I know the reach of our power and I know the power of our ideals.

We need to make America once again a beacon in the world. We need to be looked up to and not just feared.

We need to lead a global effort against nuclear proliferation—to keep the most dangerous weapons in the world out of the most dangerous hands in the world.

We need a strong military and we need to lead strong alliances. And then, with confidence and determination, we will be able to tell the terrorists: You will lose and we will win. The future doesn't belong to fear; it belongs to freedom.

And the front lines of this battle are not just far away—they're right here on our shores, at our airports, and potentially in any town or city. Today, our national security begins with homeland security. The 9-11 Commission has given us a path to follow, endorsed by Democrats, Republicans, and the 9-11 families. As President, I will not evade or equivocate; I will immediately implement the recommendations of that commission. We shouldn't be letting ninety-five percent of container ships come into our ports without ever being physically inspected. We shouldn't be leaving our nuclear and chemical plants without enough protection. And we shouldn't be opening firehouses in Baghdad and closing them down in the United States of America.

And tonight, we have an important message for those who question the patriotism of Americans who offer a better direction for our country. Before wrapping themselves in the flag and shutting their eyes and ears to the truth, they should remember what America is really all about. They should remember the great idea of freedom for which so many have given their lives. Our purpose now is to reclaim democracy itself. We are here to affirm that when Americans stand up and speak their minds and say America can do better, that is not a challenge to patriotism; it is the heart and soul of patriotism.

You see that flag up there. We call her Old Glory. The stars and stripes forever. I fought under that flag, as did so many of you here and all across our country. That flag flew from the gun turret right behind my head. It was shot through and through and tattered, but it never ceased to wave in the wind. It draped the caskets of men I served with and friends I grew up with. For us, that flag is the most powerful symbol of who we are and what we believe in. Our strength. Our diversity. Our love of country. All that makes America both great and good.

That flag doesn't belong to any president. It doesn't belong to any ideology and it doesn't belong to any political party. It belongs to all the American people.

My fellow citizens, elections are about choices. And choices are about values. In the end, it's not just policies and programs that matter; the president who sits at that desk must be guided by principle.

For four years, we've heard a lot of talk about values. But values spoken without actions taken are just slogans. Values are not just words. They're what we live by. They're about the causes we champion and the people we fight for. And it is time for those who talk about family values to start valuing families.

You don't value families by kicking kids out of after school programs and taking cops off our streets, so that Enron can get another tax break.

We believe in the family value of caring for our children and protecting the neighborhoods where they walk and play.

And that is the choice in this election.

You don't value families by denying real prescription drug coverage to seniors, so big drug companies can get another windfall.

We believe in the family value expressed in one of the oldest Commandments: "Honor thy father and thy mother." As President, I will not privatize Social Security.

I will not cut benefits. And together, we will make sure that senior citizens never have to cut their pills in half because they can't afford life-saving medicine.

And that is the choice in this election.

You don't value families if you force them to take up a collection to buy body armor for a son or daughter in the service, if you deny veterans health care, or if you tell middle class families to wait for a tax cut, so that the wealthiest among us can get even more.

We believe in the value of doing what's right for everyone in the American family.

And that is the choice in this election.

We believe that what matters most is not narrow appeals masquerading as values, but the shared values that show the true face of America. Not narrow appeals that divide us, but shared values that unite us. Family and faith. Hard work and responsibility. Opportunity for all—so that every child, every parent, every worker has an equal shot at living up to their God-given potential.

What does it mean in America today when Dave McCune, a steel worker I met in Canton, Ohio, saw his job sent overseas and the equipment in his factory literally unbolted, crated up, and shipped thousands of miles away along with that job? What does it mean when workers I've met had to train their foreign replacements?

America can do better. So tonight we say: help is on the way.

What does it mean when Mary Ann Knowles, a woman with breast cancer I met in New Hampshire, had to keep working day after day right through her chemotherapy, no matter how sick she felt, because she was terrified of losing her family's health insurance.

America can do better. And help is on the way.

What does it mean when Deborah Kromins from Philadelphia, Pennsylvania works and saves all her life only to find out that her pension has disappeared into thin air—and the executive who looted it has bailed out on a golden parachute?

America can do better. And help is on the way.

What does it mean when twenty five percent of the children in Harlem have asthma because of air pollution?

America can do better. And help is on the way.

What does it mean when people are huddled in blankets in the cold, sleeping in Lafayette Park on the doorstep of the White House itself—and the number of families living in poverty has risen by three million in the last four years?

America can do better. And help is on the way.

And so we come here tonight to ask: Where is the conscience of our country?

I'll tell you where it is: it's in rural and small town America; it's in urban neighborhoods and suburban main streets; it's alive in the people I've met in every part of this land. It's bursting in the hearts of Americans who are determined to give our country back its values and its truth.

We value jobs that pay you more not less than you earned before. We value jobs where, when you put in a week's work, you can actually pay your bills, provide for your children, and lift up the quality of your life. We value an America where the middle class is not being squeezed, but doing better.

So here is our economic plan to build a stronger America:

First, new incentives to revitalize manufacturing.

Second, investment in technology and innovation that will create the good-paying jobs of the future.

Third, close the tax loopholes that reward companies for shipping our jobs overseas. Instead, we will reward companies that create and keep good paying jobs where they belong—in the good old U.S.A.

We value an America that exports products, not jobs—and we believe American workers should never have to subsidize the loss of their own job.

Next, we will trade and compete in the world. But our plan calls for a fair playing field—because if you give the American worker a fair playing field, there's nobody in the world the American worker can't compete against.

And we're going to return to fiscal responsibility because it is the foundation of our economic strength. Our plan will cut the deficit in half in four years by ending tax giveaways that are nothing more than corporate welfare—and will make government live by the rule that every family has to follow: pay as you go.

And let me tell you what we won't do: we won't raise taxes on the middle class. You've heard a lot of false charges about this in recent months. So let me say straight out what I will do as President: I will cut middle class taxes. I will reduce the tax burden on small business. And I will roll back the tax cuts for the wealthiest individuals who make over $200,000 a year, so we can invest in job creation, health care and education.

Our education plan for a stronger America sets high standards and demands accountability from parents, teachers, and schools. It provides for smaller class sizes and treats teachers like the professionals they are. And it gives a tax credit to families for each and every year of college.

When I was a prosecutor, I met young kids who were in trouble, abandoned by adults. And as President, I am determined that we stop being a nation content to spend $50,000 a year to keep a young person in prison for the rest of their life—when we could invest $10,000 to give them Head Start, Early Start, Smart Start, the best possible start in life.

And we value health care that's affordable and accessible for all Americans.

Since 2000, four million people have lost their health insurance. Millions more are struggling to afford it.

You know what's happening. Your premiums, your co-payments, your deductibles have all gone through the roof.

Our health care plan for a stronger America cracks down on the waste, greed, and abuse in our health care system and will save families up to $1,000 a year on their premiums. You'll get to pick your own doctor—and patients and doctors, not insurance company bureaucrats, will make medical decisions. Under our plan, Medicare will negotiate lower drug prices for seniors. And all Americans will be able to buy less expensive prescription drugs from countries like Canada.

The story of people struggling for health care is the story of so many Americans. But you know what, it's not the story of senators and members of Congress. Because we give ourselves great health care and you get the bill. Well, I'm here to say, your family's health care is just as important as any politician's in Washington, D.C.

And when I'm President, America will stop being the only advanced nation in the world which fails to understand that health care is not a privilege for the wealthy, the connected, and the elected—it is a right for all Americans.

We value an America that controls its own destiny because it's finally and forever independent of Mideast oil. What does it mean for our economy and our national security when we only have three percent of the world's oil reserves, yet we rely on foreign countries for fifty-three percent of what we consume?

I want an America that relies on its own ingenuity and innovation—not the Saudi royal family.

And our energy plan for a stronger America will invest in new technologies and alternative fuels and the cars of the future—so that no young American in uniform will ever be held hostage to our dependence on oil from the Middle East.

I've told you about our plans for the economy, for education, for health care, for energy independence. I want you to know more about them. So now I'm going to say something that Franklin Roosevelt could never have said in his acceptance speech: go to johnkerry.com.

I want to address these next words directly to President George W. Bush: In the weeks ahead, let's be optimists, not just opponents. Let's build unity in the American family, not angry division. Let's honor this nation's diversity; let's respect one another; and let's never misuse for political purposes the most precious document in American history, the Constitution of the United States.

My friends, the high road may be harder, but it leads to a better place. And that's why Republicans and Democrats must make this election a contest of big ideas, not small-minded attacks. This is our time to reject the kind of politics calculated to divide race from race, group from group, region from region. Maybe some just see us divided into red states and blue states, but I see us as one America—red, white, and blue. And when I am President, the government I lead will enlist people of talent, Republicans as well as Democrats, to find the common ground—so that no one who has something to contribute will be left on the sidelines.

And let me say it plainly: in that cause, and in this campaign, we welcome people of faith. America is not us and them. I think of what Ron Reagan said of his father a few weeks ago, and I want to say this to you tonight: I don't wear my own faith on my sleeve. But faith has given me values and hope to live by, from Vietnam to this day, from Sunday to Sunday. I don't want to claim that God is on our side. As Abraham Lincoln told us, I want to pray humbly that we are on God's side. And whatever our faith, one belief should bind us all: The measure of our character is our willingness to give of ourselves for others and for our country.

These aren't Democratic values. These aren't Republican values. They're American values. We believe in them. They're who we are. And if we honor them, if we believe in ourselves, we can build an America that's stronger at home and respected in the world.

So much promise stretches before us. Americans have always reached for the impossible, looked to the next horizon, and asked: What if?

Two young bicycle mechanics from Dayton asked what if this airplane could take off at Kitty Hawk? It did that and changed the world forever. A young president asked what if we could go to the moon in ten years? And now we're exploring the solar system and the stars themselves. A young generation of entrepreneurs asked, what if we could take all the information in a library and put it on a little chip the size of a fingernail? We did and that too changed the world forever.

And now it's our time to ask: What if?

What if we find a breakthrough to cure Parkinson's, diabetes, Alzheimer's and AIDS? What if we have a president who believes in science, so we can unleash the wonders of discovery like stem cell research to treat illness and save millions of lives?

What if we do what adults should do—and make sure all our children are safe in the afternoons after school? And what if we have a leadership that's as good as the

American dream—so that bigotry and hatred never again steal the hope and future of any American?

I learned a lot about these values on that gunboat patrolling the Mekong Delta with young Americans who came from places as different as Iowa and Oregon, Arkansas, Florida and California. No one cared where we went to school. No one cared about our race or our backgrounds. We were literally all in the same boat. We looked out, one for the other—and we still do.

That is the kind of America I will lead as President—an America where we are all in the same boat.

Never has there been a more urgent moment for Americans to step up and define ourselves.

I will work my heart out. But, my fellow citizens, the outcome is in your hands more than mine.

It is time to reach for the next dream. It is time to look to the next horizon. For America, the hope is there. The sun is rising. Our best days are still to come.

Goodnight, God bless you, and God bless America.

Source: Friends of John Kerry, Inc. "Speech to the 2004 Democratic National Convention: Remarks of John Kerry." July 29, 2004. www.johnkerry.com/pressroom/speeches/spc_2004_0729.html (accessed January 30, 2005).

"Remarks Accepting the Presidential Nomination at the Republican National Convention"

Thank you all. Mr. Chairman, delegates, fellow citizens: I am honored by your support, and I accept your nomination for President of the United States.

When I said those words 4 years ago, none of us could have envisioned what these years would bring. In the heart of this great city, we saw tragedy arrive on a quiet morning. We saw the bravery of rescuers grow with danger. We learned of passengers on a doomed plane who died with a courage that frightened their killers. We have seen a shaken economy rise to its feet. And we have seen Americans in uniform storming mountain strongholds and charging through sandstorms and liberating millions with acts of valor that would make the men of Normandy proud.

Since 2001, Americans have been given hills to climb and found the strength to climb them. Now, because we have made the hard journey, we can see the valley below. Now, because we have faced challenges with resolve, we have historic goals within our reach and greatness in our future. We will build a safer world and a more hopeful America, and nothing will hold us back.

In the work we have done and the work we will do, I am fortunate to have a superb Vice President. I have counted on Dick Cheney's calm and steady judgment in difficult days, and I am honored to have him at my side.

I am grateful to share my walk in life with Laura Bush. Americans have come to see the goodness and kindness and strength I first saw 26 years ago, and we love our First Lady.

I'm a fortunate father of two spirited, intelligent, and lovely young women. I'm blessed with a sister and brothers who are my closest friends. And I will always be the proud and grateful son of George and Barbara Bush.

My father served 8 years at the side of another great American, Ronald Reagan. His spirit of optimism and good will and decency are in this hall and are in our hearts and will always define our party.

Two months from today, voters will make a choice based on the records we have built, the convictions we hold, and the vision that guides us forward. A Presidential election is a contest for the future. Tonight I will tell you where I stand, what I believe, and where I will lead this country in the next 4 years.

I believe every child can learn and every school must teach, so we passed the most important Federal education reform in history. Because we acted, children are making sustained progress in reading and math; America's schools are getting better; and nothing will hold us back.

I believe we have a moral responsibility to honor America's seniors, so I brought Republicans and Democrats together to strengthen Medicare. Now seniors are getting immediate help buying medicine; soon every senior will be able to get prescription drug coverage; and nothing will hold us back.

I believe in the energy and innovative spirit of America's workers, entrepreneurs, farmers, and ranchers, so we unleashed that energy with the largest tax relief in a generation. Because we acted, our economy is growing again and creating jobs, and nothing will hold us back.

I believe the most solemn duty of the American President is to protect the American people. If America shows uncertainty or weakness in this decade, the world will drift toward tragedy. This will not happen on my watch.

I'm running for President with a clear and positive plan to build a safer world and a more hopeful America. I'm running with a compassionate conservative philosophy, that government should help people improve their lives, not try to run their lives. I believe this Nation wants steady, consistent, principled leadership, and that is why, with your help, we will win this election.

The story of America is the story of expanding liberty, an ever-widening circle, constantly growing to reach further and include more. Our Nation's founding commitment is still our deepest commitment: In our world and here at home, we will extend the frontiers of freedom.

The times in which we work and live are changing dramatically. The workers of our parents' generation typically had one job, one skill, one career, often with one company that provided health care and a pension. And most of those workers were men. Today, workers change jobs, even careers, many times during their lives. And in one of the most dramatic shifts our society has seen, two-thirds of all moms also work outside the home.

This changed world can be a time of great opportunity for all Americans to earn a better living, support your family, and have a rewarding career. And Government must take your side. Many of our most fundamental systems, the Tax Code, health coverage, pension plans, worker training, were created for the world of yesterday, not tomorrow.

We will transform these systems so that all citizens are equipped, prepared—and thus truly free—to make your own choices and pursue your own dreams.

My plan begins with providing the security and opportunity of a growing economy. We now compete in a global market that provides new buyers for our goods but new competition for our workers. To create more jobs in America, America must be the best place in the world to do business. To create jobs, my plan will encourage investment and expansion by restraining Federal spending, reducing regulation, and making the tax relief permanent. To create jobs, we will make our country less dependent on foreign sources of energy. To create jobs, we will expand trade and level the playing field to sell American goods and services across the globe. And we must protect small-business owners and workers from the explosion of frivolous lawsuits that threaten jobs across our country.

Another drag on our economy is the current Tax Code, which is a complicated mess, filled with special interest loopholes, saddling our people with more than 6 billion hours of paperwork and headache every year. The American people deserve—and our economic future demands—a simpler, fairer, pro-growth system. In a new term, I will lead a bipartisan effort to reform and simplify the Federal Tax Code.

Another priority in a new term will be to help workers take advantage of the expanding economy to find better and higher paying jobs. In this time of change, many workers want to go back to school to learn different or higher level skills. So we will double the number of people served by our principal job training program and increase funding for our community colleges. I know that with the right skills, American workers can compete with anyone, anywhere in the world.

In this time of change, opportunity in some communities is more distant than in others. To stand with workers in poor communities and those that have lost manufacturing, textile, and other jobs, we will create American opportunity zones. In these areas, we will provide tax relief and other incentives to attract new business and improve housing and job training to bring hope and work throughout all of America.

As I've traveled the country, I've met many workers and small-business owners who have told me that they are worried they cannot afford health care. More than half of the uninsured are small-business employees and their families. In a new term, we must allow small firms to join together to purchase insurance at the discounts available to big companies.

We will offer a tax credit to encourage small businesses and their employees to set up health savings accounts and provide direct help for low-income Americans to purchase them. These accounts give workers the security of insurance against major illness, the opportunity to save tax-free for routine health expenses, and the freedom of knowing you can take your account with you whenever you change jobs. We will provide low-income Americans with better access to health care. In a new term, I will ensure every poor county in America has a community or rural health center.

As I have traveled our country, I have met too many good doctors, especially ob-gyns, who are being forced out of practice because of the high cost of lawsuits. To make healthcare more affordable and accessible, we must pass medical liability reform now. And in all we do to improve health care in America, we will make sure that health decisions are made by doctors and patients, not by bureaucrats in Washington, DC.

In this time of change, Government must take the side of working families. In a new term, we will change outdated labor laws to offer comp-time and flex-time. Our laws should never stand in the way of a more family-friendly workplace.

Another priority for a new term is to build an ownership society, because ownership brings security and dignity and independence.

Thanks to our policies, homeownership in America is at an all-time high. Tonight we set a new goal: 7 million more affordable homes in the next 10 years so more American families will be able to open the door and say, "Welcome to my home."

In an ownership society, more people will own their health care plans and have the confidence of owning a piece of their retirement. We'll always keep the promise of Social Security for our older workers. With the huge baby boom generation approaching retirement, many of our children and grandchildren understandably worry whether Social Security will be there when they need it. We must strengthen Social Security by allowing younger workers to save some of their taxes in a personal account, a nest egg you can call your own and Government can never take away.

In all these proposals, we seek to provide not just a Government program but a path, a path to greater opportunity, more freedom, and more control over your own life.

And the path begins with our youngest Americans. To build a more hopeful America, we must help our children reach as far as their vision and character can take them. Tonight I remind every parent and every teacher, I say to every child: No matter what your circumstance, no matter where you live, your school will be the path to promise of America.

We are transforming our schools by raising standards and focusing on results. We are insisting on accountability, empowering parents and teachers, and making sure that local people are in charge of their schools. By testing every child, we are identifying those who need help, and we are providing a record level of funding to get them that help. In northeast Georgia, Gainesville Elementary School is mostly Hispanic and 90 percent poor, and this year 90 percent of the students passed State tests in reading and math. The principal expresses the philosophy of his school this way: "We don't focus on what we can't do at this school. We focus on what we can do, and we do whatever it takes to get kids across the finish line." See, this principal is challenging the soft bigotry of low expectations. And that is the spirit of our education reform and the commitment of our country: *No dejaremos a ningun nino atras.* We will leave no child behind.

We are making progress—we are making progress, and there is more to do. In this time of change, most new jobs are filled by people with at least 2 years of college, yet only about one in four students gets there. In our high schools, we will fund early intervention programs to help students at risk. We will place a new focus on math and science. As we make progress, we will require a rigorous exam before graduation. By raising performance in our high schools and expanding Pell grants for low- and middle-income families, we will help more Americans start their career with a college diploma.

America's children must also have a healthy start in life. In a new term, we will lead an aggressive effort to enroll millions of poor children who are eligible but not signed up for the Government's health insurance programs. We will not allow a lack of attention or information to stand between these children and the health care they need.

Anyone who wants more details on my agenda can find them online. The web address is not very imaginative, but it's easy to remember: georgewbush.com.

These changing times can be exciting times of expanded opportunity. And here, you face a choice. My opponent's policies are dramatically different from ours. Senator Kerry opposed Medicare reform and health savings accounts. After supporting my education reforms, he now wants to dilute them. He opposes legal and medical liability reform. He opposed reducing the marriage penalty, opposed doubling the child credit, opposed lowering income taxes for all who pay them.

Wait a minute—wait a minute. To be fair, there are some things my opponent is for. He's proposed more than $2 trillion in Federal spending so far, and that's a lot, even for a Senator from Massachusetts. And to pay for that spending, he's running on a platform of increasing taxes, and that's the kind of promise a politician usually keeps.

His tax—his policies of tax and spend, of expanding Government rather than expanding opportunity, are the politics of the past. We are on the path to the future, and we're not turning back.

In this world of change, some things do not change, the values we try to live by, the institutions that give our lives meaning and purpose. Our society rests on a foundation of responsibility and character and family commitment.

Because family and work are sources of stability and dignity, I support welfare reform that strengthens family and requires work. Because a caring society will value its weakest members, we must make a place for the unborn child. Because religious charities provide a safety net of mercy and compassion, our Government must never discriminate against them. Because the union of a man and woman deserves an honored place in our society, I support the protection of marriage against activist judges, and I will continue to appoint Federal judges who know the difference between personal opinion and the strict interpretation of the law.

My opponent recently announced that he is the conservative—the candidate of "conservative values"—must have come as a surprise to a lot of his supporters. There's some problems with this claim. If you say the heart and soul of America is found in Hollywood, I'm afraid you are not the candidate of conservative values. If you voted against the bipartisan Defense of Marriage Act, which President Clinton signed, you are not the candidate of conservative values. If you gave a speech, as my opponent did, calling the Reagan Presidency 8 years of "moral darkness," then you may be a lot of things, but the candidate of conservative values is not one of them.

This election will also determine how America responds to the continuing danger of terrorism, and you know where I stand. Three days after September the 11th, I stood where Americans died, in the ruins of the Twin Towers. Workers in hardhats were shouting to me, "Whatever it takes." A fellow grabbed me by the arm, and he said, "Do not let me down." Since that day, I wake up every morning thinking about how to better protect our country. I will never relent in defending America, whatever it takes.

So we have fought the terrorists across the Earth—not for pride, not for power, but because the lives of our citizens are at stake. Our strategy is clear. We have tripled funding for homeland security and trained a half a million first-responders, because we are determined to protect our homeland. We are transforming our military and reforming and strengthening our intelligence services. We are staying on the offensive, striking terrorists abroad so we do not have to face them here at home. And we are working to advance liberty in the broader Middle East, because freedom will bring a future of hope and the peace we all want. And we will prevail.

Our strategy is succeeding.

Four years ago, Afghanistan was the home base of Al Qaida; Pakistan was a transit point for terrorist groups; Saudi Arabia was fertile ground for terrorist fundraising; Libya was secretly pursuing nuclear weapons; Iraq was a gathering threat; and Al Qaida was largely unchallenged as it planned attacks. Today, the Government of a free Afghanistan is fighting terror; Pakistan is capturing terrorist leaders; Saudi Arabia is making raids and arrests; Libya is dismantling its weapons programs; the army of a free Iraq is fighting for freedom; and more than three-quarters of Al Qaida's key members and associates have been detained or killed. We have led; many have joined; and America and the world are safer.

This progress involved careful diplomacy, clear moral purpose, and some tough decisions. And the toughest came on Iraq. We knew Saddam Hussein's record of aggression and support for terror. We knew his long history of pursuing, even using weapons of mass destruction. And we know that September the 11th requires our country to think differently. We must and we will confront threats to America before it is too late. In Saddam Hussein, we saw a threat. Members of both political parties, including. . . my opponent and his runningmate, saw the threat and voted to authorize the use of force. We went to the United Nations Security Council, which passed a unanimous resolution demanding the dictator disarm or face serious consequences. Leaders in the Middle East urged him to comply. After more than a decade of diplomacy, we gave Saddam Hussein another chance, a final chance, to meet his responsibilities to the civilized world. He again refused, and I faced the kind of decision that comes only to the Oval Office, a decision no President would ask for but must be prepared to make: Do I forget the lessons of September the 11th and take the word of a madman, or do I take action to defend our country? Faced with that choice, I will defend America every time.

Because we acted to defend our country, the murderous regimes of Saddam Hussein and the Taliban are history, more than 50 million people have been liberated, and democracy is coming to the broader Middle East. In Afghanistan, terrorists have done everything they can to intimidate people, yet more than 10 million citizens have registered to vote in the October Presidential election, a resounding endorsement for democracy. Despite ongoing acts of violence, Iraq now has a strong Prime Minister, a national council, and national elections are scheduled for January. Our Nation is standing with the people of Afghanistan and Iraq, because when America gives its word, America must keep its word.

As importantly, we are serving a vital and historic cause that will make our country safer. Free societies in the Middle East will be hopeful societies which no longer feed resentments and breed violence for export. Free governments in the Middle East will fight terrorists instead of harboring them, and that helps us keep the peace. So our mission in Afghanistan and Iraq is clear: We will help new leaders to train their armies and move toward elections and get on the path of stability and democracy as quickly as possible. And then our troops will return home with the honor they have earned.

Our troops know the historic importance of our work. One Army specialist wrote home: "We are transforming a once sick society into a hopeful place." "The various terrorist enemies we are facing in Iraq," he continued, "are really aiming at you back in the United States. This is a test of will for our country. We soldiers of yours are doing great and scoring victories and confronting the evil terrorists."

That young man is right. Our men and women in uniform are doing a superb job for America. Tonight I want to speak to all of them and to their families: You are involved in a struggle of historic proportion. Because of your service and sacrifice, we are defeating the terrorists where they live and plan, and you're making America safer. Because of you, women in Afghanistan are no longer shot in a sports stadium. Because of you, the people of Iraq no longer fear being executed and left in mass graves. Because of you, the world is more just and will be more peaceful. We owe you our thanks, and we owe you something more. We will give you all the resources, all the tools, and all the support you need for victory.

Again, my opponent and I have different approaches. I proposed and the Congress overwhelmingly passed $87 billion in funding needed by our troops doing battle in Afghanistan and Iraq. My opponent and his runningmate voted against this money for bullets and fuel and vehicles and body armor.

When asked to explain his vote, the Senator said, "I actually did vote for the $87 billion, before I voted against it." Then he said he was proud of that vote. Then, when pressed, he said it was a complicated matter. There's nothing complicated about supporting our troops in combat.

Our allies also know the historic importance of our work. About 40 nations stand beside us in Afghanistan and some 30 in Iraq. I deeply appreciate the courage and wise counsel of leaders like Prime Minister [John] Howard [of Australia], President [Aleksander] Kwasniewski [of Poland], Prime Minister [Silvio] Berlusconi [of Italy], and, of course, [British] Prime Minister Tony Blair.

Again, my opponent takes a different approach. In the midst of war, he has called American allies, quote, "a coalition of the coerced and he bribed." That would be nations like Great Britain, Poland, Italy, Japan, the Netherlands, Denmark, El Salvador, Australia, and others, allies that deserve the respect of all Americans, not the scorn of a politician. I respect every soldier from every country who serves beside us in the hard work of history. America is grateful, and America will not forget.

The people we have freed won't forget either. Not long ago, seven Iraqi men came to see me in the Oval Office. They had X's branded into their foreheads, and their right hands had been cut off by Saddam Hussein's secret police, the sadistic punishment for imaginary crimes. During our emotional visit, one of the Iraqi men used his new prosthetic hand to slowly write out, in Arabic, a prayer for God to bless America. I am proud that our country remains the hope of the oppressed and the greatest force for good on this Earth.

Others understand the historic importance of our work. The terrorists know. They know that a vibrant, successful democracy at the heart of the Middle East will discredit their radical ideology of hate. They know that men and women with hope and purpose and dignity do not strap bombs on their bodies and kill the innocent. The terrorists are fighting freedom with all their cunning and cruelty because freedom is their greatest fear. And they should be afraid, because freedom is on the march.

I believe in the transformational power of liberty. The wisest use of American strength is to advance freedom. As the citizens of Afghanistan and Iraq seize the moment, their example will send a message of hope throughout a vital region. Palestinians will hear the message that democracy and reform are within their reach, and so is peace with our good friend Israel. Young women across the Middle East will hear the message that their day of equality and justice is coming. Young men will hear the message that national progress and dignity are found in liberty, not tyranny and terror. Reformers and political prisoners and exiles will hear the message that their dream of freedom cannot be denied forever. And as freedom advances, heart by heart and nation by nation, America will be more secure and the world more peaceful.

America has done this kind of work before, and there have always been doubters. In 1946, 18 months after the fall of Berlin to Allied forces, a journalist in the *New York Times* wrote this: "Germany is a land in an acute stage of economic, political, and moral crisis. European capitals are frightened. In every military headquarters, one meets alarmed officials doing their utmost to deal with the consequences of the occupation policy that they admit has failed." Maybe that same person is still around, writing editorials. Fortunately, we had a resolute President named Truman who, with the American people, persevered, knowing that a new democracy at the center of Europe would lead to stability and peace. And because that generation of Americans held firm in the cause of liberty, we live in a better and safer world today.

The progress we and our friends and allies seek in the broader Middle East will not come easily or all at once. Yet Americans, of all people, should never be surprised by the power of liberty to transform lives and nations. That power brought settlers on perilous journeys, inspired colonies to rebellion, ended the sin of slavery, and set our Nation against the tyrannies of the 20th century. We were honored to aid the rise of democracy in Germany and Japan and Nicaragua and Central Europe and the Baltics, and that noble story goes on. I believe that America is called to lead the cause of freedom in a new century. I believe that millions in the Middle East plead in silence for their liberty. I believe that given the chance, they will embrace the most honorable form of government ever devised by man. I believe all these things because freedom is not America's gift to the world; it is the Almighty God's gift to every man and woman in this world.

This moment in the life of our country will be remembered. Generations will know if we kept our faith and kept our word. Generations will know if we seized this moment and used it to build a future of safety and peace. The freedom of many and the future security of our Nation now depend on us. And tonight, my fellow Americans, I ask you to stand with me.

In the last 4 years, you and I have come to know each other. Even when we don't agree, at least you know what I believe and where I stand. You may have noticed I have a few flaws too. People sometimes have to correct my English. I knew I had a problem when [California governor] Arnold Schwarzenegger started doing it. Some folks look at me and see a certain swagger, which in Texas is called walking. Now and then I come across as a little too blunt, and for that we can all thank the white-haired lady sitting right up there [referring to his mother, Barbara Bush].

One thing I have learned about the Presidency is that whatever shortcomings you have, people are going to notice them—[laughter]—and whatever strengths you have, you're going to need them. These 4 years have brought moments I could not foresee and will not forget. I've tried to comfort Americans who lost the most on September the 11th, people who showed me a picture or told me a story so I would know how much was taken from them. I've learned firsthand that ordering Americans into battle is the hardest decision, even when it is right. I have returned the salute of wounded soldiers, some with a very tough road ahead, who say they were just doing their job. I've held the children of the fallen, who are told their dad or mom is a hero but would rather just have their mom or dad. I've met with the parents and wives and husbands who have received a folded flag and said a final goodbye to a soldier they loved.

I am awed that so many have used those meetings to say that I'm in their prayers and to offer encouragement to me. Where does that—strength like that come from? How can people so burdened with sorrow also feel such pride? It is because they know their loved one was last seen doing good, because they know that liberty was precious to the one they lost. And in those military families, I have seen the character of a great nation, decent, idealistic, and strong.

The world saw that spirit 3 miles from here when the people of this city faced peril together and lifted a flag over the ruins and defied the enemy with their courage. My fellow Americans, for as long as our country stands, people will look to the resurrection of New York City and they will say, "Here buildings fell. Here a nation rose."

We see America's character in our military, which finds a way or makes one. We see it in our veterans, who are supporting military families in their days of worry. We see it in our young people, who have found heroes once again. We see that character in workers and entrepreneurs, who are renewing our economy with their effort and optimism. And all of this has confirmed one belief beyond doubt: Having come this far, our tested and confident Nation can achieve anything.

To everything we know there is a season, a time for sadness, a time for struggle, a time for rebuilding. And now we have reached a time for hope. This young century will be liberty's century. By promoting liberty abroad, we will build a safer world. By encouraging liberty at home, we will build a more hopeful America. Like generations before us, we have a calling from beyond the stars to stand for freedom. This is the everlasting dream of America, and tonight, in this place, that dream is renewed. Now we go forward, grateful for our freedom, faithful to our cause, and confident in the future of the greatest nation on Earth.

May God bless you, and may God continue to bless our great country. Thank you all.

Source: U.S. Executive Office of the President. "Remarks Accepting the Presidential Nomination at the Republican National Convention in New York City." *Weekly Compilation of Presidential Documents* 40, no. 36 (September 6, 2004): 1797–1804. www.gpoaccess.gov/wcomp/v40no36.html (accessed March 3, 2005).

August

2004 HISTORIC DOCUMENTS

UN Secretary General on the Democratic Republic of the Congo

August 16, 2004

INTRODUCTION

A fragile peace agreement that was supposed to end the massive, years-long war in the Democratic Republic of the Congo remained on a knife's edge all through 2004—only partially implemented and in constant danger of collapsing into another round of bloodletting. A new transitional government in Kinshasa was beset with bickering among the leaders of groups that had fought in the war. That political infighting endangered plans for the country's first-ever elections in 2005.

Actual conflict among various groups continued on a sporadic basis in the highly unstable eastern provinces, resulting in yet more rounds of killing and the displacement of thousands of people from their homes. Neighboring Rwanda, which since 1998 had been one of the chief actors in the Congo's war, threatened in December to invade the country again—a step that, if carried out, risked the resumption of large-scale fighting and the collapse of the peace process. The United Nations expanded its peacekeeping force in hopes of blocking a return to war, but that mission was plagued by underfunding, lack of manpower, and charges that some of its soldiers were preying on civilians.

Through it all, the Congo's estimated 58 million people remained the chief victims. The country's immense wealth of natural resources had been plundered by corrupt leaders, foreign governments, and armies; the war had destroyed nearly all legitimate economic activity; and thousands of people continued to die each month from disease and starvation directly linked to the war. *(Background, Historic Documents of 2002, p. 546; Historic Documents of 2003, p. 288)*

Political Infighting in Kinshasa

Under a series of peace agreements signed in 2002 and 2003, the six African nations that had sent troops to participate in the Congolese war starting in 1998 were to withdraw from the country; rebel groups were to disarm and disband; and rebel leaders were to join a transitional government, headed by President Joseph Kabila, that would make arrangements for the Congo's national elections in 2005. Some aspects of those steps had been completed by 2004, notably the withdrawal of nearly all foreign forces and the creation of a transitional government.

The political aspect of the peace process was based on the assumption that if rebel leaders were brought into the government, then they would have a stake in the government's success and thus would help end the war. In 2003 two rebel leaders became vice presidents in Kabila's government in Kinshasa, along with two civilian politicians. The government was highly unstable, however, because it was based largely on expediency rather than on a genuine acceptance of a democratic political process. Kabila and the former rebel leaders bickered constantly among themselves over matters ranging from their salaries and the size of their offices to each group's degree of political power.

Kabila faced two apparent coup attempts during the year. The first came on March 28, when armed rebels attacked several army posts and the state media headquarters in Kinshasa but failed to dislodge the government. Officials said the men were members of the guard of the country's former president, Mobutu Sese Seko, who had been ousted from power in 1997 by rebels led by Kabila's father, Laurent Kabila.

Another attempted coup attempt occurred overnight on June 10–11. Renegades in the presidential guard seized the national television station and said the army had taken power. The rebellion was quickly put down and the alleged leader—a close aide to Kabila—fled the capital. Some opposition leaders said Kabila had staged the coup in hopes of bolstering his position, a charge he denied.

The coup attempts and other forms of political intrigue did nothing to ease the daunting task facing Kabila and other leaders of preparing the Congo for elections that had been promised for June 2005. Among other things, the country needed revamped army and police forces; a new constitution; and all the elements necessary for elections, beginning with a list of voters in a country where no census had been taken in decades. None of these steps had been completed as of the end of 2004.

Instability in the Kivus

The two easternmost provinces of the Congo—North and South Kivu—were among the country's most resource-rich (with valuable minerals and timber) and were also the most troubled by conflicts among ethnic and national groups. The current round of conflict in those provinces, and in the Congo generally, resulted directly from the 1994 genocide in Rwanda, during which an estimated 800,000 Tutsis and moderate Hutus died at the hands of extremist Hutus. In the closing days of the genocide, the Hutu extremists (including elements of the then-Rwandan army) fled across the border into the Congo (then known as Zaire). In 1998 the new Tutsi-led government of Rwanda, along with Burundi and Uganda, invaded the Congo and fought armed rebel groups there, setting off what was to become the biggest and most complex war in the world since World War II. *(Rwanda, p. 115)*

The Rwandan army had occupied the Kivus for much of the time since 1998, collaborating with militia groups composed of local residents of Rwandan Tutsi origin (known as the Banyamulunge). Arrayed against these forces were militias composed at least in part of Hutu extremists who had carried out the 1994 Rwandan genocide. One of the largest militias was known as the Democratic Forces for the Liberation of Rwanda (FDLR), which was splintered into several groups. The Tutsi-led government in Kigali had justified its initial intervention in the Congo on actions of those rebels, who were said to have launched cross-border attacks into Rwanda.

As part of the peace process, Rwanda said it withdrew all its forces from the Congo by late 2003. Rwandan-supported rebel forces remained in the Kivu provinces, however, and numerous reports by UN investigators and other sources indicated that the Rwandan military retained at least indirect control over much of the region and was extracting valuable minerals and timber.

A potential crisis emerged in late May when pro-Rwanda rebels stepped up military operations in South Kivu. On June 2 a force of several thousand rebels seized control of the provincial capital, Bukavu, brushing aside a force of about 400 UN peacekeepers and a small unit from the Congolese army. Rwanda threatened to send its army back into the region to support the rebels, claiming that the Congolese army was ready to perpetrate genocide against the Banyamulunge.

After the UN dispatched a larger peacekeeping force to the region and European leaders threatened to send in a rapid-reaction force, the rebels left Bukavu on June 9 and the immediate crisis eased. Even so, the incident damaged the credibility of both the Congolese government and the UN peacekeeping force—neither of which was able to prevent the capture of the city—and it demonstrated that ethnic tensions remained dangerously volatile in that region. Several hundred people died in the fighting, and an estimated 30,000 people fled at least temporarily into Burundi or Rwanda during the crisis. The World Food Program temporarily suspended food distribution to about 3 million people because of the unrest. Subsequent investigations by Britain, South Africa, and private groups including Human Rights Watch showed that Rwanda's claim of an impending genocide against the Banyamulunge was false.

The fighting also produced a backlash against the UN mission, with local residents in Bukavu expressing bitterness about the UN's failure to prevent the brief rebel takeover. One resident, Justin Musenga, told a reporter from the *Boston Globe:* "We don't want the UN here anymore. They don't do anything." In Kinshasa, protesters attacked the UN headquarters, and UN troops fired at the protesters, killing two.

A "group of experts" appointed by the UN Security Council to investigate the council's arms embargo against Congolese rebel forces reported on July 15 that the Rwandan government had provided "direct and indirect support" to and had exercised "a degree of command and control over" the rebels who seized Bukavu. The UN panel also said the rebels had used Rwandan territory, directly across the border from the Congo, as an operating base and while there had been under the protection of the Rwandan army.

Two months after the Bukavu crisis, another event threatened momentarily to push the Congolese war back into high gear. On August 13 a group of 700 armed men attacked a UN refugee camp in Burundi, just across the border from the Congo, that housed Congolese Tutsis (the Banyamulunge), killing 152. Another 106 refugees were wounded and 8 went missing. A small Hutu militia force in Burundi, the National Liberation Force, claimed responsibility for the killings, but a subsequent UN investigation concluded that one or more of the militia groups from the Congo probably also participated. The massacre brought threats of renewed military operations, including from Rwanda, which threatened to attack Hutu rebels in the Congo if the Congolese government failed to curb them itself. The rhetoric eventually died down, but the killings once again demonstrated the fragility of the peace process, both in the Congo and in Burundi, where a related civil war was in its final stages. *(Burundi war, Historic Documents of 2003, p. 922)*

Yet another crisis came at the end of November, when Rwanda's president, Paul Kagame, suggested that he was sending his army into the Congo to clear out Hutu rebels who, he said, still posed a threat to Rwanda. The Congolese government accused Rwanda of invading with 6,000 troops—an accusation that UN officials were unable to verify—and it sent about 10,000 troops to the border region to do battle with the Rwandans. Fighting erupted in several parts of the eastern Congo between the Congolese army and pro-Rwandan militias during the first three weeks of December, and tens of thousands of people fled their homes. The fighting was halted after December 21, when the UN peacekeeping mission intervened to create a buffer zone between the combatants.

Continuing Instability in Ituri

The other center of conflict in eastern Congo was the Ituri region of Orientale province, just across the border from Uganda. This gold-producing region had been the subject of a major international uproar in 2003, when fighting between two tribes (the Hema and the Lendu) had raised fears of another genocide. The crisis was brought to halt by the rapid intervention of a French-led military force, which was succeeded by elements of the UN peacekeeping force.

Fears of renewed fighting arose in mid-January 2004 with the massacre of about 100 male passengers on a boat traveling on Lake Albert between the Congo and Uganda. A few weeks later, a convoy of UN workers traveling to investigate the massacre was fired on, and an unarmed UN military observer from Kenya was killed. Ituri was relatively calm for most of the rest of the year, although the UN reported several dozen violent incidents between the beginning of September and mid-December.

The UN Peacekeeping Mission

As was common in post-conflict situations, the UN presence in the Congo had diplomatic and military components, both under the auspices of the United Nations Organization Mission in the Democratic Republic of the Congo (MONUC, in its French acronym). William Lacy Swing, an American diplomat, was in overall charge of the UN mission, which had a budget of $709 million for its 2004–2005 fiscal year, about one-third of which came from the United States. As of early 2004, MONUC had 10,800 peacekeeping troops from nearly a dozen countries. Most of these troops were in the volatile eastern provinces: about 5,000 in Ituri and 3,100 in the Kivus.

The mission's inability to protect civilians brought widespread protests in March and again in June after the rebel seizure of Bukavu. In a report on August 16, UN Secretary General Kofi Annan asked the Security Council to more than double the size of the UN force to 23,900 troops, making it the largest UN peacekeeping force ever. Annan told the council that the current level of 10,800 troops was far too small to guarantee the peace in a country the size of Western Europe—or even in the most volatile areas of Ituri and the Kivus.

Some council members, led by France, responded positively to Annan's request, but the United States opposed it, arguing that the UN would be unable to find either the troops or the money for such a large peacekeeping force. In a compromise, on October 1 the council adopted Resolution 1565 authorizing a total of 16,700 troops for MONUC—an increase of about one-third over the 10,800 level. The resolution also extended the mandate of the force through March 2005 and broadened its authority to protect civilians. Annan expressed disappointment that the council did not accept his full recommendation, saying the 23,900 figure was the "minimum required" for the job. He suggested that he would return to the council for more troops early in 2005.

Additional troops began deploying in November, with new contingents from India, Pakistan, South Africa, and other countries. A key component of the expanded force was a reserve battalion, made up of 850 South African troops, that could be mobilized quickly to deal with emergencies, such as the Bukavu crisis.

Already under attack for its inability to prevent the Bukavu conflict, the UN mission was damaged by several reports during the year that its soldiers had committed abuses against Congolese civilians, notably the raping of women and girls. A UN investigation in midyear confirmed eight of seventy-two allegations of sexual misconduct in the vicinity of Bunia, in the Ituri region. country. The *Washington Post* reported on December 16 that investigators had documented sixty-eight allegations of rape, pedophilia, and solicitation for sex by peacekeepers from Morocco, Nepal, Pakistan, South Africa, Tunisia, and Uruguay. The UN's investigation was still under way at year's end. Annan expressed outrage and pledged strong action to enforce what he called a policy of "zero tolerance" toward sexual exploitation by UN personnel. *(UN reform issues, p. 887)*

The Faltering Disarmament

Before there could be any hope for long-term peace in the Congo, the dozens of militia armies, with an estimated total of 200,000 to 300,000 fighters, had to be disbanded and disarmed. Under the peace agreements, the process of eliminating these militias had the weighty bureaucratic name of Disarmament, Demobilization, Repatriation, Resettlement, and Reintegration (DDRRR, in UN terminology). In theory, that process was supposed to lead to militia fighters giving up their weapons and returning to their homes, whether in the Congo or in neighboring countries. Some Congolese militia leaders and fighters were to be selected for incorporation into the Congo's new national army. Limited steps in this process were carried out. For example, in March the UN mission said it had repatriated nearly 10,000 fighters, along with their dependants, to their homes in Burundi, Rwanda, and Uganda. In September the UN mission launched a new $10.5 million effort to disarm about 15,000 fighters in the troubled northeastern district of Ituri. The latter effort got off to a slow start, however, with just seven fighters disarmed on the first day, September 13.

By mid-December, the International Crisis Group—a Brussels-based think tank—was declaring the disarmament a failure. In a December 17 report, "Back to the Brink in the Congo," the International Crisis Group noted that disarmament was voluntary, and it said that neither the UN mission nor the Congolese government had the strength or fortitude to carry it out.

The War's Toll

Since 2001 the International Rescue Committee, a U.S.-based human rights organization, had been conducting studies of mortality resulting from the Congo's war. In 2001 the group estimated that about 2.5 million people had died during the war, most of them from disease and starvation. An updated study in 2003 put the estimate at 3.3 million. The group's latest estimate, published December 9, was that 3.8 million Congolese people had died since 1998—by far the largest death toll in any single conflict since World War II. The committee said an average of about 31,000 people were still dying every month from unnatural causes directly attributable to the war, which officially had been over for nearly two years. The International Rescue Committee based its estimates on mortality studies in random locations around the Congo.

Following are excerpts from the "Third Special Report of the Secretary-General on the United Nations Organization Mission in the Democratic Republic of the Congo," submitted August 16, 2004, to the United Nations Security Council by Secretary General Kofi Annan.

"Report on the United Nations Organization Mission in the Democratic Republic of the Congo"

The Bukavu Crisis

. . . 34. The Bukavu crisis in May-June is symptomatic of the lack of progress in the transitional process and, in particular, the delays in military reform and integration. The roots of the crisis can be traced to February-March 2004, when tensions rose between the Deputy Military Regional Commander, Colonel Jules Mutebutsi (formerly of the Rassemblement congolais pour la démocratie-Goma (RCD-Goma)) and the Military Regional Commander for South Kivu, Brigadier-General Prosper Nabyolwa (of the former government component) over the latter's decision to seize weapons "illegally" held by military personnel under his command. Those tensions resulted in an exchange of fire between troops loyal to them, following which both officers were suspended by the Transitional Government and recalled to Kinshasa. Brigadier-General Nabyolwa travelled to Kinshasa and was temporarily replaced by General Mbuza Mabe. Colonel Mutebutsi was allowed to remain in Bukavu and, despite concerns that the lack of resolution of his status might trigger future crises, the issue of his replacement was left pending and Colonel Mutebutsi retained control over several hundred troops.

35. Festering tensions over the unresolved problem erupted on 26 May, when clashes took place between troops loyal to the new acting Military Regional Commander, General Mabe, and those of Colonel Mutebutsi. From the outset, MONUC [United Nations Organization Mission in the Democratic Republic of the Congo] used all political means at its disposal to press the dissident forces to cease hostilities and to canton themselves under MONUC observation. In response to claims of harassment and genocide of the Banyamulenge population, MONUC, which had some 450 troops in the area at the time the crisis erupted, conducted patrols throughout the town to help reduce the heightened tensions, in particular in areas inhabited by the Banyamulenge.

36. The tensions in Bukavu took on a new dimension when, over the weekend of 29 and 30 May, "General" Laurent Nkunda, another renegade dissident ex-RCDGoma officer, who had refused to go to Kinshasa to be sworn into the FARDC [the Congolese army] pending his appointment as Military Regional Commander in the third quarter of 2003, began moving towards Bukavu from North Kivu under the pretext of preventing a genocide against the Banyamulenge population. MONUC tried to halt his advance, including by creating a buffer zone north of Bukavu, including around the airport in Kavumu, whose outer perimeter was to be defended by FARDC forces. Through an emergency redeployment, MONUC military strength was augmented by 350 troops, bringing its strength in Bukavu to 800 on 29 May. In view of the extremely volatile situation, a further reinforcement was made through the redeployment of 204 troops on 1 June, at which time the MONUC military presence on the ground numbered 1,004 all ranks.

37. The MONUC military contingent in Bukavu was nevertheless overstretched, with three major locations to protect (the airport, a MONUC engineering base on the road from the airport to the city and the city of Bukavu itself, with some 550,000 residents). As Nkunda's troops advanced towards Bukavu on 1 June, FARDC elements abandoned the buffer zone and, on 2 June, the forces belonging to Nkunda and Mutebutsi took over Bukavu. Widespread abuse and looting followed. By that time, most FARDC troops had fled the city or sought refuge in the MONUC compound. Given the attacks on MONUC personnel and property elsewhere in the Democratic Republic of the Congo, MONUC was unable to bring further reinforcements to the city. Nevertheless, the Mission was able to protect some 4,000 internally displaced persons at its premises in Bukavu and to extract individual citizens at risk to places of safety. Elsewhere in the country, MONUC also organized a number of special rescue operations to extract and protect personnel in Goma, Kinshasa, Kisangani, Lubumbashi and other hotspots.

38. What appeared initially as an act of insubordination and mutiny by two renegade officers quickly escalated into a fierce military confrontation, with a perceived ethnic overtone, alleged foreign interference and potentially heavy political consequences. The impact of the fall of Bukavu was immediate. During emergency sessions of the National Assembly called to address the crisis in early June, RCD-Goma representatives were accused of supporting what was described as a "Rwandan occupation". Elements of the Transitional Government, in particular from the former Government, supported President [Joseph] Kabila's proposal to the Council of Ministers to declare a state of emergency and called for the suspension of the transitional process. In that connection, President Kabila held a series of consultations with the signatories of the Global and All-Inclusive Agreement to seek a review of the "1+4" structure of Government. Those efforts encountered strong opposition, in particular from the Mouvement de libération du Congo (MLC) and the RCD-Goma representatives, as well as from the international community, and were subsequently abandoned.

39. At the same time, MONUC was blamed by several high-level Transitional Government officials for not using its mandate under Chapter VII of the Charter of the United Nations to prevent the capture of Bukavu by dissident elements. Violent demonstrations were staged against MONUC and United Nations agencies in Kinshasa, Lubumbashi, Kalemie, Mbandaka, Kisangani, Beni and Kindu, resulting in the destruction of over $1 million worth of equipment and property. Premises of United Nations humanitarian agencies and non-governmental organizations were also looted and damaged, resulting in the suspension of humanitarian programmes in food security, health care, water and education for some 3.3 million people in the eastern part of the country. United Nations personnel were harassed, physically attacked and their private residences looted. Non-essential staff, dependants and humanitarian workers were temporarily relocated and unarmed military observers were moved to areas of safety. However, one of them was killed by Nkunda's forces when evacuating from Kalehe. In Kinshasa, however, three demonstrators who had infiltrated MONUC premises lost their lives when MONUC troops, acting in selfdefence, were forced to open fire.

40. During the crisis I maintained close contact with regional and international leaders and members of the Security Council and encouraged them to do all they could to de-escalate the tension. The Government of Rwanda denied involvement and, on

6 June, closed its borders with the Democratic Republic of the Congo, requesting international verification of allegations of its involvement. While the borders were subsequently reopened on 2 July, their closure had an adverse effect on the delivery of humanitarian assistance in the area and on the Congolese, whose trade and supply routes were cut off.

41. Following numerous broken promises, General Nkunda's troops withdrew northwards on 6 June, while Colonel Mutebutsi's troops withdrew south towards Kamanyola on 8 June. The following morning, the FARDC, whose strength had been augmented through reinforcements from the western part of the Democratic Republic of the Congo, was able to re-enter Bukavu and regain control of the border points with Rwanda. The newly appointed Governor of South Kivu, Augustin Bulaimi, subsequently assumed his post on 11 July.

42. All sides, including FARDC troops as they entered Bukavu on 9 June, looted and abused civilians and, in some instances, raped women and girls. Between 8 and 21 June, MONUC investigated allegations of attacks on Banyamulenge in Bukavu. MONUC determined that, while the attacks did not appear to have been planned or ordered, between 26 May and 1 June, FARDC elements had perpetrated four deliberate killings and nine cases of injury of Banyamulenge civilians. It was also determined that the FARDC had unlawfully killed six Banyamulenge FARDC officers in Walungu on 3 June; the circumstances of the killings are as yet unclear. MONUC was prevented from interviewing Banyamulenge refugees in Cyangugu, Rwanda, with regard to another 12 reported killings and alleged abuses of Banyamulenge civilians in Bukavu. In addition, the MONUC investigations determined that the FARDC had deliberately killed two unarmed civilians in Bukavu who were not Banyamulenge.

43. MONUC investigations also determined that Nkunda's and Mutebutsi's troops had been responsible for dozens of cases of rape and had deliberately killed at least nine civilians while in Bukavu, which was under their control between 2 and 5 June. As many as 1,400 traders were affected by the burning of the Kadutu market by Nkunda elements and, on 4 June, a "colonel" representing Nkunda forcibly removed the equivalent of some $100,000 in francs from the Bukavu Central Bank.

44. On 11 June, about 40 presidential guards attempted a coup d'état, accusing the Transitional Government of incompetence. Following exchanges of fire in central Kinshasa, the group's leader escaped and has apparently remained at large ever since. The Commander of the Presidential Guard and the Chief of the Maison militaire du Chef de l'État were suspended and on 19 June, President Kabila replaced the Chief of Staff of the Army. On 14 July, having returned to Goma, eight RCD-Goma members of the National Assembly unilaterally suspended their membership of the Assembly and called on other RCD-Goma members to follow suit. The eight were strongly condemned by the RCD-Goma leadership, who sought to replace them. Their action was, however, contested by the President of the National Assembly as "unconstitutional". The matter remains unresolved.

45. On 20 June, a MONUC patrol came under fire believed to be from Mutebutsi's soldiers about 3 kilometres south of Kamanyola. In response, MONUC attack helicopters opened rocket fire, which scattered the men, who subsequently fled in the direction of the Rwandan border. Fighting has erupted in the Ruzizi plains following the withdrawal of Mutebutsi's troops south of Bukavu. On 21 June, Colonel Mutebutsi, along with some 300 troops, crossed into Rwanda.

46. As noted above, since the start of the crisis, the FARDC has significantly reinforced its presence in the eastern part of the Democratic Republic of the Congo, by deploying an estimated 15,000 troops (primarily former Forces armées congolaises, presidential guards, Mayi-Mayi and ex-MLC) in the provinces of Maniema, Orientale and North and South Kivu. General Nkunda's fate continues to remain unresolved. He and his troops are located between Goma and Bukavu on Lake Kivu, with reports of additional troops being recruited. The situation remains extremely tense, with concerns over the intentions of the North Kivu Military Regional Commander, General Rwibasira Obedi, given his supposed ties with General Nkunda and the fact that he has twice failed to participate in consultations of all military regional commanders held in Kinshasa during the past month. . . .

IV. The Role of the United Nations Organization Mission in the Democratic Republic of the Congo

58. The interpretation of Security Council resolution 1493 (2003) has been a major challenge for MONUC over the past year. In the resolution, the Council gave MONUC the mandate to, inter alia, provide assistance for the reform of the security forces, the re-establishment of a State based on the rule of law and the preparation and holding of elections, throughout the territory of the Democratic Republic of the Congo. It also authorized MONUC to use all necessary means to fulfil its mandate in the Ituri district and, as it deemed it within its capabilities, in North and South Kivu.

59. The establishment of the peacekeeping mandate of MONUC under Chapter VII of the Charter of the United Nations has raised expectations that the Mission will enforce the peace throughout the country. However, there is a wide gap between such expectations and the Mission's capacity to fulfil them. At the same time, the lack of specificity as to its tasks under resolution 1493 (2003) does not lend itself to the most effective use of the resources provided to the Mission.

60. The recommendations presented in the present report have been developed with the above in mind and represent my considered views on the means by which MONUC could provide more effective assistance to the peace process at this critical juncture.

61. The key role of MONUC will be to continue the provision of its good offices to build confidence among the leaders of the transition and to strengthen the Transitional Government. The Mission will also continue to build political support for the transitional process among the international community, in particular through the International Committee in Support of the Transition. . . .

VI. Observations and Recommendations

108. Following the endorsement of the Global and All-Inclusive Agreement on the Transition in the Democratic Republic of the Congo in April 2003, I presented recommendations to the Security Council on the role that MONUC could play in assisting the Government to fulfil its transitional agenda (see S/2003/566 and Corr.1).

I stressed, at the time, that the magnitude of the challenges in the Democratic Republic of the Congo should not be underestimated. The country was still divided, military hostilities were continuing in the east, the population was traumatized by years of conflict, the country was poverty-stricken and state services and infrastructure were nonexistent. In examining progress in the Democratic Republic of the Congo, it should also be remembered that the country has suffered from four decades of corrupt governance and has never enjoyed true democracy.

109. The developments of the past year should be viewed from the perspective of the starting point just one year ago. Progress has been made with the installation of the Transitional Government, which is making significant efforts to achieve unity. There is a great deal of hope among the Congolese; their anger about the events in Bukavu demonstrates their deep desire for peace, democracy and national reconciliation. Significant efforts are being made to rebuild the country's social services, administration and infrastructure. Much has been achieved over the past year and the Congolese people, their leaders and those Member States and multilateral agencies which have provided support to the Democratic Republic of the Congo deserve to be congratulated for it.

110. At the same time, as the events of the past few months have demonstrated, if the political process does not move forward, it will run off track and risk collapse. We must not allow the progress made so far to be lost. This calls for a renewed commitment by the Transitional Government, the Security Council and the international community to work in full partnership to see the transitional process through to the elections scheduled for 2005. Elections, of course, are not the end game, but they will mark a significant turning point in the history of the Democratic Republic of the Congo and put the country on the path to democracy and economic and social development.

111. While the challenges facing the Transitional Government are understandably significant, much is expected of it. For a long time, the Congolese people have suffered from most horrific human rights abuses, which have been perpetrated with impunity. This issue has been at the core of the conflict and remains a major challenge to the transitional process, including with regard to the integration of the armed forces. I urge the Transitional Government to address this issue with the seriousness it deserves and to take up, with MONUC and other concerned organizations, all instances of human rights abuses, in particular those perpetrated by members of the Transitional Government and the FARDC.

112. In the present report, I have presented my considered views on the main challenges to the transition and the critical aspects of the transitional agenda that must be addressed in order to strengthen the political process and move it towards free and fair elections. The role recommended for MONUC reflects this critical path. I call on the Security Council to endorse it and on the Transitional Government to implement it.

113. It has long been recognized that relations between the countries of the Great Lakes region is an essential factor in the stability of the Democratic Republic of the Congo. The Democratic Republic of the Congo, Rwanda and Uganda have been consistently encouraged by the United Nations, the Security Council and bilateral partners to establish good-neighbourly relations. While each has expressed its willingness to do so, their relationship remains strained. The Transitional Government continues to accuse the Government of Rwanda of providing military support to individual actors

in the east, while the Government of Rwanda continues to maintain that the Transitional Government is providing military support to ex-FAR/Interahamwe elements. Moreover, it is felt that the Government of Uganda could do more to stem the flow of arms and bring about a peaceful settlement to the ongoing crisis in Ituri.

114. Stability will allow the Democratic Republic of the Congo, a country endowed with huge natural resources, to pursue a path of strong economic development. The current situation suggests that certain Congolese and regional elements would not like to see this happen, as the legitimate exploitation of the country's natural resources would limit the illegal wealth generated by unstable conditions.

115. The Governments of the Democratic Republic of the Congo, Rwanda and Uganda must make concrete progress to ensure that the flow of arms across their borders is brought to an end; to settle the question of the foreign armed groups, in particular the ex-FAR/Interahamwe; and to legitimize the exploitation of natural resources. The Joint Verification Mechanism discussed with the parties during my meeting with them in Addis Ababa on 6 July 2004 is one means of achieving that end. Establishing normal bilateral relations, with the exchange of ambassadors, is another.

116. The steps outlined above are not difficult to take, if there is the political will to do so. In that connection, I am concerned at inflammatory statements by some officials on all sides, as well as the signs that some political figures may use the current mistrust, whether there are grounds for it or not, in pursuit of their own domestic agenda. I call on the Heads of State of the Democratic Republic of the Congo, Rwanda and Uganda to rise above such narrow interests and to demonstrate leadership by taking the specific steps necessary to strengthen their bilateral relations. I also call on those countries with the capacity to do so to continue to press them in that direction.

117. In view of the commitment made by the Governments of the Democratic Republic of the Congo and Rwanda on 27 November 2003, it is my intention to share with the Security Council by the end of October 2004 my assessment of the implementation of that commitment and of the continued threat posed by ex-FAR/Interahamwe forces in the Democratic Republic of the Congo to the security of Rwanda and the peaceful holding of elections in the Democratic Republic of the Congo.

118. As demonstrated by the analysis provided in the present report, MONUC and the Secretariat have reflected carefully on the implications of entrusting a mandate under Chapter VII of the Charter to a peacekeeping mission in a country the size of the Democratic Republic of the Congo and with the challenges it faces. The recommendations presented in the present report are based on the primary objective of finding the most effective means by which the United Nations can assist the Transitional Government in creating the environment required to implement the peace process.

119. The expectations among the Congolese people, and some international observers, of the role MONUC can play under a Chapter VII mandate far outweigh what any external partner could ever do to assist a peace process. In that connection, all concerned must be clear about one thing: MONUC cannot implement the transitional process on behalf of the Transitional Government, it can only assist. Likewise, MONUC cannot create stability; it can only assist the Transitional Government in doing so. MONUC could, however, assist the process by mobilizing the resources necessary to deter spoilers from derailing the transition.

120. I therefore recommend that the Security Council consider increasing the current military strength of MONUC of 10,800 all ranks by an additional 13,100, thus

bringing the Mission's authorized strength to 23,900, including five brigades, 230 headquarters personnel, 760 military observers and the required enabling units. I also recommend that the Council approve the expansion of the mandate of the Mission's civilian police component along the lines of paragraphs 103 and 104, which would increase the strength of the component to 507 personnel, including the current 140 civilian police officers.

121. The implementation of the Mission's revised military tasks will require the addition of formed and enabling units. It would be essential to improve its information-gathering and analysis capacity in order to better understand the threats and risks in the country. In that connection, countries from the developing world have been providing most of the Mission's military assets since its inception, some of whom have expressed their willingness to make further contributions to MONUC. I applaud them for all they have done for MONUC and other United Nations peacekeeping operations. The Security Council should not rely only on troop contributors from developing countries, however. Other troop-contributing countries must also play an active role in assisting the Congolese peace process and I call on them to seriously consider the invaluable assistance they can provide to peace in the Democratic Republic of the Congo.

122. The transitional process in the Democratic Republic of the Congo is at a critical juncture. Ultimately, the road ahead will depend on the political will of the transitional leaders. If they show the determination to move the process forward, much progress can be made. If they remain intransigent, they risk losing all the gains made to date and sinking the country, if not the region, into war. It is up to them to decide the fate of the Democratic Republic of the Congo and, in fact, of the entire region of the Great Lakes. I call on them to take advantage of the progress made to date and of the goodwill of the international community to assist them to put aside their personnel interests and fears and do what has to be done to put the Democratic Republic of the Congo on the road to peace, reconciliation and development.

123. In closing, I would like to express my admiration and deep gratitude to the women and men of MONUC, who have continued to demonstrate courage and dedication, in particular during the recent trying months, in their efforts to assist the Congolese people bring peace to their country.

Source: United Nations. Security Council. "Third Special Report of the Secretary-General on the United Nations Organization Mission in the Democratic Republic of the Congo." S/2004/650, August 16, 2004. http://daccess-ods.un.org/TMP/9227739.html (accessed March 21, 2005).

September 11 Commission on Terrorist Activity in Saudi Arabia

August 21, 2004

INTRODUCTION

The conservative kingdom of Saudi Arabia struggled again during 2004 to come to grips with Islamist terrorism, which had only recently posed dangers to the stability of that country, the world's most important source of oil. A wave of terrorist attacks in midyear appeared to be aimed at driving Americans and other foreigners out of Saudi Arabia. Those attacks had some success in achieving that goal, as the United States ordered all nonessential diplomatic personnel out of the country and strongly urged other Americans—including an estimated 30,000 employed in the oil industry—to leave as well. The United States in 2003 had closed its military bases and withdrawn nearly all its armed service personnel from the country.

The Saudi government launched a broad security crackdown that killed dozens of alleged terrorists, including the reported leader local of the al Qaeda terrorist network. Crown Prince Abdullah, the country's de facto leader, said in December that terrorists had nearly been wiped out there. Such claims were greeted with skepticism elsewhere, however, especially since the Saudi government had refused until recently to acknowledge that terrorists even existed in the country—or to acknowledge that fifteen of the nineteen hijackers who carried out the September 11, 2001, attacks against the United States were Saudi citizens.

The government also continued its limited venture into political reform, including the first elections in four decades for one-half of the seats on municipal councils. Even that step was halting, as the date for the election was pushed back twice during the year, and in October the government announced that women would not be allowed to vote. *(Background, Historic Documents of 2003, p. 227)*

Saudi Arabia and al Qaeda

Saudi Arabia experienced its first sustained rash of terrorist activity in 2003, including bombings in Riyadh, the capital, in May and November that killed more than fifty people. Despite a subsequent crackdown by the security services, 2004 saw even more sustained terrorist attacks, most of them against foreigners in the kingdom. Militants launched repeated attacks targeting the country's oil industry and the foreign workers who helped keep it running—a campaign that appeared aimed at provoking a crisis and possibly even the collapse of the government.

The government arrested dozens of suspected terrorists, captured large arsenals of weapons and explosives, and closed charities that had raised money for al Qaeda and other terrorist organizations. By the end of 2004 the government said it had captured or killed seventeen of twenty-six al Qaeda suspects of those whose names and pictures had been posted in "most wanted" posters in late 2003. Even so, terrorism experts, both in the kingdom and in Western nations, noted that thousands of Saudi men had been trained by al Qaeda and other organizations as Islamist fighters in recent years, and fundamentalist clerics were continuing to call for *jihad* (holy war) against Western influence, especially that of the United States.

A report issued August 25 by a United Nations committee examining al Qaeda and other terrorist organizations gave this summary: "Saudi Arabia has been a focus for al Qaeda from the start but now appears to have become an operational front line with determined terrorists pitched against equally determined security forces. Terrorist attacks there are designed to disrupt the economy and destabilize the State so as to create a sense of anarchy and general discontent leading to widespread insurgency and the overthrow of the government." *(UN report on al Qaeda, p. 534)*

Violent Attacks in 2004

Violent incidents in Saudi Arabia came in three waves during the year: a rash of attacks in April through June, the targeted killing of Westerners in August and September, and then two large-scale attacks in December. All attacks were aimed at the Western presence in Saudi Arabia, the country's oil industry, or at government security services.

By far the most serious in a series of incidents during the spring was an attack on May 1 that clearly was meant to damage the country's all-important oil industry. Four gunmen broke into an engineering office in the oil transportation city of Yanbu on the Red Sea, killing six Westerners, including two Americans. The body of one of the Americans was dragged through the city's streets, reportedly to the cheers of bystanders. One Saudi security officer was killed and about twenty others were wounded. Three of the gunmen, said to be employees of the company they attacked, were killed and a fourth was captured.

The attack was the first significant strike at the Saudi oil industry, and analysts said it appeared aimed at disrupting ties between Saudi Arabia and its Western oil customers. If so, the attack achieved at least part of its purpose by raising fears on world oil markets about the safety of Saudi production—and contributing to a sharp rise in oil prices that had begun earlier in the year. After the attack, U.S. ambassador James C. Oberwetter visited Yanbu and urged all remaining Americans—most of whom worked directly or indirectly for the oil industry—to leave the kingdom. Just two weeks earlier, in the wake of two days of gun battles between police and militants in Riyadh, Oberwetter had ordered all nonessential U.S. diplomatic personnel out of the country. *(Oil prices, p. 186)*

Three days after the attack in Yanbu, Crown Prince Abdullah blamed "Zionists" (a reference to Israelis and their supporters in the West) for the violence. "We can be certain that Zionism is behind everything," he told a meeting in Jeddah. "I don't say 100 percent, but 95 percent." While it might have sounded bizarre to Western ears, Abdullah's statement was in keeping with the general tendency of Saudi leaders to blame outsiders, especially Israel, for nearly everything that went wrong in the kingdom. Prince Nayef, the interior minister, had routinely blamed Zionists for terrorist incidents, including the September 11 attacks against the United States.

The Yanbu attack was followed four weeks later by one on the other side of the country, in the oil city of Khobar on the Persian Gulf. On May 29 four gunmen seized a hotel at the Oasis Resort compound for foreign workers and held several dozen people hostage. Saudi commandos stormed the compound the next day and freed most of the hostages, but not before twenty-two people in the compound had been killed, nineteen of them foreigners. Nine Saudi policemen also died.

The reported leader of the gunmen was captured, but his three colleagues escaped while still holding some of the hostages. One of the hostages, a British businessman, was killed and his body dragged through the city's streets. The ability of the gunmen to escape, despite the presence of several hundred policemen, raised questions about possible collusion between the militants and security forces. Once again, world oil prices spiked.

Also in this time period, individual Westerners came under attack for the first time. In May a German employee of an airline catering company was shot dead while withdrawing cash from a bank automated teller machine, and in June gunmen shot dead two American employees of defense contractors and a BBC television cameraman.

In mid-June Saudi Arabia experienced its first case of what was becoming a common phenomenon in Iraq: the taking of hostages, whose grisly killings were filmed and broadcast over the Internet. On June 12 Lockheed-Martin engineer Paul Johnson Jr. was kidnapped in Riyadh. He was beheaded six days later, and film of the scene was posted on the Web site of a group calling itself al Qaeda in the Arabian Peninsula. *(Iraq hijackings, p. 874)*

Immediately after Johnson's death was reported, the government said police had killed four militants in that group, and captured another dozen, in a series of raids in Riyadh. Among those killed was the local leader of al Qaeda, Abdelaziz al-Muqrin.

On June 24 Crown Prince Abdullah went on state television and read a statement offering al Qaeda limited amnesty for a one-month period, after which the government would strike "with our full might, which we derive from relying on God." Only a handful of militants surrendered as a result of the offer. One of them, Khaled Harbi, turned himself in to the Saudi embassy in Tehran. He had been shown in a videotape, released in November 2001, in which al Qaeda leader Osama bin Laden was shown praising the attacks against the United States two months earlier.

Another series of attacks against individual Westerners took place in August and September, bringing the total number of Westerners killed in such attacks to seven in a little over five months. The victims, all of whom were gunned down, included an Irish employee of a Saudi engineering firm, a British employee of the Marconi communications firm, and a French employee of a Paris-based defense contractor.

These attacks unnerved Westerners and prompted several thousand more to leave the country. Government officials, however, put the development in a different light. They said the killing of individuals showed that the terrorists were growing desperate because a security crackdown had curtailed their ability to mount large-scale attacks. By September the government was claiming near-victory in its war against al Qaeda, with Crown Prince Abdullah telling a Kuwaiti newspaper his country was "past the stages of terrorism."

On December 6 gunmen stormed the U.S. consulate in Jeddah and seized more than a dozen people in the courtyard, using eight of them as "human shields" to ward off an attack. When security forces attacked, five local employees of the consulate were killed, as were four of the attackers. Two American employees of the embassy were lightly injured. Like the earlier ones, that attack heightened fears among foreigners because it demonstrated that even heavily guarded compounds, such as the consulate, were vulnerable to at least some degree of penetration.

The consulate attack also brought praise from bin Laden. In an audiotape aired on Arabic television stations on December 16, bin Laden praised the attack, called the attackers "martyrs," demanded the overthrow of the Saudi monarchy, and predicted that the kingdom was headed "with unusual speed toward an explosion." Bin Laden's speech also specifically called for his followers to concentrate attacks on the oil industry. That same day, a group said by Saudi and Western governments to be linked to al Qaeda tried to organize antigovernment demonstrations in Jeddah and Riyadh, but the protests were blocked by an intense security clampdown in both cities.

The year's final significant incident came December 29, when militants used car bombs and suicide bombs to attack two neighborhoods of Riyadh. At least nine attackers were killed, and about twenty people, including police officers, were wounded. While the attacks caused little damage, they again unnerved the government and residents.

Al Qaeda Funding

In the minds of many westerners, Saudi Arabia was inextricably linked to Islamist terrorism because bin Laden was the son of a wealthy Saudi contractor and most of the September 11 hijackers were Saudi citizens. Ever since the 1998 terrorist bombings of U.S. embassies in Kenya and Tanzania by al Qaeda operatives, the U.S. government also had linked private individuals and organizations in Saudi Arabia—and possibly even elements of the government there—to the financial network that underpinned the al Qaeda network.

After September 11 the Bush administration focused much of its attention on a large Saudi charity, the al-Haramain Islamic Foundation. That foundation had financed thousands of schools and mosques around the world to propagate Saudi Arabia's fundamentalist sect of Islam known as Wahhabism, after an eighteenth century cleric who preached what he claimed to be a "pure" form of Islam. U.S. officials said the foundation blended support for al Qaeda and other terrorist groups in with its religious and charitable work.

Significant details about the work of the foundation, and Saudi Arabian financing of terrorism in general, were provided in two staff reports issued in 2004 by the commission that investigated the September 11 attacks. The first report, made public June 18, disputed the broadly held view in Western nations that members of the Saudi royal family, and possibly the government itself, had helped finance al Qaeda. "Saudi Arabia has long been considered the primary source of al Qaeda funding, but we found no evidence that the Saudi government as an institution or senior officials within the Saudi government funded al Qaeda," the report said. Even so, a follow-up staff report, made public August 26, said the Saudi government "turned a blind eye to the financing of al Qaeda by prominent religious and business leaders and organizations" before the September 11 attacks. Even after those attacks, the report added, "Saudi government officials appeared to be in denial that vast sums of money were flowing from Saudi Arabia to al Qaeda and related terrorist groups, or that the government had any responsibility in connection with these money flows." *(September 11 commission report, p. 450)*

The Saudi government's first serious effort to curb that financing did not come until after the May 2003 attacks in Riyadh, the report said. The government removed collection boxes for the al-Haramain foundation and similar organizations from mosques and shopping malls, and it imposed new limits on the operations of those foundations.

The spate of terrorist attacks in Saudi Arabia early in 2004, plus continued U.S. pressure, reportedly led the Saudi government to take a step Washington officials long had urged: the closing of the al-Haramain foundation. That came on June 2 when the Saudi government said it was dissolving the foundation and merging its accounts with those of other charities into a single account supervised by a recently appointed national commission. In a related step the same day, the U.S. Treasury Department announced that it had designated the foundation's former leader, Aqeel Abdulaziz Aqil, as an associate of and financier for al Qaeda; that made him subject to prosecution under U.S. antiterrorism laws. Aqil denied involvement with terrorism, telling a London-based Arabic newspaper that he had helped "the poor, the orphans, and widowed."

Terrorism experts in the United States and other countries described the dissolution of the foundation as a useful, but limited, step. They noted that the Saudi government did not make clear how it would ensure that the foundation's money was kept out of al Qaeda hands. Critics also said the government had yet to move against other major Saudi-based foundations that Western intelligence agencies had linked to al Qaeda, including the International Islamic Relief Organization and the World Assembly of Muslim Youth.

Political Developments in Saudi Arabia

In a region dominated by conservative, autocratic governments, Saudi Arabia's was one of the most conservative and autocratic of all. The country was governed by the al-Saud family of about 5,000 princes, with most of the power held by a small number of direct descendants of the founder, King ibn-Saud. The current king, Fahd, had been incapacitated by strokes in 1995, and the country was run on a day-to-day basis by his half-brother, Crown Prince Abdullah.

The Consultative Council, appointed by the al-Saud princes, served as an informal parliament with little real political power, but it did provide a conduit for public appeals to the government. In a step toward transparency, the government early in 2004 began televising council meetings. Political parties and public demonstrations were banned, and the domestic news media was tightly controlled, with only the gentlest expressions of public dissent allowed.

Hints of a slight easing of the political climate came early in 2003, when Crown Prince Abdullah held what he called a "national dialogue" with advocates of democracy and greater openness. Abdullah also announced plans to hold elections in 2004 for one-half of the seats on councils in 178 cities and towns throughout the country. They were to be the first local elections since the 1960s.

Plans for the local elections were delayed repeatedly in 2004. In July the government said the voting would be held in September. A month later another announcement said the voting had been pushed back to November, so it would not conflict with the month-long fasting holiday of Ramadan, beginning in mid-October. Finally, on September 12, the government said the elections would be delayed again until early 2005, with voting to be held in three stages in different localities in February, March, and April. As had been widely expected, the government announced in October that women—barred by Wahhabi strictures from any participation in public life—would not be allowed to vote. The first round of voter registration took place in Riyadh in November and December, but only about one-third of eligible males signed up to vote, according to a local newspaper. Saudi political analysts blamed that lackluster result on the government's modest effort to encourage voter registration, plus disenchantment with the limited nature of the elections among those who had been calling for reforms.

Reformers were disenchanted about more than the elections. Starting in mid-March, security forces arrested and jailed about a dozen of the kingdom's most prominent advocates of political change, including academics and lawyers. The men had sent several petitions to the government calling for reform and had drafted a plan for an independent organization to monitor human rights in Saudi Arabia. Several were released after they signed statements promising not to criticize the government openly. The U.S. State Department, which rarely commented on political developments in Saudi Arabia, immediately criticized the detentions, leading to a moment of tension when Secretary of State Colin Powell visited Riyadh on March 19. After meeting with Saudi leaders, Powell told reporters he had a "good, candid, and open debate" about the detentions, and foreign minister Prince Faisal pointedly said the arrests had been "an internal issue."

Three of the dissidents who remained in custody were arraigned in August on charges that included such crimes as holding a public meeting and petitioning for a constitutional monarchy. The arraignment was held in public, but subsequent sessions were held behind closed doors.

The U.S. intervention in the arrests of the reformers appeared to pose a problem as much for them as for the government. Largely because of the war in Iraq, resentment of U.S. influence had risen sharply among Saudi Arabian citizens across the country's political and religious spectrums. Some reformers said public U.S. pressure might influence the government, but it also undermined their case among the Saudi public.

In a step aimed at stabilizing the country through job security, the government in 2004 began to enforce a decade-old program called "Saudization" to put local workers in private sector jobs traditionally held by foreigners. Previously, Saudi citizens were virtually guaranteed a job with the government—and many of the jobs entitled the holders to paychecks without having to do any work. A long-term slowdown resulting from sagging oil prices during the 1990s had sent unemployment soaring and forced the government to curtail its workforce, however, and private employers were told to replace their foreign workers with local citizens. The government did little to enforce that mandate until 2004, when it began requiring employers to take on Saudi citizens. Officials said they hoped that providing work, especially for younger men, would reduce the levels of social tension and anger that created fertile recruiting ground for extremists.

Following are excerpts from chapter seven of "Monograph on Terrorist Financing: Staff Report to the Commission," prepared by the U.S. National Commission on Terrorist Attacks upon the United States and made public August 21, 2004. The monograph, written by staff members John Roth, Douglas Greenburg, and Serena Wille, explained how terrorist organizations obtained their financing and detailed U.S. government efforts to curtail that financing. Chapter seven dealt specifically with the al Haramain Islamic Foundation of Saudi Arabia.

"Monograph on Terrorist Financing: Staff Report to the Commission"

Al Haramain Case Study

The al Haramain Islamic Foundation (al Haramain or HIF) is one of the most important and prominent Saudi charities. Al Haramain has been on the radar screen of the U.S. government as a potential terrorist-financing problem since the mid- to late 1990s, when the U.S. government started to develop evidence that certain employees and branch offices might be supporting al Qaeda and related terrorist groups.

The U.S. government, however, never moved against al Haramain or pushed the Saudi government to do so until after 9/11. Terrorist financing simply was not a priority in its bilateral relationship with the Saudis before 9/11. Even when discussing terrorist financing with the Saudis, the U.S. government was more concerned about issues other than Saudi charities and al Haramain. Meanwhile, the Saudis were content to leave the issue unexplored.

After the 9/11 attacks, a more focused U.S. government sought to work with the Saudis to stem the flow of funds from al Haramain to al Qaeda and related terrorist groups. Progress was initially slow; though some U.S.-Saudi cooperation on al Haramain occurred within the first six months after 9/11, it was not until the spring of 2003 that the U.S. government and the Saudi government began to make real strides in working together to thwart al Haramain.

Background

Al Haramain, a Saudi Arabia–based nonprofit organization established in the early 1990s, has been described by several former U.S. government officials as the "United Way" of Saudi Arabia. It exists to promote Wahhabi Islam by funding religious education, mosques, and humanitarian projects around the world.

At its peak, al Haramain had a presence in at least 50 countries. Al Haramain's main headquarters are in Riyadh, Saudi Arabia, but it maintains branch offices in a number of countries to facilitate the distribution of charitable funds. Some of these offices are staffed by Saudi citizens; others are managed by the nationals of the countries involved. Estimates of its budget range from $30 to $80 million. It claims to have constructed more than 1,299 mosques, it funds imams and others to work in the mosques, and it sponsors more than 3,000 "callers to Islam" for tours of duty in different locations "to teach the people good and to warn them from wrongs." HIF provides meals and assistance to Muslims around the world, distributes books and pamphlets, pays for potable water projects, sets up and equips medical facilities, and operates more than 20 orphanages.

Although both the Saudi government and al Haramain say that it is a private organization, al Haramain has considerable ties to the Saudi government. Two government ministers have supervisory roles (nominal or otherwise) over al Haramain, and there is some evidence that low-level Saudi officials had substantial influence over various HIF offices outside of Saudi Arabia. The Saudi government has also historically provided financial support to al Haramain, although that may have diminished in recent years.

Charity and charitable organizations, like al Haramain, are extremely important to Saudi society. As discussed in more detail in chapter 2, religious and civic duty and government and religious functions in Saudi Arabia are intertwined. This dynamic creates complications for the Saudi government as it seeks to stem the flow of funds from Saudi Arabia to al Qaeda and related terrorist groups, and difficulties for the U.S. government as it seeks to engage the Saudis on terrorist financing.

Before 9/11

After the East Africa bombings in the summer of 1998 [the bombings of U.S. embassies in Kenya and Tanzania], the U.S. government began to give more attention to terrorist financing. The National Security Council established a subgroup of the Counterterrorism Security Group to focus the U.S. government's efforts on terrorist financing. As a result of this focus, and the consequent discovery that al Qaeda was not financed from Bin Ladin's personal wealth, the NSC [National Security Council in the White House] became increasingly interested in Saudi charities and Bin Ladin's use of charities to fund terrorism.

By no later than 1996, the U.S. intelligence community began to gather intelligence that certain branches of HIF were involved in financing terrorism. Later, the U.S. intelligence community began to draw links among HIF, the 1998 East Africa bombings, jihad actions in the Balkans, Chechnya, and Azerbaijan, and support for al Qaeda generally. The United States shared some of its information with the Saudis in an effort to spur action, including evidence that al Haramain officials and employees in East Africa may have been involved in the planning of the 1998 embassy bombings. The United States sought information and reports from the Saudis on employees of al Haramain around the globe and their connections to Bin Ladin, but received no substantive responses.

The Saudis took little initiative with respect to their charities. They did not make tough decisions or undertake difficult investigations of Saudi institutions to ensure that they were not being used by terrorists and their supporters. Although the Saudis did institute "Guidelines for Preventing Money Laundering" in 1995 and "Regulations on Charitable Organizations and Institutions" in 1990, these were very loose rules whose enforcement was doubtful. Moreover, the regulations covered only domestic charities, through the Ministry of Labor and Social Affairs, and exempted all charities set up by royal decree.

There may have been a number of reasons for Saudi inaction. Certainly . . . the prominence of religion-based charities in Saudi culture may have made the Saudis reluctant to entertain the idea that charities might be involved in clandestine activities. Some in the United States suspected that the Saudis were complicit or at least turned a blind eye to the problem posed by charities during this period, although others vehemently disagreed.

Ultimately, however, the U.S. government simply did not ask much of the Saudis on terrorist financing, and the Saudis were content to do little. We did not provide sufficient information for the Saudis to act against charities like al Haramain, did not push the Saudis to undertake investigations of charities like al Haramain, and did not request real cooperation from the Saudis on intelligence or law enforcement matters relating to charities like al Haramain.

Other areas of U.S. policy involving the Saudis took precedence over terrorist-financing issues such as those concerning al Haramain. The U.S. government wanted the Saudis to support the Middle East peace process, ensure the steady flow of oil, cut off support to the Taliban, continue various mutually beneficial economic arrangements, and assist in the containment of Iraq. Given these other interests, stopping the money flow to terrorists was not a top priority in the U.S.-Saudi relationship.

Saudi policy was formulated at a very high level in the U.S. government. During the late 1990s, the U.S.-Saudi relationship was handled primarily by the U.S. government's most senior officials, including the secretaries of key departments (collectively referred to as the "Principals"), and often even by the President alone. This situation reflected the significance of the U.S. interests involved, considerable Saudi ties to senior U.S. officials, and U.S. willingness to accede to the strong Saudi preference for bypassing the U.S. bureaucracy. One former NSC official noted that before 9/11, lower-level officials in both governments generally handled terrorist financing, especially given the weakness of the intelligence on terrorist financing and the issue's low priority. The officials with knowledge about it were not the ones interacting with the Saudis, and those who were interacting with the Saudis did not push the issue of terrorist financing because their concerns were different.

Moreover, the U.S. government had too little unilateral intelligence on HIF and on al Qaeda's funding mechanisms generally to press the Saudis. The Principals did not want to confront the Saudis with suspicions; they wanted firm evidence. One NSC official Terrorist Financing Staff Monograph indicated that there was some intelligence regarding charities, but it did not rise to the level of being actionable against any specific charity. As he said, "One individual could be dirty, but it would be difficult to justify closing down a charity on that basis." Occasionally the U.S. government provided select pieces of information out of context, but this method lessened the impact of the intelligence.

After 9/11

. . . [T]he 9/11 attacks generated a sudden and high-level interest in terrorist financing. Attention invariably turned to Saudi Arabia. The U.S. and Saudi governments initially agreed on a joint strategy, represented by the mutual U.S.-Saudi action against two branches of al Haramain in March 2002 designating them as financiers of terror. But it was not until the spring of 2003 that the U.S. government developed a coherent strategy on engaging the Saudis on terrorist financing and specified a senior White House official to deal with the Saudi government on these issues. These elements enabled the U.S. government to capitalize on a new Saudi commitment to countering the financing of terrorism after the Riyadh bombings on May 12, 2003. . . .

[The following sections detailed attempts by the U.S. government to respond to the September 11 terrorist attacks and to encourage Saudi Arabian government cooperation in the U.S. antiterrorism campaign.]

From 9/11 to May 2003: A lack of real cooperation from the Saudis

After 9/11, Saudi government officials appeared to be in denial that vast sums of money were flowing from Saudi Arabia to al Qaeda and related terrorist groups, or that the government had any responsibility in connection with these money flows. Some in the U.S. government thought that it simply never occurred to the Saudi government that a charity could be a conduit for terrorist financing. As well, some argued that charities' record keeping and the Saudi government's controls were insufficient for the Saudi government to know of al Haramain's links to terrorist organizations.

Even after the Saudi government froze the assets of the Bosnian office in March 2002, one senior Saudi government official denied in the press that the al Haramain office in Sarajevo was engaged in illicit activities. He claimed that the U.S. government had apologized to HIF for designating the wrong office. Another senior Saudi official characterized any terrorist financing out of the Kingdom as involving isolated cases and government controls as sufficient to prevent further problems; a third described HIF's clandestine activities as outside activities. We know these descriptions were inaccurate, as the U.S. and Saudi governments continued to take action against al Haramain and its employees.

Despite having frozen the accounts of entities and individuals listed by the United Nations under UNSCR [United Nations Security Council resolution] 1373, the Saudis did little else initially. They insisted that their then 12-year-old charities law would suffice, as would their then 7-year-old anti-moneylaundering statute. Foreign operations of charities were not regulated until 2002, when the Ministry of Islamic Affairs was put in charge of overseeing them. In the summer of 2002, the Saudis claimed that all out-of-country charitable activities had to be reported to the Foreign Ministry, but later in the year a representative of the Foreign Ministry said he knew of no such regulation. They claimed that they were reviewing all domestic charities in 2002 but took no actions and did not inform the U.S. government of any findings, even while clandestine activity continued. They repeated promises throughout 2002 to establish a High Commission that would oversee all charitable activities, and then claimed to have created such an entity in December 2002. By late fall of 2002 the Saudi government said it was moving to regulate charities further, but the U.S. government had not seen any documentation to that effect as of spring of 2003. The Saudis responded to the increase in U.S. pressure, exemplified by the delivery of the al Haramain nonpaper in early 2003, by articulating additional counterterrorism policies. The measures were to include Ministry of Islamic Affairs preclearance of transfers of charitable funds overseas, host government approval of all incoming charitable funds from Saudi Arabia, and monitoring of charities' bank accounts through audits, expenditure reports, and site visits. Also in the spring of 2003, the Saudi Arabia Monetary Authority (SAMA) was said to have instituted a major technical training program for judges and investigators on terrorist financing and money laundering.

On al Haramain, the Saudi press reported in February 2003 that the Saudi government was planning to restructure the charity. The Saudi government had also reportedly initiated an investigation of al Haramain and was examining the personal accounts of senior officers. However, the Saudis resisted taking action against a top HIF executive despite U.S. requests. In April 2003, the Saudi government said that a new Board of Directors would be appointed for al Haramain, no new offices would be permitted, no third-country nationals would be hired, all overseas offices were to have their own local lawyers and accountants, and a licensing procedure would be implemented. Again, there was a sense that the Saudis wished to take such actions quietly. On May 8, 2003, the U.S. embassy in Riyadh reported that the Saudi government would close ten al Haramain branch offices pending review of their finances. This claim was reiterated several times by Saudi or HIF officials over the summer of 2003.

Although these measures were all steps in the right direction, the Saudi government generally failed to carry out a number of the actions pledged. For instance, they did not close the branch offices of HIF as promised. As well, the Saudi government remained cautious about speaking publicly about counterterrorism issues and ramping up its reforms. Some in the U.S. government thought that public statements by the Saudi government could have gone a long way toward deterring Saudi financial support for terrorists. Admittedly, the Saudis were, and still are, cautious about how any reforms and close cooperative efforts with the United States are perceived in the Kingdom.

Underlying the Saudi government's reluctance to act against charities funneling money to terrorists lay several issues. First, at the time the Saudi government did not view al Qaeda as a domestic threat. The Saudis simply may not have believed that al Qaeda would attack it, despite the known hatred of al Qaeda and Bin Ladin for the Saudi regime. The signs were there, however, and even the U.S. government had warned the Saudis of possible upcoming attacks in the Kingdom.

Second, the Saudi government's efforts on terrorist financing were domestically unpalatable. It had been content for many years to delegate all religious activities, including those of charities, to the religious establishment and was reluctant to challenge that group. Since the Saudi government did not view al Qaeda as a domestic threat at that time, it could not justify the potential domestic rancor that would have resulted from a strong program against terrorism financing. The challenge was to find a way to increase oversight over charities, mosques, and religious donations without endangering the country's stability. Of course, by failing to reassert some measure of control over the religious establishment, the House of Saud was just as likely to endanger its stability.

Third, the Saudi government did not have the technical capabilities to stem the flow of funds to terrorists from charities in Saudi Arabia. The Mubahith lacked the necessary investigative expertise to track financial crimes. In addition, as described in an internal OFAC document from April 2002, "The SAG [Saudi Arabian government] does not have the legal or operational structures in place at this time to effectively implement the U.N. resolutions relating to the prevention and suppression of the financing of terrorist acts." Although the Saudis claimed to be developing procedures to track all donations to and from charities in October 2002, by January 2004 they were described as just starting to have such capabilities. Moreover, tighter control over money flows can be achieved only if the banks in Saudi Arabia are capable of monitoring and freezing funds. In 2002, the U.S. intelligence community was highly skeptical that Saudi banks had the necessary technical abilities.

The U.S. government was willing, and made several offers, to provide the Saudis with the necessary training. In 2002, the Saudis were described as "reluctant to host trainers from U.S. agencies on issues related to terrorist financing. This reluctance is partly cultural—an attitude that training implies a lack of equality between the parties." The U.S. government sent a Financial Services Assessment Team (FSAT) to Saudi Arabia in April 2002 to learn about Saudi financial systems and structures and ascertain opportunities for U.S. assistance and training, but the Saudis failed to schedule several key meetings during this trip.

May 2003: Turning a corner

On May 12, 2003, al Qaeda operatives detonated three explosions in an expatriate community in Riyadh, killing Westerners and Saudi Arabians. Since then, the Saudi government has taken a number of significant, concrete steps to stem the flow of funding from the Kingdom to terrorists. The Saudi government, in one of its more important actions after the bombings, removed collection boxes in mosques, as well as in shopping malls, and prohibited cash contributions at mosques. This action was important because terrorist groups and their supporters have been able to siphon funds from mosque donations. Its sensitivity cannot be overestimated. U.S. Ambassador to Saudi Arabia Jordan described the removal of the collection boxes as a "cataclysmic event." It was a real action that the Saudi public has both seen and been affected by; it has forced everyone to think about terrorist financing.

On May 24, 2003, the Saudi government followed up with comprehensive new restrictions on the financial activities of Saudi charities. These included a requirement that charitable accounts can be opened only in Saudi riyals; enhanced customer identification requirements for charitable accounts; a requirement that charities must consolidate all banking activity into one principal account, with subaccounts permitted for branches but for deposits only, with all withdrawals and transfers serviced through the main account; a prohibition on cash disbursements from charitable accounts, with payments allowed by check payable to the first beneficiary and deposited into a Saudi bank; a prohibition on the use of ATM and credit cards by charities; and a prohibition on transfers from charitable accounts outside of Saudi Arabia.

Also, after the May 12 bombings the Saudis initiated action to capture or otherwise deal with known al Qaeda operatives, financial facilitators, and financiers in Saudi Arabia. Early in this campaign, the Saudis killed a key al Qaeda leader and financial facilitator known as "Swift Sword" in a firefight. The arrests and deaths of financial facilitators such as Swift Sword have been a blow to al Qaeda and have hampered its fund-raising efforts in the Kingdom.

The May 12 bombings caused the Saudis to become more receptive to disrupting al Qaeda financing than ever before; the Saudis appeared ready to take seriously the cooperative aspect of "quiet cooperation." At the same time, the U.S. government finally developed a coherent approach to working with the Saudis on combating terrorist financing. The United States had an agenda, the Saudi strategy, and was able to engage the Saudis more forcefully on the issues than it could have otherwise. Most importantly, the U.S. government raised the terrorist-financing dialogue to the highest levels. Fran Fragos Townsend, then deputy assistant to the President and deputy national security advisor for combating terrorism, was designated the senior White House liaison on terrorist financing, and President Bush has publicly stated his confidence in her.

The U.S. government was therefore in a position to test the Saudis' new focus on terrorist financing. Townsend traveled to Saudi Arabia in early August 2003 and again in September 2003. One product of the early high-level meetings was the establishment of the joint task force on terrorist financing, described below.

Despite the positive atmosphere of the August meetings, one area of continuing concern was that the ten al Haramain branches the Saudi government had committed to closing in May 2003, before the bombings, were apparently still operating. There was apparently some question as to whether the al Haramain head office really had control over its branch offices and therefore whether closing the branch offices was the responsibility of the Saudi government or the host governments. Some in the U.S. government believe this discussion to be specious, since resources regularly flow from the head office to the branches. They argue, plausibly, that even if the Saudi government itself cannot control the flows of funds, it can pressure the headquarters to cut off these resources to the branches or pressure the heads of governments of the countries where the branch offices are located to close those offices.

In the fall of 2003, the Saudi government passed new anti-money-laundering and terrorist-financing legislation. This law updated the 1995 anti-money-laundering law and improved reporting and record-keeping requirements, created new interagency coordination mechanisms, and established a financial intelligence unit to collect and analyze suspicious financial transactions. Also that fall, the Saudi government permitted a team of assessors from the Financial Action Task Force (FATF) and the Gulf Cooperation Council to visit the Kingdom to evaluate its anti-money-laundering and terrorist-financing laws and regulations. Finally, in September 2003 the Saudi government questioned the executive director of HIF, Abd al-Rahman Bin Aqil.

The joint task force on terrorist financing started operations in the fall of 2003 as well. The task force consists of staff from both the United States and Saudi Arabia. The task force seeks to identify and financially investigate persons and entities suspected of providing financial support to terrorist groups. The U.S. government offered the Saudis training in conducting financial investigations, and the Saudis "readily accepted." This training focused on the value of tracking financial transactions in an investigation and provided practical case studies. The Saudi trainees were dedicated and enthusiastic, although very much in need of training. One FBI official said, "I cannot overemphasize the importance of this initiative and the efforts on the part of both our countries to make it work."

In November 2003, another bombing in Riyadh further jolted the Saudi government to take action on terrorist-financing issues and cooperate with the U.S. government. One U.S. government assessment described the impact of the 2003 Riyadh bombings on the Saudis, in conjunction with the May 12 bombings, as "galvanizing Riyadh into launching a sustained crackdown against al-Qaida's presence in the Kingdom and spurring an unprecedented level of cooperation with the United States." Similarly, it noted that "the attack of 9 November [2003], which resulted in the deaths of a number of Muslims and Arabs during the holy month of Ramadan, transformed Saudi public acceptance of the widespread nature of the threat in the Kingdom." As a result, the Saudi government may have more latitude to act against terrorist financing than ever before.

Similarly, FBI officials have ranked Saudi cooperation on terrorist-financing issues as "good" since the May 12 and November 8, 2003, Riyadh bombings. The Saudis have aggressively interrogated people in their custody about financial matters, including questions posed by the U.S. government, and have provided actionable intelligence to the U.S. government. A senior CIA counterterrorism official agreed that there had been progress in our cooperation with the Saudis. He described it as "not perfect" but a big improvement from the difficult days before 9/11. In a sign of the level of U.S. confidence in the Saudi effort, the U.S. government is now releasing very sensitive intelligence to the Saudis.

By late fall of 2003, Saudis confirmed that since 9/11 they had taken several significant steps to modify their rules and regulations to stem the flow of funds to terrorists. In addition to the new charities regulations, the removal of zakat boxes, and the task force, as described above, the Saudi government said it had established the High Commission to oversee all charities, contributions, and donations; required all charities to undergo audits and institute control mechanisms to monitor how and where funds are dispersed; directed all Saudi charities to suspend activities outside Saudi Arabia; and investigated numerous banks accounts suspected of having links to terrorism and frozen more than 40 such accounts. The Saudi government has apparently also regulated hawalas through a mandatory licensing requirement and legal, economic, and supervisory measures and sought to decrease demand for unlicensed hawalas.

With respect to al Haramain, the Saudi and U.S. governments took further action at the end of 2003 and into 2004. On December 22, 2003, the U.S. and Saudi governments designated Vazir, an NGO in Bosnia, and its representative a terrorist supporter. It was determined that Vazir was simply another name for the previously designated al Haramain office in Bosnia. Then, in January 2004 the United States and Saudi Arabia jointly designated four additional branches of al Haramain, in Indonesia, Kenya, Tanzania, and Pakistan. The two governments held an unprecedented joint press conference in Washington to announce the designation. The names of these branches were subsequently submitted to the United Nations, which instituted an international freeze on their assets. Also, in January 2004 Executive Director Aqil was removed from his position. One public explanation was that the firing related to recent incidents involving HIF's operations in Bosnia.

On February 19, 2004, federal law enforcement took action against both the al Haramain branch in Ashland, Oregon, and the imam of the HIF mosque in Springfield, Missouri. The FBI and the IRS conducted searches of the Ashland offices of HIF as part of an investigation into alleged money laundering and income tax and currency reporting violations. Treasury took the additional step of freezing, during the pendency of an investigation, the accounts of the branch in Oregon and the mosque in Missouri. The Saudis continue to make changes to their charities laws and regulations. Rules implementing the anti-money-laundering and terrorist-financing law were issued in February 2004. Also in February 2004, FATF issued its report indicating that Saudi Arabia was in compliance or near-compliance with international standards for almost every indicator of effective instruments to combat money laundering and terrorist financing.

On February 29, 2004, the Saudi government announced that it had approved the creation of the Saudi National Commission for Relief and Charity Work Abroad to take over all aspects of overseas aid operations and assume responsibility for the distribution of charitable donations from Saudi Arabia. Although the U.S. government had no details about this commission as of the end of March 2004, one former U.S. government counter-terrorist-financing official said that such an entity could, in theory, replace charities such as al Haramain by subsuming all of HIF's activities into its own. Al Haramain was said to be in the process of restructuring its administration and revising its financial regulations. Al Haramain was planning to refocus its charity work on Saudi Arabia, according to a statement by its new director, Sheikh Dabbas al Dabbas.

Continuing the pressure on al Haramain, the U.S. and Saudi governments jointly designated five additional branches of al Haramain (Afghanistan, Albania, Bangladesh, Ethiopia, and the Netherlands) on June 2, 2004. The United States also designated former Executive Director Aqil. These names were subsequently submitted to the United Nations for an international freeze on their assets.

Lessons Learned

The U.S. government's efforts to address issues raised by al Haramain before and after 9/11 teach some critical lessons. First, to cause the Saudi government to move against terrorist financiers, the U.S. government has to acquire and release to the Saudis specific intelligence that will enable them to take the necessary action. Thus, the U.S. government was able to get the Saudis to take concrete actions against al Haramain, and charities generally, after it released the nonpaper containing specific intelligence about al Haramain and its employees to the Saudis in January 2003. Previously, the U.S. government appears, for the most part, to have tried to encourage the Saudis to act on the basis of little more than U.S. suspicions or assurances that the United States had intelligence it could not release.

Second, counter-terrorist-financing efforts are an essential part of the overall set of counterterrorist activities and must be fully integrated into the broader U.S. counterterrorism strategy toward Saudi Arabia. Without such integration, those working on terrorist financing might not be aware of other bilateral counterterrorism issues. The U.S. government might then have the appearance of sending mixed or inconsistent messages on counterterrorism to the Saudis. Once the broader Saudi strategy was approved, the U.S. government was able to develop a consistent message across counterterrorism issues. It could push the Saudis more forcefully on terrorist-financing issues, including al Haramain, by, for example, delivering the nonpaper in January 2003 [a reference to a U.S. government document outlining for the Saudis information the United States had obtained about the foundation]. In direct response to the nonpaper, the Saudi government announced its decision to close ten branch offices of al Haramain.

Third, U.S. counter-terrorist-financing strategy must be presented to the Saudi government by a high-level U.S. government representative. The perils of not speaking through a single high-level interlocutor were clear in the case of the reopenings of the Bosnian and Somali offices of al Haramain, as discussed above, when, as one key terrorist-financing official believed, the Saudis "gamed" us. It was not until the appointment of a senior White House official that the U.S engagement of the Saudi government on terrorist financing yielded its most concrete results. A PCC [policy coordinating committee, a U.S. government intragency panel] participant said the Saudis did not take terrorist financing seriously until Townsend was appointed. She has been able to apply consistent pressure, over a period of time, with the full backing of the White House.

Fourth, the U.S. government needs a distinct interagency coordinating committee focused on terrorist financing to ensure that terrorist-financing issues are not lost in the overall counterterrorism effort. The PCC proved to be generally effective in focusing the U.S. government on terrorist financing and retaining the momentum of the immediate post-9/11 period. It enabled different branches of the U.S. government to vet the information on al Haramain and assess the options. It ensured that al Haramain-related issues were not lost in the larger counterterrorism picture but were assessed periodically with the full attention of the interagency representatives.

At the same time, the coordinating committee must be fully integrated with the overall counterterrorism effort so that terrorist financing can be made part of the high-level diplomacy necessary to win the cooperation of key allies like Saudi Arabia. One way to achieve this goal is give the NSC the lead on the PCC, as is currently the case. The NSC is better able than any individual agency to integrate terrorist financing into counterterrorism through its leadership of the Counterterrorism Security Group; the NSC is better able to see how the different terrorist-financing tools fit together; the NSC is better able to task agencies and force agencies to reallocate resources; NSC leadership is more efficient because it has the authority to resolve more issues rather than forcing them up to the DC level; the NSC has the best access to information, especially regarding covert action; and the NSC is not operational and is therefore more neutral. Throughout the interagency process on al Haramain, NSC leadership of the PCC might have been useful to expedite the process and clarify the U.S. position.

The concept of a "terrorist-financing czar" has been proposed at times; while perhaps it could have been useful before 9/11, it would serve little purpose today and could detract from the U.S. government's current efforts and recent successes. Terrorist financing is already on the agenda of senior officials, so there is no need for a czar to draw attention to the issue. Each of the relevant agencies has established new sections on terrorist financing or augmented existing groups to work on terrorist-financing issues. Further elevating the issue might overemphasize it or, at the very least, detract from current progress in the larger counterterrorism fight. Action against terrorist financing is only one tool in the fight against terrorism and must be integrated into counterterrorism policy and operations. A czar would undermine this goal. Such a position would also dilute the power of a unified message and the benefits of a single messenger on all terrorism-related issues that the leadership of the NSC seeks to provide.

Challenges Ahead

Much remains to be done to address terrorist-financing issues in Saudi Arabia and the activities of Saudi charities, such as al Haramain, around the globe. Saudi Arabia has worked hard to institute an improved legal and regulatory regime. It remains to be seen if the new laws and regulations will be fully implemented and enforced, and if further necessary legal and regulatory changes will be made. The Saudis still have not established the National Commission as they promised in February 2004 and have not demonstrated that they are willing and able to serve as the conduit for all external Saudi donations in lieu of Saudi charities. Moreover, it is imperative that the Saudi government develop its capabilities to monitor cash flows; otherwise, it will not be able to assess a given entity's or individual's compliance with the new laws and regulations. The Saudi government's acceptance of training from the United States and other countries would demonstrate its willingness to assure that gains in expertise and capabilities are ongoing.

It remains to be seen whether the Saudi government will be willing to make politically and religiously difficult decisions. The action it has taken in 2004 against several al Haramain branch offices is unquestionably significant. Although the government has frozen the assets of branches of al Haramain, it has not used its leverage with the head office to ensure that no funds flow to the designated branches. Similarly, the Saudis have yet to hold prominent individuals—like the former head of al Haramain, for instance—accountable for terrorist financing. Such actions would send a signal both to potential targets and to the Saudi public that the Saudi government is serious about stemming the flow of funds to terrorists and their supporters.

We are optimistic that the U.S. and Saudi governments are on the right track in their mutual efforts on terrorist financing. Neither country can afford to lessen the intensity of its current approach. The Saudi government has come far in recognizing the extent of its terrorist-financing problem. We cannot underplay, however, the reluctance of the Saudi government to make the necessary changes between 9/11 and late spring of 2003. It remains to be seen whether it has truly internalized its responsibility for the problem. A critical part of the U.S. strategy to combat terrorist financing will be monitoring, encouraging, and nurturing Saudi cooperation while simultaneously recognizing that terrorist financing is only one of a number of crucial issues on which the U.S. and Saudi governments need each other.

Source: U.S. National Commission on Terrorist Attacks upon the United States. "Monograph on Terrorist Financing: Staff Report to the Commission." August 21, 2004. www.9-11commission.gov/staff_statements/911_Terrfin_Monograph.pdf (accessed March 17, 2005).

United Nations on the al Qaeda Terrorist Network and the Taliban

August 25, 2004

INTRODUCTION

The al Qaeda terrorist network in 2004 appeared to be battered but still active and no less more dangerous than it had been when it carried out the September 11, 2001, attacks in New York and Washington. Numerous terrorist attacks during 2004, especially in the Middle East and Europe, indicated that al Qaeda and other extreme Islamist groups remained determined to attack Western targets and exploit local or regional grievances. The U.S. occupation of Iraq had become a prime recruiting tool for these groups, serving as a cause for disaffected Muslims from the Middle East to Southeast Asia to rally around.

The Bush administration's "war against terrorism" continued to make some inroads against al Qaeda and related groups. Mid-level operatives were arrested during the year in Britain and Pakistan, and U.S. officials said high-level al Qaeda leaders captured the previous year had provided important information about the network. Osama bin Laden, al Qaeda's founder and leader, remained at large, however, and evaded the third annual campaign by the U.S. and Pakistani militaries to capture him in his presumed hideout in northwestern Pakistan. Many international exports on terrorism said capturing bin Laden would not end the threat posed by al Qaeda, which appeared to have transformed itself into a loose, decentralized network of like-minded cells and individuals in dozens of nations around the world.

"There is no prospect of an early end to attacks from al Qaeda-associated terrorists," a United Nations monitoring team reported to the UN Security Council on August 25. "They will continue to attack targets in both Muslim and non-Muslim states, choosing them according to the resources they have available and the opportunities that occur. While they will look for ways to attack high-profile targets, soft targets [such as civilians] will be equally vulnerable." *(Background, Historic Documents of 2001, pp. 614, 802; Historic Documents of 2002, p. 1014; Historic Documents of 2003, p. 1050)*

Major Terrorist Attacks in 2004

The United States escaped any known terrorist attacks in 2004—for the third year in a row. The one possible exception was the discovery of a small amount of deadly ricin poison on Capitol Hill that did not injure anyone. For the first time in years there were few major attacks in Southeast Asia, which had become a focal point for extreme Islamist groups. *(Ricin scare, p. 442)*

Terrorism continued to take its toll, however. Major terrorist attacks of the year included:

- Bombings on four commuter trains in Madrid on the morning of May 11, killing 191 people and wounding more than 1,600. The Spanish government at first blamed the attack on a Basque separatist group despite mounting evidence that al Qaeda-affiliated terrorists were responsible. Three days after the bombing, outraged voters defeated the governing party and installed the opposition Socialist Party, which had opposed Spanish participation in the U.S. occupation of Iraq. *(Madrid bombings, p. 105)*
- Dozens of attacks in Iraq against U.S. and other coalition military units and Iraqi civilian and security force targets. By 2004 the vast majority of attacks targeted Iraqi security forces—local policemen and a new army being trained by the United States and European nations—rather than the coalition military forces led by more than 130,000 American troops. Much of Iraq was free from violence most of the time, but Baghdad and other cities in the central region known as the "Sunni triangle" were engulfed in almost daily bombings, shootings, and other attacks that killed hundreds of people, including civilians. Iraq thus became the most terrorism-afflicted country in the world. *(Iraq violence, p. 874)*
- Bombings and other attacks by extremist Palestinian groups against Israel. The Israeli army counted fifteen suicide bombing attacks during 2004—down sharply from the twenty-six such bombings a year earlier. The violence between Israel and the Palestinians was not directly related to the al Qaeda-inspired wave of terrorism elsewhere, but it derived in part from similar grievances by extreme Islamists. *(Israeli-Palestinian conflict, p. 806)*
- Near-simultaneous bombings of three Red Sea resorts in Egypt, just south of the border with Israel, on October 7. The bombings killed thirty-two people, including twelve Israelis. Egyptian officials had not pinned responsibility on any one group, as of year's end.
- Bombings and hijackings in Russia that appeared to be related to the continuing war for control of Chechnya, a Muslim-majority province in southern Russia. By far the most important was the seizing of a school in the city of Beslan, near Chechnya, in September. An estimated 360 people died on September 3, when Russian security forces attempted to rescue the more than 1,200 children and parents who had been held hostage in the school. The government also blamed Chechen terrorists for several other bombings and attacks during the year, notably the apparent suicide bombings of two airliners on August 24, in which 90 people died. *(Beslan hostage crisis, p. 564)*
- Continuing violence in Afghanistan throughout the year, especially in the weeks before the country's first-ever presidential election on October 9. Many of the attacks appeared to be carried out by remnants of the Taliban regime, which had governed Afghanistan before the U.S.-led invasion in 2001. U.S. officials said other attacks bore the hallmarks of al Qaeda, including a car bombing in Kabul on August 26 that killed ten people, including three Americans. *(Afghanistan election, p. 912)*
- A series of bombings and shootings in Saudi Arabia, including an attack on security headquarters in Riyadh in April (killing four and wounding about fifteen); attacks at a petrochemical complex in Yanbu and an oil company compound in Khobar in May (killing twenty-seven people in total); shooting attacks in Riyadh (killing two Americans and a BBC cameraman) and the abduction

and beheading of an American engineer in June; and an attack on the U.S. consulate in Jeddah (killing five local staff members) in December. *(Saudi Arabia, p. 517)*

- The sinking of a ferry in the Philippines on February 27, killing 118 people. The Philippine government on October 11 said it was seeking four members of an Islamist group, Abu Sayyaf, in connection with the sinking, which officials said was caused by the explosion of a bomb placed in a television set. It was the deadliest terrorist attack in Philippine history.

Dozens of planned terrorist attacks reportedly were thwarted in other countries that had been hit by bombings and shootings in recent years. The *Los Angeles Times* reported on August 26, for example, that two planned attacks in Morocco had been headed off at the last minute, including one on an unnamed American target. Spanish police said they had blocked another bombing just two weeks before the Madrid train bombings, and U.S. officials said they believed they had foiled attacks in the United States—but were unable or unwilling to point to specifics.

Bin Laden's Messages

Bin Laden had surfaced repeatedly since September 2001 through audiotapes and videotapes, each containing messages denouncing the United States and pledging unending "war" until all U.S. influence had been expunged from Islamic lands. In 2004 bin Laden issued five such tapes, and his chief deputy, Ayman al-Zawahiri, issued six; the combined total of eleven was more than twice as many statements as in any of the previous three years.

The first by bin Laden, an audiotape aired April 15, one month after the Madrid bombings, offered a truce for European nations that ended their operations in Islamic lands; that message brought quick denunciations from European capitals. A second audiotape made public May 7 offered rewards of 10,000 grams of gold each for the assassinations of UN Secretary General Kofi Annan; Annan's envoy to Iraq, Lakhdar Brahimi; and the head of the U.S.-led Coalition Provisional Authority in Iraq, L. Paul Bremer.

Another message came October 29, just four days before the U.S. presidential election. In a videotape, bin Laden addressed the American people directly and denounced President George W. Bush. The videotape was the first from bin Laden in a year, and it showed him standing at a lectern, apparently in good health and making a forceful presentation. It was unclear whether this tape had any impact on voters, who at the time were weighing whether Bush or his Democratic rival, John Kerry, would provide more effective leadership in the war against terrorism, among other challenges. *(U.S. election, p. 773)*

Two more audiotapes emerged in December. In a tape posted on an Islamic Internet site on December 15, bin Laden praised a December 6 shooting attack on the U.S. consulate in Jeddah, Saudi Arabia, and called on Saudi citizens to overthrow the monarchy that ruled their country. On December 28 another audiotape, apparently by bin Laden, declared a holy war against U.S. forces in Iraq and against Iraqis who supported legislative elections planned there in late January.

U.S. and international terrorism experts suggested during the year that bin Laden might no longer be actively engaged in planning specific terrorist attacks, if only because his lines of communications with al Qaeda operatives appeared to have been cut. One bit of evidence possibly contradicting this view was the October 29 videotape, which broadcast experts said showed signs of having been recorded in a studio with modern equipment. Bin Laden in the past appeared to have used taped messages to send signals to distant associates.

The UN committee said bin Laden remained important mainly by providing a symbol and inspiration for disaffected Muslims, rather than as an active plotter of individual terrorist attacks. "Even without Osama bin Laden and the rest of the core leadership, the threat would remain," the panel said.

Attacking al Qaeda

In his January 20 State of the Union address, Bush said two-thirds of al Qaeda's leadership had been captured or killed since the October 2001 U.S.-led invasion of Afghanistan. To back that figure, administration officials noted the capture of such senior al Qaeda figures as Khalid Sheikh Mohammad (said to have been the mastermind of the September 11 attacks) and the killing during the Afghanistan invasion of al Qaeda's military chief, Muhammad Atef. *(2004 State of the Union, p. 17)*

Testifying before a House International Relations subcommittee on April 1, Cofer Black, the State Department's counterterrorism coordinator, said more than 3,400 lower-level al Qaeda "operatives or associates" had been detained or killed. As a result, he said, al Qaeda "has been gravely wounded and forced to evolve in new ways to survive." Even so, he said, it remained a potent threat to Western interests.

Other experts said the U.S. claims about the damage done to Qaeda members failed to account for the recruiting success of terrorist groups as a result of the war in Iraq. The International Institute of Strategic Studies, a British think tank, on May 25 published a report estimating that more than 18,000 terrorists associated with al Qaeda were scattered around the world, with thousands more likely to swell the ranks in response to the U.S. occupation of Iraq.

A similar—and even blunter—critique came from the CIA's former top expert on al Qaeda, who went public during the year with a blistering challenge to much of the Bush administration's antiterrorism war. In a book, *Imperial Hubris,* and numerous interviews with the news media, CIA analyst Michael Scheuer said the administration was misjudging the character of al Qaeda by treating it as a traditional terrorist organization that could be dismantled by systematically arresting or killing its leaders and operatives. Instead, he said, al Qaeda was the equivalent of an insurgency that was constantly reinventing and restoring itself and so was capable of withstanding repeated attacks on its leadership. Scheuer was particularly critical of the claim by Bush and others that two-thirds of al Qaeda's leadership had been neutralized. "To say that they have only one-third of their leadership left is a misunderstanding," Scheuer told the *New York Times,* in an interview published November 7. One of al Qaeda's main tenets was to "train people to succeed leaders who are captured or killed." Scheuer resigned from the CIA later in November after the agency moved to stifle his public statements, which were highly unusual for a CIA analyst.

The Pakistani army, with U.S. logistical support, in February launched a major campaign to capture bin Laden and other al Qaeda leaders in the remote mountainous regions of Pakistan along the border with Afghanistan. That campaign quickly bogged down, however, and reportedly netted only low-level fighters rather than any leaders. *(Hunting al Qaeda, p. 1009)*

An alleged al Qaeda operative long sought by the United States was captured in Pakistan during the year—not in the wilds of the border region but living in relative comfort in the city of Gujrat, south of Islamabad. A joint operation by U.S. and Pakistani intelligence services resulted in the July 25 seizure of Ahmed Khalfan Ghailani, a Tanzanian sought by the United States because of his alleged involvement in the 1998 bombings of U.S. embassies in Kenya and Tanzania. Several weeks earlier Pakistani agents had arrested an alleged al Qaeda communications expert, Mohammed Naeem Noor Kahn, along with his extensive computer files. Khan's files reportedly provided information that contributed to an August 1 warning by Homeland Security Secretary Tom Ridge that al Qaeda was planning an attack on U.S. financial centers in the New York and Washington, D.C., areas. Several other suspected al Qaeda operatives were arrested in Britain on August 3. *(Terror alerts, p. 268)*

The captures of Khan and Ghailani also demonstrated two other facets of the post-September 11 terrorism equation. The first was that key operatives of the al Qaeda network continued to be based in the cities of Pakistan, where some had been for many years and others had moved after the U.S. invasion of Afghanistan forced the closing of al Qaeda camps in that country. The arrests showed that al Qaeda appeared to be "conducting business as usual" in Pakistan and elsewhere, RAND Corporation terrorism expert Bruce Hoffman, said. "This points to a movement with much deeper benches than we imagined, and that can build and replenish its leadership as it needs." A second factor was the continued U.S. reliance on Pakistan's cooperation in the war against al Qaeda. "The U.S. provides high-tech communication assistance in nabbing al Qaeda operatives, but completely depends on Pakistan for human intelligence," Pakistani defense analyst Aisha Agha told the *Christian Science Monitor* in August. In its July 22 report, the commission that investigated the September 11 attacks acknowledged Pakistan's vital cooperation and called for a long-term U.S. commitment to promote "stability" there. *(Commission report, p. 450)*

Changing Nature of al Qaeda

Ever since 2002 it had appeared that al Qaeda was evolving from a cohesive structure into a loose network of groups or even individuals who shared the same goals and were willing to use the same tactics to achieve them. Many intelligence officials and terrorism experts—both in Western countries and in the Middle East—had drawn attention to this transformation, and by 2004 there appeared to be a general consensus that it in fact had occurred.

In its report, the UN committee said al Qaeda "has evolved to become a global network of groups unbound by any organizational structure but held together by a set of overlapping goals. The leaders of these groups have tried to hijack and distort the basic Muslim duty of Jihad to justify terrorist campaigns against both Muslim and non-Muslim states. Perceived injustices and images of violent confrontation have ensured a steady flow of new supporters."

In his annual "worldwide threat briefing" to Congress on February 24, CIA director George Tenet had used similar language to describe al Qaeda as symbolic of a "movement" rather than as a corporate entity controlled from above. "The steady growth of Osama bin Laden's anti-U.S. sentiment through the wider Sunni [Muslim] extremist movement and the broad dissemination of al Qaeda's destructive expertise ensure that a serious threat will remain for the foreseeable future—with or without al Qaeda in the picture," Tenet said.

Tenet noted that al Qaeda and other terrorist groups could operate without official hindrance in "stateless zones" in about fifty countries. He described as "prime candidates" for these zones the "remote, rugged regions where central governments have no consistent reach and where socioeconomic problems are rife." One example was the mountainous border region between Afghanistan and Pakistan, where bin Laden and other top al Qaeda leaders were presumed to have moved after being pushed out of Afghanistan in late 2001. Gen. Charles Wald, deputy commander of U.S. forces in Europe, told Congress in May that al Qaeda-affiliated terrorist groups had moved into lawless regions of Africa, including parts of Chad, Mali, Mauritania, Niger, and Somalia.

Tenet and others identified more than one dozen extreme Islamist groups around the world as having some connections with, or at least being inspired by, al Qaeda. Among the most prominent of those groups were:

- Elements of the anti-U.S. insurgency in Iraq headed by Abu Musab al-Zarqawi, a Jordanian who had repeatedly claimed to represent al Qaeda. In 2003 U.S. officials suspected that al-Zarqawi was operating out of Iran, but by 2004 the official U.S. position was that he and his allies had taken up positions in the city of Falluja, west of Baghdad. In February U.S. officials said they had seized a letter, reportedly written by al-Zarqawi, asking al Qaeda for support and complaining about difficulties in recruiting Iraqis for terrorist attacks. U.S. officials accused al-Zarqawi of plotting or sponsoring several major attacks in Iraq, including the August 2003 bombing of UN headquarters in Baghdad that led to the UN's withdrawal from Iraq. On February 12, 2004, the United States offered a $10 million reward for information leading to the capture of al-Zarqawi. The U.S. Army and Marines moved into Falluja in November to eliminate his operations there, but al-Zarqawi and his top lieutenants appeared to have escaped the dragnet. *(Iraq developments, p. 399)*
- Ansar al-Islam, a radical Islamist group that for several years before the U.S. invasion of Iraq reportedly had been based in a remote region of northern Iraq. Some U.S. officials said the group was headed by al-Zarqawi, a contention disputed by many other experts. On February 8, 2004, the *New York Times* quoted intelligence officials as saying the group had "re-emerged in Europe as a well-organized terror threat" that helped other groups in Europe and Iraq. The *Times* noted that members of the group had been arrested the previous December in Germany and Italy.
- Jemaah Islamiyah, an al Qaeda-affiliated network based in Indonesia and operating throughout Southeast Asia, notably in the Philippines. International officials said the group was responsible for the bombing in 2002 of a nightclub in Bali, Indonesia, that killed 202 people. Experts on terrorism in the region said Jemaah Islamiyah cooperated with a Philippine secessionist group, the Moro Islamic Liberation Front, which was fighting for independence on the island of Mindanao. *(Bali bombing, Historic Documents of 2002, p. 702)*
- The Salafist Group for Call and Combat (known by its French acronym GSCP), which had been battling for an Islamist state in Algeria. GSCP had splintered from a larger guerrilla group in Algeria, the Armed Islamic Group. Terrorism experts said GSCP moved to establish ties with al Qaeda.
- Several Pakistan-based groups that since 1989 had been battling Indian control of the province of Kashmir, which was disputed between India and Pakistan. Some of these groups long had received weapons and training from the Pakistani army, which used them to harass the Indian military in the majority of Kashmir controlled by India. Pakistan officially banned some of these groups after they carried out an attack on the Indian parliament in December 2001, but by late 2002 the groups and most of their leaders reportedly had resumed their operations with little apparent interference from the Pakistani government. International terrorism experts said in 2004 that at least one of these groups, Lashkar-e-Taiaba, appeared to be recruiting and training terrorists in other

parts of South Asia and Southeast Asia, not just in Pakistan and Kashmir. *(Background, Historic Documents of 2003, p. 210)*

Terrorism Financing

In July 2001—two months before the September 11 attacks—the United Nations Security Council established a committee to monitor international compliance with an arms embargo and financial sanctions the council had imposed against al Qaeda as a result of the 1998 bombings of U.S. embassies in Africa. Headed by Michael Chandler of Britain, the panel issued regular reports both on al Qaeda's operations and on the fitful international response to the terrorist network. The panel's last report, in December 2003, said most UN member nations had done little to crack down on al Qaeda and had even failed to take such simple steps as passing onto the UN the names of suspected terrorists.

The unvarnished language of Chandler's reports apparently unsettled some Security Council members, including the United States, which quietly lobbied to have the group disbanded and replaced by a new panel. Chandler himself told the *Washington Post* that "a number of people were uncomfortable with our last report." U.S. diplomats and some UN officials told the *Post* that Chandler's reporting needlessly antagonized some nations, including Italy, Liechtenstein, and Switzerland, which had been cited in the December report for failing to crack down on terrorists.

In Resolution 1526, adopted January 30, 2004, the Security Council formally disbanded Chandler's panel and established a new one, the Analytical Support and Sanctions Monitoring Team, chaired by Heraldo Munoz, Chile's ambassador to the United Nations. Munoz said his panel would be "more effective" than the previous one and would have a more expert staff. The resolution also extended the reach of UN sanctions against al Qaeda by requiring countries to freeze the network's property and other "economic resources," not just bank accounts.

The Munoz panel issued its first report on August 25. The report sketched a picture of al Qaeda as a loose network able to carry out high-impact attacks with low budgets and also able to adapt to international sanctions and other attempts to stifle its funding. The report estimated that the March 11 bombings of four commuter trains in Madrid—which killed 191 people and contributed to the political defeat of the Spanish ruling party—cost only about $10,000. Munoz said his report showed that UN sanctions against al Qaeda needed to be strengthened, for example by getting countries to crack down on charities that channeled money to terrorist organizations and limiting the amounts of cash that could be carried across borders. The Security Council took no formal action to toughen the sanctions, however, pending specific recommendations from the Munoz panel that were expected early in 2005.

Following are excerpts from the "First Report of the Analytical Support and Sanctions Monitoring Team Appointed Pursuant to Resolution 1526 (2004) Concerning Al Qaeda and the Taliban and Associated Individuals and Entities," submitted August 25, 2004, to the United Nations Security Council by the Analytical Support and Sanctions Monitoring Team, which the council had appointed to monitor sanctions against the al Qaeda terrorist network and the former Taliban regime of Afghanistan.

Report Concerning Al Qaeda, the Taliban, and Associated Individuals

I. Summary

1. Five years after the Security Council adopted resolution 1267 (1999), the first that dealt with the Taliban and al Qaeda, the threat from al Qaeda-related terrorism remains as great as ever. But the nature of the threat has changed. The Taliban have been removed from power and the Al Qaeda leadership is dispersed. But if the leadership is less able to direct, plan and execute attacks, they have many supporters who are eager to do so. These terrorists form groups that do not wait for orders from above but launch attacks when they are ready, against targets of their own choosing. Using minimal resources and exploiting worldwide publicity, they have managed to create an international sense of crisis.

2. Al Qaeda has evolved to become a global network of groups unbound by any organizational structure but held together by a set of overlapping goals. The leaders of these groups have tried to hijack and distort the basic Muslim duty of Jihad to justify terrorist campaigns against both Muslim and non-Muslim States. Perceived injustices and images of violent confrontation have ensured a steady flow of new supporters.

3. The attacks of 11 September 2001 provided indelible images of the potential consequences of a terrorist attack and led many nations to reappraise aspects of their domestic and foreign policies, and to divert major resources to counter terrorist activity. Other States had already suffered attacks from terrorist groups and had made these adjustments much earlier. The Security Council was also already engaged, but after September 2001 it reflected a greater unity of purpose within the international community, and wider agreement on the need for action.

4. The Security Council has taken a dual approach. It has demanded that States take action against terrorists associated with Al Qaeda through a targeted sanctions regime, and it has established mechanisms to help those States that find it difficult to do so. But Security Council sanctions aimed at curbing the Taliban and Al Qaeda terrorism have achieved less than was hoped. This is partly because they address a set of circumstances that no longer apply; and partly because effective sanctions are hard to design, let alone impose, against the form of Al Qaeda associated terrorism that exists today. The sanctions measures need refining to address the ways the threat has changed.

5. In the absence of an internationally agreed definition of terrorism, Security Council sanctions against the Taliban, Al Qaeda and their associates apply to a List of designated individuals, groups and entities. To be effective, this List should reflect international agreement on which groups and individuals pose the greatest danger. For several reasons, this List has begun to lose credibility and operational value and now needs updating in terms of its relevance and accuracy.

6. While the sanctions against the financing of terrorism have had some effect, and some millions of dollars of assets have been frozen, there is scope to update them based on how Al Qaeda now raises and transfers its money. There is a similar need to improve the travel ban and the arms embargo to reflect current Al Qaeda methodology.

7. In addition the Security Council may wish to consider new measures to enhance international cooperation and to support national efforts. The Analytical Support and Monitoring Team set up to assist the 1267 Committee of the Security Council has proposals for the improvement of the current measures, and ideas from which new ones might be formulated. It believes it can generate wider support for the List by the introduction of technical improvements and the submission of new names. It also believes it can encourage closer operational cooperation between States to make the international environment still more inhospitable to Al Qaeda-related terrorism. . . .

[Sections 8 through 11 gave background on the appointment of the committee.]

III. The Threat from Al Qaeda

12. Despite international efforts, the threat from Al Qaeda terrorism remains as real today as it has been at any time since October 1999 [the date of UN sanctions against al Qaeda]. Statements by Osama bin Laden and others on behalf of Al Qaeda demonstrate that their main objective is to bring about political and social change in the Muslim world. They seek to establish a particular form of theocratic government based on a strict application of their own interpretation of Sharia [Islamic law]. They distort the teachings of the holy religion of Islam and promise those who adopt their extremist ideology, and violent methodology, a return to a time when the Islamic world was both more powerful and more pure.

13. Attacks on Western targets are designed to serve this purpose; to force the withdrawal of the West from the Islamic world, both to weaken governments that Al Qaeda regards as corrupt and seeks to overthrow, and to remove what they see as a polluting influence. Al Qaeda wishes to promote the idea that Islam and the West are now at war, and that Al Qaeda and its supporters are the true defenders of the faith. This message touches a wound felt by a large number of Muslims in all areas of the world. It appeals to a widespread sense of resentment and helplessness in the face of the West's political and economic hegemony that many believe is intrinsically and determinedly inimical to their interests. Al Qaeda's ability to strike the enemy and survive, despite the disparity in resources, taps into an ill-articulated desire for revenge and gains both recruits and donations.

14. Al Qaeda is currently a global network rather than an organization with a structure and hierarchy. In its early days it was well organized and had a formal membership in that individuals, often on behalf of a group they led, offered allegiance to Osama bin Laden; but it is unlikely that this membership ever totalled more than a few hundred. Al Qaeda's structure provided coordination and support for groups of fighters with certain objectives in common, and supplied troops for the Taliban. Membership of these groups was almost invariably determined by ethnic origin. Very few individuals have been enrolled to conduct terrorist operations under central Al Qaeda control, and although the leadership was at one time directly involved in terrorist operations, and was ready to discuss operational plans with its supporters and to offer them financial support, increasingly it withdrew from direct supervision and merely encouraged whatever activity promoted its objectives.

15. Before 2001, associated groups might nonetheless have sought central approval before launching an attack. But the ability of Al Qaeda to direct a global campaign of

terror was considerably reduced once the Taliban were ousted from power in Afghanistan and the Al Qaeda leadership was forced to disperse. Increasingly, those who sought approval were told just to do what they could when they could. Recent evidence suggests that the key leadership is too preoccupied with its own immediate problems of survival to offer more than general guidance.

16. This is not to say that the Al Qaeda leadership does not retain the intention to organize further spectacular attacks, or that it will be unable to recover the capability to do so if it is able to regroup. The leadership, through its statements, still offers strategic direction even though it leaves tactical decision-making to its supporters. Sophisticated use of the media ensures that Al Qaeda is able to preserve a clear ideological core, and that Osama bin Laden retains his position as an inspirational leader, hovering somewhere between myth and reality.

17. The Al Qaeda inspiration is both practical and religious. Any group that shares its political objectives and religious beliefs, and has the necessary initiative, resources and determination, can mount attacks in its name, using similar methodology. It is now popular to refer to "franchise" or "start-up" operations whereby groups with little or no direct contact with the central leadership can become affiliates.

18. The group responsible for bombing commuter trains in and approaching Atocha Station in Madrid on 11 March 2004 provides an example of this. A statement by Osama bin Laden in October 2003 had identified Spain as a target for attack and this seems to have inspired those responsible. But the Spanish authorities say they have discovered no clear evidence of any organizational link between the group and the Al Qaeda leadership. As a further indication of how the threat has evolved, these attacks were carried out by people who were relatively well established and integrated within their community, and were not considered by the Spanish authorities to pose an imminent threat. None had been to Afghanistan.

19. Although Al Qaeda statements continue to encourage attacks against Western targets, there has been a marked increase in attacks against local targets in Muslim countries, most notably in Saudi Arabia. Saudi Arabia has been a focus for Al Qaeda from the start but now appears to have become an operational front line with determined terrorists pitched against equally determined security forces. Terrorist attacks there are designed to disrupt the economy and destabilize the State so as to create a sense of anarchy and general discontent leading to widespread insurgency and the overthrow of the government.

20. While attacking Saudi Arabia represents an immediate Al Qaeda objective, other States in the Arabian Peninsula and beyond are also vulnerable. As there is no Muslim State that aims to introduce the sort of government that the Al Qaeda leadership would endorse, all are potential targets. The number of North Africans involved with, or supporting Al Qaeda-related terrorism, puts those countries at particular risk.

21. Currently Iraq also provides a focus for Al Qaeda activity and propaganda. To those ready to believe it, the coalition presence there appears to confirm much of what Osama bin Laden has predicted about the ambitions of the West. Although there is no good evidence to suggest that Osama bin Laden and the Al Qaeda leadership have any direct involvement in Iraq, nor any operational control of groups operating there, attacks in Iraq by supporters of Al Qaeda not only contribute to Al Qaeda objectives, but the publicity surrounding them encourages others elsewhere to mount attacks. For example, although Iraq has provided an attractive alternative to fighters who might

otherwise have gone to Afghanistan, the Afghan authorities note a correlation between the levels of activity in Iraq and the number of attacks in their own country.

22. Afghanistan was an important base for Al Qaeda before the Taliban were removed from power in November 2001. Authorities in both Afghanistan and Pakistan believe that the Taliban and Al Qaeda leaderships are still closely allied, but what evidence is available does not suggest much mutual support beyond assistance with local needs. Despite some financial help, the Afghan authorities see no evidence of direct Al Qaeda involvement in Taliban operations. Although the Afghan Government believes that many younger Taliban now question the determinedly anti-progress policy of their leaders, and have begun to withdraw their support, the Taliban remain a real threat to the reconstruction and stability of the country and their containment remains an important objective. Should the Taliban establish firm control over areas of the country, it is highly likely that they would once more offer Al Qaeda a safe haven from which to mount terrorist operations.

23. Although Al Qaeda may no longer enjoy a fixed base from which to direct its attacks, its ability to inspire acts of terror throughout the world seems limited only by the appeal of its message. Not only is the Al Qaeda leadership highly adept at the use of the media to advertise and reinforce its presence, it is also expert at exploiting modern technology and the global connectivity offered by the Internet. Apart from allowing fast and secure communication for terrorist planning, the Internet enables Al Qaeda to transmit its message to all corners of the world. This message, playing to a strong sense of injustice in the Muslim world, argues that it is the duty of every Muslim to join the battle being waged against the enemies of Islam. While it is mainly younger men who answer the call, it is striking that the appeal is equally powerful regardless of education, social background or wealth.

24. While individuals such as Osama bin Laden have a symbolic value and strong inspirational image, the survival of Al Qaeda no longer depends on its core leadership. While international action against the senior Taliban proved possible and effective, even without Osama bin Laden and the rest of the best-known Al Qaeda leaders, the threat would remain. The relevance of the Taliban was that they provided Al Qaeda in Afghanistan with the means and space to flourish. But Al- Qaida has been able to take root wherever favourable conditions exist; it will inevitably colonize States where central government tolerates its presence, or where central government is weak. Failed and failing States provide ideally fertile ground for the Al Qaeda inspiration to take hold, and will equally attract outsiders who seek a safe base from which to mount operations.

25. There is no prospect of an early end to attacks from Al Qaeda-associated terrorists. They will continue to attack targets in both Muslim and non-Muslim States, choosing them according to the resources they have available and the opportunities that occur. While they will look for ways to attack high profile targets, soft targets will be equally vulnerable.

IV. The Response

26. Effective action against Al Qaeda requires the international community to act in concert, both in its appreciation of the threat and in its willingness to combat it. As a global phenomenon, Al Qaeda demands a global response, and the Security Council,

given its responsibility for the maintenance of peace and security, has taken a leading role in the international arena by imposing a sanctions regime against its members and associates. The sanctions regime established under the 1267 Committee of the Security Council has aimed to promote a climate in which Al-Qaida will have difficulty raising, accessing and moving money, purchasing arms and crossing international borders. Its effectiveness depends on the real and sustained support of all Member States.

A. Implementation of the Sanctions

27. In order to measure the support given to the fight against the Taliban and Al-Qaida-related terrorism, and to encourage a continued commitment, Member States were required by resolutions 1390 (2002) and 1455 (2003) to report on their implementation of the sanctions regime. The reporting process was not intended as an end in itself, but designed to reveal the legal and administrative measures taken to implement the sanctions, as well as to report investigations, frozen assets and other enforcement action directed against the individuals and entities named on the Consolidated List. The reports submitted by Member States are currently the only indicator of their compliance with the resolutions.

28. As of late July 2004, 130 Member States had submitted reports pursuant to paragraph 6 of resolution 1455 (2003). While many States reported action taken against Al Qaeda, few offered specific details, or referred directly to those named on the Consolidated List maintained by the 1267 Committee. Although the true number of countries where Al Qaeda has a presence is most certainly higher, just 19 States recorded the presence of any individual or entity associated with Al Qaeda inside their borders.

29. Thirty-four Member States have reported freezing assets under the financial and economic assets sanctions imposed by the Security Council, though in some cases it has been hard to tell what this means. It is not clear from all reports of asset freezing, for example, what those assets are, their value, or who owns them. There are also inconsistencies between what some States have reported to the 1267 Committee and what they have reported to the Counter-Terrorism Committee. No State has reported stopping anyone on the 1267 Committee Consolidated List from travelling, or reported taking action against them in respect of the arms embargo.

30. Judging by the reports from Member States, and the continuing levels of Al-Qaida activity, it would appear that the sanctions regime imposed by the Security Council has had a limited impact. There appear to be several reasons for this, the most important being that the Security Council has, inevitably, reacted to events, while Al Qaeda has shown great flexibility and adaptability in staying ahead of them. The structure of Al Qaeda has evolved from its original form as an office offering support to fighters in Afghanistan, through its role as an initiator and sponsor of terrorism from an established base, to its current manifestation as a loose network of affiliated underground groups with certain goals in common. It will always be difficult to design, let alone enforce, sanctions against diverse groups of individuals who are not in one location, who can adopt different identities, and who need no special equipment to launch their attacks.

31. This may have led some Member States to question the efficacy and relevance of the sanctions. They may have found it easier in the circumstances to incorporate

the sanctions regime into their national legislation than to ensure its effective implementation on the ground. Countries with weak financial controls, or long porous borders, may regard the measures imposed by the Security Council as too difficult to enforce and of secondary importance to other counter-terrorism activity within their jurisdiction. . . .

[Paragraphs 32 through 44 discuss a UN list of al-Qaeda related terrorists, known as the "consolidated list."]

C. Financial Issues

45. Al Qaeda operations are not characterized by high cost. Only the sophisticated attacks of 11 September 2001 required significant funding of over six figures. Other Al Qaeda terrorist operations have been far less expensive. The simultaneous truck bombings of the United States embassies in Kenya and the United Republic of Tanzania in August 1998 are estimated to have cost less than $50,000; the October 2000 attack on the USS *Cole* in Aden less than $10,000; the Bali bombings in October 2002 less than $50,000; the 2003 bombing of the Marriott Hotel in Jakarta about $30,000; the November 2003 attacks in Istanbul less than $40,000; and the March 2004 attacks in Madrid about $10,000. While the centre may have provided some of this money, much of it will have been collected locally, whether through crime, or diverted from charitable donations.

46. As a result of national and international action, Al Qaeda's funding has decreased significantly. But so too has its need for money. The number of people in camps under Al Qaeda control is now far less, and Al Qaeda no longer pays the $10-20 million annually that it gave to its Taliban hosts. The only evidence of current payments to the Taliban available to the Afghan authorities is the $200 per month paid to the families of Guantanamo detainees.

47. But Al Qaeda will still need to raise and move money and, as the identities of Al Qaeda facilitators become known, the new and improved regulations will enable the appropriate authorities better to track their contacts and trace the sources and destinations of their funds. According to the reports submitted by Member States under resolution 1455 (2003), a legal basis for freezing assets related to Al Qaeda, the Taliban and associated groups and entities now exists in all but three Member States.

48. The Monitoring Team is concerned though that many States have merely amended anti-money-laundering legislation to cover terrorist crime as well. As terrorist-related financial transactions generally take place before the crime occurs, States may encounter problems when applying to terrorist financiers measures designed essentially to deal with the proceeds of crime. The Monitoring Team will look further at this issue.

49. The current focus of the international community on countering terrorist financing through the formal banking system has successfully led to the identification of individuals collecting or moving funds on behalf of suspected terrorists. These successes will encourage Al Qaeda and its associates to seek alternative means to raise and move their assets in ways that are less open to scrutiny, adapting their methods to suit local circumstances. For example, Al Qaeda may exploit the well-established trade in counterfeit currency in Somalia, just as they exploit the potential for credit card fraud in Western Europe and the Asia/Pacific region, and appear to benefit in some part from the drug trade in Afghanistan and North Africa. It is important that officials

working on regulation are in close contact with officials investigating Al Qaeda methodology on the ground.

50. There are some 32 international and regional organizations working to establish standards and agree policies to combat terrorist financing. At present, the most comprehensive regulatory regimes are those in greatest compliance with standards set by the Financial Action Task Force (FATF) 40 recommendations on Anti-Money-Laundering and eight special recommendations on Counter-Terrorist Financing. However, FATF does not attract universal support and cannot by itself achieve a properly supervised global regime for the financial sector. International financial regulation to combat terrorism is only as strong as its weakest link and there remain gaps in the universal application of recognized standards. Work should continue on achieving full acceptance.

51. Over 90 States have set up Financial Intelligence Units and in many cases these have assisted national efforts to identify Al Qaeda finances. Financial Intelligence Units analyse Suspicious Transaction Reports submitted by banks and other entities as part of national efforts against money-laundering and counter-terrorist financing. These units can play an important role in linking the work of the regulatory authorities with the work of the agencies investigating terrorism at the front line. They can also assist in ensuring that bankers dealing with financial transfers know what activity to look out for.

52. The Monitoring Team will also recommend to the Committee that Member States should circulate the Consolidated List beyond their banks to non-bank financial institutions and to any non-financial entities where assets might be held.

53. With the help of Member States, the Monitoring Team will study how Al Qaeda is now raising, holding and moving money in order to identify ways in which the financial measures might be made more effective. It will seek to identify ways in which investigating bodies can pass to the relevant regulatory authorities new information on Al Qaeda associated terrorist financing as early as possible. The Monitoring Team will also continue its engagement with other international organizations dealing with terrorist financing with a view to making recommendations to the 1267 Committee for possible further measures. . . .

Source: United Nations. Security Council. Analytical and Sanctions Monitoring Team. "First Report of the Analytical Support and Sanctions Monitoring Team Appointed Pursuant to Resolution 1526 (2004) Concerning Al Qaeda and the Taliban and Associated Individuals and Entities." S/2004/678, August 26, 2004. http://documents.un.org (accessed February 21, 2005).

Organization of American States on the Recall Vote in Venezuela

August 26, 2004

INTRODUCTION

For the third time in three years, Venezuela's left-leaning president Hugo Chavez survived an attempt to oust him from power. Venezuela's voters went to the polls in near-record numbers on August 15, 2004, and rejected, by a wide margin, an effort to recall Chavez in the middle of his second term in office. The vote solidified Chavez's hold on political power in Venezuela at least through 2006, when the next elections were scheduled and Chavez was planning to run again. The outcome also severely damaged an already wobbly coalition of opposition groups and was widely seen as a major victory for increasingly strong left-of-center political movements in South America. Argentina, Brazil, and Ecuador had elected left-leaning governments in the previous two years. Voters in Uruguay followed suit in October, electing Tabare Vazquez as the first president in 170 years who did not come from one of the country's two major centrist political parties.

The surprisingly strong victory by Chavez also caused consternation in Washington, where the Bush administration clearly had hoped for a different outcome. In addition to its disapproval of Chavez's domestic economic and political policies, the Bush administration was concerned that Chavez would use his victory to encourage leftist parties elsewhere in the region. The administration also worried about a potential threat to oil imports from Venezuela, the fourth largest source of oil for the United States.

Background

A former army colonel who had mounted a failed coup in 1992 and then spent two years in prison, Chavez won the presidency through a legitimate election in 1998. Chavez derived the bulk of his political support from Venezuela's impoverished majority—a large percentage of whom were Indians—who had not shared the benefits of the country's oil wealth. Chavez called his agenda the "Bolivarian Revolution," after the country's nineteenth-century founder, Simón Bolívar. Chavez increased his control over the machinery of government with a new constitution, ratified in a 1999 referendum, that substantially weakened the country's fractious parliament. He won a six-year term in office in 2000, and supporters in his party known as the Fifth Republic Movement controlled the parliament.

Opposition forces, ranging from business groups to labor unions that had been sidelined by Chavez, mounted a series of national strikes in 2001 that generated wide-scale protests but failed to thwart the president. In April 2002 a handful of military officers and business leaders managed to oust Chavez in a coup that lasted just two days before he regained power. The failed coup temporarily sidelined the opposition and embarrassed the Bush administration, which had eagerly endorsed the ouster of Chavez and subsequently had to deny charges that it had helped promote the coup. In the wake of the coup Chavez ousted military leaders who had opposed him, thus tightening his grip on one of the country's most important institutions. *(Failed coup, Historic Documents of 2002, p. 201)*

The opposition, calling itself the Democratic Coordinator, then sought to take advantage of a clause in Chavez's new constitution allowing for a referendum to recall the president if one was requested by 20 percent of the electorate (about 2.4 million registered voters). When the National Election Council, controlled by Chavez supporters, refused to accept the opposition's petition drive, the opposition in December 2002 mounted another national strike that shut down much of the economy, including, for a few weeks, most of the vital national oil industry. Chavez fired the striking oil workers and installed supporters in their place, a move that consolidated his control on the state-run oil company but that also entrenched the fired workers in the opposition.

In January 2003 the Venezuela Supreme Court rejected the opposition's referendum petitions on a technicality. Subsequent efforts by outside mediators—including former U.S. president Jimmy Carter (1977–1981) and the Organization of American States (OAS)—to reach a political settlement failed. Another attempt by the opposition to force a referendum was rebuffed in September 2003 by the National Election Council, again on a technicality. In November 2003 the opposition mounted its third petition drive in less than two years and collected about 3.4 million signatures demanding a recall vote. *(Background, Historic Documents of 2003, p. 279)*

A Referendum Scheduled

The early months of 2004 saw a replay of the previous scenarios, with the National Election Council using various procedural tactics to delay acceptance of the petitions and the scheduling of a referendum. The opposition faced its own internal troubles, most important an inability to agree on a candidate to pose a credible alternative to Chavez. Even the best-known opposition leaders generated support only in the single digits in public opinion polls.

In a rerun of the previous referendum attempts, the National Election Council ruled on March 2 that about one-half of the 3.4 million signatures on opposition petitions were invalid—putting the number of valid signatures well below the required 2.4 million minimum. The council said it would accept about 1.1 million of the disputed signatures, but only if those voters reported to polling centers to confirm that their signatures were valid. The opposition said that demand was meant to delay the referendum and intimidate voters.

Word of the council's ruling had leaked out in late February, and on February 27 opposition groups began mounting street barricades, called *guarimba,* that blocked traffic in Caracas, forcing some businesses to close and preventing garbage collection. In their strongest mass protest against Chavez in more than a year, an estimated half-million people turned out for a demonstration on March 6 demanding approval of the referendum petitions. At least fourteen people died in violence stemming from the demonstrations.

After a series of conflicting court rulings and negotiations between the government and the opposition, the election council agreed on a five-day period, starting May 28, during which voters whose signatures had been challenged could validate them. This *repara* (repair) period eventually produced barely enough signatures to meet the 2.4 million minimum. Chavez on June 3 announced his acceptance of a referendum, telling supporters outside his presidential palace: "Let's go to battle then."

On June 8 the election council set August 15 as the date of the referendum. The timing was crucial. Under the constitution, if Chavez lost a referendum held before the midpoint of his six year-term, another election would be held within thirty days to choose a successor. If he lost an election after the midpoint, his vice president, José Vicente Rangel, would succeed to the post for the remainder of his term. August 15 was just four days before the August 19 midpoint of Chavez's term. Court rulings left it unclear whether Chavez, if defeated on August 15, could run in the follow-up election to succeed himself.

As could be expected, headlines in the two months leading up to the referendum were dominated by Chavez, who showed up nearly everywhere in Venezuela to take credit for new schools, health clinics, and other social services paid for with the country's oil revenue. Chavez's aggressive campaign appeared to succeed. Earlier in the year opinion polls showed that only about 40 percent of the public supported him and wanted him to remain in office. By early August support for Chavez had risen to the 50 percent mark, a positive trend that led many observers to predict he would survive, although narrowly. Apparently sensing that its strong personal attacks on Chavez had been counterproductive, the opposition late in the campaign began emphasizing issues such as combating crime and the need for political unity.

A Rude Surprise for the Opposition

The voting on August 15 was monitored by several hundred domestic and international observers, including large delegations sponsored by the OAS and by former president Carter's think tank in Atlanta, the Carter Center, which had observed hundreds of elections in dozens of countries. For a country with such a polarized electorate, the voting went smoothly, with few reported cases of violence. Turnout was an exceptionally high 70 percent, and thousands of voters had to wait in line for hours. The average turnout in recent elections had been about 55 percent.

Initial results announced about 4 a.m. the next day shocked the opposition, which had assumed it would win by a wide margin. Chavez received about 58 percent of the vote, with only 42 percent voting to oust him from office. Appearing on the balcony of the presidential palace, Chavez struck a defiant pose. "The Venezuelan people have spoken, and the people's voice is the voice of God," he declared. Later in the day, Chavez adopted a more conciliatory stance, saying he wanted a dialogue with the opposition. "This is not just about Chavez, or the government, but a project for the country," he said.

Some opposition leaders immediately denounced the result as fraudulent, citing what they said were several suspicious factors, including an apparent pattern of identical results in several hundred polling stations. The opposition also cited an exit poll of voters showing that Chavez had lost by 18 points—the exact same margin as a poll by Chavez supporters showing him winning.

Former president Carter said he met with opposition leaders and appealed to them to accept the results. Carter also met with Chavez and said he had asked him to "extend the hand of reconciliation."

The final results published on August 27 were slightly better than the initial count for Chavez, who received 59.1 percent. After a partial recount and a statistical analysis of the outcome, the Carter Center reported that the Chavez victory appeared valid. In a final report made public September 30, the center said the published results "reflect the will of the Venezuelan electorate as expressed" on August 15. That finding still did not satisfy some opposition leaders, who continued to charge that the government had rigged the election.

Most independent analysts cited several reasons for Chavez's victory—or, depending on one's point of view, the opposition's loss. A central factor was Chavez's continued popularity among those he had championed, the millions of impoverished Indians and *mestizos* (those of mixed Indian and Spanish heritage). After the failed coup of 2002 Chavez worked tirelessly to bolster his political standing among this constituency. He poured millions of bolivars into public service projects in the slums of Caracas and other cities, and in rural areas. Chavez also registered nearly 2 million new voters and campaigned aggressively, portraying the opposition as representing the wealthy elite who suppressed the poor. A related factor was that many Venezuelans blamed the opposition—not Chavez—for the economic and social damage caused by the national strikes of 2001–2003 and the street barricades of early 2004. Likewise, Chavez managed to claim credit for an improvement in the economy during 2003 and 2004 generated by the worldwide spike in oil prices. The inherent instability of the opposition coalition also damaged its cause; its leaders appeared to pursue different and, at times, even conflicting agendas. Finally, Chavez benefited from the very nature of the referendum, which pitted him against an uncertain future. Because the opposition did not offer a credible, well-known candidate to oppose Chavez, a vote to oust him would have led to yet another election or even, in the worst case, renewed political instability and possibly more violence.

In Resolution 869, adopted August 26, the Permanent Council of the OAS expressed approval of the election and called on "all players to respect the results." The OAS also urged "all sectors of society to refrain from promoting violence and intolerance, in order to facilitate the necessary quest for national reconciliation." Cesar Gaviria, secretary general of the OAS, had devoted much of the previous two years to an unsuccessful mediation effort on behalf of national reconciliation in Venezuela, but he retired at the end of September.

Collapse of the Opposition

The devastating defeat created a wide rift in the opposition. Some flatly refused to accept the official results or the Carter Center findings endorsing that outcome. Some opposition leaders insisted the government had manipulated the software for the new touch-screen voting machines that were used for the first time in the referendum. One statistical study by Venezuelan academics appeared to support that claim, but another study commissioned by the Carter Center did not.

The first major crack in opposition solidarity came on September 1 when Fedecamaras, the association of large businesses, called for talks with the government. The former head of that group had been installed as president during the brief coup against Chavez in 2002. Several political parties pulled out of the opposition coalition in September, essentially leaving it a hollow shell. One of the most prominent leaders, Julio Borges of the Primero Justicia Party, said on September 24 that Venezuela had passed through "a phase" of its history and needed to move on. "It makes no sense for a country to split because of the effect of one person," he said in a reference to Chavez.

Chavez consolidated his grip on Venezuela even further in regional elections held on October 31. Candidates backed by his party won all but two of the country's twenty-three governorships. Among those defeated was one of the opposition's best-known leaders, Enrique Mendoza, who lost his governor's post to one of Chavez's former vice presidents. Unlike the August referendum, these elections were not monitored by the OAS or the Carter Center, in part because the government waited until three weeks before the voting to request outside monitoring.

The president then turned his attention to one of the most important remaining elements of the opposition: the privately owned radio and television stations that had been among his fiercest critics. Chavez submitted to the National Assembly a "Law for Social Responsibility on Radio and Television" that, he said, was intended to protect children from violent programming, but that also allowed his government to shut down media outlets that failed to adhere to vague standards of "social responsibility, social solidarity, and national security." The assembly adopted the proposal in November and Chavez signed it into law on December 8, saying it would "liberate the people of Venezuela from the dictatorship of the private media owners."

In mid-December the National Assembly approved a plan by Chavez to add twelve new justices to the Supreme Court—in effect enabling the president to take control of a court that had been sharply divided between his supporters and critics. Human Rights Watch, the U.S.-based advocacy group, denounced the move as a "severe blow to judicial independence," but Chavez supporters said it was needed to protect him against another coup attempt.

Chavez versus Washington

Chavez had been a thorn in the side of the Bush administration for several reasons. He was an active ally of Cuban president Fidel Castro and supported the ailing Cuban economy with oil, reportedly at deeply discounted prices. In exchange, Castro sent thousands of doctors and paramedics to Venezuela to provide medical care for the poor. Chavez also had worked to undermine U.S.-led negotiations toward a Free Trade Area of the Americas, which Washington said would include every country in the hemisphere except Cuba. And Chavez made clear his hopes of exporting his Bolivarian Revolution to other countries in Latin America, starting with his troubled Andean neighbor Colombia, which for decades had battled leftist rebels. *(Cuba, p. 246)*

Chavez had his own bill of particulars against the Bush administration, starting with what he said was U.S. participation in the failed 2002 coup against him. Chavez also accused Washington of backing the Venezuelan opposition with grants from the National Endowment for Democracy, a quasi-government agency that supported democratic reform around the world. Chavez's government produced evidence in February that one of the opposition groups had received $53,000 from the endowment. In an interview with the *New York Times,* published March 15, Chavez said the Bush administration had no "respect" for him or what he was trying to do in Venezuela. "I'm tired of trying to carry out the mandate of Christ, turning the other cheek," he said. "I've been slapped so many times, my cheeks are purple."

The Bush administration responded to the August 15 referendum by congratulating "the Venezuelan people" for their exercise in democracy but avoided a direct mention of Chavez. On September 10 Bush formally rebuked Venezuela for its alleged failure to curb international trafficking in women and children. That step was part of the administration's annual review of trafficking, which led Bush to impose economic sanctions against Venezuela and five other countries. In Venezuela's case,

Bush's action meant that the United States would vote against loan applications totaling $250 million that were pending before international financial institutions. *(Trafficking issues, p. 122)*

Two other matters arose late in the year to further inflame relations between the United States and Venezuela. On November 30 the Bush administration protested a plan by Chavez to buy as many as fifty Mig-29 fighter jets from Russia. Chavez had visited Moscow a week earlier and announced plans to buy dozens of helicopters and other weapons, with the purchase of the jet planes expected to follow.

Early in December a U.S.-based Web site supportive of Chavez posted documents appearing to show that the CIA was aware of planning by military officers for the April 2002 coup. Chavez cited the documents as evidence that "the government of George Bush knew" about the coup in advance.

Following is the text of Resolution 869, "Results of the Presidential Recall Referendum Held in Venezuela on August 15, 2004," adopted August 26, 2004, by the Permanent Council of the Organization of American States, commending the people of Venezuela for their peaceful referendum on the presidency of Hugo Chavez and calling on all sides in the country to respect the results.

"Results of the Presidential Recall Referendum in Venezuela"

The Permanent Council of the Organization of American States,

Having heard the oral reports by Ambassador Valter Pecly Moreira, Permanent Representative of the Federative Republic of Brazil and Head of the Electoral Observation Mission of the OAS and the Secretary General of the OAS, Dr. César Gaviria; and the statements of the Permanent Representative of Venezuela, Ambassador Jorge Valero, on the presidential recall referendum held in Venezuela on August 15, 2004;

Recognizing the wide-scale and peaceful participation of the Venezuelan people in the presidential recall referendum, held in accordance with Article 72 of the National Constitution of the Bolivarian Republic of Venezuela;

Considering that one of the essential elements of representative democracy is access to and the exercise of power in accordance with the rule of law, the holding of periodic, free, and fair elections based on secret balloting and universal suffrage as an expression of the sovereignty of the people, in accordance with the provisions of the Inter-American Democratic Charter;

Considering also that the Constitutional Government of President Hugo Chávez Frías has complied with the constitutional norms of its country and its commitments to the hemispheric community, by cooperating in the holding the aforementioned referendum, thereby strengthening democracy in the Americas; and

Bearing in mind that resolution CP/RES. 833 [adopted in 2002] urged all political and social sectors in Venezuela to promote a constitutional, democratic, peaceful, and electoral solution,

Resolves:

1. To give recognition to the people of Venezuela and its democratic political institutions for the public spirit they demonstrated in the referendum process and to President Hugo Chávez Frías for having achieved a successful ratification of his term of office.
2. To acknowledge the contribution made by the Secretary General of the OAS, Dr. César Gaviria, and by the Secretary General's Group of Friends for Venezuela, in facilitating the process leading up to the referendum.
3. To acknowledge, in particular, the responsible and effective manner in which the OAS Electoral Observation Mission chaired by Ambassador Valter Pecly Moreira, Permanent Representative of the Federative Republic of Brazil, fulfilled its mandate.
4. To express its satisfaction with the holding of the presidential recall referendum in accordance with Article 72 of the Constitution of Venezuela as well as the fulfillment of the mandate of resolution CP/RES. 833 of December 22, 2002, which urged the attainment in Venezuela of a constitutional, democratic, peaceful, and electoral solution.
5. To call upon all players to respect the results of the presidential recall referendum, issued by the National Electoral Council and endorsed by the OAS Electoral Observation Mission, the Carter Center, and other international observers. Furthermore, to urge all sectors of society to refrain from promoting violence and intolerance, in order to facilitate the necessary quest for national reconciliation.
6. To urge all sectors in Venezuela to respect human rights, the rule of law, and full enjoyment of freedom of expression and of the press as established in the Constitution of the Bolivarian Republic of Venezuela and the Inter-American Democratic Charter.
7. To welcome the offer made by President Hugo Chávez Frías to foster national dialogue. In this regard, to call for a process of reconciliation, in adherence to the principles of the Constitution of the Bolivarian Republic of Venezuela and of the Inter-American Democratic Charter, with the participation of all sectors of Venezuelan public life, in which differences are settled in the framework of the democratic system and in a spirit of transparency, pluralism, and tolerance.

Source: Organization of American States. Permanent Council. "Results of the Presidential Recall Referendum Held in Venezuela on August 15, 2004." OEA/Ser. G, CP/RES. 869 (1436/04). August 26, 2004. www.oas.org/consejo/resolutions/res869.asp (accessed March 14, 2005).

September

2004 HISTORIC DOCUMENTS

United Nations Security Council on Syrian Troops in Lebanon

September 2, 2004

INTRODUCTION

The Bush administration, with an unusual degree of cooperation from France and other countries, mounted pressure on Syria during 2004 to end its military and political control of Lebanon. The United States and France cosponsored a resolution, adopted by the UN Security Council on September 2, that called on "foreign forces" to leave Lebanon so that long-troubled country could regain its independence. The resolution was aimed directly at Syria, which had maintained thousands of troops and intelligence agents in Lebanon since 1976. Syria rejected the UN call, but the resolution focused renewed international attention on the fate of Lebanon and provided encouragement to anti-Syrian forces there.

Background

Lebanon's ethnic and religious factions—plus the Palestinian Liberation Organization (PLO), which had taken up residence there—in 1975 began a bloody civil war that quickly wrecked the country. After numerous interventions by outside powers, including Israel, France, Syria, and the United States, the war sputtered to an end when Arab leaders negotiated an agreement in Taif, Saudi Arabia, in 1989. Key provisions of that agreement required Syria to withdraw its army from Lebanon within two years and hand power to a new Lebanese government. *(Background, Historic Documents of 1991, p. 751)*

Although the Taif accord helped restore peace to Lebanon, it failed to restore control over their country to the Lebanese. Syria kept thousands of troops posted in Lebanon, arguing that their presence was necessary to prevent a recurrence of the civil war. Perhaps more important, Damascus kept a firm grip on the politics of Lebanon, partly through control of government officials and partly through the pervasive presence of Syrian intelligence agents who closely monitored Lebanon for signs of dissent and arrested hundreds, and possibly thousands, of alleged dissidents.

Over time, many outside observers suggested Syria's real reason for its continuing involvement in Lebanon was economic. Some aspects of Lebanon's postconflict economy (such as banking and tourism) boomed during the 1990s, while Syria's government-controlled economy stagnated and relied heavily on commerce with its smaller neighbor. By the late 1990s an estimated 1 million Syrians were working in Lebanon, equal to about one-fourth of Lebanon's native population.

Lebanon produced one major political figure during the 1990s who was able to exercise a limited degree of independence from Damascus. Rafiq Hariri, a Sunni Muslim who had made a fortune as a contractor in Saudi Arabia, returned to

Lebanon in 1990 and was named prime minister in 1992 after large-scale rioting in protest of the poor economy. Hariri's regime rebuilt much of Beirut, which before the civil war had been the commercial capital of the Middle East. His reconstruction helped to revive the economy, but it also put the country deeply in debt.

Hariri stepped down as prime minister in 1997 but returned to office after winning parliamentary elections in 2000. That was the same year that Israel ended its military occupation of a strip of southern Lebanon after two decades—a step that drew increased international attention to Syria's continued presence.

Weeks after Israel pulled back from Lebanon, Syria's longtime president Hafez al-Assad died. His son, Bashar, a London-trained ophthalmologist, succeeded him. At first, Bashar Assad appeared to be following a dramatically different path than his father. He ordered the release of several hundred political prisoners, allowed the long-banned Muslim Brotherhood to resume political activity, permitted the establishment of private banks, and in June 2001 redeployed most Syrian troops from Beirut to the Bekaa Valley along the Lebanese-Syrian border. Later in 2001 Assad's government sent contradictory signals about its intentions, at first arresting scores of political dissidents, then weeks later releasing more than 100 of the estimated 3,000 dissidents who had been jailed by his father, some of them for decades.

In a remarkable convergence of interests, Syria in October 2002 voted for a U.S.-sponsored resolution in the United Nations Security Council demanding that Iraq allow UN inspectors to search for the weapons of mass destruction that Baghdad allegedly had developed in violation of numerous previous Security Council resolutions. The Bush administration viewed the October 2002 resolution as a precursor to its ultimate invasion of Iraq. Damascus appeared to view its support of the resolution as a cost-free step that earned it some credit from Washington and punished Iraqi leader Saddam Hussein, who ran a rival branch of the Assad family's Ba'ath Party. *(UN resolution on Iraq, Historic Documents of 2002, p. 713)*

If Assad in fact had built up any credit with the Bush administration, he lost it in the wake of the March–April 2003 war that ousted Saddam from power. Insisting that Damascus was continuing to support terrorists and was refusing to prevent anti-U.S. insurgents from crossing into Iraq from Syria, the administration threatened new sanctions and implied that Syria might be next on the list of countries facing U.S. military action. That tension gradually faded as the administration focused its attention on the rapidly deteriorating security situation in Iraq and as it became clear that insurgents from Syria were only a minor part of that problem. Secretary of State Colin Powell visited Damascus in May 2003 and warned Assad that Congress was moving to impose sanctions against Syria unless it heeded U.S. concerns; it was the highest level contact between the United States and Syria during Bush's first term in office. *(Iraq postwar, Historic Documents of 2003, p. 933)*

Regional tensions briefly rose again in October 2003 when Israel bombed what it said was a training camp for Palestinian terrorists near Damascus. Syria denounced that attack as "aggression" but made no effort to respond militarily because of Israel's overwhelming military superiority.

The U.S. Congress added its own pressure in November 2003, adopting legislation called the Syria Accountability and Lebanese Sovereignty Restoration Act that required the president to impose sanctions against Syria because of its presence in Lebanon and its support for Hezbollah, a Lebanese Shi'ite militant group. The Israeli government had recently stepped up its allegations that Hezbollah was providing munitions and logistical support to Palestinian militant groups that sponsored suicide bombings and other attacks against Israeli citizens and troops. In response to U.S. pressure, Syria officially closed the Damascus offices of two of the Palestinian groups, Hamas and Islamic Jihad, but allowed the groups' leaders to continue operating openly.

New Pressures in 2004

As 2004 opened, some officials in the Bush administration reportedly were advocating military action against Syria. Officials wanted to punish the Syrian government for what they said was its continued failure to stop anti-U.S. insurgents from crossing the border into Iraq, its willingness to allow senior leaders of the ousted Iraq regime to live in Damascus, and its funneling of weapons from Iran to Hezbollah. Damascus denied all these charges, and the administration provided little evidence for them publicly. News reports in January 2004 said the Pentagon had drawn up plans for air strikes, and possibly even limited ground action across the Iraq-Syria border, to pressure Damascus.

Even as the Bush administration was ratcheting up its pressure, Syria was receiving entirely different—if mixed—signals from Israel, Washington's closest ally in the Middle East. Israeli president Moshe Katsav on January 12 invited Assad to visit Israel to reopen peace talks that had stalled four years earlier. He noted that Assad in December 2003 had suggested an interest in new negotiations. After the Syrian News Agency quoted government officials as rebuffing the suggestion, Katsav went on an Arabic television station, al-Jazeera, on January 14 to renew it. "The test now is a test for the Syrian president," he said. "He is required to prove his serious intentions and that he wants peace." Other Israeli officials suggested that secret talks already were under way between Israel and Syria, but if such talks did occur, nothing came of them. *(Israel-Syria diplomacy, Historic Documents of 1999, p. 890)*

Despite the failure of that brief foray into diplomacy, Israel continued its pragmatic approach to regional affairs. On January 29–30 Israel released 430 Palestinian prisoners and handed over to Hezbollah the bodies of 59 Lebanese who had been killed during the Israeli occupation of southern Lebanon; in exchange Hezbollah handed over an Israeli businessman and the bodies of three Israeli soldiers.

In mid-March Syria experienced its worst bout of domestic unrest in years when ethnic Kurds rioted in the predominantly Kurdish region along the borders with Iraq and Turkey. A brawl between Arab and Kurdish soccer fans led to several days of violence during which more than two dozen Kurds, Arabs, and policemen were killed. While mild compared to violence in the early decades of Hafez al-Assad's rule, the unrest was a potent reminder that Syria's Kurdish minority was likely to be emboldened by successes of their ethnic colleagues in neighboring Iraq following Saddam's ouster.

On May 11 Bush imposed a series of economic sanctions against Syria in compliance with the law Congress had passed five months earlier. Among other things, the sanctions barred most exports of U.S. products to Syria (food, medicine, some communications equipment, and spare parts for civilian aircraft were the exceptions); prohibited direct flights between the United States and Syria; authorized the freezing of assets of Syrian nationals involved in terrorism and other actions that Washington disapproved of; and restricted U.S. transactions by Syria's national bank. U.S. officials described most of the sanctions as symbolic since there already was only limited trade between the United States and Syria. Assad immediately denounced the sanctions, telling a group of visiting American newspaper editors two days later that Bush was wrong in claiming that Syria was aiding anti-U.S. insurgents in Iraq or was allowing Palestinian militant groups to operate in Damascus.

A Rush to Act

The pace of events quickened in late August when Damascus arranged the reelection of Lebanon's pro-Syrian president Emile Lahoud, who was nearing the end of his single six-year term allowed under the country's constitution. Syria had pressed for an extension of Lahoud's term but faced resistance from Prime Minister Hariri, who had been feuding with the president on many issues, including Syria's role in Lebanese life. After meeting with the head of the Syrian intelligence service in Damascus on August 27, Hariri backed down, and the next day his cabinet approved a bill amending the constitution to allow Lahoud to serve another three years.

In an apparent attempt to head off parliamentary approval of the bill, the Bush administration rushed ahead with long-standing plans for a UN Security Council resolution demanding Syria's withdrawal from Lebanon. Announcing the intention to introduce the resolution, along with France, State Department spokesman Richard Boucher said on August 31: "We feel the Syrian pressure to modify the Lebanese constitution to permit President Lahoud to remain in office an additional three years is an affront to Lebanon's sovereignty and political independence." That brought a protest from the Lebanese foreign minister, Jean Obeid, who said in a letter to UN Secretary General Kofi Annan that "no outside authority has a right to interfere in the details of agreements between Syria and Lebanon, or to impose changes on them."

The Security Council acted late on September 2, just a day before Lebanon's parliament was scheduled to vote on the bill extending Lahoud's term. With the minimum number of nine "yes" votes, and the other six members abstaining, the council adopted Resolution 1559, calling for the immediate withdrawal of all foreign troops from Lebanon. While this was a clear reference to Syria, it was not named. The resolution also demanded the disarming of all militias in Lebanon and declared support for "a free and fair electoral process in Lebanon's upcoming presidential election conducted according to Lebanese constitutional rules devised without foreign interference or influence." The United States and France cosponsored the resolution, a rare show of solidarity between two countries more often at odds over questions involving the Middle East. Among those abstaining were China and Russia, two permanent Security Council members with the power to veto resolutions. To avert a potential veto, the sponsors watered down some language from Washington's original version, for example modifying an original "demand" for Syrian withdrawal to a "call" for that step.

Despite its mild language, the resolution was widely seen as a significant step by the Security Council because it put new international pressure on Syria, and it addressed the internal political affairs of a UN member nation—albeit a nation effectively occupied by another UN member nation. Opponents said they viewed it as interference. Among them was Algerian ambassador Abdallah Baali, who said "the Security Council's intervention establishes a harmful precedent, which must not be repeated." U.S. ambassador John C. Danforth rejected that characterization, saying it was Syria, not the UN, which was interfering in Lebanese internal affairs.

The resolution mandated one step with potential consequences: a mechanism under which Annan would report regularly to the Security Council on the issue of Lebanon. Annan later named Norwegian diplomat Terje Roed-Larsen as his special envoy to monitor compliance with the resolution. Roed-Larsen was completing his assignment as UN special envoy for the Israel-Palestinian conflict. *(Middle East, p. 806)*

The UN resolution failed to accomplish its immediate goal of heading off the scheduled vote to extend Lahoud's term. The next day, September 3, the Lebanese parliament voted 96–29 to adopt the constitutional amendment, demanded by Syria, giving Lahoud three more years in office. Among those supporting the amendment were Hariri and his seventeen party colleagues, some of who were quoted as saying Syria had given the prime minister no choice in the matter. Government officials set off fireworks to celebrate the vote, but most Lebanese commentators across the country's wide spectrum bemoaned the action, and a poll published in a local magazine showed a strong majority against keeping Lahoud in office.

A week later, the State Department's senior Middle East envoy, William J. Burns, visited Damascus and urged Assad to begin withdrawing his troops from Lebanon and to stop supporting Hezbollah and Palestinian militant groups. "If Syria takes action on these concerns, our relationship can take a very different course, with positive results for all sides," Burns said.

Additional pressure on Syria came from an unlikely source: fellow Arab nations. Jordan announced its support for the UN resolution, and on September 13 the leaders of the Gulf Cooperation Council added their support. The council was composed of Bahrain, Kuwait, Oman, Qatar, Saudi Arabia, and the United Arab Emirates.

The first sign that Syria might be responding to the international pressure came September 11, when the Syrian army started dismantling several hilltop outposts in villages south of Beirut. Syrian officials said about 3,000 of the 20,000-some troops in Lebanon would be redeployed eastward to the Bekaa Valley.

Syria came under a different kind of pressure on September 26 when a senior Hamas official was assassinated in Damascus when his car exploded. Israel unofficially confirmed that it had carried out the killing as part of its regular "targeted assassinations" of Palestinian militants.

In his first report to the Security Council as a follow-up to its resolution, Annan on October 1 stated the obvious, that Syria had not complied with the call for it to leave Lebanon. Annan said Syria had acknowledged that about 14,000 of its troops remained in Lebanon, most of them near the Lebanon-Syria border. Annan added his personal endorsement to the thrust of the Security Council resolution, saying: "It is time, fourteen years after the end of hostilities and four years after the Israeli withdrawal from Lebanon, for all parties concerned to set aside the remaining vestiges of the past. The withdrawal of foreign forces and the disbandment and disarmament of militias would, with finality, end that sad chapter of Lebanese history." Annan also offered a personal note rebuking Lahoud's drive to stay in office: "It has long been my strong belief that governments and leaders should not hold office beyond prescribed term limits."

Responding for the first time publicly to the UN resolution and Annan's report, Assad made a rare speech on October 9 defending Syria's role in Lebanon. "In the Middle East, we have become the heart of the volcano," he said. Referring to those who sponsored the resolution, he added: "Do they want to throw this region, with no exception, in the heart of lava inside the volcano?" That statement appeared to be a warning that Lebanon would again fall into chaos if Syria withdrew.

A Political Crisis in Lebanon

In the midst of this international diplomacy, politics in Lebanon was entering a new period of ferment and potential instability. Four cabinet members aligned with Druze leader Walid Jumblatt resigned in protest after Lahoud's term was extended. One of them, former economy minister Marwan Hamadeh, was wounded in an apparent assassination attempt on October 1. His driver was killed and a bodyguard wounded when a car bomb exploded as they passed by. Many Lebanese analysts said the bombing appeared to be a warning aimed at Jumblatt, who had become one of the most vocal opponents of Syrian influence.

Nearly three weeks later, on October 20, Prime Minister Hariri and his entire cabinet resigned, citing political dissension in the country. "Facing challenges, any challenges, can only be done through a unified domestic front that meets the goals of the Lebanese people," Hariri said in a statement, adding that "these objectives have been confronted by known political realities." Hariri made it clear he would not form a new government but would remain in parliament. He was succeeded as prime minister by Omar Karami, a functionary widely assumed to be more beholden to Damascus than Hariri had been.

Although Hariri had undisguised differences with President Lahoud, the general speculation in Lebanon was that he had resigned for a practical, as much as a political, reason. In previous weeks Bush administration officials had openly discussed ratcheting up the pressure by freezing the financial assets held in the United States by Lebanese and Syrian officials. As Lebanon's richest man, with extensive holdings in the United States and elsewhere in the Middle East, Hariri would have been the principal target of such a freeze.

The first mass protest against Syria in recent years took place in Beirut on November 19, just four days before the anniversary of Lebanon's independence in 1943 from a French mandate from the League of Nations. Several thousand students and members of opposition groups demonstrated in several places in the capital, some calling for U.S. intervention against Syria. Many of the demonstrators were supporters of Michel Aoun, a Maronite Christian general who had declared himself president of Lebanon in the late 1980s but had lived in France since he lost a military battle with the Syrian army. Pro-Syrian forces mounted a counter-demonstration on November 30, featuring matching posters of Lahoud and Assad.

Parliamentary elections were scheduled in Lebanon for May 2005, providing an opportunity for supporters and opponents of Syria's role to appeal for popular support.

Following is the text of United Nations Security Council Resolution 1559, adopted September 2, 2004, calling for the withdrawal of all foreign forces from Lebanon and the disbanding and disarming of armed militias there.

Resolution 1559

The Security Council,

Recalling all its previous resolutions on Lebanon, in particular resolutions 425 (1978) and 426 (1978) of 19 March 1978, resolution 520 (1982) of 17 September 1982, and resolution 1553 (2004) of 29 July 2004 as well as the statements of its President on the situation in Lebanon, in particular the statement of 18 June 2000,

Reiterating its strong support for the territorial integrity, sovereignty and political independence of Lebanon within its internationally recognized borders,

Noting the determination of Lebanon to ensure the withdrawal of all non- Lebanese forces from Lebanon,

Gravely concerned at the continued presence of armed militias in Lebanon, which prevent the Lebanese Government from exercising its full sovereignty over all Lebanese territory,

Reaffirming the importance of the extension of the control of the Government of Lebanon over all Lebanese territory,

Mindful of the upcoming Lebanese presidential elections and *underlining* the importance of free and fair elections according to Lebanese constitutional rules devised without foreign interference or influence,

1. *Reaffirms* its call for the strict respect of the sovereignty, territorial integrity, unity, and political independence of Lebanon under the sole and exclusive authority of the Government of Lebanon throughout Lebanon;

2. *Calls upon* all remaining foreign forces to withdraw from Lebanon;

3. *Calls for* the disbanding and disarmament of all Lebanese and non- Lebanese militias;

4. *Supports* the extension of the control of the Government of Lebanon over all Lebanese territory;

5. *Declares* its support for a free and fair electoral process in Lebanon's upcoming presidential election conducted according to Lebanese constitutional rules devised without foreign interference or influence;

6. *Calls upon* all parties concerned to cooperate fully and urgently with the Security Council for the full implementation of this and all relevant resolutions concerning the restoration of the territorial integrity, full sovereignty, and political independence of Lebanon;

7. *Requests* that the Secretary-General report to the Security Council within thirty days on the implementation by the parties of this resolution and *decides* to remain actively seized of the matter.

Source: United Nations. Security Council. *Resolution 1559.* S/RES/1559 (2004), September 2, 2004. http://documents-dds-ny.un.org/doc/UNDOC/GEN/N04/498/92/pdf/N0449892.pdf (accessed March 14, 2005). Reprinted with the permission of the United Nations Security Council.

Russian President Putin on Hostage-Taking Tragedy

September 4 and 13, 2004

INTRODUCTION

Russia may have reached a turning point in 2004, although at year's end it was not entirely certain which direction the country was headed. Most indicators were not positive. Despite the Kremlin's claims of victory, a long war in Chechnya continued and resulted in Russia's worst-ever terrorist incident. Working within the flexible boundaries of Russia's nominal democracy, President Vladimir Putin took firm control of all levers of government, shutting out any effective opposition. The economy kept growing but the main stimulants appeared to be rampant corruption and a boom in international oil prices, which, as always, were subject to wild fluctuation. A narrow band of Russians continued to prosper from the decade-long rush into capitalism, but the vast majority of Russian citizens could point to few signs that their lives had improved since the collapse of communism and the Soviet state in late 1991. In addition, the Russian population was falling at an alarming rate because of emigration and a collapsed health care system overwhelmed by the nation's chronic problems of alcoholism, drug abuse, smoking, and an emerging AIDS epidemic.

A handful of optimists insisted all these problems were temporary consequences of a giant country still trying to shake off the legacy of seven decades of communist rule. Even the most wildly optimistic, however, suggested there would be many more bumpy years in Russia's transition to something different.

Many of Russia's current problems seemed to come together early in September, when Chechen militants seized a school in the southern city of Beslan and held more than 1,200 children, parents, and teachers hostage. Russian troops stormed the school after two days, driving out the militants but not before an estimated 360 people had died, nearly half of them children. Putin used the incident to justify a consolidation of political power in his own hands.

The president insisted he was acting to save democracy and ensure stability, which polls showed the Russian people craved. This step gave him more flexibility to act as he wished, but it also made him the one person whom Russians could blame for the country's travails—or credit in the event that things improved.

Putin had won election to a second four-year term in March against seven opponents, none of whom were able to command more than token attention on the state-run television networks. Putin received 72 percent of the vote, based largely on the view of many Russians that he had brought relative calm after a decade of chaos following the collapse of the Soviet Union. "At least he's not making things worse," Lyuba Smirnova, told the *New York Times* early in March. "Before him, things were unpredictable. Now they are more stable. That's the most important thing." Putin said he would not seek a third term in 2008. *(Background, Historic Documents of 2003, p. 245)*

Continuing Violence in Chechnya

Russia fought two wars to retake the small southern province of Chechnya, where an independence move emerged after the end of communism. The first war, which began in 1994, was a disaster for Moscow, which withdrew in 1996 after succeeding only in killing thousands of people, destroying much of Chechnya with bombings, and inflaming anti-Russian passions in the Muslim-majority province. Shortly after becoming prime minister to then-president Boris Yeltsin in 1999, Putin sent Russian troops back into Chechnya. The Russian military claimed victory in this second Chechen war in 2001, but the fighting continued on a sporadic basis and Chechen guerrillas resorted to frequent terrorist attacks against both the Russian military and civilians. By 2002 it had become clear that at least some rebels in Chechnya had allied themselves with the al Qaeda terrorist network, responsible for the September 2001 terrorist attacks against the United States.

The first violent event of 2004 that appeared to be related to Chechnya came on February 6 when a bomb exploded in a Moscow subway train during the morning rush hour. Forty-one people were killed and more than 130 wounded. Putin immediately blamed Chechen rebel leader Aslan Maskhadov "and his bandits" for the attack, although neither Putin nor his aides offered any hard evidence for the allegation. A previously unknown Chechen rebel group later claimed responsibility.

Two months later, on May 9, a bomb exploded at a stadium in Grozny, Chechnya's capital, killing Akhmad Kadyrov, the province's Kremlin-backed president, and five others, including the senior Russian general in the region. More than fifty people were injured. The bomb was placed in a concrete pillar immediately beneath the section where Kadyrov and other officials were watching a concert after a military parade commemorating the defeat of Nazi Germany in World War II.

A former Muslim cleric, then Chechen rebel who switched sides in the mid-1990s, Kadyrov had won election the previous October after the Kremlin pressured his main rivals to drop out. Although he still spoke of Chechen nationalism, Kadyrov was considered a Kremlin loyalist by most observers. His former colleagues in the Chechen separatist movement, who tried to assassinate him several times before they succeeded, apparently shared that view. On May 17 Chechen rebel leader Tamil Assayed claimed responsibility for the bombing, saying in an Internet posting that Kadyrov had been killed in revenge for Russian killings of Chechens. Kadyrov's interim successor survived an apparent assassination attempt in mid-July.

The assassination of Kadyrov appeared to be a major setback for Putin's strategy of calming the rebellion in Chechnya by making it appear that Chechens—not Russians in Moscow—were running the province. A referendum and the presidential election, both in 2003, had been intended to put that strategy into practice, but as so often in the past decade violence had proven to be the most effective agent of change there. Attempting to keep the situation from spiraling even further out of control, Putin flew by helicopter to Grozny on May 11 and said he was determined to continue the "reconstruction and revival of Chechnya." It was a rare visit by the leader who had unleashed the current war more than four years earlier. He acknowledged that Grozny, destroyed during years of bombings by both Russian troops and Chechen rebels, "looks horrible from a helicopter."

Yet another rebel attack took place on June 21–22, when guerrillas stormed police outposts in Ingushetia—a troubled region adjacent to Chechnya—and killed at least seventy-five people while capturing a large supply of weapons. Two more incidents took place in late August, just before an election to choose Kadyrov's successor in Chechnya. Overnight on August 21 rebels raided polling places and police stations in Grozny and killed at least two dozen security personnel. On August 24 a bomb blew up at a Moscow bus stop, wounding three people. That evening, two Russian airliners, both headed south from Moscow, blew up almost simultaneously, killing all ninety passengers and crew members. The airline bombings represented the worst-ever attack on the Russian aviation industry and exposed security flaws at Moscow's airport. A later investigation showed that one of the bombers had bribed her way onto the aircraft. The Kremlin barred domestic news coverage of the raids in Grozny and at first refused to acknowledge the possibility of terrorism in the bombing of the airliners. Putin on August 31 said Chechen rebels linked to Al Qaeda carried out the bombings. Hours after Putin spoke, a female suicide bomber blew herself up outside a Moscow subway station, killing nine other people and wounding about fifty. Women, some of them reportedly the widows of guerrillas killed by Russian security forces, carried out many of the attacks. Russians referred to them as "black widows."

The Chechen election on August 29 was won by Maj. Gen. Alu Alkhanov, who had been Chechnya's top law enforcement official. Nongovernmental agencies and foreign observers declared the election illegitimate and said it merely ratified the Kremlin's selection of Alkhanov. He made clear his allegiance in taking office on October 5, saying "We have a motherland: Russia."

Tragedy in Beslan

The dozens of bombings, guerrilla raids, and other episodes of violence during the two Chechen wars faded into the background on September 1 when a group of about two dozen men and women seized a school in the southern Russian city of Beslan, just thirty miles outside Chechnya. Hundreds of children, parents, and teachers were taken hostage. It was the most audacious attack since October 2002 when Chechen guerrillas took over a theater in Moscow and held about 750 people captive; 129 of those hostages died when Russian security forces used a poison gas in raiding the theater. *(Chechen hostages, Historic Documents of 2002, p. 763)*

In Beslan, the guerrillas took control of the school on the first day of the new school year, when dozens of parents were with their children. Russian security forces surrounded the building as the rest of the world watched in horror this latest challenge to Moscow's authority. The hostage-taking would have been serious enough in and of itself, but its impact, especially in Russia, was magnified by the series of attacks that immediately preceded it, especially the bombings of the two airliners a week earlier and the Moscow subway bombing just the day before. Suddenly, Putin's claims of success in Chechnya rang more hollow than ever. Just as damaging, the series of events illustrated yet again the weaknesses of Russian security services, which most observers said were riddled with corruption and torn by repeated purges since the Soviet era.

Initial reports from the scene were confused. The number of hostages said to have been seized ranged from about 120 to nearly 400, and reports of shootings at the beginning of the hostage-taking suggested a half-dozen or more people had been killed. Authorities attempted to negotiate with the hostage-takers, to secure the release of at least the children. That effort had a limited success on September 2, when about two dozen mothers and infants were freed.

Early in the afternoon of September 3—two days after the school was seized—explosions broke out and Russian troops stormed the building. Gunfire and explosions continued for hours, even as rescue workers brought out the dead and wounded by the dozens. In an echo of past incidents, the Kremlin's immediate reaction was to play down the extent of the disaster. For hours after the school was stormed, neither Putin nor his top aides offered any comment. At the height of the crisis the three state-controlled television networks showed regular programming (including an old soap opera) or international news, including the Republican National Convention then under way in New York City. Two days later, the main television network finally showed footage showing bloodied bodies being handed out of the school. A network anchorman apologized for broadcasting the government's inaccurate claims about the number of hostages.

Putin finally spoke out on September 4, addressing the nation with a somber speech that appeared to blame Russia's problems on the collapse of the Soviet Union a dozen years earlier. "Our country, which used to have the strongest defense system of its external borders, instantly became unprotected from either the West or the East," he said. Putin offered little in the way of condolence to the relatives of those who had died or to the broader nation.

As Putin spoke details of what had happened the day before finally began to emerge from the smoky ruins of Middle School No. 1 in Beslan. Officials said they had recovered nearly 240 bodies, another 200 remained unaccounted for, and at least 400 people were in hospitals. The official estimate of how many people had been taken hostage suddenly jumped to about 1,200—three or four times what had been suggested earlier. Remarkably, Russian security forces vanished from the scene on the evening of September 4, leaving the building open for inspection by hundreds of curious onlookers. Some of the former hostages told journalists that almost all the 1,200 children and adults had been crammed into a gymnasium, deprived of food and water, and prevented from using bathrooms. They also said the explosions that led to the final gun battle apparently were bombs set off by mistake.

The government's official tallies from the Beslan crisis were that 360 had been killed (of whom 172 were children) and about 500 were injured, out of a total of more than 1,200 hostages. Some media reports suggested the death toll as much higher, but there was no confirmation by year's end. Although the government had originally said ten of the thirty-five hostage-takers were Arabs, no Arabs were found among the bodies.

Putin on September 7 lashed out at Western critics of his policies in Chechnya, including a group of U.S. intellectuals with ties to the Bush administration who had urged negotiations with the Chechens. "Why don't you meet Osama bin Laden, invite him to Brussels or the White House, engage in talks, ask him what he wants and give it to him so he leaves you in peace?" Putin rhetorically asked a group of academics and journalists from the United States and Europe. "You find it possible to set some limits in your dealings with these bastards, so why should we [in Russia] talk to people who are child killers?" Putin also likened Western criticism of Russia's dealings with Chechnya to Washington's rhetoric against the Soviet Union during the cold war.

Putin on September 10 agreed to an inquiry into his government's handling of the crisis; it was to be conducted by the upper chamber of parliament, the Federation Council, the members of which were all appointed by him.

Chechen guerrilla leader Shamil Basayev on September 18 claimed responsibility for the Beslan attack, along with all the other attacks in Russia in August and

September. In a letter posted on the Internet, Basayev said he was "sorry" that children died at the school but insisted that Chechnya was in a "war" and would "continue waging it to the victory."

Consolidating Power in the Kremlin

Ten days after the Beslan crisis ended, Putin met with his cabinet and provincial governors at the Kremlin and announced his plans to assume much of the power of the last political institutions with any degree of independence: the eighty-nine provincial governors and the parliament. Putin's speech September 13 was broadcast live on national television and then repeated several times throughout the day.

Acknowledging that the government's fight against terrorism had failed, Putin said steps were needed to hold Russia together in the face of terrorism. "Those who inspire, organize, and carry out terrorist acts are striving to disintegrate the country," he said. "They strive for the breakup of the state, for the ruin of Russia. I am sure that the unity of the country is the main prerequisite for victory over terror."

Putin's proposal had two parts. First, he said the governors should be nominated by the president and then ratified by local legislatures. Since adoption of the Russian constitution in 1993, these officials had been elected by voters in their regions. While maintaining a semblance of democracy in the provinces, the proposal clearly was intended to increase central control over Russia's regional governments, some of which had acted with a degree of independence the Kremlin often found distressing.

Putin's second proposal called for all 450 members of the Duma, the lower house of parliament, to be elected on national party slates, in effect allowing the parties to select all candidates. Previously, half the Duma's members were elected in local districts—a process that in the most recent elections, in December 2003, had produced the only representatives who were independent or who represented smaller parties.

Putin's supporters immediately embraced the proposals. Among them were the governors who stood to lose power, several of whom said they had no choice in the matter. Independents from across the political spectrum, however, said the president was using the Beslan crisis to justify a power grab and reinstitute the central control of the Soviet era. "All these measures mean we are coming back to the USSR," independent legislator Mikhail M. Zadornov told the *New York Times.*

Although Putin's proposals appeared to contradict key portions of the 1993 constitution, he said they needed to be approved only by the parliament. Parliament duly complied and in December gave final approval to his proposals—in the face of several public demonstrations at which opposition politicians decried what they said was the "death" of democracy in Russia.

Later in the year parliament also approved a related Kremlin proposal giving the president control over the committee that appointed members of the federal courts, including the Supreme Court. Kremlin officials said the move was needed to root out corruption and improve the "effectiveness" of the judiciary, but several judges said it appeared to be aimed at limiting the independence of the judicial system.

Also in 2004 millions of ordinary Russians felt the impact of Putin's efforts to reinvent Russian government. Over the summer the Kremlin announced that a Soviet-era system providing free health care, public transportation, and other benefits for more than 30 million veterans and senior citizens would be replaced with cash payments. The plan sparked protests for weeks, but the parliament quickly approved it in August. Opinion polls appeared to show that public support for Putin dropped sharply as a result.

Oil and the Russian Economy

Official statistics showed that the Russian economy grew by about 7 percent in 2004, but at least one-third of that growth was the result in the worldwide surge in oil prices. Over the previous decade production of oil and natural gas had become Russia's one reliable industry. The Kremlin during the year consolidated government control over that industry, in effect reversing the chaotic privatization that had occurred in the mid-1990s. *(Energy prices, p. 186)*

As in 2003, the Kremlin's chief target was Yukos, once the country's largest private oil producer. Yukos chairman, Mikhail B. Khordovosky, was arrested in October 2003 and imprisoned on charges of corruption and tax evasion. Khordovosky's associates and supporters insisted he was targeted because he had begun dabbling in politics and even threatened to run against Putin.

The Kremlin methodically set about dismantling Khordovosky's empire and filed $27 billion in claims for back taxes against Yukos. That process reached its culmination on December 18 when the government auctioned off the largest subsidiary of Yukos. The buyer of record was a newly established finance company that turned out to be a front for the Kremlin.

Russia and the World

Internationally, Russian standing continued to slip as foreign governments, including the Bush administration, became more willing to criticize Putin's handling of domestic affairs. Putin also stumbled badly in November when he tried to strong-arm an electoral victory for his favored presidential candidate in Ukraine. That backfired when masses of Ukrainians rallied behind the opposition candidate, who won an election rerun. Putin also backed the losing candidate in elections in Abkhazia, the province of Georgia that for more than a decade had sought either independence or a formal alliance with Russia. *(Georgia, p. 72; Ukraine elections, p. 949)*

Ever since President George W. Bush took office in 2001 he had portrayed Putin in friendly terms and avoided any direct criticism of him. The Bush administration's first substantive challenge to Putin's domestic policies came on January 25, 2004, when the newspaper *Izvestia* published an article by Secretary of State Colin Powell criticizing limits Putin had placed on the news media and parliamentary elections the previous month. Powell, who was visiting Moscow at the time, met with Putin and reportedly expressed concerns about the arrest of Khordovosky and the seizure of his assets. The European Union also made several statements during the year criticizing developments in Russia, while acknowledging that European diplomacy had failed to have much of an effect there.

The Bush administration followed Powell's statements a month later with unusually strong remarks in the State Department's annual report on human rights worldwide. The administration also criticized, on occasion, the strong arm tactics in Chechnya by Russian security services. "We fear that the cycle of violence in Chechnya is sustained by continuing human rights abuses on the part of Russian federal and local security forces," A. Elizabeth Jones, the assistant secretary of state for European affairs told a House subcommittee on March 18. Dealing with the situation in Chechnya was difficult for Moscow, she added, "but enough is enough. More than enough blood has been spilled in Chechnya."

Despite such comments, Bush himself remained reluctant to criticize Putin. During a news conference on December 20, Bush said he and Putin "have got a good personal relationship," starting with their first meeting in Slovenia in 2001. "I intend to keep it that way." Bush said he had expressed concerns to Putin about his consolidation of political power, but he said Putin took the comments in "the spirit of two people who've grown to appreciate each other and respect each other."

Following are excerpts from two speeches by Russian president Vladimir Putin: first, a nationally televised speech on September 4, 2004, one day after the resolution of a hostage crisis at a school in Beslan, Russia; second, a nationally televised speech on September 13, 2004, to his cabinet and governors of the Russian provinces, in which he announced a series of proposals to change key components of the Russian political system.

Nationally Televised Speech by Russian President Putin

Speaking is hard. It is painful.

A terrible tragedy has taken place in our world. Over these last few days each and every one of us has suffered greatly and taken deeply to heart all that was happening in the Russian town of Beslan. There, we found ourselves confronting not just murderers, but people who turned their weapons against helpless children.

I would like now, first of all, to address words of support and condolence to those people who have lost what we treasure most in this life—our children, our loved and dear ones.

I ask that we all remember those who lost their lives at the hands of terrorists over these last days.

Russia has lived through many tragic events and terrible ordeals over the course of its history. Today, we live in a time that follows the collapse of a vast and great state, a state that, unfortunately, proved unable to survive in a rapidly changing world. But despite all the difficulties, we were able to preserve the core of what was once the vast Soviet Union, and we named this new country the Russian Federation.

We all hoped for change, change for the better. But many of the changes that took place in our lives found us unprepared. Why is this?

We are living at a time of an economy in transition, of a political system that does not yet correspond to the state and level of our society's development.

We are living through a time when internal conflicts and interethnic divisions that were once firmly suppressed by the ruling ideology have now flared up.

We stopped paying the required attention to defence and security issues and we allowed corruption to undermine our judicial and law enforcement system.

Furthermore, our country, formerly protected by the most powerful defence system along the length of its external frontiers overnight found itself defenceless both from the east and the west.

It will take many years and billions of roubles to create new, modern and genuinely protected borders.

But even so, we could have been more effective if we had acted professionally and at the right moment.

In general, we need to admit that we did not fully understand the complexity and the dangers of the processes at work in our own country and in the world. In any case, we proved unable to react adequately. We showed ourselves to be weak. And the weak get beaten.

Some would like to tear from us a "juicy piece of pie". Others help them. They help, reasoning that Russia still remains one of the world's major nuclear powers, and as such still represents a threat to them. And so they reason that this threat should be removed.

Terrorism, of course, is just an instrument to achieve these aims.

As I have said many times already, we have found ourselves confronting crises, revolts and terrorist acts on more than one occasion. But what has happened now, this crime committed by terrorists, is unprecedented in its inhumanness and cruelty. This is not a challenge to the President, parliament or government. It is a challenge to all of Russia, to our entire people. Our country is under attack.

The terrorists think they are stronger than us. They think they can frighten us with their cruelty, paralyse our will and sow disintegration in our society. It would seem that we have a choice—either to resist them or to agree to their demands. To give in, to let them destroy and plunder Russia in the hope that they will finally leave us in peace.

As the President, the head of the Russian state, as someone who swore an oath to defend this country and its territorial integrity, and simply as a citizen of Russia, I am convinced that in reality we have no choice at all. Because to allow ourselves to be blackmailed and succumb to panic would be to immediately condemn millions of people to an endless series of bloody conflicts like those of Nagorny Karabakh, Trans-Dniester and other similar tragedies. We should not turn away from this obvious fact.

What we are dealing with are not isolated acts intended to frighten us, not isolated terrorist attacks. What we are facing is direct intervention of international terror directed against Russia. This is a total, cruel and full-scale war that again and again is taking the lives of our fellow citizens.

World experience shows us that, unfortunately, such wars do not end quickly. In this situation we simply cannot and should not live in as carefree a manner as previously. We must create a much more effective security system and we must demand from our law enforcement agencies action that corresponds to the level and scale of the new threats that have emerged.

But most important is to mobilise the entire nation in the face of this common danger. Events in other countries have shown that terrorists meet the most effective resistance in places where they not only encounter the state's power but also find themselves facing an organised and united civil society. . . .

[Putin added that he soon would offer "a series of measures aimed at strengthening our country's unity."]

Source: Russian Federation. Ministry of Foreign Affairs. Information and Press Department. "Address by President Vladimir Putin." Unofficial translation from Russian. September 7, 2004. www.ln.mid.ru/brp_4.nsf/e78a48070f128a7b43256999005bcbb3/8bb02e3c693e087cc3256f08002b5fc5?OpenDocument (accessed January 12, 2005).

Speech to Cabinet and Governors by Russian President Putin

Dear colleagues,

We are meeting in this unusual format due to special circumstances. Circumstances that have deeply moved the entire country and, it may be said without exaggeration, the entire world.

I am sure that there is not a single Russian family, not a single Russian citizen, who did not feel the sorrow and suffering of the Ossetian people as their own. Not only is it impossible to speak about what happened in Beslan without tears—it is impossible to think about it without tears.

However, mere sympathy, tears and words of support are not an adequate response from the authorities. We must act. We must improve the effectiveness of power bodies in resolving all the problems that lie before the country—the entire set of problems. Because when taken out of the context of the whole, not a single issue that lies before us today, even such important issues as ensuring the security of citizens and the state, can be solved effectively.

In the situation that has arisen after the terrorist act in Beslan, I think that at this enlarged meeting it is necessary to discuss with you the problems that I raised in the address to the people of Russia on September the 4th. These are issues of ensuring the unity of the country, strengthening state structures and trust in the authorities, creating an effective system of internal security.

Not only members of federal Government are gathered here today, but also the heads of all Russian regions. I believe that in the current situation, in the current conditions, the system of executive power in the country must not simply be adapted for work in crisis situations, it must be fundamentally reorganized, in order to strengthen the unity of the country and stop crises from arising.

We must not forget that in their far-reaching plans, the people who inspire, organize and carry out terrorist acts aim for the disintegration of the country, the break-up of the state and the collapse of Russia.

I am certain that the unity of the country is the main condition for conquering terrorism. And without such unity this goal is impossible to attain.

I would like to discuss the problem in more detail.

Above all, I believe that the most important factor in strengthening the state is a unified system of executive power in the country. A unity that comes from the spirit and letter of article 77 of the Constitution of the Russian Federation. Essentially, this means that in the areas of competence of the Russian Federation, and in the areas of joint competence, the bodies of executive power in the centre and in the federal regions form a single system of power, and thus must work as an integral co-subordinate single organism.

It must be admitted that this system of power has yet to be created in the country.

The war on terrorism is a national task. It is a task that requires the mobilization of all resources. And it is clear that a unity of actions of the entire executive power vertical must be ensured here unconditionally.

I also believe that in order to ensure the unity of state power and the consistent development of federalism, the Federation and its subjects must jointly take part in forming executive bodies of power in the territories of Russia. And in connection with this, I believe that the higher regional officials of the Russian Federation subjects must be elected by legislative assemblies of the territories at the head of state proposal.

In this case, the mechanism for forming higher executive power in the regions will be organized on principles that are practically identical with the principles for forming the Government of the Russian Federation. This system of forming executive power is based on the general statutes of the Constitution and is proposed in projects presented by an entire range of heads of regions of the Russian Federation.

By the end of the year, I will submit an according draft law to the State Duma. I ask the Government, and also the heads of Russian regions together with the representative power bodies to work on preparing this document. Furthermore, I believe that nowadays the heads of regions should work more closely with municipal formations, helping them in their daily work with the people; they should also have more influence on forming bodies of local self-administration in the formats stipulated by law.

Consultations with specialists show that within the framework of the current Constitution there are such possibilities, and I ask the Government and the Presidium of the State Council to work on this and present their proposals.

Dear meeting participants,

The war on terrorism must become a national matter in all senses of the world, and so it is very important that all institutions of the political system, all Russian society take part in it.

In these tragic days, we have seen the courage and resolve of our people in opposing terror. People not only showed their solidarity, they showed their complete understanding of the situation, and a high level of civil and personal responsibility. This says a lot, and of course it is worth a great deal.

Today we must support citizens' initiatives with practical actions in their efforts to fight terrorism. Together, we must find mechanisms unifying the state. It is national parties that should become one of the mechanisms ensuring a real dialogue and cooperation between society and state in the war on terrorism. And in the interests of strengthening the political system of the country, I believe it is necessary to introduce a proportional system of State Duma elections. I will soon submit a draft law on this for examination by the Parliament.

I would also like to stress: if we are counting on society's help in the war against terrorists, people must be sure that their opinions will be heard. In connection with this, I support the idea of forming a public chamber as a platform for wide dialogue, where civic initiatives can be presented and discussed in detail. No less importantly, this chamber should become a place for conducting public examinations of key state decisions, and above all of draft laws that concern prospects for the country development of national significance.

This essentially means civilian control of the work of the state system, including the law-enforcement bodies and the special services, which in my opinion is extremely important at the moment.

I appeal especially to the representatives of the Government power bloc. In the situation that the country finds itself, in this difficult period of our development, we must establish contact with citizens and cooperate with them more closely. We must react attentively and efficiently to every appeal and concern of theirs. We must help people to learn to behave appropriately in extreme situations.

We should also support citizens' initiatives on organizing voluntary structures in the sphere of public order protection. They are capable not just of providing real assistance in collecting information and detecting signals from the people on possible crime preparations, but can also become a real factor in fighting crime and terrorism. And of course, we need help from public organizations in explaining how to behave in the threat of a terrorist act and how to assist in preventing them.

In coordination with bodies of local self-administration, a system of cooperation with people at their place of residence, at work, at schools and universities should be established, which would be adequate to the current situation.

Dear colleagues,

In my address to the people on September the 4th, I also spoke of the necessity of increasing security in the North Caucasus. The war on terrorism requires a fundamental revision of all our policies in this region. And one of the most serious, key issues is the weakness of state administration.

As you know, the socio-economic situation in the North Caucasus region remains deplorable. And the living standard there is unacceptably lower than in other Russian territories. It is enough to say that the unemployment level is several times higher than the average for Russia. In republics such as Ingushetia, Chechnya and Dagestan, it is a truly mass phenomenon. The average monthly income in the South Federal district is one and a half times lower than the average for Russia. And in Ingushetia, for example, it is almost four times lower. The child mortality rates in almost all the republics of the Northern Caucasus are extremely high.

I will put it bluntly: it is the bodies of executive power to be primarily blamed for this situation. We must not forget: the Northern Caucasus is a very important strategic region of Russia. And at the moment it is simultaneously a victim of terror, and a base for terror. It is here that ideologists of international terrorism are particularly active. And in their crimes and their criminal plans they openly and brazenly exploit our shortcomings in socio-economic policies.

In fighting manifestations of terror, we practically have not achieved visible results. Above all, we have not achieved visible results in liquidating the sources of terror. However, the roots of terror also lie in the mass unemployment that remains in the region, in the lack of effective social policies, in the low level of education of the young generation, or even the lack of opportunity to receive education. This all provides rich soil for extremist propaganda, for a growth in terror bases, and for recruiting new followers.

I would like to say that in accordance with the decree that I have signed, a special Federal commission on the North Caucasus has been created, which is headed by the Plenipotentiary Presidential envoy to the Southern Federal district. He has been given broad powers on coordinating a number of federal civic ministries, and in certain aspects—of law-enforcement authorities. I mean those aspects that primarily concern the economy and the social sphere; he also has several powers in the security sphere for swift response to the threat of terrorist acts. . . .

I also consider it necessary to make changes to the structure of the Government and create a ministry responsible for issues of regional and ethnic policy. At the agreement of the Prime Minister, Vladimir Anatol'evich Yakovlev will be appointed as minister.

And finally, the third point. The third area that I discussed on September the 4th is that we need an anti-crisis management system, effective in the conditions of the terrorist war that is being conducted against Russia. We need a full system of measures that are adequate to the situation, and which can repel the threat of terror in any form. We also need appropriate anti-crisis plans of action, for the Government, for the ministries, the departments, the regions of the Russian Federation and for local authorities. All these issues will be worked out on the basis of a special decree by the President of the Russian Federation that has been signed today.

It means that we must jointly carry out an entire range of measures, including correcting our work in the framework of the current administrative reform, providing the necessary tools and resources for effective management in crisis situations.

I repeat, this concerns the entire range of tasks—from foreign policy to specific economic tasks.

Work in the law-enforcement sphere is no exception. As you know, I have ordered a detailed analysis of the circumstances that led to the tragedy in Beslan. The law-enforcement structures have been given the necessary orders to intensify anti-terrorist operations, also by increasing the scope of international cooperation in the special services. All these are undoubtedly important and necessary measures. But they are still not enough on their own. A number of countries that have faced terrorist threats have established unified systems of security that provide comprehensive internal security and anti- terrorist actions. And here in Russia, we also need the same organizational work and the same system of national security organization which is capable of not only stopping terrorist acts and dealing with their consequences, but also of working on preventing terrorist invasions, diversions and man-made catastrophes organized by terrorists. The system that will be ahead of criminals to destroy them, so to speak, in their own lair. And if the situation requires it, to get them from abroad.

We must uncover terrorist organizations and groups, and the terrorists themselves, cut off financial channels and create a political and financial vacuum around their emissaries and lobbyists.

I also believe that extremist organizations that hide behind religious, nationalist or other slogans and that essentially breed terror must be prohibited, and their leaders and active members prosecuted in accordance with the law.

It is also necessary to punish crimes of official misconduct, which have extremely serious consequences, even though these crimes may seem insignificant at first glance. To give you an example—I mean issuing passports illegally and documents that are used in terrorist acts, which have serious consequences. These crimes should be judged accordingly by the state and the courts. The sanctions should be adequate to the consequences of the crime.

I would ask State Duma deputies to make a thorough study of all the gaps in Russian legislation and make an according decision. . . .

To end my speech, I would like once more to stress that the war on terrorism is our common and primary task, and whether we solve it depends on how effectively all the resources of state and society are mobilized.

Source: Russian Federation. Ministry of Foreign Affairs. Information and Press Department. "Address by President Vladimir Putin." Unofficial translation from Russian. September 13, 2004. www.ln.mid.ru/brp_4.nsf/e78a48070f128a7b43256999005bcbb3/7a491054ea8e0288c3256f0f0023edd5?OpenDocument (accessed January 12, 2005).

GAO on Withholding Medicare Cost Estimates from Congress

September 7, 2004

INTRODUCTION

The ink had barely dried on President George W. Bush's signature enacting the Medicare Modernization Act before the legislation providing drug benefits to seniors and making other changes in the law became mired once again in political controversy. In January 2004 the administration announced the cost would be $534 billion over ten years—$134 billion more than the $400 billion estimated when the president signed the measure into law on December 8, 2003. It then came to light that at least some administration officials had known for months of the higher estimates and had not told Congress. They instead affirmed that the $400 billion estimate was correct. Even more damning were allegations by Medicare's chief actuary, who said a superior had threatened to fire him if he gave Congress the higher estimates. That allegation resulted in several inquiries, including one by the Government Accountability Office (GAO, formerly the General Accounting Office) that said the administration had improperly tried to silence the actuary.

The Department of Health and Human Services (HHS) also ran into trouble when Democrats challenged its ad campaign to make seniors aware of the new drug benefits. Democrats said the ads were misleading and partisan. Late in the year House Majority Leader Tom DeLay, R-Texas, was admonished by the House Ethics Committee for using improper methods to try to persuade a Michigan Republican legislator to vote for the Medicare reform bill. The committee also admonished the Michigan legislator, Nick Smith, for describing DeLay's tactics as bribery; the committee said Smith had exaggerated the incident.

These incidents paled in comparison, however, to the latest report from actuaries, showing that the portion of Medicare that covered hospital costs for seniors was likely to go broke by 2019, seven years earlier than had been predicted a year earlier. Later in the year, the Bush administration announced that Medicare premiums for 2005 would increase 17 percent to $78.20 a month. That was the largest dollar increase in Medicare premiums since the program was established in 1965, and it came on top of a 14 percent increase in 2004. *(Health care costs, p. 981)*

Background

Congress had tried for several years to add a prescription drug benefit for the 40 million seniors who received their medical insurance through Medicare. Until 2003 a Republican-written bill would pass the GOP-controlled House only to die in the Senate, which was more evenly divided politically. In 2003 the dynamics shifted. Republicans were more firmly in control of both chambers, and members of both parties wanted to be able to tout the new drug benefit on the campaign trail in 2004. Republicans also wanted to give Bush a victory on his top domestic priority, and Democrats feared being tarred as obstructionists on an issue that they had long championed. Moreover, given the rising budget deficit, both parties knew that the $400 million set aside for the program in the fiscal 2004 budget resolution might not be available again for many years.

As enacted, the bill offered benefits for Medicare recipients either through stand-alone drug insurance plans, for seniors who wished to remain in the traditional fee-for-service Medicare program, or through new private managed care networks. The bill offered private insurers substantial financial incentives to establish such networks. It also included billions of dollars for hospitals, physicians, and other providers in rural areas, money that helped the measure attract bipartisan support. *(Medicare reform, Historic Documents of 2003, p. 1119)*

Philosophical differences between the two parties dominated the year-long debate. Republicans generally favored giving over to private companies the job of providing drug benefits, while most Democrats wanted the government-run Medicare program to offer a standard drug benefit to all. Republicans complained that approach would cost far more than $400 billion. Even after it passed, controversy swirled around the new law, with critics on both sides of the political spectrum raising questions about its costs, its subsidies to insurers and employers, and whether it would actually provide the benefits it promised. Fiscally conservative Republicans said the bill created a new entitlement program that taxpayers could not afford. Democrats said the bill did more for insurers and the drug companies than it did for seniors, and they promised to try to repeal parts of the measure, including a provision that prohibited the government from negotiating lower drug prices for Medicare. President Bush claimed the bill would give seniors "better choices and more control over their health care."

A first test of those choices came in mid-2004 when seniors who did not have drug coverage were allowed to apply for a prescription drug card from approved providers. The card was expected to save them as much as 25 percent on the costs of their drugs. Costs for low-income seniors would be subsidized by the government. The program, which covered those seniors that did not already have drug coverage through supplemental health plans, would be in place only until 2006, when the larger program covering all seniors would be implemented.

The initial enrollments were disappointing. By the end of the year, only 5.8 million seniors had signed up for the program. Of the 7 million low-income seniors eligible for the cards, only about 1.5 million had signed on. Medicare's Mark McClellan said that about 2 million cards were sent to low-income people in an effort to induce them to take advantage of the subsidy and drug discounts, but, he said, only about 100,000 had made the phone call necessary to activate the card. Critics said the experience confirmed their fears that the program was too confusing and too complicated. Because each provider covered some drugs but not others, and because prices varied from provider to provider, seniors on a variety of drugs might have to review several different drug card plans to find one that would cover their particular drug needs.

In part because of this confusion, many seniors appeared ambivalent about the Medicare reform. In August pollsters for the Harvard School of Public Health and the Kaiser Family Foundation reported that 47 percent of the seniors polled had an unfavorable view of the drug discount card, 26 percent had a favorable view, and 25 percent said they did not know enough about it to have an opinion. The poll also found that more seniors trusted Democratic presidential candidate John Kerry to do a better job of handling Medicare drug benefits than President Bush. A spokesman for the Harvard School of Public Health said Bush had "led an initiative that looks to be helping his challenger."

Intimidation Alleged

Legislators in both parties were stunned in January when the Bush administration's budget for fiscal 2005 estimated the ten-year cost of the new Medicare reform bill at $534 billion rather than the $400 billion that the administration had stood by throughout the debate on the bill. Legislators were even more stunned in March when they learned that administration officials had long known of the likely higher cost and that Medicare's chief actuary, Richard S. Foster, had been told he would be fired if he provided the higher estimate to Congress. Foster, who had been chief actuary since 1995, said the threat came from his boss, Thomas A. Scully, who also told Foster to funnel all congressional requests for estimates to Scully, who would decide which ones to answer. Foster said Scully told him on one occasion that he, Scully, was "acting under direct White House orders." Traditionally, Foster said, his office answered congressional requests for information in an independent, nonpartisan fashion.

Foster was eventually assured by other administration officials that his job was not in jeopardy, and he said he decided to stay in his post rather than resign in protest, but his higher estimates continued to be withheld from Congress. According to Foster those estimates ran between $500 billion and $600 billion during the five months the legislation was being actively debated. Had they been aware of those estimates during the debate, several lawmakers said they would not have voted for final passage of the measure. Scully, who left government in December 2003 to take a job in a law firm that lobbied for health care companies, acknowledged that he had directed Foster to withhold the costs estimates but denied that he had had ever threatened to fire him.

Upon hearing of Foster's complaint, Democrats cried foul and called for an investigation. Even some prominent Republicans urged the administration to clear the air. "This is very troubling and disturbing," Sen. Olympia J. Snow, R-Maine, a strong supporter of the Medicare reform law, said on March 16. "You undermine the credibility and integrity of the legislative process any time you deliberately withhold information from Congress. You hamstring our ability to do the best job we can."

HHS secretary Tommy G. Thompson announced that his Office of Inspector General would look into the incident. On July 6 that office reported that although the Medicare agency had withheld information from Congress, it had not violated any criminal statutes in doing so. Dara Corrigan, the acting principal deputy inspector general who wrote the report, confirmed that Scully had threatened to fire Foster but concluded that Scully's conduct did not violate criminal law. She suggested that Scully might have violated the department's code of ethical conduct but said that since Scully no longer worked in the government, it was a moot point.

On September 7 the Government Accountability Office issued a legal advisory on the issue in response to several Democratic members of Congress, including the party's presidential and vice presidential nominees, John Kerry and John Edwards. In the opinion, Anthony H. Gamboa, GAO's general counsel, concluded that Scully's threat to fire Foster if he released the costs estimates was a violation of federal law and that he should repay seven months of his salary as a penalty. GAO rejected the administration's argument that the cost estimates could properly be withheld under the principles of executive privilege, the separation of powers, and the president's right to control executive branch communications with Congress. Rather, Gamboa said, Scully's threats to Foster were "a prime example of what Congress was attempting to prohibit" when it enacted so-called gag rules.

The administration did not deny the facts of the incident as laid out in the GAO advisory opinion, but it disagreed with Gamboa's conclusion that it did not have a constitutional right to withhold the data from Congress and said it would not seek to recover the salary money, about $85,000, from Scully. Asked if he would repay it, Scully told the *New York Times,* "No, I'm not required to. It's a matter of principle. I never did anything wrong, and I am proud of every minute of my three years" at the Medicare agency.

HHS Ads Challenged

Democrats also asked GAO for its legal opinion on several matters related to an HHS campaign to tell Medicare recipients about the new drug benefit program, specifically whether the materials were so partisan as to violate a federal ban on tax-funded "publicity or propaganda." Although the department portrayed its efforts as an information campaign, Democrats said the materials—a brochure to be mailed to all Medicare beneficiaries and print and television ads—were misleading and designed to aid the president's reelection campaign. In particular, the Democrats questioned why HHS was running print ads in *Roll Call,* a newspaper aimed primarily at members of Congress and their staffs. Democrats also questioned the propriety of HHS using the same media firms that were handling Bush's reelection campaign. "There is no purpose for the advertisement except to convince senior citizens that the Medicare bill is good for them," said Sen. Edward M. Kennedy, D-Mass., and a leading opponent of the Medicare reform bill that was enacted. The ads, Kennedy said, "are nothing more than propaganda for the Bush reelection campaign, using $23 million of senior citizens' own money," referring to the cost of running the ads and mailing the brochures.

On March 10 Gamboa issued an advisory opinion saying that although GAO agreed that the ads contained "notable omissions and other weaknesses," they did not "constitute a purely partisan message" and thus were not illegal. In the course of its investigation, however, GAO found that the Medicare agency had prepared, as part of its information campaign, video news releases that included a news story for television broadcast that was not attributed to the U.S. government and that was narrated by an actor posing as a reporter.

On closer look, GAO found not only that the source of the video news release was unidentified, but also that the video had been designed to be run directly as a news story. Those failures, GAO said in an opinion released May 19, amounted to a violation of the prohibition on government-funded publicity or propaganda. "In a modest but meaningful way," Gamboa wrote, "the publicity or propaganda restriction helps to mark the boundary between an agency making information available to the public and agencies creating news reports unbeknownst to the receiving public." Although the Medicare agency was authorized to conduct a wide rage of informational activities, it had no authority "to produce and disseminate unattributed news stories," Gamboa concluded.

Ethics Questioned

House Majority Leader Tom DeLay was the focus during the year of a House ethics committee investigation into whether he had acted improperly when he offered to endorse Michigan Republican Nick Smith's son in his bid for a congressional seat in return for Smith's vote on the final version of the Medicare reform bill. The incident occurred in the early morning hours of November 22, 2003, as Republican leaders desperately sought support for the reform bill. The measure passed by a vote of 220–215, but only after House Speaker J. Dennis Hastert held the roll-call vote open for an unprecedented three hours while the GOP leadership rounded up enough votes to pass it. (The fifteen-minute roll calls in the House are typically held open only an extra five minutes or so to accommodate late-arriving members.)

Smith, who voted against the Medicare reform, touched off the controversy shortly after the vote when he wrote a news article saying that unnamed House members had offered financial and political support for his son Brad's race to win the Michigan House seat the older Smith was vacating at the end of his term. (Brad Smith lost the GOP primary election in August 2004.) Although Smith quickly backpedaled on his allegations of financial bribery, Democrats jumped on the issue, demanding that GOP House leaders launch an investigation. In part to quiet the Democrats, the ethics committee, formally known as the Committee on Standards of Official Conduct, announced in February that it had already begun a review of the incident. On March 17 the committee began an formal investigation.

On September 30 the committee unanimously accepted the findings of its investigating subcommittee, which concluded that DeLay had acted improperly. While it was not improper for legislators to trade legislative votes to achieve policy goals or maintain party discipline, the committee wrote, "The promise of political support for a relative of a Member goes beyond the boundaries of maintaining party discipline, and should not be used as the basis of a bargain for Members to achieve their respective goals." The panel also faulted Smith for initially making false allegations, including that he had been offered a bribe, and for failing to cooperate fully with the committee's investigation. The panel also said that another Republican legislator from Michigan, Candice S. Miller, had acted wrongly when she threatened political retaliation against Smith if he did not change his position and vote for the Medicare reform. In a statement, DeLay said he accepted the ethics committee's "guidance," on the matter, adding that he "would never knowingly violate the rules of the House."

Six days later, on October 6, the ethics committee—with bipartisan unanimity—admonished DeLay again for going "beyond the bounds of acceptable conduct" by pressuring the Federal Aviation Agency to help find Democratic state legislators who left the state in 2003 in a bid to prevent passage of a congressional redistricting plan DeLay was pushing in Texas. The ethics panel also cited Delay for sponsoring a golf fundraiser for energy company executives just before conference negotiations began on the administration's energy overhaul legislation. DeLay had been accused of soliciting campaign donations from some of the executives in return for favorable consideration of their views in writing the energy bill. (The congressional redistricting bill eventually passed and helped the Republicans win several new seats in the Texas congressional delegation; the energy bill bogged down in conference and was never passed.)

The committee also warned DeLay that it had identified a clear pattern of misbehavior by him and would be on the lookout for additional instances when he pushed the bounds of acceptable conduct in pursuing his legislative and political goals. DeLay, known as "The Hammer" for his insistence on getting his way, and other top Republican leaders quickly let it be known that the chairman of the ethics panel, Joel Hefley of Colorado, was persona non grata and might not be reappointed chairman in 2005. By year's end, a decision on the appointment had not yet been announced.

Medicare's Precarious Financial Status

In a chilling report released March 23, Medicare's board of trustees warned that rising health care costs and the costs of the new Medicare law had greatly worsened the programs financial condition. In its annual report to Congress, the board reported that based on current law and demographic and cost trends, Medicare's hospital insurance trust fund would be exhausted by 2019. That was seven years sooner than the board had forecast just a year earlier. By 2024 Medicare costs were projected to be twice those of Social Security, the trustees said. Overall, they said, Medicare would continue to grow much faster than the economy as a whole, increasing from 2.6 percent of gross domestic product in 2003 to 3.4 percent in 2006 when the prescription drug benefit program kicked in, to 7.7 percent in 2035. The trustees said that the insolvency date projected for the Social Security trust funds remained unchanged, at 2042.

John L. Palmer, one of two public representatives on the board of trustees and a former dean of the Maxwell School at Syracuse University, said the magnitude of the financing problems for Medicare was much greater than for Social Security. The problems "start sooner, get bigger, and will be much more difficult to deal with," he said. In a joint statement, the four public trustees, all administration officials, said that expanding health care costs and the new drug benefit program "raise serious doubt about the sustainability of Medicare under current financing arrangements."

HHS Secretary Thompson said that he believed the new Medicare law would introduce some cost savings in the long run that had not been fully taken into account in the projections. He specifically mentioned improvements in preventive services; greater use of generic drugs, which were typically cheaper than branded drugs; and competition among private plans for the elderly, which he said would slow the growth of Medicare spending. Palmer disagreed, however, saying that Thompson was offering "nebulous, long-term hopes" rather than potential savings "that can be quantified." Palmer added that the reform legislation "obviously made the situation somewhat worse" because it increased costs without any offsetting increases in revenue.

On September 3 the Bush administration announced the largest premium increase, measured in dollars, in Medicare's history. Starting in January 2005 the monthly premium was set at $78.20, an increase of $11.60, or 17 percent, over the 2004 cost. Premiums in 2004 were themselves 14 percent higher than in 2003. The announcement came one day after Bush, in his speech accepting the Republican nomination to run for a second term in office, took credit for helping seniors deal with the rising costs of health care. *(Bush speech, p. 493)*

Mark McClellan, the new administrator of the Medicare program, said the increase resulted largely from increased Medicare payments to doctors, and he acknowledged that a substantial portion of the increase would be used to bolster the Medicare trust fund. He also acknowledged that about one-tenth of the increase in premiums resulted from the billions of dollars Medicare was paying private insurers to entice them to offer private plans to seniors. Republicans had long argued that in the long run ensuring competition among private insurance plans would result in more benefits to seniors at less cost both to them and the government, an argument that Democrats sharply disputed.

None of the increase in the premium was attributable to the new prescription drug benefits, which were not scheduled to begin until 2006. As a result of that program, government actuaries projected that Medicare costs for the typical sixty-five-year-old would jump from 20 percent of the average Social Security benefit in 2005 to 37 percent in 2006.

Following are excerpts from an opinion by Anthony H. Gamboa, general counsel of the Government Accountability Office, dated September 7, 2004, in which he concluded that the top administrator of the Medicare program in the Department of Health and Human Services had violated federal law when he barred Medicare's chief actuary from giving adverse cost estimates and other information to Congress during its debate in 2003 on revamping the Medicare program. Gamboa recommended that the administrator forfeit seven months of his salary as a penalty.

"Department of HHS—Actuary's Communications with Congress"

By letter dated March 18, 2004, you asked for our legal opinion regarding a potential violation of the prohibitions in the Consolidated Appropriations Act of 2004 and the Consolidated Appropriations Resolution of 2003 on the use of appropriated funds to pay the salary of a federal official who prohibits another federal employee from communicating with Congress. Specifically, you ask whether alleged threats made by Thomas A. Scully, the former Administrator of the Centers for Medicare & Medicaid Services (CMS), to CMS Chief Actuary Richard S. Foster to terminate his employment if Mr. Foster provided various cost estimates of the then-pending prescription drug legislation to members of Congress and their staff made CMS's appropriation unavailable for the payment of Mr. Scully's salary.

As agreed, this opinion relies on the factual findings of the Office of Inspector General (OIG) for the Department of Health and Human Services (HHS), who conducted an independent investigation into whether Mr. Foster was prohibited from communicating with congressional offices and whether he was threatened with dismissal if he did so. The OIG concluded that CMS did not provide information requested by members of Congress and their staff, that Mr. Scully ordered Mr. Foster not to provide information to members and staff, and that Mr. Scully threatened to sanction Mr. Foster if he made any unauthorized disclosures. . . .

Background

In December 2003, Congress passed and the President signed into law the Medicare Prescription Drug, Improvement, and Modernization Act of 2003, which added a prescription drug benefit to the Medicare program. During the previous summer and fall as Congress debated various proposals, several members of Congress and committee staff asked Mr. Foster, a career civil servant and the Chief Actuary for CMS, to provide estimates of the cost of various provisions of the Medicare bills under debate.

Members and staff also made requests for technical assistance, including requests that Mr. Foster perform analyses of various provisions of the Medicare legislation.

Mr. Foster did not respond to several of these requests because Thomas Scully, CMS Administrator and Mr. Foster's supervisor, stated that there would be adverse consequences if he released any information to Congress without Mr. Scully's approval. Mr. Foster stated that the first time he felt his job was threatened was in May 2003 when he provided information on private insurance plan enrollment rates to the Majority Staff Director of the House Ways and Means Committee and Mr. Scully rebuked him for doing so. Later, on June 4, 2003, at Mr. Scully's request, Mr. Scully's special assistant instructed Mr. Foster not to respond to any requests for information from the House Ways and Means Committee and warned him that "the consequences of insubordination are extremely severe." Mr. Foster interpreted this statement to mean that Mr. Scully would terminate his employment at CMS if he released any information to Congress without Mr. Scully's approval.

The OIG Report concluded that, because of Mr. Scully's prohibition, Mr. Foster did not respond to several congressional requests for cost estimates and technical assistance, including requests from the minority staff of the House Ways and Means Committee for the total estimated cost of the legislation and for analyses of premium support provisions in the bill, and requests from Senators Mark Dayton and Edward Kennedy for premium estimates.

There is no indication in the OIG Report that Mr. Scully objected to Mr. Foster's methodology or to the validity of his estimates. Rather, Mr. Foster testified before the House Ways and Means Committee that Mr. Scully determined which information to release to Congress on a "political basis." Furthermore, Mr. Scully never objected to Mr. Foster and his staff performing the analyses required to respond to congressional requests; he simply objected to certain analyses being released to Congress. During the same time period, Mr. Foster provided similar analyses to the Office of Management and Budget.

Discussion

At issue here is the prohibition on using appropriated funds to pay the salary of a federal official who prohibits or prevents another federal employee from communicating with Congress. Specifically, this prohibition states:

> "No part of any appropriation contained in this or any other Act shall be available for the payment of the salary of any officer or employee of the Federal Government, who . . . prohibits or prevents, or attempts or threatens to prohibit or prevent, any other officer or employee of the Federal Government from having any direct oral or written communication or contact with any Member, committee, or subcommittee of the Congress in connection with any matter pertaining to the employment of such other officer or employee or pertaining to the department or agency of such other officer or employee in any way, irrespective of whether such communication or contact is at the initiative of such other officer or employee or in response to the request or inquiry of such Member, committee, or subcommittee."
>
> ["Legislative History of Section 618" omitted.]

Application of the Prohibition to the Inspector General's Findings

As noted above, section 618 prohibits an agency from paying the salary of any federal officer or employee who prohibits or prevents, or threatens to prohibit or prevent, another officer or employee from communicating with members, committees or subcommittees of Congress. The OIG report concluded that Mr. Scully both prohibited and threatened to prohibit Mr. Foster from communicating with various members of Congress and congressional committees on issues that pertained to his agency and his professional responsibilities. In May 2003, Mr. Scully rebuked Mr. Foster for providing information requested by the Majority Staff Director for the House Ways and Means Committee. In June 2003, Mr. Scully's special assistant, pursuant to Mr. Scully's direction, instructed Mr. Foster not to respond to any requests for information from the House Ways and Means Committee. Because of Mr. Scully's actions, we view HHS's appropriation as unavailable to pay his salary.

As the legislative history of section 618 demonstrates, Congress intended to advance two goals: to preserve the First Amendment rights of federal employees and to ensure that Congress had access to programmatic information from frontline employees. Mr. Scully's actions implicate the latter of these goals. Congressional offices had asked Mr. Foster for information and for technical and analytic assistance that concerned the cost and impact of proposed Medicare legislation under debate in both the House and the Senate. Many members considered such information critical to their consideration of the Medicare Prescription Drug, Improvement, and Modernization Act, a historic piece of legislation with significant implications for federal fiscal policy. This information is a prime example of the programmatic information from frontline federal employees upon which Congress focused in enacting the Lloyd-La Follette Act and its subsequent incarnations. [The Lloyd-Lafollette Act of 1912 barred imposition of so-called gag rules on federal employees.]

According to the OIG's findings, congressional offices were interested in the total estimated cost of the legislation, premium estimates, the data underlying certain premium estimates, and a technical analysis of the premium support provisions in the Medicare legislation. This information was typical of the regular, ordinary work product of Mr. Foster and the Office of the Chief Actuary, and as the frontline employee, he was competent to provide the information to Congress. Mr. Foster was more knowledgeable about the estimates than other officials within HHS and thus was able to provide information so that Congress could evaluate the Medicare program and budget.

Thus, the legislative history of section 618 and its predecessors suggest that Mr. Scully's bar on Mr. Foster responding to congressional requests is a prime example of what Congress was attempting to prohibit by those provisions. Accordingly, Mr. Scully's actions fall squarely within section 618, and HHS's appropriation was unavailable for the payment of his salary.

Constitutional Issues Raised by HHS and OLC

While the OIG Report concluded that Mr. Scully had indeed threatened Mr. Foster if he communicated with Congress, it also contained in its attachments, legal opinions by the HHS Office of General Counsel and by the Office of Legal Counsel (OLC) for the Department of Justice. These legal opinions state that the application of section 618 to the present case would be unconstitutional.

Laws passed by Congress and signed by the President come to us with a heavy presumption in favor of their constitutionality. We have long observed that it is not our role to adjudicate the constitutionality of duly enacted legislation. We apply the laws as we find them absent a controlling judicial opinion that such laws are unconstitutional. Indeed, even in such cases, we will construe a statute narrowly to avoid constitutional issues. Here, no court has found section 618 or its predecessors unconstitutional. Likewise, the courts have never held unconstitutional the Whistleblower Protection Act, which authorizes federal employees to disclose violations of law, gross mismanagement, the gross waste of funds, abuses of authority, and threats to public health or safety.

HHS and OLC first argue that section 618 is unconstitutional because it could force the disclosure of privileged, classified, or deliberative information. Constitutional concerns could be raised if Congress were to attempt to force the disclosure of classified or national security information, given the President's role as Commander in Chief. However, Mr. Foster was not asked for classified information.

Similarly, Mr. Foster was not asked for information subject to a claim of deliberative process privilege. To invoke the deliberative process privilege, the material must be both pre-decisional and deliberative, requirements that stem from the privilege's purpose of granting officials the freedom "to debate alternative approaches in private." The deliberative process privilege does not apply to the information requested of Mr. Foster because it was neither pre-decisional nor deliberative. The Administration had already formulated its Medicare prescription drug plan and had released it to the public and to the Congress in March 2003. Thus, the information requested from Mr. Foster in June through November 2003, which involved cost estimates and data formulated after the Administration's release of its Medicare plan, was not part of the deliberative process for the Administration's proposal. Furthermore, some of the information that Mr. Scully prohibited Mr. Foster from communicating to congressional offices, including the House Ways and Means Committee's request of June 13, 2003, for an analysis of the premium support provisions, was not preexisting data. Such information cannot be considered deliberative because the analysis was not preexisting nor was it tied to any decision-making process at CMS. Thus, HHS's and OLC's arguments that section 618 is unconstitutional because it could force the disclosure of classified or privileged information are inapplicable to the facts of this case.

HHS and OLC also argue that section 618 unconstitutionally limits the President's ability to supervise and control the work of subordinate officers and employees of the executive branch. In making this argument, HHS and OLC fail to balance the President's constitutional interest in managing the official communications of the executive branch with Congress's equally important need for information in order to carry out its legislative and oversight responsibilities. As OLC itself has recognized, Congress has "important oversight responsibilities and a corollary interest in receiving information [from federal employees] that enables it to carry out those responsibilities." As the Attorney General has pointed out, Congress's interest in obtaining information from the executive branch is strongest when "specific legislative proposals are in question."

HHS and OLC have overstated section 618's threat to the President's constitutional prerogatives. Executive agencies have the right to designate official spokesmen for the agency and institute policies and procedures for the release of agency information and positions to Congress and the public. Separation of powers concerns could be raised if Congress, by legislation, were to dictate to the executive branch who should communicate the official positions of the Administration, given the President's constitutional duty to "recommend to [Congress's] consideration such measures as he shall judge necessary and expedient."

Federal agencies and employees making separate legislative recommendations to Congress, without coordination with the President, could interfere with the President's constitutional duty, on behalf of the executive branch, to judge which proposals are "necessary and expedient" and make such recommendations to Congress. Designating an official agency or executive branch spokesman would be entirely appropriate in the case of legislative recommendations or a statement of the Administration's official positions. However, Mr. Foster was not asked for a CMS policy position or legislative recommendation, but rather for specific and limited technical assistance.

Thus, while certain applications of section 618 could raise constitutional concerns, application of section 618 to the facts of this case does not raise such concerns, because Mr. Foster was asked for estimates, technical assistance, and data, rather than any information which could be considered privileged. Furthermore, Congress was considering extensive changes to Medicare, and members requested cost estimates and analyses to inform debate on this legislation and to carry out the legislative powers vested by the Constitution. Indeed, if some of the Chief Actuary's estimates had been disclosed in a timely matter, Congress would have had better information on the magnitude of the legislation it was considering and its possible effect on the nation's fiscal health.

Mr. Scully's prohibitions, therefore, made HHS's appropriation, otherwise available for payment of his salary, unavailable for such purpose, because his actions are covered by section 618 of the Consolidated Appropriations Act of 2004 and section 620 of the Consolidated Appropriations Resolution of 2003. Because HHS was prohibited from paying Mr. Scully's salary after he barred Mr. Foster from communicating with Congress, HHS should consider such payments improper.

Therefore, we recommend that HHS seek to recover these payments. . . .

Sincerely yours,
Anthony H. Gamboa
General Counsel

Source: U.S. Congress. Government Accountability Office. "Department of Health and Human Services—Chief Actuary's Communications with Congress." B–302911, September 7, 2004. www.gao.gov/decisions/appro/302911.pdf (accessed February 6, 2005).

Secretary of State Powell on Genocide in Western Sudan

September 9, 2004

INTRODUCTION

A fast-spreading conflict in the Darfur region of western Sudan rose to the top of the world's diplomatic agenda in mid-2004, largely because of fears that hundreds of thousands of people might be killed. For months diplomats and lawyers debated whether to call the killings in Darfur "genocide"—a declaration of some legal significance because the post–World War II Genocide Convention required international action to stop cases of genocide. U.S. secretary of state Colin Powell on September 9 became the first major world leader to attach the genocide label to the Darfur conflict. Even so, the United States and other world powers hesitated to intervene directly beyond threatening the Khartoum government with unspecified penalties and providing food, shelter, and other humanitarian supplies to the multitude of people who had been displaced. The African Union sent 1,000 soldiers to Darfur to help contain the conflict, but a force of that size in a region the size of Texas had little power to deter violence. By year's end the United Nations was estimating that more than 2 million people had been affected by the fighting since early 2003.

The Darfur conflict was the second in a year to raise fears of a genocide in Africa and force a response by the international community. During the first half of 2003 United Nations officials and human rights activists warned of a potential genocide in the Ituri region of eastern Congo. Hundreds of people were killed there but a much broader loss of life was headed off by a quick military intervention headed by France. In both of these cases, the specter hanging over the world was that of the Rwanda genocide in 1994—a case in which some 800,000 people were slaughtered while leaders in foreign capitals failed to act. *(Rwanda genocide, Historic Documents of 1999, p. 860; Ituri conflict, Historic Documents of 2003, p. 288)*

The escalating conflict in Darfur came despite—and in some respects because of—what appeared to be the peaceful resolution of a civil war between Khartoum and rebels in the southern part of the country. That conflict had raged for more than two decades and resulted in the deaths of an estimated 2 million people but was in its concluding stages. The opposing sides signed a cease-fire in 2003 and agreed on a formal peace pact on December 31, 2004; that agreement was to be signed in January 2005. A major incentive for resolution of that fighting was a desire by both the government and rebels to expand production of oil, which had been discovered in southern Sudan in the 1990s. A fear that they would not share in the nation's new oil wealth was one of the motivating factors for the rebels in Darfur, who lived far from the oilfields. *(Southern Sudan conflict background, Historic Documents of 2003, p. 835)*

Background

Until the fighting began in March 2003, the Darfur region was barely known outside northern Africa. It became well-known worldwide only in early 2004 when UN officials, relief workers, and others began sounding the alarm about a potential tragedy there of immense proportions.

The Darfur region was composed of three provinces (northern, western, and southern Darfur) in far-western Sudan, lying along the border with Chad and the Central African Republic; the total population was estimated at 6 million. As in much of Africa, Darfur's people represent dozens of ethnic or cultural groups, with the principal division being between black Africans (many of whom were settled farmers) and Arabs (many of whom were nomadic herders of camels and cattle). Most Darfurians, both blacks and Arabs, were Sunni Muslims. Historically, the blacks exercised most of the political power in the region; even so, experts on the region said Darfurians tended to think of themselves as Sudanese rather than as members of a particular ethnic group.

The 1989 takeover of the national government in Khartoum by an Arab, Islamist faction shifted historical patterns, however, and reportedly emboldened Arab communities in Darfur and caused new resentments by black farmers. One root of the 2003–2004 conflict was the increased movement since the 1990s by Arab herders into lands previously occupied solely by black farmers. With their own homelands in northern Darfur subject to increasing desertification, the herders sought greener pasturelands for their camels and cattle. The black farmers, in turn, resented having their croplands trampled by the herders. This resentment was intensified by periodic raids in the area by Arab tribesmen, many of them reportedly armed by the Khartoum government.

With the pending resolution to the war in southern Sudan, some black Darfurians also feared they would see none of the wealth expected to be generated by increased oil exploration in that region. Early in 2003 a new rebel group, claiming to represent the blacks and calling itself the Sudanese Liberation Army (SLA), appeared on the scene in Darfur. The name caused some confusion because of its similarity to that of the long-standing rebel group in southern Sudan: the Sudan Peoples Liberation Army. According to some reports, the southern rebels provided weapons to the new group in Darfur. In March 2003 the new SLA group attacked government installations and issued a manifesto saying it was fighting Khartoum's policies of "marginalization, racial discrimination and exploitation that had disrupted the peaceful coexistence between the region's African and Arab communities." Another rebel group, called the Justice and Equality Movement, battled the SLA for a few weeks early in 2003; thousands fled their homes, some streaming into neighboring Chad but others simply escaping the fighting by moving elsewhere in Darfur. This initial conflict between the groups ended when they reached an accommodation in the face of retaliatory attacks by the government's military.

In April 2003 Sudan's president, Omar al-Bashir, declared that the government would "not negotiate" with the rebels in Darfur. Within weeks fighting between the rebels and government forces had escalated, forcing thousands more people from their homes.

Because the early stages of the conflict took place in remote regions, out of the sight of journalists and other observers, details remained hazy even more than a year later. Even so, some observers warned early on that the situation could become extremely serious. In a report issued in June 2003, for example, the International Crisis Group—a world affairs think tank headquartered in Brussels—warned: "There is credible potential for dramatic escalation in Darfur."

International concerns rose in November 2003 when fighting appeared to intensify and militias allied with the government began raiding refugee camps along the Chad-Sudan border. Often decked out in military uniforms and riding camels or horses, the militias were known as the *janjaweed,* a term historically used to describe bandits. Most of the refugees were in those camps because they had been driven from their homes by fighting between the militias and the rebels. The UN's Office for the Coordination of Humanitarian Assistance issued appeals for international aid but warned that the government was refusing access by aid workers to the hardest hit areas. On December 5, 2003, Jan Egeland, the UN's undersecretary general for humanitarian affairs and emergency relief, said the Darfur conflict "has quickly become one of the worst humanitarian crises in the world." At that point, UN officials estimated that more than 1 million people were in need of aid; about 600,000 of them had fled their homes, including about 100,000 who had taken refuge across the border in Chad. Any hope for a quick end to the conflict was crushed by the failure later in December of talks between the government and rebels.

More Warnings in 2004

As the fighting continued in Darfur during the early months of 2004, officials of UN relief agencies issued increasingly dire statements about the situation, along with appeals for food, water, and other aid. The United States in January sent its first mission to investigate the situation in Darfur; officials reported back to Washington that the government was to blame for much of the death and destruction. Amnesty International, the British-based human rights group, offered a similar conclusion in a February 3 report providing details of what it called "indiscriminate bombings, killings, torture, including rape of women and girls, arrests, abductions, and forced displacement" of civilians by the Sudanese army and the *janjaweed* militias. In many cases, the report said, government airplanes bombed villages repeatedly, then the *janjaweed* arrived and drove off the villagers, often killing the men and raping the women.

Sudan's president, Bashir, issued a statement February 9 claiming the government had "full control" of Darfur and promising to give international aid workers free access throughout the region for the first time. In response UN relief agencies stepped up deliveries of aid, both to refugees in eastern Chad and to displaced people who remained in Darfur. Despite Bashir's claim, the fighting continued in Darfur, and UN officials said aid convoys often were attacked by the *janjaweed,* who stole the supplies.

On March 19 the UN's chief aid coordinator for Sudan, Mukesh Kapila, became one of the first international officials to compare the situation in Darfur to the Rwandan genocide. "I was present in Rwanda at the time of the genocide, and I've seen many other situations around the world and I am totally shocked at what is going on in Darfur," he told the BBC. "This is ethnic cleansing, this is the world's greatest humanitarian crisis, and I don't know why the world isn't doing more about it." By that point UN agencies estimated that about 700,000 people had been displaced inside Darfur (most of them without access to aid), about 110,000 had fled into Chad, and about 10,000 had been killed.

The UN Security Council on April 2 issued the first of many statements during the year on Darfur, expressing concern about the humanitarian situation and calling for a cease-fire. The council acted after Egeland, the UN aid coordinator, described the complicity of government forces in what he called "ongoing massacres."

The level of international rhetoric was stepped up again on April 7, the tenth anniversary of the beginning of the Rwandan genocide. Commemorating that event, UN Secretary General Kofi Annan said reports from Darfur "leave me with a deep sense of foreboding. Whatever terms it uses to describe the situation, the international community cannot stand idle." President George W. Bush issued a written statement called on the Sudanese government to "immediately stop local militias from committing atrocities."

Despite these statements, the political obstacles to an aggressive international response to Darfur were made dramatically clear during the maneuvering over a resolution by the UN's Human Rights Commission. UN investigators in the region submitted a report in mid-April calling the killing of Darfurians a "war crime." The commission leadership, however, withheld that report from members debating what to say about Darfur. On April 23 the commission adopted a resolution expressing "solidarity" with Sudan but failing to detail the atrocities in Darfur. The New York-based group Human Rights released its own report on the same day; it described a "reign of terror" in Darfur and saying human rights violations there "may constitute war crimes and/or crimes against humanity."

A cease-fire signed by the government and the Darfur rebel groups on April 8 reduced the level of fighting but did not stop it. Journalists and other observers reported that the *janjaweed* militia continued to attack villages, and the rebels continued to respond with attacks on government-controlled areas.

Briefing the Security Council May 7 on his visit to Darfur the previous week, World Food Program director James T. Morris said: "It is hard to overstate the level of fear we witnessed. In fact, in all my travels as the head of the World Food Program I have never seen people who are as frightened as those displaced in Darfur." He said the Khartoum government had assigned *janjaweed* militia to "guard" displaced persons camps, "creating virtual prison camps surrounded by militias, who, on a daily basis, attack women and children in the camps or on their way to search for food, fuel, or water. It is hard to imagine a more cruel or frightening situation."

On May 17 the UN humanitarian affairs office upped to 2 million its estimate of the number of people affected by the Darfur crisis. About half of those were displaced within Sudan, about 150,000 had fled to Chad, and the rest remained at home but lacked adequate food, water, and other essentials, the UN said. The UN's estimate of the death toll had reached 30,000, but the Agency for International Development (AID) warned that more than 300,000 could die by year's end if the violence was not stopped.

Attacks against relief workers continued, including the June 4 abduction by the rebels of sixteen aid workers from five international organizations. The workers were released one day later, unharmed.

Diplomatic Pressure on Khartoum

International attention to Darfur had grown gradually during the first half of 2004 then escalated rapidly with the arrival in Sudan on June 30 of Annan and Powell, on separate but related missions. The two men met at the start of their visits, then traveled separately within Sudan and to neighboring Chad. Powell met with Bashir and other leaders in Khartoum and warned that the United States would seek UN Security Council action against Sudan if they did not stop the violence.

At the end of his trip, on July 3, Annan extracted from the Khartoum government a written promise to disarm the *janjaweed* militias, permit access by aid workers to all displaced people, and punish those responsible for human rights violations. Two days later, at Annan's urging, the African Union agreed to deploy 300 peacekeepers to Darfur and Chad to protect refugees and displaced people.

In its strongest statement yet on Darfur, the UN Security Council on July 7 called for international "sustained pressure" on the Sudan government to end the rights abuses and ease the plight of people in Darfur. The council acted after Annan, in a private briefing by satellite hook-up from Kenya, described the situation in Darfur as "totally intolerable." Despite this statement, journalists and UN officials said the situation continued to deteriorate. Especially worrisome, according to the UN, were reports that the Khartoum government was pressuring internally displaced people to return to their homes despite their fears of being attacked by the *janjaweed.* UN officials also said the militias appeared to be preventing people from escaping across the border into Chad.

In mid-July U.S. officials said Washington was preparing a resolution, for Security Council consideration, that would impose some sanctions on the *janjaweed,* including an international arms embargo. Apparently attempting to ward off such international pressure, President Bashir on July 24 said critics were "targeting the status of Islam in Sudan."

The Security Council on July 30 adopted its first formal resolution on the Darfur crisis, imposing an immediate arms embargo against the *janjaweed.* Resolution 1556 also threatened action against Khartoum if it did not disarm the militias within thirty days. However, opposition by China forced the United States to withdraw an explicit threat of sanctions and insert instead language that U.S. ambassador John C. Danforth said "means exactly the same thing." China and Pakistan abstained from even the watered-down version of the resolution, which passed 13–0.

Sudan's effort to portray U.S. pressure as being aimed at "Islam" appeared to have some success in the wake of the UN resolution. A spokesman for the Arab League denounced the United States and European nations for using Darfur as "a long lost pretext to put the [Sudan] government under the sword of international sanctions." The Sudanese government also appealed to other African nations for solidarity in the face of international pressure and appeared to win some sympathy.

Although it denounced the resolution, the Sudan government said it would comply with the demand for disarming the *janjaweed.* On August 5 Sudan's foreign minister, Mustafa Osman Ismail, signed an agreement with Jan Pronk, Annan's special envoy for Sudan, promising specific steps to disarm the *janjaweed* within a month. Bashir then announced he had ordered tribal leaders in Darfur to carry out the assignment.

Another potentially hopeful step came August 15, when 141 troops from Rwanda arrived in Darfur—the first contingent of the 300-man peacekeeping force the African Union had promised months earlier. The exact mission of the troops was unclear, however. Rwandan president Paul Kagame said the peacekeepers would stop violence against civilians, when they saw it. Sudan's government, however, said the foreign troops were authorized only to protect 80 observers who were monitoring the April 8 cease-fire and were not authorized to take action against the *janjaweed.* A contingent of 150 troops from Nigeria arrived in Darfur in late August.

The Security Council's thirty-day deadline for action by Khartoum expired August 31. The next day Annan gave the council a blistering written report saying the government had failed to comply. "Attacks against civilians are continuing and the vast majority of armed militias has not been disarmed," he said. "No concrete steps have been taken to bring to justice or even identify any of the militia leaders or perpetrators of these attacks, allowing the violations of human rights and the basic laws of war to continue in a climate of impunity." Sudan claimed it had arrested some *janjaweed,* Annan said, but in fact they appeared to be "common criminals."

Despite Annan's strong language, it had become clear that Washington's drive for sanctions against Khartoum had fizzled. China, which held veto power on the Security Council, remained adamantly opposed, as were the council's two member-nations with Islamic majorities, Algeria and Pakistan. China had direct commercial interests in Sudan; its state-owned oil company had contracts to produce oil there. As an alternative to sanctions, Annan asked the council to consider authorizing an expanded African Union force in Sudan, perhaps up to 3,000 troops—ten times the size of the current force.

Genocide or Not?

During the summer months senior State Department officials began suggesting that the attacks on civilians in Darfur amounted to genocide but refrained from calling it that specifically. The Genocide Convention broadly defined the term as an attempt to destroy a group of people "in whole or in part." One reason for the U.S. hesitation, according to news reports, was Washington's fear of upsetting progress in negotiations to end the longer conflict in southern Sudan. The Bush administration had made ending that war a major foreign policy priority and played a significant role in the negotiations since 2002.

Powell told the *New York Times* on June 11 that he was not yet prepared to call the Darfur crisis "genocide," but said "at least a million people" were in danger of dying without more aid. "And it won't make a whole lot of difference after the fact what you've called it," he said. The U.S. Congress had no such hesitations, however, and on July 22 both houses unanimously passed resolutions (S Con Res 133 and H Con Res 467) urging Bush to call the Darfur situation "by its rightful name—genocide."

European diplomats—often readier to intervene in international human rights cases than the Bush administration had been—were even more cautious than the United States about invoking the genocide term for the Darfur crisis. On August 9 a European Union fact-finding team deplored the "large-scale" violence there but refused to call it genocide. The European Parliament went a bit further, on September 16, adopting a resolution calling for action against those in Sudan who carried out war crimes and human rights violations "which can be construed as tantamount to genocide."

After reviewing reports from his own aides, Powell decided early in September to go ahead with a declaration of genocide in Darfur, reportedly in hopes that doing so would put enough pressure on the Khartoum government to keep its promises to rein in the *janjaweed.* Testifying before the Senate Foreign Relations Committee on September 9, Powell said that after reviewing all the evidence "we concluded—I concluded—that genocide has been commited in Darfur and that the government of Sudan and the *janjaweed* bear responsibility, and genocide may still be occurring." To confirm that finding, Powell called for a "full-blown and unfettered investigation" by the United Nations. Powell said he based his declaration on State Department interviews with 1,136 refugees, 61 percent of whom had witnessed the killing of a family member.

Powell defended the administration's response to the Darfur crisis, saying the United States had provided $211.3 million in food and other aid to the refugees and displaced people, had pressed both sides to halt the fighting, and had advocated sanctions against the Khartoum government at the UN Security Council. Powell also said "no new [U.S.] action is dictated" by the genocide determination. "We have been doing everything we can to get the Sudanese government to act responsibly," he said.

Powell's declaration represented the first time that the U.S. government had described a foreign crisis as genocide while it was occurring. President Bill Clinton referred to the 1994 killings in Rwanda as genocide four years afterwards; during that country's three-month rein of terror his administration refused to use the term, fearing that doing so would lead to pressure for a direct U.S. intervention. *(Clinton apology, Historic Documents of 1998, p. 159)*

Sudanese officials heatedly rejected Powell's characterization and insisted the government was attempting to calm the situation. Khartoum's chief negotiator in the Darfur crisis also said Powell was "sending a wrong signal" to the rebels, who he said would simply wait for more international pressure before reaching any agreement. Indeed, a round of peace talks collapsed on September 15.

Four days after Powell made his declaration, the UN's World Health Organization boosted its estimate of deaths resulting from the Darfur crisis to 50,000 and said 6,000 to 10,000 people were now dying each month. Most of the deaths resulted from starvation and disease in informal camps for the displaced, the organization's report said. UN agencies in mid-September estimated that about 1.45 million people remained internally displaced in nearly 150 camps in Sudan, and another 200,000 were refugees in UN camps in Chad.

World Response Still Hesitant

Armed with Powell's declaration, U.S. diplomats returned to the UN Security Council and worked to negotiate a new, stronger resolution putting pressure on Sudan. Once again, Washington was forced to water down its proposed language repeatedly. The final version, adopted September 18, again avoided use of the term "sanctions," but did threaten "additional measures" against the Khartoum government—including its oil industry—if it did not stop the *janjaweed* attacks on civilians. Washington had wanted the automatic imposition of sanctions but retreated in the face of opposition from China, Pakistan, and other members. Resolution 1564 established an international panel to determine whether genocide was occurring in Darfur, and it authorized a larger African Union force in Sudan, with greater powers than before to stop attacks on civilians. The council passed the resolution 11–0, with Algeria, China, Pakistan, and Russia abstaining. This was Russia's first formal abstention on the Darfur matter; Moscow was Sudan's largest arms supplier. The four abstaining countries said pressure on Sudan would be counterproductive, and they insisted the Khartoum government had taken steps to halt the fighting—a statement most U.S. and UN officials disputed.

Annan on October 7 appointed a commission to investigate the genocide charges. It was headed by Italian judge Antonio Cassase, who had been the first president of the International Criminal Tribunal for the former Yugoslavia. Cassase's panel began its work in November but had submitted no reports as of year's end. Several other UN experts made statements or issued reports in late 2004 that pointed to "war crimes" or "crimes against humanity" in the Darfur conflict. Among them was an October 19 report by Pamela Shifman, an adviser to the UN Children's Fund, who said every girl or woman she had spoken with during a visit to displaced persons camps in Darfur either had endured a sexual assault herself or knew someone who had.

Overnight on November 2 Sudanese army and police forcibly moved hundreds of displaced people from one camp in Darfur to another. Coupled with continuing violence by the *janjaweed,* this step heightened even further the international concerns about the safety of the estimated 1.5 million people in those camps. A week later government forces entered another camp and assaulted the residents, according to UN and other international personnel who attempted, but failed, to halt the attacks.

Citing the persistent violence, Jan Pronk, the UN's chief envoy for Sudan, on November 4 warned that the Darfur situation appeared to be deteriorating. "Darfur may easily enter a state of anarchy, a total collapse of law and order," he told the Security Council.

Under renewed diplomatic pressure, the Khartoum government and the Darfur rebels on November 9 signed what they called comprehensive agreements to end the nearly two years of fighting. The accords were signed in Abuja after talks mediated by the Nigerian government. Among other things, Sudan's government promised to ban military flights over rebel-held areas and to permit full access by relief organizations to all displaced persons camps; the rebels pledged to halt attacks on government forces.

To enforce these agreements, and previous ones that had failed, the African Union continued to send peacekeeping troops to Darfur. In November the U.S. and German military helped airlift hundreds of troops from Nigeria and Rwanda. By year's end the African peacekeeping presence stood at 1,056—about one-third of the planned total.

In mid-November the UN Security Council held one of its rare official meetings outside of New York, traveling to Nairobi, Kenya, for a series of sessions dealing with both major conflicts in Sudan—the Darfur crisis and the longer-running war in southern Sudan. The council focused most of its attention on the latter war, for which a final peace agreement was pending. The council on November 19 adopted Resolution 1574, calling for an end to both conflicts. For the third time in four months the council demanded a halt to the violence in Darfur and threatened "appropriate action against any party failing to fulfill its commitments."

As with previous Security Council resolutions, the warning—and the peace agreements—appeared to have little effect on the ground. On November 22 the two Darfur rebel groups attacked towns held by the government, and the army responded with air strikes against rebel positions and a major build-up of forces in the region. Both sides said they were no longer bound by the cease-fire agreements they had signed less than two weeks earlier. UN officials and aid agencies criticized the rebels for initiating this round of fighting. They also warned that the rebels attacks had undermined international support for their cause—and possibly blocked any chance for renewed pressure on the Khartoum government. The upsurge in violence also interrupted aid supplies to thousands of displaced people in their camps.

In an attempt to halt the escalation in fighting, the African Union set a December 18 deadline for each side to stop its attacks on the other. Both sides pulled back some of their forces and agreed to observe yet another cease-fire. Even so, the rebels and government on December 21 suspended peace talks then being held in Nigeria and promised to resume them in January 2005.

Appearing to be on the verge of despair, Annan the next day said he was calling for a "real reassessment" of the UN's entire approach to the Darfur crisis. "Quite frankly, our approach is not working" he told reporters. "What other measures can we take to hold some of the individuals who are responsible accountable, hold them individually accountable, for us to be able to move forward?" he added. Annan noted that the government had not complied with Security Council demands to disarm the *janjaweed* militias, and rebel leaders had been unwilling—or unable—to restrain their forces from attacking government-held areas.

In the meantime, the displaced people in Darfur continued to suffer. Rebel attacks forced one major aid agency—Save the Children-UK—to withdraw all its 350 relief workers from the region; that agency, which had been aiding about 250,000 people, said four of its workers had been killed by gunfire and land mines since October. On December 28 the World Food Program said it was forced to suspend its food rations to about 260,000 people because rebels had attacked aid convoys, in some cases stealing food intended for the displaced.

At year's end UN agencies estimated that 2.2 million people—more than one-third of the region's total population—were affected by the violence in Darfur. That included 1.7 million who had been forced from their homes but remained in Darfur; most were in displaced persons camps, but tens of thousands were thought to be hiding in remote areas. Another 200,000 were in refugee camps in Chad. An enormous relief effort by UN and other international aid agencies had prevented the massive death toll, exceeding 300,000, predicted earlier in the year by U.S. officials. Even so, the official estimates of deaths from violence, disease, and malnutrition exceeded 70,000. UN agencies estimated that another 100,000 were in "grave danger" unless the fighting stopped and longer-term aid and reconstruction could begin. Aid officials warned of another dangerous, long-term cycle. Because they could not plant crops or raise cattle, the hundreds of thousands of people driven from their homes would become dependent on international aid, which in turn depended on continued international concern about the situation in Darfur, which was likely to dwindle once the fighting stopped.

Following are excerpts from testimony September 9, 2004, by Secretary of State Colin Powell to the Senate Foreign Relations Committee in which he described the violence against civilians in the Darfur regions of western Sudan as "genocide" and called for a halt to the fighting there.

"The Crisis in Darfur"

Mr. Chairman, members of the committee, thank you for the opportunity to testify on the situation in Darfur. Let me start by reviewing a little history.

The violence in Darfur has complex roots in traditional conflicts between Arab nomadic herders and African farmers. The violence intensified during 2003 when two groups—the Sudan Liberation Movement and the Justice and Equality Movement—declared open rebellion against the Government of Sudan because they feared being on the outside of the power and wealth-sharing agreements in the north-south negotiations. Khartoum reacted aggressively, intensifying support for Arab militias, the so-called *jinjaweid.* The Government of Sudan supported the *jinjaweid* directly and indirectly, as they carried out a scorched-earth policy towards the rebels and the African civilian population.

Mr. Chairman, the United States exerted strong leadership to focus international attention on this unfolding tragedy. We first took the issue of Sudan to the United Nations (UN) Security Council last fall. President Bush was the first head of state to condemn publicly the Government of Sudan and to urge the international community to intensify efforts to end the violence. In April of this year, the United States brokered a ceasefire between the Government of Sudan and the rebels, and then took the lead to get the African Union (AU) to monitor that ceasefire.

As some of you are aware, I traveled to the Sudan in midsummer and made a point of visiting Darfur. It was about the same time that Congressman [Frank] Wolf [R-Va.] and Senator [Sam] Brownback [R-Kan.] were there, as well as [UN] Secretary General Kofi Annan. In fact, the secretary general and I were able to meet and exchange notes. We made sure that our message to the Sudanese government was consistent.

Senator Brownback can back me up when I say that all of us saw the suffering that the people of Darfur are having to endure. And Senator [John] Corzine [D-N.J.] was just in Darfur and can vouch for the fact that atrocities are still occurring. All of us met with people who had been driven from their homes—indeed many having seen their homes and all their worldly possessions destroyed or confiscated before their eyes—by the terrible violence that is occurring in Darfur.

During my visit, humanitarian workers from my own agency—USAID [U.S. Agency for International Development]—and from other non-governmental organizations (NGOs), told me how they are struggling to bring food, shelter, and medicines to those so desperately in need—a population of well over one million.

In my midsummer meetings with the Government of Sudan, we presented them with the stark facts of what we knew about what is happening in Darfur from the destruction of villages, to the raping and the killing, to the obstacles that impeded relief efforts. Secretary General Annan and I obtained from the Government of Sudan what they said would be firm commitments to take steps, and to take steps immediately, that would remove these obstacles, help bring the violence to an end, and do it in a way that we could monitor their performance.

There have been some positive developments since my visit, and since the visit of Senator Brownback, Congressman Wolf, and the Secretary General.

The Sudanese have met some of our benchmarks such as engaging in political talks with the rebels and supporting the deployment of observers and troops from the AU to monitor the ceasefire between Khartoum and the rebels. Some improvements in humanitarian access have also occurred though the government continues to throw obstacles in the way of the fullest provision of assistance.

The AU Ceasefire Commission has also been set up and is working to monitor more effectively what is actually happening in Darfur. The general who is in charge of that mission, a Nigerian general by the name of Okonkwo, is somebody that we know well. He is the same Nigerian general who went into Liberia last year and helped stabilize the situation there.

The AU's mission will help to restore sufficient security so that these dislocated, starving, hounded people can at least avail themselves of the humanitarian assistance that is available. But what is really needed is enough security so that they can go home. And what is really needed is for the *jinjaweid* militias to cease and desist their murderous raids against these people—and for the Government in Khartoum to stop being complicit in such raids. Khartoum has made no meaningful progress in substantially improving the overall security environment by disarming the *jinjaweid* militias or arresting its leaders.

So we are continuing to press that Government and we continue to monitor them. We continue to make sure that we are not just left with promises instead of actual action and performance on the ground. Because it is absolutely clear that as we approach the end of the rainy season, the situation on the ground must change, and it must change quickly. There are too many tens upon tens of thousands of human beings who are at risk. Some of them have already been consigned to death because of the circumstances they are living in now. They will not make it through the end of the year. Poor security, inadequate capacity, and heavy rains (which will not diminish until late September) continue to hamper the relief effort.

The UN estimates there are 1,227,000 Internally Displaced Persons (IDPs) in Darfur. In July, almost 950,000 IDPs received some form of food assistance. About 200,000 Sudanese refugees are being assisted by UNHCR and partner organizations in Chad. The World Food Program (WFP) expects two million IDPs will need food aid by October.

U.S. Government provision of aid to the Darfur crisis in Sudan and Chad totaled $211.3 million as of September 2, 2004. This includes $112.9 million in food assistance, $50.2 million in non-food assistance, and $36.4 million for refugees in Chad, $5 million for refugee programs in Darfur, and $6.8 million for the African Union mission. . . .

I am pleased to announce, Mr. Chairman, that the State Department has identified $20.5 million in FY04 funds for initial support of this expanded mission. We look forward to consulting with the Congress on meeting additional needs.

As you know, as we watched through the month of July, we felt more pressure was required. So we went to the UN and asked for a resolution. We got it on July 30.

Resolution 1556 demands that the Government of Sudan take action to disarm the *jinjaweid* militia and bring *jinjaweid* leaders to justice. It warns Khartoum that the Security Council will take further actions and measures—UN-speak for sanctions—if Sudan fails to comply. It urges the warring parties to conclude a political agreement without delay and it commits all states to target sanctions against the *jinjaweid* militias and those who aid and abet them as well as others who may share responsibility for this tragic situation. Too many lives have already been lost. We cannot lose any more time. We in the international community must intensify our efforts to help those imperiled by violence, starvation and disease in Darfur.

But the Government of Sudan bears the greatest responsibility to face up to this catastrophe, rein in those who are committing these atrocities, and save the lives of its own citizens. At the same time, however, the rebels have not fully respected the ceasefire. We are disturbed at reports of rebel kidnappings of relief workers. We have emphasized to the rebels that they must allow unrestricted access of humanitarian relief workers and supplies and cooperate fully, including with the AU monitoring mission.

We are pleased that the Government of Sudan and the rebels are currently engaged in talks in Abuja, hosted by the AU. These talks are aimed at bringing about a political settlement in Darfur. The two sides have agreed on a protocol to facilitate delivery of much-needed humanitarian assistance to rebel-held areas, and are now engaged in discussions of a protocol on security issues. We are urging both sides to intensify negotiations in order to reach a political settlement.

At midsummer, I told [senior Sudanese officials] that the United States wants to see a united, prosperous, democratic Sudan. I told them that to that end we are fully prepared to work with them. I reminded them that we had reached an historic agreement on June 5—an agreement between the Government of Sudan and the Sudan

People's Liberation Movement (SPLM). That agreement covered all the outstanding issues in the north-south process. . . .

President [Omar el-] Bashir has repeatedly pledged to work for peace, and he pledged that again when we met in midsummer. But President Bush, this Congress, Secretary General Annan and the international community want more than promises. We want to see dramatic improvements on the ground right now. Indeed, we wanted to see them yesterday.

In the meantime, we are doing all that we can. We are working with the international community to make sure that all of those nations who have made pledges of financial assistance meet those pledges. In fact, the estimated needs have grown and the donor community needs to dig deeper. America has been in the forefront of providing assistance to the suffering people of Darfur and will remain in the forefront. But it is time for the entire international community to increase their assistance. The U.S. has pledged $299 million in humanitarian aid through FY05, and $11.8 million to the AU mission, and we are well on the way to exceeding these pledges.

[Secretary General] Annan's August 30 report called for an expanded AU mission in Darfur to monitor commitments of the parties more effectively, thereby enhancing security and facilitating the delivery of humanitarian assistance. The report also highlighted Khartoum's failure to rein in and disarm the *jinjaweid* militia, and noted that the Sudanese military continued to take part in attacks on civilians, including aerial bombardment and helicopter strikes.

We have begun consultation in New York on a new resolution that calls for Khartoum to cooperate fully with an expanded AU force and for cessation of Sudanese military flights over the Darfur region. It also provides for international overflights to monitor the situation in Darfur and requires the Security Council to review the record of Khartoum's compliance to determine if sanctions, including on the Sudanese petroleum sector, should be imposed. The resolution also urges the Government of Sudan and the SPLM to conclude negotiations on a comprehensive peace accord.

And finally there is the matter of whether or not what is happening in Darfur is genocide.

Since the U.S. became aware of atrocities occurring in Sudan, we have been reviewing the Genocide Convention and the obligations it places on the Government of Sudan.

In July, we launched a limited investigation by sending a team to refugee camps in Chad. They worked closely with the American Bar Association and the Coalition for International Justice and were able to interview 1,136 of the 2.2 million people the UN estimates have been affected by this horrible violence. Those interviews indicated:

- A consistent and widespread pattern of atrocities (killings, rapes, burning of villages) committed by *jinjaweid* and government forces against non-Arab villagers;
- Three-fourths (74%) of those interviewed reported that the Sudanese military forces were involved in the attacks;
- Villages often experienced multiple attacks over a prolonged period before they were destroyed by burning, shelling or bombing, making it impossible for villagers to return.

When we reviewed the evidence compiled by our team, along with other information available to the State Department, we concluded—I concluded—that genocide has been committed in Darfur and that the Government of Sudan and the *jinjaweid* bear responsibility—and genocide may still be occurring. Mr. Chairman, we are making copies of the evidence our team compiled available to this committee today.

We believe in order to confirm the true nature, scope and totality of the crimes our evidence reveals, a full-blown and unfettered investigation needs to occur. Sudan is a contracting party to the Genocide Convention and is obliged under the Convention to prevent and to punish acts of genocide. To us, at this time, it appears that Sudan has failed to do so.

Article VIII of the Genocide Convention provides that Contracting Parties "may call upon the competent organs of the United Nations to take such action under the Charter of the United Nations as they consider appropriate for the prevention and suppression of acts of genocide or any of the other acts enumerated in Article III."

Today, the U.S. is calling on the UN to initiate a full investigation. To this end, the U.S. will propose that the next UN Security Council Resolution on Sudan request a UN investigation into all violations of international humanitarian law and human rights law that have occurred in Darfur, with a view to ensuring accountability.

Mr. Chairman, as I said the evidence leads us to the conclusion that genocide has occurred and may still be occurring in Darfur. We believe the evidence corroborates the specific intent of the perpetrators to destroy "a group in whole or in part". This intent may be inferred from their deliberate conduct. We believe other elements of the convention have been met as well.

Under the 1948 Convention on the Prevention and Punishment of the Crime of Genocide, to which both the United States and Sudan are parties, genocide occurs when the following three criteria are met:

- Specified acts are committed:
  a) killing;
  b) causing serious bodily or mental harm;
  c) deliberately inflicting conditions of life calculated to bring about physical destruction of a group in whole or in part;
  d) imposing measures to prevent births; or
  e) forcibly transferring children to another group;
- These acts are committed against members of a national, ethnic, racial or religious group; and
- They are committed "with intent to destroy, in whole or in part, [the group] as such".

The totality of the evidence from the interviews we conducted in July and August, and from the other sources available to us, shows that:

- The *jinjaweid* and Sudanese military forces have committed large-scale acts of violence, including murders, rape and physical assaults on non-Arab individuals;
- The *jinjaweid* and Sudanese military forces destroyed villages, foodstuffs, and other means of survival;
- The Sudan Government and its military forces obstructed food, water, medicine, and other humanitarian aid from reaching affected populations, thereby leading to further deaths and suffering; and
- Despite having been put on notice multiple times, Khartoum has failed to stop the violence.

Mr. Chairman, some seem to have been waiting for this determination of genocide to take action. In fact, however, no new action is dictated by this determination. We have been doing everything we can to get the Sudanese government to act responsibly. So let us not be preoccupied with this designation of genocide. These people are in desperate need and we must help them. Call it a civil war. Call it ethnic cleansing. Call it genocide. Call it "none of the above." The reality is the same: there are people in Darfur who desperately need our help.

I expect that the government in Khartoum will reject our conclusion of genocide anyway. Moreover, at this point genocide is our judgment and not the judgment of the International Community. Before the Government of Sudan is taken to the bar of international justice, let me point out that there is a simple way for Khartoum to avoid such wholesale condemnation. That way is to take action.

The government in Khartoum should end the attacks, ensure its people—all of its people—are secure, hold to account those who are responsible for past atrocities, and ensure that current negotiations are successfully concluded. That is the only way to peace and prosperity for this war-ravaged land.

Specifically, Mr. Chairman, the most practical contribution we can make to the security of Darfur in the short-term is to increase the number of African Union monitors. That will require the cooperation of the Government of Sudan.

In the intermediate and long term, the security of Darfur can be best advanced by a political settlement at Abuja and by the successful conclusion of the peace negotiations between the SPLM and the Government of Sudan.

Source: U.S. Congress. Senate. Senate Foreign Relations Committee. "The Crisis in Darfur." Prepared testimony of Secretary of State Colin L. Powell for a hearing by the Senate Foreign Relations Committee. September 9, 2004. www.state.gov/secretary/rm/36032.htm (accessed December 23, 2004).

Presidential Commission on the Need for Ocean Protection

September 20, 2004

INTRODUCTION

Pollution and overfishing were endangering U.S. coastal waters and the oceans and needed to be confronted urgently, a presidential commission reported September 20, 2004. The commission offered more than 200 recommendations for new policies and bureaucratic fixes to slow the damage to oceans.

President George W. Bush responded to the commission's report on December 17 by embracing many of its least controversial recommendations but rejecting or ignoring others of greater substance, notably an appeal for a $4 billion trust fund to pay for ocean-protection initiatives. Bush also appointed a new White House committee to review the issues raised by the commission. That committee was expected to make its own recommendations in 2005—in effect postponing action on many items the commission had considered urgent.

The report was the second major one in a year by U.S. experts to document long-term damage to the oceans. A committee sponsored by the Pew Charitable Trusts and chaired by former White House chief of staff Leon Panetta offered similar findings, but in June 2003 it put forward more far-reaching policy recommendations. Many observers said it was striking that the two reports—the Pew report written primarily by environmentalists and the government report written primarily by business executives and retired military officers—came to similar conclusions about the dire shape of the oceans.

The government itself had not conducted a full-length study of the human impact on the oceans since 1969, when a panel made recommendations that led in the 1970s to enactment of the Coastal Zone Management Act and creation of the National Oceanic and Atmospheric Administration.

Commission Report

Bush and the congressional leadership appointed the commission in 2001 in response to legislation passed by Congress the previous year. The panel was headed by retired admiral James Watkins, who had served as energy secretary under Bush's father, President George H. W. Bush (1989–1993). The fifteen other members, most of them Republicans, included academic experts and executives of oil and shipping companies but no representatives from environmental groups or the commercial and sport-fishing industries.

The panel issued a preliminary version of its report on April 20 then took comments from the public, special interest groups, governors of states, and tribal councils representing the country's native Americans. The final version released September 20 reflected many of the comments, notably a call by governors to place more emphasis on the role of states in helping set ocean policy.

The panel's 400-page report painted a generally gloomy picture about the state of U.S. coastal waters, which were defined to include the Great Lakes and coastal estuaries as well as the Gulf of Mexico and the three major oceans bordering U.S. territory: the Arctic, Atlantic, and Pacific. In general, the panel said the principal threats to the oceans were pollution and excessive development, which damaged estuaries and wetland, and overfishing, which threatened to wipe out dwindling stocks of most commercially important ocean fish. The panel also devoted much of its report to what it described as the bureaucratic gridlock among the federal, state, and local government agencies that shared responsibility for the use and protection of coastal waters.

The oceans and coastal waters were in danger of being "loved to death" by Americans, the panel said. Homes, shopping malls, and industrial plants were crowding the shorelines and being built on former wetlands, causing pollution that ran into rivers and eventually into estuaries and the oceans. "Our failure to properly manage the human activities that affect the nation's oceans, coasts, and Great Lakes is compromising their ecological integrity, diminishing our ability to fully realize their potential, costing us jobs and revenue, threatening human health, and putting our future at risk," the commission said.

The panel proposed new restrictions on runoff pollution—much of it from agricultural fertilizers and pesticides—that threatened estuaries and coastal waters. As examples, the commission pointed to the Chesapeake Bay where pollution had severely damaged once-rich blue crab and oyster fisheries. Another example was the annual summer-time "dead zone" the size of Connecticut in the Gulf of Mexico, where the Mississippi River dumped tons of nitrogen-rich fertilizer runoff that depleted oxygen in the water, killing much of the fish and plant life.

The commission cited scientific reports showing that many of the commercially valuable fish species in ocean waters had been harvested almost to the point of extinction. A 2003 Canadian study published in the scientific journal *Nature,* for example, found a 90 percent decline in the supply of cod, swordfish, tuna, and other large fish at the top of the oceanic food chain.

The panel offered several recommendations to aid in preserving the remaining fish stocks. The most controversial was a proposed shift in emphasis by the regional fisheries management councils, which set limits on catches by commercial fishing boats. These limits should be determined by scientific panels using the latest evidence about the health and size of fish stocks, the panel said, and fishermen and processors should not be allowed to serve on the councils. Once overall limits were set, the management councils would then allocate quotas among regional fishing interests.

The panel also proposed federal regulation and taxation of the hundreds of fish farms that had sprung up in coastal waters. These farms, many of which posed environmental hazards, were governed by a "confusing, inconsistent array of state and federal regulations" that should be consolidated under the National Oceanic and Atmospheric Administration (NOAA), the panel said.

Much of the commission's report dealt with ways to streamline the government's bureaucracy that handled policies and regulations related to the oceans. The panel noted that fifteen U.S. agencies shared responsibility for administering 140 federal laws dealing with ocean policy. Watkins called these overlapping jurisdictions a "Byzantine patchwork." States had their own agencies, laws, and regulations dealing with issues within their borders and three-mile coastal limits. The commission's principal recommendation for streamlining this bureaucratic stew was the creation of a National Ocean Council—similar in some respects to the National Security Council—which would bring together representatives from all affected cabinet departments and would be chaired by an assistant to the president with broad authority to coordinate federal policy on the oceans.

The panel also called for numerous changes in the operations of NOAA—described in the report as "the nation's primary ocean agency." For starters, the panel said Congress should pass legislation formally creating and giving an "ecosystem-based" mandate to NOAA, which had existed within the Commerce Department for nearly three decades solely under the authority of a presidential executive order. Ultimately, the panel said the government should consolidate all federal agencies with responsibilities for protecting natural resources—such as NOAA, the Environmental Protection Agency, parts of the Interior Department, the Forest Service, and the Fish and Wildlife Service. The panel did not formally make such a recommendation, however; Watkins said creating a Department of Natural Resources "is probably politically impossible today."

U.S. scientific research on the oceans should be doubled from the existing level of about $650 million annually, the commission said. It put the total price tag on its recommendations at $1.3 billion in the first year, $2.4 billion in the second year, and $3.2 billion in the third year. To pay that cost, the commission recommended placing into an Ocean Policy Trust Fund a total of $4 billion, over several years, from $5 billion in annual federal revenues from offshore drilling for oil and natural gas. The panel said the new fund would be comparable to the national highway trust fund, which used gas tax revenues to pay for highway maintenance and construction.

Commission members acknowledged that this recommendation would be controversial because members of Congress tended to view drilling revenues as a slush fund for projects benefiting their districts and states. "Will this be a tough sell?" Watson asked rhetorically. "You better believe it, but we're going to go for it."

In conjunction with its recommendations on bureaucracy and financing, the commission called for a fundamental shift in the government's attitude toward ocean resources. Policies and regulations should be based on their impact on entire ecosystems, the panel said, rather than narrower considerations such as political boundaries.

Reaction

Most environmental groups offered cautious praise for the report, saying that it drew high-level attention to important problems and offered some important recommendations. Several leading environmentalists criticized specific aspects of the report, however, notably the proposal that an ocean-protection trust fund be financed with revenue from offshore oil and gas leases. Such an approach might simply encourage more offshore drilling, said Richard Charter of Environmental Defense. Other environmentalists also were unhappy that the panel did not press harder for creation of marine protection areas—similar to wildlife refugees, where fish populations would be protected and given a chance to recover.

Industry representatives also generally praised the report, saying it struck a "balance" between environmental concerns and economic needs. One of the industries most affected by any changes in ocean policy would be commercial fishing, and its trade association, the National Fisheries Institute, lauded the overall tone of the report. "We are genuinely pleased that the commission recognizes that fishing is not the only human impact on our oceans," institute spokesman Linda Candler told the *New York Times.*

Legislation—called "Oceans 21"—to implement many of the commission's recommendations was introduced in both chambers of Congress and gained bipartisan support from across the political spectrum. The only formal action came in September when the Senate Commerce Committee approved a bill (S 2647) establishing a national oceans policy and endorsing some of the commissions' recommendations, including giving NOAA legal status. That bill did not reach the Senate floor, however, and comparable legislation in the House was stalled in committee.

Bush Response

The 2000 law that created the commission also required the president to file a formal response within ninety days of publication of the panel's final report. The White House beat that deadline by three days, issuing on December 17 an executive order and a thirty-seven-page document called the "U.S. Ocean Action Plan."

The executive order created a Committee on Ocean Policy, located within the White House Council on Environmental Quality, to coordinate government policy on matters related to the oceans. Bush's order offered few details about what the committee's responsibilities would be beyond a general mandate to "provide advice on establishment or implementation of policies concerning ocean-related matters." Bush also did not give the committee the bureaucratic clout the Oceans Commission had suggested was needed for the National Ocean Council it had proposed.

Watkins met with Bush at the White House when the president signed the order and then issued a noncommittal statement calling the move a "promising first step." Watkins said he and fellow commissioners would need more time to study the White House action plan. Among other things, that plan did not embrace the commission's call for creating a trust fund to pay for ocean science programs.

Environmental advocates, who had frequently clashed with the Bush administration, also offered a generally tepid response to the White House moves. Sarah Chasis, director of the coastal and water program at the Natural Resources Defense Council, praised Bush's creation of the new committee as "a good idea" but expressed disappointment that the president had not established a "clear mandate" for it. She noted, for example, that Bush's executive order did not explicitly direct the committee to work on implementing the proposals of the Ocean Commission.

Law of the Sea Treaty

After years of negotiation, the United Nations in 1982 completed the first-ever international treaty, the Convention on the Law of the Sea, governing the full range of legal issues on international ocean waters and sea beds, including commercial fishing, navigation, pollution control, and sea bed mining. The Reagan and first Bush administrations refused to sign the treaty, however, arguing that it did not guarantee adequate U.S. access to minerals and other resources in deep sea beds in international waters. A compromise to meet the objections of the United States and several other industrialized countries was reached in 1994, and the Clinton administration signed the treaty. *(Background, Historic Documents of 1982, p. 345)*

President Bill Clinton (1993–2001) never pressed the Senate for approval of the treaty, however; neither did George W. Bush during the early stages of his presidency. In 2003 a coalition of business, environmental, and defense-related groups began lobbying on behalf of the treaty and won broad support for it in the Senate.

The Foreign Relations Committee approved the treaty unanimously on February 25, 2004, and strongly urged the full Senate to support it. At that point the treaty came under renewed attack from conservatives who had opposed it ever since 1982. A typical objection came from conservative activist Phyllis Schlafly, head of the Eagle Forum, who called the treaty a "giant giveaway of American wealth, sovereignty, resources needed to maintain our economy, [and] capacity to defend ourselves.

The chairman of the Foreign Relations Committee, Sen. Richard Lugar, R-Ind., sought to counter the opposition by saying the treaty protected U.S. interests and posed none of the dangers his fellow conservatives claimed. The Bush administration expressed rhetorical support for the treaty but did not press for action, and so it never reached the Senate floor. Once the treaty won the endorsement of the Oceans Commission, the White House said Bush would ask the Senate to approve it in 2005.

Following are excerpts from the executive summary of An Ocean Blueprint for the 21st Century, *issued September 20, 2004, by the U.S. Commission on Ocean Policy.*

An Ocean Blueprint for the 21st Century

Executive Summary

Overview

America is a nation intrinsically connected to and immensely reliant on the ocean. All citizens—whether they reside in the country's farmlands or mountains, in its cities or along the coast—affect and are affected by the sea. Our grocery stores and restaurants are stocked with seafood and our docks are bustling with seaborne cargo. Millions of visitors annually flock to the nation's shores, creating jobs and contributing substantially to the U.S. economy through one of the country's largest and most rapidly growing economic sectors: tourism and recreation.

The offshore ocean area under U.S. jurisdiction is larger than its total land mass, providing a vast expanse for commerce, trade, energy and mineral resources, and a buffer for security. Born of the sea are clouds that bring life-sustaining water to our fields and aquifers, and drifting microscopic plants that generate much of the oxygen we breathe. Energy from beneath the seabed helps fuel our economy and sustain our high quality of life. The oceans host great biological diversity with vast medical potential and are a frontier for exciting exploration and effective education. The importance of our oceans, coasts, and Great Lakes cannot be overstated; they are critical to the very existence and well-being of the nation and its people. Yet, as the 21st century dawns it is clear that these invaluable and life-sustaining assets are vulnerable to the activities of humans.

Human ingenuity and ever-improving technologies have enabled us to exploit—and significantly alter—the ocean's bounty to meet society's escalating needs. Pollution runs off the land, degrading coastal waters and harming marine life. Fish populations are declining and some of our ocean's most majestic creatures have nearly disappeared. Along our coasts, habitats that are essential to fish and wildlife and provide valuable services to humanity continue to suffer significant losses. Non-native species are being introduced, both intentionally and accidentally, into distant areas, and the results are often damaging and costly. With these impacts come significant economic costs, risks to human health, and ecological consequences that we are only beginning to comprehend.

Yet all is not lost. This is a moment of unprecedented opportunity. Today, as never before, we recognize the links among the land, air, oceans, and human activities. We have access to advanced technology and timely information on a wide variety of scales. We recognize the detrimental impacts wrought by human influences. The time has come for us to alter our course and set sail for a new vision for America, one in which the oceans, coasts, and Great Lakes are healthy and productive, and our use of their resources is both profitable and sustainable.

It has been thirty-five years since this nation's management of the oceans, coasts, and Great Lakes was comprehensively reviewed. In that time, significant changes have occurred in how we use marine assets and in our understanding of the consequences of our actions. This report from the U.S. Commission on Ocean Policy provides a blueprint for change in the 21st century, with recommendations for creation of an effective national ocean policy that ensures sustainable use and protection of our oceans, coasts, and Great Lakes for today and far into the future.

The Value of the Oceans and Coasts

America's oceans, coasts, and Great Lakes provide tremendous value to our economy. Based on estimates in 2000, ocean-related activities directly contributed more than $117 billion to American prosperity and supported well over two million jobs. By including coastal activities, the numbers become even more impressive; more than $1 trillion, or one-tenth of the nation's annual gross domestic product, is generated within the relatively narrow strip of land immediately adjacent to the coast that we call the nearshore zone. When the economies throughout coastal watershed counties are considered, the contribution swells to over $4.5 trillion, fully half of the nation's gross domestic product, accounting for some 60 million jobs. . . .

Trouble in Paradise

Unfortunately, our use and enjoyment of the ocean and its resources have come with costs, and we are only now discovering the full extent of the consequences of our actions. In 2001, 23 percent of the nation's estuarine areas were considered impaired for swimming, fishing, or supporting marine species. In 2003, about 18,000 days of beach closings and advisories were issued across the nation, most due to the presence of bacteria associated with fecal contamination. Across the globe, marine toxins afflict more than 90,000 people annually and are responsible for an estimated 62 percent of all seafood-related illnesses. Harmful algal blooms appear to be occurring more frequently in our coastal waters and non-native species are increasingly invading marine ecosystems. Experts estimate that 25 to 30 percent of the world's major fish stocks are overexploited, and many U.S. fisheries are experiencing serious difficulties. Since the Pilgrims first arrived at Plymouth Rock, over half of our fresh and saltwater wetlands—more than 110 million acres—have been lost.

Coastal waters are one of the nation's greatest assets, yet they are being bombarded with pollutants from a variety of sources. While progress has been made in reducing point sources of pollution, nonpoint source pollution has increased and is the primary cause of nutrient enrichment, hypoxia, harmful algal blooms, toxic contamination, and other problems that plague coastal waters. Nonpoint source pollution occurs when rainfall and snowmelt wash pollutants such as fertilizers, pesticides, bacteria, viruses, pet waste, sediments, oil, chemicals, and litter into our rivers and coastal waters. Other pollutants, such as mercury and some organic chemicals, can be carried vast distances through the atmosphere before settling into ocean waters.

Our failure to properly manage the human activities that affect the nation's oceans, coasts, and Great Lakes is compromising their ecological integrity, diminishing our ability to fully realize their potential, costing us jobs and revenue, threatening human health, and putting our future at risk. . . .

A Vision and Strategy for the 21st Century and Beyond

The Commission began by envisioning a desirable future. In this future, the oceans, coasts, and Great Lakes are clean, safe, prospering, and sustainably managed. They contribute significantly to the economy, supporting multiple, beneficial uses such as food production, development of energy and mineral resources, recreation and tourism, transportation of goods and people, and the discovery of novel medicines, while preserving a high level of biodiversity and a wide range of critical natural habitats.

In this future, the coasts are attractive places to live, work, and play, with clean water and beaches, easy public access, sustainable and strong economies, safe bustling harbors and ports, adequate roads and services, and special protection for sensitive habitats and threatened species. Beach closings, toxic algal blooms, proliferation of invasive species, and vanishing native species are rare. Better land-use planning and improved predictions of severe weather and other natural hazards save lives and money.

In this future, the management of our impacts on the oceans, coasts, and Great Lakes has also changed. Management boundaries correspond with ecosystem regions, and policies consider interactions among all ecosystem components. In the face of scientific uncertainty, managers balance competing considerations and proceed with caution. Ocean governance is effective, participatory, and well coordinated among government agencies, the private sector, and the public.

The Commission envisions a time when the importance of reliable data and sound science is widely recognized and strong support is provided for physical, biological, social, and economic research, as well as ocean exploration. The nation invests in the needed scientific tools and technologies, including: ample, well equipped surface and underwater research vessels; reliable, sustained satellites; state-of-the-art computing facilities; and innovative sensors that can withstand harsh ocean conditions. A widespread network of observing and monitoring stations provides a steady stream of data, and scientific findings are translated into practical information and products for decision makers, vessel operators, educators, and the public.

In this hoped-for future, better education is a cornerstone of national ocean policy, with the United States once again joining the top ranks in math, science, and technology achievement. An audacious program to explore unknown reaches of the ocean inspires and engages people of all ages. An ample, diverse, well trained, and motivated workforce is available to study the oceans, set wise policies, develop and apply technological advances, and engineer new solutions. An effective team of educators works closely with scientists to learn and teach about the oceans—its value, beauty, and critical role on the planet. And, as a result of lifelong education, all citizens are better stewards of the nation's resources and marine environment.

Finally, the Commission's vision sees the United States as an exemplary leader and full partner globally, eagerly exchanging science, engineering, technology, and policy expertise with others, particularly those in developing countries, to facilitate the achievement of sustainable ocean management on an international level.

While progress has been made in a number of areas, the nation's existing system for managing our oceans, coasts, and Great Lakes is simply unable to effectively implement these guiding principles and realize the long-term vision. The Commission recommends moving toward an ecosystem-based management approach by focusing on three cross-cutting themes: (1) a new, coordinated national ocean policy framework to improve decision making; (2) cutting edge ocean data and science translated into high-quality information for managers; and (3) lifelong ocean-related education to create well-informed citizens with a strong stewardship ethic. These themes are woven throughout the report, appearing again and again in chapters dealing with a wide variety of ocean challenges.

Guiding Principles

The Commission believes the vision described above is both practical and attainable. To achieve it, however, an overarching set of principles should guide national ocean policy.

- Sustainability: Ocean policy should be designed to meet the needs of the present generation without compromising the ability of future generations to meet their needs.
- Stewardship: The principle of stewardship applies both to the government and to every citizen. The U.S. government holds ocean and coastal resources in the public trust—a special responsibility that necessitates balancing different uses of those resources for the continued benefit of all Americans. Just as important, every member of the public should recognize the value of the oceans and coasts, supporting appropriate policies and acting responsibly while minimizing negative environmental impacts.
- Ocean–Land–Atmosphere Connections: Ocean policies should be based on the recognition that the oceans, land, and atmosphere are inextricably intertwined and that actions that affect one Earth system component are likely to affect another.
- Ecosystem-based Management: U.S. ocean and coastal resources should be managed to reflect the relationships among all ecosystem components, including humans and nonhuman species and the environments in which they live. Applying this principle will require defining relevant geographic management areas based on ecosystem, rather than political, boundaries.

- Multiple Use Management: The many potentially beneficial uses of ocean and coastal resources should be acknowledged and managed in a way that balances competing uses while preserving and protecting the overall integrity of the ocean and coastal environments.
- Preservation of Marine Biodiversity: Downward trends in marine biodiversity should be reversed where they exist, with a desired end of maintaining or recovering natural levels of biological diversity and ecosystem services.
- Best Available Science and Information: Ocean policy decisions should be based on the best available understanding of the natural, social, and economic processes that affect ocean and coastal environments. Decision makers should be able to obtain and understand quality science and information in a way that facilitates successful management of ocean and coastal resources.
- Adaptive Management: Ocean management programs should be designed to meet clear goals and provide new information to continually improve the scientific basis for future management. Periodic reevaluation of the goals and effectiveness of management measures, and incorporation of new information in implementing future management, are essential.
- Understandable Laws and Clear Decisions: Laws governing uses of ocean and coastal resources should be clear, coordinated, and accessible to the nation's citizens to facilitate compliance. Policy decisions and the reasoning behind them should also be clear and available to all interested parties.
- Participatory Governance: Governance of ocean uses should ensure widespread participation by all citizens on issues that affect them.
- Timeliness: Ocean governance systems should operate with as much efficiency and predictability as possible.
- Accountability: Decision makers and members of the public should be accountable for the actions they take that affect ocean and coastal resources.
- International Responsibility: The United States should act cooperatively with other nations in developing and implementing international ocean policy, reflecting the deep connections between U.S. interests and the global ocean.

A New National Ocean Policy Framework

To improve decision making, promote effective coordination, and move toward an ecosystem-based management approach, a new National Ocean Policy Framework is needed. While this framework is intended to produce strong, national leadership, it is also designed to support and enhance the critical roles of state, territorial, tribal, and local decision makers.

National Coordination and Leadership

At the federal level, eleven of fifteen cabinet-level departments and four independent agencies play important roles in the development of ocean and coastal policy. These agencies interact with one another and with state, territorial, tribal, and local authorities in sometimes haphazard ways. Improved communication and coordination would greatly enhance the effectiveness of the nation's ocean policy.

Within the Executive Office of the President, three entities have some responsibilities relevant to oceans: the Office of Science and Technology Policy addresses government-wide science and technology issues and includes an ocean subcommittee; the Council on Environmental Quality (CEQ) oversees broad federal environmental efforts and implementation of the National Environmental Policy Act; and the National Security Council's Global Environment Policy Coordinating Committee includes a subcommittee to deal with international ocean issues. But there is no multi-issue interagency mechanism to guide, oversee, and coordinate all aspects of ocean and coastal policy.

As part of a new National Ocean Policy Framework, the Commission recommends that Congress establish a National Ocean Council (NOC) within the Executive Office of the President, chaired by an Assistant to the President and composed of cabinet secretaries of departments and administrators of the independent agencies with relevant ocean- and coastal-related responsibilities. The NOC should provide high-level attention to ocean, coastal, and Great Lakes issues, develop and guide the implementation of appropriate national policies, and coordinate the many federal departments and agencies with ocean and coastal responsibilities. The Assistant to the President should also advise OMB and the agencies on appropriate funding levels for important ocean- and coastal-related activities, and prepare a biennial report as mandated by Section 5 of the Oceans Act of 2000. A Committee on Ocean Science, Education, Technology, and Operations and a Committee on Ocean Resource Management should be created under the NOC to support its coordination and planning functions.

A President's Council of Advisors on Ocean Policy, consisting of nonfederal representatives from state, territorial, tribal, and local governments and academic, public interest, and private sector organizations, should also be created to ensure a formal structure for nonfederal input to the NOC and the President on ocean and coastal policy matters.

A small Office of Ocean Policy should provide staff support to all the bodies discussed above. Pending congressional action, the Commission recommends that the President put this structure in place through an executive order.

An Enhanced Regional Approach

Ensuring full state, territorial, tribal, and local participation in ocean policy development and implementation is a critical element of the new National Ocean Policy Framework. Many of the nation's most pressing ocean and coastal issues are local or regional in nature and their resolution requires the active involvement of state and local policy makers, as well as a wide range of stakeholders.

One of the priority tasks for the new National Ocean Council should be to develop and promote a flexible, voluntary process pursuant to which groups of states could create regional ocean councils. These regional ocean councils would serve as focal points for discussion, cooperation, and coordination. They would improve the nation's ability to respond to issues that cross jurisdictional boundaries and would help policy makers address the large-scale connections and conflicts among watershed, coastal, and offshore uses. To complement and support this effort, the President should direct all federal agencies with ocean-related functions to immediately improve their regional coordination, moving over time to adopt a common regional structure. . . .

Improved Governance of Offshore Waters

The nation's vast offshore ocean areas are becoming an increasingly appealing place to pursue economic activities. Well-established institutional frameworks exist for longstanding ocean uses, such as fishing and energy extraction; however, authorities governing new activities, such as the placement of wind farms or aquaculture facilities, need to be clarified. A comprehensive offshore management regime is needed that enables us to realize the ocean's potential while safeguarding human and ecosystem health, minimizing conflicts among users, and fulfilling the government's obligation to manage the sea in a way that maximizes long-term benefits for all the nation's citizens.

The National Ocean Council, supported by congressional action where necessary, should ensure that each current or foreseeable activity in federal waters is administered by a lead federal agency. Existing laws or authorities for well developed and enduring programs would not be supplanted, but the lead agency would be expected to continue, and perhaps enhance, coordination among all other involved federal partners. For emerging ocean activities for which authority is ill defined, dispersed, or essentially non-existent, the National Ocean Council and Congress, working with affected stakeholders, should ensure that a lead agency is providing strong coordination and should recognize the likely need for comprehensive governance structures that are integrated into a balanced, ecosystem-based offshore management regime.

Based on an improved understanding of offshore areas and their resources, the federal government should work with appropriate state and local authorities to ensure that the many different activities within a given area are compatible, in keeping with an ecosystem-based management approach. As the pressure for offshore uses grows, and before serious conflicts arise, it is critical that the National Ocean Council review the complete array of single-purpose offshore programs with the goal of achieving coordination among them. Ultimately, a streamlined management program for each potential activity should be combined with a comprehensive offshore management regime that considers all uses, addresses the cumulative impacts of multiple activities, and coordinates the many authorities with an interest in offshore waters. The National Ocean Council, President's Council of Advisors on Ocean Policy, federal agencies, regional ocean councils, and states will all have roles to play in realizing more coordinated, participatory management of offshore ocean activities.

In considering the coordination of ocean activities, marine protected areas provide one valuable tool for achieving more ecosystem-based management of both nearshore and offshore areas. Such areas can be created for many different reasons including: enhancement of living marine resources; protection of habitats, endangered species, and marine biological diversity; or preservation of historically or culturally important submerged archeological resources. Marine protected areas may also provide scientific, recreational, and educational benefits. The level of protection and types of activities allowed can vary greatly depending on the goals of the protected area.

With its multiple use, ecosystem-based perspective, the National Ocean Council should oversee the development of a flexible process—one that is adaptive and based on the best available science—to design, implement, and assess marine protected areas. Regional ocean councils, or other appropriate entities, can provide a forum for engaging all stakeholders in this process.

A Strengthened Federal Agency Structure

Improved coordination through a National Ocean Council is necessary, but not sufficient to bring about the depth of change needed. Some restructuring of existing federal agencies will be needed to make government less redundant, more flexible, more responsive to the needs of states and stakeholders, and better suited to an ecosystem-based management approach. Because of the significant hurdles involved, a phased approach is suggested.

The National Oceanic and Atmospheric Administration (NOAA) is the nation's primary ocean agency. Although it has made significant progress in many areas, there is widespread agreement that the agency could manage its activities more effectively. In addition, many of the recommendations in this report call for NOAA to handle additional responsibilities. A stronger, more effective, science-based and service oriented ocean agency is needed—one that works with others to achieve better management of oceans and coasts through an ecosystem-based approach.

As an initial step in a phased approach, Congress should pass an organic act that codifies the existence of NOAA. This will strengthen the agency and help ensure that its structure is consistent with three primary functions: assessment, prediction, and operations; management; and research and education. . . .

As a second step in the phased approach, all federal agencies with ocean-related responsibilities should be reviewed and strengthened and overlapping programs should be considered for consolidation. . . .

Ultimately, our growing understanding of ecosystems and the inextricable links between the sea, land, air, and all living things, points to the need for more fundamental reorganization of the federal government. Consolidation of all natural resource functions, including those involving oceans and coasts, would enable the federal agencies to move toward true ecosystem-based management.

Sound Science and Information for Wise Decisions

An effective national ocean policy should be based on unbiased, credible, and up-to-date scientific information. Yet the oceans remain one of the least explored and most poorly understood environments on the planet, despite some tantalizing discoveries over the last century.

Sustained investments will be required to: support research and exploration; provide an adequate infrastructure for data collection, science, and management; and translate new scientific findings into useful and timely information products for managers, educators, and the public. This is especially true as we move toward an ecosystem-based management approach that imposes new responsibilities on managers and requires improved understanding of physical, biological, social, and economic forces.

Investing in Science and Exploration

Over the past two decades, with our oceans, coasts, and Great Lakes under siege, federal investment in ocean research has stagnated while other fields have grown. As a result, ocean science funding has fallen from 7 percent of the total federal research budget twenty-five years ago to just 3.5 percent today. This lagging support in the United States, combined with growing foreign capability, has lessened the nation's preeminence in ocean research, exploration, and technology development. Chronic under-investment has also left much of our ocean-related infrastructure in woefully poor condition.

The current annual federal investment in marine science is well below the level necessary to adequately meet the nation's needs for coastal and ocean information. The Commission urges Congress to double the federal ocean and coastal research budget over the next five years. In addition, a dedicated ocean exploration program should be launched to unlock the mysteries of the deep by discovering new ecosystems, natural resources, and archaeological treasures.

A renewed U.S. commitment to ocean science and technology will require not only substantially increased funding, but also improved strategic planning, close interagency coordination, robust technology and infrastructure, and 21st century data management systems. The Commission recommends: (1) creation of a national strategy for ocean research that will guide individual agencies' ten-year science plans; (2) enhancement and maintenance of the nation's ocean and coastal infrastructure, development of new technologies, and more rapid transition of experimental technologies into operational applications; and (3) drastic improvements in our ability to archive, transfer, and manipulate research data and generate useful information products.

Launching a New Era of Ocean Data Collection

The Integrated Ocean Observing System. About 150 years ago, this nation set out to create a comprehensive weather forecasting and warning network. Today it is hard to imagine living without constantly updated and accurate weather reports. Now it is time to fully incorporate the oceans in this observational and forecasting capability. A sustained, national Integrated Ocean Observing System (IOOS) will provide invaluable economic, societal, and environmental benefits, including improved warnings of coastal and health hazards, more efficient use of living and nonliving resources, safer marine operations, and a better understanding of climate change. Our information needs are growing and the challenges we face along our coasts and in our oceans are escalating.

The nation needs to substantially advance its ability to observe, monitor, and forecast ocean conditions, and contribute to global Earth observing capabilities. The Commission recommends that the Federal government, through the National Ocean Council, make the development and implementation of the IOOS a high priority, to be organized through a formalized Ocean.US office. The United States simply cannot achieve the levels of understanding and predictive capability needed, or generate the information required by a wide range of users, without the IOOS. While implementation of the IOOS will require significant, sustained funding, estimates suggest that an operational IOOS will save the United States billions of dollars annually through enhanced weather forecasts, improved resource management, and safer, more efficient marine operations. . . .

The National Monitoring Network. Despite the growing threats to ocean, coastal, and Great Lakes waters, there is no national monitoring network in place to assess their status, track changes over time, help identify causes and impacts, or determine the success of management efforts. Increased monitoring is needed not only along the nation's coasts, but also inland where pollutants often originate, traveling downstream and ultimately affecting coastal waters. A national monitoring network is essential to support the move toward an ecosystem-based management approach that considers the impacts of human activities within the context of the broader biological and physical environment. NOAA, EPA, and USGS should lead an effort to develop a national monitoring network that coordinates and expands existing efforts by federal, state, local, and private entities. . . .

Education: A Foundation for the Future

Testing results suggest that, after getting off to a good start in elementary school, by the time U.S. students graduate from high school their achievement in math and science falls well below the international average More specifically, a 1999 study revealed that just 32 percent of the nation's adults grasp simple environmental concepts and even fewer understand more complex issues, such as ecosystem decline, loss of biodiversity, or watershed degradation. It is not widely understood that nonpoint source pollution threatens the health of coastal waters, or that mercury in fish comes from human activities via the atmosphere. From excess application of fertilizers, pesticides, and herbicides on lawns, to the trash washed off city streets into rivers and coastal waters, ordinary activities contribute significantly to the degradation of the marine environment, but without an informed and educated citizenry, it will be difficult to achieve a collective commitment to stewardship, sustained investment, and more effective policies.

A new national ocean policy should include a strong commitment to education to reverse scientific and environmental illiteracy, create a strong, diverse workforce, produce informed decision makers, and develop a national stewardship ethic for the oceans, coasts, and Great Lakes. The Commission recommends that all ocean-related agencies take responsibility for promoting education and outreach as an integral part of their missions. Ocean education at all levels, both formal and informal, should be enhanced with targeted projects and continual assessments and improvement.

A national ocean education office, Ocean.ED, should be created under the National Ocean Council to promote nationwide improvements in ocean education. As an interagency office, Ocean.ED should develop a coordinated national strategy and work in partnership with state and local governments and with K-12, university level, and informal educators. . . .

Specific Management Challenges

Building on the foundation of improved governance, new scientific information, and enhanced education, the Commission's report covers the full breadth of topics included in its charge from Congress. As a result, it includes over 200 recommendations that span the gamut of ocean and coastal issues, ranging from upstream areas to the depths of the sea, from practical problem solving to broad guidance for ocean policy.

Several important issues pose particular challenges and are highlighted in the following sections. The full report addresses these topics and a number of others in much greater depth.

Improving Management of Coasts and Watersheds

While coastal counties comprise only 17 percent of the land area in the contiguous United States, they are home to more than 53 percent of the total U.S. population. On average, some 3,600 people a day are moving to coastal counties, suggesting that by 2015 coastal populations will reach a total of 165 million. With another 180 million people visiting the coast each year, the pressure on our oceans, coasts, and Great Lakes will become ever more intense and the need for effective management greater.

Population growth and tourism bring many benefits to coastal communities and the nation, including new jobs, businesses, and enhanced educational opportunities. The great popularity of these areas, however, also puts more people and property at risk from coastal hazards, reduces and fragments fish and wildlife habitat, alters sediment and water flows, and contributes to coastal water pollution. Fortunately, we are gaining a much-improved understanding of human influences on coastal ecosystems, whether they originate locally, regionally, or in watersheds hundreds of miles upstream.

Without question, management of the nation's coastal zone has made great strides, but further improvements are urgently needed, with an emphasis on ecosystem-based, watershed approaches that consider environmental, economic, and social concerns. The Commission recommends that federal area-based coastal programs be consolidated and federal laws be modified to improve coastal resource protection and sustainable use. Congress should reauthorize and boost support for the Coastal Zone Management Act, strengthening the management capabilities of coastal states and enabling them to incorporate a watershed focus. The Coastal Zone Management Act, Clean Water Act, and other federal laws should be amended to provide financial, technical, and institutional support for watershed initiatives. . . .

The Growing Cost of Natural Hazards

Conservative estimates of damages from natural hazards, including only direct costs such as those for structural replacement and repair, put nationwide losses at more than $50 billion a year. Some experts believe this figure represents only half or less of the true costs. More accurate figures are unavailable because the United States does not consistently collect and compile such data, let alone focus specifically on losses in coastal areas or costs associated with damage to natural environments.

Many federal agencies have explicit operational responsibilities related to hazards management, while others provide technical information or deliver disaster assistance. The nation's lead agencies for natural hazards planning, response, recovery, and mitigation are the Federal Emergency Management Agency (FEMA) and the U.S. Army Corps of Engineers (USACE). These agencies implement programs that specifically target the reduction and management of risks from natural hazards. . . .

Conserving and Restoring Coastal Habitat

The diverse habitats that comprise the ocean and coastal environment provide tangible benefits such as filtering pollutants from runoff, buffering coastal communities against the effects of storms, and providing a basis for booming recreation and tourism industries. These habitats also supply spawning grounds, nurseries, shelter, and food for marine life, including a disproportionate number of endangered or commercially important species.

As more people come to the coast to live, work, and visit, coastal habitats are increasingly stressed and damaged. Over the past several decades the nation has lost millions of acres of wetlands, seen the destruction of seagrass and kelp beds, and faced a loss of significant mangrove forests. Cost-effective conservation and restoration programs should be expanded according to a national strategy that sets goals and priorities, enhances the effectiveness and coordination of individual efforts, and periodically evaluates progress. Many habitat conservation and restoration projects have been successful, but continued progress will depend on sustained funding, improved government leadership and coordination, enhanced scientific research and monitoring, better education and outreach, and solid stakeholder support.

Managing Sediment and Shorelines

From a human perspective, sediment has a dual nature—desirable in some locations and unwanted in others—making its management particularly challenging. The natural flow of sediment over land and through waterways is important for sustaining coastal habitats and maintaining beaches. Too little sediment can lead to habitat decline, damaging wetlands and allowing beaches to wash away over time. However, excess or contaminated sediment can block shipping channels, destroy habitats, poison the food chain, and endanger lives. Navigational dredging, infrastructure projects, farming, forestry, urban development, industrial operations, and many other necessary and beneficial human activities can interfere with natural sediment processes, adversely affecting the interests of other stakeholders and the environment. . . .

A national sediment management strategy is needed that balances ecological and economic needs according to an ecosystem-based management approach. Such a strategy should consider sediments on a multi-project, regional, watershed basis, and should involve all relevant parties. Participation in watershed management efforts by federal, state, and local entities, along with key stakeholders such as coastal planners and port managers, is an important step in diminishing upland sources of excess or contaminated sediment. Scientifically sound methods for characterizing contaminated sediment, combined with innovative technologies for dredging, treatment, and disposal of this material will also be critical.

Supporting Marine Commerce and Transportation

Global trade is an essential and growing component of the nation's economy, accounting for nearly 7 percent of the gross domestic product. The vast majority of our import-export goods pass through the nation's extensive marine transportation system. To meet current demands and prepare for expected growth in the future, this system will require maintenance, improvement, and significant expansion.

A first step in the process will be better coordination, planning, and allocation of resources at the federal level. As part of a national move toward an ecosystem based management approach, the efficient, safe, and secure movement of cargo and passengers should be well coordinated with other ocean and coastal uses and activities, and with efforts to protect the marine environment. . . .

Water Quality and Ecosystem Health

Coastal and ocean water quality is threatened by multiple sources of pollution, including point, nonpoint, and atmospheric sources, vessel pollution, invasive species, and trash being washed and onto beaches into the ocean. Addressing these multiple sources of pollution requires development of an ecosystem-based and watershed management approach that draws on a variety of management tools. Because water contamination problems are complex and pervasive, their solution will require substantial investments of federal resources and greatly enhanced coordination both among federal agencies (primarily EPA, NOAA, USDA, and USACE) and between the federal government and managers at state, territorial, tribal, and local levels, in addition to watershed groups, nongovernmental organizations, private stakeholders, and the academic and research communities.

Over the last few decades, great strides have been made in reducing water pollution from point sources, although further improvements can be realized through increased funding, strengthened enforcement, and promotion of innovative approaches, such as market-based incentives. Persistently troublesome point sources of pollution, including wastewater treatment plants, sewer system overflows, septic systems, industrial facilities, and animal feeding operations, must continue to be addressed.

But the widespread and growing problem of nonpoint source pollution has not seen similar success. Significant reduction of such pollution in all impaired coastal watersheds should be established as a national goal with measurable objectives set to meet water quality standards. Federal nonpoint source pollution programs should be better coordinated so they are mutually supportive. Because agricultural runoff contributes substantially to such pollution, USDA should align its conservation programs, technical assistance, and funding with EPA and NOAA programs for reducing nonpoint source pollution. State and local governments can also play central roles through better land-use planning and stormwater management.

Pollution reduction efforts should include the aggressive use of state revolving loan funds, implementation of incentives to reward good practices, and improved monitoring to assess compliance and overall progress. Congress should also amend the Clean Water Act to authorize federal financial disincentives against activities that degrade water quality and to provide federal authority to act if a state chronically fails to make progress in controlling nonpoint sources.

Given the natural functioning of hydrologic systems, watersheds are often the appropriate geographic unit within which to address water-related problems. Collaborative watershed groups have had particular success in addressing nonpoint source pollution. The federal government should strengthen collaborative watershed groups by providing them with adequate technical, institutional, and financial support.

Because contaminants can travel long distances through the atmosphere and be deposited far from their origin, EPA and states should develop and implement regional and national strategies for controlling this source of water pollution, building upon efforts such as the EPA Air-Water Interface Work Plan. In addition, the United States should participate in a vigorous international research program on the sources and impacts of atmospheric deposition and play a leadership role in negotiating international solutions.

Vessel Pollution and Vessel Safety

Ships carry more than 95 percent of the nation's overseas cargo, but their operations also present safety, security, and environmental risks. To minimize these risks, the Commission recommends that the U.S. Coast Guard work with industry partners and enhance incentive programs to encourage voluntary commitments from vessel owners and operators to build a workplace ethic that values safety, security, and environmental protection as central components of everyday vessel operations. These voluntary measures should be complemented by effective oversight and monitoring, whether conducted by the Coast Guard or third-party audit firms, and backed up by consistent enforcement efforts, including performance-based vessel inspections. . . .

Preventing the Spread of Invasive Species

The introduction of non-native organisms into ports, coastal areas, and watersheds is causing harm to marine ecosystems around the world and incurring millions of dollars in costs for monitoring, control, and remediation. The most effective weapon against invasive species is prevention. To control the introduction of invasive species through ships' ballast water, a major pathway, the U.S. Coast Guard's national ballast water management program should: incorporate sound science in the development of biologically meaningful, mandatory, and enforceable ballast water treatment standards; develop new treatment technologies, revising the standards as needed to incorporate these technologies; and allow for full consultation with EPA. . . .

Reducing Marine Debris

Marine debris refers to the enormous amount of trash, abandoned fishing gear, and other waste that can be found drifting around the global ocean and washing up along its coastlines, posing serious threats to wildlife, habitats, and human health and safety. Approximately 80 percent of this debris originates on land, either washed along in runoff, blown by winds, or intentionally dumped from shore, while 20 percent comes from offshore platforms and vessels, including fishing boats.

The Commission recommends that NOAA, as the nation's primary ocean and coastal management agency, reestablish its defunct marine debris program to build on and complement EPA's modest program. NOAA and EPA should expand their marine debris efforts, building on each agency's strengths, by pursuing: public outreach and education; partnerships with local governments, community groups, and industry; and strengthened research and monitoring efforts.

An interagency committee under the NOC should coordinate federal marine debris programs and take maximum advantage of the significant efforts conducted by private citizens, state and local governments, and nongovernmental organizations.

The United States should also remain active on the international level. An immediate priority is the development of an international plan of action to address derelict fishing gear on the high seas.

Sustainable Fisheries

Over the last thirty years, the fishing industry has evolved from being largely unregulated, with seemingly boundless opportunities, to one that is highly regulated and struggling to remain viable in some places. While the current management regime has many positive features, such as an emphasis on local participation, the pairing of science and management, and regional flexibility, it has also allowed overexploitation of many fish stocks, degradation of habitats, and negative impacts on many ecosystems and fishing communities.

The Commission's recommendations to improve fishery management can be grouped into six areas: reemphasizing the role of science in the management process; strengthening the Regional Fishery Management Council (RFMC) system and clarifying jurisdictions; expanding the use of dedicated access privileges; improving enforcement; adopting an ecosystem-based management approach; and strengthening international management.

To strengthen the link between strong science and sustainable fishery management, RFMCs should be required to rely on the peer-reviewed advice of their Scientific and Statistical Committees (SSCs), particularly in setting harvest levels. In particular, an RFMC should not be allowed to approve any measure that exceeds the allowable biological catch recommended by its SSC. Because of their importance in the process, SSC members should be nominated by the RFMCs but appointed by the Administrator of NOAA, and their credentials and potential conflicts of interest should be vetted by an external organization. An expanded research program is needed that involves fishermen where possible and is responsive to managers' requirements.

Several recommendations are made concerning the composition, responsibilities, and jurisdiction of the various federal and interstate fishery management entities. In particular, membership on the RFMCs needs to be diversified and new members should receive consistent training in the often arcane vocabulary and policies involved in U.S. fishery management.

To reverse existing incentives that create an unsustainable "race for the fish," fishery managers should explore the adoption of dedicated access privileges to promote conservation and help reduce overcapitalization. Congress should amend the Magnuson–Stevens Fishery Conservation and Management Act to affirm that RFMCs are authorized to institute dedicated access privileges, subject to meeting national guidelines, and every federal, interstate, and state fishery management body should consider the potential benefits of adopting such programs. In addition, Congress should address overcapitalization directly by revising federal programs that subsidize this practice, as well as working with NOAA to develop programs that permanently reduce overcapitalization in fisheries.

Fishery enforcement should be continually strengthened through the adoption of better technologies, such as Vessel Monitoring Systems, better cooperation among federal and state agencies, and enhanced support for the infrastructure, personnel, and programs that make enforcement possible.

Consistent with one of the major themes of this report, fishery management needs to move toward a more ecosystem-based approach to improve its effectiveness and reduce conflicts between socioeconomic forces and biological sustainability. An ecosystem-based management approach will be particularly helpful in protecting essential fish habitat and reducing the impacts of bycatch.

Finally, the U.S. should work with other countries on worldwide adoption and enforcement of international agreements that promote sustainable fisheries practices, in particular the United Nations Fish Stocks Agreement and the U.N. Food and Agriculture Organization's Compliance Agreement and Code of Conduct for Responsible Fisheries. The United States should also continue to press for the inclusion of environmental objectives—particularly those specified in international environmental agreements—as legitimate elements of trade policy.

Marine Mammals and Endangered Species

The Marine Mammal Protection Act and the Endangered Species Act are landmark laws that have protected marine mammals, sea turtles, seabirds, and other populations at risk since their passage. However, both Acts need to be updated to support the move toward a more ecosystem-based approach.

As in so many other areas of ocean policy, immediate clarification and coordination of federal agency policies is needed. The Commission recommends that Congress consolidate the jurisdiction for marine mammals within NOAA, and that the NOC improve coordination between NOAA and the U.S. Fish and Wildlife Service in implementation of the Endangered Species Act, particularly for anadromous species or where land based activities have significant impacts on marine species. Congress should also amend the Marine Mammal Protection Act to require NOAA to specify categories of activities that are allowed without a permit, those that require a permit, and those that are strictly prohibited. The permitting process itself should be streamlined by using programmatic permitting where possible. The definition of harassment in the Marine Mammal Protection Act should also be revised to cover only activities that meaningfully disrupt behaviors that are significant to the survival and reproduction of marine mammals.

The Commission recommends an expanded research, technology, and engineering program, coordinated through the National Ocean Council, to examine and mitigate the effects of human activities—including fishing, pollution, and climate change—on marine mammals, seabirds, sea turtles and all other marine endangered species. In addition,

Congress should expand federal funding for research into ocean acoustics and the potential impacts of noise on marine mammals and other species.

Coral Communities

Coral communities are among the oldest and most diverse ecosystems on the planet, rivaling tropical rainforests in biodiversity and potential economic value. Unfortunately, like the rainforests, the world's coral reefs are increasingly showing signs of serious decline, with pristine reefs becoming rare and up to one-third of the world's reefs severely damaged according to some estimates.

A strengthened Coral Reef Task Force, under the oversight of the NOC, should promote immediate actions to reverse the impacts on tropical coral communities from pollution (with EPA and USDA in the lead) and from fishing (with NOAA in the lead). NOAA should be assigned as the lead agency for assessing and protecting relatively unexplored cold water coral communities, including dedicated research on their distribution and abundance and strategies to reduce major threats to their survival.

Congress should enact a Coral Protection and Management Act that provides direct authorities to protect and manage corals, and creates a framework for research and for cooperation with international efforts. This legislation should include: mapping, monitoring, and research programs to fill critical information gaps; liability provisions for damages to coral reefs, similar to those in the National Marine Sanctuaries Act; outreach activities to educate the public about coral conservation and reduce human impacts; and mechanisms for U.S. involvement in bilateral, regional, and international coral reef programs, particularly through the sharing of scientific, technical, and management expertise.

As the world's largest importer of ornamental coral reef resources, the United States has a particular responsibility to help eliminate destructive harvesting practices and ensure the sustainable use of reef resources. In many places, harvesting methods continue to damage reefs and overexploit ornamental species. The United States should develop standards for the importation of coral species to balance legitimate trade with protection of the world's coral reefs and to ensure that U.S. citizens do not unknowingly promote unsustainable practices.

Aquaculture

Marine aquaculture has the potential to supply a significant part of the ever increasing domestic and global demand for seafood. However, two major concerns must be addressed: environmental problems associated with some aquaculture operations, particularly net-pen facilities, and a confusing, inconsistent array of state and federal regulations that hinder private sector investment.

The Commission recommends that Congress amend the National Aquaculture Act to designate NOAA as the lead federal agency for implementing a national policy on environmentally and economically sustainable marine aquaculture. Through a new Office of Sustainable Marine Aquaculture, NOAA should develop a single, multiagency federal permitting process for the aquaculture industry that ensures that aquaculture facilities meet all applicable environmental standards and protects the sustainability and diversity of wild stocks.

Additional investments in research, demonstration projects, and technical assistance can help the industry address environmental issues, conduct risk assessments, develop improved technology, select appropriate species, and create best management practices. . . .

Offshore Resources

Oil and gas development on the outer Continental Shelf (OCS) supplies over a quarter of the nation's domestic oil and gas reserves, and contributes thousands of jobs and billions of dollars to the economy. Although controversial in many locations, the process for oil and gas leasing and production is well developed, reasonably comprehensive, and could serve as a model for implementing renewable energy projects within the context of a coordinated offshore management regime.

To maintain a strong link between the use of ocean resources and their management and protection, the Commission recommends dedicating federal revenues from OCS energy leasing and production to the sustainability of ocean and coastal resources. A portion of these funds should be given to coastal states, with larger shares going to OCS producing states to help address the environmental and economic consequences of energy production.

In addition to oil and gas, other offshore energy sources are being explored. The National Ocean Council, working with the U.S. Department of Energy and others, should determine whether methane hydrates can contribute significantly to meeting the nation's long-term energy needs and, if so, what level of investment in research and development is warranted. Renewable energy sources should also be considered as part of a coordinated offshore management regime. Congress, with input from the NOC, should enact legislation to streamline the licensing of renewable energy facilities in U.S. waters, relying on an open, transparent process that accounts for state, local, and public concerns. The legislation should include the principle that the oceans are a public resource and that the U.S. Treasury should receive a fair return from any use of that resource.

International Ocean Science and Policy

The United States has historically been a world leader in international ocean policy, participating actively in the development of international agreements that govern the planet's ocean areas and resources. That leadership must now be reaffirmed and reinvigorated by (1) acceding to the United Nations Convention on the Law of the Sea; (2) enhancing the participation of all ocean-related federal agencies in international discussions and negotiations; and (3) taking a leading role in building international capacity in ocean science and management, particularly in developing countries.

The United States can advance its own interests and contribute to the health of the world's oceans by first ensuring that U.S. domestic policies and actions embody exemplary standards of wise, sustainable ocean management. The new National Ocean Policy Framework will be instrumental in setting this positive tone for the international community. Many additional recommendations for action at the international level are presented throughout the report in the context of specific ocean and coastal management issues, such as international fisheries, global transportation of air pollutants, trade in corals, ornamental fish, and other living marine resources, the worldwide spread of marine debris, and many others.

Implementing a New National Ocean Policy

There are over 200 recommendations in the Commission's report, each one calling on specific responsible parties to spearhead its implementation and be accountable for its progress. A large number of recommendations are directed at Congress, the executive branch leadership, and federal agencies. . . .

Although the Commission has generally avoided targeting recommendations at state or local governments, these entities will have critically important roles to play in the establishment of regional ocean councils, and in areas such as coastal development, water quality, education, natural hazards planning, fishery management, habitat conservation, and much more. Strong state participation is also needed in the design and implementation of regional ocean observing systems and their integration into the national IOOS, as well as in other research and monitoring activities.

A Worthwhile Investment

Implementation of the recommendations in this report will lead to tangible, measurable improvements in U.S. ocean policy and in the health of our oceans, coasts, and Great Lakes. However, significant change cannot be achieved without adequate investments—in time, money, and political will. A detailed breakdown of the cost of each recommendation is provided in Chapter 30. In summary, the Commission estimates the total additional cost for initiatives outlined in this report at approximately $1.5 billion in the first year and $3.9 billion per year in ongoing costs after full implementation. The payoff from these investments will be substantial for the United States and its citizens, benefiting our economy, health, environment, quality of life, and security.

Long Term Support: the Ocean Policy Trust Fund

As noted previously, around $5 trillion dollars, or one half of the nation's annual gross domestic product, is generated each year within coastal watershed counties. That enormous economic contribution is now being threatened by the degradation of our oceans, coasts, and Great Lakes. Modest levels of additional funding will reap significant dividends by supporting new management strategies that restore and sustain our ocean and coastal resources and maximize their long-term value.

Despite pressing needs, the Commission is mindful of the intense budgetary pressures that exist at both federal and state levels—and is sensitive to the hardships associated with unfunded federal mandates. To cover the cost of its recommendations, the Commission believes it is important to identify appropriate sources of revenue. In general, when a resource is publicly owned, its use by private profit-making entities should be contingent on a reasonable return to taxpayers. Creating a link between activities in federal waters and the cost of regulatory and management responsibilities is logical and well justified by precedents in federal land management. The Commission proposes the creation of an Ocean Policy Trust Fund in the U.S. Treasury, composed of rents generated from permitted activities in federal waters.

To start, the Trust Fund would be composed of outer Continental Shelf oil and gas revenues that are not already committed to the Land and Water Conservation Fund, the National Historic Preservation Fund, or to certain coastal states based on oil and gas production in the three nautical mile area seaward of their submerged lands. After those existing programs are funded in accordance with law, the remaining OCS monies would be deposited into the Ocean Policy Trust Fund. New offshore activities, such as renewable energy, aquaculture, or bioprospecting, may also produce revenues in time, and these would be added to the Ocean Policy Trust Fund. Creation and distribution of the Ocean Policy Trust Fund should be kept separate from any decisions about whether a particular offshore activity should be allowed.

Approximately $5 billion is generated annually from OCS oil and gas revenues. Protecting the three programs noted above would remove about $1 billion from that total.

Thus, some $4 billion would remain available for the Ocean Policy Trust Fund each year under current projections. It is not possible to estimate the level of revenue that might accompany emerging activities in federal waters, nor to predict when this income could begin to flow, but the amounts may be significant in years to come.

Trust Fund monies should be used exclusively to support the additional research, education, and management responsibilities recommended for federal and state agencies, consistent with a coordinated and comprehensive national ocean policy. Such funds would be used to supplement—not replace—existing appropriations for ocean and coastal programs, and to fund new or expanded duties.

Call to Action

This report reflects the input of hundreds of Americans from across the nation, testimony from many of the world's leading experts, and months of deliberation. The recommendations contained within can set the course to a future in which our oceans, coasts, and Great Lakes are healthy, enjoyed, and treasured by all people, and America's marine resources are restored and sustained for generations to come.

The opportunity is here and it is time to act. A new national ocean policy can be implemented that balances ocean use with sustainability, is based on sound science and supported by excellent education, and is overseen by a coordinated system of governance with strong leadership at national and regional levels. It will take great political will, significant fiscal investment, and strong public support, but in the long run all of America will benefit from these changes.

Critical Actions Recommended by the U.S. Commission on Ocean Policy

The following key recommendations provide the foundation for a comprehensive national ocean policy that will lead to significant improvements in ocean and coastal management.

Improved Governance

- Establish a National Ocean Council in the Executive Office of the President, chaired by an Assistant to the President.
- Create a President's Council of Advisors on Ocean Policy.
- Improve the federal agency structure by strengthening NOAA and consolidating federal agency programs according to a phased approach.
- Develop a flexible, voluntary process for creating regional ocean councils, facilitated and supported by the National Ocean Council.
- Create a coordinated management regime for activities in federal offshore waters.

Sound Science for Wise Decisions

- Double the nation's investment in ocean research, launch a new area of ocean exploration, and create the advanced technologies and modern infrastructure needed to support them.
- Implement the national Integrated Ocean Observing System and a national monitoring network.

Education—A Foundation for the Future

- Improve ocean-related education through coordinated and effective formal and informal efforts.

Specific Management Challenges

- Strengthen coastal and watershed management and the links between them.
- Set measurable goals for reducing water pollution, particularly from nonpoint sources, and strengthen incentives, technical assistance, enforcement, and other management tools to achieve those goals.
- Reform fisheries management by separating assessment and allocation, improving the Regional Fishery Management Council system, and exploring the use of dedicated access privileges.
- Accede to the United Nations Convention on the Law of the Sea to remain fully engaged on the international level.

Implementation

- Establish an Ocean Policy Trust Fund, based on unallocated revenues from offshore oil and gas development and new offshore activities, that is dedicated to supporting improved ocean and coastal management at federal and state levels.

Source: U.S. Commission on Ocean Policy. *An Ocean Blueprint for the 21st Century: Final Report of the U.S. Commission on Ocean Policy.* September 20, 2004. Washington, D.C.: Government Printing Office. ISBN 0-9759462-0-X. www.oceancommission.gov/documents/prepub_report/welcome.html (accessed January 22, 2005).

Defense Department Task Force on U.S. Strategic Communication

September 23, 2004

INTRODUCTION

Confronting an increasingly dangerous insurgency in Iraq, the Bush administration during 2004 sought to shift much of the debate about the Middle East to promoting democracy. President George W. Bush and his aides said bringing democracy to Iraq was a chief goal of U.S. policy there, and early in the year his administration outlined an ambitious plan to encourage democracy throughout the region. The administration scaled back the latter ambition in the face of resistance from Arab leaders. Even so, events on the ground appeared to be moving in the direction Bush wanted; Palestinians and Iraqis were offered a chance for serious elections early in 2005, and even the conservative monarchy in Saudi Arabia was laying plans for a limited experiment with democracy. *(Iraq, pp. 399, 874; Saudi Arabia, p. 517)*

Caution signals came not only from Arab leaders but also from within the Bush administration itself. A strongly worded report by a Pentagon advisory panel, written in September but withheld from the public until late November, warned that U.S. policies were alienating many in the Muslim world and that selling democracy and Western values there would be a long-term project. *(Background, Historic Documents of 2003, p. 955)*

The United States and the Muslim World

The warning about U.S. policies in the Middle East came from a seemingly unlikely source: the Defense Science Board, a Pentagon advisory panel that generally was called on to evaluate the effectiveness of weapons systems or to contemplate future directions for military policy. In May 2004 Deputy Secretary of Defense Paul Wolfowitz asked the board to address a variety of questions arising from the recent U.S. wars in Afghanistan and Iraq, including the explanation of Washington's policies to the rest of the world. A panel appointed by the science board examined that specific question over the summer and filed its report on September 23. The Pentagon did not make the report public until November 23, after the *New York Times* published a news story about it. Subsequent news reports quoted Pentagon officials as saying the administration had not wanted the panel's generally negative findings to become an issue in the presidential election campaign.

The science board panel was the latest in a long series of special committees to conclude that the U.S. government was failing to get its message across to the rest of the world, notably the Muslim world in general and the Arab world in particular. One of the previous reports, issued in October 2003 by a State Department advisory panel, said the United States had engaged in a "process of unilateral disarmament" when it came to explaining its policies and goals to overseas audiences.

The science board panel generally concurred in that conclusion and offered more than a dozen major recommendations for new programs and bureaucratic changes to improve the image of the United States in foreign lands. Among other things, the panel called on the president to appoint a top aide within his National Security Council to develop governmentwide policies and programs in the field the panel called "strategic communication." The panel noted that the incoming Bush administration had scrapped a communications policy prepared by the Clinton administration in 1999 but had failed, after nearly four years in office, to adopt a new one of its own.

The most attention-getting section of the panel's report, however, was a bluntly worded chapter arguing that the Bush administration's self-proclaimed "war against terrorism" was falling on deaf ears in much of the Muslim world—the home of the terrorists most feared by the United States. The most widely quoted section of the report was a gentle but unmistakable rebuff of President Bush's frequent statement that terrorists and other Islamist extremists were motivated primarily by opposition to Western values, most importantly political freedom. "Muslims do not 'hate our freedom,' but rather, they hate our policies," the panel said. "The overwhelming majority [of Muslims surveyed in public opinion polls] voice their objections to what they see as one-sided support in favor of Israel and against Palestinian rights, and the longstanding, even increasing support for what Muslims collectively see as tyrannies, most notably Egypt, Saudi Arabia, Jordan, Pakistan, and the Gulf states." Further, the panel said, many Muslims viewed U.S. talk of democracy in Islamic countries as "self-serving hypocrisy" because the United States long supported repressive regimes in the Muslim world. Many Muslims believed Washington was talking of democracy simply as a tactic to gain getting broader support for its policies in Afghanistan and Iraq, the panel suggested.

Citing public opinion surveys taken in six Muslim countries in 2002 and 2004, the panel noted that anti-American attitudes had hardened and become more widespread among the general population. Notably, the panel added, anti-American sentiment appeared to be greatest "in precisely those places ruled by what Muslims call 'apostates' and tyrants—the tyrants we support."

The panel did not prescribe anything resembling a cure-all for the growing U.S. unpopularity in the Muslim world. It did, however, argue that the United States needed to use private-sector commercial marketing techniques to sell the American "brand" to the rest of the world, including Muslim lands. One technique borrowed from Western political campaigns meant focusing on persuading the "undecided" and the "soft support" segment of foreign audiences. In Muslim lands, the panel said, a goal was to "drive a wedge between moderates and extremists."

Partly because it was made public on the night before the Thanksgiving holiday, the panel's report received little attention in the news media. The report did, however, ignite a widespread and prolonged debate on the Internet, both in the Muslim world and in the United States. Those opposed to Bush administration policies cited the report as evidence that the occupation of Iraq had helped spawn even more Middle East terrorism and was doomed to fail. Others said the report demonstrated that the administration was wise to focus on democracy in the Middle East, even if it meant distancing the United States from repressive states it had long supported.

At year's end it was unclear whether the report had any impact within the Bush administration. Pentagon spokesman Larry di Rita told the *New York Times* that the report had generated debate within the Defense Department, but he said no decisions had been made on the panel's recommendations. Other news reports late in the year said the science board had not received any response from the White House.

Bush's Push for Arab Democracy

In a speech in November 2003, Bush had signaled that he wanted to make promoting democracy in the Middle East a signature policy of his presidency. To put specifics behind that speech, administration officials worked over the winter on a proposal they called the "Greater Middle East Initiative." It was to be an expanded version of a "Middle East Initiative" the administration had outlined in 2002 calling for such things as expanded trade between the United States and the region, literacy programs for women, and training for judges and parliamentarians.

After consultations with diplomats from European and Middle East nations, the administration drafted a proposal in January that called for a wide range of programs, funded by the Group of Eight (G-8) industrialized countries, to promote economic growth and democracy in the Middle East. Many of these programs were similar to ones the United States and other Western countries had sponsored in other parts of the world. The proposal also was cast as meeting needs identified by Arab intellectuals in the first two reports on the Arab world published in 2002 and 2003 by the United Nations Development Programme. Those reports also contained harsh criticisms of U.S. policies in the Middle East, and the administration reportedly pushed to delay release of a follow-up report due in 2004.

The draft Middle East initiative included several ideas that were certain to generate controversy in a region where leaders were sensitive to what they viewed as outside interference. Among them were encouraging "the region's governments to allow civil society organizations, including human rights and media NGOs [nongovernmental organizations], to operate freely without harassment or restrictions" and increasing direct funding to "democracy, human rights, media, women's, and other NGOs in the region."

An Arabic-language newspaper based in London, *al Hayat,* published an Arabic version of the draft proposal on February 13, then posted an English-language version on its Web site. The negative reaction was swift and predictable, particularly from the closest U.S. allies in the Middle East. Egyptian president Hosni Mubarak and Saudi Arabian crown prince Abdullah denounced the proposal as a mandate from the United States. "Whoever imagines that it is possible to impose solutions or reform from abroad on any society or region is delusional," Mubarak said on February 25. "All peoples by their nature reject whoever tries to impose ideas on them."

The Bush administration immediately backed away from the draft proposal, emphasizing its tentative nature. Administration officials also traveled widely in the region over the next several months, seeking to gain consensus for a different approach, one that could be portrayed as originating from within the Middle East rather than being imposed on it. After meeting with top officials in Saudi Arabia on March 19, Secretary of State Colin Powell acknowledged the proposal had caused "a great deal of angst in the region" but said the debate was "part of the democratic process."

The degree of what Powell called "angst" heightened considerably after April 14, when Bush met at the White House with Israeli prime minister Ariel Sharon and essentially endorsed Israel's position on two of the basic disagreements between Israel and the Palestinians: the presence of Jewish settlements on the West Bank and the status of Palestinian refugees. Bush's stance generated widespread anger in Arab countries. A week later, Mubarak told an interviewer from the French newspaper *Le Monde* that "there is a hatred of the Americans like never before in the region. People have a feeling of injustice." Publication later in April of photographs showing U.S. soldiers abusing Iraqis at a Baghdad prison heightened the anti-U.S. outrage in the Arab world. *(U.S. policy toward Israel, p. 301; prison abuses, p. 375)*

In response to the Arab anger, the Bush administration sharply revised its proposal, including giving it an unwieldy new name: "Partnership for Progress and a Common Future with the Region of the Broader Middle East and North Africa." On a more substantive level, the new proposal emphasized repeatedly that the initiative for change had to come from within the Middle East and noted that each nation "will reach its own conclusions about the peace and scope of change." In another bow to Arab sensitivities, the final version emphasized the importance of resolving the Israeli-Palestinian conflict.

Bush and other G-8 leaders adopted the Middle East initiative on June 9, during their annual summit meeting held at Sea Island, Georgia. Mubarak and Crown Prince Abdullah were among several Arab leaders who declined an invitation to attend. Much of the attention at the meeting was focused instead on the newly named interim president of Iraq, Sheik Ghazi al-Yawar, whose attendance prompted an emotional outburst from Bush: "I never thought I'd be sitting next to an Iraqi president of a free country a year and a half ago."

Adoption by the G-8 leaders of the revised Middle East initiative appeared to have little direct impact on events in the region through the rest of the year. Even so, the debate spawned by the initiative may have contributed to political ferment in the region, embodied in several tentative moves toward democracy and a host of conferences on political "reform." Among the political developments, Saudi Arabia announced it was proceeding with long-delayed plans for local elections, postwar Iraq scheduled elections for provincial and national assemblies in January 2005, and Palestinians held their first local elections since 1976 and scheduled a presidential election for January 2005 following the death of long-time leader Yasir Arafat. *(Palestinian developments, p. 806)*

One of the concrete proposals in the approved version of the Middle East initiative was for a high-level conference on democracy called the "Forum for the Future." Largely because of continued resistance to the Bush administration's rhetoric, the conference was recast as centering on economic, rather than political, reform. The conference was held on December 11 in Rabat, Morocco, at the level of foreign ministers. Although the sessions were closed to the news media, remarks of delegates were piped to reporters, who heard the unvarnished comments of diplomats speaking off the record. Arab delegates spent much of their time complaining about what they called unrestricted U.S. support for Israel. That theme also was emphasized by German foreign minister Joschka Fischer, who said progress toward resolving the Israeli-Palestinian conflict "will lend all reform and modernization efforts in the Arab world unprecedented momentum." Powell, who represented the United States, later told reporters that progress on the Israeli-Palestinian conflict was important but "we are not sitting here today saying no reform until that is resolved."

Powell Out, Rice In

Powell's attendance at the Rabat conference was one of his last official diplomatic chores as secretary of state. He had announced his resignation from the post on November 15, and Bush had immediately named Condoleezza Rice, Bush's national security adviser, as his successor. Months earlier Powell had signaled his intention to step down at the end of Bush's first term. After Bush won the November 2 election, aides said, Powell changed his mind and decided he wanted to serve a while longer. When the two men met on November 12, however, Bush did not ask Powell to stay on, and Powell promptly submitted a resignation letter.

Many observers said the nature of Powell's departure conformed to the history of his service in the Bush administration. A retired general with more than two decades of service in top government posts, Powell was the one international celebrity in the Bush administration—much better known, and more respected, around the word than the president himself at the start of Bush's term. Over the course of the next four years Powell often found himself at odds with other senior administration officials, notably Secretary of Defense Donald H. Rumsfeld and Deputy Secretary Wolfowitz, who appeared to disdain diplomacy in favor of a more muscular, military-oriented approach to U.S. policy. Powell had been the least enthusiastic among Bush's top aides about the decision to go to war in Iraq. Ironically, however, his public justification for the war had lent an important degree of legitimacy to it. In a day-long presentation Powell made to the United Nations Security Council on February 5, 2003, Powell made a strong case, based on U.S. intelligence information, that Iraq was moving quickly to develop biological, chemical, and nuclear weapons that were banned under Security Council resolutions. Months after the war, U.S. investigations showed that evidence Powell cited was wrong.

Rice was expected to take office in January 2005. A former academic who had specialized in Soviet studies, Rice had tutored Bush in world affairs after the November 2000 election. During Bush's first term Rice often had been a staunch advocate for administration policy but, behind the scenes, appeared to be more active as a coordinator than as a setter of policy. Because she had the president's ear, it was widely expected that Rice would use her new post to enforce compliance with White House policy at the State Department.

Following are excerpts from chapter 2 of the "Report on the Defense Science Board Task Force on Strategic Communication," submitted September 23, 2004, to the acting undersecretary of defense for acquisition, technology, and logistics by William Schneider Jr., chairman of the Defense Science Board. The report outlined challenges facing the United States in explaining its foreign policy goals to the rest of the world, particularly Muslim nations, and offered recommendations for what it called a "strategic communications" policy.

"Report of the Defense Task Force on Strategic Communication"

2.1 The Cold War Paradigm

In the second half of the 20th century U.S. national security was driven by the Cold War. America and its allies faced a seemingly powerful adversary—the Soviet Union—whose strategic objectives were inimical to our own. During this long struggle we used the various elements of national power—diplomatic, informational, military and economic—to advance our interests. There is a conviction held by many that the "War on Terrorism" will have a similar influence in the 21st century. There are indeed similarities between the two struggles, and strategic communication will be as central to this war as it was to our Cold War strategy.

Throughout the Cold War the U.S. used a variety of informational and cultural means to weaken Marxist-Leninist regimes and keep alive the hope of freedom for tens of millions behind the "Iron Curtain." Over the course of the Cold War era a suite of organizations—especially the Voice of America, the United States Information Agency, and a broad program of cultural and educational exchanges—spearheaded this effort. Several Presidential decision directives staked out the central role to be played by strategic communication. When Ronald Reagan stood in Berlin in June 1987 and demanded, "Mr. Gorbachev, tear down this wall", he was speaking to a live television audience of millions behind that wall. East Germans had been watching Western TV for years, but Reagan turned this reality into a powerful metaphor that the wall's days were numbered.

The Cold War transformed the entire U.S. national security structure, and created what has been called the "national security state." The National Security Act of 1947, the web of military departments and intelligence agencies that it created, and the overriding doctrines of deterrence and containment, were integral to the Cold War. But above all the Cold War represented a conservative strategy that nurtured a conservative mindset: its strategy spoke of change, but its pervasive charge in contrast was to preserve. Despite seemingly black-and-white differences in governments and policies, over time we came to resemble our adversary, as our adversary came to resemble us. The U.S.S.R. generally acted like a normal nation state with which we could conduct diplomacy, conclude treaties, and engage in statecraft with a reasonably predictable leadership. By the 1960s the possibility of nuclear war declined as the terrible recognition of its apocalyptic consequences grew. In fact, both sides increasingly sought the assurance of stability to keep even the possibility of nuclear confrontation at arm's length. But stability encouraged—even demanded—predictability, and thus the bureaucratic activities of both sides became highly routine. The Cold War evolved over time into a ritualized struggle that sought its own comfortable perpetuation. The very idea of "victory" slowly transformed from the idea of defeating Communism to the more perfect realization of "stability." Thus the Cold War's end and outcome, with Russia in the 1990s reduced almost to a client state of the U.S., came as a shocking surprise.

Our thorough inability to grasp the final dynamic changes that led to the end of the Cold War should be unsettling to us, but after all, the outcome was also a total victory. So the Cold War template was almost mythically anointed in the decade before 9/11. Thus, with the surprise announcement of a new struggle, the U.S. Government reflexively inclined toward Cold War-style responses to the new threat, without a thought or a care as to whether these were the best responses to a very different strategic situation.

The creation of the Department of Homeland Security and the passage of the Patriot Act were two such representative organizational and legislative responses. There will surely be many more the longer the struggle goes on—because deeper expectations within the Washington policy and defense cultures still seek out Cold War models. There is an expectation that, like the Cold War, the U.S. will naturally create enduring alliances and coalitions. Moreover, if the Cold War could be described as a struggle against one form of totalitarianism—Marxist-Leninism—so too there is a desire to describe the "War on Terrorism" as a struggle against yet another form of totalitarianism—this time in the form of a radical Islamist vision. Thus the problem is presented as one of how to confront and eventually defeat another totalitarian evil. And as with the Cold War, many now also declare that it is incumbent on the U.S. to assume leadership in this struggle.

But this is no Cold War. We call it a war on terrorism—but Muslims in contrast see a history-shaking movement of Islamic restoration. This is not simply a religious revival, however, but also a renewal of the Muslim World itself. And it has taken form through many variant movements, both moderate and militant, with many millions of adherents—of which radical fighters are only a small part. Moreover, these movements for restoration also represent, in their variant visions, the reality of multiple identities within Islam.

If there is one overarching goal they share, it is the overthrow of what Islamists call the "apostate" regimes: the tyrannies of Egypt, Saudi Arabia, Pakistan, Jordan, and the Gulf states. They are the main target of the broader Islamist movement, as well as the actual fighter groups. The United States finds itself in the strategically awkward—and potentially dangerous—situation of being the longstanding prop and alliance partner of these authoritarian regimes. Without the U.S. these regimes could not survive. Thus the U.S. has strongly taken sides in a desperate struggle that is both broadly cast for all Muslims *and* country-specific.

This is the larger strategic context, and it is acutely uncomfortable: U.S. policies and actions are increasingly seen by the overwhelming majority of Muslims as a threat to the survival of Islam itself. Three recent polls of Muslims show an overwhelming conviction that the U.S. seeks to "dominate" and "weaken" the Muslim World. Not only is every American initiative and commitment in the Muslim word enmeshed in the larger dynamic of intra-Islamic hostilities—but Americans have inserted themselves into this intra-Islamic struggle in ways that have made us an enemy to most Muslims.

Therefore, in stark contrast to the Cold War, the United States today is not seeking to contain a threatening state/empire, but rather seeking to convert a broad movement within Islamic civilization to accept the value structure of Western Modernity—an agenda hidden within the official rubric of a "War on Terrorism."

But if the strategic situation is wholly unlike the Cold War, our response nonetheless has tended to imitate the routines and bureaucratic responses and mindset that so characterized that era. In terms of strategic communication especially, the Cold War emphasized:

- Dissemination of information to "huddled masses yearning to be free." Today we reflexively compare Muslim "masses" to those oppressed under Soviet rule. This is a strategic mistake. There is no yearning-to-be-liberated-by-the-U.S. groundswell among Muslim societies—*except to be liberated perhaps from what they see as apostate tyrannies that the U.S. so determinedly promotes and defends.*
- An enduringly stable propaganda environment. The Cold War was a status quo setting that emphasized routine message-packaging—and whose essential objective was the most efficient enactment of the routine. In contrast the situation in Islam today is highly dynamic, and likely to move decisively in one direction or another. The U.S. urgently needs to think in terms of promoting actual positive change.

- An acceptance of authoritarian regimes as long as they were anti-communist. This could be glossed over in our message of freedom and democracy because it was the main adversary only that truly mattered. Today, however, the perception of intimate U.S. support of tyrannies in the Muslim World is perhaps the critical vulnerability in American strategy. It strongly undercuts our message, while strongly promoting that of the enemy.

Communicating authority and persuading others has been an essential tool of statecraft since ancient times. Three millennia ago Assyrian kings carved scenes of their power and majesty into stone tableaux meant to impress their authority on peers and subjects alike. In the mid 20th century all of the major powers made extensive use of radio as a means of extending information and influence across borders. Twenty years ago the Reagan Administration had a sophisticated grasp of the power of information—especially television—characterizing information as one of the elements of national power.

Yet the current national security strategy (October 2002) says nothing about the power of information nor does it allude to the necessity of integrating all of the forms of national power and authority. We now have national strategies for securing cyberspace, protecting national infrastructures, military strategy, and others, yet a national strategy for the employment of strategic communication does not exist. This blind spot existed throughout the 1990s, abetted in part by the belief that the end of the Cold War also ended our responsibility to continue strategic communication. This critical strategic mistake was made at the same time a new threat posed by radical Islam was emerging. Strategic communication must be at the center of America's overall grand strategy in this war. But how should we begin to move in this direction? The U.S. Government does not even have a coherent statement of the problem, and refuses to address the importance of strategic communication in addressing it. Moreover, it has adopted a Cold War style response in terms of activity and organization. So where to begin?

2.2 Strategic Communication Principles

If there were a strategic communication corollary to the U.S. Military's "intelligence preparation of the battle space" it would be: *correctly analyze the combined impacts of audience, impact, message and means.* We often speak of "the audience" we wish to influence as if there were only one. The reality is that in the global information environment in which we live and work there are numerous audiences that can be affected differently by the same message. Crafting an influence campaign means precisely identifying the key audience, but also other audiences as well.

What would we like our targeted audiences to see—and what impact do we wish to have? Do we want them to "like" us? Do we want them to question and doubt the information they get from their own governments, like we did with Radio Free Europe during the Cold War? Do we wish them similarly to cease supporting militant jihadists in their midst? Or are these traditional approaches to strategic communications even the right questions? Crafting an impact that we can see, measure, and realize is surely as important as accurately analyzing the audiences we wish to influence. But how to craft a message when our target audience is unwilling even to listen to us?

What message can generate the desired impact on the targeted audience? We must begin by listening to that audience, because if we do not understand what resonates with them we have only a serendipitous chance of succeeding. Much of the current U.S. effort concentrates on delivering "the message" and omits the essential first step of listening to our targeted audiences. We can craft a message that actually gets through only by using language, symbols, and images that resonate with the targeted audience.

Each synthesis of *message-impact-audience* suggests its own best means of delivery. Whether radio, TV, Internet, or print, we must understand how these factors interrelate before we can gauge the potential influence we might have. TV may be the most ubiquitous information medium in today's world, but it is the blend of media and how they can mutually reinforce our message that is crucial.

Information Age Dynamics

We must also take the measure of new dynamics emerging from the information age. The *speed* with which information becomes available to the global audience, the *convergence* of means by which we can capture many different kinds of information (visual, audio, print, etc) in a single digital format, and the ability to get that information to a global audience all suggest some of the advantages and limitations of this information age. Often the first information to reach an audience (a global audience that is really a galaxy of niche audiences) frames how an event is perceived and discussed—and thus can shape its ultimate impact as well. Always reacting to information is tantamount to losing. For example, NATO strategists were stunned to discover that Slobodan Milosevic's most effective weapon in the air campaign against him was not, say, an air defense network, but rather the global television network. Digital convergence is only beginning to be understood by decision makers. The significance of a common news language of bit and byte simply cannot be overstated. A truly global network is reshaping politics, diplomacy, warfare—all social interaction. Just one example: the ability of a blogger in a conflict zone to capture a digital image of an atrocity, upload it, paste it on a webpage, and have it available to millions in minutes is a startling development.

Here is just one example of information age implications for old-style info-agency organization. While we focus inward our adversary is focusing outward, truly reaching and motivating those they hope to enlist against us. The U.S. has always operated from the proposition that in the "war of ideas" and the competition of ideologies, one form of governance and society functions best when the bright light of free-flowing information is pulsing—among free and democratic societies—while another—the tyrannical and fascistic—functions with difficulty, if at all, under those circumstances. Yet the paradox today is that our enemy is thriving in an environment of free and open information flows. Thus our challenge is to transcend Cold War clichés, to seek out new and creative responses—especially in the realm of strategic communication—and to do so most urgently, because at this moment it is the enemy that has the advantage.

2.3 What is the Problem? Who Are We Dealing With?

The information campaign—or as some still would have it, "the war of ideas," or the struggle for "hearts and minds"—is important to every war effort. In this war it is an essential objective, because the larger goals of U.S. strategy depend on separating the vast majority of non-violent Muslims from the radical-militant Islamist-Jihadists. But American efforts have not only failed in this respect: they may also have achieved the opposite of what they intended.

American direct intervention in the Muslim World has paradoxically elevated the stature of and support for radical Islamists, while diminishing support for the United States to single-digits in some Arab societies.

- Muslims do not "hate our freedom," but rather, they hate our policies. The overwhelming majority voice their objections to what they see as one-sided support in favor of Israel and against Palestinian rights, and the longstanding, even increasing support for what Muslims collectively see as tyrannies, most notably Egypt, Saudi Arabia, Jordan, Pakistan, and the Gulf states.
- Thus when American public diplomacy talks about bringing democracy to Islamic societies, this is seen as no more than self-serving hypocrisy. Moreover, saying that "freedom is the future of the Middle East" is seen as patronizing, suggesting that Arabs are like the enslaved peoples of the old Communist World—but Muslims do not feel this way: they feel oppressed, but not enslaved.
- Furthermore, *in the eyes of Muslims,* American occupation of Afghanistan and Iraq has not led to democracy there, but only more chaos and suffering. U.S. actions appear in contrast to be motivated by ulterior motives, and deliberately controlled in order to best serve American national interests at the expense of truly Muslim self-determination.
- Therefore, the dramatic narrative since 9/11 has essentially borne out the entire radical Islamist bill of particulars. American actions and the flow of events have elevated the authority of the Jihadi insurgents and tended to ratify their legitimacy among Muslims. Fighting groups portray themselves as the true defenders of an Ummah (the entire Muslim community) invaded and under attack—to broad public support.
- What was a marginal network is now an Ummah-wide movement of fighting groups. Not only has there been a proliferation of "terrorist" groups: the unifying context of a shared cause creates a sense of affiliation across the many cultural and sectarian boundaries that divide Islam.
- Finally, Muslims see Americans as strangely narcissistic—namely, that the war is all about us. As the Muslims see it, everything about the war is—for Americans—really no more than an extension of American domestic politics and its great game. This perception is of course necessarily heightened by election-year atmospherics, but nonetheless sustains their impression that when Americans talk to Muslims they are really just talking to themselves.

Thus the critical problem in American public diplomacy directed toward the Muslim World is not one of "dissemination of information," or even one of crafting and delivering the "right" message. Rather, it is a fundamental problem of credibility. Simply, there is none—the United States today is without a working channel of communication to the world of Muslims and of Islam. Inevitably therefore, whatever Americans do and say only serves the party that has both the message and the "loud and clear" channel: the enemy.

Arguably the first step toward mitigating and eventually even reversing this situation is to better understand the values and worldview of the target audience itself.

Target Demographics and Value

The official take on the target audience has been gloriously simple. If the enemy is a relatively small group of crazies and criminals—"Bad Muslims"—then the rest must be "Good Muslims" and thus the people we want our public diplomacy to reach: Good Muslims *(Including friendly regimes and everybody else);* Bad Muslims *(Only terrorists & sponsors).*

The difficulty of course is that the Muslim World looks nothing like this. Islam is a cacophony of competing and crosscutting groups, sub-cultures, and whole societies. A Muslim may be balancing up to five identities: as a Muslim, as a sectarian Muslim (Sunni, Sh'ia, Ismaili, etc.), as a national citizen, as an ethnic "citizen" (Arab, Kurd, Turkmen, etc.), and as a tribal or clan member. If we were to grossly simplify this picture, and yet still have a roughly accurate yardstick of Muslim sociology today—especially in terms of the dynamics of the war—it might break down like this:

- Regimes and their retainers (including the army, bigwigs, cronies, & hangers-on)
- The professional class (also known in some quarters as "technocrats")
- Establishment & activist Islamist preletes (plus social welfare & education networks)
- Regular and poor Muslims (small entrepreneurs on-down)
- Fighting groups and their networks

These broad segments represent relatively distinct social and political constituencies, with varying weight and influence in national life. The norms of national life can be seen in some ways as a balance between the first three of these segments: a rough triad of regime elites, establishment Ulama (Muslim prelates) and the technocratic class.

But the war has placed these norms under increasing stress, and conflicts below the surface in Muslim (and especially Arab) national life are emerging into a promise and anticipation of change. Change is the province of the fighting groups and the activist Islamists prelates who are not creatures of their regimes. Change means of course the vision of Islamic Restoration. Thus if we were to look at Muslim societies (again, Arab societies especially) in terms of their receptivity and support for change/restoration, the spectrum might look like this:

Regimes—Uncommitted—**Sympathizers**—Islamists—Jihadis.

This "change-spectrum" shows change constituencies in terms of a weighted mix of both numbers *and authority*. By this last measure, paradoxically, regimes may have the highest level of power but the lowest level of authority within their societies. This sort of authority is not what has been referred to as "soft power" in the foreign policy context—rather it is ultimately the foundation of political legitimacy within society. Thus a developing shift in such authority within Muslim society presages eventual changes in political power—and so in today's ruling regimes.

And of course, the regimes are the most resistant to political and social change, while the Jihadis, the fighting groups, are its most active agents. Notably the regime and *status quo* segments are quite small. Some elements within Arab regimes are actually quite committed, if subversively, to the change agenda. In Pakistan, regime support for Islamic Restoration is quite high. This sort of continuing *sub rosa* defection will be in fact a critical indicator of impending regime collapse.

Thus it is possible to show the Jihadis as having a wider degree of sympathetic (Arab majorities), indirect (Islamists), and direct support than most of the regimes. Certainly Arabs, by an overwhelming majority, sympathize with, or are active in the cause of Islamic Restoration. Therefore it is even more interesting to track the relative weight of the non-Jihadi Islamists, also called "moderate" or "New Islamists," because their professed vision of Islamic Restoration is non-violent, tolerant, and relatively pluralistic. It can be argued that the New Islamists are in fact the true center of gravity in the Muslim World today, in that they have the most authority to make change, and draw the highest levels of sympathy from less-active, but receptive and supportive Arab majorities. In this construct the Jihadis are seen as perhaps necessary to make change begin and thus become eventually inevitable, but the radicals do not appeal to the majority of Muslims in terms of practical political change if and when old regimes finally collapse.

The change spectrum reveals target demographics for U.S. public diplomacy that offer at best a highly constricted opportunity—how constricted it actually is can be shown by mapping the change-spectrum above onto the marketing construct presented in Chapter 3 which defines the "where to put your marketing effort" spectrum:

- ***Hard Support*** *(for U.S. Government):* Regimes and their retainers
- ***Soft Support:*** Regimes and their retainers, a few technocrats
- ***Neutral:*** Some of the professional class and some regular & poor
- ***Soft Opposition:*** The overwhelming majority
- ***Hard Opposition:*** A substantial minority (more than we want to admit)

This spectrum does not preclude future opportunities for us to reach key segments of these audiences. Neither, however, should we underestimate the magnitude of the problem we face. A June 2004 Zogby poll of Arab opinion shows that the audience receptive to the U.S. message is miniscule: [A chart showed "unfavorable" attitudes toward the United States in six Arab countries as of June 2004, ranging from a low of 69 percent in Lebanon to a high of 98 percent in Egypt].

But Americans believe that while the U.S. necessarily shapes foreign policies to support our national interests, those same interests are not necessarily in opposition to the interests of other nations and cultures. To the contrary, Americans are convinced that the U.S. is a benevolent "superpower" that elevates values emphasizing freedom and prosperity as at the core of its own national interest. Thus, for Americans, "U.S. values" are in reality "world values"—exemplified by the United Nations' Universal Declaration of Human Rights or the 1975 Helsinki Accords—so deep down we assume that everyone should naturally support our policies.

Yet the world of Islam—by overwhelming majorities at this time—sees things differently. Muslims see American policies as inimical to their values, American rhetoric about freedom and democracy as hypocritical, and American actions as deeply threatening. [A chart based on a July 2004 poll by Zogby International showed generally unfavorable attitudes toward U.S. policies and culture in six Arab nations].

In other words, they do not hate us for our values, but because of our policies.

But this chart suggests an even more worrisome development. A similar series of questions showed even more favorable opinion ratios in favor of U.S. culture and its values—in 2002. Thus it seems that in two years the Jihadi message—that strongly attacks American values—is being accepted by more moderate and non-violent Muslims. This in turn implies that negative opinion of the U.S. has not yet bottomed-out, but is in fact continuing to move dynamically. But the movement is now qualitative rather and quantitative, meaning that regular Muslims are moving from "soft opposition" toward "hard opposition." In Saudi Arabia, a large majority believes that the U.S. seeks to "weaken" and "dominate" Islam itself—in other words, Americans have become the enemy. It is noteworthy that opinion is hardest over against America in precisely those places ruled by what Muslims call "apostates" and tyrants—the tyrants we support. This should give us pause.

Thus it is incumbent on the U.S. strategic information campaign to first find a way to address this near-unanimity of Muslim opinion hostile to the U.S.. If we want to truly demonstrate the linkage between American power and the universal values we support, and if we want to truly build a bridge between ourselves and the Muslim World, then we must first open a working channel of communication with that world, which as of now does not exist. Furthermore, if regular Muslims are indeed moving to hard "opposition" to the U.S. then we have only so much time to open such a channel before the possibility is closed for the duration of this war.

Therefore it is not enough for us to preach to Muslims, telling them that they need to show us that they believe in our values—such as tolerance and pluralism—and that they must reject the bad values of the violent Islamists. It is patently patronizing, for example, to keep bringing up Islam's "Golden Age" as though we were scolding Muslims for some sort of civilizational backsliding. This is in fact a counter-productive approach; a non-starter. If we really want to see the Muslim World as a whole and the Arabic speaking World in particular, move more toward our understanding of "moderation" and "tolerance," we must reassure Muslims that this does not mean that they must submit to the American Way. In other words, as we seek out Islamic voices that share essential beliefs with us, we must convey an important message of reassurance to them—before we can expect to usefully talk with them.

This should not be seen as an intractable enterprise. In more moderate Muslim societies like Indonesia, Malaysia, and Bangladesh, there is markedly more support for the U.S.—albeit still small minorities—so we might look to realize some small initial success there. Furthermore, the wider task of strategic communication reaches beyond the exigencies of this war and the Muslim World. Arguably it is just as essential to renew European attitudes toward America—and this is surely a more straightforward task. Strategic communication is still a global mission. . . .

Source: U.S. Department of Defense. Office of the Undersecretary of Defense for Acquisition, Technology, and Logistics. Defense Science Board. "Report of the Defense Science Board Task Force on Strategic Communication." September 23, 2004. www.acq.osd.mil/dsb/reports/2004-09-Strategic_Communication.pdf (accessed March 7, 2004).

Government Accountability Office on the Shortage of Flu Vaccine

September 28, 2004

INTRODUCTION

Contamination kept nearly 50 million doses of influenza vaccine from the American market in 2004, causing a shortage that panicked seniors and others at risk for contracting the flu. Most people who wanted the flu vaccine were eventually able to obtain it, and some states even appeared to have a surplus on hand at the end of the year. But the crisis demonstrated how vulnerable the American population was to disruptions in the supply and distribution of vaccines. It also revealed huge shortfalls in the country's ability to cope should it be hit with a far larger health catastrophe, such as a potential flu pandemic or a massive bioterrorism attack. Health experts said, if nothing else, the shortage served as a wake-up call to policymakers.

The shortage occurred after British health officials on October 5 suspended the license of a factory in Liverpool, England, that made flu vaccine for the Chiron Corporation, a California company that was one of two major flu vaccine suppliers in the United States. The other was Aventis Pasteur, a French company that made its vaccine in Swiftwater, Pennsylvania. Chiron was to have produced 46–48 million doses of flu vaccine for the 2004–2005 flu season; Aventis was scheduled for about 52 million doses. British officials closed the Chiron plant for three months after an investigation uncovered evidence of contamination by a bacterium known as *serratia marcescens.* Although relatively common and harmless to humans on casual contact, *serratia* had been implicated in deadly blood and other infections when it was injected, as it might have been had it been in any of the doses of Fluvirin that Chiron was making.

The plant closure left the federal government, state governments, and health officials scrambling to find replacement vaccine and to redistribute the Aventis vaccine to those Americans deemed to be at highest-risk for complications from the flu. On average, influenza caused 36,000 deaths and 200,000 hospitalizations in the United States every year. Before the shortage the federal Centers for Disease Control and Prevention (CDC) Advisory Committee on Immunization Practices had recommended that 185 million Americans be immunized against the flu, including for the first time all infants six to twenty-three months old. Others at high risk were people age sixty-five and older, children and adults with chronic health problems or weak immune systems, and pregnant women. CDC also recommended vaccinations for people fifty and older, health care workers, and people who lived with or took care of people at risk of complications from the flu. Only about half the target population actually requested vaccination in any given year, and vaccine makers tried to match their production to likely demand. Based on demand in the previous year, the CDC estimated that about 100 million doses of vaccine would be available in 2004.

The Food and Drug Administration (FDA), already under fire for its slowness in recognizing safety problems with antidepressant drugs in children and with painkillers such as Vioxx and Celebrex, was also taken to task for not taking more aggressive action at the Chiron plant when the FDA first found evidence of contamination in 2003. *(Antidepressants and suicide in children, p. 746; painkillers, p. 850)*

The Unfolding of a Crisis

The first public evidence that Chiron might be having problems with its vaccine production came on August 26, when the Emeryville, California, company announced that it had temporarily stopped distribution of its vaccine, Fluvirin, after tests at its Liverpool factory found that up to 4 million doses might have been contaminated. Chiron had become the second largest supplier of flu shots in the United States after it bought a British vaccine manufacturer, PowderJect Pharmaceuticals, in July 2003 for $848 million. The company said it would retest vaccines already sent to distributors and that the contamination was likely to delay distribution of the rest of the vaccine until at least the first week in October. Distribution typically began in September.

Chiron president and chief executive Howard Pien predicted the distribution delay would have only a minimal impact on the American public, but the company's news release said "no assurances could be given that additional tests of Fluvirin will yield satisfactory results or that Chiron will be able to release Fluvirin this season." Chiron's share prices fell by nearly 10 percent the day after the announcement, but government regulators expressed little concern. Julie L. Gerberding, director of the CDC, said the announcement was "not good news" but added that the agency did not "anticipate an overall shortage."

On September 28 Pien told the Senate Special Committee on Aging that the company still expected to start supplying its vaccine in early October. At that same hearing, Janet Heinrich, director of health care and public health issues at the Government Accountability Office (GAO), offered a prescient assessment when she said that "challenges persist in ensuring an adequate and timely flu vaccine supply."

A week later, on October 5, British health authorities abruptly suspended Chiron's license for three months, citing concerns about sterility problems at the Liverpool plant. The announcement clearly caught U.S. officials off guard. "We'll be working on this fast and furiously," Gerberding told legislators at a House hearing that morning. The CDC urged that the available vaccine be reserved only for those at highest risk—the elderly, the very young, the chronically ill, and pregnant women. It immediately asked the remaining major supplier, Aventis, to try to redistribute its shipments to ensure that high-risk patients could get their vaccine first. Aventis ultimately made about 58 million doses available. (A third manufacturer, Medimmune, made a vaccine nasal spray called FluMist. Because it was made with live virus, it was recommended only for use by healthy adults. Medimmune made 2 million doses available.)

The Food and Drug Administration, which was responsible for monitoring vaccine production, immediately sent a team to the Liverpool plant to conduct its own investigation. On October 15 FDA officials confirmed that none of the Chiron vaccine could be salvaged.

Announcement of the shortage caused panic among those who wanted the vaccine and a distributional nightmare for health officials trying to obtain it. Some physicians and clinics had all the vaccine they needed because they had ordered their entire supply from Aventis. Others who had ordered from Chiron had little or none.

Across the country, the elderly and others at high risk waited for hours in line at pharmacies or supermarket health clinics, sometimes in foul weather, only to be told no vaccine was available. In a few places, people were so angered that police were called in to maintain order. A few people were arrested for disorderly conduct, and vaccine was stolen from at least one doctor's office. Some states threatened to fine or even jail health officials who gave the vaccine to anyone not at high risk.

Allegations of price gouging surfaced almost immediately. More than half of the 677 hospital pharmacy directors who responded to a survey by the American Society of Health-System Pharmacists right after the plant closure said that drug distributors had offered to sell them flu vaccine at anywhere from four to ten times the usual wholesale cost. One pharmacy director, who declined to pay the inflated prices, said the markups were "disgusting and a disgrace to the industry." On October 12 the Kansas state attorney general filed suit against a Florida supplier for trying to gouge a Kansas City pharmacy. The Department of Health and Human Services (HHS) encouraged other state attorneys general to take similarly aggressive steps against price gougers.

On October 12, as demand for the vaccine continued to grow, Gerberding announced that the government would supervise distribution of vaccine supplies that had not yet been shipped in an effort to get doses to those most in need. Officials acknowledged that large numbers of high-risk people would be unable to get the vaccine. "We're sorry for the people who need flu vaccine and may not be able to get it this year," Gerberding said.

By mid-October, when isolated cases of flu were beginning to be reported, complaints were still growing about lack of vaccine and distribution. In some areas anyone could receive the vaccine; in other areas it was unavailable or strictly monitored. In a few places, people participated in a lottery. Many Americans living near the Mexican and Canadian borders crossed over to get their flu shots abroad.

Predictably, the flu vaccine shortage became an issue in the presidential elections. President George W. Bush made his first public statement on the problem on October 19, two weeks after the plant closing was announced. At a campaign rally in St. Petersburg, Florida, Bush said he knew that people were worried about the flu season, and he wanted "to assure them that our government is doing everything possible to help older Americans and children get their shots, despite the major manufacturing defect that caused this problem."

Bush's Democratic opponent, Sen. John Kerry, D-Mass., said the administration's failure to ensure a safe supply of vaccine and distribute it to those in need underscored larger shortcomings. "If you can't get flu vaccines to Americans, how are you going to protect them against bioterrorism," Kerry asked in an interview with National Public Radio. "If you can't get flu vaccines to Americans, what kind of health care program are you running?"

Congress took a little heat after it was reported in the national media that shots were available, at no charge, to all members and employees of Congress regardless of their health status. Even after the shortage, John F. Eisold, the Capitol's attending physician, urged all lawmakers to get the shot because they shook hands with so many people and could easily transmit the virus. It appeared, however, that far fewer members and employees were getting shots than had in previous years. On October 20 Bush questioned whether members and employees of Congress should receive flu shots if they were not in the high-risk groups identified in federal guidelines and said he himself did not plan to get a shot. Eisold subsequently said that 3,000 doses would be donated to area hospitals. On October 28 government health officials announced that 300,000 doses intended for federal employees and military personnel would be diverted to high-risk groups. On November 10 Gerberding announced a plan for distributing about 10 million doses of vaccine to states, depending on how many high-risk people each state had and the number of doses already distributed.

On December 7 Tommy G. Thompson, secretary of health and human services, announced that the government had approved the purchase of up to 4 million doses of a flu vaccine, Fluarix, made in Germany by the British drug company GlaxoSmithKline. Because Fluarix had not been licensed for sale in the United States, it was being treated as an "investigational new drug," and every patient receiving the vaccine had to sign a consent form acknowledging that fact. The timing of the announcement was somewhat of an embarrassment for the administration, which had been scheduled to release a report on December 8 on the safety of importing drugs from abroad. The administration had opposed drug importation in the past. The report, which was released December 21, concluded that importation might be feasible but that the cost savings to consumers were likely to be small. *(Drug importation, p. 981)*

Ironically, Thompson's approval of the German-made vaccine came as the crisis was beginning to ease. The shortage discouraged many from even trying to get a flu shot, and a mild start to the flu season eased people's concerns. As a result, by the end of the year more than four out of five states reported having sufficient supplies of vaccine, and some even had a surplus. On December 17 the CDC advisory panel on immunization recommended that starting in January any remaining vaccine be made available to people over age fifty. "We are in danger of seesawing from a year when everybody's concerned there's no vaccine, to not using what we have," said Greg Poland, a member of the panel and a flu specialist at the Mayo Clinic in Minnesota.

A Regulatory Failure?

As the flu crisis unfolded, attention focused on whether the Food and Drug Administration should have been aware of the problems at Chiron's Liverpool plant and taken action to correct them. After investigating the plant, the British regulators made the decision to suspend Chiron's license during an internal meeting on October 4 and informed both Chiron and the FDA of the decision on October 5. Acting FDA commissioner Lester M. Crawford later said that neither Chiron or the British regulators had previously notified the FDA of a serious problem. "I want to refute as strongly as possible the contention . . . that FDA knew before October 5 that there was evidence of a problem serious enough for [British officials] to suspend Chiron's license to distribute or export influenza vaccine for the upcoming flu season," Crawford said October 11, during a telephone briefing to reporters. He also said that the FDA had relied on Chiron to disclose whether its contamination problems were serious and had been assured that the contamination was under control.

At a hearing before the House Government Reform Committee on November 18 Crawford revealed that the FDA's October investigation of the shut-down plant had found that 60 percent of the unfinished vaccine was contaminated with several different bacteria and that the contamination took place at several points along the production process, including after the vaccine had been sterilized. He also acknowledged that an FDA inspection of the plant in July 2003 had turned up higher-than-expected levels of bacteria in a "limited" number of batches of vaccine in the early stages of production. But he said that the filtering processes had removed the bacteria, and the final vaccine, used in the 2003–2004 flu season, was not contaminated.

Crawford defended the agency's decision not to reinspect the plant after finding the contamination in 2003. Typically the agency inspected plants only every two years, and in this case, Crawford said, because Chiron had fixed the problem, regular telephone conference calls and other communications were an appropriate form of "reinspection."

Rep. Henry A. Waxman of California, the ranking Democrat on the committee, sharply disagreed with that assessment, saying that the FDA "didn't do enough to stay on top" of the situation at Chiron. "This is not Rogaine," Waxman said, referring to the flu vaccine. "This is a product that is essential to the health of millions of Americans."

The Liverpool plant had a history of manufacturing problems even before Chiron bought it in 2003. In 1999 FDA inspectors found that one of the previous owners of the plant had failed to ensure that the plant's systems and equipment for making Fluvirin were free from contamination. In 2000 British health officials withdrew polio vaccines made at the plant because of possible contamination with the proteins that caused mad cow disease, and in 2002 Irish officials stopped sales of a tuberculosis vaccine made at the factory because of concerns that it did not meet required strength.

A Fragile System

Even if the FDA had found the contamination earlier in the year, a shortage of vaccine still would have occurred, because there would not have been time to manufacture a new batch in time for distribution before the flu season. The shortage also pointed up the problems of relying on two vaccine producers. The number of vaccine makers licensed by the United States had dwindled from about two dozen in the 1970s to two by 2004, largely because the vaccines were expensive to make, the profits were low, and the market was unpredictable.

The manufacturing of flu vaccine was a cumbersome and expensive process. The vaccines were made from two or three strains of influenza virus selected several months in advance of the flu season by the World Health Organization, working with experts to predict the combination likely to offer the most protection against a flu whose predominant viral strains were not yet known. The selected virus strains were injected into fertilized chicken eggs, where they multiplied rapidly and were then killed to make the vaccine. That process required millions of eggs and took five or six months, which meant that if something went wrong, such as contamination, there was generally not enough time to replace the lost production. Companies were trying to develop ways to make vaccines in cell cultures, which would eliminate the need for chicken eggs and cut the time needed to produce the vaccine. That in turn would allow companies to ramp up production if need be. But while cell culture was used for some other types of vaccine, it had not yet been successfully applied in making flu vaccine.

Another uncertainty was whether demand for the vaccine would match supply in any given year. Although there were shortages of flu vaccine in 2000 and 2003, there were surpluses in 2001 and 2002, and millions of doses of vaccine were unused and had to be destroyed.

Public health experts had been predicting a major shortage for years, warning that it was not wise to rely on only two or three companies to produce the nation's supply and faulting the government for not doing enough to encourage more companies to make the flu vaccines. The country had also experienced shortages in other vaccines, including those used to protect children against measles, chicken pox, and the mumps, because there were so few licensed manufacturers. Possible options for curing the problem were increasing the price of the vaccine to give companies more of an incentive to make it, subsidizing the manufacturers, or having the government own and operate directly or indirectly a manufacturing plant. Sen. Evan Bayh, D-Ind., proposed tax subsidies to entice vaccine producers to locate inside the United States. Only one drug maker, Aventis, currently made vaccine in the United States; other American drug companies had moved their operations overseas where wages were cheaper and taxes lower. Bayh specifically proposed giving companies a tax credit equal to 20 percent of a factory's construction costs.

Others looked to Canada as a model. Canada also had only two flu vaccine makers, but about 90 percent of all vaccine used there each year was purchased by the government, meaning the government absorbed the cost of any vaccine that was unused and had to be discarded. Although such a guarantee would not have prevented the 2004 shortage, HHS secretary Thompson said he favored a federal guarantee of a specific number of flu doses each year.

Another issue concerned distribution of vaccines. In the United States vaccine supply and distribution was largely left to the private sector. The federal and state governments were directly involved only in supplying their public health facilities with the vaccine. Most vaccine was sold by manufacturers, medical supply distributors, pharmacies, and other resellers to purchasers for use in doctors' offices, nursing homes, health clinics, and at nonmedical facilities, including workplaces and community centers. Because the federal government did not have control over vaccine distribution, Heinrich of the GAO noted on September 28, there was "no mechanism in place to ensure distribution of flu vaccine to high-risk individuals before others when the vaccine is in short supply." Although the federal government and many state governments had begun to plan for a possible bioterror attack or a pandemic, such as possible outbreak of bird flu, Heinrich said the problems could become "especially acute" in an emergency. "Until decisions are made about vaccine purchase distribution, and administration, and priority populations are designated," she said, "states will not be able to develop strategies consistent with federal priorities." *(BioShield legislation, p. 442; bird flu, p. 923)*

Investigations into Chiron

Chiron disclosed October 12 that it was the subject of a Justice Department investigation. It said it would comply with a subpoena from a New York federal grand jury for documents related to the plant shutdown. The Justice Department refused to comment, but some observers thought it likely that federal prosecutors were investigating the truthfulness of Chiron's public statements after its August announcement that it had found contamination in a few batches of Fluvirin. Just a week before the plant was closed on October 5, Pien told Congress that he expected to deliver as many as 48 million doses of the vaccine by the end of October. Chiron's stock fell 16 percent, to $33.74 a share, the day after the plant closure. On October 13 Chiron said the SEC had begun an informal investigation.

Two class-action shareholder suits against Chiron were filed in U.S. District Court for the Northern District of California on October 14, alleging that the company had misled investors about its ability to deliver the vaccine. Chiron, which entered the flu vaccine market in 2003, received more bad news on December 7 when British regulators announced they were extending their suspension of the company's license for another three months, until April 2005. That could make it impossible for the company to manufacture vaccine in time for the 2005–2006 flu season. Meanwhile, two other vaccine makers, GlaxoSmithKline of Britain and ID Biomedical Corporation of Canada, were applying to the FDA for priority review for permanent licenses to begin manufacturing flu vaccine for the American market in 2005.

Following are excerpts from "Infectious Disease Preparedness: Federal Challenges in Responding to Influenza Outbreaks," testimony delivered September 28, 2004, to the Senate Special Committee on Aging by Janet Heinrich, director of health care and public health issues at the Government Accountability Office.

"Infectious Disease Preparedness: Responding to Influenza Outbreaks"

Mr. Chairman and Members of the Committee:

I am pleased to be here today as you discuss issues regarding the annual production and distribution of flu vaccine and preparedness for a worldwide influenza epidemic—known as a pandemic. Each year, influenza viruses cause outbreaks in the United States and elsewhere in the world. Influenza is associated with an average of 36,000 deaths and more than 200,000 hospitalizations each year in the United States. Persons aged 65 and older are involved in more than 9 of every 10 deaths and 1 of every 2 hospitalizations related to influenza. The best way to prevent influenza is to be vaccinated each fall. In the 2000–01 flu season, and again in last year's flu season, this country experienced periods when the demand for flu vaccine exceeded the supply, and there is concern about the availability of vaccines for this and future flu seasons.

There has also been increased concern about the prospect of an influenza pandemic, which many experts believe to be inevitable. Pandemic influenza, which arises periodically, but unpredictably, from a major genetic change in the virus, results in a strain that can cause worldwide disease and death. Three influenza pandemics occurred in the twentieth century. The worst occurred in 1918 (Spanish flu)and killed more than 20 million people worldwide and about 675,000 people in the United States. The pandemics of 1957 (Asian flu) and 1968 (Hong Kong flu) caused fewer fatalities—70,000 and 34,000, respectively, in the United States. Some experts believe that the next pandemic could be spawned by the recurring avian flu in Asia. They estimate that the pandemic could kill up to 207,000 people in the United States and cause major social disruption. Public health experts have raised concerns about the ability of the nation's public health system to detect and respond to emerging infectious disease threats such as pandemic influenza. . . .

In summary, challenges persist in ensuring an adequate and timely flu vaccine supply. The number of producers remains limited, and the potential for manufacturing problems such as those experienced in recent years is still present. If a manufacturer's production is affected, those providers who ordered vaccine from that manufacturer could experience shortages, while providers who received supplies from another manufacturer might have all the vaccine they need. This potential for imbalance is what creates situations in which some providers might not have enough vaccine for persons at highest risk, while other providers might have enough supply to hold mass- immunization clinics even for persons at lower risk for flu-related complications. To help limit the potential for such situations, CDC [Centers for Disease Control and Prevention] and others have taken such steps as adding flu vaccine to federal stockpiles and more aggressively monitoring the projected supply of vaccine. However, there is no system in place to ensure that seniors and others at high risk for complications receive flu vaccinations first when vaccine is in short supply.

HHS's [Department of Health and Human Services'] draft "Pandemic Influenza Preparedness and Response Plan" provides a blueprint for the government's role but leaves some important decisions about the government's response unresolved. In addition to describing the federal role, responsibilities, and actions in collaboration with the states in responding to an influenza pandemic, the plan also provides planning guidance to state and local health departments and the health care system. The draft plan is comprehensive in scope, but it leaves decisions about the purchase, distribution, and administration of vaccines open for public comment and for the states to decide individually. In addition, the draft plan does not make recommendations for how population groups should be prioritized to receive vaccines in a pandemic. Difficulties encountered during the annual flu season with the purchase, distribution, and administration of flu vaccine highlight the importance of resolving these issues for pandemic preparedness.

Background

In almost every year an influenza virus causes acute respiratory disease in epidemic proportions somewhere in the world. Influenza is more severe than some of the other viral respiratory infections, such as the common cold. Most people who get the flu recover completely in 1 to 2 weeks, but some develop serious and potentially life-threatening medical complications, such as pneumonia. People who are aged 65 and older, people of any age with chronic medical conditions, children younger than 2 years, and pregnant women are more likely to get severe complications from influenza than other people. Influenza and pneumonia rank as the fifth leading cause of death among persons aged 65 and older.

For the 2004–05 flu season, CDC is recommending that about 185 million Americans in these at-risk populations and other target groups receive the vaccine, which is the primary method for preventing influenza. Flu vaccine is generally widely available in a variety of settings, ranging from the usual physicians' offices, clinics, and hospitals to retail outlets such as drugstores and grocery stores, workplaces, and other convenience locations. Millions of individuals receive flu vaccinations through mass immunization campaigns in nonmedical settings, where organizations such as visiting nurse agencies under contract administer the vaccine. It takes about 2 weeks after vaccination for antibodies to develop in the body and provide protection against influenza virus infection. CDC recommends October through November as the best time to get vaccinated because the flu season often starts in late November to December and peaks between late December and early March. However, if influenza activity peaks late, vaccination in December or later can still be beneficial.

Producing the influenza vaccine is a complex process that involves growing viruses in millions of fertilized chicken eggs. This process, which requires several steps, generally takes at least 6 to 8 months from January through August each year, so vaccine manufacturers must predict demand and decide on the number of doses to produce well before the onset of the flu season. Each year's vaccine is made up of three different strains of influenza viruses, and, typically, each year one or two of the strains is changed to better protect against the strains that are likely to be circulating during the coming flu season. The Food and Drug Administration (FDA) and its advisory committee decide which strains to include based on CDC surveillance data, and FDA also licenses and regulates the manufacturers that produce the vaccine.

In a typical year, manufacturers make flu vaccine available before the optimal fall season for administering flu vaccine. Currently, two manufacturers—one in the United States and one in the United Kingdom—produce over 95 percent of the vaccine used in the United States. According to CDC officials, for the 2002–03 flu season, manufacturers produced about 95 million doses of vaccine, of which about 83 million doses were used and 12 million doses went unused. Production for the 2003–04 flu season was based on the previous year's demand and was about 87 million doses. For the 2004–05 season, CDC estimates that about 100 million doses will be available.

Currently, flu vaccine production and distribution are largely private- sector responsibilities. Like other pharmaceutical products, flu vaccine is sold to thousands of purchasers by manufacturers, numerous medical supply distributors, and other resellers such as pharmacies. These purchasers provide flu vaccinations at physicians' offices, public health clinics, nursing homes, and less traditional locations such as workplaces and various retail outlets. Most influenza vaccine distribution and administration are accomplished within the private sector, with relatively small amounts of vaccine purchased and distributed by CDC or by state and local health departments.

HHS also has a role in planning to prepare for and respond to an influenza pandemic. Planning is key to being prepared for and mitigating the negative effects of the next influenza pandemic, including major illness, death, economic loss, and social disruption. A national pandemic influenza plan was first developed in 1978 and was revised in 1983. In 1993, efforts to revise the national plan were initiated, and these efforts picked up momentum in the late 1990s. In August 2004, HHS released a draft plan for comment entitled, "Pandemic Influenza Preparedness and Response Plan."

To foster state and local pandemic planning and preparedness, CDC first issued draft interim planning guidance to states in 1997 and posted guidance on its Web site for state and local health departments in 2001. Since that time, states have been preparing pandemic response plans, and many are integrating these plans with existing state plans to respond to public health emergencies such as natural disasters and bioterrorist attacks.

Challenges Exist in Ensuring an Adequate and Timely Flu Vaccine Supply

Ensuring an adequate and timely supply of vaccine is a difficult task. It has become even more difficult because there are few manufacturers. Problems at one or more manufacturers can significantly upset the traditional fall delivery of influenza vaccine. These problems, in turn, can create variability in who has ready access to the vaccine.

Matching flu vaccine supply and demand is a challenge because the available supply and demand for vaccine can vary from month to month and year to year. For example,

- In 2000–01, when a substantial proportion of flu vaccine was distributed much later than usual due to manufacturing difficulties, temporary shortages in the prime period for vaccinations were followed by decreased demand as additional vaccine became available later in the year. Despite efforts by CDC and others to encourage people to seek flu vaccinations later in the season, providers still reported a drop in demand in December. The light flu season in 2000–01, which had relatively low influenza mortality, probably also contributed to the lack of interest. As a result of the waning demand that year, manufacturers and distributors reported having more vaccine than they could sell. In addition, some physicians' offices, employee health clinics, and other organizations that administered flu shots reported having unused doses in December and later.
- For the 2003–04 flu season, shortages of vaccine have been attributed to an earlier than expected and more severe flu season and to higher than normal demand, likely resulting from media coverage of pediatric deaths associated with influenza. According to CDC officials, this increased demand occurred in a year in which manufacturers had produced about the same number of doses as in the previous season and that supply was not adequate to meet the demand.

If production problems delay the availability of vaccine in a given year, the timing for an individual provider to obtain flu vaccine may depend on which manufacturer's vaccine it ordered. This happened in the 2000–01 season, and it could happen again. This year, one of the two major manufacturers recently announced a delay in its shipments of vaccine. On August 26, 2004, one manufacturer announced that release of its flu vaccine would be delayed because of production problems related to sterility of a small number of doses at its manufacturing facility. The company stated that it expected to deliver between 46 million and 48 million doses to the U.S. market beginning in October, and CDC issued a notice on September 24, 2004, stating that some delays might occur for customers receiving this manufacturer's vaccine. . . .

Shortages of flu vaccine can result in temporary spikes in the price of vaccine. When vaccine supply is limited relative to public demand for flu shots, distributors and others who have supplies of the vaccine have the ability—and the economic incentive—to sell their supplies to the highest bidders rather than filling lower-priced orders they had already received. When there was a delay and temporary shortage of vaccine in 2000, those who purchased vaccine that fall—because their earlier orders had been cancelled, reduced, or delayed, or because they simply ordered later—found themselves paying much higher prices. . . .

Our work has also found that there is no mechanism in place to ensure distribution of flu vaccine to high-risk individuals before others when the vaccine is in short supply. When the supply was not sufficient in the fall of 2000, focusing distribution on high-risk individuals was difficult because all types of providers served at least some high-risk individuals. Some physicians and public health officials were upset when their local grocery stores, for example, were offering flu shots to everyone when they, the health care providers, were unable to obtain vaccine for their high-risk patients. Many physicians reported that they felt they did not receive priority for vaccine delivery, even though about two-thirds of seniors—one of the largest high-risk groups—generally get their flu shots in medical offices. In our follow-up work, we found no indication that the situation would be different if there was a shortage today.

This raises the question of what more can be done to better prepare for possible vaccine delays and shortages in the future. Because flu vaccine production and distribution largely are private-sector responsibilities, options are somewhat limited. While CDC can recommend and encourage providers to immunize high-risk patients first, it does not have control over the distribution of vaccine, other than the small amount that is distributed through public health departments.

Although HHS has limited authority to directly control flu vaccine production and distribution, it undertook several initiatives following the 2000–01 flu season. More specifically, CDC has taken actions that may encourage manufacturers to supply more vaccine because the action could lead to increased or more stable demand for flu vaccines. Actions taken by CDC and its advisory committee include the following:

- Extending the optimal period for getting a flu vaccination until the end of November, to encourage more people to get vaccinations later in the season.
- Expanding the target population to include children aged 6 through 23 months and all persons who take care of children aged 0 to 23 months.
- Including the flu vaccine in the Vaccines for Children (VFC) stockpile to help improve flu vaccine supply. For 2004, CDC has contracted for a stockpile of approximately 4.5 million doses of flu vaccine through its VFC authority.
- Beginning an annual assessment of the projected vaccine supply, and making a determination if vaccination should proceed for all persons or if a tiered approach should be used, targeting limited vaccine supplies to seniors and other high-risk individuals first.

For both last season and the upcoming flu season, CDC announced that it did not envision any need for a tiered approach. For the 2004–05 flu season, CDC issued a notice on September 24 recommending that vaccination proceed for all recommended persons as soon as vaccine is available.

HHS's Draft Pandemic Influenza Plan Defines Roles and Responsibilities But Leaves Some Important Issues Unresolved

HHS's draft pandemic influenza plan describes federal roles and responsibilities in responding to an influenza pandemic and provides planning guidance to state and local health departments and the health care system. Although the draft plan is comprehensive in scope, it leaves some important decisions about the purchase, distribution, and administration of vaccines unresolved. In addition, the draft plan does not make recommendations for how population groups should be prioritized to receive vaccines in a pandemic. Consequently, states are left to make their own decisions, potentially compromising the timing and adequacy of a response to an influenza pandemic.

Draft Plan Defines Roles and Responsibilities

HHS's draft pandemic influenza plan describes HHS's role in coordinating a national response to an influenza pandemic and provides guidance and tools to promote pandemic preparedness planning and coordination at federal, state, and local levels, including both the public and the private sectors. Pandemic influenza response activities are outlined by the different phases of a pandemic. The draft plan also provides technical background information on preparedness and response activities such as vaccine development and production.

The draft plan acknowledges that states and local areas have important roles in the national response to a pandemic. To facilitate the state and local response, the draft plan provides guidance for state and local health departments and the health care system. The draft plan states that planning for an influenza pandemic will build on HHS- supported efforts to prepare for other public health emergencies such as infectious disease outbreaks, bioterrorist events, or natural disasters, and provides important guidance on areas specific to an influenza pandemic, including disease surveillance, delivery of vaccine and other medications, and communication. According to the Council of State and Territorial Epidemiologists, currently 11 states have pandemic influenza plans. Six of these states have final plans, and five states have draft plans.

According to the draft plan, federal agencies are taking steps to ensure and expand influenza vaccine production capacity; increase influenza vaccination use; stockpile influenza medications; enhance U.S. and global disease detection and surveillance infrastructures; expand influenza-related research; support public health planning and laboratory capacity; and improve health care system readiness at the community level. Although most of these activities have not been targeted specifically to pandemic planning, according to HHS officials, spending in these areas will help prepare for the next influenza pandemic. The draft plan also encourages states to allocate funding from the CDC Bioterrorism Cooperative Agreement and 2004 Immunization Continuation Grants for pandemic preparedness planning.

Draft Plan Leaves Many Important Issues Unresolved, Making It Difficult for States to Plan

Although HHS's draft pandemic influenza plan is comprehensive in scope, it leaves many important decisions about the purchase, distribution, and administration of vaccines unresolved. These decisions include determining the public-versus the private-sector roles in the purchase and distribution of vaccines; the division of responsibility between the federal government and the states for vaccine distribution; and how population groups will be prioritized and targeted to receive limited supplies of vaccines. As we have stated previously, until these key decisions are made, states will find it difficult to plan, and the timeliness and adequacy of response efforts may be compromised.

The draft plan does not establish a definitive federal role in the purchasing and distribution of vaccine. Instead, HHS provides options for vaccine purchase and distribution that include public-sector purchase and distribution of all pandemic influenza vaccine; a mixed public-private system where public-sector supply may be targeted to specific priority groups; and maintenance of the current largely private system. Currently, approximately 85 percent of the influenza vaccine produced for annual outbreaks is purchased by the private sector, and a majority of the annual vaccinations are also delivered by the private sector. HHS states in the draft plan that such a distribution method may not be optimal in a pandemic.

Furthermore, the draft plan delegates to the states responsibility for distribution of vaccine. The lack of a clearly defined federal role in distribution complicates pandemic planning for the states. Among the current state pandemic influenza plans, there is no consistency in terms of their procurement and distribution of vaccine and the relative role of the federal government. States also approach annual vaccine procurement and distribution differently. Approximately half the states handle procurement and distribution of the influenza vaccine through the state health agency. The remainder either operate through a third- party contractor for distribution to providers or use a combination of these two approaches.

In 2003 we reported that state officials were concerned that there were no national recommendations for how population groups should be prioritized to receive vaccines. Identifying priority populations from among high-risk groups and essential health care and emergency personnel is likely to be a controversial issue. The draft plan does not identify priority groups, but HHS indicates that it has separately developed an initial list of suggested priority groups and is soliciting public comment on this list. The draft pandemic plan instructs the states to prioritize the persons receiving the initial doses of vaccine and indicates that as information about the severity of the virus becomes available, recommendations will be formulated at the national level. Prioritization will be an iterative process and will be tied to vaccine availability and the progression of the pandemic. While recognizing that this is an iterative process, state officials have consistently told us that a lack of detailed guidance makes it difficult for states to plan for the use of limited supplies of vaccine.

Concluding Observations

Ensuring an adequate and timely supply of vaccine to protect seniors and others from influenza and flu-related complications continues to be challenging. Only two manufacturers currently produce flu vaccine for seniors and others at high risk for flu-related complications, and manufacturing problems experienced in recent years illustrate the fragility of the current methods of production. Despite efforts by CDC and others, there remains no system to ensure that persons at high risk for complications receive flu vaccine first when vaccine is in short supply.

These influenza vaccine supply and distribution problems may become especially acute in a pandemic. We acknowledge the need for flexibility in planning because many aspects of an influenza pandemic cannot be known in advance. However, the absence of more detail in HHS's draft plan creates uncertainty for the states regarding how to plan for the use of limited supplies of vaccine. Until decisions are made about vaccine purchase, distribution, and administration, and priority populations are designated, states will not be able to develop strategies consistent with federal priorities. . . .

Source: U.S. Congress. Government Accountability Office. "Infectious Disease Preparedness: Federal Challenges in Responding to Influenza Outbreaks." Prepared testimony of Janet Heinrich for a hearing by the Senate Special Committee on Aging. GAO–04–1100T, September 28, 2004. www.gao.gov/new.items/d041100t.pdf (accessed March 31, 2005).

Institute of Medicine on Preventing Childhood Obesity

September 30, 2004

INTRODUCTION

Public concern with the causes and consequences of obesity among Americans continued to spread in 2004, with much of the attention focused on childhood obesity. Several new studies showed specific links between excessive weight during childhood and the onset of diseases and conditions such as diabetes and high blood pressure that formerly had been seen primarily in middle-aged adults. At least three studies released during the year, including one by the Institute of Medicine, made recommendations for reducing obesity among children and adolescents.

Some of the suggestions, such as restricting or banning junk-food ads aimed at children, met with immediate resistance from many elements of the food and restaurant industry, which argued that controlling weight gain was largely a personal responsibility. Wary of potential litigation from children's advocates similar to the campaign successfully waged against the tobacco industry, however, fast-food chains, restaurants, grocery manufacturers, and food processors were taking some steps to offer healthy alternatives to their normal high-fat, high-sugar, high-calorie offerings. McDonald's, for example, announced in March that it was phasing out its super-sized portions of drinks and french fries. *(Federal tobacco litigation, p. 280; multistate tobacco settlement, Historic Documents of 1998, p. 842)*

A Growing Problem

Excessive weight had been recognized as a national public health problem since 2001, when Surgeon General David Satcher warned that obesity among adults and children was poised to cause as much preventable disease and death as cigarette smoking. Nearly two of every three adults and one of every three children in the United States was overweight or obese. A report issued in June 2004 by the Centers for Disease Control and Prevention (CDC) showed that, in 2001–2002, 31.5 percent of children ages six through nineteen were overweight and that 16.5 percent were seriously overweight or obese. The American Heart Association reported in December 2004 that more than 10 percent of two- to five-year-olds were overweight in 2002, compared with 7 percent in 1994. (Since 1998 the federal government had used a weight-to-height ratio called body mass index, or BMI, to classify weight. A BMI between 18.5 and 25 was considered a healthy weight. People with a BMI between 25 and 30 were considered overweight, while those with a BMI above 30 were considered obese.) *(Background, Historic Documents of 2001, p. 935; Historic Documents of 2003, p. 480)*

Excessive weight in adults was linked to numerous chronic diseases and conditions, including heart failure, stroke, diabetes, asthma, arthritis, and several types of cancer, and to psychological disorders such as depression. Scientists increasingly were seeing what once were typically diseases of adulthood in younger children, including adult-onset diabetes and hypertension, or high blood pressure, which contributed to heart disease and strokes. Hypertension was associated both with excessive weight and with consumption of processed foods, which tended to have elevated levels of sodium and sugar.

Federal officials released new guidelines in 2004 for doctors to use in diagnosing and treating high blood pressure in children and adolescents. The guidelines created a "prehypertension" category for children and recommended that children in this category be put on a regimen of exercise and diet to lower their blood pressure. If that failed, the guidelines recommended that children be given drugs to reduce blood pressure.

The American Heart Association also reported that 1 million children ages twelve to nineteen—4.2 percent of the age group—had metabolic syndrome, which increased the risk of heart disease and diabetes. Metabolic syndrome was defined as the presence of three or more of five factors: high triglycerides, low "good" cholesterol, high blood sugar, high blood pressure, and a big waistline.

Causes of Childhood Obesity

The direct cause of weight gain was clear: people tended to gain weight when they ate more calories than they burned in physical activity. The more one ate and the less one exercised, the more likely one was to gain weight. The reasons that caused people, especially children, to eat more and be less active were more complex, however. Genes clearly played a role, as did parents, who had a direct influence on children's attitudes about food, nutrition, and exercise.

But the explosion in the numbers of overweight children was also linked to several societal developments that coincided with it. These included the advent of fast-food restaurants, which offered convenience and speed to families with two working parents; the easy availability of television and video games, which may have reduced children's physical activity while exposing them to hours of commercials for sugar-, salt-, and fat-filled snacks, cereals, and sodas; and Americans' growing reliance on cars to travel even short distances.

Two reports, issued within a day of each other in late February, singled out food advertising and marketing aimed at children for a closer look. The Henry J. Kaiser Family Foundation on February 24 released findings from a survey of forty studies on the media's role in obesity. According to the foundation, these studies showed a link between the amount of time children spent watching television and their weight, with those children watching the most television most likely to be overweight. Surprisingly, the studies showed that the time spent watching television, playing video games, or on computer activities did not displace time spent on physical activities.

The studies also showed that children's exposure to food advertising and marketing influenced their choices and confused them about the relative health benefits of various foods. According to the foundation, the average child was exposed to 40,000 television ads a year, at a total cost of $13 billion, and most of the ads targeted to children were for candy, cereal, and fast food. Many of the promotions for these products used popular television and movie characters, a practice that had been shown to increase a child's ability to identify a product. The foundation also cited studies showing that the food consumed by characters in children's programming was likely to consist of sweet or salty snacks, rather than well-balanced meals, and that characters were rarely shown eating fruits and vegetables.

The foundation report did not make specific policy recommendations but listed several policy options. These included reducing or regulating food ads targeted to children, expanding public education campaigns to promote healthy eating and more exercise, incorporating messages about healthy eating into television storylines, and supporting interventions that reduced the amount of time children spent watching television or playing computer games. A handful of studies had found that reduction in time spent watching television was linked with weight loss.

A day earlier, on February 23, a task force of the American Psychological Association recommended that television advertising be restricted in programming intended for children eight and under. The task force said that most children in that age group did not understand the "persuasive intent" of advertising and were not capable of evaluating whether the claims made in the advertising were truthful, accurate, or unbiased. As a result, the report said, young children were "uniquely vulnerable to commercial persuasion." Although the report was focused on advertising to children in general, it noted that several studies showed a link between increases in advertising for nonnutritious foods and increasing rates of childhood obesity. The report also noted that several countries, including Australia, Canada, Great Britain, and Sweden, had already imposed restrictions on ads aimed at children.

Institute of Medicine Report

In a report issued September 30, a committee of the National Academy of Sciences' Institute of Medicine said there needed to be changes "at many levels and in numerous environments" if the nation was to implement an effective program to reduce childhood obesity. Although personal responsibility was important, "no single factor or sector of society bears all of the blame for the problem," said Jeffrey Koplan, of Emory University, the chairman of the Committee on Prevention of Obesity in Children and Youth. In its report, entitled "Preventing Childhood Obesity: Health in the Balance," the committee called on all elements of society to respond: doctors should routinely measure children's body mass; the food industry should provide more healthful food and drink choices as well as better nutritional information; and parents should make sure their children eat better, exercise more, and spend less time playing video games and watching television. Governments at all levels should take appropriate steps to support efforts aimed at getting children to eat right and exercise more.

Specific recommendations included:

- giving the Department of Agriculture authority to develop national nutrition standards for all food and beverages sold in schools
- ensuring that all children get at least thirty minutes a day of moderate to vigorous exercise
- convening a national conference to draft voluntary guidelines aimed at curbing the advertising and marketing of junk food to children and giving the Federal Trade Commission (FTC) authority to monitor the guidelines
- improving routes to schools to encourage walking or bicycling, and building new schools within walking and biking distance of the communities they serve

- encouraging school districts to develop more nutritious meal plans and regulate more carefully soda and snack machines

The report also urged parents to encourage and support regular physical activity for their children and to limit their television time to under two hours a day.

Although the action plan laid out in the committee's report was generally applauded, several nutrition experts said the report did not go far enough. "The report is thoughtful and reasoned," said Kelly Brownell of Yale University's Center for Eating and Weight disorders. "But we've got an emergency on our hands, and I believe the science is robust enough to suggest taking more bold action." Marion Nestle, a nutrition export at New York University, also praised the report in general but said that more mandatory action was necessary to effect meaningful changes. "The government recommendations are weak because they do not include clear goals with timelines for achieving them or any system of accountability," she told the *Washington Post.* "The food industry recommendations are weak because they are voluntary, and we already know that voluntary doesn't work."

Representatives of the food industry said that more regulation was unnecessary. A spokesman for the Grocery Manufacturers of America, a lobbying group for the food and beverage industry, said manufacturers had already taken steps to fight obesity by producing healthy food alternatives and smaller package sizes. Congress had already rejected legislation to give the Agriculture Department authority to regulate the nutritional quality of food and beverages sold in schools. "Limiting food choices won't eliminate obesity," Sen. Saxby Chambliss, R-Ga., told the *Atlanta Journal and Constitution.* "We must ensure schoolchildren have access to a variety of healthy foods. However, the answer to obesity isn't in regulating the types of foods available, but encouraging children to be more active."

Giving the FTC additional authority to monitor children's food ads was also likely to run into strong opposition. In 1978 Congress temporarily halted funding for the FTC after the agency proposed a ban on food ads aimed at young children. The FTC, derisively labeled the "national nanny," was forced to shut down temporarily. Congress also passed a law barring the agency from implementing similar rules in the future.

Responses in Schools

Even before the Institute of Medicine report came out, many states and school districts were taking steps to reduce the high-fat, high-sugar foods and drinks made available in school cafeterias. Texas, for example, revamped its guidelines for the foods that public schools could serve their children. The new rules banned deep-fat fried foods, limited how often french fries could be served, and mandated how much fat and sugar could be contained in each meal, among other things.

In 2003 California became the first state to ban soft drink sales in elementary and junior high schools. A policy statement issued January 5 by the American Academy of Pediatrics calling on schools to eliminate the sale of soda also spurred action. In February 2004 the Philadelphia school system announced its was banning the sale of soft drinks in its schools; starting in July its school vending machines and cafeterias would serve only milk, water, and fruit juice. Sports drinks would be available in high school vending machines in or near athletic facilities. Milk vending machines were becoming more popular in schools. According to the Beverage Marketing Corps., an industry consultant, between 7,000 and 7,500 milk-dispensing machines had been placed in the nation's schools, most of them in the past three or four years. Still other schools were taking steps to inform their students and parents about the nutritional content of their cafeteria offerings.

The U.S. Agriculture Department announced in October that it was expanding its Healthy Lunch Pilot Program, which provided funding to buy fruits and vegetables, to fifty schools in Mississippi, Pennsylvania, North Carolina, and Washington state plus schools in the Intertribal Council of Arizona and the Ogallala Sioux Tribe in Pine Ridge, South Dakota. The initial pilot project provided $6 million for purchasing fresh fruit and vegetables to 107 schools in Iowa, Indiana, Michigan, Ohio, and Zuni Pueblo, New Mexico. The second round of funding for all the schools totaled $9 million.

Schools in Buffalo were set to begin a program in January 2005 that rewarded children who chose healthy foods such as fruit and vegetables in the school cafeteria. The rewards—perhaps bracelets or key chains—were part of a larger program to help children make better food choices and develop a positive attitude toward nutrition.

Following are excerpts from the executive summary of Preventing Childhood Obesity: Health in the Balance, *issued September 30, 2004, by the Committee on Prevention of Obesity in Children and Youth, a panel established by the Institute of Medicine in the National Academy of Sciences.*

Preventing Childhood Obesity: Health in the Balance

Despite steady progress over most of the past century toward ensuring the health of our country's children, we begin the 21st century with a startling setback—an epidemic of childhood obesity. This epidemic is occurring in boys and girls in all 50 states, in younger children as well as adolescents, across all socioeconomic strata, and among all ethnic groups—though specific subgroups, including African Americans, Hispanics, and American Indians, are disproportionately affected. At a time when we have learned that excess weight has significant and troublesome health consequences, we nevertheless see our population, in general, and our children, in particular, gaining weight to a dangerous degree and at an alarming rate.

The increasing prevalence of childhood obesity throughout the United States has led policy makers to rank it as a critical public health threat. Over the past three decades, its rate has more than doubled for preschool children aged 2 to 5 years and adolescents aged 12 to 19 years, and it has more than tripled for children aged 6 to 11 years. At present, approximately nine million children over 6 years of age are considered obese. These trends mirror a similar profound increase over the same approximate period in U.S. adults as well as a concurrent rise internationally, in developed and developing countries alike.

Childhood obesity involves immediate and long-term risks to physical health. For children born in the United States in 2000, the lifetime risk of being diagnosed with diabetes at some point in their lives is estimated at 30 percent for boys and 40 percent for girls if obesity rates level off. Young people are also at risk of developing serious psychosocial burdens related to being obese in a society that stigmatizes this condition.

There are also considerable economic costs. The national health care expenditures related to obesity and overweight in adults alone have been estimated to range from approximately $98 billion to $129 billion after adjusting for inflation and converting estimates to 2004 dollars. Understanding the causes of childhood obesity, determining what to do about them, and taking appropriate action require attention to what influences eating behaviors and physical activity levels because obesity prevention involves a focus on energy balance (calories consumed versus calories expended). Although seemingly straightforward, these behaviors result from complex interactions across a number of relevant social, environmental, and policy contexts.

U.S. children live in a society that has changed dramatically in the three decades over which the obesity epidemic has developed. Many of these changes—such as both parents working outside the home, longer work hours by both parents, changes in the school food environment, and more meals eaten outside the home, together with changes in the physical design of communities often affect what children eat, where they eat, how much they eat, and the amount of energy they expend in school and leisure time activities. Other changes, such as the growing diversity of the population, influence cultural views and marketing patterns. Use of computers and video games, along with television viewing, often occupy a large percentage of children's leisure time and potentially influence levels of physical activity for children as well as for adults. Many of the social and cultural characteristics that the U.S. population has accepted as a normal way of life may collectively contribute to the growing levels of childhood obesity. An understanding of these contexts, particularly regarding their potential to be modified and how they may facilitate or impede development of a comprehensive obesity prevention strategy, is essential for reducing childhood obesity.

Developing an Action Plan for Obesity Prevention

The Institute of Medicine Committee on Prevention of Obesity in Children and Youth was charged with developing a prevention-focused action plan to decrease the prevalence of obesity in children and youth in the United States. The primary emphasis of the committee's task was on examining the behavioral and cultural factors, social constructs, and other broad environmental factors involved in childhood obesity and identifying promising approaches for prevention efforts. The plan consists of explicit goals for preventing obesity in children and youth and a set of recommendations, all geared toward achieving those goals, for different segments of society.

Obesity prevention requires an evidence-based public health approach to assure that recommended strategies and actions will have their intended effects. Such evidence is traditionally drawn from experimental (randomized) trials and high-quality observational studies. However, there is limited experimental evidence in this area, and for many environmental, policy, and societal variables, carefully designed evaluations of ongoing programs and policies are likely to answer many key questions. For this reason, the committee chose a process that incorporated all forms of available evidence—across different categories of information and types of study design—to enhance the biological, psychosocial, and environmental plausibility of its inferences and to ensure consistency and congruency of information.

Because the obesity epidemic is a serious public health problem calling for immediate reductions in obesity prevalence and in its health and social consequences, the committee believed strongly that actions should be based on the best *available* evidence—as opposed to waiting for the best *possible* evidence. However, there is an obligation to accumulate appropriate evidence not only to justify a course of action but to assess whether it has made a difference. Therefore, evaluation should be a critical component of any implemented intervention or change.

Childhood obesity prevention involves maintaining energy balance at a healthy weight while protecting overall health, growth and development, and nutritional status. The balance is between the energy an individual consumes as food and beverages and the energy expended to support normal growth and development, metabolism, thermogenesis, and physical activity. Although "energy intake = energy expenditure" looks like a fairly basic equation, in reality it is extraordinarily complex when considering the multitude of genetic, biological, psychological, sociocultural, and environmental factors that affect both sides of the equation and the interrelationships between these factors. For example, children are strongly influenced by the food- and physical activity-related decisions made by their families, schools, and communities. Furthermore, it is important to consider the kinds of foods and beverages that children are consuming over time, given that specific types and quantities of nutrients are required to support optimal growth and development.

Thus, changes at many levels and in numerous environments will require the involvement of multiple stakeholders from diverse segments of society. In the home environment, for example, incremental changes such as improving the nutritional quality of family dinners or increasing the time and frequency that children spend outside playing can make a difference. Changes that lead to healthy communities, such as organizational and policy changes in local schools, school districts, neighborhoods, and cities, are equally important. At the state and national levels, large-scale modifications are needed in the ways in which society promotes healthful eating habits and physically active lifestyles. Accomplishing these changes will be difficult, but there is precedent for success in other public health endeavors of comparable or greater complexity and scope. This must be a national effort, with special attention to communities that experience health disparities and that have social and physical environments unsupportive of healthful nutrition and physical activity. . . .

Recommendation 1: *National Priority*

Government at all levels should provide coordinated leadership for the prevention of obesity in children and youth. The President should request that the Secretary of the Department of Health and Human Services (DHHS) convene a high-level task force to ensure coordinated budgets, policies, and program requirements and to establish effective interdepartmental collaboration and priorities for action. An increased level and sustained commitment of federal and state funds and resources are needed.

To implement this recommendation, the federal government should:

- Strengthen research and program efforts addressing obesity prevention, with a focus on experimental behavioral research and community-based intervention

research and on the rigorous evaluation of the effectiveness, cost-effectiveness, sustainability, and scaling up of effective prevention interventions
- Support extensive program and research efforts to prevent childhood obesity in high-risk populations with health disparities, with a focus both on behavioral and environmental approaches
- Support nutrition and physical activity grant programs, particularly in states with the highest prevalence of childhood obesity
- Strengthen support for relevant surveillance and monitoring efforts, particularly the National Health and Nutrition Examination Survey (NHANES)
- Undertake an independent assessment of federal nutrition assistance programs and agricultural policies to ensure that they promote healthful dietary intake and physical activity levels for all children and youth
- Develop and evaluate pilot projects within the nutrition assistance programs that would promote healthful dietary intake and physical activity and scale up those found to be successful

To implement this recommendation, state and local governments should:

- Provide coordinated leadership and support for childhood obesity prevention efforts, particularly those focused on high-risk populations, by increasing resources and strengthening policies that promote opportunities for physical activity and healthful eating in communities, neighborhoods, and schools
- Support public health agencies and community coalitions in their collaborative efforts to promote and evaluate obesity prevention interventions. . . .

Recommendation 2: *Industry*

Industry should make obesity prevention in children and youth a priority by developing and promoting products, opportunities, and information that will encourage healthful eating behaviors and regular physical activity.

To implement this recommendation:

- Food and beverage industries should develop product and packaging innovations that consider energy density, nutrient density, and standard serving sizes to help consumers make healthful choices.
- Leisure, entertainment, and recreation industries should develop products and opportunities that promote regular physical activity and reduce sedentary behaviors.
- Full-service and fast food restaurants should expand healthier food options and provide calorie content and general nutrition information at point of purchase.

Recommendation 3: *Nutrition Labeling*

Nutrition labeling should be clear and useful so that parents and youth can make informed product comparisons and decisions to achieve and maintain energy balance at a healthy weight.

To implement this recommendation:

- The Food and Drug Administration should revise the Nutrition Facts panel to prominently display the total calorie content for items typically consumed at one

eating occasion in addition to the standardized calorie serving and the percent Daily Value.
- The Food and Drug Administration should examine ways to allow greater flexibility in the use of evidence-based nutrient and health claims regarding the link between the nutritional properties or biological effects of foods and a reduced risk of obesity and related chronic diseases.
- Consumer research should be conducted to maximize use of the nutrition label and other food-guidance systems.

Recommendation 4: *Advertising and Marketing*

Industry should develop and strictly adhere to marketing and advertising guidelines that minimize the risk of obesity in children and youth.

To implement this recommendation:

- The Secretary of the DHHS should convene a national conference to develop guidelines for the advertising and marketing of foods, beverages, and sedentary entertainment directed at children and youth with attention to product placement, promotion, and content.
- Industry should implement the advertising and marketing guidelines.
- The Federal Trade Commission should have the authority and resources to monitor compliance with the food and beverage and sedentary entertainment advertising practices.

Recommendation 5: *Multimedia and Public Relations Campaign*

The DHHS should develop and evaluate a long-term national multimedia and public relations campaign focused on obesity prevention in children and youth.

To implement this recommendation:

- The campaign should be developed in coordination with other federal departments and agencies and with input from independent experts to focus on building support for policy changes; providing information to parents; and providing information to children and youth. Rigorous evaluation should be a critical component.
- Reinforcing messages should be provided in diverse media and effectively coordinated with other events and dissemination activities.
- The media should incorporate obesity issues into its content, including the promotion of positive role models. . . .

Recommendation 6: *Community Programs*

Local governments, public health agencies, schools, and community organizations should collaboratively develop and promote programs that encourage healthful eating behaviors and regular physical activity, particularly for populations at high risk of childhood obesity. Community coalitions should be formed to facilitate and promote cross-cutting programs and community-wide efforts.

To implement this recommendation:

- Private and public efforts to eliminate health disparities should include obesity prevention as one of their primary areas of focus and should support community-based

collaborative programs to address social, economic, and environmental barriers that contribute to the increased obesity prevalence among certain populations.
- Community child- and youth-centered organizations should promote healthful eating behaviors and regular physical activity through new and existing programs that will be sustained over the long term.
- Community evaluation tools should incorporate measures of the availability of opportunities for physical activity and healthful eating.
- Communities should improve access to supermarkets, farmers' markets, and community gardens to expand healthful food options, particularly in low-income and underserved areas.

Recommendation 7: *Built Environment*

Local governments, private developers, and community groups should expand opportunities for physical activity including recreational facilities, parks, playgrounds, sidewalks, bike paths, routes for walking or bicycling to school, and safe streets and neighborhoods, especially for populations at high risk of childhood obesity.

To implement this recommendation:

Local governments, working with private developers and community groups, should:

- Revise comprehensive plans, zoning and subdivision ordinances, and other planning practices to increase availability and accessibility of opportunities for physical activity in new developments
- Prioritize capital improvement projects to increase opportunities for physical activity in existing areas
- Improve the street, sidewalk, and street-crossing safety of routes to school, develop programs to encourage walking and bicycling to school, and build schools within walking and bicycling distance of the neighborhoods they serve

Community groups should:

- Work with local governments to change their planning and capital improvement practices to give higher priority to opportunities for physical activity

The DHHS and the Department of Transportation should:

- Fund community-based research to examine the impact of changes to the built environment on the levels of physical activity in the relevant communities and populations.

Recommendation 8: *Health Care*

Pediatricians, family physicians, nurses, and other clinicians should engage in the prevention of childhood obesity. Health-care professional organizations, insurers, and accrediting groups should support individual and population-based obesity prevention efforts.

To implement this recommendation:

- Health-care professionals should routinely track BMI, offer relevant evidence-based counseling and guidance, serve as role models, and provide leadership in their communities for obesity prevention efforts.

- Professional organizations should disseminate evidence-based clinical guidance and establish programs on obesity prevention.
- Training programs and certifying entities should require obesity prevention knowledge and skills in their curricula and examinations.
- Insurers and accrediting organizations should provide incentives for maintaining healthy body weight and include screening and obesity preventive services in routine clinical practice and quality assessment measures. . . .

Recommendation 9: *Schools*

Schools should provide a consistent environment that is conducive to healthful eating behaviors and regular physical activity.

To implement this recommendation:

The U.S. Department of Agriculture, state and local authorities, and schools should:

- Develop and implement nutritional standards for all competitive foods and beverages sold or served in schools
- Ensure that all school meals meet the Dietary Guidelines for Americans
- Develop, implement, and evaluate pilot programs to extend school meal funding in schools with a large percentage of children at high risk of obesity

State and local education authorities and schools should:

- Ensure that all children and youth participate in a minimum of 30 minutes of moderate to vigorous physical activity during the school day
- Expand opportunities for physical activity through physical education classes; intramural and interscholastic sports programs and other physical activity clubs, programs, and lessons; after-school use of school facilities; use of schools as community centers; and walking- and biking-to-school programs
- Enhance health curricula to devote adequate attention to nutrition, physical activity, reducing sedentary behaviors, and energy balance, and to include a behavioral skills focus
- Develop, implement, and enforce school policies to create schools that are advertising-free to the greatest possible extent
- Involve school health services in obesity prevention efforts
- Conduct annual assessments of each student's weight, height, and gender- and age-specific BMI percentile and make this information available to parents
- Perform periodic assessments of each school's policies and practices related to nutrition, physical activity, and obesity prevention

Federal and state departments of education and health and professional organizations should:

- Develop, implement, and evaluate pilot programs to explore innovative approaches to both staffing and teaching about wellness, healthful choices, nutrition, physical activity, and reducing sedentary behaviors. Innovative approaches to recruiting and training appropriate teachers are also needed

Recommendation 10: *Home*

Parents should promote healthful eating behaviors and regular physical activity for their children.

To implement this recommendation parents can:

- Choose exclusive breastfeeding as the method for feeding infants for the first four to six months of life
- Provide healthful food and beverage choices for children by carefully considering nutrient quality and energy density
- Assist and educate children in making healthful decisions regarding types of foods and beverages to consume, how often, and in what portion size
- Encourage and support regular physical activity
- Limit children's television viewing and other recreational screen time to less than two hours per day
- Discuss weight status with their child's health-care provider and monitor age- and gender-specific BMI percentile
- Serve as positive role models for their children regarding eating and physical-activity behaviors

Source: National Academy of Sciences. Institute of Medicine. Committee on Prevention of Obesity in Children and Youth. *Preventing Childhood Obesity: Health in the Balance.* September 30, 2004. ISBN 0-309-09196-9. www.nap.edu/catalog/11015.html (accessed March 17, 2005).

EPA Inspector General on the Development of Air Quality Rules

September 30, 2004

INTRODUCTION

The Bush administration made significant progress during 2004 in key aspects of its broad campaign to reduce federal environmental regulations. During the year the administration rolled back rules adopted by the Clinton administration to protect nearly 60 million acres of national forests from development and took numerous steps to pare back regulations on clean water, endangered species, wilderness protection, and other matters.

The administration continued to face intense legal and political hurdles to its proposals on other environmental issues, notably air quality. The single most controversial environmental decision of President George W. Bush's first term—a new rule reducing requirements for electric utilities and other smokestack industries to install updated pollution-control equipment at existing plants—remained tied up in a court challenge from several states. The new rule also came under fire from the inspector general of the Environmental Protection Agency (EPA), who said it would undermine efforts to get utilities to reduce their pollution levels. Bush also failed, for the third year, to get Congress to approve a broad revision of the 1970 Clean Air Act. He said the revision was needed to preserve jobs while protecting the environment, but opponents said his plan would weaken environmental protections.

Bush's victory in the November elections, coupled with Republican gains in the Senate, seemed likely to give new political impetus to the environmental agenda of the administration and its allies in private industry. Congressional Democrats, a handful of moderate Republicans, environmental advocacy groups, and leaders of several key states said they would continue trying to block as many items on that agenda as possible. Environmental issues played only a minor role in the presidential campaign, despite sharp differences between Bush and his Democratic rival, Sen. John F. Kerry. *(Election, p. 773; Background, Historic Documents of 2001, p. 212, Historic Documents of 2002, p. 894, Historic Documents of 2003, p. 173)*

"New Source Review" Rules

With few exceptions, the Bush administration's fundamental approach to environmental policy was to shift emphasis to what it called a "market-based" approach from a "rules-based" approach. In practice, that meant revising regulations, and in some cases laws, to give more flexibility to private industry, while relying less on detailed government regulations. By far the single most controversial example of the administration's new approach was in the area of air quality, largely because air pollution affected everyone and environmental regulations during the previous three decades had visible success in clearing the nation's skies.

Immediately after taking office in 2001 the Bush administration began to rewrite a key regulation under the Clean Air Act, known as "New Source Review," which Congress had added in 1977 to force the installation of improved pollution control equipment at power plants, oil refineries, steel mills, and thousands of other industrial plants that generated significant amounts of nitrogen oxide, sulfur dioxide, and other forms of air pollution harmful to human health. Under the law and subsequent regulations, companies were required to install new pollution-control equipment whenever they expanded or made significant alterations to their plants; they were not required to do so in cases of "routine maintenance," however. Over the years, many polluters used the routine maintenance exemption to expand or upgrade their plants without adding the required pollution-control equipment. The administration of President Bill Clinton (1993–2001), and several states, took some of those polluters to court and won judgments requiring them to add the new equipment; other legal cases on the matter were still pending when the Bush administration came into office and decided on a different approach.

The Bush administration's approach, first announced at the end of 2002 and then adopted as final policy in October 2003 with some revisions, set new standards for when the expansion or modernization of a plant would trigger a requirement for upgrading pollution control equipment. The key provision was that an industrial firm would be required to upgrade its pollution controls only if the cost of its proposed modernization exceeded 20 percent of the cost of replacing the plant's overall production equipment; for example, if a power plant replaced a boiler that cost more than 20 percent of the total price of replacing all the equipment needed for that unit to produce electricity, its pollution controls would have to be modernized.

EPA officials, who drafted the new rule, said it would encourage companies to install new pollution control equipment when it was needed, rather than use the routine maintenance exemption to escape the Clean Air Act requirements. While agreeing that previous regulations on the matter had failed to achieve their goals, environmental advocates said the Bush administration's new approach would reduce, rather than increase, the incentives for industry to cut back on air pollution. Attorneys general for Massachusetts, New York, and twelve other states—along with environmental advocacy groups—sued to block the new rule and in December 2003 won a temporary injunction from the federal appellate court for the District of Columbia.

While that suit was pending, the EPA announced on June 30, 2004, that it would reopen public comment for sixty days on three specific issues: the administration's legal justification for the new rule under the terms of the Clean Air act, the validity of the 20 percent threshold, and procedures under which states would incorporate the new rule into their own air quality plans. The EPA said it remained committed to the new rule, calling it "fully justified," and said it merely was responding to requests by several states and environmental advocacy groups for a reconsideration of it. The agency said it would make a final decision on the new rule in January 2005.

Three months later, on September 30, administration critics received a significant boost for their case from within the EPA. The agency's inspector general, Nikki L. Tinsley, issued a blistering report challenging the legal and policy arguments the EPA used to justify the new rule and arguing that its adoption had "seriously hampered" the government's efforts to get industry to reduce air pollution. Tinsley's report took special aim at the 20 percent threshold set by the new rule for requiring companies to upgrade their pollution equipment. EPA officials had been able to provide little evidence to justify why they chose that figure, as opposed to a lower one that would have triggered more frequent upgrading of pollution equipment, the report said. Further, the report said that 88 percent of EPA's pending lawsuits and other enforcement actions against polluters had been based on a lower threshold—meaning that the polluters had no incentive to settle those cases and, in fact, were using the new rule as grounds to ask judges to dismiss the cases against them. The report also quoted the head of the EPA's enforcement office as telling subordinates to "stop enforcing" the New Source Review regulations unless a company was violating the administration's new rule.

As inspector general, Tinsley had no authority to force the EPA to take any action in response to her report, but she suggested that the agency use her findings "to fully consider—in an open, public, and transparent manner—the environmental impact" of its new regulation. In its September 7 formal response to a draft of the report, the EPA called Tinsley's findings "inaccurate, misleading, incomplete, and superficial." In particular, the EPA challenged Tinsley's contention that the administration's new rule had encouraged several public utilities to "walk away" from negotiations to settle cases against them. The EPA said the report "misleads the public about Agency actions to reduce pollution from coal-fired power plants. We vigorously enforce the Clean Air Act and have an aggressive plan" to cut emissions.

Tinsley had based much of her report on comments and evidence provided by current and former EPA enforcement officials, several of whom resigned to protest Bush administration policies. One of them, Bruce Buckheit, former director of the agency's air enforcement division, told reporters in 2004 that "we were told to stop investigating" air pollution cases. Buckheit said about twenty companies were in negotiations with the EPA to settle claims, but after the new policy was announced "they walked away from the table" because it was clear they would not be prosecuted.

Shadow Over the "Clear Skies" Plan

The controversy over the New Source Review rules was played out in complex administration regulations and resulting court challenges to them. A related controversy was being handled in Congress because it involved a proposal by the Bush administration to change the underlying text of the Clean Air Act, not just the regulations used to enforce the law.

Bush called his proposal the Clear Skies Initiative and said it would replace detailed government regulations with what he called a "market-based" or "cap-and-trade" approach. The government would establish overall limits on acceptable levels of air pollution (a "cap") and companies could buy and sell (or "trade") credits for the right to emit certain amounts of pollution within those limits. In some cases, under this approach, individual plants might increase their output of pollution, while others would cut their pollution levels. EPA administrator Michael Leavitt said the idea was to let private industry "find the best ways, the fastest ways, the most innovative ways, and the most efficient ways to make the reductions" required by the law.

Bush's cap-and-trade concept had relatively strong bipartisan support on Capitol Hill, but other aspects of his Clear Skies plan generated strong resistance from most Democrats and some Republicans. Among the controversial provisions was a requirement that coal-fired power plants cut their overall emissions of sulfur dioxide, nitrogen oxide, and mercury by 70 percent by 2018 (or by 2020 in some cases); this was a much less modest demand than in the existing Clean Act, which required a

90 percent reduction of those pollutants ten years sooner. Administration critics also complained that the proposal failed to regulate emissions by power plants of carbon dioxide, the most important of the "greenhouse gases" that most scientists said were largely responsible for global climate change. *(Climate change issue, p. 827)*

On Capitol Hill, the Clear Skies legislation was bottled up in the Senate Environment and Public Works Committee. That panel's Republican chairman, James Inhofe of Oklahoma, halted action on the bill early in 2004 when it became clear that a narrow majority of panel members favored adding a provision regulating carbon dioxide emissions—a provision Inhofe, and the Bush administration, strongly opposed.

With the Clear Skies proposal languishing in Congress, the administration early in 2004 pledged to put a key Clear Skies provision into effect through rule making, rather than legislation. This was to be done through what the administration called the Clean Air Interstate Rule, which set new national limits on emissions of nitrogen oxide and sulfur dioxide from coal-fired power plants. The rule would have required reduction of emissions of those two pollutants by 70 percent after 2015 in twenty-eight states (most of them east of the Mississippi). Leavitt had promised to adopt it by the end of 2004, but the White House in December delayed adoption until March 2005—apparently in hopes the newly strengthened Republican majorities in Congress would win passage of the broader Clear Skies legislation instead.

Related Air Quality Issues

The year's major developments on other air pollution issues included:

- **Mercury.** The EPA appeared to be readying a final rule, to be issued early in 2005, limiting emissions by coal-fired power plants of vapors containing mercury, a toxic chemical found by scientific studies to be especially harmful to infants and children. After years of discussion, and responding to a lawsuit filed by the Natural Resources Defense Council, the Clinton administration in late 2000 had initiated action to limit mercury emissions; the Clinton plan called for reducing mercury emissions nationwide by 90 percent by 2008. Representatives of the electric power industry called the Clinton plan too drastic and expensive to implement, and they lobbied the new Bush administration to adopt a more modest plan. In late 2003 the EPA had developed a plan, favored by the power industry, to reduce mercury emissions by 70 percent by 2018. On January 31, 2004, the *Washington Post* published a report noting that the proposed EPA plan included "at least a dozen paragraphs" that "were lifted, sometimes verbatim," from memorandums prepared by the Washington, D.C., law firm Latham & Watkins, which represented power companies. Two senior EPA officials had worked at the firm before joining the Bush administration: Jeffrey Olmstead, the director of EPA's air quality enforcement office, and his chief counsel, Bill Wehrum. Nine months later, on September 22, the *New York Times* reported that other portions of the proposed EPA "mirror almost word for word" memos from the same law firm. Those passages dealt with the EPA's conclusion that other toxic chemicals emitted by coal-fired power plants—including arsenic, chromium, and lead—should not be subject to regulations because of a lack of evidence that those emissions significantly harmed human health.
- **Oil refineries.** The Bush administration on October 6 reached the latest, and one of the largest, settlements with oil refineries over air pollution requirements.

Citgo Petroleum Corporation (owned by Venezuela's state-run petroleum company), agreed to install more than $300 million worth of pollution controls at six U.S. refineries within eight years. The six Citgo plants accounted for about 5 percent of the nation's refinery capacity, and the settlement meant that about 40 percent of refinery production had reached pollution-control agreements with the government under enforcement actions initiated by the Clinton administration. The two companies with the largest oil refining capacity, ExxonMobil and Sunoco, were still in negotiations with the government.

- **Soot.** The EPA on December 17 issued regulations requiring twenty states, plus the District of Columbia, to submit plans by 2008 for reducing fine-particle air pollution, commonly known as soot. The states were to meet clean-air standards for 224 counties (home to about 95 million people) by 2010 or, in severe cases, by 2015. Many of the affected states, particularly those in the Mid-Atlantic and Northeast, contended that most of the soot came from power plants and industries in other regions, notably in the Midwest. Officials in these states had been among those most critical of the administration's proposals to change enforcement standards for power plant emissions. In other states, including California, most of the soot pollution came from diesel-burning trucks. EPA officials said soot was one of the country's most damaging types of pollution, in terms of human health, causing thousands of premature deaths from respiratory and heart illnesses. The agency estimated that development of soot-control plans for the 224 counties that exceeded federal air-quality standards would eliminate at least 15,000 premature deaths by 2010. The Clinton administration in 1997 had proposed regulations governing soot pollution, but the rules were held up for several years by legal challenges from industry groups.
- **Diesel engines.** The EPA on May 11 adopted the final version of a rule imposing pollution-control restrictions on so-called non-road diesel engines, such as those used in earthmovers, farm tractors, and similar pieces of heavy equipment. The rule required manufacturers to produce cleaner-running engines by 2008. A related EPA rule sharply reduced the amount of sulfur allowed in diesel fuel used by non-road equipment. The EPA in earlier years had mandated cleaner diesel engines for highways trucks, and it was in the early stages of proposing limits for emissions from diesel engines on marine vessels and railroad locomotives. These steps won grudging support from both manufacturers and environmental advocates.
- **Ozone.** The EPA on April 15 proposed new standards for ground-level ozone (a major component of smog) that put 474 counties (most of them in metropolitan areas) in noncompliance. Under the new standards, most counties would have to reduce ozone levels by 2010, but those areas with the most severe smog problems (notably Los Angeles) would have until 2021. The standards had been under review since 1997.

Repealing "Roadless" Rule

After three years of ambivalence on the matter, the Bush administration on July 12 staked out a clear position on the most sweeping conservation measure of the previous Clinton administration: a ban on construction of roads, and thus of logging, mining, and other commercial development, in 58.5 million acres of the national forests. Clinton had issued an executive order containing the ban at the end of his presidency; the order resulted from a years-long process of scientific studies and public hearings. The ban was strongly opposed by the logging, mining, and oil industries, and by the governors of several Western states, who said it would hurt economic development. The ban applied to about one-third of the 191 million acres in the 155 national forests.

Bush administration officials made it clear they did not like the Clinton ban, but they were hamstrung by technical procedures that made it difficult to undo the order. Instead, the administration refused to defend the ban when a lawsuit was filed against it by Idaho officials, and it took several steps to undermine enforcement of Clinton's executive order. In June 2003 the Forest Service said it would comply with Clinton's order, but it later said governors could seek exemptions to it. The first major exemption was approved in December 2003, opening up 300,000 acres of the huge Tongass National Forest in Alaska to road construction, and thus to logging.

The Bush administration completed its move away from the Clinton order on July 12, announcing a proposed new rule that gave state officials substantial leeway to determine whether national forests in their states would be developed. Once the new rule went into effect—expected in 2005—governors would have eighteen months to petition the Forest Service to protect national forests in their states from road development. After that point, the Forest Service would review those petitions, along with comments from public groups, to determine land use plans for each forest.

Agriculture Secretary Ann M. Veneman—whose department included the Forest Service—said "state governments are important partners in the stewardship of the nation's lands and natural resources." Veneman announced the policy change in a speech in Boise, Idaho, the state where opposition to Clinton's rule was strongest. Idaho's Republican governor, Dirk Kempthorne, joined officials in several other Western states and industry representatives in praising the proposal, which they said would help create jobs. Environmental advocacy groups blasted the plan, saying the national forests were owned by the nation, not by states, and should be subject to national rules. A sixty-day public comment period on the proposed new rule ended November 15, with tens of thousands of people submitting comments.

In a related development, the Forest Service on December 22 announced another regulation giving individual managers of the national forests increased responsibility for determining use of the forests. The regulation eliminated requirements that forest managers prepare assessments analyzing the environmental impact of potential uses (such as logging or mining) and placed economic goals (such as creating jobs) on an equal footing with environmental considerations (such as protecting the health of the forest). As with similar moves by the administration, the rule brought praise from commercial interests and condemnation from environmental advocates.

Other Environmental Issues

Among the numerous other environmental issues that provoked national controversy during 2004 were:

- **Salmon and dams.** Reversing a Clinton administration policy, the Bush administration on November 30 opposed the removal of eight federally owned dams on the Columbia and Snake rivers as a means of protecting endangered species of wild salmon and steelhead trout. The fisheries division of the National Oceanographic and Atmospheric Administration said the dams had become part of the environment and their removal was not justified, even to encourage the natural life cycles of the fish. Earlier, on May 28, the National Marine

Fisheries Service announced that it intended to consider hatchery-bred salmon as "wild" when determining whether the number of wild salmon had declined enough to merit protection under the Endangered Species Act.

- **Mountaintop mining.** In January the Interior Department's Office of Surface Mining proposed a ruling voiding a twenty-year ban on mining within one hundred feet of a stream. The new rule contained a milder requirement that miners take measures "to the extent possible" to protect water quality. The new rule was intended to ease restrictions on a widespread practice in Appalachian states, where mining companies sheared off the tops of mountains, mined the interior for coal, then dumped the debris into neighboring valleys, often covering up mountain streams.
- **Wetlands.** President Bush announced on April 22—Earth Day—that his administration planned to create 1 million acres of wetlands and restore another 1 million acres that had been damaged by commercial development and farming. The Natural Resources Defense Council and other environmental groups on August 11 issued a report suggesting that the Bush administration had used a 2001 Supreme Court decision to eliminate protection for millions of acres of wetlands. The Court ruling said Congress did not intend the Clean Water Act to protect small, isolated bodies of wetlands. The environmental groups said the administration had adopted an expansive interpretation of that ruling to allow development of wetlands that should have been protected. White House officials said the administration was complying with the ruling.
- **Storms and sewage.** In December the EPA prepared what it called a "final plan" allowing sewage plants to dump partially treated sewage into lakes and waterways during heavy rains or snow melts. The EPA had been developing the plan for more than a year, in response to what it said was a call by municipal water authorities for more flexibility to deal with "peak flow periods," when large quantities of rainwater entered sewage systems. EPA officials said so-called blended sewage would still have to meet Clean Water Act standards, but some environmentalists and pubic health officials said bypassing some stages of the treatment process would increase the risk of waterborne illness.
- **Oil drilling in Alaskan refuge.** Republican gains in the Senate in the November elections appeared likely to bolster the Bush administration's plan to allow drilling for oil in Alaska's Arctic National Wildlife Refuge, one of the country's last remaining pristine wilderness sites. A small majority consisting of Democrats and a few moderate Republicans had blocked the proposal in the Senate, but turnover resulting from the elections appeared to give proponents a narrow majority when the new Senate took office in January 2005.
- **Oil and gas drilling in Bridger-Teton National Forest.** In one of the few actions by the Bush administration to limit commercial development on public lands, the Forest Service on September 14 suspended plans to allow drilling for oil and natural gas in wilderness areas of the Bridger-Teton National Forest in Wyoming, just south of Grand Teton National Park. The administration had planned to lease drilling sites on 157,000 acres of the forest, more than half of which were roadless. A coalition of environmentalists, hunters, and ranchers—backed by some of the state's prominent politicians—lobbied against the drilling plan.
- **Pesticides.** In July the EPA said it was no longer consulting with wildlife agencies to determine if pesticides might be harmful to animals or plants protected by the Endangered Species Act. On December 16 outgoing EPA administrator Michael Leavitt approved a rule exempting American farmers

from an international ban on the use of methyl bromide, a pesticide shown by scientific studies to cause cancer.

Following is the text of the executive summary from "New Source Review Rule Change Harms EPA's Ability to Enforce Against Coal-fired Electric Utilities," a report issued September 30, 2004, by the Office of Inspector General of the Environmental Protection Agency.

"New Source Review Rule Change"

Purpose

The New Source Review (NSR) provisions of the Clean Air Act require that sources of air pollution, such as utilities, take steps to install and operate lower-emitting pollution control technologies at newly built major sources or modified major sources that significantly increase emissions. Controversy has surrounded implementation of NSR for years, including when the Environmental Protection Agency (EPA) issued a rule in October 2003 regarding NSR's application to existing facilities. NSR applies to stationary sources of air pollution, including the 1,032 coal-fired electric powergenerating units in the United States that produce 59 percent of all sulfur dioxide (SO_2) emissions and 18 percent of all nitrogen oxide (NO_X) emissions nationwide. Both pollutants are associated with adverse health effects, including respiratory disease and infection, and premature mortality. As a result of Congressional interest, we evaluated the basis for the rule change and the rule change's impact on EPA's enforcement policies, practices, and activities for coal-fired electric utilities. Our objectives considered the impacts on facilities that have had their enforcement cases resolved as well as those that have not.

Results in Brief

While many sources within the electric utility industry have made substantial progress in reducing emissions, some older sources have not. In 1996, EPA's Office of Enforcement and Compliance Assurance (OECA) began targeting older, dirtier utilities for compliance assessments, resulting in the identification of significant alleged violations. EPA has been taking enforcement actions against these coal-fired utilities, and this has proven to be an effective approach for requiring utilities to install pollution control devices when they are making other modifications. This has also resulted in significant reductions in harmful emissions. For example, settlements with 7 companies to date have already required owners to install emission control devices on 74 power-generating units over about a 10-year period, which is projected to reduce annual SO_2 emissions by more than 440,000 tons and NO_X by more than 210,000 tons. Further, if allowed to continue unimpeded, ongoing NSR enforcement actions may garner even greater environmental benefits. For example, by requiring lower-emitting controls on 97 power-generating units, the enforcement cases OECA is currently pursuing could reduce SO_2 emissions by 1,750,000 tons and NO_X emissions by 629,000 tons annually.

The October 2003 NSR rule change has seriously hampered OECA settlement activities, existing enforcement cases, and the development of future cases. This is due largely to EPA's revised definition of routine maintenance, which allows utilities to undertake projects up to 20 percent of the cost of the power-generating unit without being subject to NSR requirements. After the rule was issued on October 27, 2003, key officials from EPA's Office of Air and Radiation (OAR) (who wrote the 2003 NSR rule) and key enforcement officials from OECA expressed widely disparate views of the impact of the rule change.

OAR officials said the NSR rule change is not retroactive and therefore should not impact OECA's ongoing litigation with utility companies alleged to have violated NSR prior to October 2003. In OAR's opinion, the 20-percent threshold will allow utility owners to replace components under a wider variety of circumstances, provide more certainty to owners and to reviewing authorities, and enhance key operational elements such as efficiency, safety, reliability, and environmental performance.

In contrast to OAR's view that the 20-percent threshold would not impact enforcement, key OECA enforcement officials informed OIG that the exemption threshold for utilities should be no higher than 0.75 percent. Since a new 1000 megawatt coal-fired power plant could cost up to $800 million, using a 0.75-percent threshold could allow up to a $6 million project for a coal-fired electric utility before triggering NSR, as long as other NSR provisions are met, whereas a 20-percent threshold could allow as much as a $160 million project before triggering NSR.

According to key enforcement officials, the NSR rule change is so dramatic that it has impacted OECA's ongoing litigation, out-of-court settlements, and new enforcement actions against coal-fired electric utilities. This is because, even though a court in December 2003 issued a stay delaying implementation of the NSR rule, OECA's ability to obtain appropriate controls through settlements or court-imposed remedies has been weakened. Three of nine utilities in ongoing active litigation with EPA have asserted that enforcement actions should cease or be significantly reduced based on the contention that the maintenance activities in question would no longer be considered a violation under the 2003 NSR rule. Similarly, soon after the NSR rule was made public on August 27, 2003, a major utility ceased negotiations with EPA. Agency officials attributed it to the announcement of the rule as well as an adverse court ruling in an ongoing NSR enforcement case against a coal-fired utility. Similar to their views on the NSR rule change's impact on NSR enforcement, Agency officials did not agree on the extent to which the NSR rule change, as opposed to the adverse court ruling, impacted these negotiations.

No new enforcement actions have been taken against coal-fired utilities alleged to have violated the old NSR rule due to the new rule's adverse impact on OECA's leverage in settlements or court remedies. If the October 2003 rule is eventually implemented as promulgated, OECA officials estimate that, of the utilities alleged to have violated NSR in the past, only five smaller utilities, emitting a relatively small amount of SO_2 and NO_X, would still be in violation of NSR. All of OECA's other cases would be in compliance with NSR under the 20-percent threshold and thus the installation of lower emitting controls made more difficult, whether in settlements or by way of injunctive relief in court. As a result, nearly all of the projected emission reductions of 1.75 million tons of SO_2 and 629,000 tons of NO_X would not be realized under NSR enforcement efforts.

Fourteen States, several cities, and environmental groups sued EPA over the 2003 NSR rule change, resulting in the December 2003 stay. Their concerns included insufficient support for how the 20-percent threshold was selected and the adverse impact on enforcement actions. We found little basis for the 20-percent threshold, and we saw no evidence that the percent of routine maintenance in ongoing enforcement actions was considered by OAR in determining the threshold. EPA recently announced its plans to reconsider the 2003 NSR rule before the court stay is lifted. This is an excellent opportunity for EPA to fully consider—in an open, public, and transparent manner—the environmental impact of proposed NSR changes at varying levels, including the impact on OECA enforcement activities.

Recommendations

Because coal-fired electric utilities produce nearly 60 percent of all SO_2 and nearly 20 percent of all NO_X emissions nationwide, it is important that NSR enforcement against coal-fired electric utilities continue in the same manner and to the same extent as before the 2003 NSR rule was issued. This would include both the pursuit of ongoing cases and the development of new cases. As such, we recommend that:

- The EPA Administrator, through the reconsideration process of the NSR rule, specifically address the impact on enforcement activities as it relates to coal-fired electric utilities, including, if necessary, the issuance of a separate NSR rulemaking for coal-fired electric utilities that specifically considers and takes public comment on the resulting environmental impacts of a definition of routine maintenance at any threshold above the desired OECA threshold of 0.75 percent for coal-fired electric utilities, including:
  - Publishing the environmental and health impacts of different thresholds, ranging from 0.75 percent (in 1 percent increments) up to 5 percent, and at 10 percent, 15 percent, and at the 20-percent threshold, along with explicit assumptions underlying each threshold and the model inputs used for each threshold; and
  - Soliciting and accepting public comments on the proposed reconsideration rule in an open, public, and transparent manner, and fully explaining the basis for the Agency's eventual decision on any NSR rule changes as it relates to utilities, including all steps taken to minimize the impact on enforcement activities and cases.
- The Acting Assistant Administrator for Enforcement and Compliance Assurance ensure that coal-fired electric utilities found in violation of NSR requirements are brought into compliance expeditiously, and that the necessary pollution control equipment is timely installed and operated, by:
  - Vigorously pursuing ongoing court cases and settlement negotiations, including, where appropriate, prompt referrals of cases to the Department of Justice; and
  - Identifying any additional coal-fired utilities in violation of the NSR requirements prior to October 27, 2003, by fully using the site-specific utility information

obtained through Clean Air Act Section 114 information collection requests and other compliance assessment activities, and ensuring that these sources are brought into compliance in a timely manner.

Agency Comments and OIG Evaluation

EPA generally disagreed with our draft report, asserting that it contained several major flaws and that it was inaccurate, misleading, incomplete, and superficial. We met the Assistant Administrators for OAR and OECA, and obtained additional information to support the Agency's viewpoints. Many of their comments centered around other ways the Agency proposes to achieve emissions reductions from utilities, which was outside the scope of this review. Our review focused on the basis for the NSR rule change and the rule change's impact on EPA enforcement policies, practices, and activities for coal-fired electric utilities. However, we modified the report as appropriate based on the Agency's comments. . . .

We also received three sets of comments from EPA's Office of General Counsel (OGC) asserting that portions of the report involved internal, deliberative communications, and thus were exempt from disclosure under exemption #5 of the Freedom of Information Act and should not be released because of the deliberative process privilege. OGC also asserted that certain information in the draft report was enforcement sensitive, and thus should not be included in the report. OGC recommended that these portions be deleted from the report and protected from public release. At the advice of OIG Counsel, we redacted some of the enforcement information from the final report, and we redacted some of the information asserted to involve internal deliberative communications. In other instances, upon the advice of OIG Counsel, information asserted to be covered by the deliberative process privilege remained in our report. The three sets of comments from EPA's OGC asserting these exemptions and privileges were not included as appendices to the report because to do so would involve disclosing exempt and privileged information.

Source: U.S. Environmental Protection Agency. Office of Inspector General. "New Source Review Rule Change Harms EPA's Ability to Enforce Against Coal-fired Electric Utilities." Report No. 2004–P–00034, September 30, 2004. www.epa.gov/oig/reports/2004/20040930-2004-P-00034.pdf (accessed April 20, 2005).

Bush, Kerry Presidential Debates

September 30 and October 8 and 13, 2004

INTRODUCTION

Republican president George W. Bush and his Democratic opponent, Massachusetts senator John F. Kerry, met in a series of three nationally televised debates in late September and early October that gave millions of Americans their best opportunity of the campaign season to weigh the presidential candidates and their policies in the closely fought election. For ninety minutes at a time, under two different and carefully controlled formats, Bush and Kerry clashed again and again over their differing approaches to leadership, to the Iraq war and the war on terror more broadly, and to a host of domestic issues from the economy and health care to stem cell research and gay marriage.

By most accounts, Kerry was the "winner," a judgment that was confirmed by public opinion polls. Before the first debate on September 30, most polls showed President Bush in the lead by several percentage points; after the last debate Kerry had pulled even with the president. The two men remained roughly even, with Bush perhaps a bit ahead, for the rest of the campaign. Kerry, who appeared confident and focused, may have been aided in the first debate by the demeanor of the president, who frequently looked petulant and impatient as he waited for Kerry to finish his response. Bush seemed more comfortable in the second, town-hall style debate, where the two candidates answered questions from the audience. By the third debate Bush was joking about his wife's admonition "to stand up straight and not scowl."

Each of the three debates attracted more viewers than any presidential debate since 1992, when George H.W. Bush, Bill Clinton, and independent candidate Ross Perot faced off. According to Nielsen Media Research, an estimated 62.5 million viewers watched the first Bush-Kerry debate. The second debate, held on a Friday might in the middle of high-school football season, drew 46.7 million viewers. The third debate, aired opposite two baseball playoff games, drew 51.2 million viewers. An estimated 43.6 million people tuned into the October 5 vice presidential debate between Vice President Dick Cheney and Kerry's running mate, North Carolina senator John Edwards.

The private, bipartisan Commission on Presidential Debates organized the debates, as it had done for every presidential election since 1988. Unlike earlier elections, however, when one or another of the candidates had tried to change some aspect of the debate format, both the Bush and Kerry campaigns agreed to the debates without public dissent or complaint.

First Debate: Focus on Iraq

The first debate was held September 30 in the basketball arena at the University of Miami in Coral Gables, Florida, with Jim Lehrer of PBS's *The NewsHour* posing the questions while the two candidates stood next to each other at lecterns.

Although the debate was on foreign affairs and homeland security in general, the candidates spent most of their time on the war in Iraq. Both men stayed focused on the message each wanted to convey. Bush portrayed himself as a strong and resolute leader who had seen the country through the horrors of the September 11 terrorist attacks and taken swift steps to disarm terrorists and those who supported them. In contrast, the president said, Kerry would be a weak commander in chief, incapable of protecting the United States from its enemies.

As he had throughout the campaign, Bush accused Kerry of changing his position on the war out of political expediency and of sending "mixed signals" that undermined troop morale and showed that he would not be the steadfast and resolute commander in chief the country needed to protect it from terrorists. "What my opponent wants you to forget is that he voted to authorize the use of force and now says it's the wrong war at the wrong time at the wrong place," Bush said. "I don't see how you can lead this country to succeed in Iraq if you say 'wrong war, wrong time, wrong place.' What message does that send our troops? What message does that send to our allies? What message does that send the Iraqis?"

Kerry attacked the president for rushing into the war without greater support among American allies and "without a plan to win the peace." Kerry said he would strengthen relations with U.S. allies and do a better job of training Iraqi forces. Kerry also said the United States needed "to be smarter about how we wage a war on terror." He said he would do that by strengthening the military and intelligence gathering, by aggressively moving to cut off funding to the terrorists, and by "reaching out to the Muslim world," which Kerry said the president had largely failed to do.

Kerry accused Bush of making a "colossal error of judgment" when he diverted attention from "the real war on terror" against Osama bin Laden and turned it to Iraq, even though, Kerry said, there was no connection between Iraqi dictator Saddam Hussein and the terrorists responsible for the September 11 attacks on the World Trade Center and the Pentagon. "Saddam Hussein didn't attack us. Osama bin Laden attacked us," Kerry said in a statement that appeared to rankle the president.

"Of course I know Osama bin Laden attacked us. I know that," Bush shot back, then reiterated that the United States was justified in invading Iraq to prevent Iraqi dictator Saddam Hussein from manufacturing weapons of mass destruction. Linking the invasion of Iraq with the war on terror, Bush declared : "We have a duty to defeat this enemy," and "the best way to defeat them is to never waver, to be strong, to use every asset at our disposal, is to constantly stay on the offensive, and at the same time, spread liberty."

Second Debate: Town Hall Meeting

The second debate, held at Washington University in St. Louis, Missouri, on October 8, was formatted as a town hall style meeting, with the two candidates answering questions on both domestic and foreign issues from members of the audience, which was made up of voters who said they were still undecided. The debate was moderated by Charles Gibson of ABC.

The debate came at the end of a bad week for the administration. Early in the week it had been revealed that the former top American official in Iraq, L. Paul Bremer III, said that the administration had not provided enough troops to stabilize the country. That was followed by the final report of the chief U.S. weapons inspector in Iraq, Charles A. Duelfer, who concluded that Saddam Hussein had gotten rid of any weapons of mass destruction after the 1991 Persian Gulf War and had neither stockpiles of banned weapons nor the capability of producing them when the United States invaded Iraq in 2003. *(Duelfer report, p. 711)*

Although Duelfer's conclusion undercut the Bush's key justification for invading Iraq, the president nonetheless vigorously defended his decision to go to war. "I tried diplomacy, went to the United Nations," he said. "But as we learned in the same [Duelfer] report I quoted, Saddam Hussein was gaming the oil-for-food program to get rid of sanctions. He was trying to get rid of sanctions for a reason. He wanted to restart his weapons program." Everyone, including Kerry, thought there were weapons of mass destruction in Iraq, Bush continued. "Saddam Hussein was a unique threat. And world is better off without him in power."

In rebuttal, Kerry reminded listeners that during the 2000 presidential debates Bush had promised to send troops to war "with a viable exit strategy and only with enough forces to get the job done." But Bush "didn't do that. He broke that promise," Kerry said, by rushing into war "without a plan to win the peace" and by not listening to some military leaders who said more troops were needed. Bush denied that he had not given his generals everything they asked for. He said he asked them "Do we have the right plan with the right troop level?" and said that their response was "Yes." "That's what a president does," Bush said. "A president sets the strategy and relies upon good military people to execute that strategy." Kerry sharply disagreed: "The military's job is to win the war. A president's job is to win the peace."

Kerry and Bush also traded charges on a range of domestic issues. Kerry accused the president of turning his campaign into "a weapon of mass deception" by misleading the public about Kerry's record on domestic issues as well as the war in Iraq. "The president is just trying to scare everybody here with throwing labels around. I mean 'compassionate conservative,' what does that mean? Cutting 500,000 kids from after school programs, cutting 365,000 kids from health care, running up the biggest deficits in American history."

Kerry said Bush had pushed through tax cuts that benefited the wealthy at the expense of the middle class, turned budget surpluses into record deficits, failed to create jobs, and had done nothing to help the 45 million Americans who did not have health insurance. He broadly outlined his plans for providing health insurance to those who could not afford it, for stimulating jobs in the manufacturing sector, and for cutting taxes for the middle class. In response to a question, Kerry said he would pay for his initiatives by increasing income taxes on those Americans earning more than $200,000 a year, but he flatly stated that he would not raise taxes on anyone making less than that.

Bush said Kerry was "just not credible when he talks about being fiscally conservative. . . . Of course he's going to raise your taxes." Bush defended his tax cuts as the best way to "grow the economy" and said that nearly 2 million jobs had been created in the last year.

Third Debate: Domestic Issues

The third debate, held October 13 at Arizona State University in Tempe, followed the same format as the first, with both men standing at lecterns taking questions on domestic issues from moderator Bob Schieffer of CBS. The two candidates made many of the same points that they had in the second debate, but they were generally more aggressive and forceful.

Kerry asserted that Bush's economic policies had been a failure. "He's . . . the only president in seventy-two years to lose jobs—1.6 million jobs lost," Kerry said.

"He's the only president to have incomes of families go down for the last three years, the only president to see exports go down, the only president to see the lowest level of business investment in our country as it is today. Now, I'm going to reverse that. I'm going to change that. We're going to restore the fiscal discipline we had in the 1990s."

Kerry's "rhetoric doesn't match his record," Bush snapped back. "He's been a senator for twenty years. He voted to increase taxes 98 times. When they tried to reduce taxes, he voted against that 127 times. He talks about being a fiscal conservative, or fiscally sound, but he voted over—he voted 277 times to wave the budget caps [on spending], which would have cost the taxpayers $4.2 trillion."

In a softer moment, both men discussed the role of faith in their lives. The president, a born-again Christian, described his faith as "very personal" and said that "prayer and religion sustained" him. "But," he added, "I'm mindful in a free society that people can worship if they want to or not. . . . I never want to impose my religion on anybody else. But when I make decisions, I stand on principle, and the principles are derived from who I am . . . and religion is a part of me."

Kerry, a Roman Catholic who was more reserved about discussing his faith, said that he was "taught that the two greatest commandments are: Love the Lord, your God, with all your mind, your body and your soul, and love your neighbor as yourself. And frankly, I think we have a lot more loving of our neighbor to do in this country and on this planet."

The Vice Presidential Debate

The debate between the vice presidential candidates, Dick Cheney and John Edwards, was held October 5 at Case Western Reserve University in Cleveland, Ohio. The format was slightly different from that of the presidential debates, in that the candidates sat at a table across from moderator Gwen Ifill of *The NewsHour.*

Of the four debates, this one may have been in many ways the most personal, the most intense, and the most aggressive. Cheney was adamant in defending the administration's conduct of the war in Iraq and unrelenting in attacking Edwards and Kerry as incapable of leading the country. "Your rhetoric would be much tougher if you had a record to back it up," Cheney snapped at Edwards at one point. Edwards gave as good as he got, saying that the Bush ticket's descriptions of a growing economy and progress in curbing the insurgency in Iraq showed that the two men were either out of touch with reality or being dishonest with the American people.

One of the few soft spots came late in the debate when Edwards said he respected Cheney's obvious love for his family, including his openly gay daughter. Asked to respond, Cheney said, "Let me simply thank the senator for the kind words that he said about my family and our daughter. I appreciate that very much."

Following are excerpts from the transcripts of the three U.S. presidential debates, held September 30, 2004, in Coral Gables, Florida; October 8, in St. Louis, Missouri; and October 13 in Tempe, Arizona.

"The First Bush-Kerry Presidential Debate"

Presidential Candidates' Debate, Sponsored by the Miccosukee Tribe of Indians of Florida, University of Miami, Coral Gables, Florida.

Speakers: George W. Bush, president of the United States; U.S. Senator John F. Kerry (Mass.), Democratic presidential nominee; Jim Lehrer, anchor and executive editor, PBS's *The NewsHour.*

Lehrer: . . . Good evening, Mr. President, Senator Kerry. . . . Senator Kerry . . . Do you believe you could do a better job than President Bush in preventing another 9/11-type terrorist attack on the United States?

Kerry: Yes, I do. . . .

I can make American safer than President Bush has made us.

And I believe President Bush and I both love our country equally. But we just have a different set of convictions about how you make America safe.

I believe America is safest and strongest when we are leading the world and we are leading strong alliances.

I'll never give a veto to any country over our security. But I also know how to lead those alliances.

This president has left them in shatters across the globe, and we're now 90 percent of the casualties in Iraq and 90 percent of the costs.

I think that's wrong, and I think we can do better.

I have a better plan for homeland security. I have a better plan to be able to fight the war on terror by strengthening our military, strengthening our intelligence, by going after the financing more authoritatively, by doing what we need to do to rebuild the alliances, by reaching out to the Muslim world, which the president has almost not done, and beginning to isolate the radical Islamic Muslims, not have them isolate the United States of America.

I know I can do a better job in Iraq. I have a plan to have a summit with all of the allies, something this president has not yet achieved, not yet been able to do to bring people to the table.

We can do a better job of training the Iraqi forces to defend themselves, and I know that we can do a better job of preparing for elections.

All of these, and especially homeland security, which we'll talk about a little bit later.

Lehrer: Mr. President. . . .

Bush: . . . September the 11th changed how America must look at the world. And since that day, our nation has been on a multi-pronged strategy to keep our country safer.

We pursued Al Qaeda wherever Al Qaeda tries to hide. Seventy-five percent of known Al Qaeda leaders have been brought to justice. The rest of them know we're after them.

We've upheld the doctrine that said if you harbor a terrorist, you're equally as guilty as the terrorist.

And the Taliban are no longer in power. Ten million people have registered to vote in Afghanistan in the upcoming presidential election.

In Iraq, we saw a threat, and we realized that after September the 11th, we must take threats seriously, before they fully materialize. Saddam Hussein now sits in a prison cell. America and the world are safer for it. We continue to pursue our policy of disrupting those who proliferate weapons of mass destruction.

Libya has disarmed. The A.Q. Khan network has been brought to justice.

And, as well, we're pursuing a strategy of freedom around the world, because I understand free nations will reject terror. Free nations will answer the hopes and aspirations of their people. Free nations will help us achieve the peace we all want.

Lehrer: New question, Mr. President, two minutes.

Do you believe the election of Senator Kerry on November the 2nd would increase the chances of the U.S. being hit by another 9/11-type terrorist attack?

Bush: No, I don't believe it's going to happen. I believe I'm going to win, because the American people know I know how to lead. I've shown the American people I know how to lead.

I have—I understand everybody in this country doesn't agree with the decisions I've made. And I made some tough decisions. But people know where I stand.

People out there listening know what I believe. And that's how best it is to keep the peace.

This nation of ours has got a solemn duty to defeat this ideology of hate. And that's what they are. This is a group of killers who will not only kill here, but kill children in Russia, that'll attack unmercifully in Iraq, hoping to shake our will.

We have a duty to defeat this enemy. We have a duty to protect our children and grandchildren.

The best way to defeat them is to never waver, to be strong, to use every asset at our disposal, is to constantly stay on the offensive and, at the same time, spread liberty.

And that's what people are seeing now is happening in Afghanistan.

Ten million citizens have registered to vote. It's a phenomenal statistic. They're given a chance to be free, and they will show up at the polls. Forty-one percent of those 10 million are women.

In Iraq, no doubt about it, it's tough. It's hard work. It's incredibly hard. You know why? Because an enemy realizes the stakes. The enemy understands a free Iraq will be a major defeat in their ideology of hatred. That's why they're fighting so vociferously.

They showed up in Afghanistan when they were there, because they tried to beat us and they didn't. And they're showing up in Iraq for the same reason. They're trying to defeat us.

And if we lose our will, we lose. But if we remain strong and resolute, we will defeat this enemy.

Lehrer: Ninety second response, Senator Kerry.

Kerry: I believe in being strong and resolute and determined. And I will hunt down and kill the terrorists, wherever they are.

But we also have to be smart, Jim. And smart means not diverting your attention from the real war on terror in Afghanistan against Osama bin Laden and taking if off to Iraq where the 9/11 Commission confirms there was no connection to 9/11 itself and Saddam Hussein, and where the reason for going to war was weapons of mass destruction, not the removal of Saddam Hussein.

This president has made, I regret to say, a colossal error of judgment. And judgment is what we look for in the president of the United States of America.

I'm proud that important military figures who are supporting me in this race: former Chairman of the Joint Chiefs of Staff John Shalikashvili; just yesterday, General Eisenhower's son, General John Eisenhower, endorsed me; General Admiral William [Crowe]; General Tony [McPeak], who ran the Air Force war so effectively for his father—all believe I would make a stronger commander in chief. And they believe it because they know I would not take my eye off of the goal: Osama bin Laden.

Unfortunately, he escaped in the mountains of Tora Bora. We had him surrounded. But we didn't use American forces, the best trained in the world, to go kill him. The president relied on Afghan warlords and he outsourced that job too. That's wrong.

Lehrer: New question, two minutes, Senator Kerry.

"Colossal misjudgments." What colossal misjudgments, in your opinion, has President Bush made in these areas?

Kerry: Well, where do you want me to begin?

First of all, he made the misjudgment of saying to America that he was going to build a true alliance, that he would exhaust the remedies of the United Nations and go through the inspections.

In fact, he first didn't even want to do that. And it wasn't until former Secretary of State Jim Baker and General Scowcroft and others pushed publicly and said you've got to go to the U.N., that the president finally changed his mind—his campaign has a word for that—and went to the United Nations.

Now, once there, we could have continued those inspections.

We had Saddam Hussein trapped.

He also promised America that he would go to war as a last resort.

Those words mean something to me, as somebody who has been in combat. "Last resort." You've got to be able to look in the eyes of families and say to those parents, "I tried to do everything in my power to prevent the loss of your son and daughter."

I don't believe the United States did that.

And we pushed our allies aside.

And so, today, we are 90 percent of the casualties and 90 percent of the cost: $200 billion—$200 billion that could have been used for health care, for schools, for construction, for prescription drugs for seniors, and it's in Iraq.

And Iraq is not even the center of the focus of the war on terror. The center is Afghanistan, where, incidentally, there were more Americans killed last year than the year before; where the opium production is 75 percent of the world's opium production; where 40 to 60 percent of the economy of Afghanistan is based on opium; where the elections have been postponed three times.

The president moved the troops, so he's got 10 times the number of troops in Iraq than he has in Afghanistan, where Osama bin Laden is. Does that mean that Saddam Hussein was 10 times more important than Osama bin Laden—than, excuse me, Saddam Hussein more important than Osama bin Laden? I don't think so.

Lehrer: Ninety-second response, Mr. President.

Bush: My opponent looked at the same intelligence I looked at and declared in 2002 that Saddam Hussein was a grave threat.

He also said in December of 2003 that anyone who doubts that the world is safer without Saddam Hussein does not have the judgment to be president.

I agree with him. The world is better off without Saddam Hussein.

I was hoping diplomacy would work. I understand the serious consequences of committing our troops into harm's way.

It's the hardest decision a president makes. So I went to the United Nations. I didn't need anybody to tell me to go to the United Nations. I decided to go there myself.

And I went there hoping that, once and for all, the free world would act in concert to get Saddam Hussein to listen to our demands. They passed the resolution that said, "Disclose, disarm, or face serious consequences." I believe, when an international body speaks, it must mean what it says.

Saddam Hussein had no intention of disarming. Why should he? He had 16 other resolutions and nothing took place. As a matter of fact, my opponent talks about inspectors. The facts are that he was systematically deceiving the inspectors.

That wasn't going to work. That's kind of a pre-September 10th mentality, the hope that somehow resolutions and failed inspections would make this world a more peaceful place. He was hoping we'd turn away. But there was fortunately others beside himself who believed that we ought to take action.

We did. The world is safer without Saddam Hussein.

Lehrer: New question, Mr. President. Two minutes.

What about Senator Kerry's point, the comparison he drew between the priorities of going after Osama bin Laden and going after Saddam Hussein?

Bush: Jim, we've got the capability of doing both.

As a matter of fact, this is a global effort.

We're facing a group of folks who have such hatred in their heart, they'll strike anywhere, with any means.

And that's why it's essential that we have strong alliances, and we do.

That's why it's essential that we make sure that we keep weapons of mass destruction out of the hands of people like Al Qaeda, which we are.

But to say that there's only one focus on the war on terror doesn't really understand the nature of the war on terror.

Of course we're after Saddam Hussein—I mean bin Laden. He's isolated. Seventy-five percent of his people have been brought to justice. The killer—the mastermind of the September 11th attacks, Khalid Sheik Mohammed, is in prison.

We're making progress.

But the front on this war is more than just one place. The Philippines—we've got help—we're helping them there to bring—to bring Al Qaeda affiliates to justice there.

And, of course, Iraq is a central part in the war on terror. That's why [insurrection leader Abu Musab al-] Zarqawi and his people are trying to fight us. Their hope is that we grow weary and we leave.

The biggest disaster that could happen is that we not succeed in Iraq. We will succeed. We've got a plan to do so. And the main reason we'll succeed is because the Iraqis want to be free.

I had the honor of visiting with [Iraqi interim] Prime Minister [Ayad] Allawi. He's a strong, courageous leader. He believes in the freedom of the Iraqi people.

He doesn't want U.S. leadership, however, to send mixed signals, to not stand with the Iraqi people.

He believes, like I believe, that the Iraqis are ready to fight for their own freedom. They just need the help to be trained. There will be elections in January. We're spending reconstruction money. And our alliance is strong.

That's the plan for victory.

And when Iraq if free, America will be more secure.

Lehrer: Senator Kerry, 90 seconds.

Kerry: The president just talked about Iraq as a center of the war on terror. Iraq was not even close to the center of the war on terror before the president invaded it.

The president made the judgment to divert forces from under General Tommy Franks from Afghanistan before the Congress even approved it to begin to prepare to go to war in Iraq.

And he rushed the war in Iraq without a plan to win the peace. Now, that is not the judgment that a president of the United States ought to make. You don't take America to war unless [without a] plan to win the peace. You don't send troops to war without the body armor that they need.

I've met kids in Ohio, parents in Wisconsin places, Iowa, where they're going out on the Internet to get the state-of-the-art body gear to send to their kids. Some of them got them for a birthday present.

I think that's wrong. Humvees—10,000 out of 12,000 Humvees that are over there aren't armored. And you go visit some of those kids in the hospitals today who were maimed because they don't have the armament.

This president just—I don't know if he sees what's really happened [out] there. But it's getting worse by the day. More soldiers killed in June than before. More in July than June. More in August than July. More in September than in August.

And now we see beheadings. And we got weapons of mass destruction crossing the border every single day, and they're blowing people up. And we don't have enough troops there. . . .

Bush: . . . First of all, what my opponent wants you to forget is that he voted to authorize the use of force and now says it's the wrong war at the wrong time at the wrong place.

I don't see how you can lead this country to succeed in Iraq if you say "wrong war, wrong time, wrong place." What message does that send our troops? What message does that send to our allies? What message does that send the Iraqis?

No, the way to win this is to be steadfast and resolved and to follow through on the plan that I've just outlined.

Lehrer: Thirty seconds, Senator.

Kerry: Yes, we have to be steadfast and resolved, and I am. And I will succeed for those troops, now that we're there. We have to succeed. We can't leave a failed Iraq. But that doesn't mean it wasn't a mistake of judgment to go there and take the focus off of Osama bin Laden. It was. Now, we can succeed. But I don't believe this president can.

I think we need a president who has the credibility to bring the allies back to the table and to do what's necessary to make it so America isn't doing this alone.

Lehrer: We'll come back to Iraq in a moment. But I want to come back to where I began, on homeland security. This is a two-minute new question, Senator Kerry.

As president, what would you do, specifically, in addition to or differently to increase the homeland security of the United States than what President Bush is doing?

Kerry: Jim, let me tell you exactly what I'll do. And there are a long list of thing. First of all, what kind of mixed message does it send when you have $500 million going over to Iraq to put police officers in the streets of Iraq, and the president is cutting the COPS program in America?

What kind of message does it send to be sending money to open firehouses in Iraq, but we're shutting firehouses who are the first-responders here in America.

The president hasn't put one nickel, not one nickel into the effort to fix some of our tunnels and bridges and most exposed subway systems. That's why they had to close down the subway in New York when the Republican Convention was there. We hadn't done the work that ought to be done.

The president—95 percent of the containers that come into the ports, right here in Florida, are not inspected. Civilians get onto aircraft, and their luggage is X-rayed, but the cargo hold is not X-rayed.

Does that make you feel safer in America?

This president thought it was more important to give the wealthiest people in America a tax cut rather than invest in homeland security. Those aren't my values. I believe in protecting America first. . . .

The president also unfortunately gave in to the chemical industry, which didn't want to do some of the things necessary to strengthen our chemical plant exposure.

And there's an enormous undone job to protect the loose nuclear materials in the world that are able to get to terrorists. That's a whole other subject, but I see we still have a little bit more time.

Let me just quickly say, at the current pace, the president will not secure the loose material in the Soviet Union—former Soviet Union for 13 years. I'm going to do it in four years. And we're going to keep it out of the hands of terrorists.

Lehrer: Ninety-second response, Mr. President.

Bush: I don't think we want to get to how he's going to pay for all these promises. It's like a huge tax gap. Anyway, that's for another debate.

My administration has tripled the amount of money we're spending on homeland security to $30 billion a year.

My administration worked with the Congress to create the Department of Homeland Security so we could better coordinate our borders and ports. We've got 1,000 extra border patrol on the southern border; want 1,000 on the northern border. We're modernizing our borders.

We spent $3.1 billion for fire and police, $3.1 billion.

We're doing our duty to provide the funding.

But the best way to protect this homeland is to stay on the offense.

You know, we have to be right 100 percent of the time. And the enemy only has to be right once to hurt us.

There's a lot of good people working hard.

And by the way, we've also changed the culture of the FBI to have counterterrorism as its number one priority. We're communicating better. We're going to reform our intelligence services to make sure that we get the best intelligence possible.

The Patriot Act is vital—is vital that the Congress renew the Patriot Act which enables our law enforcement to disrupt terror cells.

But again, I repeat to my fellow citizens, the best way to protection is to stay on the offense.

Lehrer: Yes, let's do a little—yes, 30 seconds.

Kerry: The president just said the FBI had changed its culture. We just read on the front pages of America's papers that there are over 100,000 hours of tapes, unlistened to. On one of those tapes may be the enemy being right the next time.

And the test is not whether you're spending more money. The test is, are you doing everything possible to make America safe?

We didn't need that tax cut. America needed to be safe.

Bush: Of course we're doing everything we can to protect America. I wake up every day thinking about how best to protect America. That's my job.

I work with Director Mueller of the FBI; comes in my office when I'm in Washington every morning, talking about how to protect us. There's a lot of really good people working hard to do so.

It's hard work. But, again, I want to tell the American people, we're doing everything we can at home, but you better have a president who chases these terrorists down and bring them to justice before they hurt us again.

Lehrer: New question, Mr. President. Two minutes.

What criteria would you use to determine when to start bringing U.S. troops home from Iraq?

Bush: Let me first tell you that the best way for Iraq to be safe and secure is for Iraqi citizens to be trained to do the job.

And that's what we're doing. We've got 100,000 trained now, 125,000 by the end of this year, 200,000 by the end of next year. That is the best way. We'll never succeed in Iraq if the Iraqi citizens do not want to take matters into their own hands to protect themselves. I believe they want to. Prime Minister Allawi believes they want to.

And so the best indication about when we can bring our troops home—which I really want to do, but I don't want to do so for the sake of bringing them home; I want to do so because we've achieved an objective—is to see the Iraqis perform and to see the Iraqis step up and take responsibility.

And so, the answer to your question is: When our general is on the ground and Ambassador Negroponte tells me that Iraq is ready to defend herself from these terrorists, that elections will have been held by then, that their stability and that they're on their way to, you know, a nation that's free; that's when.

And I hope it's as soon as possible. But I know putting artificial deadlines won't work. My opponent at one time said, "Well, get me elected, I'll have them out of there in six months." You can't do that and expect to win the war on terror. My message to our troops is, "Thank you for what you're doing. We're standing with you strong. We'll give you all the equipment you need. And we'll get you home as soon as the mission's done, because this is a vital mission."

A free Iraq will be an ally in the war on terror, and that's essential. A free Iraq will set a powerful example in the part of the world that is desperate for freedom. A free Iraq will help secure Israel. A free Iraq will enforce the hopes and aspirations of the reformers in places like Iran. A free Iraq is essential for the security of this country.

Lehrer: Ninety seconds, Senator Kerry.

Kerry: Thank you, Jim.

My message to the troops is also: Thank you for what they're doing, but it's also help is on the way. I believe those troops deserve better than what they are getting today.

You know, it's interesting. When I was in a rope line just the other day, coming out here from Wisconsin, a couple of young returnees were in the line, one active duty, one from the Guard. And they both looked at me and said: We need you. You've got to help us over there.

Now I believe there's a better way to do this. You know, the president's father did not go into Iraq, into Baghdad, beyond Basra. And the reason he didn't is, he said—he wrote in his book—because there was no viable exit strategy. And he said our troops would be occupiers in a bitterly hostile land.

That's exactly where we find ourselves today. There's a sense of American occupation. The only building that was guarded when the troops when into Baghdad was the oil ministry. We didn't guard the nuclear facilities.

We didn't guard the foreign office, where you might have found information about weapons of mass destruction. We didn't guard the borders.

Almost every step of the way, our troops have been left on these extraordinarily difficult missions. I know what it's like to go out on one of those missions when you don't know what's around the corner.

And I believe our troops need other allies helping. I'm going to hold that summit. I will bring fresh credibility, a new start, and we will get the job done right. . . .

Bush: My opponent says help is on the way, but what kind of message does it say to our troops in harm's way, "wrong war, wrong place, wrong time"? Not a message a commander in chief gives, or this is a "great diversion."

As well, help is on the way, but it's certainly hard to tell it when he voted against the $87-billion supplemental to provide equipment for our troops, and then said he actually did vote for it before he voted against it.

Not what a commander in chief does when you're trying to lead troops.

Lehrer: Senator Kerry, 30 seconds.

Kerry: Well, you know, when I talked about the $87 billion, I made a mistake in how I talk about the war. But the president made a mistake in invading Iraq. Which is worse?

I believe that when you know something's going wrong, you make it right. That's what I learned in Vietnam. When I came back from that war I saw that it was wrong. Some people don't like the fact that I stood up to say no, but I did. And that's what I did with that vote. And I'm going to lead those troops to victory. . . .

Bush: . . . My opponent says we didn't have any allies in this war. What's he say to Tony Blair? What's he say to Alexander Kwasniewski of Poland? You can't expect to build an alliance when you denigrate the contributions of those who are serving side by side with American troops in Iraq.

Plus, he says the cornerstone of his plan to succeed in Iraq is to call upon nations to serve. So what's the message going to be: "Please join us in Iraq. We're a grand diversion. Join us for a war that is the wrong war at the wrong place at the wrong time?"

I know how these people think. I deal with them all the time. I sit down with the world leaders frequently and talk to them on the phone frequently. They're not going to follow somebody who says, "This is the wrong war at the wrong place at the wrong time."

I know how these people think. I deal with them all the time. I sit down with the world leaders frequently and talk to them on the phone frequently.

They're not going to follow somebody who says this is the wrong war at the wrong place at the wrong time. They're not going to follow somebody whose core convictions keep changing because of politics in America.

And finally, he says we ought to have a summit. Well, there are summits being held. Japan is going to have a summit for the donors; $14 billion pledged. And Prime Minister Koizumi is going to call countries to account, to get them to contribute.

And there's going to be an Arab summit, of the neighborhood countries. And Colin Powell helped set up that summit. . . .

Lehrer: New question. Senator Kerry, two minutes. You just—you've repeatedly accused President Bush—not here tonight, but elsewhere before—of not telling the truth about Iraq, essentially of lying to the American people about Iraq. Give us some examples of what you consider to be his not telling the truth.

Kerry: Well, I've never, ever used the harshest word, as you did just then. And I try not to. I've been—but I'll nevertheless tell you that I think he has not been candid with the American people. And I'll tell you exactly how.

First of all, we all know that in his state of the union message, he told Congress about nuclear materials that didn't exist.

We know that he promised America that he was going to build this coalition. I just described the coalition. It is not the kind of coalition we were described when we were talking about voting for this.

The president said he would exhaust the remedies of the United Nations and go through that full process. He didn't. He cut if off, sort of arbitrarily.

And we know that there were further diplomatic efforts under way. They just decided the time for diplomacy is over and rushed to war without planning for what happens afterwards.

Now, he misled the American people in his speech when he said we will plan carefully. They obviously didn't. He misled the American people when he said we'd go to war as a last resort. We did not go as a last resort. And most Americans know the difference.

Now, this has cost us deeply in the world. I believe that it is important to tell the truth to the American people. I've worked with those leaders the president talks about, I've worked with them for 20 years, for longer than this president. And I know what many of them say today, and I know how to bring them back to the table.

And I believe that a fresh start, new credibility, a president who can understand what we have to do to reach out to the Muslim world to make it clear that this is not, you know—Osama bin Laden uses the invasion of Iraq in order to go out to people and say that America has declared war on Islam.

We need to be smarter about [how] we wage a war on terror. We need to deny them the recruits. We need to deny them the safe havens. We need to rebuild our alliances.

I believe that Ronald Reagan, John Kennedy, and the others did that more effectively, and I'm going to try to follow in their footsteps.

Lehrer: Ninety seconds, Mr. President.

Bush: My opponent just said something amazing. He said Osama bin Laden uses the invasion of Iraq as an excuse to spread hatred for America. Osama bin Laden isn't going to determine how we defend ourselves.

Osama bin Laden doesn't get to decide. The American people decide.

I decided the right action was in Iraq. My opponent calls it a mistake. It wasn't a mistake.

He said I misled on Iraq. I don't think he was misleading when he called Iraq a grave threat in the fall of 2002.

I don't think he was misleading when he said that it was right to disarm Iraq in the spring of 2003.

I don't think he misled you when he said that, you know, anyone who doubted whether the world was better off without Saddam Hussein in power didn't have the judgment to be president. I don't think he was misleading.

I think what is misleading is to say you can lead and succeed in Iraq if you keep changing your positions on this war. And he has. As the politics change, his positions change. And that's not how a commander in chief acts. . . .

Kerry: I wasn't misleading when I said he was a threat. Nor was I misleading on the day that the president decided to go to war when I said that he had made a mistake in not building strong alliances and that I would have preferred that he did more diplomacy.

I've had one position, one consistent position, that Saddam Hussein was a threat. There was a right way to disarm him and a wrong way. And the president chose the wrong way.

Lehrer: Thirty seconds, Mr. President.

Bush: The only consistent about my opponent's position is that he's been inconsistent. He changes positions. And you cannot change positions in this war on terror if you expect to win.

And I expect to win. It's necessary we win.

We're being challenged like never before. And we have a duty to our country and to future generations of America to achieve a free Iraq, a free Afghanistan, and to rid the world of weapons of mass destruction. . . .

Kerry: Jim, the president just said something extraordinarily revealing and frankly very important in this debate. In answer to your question about Iraq and sending people into Iraq, he just said, "The enemy attacked us."

Saddam Hussein didn't attack us. Osama bin Laden attacked us. Al Qaeda attacked us. And when we had Osama bin Laden cornered in the mountains of Tora Bora, 1,000 of his cohorts with him in those mountains. With the American military forces nearby and in the field, we didn't use the best trained troops in the world to go kill the world's number one criminal and terrorist.

They outsourced the job to Afghan warlords, who only a week earlier had been on the other side fighting against us, neither of whom trusted each other.

That's the enemy that attacked us. That's the enemy that was allowed to walk out of those mountains. That's the enemy that is now in 60 countries, with stronger recruits.

He also said Saddam Hussein would have been stronger. That is just factually incorrect. Two-thirds of the country was a no-fly zone when we started this war. We would have had sanctions. We would have had the U.N. inspectors. Saddam Hussein would have been continually weakening.

If the president had shown the patience to go through another round of resolution, to sit down with those leaders, say, "What do you need, what do you need now, how much more will it take to get you to join us?" we'd be in a stronger place today.

Lehrer: Thirty seconds.

Bush: First of all, of course I know Osama bin Laden attacked us. I know that.

And secondly, to think that another round of resolutions would have caused Saddam Hussein to disarm, disclose, is ludicrous, in my judgment. It just shows a significant difference of opinion.

We tried diplomacy. We did our best. He was hoping to turn a blind eye. And, yes, he would have been stronger had we not dealt with him. He had the capability of making weapons, and he would have made weapons. . . .

Lehrer: New question. Two minutes, Senator Kerry.

What is your position on the whole concept of preemptive war?

Kerry: The president always has the right, and always has had the right, for preemptive strike. That was a great doctrine throughout the Cold War. And it was always one of the things we argued about with respect to arms control.

No president, through all of American history, has ever ceded, and nor would I, the right to preempt in any way necessary to protect the United States of America.

But if and when you do it, Jim, you have to do it in a way that passes the test, that passes the global test where your countrymen, your people understand fully why you're doing what you're doing and you can prove to the world that you did it for legitimate reasons. . . .

Bush: Let me—I'm not exactly sure what you mean, "passes the global test," you take preemptive action if you pass a global test.

My attitude is you take preemptive action in order to protect the American people, that you act in order to make this country secure. . . .

Lehrer: New question, President Bush. Clearly, as we have heard, major policy differences between the two of you. Are there also underlying character issues that you believe, that you believe are serious enough to deny Senator Kerry the job as commander in chief of the United States?

Bush: That's a loaded question. Well, first of all, I admire Senator Kerry's service to our country. . . .

My concerns about the senator is that, in the course of this campaign, I've been listening very carefully to what he says, and he changes positions on the war in Iraq. He changes positions on something as fundamental as what you believe in your core, in your heart of hearts, is right in Iraq.

You cannot lead if you send mixed messages. Mixed messages send the wrong signals to our troops. Mixed messages send the wrong signals to our allies. Mixed messages send the wrong signals to the Iraqi citizens.

And that's my biggest concern about my opponent. I admire his service. But I just know how this world works, and that in the councils of government, there must be certainty from the U.S. president.

Of course, we change tactics when need to, but we never change our beliefs, the strategic beliefs that are necessary to protect this country in the world.

Lehrer: Ninety second response, Senator.

Kerry: Well, first of all, I appreciate enormously the personal comments the president just made. . . . But we do have differences. I'm not going to talk about a difference of character. I don't think that's my job or my business.

But let me talk about something that the president just sort of finished up with. Maybe someone would call it a character trait, maybe somebody wouldn't.

But this issue of certainty. It's one thing to be certain, but you can be certain and be wrong.

It's another to be certain and be right, or to be certain and be moving in the right direction, or be certain about a principle and then learn new facts and take those new facts and put them to use in order to change and get your policy right.

What I worry about with the president is that he's not acknowledging what's on the ground, he's not acknowledging the realities of North Korea, he's not acknowledging the truth of the science of stem-cell research or of global warming and other issues.

And certainty sometimes can get you in trouble.

Lehrer: Thirty seconds.

Bush: Well, I think—listen, I fully agree that one should shift tactics, and we will, in Iraq. Our commanders have got all the flexibility to do what is necessary to succeed.

But what I won't do is change my core values because of politics or because of pressure.

And it is one of the things I've learned in the White House, is that there's enormous pressure on the president, and he cannot wilt under that pressure. Otherwise, the world won't be better off.

Lehrer: Thirty seconds.

Kerry: I have no intention of wilting. I've never wilted in my life. And I've never wavered in my life.

I know exactly what we need to do in Iraq, and my position has been consistent: Saddam Hussein is a threat. He needed to be disarmed. We needed to go to the U.N. The president needed the authority to use force in order to be able to get him to do something, because he never did it without the threat of force.

But we didn't need to rush to war without a plan to win the peace.

Source: Commission on Presidential Debates. "The First Bush-Kerry Presidential Debate." Transcript. Coral Gables, Florida, September 30, 2004. www.debates.org/pages/trans2004a_p.html (accessed March 4, 2005). The transcripts are strictly unofficial and the Commission does not warrant their accuracy.

"The Second Bush-Kerry Presidential Debate"

Second Presidential Candidates' Debate, Washington University, St. Louis, Missouri.
Speakers: George W. Bush, president of the United States; U.S. Senator John F. Kerry (Mass.), Democratic presidential nominee; Charles Gibson, ABC anchor.

Gibson: . . . Tonight's format is going to be a bit different. . . . Audience members will address [a] question to a specific candidate. . . . The first question is for Senator Kerry. . . .

Cheryl Otis: Senator Kerry, after talking with several co-workers and family and friends, I asked the ones who said they were not voting for you, "Why?" They said that you were too wishy-washy. Do you have a reply for them?

Kerry: Yes, I certainly do. . . . Cheryl, the president didn't find weapons of mass destruction in Iraq, so he's really turned his campaign into a weapon of mass deception. And the result is that you've been bombarded with advertisements suggesting that I've changed a position on this or that or the other.

Now, the three things they try to say I've changed position on are the Patriot Act; I haven't. I support it. I just don't like the way John Ashcroft has applied it, and we're going to change a few things. The chairman of the Republican Party thinks we ought to change a few things.

No Child Left Behind Act, I voted for it. I support it. I support the goals.

But the president has underfunded it by $28 billion.

Right here in St. Louis, you've laid off 350 teachers. You're 150—excuse me, I think it's a little more, about $100 million shy of what you ought to be under the No Child Left Behind Act to help your education system here.

So I complain about that. I've argued that we should fully funded it. The president says I've changed my mind. I haven't changed my mind: I'm going to fully fund it.

So these are the differences.

Now, the president has presided over an economy where we've lost 1.6 million jobs. The first president in 72 years to lose jobs.

I have a plan to put people back to work. That's not wishy-washy.

I'm going to close the loopholes that actually encourage companies to go overseas. The president wants to keep them open. I think I'm right. I think he's wrong.

I'm going to give you a tax cut. The president gave the top 1 percent of income-earners in America, got $89 billion last year, more than the 80 percent of people who earn $100,000 or less all put together. I think that's wrong. That's not wishy-washy, and that's what I'm fighting for, you.

Gibson: Mr. President, a minute and a half.

Bush: . . . I can see why people at your workplace think he changes positions a lot, because he does. He said he voted for the $87 billion, and voted against it right before he voted for it. And that sends a confusing signal to people.

He said he thought Saddam Hussein was a grave threat, and now he said it was a mistake to remove Saddam Hussein from power.

No, I can see why people think that he changes position quite often, because he does.

You know, for a while he was a strong supporter of getting rid of Saddam Hussein. He saw the wisdom—until the Democrat primary came along and Howard Dean, the anti-war candidate, began to gain on him, and he changed positions.

I don't see how you can lead this country in a time of war, in a time of uncertainty, if you change your mind because of politics.

He just brought up the tax cut. You remember we increased that child credit by $1,000, reduced the marriage penalty, created a 10 percent tax bracket for the lower-income Americans. That's right at the middle class.

He voted against it. And yet he tells you he's for a middle-class tax cut. It's—you've got to be consistent when you're the president. There's a lot of pressures. And you've got to be firm and consistent. . . .

Robin Dahle: Mr. President, yesterday in a statement you admitted that Iraq did not have weapons of mass destruction, but justified the invasion by stating, I quote, "He retained the knowledge, the materials, the means and the intent to produce weapons of mass destruction and could have passed this knowledge to our terrorist enemies."

Do you sincerely believe this to be a reasonable justification for invasion when this statement applies to so many other countries, including North Korea?

Bush: Each situation is different, Robin.

And obviously we hope that diplomacy works before you ever use force. The hardest decision a president makes is ever to use force.

After 9/11, we had to look at the world differently. After 9/11, we had to recognize that when we saw a threat, we must take it seriously before it comes to hurt us.

In the old days we'd see a threat, and we could deal with it if we felt like it or not. But 9/11 changed it all.

I vowed to our countrymen that I would do everything I could to protect the American people. That's why we're bringing al Qaeda to justice. Seventy five percent of them have been brought to justice.

That's why I said to Afghanistan: If you harbor a terrorist, you're just as guilty as the terrorist. And the Taliban is no longer in power, and al Qaeda no longer has a place to plan.

And I saw a unique threat in Saddam Hussein, as did my opponent, because we thought he had weapons of mass destruction.

And the unique threat was that he could give weapons of mass destruction to an organization like al Qaeda, and the harm they inflicted on us with airplanes would be multiplied greatly by weapons of mass destruction. And that was the serious, serious threat.

So I tried diplomacy, went to the United Nations. But as we learned in the same report I quoted, Saddam Hussein was gaming the oil-for-food program to get rid of sanctions. He was trying to get rid of sanctions for a reason: He wanted to restart his weapons programs.

We all thought there was weapons there, Robin. My opponent thought there was weapons there. That's why he called him a grave threat.

I wasn't happy when we found out there wasn't weapons, and we've got an intelligence group together to figure out why.

But Saddam Hussein was a unique threat. And the world is better off without him in power.

And my opponent's plans lead me to conclude that Saddam Hussein would still be in power, and the world would be more dangerous.

Thank you, sir.

Gibson: Senator Kerry, a minute and a half.

Kerry: . . . The world is more dangerous today. The world is more dangerous today because the president didn't make the right judgments.

Now, the president wishes that I had changed my mind. He wants you to believe that because he can't come here and tell you that he's created new jobs for America. He's lost jobs.

He can't come here and tell you that he's created health care for Americans because, what, we've got 5 million Americans who have lost their health care, 96,000 of them right here in Missouri.

He can't come here and tell you that he's left no child behind because he didn't fund no child left behind.

So what does he do? He's trying to attack me. He wants you to believe that I can't be president. And he's trying to make you believe it because he wants you to think I change my mind.

Well, let me tell you straight up: I've never changed my mind about Iraq. I do believe Saddam Hussein was a threat. I always believed he was a threat. Believed it in 1998 when Clinton was president. I wanted to give Clinton the power to use force if necessary.

But I would have used that force wisely, I would have used that authority wisely, not rushed to war without a plan to win the peace.

I would have brought our allies to our side. I would have fought to make certain our troops had everybody possible to help them win the mission.

This president rushed to war, pushed our allies aside. And Iran now is more dangerous, and so is North Korea, with nuclear weapons. He took his eye off the ball, off of Osama bin Laden. . . .

The president stood right here in this hall four years ago, and he was asked a question by somebody just like you, "Under what circumstances would you send people to war?"

And his answer was, "With a viable exit strategy and only with enough forces to get the job done."

He didn't do that. He broke that promise. We didn't have enough forces.

General [Eric K.] Shinseki, the Army chief of staff, told him he was going to need several hundred thousand. And guess what? They retired General Shinseki for telling him that.

This president hasn't listened. . . .

Bush: I remember sitting in the White House looking at those generals, saying, "Do you have what you need in this war? Do you have what it takes?"

I remember going down to the basement of the White House the day we committed our troops as last resort, looking at Tommy Franks and the generals on the ground, asking them, "Do we have the right plan with the right troop level?"

And they looked me in the eye and said, "Yes, sir, Mr. President." Of course, I listen to our generals. That's what a president does. A president sets the strategy and relies upon good military people to execute that strategy.

Gibson: Senator?

Kerry: You rely on good military people to execute the military component of the strategy, but winning the peace is larger than just the military component.

General Shinseki had the wisdom to say, "You're going to need several hundred thousand troops to win the peace." The military's job is to win the war.

A president's job is to win the peace. . . .

Matthew O'Brien: Mr. President, you have enjoyed a Republican majority in the House and Senate for most of your presidency. In that time, you've not vetoed a single spending bill. Excluding $120 billion spent in Iran and—I'm sorry, Iraq and Afghanistan, there has been $700 billion spent and not paid for by taxes.

Please explain how the spending you have approved and not paid for is better for the American people than the spending proposed by your opponent.

Bush: Right, thank you for that.

We have a deficit. We have a deficit because this country went into a recession. You might remember the stock market started to decline dramatically six months before I came to office, and then the bubble of the 1990s popped. And that cost us revenue. That cost us revenue.

Secondly, we're at war. And I'm going to spend what it takes to win the war, more than just $120 billion for Iraq and Afghanistan. We've got to pay our troops more. We have. We've increased money for ammunition and weapons and pay and homeland security.

I just told this lady over here we spent—went from $10 billion to $30 billion to protect the homeland. I think we have an obligation to spend that kind of money.

And plus, we cut taxes for everybody. Everybody got tax relief, so that they get out of the recession.

I think if you raise taxes during a recession, you head to depression. I come from the school of thought that says when people have more money in their pocket during economic times, it increases demand or investment. Small businesses begin to grow, and jobs are added.

We found out today that over the past 13 months, we've added 1.9 million new jobs in the last 13 months.

I proposed a plan, detailed budget, that shows us cutting the deficit in half by five years.

And you're right, I haven't vetoed any spending bills, because we work together.

Non-homeland, non-defense discretionary spending was raising at 15 percent a year when I got into office. And today it's less than 1 percent, because we're working together to try to bring this deficit under control.

Like you, I'm concerned about the deficit. But I am not going to shortchange our troops in harm's way. And I'm not going to run up taxes, which will cost this economy jobs.

Thank you for your question.

Gibson: Senator Kerry, a minute and a half.

Kerry: . . . Now with respect to the deficit, the president was handed a $5.6 trillion surplus, ladies and gentlemen. That's where he was when he came into office.

We now have a $2.6 trillion deficit. This is the biggest turnaround in the history of the country. He's the first president in 72 years to lose jobs.

He talked about war. This is the first time the United States of America has ever had a tax cut when we're at war.

Franklin Roosevelt, Harry Truman, others, knew how to lead. They knew how to ask the American people for the right things.

One percent of America, the highest one percent of income earners in America, got $89 billion of tax cut last year. One percent of America got more than the 80 percent of America that earned from $100,000 down.

The president thinks it's more important to fight for that top 1 percent than to fight for fiscal responsibility and to fight for you.

I want to put money in your pocket. I am—I have a proposal for a tax cut for all people earning less than the $200,000. The only people affected by my plan are the top income earners of America.

Gibson: I have heard you both say during the campaign, I just heard you say it, that you're going to cut the deficit by a half in four years. But I didn't hear one thing in the last three and a half minutes that would indicate how either one of you do that.

Bush: Well, look at the budget. One is make sure Congress doesn't overspend.

But let me talk back about where we've been. The stock market was declining six months prior to my arrival.

It was the largest stock market correction—one of the largest in history, which foretold a recession.

Because we cut taxes on everybody—remember, we ran up the child credit by $1,000, we reduced the marriage penalty, we created a 10 percent bracket, everybody who pays taxes got relief—the recession was one of the shortest in our nation's history.

Gibson: Senator Kerry, 30 seconds.

Kerry: After 9/11, after the recession had ended, the president asked for another tax cut and promised 5.6 million jobs would be created. He lost 1.6 million, ladies and gentlemen. And most of that tax cut went to the wealthiest people in the country.

He came and asked for a tax cut—we wanted a tax cut to kick the economy into gear. Do you know what he presented us with? A $25 billion giveaway to the biggest corporations in America, including a $254 million refund check to Enron.

Wrong priorities. You are my priority.

Gibson: Senator Kerry, the next question . . . comes from James Varner. . . .

Varner: Thank you. Senator Kerry, would you be willing to look directly into the camera and, using simple and unequivocal language, give the American people your solemn pledge not to sign any legislation that will increase the tax burden on families earning less than $200,000 a year during your first term?

Kerry: Absolutely. Yes. Right into the camera. Yes. I am not going to raise taxes.

I have a tax cut. And here's my tax cut.

I raise the child-care credit by $1,000 for families to help them be able to take care of their kids.

I have a $4,000 tuition tax credit that goes to parents—and kids, if they're earning for themselves—to be able to pay for college.

And I lower the cost of health care in the way that I described to you.

Every part of my program I've shown how I'm going to pay for it.

And I've gotten good people, like former Secretary of the Treasury Bob Rubin, for instance, who showed how to balance budgets and give you a good economy, to help me crunch these numbers and make them work.

I've even scaled back some of my favorite programs already, like the child-care program I wanted to fund and the national service program, because the president's deficit keeps growing and I've said as a pledge, "I'm going to cut the deficit in half in four years." . . .

I'm pledging I will not raise taxes; I'm giving a tax cut to the people earning less than $200,000 a year.

Now, for the people earning more than $200,000 a year, you're going to see a rollback to the level we were at with Bill Clinton, when people made a lot of money.

And looking around here, at this group here, I suspect there are only three people here who are going to be affected: the president, me, and, Charlie [Gibson].

Gibson: Mr. President, 90 seconds.

Bush: He's just not credible when he talks about being fiscally conservative. He's just not credible. If you look at his record in the Senate, he voted to break the caps—the spending caps—over 200 times.

And here he says he's going to be a fiscal conservative, all of a sudden. It's just not credible. You cannot believe it.

And of course he's going to raise your taxes. You see, he's proposed $2.2 trillion of new spending. And you say: Well, how are you going to pay for it? He says, well, he's going to raise the taxes on the rich—that's what he said—the top two brackets. That raises, he says $800 billion; we say $600 billion.

We've got battling green eye shades.

Somewhere in between those numbers—and so there's a difference, what he's promised and what he can raise.

Now, either he's going to break all these wonderful promises he's told you about or he's going to raise taxes. And I suspect, given his record, he's going to raise taxes. . . .

I think that the way to grow this economy is to keep taxes low, is have an energy plan, is to have litigation reform. As I told you, we've just got a report that said over the past 13 months, we've created 1.9 million new jobs.

And so the fundamental question of this campaign is: Who's going to keep the economy growing so people can work? That's the fundamental question. . . .

Jane Barrow: Senator Kerry, how can the U.S. be competitive in manufacturing given—in manufacturing, excuse me—given the wage necessary and comfortably accepted for American workers to maintain the standard of living that they expect?

Kerry: Jane, there are a lot of ways to be competitive. And unfortunately again I regret this administration has not seized them and embraced them. Let me give you an example.

There is a tax loophole right now. If you're a company in St. Louis working, trying to make jobs here, there is actually an incentive for you to go away. You get more money, you keep more of your taxes by going abroad.

I'm going to shut that loophole, and I'm going to give the tax benefit to the companies that stay here in America to help make them more competitive.

Secondly, we're going to create a manufacturing jobs credit and a new jobs credit for people to be able to help hire and be more competitive here in America.

Third, what's really hurting American business more than anything else is the cost of health care.

Now, you didn't hear any plan from the president, because he doesn't have a plan to lower the cost of health care.

Five million Americans have lost their health care; 620,000 Missourians have no health care at all; 96,000 Missourians have lost their health care under President Bush.

I have a plan to cover those folks. And it's a plan that lowers cost for everybody, covers all children. And the way I pay for it—I'm not fiscally irresponsible—is I roll back the tax cut this president so fiercely wants to defend, the one for him and me and Charlie.

I think you ought to get the break. I want to lower your cost to health care. I want to fully fund education, No Child Left Behind, special-needs education. And that's how we're going to be more competitive, by making sure our kids are graduating from school and college.

China and India are graduating more graduates in technology and science than we are.

We've got to create the products of the future. That's why I have a plan for energy independence within 10 years.

And we're going to put our laboratories and our colleges and our universities to work. And we're going to get the great entrepreneurial spirit of this country, and we're going to free ourselves from this dependency on Mideast oil.

That's how you create jobs and become competitive.

Gibson: Mr. President, minute and a half.

Bush: Let me start with how to control the cost of health care: medical liability reform, for starters, which he's opposed.

Secondly, allow small businesses to pool together so they can share risk and buy insurance at the same discounts big businesses get to do.

Thirdly, spread what's called health savings accounts. It's good for small businesses, good for owners. You own your own account. You can save tax-free. You get a catastrophic plan to help you on it.

This is different from saying, "OK, let me incent you to go on the government."

He's talking about his plan to keep jobs here. . . . The best way to keep jobs here in America is, one, have an energy plan. I proposed one to the Congress two years ago, encourages conservation, encourages technology to explore for environmentally friendly ways for coal—to use coal and gas. It encourages the use of renewables like ethanol and biodiesel.

It's stuck in the Senate. He and his running-mate didn't show up to vote when they could have got it going in the Senate.

Less regulations if we want jobs here; legal reform if we want jobs here; and we've got to keep taxes low.

Now, he says he's only going to tax the rich. Do you realize, 900,000 small businesses will be taxed under his plan because most small businesses are Subchapter S corps or limited partnerships, and they pay tax at the individual income tax level.

And so when you're running up the taxes like that, you're taxing job creators, and that's not how you keep jobs here. . . .

Rob Fowler: President Bush, 45 days after 9/11, Congress passed the Patriot Act, which takes away checks on law enforcement and weakens American citizens' rights and freedoms, especially Fourth Amendment rights.

With expansions to the Patriot Act and Patriot Act II, my question to you is, why are my rights being watered down and my citizens' around me? And what are the specific justifications for these reforms?

Bush: . . . I really don't think your rights are being watered down. As a matter of fact, I wouldn't support it if I thought that.

Every action being taken against terrorists requires court order, requires scrutiny.

As a matter of fact, the tools now given to the terrorist fighters are the same tools that we've been using against drug dealers and white-collar criminals.

So I really don't think so. I hope you don't think that. I mean, I—because I think whoever is the president must guard your liberties, must not erode your rights in America.

The Patriot Act is necessary, for example, because parts of the FBI couldn't talk to each other. The intelligence-gathering and the law-enforcement arms of the FBI just couldn't share intelligence under the old law. And that didn't make any sense.

Our law enforcement must have every tool necessary to find and disrupt terrorists at home and abroad before they hurt us again. That's the task of the 21st century.

And so, I don't think the Patriot Act abridges your rights at all. . . .

Kerry: Former Governor [Marc] Racicot, as chairman of the Republican Party, said he thought that the Patriot Act has to be changed and fixed.

Congressman Jim Sensenbrenner [R-Wis.], he is the chairman of the House Judiciary Committee, said over his dead body before it gets renewed without being thoroughly rechecked.

A whole bunch of folks in America are concerned about the way the Patriot Act has been applied. In fact, the inspector general of the Justice Department found that John Ashcroft had twice applied it in ways that were inappropriate.

People's rights have been abused.

I met a man who spent eight months in prison, wasn't even allowed to call his lawyer, wasn't allowed to get—finally, Senator Dick Durbin of Illinois intervened and was able to get him out.

This is in our country, folks, the United States of America.

They've got sneak-and-peek searches that are allowed. They've got people allowed to go into churches now and political meetings without any showing of potential criminal activity or otherwise.

Now, I voted for the Patriot Act. Ninety-nine United States senators voted for it. And the president's been very busy running around the country using what I just described to you as a reason to say I'm wishy-washy, that I'm a flip-flopper.

Now that's not a flip-flop. I believe in the Patriot Act. We need the things in it that coordinate the FBI and the CIA. We need to be stronger on terrorism.

But you know what we also need to do as Americans is never let the terrorists change the Constitution of the United States in a way that disadvantages our rights. . . .

Sarah Degenhart: Senator Kerry, suppose you are speaking with a voter who believed abortion is murder and the voter asked for reassurance that his or her tax dollars would not go to support abortion, what would you say to that person?

Kerry: I would say to that person exactly what I will say to you right now.

First of all, I cannot tell you how deeply I respect the belief about life and when it begins. I'm a Catholic, raised a Catholic. I was an altar boy. Religion has been a huge part of my life. It helped lead me through a war, leads me today.

But I can't take what is an article of faith for me and legislate it for someone who doesn't share that article of faith, whether they be agnostic, atheist, Jew, Protestant, whatever. I can't do that.

But I can counsel people. I can talk reasonably about life and about responsibility. I can talk to people, as my wife Teresa does, about making other choices, and about abstinence, and about all these other things that we ought to do as a responsible society.

But as a president, I have to represent all the people in the nation. And I have to make that judgment.

Now, I believe that you can take that position and not be pro- abortion, but you have to afford people their constitutional rights. And that means being smart about allowing people to be fully educated, to know what their options are in life, and making certain that you don't deny a poor person the right to be able to have whatever the constitution affords them if they can't afford it otherwise.

That's why I think it's important. That's why I think it's important for the United States, for instance, not to have this rigid ideological restriction on helping families around the world to be able to make a smart decision about family planning.

You'll help prevent AIDS.

You'll help prevent unwanted children, unwanted pregnancies.

You'll actually do a better job, I think, of passing on the moral responsibility that is expressed in your question. And I truly respect it.

Gibson: Mr. President, minute and a half.

Bush: I'm trying to decipher that.

My answer is, we're not going to spend taxpayers' money on abortion.

This is an issue that divides America, but certainly reasonable people can agree on how to reduce abortions in America.

I signed the partial-birth—the ban on partial-birth abortion. It's a brutal practice. It's one way to help reduce abortions. My opponent voted against the ban.

I think there ought to be parental notification laws. He's against them.

I signed a bill called the Unborn Victims of Violence Act.

In other words, if you're a mom and you're pregnant and you get killed, the murderer gets tried for two cases, not just one. My opponent was against that.

These are reasonable ways to help promote a culture of life in America. I think it is a worthy goal in America to have every child protected by law and welcomed in life.

I also think we ought to continue to have good adoption law as an alternative to abortion.

And we need to promote maternity group homes, which my administration has done.

Culture of life is really important for a country to have if it's going to be a hospitable society.

Thank you.

Gibson: Senator, do you want to follow up? Thirty seconds.

Kerry: Well, again, the president just said, categorically, my opponent is against this, my opponent is against that. You know, it's just not that simple. No, I'm not.

I'm against the partial-birth abortion, but you've got to have an exception for the life of the mother and the health of the mother under the strictest test of bodily injury to the mother.

Secondly, with respect to parental notification, I'm not going to require a 16-or 17-year-old kid who's been raped by her father and who's pregnant to have to notify her father. So you got to have a judicial intervention. And because they didn't have a judicial intervention where she could go somewhere and get help, I voted against it. It's never quite as simple as the president wants you to believe.

Gibson: And 30 seconds, Mr. President.

Bush: Well, it's pretty simple when they say: Are you for a ban on partial birth abortion? Yes or no?

And he was given a chance to vote, and he voted no. And that's just the way it is. That's a vote. It came right up. It's clear for everybody to see. And as I said: You can run but you can't hide the reality. . . .

Linda Grabel: President Bush, during the last four years, you have made thousands of decisions that have affected millions of lives. Please give three instances in which you came to realize you had made a wrong decision, and what you did to correct it. Thank you.

Bush: I have made a lot of decisions, and some of them little, like appointments to boards you never heard of, and some of them big.

And in a war, there's a lot of—there's a lot of tactical decisions that historians will look back and say: He shouldn't have done that. He shouldn't have made that decision. And I'll take responsibility for them. I'm human.

But on the big questions, about whether or not we should have gone into Afghanistan, the big question about whether we should have removed somebody in Iraq, I'll stand by those decisions, because I think they're right.

That's really what you're—when they ask about the mistakes, that's what they're talking about. They're trying to say, "Did you make a mistake going into Iraq?" And the answer is, "Absolutely not." It was the right decision. . . .

On the tax cut, it's a big decision. I did the right decision. Our recession was one of the shallowest in modern history.

Now, you asked what mistakes. I made some mistakes in appointing people, but I'm not going to name them. I don't want to hurt their feelings on national TV. . . .

But history will look back, and I'm fully prepared to accept any mistakes that history judges to my administration, because the president makes the decisions, the president has to take the responsibility.

Gibson: Senator Kerry, a minute and a half.

Kerry: I believe the president made a huge mistake, a catastrophic mistake, not to live up to his own standard, which was: build a true global coalition, give the inspectors time to finish their job and go through the U.N. process to its end and go to war as a last resort.

I ask each of you just to look into your hearts, look into your guts. Gut-check time. Was this really going to war as a last resort?

The president rushed our nation to war without a plan to win the peace. And simple things weren't done. . . .

Gibson: Mr. President?

Bush: He complains about the fact our troops don't have adequate equipment, yet he voted against the $87 billion supplemental I sent to the Congress and then issued one of the most amazing quotes in political history: "I actually did vote for the $87 billion before I voted against it."...

Kerry: . . . Here's what I'll say about the $87 billion.

I made a mistake in the way I talk about it. He made a mistake in invading Iraq. Which is a worse decision? . . .

Source: Commission on Presidential Debates. "The Second Bush-Kerry Presidential Debate." Transcript. St. Louis, Missouri, October 8, 2004. www.debates.org/pages/trans2004c_p.html (accessed March 4, 2005). The transcripts are strictly unofficial and the Commission does not warrant their accuracy.

"The Third Bush-Kerry Presidential Debate"

Third Presidential Candidates' Debate, Arizona State University, Tempe, Arizona.

Speakers: George W. Bush, president of the United States; U.S. Senator John F. Kerry (Mass.), Democratic presidential nominee; Bob Schieffer, CBS anchor.

Schieffer: . . . Mr. President, what do you say to someone in this country who has lost his job to someone overseas who's being paid a fraction of what that job paid here in the United States?

Bush: I'd say, Bob, I've got policies to continue to grow our economy and create the jobs of the 21st century. And here's some help for you to go get an education. Here's some help for you to go to a community college.

We've expanded trade adjustment assistance. We want to help pay for you to gain the skills necessary to fill the jobs of the 21st century.

You know, there's a lot of talk about how to keep the economy growing. We talk about fiscal matters. But perhaps the best way to keep jobs here in America and to keep this economy growing is to make sure our education system works.

I went to Washington to solve problems. And I saw a problem in the public education system in America. They were just shuffling too many kids through the system, year after year, grade after grade, without learning the basics.

And so we said: Let's raise the standards. We're spending more money, but let's raise the standards and measure early and solve problems now, before it's too late.

No, education is how to help the person who's lost a job. Education is how to make sure we've got a workforce that's productive and competitive.

Got four more years, I've got more to do to continue to raise standards, to continue to reward teachers and school districts that are working, to emphasize math and science in the classrooms, to continue to expand Pell Grants to make sure that people have an opportunity to start their career with a college diploma.

And so the person you talked to, I say, here's some help, here's some trade adjustment assistance money for you to go a community college in your neighborhood, a community college which is providing the skills necessary to fill the jobs of the 21st century. And that's what I would say to that person.

Schieffer: Senator Kerry?

Kerry: I want you to notice how the president switched away from jobs and started talking about education principally.

Let me come back in one moment to that, but I want to speak for a second, if I can, to what the president said about fiscal responsibility.

Being lectured by the president on fiscal responsibility is a little bit like Tony Soprano talking to me about law and order in this country.

This president has taken a $5.6 trillion surplus and turned it into deficits as far as the eye can see. Health-care costs for the average American have gone up 64 percent; tuitions have gone up 35 percent; gasoline prices up 30 percent; Medicare premiums went up 17 percent a few days ago; prescription drugs are up 12 percent a year.

But guess what, America? The wages of Americans have gone down. The jobs that are being created in Arizona right now are paying about $13,700 less than the jobs that we're losing.

And the president just walks on by this problem. The fact is that he's cut job-training money. $1 billion was cut. They only added a little bit back this year because it's an election year.

They've cut the Pell Grants and the Perkins loans to help kids be able to go to college.

They've cut the training money. They've wound up not even extending unemployment benefits and not even extending health care to those people who are unemployed.

I'm going to do those things, because that's what's right in America: Help workers to transition in every respect. . . .

Schieffer: . . . Both of you are opposed to gay marriage. But to understand how you have come to that conclusion, I want to ask you a more basic question. Do you believe homosexuality is a choice?

Bush: You know, Bob, I don't know. I just don't know. I do know that we have a choice to make in America and that is to treat people with tolerance and respect and dignity. It's important that we do that.

And I also know in a free society people, consenting adults can live the way they want to live.

And that's to be honored.

But as we respect someone's rights, and as we profess tolerance, we shouldn't change—or have to change—our basic views on the sanctity of marriage. I believe in the sanctity of marriage. I think it's very important that we protect marriage as an institution, between a man and a woman.

I proposed a constitutional amendment. The reason I did so was because I was worried that activist judges are actually defining the definition of marriage, and the surest way to protect marriage between a man and woman is to amend the Constitution. . . .

Kerry: We're all God's children, Bob. And I think if you were to talk to Dick Cheney's daughter, who is a lesbian, she would tell you that she's being who she was, she's being who she was born as.

I think if you talk to anybody, it's not choice. I've met people who struggled with this for years, people who were in a marriage because they were living a sort of convention, and they struggled with it.

And I've met wives who are supportive of their husbands or vice versa when they finally sort of broke out and allowed themselves to live who they were, who they felt God had made them.

I think we have to respect that.

The president and I share the belief that marriage is between a man and a woman. I believe that. I believe marriage is between a man and a woman.

But I also believe that because we are the United States of America, we're a country with a great, unbelievable Constitution, with rights that we afford people, that you can't discriminate in the workplace. You can't discriminate in the rights that you afford people.

You can't disallow someone the right to visit their partner in a hospital. You have to allow people to transfer property, which is why I'm for partnership rights and so forth. . . .

Schieffer: . . . Health insurance costs have risen over 36 percent over the last four years according to The Washington Post. We're paying more. We're getting less.

I would like to ask you: Who bears responsibility for this? Is it the government? Is it the insurance companies? Is it the lawyers? Is it the doctors? Is it the administration?

Bush: Gosh, I sure hope it's not the administration.

There's a—no, look, there's a systemic problem. Health-care costs are on the rise because the consumers are not involved in the decision-making process. Most health-care costs are covered by third parties. And therefore, the actual user of health care is not the purchaser of health care. And there's no market forces involved with health care.

It's one of the reasons I'm a strong believer in what they call health savings accounts. These are accounts that allow somebody to buy a low-premium, high-deductible catastrophic plan and couple it with tax-free savings. Businesses can contribute, employees can contribute on a contractual basis. But this is a way to make sure people are actually involved with the decision-making process on health care.

Secondly, I do believe the lawsuits—I don't believe, I know—that the lawsuits are causing health-care costs to rise in America. That's why I'm such a strong believer in medical liability reform.

In the last debate, my opponent said those lawsuits only caused the cost to go up by 1 percent. Well, he didn't include the defensive practice of medicine that costs the federal government some $28 billion a year and costs our society between $60 billion and $100 billion a year.

Thirdly, one of the reasons why there's still high cost in medicine is because this is—they don't use any information technology. It's like if you looked at the—it's the equivalent of the buggy and horse days, compared to other industries here in America.

And so, we've got to introduce high technology into health care. We're beginning to do it. We're changing the language. We want there to be electronic medical records to cut down on error, as well as reduce cost.

People tell me that when the health-care field is fully integrated with information technology, it'll wring some 20 percent of the cost out of the system.

And finally, moving generic drugs to the market quicker.

And so, those are four ways to help control the costs in health care.

Schieffer: Senator Kerry?

Kerry: The reason health-care costs are getting higher, one of the principal reasons is that this administration has stood in the way of common-sense efforts that would have reduced the costs. Let me give you a prime example.

In the Senate we passed the right of Americans to import drugs from Canada. But the president and his friends took it out in the House, and now you don't have that right. The president blocked you from the right to have less expensive drugs from Canada.

We also wanted Medicare to be able to negotiate bulk purchasing. The VA does that. The VA provides lower-cost drugs to our veterans. We could have done that in Medicare.

Medicare is paid for by the American taxpayer. Medicare belongs to you. Medicare is for seniors, who many of them are on fixed income, to lift them out of poverty.

But rather than help you, the taxpayer, have lower cost, rather than help seniors have less expensive drugs, the president made it illegal—illegal—for Medicare to actually go out and bargain for lower prices.

Result: $139 billion windfall profit to the drug companies coming out of your pockets. That's a large part of your 17 percent increase in Medicare premiums.

When I'm president, I'm sending that back to Congress and we're going to get a real prescription drug benefit.

Now, we also have people sicker because they don't have health insurance. So whether it's diabetes or cancer, they come to hospitals later and it costs America more.

We got to have health care for all Americans. . . .

Schieffer: . . . Senator Kerry, . . . You have, as you have proposed and as the president has commented on tonight, proposed a massive plan to extend health-care coverage to children. You're also talking about the government picking up a big part of the catastrophic bills that people get at the hospital.

And you have said that you can pay for this by rolling back the president's tax cut on the upper 2 percent.

You heard the president say earlier tonight that it's going to cost a whole lot more money than that.

I'd just ask you, where are you going to get the money?

Kerry: Well, two leading national news networks have both said the president's characterization of my health-care plan is incorrect. One called it fiction. The other called it untrue.

The fact is that my health-care plan, America, is very simple. It gives you the choice. I don't force you to do anything. It's not a government plan. The government doesn't require you to do anything. You choose your doctor. You choose your plan.

If you don't want to take the offer of the plan that I want to put forward, you don't have do. You can keep what you have today, keep a high deductible, keep high premiums, keep a high co-pay, keep low benefits.

But I got a better plan. And I don't think a lot of people are going to want to keep what they have today.

Here's what I do: We take over Medicaid children from the states so that every child in America is covered. And in exchange, if the states want to—they're not forced to, they can choose to—they cover individuals up to 300 percent of poverty. It's their choice.

I think they'll choose it, because it's a net plus of $5 billion to them.

We allow you—if you choose to, you don't have to—but we give you broader competition to allow you to buy into the same health care plan that senators and congressmen give themselves. If it's good enough for us, it's good enough for every American. I believe that your health care is just as important as any politician in Washington, D.C.

You want to buy into it, you can. We give you broader competition. That helps lower prices.

In addition to that, we're going to allow people 55 to 64 to buy into Medicare early. And most importantly, we give small business a 50 percent tax credit so that after we lower the costs of health care, they also get, whether they're self-employed or a small business, a lower cost to be able to cover their employees.

Now, what happens is when you begin to get people covered like that—for instance in diabetes, if you diagnose diabetes early, you could save $50 billion in the health care system of America by avoiding surgery and dialysis. It works. And I'm going to offer it to America.

Schieffer: Mr. President?

Bush: In all due respect, I'm not so sure it's credible to quote leading news organizations about—oh, never mind. Anyway, let me quote the Lewin report. The Lewin report is a group of folks who are not politically affiliated. They analyzed the senator's plan. It cost $1.2 trillion.

The Lewin report accurately noted that there are going to be 20 million people, over 20 million people added to government-controlled health care. It would be the largest increase in government health care ever.

If you raise the Medicaid to 300 percent, it provides an incentive for small businesses not to provide private insurance to their employees. Why should they insure somebody when the government's going to insure it for them?

It's estimated that 8 million people will go from private insurance to government insurance.

We have a fundamental difference of opinion. I think government- run health will lead to poor-quality health, will lead to rationing, will lead to less choice.

Once a health-care program ends up in a line item in the federal government budget, it leads to more controls.

And just look at other countries that have tried to have federally controlled health care. They have poor-quality health care.

Our health-care system is the envy of the world because we believe in making sure that the decisions are made by doctors and patients, not by officials in the nation's capital. . . .

Schieffer: Mr. President, the next question is to you. We all know that Social Security is running out of money, and it has to be fixed. You have proposed to fix it by letting people put some of the money collected to pay benefits into private savings accounts. But the critics are saying that's going to mean finding $1 trillion over the next 10 years to continue paying benefits as those accounts are being set up.

So where do you get the money? Are you going to have to increase the deficit by that much over 10 years?

Bush: First, let me make sure that every senior listening today understands that when we're talking about reforming Social Security, that they'll still get their checks.

I remember the 2000 campaign, people said if George W. gets elected, your check will be taken away. Well, people got their checks, and they'll continue to get their checks.

There is a problem for our youngsters, a real problem. And if we don't act today, the problem will be valued in the trillions. And so I think we need to think differently. We'll honor our commitment to our seniors. But for our children and our grandchildren, we need to have a different strategy.

And recognizing that, I called together a group of our fellow citizens to study the issue. It was a committee chaired by the late Senator Daniel Patrick Moynihan of New York, a Democrat. And they came up with a variety of ideas for people to look at.

I believe that younger workers ought to be allowed to take some of their own money and put it in a personal savings account, because I understand that they need to get better rates of return than the rates of return being given in the current Social Security trust.

And the compounding rate of interest effect will make it more likely that the Social Security system is solvent for our children and our grandchildren. I will work with Republicans and Democrats. It'll be a vital issue in my second term. It is an issue that I am willing to take on, and so I'll bring Republicans and Democrats together.

And we're of course going to have to consider the costs. But I want to warn my fellow citizens: The cost of doing nothing, the cost of saying the current system is OK, far exceeds the costs of trying to make sure we save the system for our children.

Schieffer: Senator Kerry?

Kerry: You just heard the president say that young people ought to be able to take money out of Social Security and put it in their own accounts.

Now, my fellow Americans, that's an invitation to disaster.

The CBO said very clearly that if you were to adopt the president's plan, there would be a $2 trillion hole in Social Security, because today's workers pay in to the system for today's retirees. And the CBO said—that's the Congressional Budget Office; it's bipartisan—they said that there would have to be a cut in benefits of 25 percent to 40 percent.

Now, the president has never explained to America, ever, hasn't done it tonight, where does the transitional money, that $2 trillion, come from?

He's already got $3 trillion, according to The *Washington Post,* of expenses that he's put on the line from his convention and the promises of this campaign, none of which are paid for. Not one of them are paid for.

The fact is that the president is driving the largest deficits in American history. He's broken the pay-as-you-go rules.

I have a record of fighting for fiscal responsibility. In 1985, I was one of the first Democrats—broke with my party. We balanced the budget in the '90s. We paid down the debt for two years.

And that's what we're going to do. We're going to protect Social Security. I will not privatize it. I will not cut the benefits. And we're going to be fiscally responsible. And we will take care of Social Security. . . .

Schieffer: Mr. President, let's go to a new question. . . . I would like to ask you, what part does your faith play on your policy decisions?

Bush: First, my faith plays a lot—a big part in my life. And that's, when I was answering that question, what I was really saying to the person was that I pray a lot. And I do.

And my faith is a very—it's very personal. I pray for strength. I pray for wisdom. I pray for our troops in harm's way. I pray for my family. I pray for my little girls.

But I'm mindful in a free society that people can worship if they want to or not. You're equally an American if you choose to worship an almighty and if you choose not to.

If you're a Christian, Jew or Muslim, you're equally an American. That's the great thing about America, is the right to worship the way you see fit.

Prayer and religion sustain me. I receive calmness in the storms of the presidency.

I love the fact that people pray for me and my family all around the country. Somebody asked me one time, "Well, how do you know?" I said, "I just feel it."

Religion is an important part. I never want to impose my religion on anybody else.

But when I make decisions, I stand on principle, and the principles are derived from who I am.

I believe we ought to love our neighbor like we love ourself, as manifested in public policy through the faith-based initiative where we've unleashed the armies of compassion to help heal people who hurt.

I believe that God wants everybody to be free. That's what I believe.

And that's been part of my foreign policy. In Afghanistan, I believe that the freedom there is a gift from the Almighty. And I can't tell you how encouraged I am to see freedom on the march.

And so my principles that I make decisions on are a part of me, and religion is a part of me.

Schieffer: Senator Kerry?

Kerry: Well, I respect everything that the president has said and certainly respect his faith. I think it's important and I share it. I think that he just said that freedom is a gift from the Almighty.

Everything is a gift from the Almighty. And as I measure the words of the Bible—and we all do; different people measure different things—the Koran, the Torah, or, you know, Native Americans who gave me a blessing the other day had their own special sense of connectedness to a higher being. And people all find their ways to express it.

I was taught—I went to a church school and I was taught that the two greatest commandments are: Love the Lord, your God, with all your mind, your body and your soul, and love your neighbor as yourself. And frankly, I think we have a lot more loving of our neighbor to do in this country and on this planet.

We have a separate and unequal school system in the United States of America. There's one for the people who have, and there's one for the people who don't have. And we're struggling with that today.

And the president and I have a difference of opinion about how we live out our sense of our faith.

I talked about it earlier when I talked about the works and faith without works being dead.

I think we've got a lot more work to do. And as president, I will always respect everybody's right to practice religion as they choose—or not to practice—because that's part of America. . . .

Source: Commission on Presidential Debates. "The Third Bush-Kerry Presidential Debate." Transcript. Tempe, Arizona, October 13, 2004. www.debates.org/pages/trans2004d_p.html (accessed March 4, 2005).

October

2004 HISTORIC DOCUMENTS

U.S. Inspector on Iraq's "Missing" Weapons of Mass Destruction

October 6, 2004

INTRODUCTION

Any lingering doubt about Iraq's alleged arsenal of weapons of mass destruction (WMD) prior to the U.S.-led invasion in 2003 was cleared away by a final report submitted to the director of central intelligence on September 30, 2004, and made public October 6, 2004. The 1,000-page report by a team of weapons experts concluded that Iraq had destroyed its biological and chemical weapons after the 1991 Persian Gulf War and had never seriously tried to restart its program to develop nuclear weapons, which also had been destroyed during and after that war.

This report, which confirmed and expanded upon preliminary findings issued a year earlier, thus undercut the principal rationale that President George W. Bush had given for the invasion to oust the regime of Iraqi leader Saddam Hussein: that Iraq possessed a vast and growing arsenal of WMDs that might either be used against the United States and its allies or turned over to Islamist terrorists. "We were almost all wrong" about Iraq's weapons, the report's author, Charles A. Duelfer, told a Senate committee October 6.

Three months earlier, on July 9, the Senate Intelligence Committee released a blistering report saying that the Central Intelligence Agency and other intelligence organizations had produced deeply flawed reports incorrectly alleging that Iraq had weapons that it did not have. Anticipating the findings, CIA director George Tenet resigned his post on June 3 after serving seven years—one of the longest tenures in the five-decade history of the agency.

Despite these revelations, Bush said the war in Iraq was justified because Iraq wanted to develop weapons of mass destruction. In his January 20, 2004, State of the Union speech, Bush had said that postwar inspections had found "weapons of mass destruction-related program activities" in Iraq—a formulation officials said was intended to convey the idea that Saddam tried to develop weapons, even if he had not succeeded. In his political campaigning later in the year Bush referred frequently to Iraq's "capability of producing weapons of mass murder." Bush also said the ousting of Saddam and the movement toward democracy in Iraq were sufficient justifications for the war. *(State of the Union speech, p. 17)*

The year's revelations apparently were richly ironic for Hans Blix, the Swedish diplomat who had headed the United Nations weapons inspection mission in Iraq just before the 2003 war. Blix had asked for more time to complete his work but had been scorned by Bush administration officials, who said he was not trying hard enough to find Iraq's weapons. Referring to U.S. and British leaders, Blix told the BBC on February 8, 2004, that "the intention was to dramatize it [the intelligence information] just as the vendors of some merchandize are trying to increase and exaggerate the importance of what they have. From politicians, our leaders in the Western world, I think we expect more than that, a bit more sincerity." In a subsequent interview with the Associated Press, Blix said "many of these politicians have put exclamation marks where we put question marks." *(Background, Historic Documents of 2003, p. 874)*

U.S. Hunt for Iraqi Arms

The U.S. search for Iraq's weapons began immediately after Saddam was ousted from power in April 2003. A team of more than four hundred weapons experts, known as the Iraq Survey Group and led by David S. Kay, a former government official, inspected nearly 1,700 of military bases, industrial plants, and munitions dumps where elements of Saddam's weapons supposedly were assembled or stored. These sites had been identified by UN weapons inspectors during their past work in Iraq or by U.S., British, and Israeli intelligence agencies.

Within weeks it became clear that the search was not turning up the vast weapons caches that had been expected, and the Bush administration began playing down expectations and, at the same time, withdrawing its inspectors or assigning them to other tasks. In October 2003 Kay gave Bush and Congress a preliminary report essentially concluding that Iraq's weapons not only were missing but probably never existed. Kay resigned his post in January 2004 and was succeeded by Duelfer, who had been the number two official in the UN weapons inspection program in Iraq during the 1990s. Before leaving office, Kay reiterated that he had concluded that Iraq did not possess the weapons the United States thought it did. "I don't think there was a large-scale production program in the '90s," he told Reuters news service on January 23. Kay repeated his assessment in other interviews and in testimony on Capitol Hill, becoming the center of a brief controversy because his conclusions were so at odds with what remained the administration's position—that Iraq's weapons eventually would be found.

In the midst of that controversy, CIA director Tenet on February 5 delivered a speech at Georgetown University, acknowledging for the first time that his agency might have overestimated Iraq's weapons but defending the integrity of his analysts' work. "When the facts on Iraq are all in, we will be neither completely right nor completely wrong," he said. U.S. intelligence had been "generally on target" in its estimates of Iraq's missile and unmanned aerial vehicle programs, but "may have overestimated the progress" of Iraq in developing nuclear weapons. Tenet denied that the CIA had been under political pressure, noting that "no one told us what to say or how to say it."

Attempting to calm controversy in an election year, Bush on February 6 named a commission to investigate U.S. intelligence gathering in Iraq. He named as cochairmen former senator Charles Robb, a Virginia Democrat, and Lawrence H. Silberman, a judge of the U.S. Circuit Court of Appeals for the District of Columbia. Bush asked the panel to submit its findings by the end of March 2005. The panel conducted its work in secrecy.

Senate Report

The Senate Intelligence Committee report, made public July 9, faulted nearly every aspect of the CIA's handling of prewar intelligence about Iraq's weapons. The report said the agency relied on unsubstantiated reports from untrustworthy sources, compiled assessments that went beyond the available hard evidence, kept important information out of the hands of those who needed it (including its own analysts), and was afflicted by "group think," an unwillingness to examine the accuracy of conventional wisdom. "Most, if not all, of these problems stem from a broken corporate culture and poor management," committee chairman Pat Roberts, R-Kan., said.

The committee was particularly critical of a classified October 2002 document known as a "National Intelligence Estimate," which made the allegations about Iraq's weapons that Bush and other officials cited to justify the war. Most of the key conclusions in that document were "either overstated or were not supported by the underlying intelligence reporting," the committee said. Key conclusions of that estimate were summarized in a White Paper the administration used to build public support for the war.

The committee acknowledged that it did not have access to what might have been one of the most important intelligence documents on the subject: a one-page summary of the National Intelligence Estimate given to Bush, who, according to aides, generally did not read lengthy reports, even on matters of such import as Iraq's weapons. The White House refused to give the summary to the Senate.

Senator Roberts, who had strongly supported the Iraq War, said upon release of the report that Congress might not have gone along with Bush's call for a resolution authorizing the Iraq War if the truth about Iraq's weapons had been known at the time. "In the end, what the president and the Congress used to send the country to war was information that was provided by the intelligence community, and that information was flawed," he said.

The report challenged the administration's other key prewar assertion: that Iraq had close ties with the al Qaeda terrorist network, which was blamed for the September 11, 2001, terrorist attacks against the United States. Bush had repeatedly linked Iraq and al Qaeda and implied that Saddam might turn his biological or chemical weapons over to terrorists, who would use them to attack the United States. Bush's statements contributed to a widely held view among the American public—according to numerous opinion polls—that Iraq had something to do with the September 11 attacks. The panel said the CIA had reached "reasonable and objective" conclusions that Iraq was not linked to al Qaeda, but the administration repeatedly tried to establish such a link. *(al Qaeda, p. 534)*

The committee's Republican majority rejected assertions by many Democrats that Bush administration officials—notably Vice President Dick Cheney, who repeatedly visited CIA headquarters in 2002—had put undue political pressure on the agency to reach its conclusions about Iraq. The committee said it found no evidence that officials "attempted to coerce, influence, or pressure analysts to change their judgment" to conform to administration policy. Instead, the report suggested that administration officials read into intelligence documents what they wanted to see. Despite this finding, Sen. John D. Rockefeller IV of West Virginia, the committee's senior Democrat, said intelligence officials had worked in an "environment of intense pressure," generated by senior administration officials.

The Republican assessment reportedly reflected an internal CIA investigation, concluded in January, which determined that agency analysts had not tailored their assessments to comply with administration pressure. Richard J. Kerr, a former CIA deputy director, said that his probe had uncovered no evidence that the administration forced the agency to make determinations for political reasons. "There was pressure and a lot of debate, and people should have a lot of debate, that's quite legitimate," the *Washington Post* quoted Kerr as saying on January 31. But the agency's assessments "were very consistent" over a period of "several years," he said. The text of Kerr's report was not made public.

Duelfer Report

When published on October 6, the Duelfer report essentially refuted President Bush's principal justification for the war: that Iraq's weapons posed a direct threat to the United States and its allies. Contrary to the assertions made before the war by Bush, Cheney, Secretary of State Colin Powell, and other administration officials, the report said Iraq did not have any stocks of biological or chemical weapons and was not working to restart its nuclear weapons program, which had ended following the 1991 Persian Gulf War. Iraq could have rebuilt at least parts of its biological and chemical weapons programs, the report said, but it was not doing so and such an effort would have taken at least one year. It would have taken several years, and possibly a decade or more, for Iraq to develop a working nuclear weapon, the report said.

Duelfer suggested that Saddam's chief priority throughout the 1990s was to win the lifting of United Nations sanctions, which had crippled Iraq's economy and made it difficult for him to rebuild his weapons programs. "Saddam wanted to recreate Iraq's WMD capability—which was essentially destroyed in 1991—after sanctions were removed and Iraq's economy stabilized, but probably with a different mix of capabilities to that which previously existed," the report said.

Duelfer also cited interviews with Saddam—who had been captured the previous December—and many of his top aides in concluding that Saddam continued to view Iran as Iraq's main threat and the main reason for any future program to rebuild weapons. Iran and Iraq fought an enormously bloody but inconclusive war between 1980 and 1988 and each side still viewed the other as a real threat.

Coming less than a month before elections, Duelfer's report prompted a predictable partisan debate on Capitol Hill. One venue for that debate was the October 6 hearing of the Senate Armed Services Committee, where Duelfer presented his report. Sen. Edward M. Kennedy, D-Mass., said the report had "basically nailed the door shut on any justification for the [Iraq] war." Republicans, however, chose to emphasize Duelfer's assessments that the Iraqi leader had a "strategic intent" to build prohibited weapons and that he would once again attempt to do so once UN sanctions were removed. "We had a situation which was rapidly deteriorating and eventually, over time, Saddam Hussein would have been relieved of or evaded those sanctions," Sen. John McCain, R-Ariz., said.

Bush said the report did not change his view that he was justified in taking the United States into war with Iraq. "Based on all the information we have to date, I believe we were right to take action, and America is safer today with Saddam Hussein in prison," Bush said. "He retained the knowledge, the materials, the means and the intent to produce weapons of mass destruction, and he could have passed that knowledge on to our terrorist enemies." John Kerry, Bush's Democratic opponent in the 2004 presidential race, said that statement showed that Bush was "still not being straight with the American people."

Nuclear Weapons

Ultimately, the Bush administration's most compelling justification for the war in Iraq had been the contention that Iraq was actively trying to rebuild a nuclear weapons program that had been destroyed, or at least severely damaged, during the 1991 Persian Gulf War. Vice President Cheney said in August 2002 that "Saddam has resumed his efforts to acquire nuclear weapons" and likely would acquire them "fairly soon." A month later he said the government had "irrefutable evidence" that

Iraq was attempting to build nuclear weapons. Bush, National Security Adviser Condoleeza Rice, and other officials made less emphatic statements but repeatedly suggested that Iraq was working on nuclear weapons and might give them to terrorists. "Facing evidence of peril, we cannot wait for the final proof, the smoking gun, that could come in the form of a mushroom cloud," Bush said in a widely publicized speech in Cincinnati in October 2002, just before the Senate voted on a resolution authorizing the war.

The administration's case was built almost entirely on a report from 2001 that Iraq had tried to purchase about 60,000 high-strength, finely calibrated aluminum tubes. CIA analysts said these tubes were intended for use in centrifuges that would convert uranium hexafluoride gas into highly enriched uranium, one of the fuels required in nuclear weapons. Energy Department experts and officials at the International Atomic Energy Agency (IAEA) reportedly doubted this and cited evidence that the tubes were for use in Iraq's short-range rockets.

The Senate Intelligence Committee devoted fifty pages of its report to discrediting the CIA's statements on the aluminum tubes, saying the agency had "lost objectivity" on the issue and prevented competing views from reaching the White House. Duelfer said his investigators had found "no indication" that the tubes were intended for centrifuges.

Duelfer said Iraq's work on nuclear weapons had been extensive before the 1991 Persian Gulf War, but the results of that work had been destroyed, either during the war or by UN inspectors afterwards. Duelfer said his inspectors had found no evidence suggesting "concerted efforts to restart the program," including research and development.

Duelfer also discounted a British report that Iraq had attempted to buy unprocessed uranium from Niger. The White House had included that report in Bush's January 2003 State of the Union address, setting off an international furor. One consequence was the illegal leaking, reportedly by senior administration officials, of the name of an undercover CIA agent. A special Justice Department investigation into that action was still under way at year's end.

Biological Weapons

In the early 1990s UN inspectors had uncovered evidence that Iraq had developed large quantities of biological weapons. After the inspectors left Iraq in 1998 they reported that Iraqi officials had failed to account for those weapons, leading to a conclusion that the weapons might still be intact. Citing the UN reports, plus allegedly new intelligence information, the Bush administration said in 2002 and 2003 that Iraq still had a large arsenal of biological weapons. In his January 2003 State of the Union address Bush said Iraq had enough anthrax to "kill several million people" and enough botulinum toxin to "subject millions of people to death by respiratory failure."

In the weeks after the start of the war, the administration trumpeted the discovery in Iraq of two truck trailers, which it said were mobile laboratories intended to produce biological weapons out of the view of weapons inspectors. Bush himself said in April 2003 that this discovery showed that "we found the weapons of mass destruction." Other officials later backtracked on that claim. The Duelfer report said the trailers could not have been used to produce biological weapons and instead were "almost certainly" intended to generate hydrogen for observation balloons.

More broadly, Duelfer said Iraq had secretly destroyed is biological weapons in the early 1990s and by 1995 had given up any attempt to create new ones. Duelfer also rejected suggestions, offered since the start of the war by some administration officials, that Iraq had hidden some of the weapons or even smuggled them abroad.

Chemical Weapons

Iraq had repeatedly used chemical weapons during the 1980s, both in Baghdad's campaign to suppress the Kurds of northern Iraq and to combat Iranian troop movements in southern Iraq during the 1980–1988 Iran-Iraq War. The use of these weapons had been well documented by independent observers, and so most experts believed right up until 2003 that Iraq retained both the capability to produce chemical weapons and probably had large quantities of them. The Bush administration left no doubt that it shared this view; Cheney in 2002 estimated that Iraq possessed at least 100 metric tons of chemical weapons "and possibly as much as 500 metric tons of CW [chemical weapons] agents, much of it added in the last year."

Duelfer said his inspectors had found old, unused munitions that once contained chemical weapons—but no actual chemical weapons agents or any evidence of a program to produce them. Iraq had destroyed its weapons in 1991, he said, and "there are no credible indications that Baghdad resumed production of chemical munitions thereafter." Moreover, he said, U.S. intelligence reports that supposedly proved the existence of Iraq's chemical weapons were wrong. Iraq did have the infrastructure necessary to make several types of chemical weapons, Duelfer said, and it was likely that it would have done so once the UN sanctions were lifted.

Delivery Systems

Iraq during the 1980s bought more than 800 short-range "Scud" missiles from the Soviet Union. Some of these missiles were fired at Israel and the U.S.-led invading forces during the Persian Gulf War, but the bulk of the Scuds were destroyed by bombing raids during that war. After the war UN sanctions barred Iraq from having any missiles with a range greater than ninety miles. The Iraqi government at first decided to keep some of the remaining missiles hidden from UN inspectors for future use in reconstituting a missile program, the report said. By late 1991, however, Iraq apparently had destroyed its remaining Scud missiles while continuing research on missiles that complied with the UN limits; this enabled Iraq to keep its engineers and scientists at work, ready for the day when the UN sanctions would be lifted.

When UN inspectors returned to Iraq in late 2002, they discovered that the military had developed a new missile, called the al Samound 2, which had a range slightly exceeding the ninety-mile limit; most versions of that missile were destroyed, under UN supervision, just before the March 2003 war.

Duelfer said his team uncovered Iraqi plans for much longer-range missiles, including a cruise missile with a range of more than 900 miles. None of those missiles had gone into production before Saddam's government was toppled, however. The Duelfer report also discounted claims by Bush and other officials that Iraq's small fleet of pilotless planes known as unmanned aerial vehicles posed a direct threat to the United States because they could be used to deliver biological or chemical weapons.

UN Oil for Food Program

The report detailed Iraq's extensive efforts to subvert UN economic sanctions throughout the 1990s, most importantly through under-the-table oil sales to other countries that generated more than $7.5 billion in revenue. Starting in 1996, the report alleged, Saddam sought to subvert the UN's Oil for Food program, which allowed Iraq to sell oil on the open market so long as the proceeds were used only to buy food and medicine for the country's civilian population. Companies in Jordan, Lebanon, Syria, Turkey, and the United Arab Emirates engaged in "deceptive trade practices" to sell weapons-related equipment and machinery to Iraq, the report said. Government agencies in Syria and Yemen were involved in these illegal sales, it added. These details in Duelfer's report also appeared to confirm long-standing rumors of corruption with the Oil for Food program, which was administered by a special UN agency. Several investigations were under way at year's end. *(UN reform issues, p. 887)*

Al Qaqaa Munitions Dump

Despite repeated efforts by Kerry, the Democratic presidential candidate, to portray Bush as having misled Americans about the need for the Iraq War, the Bush administration's misjudgments on Iraq's weapons never became a major factor in the 2004 campaign. However, a related issue emerged in the last week of the campaign that raised new questions about current U.S. military operations in Iraq.

On October 25 the *New York Times* and CBS News reported that more than 370 tons of high explosives "were stolen or looted from a government facility" in Iraq. The reports were confirmed by the IAEA, which had conducted inspections for Iraq's nuclear weapons before the war. The IAEA said it had verified the presence of the weapons the previous January but had learned from Iraqi authorities on October 10 that the munitions had disappeared. The weapons had been stored at a munitions dump in western Iraq known as al Qaqaa, an area supposedly under the control of the U.S. military since March 2003. Experts said the explosives were highly potent, and some could be used to trigger a nuclear weapon. The revelation revived concerns, expressed for more than a year by many weapons experts, that large quantities of Iraq's conventional weapons had disappeared in the chaos following the overthrow of Saddam's regime.

Kerry immediately seized on the reports of missing weapons as demonstrating Bush's "incredible incompetence" in Iraq; Bush responded by castigating Kerry for besmirching the U.S. troops who were responsible for security in Iraq. The Pentagon reported on October 29 that U.S. Army soldiers had removed about 250 tons of material from the al Qaqaa dump, but the major who commanded the operation said he did not know if that material was the same as the "missing" munitions. Television footage taken at the dump in mid-April 2003 by a Minnesota television crew appeared to show that at least some of the material was still protected by IAEA seals. The *Los Angeles Times* reported on November 2 that U.S. soldiers had later seen widespread looting at the site.

Powell's UN Presentation

Among those embarrassed by the absence of Iraq's weapons was Secretary of State Powell, who on February 5, 2003, had made the Bush administration's most dramatic case on the issue to the UN Security Council. In a day-long session broadcast live around the world, Powell had cited intelligence information, including statements by Iraqi defectors, to argue that Iraq had developed WMDs and had gone to extraordinary lengths to hide them from UN inspectors. A former general known for his independence, Powell at the time was perhaps the senior U.S. official with the greatest credibility worldwide, including in countries that were opposing Bush's plan to go to war in Iraq.

In an interview with the *Washington Post,* published on February 3, 2004, Powell said he had based his UN presentation on intelligence information available at the time, had pressed Tenet and other officials to defend that information, and had excluded some claims that he did not feel comfortable in citing as his own. The *Post* said Powell was asked if he would have recommended an invasion of Iraq if he had known at the time that Iraq did not have the weapons. "I don't know, because it was the stockpile that presented the final little piece that made it [Iraq] a more real and present danger and threat to the region and the world," Powell said, adding that the "absence of a stockpile changes the political calculus; it changes the answer you get." Even so, the *Post* quoted Powell as saying that history would judge the war as "the right thing to do."

Powell announced his resignation two weeks after Bush won the November 2 election. His resignation, which had been expected, led to another round of assessments—few of them positive—of the most highly publicized day of his four-year tenure.

Reports on British Intelligence Failures

Britain, the chief U.S. ally in the Iraq War, also relied on faulty intelligence when it made similar claims about Baghdad's weapons programs, according to the results of two major investigations in that country. British prime minister Tony Blair had mirrored the Bush administration's statements on Iraq's weapons in 2002–2003, and in 2004 those statements came under similar questioning. In Blair's case, most of the criticism centered on a widely quoted claim, in an intelligence dossier made public in late 2002, that Iraq posed a direct danger to Britain because it could mobilize its chemical weapons within forty-five minutes.

BBC radio on May 29, 2003, quoted a government weapons expert as saying Blair's office had "sexed up" the report with that information, which in fact referred to short-range battlefield weapons, not long-range weapons capable of reaching Britain. Weeks later, after the BBC had identified him, the expert, David Kelly, was found dead, apparently having committed suicide. After a resulting uproar, Blair agreed to an investigation, which was carried out by Lord Hutton, a senior appellate court judge.

Reporting January 28, 2004, on his investigation, Hutton cleared Blair and his government of any role in Kelly's suicide, saying no one else could have realized that Kelly was contemplating suicide. Instead, Hutton faulted the BBC for its report that the government had sexed up the Iraq information; the "allegation was unfounded," he said. That finding led to a major shakeup at the BBC, but it did nothing to silence critics who said Blair's government had exaggerated Iraq's weapons programs. When opposition politicians and the news media said the Hutton report left too many questions unanswered, Blair agreed to another inquiry headed by Lord Butler, who had been the private secretary to British prime ministers in the 1960s and 1970s.

Butler issued his report on July 14. Basing his conclusions, at least in part, on Kay's preliminary findings, Butler said Iraq had no stocks of biological or chemical weapons, nor was there any evidence linking Iraq to al Qaeda. Butler said the

September 2002 dossier on Iraq was at the "outer limits but not beyond" available intelligence information about Iraq's weapons and failed to mention the doubts of British weapons experts about some of the claims that it made. Even so, Butler said Blair and other British leaders had not deliberately distorted intelligence findings to justify the war. Blair immediately went before Parliament to say the report supported his contention that "no one lied, no one made up intelligence."

Following are excerpts from the executive summary of the "Comprehensive Report of the Special Advisor to the DCI [Director of Central Intelligence] on Iraq's WMD [weapons of mass destruction]," submitted to the Central Intelligence Agency on September 30, 2004, by Charles A. Duelfer and made public October 6, 2004. The report said Iraq had destroyed its biological and chemical weapons in the early 1990s and had not resumed a previous attempt to develop nuclear weapons.

"Report of the Special Advisor to the DCI on Iraq's WMD"

Regime Strategic Intent

Key Findings

Saddam Hussein so dominated the Iraqi Regime that its strategic intent was his alone. He wanted to end sanctions while preserving the capability to reconstitute his weapons of mass destruction (WMD) when sanctions were lifted.

- *Saddam totally dominated the Regime's strategic decision making.* He initiated most of the strategic thinking upon which decisions were made, whether in matters of war and peace (such as invading Kuwait), maintaining WMD as a national strategic goal, or on how Iraq was to position itself in the international community. Loyal dissent was discouraged and constructive variations to the implementation of his wishes on strategic issues were rare. Saddam was the Regime in a strategic sense and his intent became Iraq's strategic policy.
- *Saddam's primary goal from 1991 to 2003 was to have UN sanctions lifted, while maintaining the security of the Regime.* He sought to balance the need to cooperate with UN inspections—to gain support for lifting sanctions—with his intention to preserve Iraq's intellectual capital for WMD with a minimum of foreign intrusiveness and loss of face. Indeed, this remained the goal to the end of the Regime, as the starting of any WMD program, conspicuous or otherwise, risked undoing the progress achieved in eroding sanctions and jeopardizing a political end to the embargo and international monitoring.
- *The introduction of the Oil-For-Food program (OFF) in late 1996 was a key turning point for the Regime.* OFF rescued Baghdad's economy from a terminal decline created by sanctions. The Regime quickly came to see that OFF could be corrupted

to acquire foreign exchange both to further undermine sanctions and to provide the means to enhance dual-use infrastructure and potential WMD-related development.

- *By 2000–2001, Saddam had managed to mitigate many of the effects of sanctions and undermine their international support.* Iraq was within striking distance of a *de facto* end to the sanctions regime, both in terms of oil exports and the trade embargo, by the end of 1999.

Saddam wanted to recreate Iraq's WMD capability—which was essentially destroyed in 1991—after sanctions were removed and Iraq's economy stabilized, but probably with a different mix of capabilities to that which previously existed. Saddam aspired to develop a nuclear capability—in an incremental fashion, irrespective of international pressure and the resulting economic risks—but he intended to focus on ballistic missile and tactical chemical warfare (CW) capabilities.

- *Iran was the pre-eminent motivator of this policy.* All senior level Iraqi officials considered Iran to be Iraq's principal enemy in the region. The wish to balance Israel and acquire status and influence in the Arab world were also considerations, but secondary.
- *Iraq Survey Group (ISG) judges that events in the 1980s and early 1990s shaped Saddam's belief in the value of WMD.* In Saddam's view, WMD helped to save the Regime multiple times. He believed that during the Iran-Iraq war chemical weapons had halted Iranian ground offensives and that ballistic missile attacks on Tehran had broken its political will. Similarly, during Desert Storm, Saddam believed WMD had deterred Coalition Forces from pressing their attack beyond the goal of freeing Kuwait. WMD had even played a role in crushing the Shi'a revolt in the south following the 1991 cease-fire.
- *The former Regime had no formal written strategy or plan for the revival of WMD after sanctions.* Neither was there an identifiable group of WMD policy makers or planners separate from Saddam. Instead, his lieutenants understood WMD revival was his goal from their long association with Saddam and his infrequent, but firm, verbal comments and directions to them.

[The Executive Summary at this point included an explanation that many of the findings were based, in part, on the statements of former Iraqi officials (including Saddam) who had been captured following the 2003 war and had been interviewed by U.S. intelligence agents.]

Regime Finance and Procurement

Key Findings

Throughout the 1990s and up to OIF [Operation Iraqi Freedom, the war in Iraq] (March 2003), Saddam focused on one set of objectives: the survival of himself, his Regime, and his legacy. To secure those objectives, Saddam needed to exploit Iraqi oil assets, to portray a strong military capability to deter internal and external threats, and to foster his image as an Arab leader. Saddam recognized that the reconstitution of Iraqi WMD enhanced both his security and image. Consequently, Saddam needed to end UN-imposed sanctions to fulfill his goals.

Saddam severely underestimated the economic and military costs of invading Iran in 1980 and Kuwait in 1990, as well as underestimating the subsequent international condemnation of his invasion of Kuwait. He did not anticipate this condemnation, nor the subsequent imposition, comprehensiveness, severity, and longevity of UN sanctions. His initial belief that UN sanctions would not last, resulting in his country's economic decline, changed by 1998 when the UNSC did not lift sanctions after he believed resolutions were fulfilled. Although Saddam had reluctantly accepted the UN's Oil for Food (OFF) program by 1996, he soon recognized its economic value and additional opportunities for further manipulation and influence of the UNSC Iraq 661 Sanctions Committee member states. Therefore, he resigned himself to the continuation of UN sanctions understanding that they would become a "paper tiger" regardless of continued US resolve to maintain them.

Throughout sanctions, Saddam continually directed his advisors to formulate and implement strategies, policies, and methods to terminate the UN's sanctions regime established by UNSCR 661. The Regime devised an effective diplomatic and economic strategy of generating revenue and procuring illicit goods utilizing the Iraqi intelligence, banking, industrial, and military apparatus that eroded United Nations' member states and other international players' resolve to enforce compliance, while capitalizing politically on its humanitarian crisis.

- From Saddam's perspective, UN sanctions hindered his ability to rule Iraq with complete authority and autonomy. In the long run, UN sanctions also interfered with his efforts to establish a historic legacy. *According to Saddam and his senior advisors, the UN, at the behest of the US, placed an economic strangle hold on Iraq.* The UN controlled Saddam's main source of revenue (oil exports) and determined what Iraq could import.
- UN sanctions curbed Saddam's ability to import weapons, technology, and expertise into Iraq. Sanctions also limited his ability to finance his military, intelligence, and security forces to deal with his perceived and real external threats.
- In short, Saddam considered UN sanctions as a form of economic war and the UN's OFF program and Northern and Southern Watch Operations as campaigns of that larger economic war orchestrated by the US and UK. His evolving strategy centered on breaking free of UN sanctions in order to liberate his economy from the economic strangle-hold so he could continue to pursue his political and personal objectives.

One aspect of Saddam's strategy of unhinging the UN's sanctions against Iraq, centered on Saddam's efforts to influence certain UN SC permanent members, such as Russia, France, and China and some nonpermanent (Syria, Ukraine) members to end UN sanctions. *Under Saddam's orders, the Ministry of Foreign Affairs (MFA) formulated and implemented a strategy aimed at these UNSC members and international public opinion with the purpose of ending UN sanctions and undermining its subsequent OFF program by diplomatic and economic means.* At a minimum, Saddam wanted to divide the five permanent members and foment international public support of Iraq at the UN and throughout the world by a savvy public relations campaign and an extensive diplomatic effort.

Another element of this strategy involved circumventing UN sanctions and the OFF program by means of "Protocols" or government-to-government economic trade agreements. Protocols allowed Saddam to generate a large amount of revenue outside the purview of the UN. The successful implementation of the Protocols, continued oil smuggling efforts, and the manipulation of UN OFF contracts emboldened Saddam to pursue his military reconstitution efforts starting in 1997 and peaking in 2001. These efforts covered conventional arms, dual-use goods acquisition, and some WMD-related programs.

- Once money began to flow into Iraq, the Regime's authorities, aided by foreign companies and some foreign governments, devised and implemented methods and techniques to procure illicit goods from foreign suppliers.
- To implement its procurement efforts, Iraq under Saddam, created a network of Iraqi front companies, some with close relationships to high-ranking foreign government officials. These foreign government officials, in turn, worked through their respective ministries, state-run companies and ministry-sponsored front companies, to procure illicit goods, services, and technologies for Iraq's WMD-related, conventional arms, and/or dual-use goods programs.
- *The Regime financed these government-sanctioned programs by several illicit revenue streams that amassed more that $11 billion from the early 1990s to OIF outside the UN-approved methods.* The most profitable stream concerned Protocols or government-to-government agreements that generated over $7.5 billion for Saddam. Iraq earned an additional $2 billion from kickbacks or surcharges associated with the UN's OFF program; $990 million from oil "cash sales" or smuggling; and another $230 million from other surcharge impositions.

Analysis of Iraqi Financial Data

The Iraqi revenue analysis presented in this report is based on government documents and financial databases, spreadsheets, and other records obtained from SOMO, the Iraqi Ministry of Oil, and the Central Bank of Iraq (CBI), and other Ministries. These sources appear to be of good quality and consistent with other pre- and post-Operation Iraqi Freedom information. All Iraqi revenue data and derived figures in this report have been calculated in current dollars.

Saddam directed the Regime's key ministries and governmental agencies to devise and implement strategies, policies, and techniques to discredit the UN sanctions, harass UN personnel in Iraq, and discredit the US. At the same time, according to reporting, he also wanted to obfuscate Iraq's refusal to reveal the nature of its WMD and WMD-related programs, their capabilities, and his intentions.

- *Saddam used the IIS to undertake the most sensitive procurement missions. Consequently, the IIS facilitated the import of UN sanctioned and dual-use goods into Iraq through countries like Syria, Jordan, Belarus and Turkey.*
- The IIS had representatives in most of Iraq's embassies in these foreign countries using a variety of official covers. One type of cover was the "commercial attaches" that were sent to make contacts with foreign businesses. The attaches set up front companies, facilitated the banking process and transfers of funds as determined, and approved by the senior officials within the Government.
- The MFA played a critical role in facilitating Iraq's procurement of military goods, dual-use goods pertaining to WMD, transporting cash and other valuable

goods earned by illicit oil revenue, and forming and implementing a diplomatic strategy to end UN sanctions and the subsequent UN OFF program by nefarious means.

- Saddam used the Ministry of Higher Education and Scientific Research (MHESR) through its universities and research programs to maintain, develop, and acquire expertise, to advance or preserve existent research projects and developments, and to procure goods prohibited by UN SC sanctions.
- The Ministry of Oil (MoO) controlled the oil voucher distribution program that used oil to influence UN members to support Iraq's goals. *Saddam personally approved and removed all names of voucher recipients. He made all modifications to the list, adding or deleting names at will.* Other senior Iraqi leaders could nominate or recommend an individual or organization to be added or subtracted from the voucher list, and ad hoc allocation committees met to review and update the allocations.

Iraq under Saddam successfully devised various methods to acquire and import items prohibited under UN sanctions. *Numerous Iraqi and foreign trade intermediaries disguised illicit items, hid the identity of the end user, and/or changed the final destination of the commodity to get it to the region.* For a cut of the profits, these trade intermediaries moved, and in many cases smuggled, the prohibited items through land, sea, and air entry points along the Iraqi border.

By mid-2000 the exponential growth of Iraq's illicit revenue, increased international sympathy for Iraq's humanitarian plight, and increased complicity by Iraqi's neighbors led elements within Saddam's Regime to boast that the UN sanctions were slowly eroding. In July 2000, the ruling Iraqi Ba'athist paper, Al-Thawrah, claimed victory over UN sanctions, stating that Iraq was accelerating its pace to develop its national economy despite the UN "blockade." In August 2001, Iraqi Foreign Minister Sabri stated in an Al-Jazirah TV interview that UN sanctions efforts had collapsed at the same time Baghdad had been making steady progress on its economic, military, Arab relations, and international affairs.

- Companies in Syria, Jordan, Lebanon, Turkey, UAE, and Yemen assisted Saddam with the acquisition of prohibited items through deceptive trade practices. In the case of Syria and Yemen, this included support from agencies or personnel within the government itself.
- Numerous ministries in Saddam's Regime facilitated the smuggling of illicit goods through Iraq's borders, ports, and airports. The Iraqi Intelligence Service (IIS) and the Military Industrialization Commission (MIC), however, were directly responsible for skirting UN monitoring and importing prohibited items for Saddam.

Delivery Systems

Key Findings

Since the early 1970s, Iraq has consistently sought to acquire an effective long-range weapons delivery capability, and by 1991 Baghdad had purchased the missiles and infrastructure that would form the basis for nearly all of its future missile system developments.

The Soviet Union was a key supplier of missile hardware and provided 819 Scud-B missiles and ground support equipment.

Iraq's experiences with long-range delivery systems in the Iran/Iraq war were a vital lesson to Iraqi President Saddam Hussein. The successful Iraqi response to the Iranian long-range bombardment of Baghdad, leading to the War of the Cities, probably saved Saddam.

By 1991, Iraq had successfully demonstrated its ability to modify some of its delivery systems to increase their range and to develop WMD dissemination options, with the Al Hussein being a first step in this direction. The next few years of learning and experiments confirmed that the Regime's goal was for an effective long-range WMD delivery capability and demonstrated the resourcefulness of Iraq's scientists and technicians.

Iraq failed in its efforts to acquire longer-range delivery systems to replace inventory exhausted in the Iran/Iraq war. This was a forcing function that drove Iraq to develop indigenous delivery system production capabilities.

Desert Storm and subsequent UN resolutions and inspections brought many of Iraq's delivery system programs to a halt. While much of Iraq's long-range missile inventory and production infrastructure was eliminated, Iraq until late 1991 kept some items hidden to assist future reconstitution of the force. This decision and Iraq's intransigence during years of inspection left many UN questions unresolved.

- Coalition air strikes effectively targeted much of Iraq's delivery systems infrastructure, and UN inspections dramatically impeded further developments of long-range ballistic missiles.
- *It appears to have taken time, but Iraq eventually realized that sanctions were not going to end quickly.* This forced Iraq to sacrifice its long-range delivery force in an attempt to bring about a quick end to the sanctions.
- After the flight of Hussein Kamil in 1995, Iraq admitted that it had hidden Scud-variant missiles and components to aid future reconstitution but asserted that these items had been unilaterally destroyed by late 1991. The UN could not verify these claims and thereafter became more wary of Iraq's admissions and instituted a Regime of more intrusive inspections.
- *The Iraq Survey Group (ISG) has uncovered no evidence Iraq retained Scud-variant missiles, and debriefings of Iraqi officials in addition to some documentation suggest that Iraq did not retain such missiles after 1991.*

While other WMD programs were strictly prohibited, the UN permitted Iraq to develop and possess delivery systems provided their range did not exceed 150 km. This freedom allowed Iraq to keep its scientists and technicians employed and to keep its infrastructure and manufacturing base largely intact by pursuing programs nominally in compliance with the UN limitations. *This positioned Iraq for a potential breakout capability.*

- Between 1991 and 1998, Iraq had declared development programs underway for liquid- and solid-propellant ballistic missiles and unmanned aerial vehicles (UAVs).

Iraq's decisions in 1996 to accept the Oil-For-Food program (OFF) and later in 1998 to cease cooperation with UNSCOM and IAEA spurred a period of increased activity in delivery systems development. The pace of ongoing missile programs accelerated, and the Regime authorized its scientists to design missiles with ranges in excess of 150 km that, if developed, would have been clear violations of UNSCR 687.

- By 2002, Iraq had provided the liquid-propellant Al Samud II—a program started in 2001—and the solid propellant Al Fat'h to the military and was pursuing a series of new small UAV systems.
- *ISG uncovered Iraqi plans or designs for three long-range ballistic missiles with ranges from 400 to 1,000 km and for a 1,000-km-range cruise missile, although none of these systems progressed to production and only one reportedly passed the design phase. ISG assesses that these plans demonstrate Saddam's continuing desire—up to the beginning of Operation Iraqi Freedom (OIF)—for a long-range delivery capability.*

Procurements supporting delivery system programs expanded after the 1998 departure of the UN inspectors. Iraq also hired outside expertise to assist its development programs.

- ISG uncovered evidence that technicians and engineers from Russia reviewed the designs and assisted development of the Al Samud II during its rapid evolution. ISG also found that Iraq had entered into negotiations with North Korean and Russian entities for more capable missile systems.
- According to contract information exploited by ISG, Iraq imported at least 380 SA-2/Volga liquid-propellant engines from Poland and possibly Russia or Belarus. While Iraq claims these engines were for the Al Samud II program, the numbers involved appear in excess of immediate requirements, suggesting they could have supported the longer range missiles using clusters of SA-2 engines. Iraq also imported missile guidance and control systems from entities in countries like Belarus, Russia and Federal Republic of Yugoslavia (FRY). (Note: FRY is currently known as Serbia and Montenegro but is referred to as FRY in this section.)

In late 2002 Iraq was under increasing pressure from the international community to allow UN inspectors to return. Iraq in November accepted UNSCR 1441 and invited inspectors back into the country. In December Iraq presented to the UN its Currently Accurate, Full, and Complete Declaration (CAFCD) in response to UNSCR 1441.

- While the CAFCD was judged to be incomplete and a rehash of old information, it did provide details on the Al Samud II, Al Fat'h, new missile-related facilities, and new small UAV designs.
- In February 2003 the UN convened an expert panel to discuss the Al Samud II and Al Fat'h programs, which resulted in the UN's decision to prohibit the Al Samud II and order its destruction. Missile destruction began in early March but was incomplete when the inspectors were withdrawn later that month.

The CAFCD and United Nations Monitoring, Verification, and Inspection Commission (UNMOVIC) inspections provided a brief glimpse into what Iraq had accomplished in four years without an international presence on the ground.

Given Iraq's investments in technology and infrastructure improvements, an effective procurement network, skilled scientists, and designs already on the books for longer range missiles,

ISG assesses that Saddam clearly intended to reconstitute long-range delivery systems and that the systems potentially were for WMD.

- Iraq built a new and larger liquid-rocket engine test stand capable, with some modification, of supporting engines or engine clusters larger than the single SA-2 engine used in the Al Samud II.
- Iraq built or refurbished solid-propellant facilities and equipment, including a large propellant mixer, an aging oven, and a casting pit that could support large diameter motors.
- Iraq's investing in studies into new propellants and manufacturing technologies demonstrated its desire for more capable or effective delivery systems.

Nuclear

Key Findings

Iraq Survey Group (ISG) discovered further evidence of the maturity and significance of the pre-1991 Iraqi Nuclear Program but found that Iraq's ability to reconstitute a nuclear weapons program progressively decayed after that date.

- Saddam Hussein ended the nuclear program in 1991 following the Gulf war. ISG found no evidence to suggest concerted efforts to restart the program.
- Although Saddam clearly assigned a high value to the nuclear progress and talent that had been developed up to the 1991 war, the program ended and the intellectual capital decayed in the succeeding years.

Nevertheless, after 1991, Saddam did express his intent to retain the intellectual capital developed during the Iraqi Nuclear Program. Senior Iraqis—several of them from the Regime's inner circle—told ISG they assumed Saddam would restart a nuclear program once UN sanctions ended.

- Saddam indicated that he would develop the weapons necessary to counter any Iranian threat.

Initially, Saddam chose to conceal his nuclear program in its entirety, as he did with Iraq's BW program. Aggressive UN inspections after Desert Storm forced Saddam to admit the existence of the program and destroy or surrender components of the program.

In the wake of Desert Storm, Iraq took steps to conceal key elements of its program and to preserve what it could of the professional capabilities of its nuclear scientific community.

- Baghdad undertook a variety of measures to conceal key elements of its nuclear program from successive UN inspectors, including specific direction by Saddam Hussein to hide and preserve documentation associated with Iraq's nuclear program.
- ISG, for example, uncovered two specific instances in which scientists involved in uranium enrichment kept documents and technology. Although apparently acting on their own, they did so with the belief and anticipation of resuming uranium enrichment efforts in the future.

- Starting around 1992, in a bid to retain the intellectual core of the former weapons program, Baghdad transferred many nuclear scientists to related jobs in the Military Industrial Commission (MIC). The work undertaken by these scientists at the MIC helped them maintain their weapons knowledge base.

As with other WMD areas, Saddam's ambitions in the nuclear area were secondary to his prime objective of ending UN sanctions.

- Iraq, especially after the defection of Hussein Kamil in 1995, sought to persuade the IAEA that Iraq had met the UN's disarmament requirements so sanctions would be lifted.

ISG found a limited number of post-1995 activities that would have aided the reconstitution of the nuclear weapons program once sanctions were lifted.

- The activities of the Iraqi Atomic Energy Commission sustained some talent and limited research with potential relevance to a reconstituted nuclear program.
- Specific projects, with significant development, such as the efforts to build a rail gun and a copper vapor laser could have been useful in a future effort to restart a nuclear weapons program, but ISG found no indications of such purpose. As funding for the MIC and the IAEC increased after the introduction of the Oil-for-Food program, there was some growth in programs that involved former nuclear weapons scientists and engineers.
- The Regime prevented scientists from the former nuclear weapons program from leaving either their jobs or Iraq. Moreover, in the late 1990s, personnel from both MIC and the IAEC received significant pay raises in a bid to retain them, and the Regime undertook new investments in university research in a bid to ensure that Iraq retained technical knowledge.

Chemical

Key Findings

Saddam never abandoned his intentions to resume a CW effort when sanctions were lifted and conditions were judged favorable:

- Saddam and many Iraqis regarded CW as a proven weapon against an enemy's superior numerical strength, a weapon that had saved the nation at least once already—during the Iran-Iraq war—and contributed to deterring the Coalition in 1991 from advancing to Baghdad.

While a small number of old, abandoned chemical munitions have been discovered, ISG judges that Iraq unilaterally destroyed its undeclared chemical weapons stockpile in 1991. There are no credible indications that Baghdad resumed production of chemical munitions thereafter, a policy ISG attributes to Baghdad's desire to see sanctions lifted, or rendered ineffectual, or its fear of force against it should WMD be discovered.

- The scale of the Iraqi conventional munitions stockpile, among other factors, precluded an examination of the entire stockpile; however, ISG inspected sites judged most likely associated with possible storage or deployment of chemical weapons.

Iraq's CW program was crippled by the Gulf war and the legitimate chemical industry, which suffered under sanctions, only began to recover in the mid-1990s. Subsequent changes in the management of key military and civilian organizations, followed by an influx of funding and resources, provided Iraq with the ability to reinvigorate its industrial base.

- Poor policies and management in the early 1990s left the Military Industrial Commission (MIC) financially unsound and in a state of almost complete disarray.
- Saddam implemented a number of changes to the Regime's organizational and programmatic structures after the departure of Hussein Kamil.
- Iraq's acceptance of the Oil-for-Food (OFF) program was the foundation of Iraq's economic recovery and sparked a flow of illicitly diverted funds that could be applied to projects for Iraq's chemical industry.

The way Iraq organized its chemical industry after the mid-1990s allowed it to conserve the knowledge-base needed to restart a CW program, conduct a modest amount of dual-use research, and partially recover from the decline of its production capability caused by the effects of the Gulf war and UN-sponsored destruction and sanctions. Iraq implemented a rigorous and formalized system of nationwide research and production of chemicals, but ISG will not be able to resolve whether Iraq intended the system to underpin any CW-related efforts.

- The Regime employed a cadre of trained and experienced researchers, production managers, and weaponization experts from the former CW program.
- Iraq began implementing a range of indigenous chemical production projects in 1995 and 1996. Many of these projects, while not weapons-related, were designed to improve Iraq's infrastructure, which would have enhanced Iraq's ability to produce CW agents if the scaled-up production processes were implemented.
- Iraq had an effective system for the procurement of items that Iraq was not allowed to acquire due to sanctions. ISG found no evidence that this system was used to acquire precursor chemicals in bulk; however documents indicate that dual-use laboratory equipment and chemicals were acquired through this system.

Iraq constructed a number of new plants starting in the mid-1990s that enhanced its chemical infrastructure, although its overall industry had not fully recovered from the effects of sanctions, and had not regained pre-1991 technical sophistication or production capabilities prior to Operation Iraqi Freedom (OIF).

- ISG did not discover chemical process or production units configured to produce key precursors or CW agents. However, site visits and debriefs revealed that Iraq maintained its ability for reconfiguring and 'making-do' with available equipment as substitutes for sanctioned items.
- ISG judges, based on available chemicals, infrastructure, and scientist debriefings, that Iraq at OIF probably had a capability to produce large quantities of sulfur mustard within three to six months.
- A former nerve agent expert indicated that Iraq retained the capability to produce nerve agent in significant quantities within two years, given the import of required phosphorous precursors. However, we have no credible indications that Iraq acquired or attempted to acquire large quantities of these chemicals through its existing procurement networks for sanctioned items.

In addition to new investment in its industry, Iraq was able to monitor the location and use of all existing dual-use process equipment. This provided Iraq the ability to rapidly reallocate key equipment for proscribed activities, if required by the Regime.

- One effect of UN monitoring was to implement a national level control system for important dual-use process plants.

Iraq's historical ability to implement simple solutions to weaponization challenges allowed Iraq to retain the capability to weaponize CW agent when the need arose. Because of the risk of discovery and consequences for ending UN sanctions, Iraq would have significantly jeopardized its chances of having sanctions lifted or no longer enforced if the UN or foreign entity had discovered that Iraq had undertaken any weaponization activities.

- ISG has uncovered hardware at a few military depots, which suggests that Iraq may have prototyped experimental CW rounds. The available evidence is insufficient to determine the nature of the effort or the timeframe of activities.
- Iraq could indigenously produce a range of conventional munitions, throughout the 1990s, many of which had previously been adapted for filling with CW agent. However, ISG has found ambiguous evidence of weaponization activities.

Saddam's Leadership Defense Plan consisted of a tactical doctrine taught to all Iraqi officers and included the concept of a "red-line" or last line of defense. However, ISG has no information that the plan ever included a trigger for CW use.

- Despite reported high-level discussions about the use of chemical weapons in the defense of Iraq, information acquired after OIF does not confirm the inclusion of CW in Iraq's tactical planning for OIF. We believe these were mostly theoretical discussions and do not imply the existence of undiscovered CW munitions.

Discussions concerning WMD, particularly leading up to OIF, would have been highly compartmentalized within the Regime. ISG found no credible evidence that any field elements knew about plans for CW use during Operation Iraqi Freedom.

- Uday [Hussein, Saddam's son]—head of the Fedayeen Saddam—attempted to obtain chemical weapons for use during OIF, according to reporting, but ISG found no evidence that Iraq ever came into possession of any CW weapons.

ISG uncovered information that the Iraqi Intelligence Service (IIS) maintained throughout 1991 to 2003 a set of undeclared covert laboratories to research and test various chemicals and poisons, primarily for intelligence operations. The network of laboratories could have provided an ideal, compartmented platform from which to continue CW agent R&D or small-scale production efforts, but we have no indications this was planned.

- ISG has no evidence that IIS Directorate of Criminology (M16) scientists were producing CW or BW agents in these laboratories. However, sources indicate that M16 was planning to produce several CW agents including sulfur mustard, nitrogen mustard, and Sarin.
- Exploitations of IIS laboratories, safe houses, and disposal sites revealed no evidence of CW-related research or production, however many of these sites were

either sanitized by the Regime or looted prior to OIF. Interviews with key IIS officials within and outside of M16 yielded very little information about the IIS' activities in this area.

- The existence, function, and purpose of the laboratories were never declared to the UN.
- The IIS program included the use of human subjects for testing purposes.

ISG investigated a series of key pre-OIF indicators involving the possible movement and storage of chemical weapons, focusing on 11 major depots assessed to have possible links to CW. A review of documents, interviews, available reporting, and site exploitations revealed alternate, plausible explanations for activities noted prior to OIF which, at the time, were believed to be CW-related.

- ISG investigated pre-OIF activities at Musayyib Ammunition Storage Depot—the storage site that was judged to have the strongest link to CW. An extensive investigation of the facility revealed that there was no CW activity, unlike previously assessed.

Biological

Key Findings

The Biological Warfare (BW) program was born of the Iraqi Intelligence Service (IIS) and this service retained its connections with the program either directly or indirectly throughout its existence.

- The IIS provided the BW program with security and participated in biological research, probably for its own purposes, from the beginning of Iraq's BW effort in the early 1970s until the final days of Saddam Hussein's Regime.

In 1991, Saddam Hussein regarded BW as an integral element of his arsenal of WMD weapons, and would have used it if the need arose.

- At a meeting of the Iraqi leadership immediately prior to the Gulf war in 1991, Saddam Hussein personally authorized the use of BW weapons against Israel, Saudi Arabia and US forces. Although the exact nature of the circumstances that would trigger use was not spelled out, they would appear to be a threat to the leadership itself or the US resorting to *"unconventional harmful types of weapons."*
- Saddam envisaged all-out use. For example, all Israeli cities were to be struck and all the BW weapons at his disposal were to be used. Saddam specified that the *"many years"* agents, presumably anthrax spores, were to be employed against his foes.

ISG judges that Iraq's actions between 1991 and 1996 demonstrate that the state intended to preserve its BW capability and return to a steady, methodical progress toward a mature BW program when and if the opportunity arose.

- ISG assesses that in 1991, Iraq clung to the objective of gaining war-winning weapons with the strategic intention of achieving the ability to project its power over much of the Middle East and beyond. Biological weapons were part of that plan. With an eye to the future and aiming to preserve some measure of its BW capability, Baghdad in the years immediately after Desert Storm sought to save what it could of its BW infrastructure and covertly continue BW research, hide evidence of that and earlier efforts, and dispose of its existing weapons stocks.

- From 1992 to 1994, Iraq greatly expanded the capability of its Al Hakam facility. Indigenously produced 5 cubic meter fermentors were installed, electrical and water utilities were expanded, and massive new construction to house its desired 50 cubic meter fermentors were completed.
- With the economy at rock bottom in late 1995, ISG judges that Baghdad abandoned its existing BW program in the belief that it constituted a potential embarrassment, whose discovery would undercut Baghdad's ability to reach its overarching goal of obtaining relief from UN sanctions.

In practical terms, with the destruction of the Al Hakam facility, Iraq abandoned its ambition to obtain advanced BW weapons quickly. ISG found no direct evidence that Iraq, after 1996, had plans for a new BW program or was conducting BW-specific work for military purposes. Indeed, from the mid-1990s, despite evidence of continuing interest in nuclear and chemical weapons, there appears to be a complete absence of discussion or even interest in BW at the Presidential level.

Iraq would have faced great difficulty in re-establishing an effective BW agent production capability. Nevertheless, after 1996 Iraq still had a significant dual-use capability—some declared—readily useful for BW if the Regime chose to use it to pursue a BW program. Moreover, Iraq still possessed its most important BW asset, the scientific know-how of its BW cadre.

- Any attempt to create a new BW program after 1996 would have encountered a range of major hurdles. The years following Desert Storm wrought a steady degradation of Iraq's industrial base: new equipment and spare parts for existing machinery became daffy cult and expensive to obtain, standards of maintenance declined, staff could not receive training abroad, and foreign technical assistance was almost impossible to get. Additionally, Iraq's infrastructure and public utilities were crumbling. New large projects, particularly if they required special foreign equipment and expertise, would attract international attention. UN monitoring of dual-use facilities up to the end of 1998, made their use for clandestine purpose complicated and risk laden.

Depending on its scale, Iraq could have re-established an elementary BW program within a few weeks to a few months of a decision to do so, but ISG discovered no indications that the Regime was pursuing such a course.

- In spite of the difficulties noted above, a BW capability is technically the easiest WMD to attain. Although equipment and facilities were destroyed under UN supervision in 1996, Iraq retained technical BW know-how through the scientists that were involved in the former program. ISG has also identified civilian facilities and equipment in Iraq that have dual-use application that could be used for the production of agent.

ISG judges that in 1991 and 1992, Iraq appears to have destroyed its undeclared stocks of BW weapons and probably destroyed remaining holdings of bulk BW agent. However

ISG lacks evidence to document complete destruction. Iraq retained some BW-related seed stocks until their discovery after Operation Iraqi Freedom (OIF).

- After the passage of UN Security Council Resolution (UNSCR) 687 in April 1991, Iraqi leaders decided not to declare the offensive BW program and in consequence ordered all evidence of the program erased. Iraq declared that BW program personnel sanitized the facilities and destroyed the weapons and their contents.
- Iraq declared the possession of 157 aerial bombs and 25 missile warheads containing BW agent. ISG assesses that the evidence for the original number of bombs is uncertain. ISG judges that Iraq clandestinely destroyed at least 132 bombs and 25 missiles. ISG continued the efforts of the UN at the destruction site but found no remnants of further weapons. This leaves the possibility that the fragments of up to 25 bombs may remain undiscovered. Of these, any that escaped destruction would probably now only contain degraded agent.
- ISG does not have a clear account of bulk agent destruction. Official Iraqi sources and BW personnel, state that Al Hakam staff destroyed stocks of bulk agent in mid 1991. However, the same personnel admit concealing details of the movement and destruction of bulk BW agent in the first half of 1991. Iraq continued to present information known to be untrue to the UN up to OIF. Those involved did not reveal this until several months after the conflict.
- Dr. Rihab Rashid Taha Al 'Azzawi, head of the bacterial program claims she retained BW seed stocks until early 1992 when she destroyed them. ISG has not found a means of verifying this. Some seed stocks were retained by another Iraqi official until 2003 when they were recovered by ISG.

ISG is aware of BW-applicable research since 1996, but ISG judges it was not conducted in connection with a BW program.

- ISG has uncovered no evidence of illicit research conducted into BW agents by universities or research organizations.
- The work conducted on a biopesticide (*Bacillus thuringiensis*) at Al Hakam until 1995 would serve to maintain the basic skills required by scientists to produce and dry anthrax spores (*Bacillus anthracis*) but ISG has not discovered evidence suggesting this was the Regime's intention. However in 1991, research and production on biopesticide and single cell protein (SCP) was selected by Iraq to provide cover for Al Hakam's role in Iraq's BW program. Similar work conducted at the Tuwaitha Agricultural and Biological Research Center (TABRC) up to OIF also maintained skills that were applicable to BW, but again, ISG found no evidence to suggest that this was the intention.
- Similarly, ISG found no information to indicate that the work carried out by TABRC into Single Cell Protein (SCP) was a cover story for continuing research into the production of BW agents, such as *C. botulinum* and *B. anthracis,* after the destruction of Al Hakam through to OIF.
- TABRC conducted research and development (R&D) programs to enable indigenous manufacture of bacterial growth media. Although these media are suitable for the bulk production of BW agents, ISG has found no evidence to indicate that their development and testing were specifically for this purpose.

- Although Iraq had the basic capability to work with variola major (smallpox), ISG found no evidence that it retained any stocks of smallpox or actively conducted research into this agent for BW intentions.

The IIS had a series of laboratories that conducted biological work including research into BW agents for assassination purposes until the mid-1990s. ISG has not been able to establish the scope and nature of the work at these laboratories or determine whether any of the work was related to military development of BW agent.

- The security services operated a series of laboratories in the Baghdad area. Iraq should have declared these facilities and their equipment to the UN, but they did not. Neither the UN Special Commission (UNSCOM) nor the UN Monitoring, Verification, and Inspection Commission (UNMOVIC) were aware of their existence or inspected them.
- Some of the laboratories possessed equipment capable of supporting research into BW agents for military purposes, but ISG does not know whether this occurred although there is no evidence of it. The laboratories were probably the successors of the Al Salman facility, located three kilometers south of Salman Pak, which was destroyed in 1991, and they carried on many of the same activities, including forensic work.
- Under the aegis of the intelligence service, a secretive team developed assassination instruments using poisons or toxins for the Iraqi state. A small group of scientists, doctors and technicians conducted secret experiments on human beings, resulting in their deaths. The aim was probably the development of poisons, including ricin and aflatoxin to eliminate or debilitate the Regime's opponents. It appears that testing on humans continued until the mid 1990s. There is no evidence to link these tests with the development of BW agents for military use.

In spite of exhaustive investigation, ISG found no evidence that Iraq possessed, or was developing BW agent production systems mounted on road vehicles or railway wagons.

- Prior to OIF there was information indicating Iraq had planned and built a breakout BW capability, in the form of a set of mobile production units, capable of producing BW agent at short notice in sufficient quantities to weaponize. Although ISG has conducted a thorough investigation of every aspect of this information, it has not found any equipment suitable for such a program, nor has ISG positively identified any sites. No documents have been uncovered. Interviews with individuals suspected of involvement have all proved negative.
- ISG harbors severe doubts about the source's credibility in regards to the breakout program.
- ISG thoroughly examined two trailers captured in 2003, suspected of being mobile BW agent production units, and investigated the associated evidence. ISG judges that its Iraqi makers almost certainly designed and built the equipment exclusively for the generation of hydrogen. It is impractical to use the equipment for the production and weaponization of BW agent. ISG judges that it cannot therefore be part of any BW program.

Source: U.S. Central Intelligence Agency. "Comprehensive Report of the Special Advisor to the DCI on Iraq's WMD: Key Findings." October 6, 2004. www.cia.gov/cia/reports/iraq_wmd_2004/Comp_Report_Key_Findings.pdf (accessed February 18, 2005).

Pension Benefit Guaranty Corp. Director on Avoiding a Bailout

October 7, 2004

INTRODUCTION

The nation's traditional pension system, which covered about 44 million workers and retirees, remained financially troubled in 2004. Cash-strapped companies across the nation froze their plans. Other companies that had shifted to a hybrid plan known as "cash-balance" were left in legal limbo by a court ruling. Still others went out of business and turned responsibility for paying promised pensions over to a quasi-government agency, the Pension Benefit Guaranty Corporation (PBGC).

That agency announced in November that its deficit had doubled in 2004, from $11.2 billion to $23.3 billion. PBGC executive director Bradley D. Belt and others repeatedly urged Congress to fix the system quickly before the agency ran out of money and had to ask for a bailout. Belt was particularly concerned that the agency might have to take over the pension plans of at least two airlines, United and U.S. Airways, that were in bankruptcy proceedings. Both airlines said they wanted to terminate their pension plans; PBGC estimated the cost to the agency of taking over those pension plans would be $8.5 billion.

Background

Pensions did not become a common employment benefit until after World War II, and until the mid-1980s traditional defined-benefit plans were the norm. These plans, offered to workers primarily in manufacturing companies, were paid for and maintained by the company and guaranteed retirees a fixed benefit typically based on salary and years of service. There were 112,000 defined-benefit plans in the private sector, covering some 40 percent of American workers, at the plans' peak in the mid-1980s.

In 1974, in the wake of several major bankruptcies that left retirees and workers with no pensions, Congress enacted the Employee Retirement Income Security Act, which set new regulations to ensure that companies offering defined-benefit plans set aside enough money annually to cover their obligations. The measure also created the Pension Benefit Guaranty Corporation to ensure that workers and retirees continued to receive at least some of their benefits when their companies went bankrupt or out of business. The agency funded the benefits out of premiums paid by the covered companies and from returns on its investments.

In the mid-1980s companies began to turn away from defined-benefit plans to defined-contribution plans, such as 401(k)s. Under these plans, both the company and the employee contributed some set percentage of wages on a tax-free basis; that money was then invested on behalf of the employee, whose retirement benefit consisted of the contributions and any return on the investment. This system was much less expensive for employers because it shifted the investment risk to the employee. As a result, many companies that had offered traditional plans moved their employees to defined-contribution plans, and by 2004 only 20 percent of the workforce continued to participate in defined-benefit plans. Few companies were offering their employees new defined-benefit plans.

Under the 1974 federal law, every company with a defined-benefit plan was required to ensure that the company's contributions and the return on those contributions equaled 90 percent of the plan's retirement benefits commitments. Companies typically invested their pension contributions in a mix of stocks, bonds, and other financial instruments. During the stock market boom of the 1990s, many companies did not need to make any additional cash contributions to their pension plans because returns on investment were enough to cover the amounts required. But after the market collapsed in 2000 and the economy fell into recession, several major companies had to find cash to cover their pension fund obligations at the same time that they were having to cope with huge operating losses.

Most defined-benefit plans were not in jeopardy. Of about 31,000 existing plans, only 1,050 were underfunded by $50 million or more in 2003, according to PGBC. Those that were in danger tended to be offered by large corporations with unionized workers, such as the older airlines, and declining industries with many retirees, such as the steel industry.

Widening Deficit at PBGC

The Pension Benefit Guaranty Corporation reported that it incurred a net loss of $12.1 billion in fiscal 2004, for an overall deficit of $23.3 billion. In 1999 the agency had run a surplus of $9.7 billion. The agency said that, for the first time in its history, it paid retirement benefits to more than 1 million retirees and the total amount of benefits exceeded $3 billion. *(Previous deficits, Historic Documents of 2003, p. 707)*

In releasing the figures, PBGC director Belt said the agency had $39 billion in assets and could continue to meet its obligation "for a number of years." But, he added, the agency had $62 billion in liabilities and an estimated $96 billion in exposure from companies that the agency judged reasonably likely to terminate their plans. "It is imperative," Belt said, "that Congress act expeditiously so that the problem doesn't spiral out of control." Belt's warnings raised specters of the late 1980s when Congress failed to deal in a timely way with looming problems in the savings and loan industry and eventually had to approve a bailout that cost taxpayers about $200 billion.

In numerous appearances before congressional committees, business groups, and retirement analysts, Belt, who became head of PBGC in April, and his immediate predecessor Steven A. Kandarian, pressed Congress to adopt legislation proposed by the Bush administration to ensure that PBGC did not run out of money. As outlined by Belt in testimony before the Senate Commerce Committee on October 7, that legislation had three main components: changing the funding rules so that the amounts companies were required to set aside more nearly matched the benefits they had promised to pay, raising the premiums companies paid to PBGC, and requiring companies to disclose more timely and meaningful information about the status of their pension funding.

Belt said current funding rules were "Byzantine and often ineffectual," allowing companies to claim that they were "fully funded when in fact they are substantially underfunded." Funding targets were too low, Belt said, allowing companies to stop making contributions when they had funded 90 percent of "current liabilities," a measure he said had "no obvious relationship" to the amount needed if a plan were to terminate. For example, he said, although U.S. Airways said its pilots' pension plan was 94 percent funded on a current liability basis, it turned out to be only 33 percent funded on a termination basis—creating a $2.5 billion shortfall. Belt also warned that the pension insurance system could be "gamed" because it gave weak companies incentives to take excessive risks, perhaps by imprudent investments or by increasing pension benefits rather than increasing wages, in hopes of making a financial recovery, knowing that if its gamble failed the PBGC would cover its pension obligations.

Belt also said he was "particularly concerned" that companies in bankruptcy proceedings were trying to shed their pension plans as part of their effort to restructure so that they could emerge from bankruptcy and continue operating, leaving the PBGC with the burden of paying benefits under those old pension plans. Belt was referring specifically to United and U.S Airways, both of which were in bankruptcy proceedings, U.S. Air for the second time. "The pension insurance program is there to protect workers' benefits," Belt said in late July. "It shouldn't be used as a piggy bank to help companies restructure."

United announced on July 23 that it would not contribute to its pension plans while it remained in bankruptcy protection. In November both United and U.S. Airlines announced plans to terminate their pension plans so that they could escape from bankruptcy. On December 31 PBGC said it was seeking to take over United's pension plan for its 14,000 active and retired pilots, at an estimated cost of $1.4 billion. The agency moved after United's pilots agreed to a termination of the defined-benefit plan in May 2005 in return for significantly increased contributions from United into a separate defined-contribution plan. Belt said the agency was seeking immediate termination of the pilots' pension plan to save $140 million in additional losses that could occur if the plan were terminated in 2005 and to try to prevent United from ending its remaining three pension plans. Were the bankruptcy court to agree to PBGC's request, the maximum pension benefit a sixty-five-year-old retired United pilot would receive would be $44,386 a year; the pension plan promised many of them much more than that. The guaranteed PBGC benefit was scheduled to rise to $45,614 in 2005.

In his testimony to the Senate Commerce Committee, Belt stressed that the broader problem was that if United and U.S. Air were allowed to push their pension obligations onto PBGC, then other financially troubled airlines with defined-benefit plans might default on their pension plans, creating a domino effect in the industry. The agency estimated that it would lose $31 billion if that were to happen. If the airline industry could get away with such behavior, some analysts suggested, automakers—with even bigger pension obligations—might be encouraged to try a similar tactic. Belt specifically asked Congress to give the payment of pension benefits higher priority in bankruptcy proceedings.

David M. Walker, comptroller general of the United States, testifying the same day, agreed with Belt. "This moral hazard effect has the potential to escalate, with the initial bankruptcy of firms with underfunded plans creating a vicious cycle of bankruptcies and plan terminations," he said. Like Belt, Walker cautioned that any reforms would have to carefully balance the need to hold companies accountable for paying promised benefits with incentives to encourage companies to continue offering defined-benefit plans.

Congress took no action on the administration's proposals in 2004, although it did approve a stopgap measure in April to help companies cope with shortfalls caused by the slump in the stock market. The legislation (PL 108–218) temporarily replaced the rate employers used to determine the value of their defined-benefit pension plans—the interest rate on thirty-year Treasury bonds—with an index based on higher-paying corporate bonds. Assuming a higher value for the existing assets in the plan allowed companies to reduce the amount of new contributions they were required to make. Overall, the measure was expected to save companies $80 billion over two years. The bill also allowed companies with chronically underfunded pensions, including those in the airline and steel industries, to reduce their "catch-up" contributions by 80 percent in 2004 and 2005—an estimated savings of $1.6 billion.

Some legislators seemed poised to grapple with the problem in 2005. Rep. John A. Boehner, R-Ohio, chairman of the House Committee on Education and the Workforce, said in November that "we're making progress in putting together comprehensive pension legislation." The task would not be easy. Cash-strapped companies were likely to balk at any new rules that required them to make significantly larger annual contributions to their plans, while financially healthy companies might balk at higher insurance premiums. In both cases, companies that did not want to incur the higher costs might choose to terminate their plans and withdraw from the PBGC insurance plan, reducing the income the agency had to work with.

Another threat to defined-benefit plans and the financial status of the PBGC was still pending in the courts. The case involved a plan by IBM Corp. to shift its workers from defined-benefit plans to a hybrid plan known as a cash-balance plan. Such plans usually benefited younger and mobile workers, who could take their cash balances with them from job to job, but older workers who were switched from defined-benefits plans to cash-balance plans often suffered benefit cuts. In July 2003 a federal district court ruled that IBM had illegally discriminated against its older workers when it converted its pension plans. Appeals of the ruling were still under way at the end of 2004, leaving the legality of dozens, if not hundreds, of plan conversions in question. If the ruling were to be upheld, said Dallas L. Salisbury of the Employer Benefit Research Institute, and Congress did not act, many of those plans could be terminated. "A melt-down in the cash-balance area would be even more disastrous than other threats [PBGC is] facing because it would be a loss of a huge amount of premium revenue from essentially well-funded plans," Salisbury said.

Investment Policies

PBGC took steps to shore up its own finances in 2004 by changing its investment strategy, placing most of its holdings in bonds and other fixed-income investments with maturity dates that more closely matched its payment obligations. Announcing on January 29 that PBGC would reduce its stockholdings to 15–25 percent of its portfolio, then PBGC director Kandarian said the new strategy would forgo any potential for making a big killing on the stock market, but it would help protect against losses and the need for a taxpayer bailout. "If we don't match our liabilities, but just sort of shoot for the moon, if you will, the taxpayer would be providing portfolio insurance for our bets in the markets," he said. The strategy also reduced the double jeopardy that occurred when both the covered companies and their insurer were heavily invested in the same risks.

Many pension specialists argued that all pension funds should be invested in a similar fashion, as they were in earlier decades. Instead, most had roughly 60 percent invested in stocks, 30 percent in bonds, and the rest in alternative investments such as private equities that were often quite risky. One reason for the heavy investment in stocks was that accounting rules allowed companies to project the returns they expected on their pension fund investment and to calculate those projections into their bottom line, even when the projections turned out to be wrong. United, for example, projected that its pension fund would earn 9.75 percent in 2002; it used that assumption to reduce its reported labor costs, even though the pension fund lost money that year.

Investors complained that the practice was misleading, and the Securities and Exchange Commission began an investigation in 2004 of pension fund accounting practices at several big corporations, including Ford, General Motors, and Boeing. Several retirement analysts said the accounting practices were dangerous because they encouraged companies to take on greater risk than was prudent. "The accounting encourages a mismatch, because [the companies] get an earnings windfall," Zvi Bodie, a finance professor at Boston University told the *New York Times*. "It's bad for employees because it increases the chance that they won't get their promised benefits. It's bad for the PBGC. It's bad for the taxpayers. So who's it good for? It's good for the firms that manage the equities."

Following is the text of testimony given October 7, 2004, before the Senate Commerce Committee by Bradley D. Belt, executive director of the Pension Benefit Guaranty Corporation, outlining a plan for strengthening funding of corporate defined-benefit pension plans.

"Testimony of Bradley D. Belt, Pension Benefit Guaranty Corp."

. . . I welcome this opportunity to appear before you to discuss the financial and policy challenges facing the private defined benefit pension system and federal pension insurance program. Before turning to those challenges I want to emphasize that while the pension insurance fund is under increasing pressure and plan sponsors have been buffeted by a variety of forces, what is steadfast is the Administration's position that pension promises made by businesses to America's workers and retirees must be honored.

I also want to assure you and the participants in defined benefit plans that the PBGC stands ready to carry out its mission and pay benefits to participants when a pension plan is surrendered by a sponsoring company, as the agency has done since the enactment of ERISA 30 years ago last month. We currently pay monthly benefits to nearly half a million beneficiaries, and both retirees and participants with deferred benefits should know that the PBGC has sufficient resources to pay these benefits for a number of years. At the same time, the longer-term solvency of the pension insurance program, which we are here to talk about today, is at risk.

Considerable attention has been—and must be—paid to the PBGC's financial position. The Corporation's single-employer insurance fund had a record deficit at the end of the 2003 fiscal year of $11.2 billion, and we will be reporting a significantly increased deficit for the 2004 fiscal year. As you know, United Airlines has said publicly that it will not make any further contributions to its pension plans during bankruptcy and that it "likely" will have to terminate them. Those plans are now underfunded by an estimated $8.3 billion on a termination basis, $6.4 billion of which is guaranteed by the PBGC.

Likewise, US Airways, which recently re-entered bankruptcy, announced that it is suspending contributions to pension plans that are already underfunded by an estimated $2.3 billion on a termination basis, almost all of which—$2.1 billion—would be guaranteed by the PBGC. In addition, Delta has publicly indicated that the company may have to file under Chapter 11 in the near future. We estimate that the total exposure of plan participants and the pension insurance program to the airline industry was $31 billion on a termination basis as of the end of 2003.

While developments in the airline industry are cause for concern, they are symptomatic of a broader and deeper set of problems confronting the pension insurance program, plan sponsors, and beneficiaries. I believe these issues can be distilled to two central themes—corporate responsibility and retirement security. Simply put, companies should be held accountable to make good on the pension promises they have made to their workers and retirees. The consequences of not honoring these commitments are unacceptable—the retirement security of millions of current and future retirees is put at risk.

When underfunded pension plans terminate, three groups can lose: workers face the prospect of benefit reductions; other companies, including those that are healthy and have well funded plans, may face higher PBGC premiums; and, ultimately, taxpayers may be called upon by Congress to bail out the pension insurance fund, just as was the case more than a decade ago with the savings and loan bailout. (It should be noted, however, that under current law the PBGC does not have the full faith and credit backing of the U.S. government.) Of the three groups at risk, only financially robust plan sponsors have the ability to protect themselves from losses by ending their plans and exiting the system. This is the unfortunate but all too predictable result of a system that allows—and, one might even argue, sometimes encourages—companies to avoid paying for the promises they have made.

Structural Flaws in the Pension Insurance Program

I would group the structural flaws in the pension insurance program into three general categories.

The first is a Byzantine and often ineffectual set of funding rules. They are needlessly complex and fail to ensure that many pension plans are and remain adequately funded. Among the features that are impossible to square with the goal of simplicity and prudent funding: multiple liability measures, multiple discount rates, smoothing mechanisms, reclassification of contributions from one year to the prior year, credit balances, excessive discretion over actuarial assumptions, and varying amortization periods. As a result, companies can say they are fully funded when in fact they are substantially underfunded. Worse, the funding rules allow companies to avoid making contributions when they are substantially underfunded. And in some circumstances, they actually prevent companies from making contributions during good economic times. The bottom line is that we wouldn't be here today if the funding rules worked properly.

One flaw worth highlighting is that the funding targets are set too low. Employers can stop making contributions when a plan is funded at 90 percent of "current liability," a measure with no obvious relationship to the amount of money needed to pay all benefit liabilities if the plan terminates. As a result, employers can stop making contributions before a plan is sufficiently funded to protect participants. Bethlehem Steel said its plan was 84 percent funded on a current liability basis, but the plan turned out to be only 45 percent funded on a termination basis, with a total shortfall of $4.3 billion. US Airways said its pilots' plan was 94 percent funded on a current liability basis, but the plan was only 33 percent funded on a termination basis, with a $2.5 billion shortfall. No wonder the US Airways pilots were shocked to learn just how much of their promised benefits would be lost. Similarly, the funding rules allow contribution holidays even for seriously underfunded plans. Bethlehem Steel made no cash contributions to its plan for three years prior to plan termination, and US Airways made no cash contributions to its pilots' plan for four years before termination.

The second problem is what economists refer to as "moral hazard." A properly designed insurance system has various mechanisms for encouraging responsible behavior that will lessen the likelihood of incurring a loss and discouraging risky behavior that heightens the prospects of claims. That is why banks have risk-based capital standards, why drivers with poor driving records face higher premiums, why smokers pay more for life insurance than non-smokers, and why homeowners with smoke detectors get lower rates than those without.

However, a poorly designed system can be gamed. A weak company will have incentives to make generous pension promises rather than increase wages. Employees may go along because of PBGC's limited guarantee of pension benefits. If the company recovers, it may be able to afford the increased benefits. If not, the costs of the insured portion of the increased benefits are shifted to other companies through the insurance fund. Similarly, a company with an underfunded plan may increase asset risk to try to make up the gap, with much of the upside gain benefiting shareholders and much of the downside risk being shifted to other premium payers.

Unfortunately, the pension insurance program lacks basic checks and balances. There are no risk-based underwriting standards. Plan sponsors face no penalties regardless of the risk they impose on the system. And there is relatively little consequence to acting irresponsibly and not funding pension promises. As a result, there has been a tremendous amount of cost-shifting from financially troubled companies with underfunded plans to healthy companies with well-funded plans.

Bethlehem Steel presented a claim of $3.7 billion after having paid a little over $60 million in premiums, despite the fact that the company was a deteriorating credit risk and its plans were substantially underfunded for several years prior to the time the PBGC had to step in. Similarly, while United's credit rating has been junk bond status and its pensions underfunded by more than $5 billion on a termination basis since at least 2000, it has paid just $50 million in premiums to the insurance program. Yet the termination of United's plans would result in a loss to the fund of more than $6 billion. This subsidization extends across industry sectors—to date, the steel and airline industries have accounted for more than 70% of PBGC's claims by dollar amount while covering less than 5% of the insured base.

The third category of structural flaws is the lack of transparency in the system. The funding and disclosure rules seem intended to obfuscate economic reality. That is certainly their effect—to shield relevant information regarding the funding status of plans from participants, investors and even regulators. This results from the combination of stale, contradictory and often misleading information under ERISA and the accounting standards. For example, the principal governmental source of information about the 31,000 private sector defined benefit plans is the Form 5500. Because ERISA provides for a significant lapse of time between the end of a plan year and the time when the Form 5500 must be filed, when PBGC receives the complete documents the information is typically two and a half years old. It is exceedingly difficult to make informed business and policy decisions based on such dated information, given the dynamic and volatile nature of markets.

The PBGC does receive more timely information regarding a limited number of underfunded plans that pose the greatest threat to the system, but the statute requires that this information not be made publicly available. This makes no sense. Basic data regarding the funded status of a pension plan, changes in assets and liabilities, and the amount that participants would stand to lose at termination are vitally important to participants. Investors in companies that sponsor the plans also need relevant and timely information about the funded status of its pensions on a firm's earnings capacity and capital structure. While recent accounting changes are a step in the right direction, more can and should be done to provide better information to regulatory bodies and the other stakeholders in the defined benefit system.

Trends in the Defined Benefit System

These structural flaws not only threaten the solvency and undermine the integrity of the pension insurance program but are part of a broader set of forces that must be addressed to ensure the viability of the defined benefit system.

The trend lines paint a disturbing picture. Traditional defined benefit pension plans, based on years of service and either final salary or a specified benefit formula, at one time covered a significant portion of the workforce, providing a stable source of income to supplement Social Security. The number of private sector defined benefit plans grew through the 1960s and '70s before reaching a peak of 112,000 in the mid-1980s. At that time, some 40 percent of Americans workers were covered by defined benefit plans.

Since then, there has been steady erosion in the number of defined benefit plans offered. Over the past two decades, the number of defined benefit plans has fallen by 75 percent to just over 31,000 plans today. Moreover, just 1 in 5 workers—20 percent of the workforce—now participates in a private sector defined benefit plan. Notably, no new plans of significant size have been established in recent years. (An exception is the United Methodist Church, which in May created a traditional DB plan for its 25,000 American pastors and lay employees. The plan, though, does not fall under the insurance coverage of PBGC.)

But the decline in the number of plans offered and workers covered doesn't tell the whole story of how changes in the defined benefit system have impacted retirement income. There are other significant factors that can undermine the goal of a stable income stream for aging workers.

For example, in lieu of outright termination, companies are increasingly "freezing" plans. Surveys by pension consulting firms show that a significant number of their clients have or are considering instituting some form of plan freeze. PBGC is also conducting its own survey on plan freezes to obtain more comprehensive data on the phenomenon. Freezes not only eliminate workers' ability to earn additional pension benefits but often serve as a precursor to plan termination, which further erodes the premium base of the pension insurance program. Workers and retirees deserve the opportunity to have a number of options for retirement security, which is why the Administration is committed to making defined benefit plans a legally and regulatorily viable option for employers.

Mr. Chairman, given the serious challenges facing the pension insurance program, no amount of tinkering will achieve the lasting solution we need to put the PBGC on a sound footing and to restore the confidence of workers and retirees who rely on our pension protection. On the contrary, we need a considered and comprehensive approach that will improve the financial health of the defined benefit pension system, protect participants' benefits, and return the pension insurance program to financial strength.

The PBGC and others in the Administration have been hard at work identifying the challenges facing the defined benefit pension system and proposing responsible solutions for more than two years. As far back as June of 2002, my predecessor testified before Congress that PBGC was facing a big financial challenge. His warning, considered dire at the time, seems prescient today:

> "I'm concerned that our surplus may decline even further . . . [W]e still face over $9 billion in underfunding in the steel industry, nearly half of which is in companies that are in bankruptcy proceedings. We also face large amounts of underfunding in troubled companies in the airline and retail sectors."

PBGC went on to absorb most of that $9 billion in steel industry underfunding and now runs the risk of inheriting much of the airline industry's underfunding as well.

Since June of 2002, PBGC has testified seven additional times before Congress, issuing increasingly strong warnings about the dangers facing the defined benefit pension system and mapping out the major elements of reform. Moreover, in July of 2003, Assistant Labor Secretary Ann L. Combs and Treasury Undersecretary Peter R. Fisher gave testimony in which the first three elements of pension reform were detailed for Congress. The proposal is even more relevant today than it was 15 months ago.

First, as the necessary initial step toward comprehensive reform of the funding rules, the proposal would improve the accuracy of the pension liability measurement to reflect the time structure of each pension plan's benefit payments. This would be accomplished by measuring a plan's liabilities using a yield curve of highly rated corporate bonds to calculate the present value of those future payments. Second, the proposal would require better disclosure to workers, retirees, investors and creditors about the funded status of pension plans, which will improve incentives for adequate funding. Third, the proposal provides new safeguards against underfunding by requiring financially troubled companies with highly underfunded plans to immediately fund or secure backing for additional benefits, benefit improvements, and lump sum payments.

Unfortunately, no action has yet occurred on these proposals. In fact, last fall and into the early part of this year, much of the debate centered on how much funding forbearance plan sponsors should be allowed. In the end, plan sponsors received two years of a single, smoothed corporate-bond interest rate to discount their pension liabilities, which the Administration supported as a transition to use of the corporate-bond yield curve. But an extra provision exempted companies in the steel and airline industries from the special catch-up contributions designed to get plans better funded before they can terminate. As the PBGC warned last November:

> "Giving a special break to weak companies with the worst-funded plans is a dangerous gamble. The risk is that these plans will terminate down the road even more underfunded than they are today. If that happens, workers will lose promised benefits and the pension insurance program will suffer additional multibillion-dollar losses."

The members of PBGC's Board of Directors—the Secretaries of Labor, Treasury and Commerce—also issued strong warnings in November 2003 and again in January 2004 against extra funding holidays. What the Administration warned would happen is now coming to pass. Two of the airlines given a break on their required pension contributions are now in Chapter 11 and threatening to terminate their underfunded pension plans.

Comprehensive Reform Needed

Ultimately, we need comprehensive reform of the laws governing defined benefit pension plans in order to put the system on a sustainable path. The goals of reform are straightforward-to protect the pensions of the 44 million workers and retirees who are relying on the promises made by their employers; to ensure that companies adequately fund the promises they make; and to eliminate the incentive for companies to shift to others the cost of unfunded pension obligations.

To meet these goals, we need to *streamline and strengthen the ERISA funding rules.* Reform must provide sounder pension plan funding. The level of underfunding in the private defined benefit system—estimated last year to be more than $350 billion—poses a substantial risk not only to beneficiaries, but also potentially to premium payers and perhaps even eventually to taxpayers if the government is called upon to bail out the system. We need to stop the hole from getting bigger. Then, we need to make sure that the process is underway to fill the hole in a responsible and measured manner.

The current funding rules must be strengthened to ensure that accrued benefits are adequately funded. This is particularly important for those plans at the greatest risk of terminating. Various weaknesses in current law—funding holidays, so-called credit balances, unfunded benefit increases and weak liability measures—need to be fixed with a new set of rules that require sponsors falling below minimum funding levels to fund up. The rules should also be simpler and provide greater flexibility, especially for financially healthy plan sponsors. Overly prescriptive funding rules for companies that pose little or no risk of loss discourage those companies from maintaining their defined benefit plans. If we harbor any hope of keeping healthy companies in the defined benefit system we need to give them better incentives. We should allow higher tax-deductible contributions during good economic times and minimize precipitous funding increases during tough economic times.

Under existing rules, assets can be measured as multi-year averages rather than current values. Pension funding levels can only be set appropriately if both asset and liability measures are current and accurate. Failure to accurately measure assets and liabilities contributes to funding volatility. Properly structured funding rules can reduce volatility not by having the PBGC assume additional risk, but by providing better incentives for plan sponsors to adequately fund their pension promises.

We need to *rationalize PBGC's premium structure.* The objective is to implement a premium structure that meets the PBGC's long-term revenue needs and appropriately reflects the risks that it covers. Currently, PBGC's premium income is inadequate to cover projected claims, and the premium structure provides minimal incentives for plans to remain funded.

The heavy reliance of the premium structure on flat-rate charges leads to insurance that is underpriced for bad risks and that shifts wealth from healthy companies to unhealthy companies, as evidenced by the 70 percent of claims from the steel and airline industries. PBGC premiums can also play a useful role in encouraging sound plan funding and discouraging risky behavior. The premium structure should be reformed to provide sound incentives, to reflect the risks faced by the PBGC, including both potential claim incidence and claim severity, and to appropriately fund the federal insurance program.

We must *require more timely, meaningful information on pension plans' funding levels.* Too often in recent years, participants in defined benefit pension plans have mistakenly believed that their plans were well funded, only to receive a rude shock when the plan is terminated and benefits are lost. Investors are also put at risk when the true impact of a company's pension plan on its capital structure and future earnings is hidden from view. Simply put, workers, retirees, investors, and regulators need better and more timely information regarding the financial condition of pension plans.

I also believe that *the PBGC needs better tools* to carry out its statutory responsibilities in an effective way. While the PBGC is charged with administering the pension insurance program, recent events have demonstrated that the agency's ability to protect the interests of beneficiaries and premium payers is extremely limited. This is especially true when a plan sponsor enters bankruptcy. Currently, the agency has few tools at its disposal other than to move to terminate a plan. The PBGC should be given limited new authority to specifically respond to actions that pose a substantial risk of loss to the beneficiaries or the pension insurance fund, particularly in the bankruptcy context.

These are clearly complex issues and inevitably require policy trade-offs and a balancing of competing considerations. We look forward to working with Congress to resolve these issues and implement comprehensive reforms consistent with this framework that will put the pension insurance program on solid footing and strengthen the defined benefit system as a whole. The Administration's goal is not only to halt the exodus from the defined benefit system, but once again to make some form of defined benefit plan an economically and regulatory viable option for employers to offer to their employees.

I recognize that the legislative session is waning and that there is not sufficient time to give appropriate consideration to a comprehensive reform package. Moreover, comprehensive reforms, even if enacted, will need time in order to have a beneficial effect on systemic pension underfunding. However, I would encourage Congress to consider as timely a response as possible to some of the developments we have witnessed in the past few weeks. I am particularly concerned with the temptation, and, indeed, growing tendency, to use the pension insurance fund as a means to obtain an interest-free and risk-free loan to enable companies to restructure. Unfortunately, the current calculation appears to be that shifting pension liabilities onto other premium payers or potentially taxpayers is the path of least resistance rather than a last resort.

The PBGC will do all it can to protect the interests of workers and retirees, to ensure compliance with the statutory and regulatory requirements, and to discourage irresponsible behavior. However, we have relatively few arrows in the quiver, and they are not particularly sharp. The decision by United Airlines and US Airways not to make any further payments to their pension plans while in bankruptcy—and to do so without consequence, notwithstanding the fact that such payments are required by federal law—highlights the problem. In the ordinary course, if a company misses a required pension payment, a lien arises and the PBGC is able to perfect and enforce the lien on behalf of the pension plan. However, under the bankruptcy code, perfection of a lien is automatically stayed. Providing for an exception to the automatic stay would better enable the PBGC to protect the interests of the workers and retirees that it insures and make it clear that we place a high priority on meeting pension promises made to workers and retirees. Moreover, with such a change, we could expect creditors to encourage better plan funding to counteract PBGC's strengthened claim in bankruptcy.

Another needed change in the law is to provide plan participants better and more timely information regarding the funded status of their pension plan and the amount of their promised pension benefit they risk losing should the plan terminate. Participants are often the last to know what is at stake when a company enters bankruptcy. In the United Airlines situation, workers should have known much earlier that they stand to lose nearly $2 billion in benefits if the company's plans are terminated. Congress could require companies that enter bankruptcy to promptly inform their participants of the funded status of pension plans on a termination basis and of the amount of benefits that may be lost due to legal limits on PBGC's guarantees.

Conclusion

Mr. Chairman, the defined benefit system and the federal insurance program that stands behind it are being tested more severely than at any time since the enactment of ERISA 30 years ago. At stake is the viability of one of the principal means of providing stable retirement income to millions of American workers. The challenges are multi-faceted, defy easy answers, and demand a careful balancing of competing interests to achieve workable solutions.

I am confident that such solutions are achievable, and we look forward to working with Congress to find them as expeditiously as possible. Thank you for the opportunity to appear here today, and I would be pleased to answer any questions you may have.

Source: U.S. Pension Benefit Guaranty Corporation. "Testimony of Bradley D. Belt, Executive Director, Pension Benefit Guaranty Corporation." Prepared testimony of Bradley D. Belt for a hearing by the Senate Committee on Commerce, Science, and Transportation. October 7, 2004. www.pbgc.gov/news/speeches/testimony_100704.htm (accessed April 19, 2005).

FDA Advisory on Children's Use of Antidepressants and Suicide

October 15, 2004

INTRODUCTION

The federal Food and Drug Administration (FDA) on October 15, 2004, ordered the makers of all antidepressant drugs to label their products with warnings that the drugs could increase the risk of suicide in children and adolescents. Stopping short of banning the medications altogether, the so-called black-box warning was the most serious caution the FDA could impose on a drug. The agency also said that all children and adolescents being treated with antidepressants should be closely monitored for signs of worsening depression; such monitoring was particularly important, the agency said, when the patient first started taking the drug and whenever the drug dose was increased or decreased. The FDA also cautioned doctors and patients not to stop taking antidepressants abruptly. Although the studies were associated with a newer generation of antidepressants, such as Prozac, Zoloft, and Paxil, the FDA warning applied to all thirty-two antidepressant drugs on the market.

The announcement followed years of controversy over whether the drugs used to treat depression were themselves causing some youngsters to take their lives, and, if so, whether the risks of taking the drugs outweighed the benefits to be gained. The warning was seen as a major reversal in thinking for the agency, which had previously considered as inconclusive a body of studies showing that the drugs contributed to suicidal tendencies in teens and children. Most of these studies, largely conducted by the drug makers, had also failed to show that the drugs were effective in treating pediatric depression. The FDA action was likely to force members of the medical community to reexamine their belief that the benefits of antidepressants for pediatric patients far outweighed their risks.

Families of children who had committed suicide while taking the drugs had actively lobbied the FDA to issue the warning, saying that too many doctors and patients were unaware of the risks the drugs posed to pediatric patients. They were generally pleased with the decision, although some said the agency had been too slow to act and others said the warnings did not go far enough. In contrast, some physicians were concerned that the agency had gone too far. The American Psychiatric Association, for example, issued a statement reiterating its "deep concern that a black-box warning on antidepressants may have a chilling effect on appropriate prescribing for patients." Such an effect, the statement continued, "would put seriously ill patients at grave risk."

The FDA's handling of the issue was as controversial as its decision. Revelations that the agency had barred one of its own experts from presenting his findings to an advisory panel led to allegations that the agency was hiding negative data about the risk of suicide to protect the drug companies. After two congressional committees launched investigations into the allegations, the FDA made much of its data available and the drug companies began to release their scientific studies showing both negative and positive results. Both the agency and some of the drug companies acknowledged that the controversy over revealing the data had hurt their credibility with doctors and their patients.

The FDA also came under public and congressional fire late in the year when the drug manufacturer Merck decided to withdraw its popular arthritis drug Vioxx from the market because it had been shown to increase cardiovascular risk. Merck's move came after an FDA scientist challenged what he described as the FDA's reluctance to examine the safety of drugs it had already approved for market. Congress was also looking into production problems at Chiron Corp. that led to a shortage of influenza vaccine for the 2004–2005 winter season. *(Flu vaccine, p. 639; Vioxx controversy, p. 850)*

Early Concerns

Antidepressants were the second most heavily prescribed class of drugs in the United States (after pain-killing drugs containing codeine). At any one time, an estimated 1 million children were taking antidepressants. In 2002 more than 11 million pediatric prescriptions were written for antidepressants. Several studies suggested that the number of prescriptions written for children was increasing and that the medications were increasingly being prescribed for younger children. According to a study conducted by Express Scripts, a pharmacy benefit management company, the use of antidepressant drugs in children increased about 10 percent a year between 1998 and 2002. The study also found that although less than one-quarter of 1 percent of children age five and under used antidepressants, the percentage for girls in that age group doubled during the four years, while the percentage for boys rose 64 percent. Drug companies rang up $13 billion in sales of antidepressants in 2003.

Both the effectiveness of the drugs and their safety in children had been questioned since Prozac, the first of a new generation of antidepressants known as selective serotonin reuptake inhibitors (SSRIs), came on the market in 1988. Prozac was the only one of the new SSRIs that clinical trials showed to be effective in treating depression in children and was the only drug the FDA had specifically approved for that purpose. Physicians, however, could prescribe any drug legally on the market for any use not specifically disapproved, and many prescribed other antidepressants, even though several clinical trials showed that they were no more effective than sugar pills for depression in children.

The first indications that the drugs might be linked to an increased risk of suicide and other aberrant behavior in children were reported to the FDA in 1990 and 1991, but after a hearing, the FDA concluded that there was no evidence that the drugs themselves caused the suicides. The agency asked for, but did not require, more data from the drug companies. The issue simmered throughout the 1990s, as sporadic reports of teen suicides, mania, and self-mutilation attributed to the drugs became public. Critics also accused the drug companies of deliberately hiding clinical evidence showing that their antidepressants were ineffective in children and possibly contributed to suicidal tendencies.

Meanwhile, child psychiatrists, other physicians, and parents of depressed children lauded the success of the drugs in treating depressed children. These supporters frequently noted that the suicide rate among teenagers had begun to decline in the 1990s, a decline they attributed to the widespread availability of the antidepressants.

Suicide, which claimed an estimated 3,000–4,000 young lives a year, was the third leading cause of death in teens ages fifteen to nineteen. John Mann, a suicide expert at Columbia University, estimated that fewer than 20 percent of the adolescents who committed suicide were taking or had ever taken antidepressants. "It would be ludicrous to think that antidepressants could actually contribute to suicide in the United States in any kind of significant way," Mann told a reporter for the *New York Times. (Suicide prevention, Historic documents of 2001, p. 290)*

New concerns about the safety of the drugs arose in 2003, however, when GlaxoSmithKline, the British maker of Paxil, gave British and American health authorities results of three trials of its antidepressant in teens and children. The results showed that children taking Paxil appeared have an elevated risk for suicidal thoughts. In June 2003 British regulators warned doctors against prescribing Paxil to children. The FDA issued a similar warning on Paxil on June 19 and asked the makers of eight other antidepressants to submit data on the safety of their drugs.

In August 2003 Wyeth, the maker of another popular antidepressant, Effexor, warned that Effexor also appeared to increase the risk of suicide in children and asked doctors to avoid prescribing the drug to youngsters. Two months later the FDA warned all physicians to use caution in prescribing any SSRIs for children and scheduled an advisory panel meeting for early February 2004 to discuss the issue. In December British regulators added another five SSRIs to the list of prescriptions not to be used for children. The British regulators said the only antidepressant whose benefits outweighed its risk of side effects was Prozac. *(FDA, British warnings, Historic Documents of 2003, p. 507)*

Caution Issued by the FDA

On March 22, 2004, the FDA issued a public health advisory cautioning doctors, patients, and caregivers to closely monitor adults and children being treated for depression with any one of ten antidepressants. The agency also said that it was asking drug makers to include warnings on drug labels cautioning doctors to monitor patients "for the worsening of depression and the emergence of suicidal ideation, regardless of the cause of such worsening." The ten drugs were Prozac (fluoxetine), Zoloft (sertraline), Paxil (paroxetine), Luvox (fluvoxamine), Celexa (citalopram), Lexapro (escitalopram), Effexor (venlafexine), Wellbutrin (buproprion), Serzone (nefazodone), and Remeron (mirtazapine).

The agency said it was acting on the recommendation of its advisory panel, which at its February meetings heard testimony from dozens of parents and others who said the drugs caused suicides, suicide attempts, and other violent behavior among children being treated with the drugs. The FDA agency said its review of several drug studies had not been completed and stressed that it was still not clear whether the antidepressants themselves caused any additional risk of suicide among children. Nonetheless, the agency decided the new caution was "good advice whether the drugs did it or not," said Robert Temple, associate director of medical policy at the FDA. "If someone commits suicide, it doesn't really matter whether it's the drug or the underlying disease [that caused the suicide]. In either case, you need to pay attention."

A few days later, national news agencies reported that a leading scientist at the FDA had reviewed the available evidence linking antidepressants to suicide and concluded that children who took the drugs were about twice as likely to entertain serious thoughts of suicide as children who were taking a placebo. Furthermore, the report said, FDA officials had barred the expert, Andrew Mosholder, from presenting those conclusions to the advisory committee at its February meeting.

Mosholder's superiors said they withheld the report because they were not convinced of the reliability of the underlying evidence, which consisted of two dozen clinical trials conducted by the drug companies. In particular the FDA officials expressed concerns about whether the behaviors described as suicidal in the reports were accurate and consistent from report to report. The FDA, Temple said, did not want to discourage use of the medications "when we weren't sure that was the right thing to do." Temple also said the agency was awaiting the results of a study it had commissioned from Columbia University researchers who were applying consistent definitions of suicidal behavior to the behaviors reported in the twenty-four drug company studies.

FDA's squelching of the Mosholder report drew fire from several quarters, including legislators on Capitol Hill. "You don't just ask someone to clam up," said Charles E. Grassley, R-Iowa, chairman of the Senate Finance Committee, which began an investigation of the incident in late March. "If there's any doubt, they ought to put out the caution to the public at large, not try to muzzle it."

In early August news agencies reported that the Columbia researchers had reached substantially the same conclusions as Mosholder about the increased risks of suicide posed by the antidepressants. The FDA said it was still reviewing the findings and did not plan to discuss the data until a scheduled advisory committee meeting scheduled for mid-September. Grassley, among others, was clearly exasperated. "It's been almost nine months since British regulators issued new recommendations, and it's been six months since Dr. Mosholder made his determinations. Now, given this new information, it's fair to ask if the Food and Drug administration is taking too much time to draw a conclusion," he said in a statement issued August 9.

Strong Warning Adopted

Meeting just a few days later, the FDA advisory committee voted, 15–8, to recommend that a strong warning be issued linking antidepressants to an increased risk of suicide in children. One month later, on October 15, the FDA announced that it was following the recommendations of its advisory panel and ordering drug makers to warn doctors and patients that antidepressants could cause suicidal thoughts and behavior in some youngsters.

The so-called black-box warning, the strongest caution the FDA could require, was to be written in boldface type, enclosed in a black box, and placed at the top of the information sheet that physicians were to review when prescribing a drug. The warnings would also appear in advertisements for the drugs. The warnings also had to say that the drugs (except Prozac) had not been approved for treating pediatric depression because clinical trials had not shown them to be effective.

The FDA was also requiring drug manufacturers to attach a patient medication guide to the drug packaging describing the risks of suicide in plain English. Although hundreds of prescription drugs carried black-box warnings, fewer than thirty were required to have patient guides. The FDA said the warnings would be required not just for the ten newer generation antidepressants but for all thirty-two antidepressants currently on the market.

"Today's actions represent FDA's conclusions about the increased risk of suicidal thoughts and the necessary actions for physicians prescribing these antidepressant drugs and for the children and adolescents taking them," Lester M. Crawford, acting commissioner of the FDA, said in a statement. "Our conclusions are based on the latest and best science. They reflect what we heard from our advisory committee last month, as well as what many members of the public have told us."

Included in the science was FDA's analysis of the Columbia University research, which confirmed Mosholder's earlier conclusions. According to the FDA, studies from twenty-four trials, involving more than 4,400 patients, showed that during the first few months of treatment twice as many children taking the antidepressants were likely to think about committing suicide as children taking a placebo. About 4 percent of the children taking the drugs showed suicidal tendencies, compared with about 2 percent of those children taking a placebo. (No suicides occurred during the trials.)

Although virtually all parties to the debate agreed that the number of children being treated with antidepressants was likely to drop as a result of the warnings, early indications were not clear. One large drug-benefit provider reported that antidepressant prescriptions for children had dropped by about 20 percent in 2004, as concerns about the drugs' safety mounted. According to the FDA, however, antidepressant prescriptions for children had increased 8 percent in the first six months of 2004.

New Adult Studies

In September the FDA said it would examine clinical data to determine if antidepressants might be linked to suicide in adults. Earlier studies had not found such a link, but the FDA said it would reevaluate 234 clinical tests involving about 40,000 adults using the new techniques for identifying suicidal thoughts and actions developed by the Columbia University researchers to study the effects of antidepressants on children.

On December 7 British health officials advised doctors against immediately prescribing antidepressants for adults who showed signs of mild depression—estimated to be about 70 percent of all adults who complained of depression. The officials said those patients should first try alternative treatments, such as talk therapy or exercise, to avoid the possibility of adverse side effects and withdrawal symptoms associated with the antidepressants. "We are not saying 'Don't use drugs.' We are saying 'Use them appropriately,'" said Stephen Pilling, the scientist who directed the development of the new guidelines.

Following is the text of "FDA Public Health Advisory: Suicidality in Children and Adolescents Being Treated with Antidepressant Medications" a report issued October 15, 2004, by the federal Food and Drug Administration, directing drug makers to put warnings on the labels of their antidepressants to alert doctors that the drugs could increase the risk of suicide in children eighteen and under.

"Suicidality in Children Being Treated with Antidepressants"

Today the Food and Drug Administration (FDA) directed manufacturers of all antidepressant drugs to revise the labeling for their products to include a boxed warning and expanded warning statements that alert health care providers to an increased risk of suicidality (suicidal thinking and behavior) in children and adolescents being treated with these agents, and to include additional information about the results of pediatric studies. FDA also informed these manufacturers that it has determined that a Patient Medication Guide (MedGuide), which will be given to patients receiving the drugs to advise them of the risk and precautions that can be taken, is appropriate for these drug products. These labeling changes are consistent with the recommendations made to the Agency at a joint meeting of the Psychopharmacologic Drugs Advisory Committee and the Pediatric Drugs Advisory Committee on September 13–14, 2004.

The drugs that are the focus of this new labeling language are all drugs included in the general class of antidepressants; they are listed at the end of this Advisory.

The risk of suicidality for these drugs was identified in a combined analysis of short-term (up to 4 months) placebo-controlled trials of nine antidepressant drugs, including the selective serotonin reuptake inhibitors (SSRIs) and others, in children and adolescents with major depressive disorder (MDD), obsessive compulsive disorder (OCD), or other psychiatric disorders. A total of 24 trials involving over 4400 patients were included. The analysis showed a greater risk of suicidality during the first few months of treatment in those receiving antidepressants. The average risk of such events on drug was 4%, twice the placebo risk of 2%. No suicides occurred in these trials. Based on these data, FDA has determined that the following points are appropriate for inclusion in the boxed warning:

- Antidepressants increase the risk of suicidal thinking and behavior (suicidality) in children and adolescents with MDD and other psychiatric disorders.
- Anyone considering the use of an antidepressant in a child or adolescent for any clinical use must balance the risk of increased suicidality with the clinical need.
- Patients who are started on therapy should be observed closely for clinical worsening, suicidality, or unusual changes in behavior.
- Families and caregivers should be advised to closely observe the patient and to communicate with the prescriber.
- A statement regarding whether the particular drug is approved for any pediatric indication(s) and, if so, which one(s).

Among the antidepressants, only Prozac is approved for use in treating MDD in pediatric patients. Prozac, Zoloft, Luvox, and Anafranil are approved for OCD in pediatric patients. None of the drugs is approved for other psychiatric indications in children.

Pediatric patients being treated with antidepressants for any indication should be closely observed for clinical worsening, as well as agitation, irritability, suicidality, and unusual changes in behavior, especially during the initial few months of a course of drug therapy, or at times of dose changes, either increases or decreases. This monitoring should include daily observation by families and caregivers and frequent contact with the physician. It is also recommended that prescriptions for antidepressants be written for the smallest quantity of tablets consistent with good patient management, in order to reduce the risk of overdose.

In addition to the boxed warning and other information in professional labeling on antidepressants, MedGuides are being prepared for all of the antidepressants to provide information about the risk of suicidality in children and adolescents directly to patients and their families and caregivers. MedGuides are intended to be distributed by the pharmacist with each prescription or refill of a medication.

FDA plans to work closely with the manufacturers of all approved antidepressant products that are the subject of today's letters to optimize the safe use of these drugs and implement the proposed labeling changes and other safety communications in a timely manner. The labeling changes at issue will be posted on FDA's website *http://www.fda.gov/cder/drug/antidepressants/default.htm.*

- Anafranil (clomipramine HCl)
- Aventyl (nortriptyline HCl)
- Celexa (citalopram HBr)
- Cymbalta (duloxetine HCl)
- Desyrel (trazodone HCl)
- Effexor (venlafaxine HCl)
- Elavil (amitriptyline HCl)
- Lexapro (escitalopram oxalate)
- Limbitrol (chlordiazepoxide/amitriptyline)
- Ludiomil (Maprotiline HCl)
- Luvox (fluvoxamine maleate)
- Marplan (isocarboxazid)
- Nardil (phenelzine sulfate)
- Norpramin (desipramine HCl)
- Pamelor (nortriptyline HCl)
- Parnate (tranylcypromine sulfate)
- Paxil (paroxetine HCl)
- Pexeva (paroxetine mesylate)
- Prozac (fluoxetine HCl)
- Remeron (mirtazapine)
- Sarafem (fluoxetine HCl)
- Serzone (nefazodone HCl)
- Sinequan (doxepin HCl)
- Surmontil (trimipramine)
- Symbyax (olanzapine/fluoxetine)
- Tofranil (imipramine HCl)
- Tofranil-PM (imipramine pamoate)
- Triavil (Perphenaine/Amitriptyline)
- Vivactil (protriptyline HCl)
- Wellbutrin (bupropion HCl)
- Zoloft (sertraline HCl)
- Zyban (bupropion HCl)

Source: U.S. Department of Health and Human Services. Food and Drug Administration. Center for Drug Evaluation and Research. "FDA Public Health Advisory: Suicidality in Children and Adolescents Being Treated with Antidepressant Medications." October 15, 2004. www.fda.gov/cder/drug/antidepressants/SSRIPHA200410.htm (accessed February 9, 2005).

Yudhoyono on His Inauguration as President of Indonesia

October 20, 2004

INTRODUCTION

A charismatic former general won Indonesia's first-ever direct election for president, ushering in a new era in the country's troubled transition from decades of authoritarianism to democracy. Susilo Bambang Yudhoyono (known by his initials, SBY), convincingly defeated incumbent president Megawati Sukarnoputri in a runoff election held September 20, 2004. Yudhoyono took office October 20, pledging to fight corruption, terrorism, and other problems in the country of about 230 million people.

Yudhoyono's first major crisis came from an unexpected source: the ocean. A giant earthquake off the coast of Sumatra on December 26 created tsunami waves that devastated much of coastal Aceh province, along with hundreds of miles of coastline in ten other Indian Ocean countries. As of year's end authorities were estimating that at least 100,000 Indonesians had been killed by the tsunami, and tens of thousands more were made homeless. The United Nations and other international agencies rushed tons of supplies to the affected countries, but they faced enormous challenges delivering the aid because of the lack of airports, roads, and other infrastructure. *(Tsunami, p. 991)*

Victory for a Dark Horse

For nearly fifty years after achieving independence from the Netherlands in 1949, Indonesia was governed by autocratic leaders with military backgrounds. The first was Sukarno, the hero of Indonesia's struggle for independence. Then, after a transition in 1966–1967, came General Suharto, who governed for three decades before being forced from office during a popular protest in 1998 stemming from economic depression. *(Suharto overthrow, Historic Documents of 1998, p. 284)*

Swinging from one extreme to another, Indonesia experienced three weak leaders after Suharto's ouster, the last of whom was Megawati, whose political career was based entirely upon her status as Sukarno's daughter. The Indonesian parliament, chosen in the country's first free legislative elections in 1999, named Megawati as president in July 2001 after dismissing the incumbent, Abdurrahman Wahid, on charges of corruption and incompetence. Megawati showed little interest in governing and left the development and execution of policies to cabinet officials. Parliament in 2002 adopted constitutional changes intended to strengthen democracy, including the direct election of the president and vice president.

As 2004 opened, it was widely assumed that the two strongest presidential candidates would be Megawati, who retained strong loyalty among Indonesia's impoverished majority despite her passivity, and retired General Wiranto, who had headed the country's armed forces until he was forced from office under international pressure in 2000. The United States and other countries blamed Wiranto for the military's complicity in the killing in 1999 of about 1,000 people in East Timor, a province Indonesia had seized in the mid-1970s. A United Nations war crimes panel in February 2003 charged Wiranto and six other military officials with crimes against humanity during the East Timor violence, but the Indonesian government refused to hand him over to UN authorities or to charge him with crimes under national law.

Yudhoyono, who was serving as Megawati's security minister, said early in the year that he would run for the presidency. Early handicapping by political observers put Yudhoyono in the dark horse category, however, in part because he represented a minor faction, the Democrat Party, that drew support in the single digits in opinion polls.

The year's first elections were held April 5, when Indonesians went to the polls for only the second time since Suharto's overthrow to select a parliament. The voting produced a major defeat for Megawati's Democratic Party for Struggle, which secured only 18.5 percent of the overall vote. The top-ranked party was Golkar, which Suharto had used to claim democratic legitimacy and which had served as his tool for dispensing political patronage. Golkar candidates won 21 percent of the vote. Yudhoyono's Democrat Party was far behind in the field, with only 7.5 percent of the vote. The results showed that whoever was elected president would have to bargain for parliamentary support of important legislation because there was no natural majority coalition.

The parliamentary elections set the stage for the first round of voting for the president, scheduled for July 5, involving five major candidates. As election day approached, Yudhoyono—the former dark horse—was running well ahead in opinion polls. Many Indonesians seemed to view him as a safe alternative to Megawati, who was too weak, and Wiranto, who appeared to be too strong and controversial a figure. Some polls suggested that Yudhoyono might even come close to winning the 50 percent majority that would enable him to avoid a second-round runoff.

Initial results from the election showed that Yudhoyono was first, with about one-third of the vote, but Megawati and Wiranto were locked in a tight race for the number two position, each with about one-fourth of the vote. Megawati eventually won the contest, edging out Wiranto for the right to face Yudhoyono in the September 20 runoff.

Under the law, official campaigning was limited to a three-day period in the week before the election, but in the interim both candidates and their supporters were active with public appearances. This was a change of pace for Megawati, who had appeared in public rarely and seemed uncomfortable when she did. Neither candidate devoted much time to discussing specific issues, such as the still-languishing economy or the challenge posed by separatist groups in several provinces. Instead, both candidates emphasized personality: Megawati as a moralistic mother figure above the fray of petty politics, and Yudhoyono as a strong leader unafraid to tackle the country's many problems. Yudhoyono even used some time during the campaign to complete his doctorate in economics, which he was working on at a local university.

A grim reminder that Indonesia was still subject to international terrorism came September 9, when a car bomb exploded outside the Australian embassy in Jakarta, killing 9 Indonesians and wounding more than 180 others. Authorities blamed the bombing on an extreme Islamist group, Jemaah Islamiyah, which had carried out major bombings of nightclubs on the island of Bali in 2002 and of a J.W. Marriott Hotel in Jakarta in 2003. Megawati, who had been attending a royal wedding in Brunei, rushed back to Jakarta, visited victims of the bombing at a hospital, and appealed to the public for calm. Yudhoyono also visited bombing victims, presenting voters with competing images of leaders demonstrating their concern for Indonesians caught in a conflict between terrorists and Western governments. Most political commentary suggested that Yudhoyono stood to benefit politically because he had pledged an aggressive fight against terrorism and had accused Megawati of failing to do so. *(Bali bombings, Historic Documents of 2002, p. 702)*

Opinion polls taken in the days before the election predicted a landslide victory for Yudhoyono, and that is what occurred. Of the 154 million Indonesians who went to the polls on September 20, 61 percent gave their votes to Yudhoyono; just 39 percent backed Megawati. Despite her overwhelming defeat, Megawati refused to concede in the days during which the votes were being tallied. She appeared before the parliament on September 23 and offered a "deepest apology" for what she called "unresolved matters" and "shortcomings," citing in particular unemployment and the country's lagging education system.

Reluctant to claim victory while Megawati refused to acknowledge her defeat, Yudhoyono waited until October 9, when Megawati indirectly conceded by failing to file a formal challenge against the results. In a belated victory speech, Yudhoyono pledged to be "a president for all Indonesians" and called on Megawati's supporters to join him in a unity government.

Yudhoyono took office October 20 and outlined an aggressive program, promising to confront institutional problems—notably corruption and nepotism—that had been at the heart of Indonesia's failure to achieve the prosperity and stability of other southeast Asian nations. He won plaudits for his appointment of a respected supreme court judge, Abdul Rahman Saleh, as attorney general, giving him responsibility in those key areas. Yudhoyono also said he would act against terrorism and would seek a peaceful settlement of separatist conflicts that had plagued the nation of 13,000 islands, most importantly in the province of Aceh on Sumatra and in Indonesia's half of the island of New Guinea, known as Papua.

Yudhoyono also appealed for patience. "I remind us all that these complex problems cannot possibly be resolved in only 100 days. It is not easy to turn over a new leaf," he said. "But I am sure that our good intentions and hopes are far stronger than the problems we face."

Still smarting from her defeat, Megawati refused to attend Yudhoyono's inauguration. Aides said she spent the day at home, working in her garden.

SBY's Governing Challenges

If Yudhoyono expected his landslide victory to translate into overwhelming support for his initial actions as president, he surely was disappointed. In terms of politics, Yudhoyono was stymied at the outset because he could count on automatic support in the 550-seat parliament from only 57 legislators from his Democrat Party. The parties that had been aligned with Suharto and Megawati controlled nearly half the seats in parliament, and they entered into a coalition of convenience to thwart Yudhoyono on several key initiatives.

Yudhoyono also stimulated opposition with some of his key cabinet appointments, most importantly that of his economics minister, Aburizal Bakrie, a former head of the country's chamber of commerce who had run unsuccessfully for the Golkar party nomination for president. One of Indonesia's wealthiest men, Bakrie had been a close associate of the Suharto regime and, critics said, had been a beneficiary of the type of corruption Yudhoyono was now asking him to combat.

Terrorism Issues

The bombing at the Australian embassy in Jakarta in September had served as a potent reminder for Indonesians that their country had become an important battleground in the war between Islamist terrorists and Western countries. About 80 percent of Indonesian citizens were Muslim, and the vast majority were secular conservatives who, from all appearances, wanted to have nothing to do with radicals who used bombs to advance their cause. Even so, Jemaah Islamiyah and similar terrorist organizations were able to use the Indonesian archipelago as a base for operations against Western targets in the region.

Much of the attention during 2004 centered on the government's attempt to pin responsibility for terrorism on an Islamist cleric, Abu Bakar Bashir, said by officials in Australia and the United States to be the spiritual leader of Jemaah Islamiyah. Bashir was acquitted of terrorism charges in 2003 after prosecutors failed to present a strong case against him, but under U.S. pressure the Indonesian government continued to hold him and in April charged him with intellectual responsibility for the bombings in Bali and of the Marriott hotel in Jakarta. The government put Bashir on trial on October 28, and the case was still under way at year's end. The prosecution suffered a major setback on December 9, when Islamist militants who had been convicted in previous cases testified that they had not witnessed Bashir inciting terrorism.

East Timor Prosecutions

Indonesia's courts during 2004 continued the process of absolving government and military officials of responsibility for the killings of about 1,000 people in East Timor in 1999, during the territory's transition to independence. East Timor's then-governor Abillo Soares, the only senior official who had been found guilty of crimes for instigating a wave of violence against proindependence forces, was acquitted on appeal on November 5. The supreme court ruled that Soares, a civilian, had no control over the military, which was in effective control of East Timor when rioting broke out in response to a referendum vote favoring independence. *(Background, Historic Documents of 1999, p. 511)*

Sixteen military and police officials who had been charged with crimes, including the top officers in East Timor at the time, also had been acquitted. Other officials named in various reports by human rights organizations as having participated in the killings never were indicted. Indonesian courts had convicted only one other person: Eurico Guterres, the leader of a pro-Indonesian militia that had carried out much of the killing. As of the end of 2004, Guterres was free pending an appeal.

The story was different in East Timor itself, where the UN had responsibility for a court, the Serious Crimes Unit, which also was prosecuting individuals for the 1999 violence. As of 2004 that court had indicted nearly 400 people, ranging from General Wiranto down to militia fighters who had carried out much of the killing. The tribunal issued a warrant for Wiranto's arrest on May 10, but the Indonesian government refused to hand him over. The tribunal had convicted about fifty people, nearly all of them local militiamen.

The governments of East Timor and Indonesia on December 22 agreed to form a joint "truth and friendship" commission to investigate the 1999 killings and other human rights abuses committed during Indonesia's occupation of the territory. Jakarta portrayed the commission as an alternative to a "panel of experts" that UN Secretary

General Kofi Annan had been planning to appoint to review the prosecution of those responsible for the abuses. The Indonesian government wanted to avoid such a probe, and it apparently prevailed on the East Timorese government to agree to an alternative outside the UN's direct control. Annan had not announced a decision, by year's end, on whether he would go ahead with his original plan for the expert panel.

Following are excerpts from the English translation of the inaugural address, delivered October 20, 2004, by Susilo Bambang Yudhoyono, the new president of Indonesia.

"Indonesian President's Inaugural Speech"

. . . To the people of this nation, our homeland, let us give great thanks to Allah the Almighty.

After this long electoral process, today before the MPR [People's Consultative Assembly], Jusuf Kalla and I took our oaths as vice president and president of the Republic of Indonesia for our term, 2004–2009.

Our appointment today confirmed the emergence of a new government that received a mandate directly from the people. We wish to express our thanks for this great honour to all the people of Indonesia and for their participation and support and belief. Let me, personally and in the name of Jusuf Kalla and the nation, express the greatest thanks to Megawati Sukarnoputri and Hamzah Haz who served as president and vice president throughout 2001–2004, who guarded the constitution, led the government and led the nation and state well.

Their service and effort, to the nation and state, will and have been noted in history for all time. I will always safeguard these familial relations with Megawati Sukarnoputri and Hamzah Haz who I respect as great figures of this nation.

We must all hold in high esteem the statement made by (founding president) Sukarno, who said: "United we stand, divided we fall."

To all Indonesian people, today we have passed a very important historical test. First we have succeeded in holding democratic, honourable, orderly and peaceful elections. Our elections this year are the most ambitious and complex in the world. But we have succeeded in conducting them well. We are proud that our election commission was able to carry them out independently, professionally and responsibly.

Second, as we have seen today, in the ceremony at the MPR, we have taken the process to the next stage in the transfer of power constitutionally, democratically, orderly and peacefully. God willing, our nation will continue to grow in its democracy, and be able to develop its political culture with increasing maturity.

With this success, we have not only taken an important step as a great democratic nation but have also succeeded in setting an example to the global democratic community.

Our nation has conducted two elections during the reformasi [reformation] period, first in 1999 and then in 2004. In any nation holding its second democratic election, that election is usually viewed as critical, as a measure of the maturity of its democracy.

With this election we have taken an important step in advancing political modernization in Indonesia. With the success our legislative election this year we have also taken an important step in the regeneration of Indonesian politics, which we can clearly see in the appearance of fresh faces in the people's representative institutions, which we respect.

Ladies and gentlemen, God willing, the 2004 election process has come to an end and now is the time for us to advance together to meet the future.

We have passed the time of competition and now is the time to unite. The time of campaign statements and promises is now over and now is the time to take action and work. Now is the time to unite to create and work together. Now is the time for us all to rally our intentions, spirit, thoughts and awareness to confront the various challenges and problems that we face.

These challenges and problems faced by the people, the nation and the state, we must overcome in togetherness. Because indeed the government I will lead cannot overcome these challenges and problems without the support and participation of all elements of the nation.

As we all know, for the founders of this Republic, the greatest challenge was to free the people from the shackles of colonialism. For future generations, including our generation, the greatest challenge is to free the people from poverty, ignorance and backwardness and all the shackles inhibiting the development of our people. Specifically, the greatest challenge of our age is to strengthen democratization and take a clear stance on continuing reformasi.

The consolidation of democracy as it proceeds will provide a firm basis for the life of the state and nation in future. In the framework of our life together that will grow democratically, the agenda of statesmanship and the nation we can carry out well, including the resolution of various agendas of reformasi. With our perseverance, firm belief and hard work together, God willing, the nation and state will develop and the life of the people will be increasingly prosperous with the support of a more secure and just life.

In this way, I am sure our nation will be esteemed and respected by other the nations of the world.

Ladies and gentlemen of our homeland, the joyful atmosphere of today is infused with a feeling of great optimism. However, we must remember that we will pass through a difficult time and will face heavy challenges. Economic growth this year, which is still well below 7 per cent, is not enough to provide sufficient work. More than 10 million people are without work and 15 per cent of the population still lives below the poverty line. Although there has been a tendency for the debt to fall in relation to our GDP, the debt problem is a very heavy yoke that ensnares our economy.

Our kin in Aceh and Papua remain restless. The security situation in Poso and Maluku has been brought under control but has not fully returned to normal. KKN [corruption, collusion and nepotism] is still a systematic problem. The international situation remains uncertain. The price of oil has already swelled far beyond the assumptions of our state budget. And the threat of terrorism and transnational crime still haunts us.

Let us work hard to meet all these heavy challenges.

Tomorrow morning, on October 21, 2004, God willing, I will appoint cabinet members to serve their terms for 2004-2009. After this, we will roll up our sleeves to formulate and carry out the initial phases of our policies and action plans.

In the next few months, we will focus attention on domestic problems. The government will stimulate the economy in order to achieve higher growth, create employment and help to relieve poverty. The government will continue to carry out economic policies that are open, in the framework of integrating with regional and international economies. In order to do this, the government will continue to improve productivity and its competitive strengthens.

The government will encourage investment for the development of infrastructure. The government will actively speed up the eradication of corruption, which I will lead directly. The government will pay special attention to the handling of the conflicts in Aceh and Papua. The government will prioritize and make policy in the education and health sectors. The government will undertake intensive and constructive dialogue with business interests—in particular with the private sector and investors, who I hope will be the driving force of our economy.

The government will pay special attention to regional autonomy and decentralization to guarantee better government services without giving rise to a high-cost economy. And the government will work hard to form a government that is clean, good and responsive to the needs and aspirations of the people.

However, I remind us all that these complex problems cannot possibly be resolved in only 100 days. It is not easy to turn over a new leaf. But I am sure that our good intentions and hopes are far stronger than the problems we face.

It is here that our character and integrity as a great nation is being tested. For a great nation, the heavier the challenges it faces, the higher its integrity. The greater the tests it undergoes, the greater its faith and conviction. The greater the storm weathered, the greater the feeling of togetherness. And the greater the challenges to its nationhood, the greater the unity.

Let us prove and develop our greatness as a nation. God willing, with our unity and hard work, we will be able to realize better conditions in Indonesia; more secure, more just and prosperous.

Ladies and gentlemen of the nation wherever you are, with full hearts and full conviction today we turn over a new page in the history of Indonesia. Now is the time to greet the dawn.

To the people of Indonesia wherever you are, I say thank you for your support and faith given to Jusuf Kalla and myself. Although I am now the president, I am no different to you all. I am a normal citizen who was born, grew and was raised by the country and its people. With this mandate that I received directly, I intend not only to be the president of the Republic of Indonesia but also to be the president of the people of Indonesia, all the people of Indonesia. I will guard this noble political contract with the people. My thoughts, energy and time I will dedicate to advancing and protecting all Indonesia's agencies.

To the House of Representatives and Regional Representatives Council, I and Vice-President Jusuf Kalla vow to work together with you for the national interest and all the people of Indonesia in line with the mandate of the constitution and laws of Indonesia, which we all hold in high esteem. I therefore hope that we can work together to overcome the many problems we face. This clearly demands that we all stand together to create jobs, overcome poverty, re-develop our infrastructure and many more.

The people need leadership and an example to follow. To all government workers, and especially to those in the regions and centre, as well as the police, military and state-owned enterprise workers, I invite us to all greet the new government with renewed spirit, with increasing service and, with all the people of Indonesia, to create a better future. Many of the most important things in our life together are in your hands. Let us carry out our duties and obligations with full responsibility.

We are all servants of the nation. The government and civil servants indeed have the task of serving the people and the nation. Guard this spirit of service. Any nation in this world can only become great if it is supported by a government that is clean, professional and sensitive to the aspirations and the changes of society.

To Indonesia's friends in the international world, I say take the hand extended in friendship. The government that I will lead will stand firm by its "free and active" foreign policy. On the international stage Indonesia will become the voice of conscience to advance peace, increase prosperity and defend justice. Indonesia will continue to grow as a democratic nation that is modern, open, professional, pluralistic and tolerant.

In particular, I would like to express my thanks to the state visitors from friendly countries who conveyed such great respect this morning in the ceremony at the MPR. We value the attendance of the Malaysian prime minister, His Majesty the Sultan of Brunei Darussalam, the Singapore foreign minister, the prime minister of Australia and the prime minister of Timor Leste [East Timor].

I also say thank you to the leaders of friendly countries who sent special emissaries from the Netherlands, the Philippines, Japan, South Korea and Vietnam. In the name of the people of Indonesia and myself, I feel very happy and respected by your noble attention to the new government I lead.

After our appointment this morning, Jusuf Kalla and I will focus our attention on forming the cabinet, which I will, God willing, announce tonight. I will appoint them immediately in full hope that they will adapt and begin their good work.

I guarantee that we will all work hard to defend the mandate of the people. For this I ask for the support, blessing and faith of all the people and the nation to carry out this mandate over the next five years. I hope that Allah the Almighty will give us the strength and guidance to carry out our duties.

Thank you.

Source: British Broadcasting Corporation. BBC Monitoring. "Text of Indonesian President's Inaugural Speech." October 20, 2004. Laksamana.net web site, Jakarta, in English 20 Oct 04 /BBC Monitoring/ BBC.BBC Monitoring/ © BBC.

FBI Report on Crime in the United States

October 25, 2004

INTRODUCTION

Crime in the United States appeared to stabilize in 2003 at its lowest level in thirty years. According to the annual report on crime statistics produced by the Federal Bureau of Investigation, the volume of violent crime in 2003 fell 3 percent from 2002, while property crime declined slightly, by 0.2 percent. A national survey of victims of crime, conducted annually by the Justice Department's Bureau of Justice Statistics, reported different numbers but similar trends.

Overall, according to FBI statistics, murder was the only violent crime to increase in 2003; it rose 1.7 percent, to 16,503. Some criminologists found that increase troubling. "We've seen a disturbing growth in youth killings and gang killings in many cities," James Alan Fox, a professor of criminal justice at Northeastern University, told the *New York Times.* "The homicide numbers should give us reason to pay more attention to street crime than we have." Law enforcement officials in rural communities in the Midwest and West were also reporting increased crime from growing use of methamphetamine, a stimulant that caused violent behavior in some users. A key ingredient of "meth" was anhydrous ammonia, an inexpensive and plentiful agricultural fertilizer.

After peaking in the late 1980s, crime rates fell every year between 1993 and 2000 and had remained relatively stable ever since. Criminologists offered many reasons for the decline, including the end of a crack cocaine epidemic that flourished in many locales in the late 1980s, stronger and smarter policing, and tougher prison sentences that kept even petty criminals off the street for longer periods of time. The strong economy of the mid- and late 1990s, as well as a decline in the number of teenagers and young adults—the age groups most commonly involved in criminal activity—were also cited as reasons.

For several years some criminologists had been predicting a rise in the crime rates, resulting from the faltering economy and a gloomy employment picture, budget constraints that reduced the number of police officers, the diversion of some normal policing activities to counterterrorism efforts, and a large cohort of adolescents moving into their teens.

That crime had not picked up in 2000–2001 was somewhat of a mystery to experts. At least one thought the increased focus on counterterrorism might be a primary explanation. "You're after terrorists, but you're picking up other things," James Lynch, a professor at the Department of Justice, Law, and Society at American University, told the Associated Press. "That's the only thing I can think of because the economy certainly isn't robust."

FBI Report

In its annual report on crime statistics, issued October 25, the Federal Bureau of Investigation said there had been nearly 1.4 million violent crimes committed in 2003; this tally was down 3 percent from 2002 and 25.6 percent from 1994. The FBI defined violent crimes as murder and nonnegligent manslaughter, forcible rape, robbery, and aggravated assault. About 10.4 million property crimes were committed in 2003, down 14 percent from 1994. Property crimes were defined as burglary, larceny-theft, and motor vehicle theft. The FBI estimated that there were 475.0 violent crimes and 3,588.4 property crimes for every 100,000 inhabitants. *(Crime statistics for 2002, Historic Documents of 2003, p. 979)*

As in the past, the South experienced the most crime. It had 35.9 percent of the nation's population, but 41.6 percent of all violent crime and 41.2 percent of all property crime. The Northeast was the least crime-ridden region. With 18.7 percent of the population, it had 15.8 percent of the violent crime and just 12.6 percent of all property crime. The Midwest experienced the greatest drop in crime; the volume dropped 5.2 percent from 2002, with aggravated assaults and robbery both falling by nearly 6 percent. The Midwest was the only region where the number of murders declined from 2002. Murder was up slightly in the South and the West and up by 4.6 percent in the Northeast.

Although the numbers of violent and property crimes remained relatively stable overall, they shifted somewhat by size of city. For example, while murders declined somewhat or remained stable in medium-size and big cities, they increased by 20 percent in the nation's smallest cities (those under 10,000 in population). Property crimes increased 1.2 percent in those small cities, while dropping 1.2 percent in the nation's largest cities.

Of those arrested for committing violent crimes, 44.3 percent were under age twenty-five, 82.2 percent were male, and 60.5 percent were white. Of those arrested for committing property crimes, 40.1 percent were between the ages of eighteen and twenty-four, 69.2 percent were male, and 68.2 percent were white. Victims of property crime lost an estimated $17 billion, a 2.1 percent increase over 2002.

Crime Victimization Survey

The FBI based its crime statistics on reports it received from more than 17,000 city, county, state, tribal, and federal law enforcement agencies, representing 93 percent of the nation's population. Another annual report, prepared by the Bureau of Justice Statistics, was compiled from a survey of about 84,000 households with nearly 150,000 residents age twelve or older. The survey was designed to measure the public's exposure to crime as reported by victims, even if the victims had not reported the crime to the police. As a result, the survey typically reported higher crime rates than the FBI report did. Murder rates were not included.

In its September 2004 report, the FBI found that the per capita rate for violent victimizations had dropped by 55 percent since 1993, from 50 per 1,000 people over age twelve in 1993 to 23 per 1,000 people over age twelve in 2003. Property crime showed a similar decline, falling 49 percent during the same ten-year period. The property crime rate fell from about 319 incidents per 1,000 households in 1993 to about 163 per 1,000 households in 2003. Since 1993 the violent crime rate had dropped 55 percent for whites, 57 percent for blacks, and 56 percent for Hispanics. Males, blacks, and youths continued to be the groups most vulnerable to violent crimes, but all three groups were experiencing lower rates of violent crime than they had in the past.

The survey, "Criminal Victimization, 2003," also found a significant increase in the number of crimes reported to law enforcement officials. Overall, 48 percent of all violent crimes were reported to police in 2003, compared with 43 percent in 1993. However, the percentage of robberies and rape/sexual assaults reported to police decreased from 2002 to 2003. The percentage of property crimes reported to the police increased from 34 percent in 1993 to 38 percent in 2003.

Incarceration Rates

Despite the decade-long decrease in crime, incarceration rates continued to rise, although at a slower pace than in the past. As of December 31, 2003, nearly 1.5 million people were incarcerated in federal and state prisons, according to the Bureau of Justice Statistics. That was a 2.1 percent increase over 2002, compared with an average annual increase for the 1995–2003 period of 3.4 percent. Overall, counting prisoners in federal and state prisons, local jails, juvenile facilities, territorial prisons, military facilities, tribal jails, and facilities operated by the Bureau of Immigration and Customs Enforcement, 2,212,475 people were behind bars in the United States at the end of 2003.

Roughly 1 in every 109 men and 1 in every 1,613 women were sentenced prisoners under the jurisdiction of state or federal authorities. The female prison population was increasing faster than the male population. The number of women in prison rose 3.6 percent in 2003, compared with 2.0 percent for the number of men. Women made up 6.9 percent of all prison inmates at the end of 2003. Black males accounted for 44 percent of all male prisoners with sentences of one year or more, while whites accounted for 35 percent and Hispanics 19 percent. An estimated 9 percent of black males ages twenty-five to twenty-nine were in prison at the end of 2003, compared with 2.6 percent of Hispanic males and 1.1 percent of white males. White female inmates outnumbered both black and Hispanic female inmates.

More than 9,500 inmates came into the federal prison system in 2003, a 5.8 percent increase. Slightly more than 20,000 prisoners entered state prison in 2003. That was a 1.6 increase over the previous year, but less than the 2.4 percent growth in 2002. Five states with relatively small populations had the highest increases in incarceration rates: North Dakota (11.4 percent), Minnesota (10.3 percent), Montana (8.9 percent), Wyoming (7.8 percent), and Hawaii (7.5 percent). The federal government and Texas, California, Florida, and New York were the five jurisdictions with the highest number of prisoners.

The bureau's report, "Prisoners in 2003," also said that state prisons were operating at capacity to 16 percent above capacity, while the federal system was operating at 39 percent above capacity. Privately operated facilities housed 5.7 percent of state and 12.6 percent of federal inmates, while local jails housed 5 percent of all state and federal sentenced prisoners.

Much of the increase in the state and federal prison populations was attributable to tougher sentencing laws enacted since the 1990s that put many more people behind bars even for relatively minor infractions of drug and other laws. In addition to sentencing offenders to longer prison terms, these laws also reduced the opportunities for early release and parole. As a result, the prison population was aging. According to FBI statistics, 28 percent of all inmates at the end of 2003 were between the ages of forty and fifty-four. *(Sentencing guidelines, p. 358)*

Overcrowded conditions, budget cutbacks, and inexperienced and undertrained guards were several of the factors blamed for pervasive mistreatment of prisoners in the United States. Corrections officials, inmates, and human rights activists reported many instances of abuse, some of which closely paralleled the practices at the heart of the Abu Ghraib prison scandal in Iraq. At one maximum security prison in Virginia, for example, newly arriving inmates were forced to wear black hoods, ostensibly to keep them from spitting on the guards. Reports of prisoners being forced to strip naked in front of other prisoners or males being forced to wear women's underwear were not uncommon. Allegations of abusive guards, rape, and extortion were commonplace. In July a panel appointed by Gov. Arnold Schwarzenegger declared that California's prison system was "dysfunctional" and recommended that the agency running the state prisons be disbanded. The investigation had been prompted by a series of scandals, including videotaped beatings of inmates and accusations that abuses had been covered up. *(Abu Ghraib report, p. 207)*

Gun Control Issues

Neither gun rights nor gun control advocates were able to win their top legislative priority in 2004. Gun rights supporters wanted to limit the legal liability of manufacturers, distributors, dealers, and importers of firearms and ammunition. The House of Representatives passed a bill in 2003 that would have disallowed lawsuits aimed at making those businesses pay damages for the consequences of gun violence. Although such cases generally failed, defendants still had to spend large sums on legal expenses.

A similar measure, which was being pushed by the Bush administration, appeared likely to win Senate passage in 2004, until gun control advocates, leveraging some election-year momentum, succeeded in adding three amendments to the bill. One, passed 70–27, would require the sale of child safety locks or a storage box with every handgun. A second, passed 53–46, would require criminal background checks before any firearm sales at most gun shows. A third, passed 52–47, would have extended the ban on semiautomatic assault weapons for an additional ten years. The ban, first enacted in 1994, was set to expire in September.

At that point the National Rifle Association, which opposed all three amendments, directed its allies in the Senate to vote against the measure. Most gun control advocates did as well, concluding that those victories had little chance of survival in conference negotiations, and the bill went down to resounding defeat.

The gun industry managed to stave off separate attempts to reauthorize the assault weapons ban. Although President George W. Bush said he would have signed it, he did not actively lobby for its passage, and House Majority Leader Tom DeLay, R-Texas, refused to bring the measure to the floor. According to the FBI report on crime statistics, firearms were used in about 27 percent of all violent crimes—and in 71 percent of all murders—in 2003. *(Gun rights, Historic Documents of 2002, p. 959)*

Following is the text of "FBI Releases Crime Statistics for 2003," a news release issued October 25, 2004, by the Federal Bureau of Investigation summarizing the findings of its annual report, Crime in the United States, 2003.

"FBI Releases Crime Statistics for 2003"

The Federal Bureau of Investigation released crime figures for 2003 which showed that violent crime in the Nation declined 3.0 percent and property crime decreased 0.2 percent from the estimated volumes in 2002. Further, the 5- and 10-year trend data indicated that the volume of violent crime declined 3.1 percent from the 1999 estimate and 25.6 percent from the 1994 estimate. The volume of property crime rose 2.2 percent when compared to the 1999 data but fell 14.0 percent when compared to the 1994 data. A comparison of 2002 with 2003 data showed that the rate of violent crime in the Nation, estimated at 475.0 violent crimes per 100,000 inhabitants, decreased 3.9 percent in 2003. The rate of property crime occurrences nationwide in 2003, estimated at 3,588.4 property crimes per 100,000 inhabitants, decreased 1.2 percent from the 2002 property crime rate.

The FBI's Uniform Crime Reporting (UCR) Program presented the data today in its annual publication, *Crime in the United States, 2003.* More than 17,000 city, county, state, tribal, and federal law enforcement agencies representing 93.0 percent of the Nation's population voluntarily submitted crime statistics in 2003. The UCR Program presents data in two crime categories: violent crime and property crime. The violent crime category is made up of the offenses of murder and nonnegligent manslaughter, forcible rape, robbery, and aggravated assault. The property crime category is comprised of the offenses of burglary, larceny-theft, and motor vehicle theft. In this report, the FBI also provides data on arson, hate crime, and law enforcement personnel in the Nation.

Violent Crime

At nearly 1.4 million offenses, the estimated volume of violent crime in the United States in 2003 declined 3.0 percent from the 2002 figure.

In 2003, the offense of murder was the only violent crime to show an increase in volume, 1.7 percent, compared to the 2002 data.

Collectively, the Nation's cities experienced a 3.9-percent decrease in violent crime in comparison to the 2002 figure. Violent crime decreased 3.7 percent in the Nation's nonmetropolitan counties and 1.0 percent in the Nation's metropolitan counties.

More than 30 percent (30.7) of violent crimes were committed with personal weapons such as hands, fists, feet, etc. Perpetrators used firearms in 26.9 percent and knives or cutting instruments in 15.2 percent of violent crimes. Other weapons were used in 27.3 percent of violent offenses during 2003.

The UCR Program estimated that in 2003 law enforcement agencies nationwide made 597,026 arrests for violent crime. Arrests for violent crime accounted for 4.4 percent of the estimated number of all arrests.

Property Crime

The 10.4 million property crimes estimated for 2003 reflected a slight decline (–0.2 percent) when compared to the 2002 estimate.

In the Nation's cities collectively, property crime decreased 0.3 percent from the 2002 figure. In nonmetropolitan counties, property crime increased 0.6 percent and in metropolitan counties, 0.2 percent.

Victims of property crimes (excluding arson) lost an estimated $17 billion, a 2.1 percent increase from the 2002 estimated dollar loss. Of the total loss, an estimated $8.6 billion was lost as a result of motor vehicle thefts, an estimated $4.9 billion was lost as a result of larceny-thefts, and an estimated $3.5 billion was lost as a result of burglaries.

Arrests for property crime accounted for 11.8 percent of the estimated number of arrests in 2003. Most of the property crime arrests (71.3 percent) were for larceny-theft.

Clearances

Law enforcement agencies nationwide cleared 46.5 percent of violent crimes in 2003. By offense type, agencies cleared 62.4 percent of murders, 55.9 percent of aggravated assaults, 44.0 percent of forcible rapes, and 26.3 percent of robberies.

Nationally in 2003, 12.2 percent of violent crime clearances involved only juveniles. Among the population groups, 12.2 percent of violent crime clearances in cities collectively involved only juveniles; 12.7 percent of violent crime clearances in metropolitan counties and 9.8 percent in nonmetropolitan counties involved only juveniles.

Across the United States, law enforcement agencies cleared 16.4 percent of all reported property crime in 2003. By offense, agencies cleared 18.0 percent of larceny-thefts and 13.1 percent of both burglaries and motor vehicle thefts.

In 2003, 19.3 percent of all property crime clearances involved only juveniles.

Arrests

Excluding traffic offenses, law enforcement agencies in the Nation made an estimated 13.6 million arrests in 2003.

The national arrest rate was 4,695.1 arrests per 100,000 in population. The violent crime arrest rate was 205.3 per 100,000 inhabitants; the property crime arrest rate was 558.4 per 100,000 inhabitants.

In 2003, law enforcement in the Nation's cities collectively reported an arrest rate of 5,109.3 arrests per 100,000 inhabitants. Law enforcement agencies in the Nation's metropolitan counties made 3,731.0 arrests per 100,000 in population; law enforcement agencies in the Nation's nonmetropolitan counties made 3,961.2 arrests per 100,000 in population.

Compared to the data from 2002, the number of arrests in 2003 showed a slight increase, 0.2 percent. The number of arrests for violent crime in 2003 decreased 2.3 percent; the number of arrests for property crime increased 0.7 percent.

Adults comprised 83.7 percent of all arrestees in 2003.

By gender, 76.8 percent of those arrested in the Nation were male. Compared to the 2002 data, the number of males arrested in 2003 declined 0.4 percent; the number of females arrested in 2003 increased 1.9 percent.

An examination of arrestee data by race indicated that 70.6 percent of those arrested in the United States in 2003 were white.

Murder and Nonnegligent Manslaughter

The UCR Program estimated that 16,503 murders occurred in the United States in 2003. This figure represents a 1.7-percent increase from the 2002 estimate.

Law enforcement agencies provided the UCR Program with supplementary data for 14,408 murders in 2003. These data showed that most murder victims (90.6 percent) were adults and most were males (77.6 percent). Of the male murder victims, 8.2 percent were juveniles (persons under the age of 18). Juvenile females comprised 13.5 percent of female murder victims nationwide. By race, 48.7 percent of murder victims were white, 48.5 percent were black, and the remainder were of other races.

In 44.5 percent of murders, the relationship of the murder victim to the offender was unknown. Of the 55.5 percent of murders in which the victim/offender relationship was known, 77.6 percent of the victims knew their assailants.

In those murders for which law enforcement personnel reported victim and offender relationship data, 32.3 percent of females were killed by their husbands or boyfriends, and 2.5 percent of males were killed by their wives or girlfriends.

Of the murders involving a single victim and a single offender, 92.4 percent of black victims were killed by black offenders; 84.7 percent of white victims were killed by white offenders.

Of the murders in 2003 for which law enforcement identified the type of weapon, nearly 71 percent (70.9) involved firearms. Offenders used knives or cutting instruments in 13.4 percent of murders; personal weapons such as hands, fists, and feet in 7.0 percent of murders; and blunt objects in 4.8 percent of murders. Four percent of murders were committed with other types of weapons.

In 2003, law enforcement investigation was unable to determine the circumstance in 33.9 percent of murders in the Nation. The supplementary data also showed that more than 16 percent (16.4) of murders were committed during the commission of another felony such as during a robbery or a violation of a narcotic drug law.

Forcible Rape

An estimated 93,433 forcible rapes occurred in the Nation during 2003. This number represents a 1.9-percent decrease from the 2002 estimate.

The UCR Program estimated that 63.2 of every 100,000 females in the Nation were victims of forcible rape in 2003. This rate represented a 2.7-percent decrease from the 2002 rate.

By community type, the rate of forcible rape in the Nation's Metropolitan Statistical Areas (MSAs) was estimated at 64.5 forcible rapes per 100,000 females.

There were an estimated 75.1 forcible rapes per 100,000 females in cities outside MSAs and 45.7 forcible rapes per 100,000 females in the Nation's nonmetropolitan counties.

Robbery

The United States had an estimated 413,402 robbery offenses in 2003, which was 1.8 percent fewer robberies than the 2002 estimate. The rate, estimated at 142.2 robberies per 100,000 in population, decreased 2.7 percent from the 2002 estimate.

The UCR Program estimated that nearly 30 percent (29.9) of all violent crimes in 2003 were robberies.

Robbery victims collectively lost an estimated $514 million in 2003, an average dollar loss of $1,244 per offense.

Offenders used firearms in 41.8 percent of robberies, strong-arm tactics (hands, fists, feet, etc.) in 39.9 percent of robberies, and knives or cutting instruments in 8.9 percent of robberies. Other weapons were used in 9.4 percent of robberies.

Aggravated Assault

For the tenth consecutive year, the estimated number of aggravated assaults in the Nation declined. Based on law enforcement reports for 2003, the UCR Program estimated 857,921 aggravated assaults, a 3.8-percent decrease compared to the 2002 figure.

By volume, aggravated assaults comprised 62.1 percent of the estimated total number of violent crimes.

By rate, the UCR Program estimated that there were 295.0 aggravated assault offenses per 100,000 inhabitants in the Nation, a 4.7-percent decline from the 2002 estimate.

Aggravated assault offenders used personal weapons (hands, fists, feet, etc.) in 26.9 percent of offenses, firearms in 19.1 percent of offenses, and knives or cutting instruments in 18.2 percent of offenses. Other types of weapons were used in 35.9 percent of aggravated assaults.

Burglary

The Nation had an estimated 2,153,464 burglaries in 2003, a slight (+0.1 percent) increase from the 2002 estimated figure. The rate of burglary in the United States was 740.5 burglary offenses per 100,000 inhabitants, a 0.9-percent decrease from 2002 data.

Victims collectively lost an estimated $3.5 billion as a result of burglaries in 2003 with an average dollar loss of $1,626 per incident.

An examination of the burglary data indicated that forcible entry accounted for 62.4 percent, unlawful entry comprised 31.2 percent, and attempted forcible entry made up 6.3 percent of all burglary offenses.

Most burglaries (65.8 percent) occurred at residences; most residential burglaries (62.0 percent) occurred during the daytime.

Larceny-Theft

The UCR Program estimated larceny-thefts at slightly more than 7 million offenses in 2003. This represents a decrease of 0.5 percent when compared to the 2002 estimate. In 2003, larceny-theft made up 67.3 percent of the estimated volume of property crime.

By category, thefts from motor vehicles accounted for the largest portion (26.4 percent) of larceny-theft offenses in the Nation.

In 2003, the value of property taken in larceny-theft offenses collectively was an estimated $4.9 billion. Property lost to thieves had an average value of $698 per offense. The highest average dollar loss, $1,030, was associated with thefts from buildings.

Nationwide in 2003, 18.0 percent of all larceny-thefts were cleared by arrest or exceptional means; 20.2 percent of larceny-theft clearances involved only juveniles.

The estimated number of arrests for larceny-theft offenses accounted for 71.3 percent of the estimated total number of arrests for property crimes.

Motor Vehicle Theft

The UCR Program estimated that nearly 1.3 million motor vehicle thefts occurred in 2003, a 1.1-percent increase in volume when compared to the 2002 data. The rate of motor vehicle theft, estimated at 433.4 motor vehicle thefts per 100,000 inhabitants, remained virtually unchanged from the 2002 estimate.

Automobiles were stolen at a rate of 341.9 motor vehicle thefts per 100,000 in population. Commercial vehicles, such as trucks and buses, were stolen at a rate of 86.2 and other types of vehicles at a rate of 38.3.

Collectively, victims of motor vehicle thefts lost an estimated $8.6 billion in 2003, which was an average dollar value loss of $6,797 per offense.

Nationwide, law enforcement agencies made an estimated 152,934 arrests for motor vehicle theft.

Arson

In 2003, 12,776 law enforcement agencies reported 71,319 arson offenses to the UCR Program.

Of the 71,319 arsons, law enforcement agencies provided supplementary data on 64,043 offenses. Of the arsons for which additional information was provided, law enforcement reported an average dollar loss of $11,942 per offense.

By property type, residential arsons had an average dollar loss of $19,062 for single occupancy dwellings and an average dollar loss of $23,977 for other residential-type arsons per offense. The average dollar loss for a mobile property arson was $6,381, and the average dollar loss for other property type arson was $3,467 per offense.

The Nation's law enforcement agencies cleared 16.7 percent of reported arsons in 2003. Juveniles comprised 41.3 percent of all the arson clearances.

An estimated 16,163 people were arrested for arson in 2003, 84.4 percent of whom were male. More than half (50.8 percent) of arson arrestees were under the age of 18; 31.2 percent of arson arrestees were under the age of 15.

Hate Crime

In 2003, 11,909 agencies actively participated in the hate crime portion of the UCR Program, and 1,967 of those agencies reported 7,489 hate crime incidents involving 8,715 separate offenses, 9,100 victims, and 6,934 known offenders.

Of the 7,489 hate crime incidents, 7,485 were due to a single-bias, and 4 were due to a multiple-bias.

More than half (51.4 percent) of all single-bias hate crime incidents in 2003 were racially motivated. Law enforcement investigators attributed nearly 18 percent (17.9) of hate crimes to a religious bias, 16.6 percent to a sexual-orientation bias, 13.7 percent to a bias based on ethnicity/national origin, and 0.4 percent to a disability bias.

In 2003, 63.3 percent of reported hate crime offenses were classified as crimes against persons, 36.0 percent were classified as crimes against property, and 0.7 percent were classified as crimes against society.

Law enforcement agencies indicated that intimidation was the most frequently reported hate crime. Intimidation accounted for 31.5 percent of all hate crime offenses and 49.7 percent of crimes against persons.

Destruction/damage/vandalism of property, the most frequently reported hate crime against property, comprised 30.0 percent of all reported hate crime offenses and 83.4 percent of hate crimes against property.

Law Enforcement Employees

In 2003, there were 3.5 full-time law enforcement employees, including both sworn officers and civilians, per 1,000 inhabitants in the United States.

Throughout the Nation, 14,072 city, county, state, and tribal police agencies actively participated in the law enforcement segment of the UCR Program. These agencies employed 663,796 full-time officers and 285,146 civilians and furnished law enforcement services to more than 274 million inhabitants.

Law enforcement in 2003 provided services to the Nation's cities collectively at a rate of 2.3 sworn law enforcement officers for every 1,000 inhabitants. Law enforcement in the Nation's smallest cities, those with less than 10,000 inhabitants, provided services at a rate of 3.3 sworn officers per 1,000 in population, the highest rate among population groups. Law enforcement in the Nation's cities with 25,000 to 49,999 inhabitants provided services at a rate of 1.8 sworn officers per 1,000 in population, the lowest employment rate among the population groups. Law enforcement agencies providing services to metropolitan counties had 2.6 sworn officers for each 1,000 in population, and law enforcement agencies providing services to nonmetropolitan counties had 2.8 sworn officers for each 1,000 in population.

Most sworn law enforcement officers (88.6 percent) were male. Females comprised the majority (62.5 percent) of civilian law enforcement employees.

Source: U.S. Department of Justice. Federal Bureau of Investigation. "FBI Releases Crime Statistics for 2003." Press release, October 25, 2004. www.fbi.gov/pressrel/pressrel04/crimestat102504.htm (accessed March 28, 2005).

November

2004 HISTORIC DOCUMENTS

Kerry Concession Speech, Bush Victory Speech

November 3, 2004

INTRODUCTION

George W. Bush won election on November 2, 2004, to a second term as the nation's forty-third president, defeating Sen. John Kerry, D-Mass., with 51 percent of the vote. It was a banner day for Republicans, who also added three seats to their majority in the House and picked up four seats in the Senate. One of those seats had belonged to Tom Daschle of South Dakota, the soft-spoken but partisan leader of the Senate Democrats whose defeat thrilled congressional Republicans nearly as much as Bush's victory. Despite the GOP wins, political analysts cautioned that while the country might be leaning a little bit more Republican, it was still divided politically right down the middle.

Bush clearly read his victory as an endorsement of his controversial leadership of the war in Iraq and the war on terrorism—and more broadly as a mandate to move ahead with an ambitious domestic program that included overhauls of both the tax code and the Social Security system. It was likely that Bush also viewed the election as a vindication of the 2000 election, in which he lost the popular vote to then–vice president Al Gore and won the electoral college vote only after the Supreme Court barred a recount of disputed Florida ballots. *(Election dispute, Historic Documents of 2000, p. 999)*

For a few hours early in the morning of November 3, it looked as if the country might again find itself in an election dispute, this time over the balloting in Ohio, where charges and countercharges of election fraud and counting procedures had been flying for weeks. Although Bush was leading in the vote count, the Kerry camp initially said it wanted to wait for all the votes to be counted, including 150,000 or so provisional votes—votes cast by people whose eligibility was in question.

Finally, at about 2:00 P.M., Kerry formally conceded. "I would not give up this fight if there was a chance that we would prevail," Kerry said to a gathering of his supporters in Boston's historic Fanueil Hall. "But it is now clear that even when all the provisional ballots are counted, which they will be, there won't be enough outstanding votes for us to be able to win Ohio. And therefore we cannot win this election." The tired and disappointed Democrat then called on all Americans to join in "common effort without remorse or recrimination, without anger or rancor. America is in need of unity and longing for a larger measure of compassion."

"America has spoken," an obviously triumphant George Bush declared an hour or so later in a victory speech to his supporters at the Ronald Reagan Building in Washington.

Many pundits said that if Kerry had been able to speak to the American people as directly and with as much passion during the campaign as he did in his concession speech, he might have changed the outcome of the election. In the end, Kerry was unable to persuade enough voters that he, rather than Bush, would be the stronger leader and the person best able to keep the country safe from terrorists. Exit polls showed that voters preferred Kerry to Bush on several key issues, such as the economy, jobs, health care, and even the conduct of the war in Iraq. But voters gave Bush the edge on the war on terror and "moral values." Even more important, Bush won among voters who valued leadership and a clear stand on the issues. Karl Rove, the "architect" of Bush's winning campaign strategy, summarized the situation succinctly the day after the election: "We had at the top of the ticket an inspiring individual who knew what he believed and did what he said. At the end of the day, people voted for him for two reasons. One is they thought he could do the job, and two, they had deep doubts about the other guy."

Final Days of the Campaign

At the close of the last presidential debate on October 13, Bush and Kerry were running neck and neck in the public opinion polls, and the issues had narrowed down to character and leadership, particularly as they concerned the war in Iraq. The Bush campaign impugned Kerry's ability to be a strong commander in chief, while Kerry questioned Bush's judgment and his refusal to take responsibility for the mistakes he had made. Each ticket claimed that it would do a better job of protecting the American homeland from terrorists and other threats.

In the final week, Kerry might have gained from news reports that the administration could not account for the whereabouts of 380 tons of powerful explosives that had gone missing from an Iraqi ammunition dump known as Al Qaqaa. On October 29 a videotape of al Qaeda terrorist leader Osama bin Laden was released by the al Jazeera news agency. Bin Laden made no direct threat against the United States on the tape, but both Bush and Kerry interrupted their campaign schedules to declare separately that they were united in their determination to stand up to bin Laden. *(al Qaeda network, p. 534; weapons, p. 711)*

It was unclear what effect, if any, the videotape had on voters, who seemed more concerned about a repeat of the voting disputes that characterized the 2000 presidential election. A *New York Times*/CBS News poll found that 20 percent of those polled had little or no confidence that the votes for president would be counted properly, 30 percent of voters said they were worried that they might be prevented from casting a vote or that their vote would not be counted, and more than 30 percent said they thought deliberate efforts would be made to keep blacks from voting in some states.

Both campaigns enlisted thousands of poll watchers as well as attorneys at crucial polling places in Ohio, Florida, and other key states to ensure that duly registered voters were able to cast their ballots and to challenge (or, depending on party affiliation, come to the aid of) voters whose eligibility was questioned. Both camps also mounted the biggest and most aggressive get-out-the-vote drives in presidential election history in the battleground states during the weekend before the vote and on election day itself. The two campaigns, the political parties, and outside groups, such as America Coming Together, a coalition of pro-Kerry organizations, spent at least $300 million on sophisticated efforts to target and turn out the vote.

Another Long Election Night

Although Bush had a slight edge in public opinion polls going into election day, early exit polls suggested that Kerry was winning several key states. Data from the National Election Pool, a new vote projection system run by the TV networks, the Associated Press, and several major newspaper organizations, were showing Kerry beating Bush in Ohio and Pennsylvania, and two of three exit polls in Florida showed Kerry ahead there as well. By prior agreement, news agencies had promised not to project results based on exit poll data until after voting polls had closed across the country. But Kerry campaign workers with access to the data were jubilant. Bush operatives were in turn dismayed, then skeptical, and then certain that the exit polls were wrong. Rove later told reporters that he was sure something was wrong with the exit polls when he saw that they awarded Kerry South Carolina and Virginia, two states that had voted for Bush in 2000 and that both parties had conceded to Republicans early in the campaign.

As the actual vote count continued into the night, Bush increasingly looked like the winner. But Kerry was not willing to concede. Appearing in the middle of the night, at the Copley Plaza in Boston, Kerry's running mate, Sen. John Edwards, D-N.C., reminded supporters that "John Kerry and I made a promise to the American people that in this election every vote would count and every vote would be counted. Tonight we are keeping our word and we will fight for every vote. You deserve no less."

Shortly before 6:00 A.M., Andrew H. Card Jr., the White House chief of staff, announced to campaign workers in Washington that the White House was "convinced that President Bush has won reelection." By this time, the drama over the vote count had narrowed to Ohio, where Bush was running ahead of Kerry with about 150,000 provisional ballots still to be counted. After watching the count throughout the night, the Kerry campaign realized it would need to win virtually all the provisional ballots to surpass Bush's 136,000-vote lead, which was highly unlikely. Although the outcome in Iowa and New Mexico was still uncertain, Ohio's twenty votes brought Bush's electoral vote total to 274—four more than the 270 he needed to win election. Kerry called Bush late in the morning of November 3 to congratulate him on his reelection.

The Vote

Some 119 million voters, about 60 percent of those registered, went to the polls on November 2; this was the highest turnout since 1968. Turnout in 2000 was 105.4 million, slightly more than 54 percent of all registered voters. After all the votes were counted, Bush won 60.6 million popular votes and 286 electoral college votes; Kerry won 57.4 million popular votes and 252 electoral votes. The total minor party vote was less than 1 percent of the total vote cast. It was the first election since 1988 in which a third-party candidate had not figured prominently. Ralph Nader, who ran on the Green Party ticket in 2000 and who Democrats said had spoiled the election for Gore, was not a factor in 2004. He ran as in independent, did not appear on the ballot in several states, and won only 408,000 votes.

Despite the increased turnout, the state-by-state line-up barely changed. Only two states that had voted Democratic in 2004—Iowa and New Mexico—switched to vote for Bush in 2004 and then by less than a single percentage point. Only one state, New Hampshire, shifted out of the Republican "red" column into the Democratic "blue" column, and that shift reflected the absence of Nader as a factor.

Bush carried 54 percent of the white vote, about the same as he had in 2000. Despite preelection indications that the president might double his share of the black vote, nine of ten African Americans cast their ballot for Kerry, who also held onto the majority of Hispanic votes. The gender gap narrowed somewhat in 2004, with fewer men supporting the Republican than in 2000 and fewer women supporting the Democratic candidate.

Democrats worked hard to register new voters under age thirty, and about 4.6 million turned out on election day. That was only a little over 50 percent of all young voters registered, but those who did vote were strongly for Kerry. Countering the youth vote, however, was increased turnout among evangelicals, who supported Bush by a margin of better than three to one. Karl Rove had long said that Bush had lost the popular vote in 2000 because 4 million evangelicals did not vote, perhaps, he said, because of reports about an old drunk-driving charge against the president that came to light the week before the election, and perhaps because evangelicals were generally wary of politics and politicians. Rove appeared to have met his target in 2004. The evangelical influence on the vote was particularly acute in eleven states, including Ohio, that had ballot initiatives barring same-sex marriage. All eleven initiatives passed with 59 percent of the vote or more. Bush also won a majority of the Catholic vote; although a Roman Catholic, Kerry sparked opposition in the church by his positions on issues such as abortion and gay rights. *(Same-sex marriage, p. 37)*

Exit polls showed Kerry drawing more votes than the president among those who rated the economy, health care, and education as the most important issues. He also was favored by 75 percent of those who thought the Iraq War was the most important problem. But voters who were more concerned about terrorism preferred Bush by an even wider margin. Bush was also the clear preference among voters who cited strong leadership, "clear stands on the issues," and honesty and trustworthiness as the most important qualities in a candidate.

The deciding factor, however, may have been that Republicans of every stripe—conservative, moderate, and liberal—voted more solidly for Bush than Democrats voted for Kerry, and more Republicans (37 percent of the total vote) than Democrats (36 percent) voted. Kerry won 89 percent of the Democrats voting and a slim majority of independent voters, but that was not enough to overcome the turnout and cohesiveness of Republicans who gave Bush 93 percent of their vote.

Much was made after the election of the effect of moral values on the outcome. More than 20 percent of all voters said "moral values" was their top concern, and 75 percent of the moral values voters said they voted for Bush. Commentators widely identified these voters as fundamentalists or social conservatives opposed to gay marriage and abortion rights. Yet a closer look seemed to show that "moral values" had a far broader meaning. More than 75 percent of those who expressed an opinion in the national exit poll said they supported either gay marriage or civil unions. A postelection Zogby survey asking voters to identify the nation's most urgent moral problem found abortion and gay marriage far down the list. Leading the list were "greed and materialism" and "poverty and economic justice."

Campaign Financing

The 2004 elections were the most costly in history. Combined spending on the races for the White House, Senate, and House of Representatives was estimated at about $3.9 billion, according to the Center for Responsive Politics, which tracked campaign financing. That was more than 30 percent more than was spent in 2000.

The Bush campaign raised an all-time presidential record of $273 million from private contributors, but the Democrats also enjoyed record fund-raising, bringing in $249 million. Kerry was the first Democratic presidential candidate to decline public financing and its spending limits during the primary season. Bush declined public financing during the primary season in both 2000 and 2004. Both men received public financing—$75 million each—for the general election, which meant that both men had to stop taking private donations after the conventions.

Nearly as much money was raised and spent by nonparty political groups. Known as 527s for their section in the tax code, these independent groups spent nearly $550 million in the 2003–2004 election cycle. Most of this funding was devoted to the presidential election, where $266 million was spent on behalf of Kerry and $144 million on behalf of Bush. 527s emerged as a powerful force after the campaign finance reform law enacted in 2002 banned national party committees from collecting unlimited "soft money" from corporations, unions, and individuals. Democrats, who were hurt more by the soft money ban than Republicans, first realized the potential of 527s, when groups such as America Coming Together and MoveOn.org raised millions to finance voter-turnout operations aimed at targeting Democratic voters. Republicans initially challenged the legitimacy of the 527s, but after the Federal Election Commission refused to ban their activities, pro-Republican groups started to spring up. One of the more prominent was the Swift Boat Veterans for Truth, which pummeled Kerry in August with allegations that he had lied about his Vietnam service record.

By law 527s were to operate independently of the political campaigns and were barred from coordinating with them, although both campaigns charged that the other campaign had violated this restriction. Others expressed grave concern about the potential impact of unregulated and unaccountable organizations on political campaigns. The Senate authors of the 2002 campaign finance reform law, John McCain, R-Ariz., and Russell Feingold, D-Wis., indicated that they would try to close the 527 loophole with new legislation, a move that Bush had endorsed. A federal lawsuit challenging 527s was still pending at year's end. *(Campaign finance reform, Historic Documents of 2003, p. 1155)*

Voting Problems

Although voters and election officials reported plenty of problems around the country, they did not come close to matching the dire predictions made beforehand. The largest voter turnout in U.S. history caused hours-long waits throughout the country and prompted judges to order voting hours extended in some polling places. Some unknown number of would-be voters chose not to wait. Voting machines broke down, and polling places ran out of ballots. In the crucial state of Ohio, 638 voters cast ballots in one precinct, but a computer recorded 3,893 extra votes for Bush (the error was corrected in the certified vote total for the state). Constituents in minority precincts reported receiving calls designed to lead them to vote in the wrong precinct on the wrong day. While many voters remained suspicious of the final vote tallies, particularly in Florida and Ohio, where the two campaigns had been warning of potential irregularities and fraud for weeks before the election, most voters were able to cast their ballot and have it counted without incident.

The biggest complication might have been posed by provisional ballots for people whose eligibility to vote was questioned at the polls, a new mandate Congress enacted in 2002 (PL 107–252). Lawsuits challenging various aspects of the balloting were not settled in many states until days before the election. In Ohio the rules governing provisional ballots were still in contention on election day. Kerry's decision to concede the presidential race instead of contesting the results in Ohio cut off any additional litigation there. But in December Kerry asked for a statewide recount there. "It's critical that we investigate and understand any and every voting irregularity anywhere in our country, not because it would change the outcome of the election, but because Americans have to believe that their votes are counted in our democracy," he said.

At least two investigations of election problems were planned. The Government Accountability Office, responding to a request from several Democratic lawmakers, said on November 24 that it would investigate the accuracy of the vote and the methods used to count it, including the way election officials counted provisional ballots. The U.S. Election Assistance Commission, created by the election overhaul legislation passed in 2002, also said it would examine the voting results. It planned to report its findings in January 2005.

A Florida-like election did occur in 2004, not in the presidential race, but in the race for governor of the state of Washington, where Democrat Christine Gregoire, the state attorney general, ran against former GOP state representative Dino Rossi to replace retiring Democrat Gary Locke. Although Gregoire was initially a strong favorite to win, Rossi closed the gap and after the election led the race by a handful of votes. A second machine count gave Rossi a lead of 42 votes out of 2.9 million ballots cast. That also triggered a state law allowing a hand count of the ballots, which Gregoire won by 129 votes. She was certified the winner in late December and sworn into office on January 12, 2005. Rossi and the Republican Party were asking a state court to overturn the election and call for a revote.

Bush's Second Terms Plans

In his victory speech on November 3, Bush promised to put forward an ambitious agenda, which included making income tax cuts enacted in 2001 permanent and rewriting the tax code, drawing up stricter educational standards, and overhauling Social Security to allow younger workers to maintain private accounts funded through payroll taxes. "Let me put it to you this way," a confident president said at a November 4 news conference. "I earned capital in the campaign, political capital, and now I intend to spend it." Bush also said he intended to reach across party lines to win support for his agenda, but he made it clear he expected the Democrats to do most of the compromising.

Bush would start his second term in January 2005 with an almost entirely new cabinet. There had been little turnover during Bush's first term, but within days of the election, several cabinet secretaries announced they would be leaving. One of the first to announce his intentions was Attorney General John Ashcroft, who was praised by some for his stand against terrorism but criticized by others for sacrificing civil liberties in the process. Bush moved quickly to name his White House counsel, Alberto Gonzales, to take Ashcroft's place. Gonzales, who was also often mentioned as a possible Supreme Court nominee, was perhaps best known for writing a memo to Bush in January 2002 supporting the Justice Department's contention that the Geneva Conventions governing treatment of prisoners of war did not apply to captured Al Qaeda and Taliban forces. *("Torture" memo, p. 336)*

Among the other departing officials were Secretary of State Colin Powell and Secretary of Education Rod Paige. Bush replaced both men with close advisers in the White House, naming National Security Director Condoleezza Rice as Powell's successor, and Margaret Spellings, the White House chief domestic policy adviser and an author of the No Child Left Behind law, to succeed Paige. The only major cabinet member to stay on was Secretary of Defense Donald H. Rumsfeld. Rumsfeld had frequently come under fire over questions of military preparedness in Iraq, and there had been calls for his resignation during the summer over abuses of Iraqi prisoners by Americans at the Abu Ghraib prison in Iraq. *(Abu Ghraib abuses, p. 207)*

Following are the texts of two statements made November 3, 2004. The first, "Address to Supporters at Fanueil Hall," is by Sen. John Kerry, D-Mass., conceding the 2004 presidential election; the second, "Remarks in a Victory Celebration," is by George W. Bush thanking the American people for electing him to a second term as president.

"Address to Supporters: Remarks as Delivered by John Kerry"

Thank you. Thank you. Thank you so much. You just have no idea how warming and how generous that welcome is, your love is, your affection, and I'm gratified by it. I'm sorry that we got here a little bit late and a bit short.

Earlier today, I spoke to President Bush, and I offered him and Laura our congratulations on their victory. We had a good conversation and we talked about the danger of division in our country and the need—the desperate need—for unity, for finding the common ground, coming together. Today, I hope that we can begin the healing. In America it is vital that every vote count, and that every vote be counted. But the outcome should be decided by voters, not a protracted legal process.

I would not give up this fight if there was a chance that we would prevail. But it is now clear that even when all the provisional ballots are counted, which they will be, there won't be enough outstanding votes for us to be able to win Ohio. And therefore, we can not win this election.

My friends, it was here that we began our campaign for the presidency. And all we had was hope and a vision for a better America. It was a privilege and a gift to spend two years traveling this country, coming to know so many of you. I wish that I could just wrap you in my arms and embrace each and every one of you individually all across this nation. I thank you from the bottom of my heart. Thank you. Thank you. Thank you. Thank you.

Audience member: We've still got your back!

Thank you, man. And I assure you—you watch—I'll still have yours.

I will always be particularly grateful to the colleague that you just heard from who became my partner, my very close friend, an extraordinary leader, John Edwards. And I thank him for everything he did. John and I would be the first to tell you that we owe so much to our families. They're here with us today. They were with us every single step of the way. They sustained us.

They went out on their own and they multiplied our campaign, all across this country.

No one did this more with grace and with courage and candor. For that, I love than my wife, Teresa. And I thank her. Thank you. And our children were there every single step of the way. It was unbelievable. Vanessa, Alex, Chris, Andre and John, from my family, and Elizabeth Edwards who is so remarkable and so strong and so smart. And Johnny and Cate who went out there on her own just like my daughters did. And also Emma Claire and Jack who were up beyond their bedtime last night, like a lot of us.

I want to thank my crewmates and my friends from 35 years ago. That great 'band of brothers' who crisscrossed this country on my behalf through 2004. Thank you. They had the courage to speak the truth back then, and they spoke it again this year, and for that, I will forever be grateful.

And thanks also as I look around here to friends and family of a lifetime. Some from college, friends made all across the years, and then all across the miles of this campaign. You are so special. You brought the gift of your passion for our country and the possibilities of change, and that will stay with us, and with this country forever.

Thanks to Democrats and Republicans and independents who stood with us, and everyone who voted no matter who their candidate was.

And thanks to my absolutely unbelievable, dedicated staff, led by a wonderful campaign manager Mary Beth Cahill, who did an extraordinary job. There's so much written about campaigns, and there's so much that Americans never get to see. I wish they could all spend a day on a campaign and see how hard these folks work to make America better. It is its own unbelievable contribution to our democracy, and it's a gift to everybody. But especially to me. And I'm grateful to each and every one of you, and I thank your families, and I thank you for the sacrifices you've made.

And to all the volunteers, all across this country who gave so much of themselves. You know, thanks to William Field, a six-year-old who collected $680, a quarter and a dollar at a time selling bracelets during the summer to help change America. Thanks to Michael Benson from Florida who I spied in a rope line holding a container of money, and turned out he raided his piggy bank and wanted to contribute. And thanks to Alana Wexler who is 11 years old and started kids for Kerry all across our country. I think of the brigades of students and people, young and old, who took time to travel, time off from work, their own vacation time to work in states far and wide. They braved the hot days of summer and the cold days of the fall and the winter to knock on doors because they were determined to open the doors of opportunity to all Americans. They worked their hearts out, and I wish . . . you don't know how much, I could have brought this race home for you for them, and I say to them now, don't lose faith.

What you did made a difference, and building on itself—building on itself, we go on to make a difference another day. I promise you, that time will come. The time will come, the election will come when your work and your ballots will change the world, and it's worth fighting for.

I want to especially say to the American people in this journey, you have given me honor and the gift of listening and learning from you. I have visited your homes. I have visited your churches. I've visited your union halls. I've heard your stories, I know your struggles, I know your hopes. They're part of me now, and I will never forget you, and I'll never stop fighting for you.

You may not understand completely in what ways, but it is true when I say to you that you have taught me and you've tested me and you've lifted me up, and you made me stronger, I did my best to express my vision and my hopes for America. We worked hard, and we fought hard, and I wish that things had turned out a little differently.

But in an American election, there are no losers, because whether or not our candidates are successful, the next morning we all wake up as Americans. And that—that is the greatest privilege and the most remarkable good fortune that can come to us on earth.

With that gift also comes obligation. We are required now to work together for the good of our country. In the days ahead, we must find common cause. We must join in common effort without remorse or recrimination, without anger or rancor. America is in need of unity and longing for a larger measure of compassion.

I hope President Bush will advance those values in the coming years. I pledge to do my part to try to bridge the partisan divide. I know this is a difficult time for my supporters, but I ask them, all of you, to join me in doing that.

Now, more than ever, with our soldiers in harm's way, we must stand together and succeed in Iraq and win the war on terror. I will also do everything in my power to ensure that my party, a proud Democratic Party, stands true to our best hopes and ideals.

I believe that what we started in this campaign will not end here. And I know our fight goes on to put America back to work and make our economy a great engine of job growth. Our fight goes on to make affordable health care an accessible right for all Americans, not a privilege. Our fight goes on to protect the environment, to achieve equality, to push the frontiers of science and discovery, and to restore America's reputation in the world. I believe that all of this will happen—and sooner than we may think—because we're America. And America always moves forward.

I've been honored to represent the citizens of this commonwealth in the United States Senate now for 20 years. And I pledge to them that in the years ahead, I'm going to fight on for the people and for the principles that I've learned and lived with here in Massachusetts.

I'm proud of what we stood for in this campaign, and of what we accomplished. When we began, no one thought it was possible to even make this a close race. But we stood for real change, change that would make a real difference in the life of our nation, the lives of our families. And we defined that choice to America.

I'll never forget the wonderful people who came to our rallies, who stood in our rope lines, who put their hopes in our hands, who invested in each and every one of us. I saw in them the truth that America is not only great, but it is good.

So here—so with a grateful heart—I leave this campaign with a prayer that has even greater meaning to me now that I've come to know our vast country so much better. Thanks to all of you and what a privilege it has been. And that prayer is very simple: God bless America. Thank you.

Source: Friends of John Kerry, Inc. "Address to Supporters at Fanueil Hall: Remarks as Delivered by John Kerry." November 3, 2004. www.johnkerry.com/pressroom/speeches/spc_2004_1103.htm (accessed January 30, 2005).

"Remarks in a Victory Celebration"

Thank you all. Thank you all for coming. We had a long night and a great night. The voters turned out in record numbers and delivered an historic victory.

Earlier today, Senator Kerry called with his congratulations. We had a really good phone call. He was very gracious. Senator Kerry waged a spirited campaign, and he and his supporters can be proud of their efforts. Laura and I wish Senator Kerry and Teresa and their whole family all our best wishes.

America has spoken, and I'm humbled by the trust and the confidence of my fellow citizens. With that trust comes a duty to serve all Americans, and I will do my best to fulfill that duty every day as your President.

There are many people to thank, and my family comes first. Laura is the love of my life. [Applause] I'm glad you love her too. [Laughter] I want to thank our daughters, who joined their dad for his last campaign. I appreciate the hard work of my sister and my brothers. I especially want to thank my parents for their loving support.

I'm grateful to the Vice President [Dick Cheney] and Lynne and their daughters, who have worked so hard and been such a vital part of our team. The Vice President serves America with wisdom and honor, and I'm proud to serve beside him.

I want to thank my superb campaign team. I want to thank you all for your hard work. I was impressed every day by how hard and how skillful our team was. I want to thank Marc, Chairman Marc Racicot, and the campaign manager, Ken Mehlman, and the architect, Karl Rove. I want to thank Ed Gillespie for leading our party so well.

I want to thank the thousands of our supporters across our country. I want to thank you for your hugs on the ropelines. I want to thank you for your prayers on the ropelines. I want to thank you for your kind words on the ropelines. I want to thank you for everything you did to make the calls and to put up the signs, to talk to your neighbors, and to get out the vote. And because you did the incredible work, we are celebrating today.

There's an old saying, "Do not pray for tasks equal to your powers. Pray for powers equal to your tasks." In 4 historic years, America has been given great tasks and faced them with strength and courage. Our people have restored the vigor of this economy and shown resolve and patience in a new kind of war. Our military has brought justice to the enemy and honor to America. Our Nation has defended itself and served the freedom of all mankind. I'm proud to lead such an amazing country, and I'm proud to lead it forward.

Because we have done the hard work, we are entering a season of hope. We'll continue our economic progress. We'll reform our outdated Tax Code. We'll strengthen the Social Security for the next generation. We'll make public schools all they can be. And we will uphold our deepest values of family and faith.

We will help the emerging democracies of Iraq and Afghanistan so they can grow in strength and defend their freedom. And then our service men and women will come home with the honor they have earned. With good allies at our side, we will fight this war on terror with every resource of our national power so our children can live in freedom and in peace.

Reaching these goals will require the broad support of Americans. So today I want to speak to every person who voted for my opponent: To make this Nation stronger and better, I will need your support and I will work to earn it. I will do all I can do to deserve your trust. A new term is a new opportunity to reach out to the whole Nation. We have one country, one Constitution, and one future that binds us. And when we come together and work together, there is no limit to the greatness of America.

Let me close with a word to the people of the State of Texas. We have known each other the longest, and you started me on this journey. On the open plains of Texas, I first learned the character of our country, sturdy and honest and as hopeful as the break of day. I will always be grateful to the good people of my State. And whatever the road that lies ahead, that road will take me home.

The campaign has ended, and the United States of America goes forward with confidence and faith. I see a great day coming for our country, and I am eager for the work ahead.

God bless you, and may God bless America.

Source: U.S. Executive Office of the President. "Remarks in a Victory Celebration." *Weekly Compilation of Presidential Documents* 40, no. 45 (November 8, 2004): 2783–2784. www.gpoaccess.gov/wcomp/v40no45.html (accessed March 4, 2005).

GAO on Challenges in Preparing U.S. National Guard Forces

November 10, 2004

INTRODUCTION

The prolonged U.S. military deployments since the September 11, 2001, terrorist attacks—particularly the wars in Afghanistan and Iraq—put extraordinary pressures on the armed services and created concerns about the potential impact on recruitment and retention. By late 2004 about one-third of the nearly 1 million military personnel who had seen active service in the previous three years had been sent into combat zones at least twice, according to Pentagon figures. Normally, the Pentagon tried to send its personnel overseas only once in any four- or five-year period. The Pentagon also forced thousands of personnel to stay in the services even after their enlistments expired,

The military's well-publicized staffing troubles led to widespread speculation about reinstituting the draft, which the nation had abandoned at the close of the Vietnam War in 1973. Rep. Charles Rangel, D-N.Y., introduced legislation calling for a draft, arguing that soldiers from low-income families had shouldered most of the burden of recent military service. Rangel offered his proposal to underline the costs of the Iraq War, but it also helped fuel rumors that a draft was imminent. Hoping to quash the rumors during the run-up to the November elections, House leaders brought Rangel's proposal to the floor in October for a symbolic burial; it was rejected by a vote of 402–2.

Along with staffing shortages, the Bush administration found itself struggling to provide adequate equipment, training, and weapons for its troops in Iraq. This was highlighted by a controversy in December, when an Army National Guard soldier headed into Iraq publicly questioned Secretary of Defense Donald Rumsfeld about the government's failure to supply enough armor to protect U.S. military vehicles against insurgent bombs. Inadequate training and supervision of military personnel also appeared to figure in a major scandal that caused deep international embarrassment for the United States, as the abuse of Iraqis at a Baghdad prison by military police from an army reserve unit was revealed. *(Prison abuse scandal, p. 207; violence in Iraq, p. 874)*

Personnel Shortages

The military's staffing shortages that became increasingly evident in 2004 stemmed from both long- and short-term causes. The most important long-term cause was a Pentagon policy, dating from after the Vietnam War, under which certain types of job responsibilities (the Pentagon called them "skill sets") were assigned to units of the guard and reserves, rather than to the active-duty services. Important examples included civil affairs, construction, military intelligence, military police, medical corps, and transportation. This situation worked well in peace time, allowing the military to recruit doctors, lawyers, mechanics, policemen, and others who were willing to serve the country part-time—while limiting the size and expense of permanent, active-duty forces.

However, nearly all the military's deployments since a 1994–1995 peacekeeping mission in Haiti required substantial numbers of specialists from guard and reserve units, notably civil affairs officers and military police. These deployments included large peacekeeping missions in Bosnia and Kosovo in the last half of the 1990s. The same was true in Afghanistan, which the United States invaded in late 2001. Three years later, more than 18,000 U.S. troops were still there. *(Afghanistan, pp. 548, 912; Haiti peacekeeping, Historic Documents of 1994, p. 433; Bosnia peacekeeping, Historic Documents of 1995, p. 717; Kosovo peacekeeping, Historic Documents of 1999, p. 285)*

The prolonged U.S. involvement in Iraq after the 2003 war there made an already difficult situation worse. The Pentagon's original plans for the Iraq War called for nearly all of the 130,000-some U.S. forces to be withdrawn by the end of 2003 or early 2004, at the latest. With the growth of an anti-U.S. insurgency in Iraq, the Bush administration found itself adding troops to Iraq in 2004, rather than pulling them out. Among the units in greatest demand in Iraq were the civil affairs and military police units that had been stretched thin in peacekeeping missions for nearly a decade. At the end of 2004, nearly 150,000 U.S. troops were still in Iraq—and at least another 20,000 were deployed in other parts of the Middle East to support those in Iraq. About 40 percent of the troops in Iraq were from the reserve (about 38,000) and the reserves (about 22,000).

Yet another factor in the equation was the full- or part-time deployment of tens of thousands of National Guard troops within the United States since the September 11, 2001, terrorist attacks. To protect the homeland against subsequent terrorist attacks, National Guard forces at various times patrolled airports, nuclear power plants, sensitive government installations, and other places. By 2004 governors in many states were complaining that their National Guard units were so stretched from both domestic and foreign deployments that they could not be counted on for other emergencies, such as responding to hurricanes in the Southeast, wildfires in the West, and other natural disasters.

Experts on military affairs said the Pentagon was struggling to deal with the consequences of a war that lasted much longer than Bush administration planners had expected. "The Army is just running out of ideas for coping with the level of commitment that Iraq requires," Loren Thompson, a military analyst at the conservative Lexington Institute told the *New York Times* in June. "It is clear there was a fundamental miscalculation about how protracted and how intense the ground commitment in Iraq would be."

Bush Administration Policies

To meet the demands of the military, the Pentagon in 2003 and 2004 resorted to several extraordinary procedures, including:

- **"Stop-Loss" Orders.** This was a procedure under which the Pentagon forced thousands of active-duty, reserve, and National Guard personnel to stay in the military weeks or even months after their enlistments expired. Under this policy, troops could not leave the military until ninety days after their units returned home. The Pentagon began limited use of the stop-loss policy after the September 11, 2001, terrorist attacks; expanded the policy to apply to some units in Iraq in 2003; and then expanded it again on June 2, 2004, telling all soldiers headed for Afghanistan and Iraq that they would be kept in the military past their enlistment dates. Lt. Gen. Franklin L. Hagenback, chief of army personnel, said the army might have to keep issuing stop-loss orders for several years while it reorganized units to cope with the consequences of the deployments in Iraq and elsewhere.

- **Extending Tours of Duty.** Dozens of military units—including in some cases entire army divisions with up to 20,000 personnel—had their tours of duty in Iraq extended beyond the normal limits. After the war in 2003, the Pentagon boosted the Iraq duty-tours for army units from the standard six or nine months to one year; Marine Corps units remained on tour for a standard seven months. Even that step proved insufficient, however, and in April 2004 Rumsfeld said at least 20,000 army soldiers would have their one-year tours extended by as much as three months; about 25 percent of those soldiers were in Army National Guard and reserve units. This move enabled the military to keep more soldiers on the ground in Iraq while allowing units newly deployed there to serve alongside—instead of replacing—units near the end of their standard tours. Late in 2004 Rumsfeld appeared to be reconsidering the matter, however, after hearing from field commanders that the extra-long tours of duty were stretching soldiers, and their equipment, too thin. The army's acting secretary, Lee Brownlee, on October 8 ordered development of plans for shorter tours—but only after the anti-U.S. insurgency in Iraq had died down.
- **Tapping the Ready Reserve.** About 118,000 former army soldiers, who for various reasons had been discharged from service before their enlistments expired, were members of what the army called the Individual Ready Reserve, subject to activation at a moment's notice. That moment came in late June, when the Pentagon said it would call up 5,600 of the former soldiers for year-long tours of duty; most were to be sent to Iraq or Afghanistan for service in units that needed more cooks, mechanics, truck drivers, and other specialists. The army acknowledged in late September that more than 30 percent of the 4,000 Individual Ready Reserve soldiers given activation orders so far had sought delays or exemptions; some could face criminal charges if they failed to comply.
- **Expanding the Army.** After resisting congressional pressure to do so, Rumsfeld in January invoked emergency powers to increase, temporarily, the size of the army by 30,000 troops above its statutory limit of 482,000. Not all the 30,000 extra troops were to be new soldiers, officials said; that figure included many of the thousands who were kept in the army through "stop-loss" orders or who could be persuaded to stay in the military with cash bonuses. Despite this temporary step, Rumsfeld and other administration officials said they opposed a permanent increase in the active-duty army as unnecessary.
- **Tapping the "Delayed-Entry Pool."** During 2004 the army began sending new recruits into service at a faster pace than normal. This was done by reducing the amount of time between the date enlistees first signed up and when they were sent to basic training. In the past, the army deliberately postponed, by up to a year, service for thousands of new enlistees (who were put into what the army called a delayed-entry pool) so it would have a steady, predictable supply of new soldiers. To help ease its staffing shortage, the army reduced the waiting period. Some personnel experts warned that cutting the backlog of recruits could make the army's longer-term staffing problems worse.

- **Increased Bonuses.** To encourage soldiers to reenlist, the army offered better incentives than in the past, including bonuses of up to $15,000, depending on education and experience; in some cases the bonuses were more than double the previous levels. The army also added 1,000 recruiters, giving it a total force of 7,000.
- **Redeployments.** The Pentagon in mid-2004 transferred 12,500 army soldiers from South Korea to Iraq for what was called a temporary redeployment. On August 16 President George W. Bush announced that he had approved a longer-term Pentagon plan to shift as many as 70,000 service personnel from Europe and Asia to other postings, including in the Middle East; this redeployment was to take place over a ten-year period.

Stress on Soldiers and Their Families

While these and other actions helped the military keep enough troops in the field, they caused enormous stress on the individuals involved, their families, and in many cases entire military units. Opinion surveys of service members and their families showed that most were willing to make the personal sacrifice and understood the military's needs. Told in April that his unit was being kept in Iraq an extra four months past its regular one-year tour, Spc. Whitney Eargle told the *Washington Post:* "The truth is, you can be mad about it, you can let it get you down—but you're still going to be here."

An increasing number, however, said they deeply resented changes the Pentagon ordered in their lives—sometimes with little or no warning. More than 1,000 family members of personnel in an Army National Guard unit from Illinois sent a petition to the Pentagon in April asking for the return of their relatives: "Their tour in Iraq has already been extended once, and the strain of another tour of duty in Iraq is becoming a health concern for these soldiers," the petition said. Army Reserve Sgt. Catrina Hernandez, of South San Francisco, told the *San Francisco Chronicle* in May that she was proud to serve in the military but was angered by the extension of her military police unit's tour-of-duty in Iraq by four months. "I just wish that we were treated with fairness," she wrote in an e-mail to the newspaper. "We fight to keep America safe, yet when our service is done, we get stepped on."

A small number of soldiers took their complaints to a higher level than the local newspaper, filing suit to block Pentagon orders keeping them in the military past their enlistment expiration dates. Federal judges threw out most of the complaints, but several were still pending at year's end.

Soldiers and their families were not the only ones affected by the extended deployments of National Guard and reserve forces. Employers, and in some cases even entire communities, found themselves struggling to make do while soldiers were away. The burden was especially difficult in the cases of soldiers who were self-employed or worked for small companies. News organizations reported dozens of cases in which self-employed soldiers had to sell or close their businesses—or go deeply in debt—because they were away from home for months or even years. Small towns also found it difficult to cope when policemen, teachers, and even mayors were called away to Iraq for extended tours.

As could be expected, the Bush administration's struggles with military staffing requirements became an issue in the presidential election campaign. Sen. John Kerry, the Democratic presidential candidate, criticized the Pentagon stop-loss orders to soldiers as a "backdoor draft" and said it resulted from the administration's "fundamental failure" to plan for the aftermath of the war.

Stresses on the Guard and Reserves

The Afghanistan and Iraq wars were the first major recent conflicts fought by the United States in which part-time soldiers—the National Guard and reserves—were called on to serve for extended periods of time. Thousands of guard and reserve units were activated in 1990–1991 for the Persian Gulf War, but for the most part those activations lasted only a few months. By contrast, guard and reserve soldiers played a role in the Afghanistan conflict from October 2001 through the end of 2004, and in the Iraq conflict since late 2002. As of June 2004, according to the Government Accountability Office (GAO), more than 50 percent of the 350,000 Army National Guard members and 107,000 Air National Guard members had been activated for missions either overseas or at home.

Three types of specialties within the National Guard had been particularly hard hit by recent deployments: engineering, military police, and transportation units. According to guard figures published April 26 by the *Wall Street Journal,* about 74 percent of the 42,582 engineers, 80 percent of the 15,800 military policemen, and 78 percent of the 21,800 truck drivers and other transportation specialists in guard units had been deployed on various missions since late 2001. By 2004 most of these personnel already had served a full year in Iraq and could not be sent back under current policy.

A broad overview of the problems faced by the National Guard—the army guard in particular—came in a November 10 report to Congress by the GAO. The report reviewed the status of Army National Guard units in four states (Georgia, New Jersey, Oregon, and Texas)—along with national records from the Pentagon—and found that numerous deployments since the September 11 attacks had stretched the guard thin. Short-term steps taken to meet current needs—such as the transfer of more than 74,000 personnel from nondeployed units into units that had been deployed—had "degraded" the ability of the nondeployed units to respond to future needs, the report said. The army also shifted equipment from nondeployed to deployed units, further damaging the ability of nondeployed units to respond to future emergencies.

The army reserve also was under stress. An early warning came January 20 from Lt. Gen. James R. Helmly, commander of the U.S. Army Reserve, who told reporters that many of the 205,000 soldiers in his force were upset about longer tours of duties, lack of supplies and equipment, and too-short notices when they were mobilized. Helmly said the mobilization for Iraq in 2003 "was so fraught with friction that it really put a bad taste in a lot of people's mouths. We had about 10,000 [reservists] who had less than five day's notice that they were going to be mobilized. Then we had about 8,000 who were mobilized, got trained up, and never deployed." In the future, he said, individual members of the reserve should expect to be on active duty for nine to twelve months every four or five years, he said.

As of mid-September, about 43,500 of the reserve's soldiers were mobilized, half of them in Afghanistan, Iraq, or the Persian Gulf. Helmly said then that he was primarily concerned about shortages in key specialties.

Impact on Recruitment and Retention

The military's staffing problem—and the drastic steps the Pentagon took to solve it—led to predictions that recruiting and retaining soldiers would be more difficult than at any time since the end of the draft three decades earlier. As of year's end, the actual experience was mixed. The army slightly exceeded its enlistment goal of 77,000 soldiers for fiscal year 2004 (ending on September 30), and the reserve hit its target of 21,200. On a national basis, Pentagon officials said the Army National Guard fell 5,000 short of its 56,000 recruiting goal for fiscal year 2004. Commanders in many states, however, said their units had fallen much further below their goals. The recruiting shortfall was the first for the guard in a decade. Preliminary figures for the first two months of fiscal year 2005 offered evidence of potential danger for the army, as both the guard and reserve were falling further behind their recruiting goals—by about 30 percent for the guard and by about 10 percent for the reserve. As a result, the guard offered much higher bonuses of up to $15,000 for soldiers with prior military experience—three times the previous level.

In a move to ensure that it continued to meet its recruiting goals, the army slightly lowered some of its standards for new active-duty soldiers, effective October 1 of the new fiscal year. The army dropped from 92 percent to 90 percent the minimum number of new recruits who had to be high school graduates, and it raised to 2 percent (from 1.5 percent) the number of recruits who would be accepted even through they received the lowest acceptable score on the service's aptitude test. Overall, the changes meant that the army was willing to accept about 2,000 soldiers who would have been rejected in the past.

Although it had been able to meet its recruiting goals, at least until late 2004, the army for two years had experienced trouble in convincing soldiers to reenlist. The army fell short of its retention goals for both fiscal years 2003 and 2004. The National Guard was experiencing a similar problem. An internal National Guard survey, covering 5,000 soldiers from fifteen states in January 2004, showed that about 20 percent of those who had served long overseas tours of duty were planning to leave the military once their time was up. That figure was slightly higher than the historical average. Other surveys and anecdotal evidence later in 2004 appeared to indicate a higher percentage of guard soldiers would refuse to reenlist.

Although officials in Washington remained optimistic that the Iraq-related stresses would cause no long-term damage to the military, National Guard commanders in several states said they were less sanguine. "Our recruiting is down significantly from last year, and our retention rates are down also," Maine's National Guard commander, Brig. Gen. John W. Libby told the *Washington Post* in June. Of special concern, he added, was that parents were discouraging their children from joining the military: "We've got a level of reluctance with parents that we haven't seen in the past."

Following are excerpts from "Reserve Forces: Actions Needed to Better Prepare the National Guard for Future Overseas and Domestic Missions," a report submitted November 10, 2004, by the Government Accountability Office to the Senate Committee on Government Reform and the House Subcommittee on National Security, Emerging Threats and International Relations.

"Reserve Forces: Actions Needed to Better Prepare the National Guard for Future Overseas and Domestic Missions"

The September 11, 2001, terrorist attacks and subsequent launch of the global war on terrorism have resulted in the largest activation of National Guard forces—both Army and Air—since World War II. Within 1 month of the September 11 attacks, the number of Army National Guard members activated for federal missions more than quadrupled, from about 5,500 to about 23,000. By June 2004, over 50 percent of the National Guard's nearly 350,000 Army and 107,000 Air National Guard members had been activated for overseas warfighting operations in Afghanistan and Iraq, peacekeeping operations in Bosnia and Kosovo, or homeland missions, such as guarding active Air Force bases. These operations have resulted in a high demand for Guard members overall and especially for those trained with certain skills, such as security personnel and tanker pilots. As a result, National Guard personnel have experienced lengthy and repeated deployments since the September 11 terrorist attacks.

The National Guard holds a unique dual status in that it performs federal missions under the command of the President and state missions under the command of the state's governor. After September 11, the Guard's duties were expanded to include supporting new homeland missions, such as flying combat air patrols over U.S. cities, securing borders, providing radar coverage for the continental United States, and protecting civilian airports, Air Force bases, and other critical infrastructure. Governors also activated the Guard to perform additional missions, such as guarding bridges and nuclear power plants. Guard involvement in state missions almost tripled in the year after the attacks, and it has remained well above pre-September 11 levels. The Guard spent about 236,000 days performing state missions in fiscal year 2001, and that number increased to about 645,000 days in fiscal year 2002. State mission involvement subsequently declined to almost 433,000 days in fiscal year 2003, more than twice the level before September 11. This high pace of operations has raised concerns about the National Guard's ability to perform warfighting and homeland missions successfully within its existing resources and the challenges it faces in meeting these requirements in the future.

The objectives of this report are to assess the extent to which the National Guard is (1) adapting to meet current and future overseas warfighting requirements in the post-September 11 security environment and (2) supporting immediate and emerging homeland security needs. . . .

To assess the objectives, we analyzed data on National Guard utilization and readiness prior to and after September 11, 2001. We interviewed officials in the Departments of Defense (DOD), Army, and Air Force and the National Guard Bureau and supplemented this information with visits to Army and Air Force commands and Army mobilization stations. We also developed case studies of recent federal and state

National Guard operations in four states—Georgia, New Jersey, Oregon, and Texas. We selected these states because they represent a mix of geographic areas, Army and Air National Guard units with different specialties, and units that had been or were expected to be activated for federal and/or state missions. In each of these states, we visited the Adjutant General and National Guard headquarters, as well as Army and Air National Guard units that had been or will be involved in overseas or domestic missions. We also reviewed documents on planned changes to the Army Guard's force structure, such as the Army Campaign Plan and the Army Transformation Roadmap. We conducted our review in accordance with generally accepted government auditing standards between April 2003 and September 2004 and determined that the data used were sufficiently reliable for our objectives. . . .

Results in Brief

The Army and the Air National Guard have been adapting their forces to meet new warfighting requirements since the September 11 terrorist attacks, but some measures taken to meet immediate needs have made providing forces for future operations more challenging for the Army National Guard. Unlike the Air National Guard, the Army National Guard is still organized according to a post-cold war military planning strategy that provides it only a portion of the resources needed to perform warfighting missions, with the assumption that its units will have sufficient time to obtain the additional personnel and equipment before deploying. However, recent operations have required that Army National Guard units be fully manned and equipped to deploy, sometimes within short time frames. To meet warfighting needs, DOD has retrained some Army National Guard soldiers and units to perform key functions and changed the missions of some units, issuing them new equipment for their new activities. For example, to respond to a continuing demand for military police, the Army has changed some field artillery units to security forces and retrained over 7,000 soldiers to perform new duties. In addition, because the Army National Guard units do not have all of the resources they need for warfighting missions, the Army National Guard has had to transfer personnel and equipment from nondeploying units to prepare deploying units. As of July 2004, the Army National Guard had performed over 74,000 personnel transfers, shifting soldiers from one unit to another, to meet warfighting needs. Similarly, as of May 2004, it had transferred over 35,000 pieces of equipment to deploying units. While the Army National Guard has provided ready units thus far, the cumulative effect of these personnel and equipment transfers is that the readiness of nondeployed forces has declined, challenging the Army to continue to provide ready Guard forces for future missions. The Army has taken steps to begin to restructure its active, Guard, and Reserve forces into more versatile units to improve its ability to respond to the dynamic security environment, but it is still in the process of developing plans for restructuring Army National Guard forces. Under preliminary plans, Guard restructuring would not be completed until 2010. In addition, current plans do not address how the Guard's equipment will be modernized to make it compatible with active Army equipment or provide detailed time frames and costs for converting all Guard equipment. Until plans on how the Guard will fit into overall Army reorganization plans are finalized and shared with Congress, it is uncertain how they will transform the Guard for a new operational role. Further, the Army has not reevaluated its resourcing policy for the Army National Guard to mitigate the effects of increased usage on its nondeployed forces, and current Army funding plans call for continuing to maintain nondeployed Army National Guard forces with only a portion of the personnel and equipment required for warfighting operations. Like the Army National Guard, the Air National Guard has also had to adjust to the demands of recent operations and has provided forces to support current military operations by extending tours of duty. Although its readiness has declined as a result of the high use of personnel and equipment, the Air National Guard has not been as negatively affected as the Army National Guard because it has not been required to sustain the same high level of activations and is funded to maintain more fully manned and equipped units.

While the Army and the Air National Guard have supported the nation's homeland security needs by providing personnel and equipment for unanticipated missions, the Guard's preparedness to perform the homeland defense and civil support missions that may be needed in the future is unknown because (1) its role in these missions is not defined and requirements have not been established and (2) preparedness standards and measures have not been developed. Since September 11, the Army National Guard has provided security for borders, airports, and other key assets, while the Air National Guard has taken on missions such as flying air patrols over U.S. cities. The Army and the Air National Guard have conducted these missions largely using existing forces and equipment that were provided for warfighting missions. However, state officials have expressed concern about the Guard's preparedness to undertake state missions, including supporting homeland security missions, given the increase in overseas deployments and the shortages of personnel and equipment among the remaining Guard units. Moreover, some homeland security missions could require training and equipment, such as decontamination training and equipment, that differ from that provided to support warfighting missions. Because DOD, specifically the U.S. Northern Command and the Office of Assistant Secretary of Defense for Homeland Defense, has not clearly defined what the Guard's role will be or analyzed what personnel, training, and equipment may be required to support homeland missions in conjunction with the Department of Homeland Security, it is difficult to measure the Guard's preparedness for potential missions. DOD and Congress have taken some actions to strengthen the Guard's homeland capabilities, such as establishing Weapons of Mass Destruction Civil Support Teams, to support civil authorities in identifying whether chemical and biological events have occurred and the type of agent used. Moreover, the National Guard Bureau is implementing pilot programs to strengthen other capabilities to respond to weapons of mass destruction events and improve critical infrastructure protection. However, these pilot programs are in the early stages of implementation and were developed by the Guard to respond to pressing needs. They are not based on a comprehensive analysis of the full spectrum of the Guard's role and requirements for homeland security missions. Without such a comprehensive analysis, DOD and congressional policy makers may not be in the best position to assess whether additional investments are needed, and Guard personnel may lack the type of training and equipment that would facilitate an effective and timely response to future homeland security threats.

We are recommending that the Secretary of Defense develop and submit a strategy to Congress for improving the Army National Guard's structure and readiness and clearly define the Guard's role in homeland defense and providing support to civilian authorities. DOD generally agreed with our recommendations and cited several actions it is taking to develop a strategy that addresses the Army National Guard's future roles and requirements.

Source: U.S. Congress. Government Accountability Office. "Reserve Forces: Actions Needed to Better Prepare the National Guard for Future Overseas and Domestic Missions." GAO–05–21, November 10, 2004. www.gao.gov/new.items/d0521.pdf (accessed April 19, 2005).

Bureau of Justice Statistics on Capital Punishment

November 14, 2004

INTRODUCTION

Controversy over the constitutionality and fairness of the death penalty continued to swirl in the United States in 2004, even as the number of death sentences and executions declined from the highs of the late 1990s. High courts in two states declared the death penalty to be unconstitutional, five death row inmates were exonerated on the basis of DNA tests or other new evidence in their cases, and Congress passed legislation making it easier for federal inmates to obtain DNA testing of criminal evidence after their convictions. Finally, the International Court of Justice ordered American courts to review the death sentences imposed on fifty-one Mexicans in the United States, saying that their rights had been violated under an international treaty to which the United States was a signatory.

The Supreme Court in December agreed to hear arguments in a case that could determine whether the Court was willing to comply with the ruling of the international court. The Supreme Court also heard arguments in December on another issue of intense interest in the international community: the constitutionality of executing murderers who committed their crimes when they were juveniles. The United States and Somalia were the only two countries that had not formally repudiated executions of juvenile offenders. In a series of decisions, the Supreme Court indicated its displeasure with what appeared to be open defiance of several of its death penalty rulings by the top criminal court in Texas and the federal Fifth Circuit Court of Appeals.

Declining Numbers

The number of death sentences imposed and the number of executions continued to fall. In November 2004 the Bureau of Justice Statistics in the Justice Department reported that 144 death sentences were handed down in 2003—the lowest number in thirty years and well below the average annual rate of 297 between 1994 and 2000. The number of death sentences imposed in 2004 was projected to be even lower. The number of executions dropped to 65 in 2003 and to 59 in 2004. Altogether 944 people had been executed since the Supreme Court reinstated the death penalty in 1976.

Several reasons were given for the decline, including growing concerns about the reliability of the system. According to the Death Penalty Information Center, 117 death row inmates had been exonerated since 1976. The center counted pardons, acquittals after retrials, and dismissals by prosecutors. Fairness was also an issue. For example, a Texas inmate on death row since 1987 for arson and murder was released in October 2004 after expert review of the evidence showed that the fire was caused not by arson but an electrical malfunction; another Texas inmate convicted under similar circumstances was executed in 2004.

Supporters of the death penalty attributed the declining number of death sentences and executions to the falling murder rate and to changes in sentencing laws, particularly those that gave juries the option of life without parole. The only two death penalty states that lacked that option in 2004 were Texas and New Mexico. New Mexico had only 2 people on death row in late 2004; Texas had 446, second only to California, with more than 600. According to state polls, although 75 percent of Texans approved of the death penalty, 78 percent said they would like to have the option of sentencing an offender to life without parole. A Gallup Poll conducted in May found similar sentiments nationwide. Franklin Zimring, a law professor and director of the criminal justice research program at the University of California at Berkeley, neatly captured the ambivalence Americans seem to have about capital punishment. "We don't want to see innocent people executed, but we don't like murders," he told the *Christian Science Monitor.*

Texas under Scrutiny

Of the 944 persons executed in the United States between 1976 and the end of 2004, more than 35 percent—335—had been put to death in Texas; Virginia was next, with 99, and then Oklahoma, with 81. The high number of executions in Texas had long made the state's criminal justice system a subject of intense scrutiny by those opposed to the death penalty. By 2004 those concerns appeared to have reached into the Supreme Court, which handed down several rulings taking issue with the way prosecutors and judges had dealt with defendants in capital punishment cases.

On February 24 the Court ruled that Texas death row inmate Delma Banks should be allowed to appeal his murder conviction and death sentence because prosecutors had improperly withheld evidence from the defense. Banks was convicted of murdering a coworker at a Texarkana restaurant in 1980. At his trial prosecutors failed to disclose that one of two key witnesses was a paid police informant and that the other witness had received intensive coaching by prosecutors on his trial testimony. Nearly seventeen years after Bank's conviction, evidence came to light showing that prosecutors had always known the two witnesses were making false statements. A federal district court rescinded Banks's death sentence, but not his conviction, because of the false statements made during the sentencing phase of the trial. But the Fifth Circuit Court of Appeals reversed the lower court and reinstated Bank's death sentence, ruling that Bank's claims of misconduct by the prosecution were made too late and in the wrong forum. On March 12, 2003—just ten minutes before Banks was scheduled to die—the Supreme Court stayed his execution and agreed to hear his appeal of the circuit court ruling.

Writing for the majority in the case of *Banks v. Dretke,* Justice Ruth Bader Ginsburg said that it was the state's fault, not Banks's, that his claims were made so late. Both during the trial and the sentencing phase, prosecutors had assured the defense that it had been given all the information about the two witnesses to which it was legally entitled. In essence, Ginsburg wrote, the state was arguing that the defendant had the burden of proving that the state was lying and concealing evidence. "A rule thus declaring 'prosecutor may hide, defendant must seek,' is not tenable in a system constitutionally bound to accord defendants due process," she wrote.

Two justices, Clarence Thomas and Antonin Scalia, would have upheld the circuit court's ruling on the death sentence, although Thomas called it "a very close question." All nine justices agreed that the appeals court erred by not allowing Banks to appeal the underlying conviction. The facts in the Banks case and the way it was handled in the local courts had attracted high-profile attention from a group of retired federal judges, including William S. Sessions, former director of the FBI and a former federal district court judge in Texas. In their brief to the court in 2003 asking for a stay of execution, the judges wrote that "the integrity of the death penalty" was at stake. Sessions called the February 24 ruling "a clear victory for justice."

If the Banks case suggested the Supreme Court was concerned about how the lower state and federal courts were handling death penalty cases in Texas, its decision to hear arguments in a case for the second time in two years made that concern abundantly clear. The case involved Thomas Miller-El, a black man convicted of murder and sentenced to death in Texas in 2001. Miller-El was seeking to overturn his conviction on the grounds that Dallas County prosecutors had systematically kept African Americans off his jury in violation of the Fourteenth Amendment's equal protection clause. Miller-El's attorney, former solicitor general Seth Waxman, cited evidence of a long pattern of discrimination against blacks in the county, including a training manual that advised prosecutors to keep blacks off trial juries. Waxman also noted that two prosecutors who handled the jury selection in Miller-El's trial had been found by the Texas Court of Criminal Appeals to have engaged in improper racial discrimination in jury selection in other cases during the same time period.

The Fifth Circuit Court of Appeals rejected Miller-El's challenge, and in February 2003 the Supreme Court voted, 8–1, to instruct the appeals court to reconsider its ruling. In February 2004 the appeals court again rejected Miller-El's claim, again holding that prosecutors had race-neutral reasons for striking the black jurors. The circuit court also cited virtually word for word, but without attribution, several paragraphs from Justice Thomas's dissenting opinion in the 2003 ruling in *Miller-El v. Cockrell.* Miller-El again appealed to the Supreme Court.

During oral argument December 6, several justices indicated displeasure with the appeals court and sharply questioned the basis on which the appeals court made its decision. In an interview with the *New York Times* before the oral arguments, John J. Gibbons, a former chief judge of the U.S. Court of Appeals for the Third Circuit, said the Fifth Circuit "just went out of its way to defy the Supreme Court on this. The idea that the system can tolerate open defiance by an inferior court just cannot stand." Gibbons had filed a brief supporting Miller-El. The Supreme Court was expected to issue its decision in the case before it adjourned in early summer of 2005.

Flawed jury instructions were at the heart of two other cases from Texas in which the Supreme Court overturned death sentences. In 2001 the Court had ruled in the case of *Penry v. Johnson* that the jury instructions in the sentencing phase of a capital murder case were "internally contradictory" and did not allow jurors to adequately take into account the defendant's retardation. *(Penry case, Historic Documents of 2001, p. 388)*

The Fifth Circuit Court of Appeals and the Texas Court of Criminal Appeals continued to uphold some death sentences handed down under the flawed jury instructions, however, and on June 24, 2004, the Supreme Court overturned a death sentence because of the improper instructions. The Fifth Circuit's ruling approving the death sentence "has no foundation in the decisions of this court," wrote Justice Sandra Day O'Connor for the 6–3 majority in *Tennard v. Dretke.*

After arguments in the Tennard case but before the Supreme Court had issued its ruling, the Texas criminal appeals court rejected a similar appeal from another convicted murderer. Overturning that death sentence on November 15, the Supreme Court minced few words in chastising the Texas court for ignoring the problems the Supreme Court had already identified in the jury instructions. The Texas appeals court "erroneously relied on a test we never countenanced and now have unequivocally rejected," the justices said in *Smith v. Texas.*

Juvenile Executions

In other actions, the Supreme Court on June 24 ruled, 5–4, not to apply retroactively a 2002 decision in *Ring v. Arizona* that juries, rather than judges, had to decide between the death penalty and life imprisonment. The ruling affected more than 100 death row inmates in Arizona, Idaho, Montana, Nebraska, and Nevada, who had hoped retroactive application would have overturned their death sentences and given them the right to a new sentencing hearing. The case was *Schriro v. Summerlin.*

The Court also heard arguments in October on the constitutionality of executing offenders who had committed their crimes as sixteen or seventeen year olds. Although thirty-eight states allowed capital punishment for adults, only nineteen of those allowed the death penalty for juveniles. No state allowed executions of juveniles under sixteen.

The four "liberal" justices on the Supreme Court—John Paul Stevens, David H. Souter, Stephen G. Breyer, and Ginsburg—had indicated in earlier decisions that they believed the death penalty for juveniles was cruel and unusual punishment in violation of the Eighth Amendment. Chief Justice William H. Rehnquist, Thomas, and Scalia had indicated that they believed the practice was constitutional. The decision in *Roper v. Simmons* was thus likely to turn on Justices Anthony M. Kennedy and O'Connor, who had hedged on her views. Three times since 2002, the four liberal justices were unable to get a fifth vote to stop executions that presented many of the same arguments raised in *Roper v. Simmons.* That case involved a Missouri man who was seventeen when he kidnapped, duct-taped, and drowned a woman.

Opponents of the practice argued that juveniles should be held accountable for their actions but that their emotional and intellectual immaturity should bar imposing the punishment reserved for society's most heinous wrongdoers. Some scientific evidence also showed that brain development was still in flux during teenage years. Those who supported the constitutionality of imposing the death penalty on juveniles say it was a matter that should be left to juries to decide by looking at the individual circumstances of each case.

International Court Ruling

One case with international implications involved execution of foreigners in the United States. On March 31 the International Court of Justice, commonly known as the World Court, ruled that the rights of fifty-one Mexicans jailed and sentenced to death in the United States had been violated under international law and ordered the U.S. courts to undertake "an effective review" of the convictions and sentences. Under the 1963 Vienna Convention on Consular Rights, people arrested abroad had a right to meet with representatives of their own country—a right the federal government regularly invoked to meet with American citizens detained in foreign jails but that the World Court said had been denied to the Mexican defendants.

The World Court ruling was widely hailed in Mexico, which had filed the complaint in January 2003 to stop the imminent executions of three Mexican citizens. Mexico had only a very restricted death penalty that had not been used since 1961. Mexicans had been dismayed when Texas authorities executed a Mexican man in August 2002, despite a personal appeal for mercy from Mexican president Vicente Fox to President George W. Bush and Rick Perry, Bush's successor as governor of Texas. Fox called the World Court ruling "a triumph for international law, for human rights." The United States had opposed the claim as "an unjustified, unwise and ultimately unacceptable intrusion into the United States criminal justice system."

One of the first courts to respond to the ruling was the U.S. Court of Appeals for the Fifth Circuit. In May it rejected a request for a new hearing from Jose Ernesto Medellin, a Mexican on Texas's death row, ruling that because Medellin had not claimed his rights under the treaty during his state murder trial, he could not now claim them in a federal appeals court. The appeals court said it was following a ruling of the U.S. Supreme Court in 1998, which implied that the treaty was subject to a country's procedural rules. On December 10 the Supreme Court agreed to review the Fifth Circuit's ruling. The case, *Medellin v. Dretke,* was scheduled for argument in March 2005.

Action in the States

In other action in 2004, high courts in Kansas and New York declared the death penalty to be unconstitutional. On December 17 the Kansas supreme court struck down the state's capital punishment law because of flaws in the way juries weighed evidence for and against death sentences. On December 20 the court agreed to stay its ruling to give the state attorney general time to appeal the decision to the U.S. Supreme Court. The New York legislature appeared to be in no hurry to rewrite the law struck down by the high court in that state.

Moving in an opposite direction, Gov. Mitt Romney, R-Mass., a potential presidential contender in 2008, endorsed legislation at the end of the year that would reinstate the death penalty in Massachusetts but would seek to ensure that the state could not execute an innocent person. Among other safeguards, the legislation would apply the death penalty only in cases involving terrorism or torture, serial murder, the murder of police or witnesses, or murder while serving a life sentence for murder. Scientific evidence, including DNA evidence, would be required to corroborate guilt. Prosecutors would have to persuade a jury that there was "no doubt" the defendant was guilty; the current standard required that a jury could impose the death penalty only if the prosecutor had proved guilt "beyond a reasonable doubt." Romney had pledged to reinstate the death penalty in Massachusetts when he first ran for governor in 2002; the state legislature had killed death penalty legislation several times since the Supreme Court ruled in 1976 that capital punishment was constitutional.

In Illinois, the state supreme court in January upheld the mass clemencies that George Ryan had issued shortly before stepping down as the state's governor in January 2003. Ryan pardoned four death row convicts and commuted 155 death sentences, emptying the state's death row. Ryan had imposed a moratorium on executions in 2000 after several death row inmates were found to have been wrongfully convicted. Also in January Ryan's successor, Rod Blagojevich, signed into law the final piece of an extensive legislation package reforming the way the death penalty was reached in Illinois.

At the national level, the Congress passed legislation in October that made access to DNA testing easier for federal inmates to obtain. Under the law (PL 108–405), DNA testing could be ordered in cases in which an inmate asserted under penalty of perjury that he was innocent and where the test might produce new material evidence supporting the claim of innocence, raising the possibility that the inmate did not commit the crime. The time period for making such claims was limited in most cases to three years after conviction; at the same time, the government was barred from destroying DNA evidence in federal criminal cases while a defendant remained incarcerated.

Following are excerpts from "Capital Punishment, 2003," a bulletin from the Bureau of Justice Statistics released November 14, 2004, detailing a continuing decline in the number of death sentences imposed and executions carried out.

"Capital Punishment, 2003"

Eleven States and the Federal Government executed 65 prisoners during 2003. The number executed was 6 fewer than in 2002. Those executed during 2003 had been under sentence of death an average of 10 years and 11 months, 4 months longer than the period for inmates executed in 2002.

At yearend 2003, 3,374 prisoners were under sentence of death. California held the largest number on death row (629), followed by Texas (453), Florida (364), and Pennsylvania (230).

During 2003, 25 States and the Federal prison system received 144 prisoners under sentence of death.

During the year, 257 inmates had their death sentences overturned or removed, the largest number since 1976 when the Supreme Court reinstated the death penalty. Illinois accounted for 62% of these removals.

In 2003, 65 men were executed, including 41 whites, 20 blacks, 3 Hispanics (all white), and 1 American Indian. Sixty-four were carried out by lethal injection; one by electrocution.

From January 1, 1977, to December 31, 2003, 885 inmates were executed by 32 States and the Federal Bureau of Prisons. Two-thirds of the executions occurred in 5 States: Texas (313), Virginia (89), Oklahoma (68), Missouri (61), and Florida (57).

Capital Punishment Laws

At yearend 2003 the death penalty was authorized by 38 States and the Federal Government. No State enacted new legislation authorizing capital punishment in 2003.

The Missouri Supreme Court struck a portion of that State's capital statute on August 26, 2003. The Court found that evolving standards required that the minimum age for capital sentences be raised to 18 years of age rather than 16 as specified by Missouri law.

Statutory Changes

During 2003, 11 States revised statutory provisions relating to the death penalty. By State, the changes were as follows:

Colorado—Revised an aggravating factor to include use of chemical, biological or radiological weapons and added as an aggravating factor intentional killing of more than one person in more than one criminal episode, effective 4/29/2003.

Colorado also added to its list of aggravating factors deliberately killing of a pregnant woman when the defendant knew the victim was pregnant, effective 7/1/2003.

Delaware—Amended the statute to clarify that, while juries decide the existence of aggravating circumstances, sentencing is at the judge's discretion. Judges departing from a jury's recommendation must issue a written opinion specifying the reason. Both changes are effective 7/15/2003.

Idaho—Idaho amended its code of procedure to require that sentencing proceedings be held before a jury in capital cases unless a defendant waives the jury and the prosecutor consents to this waiver, effective 2/13/2003.

The Idaho legislature also added to its statute a definition of and procedures for determining if a defendant is mentally retarded, an exemption from the death penalty for any defendants who are deemed to be mentally retarded, and alternate sentencing procedures to be used under these circumstances, effective 3/27/2003.

Illinois—Amended sections of its criminal and procedural codes relating to the death penalty. These changes became effective 11/19/2003.

Illinois established procedures for courts to follow when a death sentence is deemed inappropriate in light of the facts of the case.

A new law prohibited imposition of a death sentence on any defendant found to be mentally retarded and setting forth procedures for such a determination.

The Illinois legislature also added sections regarding admissibility rules for testimony from informants, written disclosure of any information potentially relevant to witness credibility, and criteria for a court to decertify a case as a capital case.

Indiana—Revised the procedural code to require the State Supreme Court to consider during sentence review claims that the sentence is "erroneous". This law was passed in 2003, but was retroactively effective 7/1/2002.

Indiana also amended the statute to allow for post-conviction consideration of new evidence challenging the defendant's guilt or the appropriateness of the death sentence, effective 7/1/2003.

Louisiana—Amended the code of criminal procedure to prohibit capital sentencing of mentally retarded persons.

Montana—Modified the code of criminal procedure to require that a defendant either admit to or be found guilty beyond a reasonable doubt of aggravating factors in order to be sentenced to death, effective 10/1/2003.

Nevada—Revised its law to allow juries rather than 3-judge panels to determine death sentences, effective 6/9/2003; and to set alternatives to a death sentence in cases where a defendant has been found to be mentally retarded by the court, effective 10/1/2003.

Texas—Expanded its definition of criminal homicide to include murder during the commission of a terroristic threat, effective 9/1/2003.

Utah—Amended its statute to exempt mentally retarded persons from capital sentences and to specify pre-trial procedures for determining the mental retardation of defendants; and creating post-conviction procedures for defendants to prove mental retardation, effective 3/15/2003.

Virginia—Excluded mentally retarded defendants from capital sentences, effective 7/1/2003.

Automatic Review

Of the 38 States with capital statutes at yearend, 37 provided for review of all death sentences regardless of the defendant's wishes. In South Carolina the defendant had the right to waive sentence review if he or she was deemed competent by the court. Federal death penalty procedures did not provide for automatic review after a sentence of death had been imposed.

The State's highest appellate court usually conducted the review. If either the conviction or sentence were vacated, the case could be remanded to the trial court for additional proceedings or retrial. As a result of retrial or resentencing, a death sentence could be reimposed.

While most of the 37 States authorized automatic review of both the conviction and sentence, Idaho, Oklahoma, South Dakota, and Tennessee required review of the sentence only. In Idaho review of the conviction had to be filed through appeal or forfeited. In Indiana and Kentucky a defendant could waive review of the conviction.

In Virginia a defendant could waive an appeal of trial court error but could not waive review of the death sentence for arbitrariness and proportionality.

In Mississippi the question of whether the defendant could waive the right to automatic review had not been addressed. In Wyoming neither statute nor case law precluded a waiver of appeal.

Arkansas implemented a rule requiring review of specific issues relating to both capital convictions and sentences. Recent case law held waivers of this review are not permitted.

Method of Execution

As of December 31, 2003, lethal injection was the predominant method of execution (37 States).

Nine States authorized electrocution; four States, lethal gas; three States, hanging; and three States, firing squad.

Seventeen States authorized more than 1 method—lethal injection and an alternative method—generally at the election of the condemned prisoner; however, 5 of these 17 stipulated which method must be used depending on the date of sentencing; 1 authorized hanging only if lethal injection could not be given; and if lethal injection is ever ruled to be unconstitutional, 1 authorized lethal gas, and 1 authorized electrocution or firing squad.

The method of execution of Federal prisoners is lethal injection. For offenses under the Violent Crime Control and Law Enforcement Act of 1994, the method is that of the State in which the conviction took place.

Minimum Age

In 2003 seven jurisdictions did not specify a minimum age for which the death penalty could be imposed.

In some States the minimum age was set forth in the statutory provisions that determine the age at which a juvenile may be transferred to adult court for trial as an adult. Sixteen States and the Federal system required a minimum age of 18. Fifteen States indicated an age of eligibility between 14 and 17.

Characteristics of Prisoners under Sentence of Death at Yearend 2003

Thirty-seven States and the Federal prison system held a total of 3,374 prisoners under sentence of death on December 31, 2003, a decrease of 188 since the end of 2002. Illinois accounted for 84% of this decline with a net decrease of 157 prisoners. Other jurisdictions accounted for a decrease of 31 prisoners during 2003. This was the third consecutive year that the number of prisoners under a sentence of death declined, down from 3,601 on December 31, 2000.

Three States reported 43% of the Nation's death row population: California (629), Texas (453), and Florida (364). The Federal Bureau of Prisons held 23 inmates at yearend. Of the 39 jurisdictions authorizing the death penalty in 2003, New Hampshire had no one under a capital sentence, and New York, Illinois, South Dakota, Colorado, Montana, New Mexico, and Wyoming had 5 or fewer.

Among the 38 jurisdictions with prisoners under sentence of death at yearend 2003, 11 had more inmates than a year earlier, 19 had fewer inmates, and 8 had the same number. California had an increase of 16, followed by Arizona (6), and Texas and Virginia (4 each). Following Illinois, the largest decreases were in Missouri (14), North Carolina (11), and Oklahoma and Pennsylvania (10 each).

During 2003 the number of both white and black inmates under sentence of death declined (by 61 and 133, respectively) while the number of persons of other races (including American Indians, Asians, and self-identified Hispanics) rose from 72 to 78.

Men were 99% (3,327) of all prisoners under sentence of death. Whites accounted for 56%; blacks accounted for 42%; and other races (2%) included 29 American Indians, 35 Asians, and 14 persons whose race was unknown. Among those for whom ethnicity was known, 12% were Hispanic.

During 2003 the number of women sentenced to be executed decreased from 51 to 47. Two women were received under sentence of death, and six were removed from death row. Women were under sentence of death in 17 States. Two-thirds of the women on death row at yearend were being held in four States: California, Texas, Pennsylvania, and North Carolina.

The number of Hispanics under sentence of death rose from 363 to 369 during 2003. Twenty-four Hispanics were received under sentence of death, 15 were removed from death row, and 3 were executed. More than three-quarters of the Hispanics were held in 3 States: California (130), Texas (121), and Florida (30). . . .

Among all inmates under sentence of death for whom date of arrest information was available, about half were age 20 to 29 at the time of arrest for their capital offense; 13% were age 19 or younger; and less than 1% were age 55 or older. The average age at time of arrest was 28 years.

On December 31, 2003, 34% of all inmates were age 30 to 39, and 64% were age 25 to 44. The youngest offender under sentence of death was 19; the oldest was 88.

Criminal History of Inmates under Sentence of Death in 2003

Among inmates under a death sentence on December 31, 2003, for whom criminal history information was available, 64% had prior felony convictions, including 8% with at least one previous homicide conviction.

Among those for whom legal status at the time of the capital offense was available, 40% had an active criminal justice status. Less than half of these were on parole and a quarter were on probation. The remaining third had charges pending, were incarcerated, had escaped from incarceration, or had some other criminal justice status.

Criminal history patterns differed by race and Hispanic origin. More blacks (70%) than whites (62%) or Hispanics (59%) had a prior felony conviction. About the same percentage of whites, blacks, and Hispanics had a prior homicide conviction (8%). A slightly higher percentage of Hispanics (22%) or blacks (18%) than whites (14%) were on parole when arrested for their capital offense.

Since 1988, data have been collected on the number of death sentences imposed on entering inmates. Among the 4,156 individuals received under sentence of death during that time, about 1 in 7 entered with 2 or more death sentences.

Entries and Removals of Persons under Sentence of Death

Between January 1 and December 31, 2003, 25 State prison systems reported receiving 142 inmates under sentence of death; the Federal Bureau of Prisons received 2 inmates. More than half of the inmates were received in 5 States: Texas (29), California (19), Florida (11), and Arizona and Oklahoma (9 each).

Of 144 prisoners who were received under sentence of death, 143 had been convicted of murder and 1 of rape (Louisiana). Two of those admitted were female. By race, 92 were white, 44 were black, 3 were American Indian, 3 were Asian, and 2 were of unknown race. Of the 144 new admissions, 24 were Hispanic.

The 144 admissions to death row in 2003 marked a decline of 24 from the 168 admissions recorded in 2002, and represented the smallest number received in a year since 44 persons were admitted in 1973. Between 1994 and 2000, in contrast, an average 297 inmates per year were admitted. . . .

Twenty-six States and the Federal Bureau of Prisons reported 257 persons whose death sentences were removed or overturned. In addition to the 159 inmates removed in Illinois, appeals courts vacated 78 sentences while upholding the convictions and vacated 15 sentences while overturning the convictions. Pennsylvania (16 exits)had the largest number of vacated sentences. Louisiana and Ohio each reported one commutation of a death sentence. Colorado removed three inmates when the Colorado Supreme Court declared their death sentences unconstitutional.

As of December 31, 2003, 224 of 257 persons who were formerly under sentence of death were serving a reduced sentence, 11 were awaiting a new trial,12 were awaiting resentencing,7 had all capital charges dropped, and 1 had no action taken after being removed from under sentence of death. The current status of 2 inmates was not available.

In addition, 10 persons died while under sentence of death in 2003. Six of these deaths were from natural causes—2 each in Tennessee and California; and 1 each in

Ohio and Utah. Four deaths were suicides—one each in Georgia, Montana, South Dakota, and Tennessee.

From 1977, the year after the Supreme Court upheld the constitutionality of revised State capital punishment laws, to 2003, a total of 6,681 persons entered prison under sentence of death. During these 27 years, 885 persons were executed, and 2,802 were removed from under a death sentence by appellate court decisions and reviews, commutations, or death. (An individual may have been received and removed from under sentence of death more than once. Data are based on the most recent sentence.)

Among individuals who received a death sentence between 1977 and 2003, 3,266 (49%) were white, 2,723 (41%) were black, 582 (9%) were Hispanic, and 110 (2%) were other races. The distribution by race and Hispanic origin of the 3,687 inmates who were removed from death row between 1977 and 2003 was as follows: 1,910 whites (52%), 1,499 blacks (41%), 228 Hispanics (6%), and 50 persons of other races (1%). Of the 885 who were executed, 510 (58%) were white, 301 (34%) were black, 61 (7%) were Hispanic, and 13 (1%) were of other races.

Executions

According to data collected by the Federal Government, from 1930 to 2003, 4,744 persons were executed under civil authority. (Military authorities carried out an additional 160 executions between 1930 and 1961.)

After the Supreme Court reinstated the death penalty in 1976, 32 States and the Federal Government executed 885 prisoners. . . .

During this 27-year period, 5 States executed 589 prisoners: Texas (313), Virginia (89), Oklahoma (69), Missouri (61), and Florida (57). These States accounted for two-thirds of all executions. Between 1977 and 2003, 501 white non-Hispanic men, 300 black non-Hispanic men, 61 Hispanic men, 8 American Indian men, 5 Asian men, 9 white non-Hispanic women, and 1 black non-Hispanic woman were executed.

During 2003 Texas carried out 24 executions; Oklahoma executed 14 persons; North Carolina, 7; Alabama, Florida, Georgia, and Ohio, 3 each; Indiana, Missouri, and Virginia, 2 each; and Arkansas and the Federal prison system, 1 each. All 65 of the inmates executed in 2003 were male. Forty-one were white; 20 were black; 3 were Hispanic; and 1 was American Indian.

From 1977 to 2003, 7,061 prisoners were under death sentences for varying lengths of time. The 885 executions accounted for 12% of those at risk. A total of 2,802 prisoners (40% of those at risk) were removed by means other than execution. About the same percentage of whites (15%), blacks (10%), and Hispanics (10%) were executed. Somewhat larger percentages of whites and blacks (each 41%) than Hispanics (28%) were removed from under a death sentence by means other than execution.

Among prisoners executed from 1977 to 2003, the average time between the imposition of the most recent sentence received and execution was more than 10 years. White prisoners had spent an average of 10 years and 1 month, and black prisoners, 10 years and 9 months. The 65 prisoners executed in 2003 were under sentence of death an average of 10 years and 11 months.

For the 885 prisoners executed between 1977 and 2003, the most common method of execution was lethal injection (718). Other methods used included electrocution (151), lethal gas (11), hanging (3), and firing squad (2).

Among prisoners under sentence of death at yearend 2003, the average time spent in prison was 9 years and 7 months, up 6 months from that in 2002.

The median time between the imposition of a death sentence and yearend 2003 was 103 months. Overall, the average time for women was 7 years and 8 months, 23 months less than that for men (9 years and 7 months). On average, whites, blacks, and Hispanics had spent from 100 to 118 months under a sentence of death.

Source: U.S. Department of Justice. Office of Justice Programs. Bureau of Justice Statistics. "Capital Punishment, 2003." Bureau of Justice Statistics Bulletin, NCJ 206627. November 14, 2004. www.ojp.usdoj.gov/bjs/pub/pdf/cp03.pdf (accessed February 3, 2005).

UN Middle East Envoy on the Death of Yasir Arafat

November 15, 2004

INTRODUCTION

Yasir Arafat, who led the Palestinian people during both conflict and peace with Israel but failed to lead them into statehood, died November 11, 2004. Arafat's death at age seventy-five closed an era in the long-running conflict between Israel and the Palestinians but also created what leaders on both sides described as the best opportunity for peace in a decade. Palestinians chose a long-time colleague to succeed Arafat: Mahmoud Abbas, age sixty-nine, better known in the region as Abu Mazen. Abbas, who had briefly served as Arafat's prime minister in 2003, had opposed the use of violence against Israel, a tactic Arafat had condoned and possibly instigated. At year's end Abbas appeared determined to seize the new momentum toward a peaceful resolution of the conflict.

Ironically, that momentum had been created in part by Israeli prime minister Ariel Sharon, one of Arafat's bitterest foes. Sharon had spent most of 2004 aggressively pursuing a remarkable new policy of withdrawing Israeli settlements and military outposts from the small Palestinian territory known as the Gaza Strip. Sharon pushed this policy through the Israeli parliament in the face of bitter opposition from Jewish settlers and his own supporters in the Israeli right wing. He envisioned the Gaza withdrawal as a unilateral move by Israel without any role being played by the Palestinians. Once Arafat died, however, Sharon said he might be willing to cooperate more fully with the Palestinian government. *(Gaza withdrawal, p. 301)*

Briefing the United Nations Security Council on November 15, Terje Roed-Larsen, the UN's long-time Middle East envoy, called on the international community to help the Palestinians and Israelis take advantage of the changed circumstances since Arafat's death. "Now that he is gone, both Israelis and Palestinians, and the friends of both peoples throughout the world, must make even greater efforts to bring about the peaceful resolution of the Palestinian right of self-determination," he said. A former Norwegian diplomat, Roed-Larsen had helped negotiate the 1993 peace agreement between Israel and the Palestinians known as the Oslo Accords. *(Background, Historic Documents of 1993, p. 747; Historic Documents of 2003, pp. 191, 1200)*

Arafat's Death

At the time of his death Arafat had been a major international figure longer than any other current leader except Cuban president Fidel Castro. Arafat had founded the Palestine Liberation Organization (PLO) in 1964 and headed it ever since. With his scrubby beard and checkered headdress known as a *kaffiyeh,* Arafat also was one of the world's most famous people—a leader who came to symbolize the estimated 8.8 million Palestinians and their quest for a nation of their own, who inspired other nationalist movements around the world, who constantly annoyed many other world leaders (including fellow Arabs), and who infuriated and frightened two generations of Israelis.

Like many other revolutionary leaders, Arafat was considerably more successful as a rebel than as a government official. His guerrilla tactics kept Israelis on edge for the better part of four decades and eventually led Israel to sign the Oslo peace agreement with him in 1993. Arafat's government established under that agreement, the Palestinian Authority, never fully established its authority in the seven years of peace that followed, however. When presented with a chance for a permanent peace agreement in 2000, Arafat rejected it as insufficient. A new round of violence followed, which by 2004 had claimed the lives of more than 3,000 Palestinians and about 1,000 Israelis. Arafat spent the last two-plus years of his life confined to his ruined headquarters in the West Bank city of Ramallah, a virtual captive of the Israelis. His Palestinian government had long since collapsed in all but name—a victim of Israeli suppression, internal corruption and cronyism, and the growing popularity of more militant groups.

The death of Arafat capped what might have been a turning-point year for the Palestinians even had he lived. Sharon's plan to withdraw from the Gaza Strip—without even consulting the Palestinians who would have to assume responsibility there—threw the impotence of Arafat's government into view. Also during the year, younger Palestinian leaders stepped up their demands for reforms and elections that would give them a shot at power. On February 7 more than 300 members of Arafat's Fatah movement sent Arafat a mass resignation letter, protesting his failure to curb corruption and oust incompetent leaders who had risen through the ranks with him. Arafat's own prime minister, Ahmed Qureia, repeatedly threatened to resign to force similar changes, only to back down when Arafat made promises he clearly did not intend to keep. The one concession that did appear real was the calling of future municipal elections that almost certainly would have hastened the erosion of Arafat's limited power. Meanwhile, the economic plight of the 3.3 million Palestinians living in the West Bank and Gaza Strip remained difficult, with per capita income at less than $2 a day—one-third of the level before the current round of violence exploded in 2000.

Political paralysis within the Palestinian government came to a head in mid-July, when Qureia made the most emphatic of his threats to resign and the parliament overwhelmingly demanded that Arafat institute reforms. Attempting to alert the world to the dangers, Roed-Larsen, the UN Middle East envoy, warned the Security Council on July 13 that the Palestinian Authority was "in deep distress, and is in real danger of collapsing." Two weeks later, in a customary compromise that kept his opponents off guard and preserved his own power, Arafat agreed to limited changes demanded by Qureia—but then did nothing to carry them out. In a newspaper interview published October 5, Arafat compared himself to former South African president Nelson Mandela; he said he wanted to be elected president of a fully independent Palestinian state, then would retire and "leave it to others" to carry on what he had started.

Arafat did not live to fulfill that ambition. He fell ill on October 27. It was the day after his old nemesis, Sharon, survived the biggest political challenge of his long career—winning approval of his Gaza withdrawal plan in the bitterly divided Israeli parliament.

Aides at first thought Arafat was suffering from food poisoning or a digestive problem, and they gave conflicting reports about his condition. On October 29

Arafat was flown to a military hospital in Paris, but only after Sharon agreed to let him return to the West Bank after he recovered. Arafat did not recover and died November 11. The exact cause of death remained a mystery, even after his nephew made his medical records public. Arafat's aides emphatically denied rumors that he was poisoned, but the rumors spread anyway. Many Palestinians firmly believed their leader had been killed by the Israelis, who had threatened to do so on numerous occasions.

Arafat's body was flown to Cairo (his birthplace) for a brief memorial service attended by world leaders, then back to Ramallah on November 12. Tens of thousands of grieving Palestinians surrounded the two Egyptian helicopters that brought Arafat's body and Palestinian officials who accompanied it. The ensuing chaos forced authorities to cancel the formal burial ceremony they had planned as a final tribute. Instead, Arafat was interred privately in a section of the compound that had been his living prison. Palestinians insisted it was merely a temporary resting place. Eventually, they said, he would be buried at the al Aqsa mosque in Jerusalem, one of the holiest sites in Islam, but one also claimed by the Jews.

Abbas Takes Over

As Arafat lay dying in the Paris hospital, Palestinian leaders began contemplating their steps once the man who had seemed so indispensable to their cause passed from the scene. Within hours of his death, Arafat's closest colleagues in the PLO—most of whom had served with him for decades—met and selected three men to hold his three most important posts. Abbas was given the most important post as chairman of the PLO executive committee. Rawhi Fattouh, the speaker of the Palestinian parliament, temporarily succeeded to the presidency of the Palestinian Authority, as called for in the constitution. Farouk Kaddoumi, who still lived in Tunisia because he had refused to accept the 1993 peace agreement with Israel, became the senior figure in Fatah, Arafat's political party that constituted the base of the PLO. Qureia remained as prime minister. Despite the multiple leadership, it was clear that Abbas was the lead figure.

Three days later, on November 14, the Palestinian leaders announced an election on January 9, 2005, to choose a permanent successor to Arafat as president of the Palestinian Authority. Leaders of Fatah on November 22 formally selected Abbas as their presidential candidate, virtually ensuring his election.

The one Palestinian leader with the personal popularity to defeat Abbas was sitting in an Israeli prison. Marwan Barghouti, who had been a top aide to Arafat but was widely seen as the leader of the younger generation of Palestinian leaders, was convicted by an Israeli court on May 20 on five counts of murder. The court in Tel Aviv found Barghouti responsible for attacks during 2000–2002 that lead to the deaths of five Israeli civilians, one of them a Greek Orthodox monk. Barghouti had been charged with planning the deaths of twenty-one others, but the court acquitted him of those charges. Barghouti had been a popular figure in the West Bank before his arrest in 2002, but the lengthy trial and resulting convictions—on charges that supporters called trumped-up—made him a hero throughout the Palestinian community.

Barghouti on November 25 sent word from his prison cell that he would run against Abbas for the Palestinian presidency, but he reversed himself the next day. On December 1 Barghouti said he would, in fact, run against Abbas, then reversed himself once again on December 12 and supported Abbas. His withdrawal left only one prominent candidate to oppose Abbas: Mustafa Barghouti, who was a distant relative of Marwan Barghouti and one of the most vocal younger Palestinian leaders demanding reform.

Hamas and Islamic Jihad, the two Palestinian militant organizations with increasing levels of support, especially in Gaza, said they would neither participate in the presidential election nor try to block it. However, Hamas said it would participate in the separate local elections Arafat had agreed to hold.

Abbas officially opened his presidential campaign on December 25 with a speech that embraced Arafat's legacy but also looked to the future. "We are choosing the path of peace and negotiation," he said. "If there is no peace here, there will be no peace in the Middle East or the rest of the world." A relatively shy man who had always appeared in public wearing dark business suits, Abbas suddenly began wearing a *kaffiyeh* around his neck, symbolically cloaking himself in Arafat's mantle.

Palestinian newspapers on December 26 printed an open letter, signed by 559 Palestinian politicians, academics, and other opinion leaders, calling for an end to violence and for a drastic reforms in the Palestinian government once the new president took office. One of the demands was for a reform of the government's numerous security services, which had been substantially weakened in the early stages of the current Intifada. Arafat had used those services to bolster his own support and to keep potential opponents off-guard—but he had never used them to crack down on Hamas and the other militant groups, as Israel had long demanded. Controlling the security services, and using them to enforce any peace he negotiated with Israel, were certain to be among the foremost challenges facing Abbas.

The first stage of promised municipal elections got under way December 23. Voters in twenty-six West Bank towns went to the polls to select new leaders for the first time since 1976. Results released December 26 gave Fatah-backed candidates control of fourteen towns and Hamas-backed candidates control of nine towns. Three other towns had split results. The results were widely seen as a setback for Fatah, which traditionally drew its strength from the West Bank, and as an advance for Hamas, which historically was strongest in the Gaza Strip and had never before run candidates for public office. Another round of local elections was scheduled for the Gaza Strip shortly after the presidential election in January 2005.

Post-Arafat Diplomacy

When it appeared likely in early November that Arafat might not survive, diplomats and Middle East experts began discussing possible steps to revive the long-stalled peace process. Expectations for a new round of peace talks rose on November 12, the day of Arafat's burial, when President George W. Bush and British prime minister Tony Blair held a previously scheduled meeting at the White House. Afterwards, Bush said he saw a "great chance" to renew negotiations to end the conflict and lead to establishment of a Palestinian state. "We'll do what it takes to get a peace," Bush said, adding that he hoped a Palestinian state could be created by the end of his second term, in January 2009.

In years past, such statements by a president likely would have sparked multiple rounds of diplomacy: Special envoys from Washington hovering first with one side then the other, the UN Security Council passing resolutions of encouragement, the possible convening of an international peace conference in a neutral location or, alternatively, a summit meeting at Camp David hosted by the president.

High-level diplomats visited Israel, and in some cases the Palestinian territories, during the weeks after Arafat's death. Among them were European Union foreign policy chief Javier Solana, Secretary of State Colin Powell, and Prime Minister Blair. But these visits no longer had the feel of Western powers arriving on the scene to steer reluctant Middle East leaders in a certain direction. Each in his own way, Abbas and Sharon had indicated that resolving the decades-long conflict between their peoples was up to them, not to diplomats from afar.

The Toll of Violence in 2004

Public opinion polls at year's end showed that most Israelis and Palestinians were cautiously optimistic about the prospects for peace and, just as important, yearned for an end to the seemingly endless cycle of violence that had plagued their lives for more than four years. According to the polls, most people on both sides knew someone among the nearly 40,000 people who had been killed or injured in the violence.

The current round of violence began in September 2000 when Palestinians launched an uprising, which they called an Intifada, largely in response to the failure of U.S.-led peace negotiations that summer. As during a previous Intifada between 1987–1993, the violence took place in predictable patterns. Palestinian militants, generally in the form of suicide bombers or armed gunmen, would attack Israeli civilians or security forces, hoping to kill as many as possible; Israel would retaliate by demolishing the homes of the militants and attacking the Palestinian group or groups that had sponsored the original attack. In some cases Israel responded with large-scale military operations that led to many deaths and massive destruction of Palestinian homes and agricultural lands. In other cases Israel used what it called "targeted killings" to eliminate the leaders of Palestinian militant groups.

Since it began using the tactic of targeted killings in 1973, Israel had eliminated more than 140 Palestinian leaders, most of them associated with Hamas or Islamic Jihad. None of the killings, however, were as far-reaching in their consequences as Israel's actions early in 2004 against Hamas in the Gaza Strip. The single most important attack came March 22, when an Israeli helicopter fired three missiles at an entourage including the founder and spiritual leader of Hamas, Sheikh Ahmed Yassin. Yassin and seven others died in the attack, which Israeli officials said was part of a campaign to wipe out the Hamas leadership. The attack was widely popular among Israelis, who viewed Yassin as the inspiration for many of the worst terrorist attacks against Israel in recent decades. Tens of thousands of Palestinians attended Yassin's funeral the next day, and surviving Hamas leaders vowed revenge, including the assassination of Sharon. An eleven-member majority of the United Nations Security Council voted for a resolution condemning the killing, but the United States vetoed the measure.

Hamas immediately selected a new leader, Abdel Aziz Rantisi, a medical doctor who some observers had claimed to be a relative moderate among the Hamas senior cadre. An Israeli missile killed Rantisi, his son, and a bodyguard on April 17. Thereafter, Hamas declined to name its new leadership, and Israeli authorities said the two killings had thrown Hamas into disarray.

The killings of Yassin and Rantisi reflected the broader picture of the year's violence, most of which took place in the Gaza Strip, rather than in the West Bank, where much of the killing had occurred during the previous three years of the current Intifada. One reason for this shift appeared to be Sharon's determination to take a hard-line stance against militants in Gaza so his plan to withdraw Jewish settlements from that area would not be seen, by either Israelis or Palestinians, as a sign of weakness. Another reason was that several of the year's major suicide bombings and other attacks against Israel were carried out by Gazans.

Israel conducted two major military operations in Gaza during the year. The first began May 11, when the army launched "Operation Rainbow" to destroy workshops in southern Gaza where Palestinians allegedly built crude rockets that were used to attack neighboring Israeli villages. Eleven Israeli soldiers were killed in just the first two days of that operation, but over the next two weeks dozens of Palestinians died. The most serious incident occurred May 19, when an Israeli tank fired on a crowd of Palestinian protesters, killing at least eight. The army said the tank crew was being threatened, but Palestinians insisted the protesters were unarmed civilians.

An even larger Israeli military operation in Gaza began September 29, hours after two Israeli children were killed by Palestinian rockets. In "Operation Penitence," Israeli troops moved into the large Jebaliya refugee camp in northern Gaza—a place the military long had avoided because its crowded buildings and narrow streets were viewed as a death trap for soldiers. More than 100 Palestinians died in the two weeks of violence that ensued.

The killings of Hamas leaders and the incursions into Gaza eliminated some of what Israel called the "terrorism infrastructure," but by 2004 Israel was facing a new challenge. A growing number of the Palestinian attacks were financed or supported by the Iranian-backed Hezbollah, based in Lebanon and beyond Israel's direct reach. The Israeli Security Agency said Hezbollah cells had carried out about 20 percent of all attacks during the year, more than twice the rate of any previous year.

Among the major individual episodes of violence between Israelis and Palestinians during 2004 were:

- A suicide bombing of a bus in Jerusalem on January 29 killed ten Israelis and wounded about four dozen others. It was the first bombing in Israel in more than a month and appeared to be in revenge for an Israeli military raid into Gaza the previous day that killed eight Palestinians, including at least five armed militants.
- A suicide bombing of a bus in Jerusalem on February 22 killed eight Israelis and injured more than sixty others.
- An Israeli army raid into central Gaza on March 7 killed fourteen Palestinians, most of them armed fighters, but also three children. This raid was in retaliation for a failed Palestinian assault a day earlier on the Erez checkpoint between Gaza and Israel.
- Two suicide bombers crossed over from the Gaza Strip on March 14 and attacked the Israeli industrial port of Ashdod, killing themselves and ten others. This event raised special concerns in Israel because it was the first recent attack in which Palestinian militants penetrated an Israeli security fence around Gaza. Also, dangerous chemicals were stored at the port, and officials said the bombing could have caused many more casualties had the chemicals been ignited.
- Rockets fired from Gaza on June 28 killed two Israeli civilians (one of them a three-year-old boy) in the village of Sderot near the Gaza Strip. This was the first time Palestinian rockets had killed anyone.
- Palestinian suicide bombers blew up two commuter buses in the southern Israeli town of Beersheba on August 31, killing sixteen Israelis and wounding several dozen others. This attack was unusual because it took place in a city that largely had escaped violence. Israeli officials said the bombers came

from the southern portion of the West Bank, demonstrating the need to complete the fence, or security barrier, that Israel was building around much of the West Bank.
- Israeli military units on September 7 killed fourteen Hamas militants training at a soccer field in the Gaza Strip. On September 15 the military killed ten Palestinians in the West Bank towns of Jenin and Nablus; most of the dead reportedly were militants, but Palestinians said one was an eleven-year-old girl.

Responsibility for one of the year's most violent incidents had not been determined by year's end. On the night of October 7, bombs were exploded at three resorts on the coast of the Red Sea in Egypt, just south of Israeli border. The resorts were popular holiday spots for Israelis, twelve of whom died in the attacks. Twenty others, most of them Egyptian workers at the resort, also were killed. The Egyptian government at first blamed Bedouin Arabs for the attacks, but subsequent investigations failed to confirm that claim or, indeed, to prove exactly who was responsible.

Each year of the Intifada had produced at least one atrocity that generated exceptional attention amid the bloody cycle of bombings and shootings. One of those cases in 2004 was the October 5 killing by Israeli troops of a thirteen-year-old Palestinian girl near the Rafah refugee camp in southern Gaza. Soldiers said they shot the girl because they thought she was carrying explosives in a backpack. An Israeli army investigation supported her family's claim that she was on her way to school, with a load of books. The investigation also showed that the army commander at the scene pumped bullets into the girl's body to make sure she was dead. The commander faced a criminal prosecution at year's end, one of several cases in which Israeli soldiers had been prosecuted for crimes during the Intifada.

Just under 1,000 Israelis and Palestinians died in the year's violence, bringing the total for four-plus years to more than 4,000.

According to the Israel military, 117 Israelis were killed. That put the total number of Israeli deaths during the Intifada at 1,030—of whom 717 were civilians and 313 were members of security forces. B'Tselem, a left-wing human rights organization based in Israel, gave slightly different totals for Israeli casualties during the year: 107, of whom 67 were civilians and 40 were security personnel. B'Tselem said it counted 940 Israelis who had died during the Intifada, of whom 640 were civilians and 300 were security personnel.

On the Palestinian side, B'Tselem said 818 Palestinians were killed during 2004, all but two of whom were killed by Israeli security forces (those two were killed by Israeli civilians). The Palestinian Red Crescent Society (the local version of the Red Cross) said it counted 881 Palestinians killed during the year. Neither organization gave separate casualty figures for civilians and armed militants among Palestinians. The Israeli army routinely said the vast majority of Palestinians killed by its forces were armed militants, a claim generally backed by most independent news accounts.

B'Tselem said it counted 3,132 Palestinian deaths since the beginning of the Intifada, and the Red Crescent Society counted 3,518. The discrepancies in the numbers appeared to reflect the different reporting methods the organizations used. Whichever figure was used, the net result was that Palestinian deaths outnumbered Israeli deaths by about three to one.

Thousands of people on both sides also had been injured during the violence, many of them seriously. The Israeli Foreign Ministry said 6,966 Israelis had been wounded during the entire Intifada, of whom 4,855 were civilians and 2,111 were security personnel. On the Palestinian side, the Red Crescent Society counted 28,382 wounded.

Following are excerpts from a statement to the United Nations Security Council on November 15, 2004, by Terje Roed-Larsen, the UN's special coordinator for the Middle East peace process, on the death four days earlier of Palestinian leader Yasir Arafat.

"The Situation in the Middle East, Including the Palestinian Question"

Mr. Roed-Larsen:

Four days ago, a political titan passed away in a French military hospital in Paris. Three days ago, a funeral ceremony was held for Yasser Arafat in Cairo, before he was buried in Ramallah. A giant has left the world political scene. He was a giant for those who supported him and for those who opposed him, for friend and foe alike. His passing marks the end of an era.

For nearly four decades, Yasser Arafat was the leader of the Palestinian people, expressing and embodying the aspirations of his people like no other. That famous face with the trademark kaffiyeh epitomized Palestinian identity and national aspirations, even more than the Palestinian flag or the national anthem. For many, including himself, Abu Amr, the "Old Man," became one with the word Palestine. Personality and territory merged into one and became indistinguishable, a synthesis. But even more so, as a leader, he built the institutions that now are making an orderly transition possible—al-Fatah, the Palestinian Liberation Organization (PLO), and the Palestinian Authority with its President, Prime Minister, cabinet and most of all, the democratically elected Legislative Council.

Thirty years ago, Yasser Arafat became the first representative of a non-governmental organization to speak to a plenary session of the General Assembly. One year later, in 1974, the General Assembly adopted resolution 3237 (XXIX), conferring on the PLO the status of observer in the Assembly and in other international conferences held under United Nations auspices.

Yasser Arafat was also the leader who guided the Palestinians, in 1988, to accept the principle of peaceful coexistence between Israel and a future Palestinian State. He will always be remembered for doing so. President Arafat then took a giant step towards the realization of the vision of a Palestinian State living side by side in peace and security with Israel, with the signing of the Oslo Accords in 1993. Tragically, he did not live to see that vision fulfilled.

Now that he has gone, both Israelis and Palestinians, and the friends of both peoples throughout the world, must make even greater efforts to bring about the peaceful realization of the Palestinian right of self-determination.

The United Nations, together with our partners in the Quartet and in the region, must continue its work to achieve the full implementation of the road map, as endorsed by the Council in its resolution 1515 (2003) [A reference to the so-called "roadmap" to peace outlined in 2003 by the Quartet, composed of the European Union, Russia, the United Nations, and the United States]. Our shared goals must continue to be the realization of peace in the Middle East, based on Security Council resolutions 242 (1967), 338 (1973), and 1397 (2002), the end of the occupation that started in 1967, and the establishment of a sovereign, democratic, viable and contiguous Palestinian state existing side by side in peace with a secure Israel. Although Yasser Arafat did not live to see the attainment of those goals, the world must continue to strive towards them.

Our deep-felt condolences are with President Arafat's wife and young daughter Zahwa. We grieve with them. Our thoughts and prayers are also with his wider family—the Palestinian people, in the hope that they will find the strength, courage and wisdom to look to the future. They must now continue to work for the fulfilment of their aspirations through peaceful means and thus benefit succeeding generations.

These are undoubtedly momentous days in the Middle East. I am glad to say that the Palestinian leadership has reacted commendably and has taken the first firm steps towards instituting a smooth transition of power, in accordance with their Basic Law. They have, by and large, successfully prevented internal unrest in the areas under the control of the Palestinian Authority.

I am further encouraged by the great degree of coordination between the Government of Israel and the Palestinian Authority related to the arrangements for President Arafat's burial. I am particularly pleased to note the fact that Israel allowed Palestinian security forces to bear arms and that the Government of Israel has released 145 million shekels [about $32 million] in attached arrears. The extent and success of the coordination in recent days is reminiscent of earlier, happier days, and might herald a new beginning—a new beginning that would not be due to President Arafat's passing, but would be in spite of that very difficult situation.

As a first step, the Palestinians now need to organize and conduct free and fair elections for the presidency within sixty days, in accordance with the Basic Law [the Palestinian constitution]. The Palestinians also need to undertake visible, sustained, targeted and effective action on the ground to halt violence and terrorist activity. Israel, during this critical time, needs to refrain from all actions undermining trust—including settlement activity—facilitate the preparations and conduct of elections, and take steps to significantly improve the humanitarian situation by lifting curfews and easing restrictions on the movement of persons and goods. All these steps have to be taken in parallel. Only then can they mutually reinforce forward motion.

The Middle East had reached a critical juncture even before the passing of President Arafat. Less than three weeks ago, the Israeli Knesset approved Prime Minister [Ariel] Sharon's initiative to withdraw from the Gaza Strip and parts of the northern West Bank. That historic decision paves the way for the evacuation of Israeli settlements in the occupied Palestinian territory for the first time since the occupation began in 1967.

Amidst the remarkable events taking place in the region, I would like to look at the peace process from a different perspective today. In most of our briefings in recent months, we have concentrated on the events and developments on the ground, usually painting a gloomy picture of violence, deterioration, and crisis. Those pictures reflect the sad reality characterizing the Middle East. However, the potential of the present situation contains a perspective to change that reality. I would therefore like today to highlight the bigger picture, one that underlines how far the parties have moved in the past decade and what opportunities remain for them to settle their conflict.

For the past century, the Middle East has been one of the most persistent theatres of conflict in the world. As the members of the Council know better than any, the Arab-Israeli conflict is one of the greatest enduring diplomatic challenges that the world has faced since the middle of the twentieth century. At the heart of the Israeli-Palestinian conflict lies a dispute of competing and contradictory historical narratives, collective aspirations and identities. For most of its existence, Israel has remained locked in a state of war with one or more of its neighbours, and since the creation of the refugee problem, the Palestinian people have been left in limbo, struggling to find their path to a dignified existence, self-determination and independence.

For both Israelis and Palestinians, their conflict is a deeply existential struggle. Israelis feel the conflict as a constant battle for their very survival, a struggle that needs to be seen against the background of the experience of near-extermination that occurred during the lifetime of current Israeli leaders.

Palestinians feel the struggle as a battle of resistance each and every day for their identity and against the erosion of the possibility of a future as a people. Ultimately, both sides pursue similar aspirations: self-determination, peace, security, prosperity. Both sides have had, in a sense, similar leaders—leaders of war and of peace. One of those was Yitzhak Rabin, whose death we mourned this month nine years ago and who paid with his life for having taken bold and brave steps towards peace. Another is Yasser Arafat, who led the Palestinians in war and in peace and who did not live to see peace and self-determination realized.

The aspirations of both Israelis and Palestinians have long been thwarted by violence and crisis. Since September 2000, the peace process has been in reverse. Approximately 3,895 Palestinians and 983 Israelis have been killed. More than 36,620 Palestinians and 6,360 Israelis have been injured. Many of our earlier achievements have been eroded. . . .

[In the following section of his remarks, Roed-Larsen reviewed the history of the Israeli-Palestinian conflict since the signing of the so-called Oslo accords in 1993, an interim peace agreement between the two sides. He acknowledged shortcomings of the accords and criticisms of its gradual step-by-step approach, but also said they had led to progress until 1999.]

The basic principles that underlay the Oslo process remain valid and alive today. They are: the fundamental principle of land for peace, based on Security Council resolutions 242 (1967) and 338 (1973); the end of occupation; rejection of violence and terrorism; the need for security for both parties; a fair and agreed-upon solution to the plight of refugees; and Israel's legitimate right to self-defence and to exist in security. Those principles guide the vision shared by the Council, President [George W,] Bush and the Arab League, and inform and steer the key instrument we have developed and worked to implement over the past year—the road map—which was presented to Israelis and Palestinians in 2003 and was endorsed by the Council in resolution 1515 (2003).

Israel must be provided with full recognition and with real and permanent guarantees of its own security, in the form of freedom from attack and from the threat of attack. The Palestinians must be provided with real and permanent independence, in the form of a viable and secure Palestinian State established on lands occupied by Israel during the 1967 war and with economic control over its own borders. As part of the process leading to those goals, it is necessary, as the road map emphasizes, to remove Israeli settlements, reform Palestinian institutions and restore the Palestinian economy and infrastructure.

While the principles remain unchanged, the mechanics for realizing them in practice are now very different from the early days of the Oslo process. Most, if not all, agree that we must now start at the end. We require consensus about where the conflict must end. That must be agreed up front, before anything else can be done. Having agreed on the end state, we can implement its elements in an orderly sequence, but we must know where we are going. In that context, it is of great importance that we clearly define our end goal beyond the vision that we already have, while we continue to walk the road we have mapped out ahead of us.

Secondly, far from the principle of internationally facilitated bilateralism that characterized the Oslo process, at least in its early years, the principles for an end of conflict can only be introduced by the international community, as is done through the road map. The details will have to be negotiated and implemented by the parties, but we can help them and outline the end of the road that we have mapped out for them.

Thirdly, the international community must guarantee any and all agreements, and those guarantees must be firm and real. Israel must know that if it reaches final agreement, the agreement is truly final and there will be no more conflict or even the threat of conflict—no more claims and no more rejection. The Palestinians must know that provisional steps to reach an agreement will actually get there, that their gains will not be reversed and that they can begin to plan for, and count on, their own future.

There has been much talk about the demise of the road map and about the incapacity of the Quartet in the face of the continuing economic and political crisis. By contrast, I believe that the Quartet retains its validity and relevance thanks to its unique combination of legitimacy, political strength and financial and economic power represented by the Russian Federation, the European Union, the United States and the United Nations. Through consensus, it will be the most efficient and operational tool of the international community, in the best interest of the parties and of peace. The road map, as the plan accepted by both parties to find a way out of the current violence, remains equally valid. In fact, the twin mechanisms of the road map and the Quartet are now more important than ever. The implementation of the road map remains our primary goal at this stage.

As we have repeatedly stated, the implementation of Prime Minister Sharon's withdrawal initiative and the evacuation of settlements in the Gaza Strip and the northern West Bank offer an opportunity to revive the peace process, and, indeed, to move rapidly towards the realization of the principles I just talked about. For that to happen, as we have long maintained, the Israeli redeployment needs to be coordinated with the Palestinian Authority and the Quartet; be full and complete and lead to the end of the occupation of Gaza; be accompanied by similar steps in the West Bank; and be fully consistent with the road map. That is not just possible; it is a realistic expectation.

In his speech preceding the historic Knesset vote on his initiative, Prime Minister Sharon stated clearly and unequivocally that he supported the end of the Israeli occupation of the Palestinian territory and "the establishment of a Palestinian State alongside the State of Israel." He also reiterated clearly that he remained "willing to make painful compromises in order to put an end to this ongoing and malignant conflict between those who struggle over this land" and to do the "utmost in order to bring peace."

Prime Minister Sharon's statements, as well as the Knesset vote, make clear that this is a unique opportunity for the international community to engage actively in order to revive the peace process. In many ways, Mr. Sharon's initiative aims to go further than earlier Israeli Prime Ministers dared to propose. It represents nothing less than a programmatic continuation of the Oslo process, which saw a number of phases and stages of Israeli redeployment. In this sense, the implementation of Israeli disengagement is nothing but a logical step to be taken along the road towards peace. It has the potential to drive the process forward significantly, if the international community and the Palestinians are actively involved and if they contribute to it. . . .

Source: United Nations. Security Council. "Agenda: The Situation in the Middle East, Including the Palestinian Question." S/PV.5077, 5077th Meeting, November 15, 2004. http://documents-dds-ny.un.org/doc/UNDOC/GEN/N04/604/99/pdf/No460499.pdf (accessed March 19, 2005).

UN Security Council Resolution on Civil War in Ivory Coast

November 15, 2004

INTRODUCTION

Ivory Coast appeared to be sliding back toward civil war during much of 2004, endangering a peace agreement that was intended to end a bloody internal conflict that had torn the country in half two years earlier. The conflict had become a major test of an aggressive new approach by the United Nations and the international community to the wars that had plagued Africa for more than a decade. That approach involved intensive diplomacy at every sign of backsliding toward war, coupled with the stationing of international peacekeeping forces with broad authority to separate the warring parties and to protect civilians. France, the colonial power in Ivory Coast, found itself mired in the conflict in November, when its peacekeeping forces came under attack and progovernment mobs threatened the thousands of French citizens who lived there.

The conflict in Ivory Coast sprang from a potent mixture of economic collapse and long-simmering differences between the country's ethnic groups. Ivory Coast was the world's largest producer of cocoa. Revenue from the sales of that staple crop helped make the country one of the most prosperous and politically stable in all of sub-Saharan Africa after its independence from France in 1960. World cocoa prices collapsed in the late 1990s, however, sending Ivory Coast's economy into a tailspin.

A military coup against the civilian government in 1999 set in motion a series of developments that deepened underlying rifts between the country's many ethnic and tribal groups. The most important division was between those in the south (many of them Christians) who considered themselves to be the true "Ivorians," and many of those in the north and the west (predominantly Muslims) who had come to Ivory Coast from neighboring countries to work the cocoa plantations. A civil war in 2002 and early 2003 between these sides left the government, headed by President Laurent Gbagbo, in control of most of the south, and a coalition of rebel forces in control of most of the north and parts of the west.

A peace agreement, signed in the Paris suburb of Linas-Marcoussis in January 2003, called for rebel leaders to join Gbagbo in a unity government, leading to nationwide elections in late 2005. Neither side fully carried out the promises made in that agreement, however, creating a situation in which each side felt it had an excuse not to comply. Actual fighting was kept in check throughout 2003 by the presence of about 5,000 peacekeeping troops—including 4,000 from France and 1,000 from neighbors in the Economic Community of West African States. *(Background, Historic Documents of 2003, p. 237)*

UN Peacekeeping Force Authorized

The opening weeks of 2004 produced several positive developments, including a return to the unity government by rebel leaders who had been boycotting it for several months and an agreement on the process for demobilizing and disarming parts of the army and rebel forces. France, which had mediated the talks leading to the January 2003 peace agreement, resumed its diplomacy and put pressure on both sides to carry out their promises. At United Nations headquarters in New York, the United States at first opposed, then reluctantly approved, a French plan to send a 6,240-member UN peacekeeping force to Ivory Coast. As approved by the Security Council on February 27, the UN force incorporated the peacekeepers from West Africa but not the French troops, who were to remain in Ivory Coast under an independent command. Washington had been reluctant to endorse this new mission because the United States paid 27 percent of the cost of all UN peacekeeping forces, and there was growing resistance in the Republican-led Congress to the numerous UN missions in Africa.

These positive moves were counterbalanced by continuing violence—particularly in the cocoa-producing west—and infighting in the supposed unity government. Worrisome developments included a statement on February 27 by rebel leader Guillaume Soro that his soldiers—known as the New Forces—would not disarm until after the 2005 elections and the withdrawal from the government on March 5 by the Ivory Coast Democratic Party, which had been the ruling party for four years after independence but had been in opposition since the 1999 military coup. Tensions rose all through February and into March as government officials warned that the rebels and opposition politicians were plotting a coup. Youth groups affiliated with the government responded with threats against rebel leaders who were participating in the unity government.

Matters came to a head on March 25 when security forces opened fire in Abidjan on opposition demonstrators, who defied a government ban on protests. The government claimed the protesters were trying to mount a revolt. Leaders from the rebel groups and political opposition parties claimed Gbagbo and his aides were trying to eliminate all forms of dissent, and they again withdrew from the government. Initial police reports said 37 people were killed. However, a report by an inquiry sponsored by the UN Human Rights Commission put the death toll at 120, with another 20 people still missing. The report, leaked to the news media on May 3, said government forces and militias aligned with them targeted people according to their ethnic groups, in some cases attacking people in their homes. It also argued that the violence resulted from a "carefully planned and executed operation" and was not—as the government claimed—a spontaneous reaction to a banned demonstration.

In the toxic atmosphere created by the violence, advance elements of the new UN peacekeeping force began arriving on April 1. Called the UN Operation in Côte d'Ivoire (UNOCI, using the country's French name), the force took the place of a small UN mission that had been monitoring the 2003 peace agreement. The new force had a robust mandate from the Security Council to protect civilians and to keep government and rebel forces from resorting to war. In contrast to some previous UN missions, which had taken many months or even years to reach full strength, UNOCI was able to deploy nearly 5,900 troops and police officers by the end of August; most came from Bangladesh or elsewhere in Africa. The UN and French forces occupied a band of territory stretching across central Ivory Coast, dividing government forces in the south from rebel forces in the north.

Another step toward the brink of war came May 20, when Gbagbo fired from the cabinet rebel leader Soro and two other members of his New Forces group because they had been boycotting meetings. Gbagbo replaced the rebels with members of his own party, leading Soro to complain of a "coup d'etat against the peace accords."

More Peace Talks

Amid increasingly hostile rhetoric from all sides, African leaders and UN Secretary General Kofi Annan launched a new round of talks to revive the peace process. Annan and twelve African leaders met in Accra, Ghana, on July 29 with Gbagbo, civilian opposition figures, and rebel leaders. After nearly two full days of talks, Gbagbo and his opponents signed an agreement promising, yet again, to carry out the promises they made in the January 2003 peace accord. In an attempt to force action, this new agreement laid out a timetable. Gbagbo agreed to carry out political changes demanded by the opposition, including expanding the rights of immigrants, by the end of August; in turn the rebel leaders agreed to start disbanding their armed forces by October 15.

Rebel leaders rejoined the government on August 9, and both sides made optimistic promises about a new start toward peace. "It's like the first day of school. Smiles are everywhere," Prime Minister Seydou Diarra said after the first unity cabinet meeting in five months. Gbagbo also signed a decree sharing some of his powers with Diarra, a Muslim from northern Ivory Coast whose appointment had resulted from the January 2003 peace agreement. Opposition leaders had complained that Gbagbo refused to turn any real power over to Diarra—a situation the president's decree was intended to remedy.

Renewed Fighting

Whatever good feeling was created by the July agreement was dispelled when the time came for political bargaining to put the promises in place. The parliament met for six weeks during August and September but failed to adopt the laws Gbagbo had promised, including ones making it easier for immigrants to become citizens and establishing an electoral commission to run the promised elections in 2005. The October 15 deadline for the beginning of disarmament by the rebels and some government forces also passed without any real action. Rebels said they would not lay down their arms until Gbagbo pushed through the legislative changes he had promised, and Gbagbo insisted disarmament had to come first. Rebel leaders again withdrew from the government on October 28.

Several violent incidents also contributed to renewed tension, especially between government forces and the French peacekeepers. Gbagbo had implied, and some of his aides had said directly, that France favored "foreign" rebels at the expense of the native Ivorians. Pro-government gangs calling themselves "young patriots" staged repeated violent demonstrations against the French and UN missions—apparently in hopes of provoking a confrontation that would renew the fighting.

Those attacks against the foreign peacekeepers failed to generate a broader conflict, but the government initiated renewed fighting on November 4 with a series of bombing raids against positions of the rebel New Forces in the north-central part of the country. The UN called the attacks a "major violation" of cease-fire agreements, and UN relief agencies suspended their aid programs, which had been a major source of food and medical supplies for residents of the rebel-held areas.

The fighting escalated to a more dangerous phase two days later, on November 6, when government planes bombed a French peacekeeping post deep in rebel territory, killing nine French soldiers and a U.S. aid worker. Government spokesmen called the attack a mistake, but the French forces struck back quickly, destroying or severely damaging the entire government air force, consisting of the two jets said to have carried out the bombing plus five government helicopters. The French response ignited mob violence in Abidjan, where angry armed men screaming "French go home" roamed the streets in search of French citizens, or anyone else who appeared to be a foreigner. A large mob of several thousand men also marched on the airport, which the French forces had occupied. French president Jacques Chirac dispatched an additional 600 soldiers to Ivory Coast and sent three warplanes to neighboring Gabon. The UN Security Council met in emergency session and issued a statement expressing "full support" for the French actions.

Mob violence continued into the following day, November 7, as the national television station broadcast calls for Ivorians to march in the streets against "foreigners." Thousands of people responded to the appeals and attacked French businesses and schools. Hundreds of French citizens fled the country, under the protection of French forces, continuing an exodus that started during similar rounds of mob violence in 2003. An estimated 15,000 French citizens had lived in Ivory Coast before the conflict began in 2002, but most had since departed.

Gbagbo appeared on national television and expressed "regret" about the death of the French soldiers. He justified the government's attacks against the rebels, however, saying they were "compromising any hope of a negotiated peace" by refusing to disarm.

The violence threatened to escalate on November 8, when tens of thousands of people massed around the Abidjan neighborhood of Gbagbo's home in response to rumors that the French were about to mount a coup against him. French officials denied the rumors, and French troops tried to disperse the crowds, which refused to budge.

A nearby hotel became the center of action the next day, November 9, when thousands of demonstrators tried to block French efforts to evacuate about 1,000 French nationals and other foreigners who had taken refuge there. Several people were killed in an outbreak of shooting near the hotel, with each side blaming the other for the shootings. Weeks later, the French government acknowledged that its troops had killed about twenty people while trying to defend themselves during the violence. Gbagbo's government had said that French troops killed sixty people.

The violence finally abated somewhat on the fourth day, November 10, enabling France, the United States, and other foreign countries to step up the evacuation of their citizens. Over the next several days thousands of foreigners left the country, many of them after being rescued by peacekeepers or embassy security officials when their homes or businesses were attacked by mobs.

Apparently seeking to capitalize on the wave of antiFrench sentiment, Gbagbo and his aides launched a campaign to blame the French peacekeepers for the latest violence. In an interview with the *Washington Post* on November 11, Gbagbo suggested that the French had lied about their peacekeeping troops being killed in the government bombing raid five days earlier. "I haven't seen any dead bodies," he said. Gbagbo also charged that France had used the bombing as a "pretext" to pursue what he said was a policy of seeking to force him from power. "The government of Jacques Chirac never accepted that I have reached the position of president," he told the *Post.*

Leaders of key African countries met in the Nigerian capital, Abuja, on November 14 and endorsed a call for a UN arms embargo against both the Ivory Coast government and rebel groups. The leaders said they also supported imposing an international travel ban, and a freeze of personal assets, on anyone blocking the peace process there. The move was an extraordinary one for African leaders, who in the past had been wary of any action that appeared to undermine a fellow leader in the region.

With that endorsement in hand, the Security Council met the following day, November 15, and unanimously adopted Resolution 1572, imposing an immediate arms embargo, lasting thirteen months, against both sides in the Ivory Coast conflict. The council also set a one-month deadline for the parties to resume the peace process. If that deadline was missed, the council said it would impose the travel ban and asset freeze against those responsible. The resolution called on both the government and rebel leaders to resume the peace process and refrain from provocative actions. However, it also condemned the government-controlled media for "inciting hatred, intolerance and violence" and demanded that the government stop such incitements.

In a report to the Security Council on December 3, Annan said the threatened sanctions had gotten the attention of Ivory Coast leaders on both sides. He said it appeared possible that the leaders were now willing to resume the peace process. A week later Annan sent the council another report, made public on December 14, reminding all Ivory Coast leaders—"and in particular President Gbagbo"—of their obligations and "personal responsibility" for protecting civilians and conducting a "meaningful dialogue" toward peace.

In the meantime, South African president Thabo Mbeki—who had spearheaded several previous mediation efforts—met with both sides on December 6 and won yet another promise of cooperation to carry out the peace agreement signed nearly two years earlier. Based on those pledges, Mbeki asked the Security Council to hold off on the imposition of sanctions against the recalcitrant Ivory Coast leaders. In its final meeting of the year dealing with the Ivory Coast issue, the Security Council on December 16 said it still intended to impose the travel ban and assets freeze, but it offered a diplomatic excuse for inaction at that point, saying a complete list of those subject to that punishment had not yet been compiled.

Largely as a result of the international pressure, the Ivory Coast parliament on December 17 approved some parts of the constitutional changes called for in the various peace agreements. Among the changes was the revision of an anti-immigrant law the government had used to prevent opposition leader Alassane Ouattara (a former prime minister) from running for president in 2000. Gbagbo, however, said he would not sign the bill mandating the changes and would instead submit them to a public referendum. That step was denounced as a delaying tactic by the rebels, who noted that Gbagbo also said no vote could take place until the rebels disarmed. At year's end, Ivory Coast was no closer to peace—and was even more polarized because of the ongoing violence—than it had been twelve months earlier.

Following is the text of Resolution 1572, adopted unanimously by the United Nations Security Council on November 15, 2004, imposing an immediate arms embargo against all sides to the civil war in Ivory Coast and threatening personal sanctions (including an international travel ban and assets freeze) against those who blocked the peace process in that country.

Resolution 1572

The Security Council,

Recalling its resolution 1528 (2004) of 27 February 2004, as well as the relevant statements of its President, in particular those of 6 November 2004 and of 5 August 2004,

Reaffirming its strong commitment to the sovereignty, independence, territorial integrity and unity of Côte d'Ivoire, and *recalling* the importance of the principles of good neighbourliness, non-interference and regional cooperation,

Recalling that it endorsed the agreement signed by the Ivoirian political forces in Linas-Marcoussis on 24 January 2003 (the Linas-Marcoussis Agreement) approved by the Conference of Heads of States on Côte d'Ivoire, held in Paris on 25 and 26 January 2003, and the Agreement signed in Accra on 30 July 2004 (Accra III Agreement),

Deploring the resumption of hostilities in Côte d'Ivoire and the repeated violations of the ceasefire agreement of 3 May 2003,

Deeply concerned by the humanitarian situation in Côte d'Ivoire, in particular in the northern part of the country, and by the use of the media, in particular radio and television broadcasts, to incite hatred and violence against foreigners in Côte d'Ivoire,

Recalling strongly the obligations of all Ivoirian parties, the Government of Côte d'Ivoire as well as the Forces Nouvelles, to refrain from any violence against civilians, including against foreign citizens, and to cooperate fully with the activities of the United Nations Operation in Côte d'Ivoire (UNOCI),

Welcoming the ongoing efforts of the Secretary-General, the African Union and the Economic Community of Western African States (ECOWAS) towards reestablishing peace and stability in Côte d'Ivoire,

Determining that the situation in Côte d'Ivoire continues to pose a threat to international peace and security in the region,

Acting under Chapter VII of the Charter of the United Nations,

1. *Condemns* the air strikes committed by the national armed forces of Côte d'Ivoire (FANCI) which constitute flagrant violations of the ceasefire agreement of 3 May 2003 and *demands* that all Ivoirian parties to the conflict, the Government of Côte d'Ivoire as well as Forces nouvelles, fully comply with the ceasefire;
2. *Reiterates* its full support for the action undertaken by UNOCI and French forces in accordance with their mandate under resolution 1528 (2004) and with the statement of its President of 6 November 2004 (S/PRST/2004/42);
3. *Emphasizes* again that there can be no military solution to the crisis and that the full implementation of the Linas-Marcoussis and Accra III Agreements remains the only way to resolve the crisis persisting in the country;
4. *Urges* as a consequence the President of the Republic of Côte d'Ivoire, the heads of all the Ivoirian political parties and the leaders of the Forces Nouvelles immediately to begin resolutely implementing all the commitments they have made under these agreements;
5. *Expresses* its full support for the efforts of the Secretary-General, the African Union and ECOWAS [Economic Community of West African States] and *encourages* them to continue these efforts in order to relaunch the peace process in Côte d'Ivoire;

6. *Demands* that the Ivoirian authorities stop all radio and television broadcasting inciting hatred, intolerance and violence, *requests* UNOCI to strengthen its monitoring role in this regard, and *urges* the Government of Côte d'Ivoire and the Forces nouvelles to take all necessary measures to ensure the security and the safety of civilian persons, including foreign nationals and their property;
7. *Decides* that all States shall, for a period of thirteen months from the date of adoption of this resolution, take the necessary measures to prevent the direct or indirect supply, sale or transfer to Côte d'Ivoire, from their territories or by their nationals, or using their flag vessels or aircraft, of arms or any related materiel, in particular military aircraft and equipment, whether or not originating in their territories, as well as the provision of any assistance, advice or training related to military activities;
8. *Decides* that the measures imposed by paragraph 7 above shall not apply to:
   (a) supplies and technical assistance intended solely for the support of or use by UNOCI and the French forces who support them,
   (b) supplies of non-lethal military equipment intended solely for humanitarian or protective use, and related technical assistance and training, as approved in advance by the Committee established by paragraph 14 below,
   (c) supplies of protective clothing, including flak jackets and military helmets, temporarily exported to Côte d'Ivoire by United Nations personnel, representatives of the media and humanitarian and development workers and associated personnel, for their personal use only,
   (d) supplies temporarily exported to Côte d'Ivoire to the forces of a State which is taking action, in accordance with international law, solely and directly to facilitate the evacuation of its nationals and those for whom it has consular responsibility in Côte d'Ivoire, as notified in advance to the Committee established by paragraph 14 below,
   (e) supplies of arms and related materiel and technical training and assistance intended solely for support of or use in the process of restructuring defence and security forces pursuant to paragraph 3, subparagraph (f) of the Linas-Marcoussis Agreement, as approved in advance by the Committee established by paragraph 14 below;
9. *Decides* that all States shall take the necessary measures, for a period of twelve months, to prevent the entry into or transit through their territories of all persons designated by the Committee established by paragraph 14 below, who constitute a threat to the peace and national reconciliation process in Côte d'Ivoire, in particular those who block the implementation of the Linas-Marcoussis and Accra III Agreements, any other person determined as responsible for serious violations of human rights and international humanitarian law in Côte d'Ivoire on the basis of relevant information, any other person who incites publicly hatred and violence, and any other person determined by the Committee to be in violation of measures imposed by paragraph 7 above, provided that nothing in this paragraph shall oblige a State to refuse entry into its territory to its own nationals;
10. *Decides* that the measures imposed by paragraph 9 shall not apply where the Committee established by paragraph 14 below determines that such travel is justified on the grounds of humanitarian need, including religious obligation, or

where the Committee concludes that an exemption would further the objectives of the Council's resolutions, for peace and national reconciliation in Côte d'Ivoire and stability in the region;

11. *Decides* that all States shall, for the same period of twelve months, freeze immediately the funds, other financial assets and economic resources which are on their territories at the date of adoption of this resolution or at any time thereafter, owned or controlled directly or indirectly by the persons designated pursuant to paragraph 9 above by the Committee established by paragraph 14 below, or that are held by entities owned or controlled directly or indirectly by any persons acting on their behalf or at their direction, as designated by the Committee, and *decides further* that all States shall ensure that any funds, financial assets or economic resources are prevented from being made available by their nationals or by any persons within their territories, to or for the benefit of such persons or entities;
12. *Decides* that the provisions of paragraph 11 do not apply to funds, other financial assets and economic resources that:
    (a) have been determined by relevant States to be necessary for basic expenses, including payment for foodstuffs, rent or mortgage, medicines and medical treatment, taxes, insurance premiums, and public utility charges, or exclusively for payment of reasonable professional fees and reimbursement of incurred expenses associated with the provision of legal services, or fees or service charges, in accordance with national laws, for routine holding or maintenance of frozen funds, other financial assets and economic resources, after notification by the relevant States to the Committee established by paragraph 14 below of the intention to authorize, where appropriate, access to such funds, other financial assets and economic resources and in the absence of a negative decision by the Committee within two working days of such notification,
    (b) have been determined by relevant States to be necessary for extraordinary expenses, provided that such determination has been notified by the relevant States to the Committee and has been approved by the Committee, or
    (c) have been determined by relevant States to be subject of a judicial, administrative or arbitral lien or judgement, in which case the funds, other financial assets and economic resources may be used to satisfy that lien or judgement provided that the lien or judgement: was entered prior to the date of the present resolution, is not for the benefit of a person referred to in paragraph 11 above or an individual or entity identified by the Committee, and has been notified by the relevant States to the Committee;
13. *Decides* that, at the end of a period of 13 months from the date of adoption of this resolution, the Security Council shall review the measures imposed by paragraphs 7, 9 and 11 above, in the light of progress accomplished in the peace and national reconciliation process in Côte d'Ivoire as defined by the Linas-Marcoussis and Accra III Agreements, and expresses its readiness to consider the modification or termination of these measures before the aforesaid period of 13 months only if the Linas-Marcoussis and Accra III Agreements have been fully implemented;

14. *Decides* to establish, in accordance with rule 28 of its provisional rules of procedure, a Committee of the Security Council consisting of all the members of the Council (the Committee), to undertake the following tasks:
    (a) to designate the individuals and entities subject to the measures imposed by paragraphs 9 and 11 above, and to update this list regularly,
    (b) to seek from all States concerned, and particularly those in the region, information regarding the actions taken by them to implement the measures imposed by paragraphs 7, 9 and 11 above, and whatever further information it may consider useful, including by providing them with an opportunity to send representatives to meet the Committee to discuss in more detail any relevant issues,
    (c) to consider and decide upon requests for the exemptions set out in paragraphs 8, 10 and 12 above,
    (d) to make relevant information publicly available through appropriate media, including the list of persons referred to in subparagraph (a) above,
    (e) to promulgate guidelines as may be necessary to facilitate the implementation of the measures imposed by paragraphs 11 and 12 above,
    (f) to present regular reports to the Council on its work, with its observations and recommendations, in particular on ways to strengthen the effectiveness of the measures imposed by paragraphs 7, 9 and 11 above;
15. *Requests* all States concerned, in particular those in the region, to report to the Committee, within ninety days from the date of adoption of this resolution, on the actions they have taken to implement the measures imposed by paragraphs 7, 9 and 11 above, and *authorizes* the Committee to request whatever further information it may consider necessary;
16. *Urges* all States, relevant United Nations bodies and, as appropriate, other organizations and interested parties, to cooperate fully with the Committee, in particular by supplying any information at their disposal on possible violations of the measures imposed by paragraphs 7, 9 and 11 above;
17. *Expresses its determination* to consider without delay further steps to ensure the effective monitoring and implementation of the measures imposed by paragraphs 7, 9 and 11 above, in particular the establishment of a panel of experts;
18. *Requests* the Secretary-General to submit a report to the Council by 15 March 2005, drawing on information from all relevant sources, including the Government of National Reconciliation in Côte d'Ivoire, UNOCI, ECOWAS and the African Union, on progress made towards the goals described in paragraph 13 above;
19. *Decides* that the measures imposed by paragraphs 9 and 11 above shall enter into force on 15 December 2004, unless the Security Council shall determine before then that the signatories of the Linas-Marcoussis and Accra III Agreements have implemented all their commitments under the Accra III Agreement and are embarked towards full implementation of the Linas-Marcoussis Agreement;
20. *Decides* to remain actively seized of the matter.

Source: United Nations. Security Council. Resolution 1572 (2004). S/RES/1572 (2004), November 15, 2004. http://documents-dds-ny.un.org/doc/UNDOC/GEN/N04/607/37/pdf/ N0460737.pdf (accessed March 21, 2005).

Arctic Climate Impact Assessment Study on Global Warming

November 16, 2004

INTRODUCTION

Scientists continued during 2004 to produce more studies indicating that the burning of fossil fuels (coal, gas, and oil) was contributing to changes in the global climate, and that those changes would have significant consequences—many of them negative—for plants, wildlife, and humans in many parts of the world. Among the studies was the first-ever comprehensive analysis of the impact of climate change on the Arctic region around the North Pole. A four-year study released in November said human-caused climate change was partly responsible for the recent melting of sea ice and other trends that appeared to signal a dramatic shift in the Arctic's environment.

Against the odds, the most significant and controversial international effort to combat climate change took on new life during the year. The Kyoto Protocol, a United Nations treaty negotiated in 1997, was ratified in November by Russia, clearing the last major hurdle to its taking effect. The Bush administration had staunchly opposed the treaty, and in recent years it had appeared likely that Russia would reject it as well, preventing the treaty from taking force as international law. Russian president Vladimir Putin ultimately decided that ratifying the treaty, over U.S. objections, served his country's interests. The Kyoto Protocol was scheduled to take effect in February 2005. *(Kyoto treaty, Historic Documents of 1997, p. 859; climate change background, Historic Documents of 2003, p. 861)*

The Arctic Assessment

The study of the Arctic was the most detailed scientific survey ever made of the effects of climate change in a specific region of the world. Launched in 2000, the study—formally known as the Arctic Climate Impact Assessment—was commissioned by the Arctic Council, an intergovernmental forum including Canada, Denmark, Finland, Iceland, Norway, Russia, Sweden, and the United States, all of which had territory bordering on or included in the Arctic Ocean region. The study was conducted by a team of three hundred scientists, other experts on climate and the environment, and elders from the indigenous peoples who inhabited the Arctic region. Robert W. Corell, a Harvard University oceanographer and senior fellow of the American Meteorological Society, chaired the study panel.

A 140-page summary of the study's findings was released November 8 at the opening of a forum in Reykjavik, Iceland. A 1,200-page technical report, containing the results of numerous scientific studies related to climate change in the Arctic, was scheduled for release early in 2005. Corell described both reports in testimony on November 16 to the Senate Commerce Committee.

A third related section was to have contained specific policy recommendations for dealing with the effects of climate change in the Arctic. For more than a year that section had been the subject of intense political bargaining among the eight member-nations of the Arctic Council, with the Bush administration opposing all recommendations for curbing the emissions of the so-called greenhouse gases (such as carbon dioxide, created by the burning of fossil fuels), said to be largely responsible for recent climate change. After a high-level diplomatic meeting in Reykjavik to complete the recommendations, the Arctic Council on November 24 released a statement expressing concern about the effects of climate change in the Arctic and calling for "effective measures" to confront it. At U.S. insistence, however, the council offered no concrete recommendations for mandatory actions by governments to confront the problem. Paula Dobriansky, undersecretary of state for global affairs and the leader of the U.S. delegation at the Reykjavik negotiations, said the Bush administration was waiting for publication of the scientific study in 2005 and would take those findings "into account" as it developed U.S. policy.

The summary released November 8, and explained to the Senate committee by Corell on November 16, said temperatures were warming in the Arctic region at about twice the rate of the rest of the globe—and would continue on an upward path because of atmospheric changes caused by the burning of fossil fuels. In Alaska, eastern Russia, and Western Canada, the summary said, average winter temperatures had increased in the range of 4 to 7 degrees Fahrenheit during the previous five decades and would rise another 7 to 13 degrees during the next century.

The many consequences of this warming included the continued melting of summer sea ice (at least half of which might disappear by the end of the twenty-first century) and of the massive ice sheet that covered most of Greenland. The melting of sea ice in the Arctic would have positive benefits for the shipping and tourism industries, the summary said, but wildlife (notably polar bears and some species of seals) and indigenous peoples who depended on the ice to reach food sources could be seriously harmed. The melting of the Greenland ice sheet had the potential to affect coastal areas worldwide, the study said. The ice sheet contained enough water to raise the sea level by about 23 feet, thus submerging many low-lying coastal areas. Even a partial melting of the ice sheet could raise the sea level and threaten some areas. Rising temperatures also were causing permafrost to thaw in parts of the Arctic region, the summary said, damaging ecological systems (such as lakes and rivers) and destabilizing man-made structures on the previously frozen ground (including airports, buildings, and roads).

In his testimony to the Senate Commerce Committee, Corell said the findings of his panel were important for the rest of the world, providing "an early indication of the environmental and societal significance of global warming." In addition to the rising sea level, he noted that climate change in the Arctic region would adversely affect the production of natural resources—including fish, gas, and oil—that were exported to the rest of the world.

Kyoto Takes Effect

Ever since President George W. Bush definitively rejected U.S. acceptance of the Kyoto protocol in 2001, Russia had been in the position of determining whether the treaty would take legal effect, thus requiring countries that ratified it to abide by its terms. This was because the treaty specified that it would become operable only when it had been ratified by nations that in 1990 had generated at least 55 percent of the industrialized world's emissions of the six greenhouse gases. The United States, by itself, accounted for about one-third of all greenhouse gas emissions by the thirty-six nations considered to be "industrialized" (this excluded several major developing countries, such as Brazil, China, and India). After European countries ratified the treaty, Russia (with about 17 percent of the 1990 emissions total) was the only country left that could push the treaty over the 55 percent threshold.

Over the previous two years, Russian officials had engaged in an unusually open debate about whether to ratify the treaty. Some senior figures in the country's economic ministries argued that ratifying the treaty might damage long-term economic growth because of Russia's heavy reliance on oil and gas production and on major smokestack industries, such as steel and heavy machinery. Other officials argued, however, that Russia stood to gain by accepting the Kyoto treaty. They noted that because of the decline of heavy industry during the 1990s, Russia's greenhouse gas emissions already were well below the 1990 levels, as required by the treaty. Russia thus could make millions or even billions of dollars by selling emissions "credits" to European countries; the treaty allowed countries with excess greenhouse gas emissions to buy credits from countries that were below their limits, so long as the overall global levels fell below the 1990 figure.

Putin himself had been silent in this debate, although by 2003 many observers had concluded that he ultimately would decide against ratifying the treaty, thus allowing it to die. By mid-2004, however, Kremlin aides were suggesting that Russia would ratify the treaty, and Putin's cabinet made that position formal on September 30. Action followed quickly. The necessary ratification legislation was approved by the lower house of parliament on October 22 and by the upper house on October 27. The Kremlin announced on November 6 that Putin had signed the legislation. That announcement reviewed the arguments for and against the treaty and suggested that Putin's positive decision had been influenced by Russia's key role in deciding the future of the treaty. "The decision on ratification was passed taking into account the significance of the protocol for the development of international cooperation and, likewise, taking into account the protocol will take effect only under the condition of the Russian Federation's participation in it."

Russia submitted its ratification documents to the UN on November 16, starting a timetable that would lead to the treaty entering into force on February 16, 2005. After that point, ratifying countries would have seven years to reduce their greenhouse gas emissions to the levels that prevailed in 1990.

The Bush administration made it clear that Putin's endorsement of the treaty would not influence U.S. policy. "President Bush strongly opposes any treaty or policy that would cause the loss of a single American job, let alone the nearly 5 million jobs Kyoto would cost," said James Connaughton, chairman of the White House Council on Environmental Quality. The figure of 5 million jobs was based on Energy Department estimates of how many manufacturing jobs would be lost if the United States was forced to reduce its greenhouse gas emissions. Kyoto supporters said the estimate was grossly exaggerated.

With the Kyoto treaty set to take effect, the next matter on the international climate change agenda was the tenth annual follow-up session, known as the Conference of the Parties (or COP-10), of the countries that had signed the original treaty on the subject, the UN Framework Convention on Climate Change, better known as the Rio treaty because it was negotiated in Rio de Janeiro in 1992. Once it appeared that Russia would ratify the Kyoto treaty, organizers of the COP-10 meeting in Buenos Aires expressed hope that world leaders could agree to begin negotiations toward some kind of measures to be taken once Kyoto expired in 2012. *(Rio treaty, Historic Documents of 1992, p. 499)*

At the outset, Bush administration representatives made clear that Washington was not willing to consider any measures that required the United States to reduce its greenhouse gas emissions. Henry L. Watson, the senior U.S. climate negotiator, told a news conference on December 7 that the U.S. approach of seeking cleaner energy sources was more effective than the treaty's mandate to reduce emissions by certain levels. "We match or exceed what any other country is doing to address this issue," he said. "I would challenge any of the Kyoto parties to match us both internationally and domestically."

In subsequent negotiations, administration officials opposed a call by European nations for meetings in 2005 that might launch the process of developing a post-Kyoto treaty. In a compromise, negotiators settled on one "seminar" in May 2005 where countries would exchange information on climate change.

Other Scientific Studies

The Arctic study was one of dozens of scientific reports issued during the year on climate change topics. Other studies dealt with such matters as the potential impact of climate change on other specific geographical regions, on certain types of wildlife or plants, or on specific weather patterns. As had become the case in recent years, nearly all the studies were based on the assumptions that human activities were among the main causes of climate change and that mankind needed to alter its behavior before climate change caused irreversible environmental damage.

For European leaders, one of the year's most important studies was issued in September by the European Environment Agency, an arm of the European Union. Titled "Impacts of Europe's Changing Climate," the report analyzed trends in twenty-two indicators (such as ocean temperatures, precipitation levels, and crop yields) to make projections for the near-term future of the European climate. As with most other projections, the report offered a complex picture of changing weather patterns and their effects on agriculture, economies, human health, and ecosystems. The report predicted a continuation of a trend during the latter half of the twentieth century of increased precipitation in central and northern Europe and decreased precipitation in southern Europe. The latter region was expected to suffer severe consequences, such as more frequent droughts, with "considerable impacts" on agriculture and water resources, the report said. The conflicting nature of the impact of climate change was illustrated by the likely effects on agricultural production. Warmer temperatures would result in longer growing seasons and increased crop yields in some cases but also would require more water, thus straining water resources, especially in southern Europe. The overall result might be "a northward shift of agriculture," the report said.

One report on climate change received exceptionally broad attention because of its source: the Pentagon. News organizations reported in late February that Andrew Marshall, the head of a Defense Department think tank called the Office of Net Assessment, had commissioned two California futurologists, Peter Schwartz and Doug Randall, to envision the possible consequences for international affairs should the most extreme predictions for global climate change come true. After interviewing climate scientists, the two men in October 2003 produced a report outlining the results should there be a "relatively abrupt" change in the global ocean current known as the thermohaline conveyor (including the Atlantic Ocean's Gulf Stream), which carried warm water from the topics into colder latitudes. The nature of the ocean conveyor had been changing in recent decades as the melting of glaciers and Greenland's ice sheet dumped fresh water into the ocean. Envisioning a gradual collapse of the ocean conveyor beginning around 2010, Schwartz and Randall described major changes in weather patterns in much of the world, leading to crop failures and water shortages in some places but surpluses in others, followed by conflicts over food and water supplies, mass migrations from countries suddenly afflicted with extreme temperatures, border conflicts in Asia and Europe, and even civil war in China. The authors did not predict any of these events but said the United States needed to be better prepared to deal with them as potential consequences of climate change. Several newspapers ran stories about the report under scare headlines, leading the Pentagon's Marshall to issue a statement saying the scenarios in it were based on "speculation."

Climate change could prove fatal for many endangered animal and plant species, a study published in the journal *Nature* on January 8 said. Written by eighteen biological researchers, the study assessed the potential impact on 1,103 fragile species in Australia, Latin America, and South Africa from several climate change models estimating a range of increases in global temperatures during the twenty-first century. Depending on how much temperatures increased, the study estimated that 15 to 37 percent of the species in the analysis would become extinct, or be near extinction, by 2050.

An exceptionally severe hurricane season in the southeastern United States generated increased interest in reports suggesting that climate change could produce even more intense hurricanes in future decades. Several academic studies had suggested that rising ocean temperatures likely would produce more powerful, and wetter, hurricanes, which drew their strength from the warmth of ocean waters. The most comprehensive study of the question to date was published on September 28 by the *Journal of Climate.* A half-dozen computer models developed at the Commerce Department's Geophysical Fluid Dynamics Laboratory in Princeton, New Jersey, predicted that by the 2080s typical hurricanes would be more powerful and would contain more moisture than those earlier in the century.

Bush Administration Policy

The Bush administration on August 25 sent Congress its latest summary of studies being conducted under the new round of government-funded climate research. Most of the summary contained routine information, but one page offered what appeared to be a sharp departure from the administration's standard line that it was too early to know whether human activities had caused the perceived rise in global temperatures. A summary of simulations of global temperatures during the twentieth century noted that an upward trend in temperatures—especially since the 1970s—could be reproduced in the computer models only by including what scientists called "anthropogenic forcings": greenhouse gases, ozone concentrations, and tiny particles of pollution from automobiles and power plants known as "sulfate aerosols." The administration summary, "Our Changing Planet: The U.S. Climate Change Science Program," cited two computer model studies showing that human activities were at least partly responsible for rising temperatures. One study was on a global scale; the other measured the effects only in North America. The document was signed by the secretaries of commerce and energy and by the president's science adviser.

James R. Mahoney, the administration's director of climate research, said the August 25 science summary did not represent a change of policy but simply was "the best possible scientific information" on the subject of climate change. Environmental advocates said they found it disturbing that the administration had access to information pointing to man-made causes of climate change but refused to adopt policies in line with that information. Industry groups and scientists who remained skeptical on climate change matters said the studies cited in the new summary were based on flawed computer models, and so offered no valuable information.

The study was the second government report in a little over two years that took a position at odds with Bush administration policy. In May 2002 the State Department sent the United Nations a report—written largely by the Environmental Protection Agency—that appeared to blame human causes for climate change. Bush dismissed the report as "something put out by the bureaucracy" and portions of it later were rewritten. *(Historic Documents of 2002, p. 300)*

California Initiative

In recent years many state governments had been much more aggressive than the federal government in adopting policies intended to reduce emissions of greenhouse gases. The Pew Center on Global Climate Change said nearly thirty states had taken various steps, as of late 2004, to combat global warming.

California, which for decades had some of the nation's toughest environmental laws, jumped out front on the climate change issue on September 24 when its Air Resources Board established rules intended to reduce automotive tailpipe emissions over an eleven-year period. The rules were the first ever adopted by any major governmental body in the world to limit emissions of carbon dioxide, and they were seen as a means of forcing automakers to increase the fuel efficiency of their products. The rules required an overall reduction of about 30 percent in emissions of carbon dioxides and other greenhouse gases in California, phased in between the 2009 and 2016 model years. The board acted on an 8–0 vote, with strong support from Republican governor Arnold Schwarzenegger.

California was able to establish its own air quality rules because it already had acted on the subject when Congress passed the Clean Air Act in 1970. Seven other states, known collectively as the Northeast States for Coordinated Air Use Management—Connecticut, Maine, Massachusetts, New Jersey, New York, Rhode Island, and Vermont—generally followed California's lead on air quality matters. As of year's end, Connecticut, Massachusetts, and New York indicated that they were planning to adopt the California rules; other states appeared to be considering the matter, as was Canada, which often adopted similar positions to those of California on air quality issues.

Auto manufacturers opposed the rules, arguing that they would add an average of $3,000 to the cost of new vehicles—three times the estimate made by the California board. On December 7 ten major auto companies joined a group of California auto dealers who had filed suit seeking to block the rules. All major U.S., European, and Japanese automakers were part of the suit except for Honda and Nissan, which were not members of the Alliance of Automobile Manufacturers; both of those companies said they opposed the rules, as well. The Bush administration, which had ruled in 2003 that carbon dioxide was not a pollutant governed by the Clean Air Act, also opposed the California rules.

Another significant action at the state level came in Colorado, where voters on November 2 approved an initiative requiring new electrical utilities to produce at least 10 percent of their energy from renewable sources, such as wind power, by 2015. Sixteen other states had adopted similar rules, but Colorado was the first to do so through a voter initiative.

Global Warming Continues

For most people, climate change meant "global warming," and 2004 provided yet more evidence that most of the Earth was getting noticeably warmer. The World Meteorological Organization reported December 15 that 2004 was the fourth-warmest year since modern record-keeping began in 1861. The average world temperature was 0.8 degrees Fahrenheit above the 57 degree long-term average, the UN agency said. Counting 2004, nine of the ten past years were among the warmest on record. The single hottest year remained 1998.

Weather extremes during 2004 ranged from exceptionally severe winter cold spells in parts of South America to above-average summer temperatures in much of Europe, particularly southern Portugal and Spain. Four major hurricanes hit the Caribbean region in September and October, causing extensive damage, especially in Haiti. Japan and the Philippines also were hit with record numbers of typhoons.

Following are excerpts from "Senate Committee Hears Testimony on Arctic Assessment: Arctic Warming Is the Result of Human Activity, Scientists Say," testimony to the Senate Commerce Committee on November 16, 2004, by Robert Corell, chairman of the Arctic Climate Impact Assessment Study, in which he described the general findings of a four-year study of the effects of climate change on the Arctic region.

"Senate Testimony: Arctic Warming Is the Result of Human Activity"

Mr. Chairman, Members of the Committee, thank you for the opportunity to participate in today's Full Committee hearing on the release of the Arctic Climate Impact Assessment's report entitled, "Impacts of a Warming Arctic ." I am Dr. Robert W. Corell, Chair of the Arctic Climate Impact Assessment (ACIA) and I am honored to testify before you today on behalf of an international team of 300 scientists, other experts, and elders and other insightful indigenous residents of the Arctic region who have prepared this comprehensive analysis of the impacts and consequences of climate variability and changes across the Arctic region, including the impacts induced by increases in UV radiation arising from depletion of stratospheric ozone in the region.

The scientific analysis and assessment conducted in the ACIA is documented in two reports, both published by Cambridge University Press.

- *A Scientific Report:* A series of assessment reviews and analyses has lead to a more integrated understanding of climate variability and change for the Arctic region (across sectors, sub-regions, indigenous and local interests). This scientific document is fully referenced, and is composed of detailed scientific and technical information describing current understanding of climate change, climate variability and increased UV radiation and their consequences over the entire Arctic region. This 1200 plus page report has been completed and is in final production for release in the weeks ahead. This report provides the scientific foundations for the Overview Document.

- *An Overview Report:* This 140 page document, which is titled "Impacts of a Warming Arctic," is a comprehensive plain language summary of the scientific aspects of the assessment and is designed to synthesizes the key findings of the assessment and place those insights in a policy-makers framework. It states our collective consensus of understanding and knowledge concerning the consequences of climate change over the entire Arctic region. This report was released last week in Reykjavik, Iceland at the ACIA Scientific Symposium (Nov. 9–12) and provides the foundations for our discussions here today.

The ACIA is a comprehensively researched, fully referenced, and independently reviewed evaluation of arctic climate change and its impacts for the region and for the world. It is the first such assessment ever conducted for the Arctic. As we reported to you and your committee in March of this year, the Arctic Council (2) called for this assessment in 2000, and charged two of its working groups, the Arctic Monitoring and Assessment Programme (AMAP) and the Conservation of Arctic Flora and Fauna (CAFF), to conduct this assessment in cooperation with the International Arctic Science Committee (IASC).

The Scientific Report

The scientific report is organized around eighteen chapters that address a broad range of issues concerning climate and UV changes across the circumpolar Arctic. These chapters are:

1. Introduction
2. Arctic Climate—Past and Present
3. The Changing Arctic: Indigenous Perspectives
4. Future Climate Change: Modeling and Scenarios for the Arctic Region
5. Ozone and Ultraviolet Radiation
6. Cryospheric and Hydrologic Variability
7. Arctic Tundra and Polar Desert Ecosystems
8. Freshwater Ecosystems and Fisheries
9. Marine Systems
10. Principles of Conserving the Arctic's Biodiversity
11. Management and Conservation of Wildlife in a Changing Arctic Environment
12. Hunting, Herding, Fishing and Gathering: Indigenous Peoples and Renewable Resource Use in the Arctic
13. Fisheries and Aquaculture
14. Forests, Land Management and Agriculture
15. Human Health
16. Infrastructure: Buildings, Support Systems, and Industrial Facilities
17. Climate Change in the Context of Multiple Stressors and Resilience
18. Summary and Synthesis

The Overview Report

The Overview Report, entitled, "Impacts of a Warming Arctic," provides the foundations for our discussions today and concludes that:

- "The Arctic is now experiencing some of the most rapid and severe climate change on Earth. Over the next 100 years, climate change is expected to accelerate, contributing to major physical, ecological, social, and economic changes, many of which have already begun. Changes in arctic climate will also affect the rest of the world through increased global warming and rising sea levels."

These climate changes are being experienced particularly intensely in the Arctic. Arctic average temperature has risen at almost twice the rate as the rest of the world in the past few decades. Widespread melting of glaciers and sea ice and rising permafrost temperatures present additional evidence of strong arctic warming. These changes in the Arctic provide an early indication of the environmental and societal significance of global warming.

An acceleration of these climatic trends is projected to occur during this century, due to ongoing increases in concentrations of greenhouse gases in the earth's atmosphere. While greenhouse gas emissions do not primarily originate in the Arctic, they are projected to bring wide-ranging changes and impacts to the Arctic. These arctic changes will, in turn, impact the planet as a whole. For this reason, people outside the Arctic have a great stake in what is happening there. For example, climatic processes unique to the Arctic have significant effects on global and regional climate. The Arctic also provides important natural resources to the rest of the world (such as oil, gas, and fish) that will be affected by climate change. And melting of arctic glaciers is one of the factors contributing to sea-level rise around the globe.

Climate change is also projected to result in major impacts inside the Arctic, some of which are already underway. Whether a particular impact is perceived as negative or positive often depends on one's interests. For example, the reduction in sea ice is very likely to have devastating consequences for polar bears, ice-dependent seals, and local people for whom these animals are a primary food source. On the other hand, reduced sea ice is likely to increase marine access to the region's resources, expanding opportunities for shipping and possibly for offshore oil extraction (although operations could be hampered initially by increasing movement of ice in some areas). Further complicating the issue, possible increases in environmental damage that often accompanies shipping and resource extraction could harm the marine habitat and negatively affect the health and traditional lifestyles of indigenous people.

Another example is that increased areas of tree growth in the Arctic could serve to take up carbon dioxide and supply more wood products and related employment, providing local and global economic benefits. On the other hand, increased tree growth is likely to add to regional warming and encroach on the habitat for many birds, reindeer/caribou, and other locally beneficial species, thereby adversely affecting local residents. Potential complications include projected increases in forest disturbances such as fires and insect outbreaks that could reduce expected benefits.

Climate change is taking place within the context of many other ongoing changes in the Arctic, including the observed increase in chemical contaminants entering the Arctic from other regions, overfishing, land use changes that result in habitat destruction and fragmentation, rapid growth in the human population, and cultural, governance, and economic changes. Impacts on the environment and society result not from climate change alone, but from the interplay of all of these changes.

One of the additional stresses in the Arctic that is addressed in this assessment results from increasing levels of ultraviolet radiation reaching the earth's surface due to stratospheric ozone depletion. As with many of the other stresses mentioned, there are important interactions between climate change and ozone depletion. The effects of climate change on the upper atmosphere make continued ozone depletion over the Arctic likely to persist for at least a few more decades. Thus, ultraviolet radiation levels in the Arctic are likely to remain elevated, and this will be most pronounced in the spring, when ecosystems are most sensitive to harmful ultraviolet radiation. The combination of climate change, excess ultraviolet radiation, and other stresses presents a range of potential problems for human health and well-being as well as risks to other arctic species and ecosystems. To communicate the results contained in the 1200 page Scientific Report of this assessment, the more non-technical and plain language Overview Report we are discussing today, integrates the scientific aspects of the assessment through ten Key Findings. . . .

We appreciate the opportunity to meet with the Committee and to outline some aspects of these ten Key Findings contained "Impacts of a Warming Arctic." This Overview Report details the major findings of the assessment. For example, the reductions in sea ice . . . [are] based on the analyses conducted in this assessment which show that September sea-ice extent, already declining markedly, is projected to decline even more rapidly in the future. . . . As the century progresses, sea ice moves further and further from the coasts of arctic land masses, retreating to the central Arctic Ocean. Some models project the nearly complete loss of summer sea ice in this century.

Further, sea level rise has the potential for significant impacts on societies and ecosystems around the world. Climate change causes sea level to rise by affecting both the density and the amount of water in the oceans. The primary factors contributing to this rise are thermal expansion due to ocean warming and melting of land-based ice that increases the total amount of water in the ocean. Global average sea level is projected by IPCC to rise 10 to 90 centimeters during this century, with the rate of rise accelerating as the century progresses. However, recent studies suggest the potential of up to 1 meter (~3 feet) by the end of the century.

This would have profound impacts for Florida. . . . Over the longer term, much larger increases in sea level are projected. Sea-level rise is expected to vary around the globe, with the largest increases projected to occur in the Arctic, in part due to the projected increase in freshwater input to the Arctic Ocean and the resulting decrease in salinity and thus density. Sea-level rise is projected to have serious implications for coastal communities and industries, islands, river deltas, harbors, and the large fraction of humanity living in coastal areas worldwide. Sea-level rise will increase the salinity of bays and estuaries. It will increase coastal erosion, especially where coastal lands are soft rather than rocky.

[Also projected are] . . . major changes in both the landscape and the Arctic oceanic basin. As Larisa Avdeyeva of Lovozero, Russia has indicated "Nowadays snows melt earlier in the springtime. Lakes, rivers, and bogs freeze much later in the autumn. Reindeer herding becomes more difficult as the ice is weak and may give way. All sorts of unusual events have taken place. Nowadays the winters are much warmer than they used to be. Occasionally during winter time it rains. We never expected this; we could not be ready for this. It is very strange. The cycle of the yearly calendar has been disturbed greatly and this affects the reindeer herding negatively for sure." These changes observed by this elder in Russia are also consistent with and documented by the scientific analyses of this assessment and are projected to continue in the coming decades.

I'd like to conclude by noting that the impacts of climate change in the Arctic addressed in this assessment are largely caused from outside the region, and will reverberate back to the global community in a variety of ways. The scientific findings reported here can inform decisions about actions to reduce the risks of climate change. As the pace and extent of climate change and its impacts increase, it will become more and more important for people everywhere to become aware of the changes taking place in the Arctic, and to consider them in evaluating what actions should be taken to respond. The IPCC [Intergovernmental Panel on Climate Change] concluded in 2001 that "There is new and stronger evidence that most of the warming observed over the last 50 years is attributable to human activities." The findings of this assessment are consistent with this perspective. Based on both our analyses and those of the IPCC, carbon dioxide concentrations in the atmosphere will remain elevated above historic levels for centuries, even if emissions were to cease immediately. Some continued warming is thus inevitable. However, the speed and amount of warming can be reduced if future emissions are limited sufficiently to stabilize the concentrations of greenhouse gases. The more than 30 scenarios developed by the IPCC assume a variety of different societal developments, resulting in various plausible levels of future emissions. Of these scenarios, the ACIA used a moderate IPCC scenario, B2, for all of its model simulations of future climate change in the Arctic, adding in some cases the A2 scenario to explore additional aspects of climate change across the circumpolar Arctic. None of these scenarios assume implementation of explicit policies to reduce greenhouse gas emissions. Thus, atmospheric concentrations do not level off in these scenarios, but rather continue to rise, resulting in significant increases in temperature and sea level and widespread changes in precipitation. The costs and difficulties of adapting to such increases are very likely to increase significantly over time.

If, on the other hand, society chooses to reduce emissions substantially, the induced changes in climate would be smaller and would happen more slowly. This would not eliminate all impacts, especially some of the irreversible impacts affecting particular species. However, it would allow ecosystems and human societies as a whole to adapt more readily, reducing overall impacts and costs. The impacts addressed in this assessment assume continued growth in greenhouse gas emissions. Although it will be very difficult to limit near-term consequences resulting from past emissions, many longer-term impacts could be reduced significantly by reducing global emissions over the course of this century. This assessment did not analyze strategies for achieving such reductions, which are the subject of efforts by other bodies.

Key Findings of the Arctic Climate Impact Assessment

1. Arctic climate is now warming rapidly and much larger changes are projected.
    - Annual average arctic temperature has increased at almost twice the rate as that of the rest of the world over the past few decades, with some variations across the region.

- Additional evidence of arctic warming comes from widespread melting of glaciers and sea ice, and a shortening of the snow season.
- Increasing global concentrations of carbon dioxide and other greenhouse gases due to human activities, primarily fossil fuel burning, are projected to contribute to additional arctic warming of about 4–7°C over the next 100 years.
- Increasing precipitation, shorter and warmer winters, and substantial decreases in snow cover and ice cover are among the projected changes that are very likely to persist for centuries.
- Unexpected and even larger shifts and fluctuations in climate are also possible.

2. Arctic warming and its consequences have worldwide implications.
   - Melting of highly reflective arctic snow and ice reveals darker land and ocean surfaces, increasing absorption of the sun's heat and further warming the planet.
   - Increases in glacial melt and river runoff add more freshwater to the ocean, raising global sea level and possibly slowing the ocean circulation that brings heat from the tropics to the poles, affecting global and regional climate.
   - Warming is very likely to alter the release and uptake of greenhouse gases from soils, vegetation, and coastal oceans.
   - Impacts of arctic climate change will have implications for biodiversity around the world because migratory species depend on breeding and feeding grounds in the Arctic.
3. Arctic vegetation zones are very likely to shift, causing wide-ranging impacts.
   - Treeline is expected to move northward and to higher elevations, with forests replacing a significant fraction of existing tundra, and tundra vegetation moving into polar deserts.
   - More-productive vegetation is likely to increase carbon uptake, although reduced reflectivity of the land surface is likely to outweigh this, causing further warming.
   - Disturbances such as insect outbreaks and forest fires are very likely to increase in frequency, severity, and duration, facilitating invasions by non-native species.
   - Where suitable soils are present, agriculture will have the potential to expand northward due to a longer and warmer growing season.
4. Animal species' diversity, ranges, and distribution will change.
   - Reductions in sea ice will drastically shrink marine habitat for polar bears, ice-inhabiting seals, and some seabirds, pushing some species toward extinction.
   - Caribou/reindeer and other land animals are likely to be increasingly stressed as climate change alters their access to food sources, breeding grounds, and historic migration routes.
   - Species ranges are projected to shift northward on both land and sea, bringing new species into the Arctic while severely limiting some species currently present.
   - As new species move in, animal diseases that can be transmitted to humans, such as West Nile virus, are likely to pose increasing health risks.
   - Some arctic marine fisheries, which are of global importance as well as providing major contributions to the region's economy, are likely to become more productive. Northern freshwater fisheries that are mainstays of local diets are likely to suffer.
5. Many coastal communities and facilities face increasing exposure to storms.
   - Severe coastal erosion will be a growing problem as rising sea level and a reduction in sea ice allow higher waves and storm surges to reach the shore.

- Along some arctic coastlines, thawing permafrost weakens coastal lands, adding to their vulnerability.
- The risk of flooding in coastal wetlands is projected to increase, with impacts on society and natural ecosystems.
- In some cases, communities and industrial facilities in coastal zones are already threatened or being forced to relocate, while others face increasing risks and costs.

6. Reduced sea ice is very likely to increase marine transport and access to resources.
   - The continuing reduction of sea ice is very likely to lengthen the navigation season and increase marine access to the Arctic's natural resources.
   - Seasonal opening of the Northern Sea Route is likely to make trans-arctic shipping during summer feasible within several decades. Increasing ice movement in some channels of the Northwest Passage could initially make shipping more difficult.
   - Reduced sea ice is likely to allow increased offshore extraction of oil and gas, although increasing ice movement could hinder some operations.
   - Sovereignty, security, and safety issues, as well as social, cultural, and environmental concerns are likely to arise as marine access increases.
7. Thawing ground will disrupt transportation, buildings, and other infrastructure.
   - Transportation and industry on land, including oil and gas extraction and forestry, will increasingly be disrupted by the shortening of the periods during which ice roads and tundra are frozen sufficiently to permit travel.
   - As frozen ground thaws, many existing buildings, roads, pipelines, airports, and industrial facilities are likely to be destabilized, requiring substantial rebuilding, maintenance, and investment.
   - Future development will require new design elements to account for ongoing warming that will add to construction and maintenance costs.
   - Permafrost degradation will also impact natural ecosystems through collapsing of the ground surface, draining of lakes, wetland development, and toppling of trees in susceptible areas.
8. Indigenous communities are facing major economic and cultural impacts.
   - Many Indigenous Peoples depend on hunting polar bear, walrus, seals, and caribou, herding reindeer, fishing, and gathering, not only for food and to support the local economy, but also as the basis for cultural and social identity.
   - Changes in species' ranges and availability, access to these species, a perceived reduction in weather predictability, and travel safety in changing ice and weather conditions present serious challenges to human health and food security, and possibly even the survival of some cultures.
   - Indigenous knowledge and observations provide an important source of information about climate change. This knowledge, consistent with complementary information from scientific research, indicates that substantial changes have already occurred.
9. Elevated ultraviolet radiation levels will affect people, plants, and animals.
   - The stratospheric ozone layer over the Arctic is not expected to improve significantly for at least a few decades, largely due to the effect of greenhouse gases on stratospheric temperatures. Ultraviolet radiation (UV) in the Arctic is thus projected to remain elevated in the coming decades.
   - As a result, the current generation of arctic young people is likely to receive a lifetime dose of UV that is about 30% higher than any prior generation.

Increased UV is known to cause skin cancer, cataracts, and immune system disorders in humans. Elevated UV can disrupt photosynthesis in plants and have detrimental effects on the early life stages of fish and amphibians.
- Risks to some arctic ecosystems are likely as the largest increases in UV occur in spring, when sensitive species are most vulnerable, and warming-related declines in snow and ice cover increase exposure for living things normally protected by such cover.

10. Multiple influences interact to cause impacts to people and ecosystems.
    - Changes in climate are occurring in the context of many other stresses including chemical pollution, overfishing, land use changes, habitat fragmentation, human population increases, and cultural and economic changes.
    - These multiple stresses can combine to amplify impacts on human and ecosystem health and well-being. In many cases, the total impact is greater than the sum of its parts, such as the combined impacts of contaminants, excess ultraviolet radiation, and climatic warming.
    - Unique circumstances in arctic sub-regions determine which are the most important stresses and how they interact.

Source: U.S. Department of State. "Senate Committee Hears Testimony on Arctic Assessment: Arctic Warming is the Result of Human Activity, Scientists Say." Prepared testimony of Dr. Robert W. Corell for a hearing by the Senate Committee on Commerce, Science, and Transportation. November 16, 2004. http://usinfo.state.gov/gi/Archive/2004/Nov/17-685964.html (accessed April 8, 2005).

Government Panel on Science and Technology Appointments

November 17, 2004

INTRODUCTION

The intersection of science and politics in the United States drew greater public attention during 2004 than at any other time in recent history—almost entirely because of conflicts between many leading scientists and the administration of President George W. Bush. The president and his administration had taken policy positions on a host of science-related issues that were at odds with the views of many in the mainstream scientific community. Those disagreements came to the fore in an election year, as dozens of well-known scientists accused the administration of manipulating science to suit its ideological or moral agendas, and the administration responded by accusing the scientists of parallel distortions.

The conflict came into play during the presidential election campaign when several dozen Nobel laureates and other prominent scientists publicly attacked Bush and endorsed Sen. John Kerry, his Democratic opponent. This dispute roiled the waters in academic and political circles and made the newspaper headlines but appeared to have little influence on the election outcome. Opinion polls showed the voters were concerned about the economy and the U.S. position in Iraq and paid little attention to the use of science to determine public policy. *(Election, p. 773)*

Background

Throughout the nation's history, science had influenced governmental decision making, generally on such questions as where to place roads and dams, or how to build more powerful weapons or send astronauts to the moon. Ever since the mid-twentieth century, when the federal government's role in society grew and scientific matters simultaneously appeared to become more complex, the government's use of science gradually became more controversial. The controversy quite often was greatest when Republicans were in the White House, if only because a significant portion of scientists in academic circles were Democrats. Until George W. Bush appeared on the scene, the high watermark of political disputes between the White House and the scientific community was during the presidency of Ronald Reagan (1981–1989).

The quantity and intensity of political debate on scientific matters escalated almost immediately after Bush took office. Many of the early disputes were over environmental issues, notably Bush's rollback of several major environmental regulations initiated by President Bill Clinton (1993–2001) and the president's skepticism about scientific reports pointing to human causes (notably the burning of oil and other fossil fuels) of climate change. *(Background, Historic Documents of 2001, p. 109)*

Scientists Take on Bush

Over the course of Bush's first term, many scientists and Democrats in Congress charged that the administration either ignored scientific opinion, or distorted it, on a broad range of other issues, including health care, family planning, a proposed missile defense system, and the presence of weapons in Iraq. These complaints reached a crescendo in 2004 with two widely publicized statements by scientists condemning Bush and his administration. *(Missile defense, p. 176; Iraq weapons, p. 711)*

The first statement was issued February 18 under the auspices of the Union of Concerned Scientists, a liberal organization that advocated for arms control, strict environment standards, and other causes. A statement signed by sixty-two scientists said: "When scientific knowledge has been found to be in conflict with its political goals, the administration has often manipulated the process through which science enters into its decision." As examples, the statement said independent scientists had been removed from federal advisory panels and replaced with industry representatives, some scientists had been rejected for these panels because they had not voted for Bush, career scientists in government agencies had been forbidden to air their views publicly if they disagreed with administration policy, former industry lobbyists had become key administration officials whose decisions affected their former employers, and the administration had "misrepresented" or "suppressed" scientific studies that were at odds with White House policies. Among the signers of this statement were twenty recipients of the Nobel Prize and nineteen recipients of the National Medal of Science.

A more overtly partisan statement by prominent scientists came June 21 when forty-eight Nobel laureates signed a paper endorsing Kerry for president and condemning Bush for manipulating science. "Unlike previous administrations, Republican and Democratic alike, the Bush administration has ignored scientific advice in the policy-making that is so important to our collective welfare," the statement said. Kerry used that statement to bolster his own contention that Bush had allowed ideology to override scientific conclusions, notably in his opposition to using stem cells for scientific research.

White House officials and Bush presidential campaign spokesmen repeatedly rejected such charges, saying the administration had not manipulated scientific advice and instead had based all its decisions on what the White House called "sound science." The most detailed rebuttal came in a pair of documents released by the White House on April 2: a letter to Congress from Bush's science adviser, John H. Marburger III, and a four-color brochure, "Bush Administration Science and Technology Accomplishments: Promoting Innovation for a Stronger, Safer America."

The letter from Marburger, a Democrat, was a point-by-point response to the charges in the Union of Concerned Scientists statement. "I can attest from my personal experience and direct knowledge that this administration is implementing the president's policy of strongly supporting science and applying the highest scientific standards in decision-making," he said. Marburger acknowledged some errors by the administration, notably a case earlier in 2004 when a proposed Environmental Protection Agency (EPA) rule governing emissions of mercury from power plants contained a dozen paragraphs taken from a legal brief written by lawyers for the electric power industry. Marburger said the use of that material in the EPA rule "should not have occurred," but he argued that the industry-supplied text "had nothing to do with the integrity of the science used by EPA."

Marburger's defense failed to quell the debate and, in fact, added even more fuel to the fire. Rep. Henry Waxman, D-Calif., who had been a leading critic of the

Bush administration's use of science, on April 13 issued his own rebuttal to Marburger's rebuttal. Waxman said Marburger omitted "relevant facts," failed to substantiate his claims, and failed to address nineteen specific incidents in which the Union of Concerned Scientists had alleged scientific manipulation by the White House.

Advisory Panels

Nearly every major agency of the federal government relied on independent committees of experts to provide information on public policy matters. As of 2004, according to the Government Accountability Office (GAO), the government had about 950 of these "advisory" panels, composed of about 62,000 members. Some panels were permanent bodies that gave advice on such broad issues as food safety, environmental protection, and the gathering of foreign intelligence. Others were temporary bodies, appointed to examine a narrow question of immediate urgency. Each president was free to choose the experts serving on these panels, and every president had used at least some of these appointments to reward political supporters or to advance a particular policy agenda.

Federal advisory councils rarely had generated much public controversy until the Bush administration revamped many of them. Administration critics offered two major complaints: that some appointees to scientific advisory panels were unqualified—except for their known support of administration policy, and that the administration routinely applied a political litmus test for appointees to these panels.

One of the most controversial cases came in late February, when the White House dismissed two members from the Council on Bioethics, which he had formed in 2001 to provide advice on such controversial matters as cloning and research on stem cells. The terms of all members of the council expired at the end of 2003, and the White House reappointed all the members except for two, Elizabeth Blackburn and William May, who had occasionally been at odds with administration policy. The White House replaced them with members who had expressed public support for Bush's policies, but a spokeswoman said the switch was unrelated to politics. *(Bioethics panel, Historic Documents of 2002, p. 512)*

Another case that attracted broad attention involved William Miller, a well-known drug addiction expert at the University of New Mexico. He said he had been dropped from consideration for a place on the National Advisory Council on Drug Abuse because he had not voted for Bush and he supported abortion rights.

In its February 18 statement, and again in a follow-up report in July, the Union of Concerned Scientists cited other cases in which, it said, the administration had quizzed nominees for advisory council positions about whether they had voted for Bush in the 2000 election. Several well-known scientists who refused to answer the question, or who said they had not voted for Bush, were then told their nominations had been rejected, the reports said.

Donald Kennedy, editor of the journal *Science* and former president of Stanford University, wrote in an editorial: "What is unusual about the current epidemic is not that the Bush administration examines candidates for compatibility with its 'values.' It's how deep the practice cuts, in particular, the way it now invades areas once immune to this kind of manipulation."

The administration's track record on appointments to advisory councils was examined, and found wanting, by two independent examinations during the year. The first was by the GAO, which issued a detailed report on May 20, "Federal Advisory Committees: Additional Guidance Could Help Agencies Better Ensure Independence and Balance." The GAO said it found that agencies had no uniform rules for determining whether the members of advisory councils had conflicts of interest, were truly independent of the government, or represented a "balance" of views. The GAO recommended detailed procedures to ensure that advisory council members met these qualifications.

A broader analysis was published November 17 by a panel appointed by the National Academy of Science, which examined federal advisory panels on scientific and technical issues and updated previous studies that had been conducted in 1992 and 2000. The panel was chaired by former representative John Edward Porter, an Illinois Republican. Among its members was Christine Todd Whitman, who had served as administrator of the Environmental Protection Agency early in Bush's term.

The panel offered six specific recommendations for improving the process of selecting government advisers on scientific matters, ranging from the president's full-time science adviser to the experts who serve on the hundreds of part-time advisory panels. The panel did not directly comment on the controversies over the Bush administration's selections for advisers, but its central recommendation appeared to address many of the criticisms of administration appointments. The panel said members should be chosen "for their scientific and technical knowledge and credentials and for their professional and personal integrity." The administration should not ask potential advisers for "nonrelevant information" such as their voting records, political party affiliation, or positions on particular policies.

"Peer Review"

For nearly a year scientists, industry lobbyists, and the Bush administration engaged in a tussle over an even more obscure issue: the process by which government agencies selected scientific information in their decision making. The debate began in August 2003, when the Office of Management and Budget (OMB), drafted a proposal known as a "bulletin" revising the guidelines under which government agencies chose the experts who would evaluate the scientific underpinnings of proposed regulations on matters such as acceptable levels of air pollution or food safety standards. Such evaluations, known as peer reviews, were common in the academic world and long had been used in the government, as well. What was different about the OMB's proposal was that it required peer reviews for all regulations involving scientific matters. In what was described as a step to eliminate conflicts of interest, the proposal also required that all peer reviewers be "independent of the agency" involved, thus barring the use of academic experts who had received grants from that agency. There was no comparable prohibition on the use of experts associated with industries affected by the regulations.

Dozens of scientists and former executive branch officials wrote to oppose the OMB proposal, arguing that it imposed new layers of bureaucracy and could allow affected industries too great a voice in the regulatory process. Support for the proposal came from major industry groups, including the National Association of Manufacturers and the National Petrochemical and Refiners Association. John Graham, who crafted the new guidelines as head of OMB's office on regulations, said the proposal was intended to "increase the technical quality and credibility of regulatory science."

Responding to the criticism, OMB on April 15 issued a revised rule that softened many of the proposals that had brought the most criticism. The revised rule dropped the conflict of interest language that critics said would have given preference to industry representatives over academic experts. The rule also allowed exemptions to the requirement for peer reviews in cases of emergencies, such as a recall of tainted beef by the Agriculture Department.

Following is the text of the executive summary of Science and Technology in the National Interest: Ensuring the Best Presidential and Advisory Committee Science and Technology Appointments, *a report issued November 17, 2004, by an ad hoc panel of the National Academies of Science Committee on Science, Engineering and Public Policy.*

Science and Technology in the National Interest

The security, economic well-being, and safety and health of the United States depend on the strength and vitality of the nation's science and technology (S&T) enterprise. Almost every aspect of modern public policy is touched by S&T, including those involving national security, economic development, health care, the environment, education, energy, and natural resources. The US research enterprise is the largest in the world and leads in innovation in many fields. For these reasons, it is critical to attract scientists and engineers into the highest levels of public service, either as political appointees in top leadership positions or as members of the many advisory committees providing scientific and technical advice to executive agencies.

In 2004, an ad hoc committee of the National Academies Committee on Science, Engineering, and Public Policy was charged with preparing this third report examining the most senior S&T appointments to federal government positions and updating the accompanying list of the most urgent S&T presidential appointments. Sufficient changes have occurred since the National Academies 2000 report on presidential appointments—including the 2001 terrorist attacks, the anthrax deaths, the reorganization of homeland-security activities in the federal government, new developments in S&T, and concerns about the politicization of S&T decision making and advice—to warrant this new edition. In contrast with previous reports on the subject, this one covers not only presidential appointments to top S&T leadership positions but also the appointment of scientists, engineers, and health professionals to serve on federal advisory committees that focus on science-based policy or on the review of research proposals. The committee recognizes that other areas of federal responsibility are as important as S&T, but S&T appointments are the only ones within its purview. This summary presents the committee's recommendations on the two major topics in its charge: presidential S&T appointments and appointments of scientists and engineers to federal advisory committees.

Presidential Science and Technology Appointments

1. Shortly after the election, the President or President-elect should identify a candidate for the position of Assistant to the President for Science and Technology (APST) to provide advice, including suggesting and recruiting other science

and technology presidential appointees. After inauguration, the president should promptly both appoint this person as APST and indicate the intent to nominate him or her as the director of the White House Office of Science and Technology Policy (OSTP).

Selection of a confidential adviser on S&T immediately after the election, if one is not already in place, is essential to ensure that assistance is available to the incoming president in identifying the best candidates for key S&T appointments and to provide advice in the event of a crisis. That person should be named the Assistant to the President for Science and Technology (APST) immediately after the inauguration so that he or she will have the stature that the S&T portfolio warrants.

Ideally, the APST will have credibility and the respect of the S&T community; an understanding of large research and educational enterprises; background as a practicing researcher (academic or nonacademic); awareness of a wide variety of public policy issues; familiarity with issues in technology and national security, economic development, health and the environment, and international affairs; and the ability to work and communicate with others, including policy makers.

Because the APST does not require Senate confirmation, the nominee should be appointed immediately after the presidential inauguration. However, because the APST cannot undertake the duties of OSTP director without Senate confirmation, the President should seek his or her rapid confirmation to facilitate a continuous connection between the two roles.

2. The President and the Senate should streamline and personnel—indeed, all key personnel—to reduce the personal and financial burdens on nominees and to allow important positions to be filled promptly.

Because of the critical need for input by high-level S&T leadership in program implementation and current policy debates, it is imperative that key positions not sit vacant for long periods. In addition to identifying candidates early in a new administration or replacements in an existing one, efforts must be made to streamline and accelerate the appointment process.

Streamlining could involve such mechanisms as relying on one system of background checks rather than separate systems for the White House and the Senate, clarifying the criteria for the position in question and the principles for questioning nominees, requesting only relevant and important background information, and keeping the process timely and on track with the goal of completing the appointment process within 4 months from first White House contact to Senate confirmation.

3. Congress and the Office of Government Ethics should consolidate and simplify appointment policies and procedures to reduce the financial and vocational obstacles to government service.

Some mechanisms for consolidating and simplifying the process are standardizing and clarifying pre-employment requirements and postemployment restrictions, reducing unreasonable financial and professional losses for those who serve by simplifying financial-disclosure reporting requirements (for example, evaluating a de minimis rule), eliminating many of the restrictions associated with the use of blind trusts, and ensuring continuing health insurance and pension-plan coverage.

4. The APST and other senior administration leadership should actively seek input from accomplished and recognized S&T leaders and from a broad and diverse set of constituencies when seeking candidates for S&T appointments.

As a means of seeking this input and to build a strong pool of candidates with policy experience now and in the future, accomplished and recognized S&T leaders and professional science, engineering, and health societies should propose emerging leaders in their fields to serve in government positions and should expand junior and senior internship and fellowship programs that provide their members with government and policy experience. Continuing efforts should be made to identify women and members of underrepresented groups for such positions.

Science and Technology Appointments to Federal Advisory Committees

5. When a federal advisory committee requires scientific or technical proficiency, persons nominated to provide that expertise should be selected on the basis of their scientific and technical knowledge and credentials and their professional and personal integrity. It is inappropriate to ask them to provide nonrelevant information, such as voting record, political-party affiliation, or position on particular policies.

S&T issues frequently pose ethical and societal questions that may require regulation or policy solutions, and many critical policy choices in national security, the environment, the economy, agriculture, energy, and health depend on a deep understanding of S&T. Many factors—including societal values, economic costs, and political judgments—come together with technical judgments in the process of reaching advisory committee recommendations. Essential viewpoints needed for appropriate committee balance and scope should be represented by accomplished people in that policy arena, but scientists, engineers, and health professionals nominated primarily to provide S&T input should be selected for their scientific and technological knowledge and credentials and for their professional and personal integrity.

Achieving a balance of policy perspectives may be appropriate for those placed on committees for their policy insights, but it is not a relevant criterion for selecting members whose purpose is to provide scientific and technical expertise. Therefore, it is no more appropriate to ask S&T experts to provide nonrelevant information—such as voting record, political-party affiliation, or position on particular policies—than to ask them other personal and immaterial information, such as hair color or height. This type of information has no relevance in discussions related to S&T.

Furthermore, even for committee members selected for reasons unrelated to expertise, political-party affiliation and voting record do not necessarily predict their position on particular policies and should not be used as a means to balance committee perspectives.

Finally, most people are likely to form opinions on S&T issues with which they are experienced and familiar. For that reason, excluding S&T experts from serving on advisory committees solely on the grounds that their opinions are known is inappropriate and could leave the federal advisory committee system devoid of qualified candidates. The government would be better served by a policy in which the best scientists, engineers, and health professionals are selected because of their expertise with their opinions disclosed to staff and other committee members in closed session than by a policy that excludes them because of their presumed opinions on S&T issues.

Disclosing perspectives, relevant experiences, and possible biases serves two important purposes: it provides a context in which committees can assess and consider the views of individual committee members, and it provides an opportunity to balance strong opinions or perspectives through the appointment of additional committee members.

The National Academies uses such a policy: people asked to serve on committees are obliged to reveal any possible sources of bias that they have so that others on the committee can discount or ignore their advice on a given subject. That approach promotes the inclusion of people who potentially can make important contributions to the work at hand. It does not, however, prevent or guard against appointing people who have conflicts of interest—a separate but equally important concern.

6. Presidential administrations should make the process for nominating and appointing people to advisory committees more explicit and visible and should examine current federal advisory committee appointment categories to see whether they are sufficient to meet the nation's needs.

Administration officials should broadly announce the intent to create an advisory committee or appoint new members to an existing committee and should provide an opportunity for relevant and interested parties to suggest nominees they believe would be good committee members.

A model for this process is that used by the Environmental Protection Agency Science Advisory Board, which provides information on its Web site on the method and selection criteria related to its advisory committees and *Federal Register* notices requesting nominations for a particular committee and later describing how a particular committee was formed. It also posts biographic and some general financial information (such as sources of research support) on a committee's membership before the committee's initial meeting and provides timely announcements of the committee's meeting agenda and follow-up on a short-term basis with the minutes of committee meetings' open sessions (although the latter are required by the Federal Advisory Committee Act [FACA], timeliness is not enforced). Procedural mechanisms of this type should be in place for all federal advisory committees.

Efforts are also needed to clarify and identify the conflict-of-interest principles that will be applied to committee membership. As a first step toward public disclosure, the General Service Administration should post on its Web site and elsewhere the appointment status of appointees—that is, whether a committee member is to be classified as a special government employee, a regular government employee, a consultant, or a representative since there can be great variance in conflict-of-interest procedures.

As a second step, the appointment classification should be re-examined to determine whether it meets the needs of federal agencies' activities. Of particular concern is the classification of committee members who review research proposals or provide direction on federal research programs. Care needs to be taken to ensure that conflict-of-interest requirements for such federal advisory committees are not so burdensome that the best scientists, engineers, and health professionals are unwilling to serve on them.

7. To build confidence in the advisory committee system and increase the willingness of scientists and engineers to serve, department and agency heads should establish an appointment process supported by explicit policies and procedures and hold staff accountable for its implementation.

Staff who process advisory committee membership nominations and who manage advisory committee operations should be properly trained senior employees familiar with the importance and nuances of the advisory committee process, including a clear understanding of the appropriateness of the questions that candidates should and should not be asked.

Conclusion

The nation is in need of exceptionally able scientists, engineers, and health professionals to serve in executive positions in the federal government and on federal advisory committees. Such persons, when serving as presidential appointees, make key programmatic and policy decisions that will affect our lives and those of our children. Similarly, skilled scientists and engineers are needed for advisory committees to provide advice on the myriad issues with complex technologic dimensions that confront government decision makers. Our nation has long been served by its ability to draw qualified S&T candidates to government service because of the opportunities for intellectually challenging work that affects the world in which we live and that encourages and protects the scientific process. We must continue to enlist the best candidates for these important positions and ensure that the obstacles to their service are minimized.

Source: National Academy of Sciences. Committee on Science, Engineering, and Public Policy. Committee on Ensuring the Best Presidential and Federal Advisory Committee Science and Technology Appointments. *Science and Technology in the National Interest: Ensuring the Best Presidential and Federal Advisory Committee Science and Technology Appointments.* Washington: National Academies Press, 2004. www.nap.edu/catalog/11152.html (accessed February 5, 2005).

FDA Officials on Protecting Patients from Unsafe Drugs

November 18, 2004

INTRODUCTION

The safety of a best-selling type of pain reliever was called into question in late 2004 when Merck, the maker of Vioxx, abruptly pulled it from the market on September 30 and Pfizer, the maker of Celebrex, suspended advertising that medication directly to consumers. Studies of both drugs showed that they could cause an increased risk of heart attack and stroke. The safety of a third drug in the category, Pfizer's Bextra, was also under scrutiny.

The announcements were major blows to the financial status and reputations of the two drug makers. They also left millions of pain sufferers and their physicians in a quandary. The drugs were a relatively new type of anti-inflammatory medication that provided the same pain relief as earlier versions such as ibuprofen and naproxen but supposedly without the damage to the gastrointestinal system that those drugs sometimes caused, especially in patients who took high doses of painkillers over long periods of time to relieve chronic pain.

The announcements also raised questions about whether the drug companies should have acted sooner, whether the federal Food and Drug Administration (FDA) should have approved the drugs in the first place, and whether the agency was adequately monitoring the safety of drugs after they were on the market. A claim from one of FDA's own researchers that the agency had tried to suppress his findings about problems with Vioxx further inflamed the controversy.

Earlier in the year the FDA was widely criticized for moving too slowly on reports linking antidepressant drugs to an increased risk of suicide among adolescents and for trying to suppress the findings of one of its own scientists verifying those reports. The FDA was also under fire for failing to monitor more closely a factory that was supposed to have manufactured half of the United States's annual vaccine supply for the 2004–2005 flu season. The American-owned plant in Liverpool, England, was closed down on October 5 by British health regulators after they found bacterial contamination in the manufacturing process. *(Flu vaccine shortage, p. 639; antidepressants and suicide in children, p. 746)*

Vioxx Withdrawal

Merck's September 30 announcement that it was pulling Vioxx from the worldwide market came as a surprise. The company said it was withdrawing the drug because data from a clinical trial showed that patients taking Vioxx for eighteen months or more were twice as vulnerable for heart attack than patients taking a placebo. "Although we believe it would have been possible to continue to market Vioxx with labeling that would incorporate these new data, given the availability of alternative therapies, and the questions raised by the data, we concluded that a voluntary withdrawal is the responsible course to take," said Raymond V. Gilmartin, Merck's chief executive officer. The FDA followed up Merck's announcement with a public health advisory suggesting people taking Vioxx consult their physicians about alternative medications.

Vioxx won FDA approval in 1999 for the reduction of pain and inflammation caused by osteoarthritis, as well as for acute pain in adults and for menstruation pain. In August 2004, less than two months before the drug was pulled off pharmacy shelves, the FDA approved Vioxx for adults and children with rheumatoid arthritis.

Vioxx was the second of a new class of painkillers, known as selective COX-2 inhibitors, approved by the FDA. The first was Pfizer's Celebrex. Although none of these COX-2 inhibitors had been shown to reduce pain any more effectively than earlier pain relievers such as ibuprofen and naproxen (sold under the brand name Aleve), there was some evidence that these new drugs would reduce the risk of gastrointestinal ulcers and bleeding. Of the COX-2 inhibitors, however, only Vioxx had been shown to have this effect. An estimated 10–25 percent of regular users of the earlier class of pain relievers suffered from ulcers, and an estimated 16,500 died each year from gastrointestinal problems associated with use of pain relievers.

Long-time critics of Vioxx said they were surprised—not that Merck had withdrawn the drug but that the company took so long to do it. Evidence that Vioxx increased the risk of heart attack and stroke began accumulating almost as soon as the drug was approved. In 2000 the so-called VIGOR study, funded by Merck, showed that patients taking Vioxx had a significantly higher risk of suffering a cardiovascular event than patients taking naproxen. The authors of the study suggested that the results were related to naproxen's protective effect against heart problems, not to any heightened risk posed by Vioxx.

Other epidemiological studies uncovered additional evidence that Vioxx, particularly at higher doses, was linked to heart and stroke problems; one study also challenged the finding that naproxen protected the heart. In August Kaiser Permanente, a nonprofit health maintenance organization, announced that a review of patient records, conducted by FDA scientist David Graham, showed that those taking high doses of Vioxx suffered more heart attacks and strokes than patients on other medications. Merck rejected these findings as inconclusive because they were surveys of patient records and not clinical trials where a drug's effects were carefully monitored against a control group taking a placebo.

Ironically, it was Merck's own clinical trial that proved Vioxx's undoing. In an effort to find other medical conditions that the drug might treat, Merck had begun a clinical trial to assess whether Vioxx was effective in preventing a recurrence of polyps in patients with a history of benign colorectal tumors. The company stopped the trial when it found evidence that people taking Vioxx for eighteen moths were twice as likely to suffer heart attacks, strokes, or blood clots as those taking a placebo. Although the actual number of cases was small—fifteen out of one thousand people taking the drug—Merck judged the risk to be unacceptable. (In late December, the *New York Times* reported that further analysis of the study data showed that Vioxx apparently *was* effective in preventing precancerous colon polyps.)

The financial impact for Merck and its shareholders was enormous. Vioxx was sold in eighty countries, earning the company $2.5 billion worldwide in 2003. About 2 million people were taking the prescription drug at the time of its withdrawal, and an estimated 20 million Americans had taken the drug since it came on the market in 1999. Many of those consumers had been lured to the medication by Merck's intense direct-to-consumer commercial advertising that featured former ice skater Dorothy Hamill and music by the Rascals to appeal to the middle-age baby boom generation beginning to suffer from the pains of osteoarthritis and other conditions associated with aging. The company spent $160 million advertising Vioxx directly to consumers in 2003 and reportedly even more promoting the drug to physicians. Such advertising, critics said, led to widespread overuse and misuse of the drug. The fact that it took so long for the drug to be withdrawn was "a terrifying testimony to the power of marketing," one physician who had studied the drug told the *New York Times.*

The value of Merck stock plunged 17 percent on the New York Stock Exchange immediately after the announcement and fell more than 40 percent by mid-November. The company was facing at least two class-action suits alleging damage from taking Vioxx. Merck also said that, as of October 31, it had been named in about 375 lawsuits involving 1,000 plaintiff groups alleging that they had been adversely affected by taking the drug. Some Wall Street analysts estimated Merck's potential liability at more than $10 billion. On November 8 Merck disclosed that it was also under investigation by both the Securities and Exchange Commission (SEC) and the Justice Department. Reporters said the SEC investigation was likely probing whether Merck had misled investors about the potential problems with Vioxx. The Justice Department had issued a subpoena "requesting information related to the Company's research, marketing and selling activities with respect to Vioxx in a federal healthcare investigation under criminal statutes."

Problems with Celebrex, Bextra

Two weeks after Merck pulled Vioxx off the market, Pfizer warned doctors that Bextra might increase risk of heart attack or stroke in coronary artery bypass patients and that it could cause rare but potentially fatal skin reactions. Pfizer also announced that it would undertake a worldwide clinical trial of Celebrex to determine if it was safe for long-term use. Pfizer added that some characteristics of Celebrex suggested that it might actually help people with coronary artery disease. Neither Bextra nor Celebrex had been shown to be any more effective than earlier drugs at easing pain or preventing stomach bleeding, although individual patients sometimes tolerated one of the newer drugs better than the older varieties.

On December 17 Pfizer announced that a long-term study of Celebrex by the National Cancer Institute had been stopped after researchers discovered a heightened risk of heart problems in patients taking the drug at two to four times the recommended dosage over long periods of time. It was the first time that Celebrex had been linked to heart attacks.

Later in the day FDA issued a warning to physicians urging them to consider alternatives to Celebrex for their patients. The agency also said it might take other actions soon, including stronger warnings on the label or even ordering the drug off the market. In October the agency had announced that it planned to convene an expert advisory panel to review the safety evidence on the COX-2 inhibitors and make recommendations on continuing their use.

On December 19 Pfizer announced that it would stop advertising Celebrex directly to consumers, although it would continue marketing the pain reliever to doctors. Pfizer executives also said they had no plans to take Celebrex off the market. They maintained that the drug was safe when taken at the prescribed dosage and that it remained an "appropriate option" for thousands, perhaps millions, of patients.

Some analysts said Pfizer was making a mistake by leaving Celebrex on the market. "Pfizer will inevitably have to recall Celebrex, and I believe they are making a strategic error not doing it immediately," George Sard, chairman of a crisis communications firm, told the *New York Times*. "Their current position is untenable—and the price of waiting will be increased legal, financial and reputational costs." Sales of Celebrex and Bextra had been expected to bring in more than $4 billion in 2004, about 10 percent of Pfizer's total revenues. Those totals were expected to fall in the wake of safety concerns about the drugs.

FDA Scrutiny

Merck's decision to remove Vioxx from the market appeared to catch even the FDA by surprise, prompting new questions about whether the agency was capable of protecting American consumers from unsafe drugs. Many critics said the FDA had known of concerns about the medication's safety for some time. They pointed to an FDA warning to Merck in 2001 to stop downplaying the cardiovascular risks of the drug in its promotional materials and the agency's requirement in 2002 that Merck change the Vioxx label to indicate that the drug had been implicated in an increased risk of heart attack and stroke.

Criticisms of FDA's actions, or inactions, were heightened in early October when David Graham, associate science director of the Office of Drug Safety at the FDA, said that his superiors had tried to suppress the results of his Vioxx study, done in collaboration with Kaiser Permanente, that showed increased risk of heart attack and stroke. Graham's allegations were made public by Sen. Charles E. Grassley, R-Iowa, chairman of the Senate Finance Committee, who earlier in the year had investigated allegations that the FDA had tried to cover up one of its researcher's findings linking a certain class of antidepressants to increased risk of suicide in children. Steven Galson, the acting director of FDA's Office of Drug Evaluation and Research, called the accusations "baloney" and said that Graham had never turned over the data for review as he had promised.

Grassley was not persuaded. "It seems that while Merck was taking a fresh look at its clinical data in search of trouble, the FDA was challenging its own researcher," he said in a news release. "Merck knew it had trouble on its hands and took action. At the same time, instead of acting as a public watchdog, the Food and Drug Administration was busy challenging its own expert and calling his work "scientific rumor."

The situation grew more explosive on November 18, when Graham appeared before the Finance Committee, where he called the FDA's handling of Vioxx "a profound regulatory failure" and said the agency was "incapable of protecting America against another Vioxx." During questioning, Graham listed five other drugs that he said had dangerous side effects and should be withdrawn from the market or whose use should be restricted. The five were Bextra; Crestor, a cholesterol-lowering drug; Meridia, a weight-loss medication; Accutane, a treatment for severe acne; and Serevent, an asthma medication. (Makers of all five medications defended their safety in statements released after the hearing.)

Graham cited several reasons for his lack of confidence in the FDA's ability to protect against unsafe drugs, including the inherent conflict of interest in expecting the same people that approved the drugs to later admit they had made a mistake, and an agency "culture" that viewed the pharmaceutical industry "as its client." As a result, Graham said, the agency "over-values the benefits of the drugs it approves and seriously under-values, disregards, and disrespects drug safety." Graham again charged that the agency had tried to prevent him from publishing his own study of safety problems with Vioxx.

FDA acting commissioner Lester M. Crawford denied that the agency had tried to suppress Graham's findings. In a statement released before the Senate hearing, Crawford said FDA officials should not be faulted for failing to act on Graham's recommendation that Vioxx be withdrawn from the market because they did not see his report until after Merck had withdrawn the drug.

At the hearing, Sandra L. Kweder, deputy director of the FDA's Office of New Drugs, disputed Graham's view of the way the agency operated, saying his description was "not the FDA I know." She acknowledged, however, that there was "clearly . . . concern by the public and this committee that the system isn't working as well as it should, and we need to address that." Kweder then explained a five-step plan the FDA had announced earlier in November to strengthen its drug safety program. That plan included a study by the Institute of Medicine of the agency's drug safety system, in particular the effectiveness of its safety monitoring after a drug reached the market. Kweder also said the agency planned to set up a transparent system for adjudicating differences of opinion among its scientists. Asked to comment on Graham's list of drugs needing immediate attention from the FDA, Kweder said she had no "reason to believe that set of five drugs gives more reason for concern than any other set."

In the aftermath of the hearings, Grassley warned the FDA not to take punitive action against Graham, including transferring him within the agency or firing him.

The hearings also brought forth numerous proposals for fixing the agency. The most common were establishing an independent drug safety board to monitor the safety of drugs and medical devices after they were approved and in wide use, ensuring adequate funding for monitoring safety of drugs once they were on the market, and giving the FDA authority to require drug companies to complete requested safety studies. Several policy makers and others said it was time to end the user fees pharmaceutical companies paid to the FDA. Those fees were authorized in 1992 after drug makers complained that the agency was taking too long to approve new drugs. Drug approvals speeded up after the user fees were in place, but so did the number of drug recalls once they were on the market. The FDA also had to shift money from other activities, including monitoring postmarketing drug safety, to meet legislated funding minimums for new drug approvals.

Others also called for naming a permanent FDA commissioner. The position had been filled by an acting commissioner for most of President George W. Bush's first term. "Much of this can be fixed by strong leadership," David A. Kessler, the FDA commissioner from 1990 to 1997, told the *Boston Globe.* "You don't need a change in statute to give greater prominence to drug safety review. An FDA commissioner on his or her own could give greater independence to an office of drug safety . . . overnight."

Others proposed giving the FDA authority to require drug companies to study widespread unapproved uses of a drug and to limit physicians' ability to prescribe a drug for unapproved uses when it was known that such uses could lead to severe injuries. Senator Grassley, who planned to introduce legislation to create an independent office of drug safety, also proposed a review of the FDA by an independent commission similar to the commission that investigated U.S. intelligence failures surrounding the September 11 terrorist attacks on the United States. Speaking on ABC's *This Week,* White House chief of staff Andrew H. Card Jr. pooh-poohed the commission proposal, saying he thought the FDA was doing a "spectacular" job and should "continue to do the job they do." *(9/11 commission report, p. 450)*

Meanwhile, the FDA appeared to be stepping up its scrutiny of drugs suspected of having safety problems. In addition to warning doctors to use caution in prescribing Celebrex, the agency on December 22 said it had warned AstraZeneca that its newspaper advertisements claiming that the FDA "has confidence in the safety and efficacy" of its cholesterol-lowering drug Crestor were untrue. AstraZeneca had already stopped running the ads, which had appeared after Graham challenged the drug's safety at the November 18 Senate hearing. Public Citizen, a consumer advocacy group, had petitioned the FDA to remove Crestor from the market because it appeared to be linked to increased risk of kidney failure.

In more bad news for pain sufferers, preliminary results from a study by the National Institute of Aging announced on December 20 that preliminary results of a study showed that Aleve (naproxen), one of the main alternatives to Celebrex, also appeared to increase risk of heart attack and stroke. The study, which began in 2001, was trying to determine whether naproxen helped reduce the risk of Alzheimer's disease; the 2,400 volunteers were all age seventy or older. Federal health officials urged consumers to follow the directions for using over-the-counter versions of naproxen and to consult their physicians if they were using the prescription versions Naprosyn and Anaprox.

Following are excerpts from testimony before the Senate Finance Committee on November 18, 2004, from David Graham, associate director for science and medicine in the Office of Drug Safety at the Food and Drug Administration (FDA), and from Sandra Kweder, deputy director of the Office of New Drugs at the FDA. Kweder defended the agency against Graham's assertion that it was "incapable" of protecting the American public from unsafe drugs.

"FDA, Merck and Vioxx: Putting Patient Safety First?"

Testimony of David J. Graham, MD, MPH

Mr. Chairman and members of the Committee,

Introduction. Good morning. My name is David Graham, and I am pleased to come before you today to speak about Vioxx, heart attacks and the FDA. By way of introduction, I graduated from the Johns Hopkins University School of Medicine, and trained in Internal Medicine at Yale and in adult Neurology at the University of Pennsylvania. After this, I completed a three-year fellowship in pharmacoepidemiology and a Masters in Public Health at Johns Hopkins, with a concentration in epidemiology and biostatistics. Over my 20 year career in the field, all of it at FDA, I have served in a variety of capacities. I am currently the Associate Director for Science and Medicine in FDA's Office of Drug Safety [ODS].

During my career, I believe I have made a real difference for the cause of patient safety. My research and efforts within FDA led to the withdrawal from the US market of Omniflox, an antibiotic that caused hemolytic anemia; Rezulin, a diabetes drug that caused acute liver failure; Fen-Phen and Redux, weight loss drugs that caused heart valve injury; and PPA (phenylpropanolamine), an over-the-counter decongestant and weight loss product that caused hemorrhagic stroke in young women. My research also led to the withdrawal from outpatient use of Trovan, an antibiotic that caused acute liver failure and death. I also contributed to the team effort that led to the withdrawal of Lotronex, a drug for irritable bowel syndrome that causes ischemic colitis; Baycol, a cholesterol-lowering drug that caused severe muscle injury, kidney failure and death; Seldane, an antihistamine that caused heart arrhythmias and death; and Propulsid, a drug for night-time heartburn that caused heart arrhythmias and death. I have done extensive work concerning the issue of pregnancy exposure to Accutane, a drug that is used to treat acne but can cause birth defects in some children who are exposed in-utero if their mothers take the drug during the first trimester. During my career, I have recommended the market withdrawal of 12 drugs. Only 2 of these remain on the market today—Accutane and Arava, a drug for the treatment of rheumatoid arthritis that I and a co-worker believe causes an unacceptably high risk of acute liver failure and death.

Vioxx and heart attacks. Let me begin by describing what we found in our study, what others have found, and what this means for the American people. Prior to approval of Vioxx, a study was performed by Merck named 090. This study found nearly a 7-fold increase in heart attack risk with low dose Vioxx. The labeling at approval said nothing about heart attack risks. In November 2000, another Merck clinical trial named VIGOR found a 5-fold increase in heart attack risk with high-dose Vioxx. The company said the drug was safe and that the comparison drug naproxen, was protective. In 2002, a large epidemiologic study reported a 2-fold increase in heart attack risk with high-dose Vioxx and another study reported that naproxen did not affect heart attack risk. About 18 months after the VIGOR results were published, FDA made a labeling change about heart attack risk with high-dose Vioxx, but did not place this in the "Warnings" section. Also, it did not ban the high-dose formulation and its use. I believe such a ban should have been implemented. Of note, FDA's label change had absolutely no effect on how often high-dose Vioxx was prescribed, so what good did it achieve?

In March of 2004, another epidemiologic study reported that both high-dose and low-dose Vioxx increased the risk of heart attacks compared to Vioxx's leading competitor, Celebrex. Our study, first reported in late August of this year found that Vioxx increased the risk of heart attack and sudden death by 3.7 fold for high-dose and 1.5 fold for low-dose, compared to Celebrex. A study report describing this work was put on the FDA website on election day. Among many things, this report estimated that nearly 28,000 excess cases of heart attack or sudden cardiac death were caused by Vioxx. I emphasize to the Committee that this is an extremely conservative estimate. FDA always claims that randomized clinical trials provide the best data. If you apply the risk-levels seen in the 2 Merck trials, VIGOR and APPROVe, you obtain a more realistic and likely range of estimates for the number of excess cases in the US. This estimate ranges from 88,000 to 139,000 Americans. Of these, 30–40% probably died. For the survivors, their lives were changed forever. It's important to note that this range does not depend at all on the data from our Kaiser-FDA study. Indeed, Dr. Eric Topol at the Cleveland Clinic recently estimated up to 160,000 cases of heart attacks and strokes due to Vioxx, in an article published in the *New England Journal of*

Medicine. This article lays out clearly the public health significance of what we're talking about today.

So, how many people is 100,000? . . .

. . . Imagine that instead of a serious side-effect of a widely used prescription drug, we were talking about jetliners. Please ignore the obvious difference in fatality rates between a heart attack and a plane crash, and focus on the larger analogy I'm trying to draw. If there were an average of 150 to 200 people on an aircraft, this range of 88,000 to 138,000 would be the rough equivalent of 500 to 900 aircraft dropping from the sky. This translates to 2–4 aircraft every week, week in and week out, for the past 5 years. If you were confronted by this situation, what would be your reaction, what would you want to know and what would you do about it?

Brief history of drug disasters in the US. Another way to fully comprehend the enormity of the Vioxx debacle is to look briefly at recent US and FDA history. The attached figure shows a graph depicting 3 historical time-points of importance to the development of drug safety in the US. In 1938, Congress enacted the Food, Drug and Cosmetic [FD&C] Act, basically creating the FDA, in response to an unfortunate incident in which about 100 children were killed by elixir of sulfanilamide, a medication that was formulated using anti-freeze. This Act required that animal toxicity testing be performed and safety information be submitted to FDA prior to approval of a drug. In 1962, Congress enacted the Kefauver-Harris Amendments to the FD&C Act, in response to the thalidomide disaster in Europe. Oversees, between 1957 and 1961, an estimated 5,000 to 10,000 children were born with thalidomide-related birth defects. These Amendments increased the requirements for toxicity testing and safety information preapproval, and added the requirement that "substantial evidence" of efficacy be submitted. Today, in 2004, you, we, are faced with what may be the single greatest drug safety catastrophe in the history of this country or the history of the world. We are talking about a catastrophe that I strongly believe could have, should have been largely or completely avoided. But it wasn't, and over 100,000 Americans have paid dearly for this failure. In my opinion, the FDA has let the American people down, and sadly, betrayed a public trust. I believe there are at least 3 broad categories of systemic problems that contributed to the Vioxx catastrophe and to a long line of other drug safety failures in the past 10 years. Briefly, these categories are 1) organizational/structural, 2) cultural, and 3) scientific. I will describe these in greater detail. . . .

My Vioxx experience at FDA. To begin, after publication of the VIGOR study in November 2000, I became concerned about the potential public health risk that might exist with Vioxx. VIGOR suggested that the risk of heart attack was increased 5-fold in patients who used the high-dose strength of this drug. Why was the Vioxx safety question important? 1) Vioxx would undoubtedly be used by millions of patients. That's a very large number to expose to a serious drug risk. 2) heart attack is a fairly common event, and 3) given the above, even a relatively small increase in heart attack risk due to Vioxx could mean that tens of thousands of Americans might be seriously harmed or killed by use of this drug. If these three factors were present, I knew that we would have all the ingredients necessary to guarantee a national disaster. The first two factors were established realities. It came down to the third factor, that is, what was the level of risk with Vioxx at low- and high-dose.

To get answers to this urgent issue, I worked with Kaiser Permanente in California to perform a large epidemiologic study. This study was carefully done and took nearly

3 years to complete. In early August of this year, we completed our main analyses and assembled a poster presentation describing some of our more important findings. We had planned to present these data at the International Conference on Pharmacoepidemiology, in Bordeaux, France. We concluded that high-dose Vioxx significantly increased the risk of heart attacks and sudden death and that the high doses of the drug should not be prescribed or used by patients. This conclusion triggered an explosive response from the Office of New Drugs, which approved Vioxx in the first place and was responsible for regulating it postmarketing. The response from senior management in my Office, the Office of Drug Safety, was equally stressful. I was pressured to change my conclusions and recommendations, and basically threatened that if I did not change them, I would not be permitted to present the paper at the conference. One Drug Safety manager recommended that I should be barred from presenting the poster at the meeting, and also noted that Merck needed to know our study results.

An email from the Director for the entire Office of New Drugs, was revealing. He suggested that since FDA was "not contemplating" a warning against the use of high-dose Vioxx, my conclusions should be changed. CDER [Center for Drug Evaluation and Research] and the Office of New Drugs have repeatedly expressed the view that ODS should not reach any conclusions or make any recommendations that would contradict what the Office of New Drugs [OND] wants to do or is doing. Even more revealing, a mere 6 weeks before Merck pulled Vioxx from the market, CDER, OND and ODS management did not believe there was an outstanding safety concern with Vioxx. At the same time, 2–4 jumbo jetliners were dropping from the sky every week and no one else at FDA was concerned.

There were 2 other revelatory milestones. In mid-August, despite our study results showing an increased risk of heart attack with Vioxx, and despite the results of other studies published in the literature, FDA announced it had approved Vioxx for use in children with rheumatoid arthritis. Also, on September 22, at a meeting attended by the director of the reviewing office that approved Vioxx, the director and deputy director of the reviewing division within that office and senior managers from the Office of Drug Safety, no one thought there was a Vioxx safety issue to be dealt with. At this meeting, the reviewing office director asked why had I even thought to study Vioxx and heart attacks because FDA had made its labeling change and nothing more needed to be done. At this meeting a senior manager from ODS labeled our Vioxx study "a scientific rumor." Eight days later, Merck pulled Vioxx from the market, and jetliners stopped dropping from the sky.

Finally, we wrote a manuscript for publication in a peer-reviewed medical journal. Senior managers in the Office of Drug Safety have not granted clearance for its publication, even though it was accepted for publication in a very prestigious journal after rigorous peer review by that journal. Until it is cleared, our data and conclusions will not see the light of day in the scientific forum they deserve and have earned, and serious students of drug safety and drug regulation will be denied the opportunity to consider and openly debate the issues we raise in that paper.

Past experiences. My experience with Vioxx is typical of how CDER responds to serious drug safety issues in general. This is similar to what Dr. Mosholder went through earlier this year when he reached his conclusion that most SSRIs [selective serotonin reuptake inhibitors] should not be used by children. I could bore you with a long list of prominent and not-so-prominent safety issues where CDER and its Office of New Drugs proved to be extremely resistant to full and open disclosure of safety information, especially when it called into question an existing regulatory position. In these situations, the new drug reviewing division that approved the drug in the first place and that regards it as its own child, typically proves to be the single greatest obstacle to effectively dealing with serious drug safety issues. The second greatest obstacle is often the senior management within the Office of Drug Safety, who either actively or tacitly go along with what the Office of New Drugs wants. Examples are numerous so I'll mention just a few.

With Lotronex, even though there was strong evidence in the pre-approval clinical trials of a problem with ischemic colitis, OND approved it. When cases of severe constipation and ischemic colitis began pouring into FDA's MedWatch program, the reaction was one of denial. When CDER decided to bring Lotronex back on the market, ODS safety reviewers were instructed to help make this happen. Later, when CDER held an advisory committee meeting to get support for bringing Lotronex back on the market, the presentation on ways to manage its reintroduction was carefully shaped and controlled by OND. When it came to presenting the range of possible options for how Lotronex could be made available, the list of options was censored by OND. The day before the advisory meeting, I was told by the ODS reviewer who gave this presentation that the director of the reviewing office within OND that approved Lotronex in the first place came to her office and removed material from her talk. An OND manager was "managing" an ODS employee. When informed of this, ODS senior management ignored it. I guess they knew who was calling the shots.

Rezulin was a drug used to treat diabetes. It also caused acute liver failure, which was usually fatal unless a liver transplant was performed. The pre-approval clinical trials showed strong evidence of liver toxicity. The drug was withdrawn from the market in the United Kingdom in December 1997. With CDER and the Office of New Drugs, withdrawal didn't occur until March 2000. Between these dates, CDER relied on risk management strategies that were utterly ineffective and it persisted in relying on these strategies long after the evidence was clear that they didn't work. The continued marketing of Rezulin probably led to thousands of Americans being severely injured or killed by the drug. And note, there were many other safer diabetes drugs available. During this time, I understand that Rezulin's manufacturer continued to make about $2 million per day in sales.

The big picture. The problem you are confronting today is immense in scope. Vioxx is a terrible tragedy and a profound regulatory failure. I would argue that the FDA, as currently configured, is incapable of protecting America against another Vioxx. We are virtually defenseless.

It is important that this Committee and the American people understand that what has happened with Vioxx is really a symptom of something far more dangerous to the safety of the American people. Simply put, FDA and its Center for Drug Evaluation and Research are broken. Now, I'm sure you have read the recent proposal to have the Institute of Medicine perform a review of CDER and its drug safety program and make recommendations for fixing things up. Don't expect anything meaningful or effective from this exercise. Over the history of CDER's drug safety program, a number of similar reviews have been done. In the late 1970's, I believe that a blue ribbon panel recommended that there be an entirely separate drug safety operation in FDA with full regulatory authority. It wasn't implemented. During the 1980's and early

1990's, CDER organized its own "program reviews" of drug safety. The basic premise underlying each of these reviews was that the "problem" was with the drug safety group; it didn't fit into the Center. So, the charge given to the review panel members was always framed as "figure out what's wrong with drug safety, and tell us what to do to get it to fit in." There was and is an implicit expectation that the status quo will remain unaltered.

The organizational structure within CDER is entirely geared towards the review and approval of new drugs. When a CDER new drug reviewing division approves a new drug, it is also saying the drug is "safe and effective." When a serious safety issue arises post-marketing, their immediate reaction is almost always one of denial, rejection and heat. They approved the drug so there can't possibly be anything wrong with it. The same group that approved the drug is also responsible for taking regulatory action against it post-marketing. This is an inherent conflict of interest. At the same time, the Office of Drug Safety has no regulatory power and must first convince the new drug reviewing division that a problem exists before anything beneficial to the public can be done. Often, the new drug reviewing division is the single greatest obstacle to effectively protecting the public against drug safety risks. A close second in my opinion, is an ODS management that sees its mission as pleasing the Office of New Drugs.

The corporate culture within CDER is also a barrier to effectively protecting the American people from unnecessary harm due to prescription and OTC [over the counter] drugs. The culture is dominated by a world-view that believes only randomized clinical trials provide useful and actionable information and that postmarketing safety is an afterthought. This culture also views the pharmaceutical industry it is supposed to regulate as its client, over-values the benefits of the drugs it approves and seriously under-values, disregards and disrespects drug safety.

Finally, the scientific standards CDER applies to drug safety guarantee that unsafe and deadly drugs will remain on the US market. When an OND reviewing division reviews a drug to decide whether to approve it, great reliance is placed on statistical tests. Usually, a drug is only approved if there is a 95% or greater probability that the drug actually works. From a safety perspective, this is also a very protective standard because it protects patients against drugs that don't work. The real problem is how CDER applies statistics to post-marketing safety. We see from the structural and cultural problems in CDER, that everything revolves around OND and the drug approval process.

When it comes to safety, the OND paradigm of 95% certainty prevails. Under this paradigm, a drug is safe until you can show with 95% or greater certainty that it is not safe. This is an incredibly high, almost insurmountable barrier to overcome. It's the equivalent of "beyond a shadow of a doubt." And here's an added kicker. In order to demonstrate a safety problem with 95% certainty, extremely large studies are often needed. And guess what. Those large studies can't be done.

There are 2 analogies I want to leave you with to illustrate the unreasonableness of CDER's standard of evidence as applied to safety, both pre- and post-approval. If the weather-man says there is an 80% chance of rain, most people would bring an umbrella. Using CDER's standard, you wouldn't bring an umbrella until there was a 95% or greater chance of rain. The second analogy is more graphic, but I think it brings home the point more clearly. Imagine for a moment that you have a pistol with a barrel having 100 chambers. Now, randomly place 95 bullets into those chambers. The gun represents a drug and the bullets represent a serious safety problem. Using

CDER's standard, only when you have 95 bullets or more in the gun will you agree that the gun is loaded and a safety problem exists. Let's remove 5 bullets at random. We now have 90 bullets distributed across 100 chambers. Because there is only a 90% chance that a bullet will fire when I pull the trigger, CDER would conclude that the gun is not loaded and that the drug is safe.

Statement of Sandra Kweder, M.D

Mr. Chairman and Members of the Committee, I am Dr. Sandra Kweder, Deputy Director of the Office of New Drugs at the Center for Drug Evaluation and Research (CDER), U.S. Food and Drug Administration (FDA or the Agency). We appreciate the opportunity to participate in this hearing regarding drug safety and the worldwide withdrawal by Merck & Co., Inc. of Vioxx.

I. Background on Drug Safety

Modern drugs provide unmistakable and significant health benefits. It is well recognized that FDA's drug review is a gold standard. Indeed, we believe that FDA maintains the highest worldwide standards for drug approval. FDA grants approval to drugs after a sponsor demonstrates that they are safe and effective. Experience has shown that the full magnitude of some potential risks do not always emerge during the mandatory clinical trials conducted before approval to evaluate these products for safety and effectiveness. Occasionally, serious adverse effects are identified after approval either in post-marketing clinical trials or through spontaneous reporting of adverse events. That is why Congress has supported and FDA has created a strong post-market drug safety program designed to assess adverse events identified after approval for all of the medical products it regulates as a complement to the pre-market safety reviews required for approval of prescription drugs in the United States. Monitoring the drug safety of marketed products requires close collaboration between our clinical reviewers and drug safety staff to evaluate and respond to adverse events identified in ongoing clinical trials or reported to us by physicians and their patients. The most recent actions concerning the drug Vioxx (rofecoxib) illustrates the vital importance of the ongoing assessment of the safety of a product once it is in widespread use.

It is important to understand that all approved drugs pose some level of risk, such as the risks that are identified in clinical trials and listed on the labeling of the product. Unless a new drug's demonstrated benefit outweighs its known risk for an intended population, FDA will not approve the drug. However, we cannot anticipate all possible effects of a drug during the clinical trials that precede approval. An adverse drug reaction can range from a minor, unpleasant response to a drug product, to a response that is sometimes life-threatening or deadly. Such adverse drug reactions may be expected (because clinical trial results indicate such possibilities) or unexpected (because the reaction was not evident in clinical trials). It may also result from errors in drug prescribing, dispensing or use. The issue of how to detect and limit adverse reactions can be challenging; how to weigh the impact of these adverse drug reactions against the benefits of these products on individual patients and the public health is multifaceted and complex, involving scientific as well as public policy issues.

II. Vioxx

The Vioxx Approval

FDA approved Vioxx in May 1999 for the reduction of signs and symptoms of osteoarthritis, as well as for acute pain in adults and for the treatment of primary dysmenorrhea. Vioxx received a six-month priority review because the drug potentially provided a significant therapeutic advantage over existing approved drugs due to fewer gastrointestinal side effects, including bleeding. A product undergoing a priority review is held to the same rigorous standards for safety, efficacy, and quality that FDA expects from all drugs submitted for approval.

As with many other new molecular entities, this product was taken before the Arthritis Advisory Committee, April 20, 1999, prior to its approval. It was the second of a new class (COX-2 selective) of non-steroidal anti-inflammatory drugs (NSAIDs) approved by FDA. The original safety database for this product included approximately 5,000 patients on Vioxx and did not show an increased risk of heart attack or stroke.

In the clinical trials conducted before approval, the risk of gastrointenstinal (GI) side effects was determined through the use of endoscopy. At the time that FDA approved Vioxx, the available evidence from these endoscopy studies showed a significantly lower risk of gastrointestinal ulcers, a significant source of serious side effects such as bleeding and death, in comparison to ibuprofen.

The VIGOR Study

After Vioxx was approved in 1999, Merck continued studies of Vioxx designed to look at clinically meaningful GI effects, such as stomach ulcers and bleeding (VIOXX Gastrointestinal Outcomes Research, or VIGOR study). This study was designed to provide longer term clinical outcome data to confirm the shorter term endoscopy findings and to evaluate overall safety. The VIGOR study was a large (8,000-patient) study designed to evaluate the GI safety of Vioxx as compared to naproxen. This study was done in a rheumatoid arthritis population who typically require a higher dose (50 mg was used) of antiinflammatory medication.

VIGOR did not have a placebo group because to do so would have meant patients with rheumatoid arthritis would have been randomized to receive no pain relief. Use of a placebo would have been intolerable, because untreated patients would have suffered and left the study. The study also excluded subjects taking low dose aspirin for cardiovascular (CV) prevention because use of aspirin might have contributed to increased rates of GI bleeding in the study and confound the results. However, the exclusion of patients on low dose aspirin may have influenced CV events in the study, since low dose aspirin has been shown to reduce CV risk.

In April 2002, FDA approved extensive labeling changes to reflect the findings from the VIGOR study. FDA also approved a rheumatoid arthritis indication at the 25 mg dose based on separate efficacy trials. The new label provided additional information to the Clinical Studies, Precautions, Drug Interactions and Dosage and Administration sections to reflect all that was known at the time about the potential risk of cardiovascular effects with Vioxx. These labeling changes included detailed information about the increase in risk of cardiovascular events relative to naproxen, including heart attack. It also included data from the ongoing placebo controlled Alzheimer's study at the 14 month time point which did not show an increase in CV risk. The new labeling change also noted that Vioxx 50 mg was not recommended for chronic use.

Other Vioxx Studies

In the years following the 1999 FDA approval of Vioxx, Merck began conducting a series of clinical trials exploring other potential indications of this product. All trials for chronic use were designed to monitor carefully for CV safety and included data safety monitoring committees as well as blinded experts to assess all CV events in the trials. Some of these studies included placebo-controlled studies of Vioxx in Alzheimer's disease, prostate cancer, and colon polyps. Following the 2001 Advisory Committee meeting and the 2002 labeling changes, FDA focused on ensuring that all clinical trials conducted with Vioxx were designed to include careful monitoring of CV risk, and required that Merck submit all available CV data in ongoing trials.

In the period following the 2002 Vioxx labeling changes, FDA also continued to monitor the scientific literature reviewing several retrospective epidemiologic studies. Some of these studies suggested an increased risk for CV events with Vioxx, primarily with the 50 mg dose, while others did not. Epidemiologic studies in real world populations of conditions such as heart attack or stroke are difficult to conduct and interpret because of the need to carefully and adequately account for the many known powerful risk factors for these diseases. Merck, or Pfizer, the manufacturer of Celebrex (another COX-2 inhibitor), sponsored, directly or indirectly, many of these epidemiology studies.

Given the need for data to distinguish the impact of the use of these drugs on cardiovascular risk from factors such as smoking, hypertension, diabetes, low dose aspirin use, high cholesterol and others, the long-term, placebo-controlled trials that were being conducted offered the best opportunity to carefully assess both the existence of and the magnitude of these cardiovascular effects.

III. Merck's Worldwide Withdrawal of Vioxx

Merck contacted FDA on September 27, 2004, to request a meeting to discuss with the Agency the Data Safety Monitoring Board's decision to halt Merck's long-term study of Vioxx in patients at increased risk of colon polyps. Merck and FDA officials met the next day, September 28, and during that meeting the company informed FDA of its decision to remove Vioxx from the market voluntarily. The data presented demonstrated an increase in risk in cardiovascular risk and stroke starting at the eighteen month time point compared to placebo. This was the first demonstration of a difference in comparison to a placebo group and supported the previous signal seen in the VIGOR trial and some of the epidemiologic studies.

IV. The Kaiser Study on Vioxx

In follow up to the VIGOR findings, FDA worked with Kaiser Permanente California HMO as part of a collaborative agreement to provide an alternative means of evaluating the CV safety signal using a managed care database. In 2001, the forerunner of the Office of Drug Safety (ODS) and Dr. David Graham began informal discussions with Kaiser Permanente about projects of mutual interest. At the same time, FDA's Arthritis Advisory Committee was reviewing the cardiovascular risk observed in clinical trials for Vioxx and recommended the need to collect additional information regarding this risk. Dr. Graham indicated that Kaiser was interested in the CV safety of the COX-2 agents in general and in pursuing a scientific collaboration with ODS on this topic even if Agency funding were not available for the full study. FDA provided funding to partially support this pilot scientific collaboration in August 2001 and again in August 2002. A protocol for the study was developed to study the risk of myocardial infarction among users of selective (COX-2) and non-selective non-steroidal antiinflammatory agents (NSAIDs). Dr. Graham was designated the ODS project officer for this study to work with his counterparts at Kaiser Permanente. Dr. Wayne Ray, an epidemiologist at Vanderbilt University and a cooperative agreement grantee of FDA, was added to the study team during the course of the study. Dr. Graham periodically discussed his work with his supervisors to provide updates on the progress of the study.

In February 2004, Dr. Graham and his coauthors submitted an abstract to the International Society for Pharmacoepidemiology (ISPE) for possible presentation at the August 2004 meeting in Bordeaux, France. No study results were included in this abstract, which was accepted for a poster presentation in August 2004. In May 2004, Dr. Graham and his coauthors submitted an abstract of their study findings to the American College of Rheumatology (ACR) for possible presentation at their October 2004 meeting in San Antonio. The deadline for submitting abstracts for the San Antonio meeting was May 13, 2004. Dr. Graham informed his supervisor about his authorship role in the ACR abstract in early September 2004.

On August 11, 2004, David Graham first shared a draft of his ISPE poster presentation with his supervisors to obtain their review and clearance, as is required of any FDA author or presenter. At that time, Dr. Graham's supervisors in ODS informed him of the importance of this work and the need to promptly complete a study report for circulation within the Agency and for broader dissemination in a scientific journal. In reviewing the poster presentation, scientists within ODS and within the Office of New Drugs with specific expertise in COX-2s provided comments and raised questions regarding the study design and statistical modeling, which were not detailed in the poster. The conclusion that high dose Vioxx should never be used was questioned, as the label for the drug already recommended limiting high dose use to no more the five days based on the cardiovascular risks identified in clinical trials. A concern was expressed that the data presented in the poster and in the medical literature did not support the recommendation of never using high dose Vioxx. These comments and concerns were shared with Dr. Graham who chose to revise his conclusions voluntarily. A disclaimer was placed on the poster to reflect that some of the conclusions and statements in the poster were those of the authors and did not necessarily reflect Agency policy.

Dr. Graham presented his poster in Bordeaux, France, on August 23–24, 2004, and participated in press coverage that discussed the findings. . . .

Upon Dr. Graham's return from Bordeaux in late August, given the data's potential application to regulatory actions, Dr. Graham was asked to submit a draft report for Agency review within two weeks. He asked for a September 30, 2004, deadline and on that date, Dr. Graham provided a first draft of his report to his supervisors. Discussions concerning the report are ongoing between Dr. Graham and his supervisors. Dr. Graham has meanwhile submitted a manuscript version of the report to *Lancet* for publication.

V. FDA Initiatives to Strengthen Drug Safety

At FDA, we are constantly searching for ways to improve our processes and methods, and thereby better serve the public health. On November 5, 2004, FDA announced a five-step plan to strengthen its drug safety program. First, CDER will sponsor an Institute of Medicine (IOM) study on FDA's drug safety system. An IOM committee will study the effectiveness of the United States' drug safety system, with an emphasis on the post-market phase, and assess what additional steps could be taken to learn more about the side effects of drugs as they are actually used. We will ask IOM to examine FDA's role within the health care delivery system and recommend measures to enhance the confidence of Americans in the safety and effectiveness of their drugs.

Second, CDER will implement a program for addressing differences of professional opinion. Currently, in most cases, free and open discussion of scientific issues among review teams and with supervisors, managers and external advisors, leads to an agreed course of action. Sometimes, however, a consensus decision cannot be reached, and an employee may feel that his or her opinion was not adequately considered. Such disagreements can have a potentially significant public health impact.

In an effort to improve the current process, CDER will formalize a program to help ensure that the opinions of dissenting scientific reviewers are formally addressed and transparent in its decision-making process. An ad hoc panel, including FDA staff and outside experts not directly involved in disputed decisions, will have 30 days to review all relevant materials and recommend to the Center Director an appropriate course of action.

Third, CDER will conduct a national search to fill the currently vacant position of Director of the Office of Drug Safety, which is responsible for overseeing the post-marketing safety program for all drugs. The Center is seeking a candidate who is a nationally recognized drug safety expert with knowledge of the basic science of drug development and surveillance, and has a strong commitment to the protection of public health.

Fourth, in the coming year, CDER will conduct workshops and Advisory Committee meetings to discuss complex drug safety and risk management issues. These consultations may include emerging concerns for products that are investigational or already marketed. Examples of areas where FDA may seek input include:

- Whether a particular safety concern alters the risk-to-benefit balance of a drug;
- Whether FDA should request a sponsor to conduct a particular type of study to further address an issue;
- What types of studies would best answer safety questions;
- Whether a finding is unique to one product or seems to be a drug class effect;
- Whether a labeling change is warranted and, if so, what type; and
- How to otherwise facilitate careful and informed use of a drug.

These consultations will include experts from FDA, other federal agencies, academia, the pharmaceutical industry, and the healthcare community.

Finally, by the end of this year, FDA intends to publish final versions of three guidances that the agency developed to help pharmaceutical firms manage risks involving drugs and biological products. These guidances should assist pharmaceutical firms in identifying and assessing potential safety risks not only before a drug reaches the market and but also after a drug is already on the market. These guidances will rely on the use of good pharmacovigilance practices and pharmacoepidemiologic assessment. These documents are:

- "Premarketing Guidance," which covers risk assessment of pharmaceuticals prior to their marketing;

- "RiskMAP Guidance," which deals with the development and use of risk-minimization action plans; and
- "Pharmacovigilance Guidance," which discusses post-marketing risk assessment, good pharmacovigilance practices and pharmacoepidemiologic assessment.

VI. Conclusion

In summary, FDA worked actively and vigorously with Merck to inform public health professionals of what was known regarding CV risk with Vioxx, and to pursue further definitive investigations to better define and quantify this risk. FDA also reviewed and remained current on new epidemiologic studies that appeared in the literature. Indeed, the recent study findings disclosed by Merck, leading to its decision to voluntarily withdraw Vioxx from the marketplace, resulted from FDA's vigilance in requiring these long-term outcome trials to address our concerns.

Detecting, assessing, managing and communicating the risks and benefits of prescription and over-the-counter drugs is a highly complex and demanding task. FDA is determined to meet this challenge by employing cutting-edge science, transparent policy, and sound decisions based on the advice of the best experts in and out of the agency. We are confident that the additional activities discussed above will strengthen the agency's program to greater ensure the safety of medical products that make a major contribution to the health and quality of life of millions of Americans. Medicines that receive FDA approval are among the safest in the world, and the measures we are taking are designed to strengthen this quality, as well as consumer confidence that FDA's processes ensure the highest protection of the public health.

Source: U.S. Congress. Committee on Finance. "FDA, Merck and Vioxx: Putting Patient Safety First?" Prepared statements of Sen. Charles Grassley, R-Iowa; Sen. Max Baucus, D-Mont.; Dr. David J. Graham; Dr. Gurkirpal Singh; Dr. Bruce M. Psaty; Dr. Sandra L. Kweder; and Mr. Raymond V. Gilmartin. 108th Cong., 2nd sess. November 18, 2004. http://finance.senate.gov/sitepages/hearing111804.htm (accessed March 8, 2005).

Atomic Energy Agency on Nuclear Programs in Iran

November 29, 2004

INTRODUCTION

For the second year in a row, key European nations used diplomacy to try to convince Iran to stop its work to develop nuclear weapons; for the second year in a row, Iran signed an agreement pledging to meet the European demands. The Bush administration, which had little international support for its preferred tougher policy of penalizing Iran, was forced to sit on the sidelines and complain that diplomacy was failing to put a serious brake on Iran's nuclear weapons ambitions.

President George W. Bush in 2002 had listed Iran—along with Iraq and North Korea—as one of the "axis of evil" nations he said threatened the rest of the world through their support of terrorism and their programs to build biological, chemical, and nuclear weapons (the so-called weapons of mass destruction). The United States a year later invaded Iraq and overthrew its government, only to discover that Baghdad did not have any of the weapons Bush claimed had posed a "gathering threat" to world peace. Iran and North Korea both presented much more formidable obstacles to a U.S. military invasion, however, and the Bush administration in 2003 and 2004 was confined to uttering threats against them while relying on multilateral diplomacy—something administration hawks insisted would never work. The hawks appeared correct on at least one score: while the diplomats talked, at least some work continued on the nuclear weapons programs in both countries. *(Nuclear weapons proliferation, p. 323; Iraq weapons, p. 711; North Korea background, Historic Documents of 2002, p. 731; Iran background, Historic Documents of 2003, p. 1025)*

More Surprise Discoveries in Iran

Revelations by an Iranian exile opposition group led to the discovery early in 2003 of secret facilities in Iran to develop key components for nuclear weapons. A plant near the city of Natanz, south of Tehran, produced highly enriched uranium (one of two fuels for weapons), and a plant near the city of Arak, in central Iran, produced heavy water, which is used to make plutonium (the other fuel for weapons). After much diplomatic bargaining, Iran agreed to open these facilities to inspections by the International Atomic Energy Agency (IAEA), the United Nations agency charged with enforcing the Nuclear Nonproliferation Treaty, which was intended to halt the spread of nuclear weapons and which Iran had signed. These inspections led to further revelations about Iran's weapons program and to yet more diplomacy, resulting in Iran's promise in November 2003 to allow even broader IAEA inspections under an agreement called an "Additional Protocol." Iran also promised to suspend its work to enrich uranium. These steps appeared to offer at least some hope that Iran's nuclear program would be revealed and thus halted, if not permanently stopped.

IAEA inspectors visited Iranian nuclear installations over the winter and reportedly found numerous weapons-related items the government had failed to disclose. In mid-February 2004 IAEA director general Mohammed ElBaradei outlined these findings to Hassan Rohani, head of Iran's Supreme National Security Council. On February 21 the Iranian foreign ministry issued a statement acknowledging that Iran had "bought some things from some dealers" but claiming that it did not know the exact sources.

ElBaradei on February 24 issued a report saying the IAEA inspectors had uncovered several important items Iran had neglected to mention in what it had called a "full disclosure" of its nuclear programs. These items included traces of highly enriched uranium on centrifuges that Iran had built itself and previously had hidden, as well as traces of polonium, a radioactive element used to trigger nuclear explosions. ElBaradei said these findings raised questions about Iran's "stated policy of transparency." The IAEA board of governors—with U.S. support—on March 13 adopted a resolution expressing "serious concern" about Iran's past failures to disclose its nuclear programs and urging Iran to keep its promises.

Iran responded to this mild censure by barring IAEA inspectors from its facilities for a month and announcing that it was resuming production of uranium hexafluoride (a gas used to make highly enriched uranium for weapons) at a plant in Isfahan, south of Tehran. This announcement brought a rebuke on March 31 from the foreign ministers of Britain, France, and Germany—the three countries that had negotiated directly with Tehran on its weapons program. Restarting uranium enrichment, the diplomats said, "sends the wrong signal regarding Iran's readiness to implement a suspension of its [weapons] activities."Iran heightened international concerns even further on April 7 when it confirmed plans to build a new nuclear reactor in Arak, which it said would produce radioisotopes for medical research. Western experts said the reactor also could produce enough plutonium annually for one nuclear bomb.

Once again, the IAEA board reacted with a resolution, adopted June 18, complaining that Iran's cooperation "has not been as full, timely, and proactive as it should have been." The resolution noted several cases in which Iran had opened facilities to inspections and answered questions only after lengthy delays. The board turned aside the Bush administration's demand that Iran's case be referred to the United Nations Security Council, which had the power to impose economic or other sanctions as punishment. The State Department's chief weapons negotiator, John R. Bolton, told a House International Relations subcommittee on June 24 that hauling Iran before the Security Council "is long overdue."

On July 27 diplomats at IAEA headquarters in Vienna said Iran had resumed making centrifuges used to enrich uranium—reversing one of the promises it made to the Europeans the previous fall. The move reportedly stopped short of actually enriching uranium, but it did represent a setback for diplomatic efforts to halt Iran's nuclear program.

Apparently attempting to seize the diplomatic initiative, the Bush administration began lobbying for a what it called "isolation" of Iran as opposed to the "engagement" represented by the European negotiations. In August, for example, Bush's national security adviser, Condoleezza Rice, said she expected that an IAEA board meeting in September would produce a "very strong statement" essentially forcing Iran to choose between international isolation or abandoning its weapons program.

The IAEA on September 1 circulated its latest report on Iran. The report appeared to confirm that Iran had received weapons-related equipment from Pakistan and said Iran was planning to convert about thirty-seven tons of raw uranium (called yellowcake) into the uranium hexafluoride gas used to make highly enriched uranium for weapons. Iran insisted the uranium was for production of electricity, not weapons. Despite these findings, the report said Iran appeared to be cooperating more fully with IAEA inspectors than in the past. Once again Bush administration officials expressed concerns, noting that the amount of raw uranium Iran planned to process might be enough for four small nuclear weapons. Iranian officials insisted they had disclosed the processing plans months earlier.

European Negotiations with Tehran

With Iran appearing determined to move ahead with its uranium enrichment program, top European diplomats stepped back into the picture with the stated goal of getting Tehran to halt that work indefinitely. On September 8 the foreign ministers from Britain, France, and Germany met in the Netherlands with senior Iranian officials and demanded that Iran stop its enrichment work within two months. Ten days later the IAEA board of governors adopted its third resolution of the year criticizing Iran for failing to keep its promises. The agency again called on Iran to suspend all its uranium enrichment activities, and it warned that Iran's actions would be examined again in mid-November.

At least initially, these additional pressures appeared to have the opposite of their intended affect. Iranian president Mohammad Khatami said on September 21 that Iran had a right to produce nuclear fuel "and we will not give it up" regardless of the international consequences. The Iranian parliament also said it would not ratify the Additional Protocol, which Iran had accepted in late 2003, granting the IAEA broad access to the country's nuclear facilities. Early in October the parliament debated a bill requiring the government to continue the uranium enrichment program, and the government said on October 6 that it had processed several tons of the raw uranium into uranium hexafluoride.

Negotiations between the Europeans and Iranians continued throughout October and into November. European diplomats made repeated variations of the demand that Iran stop its uranium enrichment, and the Iranians responded with demands of their own, reportedly including a promise of aid for Iran's nuclear power program and a pledge that the United States would not pursue "regime change" in Tehran, as it had in Baghdad a year earlier.

On November 14 the European diplomats announced that Iran had formally promised to halt its uranium enrichment work, starting November 22, while negotiations continued on what benefits Tehran would receive in return. The agreement was not the "comprehensive" settlement of all issues surrounding Iran's nuclear program that the Europeans had sought, but it did appear to meet the minimal demands of both sides. British foreign secretary Jack Straw said: "We believe that the conclusion of this agreement can both allow for confidence-building with respect of Iran's nuclear program and represent a significant development in relations between Europe and Iran." This last phrase was a reference to a broad European desire not to jeopardize commercial trade with Iran, a major oil producer. Bush administration officials remained skeptical of any promise by Iran to stop its nuclear weapons work.

The Iran-Europe agreement was timed to coincide with the latest report by ElBaradei, details of which were made public November 15. Citing the results of inspections over the summer, ElBaradei's report was the most upbeat of the year. All the nuclear material that Iran had declared to the IAEA "has been accounted for, and therefore such material is not diverted to prohibited activities," he wrote. It was possible that Iran still had nuclear programs it had not revealed to the IAEA, ElBaradei conceded.

Yet Another Diplomatic Hurdle

In keeping with its deal with the Europeans, Iran announced on November 22 that it had suspended all its work to enrich uranium. ElBaradei said initial reports of his inspectors appeared to verify that announcement.

As diplomats gathered in Vienna a week later for another IAEA board meeting on Iran, however, Tehran had one more surprise. In a last-minute letter, Tehran said it was reserving the right to continue operating twenty of its uranium-enriching centrifuges for "research and development purposes." Because thousands of the machines were needed to process enough highly enriched uranium for a weapon, the continued operation of twenty centrifuges was seen as more of a symbolic than a practical step by Iran. Even so, it raised new questions about Tehran's determination to stick to the promises it had made, and European governments said Iran could not go back on the agreement it had signed just a week earlier.

After yet another round of last-minute negotiations, Iran appeared to back down. On November 28 Tehran sent ElBaradei a letter agreeing to place the twenty centrifuges under IAEA "surveillance" and pledging not to test them. ElBaradei told the IAEA board the next day the machines were being monitored by agency surveillance cameras but, in an apparent concession to Iran, would not be sealed.

With the latest hurdle out of the way, the IAEA board on November 29 adopted its fourth resolution of the year—and its sixth since early 2003—on Iran's nuclear program. The resolution was the mildest yet, reflecting Tehran's latest promises to suspend all its enrichment work. The resolution noted the "many breaches" in Iran's compliance with IAEA rules prior to October 2003 but added that "good progress has been made since that time in Iran's correction of those breaches and in the Agency's ability to confirm certain aspects of Iran's current declarations."

The United States, which was just one of thirty-five nations represented on the IAEA board, made no attempt to block the resolution but afterwards issued an angry statement cataloging what it called Iran's "deceit" and castigating the IAEA for failing to hold Iran to account. The statement said Washington "reserves all its options with respect to Security Council consideration of the Iranian nuclear weapons program." That was a threat to ask the council to take up the issue and impose sanctions against Iran—but even U.S. officials admitted that Washington lacked the international support for such a step.

One of the U.S. complaints was that Iran viewed its suspension of uranium enrichment as a temporary ploy to gain trade concessions from Europe. Iran's chief negotiator, Hassan Rohani, appeared to confirm that charge. Iran had suspended its enrichment only so long as its negotiations continued with the Europeans over future trade benefits, he said. "We are talking months, not years." Those negotiations began in December but had not concluded by year's end.

A sidelight to the international struggle over Iran was the Bush administration's determination to oust ElBaradei from his job at the IAEA. An Egyptian, ElBaradei's second five-year term was due to expire in 2005. Washington was actively lobbying to replace him, arguing that he had failed to move aggressively enough in Iran,

Iraq, and North Korea, among other cases. On December 13 the *Washington Post* reported that U.S. intelligence agencies had monitored ElBaradei's telephone conversations, including those with Iranian officials. Administration officials refused to comment on the report. ElBaradei said such spying would violate his personal privacy and constitute interference with an international organization, but added: "If anyone wants to listen in, then listen in. I don't have anything to hide."

Iranian Reform Movement Collapses

The extended international haggling over Iran's nuclear weapons program overshadowed what appeared to be the final collapse of a years-long effort by moderates in Iran to pry political power from the hands of the conservative Islamist clerics who had run the country since the 1979 revolution. President Khatami, a moderate cleric, had won two elections (in 1997 and 2001), riding a wave of public dissatisfaction with religious restrictions on most aspects of daily life and the clerics' mishandling of the economy. Khatami's influence appeared to wane, however, after hard-line security services answering to the clerics used violence to put down large student demonstrations in 1999.

Reformers aligned with Khatami won elections for the parliament (the Majlis) in 2001 but were unable to enact any serious political or economic changes because of opposition from the clerics, led by Iran's supreme leader, Ayatollah Ali Khamenei. Elections for a new parliament were scheduled for February 2004, and in January Khamenei's Guardian Council (which had the final word on political matters) disqualified more than 3,600 of the 8,200 people who had filed as candidates. After protests, Khamenei and the council relented somewhat, restoring about one-third of the potential candidates. More than 500 reform candidates, including most of those currently serving in parliament, eventually withdrew from the election, leaving only a handful of moderates still in the race. As a result, conservatives took control of the parliament in the February 20 elections.

On March 17 Khatami gave up pressing for his reform platform, which had stalled for several years. He withdrew two proposals pending in the parliament that sought to curb the political power of the Guardian Council and other institutions dominated by the conservative clerics. "I withdraw the bills and declare that I have met with defeat," he told reporters.

During the rest of the year Khatami's conservative foes consolidated their grip on power, closing newspapers and Internet sites that had sided with the reformers, jailing journalists and other critics, and repealing laws and regulations that had loosened restrictions on the social freedoms of women. In an address to students at Tehran University on December 6, Khatami said he had given in to Khamenei and the conservative establishment to avoid riots and violence. Elections for Khatami's successor were to be held early in 2005.

No Progress on North Korea

The start-stop-start character of the diplomatic maneuvering over Iran produced enormous progress during 2004 compared with international efforts to confront North Korea's nuclear weapons program. North Korea in late 2002 had expelled IAEA inspectors and resumed work to develop nuclear weapons, according to reports by U.S. and other officials. During the last half of 2003 the United States and four other nations (China, Japan, Russia, and South Korea) held a series of negotiations with North Korea in hopes of bringing its weapons program under control. Those "six-party" talks stalled, however, over North Korea's demands for economic concessions and a guarantee that the United States would not attack it. *(Background, Historic Documents of 2003, p. 592)*

On December 3, 2004, ElBaradei told the *New York Times* he was convinced that North Korea had reprocessed sufficient plutonium to develop four to six nuclear weapons. The plutonium would have come from some 8,000 spent nuclear fuel rods that the IAEA had monitored between 1994 and 2002, when North Korea ordered the agency's inspectors to leave the country.

Following is the text of a resolution adopted November 29, 2004, by the International Atomic Energy Agency board of governors concerning the alleged nuclear weapons programs in Iran.

"NPT Safeguards Agreement in the Islamic Republic of Iran"

The Board of Governors,

(a) *Recalling* the resolutions adopted by the Board on 18 September 2004, 18 June 2004, 13 March 2004, 26 November 2003, and on 12 September 2003 and the statement by the Board of 19 June 2003,

(b) *Noting* with appreciation the Director General's report of 15 November 2004 on the implementation of Iran's NPT [Nuclear Non-Proliferation Treaty] Safeguards Agreement,

(c) *Noting* specifically the Director General's assessment that Iranian practices up to October 2003 resulted in many breaches of Iran's obligations to comply with its Safeguards Agreement, but that good progress has been made since that time in Iran's correction of those breaches and in the Agency's ability to confirm certain aspects of Iran's current declarations,

(d) *Also noting* specifically the Director General's assessment that all the declared nuclear material in Iran has been accounted for, and that such material is not diverted to prohibited activities, but that the Agency is not yet in a position to conclude that there are no undeclared nuclear materials or activities in Iran,

(e) *Recalling* the Board's previous requests to Iran to suspend all enrichment related and reprocessing activities as a voluntary confidence building measure,

(f) *Noting* with concern that Iran has continued enrichment related activities, including the production of UF6 up to 22 November 2004, in spite of the request made by the Board in September that Iran immediately suspend all such activities,

(g) *Noting* with interest the agreement between Iran, France, Germany and the UK with the support of the High Representative of the EU, made public on 15 November, in which Iran states its decision to continue and extend its suspension of all enrichment related and reprocessing activities; and noting with satisfaction that, pursuant to this agreement, notification of this decision was sent by Iran to the Director General on 14 November with the Agency invited to verify the suspension with effect from 22 November 2004,

(h) *Recognizing* that this suspension is a voluntary confidence building measure, not a legal obligation,

(i) *Recognizing* the right of states to the development and practical application of atomic energy for peaceful purposes, including the production of electric power, consistent with their Treaty obligations, with due consideration for the needs of the developing countries,

(j) *Stressing* the need for effective safeguards to prevent nuclear material being used for prohibited purposes, in contravention of agreements, and underlining the vital importance of effective safeguards for facilitating cooperation in the field of nuclear energy, and

(k) *Commending* the Director General and the Secretariat for the work they have done to date to resolve all questions relevant to safeguards implementation in Iran,

1. *Welcomes* the fact that Iran has decided to continue and extend its suspension of all enrichment related and reprocessing activities, and underlines that the full and sustained implementation of this suspension, which is a voluntary, non-legally-binding, confidence building measure, to be verified by the Agency, is essential to addressing outstanding issues;
2. *Welcomes* the Director General's statements of 25 and 29 November 2004 that the above decision has been put into effect, and requests the Director General to continue verifying that the suspension remains in place and to inform Board members should the suspension not be fully sustained, or should the Agency be prevented from verifying all elements of the suspension, for as long as the suspension is in force;
3. *Welcomes* Iran's continuing voluntary commitment to act in accordance with the provisions of the Additional Protocol, as a confidence building measure that facilitates the resolution of the questions that have arisen, and calls on Iran once again to ratify its Protocol soon;
4. *Reaffirms* its strong concern that Iran's policy of concealment up to October 2003 has resulted in many breaches of Iran's obligations to comply with its NPT Safeguards Agreement; at the same time acknowledges the corrective measures described in the Director General's report;
5. *Welcomes* the Director General's intention to pursue his investigations into the remaining outstanding issues, in particular the origin of contamination and the extent of Iran's centrifuge programme, as well as the full implementation of Iran's Safeguards Agreement and Additional Protocol, with a view to providing credible assurances regarding the absence of undeclared nuclear material and activities in Iran;
6. *Underlines* the continuing importance of Iran extending full and prompt cooperation to the Director General in the above pursuit, and requests Iran as a confidence building measure to provide any access deemed necessary by the Agency in accordance with the Additional Protocol; and
7. *Requests* the Director General to report to the Board on his findings, as appropriate.

Source: United Nations. International Atomic Energy Agency. Board of Governors. "Implementation of the NPT Safeguards Agreement in the Islamic Republic of Iran." GOV/2004/90, November 29, 2004. www.iaea.org/Publications/Documents/Board/2004/gov2004-90_derestrict.pdf (accessed January 18, 2004).

Iraqi Prime Minister Allawi on Security Challenges

November 30, 2004

INTRODUCTION

Iraq was one of the most dangerous places in the world during 2004 despite the ouster a year earlier of a tyrannical regime and the subsequent presence of about 150,000 troops from the United States, Great Britain, and other countries. Thousands of people—including more than 700 U.S. troops and about that many recruits for Iraq's new security services—were killed in daily suicide bombings, roadside bombings, shootings, and other acts of violence. Most of the violence was initiated by insurgents opposed to the United States and the new government in Baghdad. Hundreds of insurgents and civilians also died as a result of U.S.-led military operations to gain control of rebel-held cities. At least thirty of the nearly two hundred foreigners taken hostage in Iraq by insurgents also were killed.

At year's end the United States, its allies, and an interim Iraqi government were facing a major challenge in mounting and protecting elections scheduled for January 2005. It appeared likely that one of the country's main minority groups—the Sunni Muslims, who had ruled Iraq until the U.S. invasion in 2003—would boycott the election, partly due to the violence. *(Political developments in Iraq, p. 399)*

The U.S. Presence

In its original plans for the Iraq War, the Bush administration had assumed that a new Iraqi government headed by U.S.-backed exiles would take over in Baghdad and quickly restore order, thus enabling nearly all the U.S. and allied forces who had invaded Iraq in March 2003 to be withdrawn by the end of that year. The plan to invade Iraq and oust the regime of Saddam Hussein went according to schedule. Little else in Iraq went according to any plan, however, especially the idea that the country would calm down.

The rapid growth of an insurgency against the U.S. occupation meant that more than 130,000 U.S. troops were still in Iraq at the end of 2003. A year later, about 138,000 troops were there, and the military was planning to boost the total to 150,000 early in 2005 to protect the planned elections. A United Nations mandate for the U.S. forces was set to expire at the end of 2005, but Pentagon planners were assuming that a major foreign military presence would be necessary in Iraq at least through 2006. Secretary of Defense Donald H. Rumsfeld went even further, saying some U.S. troops might still be in Iraq through 2008. In addition to the U.S. presence inside Iraq, another 30,000-some support personnel were stationed in Kuwait and elsewhere in the Middle East, putting the total U.S. military commitment for the Iraq mission during 2004 at about 170,000.

The size of that commitment strained the U.S. military to the limit, forcing the Pentagon to keep tens of thousands of troops from National Guard and reserve units on active duty. At several points in 2004 the Pentagon also resorted to extraordinary steps, such as extending tours of duty in Iraq beyond normal rotations and prohibiting soldiers from leaving the military at the legal expiration of their sign-ups (a procedure known as "stop-loss"). While these actions solved short-term problems, they created longer-term difficulties by discouraging soldiers from reenlisting and hurting efforts to recruit new soldiers. The Pentagon addressed these problems by offering enlistment bonuses, thus adding to the overall cost of the war, which had reached about $220 billion by year's end.

The continuing violence in Iraq meant mounting casualties for U.S. forces, as well as for Iraqis. By the end of 2004, the Pentagon said 1,331 U.S. military personnel had died in the campaign since the March 2003 invasion. Of those, 1,033 were killed in combat and 298 died from accidents or other causes.

Many more Americans died in 2004, when Pentagon plans had called for Iraq to be at peace, than had died during the brief war. According to Pentagon figures, 713 of the 1,033 U.S. troops killed in combat and 132 of the 298 that died from accidents and other causes—a total of 845, or 63 percent of all deaths—took place in 2004. April and November were the bloodiest months because of large-scale military operations to take control of the city of Falluja. In April 135 Americans died, all but 9 of them in combat; 147 were killed in November, all but 12 of them in combat. Another 10,358 U.S. troops had been wounded in action in Iraq since the beginning of the war; the majority—7,950 of them—during 2004.

The single deadliest day of the year for U.S. forces was December 21, when an explosion at an army mess tent in Mosul killed 22 people, including 13 U.S. military personnel, 5 civilian contractors, 3 Iraqi national guardsmen, and 1 unidentified person. More than 50 troops and civilians were wounded. Officials said the blast was caused by a suicide bomber wearing an Iraqi national guard uniform.

Throughout its operations in Iraq, the Pentagon was plagued by reports that soldiers had been sent into dangerous situations without adequate armament and equipment, particularly bullet-proof vests and armor for the large jeeps known as Humvees. A question by one soldier created a major controversy when he addressed it to Secretary Rumsfeld. Meeting in Kuwait on December 8 with soldiers who were headed into Iraq, Rumsfeld was asked by Spc. Thomas Watson why soldiers were forced to scavenge in landfills for scrap metal and bulletproof glass to protect their vehicles. "Why don't we have those resources readily available to us?" he asked. Obviously taken aback, Rumsfeld at first stalled for time, then eventually admitted shortages were likely to continue. "You go to war with the army you have, not the army you might want or wish to have at a later time," he said. That comment, replayed endlessly on television for days afterward, deepened the controversy. The army quickly placed an order with a contractor to speed up production of fully protected Humvees, from the current output of 450 a month to 550 a month.

A Growing Insurgency

The insurgency faced by the troops in Iraq appeared to grow stronger and more lethal during the course of 2004—debunking another key Pentagon assumption that violent opposition to the U.S. presence would diminish rapidly. Every major city was plagued by at least some form of political violence, and the cities in the central section of Iraq known as the "Sunni Triangle" witnessed a relentless barrage of suicide bombings and other attacks. Baghdad, the capital and largest city, was hit with more than a dozen major attacks and scores of smaller violent incidents that killed hundreds of people.

In addition to growing stronger, the character of the violence carried out by the insurgency changed during the year. In the months after the 2003 war, insurgents had mounted several large-scale bombings against symbols of the occupation, including the headquarters in Baghdad of the United Nations and the International Red Cross. In 2004 the chief aim of insurgents appeared to be intimidating Iraqis who were cooperating with the occupation, notably newly recruited police officers and soldiers. The tactic of choice was the suicide bomber, who would drive a car packed with explosives into a crowd of recruits at a police station or Iraqi army post, killing as many of them as possible. Dozens of these attacks during the year killed at least 500 recruits and newly trained security personnel. The effectiveness of the tactic was difficult to judge. Thousands of unemployed Iraqi men continued to volunteer for jobs with the security services despite the violence, but it was unknown how many potentially qualified people had been intimidated.

Several major attacks also targeted Shi'ites and Kurds. Twin suicide bombings took place on February 1 aimed at Kurdish political parties, killing 109 people. Coordinated bombings of Shiite shrines in Karbala and Baghdad on March 2 killed a combined total of at least 181 people. Shi'ite Muslims constituted about 60 percent of the population in Iraq, with Kurds (non-Arabic Muslims) and Sunni Muslims each constituting about 20 percent. Most of the insurgents were assumed to be Sunnis.

Insurgents tried another tactic to discourage foreign involvement in Iraq: hostage taking. Nearly 200 hostages, most of them laborers for international companies hired by the United States to provide goods and services, were taken. Most hostages eventually were released unharmed, but at least 30 were killed, often in gruesome beheadings that were videotaped and then broadcast on the Internet. The highest-profile hostage of the year was Margaret Hassan, an Irish native who had lived in Iraq for three decades and was the local director for Care International. Hassan was taken hostage October 20. After she appeared in a videotape appealing for her life, her body was found in a Baghdad street a month later. Three of the murdered hostages were Americans working on construction projects in Iraq: Nicholas Berg, a Pennsylvania radio tower contractor, whose grisly beheading was shown on an Islamic militant Web site on May 11; Eugene "Jack" Armstrong, a contractor formerly of Hillsdale, Michigan, found beheaded on September 20; and Jack Hensley, a civil engineer from Marietta, Georgia, taken hostage in September and found beheaded on September 22.

At least some of the hostage-takings appeared to produce the desired goal of discouraging foreign involvement in Iraq. After a Turkish truck driver was shown being shot to death on August 2, his colleagues temporarily stopped hauling freight into Iraq. The kidnapping of a Filipino truck driver in July led Manila to withdraw its small peace-keeping force.

Identifying the Insurgents

In the months after the 2003 war, senior Bush administration officials claimed that many, if not most, of the insurgents were Islamist terrorists from other countries who had infiltrated into Iraq to wage holy war against the U.S. occupation. Military commanders in Iraq were skeptical of such claims, however, noting that only a small percentage of the insurgents who had been captured came from outside Iraq. It was not until late 2004 that significant numbers of foreign insurgents appeared on the scene. U.S. intelligence officers reported that groups of Islamic extremists were entering Iraq from Iran, through remote sections of the mountainous border between the two countries.

Among the native Iraqi insurgents, some appeared to be former members of the military or Saddam's outlawed Ba'ath Party, while others either were common criminals taking advantage of the chaos or simply men who were enraged by the U.S. presence.

U.S. military officials said it was clear that many of the insurgent attacks were being planned and directed by one or more central commands, probably consisting of senior officials from Saddam's regime. The Iraqi leader himself might have participated in this command structure until his capture in December 2003. Gen. George W. Casey Jr., who took over command of U.S. forces in Iraq in July, told reporters in December that former senior Ba'ath Party officials, operating in Syria, appeared to be commanding much of the insurgency. Casey said the insurgent leaders called themselves the New Regional Command and appeared to be operating without any hindrance from the Syrian government.

The United States also blamed many of the attacks on Abu Musab al-Zarqawi, a Jordanian militant who asserted loyalty to the al Qaeda terrorist network and its leader, Osama bin Laden. U.S. officials in February said they had intercepted a detailed letter from Zarqawi to bin Laden appealing for support. Zarqawi's location, and the extent of his control over the insurgency, remained mysteries, both to the public and, by all indications, to the U.S. military. In midyear officials said they assumed Zarqawi had established his headquarters in the rebel-held city of Falluja, west of Baghdad. That city was captured in a major U.S.-led invasion in November, but by then Zarqawi had disappeared. *(al Qaeda, p. 534)*

A Daily Drumbeat of Violence

The vast majority of the violent attacks in Iraq received no attention beyond the neighborhoods where they occurred. In most cases, only a handful of people were killed or injured. Over the course of the year, however, the cumulative effect of these "minor" attacks, which took place on a daily basis, was to create an acute sense of insecurity among Iraqis in the affected cities, especially in the Sunni Triangle bounded by Baghdad, Falluja, and Tikrit.

More attention was paid to the several dozen major bombings and other attacks during the year that each killed 20 or more people. Most of these attacks took place in central and southern Iraq, and the majority of victims were recruits for the Iraqi security services and Shi'ite Muslims. But no area of Iraq was entirely free of violence, even the three provinces of northern Iraq controlled by Kurds, who had their own powerful militias. The first large-scale attack of the year was on February 1, when two suicide bombers attacked Kurdish political offices in Irbil, killing 109 people. For much of the year it seemed that the safest place in Iraq was the so-called Green Zone in central Baghdad, where U.S. officials and the interim Iraqi government worked under tight security. Even so, insurgents repeatedly reached the gates of the Green Zone, including on December 13 when two suicide bombers blew up cars waiting to enter the Green Zone, killing 20 people and wounding more than a dozen.

Many of the major attacks required a degree of coordination that demonstrated extensive planning by insurgents. Examples included:

- On March 2 coordinated attacks using suicide bombs, mortars, and grenades killed at least 181 people at Shi'ite mosques in Baghdad and Karbala. It was the highest death toll on any single day since the war began almost a year earlier. U.S. officials blamed al-Zarqawi and said he had planned another attack the same day in Basra, which had been foiled.

- On April 21 five suicide bombings at police stations in Basra killed 74 people. Among the victims were about two dozen school children on a bus.
- On June 24 a surge of apparently coordinated attacks in central and northern Iraq killed 89 people, including 3 U.S. soldiers, and wounded more than 300 people. Five cities were engulfed with violence as insurgents mounted an effort to disrupt the transition to the new Iraqi regime.
- On August 1 car bombs were set off near four Christian churches in Baghdad and another church in Mosul, killing a dozen people and wounding about 30 others. These were the first major attacks against Iraq's minority Christian community.
- On September 4 several attacks around the country killed about 30 people. The largest was a suicide car bomb outside a police academy in Kirkuk, killing 20 and wounding 36.
- On September 12 a series of car bombings and other attacks in Baghdad killed at least 25 people; another 30 died in violence elsewhere in the country.
- On September 14 a suicide car bomb exploded outside police headquarters in Baghdad, where hundreds of young men were seeking jobs; the bomb killed at least 47 people and wounded more than 100 others. Several hours later another 12 were killed in Baqouba when gunmen opened fire on a van carrying policemen.
- On September 30 three car bombs exploded in western Baghdad during a ceremony marking the opening of a new sewage treatment plant, killing 35 children and 7 Iraqi adults. Dozens of people were wounded, including 10 U.S. soldiers. Soldiers were handing out candy to children when the bombs went off. A roadside bomb at another location in Baghdad the same day killed 1 U.S. soldier and 2 Iraqi policemen.
- On October 4 two car bombs exploded: one at the gates to the Green Zone and one in Mosul, killing a total of at least 26 people.
- On November 7 coordinated attacks on police stations throughout Iraq, with car bombs, mortars, and rockets, killed more than 50 people and wounded about 60 others, including two dozen Americans.
- On November 11, the fourth day of the U.S. offensive in Falluja, car bombs in Baghdad and Kirkuk killed 18 people and wounded more than 40. The bombings appeared to be aimed at convoys carrying U.S. and Iraqi troops but killed bystanders instead.
- On December 19 car bombs in a central square in Najaf and at the main bus station in Karbala killed at least 60 people and wounded more than 120.

Civilian Casualties

One of the unknown features of the year's violence was the true extent of casualties among Iraqi civilians. The United States maintained no official records of civilian casualties in Iraq, either during or after the war. Records compiled by Iraqi government agencies were fragmentary, based on reports from hospitals and morgues in just a few cities. Several news organizations, human rights groups, and independent monitors with Web sites attempted to compile statistics using various methods and came up with figures ranging from several thousand to approximately 100,000.

On May 23 the Associated Press reported that morgue records showed that 5,500 Iraqis had died violent deaths in Baghdad and the provinces of Karbala, Kirkuk, and

Tikrit in the period from May 1, 2003, through April 30, 2004. The most comprehensive official record from the Iraqi government was an estimate in November by the Iraqi Ministry of Health, based on hospital reports, that 2,853 people had died and 15,517 people were injured from violence in Iraq between April and October.

The *New York Times* on October 18 documented Iraqi civilian deaths for just one week, October 11 through 17, and estimated that 208 were killed in war-related incidents. The *Times* said that figure appeared to be "significantly higher" than the weekly average, which for the twenty-two-week period of April 5 through September 6 had been 138 weekly deaths, based on the Health Ministry estimate. The *Times*'s figures excluded the Kurdish regions in northern Iraq.

One of the few systematic efforts to estimate Iraqi civilian deaths on a regular basis was by a British-based Web site, iraqbodycount.net. Citing news reports of daily casualties, that site put the death total from March 2003 through December 2004 at about 15,000 to 17,000. The British medical journal *Lancet* published an epidemiological study on October 3 estimating that 98,000 civilians had died since the war began. That study was widely criticized, in part because the 98,000 figure was the midpoint of a wide range of about 8,000 to 194,000.

Confronting Sadr and His Militia

Although insurgents who were presumed to be Sunnis created most of the violence in Iraq, a rebel Shi'ite cleric with a broad following also posed a serious challenge to U.S. and Iraqi officials for much of the year. Moqtada al-Sadr, the son of a revered Shi'ite cleric murdered by Saddam's regime in 1999, had gathered thousands of supporters and built a personal militia, which he called the Mahdi Army, in the months after the U.S. invasion. Much of Sadr's following was based in the cities of Karbala and Najaf, which were home to important Shi'ite shrines, and in a huge slum in Baghdad, formerly called Saddam City but since the war called Sadr City after the murdered senior cleric.

On March 28 the U.S.-led Coalition Provisional Authority closed *al-Hawza,* a newspaper published by Sadr's group, on the grounds that it was inciting Iraqis to commit violence against U.S. forces. A week later, thousands of Sadr's supporters took to the streets in cities in southern Iraq, generating fears among U.S. officials of a widespread Shi'ite uprising. Sadr took over mosques in Kufa and Najaf, and the U.S. occupation said Iraqi officials had issued a warrant for his arrest.

A stand-off ensued, during which Sadr's guerrillas essentially controlled Kufa and Najaf, along with Sadr City in Baghdad. This challenge by Sadr threatened to undermine the U.S.-led occupation of all of southern Iraq and to further destabilize an already tenuous situation in the central region. U.S. forces moved into Najaf in mid-May, putting pressure on Sadr, who had moved into the Imam Ali shrine, one of the holiest sites for Shi'ite Muslims. Aides to Iraq's senior Shi'ite cleric, Ayatollah Ali al-Sistani, brokered an agreement, accepted by both Sadr and U.S. authorities on May 27, under which Sadr agreed to leave Najaf and take most of his militiamen with him. The agreement ended the confrontation but left Sadr's militia intact, with his thousands of fighters armed and dangerous.

Sadr on June 16 ordered his militiamen to disband and return to their homes, and thousands of them appeared to comply. Sadr himself was said to be preparing to focus his attention on political matters, but aides said he had no immediate plans to run for office in the elections scheduled for January 2005. By early July Sadr's militia appeared to be regrouping, having captured ten Iraqi policemen in Najaf. The U.S. military began another push into Najaf early in August, and Sadr called for a national uprising against the interim government and U.S. forces on August 5. Another potential conflict was avoided at the end of August when Sistani again intervened and convinced Sadr to withdraw his militia from Najaf. Sadr agreed in October to encourage his militia members in Baghdad's Sadr City to hand over their weapons for cash from the United States, and hundreds did so starting on October 11. Many, however, reportedly took the money and bought newer weapons.

Battles for Falluja

By early 2004 U.S. military officials had concluded that much of the insurgency was based in Falluja, a predominantly Sunni city of nearly 300,000 people west of Baghdad. Falluja had been the site of the worst killing of Iraqi civilians after the 2003 war, when frightened U.S. soldiers opened fire on an angry crowd, killing 20 people.

Falluja was again the scene of violence in 2004, beginning March 31 with the grisly murder and desecration of the bodies of four employees of Blackwater Security Consulting, a private security firm that was guarding food deliveries in the city. The bodies of the civilians were dragged from their vehicles and burned; two of them were hung on a bridge across the Euphrates River. The scene was televised worldwide and, for a moment at least, symbolized both the chaos in much of Iraq and the inability of the world's most powerful military to bring it to an end.

U.S. marines advanced on Falluja on April 6 and engaged in fierce battles that gave them control of much of the city. By mid-April, however, rumors spread throughout Iraq that hundreds or even thousands of civilians had died in the fighting. These rumors sparked hostile anti-American demonstrations in many cities, leading several prominent Sunni political leaders to threaten to resign from the government. Faced with the prospect of a general revolt, the Bush administration ordered a halt to the siege of Falluja on April 22. In a face-saving gesture, the U.S. military said it was turning control of the city over to a former Iraqi general, but he was replaced after about ten days when questions were raised about his ties to Saddam's regime. By late May reporters who visited the city said hard-line Islamic militants had regained control.

By late summer U.S. officials concluded that Zarqawi was using Falluja as his headquarters. The military developed, and the White House approved, plans to return to Falluja with a massive invasion that would seize control of the city from the insurgents.

As those plans were being laid, the military on October 1 launched a major assault on another city controlled by the insurgents: Samarra, about sixty miles north of Baghdad. Soldiers from the army's First Infantry Division and a contingent of Iraqi soldiers assaulted insurgent positions, and the Iraqi soldiers captured a famed Shi'ite shrine, the Golden Mosque. The combined forces drove the insurgents from the city in three days of fighting. The taking of city, and the successful participation of Iraqi troops, was a significant psychological boost for the new interim Iraqi government amid relentless carnage elsewhere in the region.

Interim prime minister Ayad Allawi signaled that the second battle of Falluja was imminent by taking two steps: first, he issued a formal authorization for it on November 3; four days later he issued a declaration of martial law throughout Iraq except for the northern Kurdish areas. The latter step followed two days of apparently coordinated attacks on police stations in central Iraq that killed more than 50 Iraqi policemen.

The second U.S. campaign of the year to take control of Falluja began on November 8 with a massive assault from the north of the city by nearly 15,000 soldiers and marines. Because of warnings by Allawi and others that the battle was imminent, an estimated 90 percent of the city's 300,000 residents had left. U.S. officials said they assumed that many of the insurgent leaders, including Zarqawi, were among those who fled the city in anticipation of the fighting.

U.S. forces, with help from Iraqi units, gained effective control of the streets of Falluja within a week, but sporadic fighting continued for several more days. By late November the military was taking Iraqi government officials and journalists on tours of the city, which had suffered massive damage during its occupation by the insurgency and two major battles in six months. The Pentagon produced detailed plans for rebuilding the city and luring the population back, sector by sector, as repairs were made. Those plans were based on the assumption that Iraqi contractors would do much of the reconstruction, an assumption that had proven faulty elsewhere in the country since the 2003 invasion.

In the wake of the battle for Falluja, the videotaped shooting by a U.S. marine of a wounded Iraqi prisoner set off another round of protests. NBC News on November 15 aired footage appearing to show the marine shooting an unresisting prisoner at a mosque in Falluja. The videotape was televised repeatedly in Iraq and the rest of the Arab world in the following days, sparking a round of outrage similar to that resulting from the Abu Ghraib prison abuse scandal earlier in the year. *(Abu Ghraib scandal, p. 207)*

In a speech to the interim Iraqi assembly on November 30, Allawi said inspections of Falluja after the fighting had turned up large quantities of weapons, improvised bombs, and locations where hostages had been held and tortured. "All these facts confirm our right decision to uproot terrorism," he said.

Iraqi Security Forces

A key assumption of the Bush administration's original plan for postwar Iraq was that thousands of Iraqi men would be eager to serve in a new army and police force, and thus would provide the security that would enable the United States and its allies to withdraw their troops quickly. Nearly every aspect of this assumption proved to be faulty. Thousands off Iraqis signed up for army and police jobs, but a large percentage of them failed to finish training courses organized by the U.S. military or fled in the face of violence targeting them. Hopes of turning full security responsibility over to the Iraqi services any time soon vanished in the face of the rapid growth of the insurgency.

Officials in Washington repeatedly made optimistic pronouncements, but U.S. commanders in Iraq said the facts on the ground were not so rosy. Army Maj. Gen. Paul D. Eaton, who commanded U.S. security training efforts in Iraq for the first year after the war, left in early June after telling reporters "it hasn't gone well. We've had almost one year of no progress." Eaton cited misguided U.S. policies, such as failing to concentrate on training leaders, and unrealistic expectations, including a hope that new Iraqi army units would take the lead in the spring offensive against insurgent forces in Falluja. Eaton was replaced by Lt. Gen. David Petraeus, the former commander of the 101st Airborne Division, who was given responsibility for training all Iraqi security forces.

The difficult position of Iraqi soldiers and policemen was evident on an almost daily basis because they were the principal targets of violence during 2004. At least 500—and probably more than 1,000—Iraqi security personnel were killed in insurgent attacks during the year. Even when they were not the targets, Iraqi police officers or soldiers often stood by and watched acts of violence, unable or unwilling to intervene. A typical case occurred in Baghdad on June 14 when a suicide bomber drove a truck full of explosives into a convoy of vehicles carrying foreign contractors, killing more than a dozen people. A mob of young men then emerged, doused the wreckage with gasoline and lit it, creating a huge fireball; they then threw bricks at a nearby squad of U.S. soldiers. About fifty Iraqi policemen stood by, taking no action. "What are we to do?" an Iraqi police lieutenant told a reporter. "If we try to stop them, they will think we are helping the Americans. Then they will turn on us."

Iraqi soldiers did participate in major U.S. military operations in Falluja, Najaf, and Samarra. U.S. officials said some units, notably elite commando units working closely with U.S. troops, performed well. Hundreds of Iraqi soldiers deserted just before the Falluja and Samarra offensives were launched, however, apparently indicating that many Iraqis were unwilling to act against their fellow countrymen, especially when that action was directed by the United States. Another ominous sign came in Mosul in mid-November, when most of the Iraqi police force and hundreds of soldiers deserted in the face of an anti-American uprising. That situation was calmed only through the use of Kurdish soldiers—itself a controversial step in a city rife with tensions between Arabs and Kurds. U.S. news reports quoted American soldiers as repeatedly expressing frustration with the performance of Iraqi troops—one of many examples of the cultural differences that afflicted many aspects of what officials in Washington claimed was a joint venture to secure Iraq's future.

A related problem of unknown dimension was the penetration of Iraqi security units by informants for the insurgents. U.S. officials said suicide bombers clearly had inside information enabling them to attack groups of army or police recruits when they were most vulnerable. Many Iraqi soldiers and policemen reportedly were so worried about this problem that they lied to their friends and families—even their wives—about where they were working.

A Faltering Coalition

The Bush administration in 2003 had trumpeted the participation of about three dozen countries in the invasion and immediate aftermath of the war, saying this "coalition of the willing" demonstrated broad international support. In 2004 the coalition was weakened—in political terms and possibly militarily as well—by the defections of several allies.

Spain pulled its 1,300 troops from Iraq after the Socialist opposition, which had opposed the war, defeated the government that supported it in national elections held three days after the March 11, 2004, terrorist bombings aboard four commuter trains in Madrid. Other countries that withdrew most or all of their forces from Iraq included the Dominican Republic (320 troops), Honduras (370 troops), Nicaragua (115 troops), Norway (140 troops), and Singapore (160 troops). The Philippines announced in mid-July that it would withdrew its small force to obtain the release of a Filipino truck driver who had been held hostage. Several other countries scaled back their contingents. The most significant addition during the year came from South Korea, which boosted its presence from 600 to 3,700 troops, the third largest after the U.S. and British contingents. Other large contingents, as of mid-August, were Italy, with 3,000 troops; Poland, with 2,400 troops; and the Netherlands, with 1,400 troops. The Dutch government said in October that its troops would be withdrawn early in 2005, and Poland on December 14 said 700 of its troops would be withdrawn in mid-February 2005. *(Madrid terrorist bombings, p. 105)*

Following is the text of an address November 20, 2004, by Iraq's interim prime minister, Ayad Allawi, to the interim parliament known as the National Council, describing the recent capture by U.S. and Iraqi forces of the city of Falluja and outlining challenges facing the country. The translation from Arabic to English was provided by the Iraqi government.

"Speech by Prime Minister Ayad Allawi to the National Council"

The head of the National Council

Ladies and gentlemen members of the National Council

It is my pleasure to meet you and at the same time to inform you about the events happening in our dear country. I have just come back from Falluja after we put the basis to reconstruct the city. We confirm that force in solving problems is our last choice. We were forced to resort to political operations after we waited for a long time but the terrorists continued in their wrong doings, and considered our patience as weakness which made them exaggerate their criminal acts.

So, we are determined to clean the Iraqi cities from terrorists. I have told you all about Falluja after the end of the political operations. We found hundreds of weapon storages, many of improvised explosive devices factories and places for kidnapping and torturing. All these facts confirm our right decision to uproot terrorism.

It is our pleasure to tell you that we made progress concerning this matter. At the same time, we confirm our determination to work forward in order that civilians return to cities which were cleaned up from terrorists and reconstructing them so they would return safe to their houses.

We, motivated by our responsibility and adherence on the citizen's comfort, directed ministers to exert all efforts to reconstruct the cities that are cleaned from terrorists and provide what they need of equipment.

Ladies and gentlemen

The most dangerous thing terrorism aims at is encouraging separation among the Iraqi people sects. Terrorists want to set Iraqi people against each other and expose the national unity to danger. It is very well-known to you all that this method is very dangerous [to] the national unity.

As we believe that Iraq is the country for all, the national unity represents the base of national existence. So, we are determined to strengthen it and defeat all who try to play with it.

Hence, all Iraqi people have the equal rights that guarantee their dignity and security, without distinction, so that each will have a share and heard opinion through participation in the political process. This was a basic aim for our encouragement for all Iraqi people sects to take part in the political process.

During our visit to the Kurdish region this week, we held meetings with religious figures. The last one was this morning, we listened to viewpoints of Sunni and Shiite clerics. Similar meetings will be held to get acquainted with opinions of different segments of Iraqi people.

Ladies of the National Council
Gentlemen of the National Council

It is pretty sad to notice, through the past period, that some of the clerics (especially those loyal to the former regime) encourage violent actions that only harm the innocent unarmed people, women and children. From this platform, I call upon those who misunderstood ideas and did not find the right way to the light that we seek for the sake of the welfare of our country and our people. I call upon them to realize that their attempts led to nothing but disunity and disorder. We, and all the good Iraqi people, do not accept this way because it brings about harm to Iraq and the brotherhood of its people. Therefore we will stand firmly against these intentions. Not only because they are illegal intentions, but also because they bring destruction and ravage to our people and our country.

Those who spur on hatred and terrorism do not want this country to achieve stability and progress. Moreover, this behavior reflects strict and severe minds that stab the Islamic religion in its justice and lenience and offend the humanitarian core of Islam and its valuable principles.

Sisters and Brothers, I find it a must to tell you that we are proceeding in developing the economical realm and creating work opportunities through the reconstruction process and giving chances for local and international investment. Here I should refer to the improvement of the living standard of the Iraqi people and we are looking forward in achieving a lot more than that. We would like to point out that 80% of the Iraqi debts have been written off by Paris Club. This is considered as an important and great success through which we are looking forward to similar approvals and more by the Arab brothers. I would like to inform you as well that some Iraqis who live abroad aspire to play a political role in their country. And we have no objection of that on condition that their work comes under the current legal framework and in a peaceful and democratic method.

In conclusion, I would like to inform you that I will travel this week in a tour to a number of countries in order to develop and enhance our relations with our major allies like Jordan, Germany and Russia adopting the fact that the good relations with these countries enable us to gain new interests in all realms; policy, economy and security. I will notify you of the outcomes of these talks after coming back.

I wish you good luck and may Allah help us all for the purpose of Iraq's welfare and progress.

Peace be upon you. . . .

Source: Office of the Prime Minister of Iraq. "Text of speech by Prime Minister Ayad Allawi to the National Council." Baghdad, Iraq, November 30, 2004. www.iraqigovernment.org/archive.htm (accessed March 9, 2005).

December

2004 HISTORIC DOCUMENTS

Secretary General's Panel on Reform of the United Nations

December 1, 2004

INTRODUCTION

United Nations Secretary General Kofi Annan called 2004 an *annus horribilus*—horrible year—for the often-troubled body he led. The year was difficult for him personally, bringing demands for his resignation from conservatives in the United States and allegations that officials under his supervision had mismanaged a multibillion dollar program of oil sales by Iraq. The year also brought renewed conflicts between the United Nations and the Bush administration, with Iraq again being the main sore point.

The year also offered new opportunities for the UN that would be played out in 2005 and beyond. One opportunity emerged from the enormous tragedy caused by a giant tsunami that devastated Indian Ocean coastal areas on December 26, killing tens of thousands of people. The UN responded quickly with what was likely to become its biggest relief effort ever—one that either could visibly demonstrate the UN's key role in humanitarian affairs or reinforce a reputation for bureaucratic inefficiency and sluggishness. *(Tsunami, p. 991)*

Over the long term, a potentially even more important opportunity came with the publication on December 1 of a report by a panel of experts, appointed by Annan, identifying many of the UN's chronic institutional problems and suggesting sweeping changes, including expanding the Security Council. Annan broadly endorsed the panel's recommendations and said he would incorporate them into his own plan for consideration by world leaders at the next opening session of the General Assembly in September 2005.

Changing the UN

After a confrontation early in 2003 over Iraq between the Bush administration and other UN Security Council members, Annan appointed a sixteen-member panel to examine the role of the world body. The High-Level Panel on Threats, Challenges, and Change was chaired by Anand Panyarachun, a former prime minister of Thailand, and included many senior figures with the word *former* as part of their titles. The U.S. representative was Brent Scowcroft, a retired air force lieutenant general who had been national security adviser to President George H.W. Bush (1989–1993), father of the current president, George W. Bush. The panel held more than fifty seminars and six formal meetings around the world from late 2003 through 2004 and gave its report to Annan in November; Annan made it public on December 1. The 115-page report made 101 recommendations, some of which Annan had authority to act on himself but most of which would require approval by the General Assembly.

Annan said he would combine the recommendations with his own proposals for helping the UN meet an ambitious humanitarian agenda, called the Millennium Development Goals, into a broad document by March 2005 and would ask the General Assembly to consider it the following September. "It is hardly possible to overstate what is at stake, not only for this organization for but all the peoples of this world, for whose safety this organization was created," Annan told the General Assembly on December 8. "If we do not act resolutely, and together, the threats described in the report can overwhelm us." *(Millennium goals, Historic Documents of 2000, p. 477)*

Most of the public attention focused on the one key question about which the panel could not come to total agreement: the makeup of the Security Council. The council was the UN's most visible and potentially powerful body but often had been stifled by dissension or indecision when member nations could not agree on a course of action. Panel members reportedly had been reluctant to take on the question of revising the Security Council but did so at Annan's request. In its report, the panel said the Security Council had been "slow to change" to meet current world needs and had regularly made inconsistent or unrealistic decisions that failed to produce any meaningful action.

The panel concluded that expanding the Security Council was a "necessity" to generate increased international support for the council's decisions. The UN Charter, dating from the closing days of World War II, gave permanent Security Council membership (and the right to veto resolutions) to the five major victors in that war: Britain, China, France, the United States, and the Soviet Union (later, Russia). Ten other countries served two-year, nonrenewable terms. The panel was unable to agree on a single proposal to change that system and instead offered two options, each of which would retain the five veto-bearing permanent members but expand the Security Council to twenty-four seats:

- Adding six new permanent members but not giving any of them veto power. The panel did not name candidates for the six new permanent members but suggested two each from Asia and Africa and one each from the Americas and Europe. The seven potential countries mentioned most often (because of their size and economic or political influence) were Brazil, Egypt, Germany, India, Japan, Nigeria, and South Africa. The number of rotating members, each serving two-year terms, would be expanded from ten to thirteen.
- Creating a new category of eight "semi-permanent" member countries, which would serve four-year terms that could be renewed. Each of the four regions (Africa, the Americas, Asia, and Europe) would get two of these seats. To bring the total council membership to twenty-four, the panel proposed adding one seat with a two-year, nonrenewable term.

Noting that it had been nearly sixty years since the current membership formula was put in place, the panel called for another review of the issue by 2020. A major part of that review should be examining the contributions that member nations made to the United Nations, both in terms of financial contributions and in manpower for peacekeeping operations.

As could be expected, the nations that had been the most active candidates for permanent slots on the council preferred the first option. Even so, leaders of some of these countries expressed disappointment that the proposal would not give new permanent members the veto power. Those countries received at least verbal backing from Russian president Vladimir Putin, who said all new permanent members of the council should be given the veto. "Otherwise, it will be a one-sided reform of the United Nations," he said on December 4, while visiting India.

Some UN critics denounced the plan for expanding the Security Council. Such a step "would probably make UN paralysis worse, not better, because it would mean having to get the agreement of even more states before taking action," Max Boot, a senior fellow at the Council on Foreign Relations, wrote in a column published by the *Los Angeles Times* on December 9.

Panel members said one of the most difficult questions they had faced involved the seemingly simple matter of defining terrorism. The panel noted that even though terrorism had risen to the top of the world's agenda as a result of the September 11, 2001, attacks against the United States, the UN had not developed a comprehensive treaty to combat it and had been unable even to define what it was.

After much internal debate, the panel agreed on a definition of terrorism as any act "that is intended to cause death or serious bodily harm to civilians or non-combatants, when the purpose of such act, by its nature or context, is to intimidate a population, or to compel a government or an international organization to do or abstain from doing any act."

The panel attempted to settle two related controversies over the definition of terrorism. First, it said that the killing or abuse of civilians by a government-sanctioned military force was a war crime under the Geneva Conventions and numerous other treaties—but was not terrorism. Second, the panel included in its definition of terrorism the targeting of civilians by rebels battling an occupying power. "There is nothing in the fact of occupation that justifies the targeting and killing of civilians," the panel said. The panel did not cite specific examples, but its definition appeared to cover such acts as the suicide bombings of civilian targets by the insurgents who opposed the U.S. occupation of Iraq and by Palestinian militants who opposed Israeli occupation of the West Bank and Gaza Strip.

The Bush administration applauded the panel's statements on terrorism but appeared less pleased by another statement by the panel on the concept of "preemption" as military action by nations to head off potential threats. As part of its intellectual justification for the impending war in Iraq, the administration in 2002 had published a National Security Strategy suggesting the United States would eliminate threats to its vital national interests when they were still developing—not after they had occurred. That strategy generated controversy at the time, and the controversy grew when it was discovered that Iraq did not possess the weapons of mass destruction that Bush had said threatened the United States and its allies, thus justifying the invasion of Iraq in 2003. *(Iraq weapons, p. 711; Preemption policy, Historic Documents of 2002, p. 633)*

In its report, the UN panel acknowledged the potential need for what it called "anticipatory self-defense" against such threats as the acquisition of a nuclear weapon by a hostile power or terrorists. Even so, the panel said, a nation anticipating such a threat should take its case, "with good evidence" to support it, to the Security Council. The panel rejected what it called "unilateral preventive action" because allowing it in one case meant allowing it in all cases. The panel also listed five criteria for the Security Council to use when considering whether to authorize individual countries or groups of countries to use force:

- the seriousness of the threat
- the purpose of the action to be taken against it
- the use of force as the last resort

- the proportionality of the response to the threat
- the likelihood that military action would produce a better result than inaction

U.S. officials objected to the panel's argument, saying that forcing a threatened nation to go to the Security Council imposed an unjustified limit on the right of self-defense. "Such constraints will never be acceptable to the United States," Kim R. Holmes, the assistant secretary of state for international affairs told a conference in Baltimore on December 6.

Many of the panel's dozens of other recommendations dealt with specific issues, such as streamlining the UN bureaucracy and tightening international restraints on the development of nuclear weapons. One controversial proposal would give all countries automatic membership on the Commission on Human Rights. The panel said that step would reinforce the obligation by all countries to adhere to international human rights standards and would eliminate biennial disputes over commission membership. One of those disputes had occurred early in 2004 when African nations forced the selection of Sudan as a member of the commission despite allegations that the Khartoum government participated in, or at least allowed, mass killings and displacement of residents in the Darfur region. *(Sudan, p. 588)*

Bush and the UN

For a few weeks early in 2004 it appeared some of that ill-feeling generated by the dispute in 2003 over the Security Council's refusal to authorize the U.S. war in Iraq might be dissipating. In February the Bush administration turned to Annan for help in resolving a deadlock over the shape of Iraq's interim government. Annan called on one of his most trusted troubleshooters, former Algerian diplomat Lakhdar Brahimi, who succeeded in negotiating an arrangement that met the minimal demands of Iraq's key actors and enabled a new government to take office in June. This was a case where the UN imprimatur, coupled with Brahimi's personal prestige, provided the credibility, both in Iraq and internationally, that the Bush administration lacked. Brahimi also had led UN efforts to develop a new government in Afghanistan between November 2001 and January 2004. *(Iraq political developments, p. 399; Afghanistan, p. 912)*

The tentative U.S.-UN cooperation on Iraq did not last, however, in part because of undiplomatic remarks made by UN diplomats. The first came from Brahimi, who described L. Paul Bremer III, the chief U.S. official in Iraq, as a "dictator," apparently because he had rejected some of Brahimi's proposals. A second remark came in September when Annan told an interviewer that the U.S.-led invasion of Iraq had been "illegal." Washington's resentment of that characterization was heightened in October when Annan sent the administration a letter warning against an impending invasion of Falluja, where some of Iraq's anti-American insurgents were said to be based. *(Falluja, p. 874)*

The strain in relations deepened later in the fall when the Bush administration pressed Annan to send a large delegation of experts to Iraq to plan and manage the provincial and national elections scheduled for January 2005. UN staff designed the format for the elections, and Annan stationed a handful of election experts in Iraq during the last months of 2004. However, Annan resisted Washington's pressure for a larger UN presence, citing security reasons. After the August 2003 bombing of the UN headquarters in Baghdad, killing twenty UN employees, Annan had vowed never again to send his workers into an unsafe environment without adequate protection. Bush administration officials were angered by Annan's stance and voiced suspicion that he simply was reinforcing his point that the U.S. invasion of Iraq had been misguided.

Yet another dispute involved what had become a recurring controversy over the International Criminal Court, a new entity to handle war crimes cases. The Bush administration refused to have anything to do with the court, arguing that it would be used to target U.S. personnel serving overseas. At Washington's insistence, the Security Council in 2002 and again in 2003 had granted one-year exemptions from the court's jurisdiction for U.S. troops participating in international peacekeeping missions. In late April, just three months before the current exemption was to expire, news organizations published photographs of U.S. soldiers cruelly abusing Iraqis at a prison in Baghdad. The graphic photographs cause a worldwide scandal and doomed any chance for the Bush administration to get another exemption from the criminal court. Instead, the administration said early in July that all U.S. soldiers would be withdrawn from UN missions in Ethiopia, Eritrea, and Kosovo. *(International Criminal Court background, Historic Documents of 2003, p. 99)*

At year's end Bush was weighing one decision of potential importance to Washington's role at the United Nations: the appointment of a new ambassador. Former senator John Danforth, R-Mo., had taken that job in June after his predecessor, John Negroponte, became U.S. ambassador to Iraq. After serving less than six months, Danforth announced on December 2 that he was leaving to return to his home in St. Louis. In interviews, Danforth expressed frustration with the diplomatic life, noting that as a senator he was not accustomed to having the State Department transform his speeches into "mush" before he could give them. He voiced even greater frustration with the Security Council, in particular the requirement for unanimity among the five permanent members. Danforth spent much of his short tenure in New York pushing for stronger international action to halt fighting in the Darfur region of western Sudan, only to be blocked by resistance from China and other council members. Bush had not announced a replacement for Danforth as of year's end. *(Sudan, p. 588)*

Yet another potential conflict arose at the very end of the year over the international response to the major disaster caused by the tsunami in the Indian Ocean. UN relief agencies responded immediately, but on December 31 Bush said the United States—along with Australia, India, and Japan—would create a "core group" to coordinate rescue and recovery efforts, implying a lack of confidence in the UN agencies.

"Oil for Food" Scandals

Of all the challenges faced by the United Nations during the year, none had as much potential for immediate damage to the institution as a rapidly blossoming scandal over its handling of Iraq's oil sales between 1996 and the U.S. invasion in 2003. Critics of the UN, especially conservatives in the United States, cited the scandal as evidence that the world body was corrupt as well as incompetent, and they used it to denounce Annan, whose willingness to defy the Bush administration infuriated them. Even strong UN supporters were distressed to learn that Annan had not exercised more discipline over the high-profile office that administered the Iraqi oil sales.

The Security Council had banned Iraqi oil sales after that country invaded neighboring Kuwait in 1990. That ban, along with other economic sanctions and curbs on Iraq's military programs, remained in place after the 1991 Persian Gulf War that ousted Iraq from Kuwait. In 1996 Iraqi leader Saddam Hussein accepted a UN offer to allow resumed oil sales—if the money was used to by food and medicine for the Iraqi people, and for a limited amount of industrial equipment, including replacement parts for the country's oil industry. The United Nations ran this program, called "Oil for Food," under the close supervision of the Security Council until November 2003. *(Oil for Food background, Historic Documents of 1999, p. 146)*

During the late 1990s numerous news reports indicated that Iraq was getting around some of the UN's restrictions on oil sales, notably by smuggling oil, outside the control of the UN program, to neighboring countries, including Jordan, Syria, and Turkey. Neither the Security Council, nor any of its member nations, ever made a serious attempt to stop this smuggling.

After Saddam's regime was ousted in the U.S.-led invasion of Iraq early in 2003, new allegations arose that Iraq had subverted the Oil for Food program in other ways, including by bribing the UN officials who ran it. The General Accounting Office (GAO, later renamed the Government Accountability Office) reported March 18, 2004, that its investigations had uncovered $10.1 billion in illegal revenues for Iraq under the program: $5.7 billion from the smuggling of oil and $4.4 billion in improper surcharges or kickbacks on the sale of oil and purchase of commodities under the Oil for Food program. Sen. Norm Coleman, R-Minn., who chaired the Senate Government Affairs investigating subcommittee, said on November 15 that new figures put Iraq's illegal oil revenues at more than $21 billion. Coleman was one of several Republicans who demanded that Annan resign because of the scandal.

Five congressional committees launched investigations during the year, and Annan on March 31 appointed an independent panel to investigate the matter, headed by Paul Volcker, a former chairman of the U.S. Federal Reserve. Volcker planned to issue an interim report on his findings early in 2005, but aides said in December that the Russian government was hampering the inquiry by refusing access to documents and potential witnesses.

Three separate but related issues were under investigation:

- The UN's administration of the Oil for Food program, including allegations that program administrator Benon V. Sevan was among those who personally profited from deals with Iraq. A report issued in October by the CIA task force that searched for illegal weapons in Iraq detailed a series of arrangements under which Iraqi officials, foreign companies, and officials in France, Indonesia, Russia, the United States, and elsewhere accepted vouchers that enabled them to make profits before Iraq's oil was sold on the international market. Volcker's panel on October 22 published a list of 4,734 companies that had traded with Iraq using the vouchers. The CIA report said Sevan was among those who profited by accepting vouchers through firms he had recommended to Baghdad. The report alleged that Sevan might have earned between $730,000 and $2 million from these deals. Sevan denied the charges. Related to this was an allegation that Annan's son, Kojo, received up to $150,000 in payments over five years from a Swiss-based company, Cotecna Inspection S.A., which had been hired by the UN to inspect shipments of food and other items to Iraq under the Oil for Food program. Kojo Annan said he left the firm at the beginning of the Oil for Food program and the payments were made under a standard severance arrangement having nothing to do with Iraq. Kofi Annan said on November 29 that he had not known of his son's continuing payments from the firm.
- The ease with which Saddam's government subverted the intended purpose of the program and instead earned billions of dollars for military programs,

construction of palaces and other buildings in his own honor, and other purposes. This was accomplished in three ways: through the voucher system, which generated kickbacks in exchange for oil contracts; through surcharges of 25 to 30 cents for each barrel of oil purchased by foreign companies; and through the smuggling of oil to other countries in the region.

- The administration of Iraq's oil industry by the U.S.-led Coalition Provisional Authority in the period after the 2003 Iraq War and before the transfer of sovereignty to an interim Iraqi government on June 28, 2004. The Security Council established an agency, the International Advisory and Monitoring Board for Iraq, to audit the U.S. spending of about $20 billion in a UN-approved Development Fund for Iraq, most of which came from oil sales. That board issued an interim report on December 14 alleging numerous faults in the U.S. administration of the fund, including a failure to keep track of the amount of oil produced by Iraqi fields, the use of noncompetitive and sole-source bidding in awarding contracts worth millions or even billions of dollars, and the use of vague barter deals with neighboring countries that might have shortchanged Iraq's interests. By far the most controversial matter was the awarding by the U.S. authority of sole-source contracts to subsidiaries of the Halliburton Company, a Texas oil services firm headed during the 1990s by Vice President Dick Cheney. Some of these contracts were paid for with Iraqi oil revenue. The monitoring board complained repeatedly during 2004 that the Pentagon had delayed or refused to provide documents for its investigation.

After Senator Coleman and other congressional Republicans began demanding Annan's resignation, British prime minister Tony Blair, the European Union, Russian president Putin, and many other world leaders rallied to Annan's side, and the Bush administration on December 9 issued a tepid endorsement. A small delegation of influential U.S. foreign policy experts met privately with Annan and warned him that the always tenuous American support for the United Nations was in danger of collapsing unless he cleaned out bureaucratic dead wood and stepped up the pace of reforms he had been promising since his appointment in 1997. Annan responded with several changes still under way at year's end, starting with the appointment of a new chief of staff with broad experience in crisis management, Mark Malloch Brown, the head of the United Nations Development Programme.

Sexual Abuse Scandals

The oil for food scandal generated headlines in the United States and a handful of other countries, but in at least three of the world's chronically troubled countries the year's big UN-related issue was sexual abuse by peacekeepers. Soldiers and police officers assigned to UN missions in Burundi, the Democratic Republic of the Congo, and Kosovo had been accused of using their privileges to abuse girls and women.

The allegations of abuses in Kosovo were lodged in a May 6 report by Amnesty International, the British-based human rights organization. The report said troops assigned to NATO's peacekeeping force and policemen working for the UN mission that had ultimate responsibility for Kosovo had engaged in trafficking of women or had failed to stop trafficking networks run by criminal networks. Amnesty said about two dozen NATO peacekeepers had been investigated for such crimes between 2002–2003, and ten UN police officers had been dismissed or sent home because of alleged involvement in trafficking. None of these infractions had been made public by NATO or the UN, the report said. *(Kosovo, p. 949)*

On May 7 the UN peacekeeping mission in the Congo said it had begun investigating charges that peacekeepers had sexually exploited and abused civilians, including minors, in Bunia, in the eastern part of the country. The *Washington Post* reported on December 16 that investigators had documented sixty-eight allegations of rape, pedophilia, and solicitation for sex by peacekeepers from Morocco, Nepal, Pakistan, South Africa, Tunisia, and Uruguay. Annan said he was "outraged" by what he called "acts of gross misconduct" and pledged action when the investigation was completed. In a related case, Annan's office announced on December 17 that two UN peacekeepers in Burundi had been suspended because of alleged sexual misconduct.

Even more embarrassing for the UN was the revelation in mid-May that a senior UN official was under investigation for alleged sexual misconduct toward a female aide. The *New York Times* reported on May 18 that an aide to Ruud Lubbers, the United Nations High Commissioner for Refugees, had filed a complaint about an incident the previous December in which she said he had harassed her. Lubbers denied the charge. On October 28 the *Washington Post* reported that a UN investigator had concluded that Lubbers had harassed his aide. Annan, however, closed the case after concluding that the evidence would not hold up in a court of law. Nevertheless, Annan reportedly expressed concerns "in the strongest terms" to Lubbers about his behavior. A former prime minister of the Netherlands, Lubbers had headed the UN refugee agency since 2000.

Implementing Previous UN Reforms

When he took office in 1997, Annan made a high priority the streamlining and reforming of a host of UN operations, starting with his own office (known as the secretariat) but including virtually every aspect of the UN's many agencies and missions. Annan's efforts came at the same time as congressional leaders were demanding major reforms in exchange for payment of millions of dollars in dues that Congress had routinely withheld over the years. In 1999 Congress agreed to release more than $1 billion in past-due money after Annan pledged aggressive action on reforms. *(Historic Documents of 1999, p. 700)*

The GAO on February 13 published a detailed assessment of the implementation of the promised reforms. In general, the GAO found that Annan had carried out many of the significant reforms in areas under his direct control (for example, revamping personnel policies so he could gain more control over the UN's sluggish bureaucracy). Many reforms that required action by or approval from member states had not been implemented, however, the GAO said. Most notable were those requiring approval of the General Assembly, which set the UN's annual budget. One example was a proposal to revamp the UN's scattered offices dealing with human rights issues, many of which suffered from weak management but were outside of Annan's direct control.

Following are excerpts from "A More Secure World: Our Shared Responsibility," a report submitted to United Nations Secretary General Kofi Annan by the High-Level Panel on Threats, Challenges, and Change and made public on December 1, 2004.

"A More Secure World: Our Shared Responsibility"

Synopsis

Towards a New Security Consensus

The United Nations was created in 1945 above all else "to save succeeding generations from the scourge of war"—to ensure that the horrors of the World Wars were never repeated. Sixty years later, we know all too well that the biggest security threats we face now, and in the decades ahead, go far beyond States waging aggressive war. They extend to poverty, infectious disease and environmental degradation; war and violence within States; the spread and possible use of nuclear, radiological, chemical and biological weapons; terrorism; and transnational organized crime. The threats are from non-State actors as well as States, and to human security as well as State security.

The preoccupation of the United Nations founders was with State security. When they spoke of creating a new system of collective security they meant it in the traditional military sense: a system in which States join together and pledge that aggression against one is aggression against all, and commit themselves in that event to react collectively. But they also understood well, long before the idea of human security gained currency, the indivisibility of security, economic development and human freedom. In the opening words of the Charter, the United Nations was created "to reaffirm faith in fundamental human rights" and "to promote social progress and better standards of life in larger freedom."

The central challenge for the twenty-first century is to fashion a new and broader understanding, bringing together all these strands, of what collective security means—and of all the responsibilities, commitments, strategies and institutions that come with it if a collective security system is to be effective, efficient and equitable. If there is to be a new security consensus, it must start with the understanding that the front-line actors in dealing with all the threats we face, new and old, continue to be individual sovereign States, whose role and responsibilities, and right to be respected, are fully recognized in the Charter of the United Nations. But in the twenty-first century, more than ever before, no State can stand wholly alone. Collective strategies, collective institutions and a sense of collective responsibility are indispensable.

The case for collective security today rests on three basic pillars. Today's threats recognize no national boundaries, are connected, and must be addressed at the global and regional as well as the national levels. No State, no matter how powerful, can by its own efforts alone make itself invulnerable to today's threats. And it cannot be assumed that every State will always be able, or willing, to meet its responsibility to protect its own peoples and not to harm its neighbours.

We must not underestimate the difficulty of reaching a new consensus about the meaning and responsibilities of collective security. Many will regard one or more of the threats we identify as not really being a threat to international peace and security. Some believe that HIV/AIDS is a horrible disease, but not a security threat. Or that terrorism is a threat to some States, but not all. Or that civil wars in Africa are a humanitarian tragedy, but surely not a problem for international security. Or that poverty is a problem of development, not security.

Differences of power, wealth and geography do determine what we perceive as the gravest threats to our survival and well-being. Differences of focus lead us to dismiss what others perceive as the gravest of all threats to their survival. Inequitable responses to threats further fuel division. Many people believe that what passes for collective security today is simply a system for protecting the rich and powerful. Such perceptions pose a fundamental challenge to building collective security today. Stated baldly, without mutual recognition of threats there can be no collective security. Self-help will rule, mistrust will predominate and cooperation for long-term mutual gain will elude us.

What is needed today is nothing less than a new consensus between alliances that are frayed, between wealthy nations and poor, and among peoples mired in mistrust across an apparently widening cultural abyss. The essence of that consensus is simple: we all share responsibility for each other's security. And the test of that consensus will be action.

Collective Security and the Challenge of Prevention

Any event or process that leads to large-scale death or lessening of life chances and undermines States as the basic unit of the international system is a threat to international security. So defined, there are six clusters of threats with which the world must be concerned now and in the decades ahead:

- Economic and social threats, including poverty, infectious disease and environmental degradation
- Inter-State conflict
- Internal conflict, including civil war, genocide and other large-scale atrocities
- Nuclear, radiological, chemical and biological weapons
- Terrorism
- Transnational organized crime

In its first 60 years, the United Nations has made crucial contributions to reducing or mitigating these threats to international security. While there have been major failures and shortcomings, the record of successes and contributions is underappreciated. This gives hope that the Organization can adapt to successfully confront the new challenges of the twenty-first century.

The primary challenge for the United Nations and its members is to ensure that, of all the threats in the categories listed, those that are distant do not become imminent and those that are imminent do not actually become destructive. This requires a framework for preventive action which addresses all these threats in all the ways they resonate most in different parts of the world. Most of all, it will require leadership at the domestic and international levels to act early, decisively and collectively against all these threats—from HIV/AIDS to nuclear terrorism—before they have their most devastating effect.

In describing how to meet the challenge of prevention, we begin with development because it is the indispensable foundation for a collective security system that takes prevention seriously. It serves multiple functions. It helps combat the poverty, infectious disease and environmental degradation that kill millions and threaten human security. It is vital in helping States prevent or reverse the erosion of State capacity, which is crucial for meeting almost every class of threat. And it is part of a long-term strategy for preventing civil war and for addressing the environments in which both terrorism and organized crime flourish.

Collective Security and the Use of Force

What happens if peaceful prevention fails? If none of the preventive measures so far described stop the descent into war and chaos? If distant threats do become imminent? Or if imminent threats become actual? Or if a non-imminent threat nonetheless becomes very real and measures short of the use of military force seem powerless to stop it?

We address here the circumstances in which effective collective security may require the backing of military force, starting with the rules of international law that must govern any decision to go to war if anarchy is not to prevail. It is necessary to distinguish between situations in which a State claims to act in self-defence; situations in which a State is posing a threat to others outside its borders; and situations in which the threat is primarily internal and the issue is the responsibility to protect a State's own people. In all cases, we believe that the Charter of the United Nations, properly understood and applied, is equal to the task: Article 51 needs neither extension nor restriction of its long-understood scope, and Chapter VII fully empowers the Security Council to deal with every kind of threat that States may confront. The task is not to find alternatives to the Security Council as a source of authority but to make it work better than it has.

That force *can* legally be used does not always mean that, as a matter of good conscience and good sense, it *should* be used. We identify a set of guidelines—five criteria of legitimacy—which we believe that the Security Council (and anyone else involved in these decisions) should always address in considering whether to authorize or apply military force. The adoption of these guidelines (seriousness of threat, proper purpose, last resort, proportional means and balance of consequences) will not produce agreed conclusions with push-button predictability, but should significantly improve the chances of reaching international consensus on what have been in recent years deeply divisive issues.

We also address here the other major issues that arise during and after violent conflict, including the needed capacities for peace enforcement, peacekeeping and peacebuilding, and the protection of civilians. A central recurring theme is the necessity for all members of the international community, developed and developing States alike, to be much more forthcoming in providing and supporting deployable military resources. Empty gestures are all too easy to make: an effective, efficient and equitable collective security system demands real commitment.

A More Effective United Nations for the Twenty-First Century

The United Nations was never intended to be a utopian exercise. It was meant to be a collective security system that worked. The Charter of the United Nations provided the most powerful States with permanent membership on the Security

Council and the veto. In exchange, they were expected to use their power for the common good and promote and obey international law. As Harry Truman, then President of the United States, noted in his speech to the final plenary session of the founding conference of the United Nations Organization, "we all have to recognize—no matter how great our strength—that we must deny ourselves the licence to do always as we please."

In approaching the issue of United Nations reform, it is as important today as it was in 1945 to combine power with principle. Recommendations that ignore underlying power realities will be doomed to failure or irrelevance, but recommendations that simply reflect raw distributions of power and make no effort to bolster international principles are unlikely to gain the widespread adherence required to shift international behaviour.

Proposed changes should be driven by real-world need. Change for its own sake is likely to run the well-worn course of the endless reform debates of the past decade. The litmus test is this: does a proposed change help meet the challenge posed by a virulent threat?

Throughout the work of the High-level Panel on Threats, Challenges and Change, we have looked for institutional weaknesses in current responses to threats. The following stand as the most urgently in need of remedy:

- The General Assembly has lost vitality and often fails to focus effectively on the most compelling issues of the day.
- The Security Council will need to be more proactive in the future. For this to happen, those who contribute most to the Organization financially, militarily and diplomatically should participate more in Council decision-making, and those who participate in Council decision-making should contribute more to the Organization. The Security Council needs greater credibility, legitimacy and representation to do all that we demand of it.
- There is a major institutional gap in addressing countries under stress and countries emerging from conflict. Such countries often suffer from attention, policy guidance and resource deficits.
- The Security Council has not made the most of the potential advantages of working with regional and subregional organizations.
- There must be new institutional arrangements to address the economic and social threats to international security.
- The Commission on Human Rights suffers from a legitimacy deficit that casts doubts on the overall reputation of the United Nations.
- There is a need for a more professional and better organized Secretariat that is much more capable of concerted action.

The reforms we propose will not by themselves make the United Nations more effective. In the absence of Member States reaching agreement on the security consensus contained in the present report, the United Nations will underachieve. Its institutions will still only be as strong as the energy, resources and attention devoted to them by Member States and their leaders. . . .

[Part 1 Omitted.]

Part 2: Recommendations

Poverty, Infectious Disease and Environmental Degradation

1. All States must recommit themselves to the goals of eradicating poverty, achieving sustained economic growth and promoting sustainable development.
2. The many donor countries which currently fall short of the United Nations 0.7 per cent gross national product target for official development assistance should establish a timetable for reaching it.
3. World Trade Organization members should strive to conclude the Doha development round of multilateral trade negotiations at the latest in 2006.
4. Lender Governments and the international financial institutions should provide highly indebted poor countries with greater debt relief, longer rescheduling and improved access to global markets.
5. Although international resources devoted to meeting the challenge of HIV/AIDS have increased from about $250 million in 1996 to about $2.8 billion in 2002, more than $10 billion annually is needed to stem the pandemic.
6. Leaders of countries affected by HIV/AIDS need to mobilize resources, commit funds and engage civil society and the private sector in disease-control efforts.
7. The Security Council, working closely with UNAIDS, should host a second special session on HIV/AIDS as a threat to international peace and security, to explore the future effects of HIV/AIDS on States and societies, generate research on the problem and identify critical steps towards a long-term strategy for diminishing the threat.
8. International donors, in partnership with national authorities and local civil society organizations, should undertake a major new global initiative to rebuild local and national public health systems throughout the developing world.
9. Members of the World Health Assembly should provide greater resources to the World Health Organization Global Outbreak Alert and Response Network to increase its capacity to cope with potential disease outbreaks.
10. States should provide incentives for the further development of renewable energy sources and begin to phase out environmentally harmful subsidies, especially for fossil fuel use and development.
11. We urge Member States to reflect on the gap between the promise of the Kyoto Protocol and its performance, re-engage on the problem of global warming and begin new negotiations to produce a new long-term strategy for reducing global warming beyond the period covered by the Protocol.

Conflict between and within States

12. The Security Council should stand ready to use the authority it has under the Rome Statute to refer cases of suspected war crimes and crimes against humanity to the International Criminal Court.
13. The United Nations should work with national authorities, international financial institutions, civil society organizations and the private sector to develop norms governing the management of natural resources for countries emerging from or at risk of conflict.

14. The United Nations should build on the experience of regional organizations in developing frameworks for minority rights and the protection of democratically elected Governments from unconstitutional overthrow.
15. Member States should expedite and conclude negotiations on legally binding agreements on the marking and tracing, as well as the brokering and transfer, of small arms and light weapons.
16. All Member States should report completely and accurately on all elements of the United Nations Register of Conventional Arms, and the Secretary-General should be asked to report annually to the General Assembly and Security Council on any inadequacies in the reporting.
17. A training and briefing facility should be established for new or potential special representatives of the Secretary-General and other United Nations mediators.
18. The Department of Political Affairs should be given additional resources and should be restructured to provide more consistent and professional mediation support.
19. While the details of such a restructuring should be left to the Secretary-General, it should take into account the need for the United Nations to have:
    (a) A field-oriented, dedicated mediation support capacity, comprised of a small team of professionals with relevant direct experience and expertise, available to all United Nations mediators;
    (b) Competence on thematic issues that recur in peace negotiations, such as the sequencing of implementation steps, the design of monitoring arrangements, the sequencing of transitional arrangements and the design of national reconciliation mechanisms;
    (c) Greater interaction with national mediators, regional organizations and non-governmental organizations involved in conflict resolution;
    (d) Greater consultation with and involvement in peace processes of important voices from civil society, especially those of women, who are often neglected during negotiations.
20. National leaders and parties to conflict should make constructive use of the option of preventive deployment of peacekeepers.

Nuclear, Radiological, Chemical and Biological Weapons

21. The nuclear-weapon States must take several steps to restart disarmament:
    (a) They must honour their commitments under Article VI of the Treaty on the Non-Proliferation of Nuclear Weapons to move towards disarmament and be ready to undertake specific measures in fulfilment of those commitments;
    (b) They should reaffirm their previous commitments not to use nuclear weapons against non-nuclear-weapon States.
22. The United States and the Russian Federation, other nuclear-weapon States and States not party to the Treaty on the Non-Proliferation of Nuclear Weapons should commit to practical measures to reduce the risk of accidental nuclear war, including, where appropriate, a progressive schedule for de-alerting their strategic nuclear weapons.
23. The Security Council should explicitly pledge to take collective action in response to a nuclear attack or the threat of such attack on a non-nuclear weapon State.

24. Negotiations to resolve regional conflicts should include confidence-building measures and steps towards disarmament.
25. States not party to the Treaty on the Non-Proliferation of Nuclear Weapons should pledge a commitment to non-proliferation and disarmament, demonstrating their commitment by ratifying the Comprehensive Nuclear-Test-Ban Treaty and supporting negotiations for a fissile material cut-off treaty, both of which are open to nuclear-weapon and non-nuclear-weapon States alike. We recommend that peace efforts in the Middle East and South Asia launch nuclear disarmament talks that could lead to the establishment of nuclear-weapon-free zones in those regions similar to those established for Latin America and the Caribbean, Africa, the South Pacific and South-East Asia.
26. All chemical-weapon States should expedite the scheduled destruction of all existing chemical weapons stockpiles by the agreed target date of 2012.
27. States parties to the Biological and Toxin Weapons Convention should without delay return to negotiations for a credible verification protocol, inviting the active participation of the biotechnology industry.
28. The Board of Governors of the International Atomic Energy Agency (IAEA) should recognize the Model Additional Protocol as today's standard for IAEA safeguards, and the Security Council should be prepared to act in cases of serious concern over non-compliance with non-proliferation and safeguards standards.
29. Negotiations should be engaged without delay and carried forward to an early conclusion on an arrangement, based on the existing provisions of Articles III and IX of the IAEA statute, which would enable IAEA to act as a guarantor for the supply of fissile material to civilian nuclear users.
30. While that arrangement is being negotiated, States should, without surrendering the right under the Treaty on the Non-Proliferation of Nuclear Weapons to construct uranium enrichment and reprocessing facilities, voluntarily institute a time-limited moratorium on the construction of any further such facilities, with a commitment to the moratorium matched by a guarantee of the supply of fissile materials by the current suppliers at market rates.
31. All States should be encouraged to join the voluntary Proliferation Security Initiative.
32. A State's notice of withdrawal from the Treaty on the Non-Proliferation of Nuclear Weapons should prompt immediate verification of its compliance with the Treaty, if necessary mandated by the Security Council. The IAEA Board of Governors should resolve that, in the event of violations, all assistance provided by IAEA should be withdrawn.
33. The proposed timeline for the Global Threat Reduction Initiative to convert highly enriched uranium reactors and reduce HEU stockpiles should be halved from 10 to five years.
34. States parties to the Biological and Toxin Weapons Convention should negotiate a new bio-security protocol to classify dangerous biological agents and establish binding international standards for the export of such agents.
35. The Conference on Disarmament should move without further delay to negotiate a verifiable fissile material cut-off treaty that, on a designated schedule, ends the production of highly enriched uranium for non-weapon as well as weapons purposes.

36. The Directors-General of IAEA and the Organization for the Prohibition of Chemical Weapons should be invited by the Security Council to report to it twice-yearly on the status of safeguards and verification processes, as well as on any serious concerns they have which might fall short of an actual breach of the Treaty on the Non-Proliferation of Nuclear Weapons and the Chemical Weapons Convention.
37. The Security Council should consult with the Director-General of the World Health Organization to establish the necessary procedures for working together in the event of a suspicious or overwhelming outbreak of infectious disease.

Terrorism

38. The United Nations, with the Secretary-General taking a leading role, should promote a comprehensive strategy against terrorism, including:
    (a) Dissuasion, working to reverse the causes or facilitators of terrorism, including through promoting social and political rights, the rule of law and democratic reform; working to end occupations and address major political grievances; combating organized crime; reducing poverty and unemployment; and stopping State collapse;
    (b) Efforts to counter extremism and intolerance, including through education and fostering public debate;
    (c) Development of better instruments for global counter-terrorism cooperation, all within a legal framework that is respectful of civil liberties and human rights, including in the areas of law enforcement; intelligence-sharing, where possible; denial and interdiction, when required; and financial controls;
    (d) Building State capacity to prevent terrorist recruitment and operations;
    (e) Control of dangerous materials and public health defence.
39. Member States that have not yet done so should actively consider signing and ratifying all 12 international conventions against terrorism, and should adopt the eight Special Recommendations on Terrorist Financing issued by the Organization for Economic Cooperation and Development (OECD)-supported Financial Action Task Force on Money-Laundering and the measures recommended in its various best practices papers.
40. The Al-Qaida and Taliban Sanctions Committee should institute a process for reviewing the cases of individuals and institutions claiming to have been wrongly placed or retained on its watch lists.
41. The Security Council, after consultation with affected States, should extend the authority of the Counter-Terrorism Executive Directorate to act as a clearing house for State-to-State provision of military, police and border control assistance for the development of domestic counter-terrorism capacities.
42. To help Member States comply with their counter-terrorism obligations, the United Nations should establish a capacity-building trust fund under the Counter-Terrorism Executive Directorate.
43. The Security Council should devise a schedule of predetermined sanctions for State non-compliance with the Council's counter-terrorism resolutions.

44. The General Assembly should rapidly complete negotiations on a comprehensive convention on terrorism, incorporating a definition of terrorism with the following elements:
   (a) recognition, in the preamble, that State use of force against civilians is regulated by the Geneva Conventions and other instruments, and, if of sufficient scale, constitutes a war crime by the persons concerned or a crime against humanity;
   (b) restatement that acts under the 12 preceding anti-terrorism conventions are terrorism, and a declaration that they are a crime under international law; and restatement that terrorism in time of armed conflict is prohibited by the Geneva Conventions and Protocols;
   (c) reference to the definitions contained in the 1999 International Convention for the Suppression of the Financing of Terrorism and Security Council resolution 1566 (2004);
   (d) description of terrorism as "any action, in addition to actions already specified by the existing conventions on aspects of terrorism, the Geneva Conventions and Security Council resolution 1566 (2004), that is intended to cause death or serious bodily harm to civilians or non-combatants, when the purpose of such act, by its nature or context, is to intimidate a population, or to compel a Government or an international organization to do or to abstain from doing any act."

Transnational Organized Crime

45. Member States that have not signed, ratified or resourced the 2000 United Nations Convention against Transnational Organized Crime and its three Protocols, and the 2003 United Nations Convention against Corruption should do so, and all Member States should support the United Nations Office on Drugs and Crime in its work in this area.
46. Member States should establish a central authority to facilitate the exchange of evidence among national judicial authorities, mutual legal assistance among prosecutorial authorities and the implementation of extradition requests.
47. A comprehensive international convention on money-laundering that addresses the issues of bank secrecy and the development of financial havens needs to be negotiated, and endorsed by the General Assembly.
48. Member States should sign and ratify the Protocol to Prevent, Suppress and Punish Trafficking in Persons, Especially Women and Children, and parties to the Protocol should take all necessary steps to effectively implement it.
49. The United Nations should establish a robust capacity-building mechanism for rule-of-law assistance.

The Role of Sanctions

50. The Security Council must ensure that sanctions are effectively implemented and enforced:
   (a) When the Security Council imposes a sanctions regime—including arms embargoes—it should routinely establish monitoring mechanisms and provide them with the necessary authority and capacity to carry out high-quality,

in-depth investigations. Adequate budgetary provisions must be made to implement those mechanisms;

(b) Security Council sanctions committees should be mandated to develop improved guidelines and reporting procedures to assist States in sanctions implementation, and to improve procedures for maintaining accurate lists of individuals and entities subject to targeted sanctions;

(c) The Secretary-General should appoint a senior official with sufficient supporting resources to enable the Secretary-General to supply the Security Council with analysis of the best way to target sanctions and to assist in coordinating their implementation. This official would also assist compliance efforts; identify technical assistance needs and coordinate such assistance; and make recommendations on any adjustments necessary to enhance the effectiveness of sanctions;

(d) Donors should devote more resources to strengthening the legal, administrative, and policing and border-control capacity of Member States to implement sanctions. Capacity-building measures should include efforts to improve air-traffic interdiction in zones of conflict;

(e) The Security Council should, in instances of verified, chronic violations, impose secondary sanctions against those involved in sanctions-busting;

(f) The Secretary-General, in consultation with the Security Council, should ensure that an appropriate auditing mechanism is in place to oversee sanctions administration.

51. Sanctions committees should improve procedures for providing humanitarian exemptions and routinely conduct assessments of the humanitarian impact of sanctions. The Security Council should continue to strive to mitigate the humanitarian consequences of sanctions.

52. Where sanctions involve lists of individuals or entities, sanctions committees should establish procedures to review the cases of those claiming to have been incorrectly placed or retained on such lists.

Part 3: Collective Security and the Use of Force

Using Force: Rules and Guidelines

53. Article 51 of the Charter of the United Nations should be neither rewritten nor reinterpreted, either to extend its long-established scope (so as to allow preventive measures to non-imminent threats) or to restrict it (so as to allow its application only to actual attacks).

54. The Security Council is fully empowered under Chapter VII of the Charter of the United Nations to address the full range of security threats with which States are concerned. The task is not to find alternatives to the Security Council as a source of authority but to make the Council work better than it has.

55. The Panel endorses the emerging norm that there is a collective international responsibility to protect, exercisable by the Security Council authorizing military intervention as a last resort, in the event of genocide and other large-scale killing, ethnic cleansing or serious violations of humanitarian law which sovereign Governments have proved powerless or unwilling to prevent.

56. In considering whether to authorize or endorse the use of military force, the Security Council should always address—whatever other considerations it may take into account—at least the following five basic criteria of legitimacy:
    (a) *Seriousness of threat.* Is the threatened harm to State or human security of a kind, and sufficiently clear and serious, to justify *prima facie* the use of military force? In the case of internal threats, does it involve genocide and other large-scale killing, ethnic cleansing or serious violations of international humanitarian law, actual or imminently apprehended?
    (b) *Proper purpose.* Is it clear that the primary purpose of the proposed military action is to halt or avert the threat in question, whatever other purposes or motives may be involved?
    (c) *Last resort.* Has every non-military option for meeting the threat in question been explored, with reasonable grounds for believing that other measures will not succeed?
    (d) *Proportional means.* Are the scale, duration and intensity of the proposed military action the minimum necessary to meet the threat in question?
    (e) *Balance of consequences.* Is there a reasonable chance of the military action being successful in meeting the threat in question, with the consequences of action not likely to be worse than the consequences of inaction?
57. The above guidelines for authorizing the use of force should be embodied in declaratory resolutions of the Security Council and General Assembly.

Peace Enforcement and Peacekeeping Capability

58. The developed States should do more to transform their existing force capacities into suitable contingents for peace operations.
59. Member States should strongly support the efforts of the Department of Peacekeeping Operations, building on the important work of the Panel on United Nations Peace Operations of the United Nations Secretariat, to improve its use of strategic deployment stockpiles, standby arrangements, trust funds and other mechanisms in order to meet the tighter deadlines necessary for effective deployment.
60. States with advanced military capacities should establish standby high readiness, self-sufficient battalions at up to brigade level that can reinforce United Nations missions, and should place them at the disposal of the United Nations.
61. The Secretary-General should recommend and the Security Council should authorize troop strengths for peacekeeping missions that are sufficient to deter and repel hostile factions.
62. The United Nations should have a small corps of senior police officers and managers (50–100 personnel) who could undertake mission assessments and organize the start-up of police components of peace operations, and the General Assembly should authorize this capacity.

Post-Conflict Peacebuilding

63. Special representatives of the Secretary-General should have the authority and guidance to work with relevant parties to establish robust donor-coordinating mechanisms, as well as the resources to perform coordination functions effectively,

including ensuring that the sequencing of United Nations assessments and activities is consistent with Government priorities.

64. The Security Council should mandate and the General Assembly should authorize funding for disarmament and demobilization programmes from assessed budgets for United Nations peacekeeping operations.
65. A standing fund for peacebuilding should be established at the level of at least $250 million that can be used to finance the recurrent expenditures of a nascent Government, as well as critical agency programmes in the areas of rehabilitation and reintegration.

Protecting Civilians

66. All combatants must abide by the Geneva Conventions. All Member States should sign, ratify and act on all treaties relating to the protection of civilians, such as the Genocide Convention, the Geneva Conventions, the Rome Statute of the International Criminal Court and all refugee conventions.
67. The Security Council should fully implement resolution 1265 (1999) on the protection of civilians in armed conflict.
68. The Security Council, United Nations agencies and Member States should fully implement resolution 1325 (2000) on women, peace and security.
69. Member States should support and fully fund the proposed Directorate of Security and accord high priority to assisting the Secretary-General in implementing a new staff security system in 2005.

Part 4: A More Effective United Nations for the Twenty-First Century

The General Assembly

70. Members of the General Assembly should use the opportunity provided by the Millennium Review Summit in 2005 to forge a new consensus on broader and more effective collective security.
71. Member States should renew efforts to enable the General Assembly to perform its function as the main deliberative organ of the United Nations. This requires a better conceptualization and shortening of the agenda, which should reflect the contemporary challenges facing the international community. Smaller, more tightly focused committees could help to sharpen and improve resolutions that are brought to the whole Assembly.
72. Following the recommendation of the report of the Panel on Eminent Persons on United Nations-Civil Society Relations, the General Assembly should establish a better mechanism to enable systematic engagement with civil society organizations.

The Security Council

73. Reforms of the Security Council should meet the following principles:
    (a) They should, in honouring Article 23 of the Charter of the United Nations, increase the involvement in decision-making of those who contribute most to the United Nations financially, militarily and diplomatically—specifically in terms of contributions to United Nations assessed budgets, participation

in mandated peace operations, contributions to the voluntary activities of the United Nations in the areas of security and development, and diplomatic activities in support of United Nations objectives and mandates. Among developed countries, achieving or making substantial progress towards the internationally agreed level of 0.7 per cent of gross national product for official development assistance should be considered an important criterion of contribution;

(b) They should bring into the decision-making process countries more representative of the broader membership, especially of the developing world;

(c) They should not impair the effectiveness of the Security Council;

(d) They should increase the democratic and accountable nature of the body.

74. A decision on the enlargement of the Council, satisfying these criteria, is now a necessity. The presentation of two clearly defined alternatives, of the kind described below as models A and B, should help to clarify—and perhaps bring to resolution—a debate which has made little progress in the last 12 years.

75. Models A and B both involve a distribution of seats as between four major regional areas, which we identify, respectively, as "Africa," "Asia and Pacific," "Europe" and "Americas." We see these descriptions as helpful in making and implementing judgements about the composition of the Security Council, but make no recommendation about changing the composition of the current regional groups for general electoral and other United Nations purposes. Some members of the Panel, in particular our Latin American colleagues, expressed a preference for basing any distribution of seats on the current regional groups.

76. Model A provides for six new permanent seats, with no veto being created, and three new two-year term non-permanent seats, divided among the major regional areas. Model B provides for no new permanent seats, but creates a new category of eight four-year renewable-term seats and one new two-year nonpermanent (and non-renewable) seat, divided among the major regional areas.

77. In both models, having regard to Article 23 of the Charter, a method of encouraging Member States to contribute more to international peace and security would be for the General Assembly, taking into account established practices of regional consultation, to elect Security Council members by giving preference for permanent or longer-term seats to those States that are among the top three financial contributors in their relevant regional area to the regular budget, or the top three voluntary contributors from their regional area, or the top three troop contributors from their regional area to United Nations peacekeeping missions.

78. There should be a review of the composition of the Security Council in 2020, including, in this context, a review of the contribution (as defined in paragraph 249 of the main report) of permanent and non-permanent members from the point of view of the Council's effectiveness in taking collective action to prevent and remove new and old threats to international peace and security.

79. The Panel recommends that under any reform proposal, there should be no expansion of the veto.

80. A system of "indicative voting" should be introduced, whereby members of the Security Council could call for a public indication of positions on a proposed action.

81. Processes to improve transparency and accountability in the Security Council should be incorporated and formalized in its rules of procedure.

A Peacebuilding Commission

82. The Security Council, acting under Article 29 of the Charter of the United Nations and after consultation with the Economic and Social Council, should establish a Peacebuilding Commission.
83. The core functions of the Peacebuilding Commission should be to identify countries that are under stress and risk sliding towards State collapse; to organize, in partnership with the national Government, proactive assistance in preventing that process from developing further; to assist in the planning for transitions between conflict and post-conflict peacebuilding; and in particular to marshal and sustain the efforts of the international community in post-conflict peacebuilding over whatever period may be necessary.
84. While the precise composition, procedures and reporting lines of the Peacebuilding Commission will need to be established, they should take account of the following guidelines:
    (a) The Peacebuilding Commission should be reasonably small;
    (b) It should meet in different configurations, to consider both general policy issues and country-by-country strategies;
    (c) It should be chaired for at least one year and perhaps longer by a member approved by the Security Council;
    (d) In addition to representation from the Security Council, it should include representation from the Economic and Social Council;
    (e) National representatives of the country under consideration should be invited to attend;
    (f) The Managing Director of the International Monetary Fund, the President of the World Bank and, when appropriate, heads of regional development banks should be represented at its meetings by appropriate senior officials;
    (g) Representatives of the principal donor countries and, when appropriate, the principal troop contributors should be invited to participate in its deliberations;
    (h) Representatives of regional and subregional organizations should be invited to participate in its deliberations when such organizations are actively involved in the country in question.
85. A Peacebuilding Support Office should be established in the Secretariat to give the Peacebuilding Commission appropriate Secretariat support and to ensure that the Secretary-General is able to integrate system-wide peacebuilding policies and strategies, develop best practices and provide cohesive support for field operations.

Regional Organizations

86. In relation to regional organizations:
    (a) Authorization from the Security Council should in all cases be sought for regional peace operations;
    (b) Consultation and cooperation between the United Nations and regional organizations should be expanded and could be formalized in an agreement,

covering such issues as meetings of the heads of the organizations, more frequent exchange of information and early warning, co-training of civilian and military personnel, and exchange of personnel within peace operations;

(c) In the case of African regional and subregional capacities, donor countries should commit to a 10-year process of sustained capacity-building support, within the African Union strategic framework;

(d) Regional organizations that have a capacity for conflict prevention or peacekeeping should place such capacities in the framework of the United Nations Standby Arrangements System;

(e) Member States should agree to allow the United Nations to provide equipment support from United Nations-owned sources to regional operations, as needed;

(f) The rules for the United Nations peacekeeping budget should be amended to give the United Nations the option on a case-by-case basis to finance regional operations authorized by the Security Council with assessed contributions.

The Economic and Social Council

87. The Economic and Social Council should provide normative and analytical leadership in a time of much debate about the causes of, and interconnections between, the many threats we face. To that end, the Economic and Social Council should establish a Committee on the Social and Economic Aspects of Security Threats.

88. The Economic and Social Council should provide an arena in which States measure their commitments to achieving key development objectives in an open and transparent manner.

89. The Economic and Social Council should provide a regular venue for engaging the development community at the highest level, in effect transforming itself into a "development cooperation forum." To that end:

(a) A new approach should be adopted within the Economic and Social Council agenda, replacing its current focus on administrative issues and programme coordination with a more focused agenda built around the major themes contained in the Millennium Declaration;

(b) A small executive committee, comprising members from each regional group, should be created in order to provide orientation and direction to the work of the Economic and Social Council and its interaction with principal organs, agencies and programmes;

(c) The annual meetings between the Economic and Social Council and the Bretton Woods institutions should be used to encourage collective action in support of the Millennium Development Goals and the Monterrey Consensus;

(d) The Economic and Social Council, with inputs from its secretariat and the United Nations Development Group, should aim to provide guidance on development cooperation to the governing boards of the United Nations funds, programmes and agencies;

(e) The Economic and Social Council should provide strong support to the efforts of the Secretary-General and the United Nations Development

Group to strengthen the coherence of United Nations action at the field level and its coordination with the Bretton Woods institutions and bilateral donors.

The Commission on Human Rights

90. Membership of the Commission on Human Rights should be made universal.
91. All members of the Commission on Human Rights should designate prominent and experienced human rights figures as the heads of their delegations.
92. The Commission on Human Rights should be supported in its work by an advisory council or panel.
93. The United Nations High Commissioner for Human Rights should be called upon to prepare an annual report on the situation of human rights worldwide.
94. The Security Council and the Peacebuilding Commission should request the High Commissioner for Human Rights to report to them regularly on the implementation of all human rights-related provisions of Security Council resolutions, thus enabling focused, effective monitoring of those provisions.

The Secretariat

95. To assist the Secretary-General, an additional Deputy Secretary-General position should be created, responsible for peace and security.
96. The Secretary-General should be provided with the resources he requires to do his job properly and the authority to manage his staff and other resources as he deems best. To meet the needs identified in the present report, the Panel recommends that:
    (a) Member States recommit themselves to Articles 100 and 101 of the Charter of the United Nations;
    (b) Member States review the relationship between the General Assembly and the Secretariat with the aim of substantially increasing the flexibility provided to the Secretary-General in the management of his staff, subject always to his accountability to the Assembly;
    (c) The Secretary-General's reform proposals of 1997 and 2002 related to human resources should now, without further delay, be fully implemented;
    (d) There should be a one-time review and replacement of personnel, including through early retirement, to ensure that the Secretariat is staffed with the right people to undertake the tasks at hand, including for mediation and peacebuilding support, and for the office of the Deputy Secretary-General for peace and security. Member States should provide funding for this replacement as a cost-effective long-term investment;
    (e) The Secretary-General should immediately be provided with 60 posts—less than 1 per cent of the total Secretariat capacity—for the purpose of establishing all the increased Secretariat capacity proposed in the present report.

The Charter of the United Nations

97. In addition to any amendment of Article 23 of the Charter of the United Nations required by proposed reform of the Security Council, the Panel suggests the following modest changes to the Charter:

98. Articles 53 and 107 (references to enemy States) are outdated and should be revised.
99. Chapter XIII (The Trusteeship Council) should be deleted.
100. Article 47 (The Military Staff Committee) should be deleted, as should all references to the Committee in Articles 26, 45 and 46.
101. All Member States should rededicate themselves to the purposes and principles of the Charter and to applying them in a purposeful way, matching political will with the necessary resources. Only dedicated leadership within and between States will generate effective collective security for the twenty-first century and forge a future that is both sustainable and secure.

Source: United Nations. The Secretary-General's High-Level Panel on Threats, Challenges, and Change. "A More Secure World: Our Shared Responsibility." December 1, 2004. http://www.un.org/secureworld (accessed March 4, 2005).

Karzai on His Inauguration as President of Afghanistan

December 7, 2004

INTRODUCTION

The people of Afghanistan on October 9, 2004, voted for the first time ever in a free election and selected Hamid Karzai as president for a five-year term. Karzai had been interim president since late 2001, following a U.S.-led invasion that ousted the autocratic government of an Islamist faction known as the Taliban. Parliamentary elections, which had been postponed earlier in 2004 because of continued violence, were scheduled for April or May 2005 but were almost certain to be postponed again. Both sets of elections were authorized in a new constitution approved by a traditional national assembly on January 4.

The election of Karzai, a moderate leader of Afghanistan's Pashtun ethnic plurality, gave the Bush administration an opportunity to claim at least short-term success for its invasion of Afghanistan and subsequent policy of promoting democracy there. Indeed, Afghanis from across the country's broad ethnic patchwork appeared enthusiastic about the election and hopeful that it would lead to peace and a measure of prosperity in their long-troubled land.

Even so, the largely ethnic-based outcome of the election appeared to indicate that the drive to unify Afghanistan was still in the very early stages. Regional warlords continued to exercise the real political and military power in much of outlying Afghanistan, although Karzai began in 2004 to curb their influence. Some ran against him in the election. Despite this resort to the ballot box, rather than guns, it was far from clear that all the warlords were willing to disband their private armies and accept rule by a national civil government. Some warlords benefited from the country's booming narcotics trade, which threatened to overwhelm the economy and possibly even the fragile new political system. Cultivation of opium poppies soared during the year, keeping Afghanistan as the world's dominant source of opium.

Afghanistan's move toward peace and democracy also remained under challenge from the defeated Taliban and its supporters in the al Qaeda terrorist network. These groups continued to mount hundreds of attacks during 2004 against the Afghan government, U.S. troops, a NATO-led peacekeeping force, and even international aid agencies. The violence hampered reconstruction efforts but did not derail the elections, offering some hope that Afghanistan's twenty-five-year period of seemingly endless wars might finally be nearing an end. *(Background, Historic Documents of 2003, p. 1089)*

The Security Situation

The lack of security remained Afghanistan's most urgent problem, as it had been since the ouster of the Taliban. During the first part of the year, violence increased from an already high level as the Taliban and other rejectionist forces tried to disrupt a voter registration drive and then the election itself. The *New York Times* reported August 1 that 179 Afghans—most of them policemen and soldiers—had been killed in attacks during the first half of 2004, compared to 119 killed during the same period in 2003. The single deadliest attack came in late June when Taliban guerrillas captured a bus carrying 17 civilians in the central province of Uruzgan and killed all but one of them when they were found to be carrying voter registration cards.

U.S. soldiers and personnel working for government contractors also were victims of violence During the first seven months twenty-three U.S. troops had been killed in hostile action, nearly twice as many as had been killed in all of 2003.

The Taliban appeared to be winning fresh recruits from rural provinces in Afghanistan. The new fighters appeared to be angered by what many Afghans saw as the heavy-handed U.S. military presence and the Kabul government's inability to provide services in remote regions. In previous years most of the new Taliban recruits had come from neighboring Pakistan, where Islamist clerics continually preached against the United States and the West.

The safe conduct of the presidential election was made possible only through an intense law enforcement effort by the U.S. military, an international peacekeeping force run by NATO, and Afghanistan's fledgling new Western-trained army and police force. Partly because of this security clampdown the Taliban's campaign against the election ultimately failed. During a year-long registration process, an estimated 10 million people registered to vote, and nearly 8 million of them went to the polls on election day. Even so, a dozen election workers were killed, and presidential candidates could not safely campaign outside their home regions.

Kabul was by far the safest place in Afghanistan. Its security was provided by about 6,000 NATO peacekeepers, called the International Security Assistance Force (ISAF), and the bulk of the new Afghan army. Despite this level of security, violence struck even in Kabul. On August 29 6 people, including 3 Americans working for a U.S. security contractor, were killed in a bombing there; it was the deadliest attack in the capital in nearly two years.

U.S. troops operated in much of the rest of Afghanistan, especially in the southern and eastern provinces where remnants of the Taliban and al Qaeda were most prevalent. The United States had about 11,500 troops in Afghanistan at the beginning of 2004 but gradually raised the number to nearly 20,000 in the weeks before the election; by year's end the total was down slightly to about 18,000. In late November United Nations Secretary General Kofi Annan pleaded with the United States and other NATO countries not to reduce their troop commitments in Afghanistan. Annan had tried, unsuccessfully, ever since 2002 to convince the Bush administration and other Western governments to provide more security in the Afghan countryside.

Afghanistan would eventually have to provide its own security. A new Afghan army was being trained by United States and Germany. Karzai had set a goal of 70,000 soldiers in the army; by late November 2004 the total had grown to about 15,000 trained soldiers, although many recruits were unable to deal with army life and deserted. Nearly half the army—three full brigades totaling about 7,000 soldiers—was deployed in and around Kabul. The army's main task during the year was providing security for the election—guarding polling stations, securing roads and searching for road-side bombs, and generally giving the Afghan people a sense of safety as they went to the polls.

The United States also was training a new police force for Afghanistan. As of late in the year nearly 30,000 policemen—and a few dozen policewomen—had been trained, a good start toward the goal of having a total force of 50,000.

The creation of new security services was taking place at the same time as Afghanistan's ubiquitous private armies were slowly being disarmed and demobilized. The UN estimated that 60,000 to 100,000 men belonged to militias commanded by various warlords, and tens of thousands more armed men served in various informal militias. Under a UN program begun in late 2002, these men were offered job training and small cash payments when they gave up their weapons and mustered out of the militias. By the end of 2004 about 30,000 militiamen had gone through the demobilization process; about 4,000 of them were teenage boys who were given training in agriculture, carpentry, or other forms of manual labor.

Despite the many steps to provide security, much of southern and southeastern Afghanistan remained conflicted areas in 2004, scenes of repeated attacks on anyone remotely connected to Karzai's government or the international agencies that supported it. The violence disrupted reconstruction projects. For example, ten Chinese road construction workers were killed on June 10; it was the largest number of foreign noncombatants killed in a single incident in the country. Humanitarian aid work also was disrupted, particularly in southern regions, which aid agencies had avoided since the murder of a UN worker in 2003. One of the highest profile attacks of 2004 came on June 2 when five employees of the Dutch branch of Médecins sans Frontières (Doctors without Borders) were shot dead in an ambush in northwest Afghanistan. It was the deadliest attack against an aid agency since the fall of the Taliban and brought the total number of aid workers killed in Afghanistan to thirty-two. A Taliban spokesman claimed responsibility, but Afghan security officials said the real culprit was a former local police chief who had been fired. Protesting the government's failure to arrest the alleged assassin, Médecins sans Frontières on July 28 said it was withdrawing all its remaining staff from Afghanistan. The agency had worked in Afghanistan, despite raging wars, for more than two decades, and its withdrawal was a major blow to the international reputation of Karzai's government.

Aside from protecting the election process, the biggest single security challenge of the year for Karzai's government came in mid-August when a rival militia commander launched an attack against one of Afghanistan's most powerful and independent warlords: Ismail Kahn, the governor of western Herat province adjacent to Iran. At least two dozen fighters were killed in four days of fighting before the Afghan army—with advice from U.S. military trainers—was able to bring the situation under control.

Karzai's aid to Kahn had a certain degree of irony because the Herat warlord had insisted on independent control of his own region and had refused to give the Kabul government more than a token share of the millions of dollars in taxes he extracted from travelers at the Iran-Afghan border. Two weeks after the attacks, Karzai finally moved directly against Kahn, firing him as Herat governor and appointing him instead to a cabinet post as minister of mines and industry. That move set off a round of violent clashes in Herat, during which local UN offices were looted and several people were killed.

Earlier in the year, Kahn's son, who was serving as Karzai's aviation minister, was assassinated in Herat, reportedly by soldiers loyal to another rival warlord. That killing, on March 21, set off set off a gun battle in which about 100 people died.

The Election "Campaign"

A political agreement negotiated among Afghanistan's factions in late 2001 had envisioned simultaneous parliamentary and presidential elections by 2003 or 2004. It was clear by 2003, however, that the lack of security, and the logistical challenges of holding legislative elections, would make simultaneous elections impossible. As a result, Afghan and UN officials decided to move ahead with presidential elections in 2004 and follow up with parliamentary elections in 2005. Even that plan proved unduly optimistic, as it called for presidential elections by June 2004; security concerns forced a postponement to October.

Registering Afghanistan's voters was an enormous logistical task. The country lacked a census or any other listing to identify potential voters, and ignorance of voting procedures was nearly universal in a country that had never experienced democracy of any kind. The United Nations was in charge of organizing the election, but since the violence made it dangerous for UN officials to travel into outlying areas much of the registration work was handled by private contractors and local employees. Despite these difficulties, 10.5 million potential voters were registered by June. That figure nearly matched UN estimates of the total number of eligible voters, lending credence to reports that many people had registered multiple times. Another 1.5 million Afghan refugees in Iran and Pakistan also were eligible to vote. The level of registrations was lowest in the southern provinces where the Taliban presence was concentrated.

From the outset it was clear that Karzai was the front-runner. An ethnic Pashtun from a prominent family, Karzai had a natural base of support in Afghanistan's largest ethnic group. He also had the full backing of the Bush administration and other Western governments that were financing much of the postwar reconstruction. An opinion poll conducted in the spring—the first-ever in Afghanistan—gave him an approval rating of about 85 percent.

At first, Karzai seemed determined to try to assemble a broad coalition by wooing the regional warlords and the Islamist fighters, known as *mujahideen*, who had led the guerrilla war against Soviet occupation in the 1980s. By early June Karzai had won pledges of support from most of the key warlords, including Muhammad Qasim Fahim, who served both as his defense minister and vice president. An ethnic Tajik, Fahim also commanded a private militia that controlled much of Kabul. Also supporting Karzai at that stage were Kahn (then-governor of Herat) and Yonous Qanooni, an ethnic Tajik who was the education minister and had been a leader of the Northern Alliance army based in the Panjshir Valley of northeastern Afghanistan. Karzai's decision to include the warlords—rather than attempting to sideline them—reportedly angered Afghans who had hoped a new national government finally would rein in the men who used private armies for personal and regional gain.

Karzai's inclusive approach came under pressure, however, when many of the warlords continued to resist demands that they demobilize their armies. Early in July UN elections experts warned the government that the presidential election might have to be delayed again because of the threats posed by the warlord armies. At that point only about 10,000 of the estimated 100,000 militiamen in the various warlord armies had been disarmed under a UN-sponsored program.

In a dramatic reversal of his earlier position, Karzai on July 26 dumped defense minister Fahim as his vice president. Instead, he chose as his running mate Ahmed Zia Massoud, the younger brother of the charismatic leader of the Northern Alliance, Ahmed Shah Massoud, who had been assassinated by al Qaeda suicide bombers two days before the September 11, 2001, terrorist attacks against the United States. The younger Massoud had been Karzai's ambassador to Moscow.

Karzai's decision to jettison Fahim was widely seen, both in Afghanistan and in Western capitals, as his most important step yet to curb the influence of the warlords. Not surprisingly, the move angered the warlords, several of whom withdrew their earlier support of Karzai and announced they would challenge him in the election. Among them was Qanooni, who resigned as education minister. Qanooni quickly won high-profile support from fellow ethnic Tajiks, including Fahim and the foreign minister, Abdullah Abdullah.

On August 10 the Afghan electoral commission announced that eighteen candidates had been certified for the presidential election. In addition to Karzai, the most prominent candidates were Qanooni; Mohammad Mohaqeq, a Shiite warlord leader who Karzai had fired in March as planning minister; and Abdul Rashid Dostum, a warlord who led an ethnic Uzbek faction in the Northern Alliance army and had fought on just about every possible side during Afghanistan's many wars. Karzai was the only candidate who appeared to have broad national support. One other candidate stood out simply because she was a woman. Masooda Jalal was an important symbol of how much had changed in Afghanistan since the days of the Taliban, which had severely repressed the rights of women and would never have allowed a woman to speak out in public, much less aspire to a political office. Jalal campaigned little, however, and ultimately endorsed Karzai.

Because of the continuing violence throughout the country, election "campaigning" was very limited—generally confined to such low-tech techniques as the posting of billboards. Each candidate also was given free television airtime. Karzai made just one formal campaign speech—in Kabul on the September 7 official start of the campaign. On September 16 Karzai was forced to cancel a campaign rally, which had been scheduled in the city of Gardez, when a rocket was fired near his helicopter as it was about to land. No one was hurt, but the incident appeared to demonstrate both that Karzai remained in danger and that his security guards had the final say over his movements. Karzai had survived two assassination attempts in 2003, and he spent most of his time in the heavily guarded presidential palace in Kabul. Both of Karzai's vice presidential running mates survived car bomb attacks, one of which came just three days before the election.

Afghans Vote

Afghan and international officials had feared that Taliban and al Qaeda fighters would attack voters and polling places October 9. Violence did break out on election day and fourteen people were killed, most of them policemen and soldiers, but the mass attacks the Taliban had threatened did not occur. Instead, election day turned out to be a day of national celebration as people lined up, many of them for hours, to vote.

The major problem proved to be a technical one. The supposedly indelible ink used to mark voters' fingers washed off easily, theoretically enabling people to vote repeatedly. As the voting was under way opposition candidates appealed to voters to stay away from the polls to protest what they called a fraudulent election. That last-minute appeal seemed to have little effect, however. Slightly more than 8.1 million ballots were cast, about three-fourths of the total voter registrations. A joint panel of international election experts and Afghan officials investigated the opposition complaints and confirmed that some irregularities had occurred but not enough to have an effect on the outcome.

On November 3 Karzai was declared the winner with 55.4 percent of the vote; he had needed a bare majority to avoid a second-round runoff. Qanooni finished second with 16.3 percent, followed by Mohaqeq with 11.6 percent and Dostum with 10 percent. The other fourteen candidates received a total of 6 percent of the vote. Karzai's vote was pushed over the 50 percent minimum with the help of 450,000 votes from Afghan refugees in Pakistan, who were to be excluded from voting in the parliamentary elections.

Each of the four major candidates received nearly unanimous support from his own ethnic group in rural areas: Karzai from Pashtuns, Qanooni from Tajiks, Mohaqeq from Hazaras, and Dostum from Uzbeks. The ethnic breakdown was not as uniform in the cities, however. Qanooni at first refused to accept the results but gave in the next day, saying he would abide by the outcome "with bitterness" and would participate "in the spiritual and material reconstruction of our country."

Karzai's victory was somewhat shadowed by the kidnapping, five days earlier, of three UN election workers in Kabul. The workers, from Kosovo, Northern Ireland, and the Philippines, were released unharmed on November 23. The kidnapping served as yet another reminder of the difficult challenges facing Afghanistan's parliamentary and local elections, which were scheduled for April or May 2005. Those elections would involve hundreds or even thousands of candidates competing nationwide. Providing security for that many candidates was certain to be a daunting task. At the end of 2004 UN officials suggested the elections probably would have to be delayed by at least two months.

Karzai's Inauguration, Cabinet Selections

Karzai was sworn in as Afghanistan's first elected president on December 7, at a heavily guarded ceremony in Kabul attended by several hundred invited Afghans and foreign dignitaries, including U.S. vice president Dick Cheney and Secretary of Defense Donald H. Rumsfeld. Karzai was accompanied to the ceremony by Afghanistan's former king, ninety-year-old Mohammed Zahir Shah, whose ouster in 1973 set in motion the years of war that brought the country to ruin.

In his inaugural address, Karzai acknowledged that Afghanistan remained plagued by violence, corruption, narcotics production, and other problems—all of which he pledged to tackle aggressively. Karzai also celebrated his country's emergence as a democracy. "Every vote that was cast in the elections was a vote for Afghanistan, whether I received it or another candidate," he said. Karzai spoke alternately in Dari (a form of Persian) and Pashto, the two main languages in Afghanistan.

Armed with a popular mandate, Karzai used the formation of a new cabinet to accelerate his campaign to undermine the influence of regional warlords. He dumped two of the most important warlords from the Panjshir Valley, including his former defense minister, Muhammad Fahim, who had maintained his own private armies despite his government responsibilities. Karzai also ejected Qanooni, his closest rival in the election. Most observers had expected Karzai would find a way to keep Qanooni in the cabinet as a nod to the ethnic Tajiks in the Panjshir valley. Instead, Karzai said he had asked Qanooni to form a national political party for the parliamentary elections. Qanooni announced December 26 that he would form such a party, New Afghanistan, and Karzai said he would support it so long as it represented national, rather than ethnic or regional, interests.

Karzai also dumped his finance minister, Ashraf Ghani, a former World Bank official who had been largely responsible for developing reconstruction plans and winning the confidence of international donors. Donor nations had pressed Karzai to keep Ghani, but Karzai reportedly eased him out as a concession to regional governors who had resented Ghani's Western orientation and influence with the donors. In his place Karzai named Anwar ul-Haq Ahadi, the director of the central bank. The other cabinet member who was well-known and highly regarded internationally, Foreign Minister Abdullah Abdullah, kept his job even though he had supported Qanooni in the election.

Rebuilding Afghanistan

After nearly three decades of war much of Afghanistan was still in ruins. The few schools, hospitals and medical clinics, roads, public utilities, and governmental services that survived were rudimentary and unable to meet the overwhelming demand. The United States, European nations, the World Bank, and other aid agencies and donors pledged billions for reconstructions, but much of it never reached Afghanistan. The aid that did arrive had barely scratched the surface. An annual conference of aid donors, held in Berlin in late March, generated $4.4 billion in promised loans and grants for Afghanistan over the following year. Just more than half that amount, $2.3 billion, was pledged by the United States.

For many of the Afghan people, the ravages of war were compounded by a prolonged drought, which was in its sixth year in 2004. The UN estimated that 4 million people, most of them in the violence-prone southern, southeastern, and western provinces, were affected by drought and were dependent on at least some level of food aid.

Providing education remained one of the biggest challenges, but by 2004 a major effort spearheaded by UNICEF had resulted in a slight majority of children ages seven to thirteen being enrolled in school. Enrollment of girls still was only about half that of boys, particularly in rural areas. UNICEF launched a new program to create 1,500 informal "community schools" in remote villages that lacked formal schools.

Afghanistan remained a place where international concepts of human rights were observed rarely, especially in rural areas. After visiting the country in August, a UN human rights monitor expressed concern about many issues, notably the almost total lack of rights for women in many parts of the country and the abduction of children, who were exported by criminal gangs into the worldwide sex and slave markets.

Refugees and Displaced People

Before the U.S. invasion, Afghanistan had the largest population of refugees and displaced people in the world. An estimated 5.5 million had fled their homes during the country's various wars and fled across the borders, mostly into Pakistan and Iran.

By the end of 2004 more than 3.5 million of the refugees had returned—not all of them to their original homes (many of which had been destroyed), but most to their home regions. Of these, nearly 700,000 returned during 2004; each received a modest stipend and travel allowance. At least 1 million were still living in refugee camps in Pakistan, and an unknown number had moved into Pakistan's cities; many of the refugees had been in Pakistan ever since the Soviet Union invaded Afghanistan at the end of 1979. Just under 1 million were still in Iran, according to the United Nation High Commissioner for Refugees. Several hundred thousand more people had fled their homes but remained within Afghanistan's borders. Of these, 145,000 were in camps in southern Kandahar province—more than one-third of them at an enormous camp called Zhari Dasht.

Narcotics Production Booming

In a November 26 report to the UN Security Council, Secretary General Annan expressed the fear that Afghanistan's economy "may well be subsumed by the illicit-drugs industry" unless there was "substantial progress" in improving security and rebuilding the legitimate aspects of society.

According to UN figures, more than 300,000 acres were in poppy production in 2004, a record that kept Afghanistan as the source of about 75 percent of the world's opium. The opium market also made Afghanistan one of the few countries in the world whose economy absolutely depended on narcotics. About two-thirds of the country's gross domestic product came from the illegal opium industry. Many of the regional warlords were either directly involved in the narcotics trade or earned money protecting it.

In his inaugural address, Karzai blamed the narcotics trade for many of Afghanistan's problems and noted "the relationship between terrorism and narcotics." At an antinarcotics conference shortly after the inauguration, Karzai pledged to eradicate poppy fields over a two-year period by helping farmers plant substitute crops, such as sugar.

Following is the text of the inaugural address given December 7, 2004, by Hamid Karzai, the president of Afghanistan.

"H.E. President Hamid Karzai's Inaugural Speech"

[IN ARABIC]
In the name of Allah, the Merciful, the Compassionate
Praise Be to Allah, the Lord of All Worlds
And Peace and Prayers Be to the Last of God's Prophets

[IN PASHTO]
Dear compatriots,
Distinguished guests,
Ladies and gentlemen,

I am pleased that this grand occasion has brought such a distinguished audience together. I welcome you all here.

On this historical day, many distinguished guests from countries around the world have joined us in Kabul. This is a testament to the sense of solidarity, cooperation and deepening relations between us, Afghans, and the international community. The people of Afghanistan cherish this friendship.

Today, as I take oath as Afghanistan's president, I reflect on the past three years—on ups and downs, on moments of both joy and gloom. During the past three years, I took encouragement and strength from our people—from the meetings I held several times a week with elders and youth, women and men, coming from the provinces;

from the strong atmosphere of national unity at the two Loya Jirgas; from the love I found in this nation for progress and prosperity; from the resilience of those fellow Afghans who were determined to leave behind the suffering and oppression they once endured, and move forward to rebuild this great nation. Nothing makes me more hopeful to the future of this country—and my ability to serve it—than the incredible experience of our people's participation in the recent elections. So it is with God's blessing, and our people's support, that I resolve to fulfill this great responsibility that has been put on my shoulders today.

My brothers and sisters,

I have heard, over the past month or so, many extraordinary stories of the Afghan people's participation in the elections. Someone told me the story of an elderly woman in Farah province who arrived at a polling station with two voter's cards. She went up to an election worker and declared that she wanted to vote twice, once for herself, and again for her daughter who, she said, was about to deliver her child and unable to come to the polling station to vote. "We are sorry, but no one can vote for another person, this is the rule", the elderly lady was told. So she voted—for herself—and left the station. Later in the day, the election worker was shocked to see the elderly women back, this time accompanying her young daughter to the polling station. Her daughter carried her newborn baby, as well as her voting card which she used to cast her vote.

Tens of other stories like this exist that I cannot tell you today. Each of these is remarkable and distinct, but they all tell one truth—the truth of the Afghan people's love for their country and concern for their future.

Every vote that was cast in the elections was a vote for Afghanistan, whether I received it or another candidate. Every voter had Afghanistan's best interests at heart. I thank all the voters who participated in the elections, and I respect their vote. I am confident, and proud, that this nation is determined to rebuild Afghanistan, and rebuild it fast; to live in security, and to stand on its own feet.

I and my colleagues in the new government feel deeply compelled, not only by your votes in the elections but also by your determination, to respect your aspirations and serve your goals. We will stand by the promises which we have made for the good of this nation. We will be steady and unflinching; we will invoke Allah the Almighty for His blessing, and will depend on you for courage and support.

[IN DARI]

During our election campaign, we presented a manifesto for the future to the people of Afghanistan. Our principal promises are concerning the strengthening of security sector and ensuring lasting stability throughout the country; the elimination of poppy cultivation and the fight against processing and trafficking of drugs; the disarmament and demobilisation of former combatants; the eradication of poverty, generation of wealth and the provision of public services especially to the rural areas; the rule of law, and the protection of civil liberties and human rights; the acceleration of administrative reform to strengthen administration, root out corruption, stop the abuse of public funds, and ensure meritocracy; the strengthening of national unity; the rebuilding and building of the country's infrastructure; and of course the strengthening of understanding and cooperation with the international community. We feel obliged to work to deliver on these promises, with the help of God the Almighty, over the next five years.

In addition to the above, a significant challenge facing us over the next few months is conducting parliamentary elections. Again with help of the Almighty, and participation of the people of Afghanistan, this challenge will also be overcome and parliamentary elections will be held on schedule, in a safe and free environment. The election of the legislature will complete the establishment of the third branch of power in our state, paving the way for a law-abiding, progressive and prosperous Afghanistan.

I and my colleagues have a duty before the people of Afghanistan to remain steady and persistent as we work to realise their aspirations. We have a duty before our people to deliver, to the best of our ability, an Afghanistan that is free, stable, prosperous and enjoying a dignified place in the family of nations.

Distinguished guests,

I must hasten to say that our fight against terrorism is not yet over, even though we have succeeded to reduce this common enemy of humanity to a lesser threat in this country. The relationship between terrorism and narcotics, and the continued threat of extremism in the region and the world at large, are a source of continued concern. A decisive victory over terrorism requires serious and continued cooperation at regional and international levels.

Three years ago, the firm and productive cooperation of the international cooperation rid Afghanistan from the rule of terrorism. The same cooperation has led to the rebuilding of the Afghan state, and significant progress in restoring peace, stability and security to our country. As a result, we have now left a hard and dark past behind us, and today we are opening a new chapter in our history, in a spirit of friendship with the international community.

May I take this opportunity to thank the United States of America for helping us so generously in so many different ways. I would also like to thank the United Nations, the European Union, Japan, Canada, some of our neighbours and many others. These countries have extended to us a helping hand when we needed it most. The help from the international community has taken us step by step over the past three years to where we are today. I thank them all for their generosity and friendship. And I am joined in this feeling of gratitude by all my fellow Afghans.

With our neighbours, Afghanistan has enjoyed an ever flourishing partnership and cooperation in trade, economic and other fields, over the past three years—thanks to the relative stability in Afghanistan and the region. A peaceful, strong and stable Afghanistan is in the interest of our neighbours and our region—I invite them to take maximum advantage of our trade and investment potential. I pledge that, mindful of our own national interests as well as theirs, we will remain a friend and a partner to all our neighbours.

Ladies and gentlemen,

Last week, during a meeting with the elders of Badghis province, as I went around greeting the guests individually, I saw an elderly man who had tears in his eyes and said to me as I shook his hand: "We want a clean and efficient government from you!" I would like all of you to leave this gathering today having heard one pledge from me: I will do everything it takes to turn that elderly man's tears of hope into the smile of fulfillment.

Once again, my fellow Afghans, I congratulate you on this historical day, on your courage to bring this day about, and on this dawn of a new peaceful and prosperous era for our country.

Oh God, make good the conclusion of our endeavour
Such that leads to your approval, and to our success

Source: Afghanistan. Embassy of Afghanistan in Washington, D.C. "H.E. President Hamid Karzai's Inaugural Speech" (English translation). December 7, 2004. www.embassyofafghanistan.org/pdf's/Events/InauguralSpeechHEPresidentHamidKarzai.pdf (accessed December 23, 2004).

World Health Organization on Preparing for a Flu Pandemic

December 8, 2004

INTRODUCTION

Health officials around the world closely monitored outbreaks of an especially virulent form of avian, or bird, influenza during the year, amid growing concerns that the virus was on the verge of transmuting to a strain that could cause a pandemic among humans. Experts warned that such an outbreak could affect 20–50 percent of the world's population and kill as many as 50 million or more. At the end of the year, the World Health Organization (WHO) urged all countries to develop or update plans for dealing with the social and economic disruptions that a pandemic of such magnitude would cause. "The global spread of a pandemic cannot be stopped but preparedness will reduce its impact," WHO said in a December 8 press release.

Avian influenza was caused by viruses that normally affected birds and, less often, pigs and possibly cats. Although all species of birds were thought to be susceptible to these viruses, domestic chickens and ducks appeared to be especially vulnerable. There were two types of avian influenza, with several strains of virus in each type. One type was a mild form that caused little damage to the birds. The other, known as "highly pathogenic avian influenza," was extremely contagious and virulent, with birds often dying the same day that they showed symptoms of the disease. This virulent form of bird flu was controlled by killing all exposed birds, disposing of their carcasses, and quarantining and decontaminating involved farms.

First recognized in Italy in 1848, bird flu periodically decimated bird populations in various parts of the world, at great economic loss to the affected farmers and countries. An outbreak of a mild version in Pennsylvania in 1983–1984 resulted in the destruction of 17 million birds, for example, at a cost of nearly $65 million. Controlling an outbreak was also difficult. In Mexico, for example, an avian flu epidemic that began in 1992 was not brought under full control until 1995.

The most recent outbreak of highly pathogenic bird flu began in December 2003, when South Korean authorities reported an epidemic at a chicken farm. Within six days 19,000 of the 24,000 chickens on the farm died; the remaining 5,000 birds were destroyed in an effort to stop the disease from spreading. Health authorities were immediately alerted because the flu was caused by the H5N1 strain of virus, which had already shown a capacity to jump from species to species, including humans, where it caused severe illness and high mortality. Even more alarming was the possibility that, in a person infected with both bird and human flu viruses, the viruses would exchange genes and create a new strain of flu virus to which humans had virtually no immunity. If such a virus contained enough human genes, it could be transmitted from human to human (rather than bird to human), creating the conditions for a potential flu pandemic.

Scientists believed just such a transmutation caused the Spanish flu pandemic in 1918, when a new strain of flu virus spread around the world in four to six months. Although estimates varied, that pandemic killed at least 20 million people worldwide and possibly as many as 50 million. About 675,000 people died in the United States. The Asian flu pandemic of 1957 killed about 70,000 people in the United States, and the Hong Kong flu pandemic of 1968 caused about 34,000 deaths in the United States.

The outbreak in Asia in late 2002 of a previously unknown, highly infectious respiratory disease alarmed the world health community, which thought it might be the start of the next flu pandemic. Led by WHO, medical scientists and health experts around the world immediately collaborated on identifying the cause of the disease, Severe Acute Respiratory Syndrome, known as SARS; treating it; and stopping its spread. In part because of the quick world reaction to the problem, SARS was contained within seven months and did not develop into a full-blown outbreak. Even so, the SARS virus infected more than 8,000 people and killed about 800, mostly in Asia. It also sent several economies into recession and caused political unrest in China, which initially tried to cover up the infections. *(SARS, Historic Documents of 2003, p. 121)*

Bird Flu Outbreak

Despite major control efforts, avian flu appeared to be firmly entrenched in bird populations in Asia at the end of 2004. The outbreak in South Korea in December 2003 was quickly followed by an outbreak in Vietnam. By the end of January 2004 Cambodia, China, Japan, Indonesia, Laos, Pakistan, Taiwan, and Thailand had all announced confirmed or suspected cases of the bird flu, although they were not all the same strain of virus. WHO said in early February that the simultaneous appearance of avian influenza in so many countries in one region was "unprecedented." The spread of the bird flu appeared to wane for a few months, but China, Indonesia, Thailand, and Vietnam were again reporting outbreaks of the disease in poultry by July. In September Malaysia became the ninth country with confirmed cases of H5N1 virus, the only strain of the bird flu so far known to infect humans.

Thailand and Vietnam were the only countries to report human illness and deaths from the bird flu in 2004, although Japan reported late in December that it suspected five people there might be infected. Altogether forty-four people in Thailand and Vietnam were infected with the H5N1 viral strain and thirty-two of them had died. Although several of these deaths had initially been feared to have been human-to-human transmission of the deadly H5N1 strain, further investigation and testing showed that the virus had been contracted directly from exposure to infected birds.

By the end of the year, bird flu had been discovered in several other countries, including the United States, where mild strains erupted in Delaware, Maryland, New Jersey, and Pennsylvania. Another strain of the flu virus that was much more infectious and fatal to poultry was found on a farm in Texas in February. The flock was immediately destroyed and the surrounding area quarantined. It was the first outbreak of that particular strain in the United States since 1984. Although this virus had never been found to have transferred to humans, the federal Centers for Disease Control and Prevention nonetheless warned people who had been exposed to the Texas poultry to see a doctor if they developed a fever and respiratory symptoms.

After the Texas outbreak was made public, the European Union ordered a one-month ban on live poultry and egg imports from the United States. Several other countries including Brazil, China, Japan, Malaysia, Mexico, Singapore, and South Korea imposed temporary bans either on all American poultry or on poultry from affected states, dampening any hopes the American poultry industry had for filling the gaps in the world market caused by the crisis in Asia.

Asia's poultry industry was devastated by the bird flu outbreak. By the end of the year at least 200 million birds had either died or been destroyed to stop the disease from spreading. Most countries that imported poultry, either live or dead, from Asia had halted the imports. Thailand, the fourth largest poultry exporter in the world, was especially hard hit, as was Vietnam, which was already experiencing acute economic hardship. The bird flu epidemic was also difficult for poorer families in these countries who were dependent on poultry for food as well as income.

Preparing for a Pandemic

Public health officials, veterinarians, government officials, and farmers, particularly in the affected Asian countries, cooperated to a remarkable degree to monitor individual outbreaks of bird flu in poultry and to take the necessary steps to eradicate it. This included destroying exposed birds, instituting quarantines, and initiating some limited vaccination of poultry. WHO also recommended that individuals involved in slaughtering and disposing of exposed poultry wear protective clothing and be vaccinated with the current human influenza vaccine to prevent the possibility of being infected with human and avian flu at the same—the condition that many experts thought could lead to a pandemic flu virus.

The United Nation's Food and Agricultural Organization set up a veterinary network in ten Southeast Asian countries, included some that had not yet been affected by the avian flu, to train veterinary workers in detecting and controlling the disease, speed up exchange of information, and better link veterinary and human health services.

At the same time, WHO stepped up its warnings that countries were unprepared to cope with a potential bird flu pandemic in humans and needed to take immediate action. On November 11–12 WHO convened an unprecedented summit at its headquarters in Geneva of about fifty officials from public health agencies, drug regulatory agencies, and drug companies to impress upon them the urgency of the situation and to explore what was needed to ensure a supply of vaccine against the bird flu as well as antiviral drugs. "We have a unique window of opportunity now to get our homework done to ensure that, when it matters most, vaccine production can happen immediately," said Klaus Stohr, the head of WHO's influenza division and the chairman for the two-day meeting.

WHO's message was reinforced by a flu vaccine shortage in the United States, caused when nearly 50 million doses of the 2004–2005 flu vaccine were lost to contamination. The shortage caused alarm and even panic among Americans who could not get the vaccine and pointed up the fragility of the system for supplying and distributing even annual flu vaccine and rationing it when necessary. *(Flu vaccine shortage, p. 639)*

The United States was the only country working on an experimental bird flu vaccine, Stohr said at the WHO November meeting. Aventis Pasteur and Chiron Corp., the United States's two major flu vaccine suppliers, were working on prototype bird flu vaccines that were expected to be ready for human tests in spring 2005. (Chiron's bird flu vaccine was being developed at a plant in Europe, not the factory in Liverpool, England, that was closed down after British authorities discovered contamination in its annual flu production operations.)

Although Stohr lamented that there was not more "momentum" to develop a bird flu vaccine, such efforts were a sort of a "Catch-22" for drug makers. Aventis and Chiron, for example, had contracts from the federal government to produce about 2 million doses of bird flu vaccine. That was obviously nowhere near enough if a pandemic should develop. Asked who would need to be vaccinated in a pandemic, Stohr said "practically everybody." Because humans would have no natural antibodies to the virus, experts thought it likely everyone who received the vaccine would need two shots. Whether that much vaccine could be produced quickly enough was highly problematic given current production practices. "The ability to respond with the production of billions of doses of vaccine is quite limited," said Wendy Keitel of Baylor College of Medicine in Houston.

For one thing, only about a dozen companies in the world were equipped to make flu vaccine, and total annual production worldwide was about 300 million doses. Flu vaccine production also took several months. "Production capacity cannot be doubled overnight," an executive at Aventis said, and "you cannot switch from [making] measles vaccine to a flu vaccine" because the production processes were very different. But stockpiling vaccine did not appear to be a viable option, either. Any vaccine produced now might become outdated, might never be needed, or might turn out to be the wrong one if a pandemic was caused by a different strain of the bird flu virus.

In the absence of a vaccine, antiviral drugs could prove useful in controlling the spread of bird flu in humans. But the antivirals likely to protect against bird flu were also in short supply. Stohr said in November that WHO had about 120,000 packages of Tamiflu (oseltamivir), the one antiviral that had been shown to have some effect against bird flu on laboratory tests. The United States was also stockpiling several million doses. "That will not go very far," Stohr said, but if targeted effectively, he added, it might be enough to "buy time" while a vaccine was being prepared. The conference did not deal with other issues that would arise in a health care crisis, such as distributing necessary medical supplies and rationing medicines in short supply.

In its December 8 news release, WHO urged national policymakers to make plans for dealing with a pandemic. Planning to maintain health care systems would be "especially crucial," the agency said, particularly if essential medicines were in short supply and health care workers fell ill in large numbers. The agency said that even under the best scenarios, experts predicted that "2 to 7 million people would die and tens of millions would require medical attention." Yet, WHO said, many countries had only incomplete plans for dealing with the effects of a pandemic and some had not even begun to plan. "While it is impossible to forecast the magnitude of the next pandemic," the agency said, "we do know that much of the world is unprepared for a pandemic of any size."

Following is "Estimating the Impact of the Next Influenza Pandemic: Enhancing Preparedness," a press release issued December 8, 2004, by the World Health Organization in Geneva, Switzerland, on preparing for an influenza pandemic.

"Estimating the Impact of the Next Influenza Pandemic"

Influenza pandemics are recurring and unpredictable calamities. WHO and influenza experts worldwide are concerned that the recent appearance and widespread distribution of an avian influenza virus, Influenza A/H5N1, has the potential to ignite the next pandemic.

Give the current threat, WHO has urged all countries to develop or update their influenza pandemic preparedness plans . . . for responding to the widespread socioeconomic disruptions that would result from having large numbers of people unwell or dying.

Pandemic Preparedness

Central to preparedness planning is an estimate of how deadly the next pandemic is likely to be. Experts' answers to this fundamental question have ranged from 2 million to over 50 million. All these answers are scientifically grounded. The reasons for the wide range of estimates are manyfold.

- Some estimates are based on extrapolations from past pandemics, but significant details of these events are disputed, including the true numbers of deaths that resulted. The most precise predictions are based on the pandemic in 1968, but even in this case estimates vary from one million to four million deaths. Similarly, the number of deaths from the Spanish flu pandemic of 1918 is posited by different investigators to range from 20 million to well over 50 million.
- Extrapolations are problematic because the world in 2004 is a different place from 1918. The impact of greatly improved nutrition and health care needs to be weighed against the impact the increase in international travel would have in terms of global spread.
- The specific characteristics of a future pandemic virus cannot be predicted. It may affect between 20–50% of the total population. It is also unknown how pathogenic a novel virus would be, and which age groups will be affected.
- The level of preparedness will also influence the final death toll. Even moderate pandemics can inflict a considerable burden on the unprepared and disadvantaged. Planning to maintain health care systems will be especially crucial. Good health care will play a central role in reducing the impact, yet the pandemic itself may disrupt the supply of essential medicines and health care workers may fall ill.

Because of these factors, confidently narrowing the range of estimates cannot be done until the pandemic emerges. Therefore, response plans need to be both strong and flexible.

Even in the best case scenarios of the next pandemic, 2 to 7 million people would die and tens of millions would require medical attention. If the next pandemic virus is a very virulent strain, deaths could be dramatically higher.

The global spread of a pandemic cannot be stopped but preparedness will reduce its impact. WHO will continue to urge preparedness and assist Member States in these activities. In the next few weeks, WHO will be publishing a national assessment tool to evaluate and focus national preparedness efforts. WHO will also be providing guidance on stockpiling antivirals and vaccines. Next week, WHO will be convening an expert meeting on preparedness planning. WHO is also working to advance development of pandemic virus vaccines, and to expedite research efforts to understand the mechanisms of emergence and spread of influenza pandemics.

It is of central importance that Member States take the necessary steps to develop their own preparedness plans. Some have already developed structures and processes to counter the threat of a pandemic, but some plans are far from complete and many Member States have yet to begin.

WHO believes the appearance of H5N1, which is now widely entrenched in Asia, signals that the world has moved closer to the next pandemic. While it is impossible to accurately forecast the magnitude of the next pandemic, we do know that much of the world is unprepared for a pandemic of any size.

Source: World Health Organization. "Estimating the Impact of the Next Influenza Pandemic: Enhancing Preparedness." Press release, December 9, 2004. www.wpro.who.int/public/press_release/press_view.asp?id=473 (accessed March 30, 2005).

Wangari Maathai on Receiving the Nobel Peace Prize

December 10, 2004

INTRODUCTION

The Nobel Peace Prize for 2004 was awarded to Wangari Maathai, a Kenyan and the first African woman to win the prestigious award, for her "contribution to sustainable development, democracy, and peace." Maathai, currently the deputy environment minister of Kenya, was the founder of the Green Belt Movement, which began in 1977 as a campaign to plant trees as a source of firewood and soon became a voice in Kenya protesting government corruption and promoting women's rights and democracy.

"Peace on earth depends on our ability to secure our living environment," the Norwegian Nobel committee said in announcing the award on October 8. "Maathai stands at the front of the fight to promote ecologically viable social, economic and cultural development in Kenya and Africa. She has taken a holistic approach to sustainable development that embraces democracy, human rights and women's rights in particular. She thinks globally and acts locally." Maathai celebrated the announcement by planting a Nandi flame tree in her home town of Nyeri near the base of Mt. Kenya.

Maathai was the twelfth woman and the sixth African to receive the peace prize, which was created in 1901 and was worth about $1.5 million. The committee had received a record 194 nominations for the 2004 award, among them Hans Blix and Mohamed ElBaradei, the two men who had headed weapons inspections missions in Iraq in 2002 and 2003. The winner of the 2003 award was also a woman, Shirin Ebadi, a lawyer and human rights activist in Iran. *(2003 award, Historic Documents of 2003, p. 1129)*

Like many previous peace prizes, this one came in for its share of criticism. The Nobel committee's decision to grant the peace prize to an environmental activist was sharply questioned by some, who said it should have been given to someone fighting more directly for peace. Others were upset by a report in the *East African Standard,* a daily newspaper in Nairobi, quoting the often-outspoken Maathai as saying on August 30 that "AIDS is not a curse from God to Africans or the black people. It is a tool to control them designed by some evil-minded scientists."

In a statement released by the Nobel committee on November 23, Maathai said she was "shocked" by the AIDS controversy. "I neither say nor believe that the virus was developed by white people or white powers in order to destroy the African people," Maathai said in the statement. She added that she was "sure the scientists will continue their search for concluding evidence so that the view, which continues to be quite widespread, that the tragedy could have been caused by biological experiments that failed terribly in a laboratory somewhere, can be put to rest." Although one theory, widely rejected by most scientists, suggested that the AIDS virus came from a botched experiment to develop a polio vaccine in the Belgian Congo in the 1950s, the most prominent scientific theory held that a virus common in African apes mutated naturally and passed to humans in the mid-twentieth century, where it eventually erupted into a pandemic. *(AIDS, p. 429)*

"The Tree Woman"

Maathai was born in 1940, the daughter of farmers. At a time when few girls in Kenya even had the opportunity to finish primary school, Maathai completed school in her native country before going to the United States, where she received a bachelor's degree in biology from Mount St. Scholastica College in Atchison, Kansas, and a master's degree in biological sciences from the University of Pittsburgh. She studied for a doctorate in Germany before returning to Kenya, where she earned a Ph.D. in anatomy at the University of Nairobi in 1971. In 1976 she was named chair of the Department of Veterinary Anatomy at the University of Nairobi, and a year later she became an associate professor there. She reportedly was the first woman in Kenya to obtain such positions.

Maathai founded the Green Belt Movement in 1977 when her work with the National Council of Women of Kenya brought her into contact with many women from rural areas. These women told of how they were having to walk farther and farther each day to find clean drinking water and firewood for cooking and heating. Maathai realized that a tree planting campaign would supply not only precious firewood, but that the trees themselves, by slowing soil erosion and retaining water in the soil, could help stop the desertification that was spreading across Kenya.

Beginning with seven seedlings planted in her own backyard, Maathai and her colleagues over the years set up tree nurseries, operated primarily by women, who in turn showed other women how to plant and care for the trees. The new trees pumped precious nutrients into the soil, offered shade for people and habitat for wildlife, and provided a steady source of firewood, timber, and construction material. The improved soil and watersheds also improved the ability of the women to grow household crops, which provided food for their families and in some cases another source of income. The tree-planting project also helped empower women, who were generally relegated to a second-class existence even in poor rural villages. Since 1977 the movement had planted some 30 million trees and provided incomes to 10,000 women who were paid small sums to plant the seedlings and ensure that they survived. Groups in several other countries in Africa had begun similar programs based on the Green Belt Movement's model.

A new dimension of the movement began in the mid-1980s, when Maathai and the Green Belt Movement began to protest what they saw as blatant land grabs, corruption, and environmental mismanagement by the government of Kenya's autocratic president Daniel arap Moi. Maathai accused Moi, other government officials, and companies connected to them of seeking to benefit financially by allowing unnecessary development and commercialization.

Maathai's protests were as legendary as her outspokenness. In 1989 she led a campaign to stop the government from building a sixty-story skyscraper in Nairobi's Uhuru Park, the only green space in the capital city. Moi called her "subversive." She and her movement were vilified in parliament, and she was threatened physically and forced to leave the country temporarily. The protests, however, raised public opposition to the park project and scared away foreign investors. In 1992 she and other women stripped naked in downtown Nairobi to protest police abuses.

In January 1999 Maathai again caught public attention after she was arrested by security forces allegedly hired by Moi to disperse members of the Green Belt Movement who were protesting the cutting down of a forest near Nairobi to make way for a luxury housing development. Maathai was beaten during the arrest, and she insisted on signing the police report in blood from the wound on her head. The housing development was never built.

Maathai and the Green Belt Movement were among those who began pressing for political reform and multiparty elections in the early 1990s. "As we progressively understood the causes of environmental degradation," Maathai said in her speech December 10 accepting the peace prize, "we saw the need for good governance. Indeed, the state of any country's environment is a reflection of the kind of governance in place, and without good governance there can be no peace. Many countries, which have poor governance systems, are also likely to have conflicts and poor laws protecting the environment."

In 2002 Moi finally stepped aside and allowed the opposition coalition to win an election for the first time since Kenya gained independence from Britain in 1963. Maathai won a seat in parliament in the same election, and in 2003 was named assistant minister for environment, natural resources, and wildlife. Maathai had three children. She was divorced by her husband, who said she was "too educated, too strong, too successful, too stubborn, and too hard to control." *(Kenyan elections, Historic Documents of 2002, p. 1044)*

Defining Peace

Controversy over giving the peace prize to an environmental activist erupted almost as soon as the award was announced. "I thought the intention of Alfred Nobel's will was to focus on a person or organization who had worked actively for peace," said Carl I. Hagan, the leader of the Progress Party in Norway. "It is odd that the committee has completely overlooked the unrest that the world is living with daily, and given the prize to an environmental activist," he said. A former deputy foreign minister of Norway, Espen Barth Elde, said that if the Nobel committee expands the definition of peace too much, "they risk undermining the core function of the Peace Prize; you end up saying that everything that is good is peace."

Others defended the committee's choice. One of those was David B. Sandalow, a scholar at the Brookings Institution and senior director for environmental affairs on the National Security Council during the Clinton administration. In an opinion piece in the *Washington Post,* Sandalow argued that environmental degradation was often a "precursor of violence." He pointed specifically to the Darfur region of Sudan, where he said "extended drought and poor land management have pushed the desert southward year after year, forcing Arab nomads from the north deeper into southern farmlands while breeding resentment and conflict." In Mexico, he said, soil erosion and deforestation contributed to a rebellion in Chiapas in the mid-1990s that in turn rocked the national government and fueled a currency crisis that had international repercussions. *(Darfur conflict, p. 588)*

The Nobel committee itself did not appear to have any second thoughts. "It is often the underlying ecological circumstances that bring the more readily visible factors to the flashpoint," said Ole Danbolt Mjøs, chairman of the Nobel committee. Mjøs acknowledged that wars and conflicts have many causes. "But who would deny that inequitable distribution [of natural resources], locally and internationally, is relevant in this connection? I predict that within a few decades, when researchers have developed more comprehensive analyses of many of the world's conflicts, the relation between the environment, resources and conflict may seem almost as obvious as the connection we see today between human rights, democracy and peace."

Maathai perhaps offered the most eloquent defense of the award in her Nobel lecture: "There can be no peace without equitable development; and there can be no development without sustainable management of the environment in a democratic and peaceful space. This shift [in the understanding of peace] is an idea whose time has come."

Postscript

In late October, Shirin Ebadi, the Iranian lawyer who won the 2003 peace prize, filed suit against the U.S. government for blocking publication of her memoirs in the United States. Treasury Department regulations restricted publication of books by authors in Iran, Cuba, and Sudan because the countries were subject to a U.S. economic embargo. American publishers were also prohibited from promoting or marketing works from the three countries unless they obtained a license from Treasury. Ebadi said in her suit that blocking publication of her book would be a "critical missed opportunity both for Americans to learn more about my country and its people from a variety of Iranian voices and for a better understanding to be achieved between our two countries." A federal district judge in New York agreed on November 2 to add Ebadi's suit to several similar cases.

Before any further court action, however, the Office of Foreign Assets Control (OFAC) in the Treasury Department announced that it was changing the regulation to allow U.S. publishers to engage in "most ordinary publishing activities" with residents of Iran, Cuba, and Sudan while still maintaining economic sanctions against the three governments and their officials or agents. "OFAC's previous guidance was interpreted by some as discouraging the publication of dissident speech from within these three oppressive regimes. That is the opposite of what we want," the Treasury Department said in a statement issued December 15. "This new policy will ensure those dissident voices and others will be heard without undermining our sanctions policy."

Following is the text of the speech delivered December 10, 2004, in Oslo, Norway, by Wangari Maathai, a Kenyan environmental and human rights activist, upon accepting the 2004 Nobel Peace Prize.

"Nobel Lecture by Wangari Maathai"

Your Majesties
Your Royal Highnesses
Honourable Members of the Norwegian Nobel Committee
Excellencies
Ladies and Gentlemen

I stand before you and the world humbled by this recognition and uplifted by the honour of being the 2004 Nobel Peace Laureate.

As the first African woman to receive this prize, I accept it on behalf of the people of Kenya and Africa, and indeed the world. I am especially mindful of women and the girl child. I hope it will encourage them to raise their voices and take more space for leadership. I know the honour also gives a deep sense of pride to our men, both old and young. As a mother, I appreciate the inspiration this brings to the youth and urge them to use it to pursue their dreams.

Although this prize comes to me, it acknowledges the work of countless individuals and groups across the globe. They work quietly and often without recognition to protect the environment, promote democracy, defend human rights and ensure equality between women and men. By so doing, they plant seeds of peace. I know they, too, are proud today. To all who feel represented by this prize I say use it to advance your mission and meet the high expectations the world will place on us.

This honour is also for my family, friends, partners and supporters throughout the world. All of them helped shape the vision and sustain our work, which was often accomplished under hostile conditions. I am also grateful to the people of Kenya-who remained stubbornly hopeful that democracy could be realized and their environment managed sustainably. Because of this support, I am here today to accept this great honour.

I am immensely privileged to join my fellow African Peace laureates, Presidents Nelson Mandela and F.W. de Klerk, Archbishop Desmond Tutu, the late Chief Albert Luthuli, the late Anwar el-Sadat and the UN Secretary General, Kofi Annan.

I know that African people everywhere are encouraged by this news. My fellow Africans, as we embrace this recognition, let us use it to intensify our commitment to our people, to reduce conflicts and poverty and thereby improve their quality of life. Let us embrace democratic governance, protect human rights and protect our environment. I am confident that we shall rise to the occasion. I have always believed that solutions to most of our problems must come from us.

In this year's prize, the Norwegian Nobel Committee has placed the critical issue of environment and its linkage to democracy and peace before the world. For their visionary action, I am profoundly grateful. Recognizing that sustainable development, democracy and peace are indivisible is an idea whose time has come. Our work over the past 30 years has always appreciated and engaged these linkages.

My inspiration partly comes from my childhood experiences and observations of Nature in rural Kenya. It has been influenced and nurtured by the formal education I was privileged to receive in Kenya, the United States and Germany. As I was growing up, I witnessed forests being cleared and replaced by commercial plantations, which destroyed local biodiversity and the capacity of the forests to conserve water. . . .

In 1977, when we started the Green Belt Movement, I was partly responding to needs identified by rural women, namely lack of firewood, clean drinking water, balanced diets, shelter and income.

Throughout Africa, women are the primary caretakers, holding significant responsibility for tilling the land and feeding their families. As a result, they are often the first to become aware of environmental damage as resources become scarce and incapable of sustaining their families.

The women we worked with recounted that unlike in the past, they were unable to meet their basic needs. This was due to the degradation of their immediate environment as well as the introduction of commercial farming, which replaced the growing of household food crops. But international trade controlled the price of the exports from these small-scale farmers and a reasonable and just income could not be guaranteed. I came to understand that when the environment is destroyed, plundered or mismanaged, we undermine our quality of life and that of future generations.

Tree planting became a natural choice to address some of the initial basic needs identified by women. Also, tree planting is simple, attainable and guarantees quick, successful results within a reasonable amount time. This sustains interest and commitment.

So, together, we have planted over 30 million trees that provide fuel, food, shelter, and income to support their children's education and household needs. The activity also creates employment and improves soils and watersheds. Through their involvement, women gain some degree of power over their lives, especially their social and economic position and relevance in the family. This work continues.

Initially, the work was difficult because historically our people have been persuaded to believe that because they are poor, they lack not only capital, but also knowledge and skills to address their challenges. Instead they are conditioned to believe that solutions to their problems must come from 'outside'. Further, women did not realize that meeting their needs depended on their environment being healthy and well managed. They were also unaware that a degraded environment leads to a scramble for scarce resources and may culminate in poverty and even conflict. They were also unaware of the injustices of international economic arrangements.

In order to assist communities to understand these linkages, we developed a citizen education program, during which people identify their problems, the causes and possible solutions. They then make connections between their own personal actions and the problems they witness in the environment and in society. They learn that our world is confronted with a litany of woes: corruption, violence against women and children, disruption and breakdown of families, and disintegration of cultures and communities. They also identify the abuse of drugs and chemical substances, especially among young people. There are also devastating diseases that are defying cures or occurring in epidemic proportions. Of particular concern are HIV/AIDS, malaria and diseases associated with malnutrition.

On the environment front, they are exposed to many human activities that are devastating to the environment and societies. These include widespread destruction of ecosystems, especially through deforestation, climatic instability, and contamination in the soils and waters that all contribute to excruciating poverty.

In the process, the participants discover that they must be part of the solutions. They realize their hidden potential and are empowered to overcome inertia and take action. They come to recognize that they are the primary custodians and beneficiaries of the environment that sustains them.

Entire communities also come to understand that while it is necessary to hold their governments accountable, it is equally important that in their own relationships with each other, they exemplify the leadership values they wish to see in their own leaders, namely justice, integrity and trust.

Although initially the Green Belt Movement's tree planting activities did not address issues of democracy and peace, it soon became clear that responsible governance of the environment was impossible without democratic space. Therefore, the tree became a symbol for the democratic struggle in Kenya. Citizens were mobilised to challenge widespread abuses of power, corruption and environmental mismanagement. In Nairobi's Uhuru Park, at Freedom Corner, and in many parts of the country, trees of peace were planted to demand the release of prisoners of conscience and a peaceful transition to democracy.

Through the Green Belt Movement, thousands of ordinary citizens were mobilized and empowered to take action and effect change. They learned to overcome fear and a sense of helplessness and moved to defend democratic rights.

In time, the tree also became a symbol for peace and conflict resolution, especially during ethnic conflicts in Kenya when the Green Belt Movement used peace trees to reconcile disputing communities. During the ongoing re-writing of the Kenyan constitution, similar trees of peace were planted in many parts of the country to promote a culture of peace. Using trees as a symbol of peace is in keeping with a widespread African tradition. For example, the elders of the Kikuyu carried a staff from the thigi tree that, when placed between two disputing sides, caused them to stop fighting and seek reconciliation. Many communities in Africa have these traditions.

Such practises are part of an extensive cultural heritage, which contributes both to the conservation of habitats and to cultures of peace. With the destruction of these cultures and the introduction of new values, local biodiversity is no longer valued or protected and as a result, it is quickly degraded and disappears. For this reason, The Green Belt Movement explores the concept of cultural biodiversity, especially with respect to indigenous seeds and medicinal plants.

As we progressively understood the causes of environmental degradation, we saw the need for good governance. Indeed, the state of any county's environment is a reflection of the kind of governance in place, and without good governance there can be no peace. Many countries, which have poor governance systems, are also likely to have conflicts and poor laws protecting the environment.

In 2002, the courage, resilience, patience and commitment of members of the Green Belt Movement, other civil society organizations, and the Kenyan public culminated in the peaceful transition to a democratic government and laid the foundation for a more stable society. . . .

It is 30 years since we started this work. Activities that devastate the environment and societies continue unabated. Today we are faced with a challenge that calls for a shift in our thinking, so that humanity stops threatening its life-support system. We are called to assist the Earth to heal her wounds and in the process heal our own—indeed, to embrace the whole creation in all its diversity, beauty and wonder. This will happen if we see the need to revive our sense of belonging to a larger family of life, with which we have shared our evolutionary process.

In the course of history, there comes a time when humanity is called to shift to a new level of consciousness, to reach a higher moral ground. A time when we have to shed our fear and give hope to each other.

That time is now.

The Norwegian Nobel Committee has challenged the world to broaden the understanding of peace: there can be no peace without equitable development; and there can be no development without sustainable management of the environment in a democratic and peaceful space. This shift is an idea whose time has come.

I call on leaders, especially from Africa, to expand democratic space and build fair and just societies that allow the creativity and energy of their citizens to flourish.

Those of us who have been privileged to receive education, skills, and experiences and even power must be role models for the next generation of leadership. In this regard, I would also like to appeal for the freedom of my fellow laureate Aung San Suu Kyi so that she can continue her work for peace and democracy for the people of Burma and the world at large.

Culture plays a central role in the political, economic and social life of communities. Indeed, culture may be the missing link in the development of Africa. Culture is dynamic and evolves over time, consciously discarding retrogressive traditions, like female genital mutilation (FGM), and embracing aspects that are good and useful.

Africans, especially, should re-discover positive aspects of their culture. In accepting them, they would give themselves a sense of belonging, identity and self-confidence. . . .

There is also need to galvanize civil society and grassroots movements to catalyse change. I call upon governments to recognize the role of these social movements in building a critical mass of responsible citizens, who help maintain checks and balances in society. On their part, civil society should embrace not only their rights but also their responsibilities.

Further, industry and global institutions must appreciate that ensuring economic justice, equity and ecological integrity are of greater value than profits at any cost.

The extreme global inequities and prevailing consumption patterns continue at the expense of the environment and peaceful co-existence. The choice is ours.

I would like to call on young people to commit themselves to activities that contribute toward achieving their long-term dreams. They have the energy and creativity to shape a sustainable future. To the young people I say, you are a gift to your communities and indeed the world. You are our hope and our future.

The holistic approach to development, as exemplified by the Green Belt Movement, could be embraced and replicated in more parts of Africa and beyond. It is for this reason that I have established the Wangari Maathai Foundation to ensure the continuation and expansion of these activities. Although a lot has been achieved, much remains to be done. . . .

As I conclude I reflect on my childhood experience when I would visit a stream next to our home to fetch water for my mother. I would drink water straight from the stream. Playing among the arrowroot leaves I tried in vain to pick up the strands of frogs' eggs, believing they were beads. But every time I put my little fingers under them they would break. Later, I saw thousands of tadpoles: black, energetic and wriggling through the clear water against the background of the brown earth. This is the world I inherited from my parents.

Today, over 50 years later, the stream has dried up, women walk long distances for water, which is not always clean, and children will never know what they have lost. The challenge is to restore the home of the tadpoles and give back to our children a world of beauty and wonder.

Thank you very much.

Source: Nobel Foundation. "Nobel Lecture by Wangari Maathai." December 10, 2004. Oslo, Norway. http://nobelprize.org/peace/laureates/2004/maathai-lecture.html (accessed January 15, 2005).

U.S. Trade Representative on China's Trading Practices

December 11, 2004

INTRODUCTION

China continued its relentless economic expansion during 2004—so much so that the government intervened to try to cool things off in hopes of averting inflation and a potentially dangerous overheating of the economy. Wrestling with the rambunctious economy was just one of the challenges for China's new leaders who had come to power in the previous two years.

President Hu Jintao, Prime Minister Wen Jiabao, and their colleagues in the fourth generation of Chinese leadership since the 1949 revolution also faced rising political dissent due to growing social troubles. The social distress resulted from the country's inefficient bureaucracy, systemic corruption, a troubled banking system, a widening gulf between urban and rural residents, extreme environmental degradation, and shortages in important resources (notably electricity, oil, and raw materials) needed to maintain economic growth for the long haul. *(Background, Historic Documents of 2003, p. 1173)*

China's Growing Role in the World

Since taking over as Communist Party chairman in 2002, Hu gradually had stepped further onto the world stage—asserting his own personal authority and, perhaps more important, increasingly asserting China's role as a rising power in international economic and political affairs. Hu's predecessors had made trips to other world capitals as supplicants, seeking investments and trade agreements to spur the Chinese economy or attempting to make sure that China's interests on such matters as the future of Taiwan were not ignored. Backed by his country's fast-growing economic clout, Hu often was in the opposite position, able to dispense investments and trade agreements on his own terms or able to insist—not request—that China's views be taken into account.

Increasingly, China was appearing to edge out Japan and the United States as the dominant forces in Asia. The Japanese economy had been stagnant since 1990, and a new surge of growth there since 2003 was attributable in large part to a growing dependence on China as an export market. According to most estimates, China was expected to overtake Japan as the world's second-largest economy within another two decades. By 2004 there already were indications that Beijing was supplanting Tokyo in some aspects of regional affairs (for example. its sponsorship of periodic, six-party negotiations over North Korea's presumed efforts to acquire nuclear weapons).

China also was moving alongside the United States as a major force in all aspects of Asian life. For many years the United States had been the first- or second-largest export market for many Asian countries—but by the early part of the twenty-first century China was taking over the first position. Most of the growth in exports by most countries in the region since the 1997–1998 Asian financial crisis resulted from Chinese demand for raw materials and finished goods, not from American consumers. *(Asian financial crisis, Historic Documents of 1998, p. 722)*

Most Asian countries watched these developments warily, especially those most closely aligned with the United States on political and security matters, such as Japan, the Philippines, and Taiwan. "If China's objective is economic prosperity, then it is no problem to Japan. But if this is a means to military hegemony, then there is a problem," the *Asia Times* on February 10 quoted Tomohide Murai, chairman of the program of international relations at the National Defense Academy in Tokyo, as saying.

China also began reaching out to India, the other emerging Asian giant with more than a billion people. The two countries fought a border war in 1962 and had been wary rivals ever since, but in a new era they were finding ways to benefit from each other's economic strengths: China as a mass-producer of consumer goods and India as an increasingly important source of computer software and back-office services for the world's businesses.

Extending its reach into the region traditionally considered America's back yard, China in 2004 made a concerted effort to strengthen its business and political ties with Latin America. Brazilian president Luiz Inacio Lula da Silva led a 450-member trade mission to China in May, and in November president Hu—along with more than 200 Chinese business leaders—spent nearly two weeks in Latin America. China's vast appetite for raw materials and other goods needed for its industries made it an appealing trade partner for many countries in the region. Chile, for example, was negotiating a trade deal with China, which had become the world's biggest importer of copper—Chile's most important export product.

Hu announced plans by Chinese businesses to invest billions of dollars in the region, including nearly $20 billion over ten years in Argentina, which was still struggling to recover from its financial collapse of 2001–2002. There even were reports that China had offered to finance a modernization of the Panama Canal, the crucial international waterway that the United States built a century earlier and had turned over to Panama at the end of 1999. *(Panama canal handover, Historic Documents of 1999, p. 850; Argentina collapse, Historic Documents of 2002, p. 80)*

For China, the highlight of Hu's trip was the November 12 announcement by president Lula that Brazil was designating China as a "market economy" under the terms of trade agreements administered by the World Trade Organization (WTO). In practical terms, this meant that Brazil renounced most of the standard tools for retaliating unilaterally against China because of unfair trading practices; under WTO rules, any country that considered China as a "non-market economy" could impose quotas or take other steps to protect its domestic industry on the grounds that China was "dumping" goods at below-market prices. Lula's step had much greater political significance, however, because it made Brazil by far the world's largest and most important nation so far to put China into the "market economy" category. Previously, Australia had been the only major country to do so.

Hu wound up his visit to South America by participating in the annual summit meeting of the Asia-Pacific Economic Cooperation forum, held in Santiago, Chile, on November 20–21. Among the other participants was U.S. president George W. Bush, who—in contrast to the enthusiastic reception Hu had received throughout the region—was greeted by street protests against the U.S. war in Iraq.

In symbolic terms, one of the year's most important signs of China's emergence as a global economic force was the December 8 announcement that Chinese computer maker Lenovo had signed $1.75 billion deal to buy the personal computer hardware business of IBM. The giant U.S. firm had developed the personal computer more than two decades earlier but had since shifted its business emphasis from hardware to services.

Another small step of potentially great diplomatic and political significance was China's decision to send a unit of riot-control police to take part in the United Nations peacekeeping mission in strife-torn Haiti. A November 15 article in the official Chinese newspaper, *People's Daily*, said this step—China's first-ever peacekeeping mission in the Western Hemisphere—"has greatly enhanced China's international prestige." *(Haiti developments, p. 94)*

China and the United States

By 2004 relations between China and the United States had become remarkably stable and predictable—in contrast to much of the past half century, when the two countries routinely eyed each other with suspicion and often allowed seemingly minor incidents to blow up into major confrontations. Prime Minister Wen had received a warm reception in Washington in December 2003, and in turn Vice President Dick Cheney visited China in April for talks that both sides described in friendly terms.

Ever since a new U.S.-China trade agreement went into effect in 2001 as part of China's entry into the WTO, economics had replaced politics at the core of the relationship between the two countries. By 2004 China and the United States had become major trading partners; the United States was China's single-biggest export market, and China the fifth largest export market for the United States. The balance of trade was decidedly in China's favor, posting a net of $124 billion in 2003 that grew to $162 billion in 2004. In part because of that imbalance, China also had become the second biggest holder of American dollars, after Japan. *(China trade agreement, Historic Documents of 2001, p. 738)*

Largely because of the trade imbalance, this expansion of trade was not friction-free. American manufacturers and labor unions for years had complained that China's low-wage economy was competing unfairly—sending billions of dollars worth of clothing, electronic gadgets, and household goods to the United States at prices that made American-made products uncompetitive. The Bush administration generally brushed these complaints aside, pointing to the benefits for American consumers of U.S. trade with China. At the outset of an election year, however, the Bush administration on March 18 filed the first formal trade complaint against China, by any country, since its entry into the WTO in 2001. The complaint said China was using its tax code to give preference to local manufacturers of semiconductor chips, primarily at the expense of U.S. manufacturers. After negotiations, China agreed on July 9 to phase out the tax preferences in a series of year-long steps.

In its annual report to Congress on China, dated December 11, the office of the U.S. Trade Representative said China had made "tremendous efforts" to comply with WTO trading rules. Even so, the report said, China's efforts at compliance "are far from complete and have not always been satisfactory, and China at times has demonstrated difficulty in adhering to WTO rules." A prime example, the report said, was China's long-time failure to follow through on its obligations to curb the unrestrained piracy there of American computer software, movies, and music (known under trading rules as "intellectual property"). After the United States launched another series of complaints about the matter, China agreed on April 21 to crack down on counterfeiters, who made hundreds of millions of dollars annually from illegal copies of American products.

The Bush administration also pushed China during 2004 to allow a revaluation of its currency, the yuan, which was linked to the value of the U.S. dollar. Economists said this yuan-dollar link meant that the Chinese currency traded at an artificially low value, perhaps by as much as 40 percent. That meant China's exports were cheaper than they would have been if the currency was allowed to float on the free market. China resisted U.S. pressure on this score, but the matter was certain to remain at least a modest sore point in China's relations with many of its trading partners, not just the United States. *(U.S. trade deficits, p. 235)*

Attempting to Manage Economic Growth

China's leaders acted at several points during the year to cool economic growth—which had reached 9.1 percent in 2003—to a slightly more modest level in hopes of avoiding inflation and other negative consequences of an overheated expansion. Government officials, China's central bankers, and economists from the International Monetary Fund and other agencies all said China needed a modest slowdown of its economy (known as a "soft landing") rather than the "hard crash" of a recession that could damage the country's hard-won economic reforms and hurt the economies of other countries that had become increasingly dependent on China's expansion.

Officials were concerned in particular about rising energy prices and shortages in raw materials, which had stymied production in some cases and posed the danger of general inflation. One of the most direct expressions along this line came on March 5, when Prime Minister Wen gave the opening speech to the People's National Congress—the functional equivalent of China's state-of-the-union address. Wen laid out a 7 percent growth rate as the government's goal for 2004, saying this would be accomplished in part by reducing investments in industries (such as automobiles and steel) and in regions that were expanding too quickly and were oversaturated with state financing. Wen also said the government would tamp down investment by increasing bank-reserve deposits.

In a move that took the rest of the world by surprise, the Chinese central bank on October 28 boosted interest rates for the first time in ten years. The increase of the one-year lending rate was small—from 5.31 percent to 5.58 percent—but it was widely seen as the first of several additional steps to put economic growth on a more moderate, and possibly sustainable, path. Despite the investment cutbacks and the interest rate hike, the economy grew even faster in 2004—at an annual rate of 9.5 percent—than the torrid pace of 2003. The latest projections were that growth would fall into the range of 7 percent for 2005, however.

In addition to attempting to cool the economy, the new Chinese leaders continued a campaign, launched in 2003, to broaden the benefits of the country's economic growth. Wen told the parliament that the government's past practice of concentrating investments in a limited number of coastal urban areas had led to a situation in which rural populations had been left behind and "development in different regions of the country is not balanced." To help improve the lives of China's 700-million plus rural poor, Wen said the government would boost its investment in agricultural production, would reduce or even eliminate many taxes on farmers, and would move to ensure payment of wages to rural migrant workers (millions of whom often went unpaid for months at a time).

Completing the Transition

A multistep transition from China's third to fourth generation of leaders since the 1949 revolution appeared to be completed in 2004. Jiang Zemin, who had led China during the 1990s, stepped down as chairman of the China's Central Military Commission on September 19, three years ahead of schedule. Jiang had given up his other top posts to Hu in 2002 (as Communist Party leader) and in 2003 (as president of the government), in the first phases of the transition. Jiang had been expected to hold onto the military chairmanship, a post that gave him significant residual power. He submitted his resignation early in September, however, and the state media on September 19 published a statement from him saying he had been looking forward to retirement and expressing confidence in Hu's qualifications to take the military job.

News reports suggested that the seventy-eight-year-old Jiang may have come under pressure from other party leaders—including Hu—to retire while he was still in relatively good health. Hu, a young leader for China at age sixty-one, thus consolidated his grip on all major levers of power and was in a position to shape the country's future for many years to come.

Maintaining Party Control

If anything, the secrecy and suddenness of Jiang's resignation from his last post demonstrated that the government was making little effort to open its decision-making processes to public scrutiny—much less to real democracy. Hu and Wen had made many more public appearances, especially in the hinterlands, than had their predecessors, and Wen told the parliament in March that some democracy would be allowed "at the lowest levels" of government. There was no evidence, however, that the new leadership was planning any serious political reforms that would erode the Communist Party's total grip on political power.

Especially in the early months of the year, the government continued to crack down on individuals who breached acceptable boundaries on dissent. One prominent case was that of Du Daobin, who was arrested in late 2003 after he used the Internet to call for political changes. A small group of protesters gathered signatures in January and February for an online petition calling for his release; the pressure won Du a sentence of house arrest, rather than imprisonment, but it did not curtail the government's campaign to control Internet use by citizens. The government also rounded up dissidents in the days before the fifteenth anniversary of the June 4, 1989, crackdown against thousands of student pro-democracy protesters who had gathered at Tiananmen Square. *(Tiananmen Square background, Historic Documents of 1989, p. 275)*

Chinese leaders in 2004 appeared to face no immediate threat of another broad Tiananmen Square-type uprising. However, there were hundreds of smaller scale protests in rural areas centering on local grievances, many of them with national implications, such as environmental damage, nonpayment of wages and pensions, or general neglect by the central government. A series of labor strikes and protest demonstrations in central China in the last half of the year drew wide attention internationally—but not in China outside the local areas where they occurred—because of the government's tight strict censorship of the news media. One of the largest protests took place in southwest Sichuan province, where in late October and early November tens of thousands of people showed up for two demonstrations against government plans for a hydroelectric dam.

The leadership took two steps toward reform with potential long-term significance. On March 14 the government pushed through the rubber-stamp National People's Congress two constitutional amendments creating private property rights and guaranteeing basic human rights in China. China already had legal protections for human rights, which were routinely ignored, and it was unclear what difference the constitutional change would make in the near future; the new law simply declared that "the state respects and protects human rights." The guarantee of protection for "legally obtained private property," on the other hand, was widely seen as having more immediate importance because it overturned official communist policy in effect since the 1949 revolution. The change offered potential benefits not only for Chinese citizens, who had faced confiscation of their property for state purposes (often with little or no reimbursement), but also for foreign investors, who had pumped hundreds of billions of dollars into China in the previous twenty years without formal legal protections.

Hong Kong and Taiwan

The Beijing government made it clear during the year that it was not ready to allow a rapid move toward democracy in Hong Kong—the semi-autonomous province that had reverted to Chinese control in 1997 after more than a century as a British colony. Pro-democracy demonstrations attracted tens of thousands of people in 2003, in part because of a long-term slowdown in the province's once-booming economy. Hong Kong was a major victim of the Asian financial crisis of 1997–1998. The failure of pro-democracy demonstrations to achieve any substantial gains—coupled with stern warnings from Beijing—cooled the fervor in 2004.

Early in the year Chinese officials made numerous statements intended to discourage the demands for democracy. In February Beijing listed Hong Kong groups that it considered to be unpatriotic, and said all leaders in the province would be subject to a test of their patriotism. Chinese officials were angered early in March when Martin Lee, a prominent Hong Kong democracy advocate, testified to the U.S. Senate Foreign Relations Committee and later met with Bush's national security adviser, Condoleezza Rice. That brought a stern warning from Chinese foreign minister Li Zhaoxing that "we do not welcome, nor do we need, any outside intervention in Hong Kong affairs."

On April 7 the National People's Congress published a statement asserting that "central authorities" (meaning Beijing, not Hong Kong) would determine if and when the province could move toward democracy. That statement brought harsh complaints from democracy advocates that the central government was reneging on its promise of fifty years of autonomy—a promise that coincided with the 1997 handover of the province from Britain to China. *(Background, Historic Documents of 1997, p. 501)*

On September 12 pro-democracy candidates failed to made significant headway in elections for Hong Kong's legislature, which exercised only limited power. Under a system tilted in favor of the government, pro-Beijing candidates won a majority of the legislature's sixty seats—even though opposition candidates won about 60 percent of the popular vote. The two dozen seats won by opposition groups appeared to be the upper limit of what they could secure under the system.

Late in the year, the Chinese government also began to compile a legal justification for action against Taiwan in the event that the island's leaders adopted a formal declaration of independence from the mainland. Officials said the National People's Congress in 2005 would pass "antisecession" legislation claiming that such a move by Taiwan would be illegal. Taiwan's pro-independence president, Chen Shui-Bian, won reelection in March but did not appear to be ready, or even politically strong enough, to press for a formal split from China. Even so, Beijing's leaders seemed determined to head off the prospect by whatever means necessary. *(Taiwan, p. 258)*

Following is the executive summary of the "2004 Report to Congress on China's WTO [World Trade Organization] Compliance," submitted December 11, 2004, by the Office of the U.S. Trade Representative.

"2004 Report to Congress on China's WTO Compliance"

The publication of this Report marks three years since China's accession to the WTO on December 11, 2001. That event was in many ways the culmination of two decades of economic reform that saw China move from a strict command economy to one in which market forces have played an increasing role. Through an accession agreement founded on the key WTO principles of market access, non-discrimination, national treatment and transparency, China committed to overhaul its trade regime and, more fundamentally, to open its market to greater competition.

The United States and other WTO members negotiated with China for 15 years over the specific terms pursuant to which China would enter the WTO. As a result of those negotiations, China agreed to extensive, far-reaching and often complex commitments to change its trade regime, at all levels of government. China committed to implement a set of sweeping reforms that required it to lower trade barriers in virtually every sector of the economy, provide national treatment and improved market access to goods and services imported from the United States and other WTO members, and protect intellectual property rights (IPR). China also agreed to special rules regarding subsidies and the operation of state-owned enterprises, in light of the state's large role in China's economy. In accepting China as a fellow WTO member, the United States also secured a number of significant concessions from China that protect U.S. interests during China's WTO implementation stage. Implementation should be substantially completed—if China fully adheres to the agreed schedule—by December 11, 2007. By contrast, the United States did not make any specific new concessions to China, other than simply to agree to accord China the same treatment it accords the other 146 members of the WTO.

China deserves due recognition for the tremendous efforts made to reform its economy to comply with the requirements of the WTO. It is beyond the scope of this Report, however, to detail all the ways in which China is in compliance with its commitments. This Report sets out to reflect the significant concerns raised by U.S. stakeholders regarding China's efforts to implement its WTO commitments and China's adherence to WTO rules. As the Report shows, while China's efforts to fulfill its WTO commitments are impressive, they are far from complete and have not always been satisfactory, and China at times has demonstrated difficulty in adhering to WTO rules.

As described in our 2002 Report, the first year of China's WTO membership saw significant progress, as China took steps to repeal, revise or enact more than one thousand laws, regulations and other measures to bring its trading system into compliance with WTO standards. However, that year also saw uneven implementation of many of China's WTO commitments.

In the 2003 Report, we concluded that China's WTO implementation efforts had lost a significant amount of momentum, and we identified numerous specific WTO-related problems. As those problems mounted in 2003, the Administration responded by stepping up its efforts to engage China's senior leaders. The Administration's efforts culminated in December 2003, when President [George W.] Bush and China's Premier, Wen Jiabao, committed to upgrade the level of economic interaction and to undertake an intensive program of bilateral interaction with a view to resolving problems in the U.S.-China trade relationship. Premier Wen also committed separately to facilitate the increase of U.S. exports to China.

This new approach was exemplified by the highly constructive Joint Commission on Commerce and Trade (JCCT) meeting in April 2004, with Vice Premier Wu Yi chairing the Chinese side and Secretary of Commerce [Donald] Evans and United States Trade Representative [Robert] Zoellick chairing the U.S. side, with leadership from Secretary of Agriculture [Ann] Veneman on agricultural issues. At that meeting, which followed a series of frank exchanges covering a wide range of issues in late 2003 and early 2004, the two sides achieved the resolution of no fewer than seven potential disputes over China's WTO compliance.

In July 2004, the United States was able to successfully resolve the first-ever dispute settlement case brought against China at the WTO. In that case, the United States, with support from four other WTO members, had challenged discriminatory value-added tax (VAT) policies that favored Chinese-produced semiconductors over imported semiconductors. The United States also effectively used other mechanisms at the WTO throughout the year, including the transitional review process for China, to draw attention to a variety of areas where China needed to make progress.

U.S. stakeholders were significantly more satisfied with China's WTO performance in 2004 than in the previous two years. For example, in September 2004, two U.S. trade associations representing many U.S. businesses doing business in China explained in a written submission:

> It has been a good year for American companies in China . . . . We believe China is now substantially in compliance with its [WTO] obligations—a marked improvement over last year.

At the same time, U.S. exports to China continued to increase dramatically in 2004, as they have done in every year since China joined the WTO. U.S. exports to China totaled $35 billion for the most recent twelve-month period, more than double the total for 2001. In fact, from 1999 to 2004, U.S. exports to China increased nearly ten times faster than U.S. exports to the rest of the world. As a result, China has risen from our 11th largest export market five years ago to our fifth largest export market today.

The reports from the private sector and improved export statistics are heartening. Nevertheless, serious problems remain, and new problems regularly emerge. Most seriously,

China's implementation of its WTO commitments has lagged in many areas of U.S. competitive advantage, particularly where innovation or technology play a key role.

The areas of particular concern to the United States are summarized below.

Intellectual Property Rights

Upon joining the WTO, China agreed to overhaul its legal regime to ensure the protection of intellectual property rights in accordance with the WTO's Agreement on Trade-Related Aspects of Intellectual Property Rights (TRIPS Agreement). China has undertaken substantial efforts in this regard, as it has revised or adopted a wide range of laws, regulations and other measures. While some problems remain, China did a relatively good job of overhauling its legal regime.

However, China has been much less successful in ensuring effective IPR protection, as IPR enforcement remains problematic. Indeed, counterfeiting and piracy in China are at epidemic levels and cause serious economic harm to U.S. businesses in virtually every sector of the economy. One U.S. trade association reports that counterfeiting and piracy rates in China remain among the highest in the world, exceeding 90 percent for virtually every form of intellectual property.

The Administration places the highest priority on improving the protection of IPR in China. At the April 2004 JCCT meeting, in response to concerns raised by the United States, Vice Premier Wu presented an "action plan" to address the IPR problem in China. Intended to "substantially reduce IPR infringement," this action plan calls for improved legal measures to facilitate increased criminal prosecution of IPR violations, increased enforcement activities and a national education campaign. The Administration is monitoring implementation of this action plan closely and will conduct an out-of-cycle review early next year under the Special 301 provisions of U.S. trade law to assess China's implementation of its IPR commitments. The Administration has called on U.S. companies to submit a range of information to enhance its monitoring of China's enforcement efforts in every industry and in all regions of China. In addition, the Administration has taken comprehensive action—under the Strategy Targeting Organized Piracy (STOP!)—to block trade in counterfeit and pirated goods, regardless of their origin. The Administration will take whatever action is necessary at the conclusion of the out-of-cycle review to ensure that China develops and implements an effective system for IPR enforcement, as required by the TRIPS Agreement.

Trading Rights and Distribution Services

Of key importance during 2004 was China's implementation of its commitments to full liberalization of trading rights and distribution services, including wholesaling services, commission agents' services, retail services and franchising services, as well as related services. As agreed at the JCCT meeting in April 2004, China implemented its trading rights commitments nearly six months ahead of schedule, permitting companies and individuals to import and export goods in China directly without having to use a middleman. China is scheduled to implement its distribution services commitments by

December 11 of this year and thereby allow foreign enterprises to freely distribute goods within China. While China has issued regulations that call for timely implementation of these commitments, China has not made clear the precise means by which foreign enterprises will actually be able to apply for approval to provide any of the various types of distribution services. In addition, China has not yet fulfilled its commitment to open its market for sales away from a fixed location, or direct selling, by December 11, 2004, as none of the measures necessary to allow foreign participants have been issued. The Administration will pay particular attention to these areas over the coming months to ensure that China fully meets these important WTO commitments.

Services

The United States enjoys a substantial surplus in trade in services with China, and the market for U.S. service providers in China is increasingly promising. However, the expectations of the United States and other WTO members when agreeing to China's commitments to open China's service sectors have not been fully realized in all sectors. Indeed, through an opaque regulatory process, overly burdensome licensing and operating requirements, and other means, Chinese regulatory authorities continue to frustrate efforts of U.S. providers of insurance, express delivery, telecommunications and other services to achieve their full market potential in China. At the April 2004 JCCT meeting, China committed to abandon problematic proposed express delivery restrictions and to resume a dialogue on insurance issues, although it has been slow to follow through on these commitments.

Agriculture

With U.S. agricultural exports totaling $5.4 billion in 2003, China has become one of the fastest growing overseas markets for U.S. farmers. U.S. soybeans, cotton and other agricultural commodities have found ready customers in China, largely fulfilling the potential recognized by U.S. negotiators during the years leading up to China's WTO accession.

Despite the impressive export figures, China's WTO implementation in the agricultural sector is beset by uncertainty. Capricious practices by Chinese customs and quarantine officials can delay or halt shipments of agricultural products into China, while sanitary and phytosanitary standards with questionable scientific bases and a generally opaque regulatory regime frequently bedevil traders in agricultural commodities. Like all commodity markets, agricultural trade requires as much predictability and transparency as possible in order to reduce the already substantial risks involved and preserve margins. Agricultural trade with China, however, remains among the least transparent and predictable of the world's major markets.

In 2004, the United States was able to make substantial headway on a number of key issues in agricultural trade, particularly in the area of biotechnology approvals and the removal of problematic sanitary and phytosanitary measures that had been curtailing trade. Given past experiences, however, maintaining and improving China's adherence to WTO rules in the area of agriculture will require continued high-level attention in the months and years to come.

Industrial Policies

Since acceding to the WTO, China has increasingly resorted to policies that limit market access by non-Chinese origin goods and that aim to extract technology and intellectual property from foreign rights-holders. The objective of these policies seems to be to support the development of Chinese industries that are higher up the economic value chain than the industries that make up China's current labor-intensive base, or simply to protect less-competitive domestic industries.

Prime examples of these industrial policies in 2004 included China's discriminatory semiconductor VAT [value-added tax] policies, China's efforts to promote unique Chinese standards for wireless encryption and third generation (3G) wireless telephony and, more recently, a government procurement policy that mandates purchases of Chinese-produced software. These are among an array of steps that China has taken to encourage or coerce technology transfer or the use of domestic content across many sectors. Some of these policies stray dangerously close to conflict with China's WTO commitments in the areas of market access, national treatment and technology transfer.

In 2004, the United States and China made important progress toward resolving conflicts over a number of these and other industrial policies, such as China's export restrictions on coke. However, more work needs to be done, and the advent of new or similar policies in the future will require continued vigilance by the United States and other WTO members.

Transparency

The foundation of WTO compliance is transparency, which permits markets to function effectively and reduces opportunities for officials to engage in trade-distorting practices behind closed doors. China has not traditionally operated according to the WTO's transparency principles, and thus its commitments in this area in many ways represent a profound historical shift. By that scale, China has come a great distance toward achieving transparency in its official decision-making and regulatory regimes. Indeed, in the last several years, China has made important strides to improve transparency across a wide range of national and provincial authorities. China's Ministry of Commerce (MOFCOM) is most notable for its impressive moves toward adopting WTO transparency norms. However, many other ministries and agencies have made less than impressive efforts to improve their transparency. As a result, China's regulatory regimes continue to suffer from systemic opacity, frustrating efforts of foreign—and domestic—businesses to achieve the potential benefits of China's WTO accession.

Conclusion

Most of China's key commitments—including trading rights and distribution services—were scheduled to be phased in fully by December 11, 2004. This coming year—2005—will therefore provide a critical glimpse at what to expect of China as a WTO member once its full range of commitments are in place.

In 2005, the Administration will continue to be relentless in its efforts to ensure China's full compliance with its WTO commitments, with particular emphasis on ensuring effective protection of U.S. patents, trademarks and copyrights in China. This work will be facilitated by additional funding from the Congress in 2004 that has allowed USTR and other agencies to increase their level of engagement and enforcement vis-à-vis China. With this additional funding, USTR established a separate office focused solely on China trade issues and doubled the resources devoted to those issues, while other agencies increased staffing levels in Washington and Beijing.

As in 2004, the Administration is committed to working with China to ensure that all of the benefits of China's WTO membership are fully realized by U.S. workers, businesses, farmers, service providers and consumers. The Administration is also committed to working with China to resolve problems in our trade relationship before they become broader bilateral irritants. When this process is not successful, however, the Administration will not hesitate to employ the full range of dispute settlement and other tools available through China's WTO accession agreement. At the same time, the Administration will continue to strictly enforce its trade laws to ensure that U.S. interests are not harmed by unfair trade practices.

Source: U.S. Office of the United States Trade Representative. "2004 Report to Congress on China's WTO Compliance." December 11, 2004. www.ustr.gov/assets/Document_Library/Reports_Publications/2004/asset_upload_file281_6986.pdf (accessed April 20, 2005).

UN Special Envoy on Ethnic Violence in Kosovo

December 16, 2004

INTRODUCTION

The worst ethnic violence in the Balkans in five years broke out in Kosovo in mid-March 2004, underlining the continuing fragility of international efforts to bring harmony to the troubled lands of the former Yugoslavia. Two days of mob violence by ethnic Albanians drove several thousand ethnic Serbs from their homes and killed nineteen people. While mild compared with the wide-scale killings and ethnic purges that characterized Kosovo's 1998–1999 war, the violence represented a major setback for the United Nations–led campaign to make Kosovo stable enough for the opening of negotiations in 2005 on its long-term future. A special UN envoy reported that Kosovo was in danger of lapsing back into more violence and instability—potentially endangering its neighbors in the Balkans—unless theinternational community made major changes in its approach to the province.

Other areas of the former Yugoslavia also struggled during 2004 to deal with the lingering consequences of ethnic conflicts that seized the region during the 1990s. In Bosnia and Serbia, new generations of ethnic nationalist politicians had learned to use elections to advance their sectarian causes, and in Macedonia an attempt to subvert a three-year-old peace agreement was narrowly avoided.

Violence in Kosovo

Ever since NATO forces snatched Kosovo from the former Yugoslav government in 1999, the province had been a ward of the international community. Its security was provided by NATO peacekeepers and UN-recruited police. Its economy was heavily dependent on international aid, and its government was supervised closely by a UN administration. Kosovo's 1.8 million ethnic Albanian Muslims and 100,000 remaining ethnic Serbs were segregated into their own communities, with the Serbs dependent on NATO troops and UN police for protection. Technically, Kosovo still remained a province of Serbia, which had been the heart of Yugoslavia until it dissolved in the early 1990s, eventually to be replaced by the fragile union of Serbia and Montenegro. It seemed highly unlikely, however, that the Serbian government in Belgrade would ever regain anything more than a symbolic link with Kosovo. *(Background, Historic Documents of 1999, p. 119; Historic Documents of 2003, p. 1138)*

For the most part, Kosovo had been relatively peaceful since the 1998–1999 war, although there had been numerous limited cases of violence between Albanians and Serbs, whom the war had had driven apart. Latent hostilities broke into the open on March 17 when Albanians rioted after three Albanian boys drowned when they allegedly were being chased by Serbs in the northern city of Mitrovica. The rioting quickly spread throughout the province and developed into a campaign of "ethnic cleansing" of Serbs by the Albanian majority.

In nearly three dozen locations, Albanian mobs totaling 30,000 to 50,000 (according to varying police reports) attacked Serbs, other minorities (such as Roma, or gypsies), and even UN officials. More than 900 houses and 45 churches and monasteries were burned, many of them totally destroyed. Some 4,000 Serbs were forced from their homes, according to UN figures. Casualty figures varied, but the UN eventually settled on an estimate that 19 people were killed and nearly 1,000 were wounded in two days of violence. Britain, France, Germany, Italy, and other countries rushed nearly 2,000 additional soldiers to Kosovo to bolster the NATO peacekeeping force, which at the time had about 17,000 troops.

The worst violence targeted Serbs who lived in isolated towns and villages. One example was the village of Obilic, which before the war was mainly Serbian; most Serbs left during or after the war, and all the remaining ones fled as a result of the violence in March.

UN officials and other observers said the riots appeared to reflect mass frustration in the Albanian community about high unemployment (estimated at about 60 percent), the unresolved political status of Kosovo, and continuing fears that the Belgrade government might somehow regain control of the province. "This isn't what we fought for, to be half-free," one former Kosovar Albanian guerrilla, Bajram Redenica, told the *Christian Science Monitor.*

Albanian political leaders denounced the violence, but only under international pressure. Harri Holkeri, who headed the UN mission in Kosovo at the time, later told the Security Council that Albanian leaders had been "tardy" in condemning attacks on Serbs. Holkeri also appeared to endorse the view of some observers who said the violence was orchestrated by Albanian hard-liners whose ultimate aim was to drive all remaining Serbs out of the province. He said the violence was perpetrated by a small minority determined to "govern through violence and intimidation, holding all the people of Kosovo hostage to their aims." Human Rights Watch reported cases in which Albanian rioters specifically targeted Serbs who had recently returned to Kosovo after having been driven out during the 1998–1999 war. More than 270 people were arrested on charges related to the riots, but Kosovo's Albanian-led government was slow in bringing them to justice.

The Kosovo government agreed to rebuild the Serb houses damaged during the violence and had completed much of that work by November. Even so, only about half of the Serbs who had been driven from their homes had returned. The government also allocated money to rebuild the Serb Orthodox churches and shrines damaged in the rioting, but the church disputed some details of the rebuilding program, so little of that work had been done by year's end.

In addition to hurting people and damaging buildings, the March violence threatened to set back the already halting process of establishing democracy in Kosovo in anticipation of negotiations on the province's political future—called "final status" in the UN's language. In 2003 the UN mission announced a series of eight "standards" on adherence to democracy and the rule of law that would be used to determine whether Kosovo was ready to govern itself, either as an independent nation or under some kind of loose affiliation with Serbia or possibly even Albania. The UN's slogan was "standards before status," which implied that Kosovo had to make substantial progress in reaching the standards before its final status could be determined. Many Kosovar Albanians said that approach set an impossibly high goal, in effect requiring the province to become a mini-Switzerland in just a few years.

On March 31, two weeks after the riots, UN administrator Holkeri and prime minister Bajram Rexhepi launched an ambitious program to implement the eight standards. In a sign that Serbs saw little chance that the program would benefit them, Serbian politicians refused to participate.

A UN Reassessment in Kosovo

Citing health reasons, Holkeri, a former Finnish prime minister, resigned from the UN mission in April after serving less than a year; news reports said he was suffering from stress and fatigue related to the violence. He was succeeded in August by Danish diplomat Soren Jessen-Petersen, who had been the representative of the European Union (EU) in Macedonia.

During the transition, United Nations Secretary General Kofi Annan commissioned Kai Eide, Norway's ambassador to the UN, to review international policy toward Kosovo. Eide submitted a confidential report on July 23; it was made public on December 16. The unusually caustic report was sharply critical of UN policies that were seen widely in Kosovo as thwarting the desires of all parties there. The opening paragraph of the report's summary described "growing dissatisfaction and frustration" on both sides of Kosovo's ethnic divide:

> Seen from the Kosovo Albanian majority, the main cause is not of inter-ethnic nature, but stems from what is rightly seen as a serious lack of economic opportunities and an absence of clear political perspective [diplomatic language for the future political status of Kosovo]. As a Kosovo Albanian student said, "You gave us freedom, but not a future." The Kosovo Serbs believe—also rightly—that they are victims of a campaign to reduce their presence in Kosovo to a scattered rural population.

Eide's report also had harsh words for the UN administration in Kosovo, saying it had given "an impression of being in disarray" at the time of the March violence. The "international community" (by which he meant the UN, the EU, and the United States—the principal actors on Kosovo) "had failed to read the mood of the population" in Kosovo, Eide said. The international community, he added, "is today seen by Kosovo Albanians as having gone from opening the way to now standing in the way. It is seen by Kosovo Serbs as having gone from securing the return of so many to being unable to ensure the return of so few." Eide also criticized the "standards before status" policy as lacking credibility because it was widely seen in Kosovo as "unachievable." Everyone in Kosovo, he said, suffered because of uncertainty about the region's political future. That uncertainty would be resolved, however, only if the UN mission—with the backing of the Security Council—could exert "strong pressure" on both Albanians and Serbs to cooperate with one another.

With Eide's report in hand, Annan met on September 20 with key officials from the European Union for a reconsideration of basic elements of international policy toward Kosovo. Following that meeting Annan reportedly pressed his new envoy, Jessen-Petersen, to speed up the process of turning administrative functions over to the Kosovo government. Jessen-Petersen told the UN Security Council on November 29 that he was establishing three new ministries for the Kosovo government and planning further ones to handle purely local functions.

The Kosovo government that was to get these new powers would have a significantly different look as the result of parliamentary elections on October 23. As in Kosovo's first election in 2001, two main ethnic Albanian parties dominated the outcome: the Democratic League of Kosovo (headed by President Ibrahim Rugova), with 45.4 percent, and the Democratic Party of Kosovo with 28.9 percent. But a third party, the Alliance for the Future of Kosovo, headed by Ramush Haradinaj, proved to be the kingmaker with its 8.4 percent of the vote. Only about 2,000 ethnic Serbs had voted in the October 23 election; the rest had boycotted the voting in response to the urgings of some Serb leaders in Belgrade or because they were afraid to go to the polls.

Haradinaj on November 19 struck a deal with Rugova that put their two parties in charge of the government and gave Haradinaj the job of prime minister. The arrangement was controversial, both in Kosovo and internationally, for two reasons. First, it meant that power would be shared by two Kosovar Albanian leaders who had taken opposite positions at the outset of the 1998–1999 conflict. Rugova had opposed the use of violence, while Haradinaj had been a popular leader of the Albanian guerrilla organization, the Kosovo Liberation Army, which had fought Yugoslav control of the province. In addition, Haradinaj himself was a controversial figure because of his alleged participation in anti-Serb atrocities during the war. Just two weeks after the election, on November 6, the UN war crimes tribunal said it wanted to interview Haradinaj about his activities in the war—a step that threatened the political negotiations then under way in Kosovo. Carla Del Ponte, chief prosecutor for the UN panel, later backed away from issuing an indictment of Haradinaj, clearing the way for the deal that put him in office.

Jessen-Petersen adopted a hands-off stance toward the formation of the new government. Even so, he used a speech to the new parliament on December 3 to issue a thinly veiled warning to Haradinaj and other hard-line Albanian politicians: "I am prepared to challenge officials who fail to carry out their duties responsibly, or who block attempts to make improvements in key areas such as minority rights, freedom of movement, returns of displaced persons, equal provision of services, responsible media, and security."

Annan on November 17 sent the Security Council a set of recommendations incorporating recommendations from Eide's report and the results of the September consultations with European officials. The UN made the documents public on December 16. The key change from past policy appeared to be the setting of priorities among the eight standards that were being used to judge Kosovo's progress. This in effect represented a recognition by the UN that Kosovo could not achieve uniform progress toward all eight standards. On December 17 Jessen-Petersen announced that he and prime minister Haradinaj had agreed on priorities among the standards—but he did not make them public.

UN officials said another priority was to gain cooperation from Serbian leaders in Belgrade, who still had the potential to undermine any agreements on Kosovo's long-term future. Serbia's new prime minister, Vojislav Kostunica, left no doubt that Belgrade opposed any form of independence for Kosovo, which had deep historical significance for Serbs going back six centuries. "I can't imagine independence for Kosovo would happen without very serious consequences for peace in the region," he told the BBC on September 17.

Bosnia

Of all the Balkan wars of the 1990s, by far the most damaging was in Bosnia-Herzegovina. An interethnic conflict among Croats, Muslims, and Serbs between 1992 and 1995 killed an estimated 200,000 people, pushed at least 2 million people from their homes, and shredded the fabric of what had been remarkable harmony among the three disparate communities. A peace agreement signed near Dayton, Ohio, under U.S. supervision in 1995 ended the war but left Bosnia into two distinct parts: a Croat-Muslim federation and a Bosnian Serb republic. In theory, these parts were united by a weak central government. In practice, the real unifying forces were a strong NATO peacekeeping contingent and a United Nations supervisory administration with wide powers to impose its will. *(Background, Historic Documents of 2003, p. 460)*

By 2004 Bosnia had been at peace for nine years, but the economy remained a shambles and the UN authority's attempts to build a viable national government had met with only limited success. Perhaps the most vigorous actor in Bosnian affairs remained the head of the UN mission—British politician Paddy Ashdown, who had taken over the job in 2002 and had not hesitated to use his powers to nudge Bosnia's leaders down the path he said would lead to a brighter future, including admission to the EU.

Ashdown clearly had lost his patience with the leaders of the Bosnian Serb republic (known as the *Republika Srpska*, in Serbo-Croatian), who had refused to hand over any of the Serbian suspects who had been indicted by a United Nations tribunal on war crimes charges. Chief among these suspects was the former Bosnian Serb leader, Radovan Karadzic, who faced several war crimes indictments but reportedly lived with local government protection in the Bosnian Serb republic.

On June 3 Ashdown targeted the leadership of the Serbian Democratic Party, firing sixty officials, including the speaker of the Bosnian Serb parliament, Dragan Kalinic; the interior minister; the police chief; and other officials. "We have to get rid of the cancer of obstructionism and corruption in the [Bosnian Serb] structures and nothing less than major surgery will do," he said. Ashdown froze the party's bank accounts and imposed sanctions against private businessmen.

If Ashdown had any expectation that his action would force the Serbs to hand over Karadzic, he was disappointed. Kalinic was defiant, saying that "Karadzic is most likely protected by God and angels." Four months later, Ashdown took his message directly to the Bosnian Serb parliamentarians. In a tough speech to the assembly on November 2 Ashdown accused the Bosnian Serb republic of violating the Dayton peace agreement for nine years through its refusal to hand over war crimes suspects. That refusal was the single most important impediment to the aspirations of Bosnia, as a whole, to join the EU and NATO, he told the Serb assembly. "One major barrier—only one—now separates you, your children, and your grandchildren from the path to success, which you have done so much to win," Ashdown said. "You know what it is. You have to remove it. Don't delay. Just do it."

Ashdown stepped up the pressure on December 16, firing nine more Bosnian Serb government officials. In what appeared to be a coordinated move, on that same day the United States imposed a travel ban on the Serb region's ruling party. Protesting those moves, Bosnian Serb prime minister Dragan Mikerevic and his foreign minister, Mladen Ivani, both resigned.

The closest the Bosnian Serbs came to meeting Ashdown's demands was a limited apology by the Serb assembly for the 1995 massacre at Srebrenica, in which about 8,000 Muslim men and boys were killed by Serb forces. Mikerevic attended the annual commemoration of the massacre on July 11 and said, "I am here to pay tribute to the victims." *(Srebrenica massacre, Historic Documents of 1999, p. 735)*

In both halves of Bosnia—the Serb republic and the Croat-Muslim federation—2004 saw a further consolidation of political gains by the nationalist political parties that had led Bosnia into the war. Karadzic and his Croat and Muslim counterparts from the war years were no longer in power, but a new generation of nationalist leaders had come to office because many voters in each of the three communities were frustrated by the lack of progress on their own demands. Although Ashdown had persuaded those parties to sign onto a joint "jobs and justice" platform that promised programs to benefit the entire nation, it was clear that key leaders remained primarily interested in advancing the causes of each of their ethnic communities. Local elections held October 2 produced victories for the nationalist parties in most jurisdictions. These were the first elections since the war to be organized by the Bosnians themselves, rather than by the UN administration.

Another turning point for Bosnia came December 2, when the European Union took over command from NATO of the 7,000-strong peacekeeping force. In essence, most of the troops in NATO's mission (called SFOR, for Stabilization Force), simply switched patches on their uniforms to EUFOR (for European Union Force). The transfer of power had been authorized on November 22 by the UN Security Council in Resolution 1575.

Even after the transfer, NATO kept a small U.S.-led headquarters in Sarajevo, focusing on pursuing war criminals, helping unite Bosnia's two separate armies, preparing the country for eventual NATO membership, and continuing NATO's search for Karadzic. NATO troops made several attempts during the year to capture Karadzic but failed each time. The United States also retained a semi-permanent base at Tuzla in northeast Bosnia, with about 200 troops, described as a platform for staging operations elsewhere in the region.

In terms of symbolism, one of the year's most important events was the formal reopening on July 23 of the famous stone bridge that crossed the Neretva River in Mostar, in south-central Bosnia. The graceful arch, built by the Turkish Ottoman Empire in the sixteenth century, was destroyed by Croatian artillery in November 1993, during the height of fighting between Croat and Muslim forces. The destruction of the bridge left Mostar as a divided city, with Croats living on one side of the river and most Muslims on the other. European nations and other donors spent more than $13 million rebuilding the bridge to be an exact duplicate of the original. The official opening was marked with a celebration of song and dance, but there seemed little chance that even the rebuilt bridge would restore Mostar's long-lost ethnic harmony.

Yet another milestone was reached September 21 when the United Nations High Commissioner for Refugees (UNHCR) announced that the number of Bosnian refugees who had returned to their homes finally topped 1 million. That figure represented about one-half of all the people of Bosnia who had fled their homes during the war. Of the returnees, 440,000 were people who had fled into neighboring countries during the war; the rest had fled their homes but taken refuge elsewhere in Bosnia. About 447,000 of the 1 million returnees had gone back to places where they were in the minority; for example, Croats living in Muslim areas, and vice versa. Of the 1 million people who had not yet returned to their homes, the UNHCR said, more than 300,000 were still living elsewhere in Bosnia, and about 500,000 were "thought to have found a solution," including by gaining citizenship or permanent residency in other countries.

Despite such symbolic steps, the daily lives of people in Bosnia remained difficult. Officially, the unemployment rate was about 40 percent, but the real jobless level was said to be much higher. Much of the infrastructure damaged in the war—roads, bridges, power lines, and other public utilities—had been replaced, but tens of thousands of private houses and even some public buildings still bore the scars of fires and bullets that each ethnic group had used to drive out people of other ethnic groups. Few of the signs of ethnic harmony for which Bosnia was famous before the war had survived the conflict and its aftermath. People of different ethnic groups no longer socialized with one another or shared neighborhoods. Intermarriage, once common, had almost ceased to exist. Schools were segregated. The three economic pillars of Bosnia were corruption, crime, and foreign aid.

There were increasing calls in the Croat and Muslim communities for a new system to replace the political structure put in place by the Dayton Accords. Agreement on an alternative did not appear in sight, however, because each of Bosnia's communities—and the country's international overseers—had differing views on what the future structures should be and when the country would be ready for change. Least ready for change were the Serb leaders, both in Bosnia and in Serbia proper, who appeared to prefer the current system because it allowed for an effectively independent Serbian republic in Bosnia.

Serbia-Montenegro

Serbia—the powerful central force in the former Yugoslavia during the Balkan wars—continued to lurch from one crisis to another during the year. A popular revolution that swept Yugoslav Slobodan Milosevic from power in October 2000 led to a pro-Western government that promised, but had trouble delivering, economic and political reforms. The assassination in February 2003 of the leading reform politician, Prime Minister Zoran Djindjic, created new doubts about whether Serbia could shake off the demons of tyranny from the Milosevic era. *(Background, Historic Documents of 2003, p. 55)*

The first two months of 2004 were lost to wrangling among political parties in an attempt to form a new government following inconclusive parliamentary elections that had been held late in December 2003. The central actor was Vojislav Kostunica, who had defeated Milosevic in the disputed 2000 elections. Kostunica was a Serbian nationalist who opposed Milosevic's authoritarian tactics and the wars that were waged unsuccessfully in the 1990s to impose Serbian dominance on the Balkans. Kostunica headed the Democratic Party of Serbia, which had won about 18 percent of the vote in the elections—enough to make him the power broker and the likely prime minister in a new center-right government.

Kostunica ruled out an alliance with the strongly pro-Western party (also called the Democratic Party) of his old rival Djindjic. Instead, he turned to more conservative parties for support, including the Milosevic's old Socialist Party. A new government with Kostunica as the prime minister took office on March 3; lacking a true majority in parliament, it was forced to cobble together ad hoc deals to stay in office.

The new government managed to pass several pieces of legislation that had been demanded by the World Bank and other international lenders in exchange for economic aid to Serbia; among other things these bills called for selling off major state-owned enterprises and established the legal basis for a return to private enterprise after years of communism.

The government also adopted a key measure that enabled Serbs to elect a new president. In 2002 Kostunica had given up the figurehead presidency of Yugoslavia so he could run for the somewhat more powerful presidency of Serbia—the dominant partner of the two republics (along with Montenegro) that made up Yugoslavia at that point. Kostunica won a majority of the vote in two elections in 2002 but failed to gain the Serbian presidency because voter turnout fell below the required level of 50 percent. Another attempt to elect a president, this time without Kostunica's participation, failed in November 2003. After taking office as prime minister, Kostunica pushed through legislation eliminating the 50 percent-turnout requirement.

Two rounds of presidential elections in June produced a result that Kostunica clearly did not want: a victory for Boris Tadic, who had taken over leadership of the rival Democratic Party formerly headed by the assassinated Djindjic. Tadic won nearly 54 percent of the vote, defeating Tomislav Nikolic, the nominal head of an ultranationalist party; the real head of that party, Voijislav Seselj, was in prison at The Hague, waiting trial on war crimes charges.

Tadic took office on July 11 and promised to promote reform policies that eventually would gain membership for Serbia in the EU. As president he had little real governing power, however, and he was unable to win adoption of key proposals for which he had campaigned. On December 1 Tadic survived an incident in which his car was rammed repeatedly by another car in Belgrade. Police described the incident as "road rage," but Belgrade newspapers called it an assassination attempt.

The ambivalent nature of post-Milosevic Serbian politics appeared to be confirmed by local elections on October 3. Voters handed victories to the two parties representing the opposite extremes of Serbia's political spectrum: Tadic's pro-Western Democratic Party, and the hard-line nationalist Serbian Radical Party led by Tomislav Nikolic. Turnout was exceptionally low, only about 23 percent.

None of the year's elections or other developments fully resolved the question of whether Serbia would again cooperate with the UN tribunal that was prosecuting Milosevic and others for crimes during the Balkan wars. The Djindjic government had handed Milosevic over to The Hague tribunal in 2001, provoking cries of treason from the former dictator's allies and other Serbian nationalists, including Kostunica. Since then Belgrade had halted its cooperation with the tribunal, refusing to extradite former Bosnian Serb general Ratko Mladic (who was believed to be living in Serbia and was receiving a Serbian government pension) or three former Yugoslav generals who had been indicted on war crimes charges stemming from the Kosovo conflict. Instead, Serbia set up its own war crimes court, which handled several cases during the year, including the conviction in March of a Serb policeman for killing fourteen Kosovar Albanians in 1999. Kostunica appeared to rule out any further cooperation with the UN court, telling the BBC in September: "The Serbian government has done all it can in this situation."

Serbia's internal and international troubles appeared likely to play a role in a vote, expected in 2006, on whether Serbia and Montenegro should continue their shotgun marriage as a country that was unified primarily in name. Under strong international pressure to avoid a final breakup of the Yugoslav state, Serbia and Montenegro in 2002 agreed to discard the name "Yugoslavia" and establish a new entity known simply as Serbia and Montenegro. That union became official in 2003, but it included a provision that either side could hold an independence referendum after three years. By 2004 it appeared ever more likely that one or both of the republics would vote for a divorce, thus resulting in seven independent Balkan states in place of the former Yugoslavia.

Macedonia

An effort to block intercommunal harmony in yet another of the Balkan states—Macedonia—failed in November, much to the relief of the Western powers that had intervened to quell a bloody seven-month civil conflict in 2001. That conflict had been started by ethnic Albanian Muslim guerrillas who demanded concessions from the government run by the ethnic Slav majority. The war ended after Western diplomats negotiated a compromise agreement that gave the Muslim minority greater civil and political rights. *(Background, Historic Documents of 2001, p. 554)*

A key element of the 2001 agreement came under challenge in 2004 by Slav hard-liners who had opposed concessions to the Muslims. That element was a Western-sponsored plan to consolidate many of the country's municipalities to reduce the gerrymandering that had arbitrarily reduced the political influence of the Muslim minority. Slav opponents said the plan would disadvantage the majority and split the country in two, and they called for a referendum to overturn it. Only 26 percent of the population, well below a required quorum, voted in the November 7 referendum, thus preserving the original plan. Three days later politicians from across the country's spectrum met and affirmed the reconciliation process.

In the run-up to the vote, the Bush administration had taken an important symbolic step to assuage Slavic hard-liners. The administration formally recognized the country as the Republic of Macedonia—thus dispensing with the "Former Yugoslav Republic of Macedonia" title that Greece had insisted on because of its historic claims to the name of Macedonia. The reaction from Athens was muted, especially in contrast to Greek anger in 1992 when Skopje declared independence from Yugoslavia and demanded the right to be called Macedonia.

Following are excerpts from the summary and recommendations of "Enclosure: Report on the Situation in Kosovo" a report submitted July 23, 2004, by Norwegian diplomat Kai Eide, to United Nations Secretary General Kofi Annan, who had appointed Eide to investigate the UN mission in the province of Kosovo. Annan sent his own recommendations based on Eide's report to the UN Security Council on November 17. Both documents were made public on December 16.

"Enclosure: Report on the Situation in Kosovo"

Summary and Recommendations

Summary

Kosovo (Serbia and Montenegro) is characterized by growing dissatisfaction and frustration. Seen from the Kosovo Albanian majority, the main cause is not of an inter-ethnic nature, but stems from what is rightly seen as a serious lack of economic opportunities and an absence of a clear political perspective. As a Kosovo Albanian student said, "You gave us freedom, but not a future". The Kosovo Serbs believe—also rightly—that they are victims of a campaign to reduce their presence in Kosovo to a scattered rural population.

The international community was taken by surprise by the violence in March. It had failed to read the mood in the population and to understand the depth of the dissatisfaction of the majority and the vulnerability of the minorities. The international community, with the United Nations Interim Administration Mission in Kosovo

(UNMIK) in the lead, gave an impression of being in disarray, without direction and internal cohesion. UNMIK has become the main target of criticism from all sides, although it has also been a victim of the lack of a clear political perspective.

However, during our visits, positive trends were noticed. This new tone has come as a result of clear messages given by the international community. The Kosovo Albanians now seem to accept that they did "too little, too late" to stem the violence that occurred in March. They understand that this violence damaged their reputation and support in the international community. Now, they must make a serious effort to reassure the international community and the Serbs that they will act to repair the damage caused by the violence as well as develop meaningful local government, giving the Serbs more authority in areas where they have a more concentrated population, and mechanisms enabling them to protect and promote their identity. If implemented, these commitments would facilitate the return of those who fled and the return of the Serb leaders to the political process. The Serbs understand that they cannot and should not remain outside the political process when their Kosovo Albanian counterparts are seen to take steps to accommodate their demands. The Serbs therefore seem more willing to participate in common efforts, although a decision to take part in elections and return to the Provisional Institutions of Self-Government has not been made. Remaining outside would also cost them support they now enjoy from the international community. The joint declaration signed on 14 July reflects these positive trends. In these efforts, the interests of other minorities must also be borne in mind.

The first test we now face is to maintain the strong pressure required to bring the work forward in the above-mentioned priority areas. If there is insufficient progress, it will be very hard—if not impossible—to repair the damage caused by the March violence. It will be extremely difficult for the international community to regain the initiative and the credibility it has lost. Even more important, it will be hard for the Kosovo Albanian leaders to repair their image and for the Kosovo Serbs to return gradually to the political processes and participate in the October elections. The deadlines are indeed very tight.

The second test relates to managing the interim—including increased transfer of competencies and authority to the institutions of Kosovo and a more dynamic standards policy. The question of transfer represents a key demand from the Kosovo Albanian side. The international community should be forthcoming, transferring competencies where possible and involving the Kosovo Provisional Institutions as much as possible in core reserved areas in order to enhance a sense of ownership and transfer of relevant experience.

An ambitious policy of transfer should, however, be accompanied by two other critical elements: the new Special Representative of the Secretary-General should be prepared to introduce a robust policy of interventions and sanctions in cases of inappropriate performance. Furthermore, a more ambitious and systematic policy of capacity-building should be implemented.

The current "standards before status" policy lacks credibility. The implementation of a highly ambitious set of standards before status talks begins is seen as unachievable. The implementation of the standards should be seen as an integral part of a wider policy and continue to guide efforts to bring Kosovo closer to European standards even after the conclusion of future status negotiations. This would enable all to concentrate attention on a set of more immediate priorities reflecting urgent requirements, coupled with a longer-term perspective. It would increase the chances of having met certain key conditions when future status talks begin. These priorities must be achievable and the results visible, leading to concrete results on the ground, a better climate between the majority and the minorities and greater credibility for the international community. A priority-based and realistic standards policy would facilitate our efforts to mobilize pressure and send a more convincing message to all of what is expected of them. A series of standards reviews under the leadership of the Special Representative of the Secretary-General, and with the full participation of the Contact Group, could be held before the scheduled mid-2005 review.

The third test relates to preparations for future status discussions. They cannot be postponed much longer. There will not be any ideal moment for starting such preparations—not even a good moment. However, while a gradual reduction of the international presence in Kosovo can be expected, the economic situation will continue to worsen and the frustrations and dissatisfaction inside Kosovo will grow. Raising the future status question soon seems—on balance—to be the better option and is probably inevitable.

Therefore, the United Nations should initiate its own thinking with key Member States. Some key considerations for thinking on future status are outlined in the main part of the report.

The international community should intensify its dialogue with Belgrade. The authorities in Belgrade have a sense of not being sufficiently included. That impression should be corrected as soon as possible. Belgrade will, of course, be one of the parties to the future status negotiations. Belgrade's support and participation will also be a key to success at each and every stage of the process.

A restructuring of UNMIK is unavoidable, to re-energize the Mission, bring its various components more closely together and concentrate on key priorities in a more organized way. Particular attention should at this stage be given to highlighting community issues, reflecting pressing challenges. However, a complete overhaul would at this stage be counterproductive, leading to more internal discussion and confusion at a time when a concentrated effort on urgent priority issues of substance is required. An immediate streamlining and realigning of UNMIK—maintaining the pillar structure—should be undertaken first, to be followed by preparations for a major restructuring, which would have to take place next year and be prepared in early 2005. With the future status question approaching, the United Nations should prepare for a gradual reduction of its presence to be accompanied by a parallel increase in the European Union and a continuation of the presence of the Organization for Security and Cooperation in Europe (OSCE). The pillar structure would then be eliminated. Handing over the responsibility for the police to the European Union or OSCE as part of the major restructuring should be discussed early.

The international community faces important challenges in several stages: the immediate and urgent requirements following the March violence; the interim challenges of revising the "standards before status" policy and transferring greater competencies; the critical phase of preparing for future status negotiations; and finally, for supporting the outcome of such negotiations. It is obvious that these challenges—many of them having to be dealt with in parallel—will require an integrated, comprehensive strategic plan. It will have to be based on commitments from all major international organizations and Member States involved. UNMIK will not be able to mobilize the strength and credibility required for carrying out its responsibilities without strong support from the international community at large.

A more concerted effort is therefore urgently required to ensure that the international community can regain the initiative and maintain it through 2005. A coordinated strategy will have to be elaborated. A comprehensive and cohesive engagement from the European Union, in the political as well as the economic areas, would be of great importance. A set of economic and political incentives and disincentives will have to be formulated. OSCE and the Council of Europe should play prominent roles in a more robust capacity-building effort. In addition, the North Atlantic Treaty Organization (NATO) should ensure that it maintains an adequate presence through the most sensitive periods ahead of us, which will be related to the future status process.

Furthermore, UNMIK will not be able to operate in an efficient manner without constant and strong support from the Security Council and the Contact Group. The international community cannot afford to perform in a fragmented, uncoordinated and often competitive way. The stakes are too high and the challenges too demanding.

Recommendations

The main recommendations of the report are therefore as follows:

- A comprehensive and integrated strategy covering the period from now until the end of 2005 should be elaborated and consulted on with relevant partners. This report contains elements for such a strategy. Discussions with the Security Council, other organizations and key Member States should be undertaken in early fall to secure commitment for the resources and support required to implement that strategy.
- Pressure must be maintained in order to strengthen current positive trends and ensure that immediate challenges are met in a convincing way. This includes demonstrable progress in the area of security, reconstruction, prosecution of those responsible for the March events and reform of local government. This relates to reassuring the Serbs in a way that could bring those who fled back to their homes and their leaders back to the political processes.
- The "standards before status" policy should be immediately replaced by a dynamic priority-based standards policy within the overall framework of the integrated strategy in order to facilitate orderly future status discussions as well as regional and European integration efforts. Three intermediary standards reviews should be scheduled before the mid-2005 review.
- An ambitious policy of transferring further competencies should be launched without delay, giving the Provisional Institutions of Self-Government a greater sense of ownership and responsibility as well as accountability. This should include establishing new ministries of energy, of justice and of community matters, human rights and returns.
- A process of handing operational control of the Kosovo Police Service (KPS) gradually over to the Provisional Institutions of Self-Government, while UNMIK maintains overall executive policing authority, should be elaborated and implemented. Units of KPS should immediately be given proper training and equipment to meet

challenges relating to civil disturbances. The handover of remaining United Nations police responsibilities to the European Union or OSCE should be explored.

- The Special Representative of the Secretary-General should be ready to make greater use of sanctions and interventions without delay. An inventory of possible measures should be drawn up.
- A more coherent and ambitious policy of capacity-building is urgently needed and should be elaborated and implemented under the leadership of OSCE.
- UNMIK should be streamlined and realigned this summer with the aim of providing new energy and a more concentrated effort on key challenges. A more comprehensive restructuring of the international presence as a whole should be undertaken in 2005 with a gradual reduction of UNMIK as it moves towards a completion of its mandate and a handover of responsibilities to other authorities and organizations. Preparations for such a handover to regional organizations should begin well in advance, based upon agreements reached and as part of the overall strategy.
- The European Union should urgently develop an economic development strategy and should consolidate its various presences in Kosovo and strengthen its overall commitment.
- NATO should maintain the presence of the Kosovo Force required to ensure a safe and secure environment, with a view to ensuring an adequate force level during the future status process.
- The broader international community should provide a more concerted and coordinated engagement.
- A more intense and comprehensive dialogue with Belgrade should be initiated without delay.
- A high-level international consultative mechanism for Kosovo involving key capitals and headquarters should be established.
- Serious exploratory discussion of the future status question should be undertaken by the United Nations beginning this autumn.

Annex II: The way forward in Kosovo

Recommendations of the Secretary-General

1. As stated in my report to the Security Council on the United Nations Interim Administration Mission in Kosovo (UNMIK) following the events of March, I requested that a comprehensive review of the policies and practices of all actors in Kosovo (Serbia and Montenegro) be conducted and that options and recommendations be provided as a basis for further thinking on the way forward, in accordance with Security Council resolution 1244 (1999). Ambassador Kai Eide of Norway, whom I asked to conduct the review, submitted his assessment and recommendations for my consideration. In his excellent report he outlined a comprehensive and integrated strategy that provides a basis to take us from the present into the process that will determine the future status of Kosovo. On 6 August, I conveyed a copy of the report to the President of the Security Council, with a request that it be brought to the attention of the members of the Council. I also stated that I was considering the recommendations contained in the report and that, in due course, I would revert to the Council with my recommendations after appropriate consultations, including with my Special Representative for Kosovo, Søren Jessen-Petersen.

2. Consultations with key Member States—the Contact Group plus the other European members of the Security Council—as well as the leadership of our partner organizations in Kosovo, the European Union, the Organization for Security and Cooperation in Europe (OSCE) and the North Atlantic Treaty Organization (NATO), were held on 20 September. We felt that those constructive meetings resulted in a general understanding of and support for an integrated strategy for the way forward in Kosovo from now to mid-2005 and in preparation for the future status process. There was broad agreement on the need to focus on the economy and on security, the need to engage with Belgrade and to bring the Kosovo Serbs into the process, and the importance of the standards process. There was also broad support for a subregional approach that would not focus exclusively on Kosovo. My Special Representative has also consulted with the parties on the ground.

3. I would like to emphasize that all processes in Kosovo must remain within the parameters of Security Council resolution 1244 (1999). In order to move beyond the current situation, we find it is essential that a comprehensive and integrated strategy be put in place to take us into the future status process based on a decision by the Security Council. At that time, the international community will need to be prepared and the United Nations will lead the preparations in coordination with key Member States and partner organizations.

4. Such an integrated strategy includes several main components: strengthening current efforts to deal with the causes and consequences of the March violence; improving dialogue at all levels; initiating a more comprehensive dialogue with Belgrade; recalibrating the standards policy; transferring further competences to the Provisional Institutions of Self-Government; increasing accountability of the Provisional Institutions; increasing oversight and intervention, as necessary, by UNMIK; enhancing capacity-building for the Provisional Institutions; implementing a stronger economic development policy with short- and long-term measures; and realigning and streamlining UNMIK. My Special Representative has already taken significant initiatives while moving forward with the integrated strategy.

5. Achieving progress on the eight standards remains the basis of our policy, and this process be carried out in a dynamic and priority-based way within the overall framework of the integrated strategy in order to give momentum and direction to the political process. The Provisional Institutions must make substantial progress on meeting the standards in order to move forward. I must emphasize that all the standards are important. The focus of this refined policy is not to diminish any of the eight standards but to focus on priority areas. We should bear in mind that the standards are of value in and of themselves. Achieving the standards will not only lead to a qualitative change in society in Kosovo, but will also provide a political perspective for Kosovo within Europe. UNMIK will lead the reviews of progress achieved in implementing the standards by providing quarterly technical assessments, which are discussed with the Provisional Institutions and local representatives of the Contact Group. These technical assessments provide the basis for the political assessments contained in my reports to the Security Council that focus on priority actions within each standard considered necessary to facilitate orderly future status discussions, to contribute to ensuring the sustainability of an eventual political settlement, to further regional and European integration efforts and to ensure measures crucial for security and the inclusion of all communities in Kosovo. A comprehensive review may be conducted in

mid-2005 on the basis of which the Security Council will determine whether to initiate the political process leading to a determination of the future status of Kosovo.

6. Another element of the integrated strategy is the transfer to the Provisional Institutions of those additional competencies which are not inherent attributes of sovereignty. We must also take into account reserved powers and responsibilities in areas of key importance for the implementation of the mandate of the international civil presence. In this regard, I would recall that, in accordance with resolution 1244 (1999), my Special Representative is vested with full authority and accountability for the implementation of the duties and responsibilities of the international civil presence. This ultimate authority cannot be delegated or transferred. UNMIK has undertaken a comprehensive review of the competencies it currently manages and has identified a number of competencies that do not impinge on sovereignty that may be transferred to the Provisional Institutions. UNMIK has also identified areas of enhanced operational involvement of the Provisional Institutions in certain reserved fields.

7. This transfer policy is strongly linked to the need for greater accountability and responsibility of the Provisional Institutions, which must ensure the delivery of essential services to all communities. The representatives of the Provisional Institutions, and in particular the political leaders of the majority community, are responsible for demonstrating that they will exercise their powers and responsibilities for the benefit of all people in Kosovo. This requires that all communities actively and meaningfully participate in the Provisional Institutions. In order to further this process, there is a need to build additional capacities within the Provisional Institutions. A more coherent and ambitious capacity-building policy will therefore be essential, and action by UNMIK in this regard is already under way.

8. Furthermore, the transfer policy outlined above cannot work without greater accountability of the Provisional Institutions and a robust oversight, intervention and sanctioning policy implemented by UNMIK. This requires that the Provisional Institutions accept that the transfer of further competencies is necessarily coupled with a greater degree of oversight and that they cooperate with UNMIK in this regard. In addition, UNMIK is putting in place more effective mechanisms for oversight and remedial interventions to ensure the full implementation of resolution 1244 (1999) and compliance with the Constitutional Framework and applicable legislation.

9. Progress on the reform of local government is essential. Active steps will be necessary to ensure consensus on the way forward and to begin implementation. As requested by the Council, I will in due course submit recommendations on possible new institutional arrangements for more effective local government through the devolution of central non-reserved responsibilities to local authorities and communities in Kosovo.

10. We also cannot lose sight of the fact that, despite some progress, much remains to be done in response to the violence that occurred in March. It is important to ensure sustained action to deal with the consequences and causes of the March events by creating institutions that are responsive to those needs and by ensuring the active engagement of the leaders and people of Kosovo for a multi-ethnic society. The focus on priority actions within the standards that relate to the causes of that violence will help to ensure that the consequences are addressed. Current efforts—through action by the Provisional Institutions of Self-Government, with the support of UNMIK and the Kosovo Force (KFOR)—aimed at ensuring the prosecution of those responsible, the improvement of security and the reconstruction of destroyed homes and religious

sites must be reinforced. Furthermore, the conditions necessary for the safe and sustainable return of those newly displaced, as well as those displaced for a number of years, need to be put in place. UNMIK will work with local partners to ensure the continuation of improved security and freedom of movement, which are key factors needed for accelerating the return of displaced persons to Kosovo.

11. While security underlies all other activities in Kosovo, revitalization of the economy remains an overriding concern. Economic development should improve not only general social and economic conditions, but also the social context for security and stability. A midterm and long-term economic strategy must be complemented by effective short-term measures. I call upon the European Union urgently to design and implement an economic development strategy and ensure that there is a regional perspective for the economic development of Kosovo.

12. Multi-channel dialogue is essential. There needs to be intensified dialogue between the communities in Kosovo as well as between Belgrade and Pristina. In addition, a more intense and comprehensive dialogue with Belgrade is being initiated, taking into account Belgrade's legitimate interest and concerns. Further, it is imperative to enhance the involvement of Kosovo in regional dialogue and initiatives if European standards are to be achieved.

13. Meanwhile, UNMIK is being streamlined and realigned now within the existing pillar structure to ensure a more concentrated effort and to focus on the key challenges and priorities. This could involve our partners in UNMIK—the European Union and OSCE—taking on additional competences (including financial commitments) in different areas within UNMIK and strengthening their overall commitment. A more comprehensive restructuring of the international presence as a whole could be undertaken in 2005, based on the decisions of the Security Council and its priorities at that time. Furthermore, I call upon NATO to maintain the KFOR presence required to implement its responsibilities under resolution 1244 (1999), particularly to ensure a safe and secure environment, including with the provision of an adequate force level during the future status process and the implementation of an eventual political settlement.

14. Finally, I would like to emphasize that the unified and coordinated support of the broader international community, particularly that of key Member States, such as those in the Security Council and in the Contact Group, is essential for success in our common endeavour. While UNMIK and our key international partners play a central role in the implementation of the integrated strategy, it is the people of Kosovo from all communities and their representatives in the Provisional Institutions and political leaders that must work towards the goals set out in the strategy in their areas of responsibility and ensure that there is progress. Progress in all these aspects is essential for the success and sustainability of any future status process, and only if progress is sufficient will it be possible to consider moving gradually into talks on the future status of Kosovo.

Source: United Nations. Security Council. Letter dated 17 November 2004 from the Secretary-General Addressed to the President of the Security Council. "Enclosure: Report on the Situation in Kosovo." S/2004/932, December 16, 2004. www.un.org/Docs/journal/asp/ws.asp?m=s/2004/932 (accessed February 3, 2005).

President Bush on the Overhaul of U.S. Intelligence Agencies

December 17, 2004

INTRODUCTION

U.S. intelligence agencies—frequently a collective scapegoat when American national security policies failed—suffered their most intense criticism in a generation during 2004. The Senate Intelligence Committee on July 9 denounced failures that had led the Central Intelligence Agency and other organizations to conclude erroneously in 2002 that Iraq possessed biological and chemical weapons and was actively trying to develop nuclear weapons. On July 22 a commission that investigated the September 11, 2001, terrorist attacks against the United States concluded that a sweeping overhaul of the intelligence services was needed to correct the systemic flaws that had made the United States vulnerable to terrorism.

George Tenet, who had led the CIA and served as nominal head of all intelligence services for seven years, resigned on June 3, a month before the Senate committee issued its scathing report. More important, Congress responded with unusual speed to the September 11 commission report and enacted legislation incorporating many of its recommendations. The keystone of that legislation was the creation of the post of director of national intelligence. The new director would control the budgets of most of the fifteen government intelligence agencies and, in theory at least, be able to improve the quality of information they provided the president and other policy makers.

The congressional action was far from easy. Political pressures forced Congress to begin its work on the recommendations of the September 11 commission in the hectic weeks of campaigning before election day, November 2. Work stalled after the election, however, and only sustained pressure by a broad coalition of forces, ultimately including President George W. Bush, resulted in the adoption of the landmark legislation in December. *(September 11 commission report, p. 450; Iraq weapons issues, p. 711; election results, p. 773)*

Background

The general framework of the U.S. intelligence community was created in 1947 when Congress and the Truman administration transformed a World War II spy service into the CIA. By 2004 legislative changes and bureaucratic realignments had produced a complex system of fifteen intelligence agencies, most of them controlled by the Department of Defense but all at least nominally under the supervision of the CIA director, wearing his second hat as director of central intelligence. In actual practice the CIA director had virtually no operational control over the other agencies, largely because the Pentagon and other agencies zealously guarded their own turf.

Repeated foreign policy and national security disasters over the decades had led to frequent charges that an "intelligence failure" had been responsible or at least had been a contributing cause. Notable examples included the failure of a CIA-financed invasion of communist Cuba by Cuban exiles in 1961; numerous lapses during the Vietnam War that led to embarrassing disclosures by congressional investigating committees in the mid-1970s; the CIA's involvement in the Iran-contra abuses of the mid-1980s; and the inability by intelligence agencies to anticipate such major international changes as the Iranian revolution in 1979 and the collapse of communism in Eastern Europe and the Soviet Union between 1989 and 1991. Several high-level commissions and study groups over the years suggested revamping the intelligence community, starting with giving the CIA director (or some other official) real budgetary and bureaucratic power over all the intelligence agencies. Many less far-reaching changes were adopted at various points, but the Pentagon successfully fought off all schemes to force it to give up control of its intelligence agencies. *(Background, Historic Documents of 1996, p. 796)*

Serious as they were, all the past failures appeared to pale in comparison to the problems with the nation's intelligence-gathering that became evident after the September 11 attacks and the U.S.-led invasion of Iraq in 2003. Suddenly, it became clear—in hindsight—that the tens of billions of dollars spent each year on spy satellites, electronic surveillance, espionage, and intelligence analysis once again had failed to give decision makers the information they needed. Repeating the pattern of past experiences, the House and Senate Intelligence committees launched investigations and issued reports, Washington think tanks offered their evaluations, and the intelligence agencies began their own internal reassessments.

September 11 Panel Recommendations

None of the previous problems or recommended solutions had the impact of the September 11 commission, which used its highly visible bully pulpit to advocate a basic rethinking of the intelligence structures in place since 1947. A constant theme of its 357-page report was the inability of U.S. government agencies to pool the intelligence information that had been gathered on the al Qaeda terrorist network that had launched the September 11 attacks. The government missed numerous opportunities to catch the nineteen al Qaeda hijackers before they boarded the four airplanes used in the September 11 attacks, the commission said, largely because agencies did not share the information that might have alerted them to the terrorist plot.

The commission offered four major recommendations on intelligence-related matters:

- All fifteen U.S. intelligence agencies should be put under the control of a national intelligence director. This executive, the commission said, would review and submit to the president the budgets of all the agencies, would be the principal adviser to the president on intelligence matters, and would ensure that the agencies shared vital information.
- All the government's efforts to combat terrorism should be coordinated by a new office, the National Counterterrorism Center. The commission said this center would pool all the government's information about terrorist threats and would take charge of planning operations to defeat those threats. Actual operations, however, would be carried out by the military services, the intelligence agencies, or the other offices with those responsibilities.

- The government should create an unspecified number of other national intelligence centers, overseen by the national intelligence director, which would bring together information and analysis on specific major topics other than terrorism. In a flow chart, the commission showed five examples of topics for these centers— proliferation of weapons of mass destruction, international crime and narcotics, China and East Asia, the Middle East, and Russia and Eurasia—but said others might be needed as well.
- The total annual figure for the nation's overall intelligence spending should be made public, rather than kept secret. According to most independent estimates, the intelligence budget ran around $40 million, but the actual figure had been one of the government's most closely guarded secrets.

The commission specifically rejected another proposal that had been widely considered in the aftermath of the September 11 attacks: creation of a domestic intelligence service to replace some functions of the FBI. The panel said the FBI had missed many opportunities to catch the September 11 terrorists, but it praised the bureau for numerous reforms put in place since the attacks.

The panel's proposal for a national intelligence director won an immediate endorsement from Sen. John Kerry, D-Mass., who at the time was within two weeks of getting the Democratic Party's formal presidential nomination. Many other leading Democrats in Congress, and a handful of Republicans, also endorsed the plan. Bush praised the commission's report overall but hesitated, at first, to endorse any of its specific proposals. White House officials said Bush would instead issue an executive order making several less sweeping changes, in hopes of easing the pre-election pressure for adoption of the commission's proposals.

Bush Signs On

What was expected to be a bruising debate over the commission recommendations got under way July 30 when the Senate Governmental Affairs Committee held the first congressional hearing on the panel's report. Chairman Thomas Kean and Vice Chairman Lee H. Hamilton made impassioned pleas for urgent action. "These people are planning to attack us again, and trying to attack us sooner rather than later," Kean told the panel, referring to the al Qaeda terrorists. "Every delay we have in changing structures or changing people, or whatever it is, to make that less likely is a delay the American people can't tolerate." Hamilton said the recommendation for a national intelligence director was central to the commission's concept of reform. "We have concluded that the intelligence community is not going to get its job done unless somebody is really in charge," he said. "That is just not the case now, and we paid the price."

As the commissioners anticipated, members of Congress in both parties raised objections. Some Republicans expressed concerns that the panel's proposed changes would weaken the military's intelligence agencies, and some Democrats said they feared that putting the national intelligence director in the White House—as the commission recommended—would undermine his or her independence from political considerations. Despite these concerns, it was clear that the commission's report had tapped into a deep well of public support for changing the business-as-usual practices of the nation's capital. The Senate committee's Republican chairman, Susan Collins of Maine, and ranking Democrat, Joseph I. Lieberman, said they were preparing legislation to implement the recommendations and would push for action before the election.

Apparently deciding to ride with, rather than against, the political winds, Bush on August 2 announced that he was supporting the commission's two key recommendations for a national intelligence director and a counterterrorism center. Under a proposal he would send Congress, Bush said, the new director "will serve as the president's principal intelligence adviser and will oversee and coordinate the foreign and domestic intelligence activities of the intelligence community." Bush appeared to reject key details of the commission's plans, however, by suggesting that the new director would have only a limited role in setting the intelligence budget and in selecting the heads of the various intelligence agencies. The president also rejected outright the commission's plan to locate the intelligence director within the White House. Kean and Hamilton responded with a statement welcoming Bush's proposal as "an important step" but noting that many items of "substance" needed to be discussed.

Bush's proposal came under immediate attack on Capitol Hill from Democrats and some Republicans who said it fell short of what the commission had recommended. Lieberman said the president's plan "would create a kind of Potemkin national intelligence director, where you see the facade but there's no authority behind it." Others urged caution, among them the chairman of the House Intelligence Committee, Republican Porter Goss of Florida: "We cannot afford to make changes blindly or in an unnecessary haste. We can ill afford to rush to judgment any more than we can tolerate needless delay." While this debate was under way, Secretary of Defense Donald H. Rumsfeld and other Pentagon officials launched an all-out lobbying effort to slow down the rush toward action or, failing that, to ensure that military intelligence operations would not be put under the control of the new intelligence director.

Bush threw a new element into the political equation on August 10, nominating Representative Goss to succeed Tenet as the head of the CIA. Goss had been an army intelligence officer and had worked in the CIA's covert operations bureau before his election to Congress in 1988. He had chaired the House intelligence panel since 1997. Bush called Goss "a reformer" who was "well prepared" for the job of leading the CIA. The appointment brought criticism from some Democrats, who said Goss in recent years had been too partisan on many issues, and from supporters of the September 11 commission recommendations, who said Goss did not appear committed to those changes. Bush followed the appointment with an executive order giving the CIA director some, but not all, of the new powers the September 11 commission had envisioned for the new national intelligence director.

Goss won Senate confirmation on September 22, by a 77–17 margin, with all the no votes cast by Democrats; he took office two days later. Goss moved quickly to put his stamp on the agency, forcing out senior career CIA officials, including Deputy Director John E. McLaughlin (whom Bush had bypassed for the top job), the director and deputy director of the agency's clandestine service, and the director of the analysis branch. He also sent CIA employees a memo telling them to "support the administration and its policies in our work"—a message that brought criticism from some employees and Democrats on Capitol Hill, who said it appeared to politicize the agency.

Congress Begins Work

Several leading members of Congress, including Goss, introduced legislation to shake up the intelligence agencies just before, or immediately after, the September 11 commission published its report. The first truly dramatic proposal for change came

August 22 from Kansas Republican Pat Roberts, the chairman of the Senate Intelligence Committee, and several of his Republican colleagues. That plan called for consolidating all the intelligence agencies into one National Intelligence Service, headed by a cabinet-level national intelligence director with broad powers. Its headline-grabbing aspect, however, was breaking up the CIA into four branches of the new intelligence service. Roberts said he drafted the proposal because he had become angry with the CIA's repeated failures, most recently its wrong analyses of weapons programs in Iraq. The Roberts plan came under harsh attack from across the political spectrum in Washington, and especially from the intelligence agencies and its remaining allies. In political terms, the plan also made all other proposals under discussion appear moderate in comparison.

Collins and Lieberman on September 15 introduced bipartisan legislation to implement the September 11 commission recommendations. They had support from the Senate leadership, which chose the bill as the chamber's main bill on the matter, and from the commission itself. The next day the White House finally sent its own draft of legislation to Capitol Hill; it incorporated many of the same changes but explicitly exempted key parts of the Pentagon's intelligence work from supervision by the new national intelligence director. By that point, however, Bush had shifted his position on another key question and agreed that the new director should have what he called "full budgetary authority" over the intelligence agencies. Once again, Bush did not spell out exactly what he meant.

The House Republican leadership introduced its proposal on September 24; it also created the post of national intelligence director but assigned the director fewer powers than did the Senate bill. The House proposal also contained numerous provisions giving expanded powers to domestic law enforcement agencies, made it easier for the government to deport illegal aliens without judicial review, and prohibited states from issuing drivers licenses to people in the country illegally. The September 11 commission leaders objected to the immigration and law enforcement provisions, saying they would create unnecessary controversy and endanger the underlying legislation.

The Senate began its work on the intelligence legislation (S 2845) on September 27 and plowed through dozens of amendments. A key vote came September 29 when Roberts and his two immediate predecessors as committee chairman offered an amendment to give the new director total control over all intelligence spending—including that by all Pentagon agencies. They lost on a 78–19 vote after the Pentagon mounted a full-scale offensive against them. The Senate passed the bill on October 6, by a 96–2 vote. The House began work on its bill (HR 10) the next day and immediately defeated a Democratic attempt to adopt the Senate version. The House then passed the Republican leadership version on October 8 by a 282–134 margin.

House-Senate conferees began work October 20 to reconcile the two bills but made little progress before the November 2 election. A breakthrough came November 20 when the conferees accepted a draft agreement that dropped some of the most controversial immigration proposals of the House bill and limited the new national intelligence director's operational control of Pentagon programs. Conferees also dropped a Senate provision making the overall intelligence budget figure public, which had been one of the September 11 commission's recommendations.

Action came to a sudden stop, however, when two key House committee chairmen raised objections. Armed Services Committee Chairman Duncan Hunter, R-Calif., objected that the new intelligence director would have too much power over Pentagon programs. Judiciary Committee Chairman F. James Sensenbrenner,

R-Wis., said the House immigration law provisions had been weakened too much. House Speaker J. Dennis Hastert of Illinois then pulled the bill from consideration, setting off a high-stakes political battle that lasted more than two weeks. Among other things, the battle brought into question whether senior Pentagon officials—who supported Hunter—were taking a different position from the White House, which officially supported the conference committee bill.

After advocates of the bill complained that the White House had taken a hands-off approach, Bush on November 30 called on Congress to pass the conference bill. Hunter's concerns eventually were satisfied with cosmetic wording changes, and Sensenbrenner was forced to accept the bill as it stood. The House passed the final bill on December 7 by a 366–75 vote, and the Senate cleared it for the president the next day, 89–2.

The final bill created a National Intelligence Authority, headed by a director who would oversee eleven of the fifteen intelligence agencies (the exceptions being the intelligence operations of the military branches). The director was described as the president's principal intelligence adviser, with budgetary authority over the nonmilitary intelligence agencies and the right to "participate" with the defense secretary in developing the military intelligence budget.

The bill also created the National Counterterrorism Center recommended by the September 11 commission, thereby putting into law an agency that Bush had created by executive order. The bill also included numerous domestic security provisions, such as setting minimum national standards for birth certificates and drivers licenses, denying bail for terrorism suspects in most cases, and giving law enforcement agencies expanded powers to use wiretapping and other investigative tools against so-called lone wolf terrorists not affiliated with terrorist groups.

Bush signed the Intelligence Reform and Terrorism Prevention Act of 2004 into law (PL 108–458) on December 17. "The many reforms in this act have a single goal, to ensure that the people in government responsible for defending America have the best possible information to make the best possible decisions," Bush said.

Speculation in Washington immediately centered on who Bush would appoint to the new post, which required Senate confirmation. Kean and Hamilton were among the names widely mentioned, as were those of several current and former senior government officials. Goss did not appear to be in the running for the job and was expected to remain at the CIA. Bush had not announced his decision by year's end.

Passage of the legislation left one other task for Congress: reorganizing its own oversight of the intelligence agencies, as recommended by the September 11 commission. The Senate briefly considered but then rejected one major part of the commission's proposal: consolidating within its Intelligence Committee the functions of both authorizing and appropriating funds. Instead, the Senate created a new subcommittee of the Appropriations Committee to handle the actual spending bills. The Senate made several smaller changes in the makeup of its Intelligence Committee, however. The House had taken no action to overhaul its oversight of intelligence matters by year's end.

Following are excerpts from remarks by President George W. Bush on December 17, 2004, on signing into law the Intelligence Reform and Terrorism Prevention Act of 2004, which overhauled U.S. intelligence agencies.

"The Intelligence Reform and Terrorism Prevention Act of 2004"

Nearly six decades ago, our Nation and our allies faced a new—the new world of the cold war and the dangers of a new enemy. To defend the free world from an armed empire bent on conquest, visionary leaders created new institutions such as the NATO Alliance. The NATO Alliance was begun by treaty in this very room. President Truman also implemented a sweeping reorganization of the Federal Government. He established the Department of Defense, the Central Intelligence Agency, and the National Security Council.

America, in this new century, again faces new threats. Instead of massed armies, we face stateless networks. We face killers who hide in our own cities. We must confront deadly technologies. To inflict great harm on our country, America's enemies need to be only right once. Our intelligence and law enforcement professionals in our Government must be right every single time. Our Government is adapting to confront and defeat these threats. We're staying on the offensive against the enemy. We'll take the fight to the terrorists abroad so we do not have to face them here at home.

And here at home, we're strengthening our homeland defenses. We created the Department of Homeland Security. We have made the prevention of terror attacks the highest priority of the Department of Justice and the FBI. We'll continue to work with Congress to make sure they've got the resources necessary to do their jobs. We established the National Counterterrorism Center, where all the available intelligence on terrorist threats is brought together in one place and where joint action against the terrorists is planned.

We have strengthened the security of our Nation's borders and ports of entry and transportation systems. The bill I sign today continues the essential reorganization of our Government. Those charged with protecting America must have the best possible intelligence information, and that information must be closely integrated to form the clearest possible picture of the threats to our country.

A key lesson of September the 11th, 2001, is that America's intelligence agencies must work together as a single, unified enterprise. The Intelligence Reform and Terrorism Prevention Act of 2004 creates the position of Director of National Intelligence, or DNI, to be appointed by the President with the consent of the Senate.

The Director will lead a unified intelligence community and will serve as the principle adviser to the President on intelligence matters. The DNI will have the authority to order the collection of new intelligence to ensure the sharing of information among agencies and to establish common standards for the intelligence community's personnel. It will be the DNI's responsibility to determine the annual budgets for all national intelligence agencies and offices and to direct how these funds are spent. These authorities, vested in a single official who reports directly to me, will make all our intelligence efforts better coordinated, more efficient, and more effective.

The Director of the CIA will report to the DNI. The CIA will retain its core of responsibilities for collecting human intelligence, analyzing intelligence from all sources, and supporting American interests abroad at the direction of the President.

The new law will preserve the existing chain of command and leave all our intelligence agencies, organizations, and offices in their current Departments. Our military commanders will continue to have quick access to the intelligence they need to achieve victory on the battlefield. And the law supports our efforts to ensure greater information sharing among Federal Departments and Agencies and also with appropriate State and local authorities.

The many reforms in this act have a single goal, to ensure that the people in Government responsible for defending America have the best possible information to make the best possible decisions. The men and women of our intelligence community give America their very best every day, and in return, we owe them our full support. As we continue to reform and strengthen the intelligence community, we will do all that is necessary to defend its people and the Nation we serve.

I'm now pleased and honored to sign into law the Intelligence Reform and Terrorism Prevention Act of 2004.

Source: U.S. Executive Office of the President. "Remarks on Signing the Intelligence Reform and Terrorism Prevention Act of 2004." *Weekly Compilation of Presidential Documents* 40, no. 51 (December 20, 2004): 2985–2987. www.gpoaccess.gov/wcomp/v40no51.html (accessed February 15, 2005).

European Union President on a Membership Invitation to Turkey

December 17, 2004

INTRODUCTION

More than four decades after it began making overtures to Europe, Turkey in 2004 finally won an invitation to open negotiations for membership in the European Union (EU). Even under the best of circumstances, Turkey was not expected to be able to join the EU for another ten to fifteen years, but the invitation itself was a major psychological boost for the Muslim-majority country that straddled the geographical and cultural lines between Europe and Asia. The invitation also was a major victory for Turkey's prime minister, Recep Tayyip Erdogan, who had been in office just two years. The leader of an openly Islamic party whose rise to power in 2002 stirred fears both in Europe and among Turkey's traditionally secular leadership, Erdogan had proven to be an adept politician at home and a sure-footed diplomat abroad. *(Background, Historic Documents of 2002, p. 906)*

Left behind, at least for the moment, was the Turkish population on the northern part of Cyprus. Under pressure from Erdogan and the United Nations, the Turkish Cypriots moved in 2004 toward a political resolution of their thirty-year dispute with the Greek majority on the southern part of the island. But this time it was the Greek Cypriots—focused on their own new membership in the European Union—who blocked a settlement.

EU Commission Acts

Turkey had been trying since the late 1950s to join the predecessor organizations of the European Union, starting with the European Economic Community (EEC), the predecessor of the European Common Market. European leaders for many years refused even to entertain the idea of Turkey's membership, saying at various points that the country was Asian rather than European, lacked political stability, failed to meet European standards of democracy, and was too far behind Europe economically. Only occasionally did European officials acknowledge that, with nearly 70 million people, almost all of them Muslim, Turkey was too big and too poor to be absorbed easily into the rest of Europe.

Turkey had been able to join the North Atlantic Treaty Organization (NATO) in 1952, but that was a decision made in Washington for strategic reasons at the height of the cold war—not an embrace by Europeans of Turkey or its civilization. In 1963 the EEC made Turkey an "associate" member; that step was seen at the time as an indefinite postponement of Turkey's aspirations for European membership rather than as a step toward it. European leaders offered Turkey a momentary chance at membership in 1978, but the government in Ankara at the time was unwilling to risk the domestic upheaval that would have ensued if the country opened its economy to unrestricted trade with the rest of Europe. Turkey came back to Europe with a membership appeal in 1987, but it took another dozen years before EU leaders grudgingly agreed to start the process of considering Ankara's application. That was followed, in 2002, by a promise that Turkey would get a date for the start of membership negotiations by 2004. *(Turkey's EU efforts, Historic Documents of 1999, pp. 158, 466; Historic Documents of 2002, p. 906)*

In the meantime a succession of Turkish governments moved to rewrite the country's laws, and update its economic and political institutions, to bring them into compliance with an elaborate series of EU membership standards known as the "Copenhagen criteria" (after the EU summit meeting where they were adopted). The basic thrust of the Copenhagen standards was to ensure that new EU members would be fully functioning democracies with free-market economies that provided adequate standards of living for their citizens.

Significant moves toward adoption of the political criteria began in 2002 (even before the election of Erdogan's government), when Ankara abolished the death penalty for peace-time offenses and moved to allow use of the minority Kurdish language in broadcasts and schools. After taking office at the end of 2002, the Erdogan government moved on other human rights issues, such as by enacting procedures to curb the widespread use of torture by police and other security services, and by instructing the nation's clerics to use their Friday sermons to preach the benefit of women's rights. The latter step was an extraordinary one, considering that Erdogan's party had deep roots in conservative Islam, often seen as one of the world's most male-dominated religions.

It had been clear that 2004 would be a landmark year for the question of Turkey's membership because of developments both in Europe and in Turkey. Perhaps the most important development was the May 1 addition of ten new members to the EU, one of which was the Greek-dominated Republic of Cyprus. In terms of geography, Cyprus was no more European than was Turkey; in political terms, Erdogan's unstinting efforts to settle a long-running dispute between Greeks and Turks on Cyprus gave him a powerful argument for admitting Turkey to the EU, as well. *(EU expansion, p. 197)*

There also was a sense among many European intellectuals, business leaders, and politicians that Turkey's time finally had arrived. Turkey was too big and important to ignore any longer, was making the economic and political changes Europe had long demanded, and deserved the chance to prove that it could be part of the modern world.

A powerful related argument was that Europe should seize the opportunity offered by Erdogan who, in the eyes of many Europeans, was a "moderate" Islamist trying to drag his country into modernity. By 2004 opinion polls showed that most Turks were becoming impatient, even angry, with what they viewed as Europe's foot dragging. If Erdogan was rebuffed by Europe after expectations had risen so high, according to this argument, more radical Islamists might come to power in Turkey, end the country's secular traditions, and even threaten the stability of European countries with their millions of Muslim immigrants from Turkey, the Middle East, and North Africa.

Ironically, this argument also played into the lingering reluctance in Europe to spread the European Union net too far. Former French president Valery Giscard d'Estaing was perhaps the most prominent person to articulate the view that Turkey belonged to Asia, not Europe. While chairing a commission that drafted a new EU constitution, Giscard said in 2003 that Turkish membership would mean "the end of Europe."

That statement by a senior statesman expressed what many ordinary Europeans were saying even more bluntly: Europe already had too many Muslims, and Turkey, with its population of about 70 million, would add way too many more. Anti-immigrant parties had been growing in influence in Austria, France, Germany, the Netherlands, and other countries in recent years. In 2004 Turkey's EU application even became entangled in a controversy over the killing by a Dutch citizen, of Moroccan roots, of a Dutch filmmaker who had been critical of Islam. The murder became a *cause celebre* for Europeans fearful of everything having to do with Islam, including Turkey. Yet another argument that gained new prominence in 2004 was that Turkey was too poor to qualify for EU membership. The crux of this argument was that Turkey would drain the EU budget of subsidies intended to raise the union's poorer members closer to the standards of its richer ones.

Under EU procedures, Europe's invitation to Turkey came through a two-step process: action by the European Commission (the EU's highest-ranking executive body), then a formal endorsement by the European Council, composed of the top leaders of the twenty-five EU nations. Approval by the European Commission appeared to be on track until the late summer, when Erdogan's government put forward a new criminal code, as demanded by the EU, but included in it was a proposal to criminalize adultery. That plan raised international concerns that Turkey was moving backward on women's rights. Erdogan backed down in September after he visited Brussels and heard that the plan might jeopardize Turkey's EU membership chances. Turkey's parliament adopted the new code, without the adultery provision, on September 26.

The European Commission acted on October 6, endorsing a report by Gunter Verheugen, its commissioner for EU enlargement, that Turkey was moving to meet the necessary criteria for membership, although it still had much work to do. The commissioners added what they called an "emergency brake," saying that Turkey had to make sustained progress on democracy, human rights, and the rule of law. Any breakdown in those areas "will automatically bring negotiations to a halt," outgoing European Commission President Romano Prodi said, noting that the commission's overall response to Turkey was a "qualified yes." Responding to widespread concerns about the potential for massive flooding of Turks across European borders, the commission also said the EU should consider "permanent safeguard measures" limiting Turkish emigration to other member countries. The union had imposed temporary emigration limits when it accepted some other poor countries but had never before made them permanent.

Erdogan called the commission plan "generally balanced" but warned that Turkey was not interested if the EU wanted to remain a "Christian club." Despite that bravado, the *Economist* magazine, in its October 9 issue, quoted one Turkish diplomat: "The truth is that there won't be negotiations. The EU will lay down the law, and we will have to abide by it."

An Invitation, At Last

As European leaders prepared for their annual December summit, it was almost certain that Turkey would get a formal invitation—but it was not clear for what, under what terms, and whether the terms would be acceptable to Turkey. To take any action, the twenty-five EU leaders had to be unanimous, a requirement that gave significant leverage to the leaders of countries were public opposition was greatest, notably Austria, Denmark, and France. Some European leaders talked of offering Turkey a vaguely defined status of "privileged partnership" rather than full membership, a suggestion Erdogan rebuffed as unacceptable. Another potential hitch appeared to be the attitude of Cyprus, one of the EU's new members, which demanded that Turkey formally recognize its government before starting its EU membership negotiations. Last-minute backing for Turkey came from the European Parliament, which on December 15 passed a nonbinding resolution urging the leaders to open membership talks with Turkey as soon as possible.

After the years of delay, and the recent months of rhetoric on all sides, the decision came quickly as the European leaders met in Brussels. Over dinner on December 16, and then in meetings the following day, Erdogan and the twenty-five EU leaders worked out a deal under which Turkey was invited to begin formal negotiations on October 3, 2005, toward full membership. The sensitive issue of Turkey's relations with Cyprus was settled with a compromise: Erdogan would sign an agreement, before October 3, 2005, acknowledging that Cyprus and the other new EU members were part of the European customs union (Turkey for years had participated in that union as a non-EU member). In turn, Erdogan issued a statement declaring that signing the agreement would not constitute formal diplomatic recognition of Cyprus. The leaders toasted their hard-won agreement with champagne (and orange juice for Erdogan).

Making the formal announcement, the current president of the European Council, Dutch prime minister Jan Peter Balkenende, said: "I believe we can say that we have made history with one another today." Balkenende was careful to emphasize the EU's standard language that the outcome of the negotiations on Turkey's membership "cannot be guaranteed."

Erdogan emerged from the meetings claiming victory for his country's position. "This is a win-win agreement," he said. "We're at a point where we [are] reaping the reward of forty-one years of work." He acknowledged that Turkey's future steps to meet EU standards "will be even more difficult" than those taken in the past, but added: "I strongly believe Turkey will be able to achieve this."

British prime minister Tony Blair, a staunch supporter of Turkey's membership, said the agreement sent a much broader message to the world than the timing of negotiations. "It shows that those who believe there is some fundamental clash in civilizations between Christian and Muslim are actually wrong, that we can work together and we can cooperate together."

Leaders from the countries most resistant to Turkish membership expressed considerably less enthusiasm. Austrian chancellor Wolfgang Schuessel, for one, suggested he would submit the question to a referendum back home. The decision on Turkey's membership "cannot be decided in an ivory tower," he said. "We cannot be indifferent about public opinion."

The new president of the European Commission, former Portuguese prime minister Jose Manuel Barroso, put the matter in different terms. "The challenge for Turkey is to win the hearts and minds of those in Europe who do not recognize Turkey's European destiny," he said. If so, recent opinion polls showed that Turkey had a big task ahead. By margins of more than 60 percent, those polled in Austria, France, and Germany opposed Turkish membership in the EU.

Returning home to Ankara later on December 18, Erdogan told a crowd that Turkey had "turned the critical junction" in its future as a modern, European state. "From now on, democracy will have a different meaning and human rights and freedoms will be practiced in a more meaningful manner, the economy will perform better," he said. "By this, Turkey will take its rightful place among modern and civilized countries."

Three other countries received positive news from the EU leaders at the summit. Croatia, which also had been waiting for an invitation to negotiate for membership, was told that its talks could start in March 2005—but only if it handed important war crimes suspects over to a UN tribunal that was handling cases from the Balkan conflicts of the early 1990s. Bulgaria and Romania were told their membership would become official at the beginning of 2007 if they continued to make progress on their economic and political reforms.

Failure in Cyprus

As the last-minute hitch over Cyprus demonstrated, the fate of that island remained a source of contention in European politics. For a few weeks earlier in 2004, it finally seemed possible that the division of Cyprus—one of Europe's longest-running conflicts—was about to be resolved. Cyprus had been divided since 1974, when Turkey invaded, and then occupied, the northern part of the island, saying it intended only to protect the ethnic Turkish minority there from an alleged plot by the ethnic Greek majority to unite the island with Greece. Under Turkey's sponsorship, the Turkish Cypriot community declared its own government (recognized only by Turkey), and for nearly three decades resisted numerous diplomatic efforts to reunite the island.

Early in 2004 the pending EU membership of the Republic of Cyprus—the relatively prosperous Greek half of the island—offered the latest opportunity for a solution. Settlement prospects also were enhanced by the position of Erdogan's government, which viewed closing the Cyprus dispute as a way of enhancing Turkey's own application for EU membership. Erdogan applied consistent pressure to the Cypriot Turkish leadership and won grudging support for the bulk of a peace plan advanced a year earlier by UN Secretary General Kofi Annan. That plan called for a single state of Cyprus unified by a weak federal government, with the Greek and Turkish communities retaining strong powers in their local areas. The chances for Annan's plan had been given a boost by elections in December 2003 that led to formation of a new Turkish Cypriot government committed to a peace deal.

By 2004, however, the center of resistance to a settlement had shifted to the Greek portion of Cyprus. A newly elected hard-line government there argued that the Greek community would lose some of its advantages if Annan's peace plan took effect; moreover, the Republic of Cyprus would enter the EU on May 1 regardless of the status of the peace agreement. The latest of a series of negotiations, mediated by Annan, failed on April 1, with the Greek Cypriot side blocking progress. That left the future of Annan's plan up to an already scheduled referendum, held in both communities on April 24. Turkish voters approved the plan, but Greek voters went along with their government's urging of a "no" vote, effectively killing it for the time being. Two days later, the European Commission issued a statement expressing regret at the rejection by the Greek Cypriots but "warmly" praising the outcome on the Turkish side. "A unique opportunity to bring about a solution to the long-lasting Cyprus issue has been missed," the commission said. Even so, Erdogan's labors on behalf of the peace agreement had won him—and Turkey generally—much credit at the UN and in European capitals, where Turkey in the past had been the bogeyman on the Cyprus issue.

Turkey and the United States

Relations between Ankara and Washington swung like a pendulum during the year, largely because of differing views over the Iraq War and its aftermath. Relations had fallen to a low point during the run-up to the war early in 2003. As the U.S.

military was preparing its massive invasion of Iraq, the Turkish parliament narrowly blocked an agreement—made by Erdogan's government—allowing the U.S. Army to mount the northern pincer of the invasion through Turkish territory. The decision embarrassed Erdogan, forced a massive reshuffling of the Pentagon's war plans, and raised questions in Washington about Turkey's reliability as an ally. Ankara later eased the sting of its action by allowing the U.S. military to use bases in Turkey for "logistical" support of its operations in Iraq. Although it temporarily strained relations with Washington, Turkey's initial rebuff enhanced its credibility among some Arab countries in the Middle East, which long had been suspicious of Turkey's NATO membership and its warm relations with Israel, America's closest ally in the region. *(Iraq War, Historic Documents of 2003, p. 135)*

A major step toward better U.S.-Turkish relations came in late January 2004, when Erdogan visited Washington for meetings with senior officials, including President George W. Bush, who gave him a warm welcome at the White House on January 28. Iraq one again was a major topic of discussion, in particular the fate of Kurds in northern Iraq, adjacent to Turkey. Turkey adamantly opposed any move by Iraq's Kurds toward independence or even increased autonomy from Baghdad, fearing that Turkey's own restive Kurdish population would be inspired to seek a similar status. Bush administration officials assured Erdogan that the United States opposed the division of Iraq; in Bush's language, Washington wanted Iraq to remain "territorially intact."

Bush visited Turkey in late June for a NATO summit hosted by Erdogan. The significance of that visit was overwhelmed, however, by another development: the nominal handover of power by U.S. authorities in Iraq to a new, U.S.-appointed government there. Bush received formal word of the transfer as he was meeting with his fellow NATO leaders on June 28. Bush used his visit to press the case for Turkey's membership in the EU, saying it would be an important sign to Muslims that Europe was not an "exclusive club" of Christian nations. At least one EU leader—France's Chirac—made it clear that he did not appreciate Bush's advice, saying it was up to Europe, not the United States, to determine which countries would become EU members.

Relations between Ankara and Washington chilled later in the year when Erdogan and lawmakers from his Justice and Development Party made statements clearly intended to distance Turkey from the continuing U.S. military occupation of Iraq. Erdogan said in November that Turkey was prepared to lead the Muslim world "against powers that are seeking to assert their hegemony" in the Middle East—a clear reference to Washington. The U.S. ambassador to Turkey, Eric S. Edelman, sought a meeting with Erdogan to discuss that language but was forced to wait six weeks for an appointment. After the two men met on December 13, Edelman described their talks as "constructive, thorough, and frank"—diplomatic language for a less-than-pleasant exchange of views.

Following is the text of a statement made December 17, 2004, by Jan Peter Balkenende, the prime minister of the Netherlands who was serving at the time as president of the European Council, following a meeting during which European leaders extended an invitation to Turkey to begin negotiations in October 2005 toward Turkish membership in the European Union.

"European Council President's Press Conference"

Yesterday evening I gave you the preliminary results of the talks and discussions during the working dinner of the heads of state and government. There we had reached a consensus on the decisions which we had to make with regard to enlargement, in particular the decision on Turkey. Today the debate continued. When I think back on today's events and the decisions which we have made, I believe that we can say that we have made history with one another today.

The agreement which we are in the process of making will be of great significance in the coming years. I am happy to report that the European Council has made the decision to begin accession negotiations with Turkey and Croatia and on wrapping up the accession negotiations with Bulgaria and Romania.

Yesterday evening I was able to report to you that the 25 Member States of the EU reached unanimity on the beginning of accession negotiations with Turkey. And today I can add that Turkey has accepted the offer.

In our capacity as the Presidency, we have always said that we are working towards a decision—a decision which are now making not only based on firm conviction, but also a decision which is sustainable in the future.

With regard to Turkey, we have decided that the negotiations will begin on 3 October 2005. Guarantees have been made on the democratic rule of law and respecting human rights. Accession is the goal, but this outcome cannot be guaranteed. The "anchoring" of Turkey into European structures has been assured in all cases.

As you know, Cyprus is perhaps the most sensitive issue. We spoke here about this extensively last night and today. Ultimately Prime Minister [Recep Tayyip] Erdogan indicated in a statement that he will sign the Protocol of the Ankara Agreement [this document dealt with Turkey's relations with the European Union's customs union; by singing it Erodgan would recognize that the EU's ten new members, including Cyprus, also were members of that customs union]. Paragraph 19 of the conclusions of the Council states that the European Council welcomes this decision. It is important for me to emphasise that this agreement must be signed before the negotiations can begin on 3 October 2005.

As for Bulgaria and Romania, the European Council has decided that these countries can join the Union under certain conditions on 1 January 2007.

With respect to Croatia, the European Council has decided to open accession negotiations on 17 March 2005. In light of the efforts made by Croatia, this is a well-deserved result.

These were the most important issues which were on the agenda today. We of course have debated other issues as well: fighting terrorism, the financial framework, and the financial outlook. We stalled on the issue of "values in Europe". These are all matters which were on the agenda during the Dutch Presidency [the six-month rotating presidency of the European Council, held by the Netherlands during the last half of 2004]. Above all though, the feeling and conviction that we have made historical decisions prevails today—decisions that affect the future of Europe and the Europe of the 21st century. Of course, much more must happen. This holds, in particular, with respect to Turkey, because the negotiations on many issues should go on and will also take time. Nevertheless, today was an important day and as President of the European Council I am glad that we were able to make the decision unanimously, so that we can move on. It was not an easy process, but it has been successfully wrapped up today and I am indeed delighted about that.

At the end of the Dutch Presidency, I would also like to express my gratitude for the cooperation with all those who made today's decisions possible. With this I mean the Member States, but I would also like to mention the support from the General Secretariat. And I would also like to mention, in particular, the good cooperation with the European Commission and recently the new President of the European Commission, Mr. [Jose Manuel] Barroso. A successful European Council with an important decision. That was what was on the agenda today.

Source: European Union. European Council. "Prime Minister and President of the European Council Jan Peter Balkenende at the Press Conference Following the European Council." December 17, 2004. www.eu2004.nl/default.asp?CMS_TCP=tcpPrint_EU2004&CMS_ITEM=49EDDD8211FD4B5696876C6305BF806DX1X68016X77 (accessed March 29, 2005).

Task Force Report on Prescription Drug Importation

December 21, 2004

INTRODUCTION

The rising cost of health care was a potent issue for many voters during the 2004 presidential election season, but little immediate relief was forthcoming. Several members of Congress, state elected officials, and even a leading pharmacy joined in calls for the federal government to allow consumers to save money by importing prescription drugs. But a Bush administration task force issued a report at the end of the year saying that the costs of ensuring the safety of drug imports were likely to wipe out any savings consumers could reap. The Bush administration, backed by the pharmaceutical industry, had long opposed legalizing drug imports.

Two important organizations—the Institute of Medicine and a bipartisan coalition of businesses, unions, health care associations, and consumer groups—also said it was time to consider enacting guaranteed health care coverage for all Americans. Despite widespread opposition to universal health care coverage in the past, both organizations said they thought the country could be reaching a tipping point where some sort of universal program might be acceptable if it could hold down costs and ensure quality care.

Rising Health Care Costs

The Department of Health and Human Services (HHS) reported on January 8, 2004, that spending on health care rose 9.3 percent in 2002, to a total of $1.55 trillion, accounting for nearly 15 percent of the national economy. It was the largest single-year increase in health care spending in eleven years. 2002 was the latest year for which complete figures were available. Estimates for 2003, released by HHS in February, reported that growth in health care spending apparently slowed that year, rising an estimated 7.8 percent, to $1.7 trillion, or more than $5,800 for every American. Health care spending was expected to grow faster than the rest of the economy for at least the next ten years, reaching an estimated $3.4 trillion in 2013 and accounting for more than 18 percent of gross domestic product.

Rising health care costs and a continuing decline in the number of workers in employer-sponsored health insurance plans pushed the number of those without health insurance up by 1.4 million in 2003 to a record high of 45 million. More than one-quarter of all young adults ages eighteen to thirty-four were uninsured in 2003, according to a Census Bureau report released August 26. This age group also sustained the greatest decline in median annual income. Typically, members of this age group were healthier than older Americans but also less able to afford health insurance. The Census Bureau reported that 3.2 million people were added to government health programs, including Medicare, Medicaid, and state coverage for children. More than one-fourth of the 243 million Americans with health insurance were covered under a public program.

Health insurance coverage was declining in part because many employers were asking their employees to pick up a bigger share of the tab or dropping employer-sponsored plans altogether. In September the Kaiser Family Foundation and Health Research and Education Trust released results of an annual survey the two groups conducted, which showed that health insurance premiums for employer-sponsored plans had gone up an estimated 11.2 percent in 2004. That was an improvement over the 13.9 percent increase recorded in 2003. The survey also found that the share of all companies offering health benefits to their employees had declined from 65 percent in 2001 to 61 percent in 2004. As a result, said John Gabel, vice president of Health Research and Education Trust, the number of workers with access to employer health care coverage dropped by an estimated 5 million between 2001 and 2004.

Guaranteed Health Care

Ever since President Bill Clinton's health care reform proposal was declared dead in 1994, the victim of overambition and intense opposition, politicians in Washington had shied away from talk about universal health care coverage. But that was beginning to change as health care costs and the number of uninsured continued to rise. Although the words *universal health care* were often avoided, a scattering of legislators and other policy makers were beginning to explore proposals to guarantee all Americans basic health care services. *(Clinton health care plan, Historic Documents of 1993, p. 781)*

That effort got a boost in January when the prestigious Institute of Medicine (IOM), an arm of the National Academy of Sciences, formally recommended for the first time that the government guarantee health insurance coverage for everyone by 2010. "The lack of health insurance for tens of millions of Americans has serious negative consequences and economic costs not only for the uninsured themselves but also for their families, the communities they live in, and the whole country," wrote the IOM's Committee on the Consequences of Uninsurance. "The situation is dire and expected to worsen. The committee urges Congress and the Administration to act immediately to eliminate this longstanding problem."

The committee's recommendation, released January 14, was contained in the sixth and final report the panel had issued during a three-year study of the uninsurance problem. In earlier reports, the committee found that about 18,000 people died prematurely each year because they lacked health insurance; that the uninsured received only about half the medical care as the insured, leaving the uninsured sicker and likely to die younger; and that the poor health and premature deaths of uninsured Americans cost the nation between $65 billion and $130 billion every year. *(Early reports, Historic Documents of 2001, p. 710; Historic Documents of 2002, p. 669; Historic Documents of 2003, p. 848)*

The committee did not recommend a specific plan for guaranteeing health care for everyone, but it did propose five principles for guiding and judging such proposals. Health care coverage should be universal, continuous, affordable to individuals and families, and affordable and sustainable to society, the panel said. It should also "enhance health and well-being by promoting access to high-quality care that is effective, efficient, safe, timely, patient-centered, and equitable," the committee wrote. "We're calling for action. We're calling for universal coverage by 2010,"

Mary Sue Coleman, president of the University of Michigan, Ann Arbor, and a cochair of the IOM panel, told the *New York Times*. "There have been times in our history when we have galvanized ourselves to action. This may be one of those points in history."

The IOM recommendation was followed in July by a similar proposal from the bipartisan National Coalition of Health Care, a diverse group of health care, business, labor, religious, and civic groups. The organization said Congress should require everyone to have basic health insurance, with subsidies for those who could not afford it.

The coalition noted that if no action was taken to relieve the situation, the number of Americans without insurance was projected to be 51 million by 2006 and that the average annual premium for employer-sponsored coverage for a family would be $14,565. "Small changes, incremental changes are not sufficient," said Henry E. Simmons, the president of the coalition and a physician who had served in three Republican administrations.

Action on legislation of the magnitude envisioned by the coalition and IOM seemed unlikely without the support of the Bush administration, however. In his State of the Union message on January 20, President George W. Bush said that "a government-run health care system is the wrong prescription." He called instead for Congress to approve tax credits to help the uninsured buy coverage; to allow small employers to band together so that they could negotiate lower insurance premiums; and to expand tax deductions under the health savings account program, enacted as part of the 2003 Medicare overhaul, to cover 100 percent of the premiums for catastrophic health insurance. Bush's Democratic presidential opponent, Sen. John Kerry of Massachusetts, proposed an expansion of health insurance coverage that included opening to the public the federal program that insured members of Congress and providing tax credits to laid-off workers. Kerry would have paid for his initiative by rolling back tax cuts for those earning more than $200,000 a year. *(State of the Union address, p. 17; Medicare overhaul, Historic Documents of 2003, p. 1119)*

Drug Imports

Allowing American to legally import cheaper prescription drugs from abroad gained increasing support among members of Congress and state officials as one way to curb rising medical costs. The Bush administration, with strong backing from the pharmaceutical industry, opposed the idea, saying it would open the market to a flood of unsafe and counterfeit drugs. The issue had gained political urgency in part because it was an election year and in part because Americans were paying more out of their own pockets for prescription drugs every year. According to the HHS report on health care spending issued in January, out-of-pocket spending for prescription drugs totaled $48.6 billion in 2002, up $6.1 billion from 2001.

For the past several years more and more American consumers had been turning abroad, primarily to Canada, to buy brand-name prescription drugs that often were one-third to one-half as expensive as the same drugs in the United States. A commonly offered example illustrating the price savings was Lipitor, the cholesterol-reducing drug made by Pfizer. Lipitor was the leading prescription drug in the United States, with $6.8 billion in sales in 2003. A bottle of ninety, 20 milligram pills sold for about $280 in American pharmacies and for about $180 on Canadian pharmacy Internet sites. Canadian and other foreign pharmacies could charge lower prices for the drugs because, unlike the United States, their governments essentially controlled drug prices. According to IMS Health, an international consulting firm that monitored the pharmaceutical industry, Americans spent $695 million on Canadian drugs in 2003, up from $414 million in 2002. About two-thirds of the 2003 sales were conducted over the Internet.

Such purchases were illegal, however. Federal law prohibited the importation of drugs unless and until the federal government certified that the drugs being imported were made according to U.S. standards. Government officials said without such certification consumers could not be sure that the drugs they were purchasing were real or counterfeit, whether they were the stated strength, and whether they had been manufactured under clean and safe conditions. Pharmaceutical companies, which opposed the imports, began in 2004 to restrict or cut off sales of their drugs to Canadian and other foreign drug wholesalers. For example, in a letter dated February 12, Pfizer notified several Canadian Internet pharmacies that it would no longer sell them Pfizer drugs. Pfizer said it was taking the action to protect patents and the integrity of the pharmaceutical supply system. A spokesman for one of the Internet companies disagreed. "This is all about Pfizer sales, profits, and the bottom line," Jeff Uhl, president of Universaldrugstore.com, told the Associated Press.

Pressure to allow the imports came from a variety of sources. Several states began to sponsor Web sites listing Canadian and European pharmacies that state health officials deemed safe and reliable. Officials in Springfield, Massachusetts, the first city to buy Canadian prescription drugs for its city workers and retirees, said in April that the city had saved $2 million during the first nine months of the program. In May Minnesota went a step further and set up a state program that allowed state employees to obtain certain drugs for free if they ordered the medications from a state-inspected Canadian pharmacy. The state estimated it would save $1.4 million a year on the cheaper Canadian versions of the drugs. Also in May Thomas Ryan, chairman and chief executive officer of the CVS pharmacy chain, said he supported legalizing importation of drugs.

In August Vermont governor Jim Douglas, a Republican, sued the federal Food and Drug Administration (FDA) in federal district court in an effort to force the agency to write regulations governing legal importation of prescription drugs. In early December the American Medical Association endorsed importation of drugs so long as they carried electronic tracking devices to distinguish them from counterfeit drugs.

Pressure was also building in Congress for legislation legalizing drug imports. In 2003 the House passed such legislation by a surprisingly strong 243–186 vote. The legislation would have allowed FDA-approved drugs made in FDA-approved factories in twenty-five industrialized countries to be imported.

Several bills to allow imports were introduced in the Senate, but none of them saw committee or floor action. One of the measures was a bipartisan plan that would have directed the FDA to implement a system to import drugs from Canada and that would have imposed penalties on manufacturers that interfered with importation by restricting supply or raising prices. Backers of the measure, including the powerful senior lobby AARP, had hoped to bring the measure straight to the Senate floor without it first going through committee. Senate Finance Committee chairman Charles E. Grassley, R-Iowa, insisted that the measure would pass by a wide margin if it reached the floor. But Majority Leader Bill Frist, R-Tenn., refused to cooperate, apparently not wanting to risk a floor fight over a popular bill that could potentially embarrass the president and the GOP congressional leadership during an election year.

Task Force Study

Supporters also tried to include drug importation provisions in the landmark 2003 overhaul of the Medicare program, which authorized a new prescription drug benefit for seniors. They were unsuccessful and instead settled for directing HHS to study the issue and report its findings to Congress within a year. The study got off to a rocky start, when HHS secretary Tommy G. Thompson announced that he was naming Mark B. McClellan, the outgoing head of the FDA who was awaiting confirmation as the new administrator of the Medicare program, to chair the task force. The appointment was criticized by members of both parties. "It's like putting the fox in charge of the chicken house," said Sen. Byron L. Dorgan, D-N.D., a strong advocate of importation. "Dr. McClellan has clearly made up his mind not to allow importation and done everything in his power to stop it," Dorgan said. Republican senator John McCain of Arizona registered his concern though a spokesperson who said, "Dr. McClellan has already displayed a personal bias" against drug imports. After several senators indicated they would hold up McClellan's nomination as head of the Medicare agency, Thompson backed down and announced March 16 that Richard H. Carmona, the surgeon general, would chair the task force and McClellan would remain a member.

The task force, which was widely expected to oppose drug importation, was to have made its report by December 8, but the release was postponed to December 21. Thompson said the postponement was required because he was traveling overseas and was not able to review the final document until he returned. Skeptics noted that it was more likely the department was trying to avoid embarrassment. On December 7 Thompson announced that the government would import 1.2 million doses of influenza vaccine from a British-owned factory in Germany to help ease the vaccine shortage that occurred when one of the two U.S. suppliers lost its entire production of vaccine to contamination. "Here we are buying flu vaccine from Germany and yet [HHS is] sitting on a report that probably says it's dangerous to purchase medicines from other countries," said Rep. Gil Gutknecht, R-Minn., sponsor of the drug importation legislation in the House. "Why is it that the FDA can do this safely but your local pharmacist can't?" *(Flu vaccine shortage, p. 639)*

In its report, the thirteen-member task force warned that consumers were taking a "significant risk" by buying largely unregulated prescription drugs from overseas suppliers. The panel said that ensuring the safety of individual drug imports for personal use was unworkable but that legalizing commercial imports by pharmacies and drug wholesalers might be feasible. The panel added, however, that ensuring the safety of such drugs would be expensive, that middlemen would reap much of the benefit, and that overall savings to consumers were likely to be modest. The panel suggested that consumers could save up to $17 billion a year simply by using generic drugs, bought in the United States, whenever possible. The panel also said that drug imports were likely to prove a disincentive for development of new drugs by pharmaceutical companies.

In a letter submitting the report to Congress, Secretary Thompson and Commerce Department Secretary Donald L. Evans were even stronger in opposing legitimizing drug imports. They listed several "significant safety and economic issues" that they said "must be addressed before importation of prescription drugs is permitted." The net effect would limit importation to "a discrete number of high-volume, high-cost prescription drugs from a country with equivalent drug safety protections," namely, Canada. Thompson and Evans said that if Congress were to pass legislation that did not address the concerns listed or that "discouraged innovation or stifled competition," their departments would recommend that Bush veto the measure.

Supporters of drug importation legislation said they would continue to push for the legislation in the 109th Congress.

Following are excerpts from the executive summary of the "Report on Prescription Drug Importation," prepared by the HHS Task force on Drug Importation and released December 21, 2004.

"Report on Prescription Drug Importation"

Overview

Introduction

In 2003, Congress passed the Medicare Prescription Drug, Improvement and Modernization Act of 2003, Pub. L. 108–173 (Medicare Modernization Act or MMA), which for the first time provided a prescription drug benefit for seniors and people with disabilities. The MMA also contained provisions that would permit the importation of prescription drugs into the U.S. if the Secretary of the Department of Health and Human Services (HHS) certifies that drugs imported from Canada pose no additional risk to public health and safety and that such imports would provide significant cost savings to American consumers. The MMA also requires the Secretary to conduct a study on the importation of drugs. The conference agreement for MMA included eleven issues for consideration. The Surgeon General of the U.S. Public Health Service, Dr. Richard H. Carmona, was charged with leading a task force of senior executives across the Federal government to conduct the analysis required by the MMA. The Task Force met with key constituencies numerous times throughout 2004 in public forums, received testimony from over one hundred presenters from around the world with all types of backgrounds, and received over one hundred written comments providing insight into these issues. This report is a summary of what the Task Force reviewed from the testimony and written comments for the specific questions posed in the MMA conference agreement and their findings based on this evaluation.

Background

In the early years of the twentieth century, pharmaceuticals in the U.S. were characterized by a large number of ineffective, often dangerous, compounds, the principal ingredient of which was often alcohol. The invention of penicillin in the 1930s marked the beginning of the modern era of drug development, when scientists were able to create powerful new chemicals that were safe and effective in killing bacteria. Since then, the world's investment in research and development (R&D) has produced many more safe and effective treatments to reduce pain and inflammation, regulate the cardiovascular system, impede the growth of cancer cells, and provide a host of other effective therapies for disease. The resulting discovery of new medications has enabled doctors to offer comfort for the sick and to prescribe from an extensive array of drugs to treat most human afflictions.

As this innovation began in the 1930s, Congress recognized the need for a strong oversight body to ensure that drugs were properly tested before being given to patients. The manufacturing of drugs needed equally rigorous oversight to ensure that drugs were made in a safe and consistent way. The Federal Food, Drug, and Cosmetic (FD&C) Act of 1938 and its 1962 amendments provided that oversight, by requiring that the U.S. Food and Drug Administration (FDA) approve each new drug as safe and effective before marketing and authorizing FDA to oversee the production of drugs, whether manufactured in a U.S. facility or imported from abroad.

By the 1980s, Congress recognized that some entities not subject to U.S. law were importing counterfeit drugs as well as improperly handled and stored drugs. For example, at that time, counterfeit birth control pills found their way into the U.S. drug distribution system. These types of activities posed significant risks to American consumers. Therefore, in 1987, Congress passed the Prescription Drug Marketing Act (PDMA), which, among other things, strengthened oversight of domestic wholesalers and added the "American goods returned" provision to the FD&C Act, which prohibits anyone U.S. a prescription drug that was originally manufactured in the U.S. and then sent abroad.

We recognize that there are different categories of "imported drugs" that potentially have different levels of associated risk. Currently, the only types of legally imported drugs are: 1) those that are manufactured in foreign FDA-inspected facilities and adhere to FDA-approval standards, or 2) those that are U.S.-approved and manufactured in the U.S., sent abroad, then imported back into the U.S. by the manufacturer under proper controls and in compliance with the FD&C Act. This latter category includes products that are truly re-imported. In both cases, the manufacturing process is subject to direct FDA oversight and the drug distribution system is "closed," and the manufacturer complies with FDA and other regulations to assure that the drug delivered to the pharmacy is of high quality.

Another category of imported drugs are those that are manufactured in a foreign facility that also manufactures the U.S.-approved version. In such a case, FDA would have inspected the U.S.-approved manufacturing process, but not the unapproved production lines; in this case, the foreign version may differ in certain respects from the U.S.-approved version. Although there may be significant similarities between the two versions, because of the potential differences and the fact that only the U.S.-approved drugs have been shown to meet U.S standards enforced by FDA, the foreign version cannot necessarily be considered equivalent to the U.S.-approved version.

A final category of imported drugs are unapproved drugs that are produced in foreign facilities that FDA has not inspected and, therefore, has no knowledge of, or experience with, the facility. Consequently, the safety and effectiveness of these drugs and the safety and security of their distribution systems are unknown. These drugs pose the greatest level of concern because they are not regulated within the U.S. drug safety system and little is known to U.S. regulators about the specifications to which they are made, the processes used to ensure their safety, and the integrity of their distribution. As the report describes, there is ample evidence that these are the types of drugs that consumers have received when they order prescription drugs from some international sources over the internet.

When a drug is imported into the U.S., FDA inspectors are required to confirm that the drug meets the necessary approval requirements. Such review of imported drugs is limited by the amount of resources available, given the substantial amount of legal and illegal prescription drugs that are imported daily. If there is a question of whether the drug can legally be imported and, thus, raises safety questions, FDA has the authority to detain the product and gives the importer several days to demonstrate the drug's acceptability (or, failing that, the drug is either refused admission and returned to its foreign source, if known, or destroyed.)

The conclusion of Congress reflected in current law is that the safety and effectiveness of imported drugs can only be assured for drugs legally imported into the U.S., as described above. In these cases, the chain of custody is known for a U.S.-approved drug manufactured in an FDA-inspected facility using FDA-approved methods as it travels through the U.S. distribution system. Much of the current public debate about the safety of broader importation comes down to issues regarding the additional oversight authorities, resources, and foreign government support that would be needed to assure the safety and effectiveness of other types of drugs, principally foreign drug purchases from international internet operations that are not subject to FDA's regulatory oversight.

Since the FD&C Act's passage in 1938, American citizens returning from overseas with foreign drugs have been advised that most of these drugs are not legal, but, as a matter of enforcement discretion, FDA has generally allowed those citizens to bring in small quantities for their personal use and advised them to consult with their physician. FDA created this enforcement discretion policy to allow American residents who became ill in another country to continue the treatment prescribed by a foreign healthcare practitioner until they could receive medical attention back home. That policy was not controversial until the latter part of the 1990's, when some citizens began traveling regularly to other countries to fill their prescriptions, and especially when more Americans began ordering drugs via internet pharmacies located in other countries.

The Task Force understands what motivates more and more Americans to import drugs. Access to affordable prescription drugs, many of which are needed to treat life-threatening and serious conditions, is a daily concern and challenge for many Americans. As there has been a significant increase in drug utilization and in list prices for drugs in the U.S. over the last few years, spending by American consumers on prescription drugs has risen significantly. Over 40 percent of Americans take at least one prescription drug and, in an effort to lower their prescription drug bill, a relatively small but increasing number have turned to importing drugs.

Consequently, the Task Force believes that access to drugs that are safe and effective, as well as affordable, is a critical policy goal, and that all approaches to achieving this challenging goal should be explored thoroughly. Drugs that are affordable, but not safe and effective, could be more harmful to patients than not having the drugs at all. The difficult balance between the need for affordable prescription drugs and concerns over potential safety hazards that many imported drugs may pose is reflected in the public debate and controversies regarding drug importation policy in the U.S. The Task Force report presents a comprehensive overview of the evidence related to this balance, as well as a number of other critical issues, as requested by Congress, on the subject of prescription drug importation. . . .

Key Findings

This report details the diverse opinions expressed, the data collected, and Task Force findings based on the information presented. Some of the key findings of the Task Force are:

1) **The current system of drug regulation in the U.S. has been very effective in protecting public safety, but is facing new threats. It should be modified only with great care to ensure continued high standards of safety and effectiveness of the U.S. drug supply.** Americans have the benefit of one of the safest drug supplies in the world and generally have first access to the newest breakthrough drug treatments. Any legislation to permit the importation of foreign drugs should only be done in a way that provides the statutory authority and substantial resources needed to effectively regulate imported drugs and, most importantly, protect the public health by providing the same level of safety assurances available for drugs sold in the U.S.

2) **There are significant risks associated with the way individuals are currently importing drugs.** While some means of drug importation (e.g., traveling to Canada for certain brand name drugs available in both countries) may be relatively safe in specific instances, this is not the only way "importation" into the U.S. is occurring today. Many transactions are occurring via poorly-regulated and occasionally bogus internet operations that have been documented in some cases to provide consumers with inferior products that are not the same as the U.S.-approved versions. Also, treatment failures, which are not obvious adverse events, are a real concern with substandard drug products.

3) **It would be extraordinarily difficult and costly for "personal" importation to be implemented in a way that ensures the safety and effectiveness of the imported drugs.** While wholesalers and pharmacists purchase, transport, and dispense imported drugs within our regulatory framework, American consumers making individual purchases from foreign sources outside our regulatory system, in particular those making long-distance purchases from internet sites or by fax or phone, face safety hazards that would be extraordinarily difficult to effectively address and prevent.

4) **Overall national savings from legalized commercial importation will likely be a small percentage of total drug spending and developing and implementing such a program would incur significant costs and require significant additional authorities.** The public rightly expects that, under any legal importation program, the imported drugs will be safe and effective. To accomplish this, additional safety protections would need to be added that would increase the costs of the program in an additive way as more safety measures are put in place. Substantial resources would also be needed to ensure adequate inspection of imported drug products. In addition to other factors that are likely to reduce potential consumer savings, these increased regulatory and program costs will also impact potential savings to consumers. Furthermore, intermediaries will likely capture at least half of any savings between the U.S. and price-controlled countries and potential quantity constraints imposed by foreign governments and manufacturers will likely further limit the supply of these drugs to U.S. consumers.

5) **The public expectation that most imported drugs are less expensive than American drugs is not generally true.** Generic drugs account for most prescription

drugs used in the U.S. and are usually less expensive in the U.S. than abroad. Shopping around for price comparisons, asking a doctor or pharmacist for a generic alternative to a prescribed brand name drug, or using a Medicare or other prescription drug discount card is a proven method to save American consumers money on domestic prescription drugs while retaining the protections of a comprehensive safety regime.

6) **Legalized importation will likely adversely affect the future development of new drugs for American consumers.** This report estimates that R&D incentives will be lowered by legalized importation, resulting in roughly between four and eighteen fewer new drugs introduced per decade.

7) **The effects of legalized importation on intellectual property rights are uncertain but likely to be significant.** A host of legal and constitutional challenges are probable, and the effects on enforcement of intellectual property rights and on agreements with foreign countries are likely to be problematic. These effects could create additional disincentives to develop breakthrough medicines and further limit any potential savings that might have been realized.

8) **Legalized importation raises liability concerns for consumers, manufacturers, distributors, pharmacies, and other entities.** Consumers harmed by imported drugs may not have legal recourse against foreign pharmacies, distributors, or others suppliers. Entities in the pharmaceutical supply chain may take actions to protect themselves from liability that could ultimately raise the cost of drugs.

Source: U.S. Department of Health and Human Services. HHS Task Force on Drug Importation. "Report on Prescription Drug Importation." December 21, 2004. www.hhs.gov/importtaskforce/Report1220.pdf (accessed March 17, 2005).

United Nations Reports on Tsunami in Indian Ocean Region

December 26, 27, and 29, 2004

INTRODUCTION

A powerful undersea earthquake off the Indonesian island of Sumatra generated a series of enormous tsunami waves on December 26, 2004, that swept across the Indian Ocean, killing tens of thousands of people and devastating hundreds of miles of Asian coastlines. The United Nations and aid agencies from around the world rushed food, medicine, shelter, and other supplies to eleven countries in what was certain to become the biggest emergency relief effort of modern times. At year's end there even appeared to be a degree of one-upmanship among donors, with individual nations engaging in a virtual bidding war to exceed each other's contributions. Millions of people around the world also flooded nongovernmental aid groups with money, collectively creating the single greatest outpouring of private charity in recent memory.

At year's end the total estimated death toll stood at about 145,000 and was certain to rise significantly as rescue teams reached remote regions and as bodies continued to wash ashore. Indonesia was closest to the epicenter of the earthquake and was hardest hit with at least 100,000 people dead in its Aceh province. Sri Lanka was second in damage, with an estimated 30,000 people dead. Other major casualty centers were southern India, with about 10,000 dead, and Thailand, with more than 4,500 dead. Bangladesh, Burma, Malaysia, the Maldives, and even the distant African coastal areas of Kenya, Mauritius, and Somalia also suffered damage and lost lives.

Depending on the eventual death total, the tsunami was likely to be rated as one of the deadliest half-dozen natural disasters in a century. Recent record holders were a 1975 cyclone and subsequent flooding in Bangladesh that killed about 500,000 people; a 1976 earthquake in China that killed about 255,000 people; earthquakes in China in 1920 and 1927 that killed about 200,000 each; a 1927 earthquake in Japan that killed 143,000 people; and a 1991 cyclone and flooding that killed about 138,000 people in Bangladesh.

Speaking the day after the event, Jan Egeland, the UN's emergency relief coordinator, said the tsunami was not the biggest in recorded history "but the effects may be the biggest because many more people live in exposed areas than ever before." Scientists and demographers had been warning for years that the world was becoming more vulnerable to natural disasters and the effects of climate change because of the overcrowding of low-lying coastal areas and the deliberate destruction of barrier reefs, mangrove forests, and sand dunes, which once softened the ocean's blows on beachfronts. Everyone killed by the December 26 tsunami was living—or visiting—within a few hundred feet of the ocean shoreline.

Earthquakes, Then Walls of Water

Shortly before 7 A.M. local time on December 26, an earthquake rated at a magnitude of 8.5 on the Richter scale, took place deep beneath the seabed of the Indian Ocean, about 150 miles southeast of the province of Aceh, on the northwest coast of Sumatra. The combined effect made the event the world's most powerful earthquake in forty years and the fourth most powerful in a century.

The earthquake pushed a 625-mile section of the Earth's crust about 50 feet upward into the ocean. The immense force of that motion generated a tsunami—a series of waves that eventually reached speeds of nearly 500 miles an hour traveling across the ocean. When they reached coastal areas, the tsunami waves slowed but rose to heights of as much as 30 feet.

The first waves hit a 115-mile stretch of coastline on Sumatra less than an hour after the earthquake, engulfing fishermen in their boats and people at the beachfront. The waves uprooted trees and demolished buildings, turning them into battering rams that created a broad path of devastation up to several hundred feet from the shore. The coasts of Malaysia and Thailand, and the Indian island chains of Andaman and Nicobar, were next as the waves traveled their deadly course. Then coastal areas of Burma (Myanmar), Sri Lanka, and nearly the entire low-lying island nation of the Maldives were hammered by walls of water. Hours later, the tsunami waves finished their travels across the 3,000 miles of the Indian Ocean and crashed onto the island nation of Mauritius and then the African coast, much diminished in power but still deadly for those unfortunate enough to be in their path.

Still attempting to recover from the shock hours afterward, survivors in various locations thousands of miles apart told almost identical stories. "It was very fast," said Montri Charnvichai, a resident of the tourist town of Phuket, Thailand, in describing the approach of the tsunami about 10 A.M. local time. "It swept up the beach, carrying everything with it. There were many, many people in the sea at this time, and many of them were tourists. I have no idea what happened to them."

Some survivors told stories of courage—rescuers who endangered their own lives to pluck people from exposed positions and neighbors who came to warn them. Many more survivors had stories of tragedy—parents who, while clinging to trees or rooftops, lost hold of their children, who were swept away by the waves. Still others had stories of incredible fortune, including some who had been carried out to sea but somehow managed to survive.

Nearly all the early news reporting centered on tourist areas in the Maldives, Malaysia, Sri Lanka, and Thailand that were crowded with Europeans and North Americans on Christmas holidays. These areas were served by airports and advanced telecommunication facilities, enabling rescue teams, along with reporters and television camera crews, to reach the scene quickly. Only days later did the rest of the world begin to learn the extent of the devastation in distant areas where tourists rarely ventured.

Early Relief Efforts

Local governments across the Indian Ocean region organized themselves as best they could to recover bodies and tend to the injured, but it was clear that a rescue and relief effort of giant proportions would be necessary. The United Nations put its first relief experts on airplanes to Sri Lanka within hours after the reports of the tsunami, and UN officials issued warnings that hundreds of thousands of people could be endangered by disease and the lack of food and clean water resulting from the destruction.

The first shipments of international relief supplies began arriving in the most accessible parts of the region within thirty-six hours. On December 28 UNICEF sent an airplane from Denmark to Sri Lanka stocked with enough medicines and other health supplies to care for 150,000 people for three months. Aid agencies quickly encountered logistical difficulties in distributing the supplies, however, including a lack of airplanes and helicopters to reach remote areas, and heavy damage to roads and electrical and telephone lines.

Many world leaders went on radio and television to express their condolences and pledge aid for the victims. Curiously absent from this immediate outpouring was U.S. President George W. Bush, who was clearing brush and bicycling while on vacation at his ranch in Crawford, Texas. A White House spokesman said Bush was being briefed on the situation but felt no need "to make a symbolic statement about 'We feel your pain.'"

The first official U.S. response to the tsunami came from the Agency for International Development, which was responsible for giving aid in international disasters. It pledged $15 million on December 27.

On the ground in Asia, rescue workers began retrieving bodies, and relief workers provided the first limited quantities of food and medicine for survivors. The reported death toll throughout the region reached about 25,000 on December 28, then 57,000 on December 29, and then doubled to about 117,000 on December 30. At year's end the estimated total stood at about 145,000. Officials warned of a potential for more people to die of disease than had been killed by the impact of the tsunami waves.

It was not until December 28—two days after the tsunami—that the first international aid workers and news reporters reached Banda Aceh, the capital of Indonesia's Aceh region, which was closest to the epicenter of the earthquake. Rebels in Aceh province for years had been fighting for independence from Indonesia, and the province had been under martial law since May 2003, when peace talks between the government and rebels collapsed. That conflict was set aside at least momentarily in the face of the more urgent relief needs. "The soldiers that were sent to Aceh to fight rebels now have a new task, disposing of the dead," BBC correspondent Rachel Harvey reported after arriving in the capital on December 29. "The conflict is now at the back of everyone's minds. People are fighting for survival, they haven't got time to fight among themselves."

A similar story was played out in Sri Lanka, were a fragile cease-fire was in effect between the government and rebels representing the Tamil minority. The government and rebels set aside their differences and worked side-by-side to respond to the tragedy of the moment. *(Sri Lanka peace, Historic Documents of 2002, p. 92)*

An Aid Bidding War

Speaking to reporters one day after the tsunami, UN relief coordinator Egeland put the world response to the tragedy in the broader context of aid from the rich countries to the poorer ones. "It is beyond me why we are so stingy," he said. "Really, Christmas time should remind many Western countries at least, how rich we have become. There are several donors who are less generous than before, in a growing world economy."

Egeland's comment brought a caustic response on December 28 from Secretary of State Colin Powell, who made the rounds of morning television shows to rebut the remark and demonstrate U.S. concern about the situation in Asia. "The United States is not stingy," he said. Later that day the U.S. boosted its contribution by $20 million, and the Pentagon announced that the aircraft carrier *Abraham Lincoln* had been dispatched to provide aid to Indonesia.

Egeland immediately said his remark had been misinterpreted and that he had referred to the shortage of Western aid in general for developing countries. "This has nothing to do with any particular country or the response to this emergency," he said.

Egeland also appealed on December 29 for "coordination" of relief to avoid unnecessary duplication and excessive strain on transportation facilities in the affected areas. "There are few airstrips in many of these areas, and airspace and airstrip space is very, very precious," he said. He also appealed for $130 million in aid to be funneled through the UN and said a larger appeal would be issued early in January after more extensive assessments had been made of needs in remote regions. UN officials noted that Secretary General Kofi Annan, who had been on vacation, was returning to his New York office to oversee the UN's emergency work.

President Bush made his first public appearance since the tsunami on December 29 and said the $35 million promised so far by the United States was "only the beginning" of the aid. Bush also responded heatedly to Egeland's "stingy" remark, saying: "Well, I felt like the person who made that statement was very misguided and ill-informed. We're a very generous, kindhearted nation, and, you know, what you're beginning to see is a typical response from America." Aides later said Bush had "accepted" Egeland's clarification that his remark was not directed at the U.S. response to the tsunami crisis.

Some of Bush's domestic critics could not resist the temptation to fault his administration for what they said was a slow response to the disaster. "I just about went through the roof when I heard them bragging about $35 million," Sen. Patrick J. Leahy. D-Vt., said. "We spent $35 million before breakfast in Iraq," where more than 130,000 U.S. troops were battling an insurgency.

Annan and Egeland held a joint news conference at the UN on December 30 and said donations pledged by governments and private agencies had reached about $500 million. "This is an unprecedented, global catastrophe, and it requires an unprecedented, global response," Annan said.

Officials at the UN and other agencies on December 30 issued their first comprehensive estimates of how many people had been affected by the earthquake and tsunami, beyond the number of people killed. Reporting on initial assessments from the field, the World Health Organization said as many as 5 million people lacked such essentials as food, clean water, shelter, and basic medical supplies.

By December 30 it appeared that Western nations and aid agencies were competing with each other to up the ante on aid pledges. The U.S. total of $35 million as of that date was far down the list of major contributions, headed by the World Bank at $250 million, and Britain at $100 million. France and the United States—still engaged in diplomatic tussles resulting from their differences over the war in Iraq—publicly disputed each other's generosity. Appearing on ABC's *Nightline* program that evening, Powell expressed irritation at the news media's focus on the aid totals: "I don't know yet what the United States contribution will be, and what we have to do is make a needs assessment and not just grasp at numbers or think we're in some kind of an auction house where every day somebody has to top someone else."

Even so, the United States finally jumped into the bidding the next day, December 31, when the White House issued a statement, under Bush's name, raising the U.S. commitment to $350 million. The White House also said Powell and the president's brother, Florida governor Jeb Bush, would travel to some of the affected countries in the region to make quick assessments of continuing needs.

Another aspect of the White House statement generated questions about administration intentions. It said the United States had formed a "core group," along with Australia, India, and Japan, to coordinate tsunami aid. Annan publicly welcomed the announcement, but some officials at the Untied Nations and private aid agencies said the approach appeared to represent an attempt by the Bush administration to wrest control away from the United Nations, which traditionally coordinated aid in such situations. Powell insisted this was not the administration's intent. Instead, he said, the United States and the other "core group" nations would coordinate their immediate aid but eventually would rely on the "overall supervision and leadership of the United Nations."

It was routine for governments to respond quickly to natural disasters in other countries with offers of help, but perhaps the most remarkable aspect of the world response to the Indian Ocean tsunami was an exceptionally generous outpouring of support from private individuals. Western aid agencies were swamped with letters and telephone calls offering donations, and the Internet traffic was so heavy that the Web sites of some agencies crashed. Many aid agencies said they had raised record amounts of money, in some cases into the millions of dollars without even having issued public appeals.

By year's end—five days after the earthquake and tsunami—small quantities of public and private aid had reached the most accessible areas hit by the tsunami, notably the tourist resorts of Sri Lanka and Thailand. However, very little outside help had arrived in more remote areas, including rural regions of Indonesia's Aceh province and distant islands in the Maldives archipelago. Poor roads, damage to the roads that did exist, a shortage of trucks and fuel, and inadequate air transportation were the major problems. News reports said tons of relief supplies were sitting at staging areas in Indonesia, Thailand, Sri Lanka, and other countries waiting to be transported to those in need. The needy were becoming increasingly desperate for food, water, and medical supplies, according to relief workers and journalists on the scene. The grisly task of collecting bodies was proceeding slowly, and local officials said they feared it might be weeks or even months before all the dead had been located. One bright spot was that diseases such as cholera had not yet set in, but aid workers warned that epidemics were possible if supplies of fresh water and medicine did not reach remote locations quickly.

Tsunami Warnings

The enormity of the devastation in the Indian Ocean region focused new attention on the absence of a tsunami warning system there. After a tsunami hit Alaska in 1965, the United States, Japan, and other nations established an electronic communications network to warn of tsunamis in the Pacific rim. No such system existed in the Indian Ocean, however, and officials in the region immediately began talking of building one.

Officials from the United Nations and several of the affected countries called for urgent studies of a tsunami warning system for the region. Japan offered to help finance the cost, but as of year's end no formal cost estimates had been made.

Following are three news reports by the United Nations, issued December 26, December 27, and December 29, 2004, in response to an undersea earthquake and resulting tsunami that caused vast devastation across the Indian Ocean region.

"UN Experts Rush to Countries Devastated by Quake, Tidal Waves"

United Nations relief experts are headed to Sri Lanka to help coordinate the international response to the massive tidal waves that struck the Indian Ocean nation after a series of earthquakes rocked the western coast of Northern Sumatra in Indonesia as well as the Andaman and Nicobar Islands.

Additional UN emergency staff are being sent to other affected countries to reinforce the world body's capacity to support government response efforts. Immediate humanitarian needs include portable sanitation facilities, medical supplies, tents and helicopters to evacuate people in the crisis spots.

The UN Office for the Coordination of Humanitarian Affairs (OCHA) announced that it will provide initial emergency cash grants to help the affected countries.

"This is the first step in what will surely be a larger United Nations response to catastrophic losses suffered as a result of earthquakes and tidal waves this morning," said UN Emergency Relief Coordinator Jan Egeland.

According to information from the United States Geological Survey, the two strongest earthquakes had the magnitude of 8.9 on the Richter Scale and 7.3 on the Richter Scale. The quakes caused tsunamis—massive tidal waves—impacting several countries in the region. Media reports place the death toll throughout the region at some 7,000 people.

The Government of Sri Lanka has declared a state of emergency and requested international assistance. The Maldives Government is also seeking international help.

The UN pledged to work closely with all affected countries in order to help the victims.

"The United Nations stands ready to provide the assistance necessary to meet the needs created by these natural disasters," a spokesman for Secretary-General Kofi Annan said in a statement released in New York, extending "sincere condolences to the people and governments of the countries affected as they cope with their catastrophic losses."

"The power of this earthquake, and its huge geographical reach, are just staggering," said Carol Bellamy, Executive Director of the UN Children's Fund (UNICEF). "Hundreds of thousands of children in coastal communities in six countries may be in serious jeopardy," she said. "We're supporting governments in their damage assessments, and we're prepared to respond wherever help is needed."

All UNICEF offices in the region have been mobilized to support relief efforts. Emergency supplies are on stand-by at the UNICEF global supply hub in Copenhagen and relief flights can be launched at any hour.

Source: United Nations. UN News Service. "UN Experts Rush to Indian Ocean Countries Devastated by Quake and Tidal Waves." December 26, 2004. www.un.org/apps/news/story.asp?NewsID=12912&Cr=earthquake&Cr1= (accessed March 14, 2005).

"UN Launches Effort to Aid Victims of Asia's Devastating Tsunami"

The United Nations today rushed in more aid to the victims of the devastating tsunami that struck south Asia as it prepared to launch a flash appeal in what relief officials called an unprecedented effort by the world body to forestall the dangers of disease threatening millions of people.

"An enormous relief effort is on its way," UN Emergency Relief Coordinator Jan Egeland said, as UN Disaster Assessment Coordination (UNDAC) teams fanned out to the stricken countries and local branches of the world body's various agencies began releasing emergency material.

This tsunami "is not the biggest in recorded history, but the effects may be the biggest ever because many more people live in exposed areas than ever before," he told a news conference at UN Headquarters in New York, appealing to donor countries to respond generously to what he called a "tremendous emergency."

While "the first wave" of the disaster has already brought tens of thousands of casualties, Mr. Egeland stressed the "second wave"—the after-effects which will affect millions of people. "Drinking water for millions has been polluted," he said. "Disease will be a result of that and also acute respiratory disease always comes in the wake of disasters."

He paid tribute to local relief bodies in the affected nations for their immediate response to the catastrophe, estimated that total costs would be in "the many billions of dollars," and stressed that it was imperative to have a tsunami early warning system established in the Indian Ocean.

Sálvano Briceño, Director of the International Strategy for Disaster Reduction (ISDR), said the catastrophe showed that Indian Ocean nations are not prepared—as most countries in the Pacific basin are—for alerting their citizens about imminent tsunamis.

"A simple and timely message can go a long way and can mean the difference between life and death, not to mention economic survival or ruin," he said. Next month the World Conference on Disaster Reduction will be held in Kobe, Japan, will focus on improving early warning systems.

The Assistant Emergency Relief Coordinator and Director of the UN Office for the Coordination of Humanitarian Affairs (OCHA) Yvette Stevens told a news conference in Geneva that that the situation was particularly challenging given that widespread disaster has occurred in several countries. The UN was "used to dealing with disasters in one country," she said. "But I think something like this spread across many countries and islands is unprecedented. We have not had this before."

She added that the UN would launch a flash appeal in the coming days to fund aid to all the affected regions, where media reports put the latest death toll at over 20,000, with more than 10,000 in Sri Lanka alone.

In Sri Lanka, the UN refugee agency opened up its relief stockpiles to deliver immediate emergency assistance to the Indian Ocean island, where thousands were killed, injured or displaced by the catastrophe, while the UN World Food Programme (WFP) took steps to feed some 400,000 people displaced by the catastrophe.

"The magnitude of this disaster is so enormous and shocking that we will do everything we can to join the international community in bringing help as rapidly as possible to the victims of these gigantic waves," UN High Commissioner for Refugees (UNHCR) Ruud Lubbers said. "Our supplies are usually for displaced people, but this is an emergency and the local population needs help right now."

WFP issued an initial call, ahead of the flash appeal, for $1.5 million for the most immediate food needs of hundreds of thousands of victims in Sri Lanka, Indonesia and Thailand. The agency has already identified available stockpiles from projects in the region, but urgently needs $500,000 in cash for each country to quickly purchase food as near to the disaster zones as possible, from where it can be rapidly transported.

The number of internally displaced people in Sri Lanka continues to swell, with some 400,000 having taken refuge in public buildings, schools and makeshift camps and WFP is poised to start distributing some 4,000 tons of rice, wheat flour, lentils and sugar—enough to provide an emergency ration to 500,000 people for two weeks.

At an emergency meeting today with the Government and other UN agencies in the country's capital, Colombo, it was decided that UNHCR would concentrate on delivering relief items in the east of the country, where it has offices and access in a region that has been torn by a war with Tamil separatists.

Overall, UNHCR has seven offices in Sri Lanka, where it has worked for nearly two decades helping displaced populations as well as returning refugees.

The agency will provide 18,000 pieces of plastic sheeting, 17,000 plastic mats, rope, and non-food relief packages for 2,000 families, including cooking sets, plastic jerry cans, mosquito nets and clothing.

Stichting Vluchteling, a Dutch non-governmental organization (NGO) that works closely with UNHCR on refugee programmes, today told UNHCR it would cover at least $200,000 of the approximate $280,000 cost of the relief items through its special fund-raising efforts for the disaster victims.

The agency will also assist the UN country team in strengthening the Government's response to the disaster and actively support emergency coordination at the district level.

OCHA has already deployed UNDAC teams to Sri Lanka and the Maldives to work closely with national governments and relief workers in coordinating support from all over the world, and plans are underway to send additional teams to Indonesia and Thailand.

Adding his condolences to those of other UN officials, Under-Secretary-General and High Representative for the Least Developed Countries, Landlocked Developing Countries and Small Island Developing States Anwarul K. Chowdhury said the catastrophe "highlights the vulnerability" of such nations to these events.

Mr. Chowdhury, who is Secretary-General of next month's UN International Meeting on Small Island Developing States, which will be held in Mauritius, urged affluent countries to work together to support small island States as they try to recover from natural disasters such as the tsunami that struck southern Asia and to cope with the effects of climate change.

Source: United Nations. UN News Service. "UN Launches Unprecedented Multiple Effort to Aid Victims of Asia's Devastating Tsunami." December 27, 2004. www.un.org/apps/news/story.asp?NewsID=12914&Cr=tsunami&Cr1= (accessed March 14, 2005).

"UN's Tsunami Relief Takes Various Forms in Worst-Hit Countries"

As the United Nations system moves into high gear to identify the immediate needs of the countries devastated by the South Asian tsunami that has reportedly claimed nearly 70,000 lives and affected millions more, initial actions have been tailored to help each of the worst-hit nations.

- **Sri Lanka**—The World Food Programme (WFP), which says at least 1 million people have been displaced from their homes, is providing food aid for 500,000 people for two weeks. The Office for the Coordination of Humanitarian Affairs (OCHA) is organizing an airlift of relief items from its UN Humanitarian Response Depot located in Brindisi, Italy, and the UN Children's Fund (UNICEF) will bring in medical supplies for 150,000 people for three months after already providing more than 30,000 blankets. The World Health Organization (WHO) is shipping four emergency health kits for hospitals with medicines, disposables and instruments sufficient to support 40,000 people for three months. The UN High Commissioner for Refugees (UNHCR) is initially distributing $380,000 worth of supplies, including 23,500 plastic sheets for shelter, 24,500 plastic mats, clothing, towels and 20,000 kitchen sets.
- **Indonesia**—UNHCR is set to airlift emergency shelter supplies for up to 100,000 people in the province of Aceh, including 3,500 lightweight tent, 20,000 kitchen sets, plastic sheeting for 20,000 families and 100,000 blankets. UNICEF is sending emergency health kits to supply 200,000 people for two weeks. UNICEF will also send tarpaulins and family sets for 8,000 households. The UN Development Programme (UNDP) will deploy a recovery expert and WFP will purchase food for immediate distribution.
- **India**—UNICEF is providing hundreds of thousands of water purification tablets, 1,600 community water tanks containing 500 litres each, 200,000 sachets of oral rehydration salts, medical supplies sufficient to serve 30 health centres, and 30,000 blankets. WHO staff working on polio and tuberculosis prevention have already been mobilized to support government efforts in surveillance and relief work.
- **Maldives**—UNDP released a $100,000 emergency grant. OCHA is organizing a 15-ton airlift of relief items from its Brindisi depot including tents, water containers, jerry cans, as well as emergency health kits. WHO is procuring supplies of water purifying tablets, oral rehydration salts and antibiotics. UNICEF is working with the government on the immediate provision of water purification supplies, food, clothing for children, shelter and other basics.
- **Thailand**—UNDP released an emergency grant of $100,000, while WFP allocated $500,000 to purchase food for immediate distribution to the affected population.
- **Somalia**—OCHA is organizing an aerial assessment of affected coastal areas while WFP has started moving more than 30 tons of food. A total of 1,000

tons of food is currently available in WFP stocks in the northern Puntland area and a ship with another 1,300 tons will be dispatched soon from Mombassa, Kenya.

Source: United Nations. UN News Service. "UN's Initial Tsunami Relief Takes Various Forms in Worst-Hit Countries." December 29, 2004. www.un.org/apps/news/story.asp?NewsID=12928&Cr=tsunami&Cr1= (accessed March 14, 2005).

Yushchenko on His Victory in Ukrainian Presidential Election

December 27, 2004

INTRODUCTION

Ukraine in late 2004 joined Yugoslavia and Georgia on the list of formerly communist countries where popular protests—encouraged by the United States and other Western nations—toppled autocratic leaders who tried to used rigged elections to hold onto power. Viktor A. Yushchenko, a former prime minister, won the presidency late in December after a full month of peaceful mass protests forced a retreat by the current prime minister, Viktor F. Yanukovich. Yanukovich had the backing of outgoing president Leonid Kuchma and the government of Ukraine's big-brother neighbor, Russia.

The month of protests leading to Yushchenko's victory was full of drama and—until near the very end—uncertainty about whether the outcome would be peaceful or end in tragedy. Important elements of the drama included allegations that the government had tried to poison Yushchenko, an increasingly bitter political and social division among Ukrainians over their country's future, and the possibilities that Russia might intervene directly or the Ukrainian security services might use force to impose a solution. The peaceful resolution brought a sense of relief to most Ukrainians and boosted the ambitions of those, led by Yushchenko, who wanted the country to orient itself westward, toward Europe, and away from its historical dependence on Russia. Ukraine still faced a multitude of problems that were certain to pose daunting challenges long after the excitement of the peaceful revolution in late 2004 had faded.

For object lessons, Ukrainians had only to look at two other countries where similar public protests had topped autocratic regimes in recent years. In Serbia, the heart of the former Yugoslavia, the ouster in 2000 of President Slobodan Milosevic had led to four straight years of intense political discord, fostered in large part by the divergent views of opposition leaders whose marriage-of-convenience unity had led to Milosevic's downfall. In Georgia, opposition leaders who in 2003 had driven President Eduard Shevardnadze from office struggled all through 2004 to deal with the endemic corruption and sense of malaise that had infected their country since the collapse of communism a decade earlier. *(Georgia, p. 72; Serbia, p. 949)*

The Election

With a population of nearly 50 million, a strategic location, strong agricultural production, and abundant natural resources, Ukraine had the potential to be one of the most successful of the fifteen former republics of the Soviet Union, which collapsed at the end of 1991. In the following decade, however, Ukraine's leaders appeared unable, or unwilling, to chart a steady course away from the failures of the Soviet era. Elections were held and some aspects of the rigid communist economic system were dismantled, but each step away from the past was accompanied by another step backward. Kuchma, the former head of a missile factory, won the presidency in 1994 elections generally regarded as free and fair. He had campaigned on a platform of economic change, including selling back to farmers the massive agricultural collectives created during the Soviet era. Kuchma faced intense opposition from communist hard-liners who opposed such changes, and his ambivalent leadership left the country stuck in a rut. His reelection in 1999 was tainted by accusations that his government pressured the news media and misused its powers to ensure his victory. A turning point came in April 2001, when Kuchma acquiesced in the ouster of his reform-minded prime minister, Yushchenko, who then went into opposition. Kuchma himself was on the defensive because of accusations that he ordered the murder in 2000 of a prominent journalist.

With his second five-year term set to expire at the end of 2004, Kuchma at first appeared to be maneuvering to stay in office. Early in the year his parliamentary allies began the process of amending the constitution to shift power from the president to the prime minister. Such a move would have allowed Kuchma to remain as president, and thus protected from prosecution for the murder of the journalist or on charges that he had amassed enormous personal wealth while serving as president. Opposition parties blocked that amendment in parliament in April, however, and so Kuchma adopted a fall-back position of supporting Yanukovich for the presidency. Yanukovich, a former Communist Party functionary, had taken over as prime minister in 2002.

Yushchenko's announcement that he would seek the presidency set up a confrontation between two starkly different views of Ukraine's future. Yanukovich drew the bulk of his support from the eastern half of the country (including the Crimea), where the Soviet Union had built enormous industrial complexes that produced heavy machinery and weapons. This region also was the site of the Chernobyl nuclear plant, part of which exploded in 1986, causing the world's worst leak of radioactivity. Many Ukrainians in this region feared that further economic reforms would force the closing of inefficient industries that no longer had Moscow as a reliable customer. Yushchenko appealed primarily to Ukrainians in western regions who had watched with envy—and more than a little resentment—as Czechoslovakia, Hungary, Poland, and other countries once dominated by Moscow had adopted a European outlook and even—as of May 1—become members of the European Union. *(EU expansion, p. 197; Chernobyl disaster, Historic Documents of 1986, p. 386)*

As in several other former Soviet republics, language was a basic point of contention between the two halves of Ukraine. Many people in eastern Ukraine, Yanukovich among them, were ethnic Russians and were uncomfortable with the Ukrainian language; these people resented a post-Soviet law that downgraded Russian from its status as one of the country's two official languages. Many people in western Ukraine resented Moscow's importation of Russians during the Soviet era and insisted on the use of Ukrainian in public affairs.

The presidential campaign got under way in July and quickly developed into a competitive race, with opinion polls showing Yanukovich and Yushchenko drawing about equal levels of support, although from different regions. The campaign took an unexpected turn on September 6, when Yushchenko fell ill from mysterious causes and spent nearly two weeks attempting to recover in a Vienna hospital. He briefly resumed campaigning on September 18 and charged that the government had attempted to kill him with poison. Yushchenko returned to the Vienna hospital for the first week of October, and resumed his campaign on October 10 appearing visibly weaker.

Yanukovich also suffered a collapse while campaigning. On September 24 he stumbled while getting off a campaign bus and was taken to a hospital. A videotape showed that he had been hit in the chest by an egg.

As these events were played out, the country appeared to become even more polarized than in the past, and each side charged that the other was planning to steal the election. Yushchenko's supporters insisted the government was deploying all its resources to guarantee a victory by Yanukovich, citing pressure on public employees to support him. Yanukovich supporters countered that Yushchenko was being openly backed by the United States, which had spent more than $50 million to support what it said were "grass-roots" organizations working on behalf of free and fair elections. Russian president Vladimir Putin heaped praise on Yanukovich, making his sympathies clear.

Despite the polarized atmosphere, the voting, held October 31, went off without serious incident. However, a monitoring team from the Organization for Security and Cooperation in Europe (which routinely observed elections in the former Soviet republics) issued a statement the next day saying the election did not meet "European standards for democratic elections." The European observers cited numerous actions by government agencies in support of Yanukovich, the failure of the Central Elections Commission to act on behalf of voters turned away from the polls, and persistent bias against Yushchenko by the state-controlled broadcast media (Ukraine had only one independent television station). An observer group from other former Soviet republics found no irregularities in the election.

Official results from the first round gave Yushchenko 39.9 percent of the vote and Yanukovich 39.3 percent, with the balance split among twenty-two other minor candidates. Because neither leading candidate won a majority, a second round was required.

That round was held November 21 in an atmosphere of rising tension, generated in part by accusations from each side about the other side's candidate. Yanukovich supporters insisted Yushchenko had poisoned himself and was too sick to serve as president. Yushchenko's supporters—and Yushchenko himself—drew attention to the fact that Yanukovich, as a young man, had served time in prison on charges of assault and robbery. Russian president Putin again intervened, traveling to Ukraine to praise Yanukovich.

Exit polls on election day suggested that Yushchenko would win by a wide margin, but initial results announced the next day by the Central Elections Commission put Yanukovich in first place with 49.4 percent and Yushchenko trailing with 46.3 percent. Again, election monitors from Western countries cited numerous irregularities. Among the monitors was U.S. senator Richard G. Lugar, R-Ind., the chairman of the Foreign Relations Committee, who also was serving as a special envoy for President George W. Bush. "It is now apparent that a concerted and forceful program of election-day fraud and abuse was enacted with either the leadership or cooperation of governmental authorities," Lugar said.

Mounting Protests

At the urging of Yushchenko's Our Ukraine Party, tens of thousands of people gathered on the night of November 22 at Independence Square in central Kiev, the capital. Many wore orange, Yushchenko's official campaign color. Yushchenko addressed the crowd, saying its presence was necessary to prevent "a terrible evil" from taking place. At least 1,000 Yushchenko supporters remained in the square overnight, braving freezing temperatures. One of the protesters, an accountant named Olga Homenka, told a reporter from the *Chicago Tribune:* "I'm willing to stand up to whatever force they put up, because as it stands right now, there's no way back. I feel that if we do not do this now, we'll never have another chance." Yanukovich also addressed his supporters but stopped short of declaring victory. Putin was not so hesitant, sending official congratulations to Yanukovich as the victor.

Attitudes hardened on both sides the following day, November 23, as the two candidates escalated their rhetoric. Yanukovich accused Yushchenko's supporters of "splitting Ukraine," and Yushchenko warned that the country was "on the threshold of a civil conflict." Each man also tried to establish himself as the victor. Yanukovich's office declared victory on his behalf and Yushchenko tried, without success, to get the parliament to declare no confidence in the official count. Yushchenko then staged an unofficial swearing-in ceremony at the parliament, claiming that he was the victor and the new president. Kuchma, who had stayed in the background during the first two days, intervened with a call for "consultations" between the two sides.

The throng of Yushchenko supporters in Kiev developed into a mobile demonstration of thousands of people who marched in the snow from Independence Square to the nearby presidential building, which was protected by police. The dramatic standoff of protesters peacefully confronting policemen in central Kiev was broadcast around the world. One of many signs that the world was paying attention to events in Ukraine was a statement by Secretary of State Colin Powell that the United States did not accept the election as legitimate "because it does not meet international standards and because there has not been an investigation of the numerous and credible reports and fraud and abuse."

Another escalation came November 24, when the Central Election Commission formally declared Yanukovich the winner with 49.5 percent of the vote to Yushchenko's 46.6 percent. Kuchma again appeared on television to appeal for calm and to warn of the risks of civil war. Yushchenko appealed to his supporters to keep up the pressure on the government, and he challenged the army and police to remain neutral. "Don't turn the weapons against the people," he said. Again, outside actors were making their views known, as well. The lower house of the Russian parliament passed a resolution congratulating Yanukovich on his victory, and European and U.S. officials demanded new elections under tighter international supervision.

As the massive street protests continued, the momentum appeared to break slightly toward Yushchenko on November 25. The Ukrainian Supreme Court ordered a delay in formal publication of the election results, saying it wanted to examine opposition claims of fraud. That step, which raised the first official concerns about the validity of the vote, led the two candidates the next day to agree to work toward a peaceful solution.

Yet another step in Yushchenko's direction came November 27, a Saturday, when the parliament held a stormy session and adopted two resolutions. One, passed by a narrow margin, declared the election results invalid; another, passed by a much broader margin, said the published results "did not meet the will of the people." The resolutions had no official meaning because the parliament technically had no control over the election commission, but they represented a major symbolic victory for Yushchenko. The parliament's votes also heightened the potential for some kind of split in the country. Leaders from the eastern regions, where

Yanukovich's support was strongest, called for autonomy from the central government, and several threatened an outright split of the country if Yushchenko was given the presidency.

Kuchma again intervened on November 29, calling for new elections. He did not make it clear, however, whether he meant another runoff between Yushchenko and Yanukovich or an entirely new election. Kuchma insisted that he was not trying to hold onto power himself: "I have had enough," he said. Kuchma's call for new voting appeared to signal a split in what had been solidarity between him and Yanukovich, who continued to insist he had won the election. Also on November 29 the Ukrainian Supreme Court began its inquiry into the voting and accepted a box of audiotapes and videotapes from Yushchenko's camp as evidence of ballot rigging. One of the tapes reportedly was of a telephone conversation in which Yanukovich campaign officials discussed plans for ballot rigging. News reports said the tape had been made by the powerful Ukrainian intelligence agency, suggesting that the agency's leaders were hedging their bets on the ultimate outcome of the political struggle.

Another lurch forward came December 1, when the parliament narrowly passed a motion of no-confidence in the government headed by Yanukovich. The two candidates also met with Kuchma and European mediators and agreed to draft plans for a new election. As part of the agreement, Yushchenko called on his supporters to end a blockade of government offices. Another ominous sign for Yanukovich was a statement by Viktor M. Pinchuk, a well-connected businessman (he was Kuchma's son-in-law) that Yushchenko likely would win any new election. The statement appeared to indicate that even some of Ukraine's leaders with a vested interest in a Yanukovich victory had given up on that prospect.

One important Yanukovich supporter who did not appear willing to budge was Putin, who met at the Moscow airport the next day with Kuchma and derided the calls for another round of elections. "A rerun of the second round may also produce nothing," he said in remarks broadcast on Russian television. "What happens then? Will there be a third, a fourth, a twenty-fifth round until one of the sides obtains the necessary result?" Putin then set off on an official trip to India, where he accused the United States of intervening in Ukraine's politics in hopes of establishing a "dictatorship of international affairs."

Calling a New Election

The key step toward resolution of the standoff came December 3, when the Ukrainian Supreme Court threw out the official results of the November 21 runoff election and ordered a new round before December 26 between Yanukovich and Yushchenko. The court cited violations by the government and the election commission at nearly every stage of the runoff election, "which makes it impossible to ascertain the true result of voters' choice." In the only positive sign for Yanukovich, the court rejected Yushchenko's petition that he be declared the actual winner.

The focus of attention then shifted to the parliament, where Yanukovich sought agreement on a plan, which had been debated earlier in the year, to change the constitution to replace the current system of government with a new one transferring key powers from the president to the prime minister. Some opposition leaders long had supported such a plan as a step toward the type of parliamentary democracy common in Western Europe—but they viewed its adoption at this stage as a ploy to allow Kuchma to name a new, more powerful prime minister.

The constitutional changes became the centerpiece of a political deal approved by parliament on December 8. In exchange for agreement on a new runoff election on December 26 under procedures intended to produce an honest result, Yushchenko's supporters accepted the constitutional changes reducing some of the powers of the presidency. Under the new arrangement, the president would appoint the prime minister and the defense and foreign ministers, but parliament would choose other cabinet ministers. The changes were to take place following the next parliamentary elections, scheduled for 2006. Parliament's vote for the changes was overwhelming, with the only opposition coming from the opposition party headed by Yushchenko's closest ally, Yulia V. Tymoshenko, who said there was no need for compromise with the government.

As the two sides prepared to kick off another round of campaigning—the third in the election cycle—Yushchenko's doctors in Vienna announced on December 11 that new tests indicated that the candidate had been poisoned with dioxin, an extremely toxic chemical. Michael Dimpfer, director of the private Rudolfinerhaus Clinic, said Yushchenko's blood and tissue showed levels of dioxin about 1,000 times above normal levels. Yushchenko was "in a critical stage," Zimpfer said, but was not in danger of dying. Yushchenko's health had been the subject of intense international interest and speculation. As the political campaign, and then the rounds of postelection protests, continued, Yushchenko's face became increasingly blotchy and took on a yellow-green hue, and the fifty-year-old Yushchenko was forced to limit his public appearances and other types of activity to short periods. The announcement that Yushchenko suffered from dioxin poisoning heightened the mystery about the cause. Yushchenko continued to maintain that unidentified Ukraininian officials were responsible, but some supporters pointed the finger of blame at Moscow, as well.

The election campaign got under way on December 14. Just two days later Yanukovich insisted neither he nor his supporters would accept a victory by Yushchenko. "The people who voted for me, they will never recognize him," he said. "They are talking about it, even now." Despite such rhetoric, signs already were emerging that Yanukovich's support had slipped. Yushchenko drew increasingly large crowds in the eastern regions, which had been the source of Yanukovich's strength.

The two men held their only televised debate of the third round on December 20 and managed to keep a civil tone for the most part, even while accusing each other of misdeeds. By this point Yanukovich appeared to have become reconciled to his likely defeat, calling on Yushchenko to join him in a "normal government of national concord."

The campaign came to an official end on December 24 and was followed the next day by a ruling from the country's Constitutional Court striking down one of the reforms the parliament had adopted two weeks earlier: a ban on voting from home. Yushchenko's aides had said the government stuffed the ballot boxes with thousands of fraudulent votes it said had been cast by people at home, but Yanukovich said the ban on home-voting discriminated against the disabled and elderly.

The voting on December 26 took place in a much calmer atmosphere than the previous two rounds, with international observers generally praising the conduct of the balloting and the new procedures parliament had put in place. The overall situation was a sharp reversal, however. Initial results gave Yushchenko a convincing win, and Yanukovich reacted by refusing to accept the outcome and saying he would challenge it in the courts. Preliminary results made public December 27 gave

Yushchenko just more than 52 percent of the vote to Yanukovich's 44 percent. The eight-point lead was less than what many independent observers had expected, based on opinion polls, and it showed continuing divisions between eastern and western Ukraine. Even so, Yushchenko told supporters it was a "victory for the Ukrainian people and the Ukrainian nation." Noting the enormous international attention that had focused on the country, he said: "Probably three, four months ago, many people had no idea where Ukraine was located. Today the world starts almost every morning with the question: 'What's going on in Ukraine?'"

For at least a couple more days, the answer to that question was: yet more political conflict. Yanukovich called for a cabinet meeting on December 28, only to cancel the session when Yushchenko again called on his supporters to block government buildings in protest. On December 29 Yanukovich filed a complaint with the election commission, citing what he said were illegal actions by the Yushchenko camp. For his part, Yushchenko began the process of taking the reins of power, drawing up plans for his cabinet appointments and for replacing regional governors in the eastern part of the country.

The last acts in the year's drama came December 30, when the election commission rejected Yanukovich's complaints against the election, and on December 31, when a still-defiant Yanukovich said in a New Year's Eve address to the nation that he was resigning as prime minister. "I believe it is impossible to have any position in a state that is ruled by such individuals," he said, in a reference to Yushchenko and his supporters.

Yushchenko was expected to take office in late January 2005. He had not appointed a new prime minister as of the end of 2004, but it appeared increasingly likely that he would select the charismatic Tymoshenko, who had stirred the massive crowds in Kiev's streets with fiery rhetoric against Kuchma, Yanukovich, and the Russian government.

Following is the text of an address given December 27, 2004, by Viktor A. Yushchenko, the newly elected president of Ukraine.

"Victor Yushchenko's Address at the Election Press Center"

Dear friends!

We've done it. This is victory, victory for the Ukrainian people and the Ukrainian nation. It took us several hundred years to get here. We had 14 years of independence, but now . . . we are free.

Today, Ukraine has started a new political year. The era of [President Leonid] Kuchma, [Viktor] Medvedchuk [Kuchma's chief of staff] and Kuchma is history. Today we are turning the page of our history, full of disrespect for the people, lies, censorship and brutality. Those who brought Ukraine to the brink of this chasm are going away these minutes. Everyone has contributed to this immense achievement.

A new era of great democracy is beginning. Dozens of millions of Ukrainians dreamed about it. Today it is fashionable, stylish and beautiful to be a Ukrainian. It's you who laid the basis for the entire world to talk about Ukraine, to deliver the truth. Probably, 3–4 months ago many people had no idea where Ukraine was located. Today the world starts almost every morning with the question: "What's going on in Ukraine?"

Thank you, dear friends, each of you personally, independently of political forces you've preferred. I believe that it would be impossible for the world to see the real Ukraine without independent and unbiased journalists, as it is seen through your eyes.

My team has received a great credit of trust today. I understand the responsibility and will deserve your support, from each of you, of those hundreds of thousands people on Maydan [Independence Square in Kiev], of dozens of millions of Ukrainians, who not only waited but forged this victory and proved the historic words: this is our Ukraine and I'm proud to be citizen of it.

Congratulations on our victory! Happiness and all the good things to you all!

Source: Ukraine. My Ukraine: Personal Website of Viktor Yushchenko. "Victor Yushchenko's Address at the Election Press Center." December 27, 2004. ww2.yuschenko.com.ua/eng/present/News/1970 (accessed March 29, 2005).

Pakistan President Musharraf on Retaining His Military Role

December 30, 2004

INTRODUCTION

Pakistan's president, Pervez Musharraf, backtracked during the year on his promise—made at the end of 2003—to give up his other position as army chief of staff. Musharraf said his decision to remain in uniform was based on the need to maintain stability, and stability did appear likely for Pakistan in the short term. Opposition groups said Musharraf was risking longer-term instability, however, by frustrating a return to full-scale democracy.

Musharraf seized power in a 1999 military coup, the latest in a string of coups that had repeatedly interrupted the growth of democracy in Pakistan. Musharraf's rule coincided with one of the most difficult periods in Pakistan's five decades of existence. Pakistan had exploded a nuclear bomb in 1998, and a year later almost went to war with neighboring India—the event that led to Musharraf's coup. Then in late 2001 Musharraf came under intense pressure from the Bush administration to side with the United States in its war against the al Qaeda terrorist network based in neighboring Afghanistan. Musharraf complied, but at the risk of provoking a reaction from extreme Islamist groups in his own country. That reaction came in stages: first, a victory by Islamist political groups in two provincial elections in 2002, and then, more violently, in two failed assassination attempts against Musharraf in late 2003.

Musharraf also struggled to keep a lid on sectarian violence between the two rival Muslim groups, the Sunnis, who constituted about 80 percent of the population, and the minority Shi'ites. More than 1,200 Pakistanis had been killed in violent clashes between the two factions since the late 1980s, and dozens more were killed in several major incidents during 2004. Two bombings early in May killed more than 30 Shi'ite Muslims and set off several days unrest in the city of Karachi. On October 4 two bombs exploded at a gathering of several thousand Sunni militants in the central city of Multan, killing 39 people and wounding more than 100. In response the government decreed a ban on political and religious meetings.

Yet another controversy that dogged Musharraf throughout the year was the fallout from revelations that Abdul Qadeer Kahn, considered by Pakistanis as the "father" of the nation's nuclear bomb, had run an international black market in nuclear materials and equipment. Kahn's activities came to light as a result of Libya's decision to give up its nuclear weapons program, which had benefited from Pakistani technology. Kahn publicly apologized for his actions on February 4 and was pardoned the following day by Musharraf. New details about Kahn's actions continued to emerge, however, raising questions about the extent of involvement by the Pakistani military under Musharraf's leadership. *(Kahn activities, p. 323)*

In the midst of this maneuvering over domestic matters, Musharraf continued negotiations with India over Kashmir, a region that both countries claimed and that had been the cause of three major wars between them. The negotiations were delayed for a few months in midyear after Indian prime minister Atal Bahari Vajpayee and his ruling party were defeated. *(India elections and Kashmir, p. 348)*

Musharraf's Political Role

Musharraf ousted the elected prime minister, Nawaz Sharif, in 1999 and two years later formally took the title of president. In April 2002 he submitted his presidency to a referendum and received 98 percent of the vote—an outcome that opposition parties and most international election observers said was rigged. Parliamentary elections later in 2002 resulted in the installation of a civilian government over which Musharraf exercised ultimate control. *(Background, Historic Documents of 2002, p. 165)*

In December 2003 Musharraf reached a political accommodation with his Islamist opposition, a coalition known as the Muttahida Majlis-e-Amals. Under the agreement, Musharraf won indemnity from future prosecution for his role in the 1999 coup; in return he agreed to step down as army chief within one year. The deal also allowed Musharraf to dismiss the parliament and the prime minister, but only with the permission of the supreme court, which he controlled. On January 1, 2004, a week after that deal was sealed, Pakistan's electoral college—consisting of parliament and the four provincial assemblies—ratified Musharraf's term in office until 2007. Most opposition lawmakers boycotted this vote. *(Background, Historic Documents of 2003, p. 214)*

As president, Musharraf said he was following a policy of "enlightened moderation," which he defined as confronting Islamist extremists, reforming the economy to encourage Western aid and investment, and promoting democracy at the national level—but with the military as a guiding hand. On January 17, 2004, Musharraf made his first speech to parliament since taking power in 1999. He called for "moderation" and denounced "extremism," which he defined as "ultra modernized westernized people who wish to end the religious system in the country," versus "hard liners who interpret Islam in a wrong way and want to impose their views on all." Those words were not greeted with broad approval in the chamber. Members from the Islamist parties walked out, and members from the secular opposition parties jeered.

Two developments on April 14 offered evidence that the military would remain deeply engaged in Pakistan's political future. Musharraf suggested that he was reconsidering his promise to give up his army position, telling the BBC that he had not yet made a decision on what he called "a contentious issue." On the same day, Pakistan's senate gave final approval to a bill giving the military a formal role in most major government decisions. The bill created a thirteen-member national security council, including the four senior military officers, which would advise the government on a broad range of issues. The military had long sought such a role, but parliament had rejected previous efforts to put it into law. Most political analysts in Pakistan said Musharraf appeared to view the council as insurance of a military role in the government even if he gave up his army post. Opposition lawmakers boycotted the votes in both chambers of parliament, with some saying it created permanent martial law.

Both of these developments reportedly played a role in the June 26 resignation of Mir Zafarullah Khan Jamali, who had served as Musharraf's prime minister since shortly after the 2002 parliamentary elections. Jamali had publicly called on

Musharraf to keep his promise to step aside as army chief, and news reports indicated that he had opposed formation of the national security council. Musharraf eventually named one of his closest civilian allies, Shaukat Aziz, to succeed Jamali. A former executive of the U.S.-based Citibank, Aziz had been serving as finance minister and had won wide praise for stabilizing the economy and pushing through economic reforms that brought new loans and debt relief from international banks. Aziz on July 30 survived a suicide bomb attack on his motorcade when he was traveling in a town near Islamabad. At least nine other people died in the attack, which appeared to be the work of a Pakistani group allied with al Qaeda. At the time, Aziz was campaigning for a seat in the lower house of parliament, which he needed to take the post of prime minister. He won that seat in an August 18 election, which opposition leaders said was rigged, and was confirmed as prime minister on August 27.

In subsequent months Musharraf, his aides, and political allies laid the groundwork for reversal of his promise to give up the army post. Cabinet members publicly called on Musharraf to continue in uniform, and in mid-September the regional parliament in Punjab province—overwhelmingly controlled by pro-Musharraf parties—passed a resolution seconding that call. Again using an interview with a Western reporter to signal his intentions, Musharraf on September 16 told a *Washington Post* reporter that he was reconsidering his promise because "the vast majority" of the Pakistani people "want me in uniform." He said he based that conclusion on letters and telephone calls his office had received. Musharraf also told a Dubai-based television station that "96 percent" of the Pakistani people wanted him to remain in uniform.

Musharraf on September 22 received what he appeared to interpret as a green light for his impending decision from President George W. Bush. During an hour-long meeting in New York, where both men were attending the opening session of the United Nations General Assembly, Bush urged continued democratic reform in Pakistan but did not mention the question of Musharraf's military role.

Shortly after his meeting with Bush, Musharraf began taking the formal steps necessary to keep his military job. First, on October 2, he named new commanders for several senior army posts—but not a successor for his own job as chief of staff. Then in November the parliament began considering legislation specifically authorizing Musharraf to continue holding both jobs. That measure was signed into law on November 30 by the chairman of the senate, who was filling in for Musharraf during a trip by the president to Latin America and the United States. During that trip, on December 4, Musharraf met again with Bush, this time at the White House. After the meeting Bush praised Musharraf and the Pakistan army for its hunt for terrorists.

In a television interview on December 18, Musharraf said for the first time that he would "remain in uniform." He repeated his earlier assertion that 96 percent of Pakistanis wanted him to keep both jobs, but, again, he did not say how his countrymen had expressed that view. Giving up his uniform, he said, would "weaken the democracy and economic stability in the country."

Musharraf finally made his stance official on December 30 with a lengthy televised speech to the nation, in which he repeatedly stressed the need for "continuity" of government policy. "In my view, any change in the internal and external policies can be extremely dangerous to Pakistan," he said. Seeking to counter certain criticism, Musharraf appealed to the opposition "to accept the democratic verdict of the [parliament] and avoid [an] undemocratic attitude."

If he harbored any illusions that the opposition would heed his call, Musharraf quickly learned otherwise. The acting chairman of the opposition Pakistan People's

Party said Musharraf's decision demonstrated that he remained beholden to the army. "Our struggle will continue until he resigns and goes back to the barracks," Makhdoom Amin Fahim said. The coalition of Islamic parties, Muttahida Majlis-i-Amal, held demonstrations in several regions the next day.

Searching for al Qaeda

Pakistan in late February mounted a major military offensive intended to clear out remnants of the al Qaeda terrorist network and the former Taliban regime of Afghanistan. Fighters for both groups reportedly had been hiding in the remote, mountainous regions of Pakistan's Northwest Province, along the border with Afghanistan, ever since the United States and its allies drove the Taliban from power in late 2001. Among those thought to be in hiding in the area was Osama bin Laden, the head of al Qaeda and the man with overall responsibility for the September 11, 2001, terrorist attacks against the United States. *(September 11 attacks, Historic Documents of 2001, p. 614)*

Bin Laden's continued at-large status was a major embarrassment for President Bush, who had pledged in 2001 to capture him "dead or alive." Bagging bin Laden before the U.S. presidential elections in November would have been a significant political boost for the president—but it was not to be. Working along both sides of the Afghanistan-Pakistan border, U.S. and Pakistani troops sought to trap the hundreds of al Qaeda and Taliban fighters assumed to be in the area. The manhunt, which lasted for much of the year, netted dozens of militants but did not produce either bin Laden or his top deputy, Ayman al-Zawahiri. Also still at large, possibly in Afghanistan, was the former leader of the Taliban, Mullah Omar.

The early stages of the manhunt went awry when Pakistani militants captured several dozen soldiers, other security workers, and government officials. At least eight of the soldiers were executed in late March. The military operation also led thousands of civilians to flee their homes, generating widespread anger against the government.

Al Qaeda appeared to strike back at Musharraf for his cooperation with the United States. On March 25 the pan-Arab satellite television channel Al Jazeera broadcast an excerpt of a videotape, reportedly of Zawahiri, denouncing Musharraf as a "traitor" and calling on Pakistanis to overthrow him.

On September 26 the Pakistani government reported that police had killed Amjad Hussain Farooqi, who authorities had linked to the assassination attempts against Musharraf and to the killing in 2002 of *Wall Street Journal* reporter Daniel Pearl. Farooqi reportedly was killed during a four-hour gun battle in the southern city of Nawabshah.

The highest profile al Qaeda operative captured in Pakistan during the year was Ahmed Khalfan Ghailani, a Tanzanian who had been accused by the United States of involvement in the 1998 bombing of the U.S. embassies in Kenya and Tanzania. Ghailani was captured July 25 in the eastern city of Gujrat. *(Embassy bombings, Historic Documents of 1998, p. 555)*

September 11 Panel Recommendations

The commission that investigated the September 11, 2001, attacks against the United States suggested that Pakistan would continue to play a central role in the U.S.-led fight against Islamist terrorism. In its report released July 22 the commission painted a decidedly mixed picture of Pakistan as a country that possessed nuclear weapons and was ripe for Islamist extremism, in large part because the government had relied on religious schools, known as *madrassas,* as the main source of education for most lower-class families. *(Commission report, p. 450)*

The commission also was ambivalent about Musharraf, noting that he at least had stood by while Kahn created his nuclear black market and had made "little progress" toward democracy at the national level. Even so, the commission said, Musharraf's government "remains the best hope for stability in Pakistan and Afghanistan." The commission recommended that the U.S. government make a "long-term commitment" to Pakistan in the form of a "comprehensive effort" including military aid and support for improved education there.

Congress and the Bush administration, which had provided more than nearly $2 billion in economic and military aid since 2001, heeded the commissions' call by providing another $700 million for the next fiscal year, 2005; this was the first installment on a five-year, $3 billion commitment Bush had first requested in June 2003.

Following are excerpts from a televised address to the nation by Pakistan's president, Pervez Musharraf, delivered December 30, 2004, in which he explained his reversal of an earlier promise to give up his other post as army chief of staff by the end of 2004.

"Text of President's Address to the Nation"

My Dear Pakistani brothers and sisters:

It's been long since I addressed you last time. This delay has been due to a busy schedule of engagements and some developments.

But today, a few days after Quaid-e-Azam's [nickname for Mohammad Ali Jinnah, the founder of Pakistan] birth anniversary, I think it is appropriate that we review collectively what has happened to Pakistan of the Quaid-e-Azam, how we are correcting the situation and what does future hold for the country.

First of let us see what conditions prevailed before October 1999. Here, first of all I would like to dilate on the economic state. The economy was in shambles. It was bankrupt. The national wealth had been looted and the exchequer was empty. We were confronting darkness all around with hardly any ray of hope in sight. . . .

Extremism and terrorism were on the rise, corruption and nepotism were the order of the day. The system of the government was that of loot and plunder. All national corporations and institutions were headed by flattering government officials. These corporations and institutions were badly damaged. Transparency International had rated Pakistan as the second most corrupt country. It was a shameful situation. Political tussles were rife. On the one hand, the political dictatorship of the government was being let loose in the form of the 14th Amendment in the Constitution, which had bereft the parliamentarians of their right to express their will.

On the other hand, the Opposition, at the very outset, engaged itself in toppling the government. They would go GHQ [army general headquarters] and ask the Army Chief to take over or remove the prime minister.

Such was the state of democracy at that time. The vital national interests were compromised and bargained. We faced isolation in the world. Nobody was willing to interact with us. Resultantly, we were being dubbed as a defaulted state, a terrorist state and a failed state. This, in brief, was the pre-October 1999 scenario [prior to the coup that brought Musharraf to power]. Now let us see what have been our achievements and what have we set upon to achieve in the future.

First of all, let us see Pakistan's international stature. Previously, we were called a pariah state, whom nobody was willing to interact with. Now the world leaders, meet us, seek our views, listen to our views and accept our views. The world leaders visit Pakistan to meet us. Pakistan holds a special status in the Muslim Ummah [the Muslim world]. We have a lead role to play in the Ummah. We have friendship with all leaders. We are in touch with them on important issues. In this context, we have put forward the strategy of enlightened moderation, which has been widely received. *Inshallah* ["If Allah wills it"], I am hopeful that this strategy would help take the Muslims forward on the path of socio-economic development.

Let us look at our region and view our relations with Afghanistan. In the beginning, we faced some difficulties with Afghanistan but now the two countries enjoy excellent diplomatic, political and trade ties. The government and the people of Afghanistan are extremely thankful to Pakistan for our cooperation in political developments and the Afghan election process. *Inshallah,* Pakistan's trade with Afghanistan will cross one billion US dollars this year. Our relations with Afghanistan are progressing Well. It is only because of some terrorists going for terrorist activities from our tribal region, that bring us a bad name. Otherwise, our bilateral relations remain excellent.

Let us look at our relations with India. Our relations have seen a great improvement. But, now we are dealing with them on the basis of sovereign equality. We are not compromising on principles as was being done before. We are moving forward our relations at two levels: confidence building measures and the dialogue process.

We have made it clear that the Kashmir issue is central to the whole process of bilateral relations and resolving this dispute is absolutely imperative. We have also stated that we will show flexibility for the resolution of the dispute. But we have never said that we will demonstrate this flexibility unilaterally, that we shall leave aside our principled stand and move forward. I have neither stated this nor shall I ever say that. Our stand today is the same as it was in 1948, that is the UN resolutions and plebiscite as a solution. But, we have shown flexibility to the extent that we would show flexibility, if India also reciprocates.

If both countries step back, we will be able to move forward to the resolution of the Kashmir dispute somewhere from the middle path. This is what I have said and this is the purpose of demonstrating flexibility. We shall never show flexibility unilaterally. We have also made it clear that the dispute cannot be resolved against the wishes of Kashmiri people. The will of Kashmiris has be taken into account The Kashmiris will have to be included in the dialogue process at some stage. We have made it clear. Therefore, I say that I see a ray of hope. It will be our endeavour that our relations with India improve and all outstanding issues, particularly the Kashmir dispute, move toward their resolution. . . .

A lot of improvement has been brought in the system of governance. Corruption and nepotism have been reduced at top level of the government The fear of God has been put in the hearts and minds of the rich and powerful. . . .

I want to say something about myself. I have always fulfilled my pledges in the political sphere. I remain true to all commitments I have made. Now I would like to talk in the context of politics. I had promised that we will empower the people through devolution. I had promised to introduce local government system and I had committed to hold elections in the year 2002.

With the Grace of Almighty Allah, the system of local governments, introduced on August 14, 2002 is functioning well in the country. Then a Supreme Court verdict had mandated me to run the government for three years. Thankfully, general elections were held in October 2002, exactly after three years. Secondly, I voluntarily handed over the government to the elected government and an elected prime minister.

Here, I would like to state that a situation had been created in the aftermath of 9/11 that a justification arose that I could seek extension in the period of government from the Supreme Court. And a number of suggestions to that effect were floated at that time, asking me to seek extension. But I listened to my inner conscience which said that I had made a pledge to steer the country forward on the path of democracy. Therefore, I fulfilled that commitment. And we held free and fair elections in the year 2002. Some people had even doubted that. Look at the strong Opposition presence in National Assembly, the Senate and the provincial assemblies.

This strength of the Opposition evidences that elections were free and fair. I voluntarily handed over the government to the Prime Minister. That happened for the first time in the history of Pakistan. I have always taken the people into confidence on important national matters, I have been talking to you on TV, I have been giving interviews to the newspapers and have been taking you along on national issues.

I had decided to leave the office of the Army Chief and also announced it. But I had announced this decision with some hopes and expectations. I had made it with good intentions but also with some hopes and expectations. I had decided this voluntarily. It is not mentioned in the Government's accord with the MMA [the Islamist opposition coalition] and nor has the 17th Amendment of the Constitution touched it. I decided this on my own. But this decision was made with some hopes and expectations.

First of all, the 17th Amendment should be passed and thankfully it was passed. Secondly, I had thought that the Opposition will engage in positive politics. Thirdly, the elected government will be allowed to complete its tenure and the Government will be supported amicably. Fourthly, the political system will run smoothly and strengthen Pakistan's integrity.

But let us view the situation after I had announced the decision in December 2003 [a reference to his decision to step down as army chief of staff by the end of 2004]. One year has passed. Let us see the situation on ground.

First of all, after having signed the accord, the MMA time and again went back on its words. Secondly, the Opposition's attitude went from bad to worse as they indulged in undemocratic activities. They want the rule of minority. They want to suppress majority through minority, which is contrary to the demands of democracy. In addition, they are threatening that taking off the uniform is the first step, after which they will take more actions. Instead of strengthening democracy they are posing a danger to democracy. After looking into the political side, I reviewed the situation internally, regionally and internationally. I want to inform you about that as well.

In my opinion, it is absolutely imperative that the Parliament and the Government completes their tenure. Continuity of policies and strengthening of democracy are absolute requirements for Pakistan. Thirdly, there is a military action against foreign terrorists and their local abettors and political dialogue going on in the South Waziristan agency of tribal areas. The continuation of this process is vitally important. Then, continuity in the process of improvement in relations with India is very important in the context of resolution of Kashmir issue. Continuity in Pakistan's foreign policy is very important in view of the developments taking place in the world including Palestine, Iraq, Afghanistan, and Islamic Ummah.

Then, improving Pakistan's perception internationally, is also vitally important for us as the country is wrongly perceived in the world as an extremist, militant, intolerant society. We also have to deal with extremism internally as we need unity to take our society forward towards moderation.

Then we have to safeguard our vital national interests. It is the voice of the Pakistani nation. In view of this situation, Pakistan direly needs harmony among political, bureaucracy and military institutions. I have viewed the issue of my holding dual office both legally and constitutionally. The Constitution of Pakistan allows me to retain both the offices until 2007. And I shall never violate the Constitution. The National Assembly and the Senate, the two premier democratic institutions of Pakistan, have passed a bill that I should keep both the offices. This is the voice of the majority. Democracy demands that minority should accept the ruling of the majority. I know that uniform is a non-issue for the people of Pakistan. They are doing it take political mileage out of it.

I have informed you about the entire situation. Therefore, I have decided to retain both the offices [as president and army chief of staff]. In my view, any change in the internal and external policies can be extremely dangerous for Pakistan. Therefore, I appeal to the opposition to accept the democratic verdict of the National Assembly and the Senate and avoid undemocratic attitude.

Pakistan faces internal challenge in the form of extremism and terrorism. I would like to talk about the culture of hatred and violence being spread by some elements in the country. If we do not check it, which we are doing, then internally this menace will eat us like termites.

Here I would like to quote a favourite verse of mine: *"I have high ambitions and I do not fear flames from outside; What I fear is that the fire of flower may not set this garden ablaze."*

We have to face it collectively and boldly and not fearfully. We have to face it wisely and with a strategy. I know that the majority of Pakistanis are moderate Muslims and I call Jaish, Sipah, Lashkar as extremists. In my view, they have no place in the society. Nobody should have any doubt that Pakistan is an ideological state. It is an Islamic Republic of Pakistan. It is the only country which came into existence in the name of Islam and it is home for Muslims of this part of the region. Nobody should doubt that.

Muslims of strong faith inhabit this country, Nobody should doubt that as well. It is not a question of being Muslim or non-Muslim, the question is what kind of ideology should be in place in Pakistan. An ideology of ignorance, backwardness, a retrogressive ideology, which is given the name of Islam. Or we should have an ideology of high values, justice and progressiveness. The answer is clear. Pakistan wants a system, having ideology of Allama Iqbal, and vision of Quaid-e-Azam Let us all of us pledge today that we shall boldly confront those who want to push us to darkness and will make efforts for prevailing the majority of moderates on the minority of extremists.

My dear countrymen,

I assure you at the start of the year 2005 that I fully stand for democracy. Democracy will continue to function in the country and assemblies will complete their tenure. Local bodies elections will begin in April next year. The fight against extremism, terrorism and anti-national interests will continue unabated. The writ of the government will be established firmly. *Inshallah.*

All mega development projects will be completed, *Inshallah.* About large dams, I would like to say that I will give the nation a good news shortly. The national economy will be further strengthened. *Inshallah,* and poverty will be reduced. And all efforts will be made for poverty alleviation. We will address the Kashmir dispute and improve relations with India honourably. Our nuclear and missile power will be further strengthened. . . .

My dear Pakistani brothers and sisters,

Today's Pakistan is not the Pakistan of pre-1999, not an asleep, lost, drowning, begging around, surrounded in despairs. It is a wakeful, progressing Pakistan, respected in the Muslim Ummah and a hopeful Pakistan. We should take pride in our country. We should be united for sake of its prestige, honour and security. I extend hand of friendship to the opposition. Come forward and let us take Pakistan forward towards light, give up confrontation, strengthen democracy and do not weaken it. Our youth and coming generation demand a bright future from us. *Inshallah.*

I shall never disappoint them. . . .

Source: Government of Pakistan. Ministry of Foreign Affairs. "Text of President's Address to the Nation." Speech, December 30, 2004; English translation released January 5, 2005. www.pakistan.gov.pk/foreignaffairs-ministry/news-des.jsp?div=ForeignAffairs_Ministry&file=mofa05012005speech.xml&path=foreignaffairs-ministry/ (accessed April 27, 2005).

Credits

Credits are a continuation from page iv.

A Report on the Crisis in the Catholic Church in the United States. © 2004 United States Conference of Catholic Bishops, Washington, D.C. Reprinted with permission. All rights reserved.

Resolution 1529, "Rwanda Genocide 'Must Leave Us Always with a Sense of Bitter Regret and Abiding Sorrow,' Says Secretary-General to New York Memorial Conference," "Third Special Report of the Secretary-General on the United Nations Organization Mission in the Democratic Republic of the Congo," "First Report of the Analytical Support and Sanctions Monitoring Team Appointed Pursuant to Resolution 1526 (2004) Concerning Al Qaeda and the Taliban and Associated Individuals and Entities," *Resolution 1559,* "Agenda: The Situation in the Middle East, Including the Palestinian Question," *Resolution 1572,* "A More Secure World: Our Shared Responsibility," "Estimating the Impact of the Next Influenza Pandemic: Enhancing Preparedness," "Enclosure: Report on the Situation in Kosovo," "UN Experts Rush to Indian Ocean Countries Devastated by Quake and Tidal Waves," "UN Launches Unprecedented Multiple Effort to Aid Victims of Asia's Devastating Tsunami," and "UN's Initial Tsunami Relief Takes Various Forms in Worst-Hit Countries." Copyright © United Nations 2004. All rights reserved. The United Nations is the author of the original material.

"Mr. Bertie Ahern, Mr. Pat Cox and Mr. Romano Prodi Address Accession Day Conference of the Three Presidents" and "Prime Minister and President of the European Council Jan Peter Balkenende at the Press Conference Following the European Council." © European Communities, 1995–2005.

"The First Bush-Kerry Presidential Debate," "The Second Bush-Kerry Presidential Debate," and "The Third Bush-Kerry Presidential Debate." © 2004 Commission on Presidential Debates. All rights reserved.

Preventing Childhood Obesity: Health in the Balance and *Science and Technology in the National Interest: Ensuring the Best Presidential and Federal Advisory Committee Science and Technology Appointments.* Copyright © 2004 National Academy of Sciences.

All rights reserved. Reprinted with permission from the National Academy of Sciences, courtesy of the National Academies Press.

"Text of Indonesian President's Inaugural Speech." Laksamana.net web site, Jakarta, in English 20 Oct 04 /BBC Monitoring/ BBC.BBC Monitoring/ © BBC.

"Estimating the Impact of the Next Influenza Pandemic: Enhancing Preparedness." © World Health Organization 2005. All rights reserved.

"Nobel Lecture by Wangari Maathai." © The Nobel Foundation.

"Victor Yushchenko's Address at the Election Press Center." My Ukraine. Personal Web site of Viktor Yushchenko. Copyright © 2005. All rights reserved.

Cumulative Index, 2000–2004

H

K

P

X

Y